ENCYCLOPEDIA
of
ECONOMICS

Douglas Greenwald
EDITOR IN CHIEF

McGraw-Hill Book Company

New York   St. Louis   San Francisco   Auckland   Bogotá
Hamburg   Johannesburg   London   Madrid   Mexico
Montreal   New Delhi   Panama   Paris   São Paulo
Singapore   Sydney   Tokyo   Toronto

Library of Congress Cataloging in Publication Data

Main entry under title:
Encyclopedia of economics.

Includes index.
1.Economics—Dictionaries.   I.Greenwald,
Douglas.
HB61.E55   330′.03′21   81-4969
                                  AACR2

ISBN 0-07-024367-0

234567890   KPKP   898765432

The editors for this book were Kiril Sokoloff, Nancy Warren, and
Ann Gray; the designer was Mark E. Safran; and the production
supervisor was Sally Fliess. It was set in Melior by University
Graphics, Inc.

It was printed and bound by The Kingsport Press.

Contents

Contributors

Name and Affiliation	Articles
Clopper Almon, Jr. Professor of Economics, University of Maryland; author, *1985: Inter-industry Forecasts of the American Economy.*	Distributed lags in economics; Input-output analysis
Henry C. F. Arnold Associate Professor of Finance, Pace University; former Economist, McGraw-Hill Publications' Economics Department, and coauthor, *McGraw-Hill Dictionary of Modern Economics.*	Bond; Bond rating agencies; Price-earnings ratio; Securities and Exchange Commission; Stock; Stock exchange; Stock price averages and indexes; Yield curve.
Irving M. Auerbach Vice President and Economist, Aubrey G. Lamston & Co., Inc.; former Manager, Statistics Department, Federal Reserve Bank of New York.	Monetary policy
Jules Backman Research Professor Emeritus of Economics, New York University's School of Business; Editor, *Business Problems of the Eighties.*	Integration
Theodore Bakerman Professor of Business, School of Business, Indiana State University; Fellow of Financial Analysts Federation.	Fringe benefits
Sam Barone Dean, College of Business and Administration, University of Detroit; author, "The Impact of Recent Developments in Civil Rights Legislation on Employers and Unions," in *Labor Law Journal.*	Collective bargaining; Labor-management relations

Name and Affiliation	Articles
Jere Behrman Professor of Economics, University of Pennsylvania; Consultant to United Nations.	Coauthor, Human capital
Lewis Beman Economics associate, *Business Week;* former associate editor, *Fortune.*	Supply-side economics
Anita M. Benvignati Brookings Economic Policy Fellow, U.S. Department of Treasury; project coordinator and author, *Wharton School Study of Foreign Investment in Pennsylvania.*	Barriers to trade; Dumping
Peter L. Bernstein President, Peter L. Bernstein, Inc.; Editor, *Journal of Portfolio Management.*	Mutual funds
Stanley W. Black Professor of Economics, Vanderbilt University; author, *Floating Exchange Rates and National Economic Policy.*	Foreign exchange rates
David M. Blank Vice President and Chief Economist, CBS Inc.; member, Board of Directors, Advertising Research Foundation.	Advertising, economic aspects
Mark Blaug Professor of the Economics of Education, University of London Institute of Education; former Visiting Professor in the History of Economic Thought, University of Manchester.	Cambridge school; Comparative advantage theory; Labor theory of value; Manchester school.
Arthur I. Bloomfield Professor of Economics, Wharton School, University of Pennsylvania; contributor, *The Economics of International Adjustment.*	Gold standard
Charlotte Boschan Senior Economist in Charge of Citibase, Citibank's Economic Database; coauthor, *Cyclical Analysis of Time Series— Selected Procedures and Computer Programs.*	Data banks
George E. P. Box Vilas Research Professor of Statistics,	Time series analysis

Name and Affiliation	**Articles**

University of Wisconsin; coauthor, *Time Series Analysis, Forecasting and Control.*

Thomas F. Brady
Economist, Division of Research and Statistics, Board of Governors of the Federal Reserve System; former Assistant Chief, Department of Banking and Financial Analysis, Bank of Canada.

Coauthor, Federal Reserve policy; coauthor, Federal Reserve System

George H. Brown
Corporate Secretary and Consultant to the President, Conference Board, Inc.; former Director, Bureau of the Census.

Conference Board, Inc.

William J. Brown
Professor of Finance, Northern Illinois University; former Senior Financial Economist, Office of the Comptroller of the Currency.

Bank deposits; Banking system; Federal Trade Commission; Financial institutions; Financial instruments

Brian C. Brush
Chariman, Department of Economics, Robert A. Johnson College of Business Administration, Marquette University; author of articles in *Journal of Industrial Economics.*

Economies of scale

M. L. Burstein
Visiting Professor of Economics, State University of New York at Buffalo; former Founding Professor of Economics, University College at Buckingham, England.

Business inventory; Change in business inventories in GNP; Stock-flow analysis

James L. Burtle
Vice President, Economics Group, W. R. Grace & Company; coauthor, *The Great Wheel, The International Monetary System.*

Exports; Foreign exchange management; Imports; Net exports in GNP

Gwen J. Bymers
Professor Emeritus, Department of Consumer Economics and Housing, New York State College of Human Ecology, Cornell University; former Chairman, Consumer Interests Committee, New York State.

Consumerism

Name and Affiliation	Articles
Colin D. Campbell Loren M. Berry Professor of Economics, Dartmouth College; Adjunct Scholar of American Enterprise Institute.	Chicago school
Jack Carlson Executive Vice President and Chief Executive Officer, National Association of Realtors; former Chief Economist, U.S. Chamber of Commerce.	Trade and professional associations
Benjamin Chinitz Vice President for Regional Development Research, ABT Associates; former President, Regional Science Association.	Regional economics; Urban economics
Ewan Clague Consulting Economist; former Commissioner of Labor Statistics, Bureau of Labor Statistics, U.S. Department of Labor.	Bureau of Labor Statistics
Bernard Clyman Economic Consultant; former Vice President, Office of Social Security Affairs, Equitable Life Assurance Society of the United States.	Social Security programs
Willard W. Cochrane Professor of Agricultural Economics and Public Affairs, University of Minnesota; former Director, Agricultural Economics, U.S. Department of Agriculture and Economic Adviser to Secretary of Agriculture.	Agricultural economic policy
Richard N. Cooper Under Secretary of State for International Economics, former Frank Altschul Professor of International Economics, Yale University.	Value of the dollar
John Cornwall Professor of Economics, Dalhousie University, Halifax, Canada; author, *Modern Capitalism: Its Growth and Transformation*.	Capitalism

Name and Affiliation

Articles

Bernard A. Corry
Head, Department of Economics, Queen Mary College, University of London; coeditor, *Essays in Honour of Lord Robbins.*

Consumers' surplus; Marshallian economics

Reavis Cox
Kresge Professor Emeritus of Marketing, University of Pennsylvania; author, *Distribution in a High Level Economy.*

Channels of marketing

Camilo Dagum
Professor of Economics, University of Ottawa; former Guest Scholar at Brookings Institution.

Coauthor, Index numbers; coauthor, Secular trend

Estela Bee Dagum
Director, Seasonal Adjustment and Time Series Analysis Staff, Statistics Canada; Adviser to Bureau of Labor Statistics and Bureau of the Census.

Coauthor, Index numbers; Seasonal adjustment methods; Seasonal variations; coauthor, Secular trend

Michael R. Darby
Professor of Economics, University of California at Los Angeles; author, *Intermediate Macroeconomics.*

Consumption function; Dynamic analysis; Dynamic macroeconomic models; IS-LM model; Permanent income hypothesis; Static analysis

Paul Davidson
Professor of Economics, Rutgers University; Editor, *Journal of Post-Keynesian Economics.*

Post-Keynesian economics

Thomas F. Dernburg
Staff Director, Subcommittee on Economic Stabilization, U.S. Senate Committee on Banking, Housing, and Urban Affairs; coauthor, *Macroeconomics.*

Automatic stabilizers; Macroeconomics

Ronald W. Dickey
Associate Dean, and Associate Professor of Economics and Finance, Samuel J. Silberman College of Business Administration, Fairleigh Dickinson University; coauthor, *Investing in New Jersey: A Guide to Common Stocks with Significant Growth Potential.*

Small business

Name and Affiliation	Articles
Dudley Dillard Professor of Economics, University of Maryland; author, *The Economics of John Maynard Keynes*.	Keynesian economics; Neo-Keynesian economics
Joseph W. Duncan Chief Statistician and Director, Office of Federal Statistical Policy and Standards, U.S. Department of Commerce; U.S. Representative to United Nations Statistical Commission.	Coauthor, Economic statistics
A. Ross Eckler Consultant; former Director, Bureau of the Census.	Bureau of the Census
M. Kathryn Eickhoff Vice President and Treasurer, Townsend-Greenspan and Company, Inc; coauthor, chapter in *Methods and Techniques of Business Forecasting*.	Anticipation surveys, business
Robert Eisner Walter R. Kenan Professor of Economics, Northwestern University; author, *Factors in Business Investment*.	Business investment in new plants and equipment; Capital formation; Investment function; Profits in economic theory
Holgar L. Engberg Professor of Economics, Graduate School of Business Administration, New York University; coauthor, *World Business Systems and Environment*.	Money markets
Martin Feldstein President, National Bureau of Economic Research; Professor of Economics, Harvard University.	National Bureau of Economic Research
Robert Ferber Professor of Economics and Director, Survey Research Laboratory, University of Illinois; editor, *Handbook of Marketing Research*.	Marketing research and business economics; Sampling in economics
Stanley Fischer Professor of Economics, Massachusetts Institute of Technology; Coauthor, *Macroeconomics*.	Indexation

Name and Affiliation	Articles
Karl A. Fox Distinguished Professor in Sciences and Humanities and Professor of Economics, Iowa State University; author, *Econometric Analysis for Public Policy*.	Coauthor, Cross-sectional analysis in business and economics; coauthor, Game theory, economic applications; coauthor, Regression analysis in business and economics; coauthor, Simultaneous equation estimates in business and economics
Arthur M. Freedman Professor of Economics, Wharton School, University of Pennsylvania, coauthor, *Money and Banking: Analysis and Policy*.	Gresham's law
Bernard S. Friedman Professor of Economics, Northwestern University.	Debt; Debt management; Scarcity; Subsidies
Gary Fromm Director, Center for Economic Policy Research, SRI International; coauthor, *Policy Simulations with an Econometric Model*.	Coauthor, Simulation in business and economics
Norman Frumkin Senior Statistician, Economic Statistics Branch, Office of Federal Statistical Policy and Standards; contributor to the Gross National Product Data Improvement Project.	Coauthor, Economic statistics
John Kenneth Galbraith Paul M. Warburg Professor of Economics Emeritus, Harvard University; author, *The New Industrial State*.	Countervailing power
Clayton Gehman Consultant; former Chief, Business Conditions Section, Division of Research and Statistics, Federal Reserve Board.	Industrial production index
Nicholas Georgescu-Roegen Distinguished Professor of Economics Emeritus, Vanderbilt University; author, "Utility and Value in Economic Thought," in *Dictionary of the History of Ideas*.	Utility

Name and Affiliation	Articles
William E. Gibson Senior Vice President, Economics and Financial Policy, McGraw-Hill, Inc.; former Director, Fixed-Income Research, Smith, Barney, Harris & Upham Co., Inc.	Portfolio management theories
Margaret S. Gordon Associate Director, Institute of Industrial Relations, University of California at Berkeley; author, *The Economics of Welfare Policies.*	Negative income tax
Peter T. Gottschalk Project Associate, Institute for Research on Poverty, University of Wisconsin; former Brookings Economic Policy Fellow, Office of Assistant Secretary for Planning and Evaluation, U.S. Department of Health, Education, and Welfare.	Poverty
John P. Gould Professor of Economics, Graduate School of Business, University of Chicago; coauthor, *Microeconomic Theory.*	Price theory
Edward M. Graham Principal Administrator, Planning and Evaluation Unit, Organization for Economic Cooperation and Development; principal author, *Technology, Trade, and the U.S. Economy.*	Foreign direct investment; General Agreement on Tariffs and Trade; Joint venture; Multinational corporation; Nationalization of industry; Protectionism
Douglas Greenwald Chief Editor, *Encyclopedia of Economics;* Chief Editor and coauthor, *McGraw-Hill Dictionary of Modern Economics.*	Council of Economic Advisers; Disposable personal income; Distribution theory; Government expenditures in GNP; Gross private domestic investment; Linear programming; Mercantilism; Personal consumption expenditures in GNP
John I. Griffin Dean, School of Business, Fairfield University; author, *Statistics, Methods and Applications.*	Statistical techniques in economics and business, an overview

Name and Affiliation	Articles
Jeanne L. Hafstrom Associate Professor and Acting Head, Department of Family and Consumer Economics, School of Human Resources and Family Studies, College of Agriculture, University of Illinois; former Office Manager, Department of Home Economics, University of Illinois.	Standard of living
George Harben Associate, Economics Department, Dean Witter; former Sales Manager, Hemphill, Noyes.	Coauthor, Closed-end investment companies; coauthor, Random walk hypothesis
Albert Gailord Hart Professor of Economics, Columbia University; author, *Anticipations, Uncertainty and Dynamic Planning.*	Economics
William J. Hausman Associate Professor of Economics, University of North Carolina at Greensboro; coauthor, "Structural Change in the Eighteenth Century British Economy," in *Explorations in Economic History.*	Industrial revolution
H. Robert Heller Vice President, International Economics, Bank of America; author, *International Monetary Economics.*	European Economic Community; International Monetary Fund; Organization for Economic Cooperation and Development; Special drawing rights
James M. Henderson Professor of Economics, University of Minnesota; author, *Microeconomics.*	Isoquant; Microeconomics; Production function
Walter G. Hoadley Executive Vice President and Chief Economist, Bank of America; former Chairman, Federal Reserve Bank of Philadelphia.	International economics, an overview
Werner Hochwald Tileston Professor Emeritus of Political Economy, Washington University in St. Louis; author, "An Economist's Image of History," in *Southern Economic Journal.*	Economic history and theory

Name and Affiliation	Articles

Charles Hoffman
Dean of Social Sciences and Professor of Economics, Queens College of the City University of New York; author, *Modern China.*

Maoism

Richard Hoffman
Consultant on Health Care Financing Cost Containment and Health Maintenance Organizations; Fellow, Society of Actuaries.

Medicare programs

Janos Horvath
John A. Arbuckle Professor of Economics and Research Scholar, Holcombe Research Institute, Butler University; author, *Chinese Technology Transfer to the Third World: A Grants Economy Analysis.*

Grants economics

Thomas M. Humphrey
Research Officer, Federal Reserve Bank of Richmond; author, *Essays on Inflation.*

Banking school; Currency school

A. J. Jaffe
Senior Research Associate, Graduate School of Business, Columbia University; Fellow, American Statistical Association.

Malthusian theory of population

George Jaszi
Director, Bureau of Economic Analysis, U.S. Department of Commerce; Fellow, National Association of Business Economists.

Bureau of Economic Analysis

Paul D. Johns
Executive Vice President, Market and Product Development, Chicago Board of Trade; Former Regional Marketing Manager, Midwest Region, IBM.

Commodity exchanges

D. Gale Johnson
Eliakim Hastings Moore Distinguished Service Professor of Economics and Provost, University of Chicago; editor, *Developments in American Farming: An Original Anthology.*

Agricultural productivity

Name and Affiliation	Articles

Robert W. Johnson
Director, Credit Research Center, Krannert Graduate School, Purdue University; former Presidential Appointee to National Commission on Consumer Credit.

Consumer credit

F. Thomas Juster
Director, Institute for Social Research, and Professor of Economics, University of Michigan; author, *Anticipations and Purchases: An Analysis of Consumer Behavior.*

Consumer theory; Expectations; Income

George Katona
One of Founders of and Research Coordinator of Survey Research Center, Institute for Social Research, University of Michigan; author, *Psychological Analysis of Economic Behavior.*

Anticipation surveys, consumer; Behavioral economics

Bernard S. Katz
Head, Department of Economics and Business, Lafayette College; author, *The Basic Theory and Policy of International Economics.*

Bretton Woods Conference; Infrastructure; Smithsonian Agreement; Stages theory of economic development

Tej K. Kaul
Post Doctoral Research Associate, Department of Economics, Iowa State University; coauthor, *Intermediate Economic Statistics,* vol. II: *A Guide to Recent Developments and Literature, 1968–78.*

Coauthor, Cross-sectional analysis in business and economics; coauthor, Game theory, economic applications; coauthor, Regression analysis in business and economics; coauthor, Simultaneous equation estimates in business and economics

John W. Kendrick
Professor of Economics, George Washington University; former Chief Economist, U.S. Department of Commerce.

Productivity; Wealth

Saul B. Klaman
President, National Association of Mutual Savings Banks; former member of Economic Advisory Board to the Secretary of Commerce.

Coauthor, Mortgage credit; coauthor, Thrift institutions

Name and Affiliation	Articles
John J. Klein Professor of Economics, Georgia State University; author, *Money and the Economy*.	Interest, economic theory; Real balance effect theory
Lawrence R. Klein Benjamin Franklin Professor of Economics, University of Pennsylvania; author, *An Introduction to Econometrics*.	Computers in economics; Econometrics; Economic models
Philip A. Klein Academic Visitor, London School of Economics and Political Science; Professor of Economics, Pennsylvania State University.	German historical school; Institutional economics; Kuznets cycles
Fred H. Klopstock U.S. Representative of the Caisse Centrale des Banques Populaire; former Adviser in the Foreign Function, Federal Reserve Bank of New York.	Eurodollar market
Robert E. L. Knight Associate Professor of Economics, University of Maryland; author. *Industrial Relations in the San Francisco Bay Area*.	Zero population growth
James W. Knowles Consulting Economist; former Executive Director, Joint Economic Committtee of the U.S. Congress.	Joint Economic Committee of Congress
Lewis Koflowitz Financial editor, *Metalworking News;* former Economist, McGraw-Hill Publications' Economics Department, and coauthor, *McGraw-Hill Dictionary of Modern Economics*.	Acceleration principle; Division of labor
John L. Komives President, Lakeshore Group Ltd.; Adjunct Professor, Graduate School of Management, Northwestern University.	Venture capital
Walther Lederer Contributor to a study on Capital Investment and Savings, Sponsored by the American Council of Life Insurance; former Senior Advisor for Balance of Payments Analysis and Projections, Office of the Assistant Secretary of International Affairs, U.S. Department of the Treasury.	Balance of international payments; Balance of international trade

Name and Affiliation	**Articles**
Joong-Koon Lee Associate Professor of Economics, University of Cincinnati; former Assistant Professor of Economics, New York University.	Money illusion
Brian E. Leverich Operations Research Consultant, Rand Corporation; Operations Research Consultant, Institute for Defense Analysis.	Operations research
Michael E. Levy Director, Economic Policy Research, The Conference Board; editor and senior author, *The Federal Budget: Its Impact on the Economy.*	Federal budget; Federal budget process; Fiscal policy
Fred J. Levin Manager, Securities Department, Federal Reserve Bank of New York; author of articles on money stock control.	Coauthor, Open-market operations
Robert E. Lewis Vice President, Economics Department, Citibank, and responsible for Citibank's corporate profit surveys; former Chairman of the Federal Statistics Users Conference.	Profits measurement
Herman I. Liebling Frank Lee and Edna Smith Professor of Economics and Business, Lafayette College; former Senior Economic Adviser, U.S. Treasury Department.	Economic forecasts; Forecasting methods; Gross national product; Phillips curve; Stagflation
Fabian Linden Director, Consumer Research, Conference Board; author, *Consumer of the Seventies.*	Demographics and economics
Richard W. Lindholm Director, Business Regulation Study Center and Professor of Finance and Dean Emeritus College of Business, University of Oregon; author, *Value Added Tax and Other Tax Reforms.*	Value-added tax
Hugh Macauley Alumni Professor of Economics, College of Industrial Management and Textile Science, Clemson University; coauthor, *Environmental Use and the Market.*	Externalities

Name and Affiliation	Articles

Fritz Machlup
Professor of Economics, New York University; former President, American Economic Association.

Austrian economics; Marginal revenue

H. Michael Mann
Professor of Economics, Boston College; contributor of article, "Advertising, Concentration and Profitability: The State of Knowledge and Directions for Public Policy," in *Industrial Concentration: The New Learning.*

Concentration of industry

Stephen Martin
Assistant Professor of Economics, Michigan State University.

Cartel

G. H. Mattersdorff
Professor of Economics and Public Administration, Lewis and Clark College; former Economist, McGraw-Hill Publications' Economics Department, and coauthor, *McGraw-Hill Dictionary of Modern Economics.*

Diminishing returns law; Economic rent; Physiocrats

Edward G. Mayers
Coauthor, *McGraw-Hill Dictionary of Modern Economics;* former Senior Economist, McGraw-Hill Publication Company's Department of Economics, and responsible for McGraw-Hill's pension fund management surveys.

Monopoly and oligopoly; Monopsony and oligopsony; Pension funds

Roger A. McCain
Associate Professor of Economics, School of Business Administration, Temple University; author, *Markets, Decisions and Organizations: Intermediate Microeconomic Theory.*

Firm theory

Martin C. McGuire
Professor of Economics, University of Maryland; former Ford Foundation Visiting Research Professor, University of California, Berkeley.

Normative economics

Robert L. McLaughlin
President, Micrometrics, Inc.; Author, "A New Five-Phase Economic Forecasting System," in *Business Economics.*

Leading indicator approach to forecasting

Name and Affiliation	**Articles**
Gardiner C. Means Retired; author, *Administrative Inflation and Public Policy.*	Administered prices
A. James Meigs Chairman of the Board, Claremont Economics Institute and Professor of Economics, Claremont Men's College; author, *Money Matters: Economics, Markets, Politics.*	Money supply; Quantity theory of money; Velocity of circulation of money
Paul A. Meyer Associate Professor of Economics, University of Maryland; coauthor, *Probabilities and Potential.*	Say's law of markets
Geoffrey H. Moore Director, Center for International Business Cycle Research, Rutgers University; author, *Business Cycles, Inflation and Forecasting.*	Business cycles; Diffusion indexes
Arnold X. Moskowitz Vice President, Research and Economics, Dean Witter Reynolds, Inc.; author, *Security Selection and Active Portfolio Management.*	Coauthor, Closed-end investment companies; coauthor, Random walk hypothesis
Laurence S. Moss Associate Professor of Economics, Babson College; editor, Karl Pribram's manuscript, *History of Economic Reasoning.*	Classical liberalism; Classical school; Laissez faire; Liberalism; Neoclassical economics; Reform liberalism
Charles H. Movit Research Associate, Center for Economic Policy Research, SRI International; author, articles on modeling of planned economies.	Coauthor, Simulation in business and economics
R. Charles Moyer Professor of Finance, Robert O. Anderson Graduate School of Management, University of New Mexico; Coauthor, *Contemporary Financial Management.*	Opportunity cost
John G. Myers Professor of Economics, Southern Illinois University at Carbondale; former Research Director, The Conference Board.	Energy costs

Name and Affiliation	Articles
Egon N. Neuberger Professor of Economics, State University of New York at Stony Brook; coauthor, *Comparative Economic Systems: A Decision Making Approach.*	Comparative economic systems, an overview
John B. Nicholson Director, Consumer and Regulatory Affairs, Washington Office, National Association of Realtors; former Executive Vice President, National Association of Real Estate Investment Trusts.	Real estate investment trusts
John H. Niedercorn Associate Professor of Economics and Urban and Regional Planning, University of Southern California; coauthor, *Recent Land Use Trends in Forty-Eight Large American Cities.*	Location theory
Arthur M. Okun Senior Fellow, Economic Studies Program, Brookings Institution; former Chairman, Council of Economic Advisers to the President.	Potential gross national product
James J. O'Leary Economic Consultant and former Vice Chairman, United States Trust Company; former President, American Finance Association.	Capital markets and money markets
Robert W. Oliver Professor of Economics, California Institute of Technology; author, *International Economic Cooperation and the World Bank.*	World Bank
Janusz A. Ordover Associate Professor of Economics, New York University; Member, Technical Staff, Bell Laboratories.	Marginal cost
Rudolph Oswald Director, Department of Research, American Federation of Labor and Congress of Industrial Organizations; President, Industrial Relations Research Association.	Labor unions

Name and Affiliation	Articles
William N. Parker Professor of Economics, Yale University; former President, Economic History Association.	Agricultural revolution
Henry M. Peskin Senior Fellow, Resources for the Future; Adviser to Environmental Directorate, OECD.	Environmental costs
William H. Peterson Holder of the Scott L. Probasco Jr. Chair of Free Enterprise, and Director, Center for Economic Education, University of Tennessee at Chattanooga; former Economist and Assistant to the Chairman of the Finance Committee, United States Steel Corporation.	Capital-intensive industry; Government regulation of business; Return on investment; Right-to-work law
Solomon Polachek Associate Professor of Economics and Fellow at the Carolina Population Center, University of North Carolina; Hoover Institution National Fellowship at Stanford University.	Discrimination economics
Joel Popkin Owner, Joel Popkin Company; former Assistant Commissioner for Prices, Bureau of Labor Statistics, U.S. Department of Labor.	Consumer price index; Cost of living; Escalator clause; Implicit price deflator; Price measurement; Producer price index
Rosemary Rainey Economist, Board of Governors of the Federal Reserve System; former Staff Economist, Council of Economic Advisers to the President.	Coauthor, Incomes policy
Roger L. Ransom Professor of Economics, University of California at Riverside; coauthor, *One Kind of Freedom: The Economic Consequences of Emancipation.*	Great Depression
Richard Roehl Chairman, Department of Social Sciences and Professor of Economics and History, University of Michigan at Dearborn; author, *French Industrialization: A Reconsideration.*	Fascism

Name and Affiliation	Articles

Joshua Ronen
Assistant Director, the Vincent C. Ross Institute of Accounting Research, College of Business and Public Administration, New York University; Professor of Accounting, New York University Graduate School of Business Administration.

Break-even analysis; Financial statements

Sally S. Ronk
Financial Economist, U.S. Department of the Treasury; former Vice President and Chief Economist, Drexel Burnham & Co.

Flow of funds; Saving

Jack Rubinson
Director of Research and Economics, National Association of Mutual Savings Banks; coauthor "Mortgage Market: Structure and Characteristics," *Financial Analysts Handbook.*

Coauthor, Mortgage credit; coauthor, Thrift institutions

Nancy Ruggles
Coauthor, *National Income Accounting and Income Analysis;* coauthor, *The Design of Economic Accounts.*

Coauthor, Factor cost; coauthor, National income accounting

Richard Ruggles
Professor of Economics, Yale University; coauthor, *National Income Accounting and Income Analysis.*

Coauthor, Factor cost; coauthor, National income accounting

R. Robert Russell
Director, Council on Wage and Price Stability; former Professor of Economics, University of California, San Diego.

Council on Wage and Price Stability

Peter G. Sassone
Associate Professor, College of Industrial Management, Georgia Institute of Technology; coauthor, *Cost Benefit Analysis: A Handbook*

Cost-benefit analysis; Welfare economics

Raymond J. Saulnier
Professor Emeritus of Economics, Barnard College, Columbia University; former Chairman of Council of Economic Advisers to the President.

Credit, an overview; Selective credit controls

Name and Affiliation	**Articles**
Francis H. Schott Vice President and Chief Economist, the Equitable Life Assurance Society of the U.S.; former Adjunct Professor of Economics, Baruch College, City University of New York.	Disintermediation; Interest rates; Variable annuity
Eli Shapiro A. P. Sloan Professor of Management, MIT; former Professor of Finance, Harvard University.	Business credit
Howard J. Sherman Professor of Economics, University of California at Riverside; author, *The Soviet Economy*.	Communism; Marxism; Socialism
Mark Sherwood Economist, Prices and Living Conditions, Bureau of Labor Statistics, U.S. Department of Labor.	Family budgets
Richard E. Slitor Economic Consultant; author, *Tax Incentives*.	Depletion allowance; Depreciation allowance
Dan Throop Smith Director, Cambridge Research Institute; author, *Federal Tax Reform*.	Capital gains; Taxation, an overview
Arthur Smithies Professor of Economics, Harvard University; coeditor, *Public Policy Yearbook*, vols. 13 and 15.	Propensity to consume or to save and inducement to invest; Stagnation thesis
Charles W. Smithson Assistant Professor of Economics, Texas A.&M. University; coauthor, *The Economics of Mineral Extraction*.	Factors of production; Capital; Entrepreneurial ability; Labor; Land
Eugene Smolensky Chair, Department of Economics, University of Wisconsin; coauthor, *Aggregate Supply and Demand Analysis*.	Income distribution; Lorenz curve
Ira Sohn Adjunct Assistant Professor of Economics and affiliated with the Institute for Economic Analysis, New York University; author, articles integrated with the input-output technique.	Economic planning

Name and Affiliation	Articles
Robert Solomon Senior Fellow, Foreign Policy Studies Program, Brookings Institution; former Director, Division of International Finance, Board of Governors of the Federal Reserve System as well as Adviser to the Board.	Liquidity, International
Hugo Sonnenschein Professor of Economics, Princeton University; Editor, *Econometrica*.	General equilibrium
Joseph B. Starshak Second Vice President, Corporate Finance Division, Northern Trust Company.	Risk premium on investment
Peter D. Sternlight Senior Vice President, Open-Market Operations, and Treasury Issues Functions, Federal Reserve Bank of New York; Deputy Under Secretary for Monetary Affairs, U.S. Department of Treasury.	Coauthor, Open-market operations
Charles D. Stewart Consultant; former Director, OECD Affairs, U.S. Department of Labor.	Employment and unemployment; Labor force
Theodore Suranyi-Unger, Jr. Research Professor of Economics, George Washington University; former Economist, National Science Foundation.	Innovation; Research and development; Technology
Alan Sweezy Professor of Economics, California Institute of Technology; former Professor of Economics, Williams College.	Multiplier
Paul J. Taubman Professor of Economics, University of Pennsylvania; author, *Income Distribution and Redistribution*.	Coauthor, Human capital
Lester G. Telser Professor of Economics, University of Chicago; author, *Competition, Collusion and Game Theory*.	Arbitrage; Competition

Name and Affiliation	Articles

Nestor E. Terleckyj
Vice President and Director of Domestic Research Centers, National Planning Association; author, *Household Production and Consumption*.

Economic growth

James Tobin
Sterling Professor of Economics, Yale University; former President of The American Economic Association.

Inflation

Lloyd M. Valentine
Professor of Economics, University of Cincinnati; coauthor, *Business Cycles and Forecasting*.

Juglar cycle; Kitchin cycle; Kondratieff cycle

Henry C. Wallich
Member, Board of Governors of the Federal Reserve System; former Seymour H. Knox Professor of Economics, Yale University.

Coauthor, Federal Reserve policy; coauthor, Federal Reserve System; coauthor, Incomes policy

Donald S. Watson
Professor of Economics, Emeritus, George Washington University; coauthor, *Price Theory and Its Uses*.

Cobweb theorem; Demand; Elasticity; Supply

C. Edward Weber
Professor of Policy and Management Studies, School of Business Administration, University of Wisconsin; former Dean, School of Business Administration, University of Wisconsin at Milwaukee.

Decision making in business: a behavioral approach

Edgar Weinberg
Senior Labor Economist, Office of the Assistant Secretary for Policy, Evaluation and Research, U.S. Department of Labor; former Assistant Director, National Center for Productivity and Quality of Working Life.

Automation

Thomas E. Weisskopf
Professor of Economics, University of Michigan; coauthor, *The Capitalist System: A Radical Analysis of American Society*.

Radical economics

Name and Affiliation	Articles
J. Fred Weston Professor of Managerial Economics and Finance and Director, Research Program in Competition and Business Policy, Graduate School of Management, University of California at Los Angeles; author, *The Impact of Large Firms on the U.S. Economy.*	Conglomerate; Liquidity, corporate; Mergers
Simon N. Whitney Adjunct Professor, Graduate Division of Business Administration, Iona College; author, *Antitrust Policies.*	Antitrust policy; Restraint of trade
William C. Young Research Analyst, Economics Division, National Association of Home Builders; author of articles for NAHB's *Economic News Notes.*	Housing economics
Victor Zarnowitz Professor of Economics and Finance, Graduate School of Business, University of Chicago; author, "How Accurate Have the Forecasts Been," in *Methods and Techniques of Business Forecasting.*	Accuracy of economic forecasts
Howell H. Zee Teaching Fellow, University of Maryland; former Economist, International Monetary Fund.	Zero economic growth
Arnold Zellner H. G. B. Alexander Professor of Economics and Statistics, Graduate School of Business, University of Chicago; editor, *Bayesian Analysis in Econometrics and Statistics: Essays in Honor of Harold Jeffreys.*	Bayesian inference

Preface

The purpose of the *Encyclopedia of Economics* is to bring together the expertise of distinguished contributors from the academic, business, and government sectors in order to provide a reference book of highest-quality authorship.

An encyclopedia is essentially a reference book. Its scope and contents should, therefore, be suitable for the needs of the readers. The articles in the *Encyclopedia* are written for readers with widely varying levels of knowledge and sophistication.

In order to serve both the student who merely is looking up something and the serious scholar who is looking for an authoritative statement on a subject of great importance to him or to her, we have attempted to provide a list of the most important subjects and articles written on those subjects that are meaningful and useful.

The idea for the *Encyclopedia of Economics* was generated by Joseph Dooher, a former economics editor of and more recently a consultant to the McGraw-Hill Book Company. He had felt for some time that it was important for McGraw-Hill to publish a completely new reference book of economics, a one-volume encyclopedia.

He came to me with the idea because, at the time, I was Vice President, Economics, of the McGraw-Hill Publications Company and was chief editor and coauthor of the successful and useful *McGraw-Hill Dictionary of Modern Economics*. I thought the idea was good, so we brought it to the attention of William Mogan, who was at the time the economics editor for the Professional and Research Book Division of the McGraw-Hill Book Company. He, and subsequently, other members of the Book Company staff thought the idea had great merit. Then they asked me to serve as chief editor of the *Encyclopedia*, to which I agreed. Thus, the project was launched.

The first step in organizing the *Encyclopedia* was to decide on the subjects that should be included. When the project was started, it was agreed that the *Encyclopedia of Economics* would cover important subjects from the related fields of econometrics and statistics, no matter how complex these subjects were.

A basic list of about 200 subjects was compiled from the roughly 1400 terms covered in the *McGraw-Hill Dictionary of Modern Economics*. The 200 subjects were chosen because they were important in economics and because they could be expanded well beyond their brevity in the *Dictionary*.

This list was then circulated among 50 economists in business, academia, and government for suggestions of additional subjects or deletions. The list of economists who cooperated in compiling the final list of subjects for the *Encyclopedia* follows:

Henry Arnold (*Pace College*), Kenneth Boulding (*University of Colorado*), William Brown (*Northern Illinois University*), Daniel Creamer (*Conference Board*), James Dawson (*National City Bank of Cleveland*), Robert Eggert (*Eggert Economic Enter-*

prise), Robert Eisner (Northwestern University), Richard Everett (Chase Manhattan Bank), William Hoppe (Bethlehem Steel Corporation), Dawson Johnson (Office of Management and the Budget), Richard Karfunkle (Econoviews International), Dexter Keezer (Retired), John Kendrick (George Washington University), L. Douglas Lee (Joint Economic Committee), Robert E. Lewis (Citibank), Herman I. Liebling (Lafayette College), Richard W. Lindholm (University of Oregon), Alfred Litwak (Johns Manville Corporation), G. H. Mattersdorff (Lewis and Clark College), Lawrence Mayer (Council on Economic Education), Edward Mayers (McGraw-Hill), Donald McCloskey (University of Chicago), Gordon McKinley (McGraw-Hill), George McKinney (Irving Trust Company), Robert McLaughlin (Micrometrics, Inc.), Paul McCracken (University of Michigan), Lynn Michaelis (Weyerhauser, Inc.), David Munro (Council of Economic Advisers), Robinson Newcomb (Consultant), Richard Parry (Skogmo), Richard Peterson (Continental Bank), William Peterson (University of Tennessee, Chattanooga), Charles Reeder (E. I. du Pont de Nemours & Company), Joseph Zeisel (Board of Governors, Federal Reserve System)

At the end of this phase of the project, a consensus developed and 310 subjects were selected for the Encyclopedia.

At this stage of the organization of the Encyclopedia, I had to decide on the length of each article. I decided on the number of pages for each article based on my notion of the relative importance of the subject and what would be appropriate for a one-volume encyclopedia. However, authors often find it difficult to keep their articles within prescribed page limits. On one hand, I was limited by the size of the volume, but on the other hand, I wanted the highest quality of authorship. Thus, it turned out that when the articles came in I was more flexible about length of article than I might have been.

A dictionary of economics can be written by one economist or very few since it usually merely defines economic terms. But many experts in specific fields of economics are needed to write articles for an encyclopedia of economics in which subjects are dealt with in great detail. So the next step in organizing the Encyclopedia was to select for each of the 310 articles the most qualified economist, econometrician, or statistician we could find in order to make the Encyclopedia a very authoritative volume.

This was carried out by sending the list of 310 subjects to about 75 business, academic, and government social scientists and asking them to suggest one or more experts who could write on each of the subjects to be covered in the Encyclopedia. None of the respondents to this questionnaire listed names for every subject. But some did list names for as many as 100 subjects, while, at the other extreme, one or two respondents provided names for only one or two subjects. And some of the members of this advisory panel listed themselves as experts on specific subjects. The list of people who provided the names of qualified potential authors for subjects in the Encyclopedia follows:

Walter Adams (Michigan State University), Henry Arnold (Pace College), Kathryn Arnow (Consultant), Jere R. Behrman (University of Pennsylvania), Bela Belassa (World Bank), Kenneth Boulding (University of Colorado), William Brown (Northern Illinois University), Hollis Chenery (World Bank), Robert Clower (University of California at Los Angeles), Don R. Conlan (Capital Strategic Services), Daniel

Creamer (Conference Board, Inc.), George Dantzig (Stanford University), James Dawson (National City Bank of Cleveland), Gerard Debreu (University of California at Berkeley), Rudiger Dornbusch (Massachusetts Institute of Technology), Robert Eggert (Eggert Economic Enterprise), Robert Eisner (Northwestern University), Edgar R. Fiedler (Conference Board, Inc.), Irwin Friend (University of Pennsylvania), Tilford Gaines (Manufacturers Hanover Trust Company), Glenn Hueckel (Purdue University), George Jaszi (U.S. Department of Commerce), John Kendrick (George Washington University), Avram Kisselgoff (Consultant), Saul Klaman (National Association of Mutual Savings Banks), Nathan Koffsky (International Food Policy Research), Irving Kravis (University of Pennsylvania), Leo Leiderman (Boston University), Wassily Leontief (New York University), Michael Levy (Conference Board, Inc.), Robert E. Lewis (Citibank), Herman I. Liebling (Lafayette College), Edward Lucas (University of California), Edward Mansfield (University of Pennsylvania), Martin Marimont (U.S. Department of Commerce), G. H. Mattersdorff (Lewis and Clark College), Lawrence Mayer (Council on Economic Education), Edward Mayers (McGraw-Hill), Donald McCloskey (University of Chicago), Paul McCracken (University of Michigan), David Meiselman (Virginia Polytechnic Institute), Marcus Miller (University of Warwick), Edward Mishan (London School of Economics and Political Science), John Montias (Yale University), Geoffrey H. Moore (Rutgers University), Mancur Olson (University of Maryland), Joel Popkin (Joel Popkin and Company), Charles Reeder (E. I. du Pont de Nemours & Company), Sally S. Ronk (Treasury Department), Robert Roosa (Brown Harriman), Arnold Sametz (New York University), Raymond J. Saulnier (Barnard College), F. M. Scherer (Northwestern University), Gary Seevers (Goldman Sachs), William Shepherd (University of Michigan), Herbert Simon (Carnegie-Mellon University), Robert M. Solow (Massachusetts Institute of Technology), Milton Spencer (Wayne State University), Joseph S. Spengler (Duke University), William H. Starbuck (University of Wisconsin), George J. Stigler (University of Chicago), Conrad Taeuber (Joseph and Rose Kennedy Institute of Ethics), William Vickery (Columbia University), Murrary Weidenbaum (Washington University in St. Louis), William Wolman (Business Week)

This survey provided at least two names of qualified potential authors for each subject and, in some cases, perhaps as many as 15 names for a subject. I selected the name of the expert to whom the panel had given the most votes for a specific subject. In some cases the same person was chosen for several subjects.

I then wrote to these people and asked them to prepare the article or articles for the *Encyclopedia*. Replies came back quickly. The rate of acceptance among the group of invited contributors was very high. Often when my number 1 choice could not write the article or articles because of time restraints, he or she would suggest a qualified candidate to prepare the article or articles. In turn, I would write to them to cooperate in this project, and most of them agreed to contribute to the *Encyclopedia*. Thus the *Encyclopedia* consists mainly of articles prepared expressly for it at the request of the chief editor. However, some articles were dropped from the list when a topic was deemed inappropriate or when a qualified contributor could not be found.

Incidentally, no one declined to contribute because he or she saw no need for an encyclopedia. Rather, most of the people who agreed to contribute articles indicated that they thought it was a very good idea to publish a one-volume *Encyclopedia of Economics*.

There are 178 authors for the 303 articles in the *Encyclopedia* and each of the contributors is an expert or is extremely knowledgeable about the subject or subjects on which he or she wrote for the *Encyclopedia*. A listing of authors with a bit more biographical material than just their current affiliations follows the table of contents.

Authors took their assignments serious. Several asked about the level of the audience which the *Encyclopedia* was expected to reach. I thought it best not to insist that the contributors aim at a particular intellectual level, but I often suggested that their articles should be aimed at the graduate level. One thing I did not want the authors to do was to write down to the readers. Other authors asked for clarification on the direction an article should take. Still others asked how the article they were preparing would fit in with other articles covered in the *Encyclopedia*.

Some authors procrastinated. But most contributors were conscientious about meeting delivery dates, getting their articles in within a month or two of the deadlines I had set. However, a few of them never delivered articles that they had agreed to prepare. I am very grateful to those contributors who stepped in and completed articles that others had promised previously but never delivered. At the very last minute, I personally prepared several articles that I felt could not be omitted from the *Encyclopedia*.

All articles were edited and reviewed by myself and Margaret Sylvester, former business economist and editor in the McGraw-Hill Publications Company's Department of Economics. Some articles were reviewed by Martin J. Pring of Pring Research Associates, Inc.; Robert Schultz, consulting economist; Avram Kisselgoff, consulting economist; Lawrence Mayer of the Joint Council on Economic Education; Donald Adams, Assistant Vice Preisdent of Financial Policy, McGraw-Hill, Inc.; and John Stodden, Director of Editorial Services, McGraw-Hill Publications Company's Department of Economics.

The articles were reviewed primarily for clarity and for the appropriateness of content. Since the articles were written by experts or knowledgeable people in their specific fields, our criticisms were generally minor. Virtually all of the editors' suggestions for revisions were agreed upon by the authors.

The subjects and the written articles in the *Encyclopedia* vary widely in degree of complexity. It is obvious that many technical subjects are difficult to write about. No matter how hard they try, experts cannot make very complex subjects simplistic without distorting some of the meaning. The editors, as well as the reviewers, recognized this problem. However, we called attention to some very complex sections of complex articles, which were probably well beyond the level of comprehension of readers with limited technical training. Even so, we decided that readers with limited technical training would probably not look up articles on those complex subjects in the first place.

Largely because biographical source material is hard to find, there are no biographical articles in the *Encyclopedia*. References are made throughout to individual economists who founded, helped to develop, and popularized economic schools and economic theories. A volume on biographies of economists, living and dead, may be organized for the future.

The subject matter of the *Encyclopedia of Economics* does not easily lend itself to an alphabetical arrangement. But it was decided early on that an alphabetic order would be the most useful to readers since they generally first consult an alphabetically located entry. Thus, in alphabetizing the subjects we have tried to list the articles by the subject we think the reader would look up. However, other guides to the location of articles in the *Encyclopedia* are provided. For example, an alternative entry to the subject "Profits in economic theory" is the line entry "Economic theory of profits."

No one reads a dictionary from cover to cover and I am certain that no one reads an encyclopedia from cover to cover. Readers, however, expect to learn considerably more about a specific subject from a more important reference book such as an encyclopedia than they would from a dictionary. And the *Encyclopedia of Economics* is no exception.

Moreover, the *Encyclopedia* is thoroughly cross-referenced and indexed, with extensive bibliographical references to guide the reader who wants to know more about the subject and how it relates to other subjects. And each article in the *Encyclopedia* is self-contained.

Thus, the *Encyclopedia of Economics* is an indispensable tool for practitioners, teachers, and graduate and undergraduate students in economics, econometrics, and statistics.

I would like to thank all of the economists who helped in providing additional subjects for the *Encyclopedia* and those who provided the names of qualified contributors as well as those who reviewed the various articles.

I would also like to acknowledge exceptional secretarial help, in the course of organizing and preparing the *Encyclopedia* for publication, from Dianne Brennan, Carol Mann, Margaret DeJoy, and Mary McGee of McGraw-Hill.

The McGraw-Hill Library and its helpful staff also deserve thanks. Members of the staff contributed mightily to the preparation of the bibliographies in the *Encyclopedia.*

I must also thank my wife Mickey for her enthusiastic support and encouragement while I was organizing and editing the *Encyclopedia.* In an emergency, she even did some typing for me.

Finally, I thank the authors of all the excellent articles that make up this encyclopedia. Although their financial rewards were relatively small, their contribution in terms of time and effort was very large. In particular, I would like to thank Werner Hochwald, who wrote the article on economic history and theory, for an illuminating timetable of economic events, technological developments, financial developments, and economic thought to go along as background for his article, but which I found so outstanding that I have included it as the *Encyclopedia*'s Appendix II. Please be sure to look at this comprehensive timetable. Appendix I consists of a listing of the articles classified by economic field.

Douglas Greenwald

Acceleration principle

The acceleration principle received its name from the accelerated effect of a change in production or income on levels of investment—equipment or inventory. Acceleration can work in both positive and negative directions. When output grows, acceleration in investment is positive; when output declines, acceleration is negative. Thus, net investment—additions to the capital stock—will occur only when production or income is growing.

Only machinery replacement needs are determined by the absolute level of output in the user industry. The demand for additional machinery capacity depends on the rate of growth of user-industry output.

Let us assume that a manufacturer of paper machinery needs $3 of capital for every $1 of production and that the manufacturer has annual replacement cost equal to 10 percent of the previous year's capital stock. The accompanying table shows that output rises by $5 million between periods 1 and 2, while capital stock must be expanded by $15 million. Then between periods 2 and 3, output increases by $15

Period	Output of paper	Capital stock required	Net investment	Replacement investment	Gross investment
1	$100*	$300	$ 0	$30.0	$ 30.0
2	105	315	15	30.0	45.0
3	120	360	45	31.5	76.5
4	150	450	90	36.0	126.0
5	150	450	0	45.0	45.0
6	130	390	−60	45.0	−15.0

*All figures are in millions of dollars.

1

million, while capital stock goes up $45 million. Thus, a less than 15 percent increase in paper output induces a 200 percent increase in net investment in paper machinery and a 70 percent increase in gross investment. Between periods 3 and 4, paper output increases 25 percent, while net investment doubles and gross investment rises about 65 percent. If demand for paper were to continue to rise in future periods, increases in paper equipment orders would take place in every year. But paper output has to keep growing every year in order for paper machinery investment to grow.

If paper production stabilizes at the high level of $150 million, as in period 5, net investment will drop to zero for a decline of 100 percent, and gross investment will drop about 64 percent. A shrinkage in the rate of growth of paper production, as in period 6, results in sharply reduced demand for paper machinery. Both net investment and gross investment become negative.

Inventory Accumulation

Inventory accumulation is another example of the acceleration principle that helps to explain short inventory cycles and inventory recessions.

Basically, stocks of goods tend to be held in some proportion to sales per time unit. If the marketable output of each seller rises at a rate Y, sellers will usually place orders at the firms from whom they buy, not only for the increase in marketable output but also for an increase due to planned inventory levels. If at a later date sales stabilize at a high level, then orders placed by the sellers will diminish, not stabilize, at the high level. This is because the sellers will then order the same quantity of goods for sales to their customers as they did earlier, but they will not order the additional goods for further increases in inventories. If at a still later date sales decline from peak levels, in order to reduce their stocks sellers will cut their levels of ordering sharply.

The acceleration principle has some limitations. Among them are the following:

1. The principle assumes full-capacity operations at all times, which obviously is not the case.

2. The theory assumes that gross investment can fall below zero, which is impossible.

3. The theory does not take account of expectations, which may raise or lower capital investment.

4. The principle ignores the fact that complex machinery sometimes takes as long as 5 years to build, not 1 year.

5. The principle assumes a fixed relationship between output and capital stock, which may not be true.

John M. Clark introduced the acceleration principles in 1917 to explain proportionately larger variations in investment over the course of a business cycle than those which occurred in consumer goods output. Interest in the accelerator as a theoretical tool expanded after 1936, when it was combined with the Keynesian consumption function to formulate self-generating models of the business cycle.

References

Clark, John M., "Business Acceleration and the Law of Demand: A Technical Factor in Economic Cycles," *Journal of Political Economy*, vol. xxv, no. 3, 1917, pp. 217–235, reprinted in

Readings in Business Cycle Theory, Irwin, Homewood, Ill., 1951, pp. 235–260; Dernburg, Thomas F., and Duncan M. McDougall, *Macroeconomics*, 5th ed, McGraw-Hill, New York, 1976, pp. 272–280; Fellner, William, *Modern Economic Analysis*, McGraw-Hill, New York, 1960; Samuelson, Paul A., "Interactions Between the Multiplier Analysis and the Principle of Acceleration," *Review of Economics and Statistics*, vol. 21, 1939, pp. 78–88.

(*See also* Investment function)

Lewis Koflowitz

Accuracy of economic forecasts

That forecasts be verifiable is an essential requirement of evaluating their accuracy. Some predictions are so vague, broad, or hedged as to be trivial. Some have the opposite fault of being pretentious—spuriously precise, given the quality of the measurements to which they refer. Still others rely on entirely improbable conditions, which render them meaningless. But such gross defects are no longer widely ignored or tolerated, and they seem to be relatively uncommon among present-day economic forecasts.

The main purpose of economic forecasts is to help formulate and improve public and private plans and decisions. Thus it seems reasonable to evaluate the forecasts principally by their relative accuracy. It seems natural to most people to discriminate among forecasting sources, methods, or models according to past accuracy: the lower the errors, the higher the given set of predictions is ranked. In effect, the accuracy of a set of predictions is frequently viewed as the principal single aspect of its quality.

In any event, it is clear that forecasts must be properly evaluated if the makers of forecasts are to learn from past errors and if the users of forecasts are to choose intelligently among the available sources and methods. Without dependable accuracy assessments, informed comparisons of costs and returns associated with forecasting are impossible.

Types of Forecasts and Assessments

The forecasting procedures that are most widely used can be broadly classified as follows:

1. Various types of extrapolation of past values or behavior of time series, ranging from simple projections of levels, changes, or trends to sophisticated stochastic models

2. Observations from the evidence of series with systematic properties of timing in the business cycle, particularly the leading indicators in relation to others that tend to move more sluggishly

3. Econometric models, that is, single-equation regression and multiequation simulation models designed to represent certain quantitative relationships among the pertinent economic variables and estimated primarily with time series or other statistical data

4. Surveys of intentions and anticipations by units making economic decisions.

These methods and techniques serve different purposes but may often complement each other; for example, regressions with distributed lags may be used to predict the coincident from the leading indicators; indexes based on anticipation surveys may be incorporated in econometric models; a time series model may be developed to explain the residuals, i.e., error terms, in a regression equation. Forecasters may favor one or another of these approaches, depending on their purposes, interests, etc., but, they typically use various combinations of them in a more or less judgmental fashion. Judgment, of course, enters the forecasting process at several stages, in the choice of data, models, and methods as well as in the assessment and use of the results.

Depending on the type of the forecast, different appraisals of the predictive process and its results can be made. These include (1) ex ante and ex post model evaluations; (2) checks on the data inputs and estimation procedures; (3) monitoring, measuring, and analyzing errors of forecasts; (4) comparisons with a hierarchy of standards of predictive performance; and, (5) combinations of different predictors and assessment of their respective contributions to the joint forecasts.

Econometric and Time Series Models   If a forecast is based on a model of relations among economic variables, it is desirable and usually possible to assess that model in the light of economic theory. However, the forecaster probably will have selected the model specifications after experimentation with alternatives. This is because the clues from theory and prior beliefs of the forecaster seldom are sufficient for the forecaster to choose a model that could not be improved upon with the aid of the available and potentially relevant data. But the experimentation creates the danger of choosing an incorrect model that for accidental reasons happens to fit the data well. For this reason, it is important that a record be kept of the various steps taken in developing the model. The same applies to any subsequent model changes and also to any approximations and ad hoc procedures that may have been used, particularly the adjustments of constant terms which are typically applied to equations in econometric forecasting models in efforts to reduce the size and interdependence of errors. The information is, of course, valuable to forecast users and reviewers as well, and is increasingly provided to them by the forecasters.

In addition to the model's logical consistency, theoretical adequacy, and residual properties, it is well to check the statistical estimation procedures and the inputs used. It is important to keep in mind that the reported (ex ante) forecasts of econometric variety involve judgmental predictions of the exogenous inputs, recurrent revisions of the model, and frequent adjustments of the constant terms ("fine tuning")—all subject to modifications in the light of whatever current information is available to the forecaster. Such results, therefore, tell us something about how well the forecaster uses the model, other information, and judgment rather than about how well the model per se forecasts. To examine the forecasting performance of both the models and their operators, and how the two interact, it is necessary to analyze not only the ex ante forecasts but also the ex post forecasts which use the actual historical values for the exogenous variables; also, one must take into account the adjustments of the constant terms.

Although the widest range of such tests and evaluations is available for econometric models (provided they are well documented and accessible), some of the above or similar assessments can be applied to other forecasting approaches. Thus, there are established methods for the specification, estimation, and diagnostic checking of linear stochastic time series models. Different forms of such models can be used to predict a given variable, and the results can be compared with their relative accuracy. Predictions from such models have been used as standards against which to compare genuine ex ante forecasts, with the models being fitted ex post to currently available data. These are not fair tests but it is possible (though laborious) to revise and reestimate the time series models to produce benchmark predictions comparable to the actual forecasts (i.e., fitted to the data that were available at the time the forecasts were made).

Where costs matter, as in forecasting sales and managing inventory systems, simple mechanical techniques such as moving averages or exponential smoothing are widely used. Such projections are akin to the naive models often employed as minimal standards of forecast evaluation in that they are not grounded in economic and statistical theory, but they may well be useful when properly applied and monitored. The selection and updating of the models are roughly guided by the properties of the series to be predicted and the accumulated error records, but they are made as automatic as possible in the interest of keeping the costs acceptably low.

Surveys and Indicators   Periodic surveys of economic agents are the source of basic data on micropredictions, plans, or intentions, and sometimes, as in the case of business expenditures for plant and equipment, also of the corresponding realizations. Such data have manifold uses—in studies of errors and changes in economic expectations, in tests of hypotheses on the formation and properties of expectations, and in analyses of predictive performance of aggregate series of business investment anticipations and consumer attitudes and buying plans. Presumably, expectations incorporate elements of extrapolation of past behavior of the given series and inferences from observed relations with other series; however, they may also include some additional information as a result of insider knowledge, expert insight, or mere hunches. Hence, even where an anticipations series is not very efficient as a single direct predictor, it may make a significant net contribution as an ingredient in a forecasting process that combines expectational with other inputs.

Similarly, the net predictive value of a leading indicator can be assessed by using that series as one of the explanatory variables in an econometric model; e.g., contracts and orders for plant and equipment may help determine and forecast nonresidential fixed investment. However, the task to which these indicators are put in the first place is to signal business cycle turning points—recessions and recoveries. The selection of series for this purpose is based on a system of scoring for such characteristics as economic significance, statistical adequacy, cyclical conformity and timing, smoothness, and currency. Composite indexes are constructed which incorporate the best-scoring series from different economic-process groups (e.g., employment, production, consumption, investment, money and credit) and combine those with similar timing behavior, using as weights their overall performance scores. Such indexes outperform the individual indicators because of their greater smoothness and diversified economic coverage. In addition to comprehensive historical studies of the behavior of indicators, some tests of their predictive performance or value are available. These include evaluations of forecasts that relied on this approach and measures of types of error ("missed turns" and "false warnings") that would have been made under certain prespecified rules of using the indexes or the individual indicators to predict business cycle turns.

Criteria and Measures of Accuracy

The computational simplicity of measuring the accuracy of forecasts, given comparable data on actual values, hides a number of conceptual and practical problems.

1. Isolated successes or failures can be due to chance; hence, they do not prove that a source or type of forecast is (or is not) accurate with a fair degree of reliability. Thus, the average performance of a predictor should be examined over sufficient time to include different economic developments; the longer and the more varied the period covered, the more informative is the analysis of forecast errors. Unfortunately, few forecasters have produced long, consistent series of verifiable predictions, and the evaluation of forecasts suffers considerably from small sample problems for which no good statistical solutions are available.

2. The period covered should be varied because different types of economic change confront the forecaster with problems of differing nature and degree of difficulty. If a business expansion has taken hold and is gathering speed, it is safe and easy to predict that the expansion will continue, but a reasonably accurate forecast of the end of such a movement (of peaks in real gross national product, industrial production, employment) is much more difficult even over short spans. Many forecasters and users of predictions recognize this, which explains why they pay much attention to turning-point errors.

3. Individual predictions can suffer from excusable errors in assumptions about exogenous, often noneconomic, events, or, conversely, they can be relatively accurate in spite of being based on wrong assumptions (i.e., they are correct for wrong reasons because of offsetting errors). Thus, forecasting assumptions should be reported and their analysis included in the process of forecast evaluation. However, if a forecaster's record is poor on the average over time, it is unlikely to be so only because of consistently wrong assumptions.

4. Conceivably, the effectiveness of forecasts could seriously complicate their evaluation. Forecasts may influence economic behavior and, in particular, the variables being predicted; to the extent that this happens, the forecasts may validate or invalidate themselves. For example, universally optimistic predictions and expectations would presumably contribute to a high growth rate for the economy. Conversely, widespread recession forecasts may act as a depressant and prompt the government to adopt policies designed to avert or postpone the apprehended downturn. The interaction of expectations, behavior, and policies (which are themselves in part anticipated) is an intricate subject about which there is little knowledge, but it is easy to exaggerate or misjudge such feedback effects. In particular, the macroeconomic forecasts in the United States are probably too numerous and differentiated to have strong effects of this kind, which indeed are hardly in evidence.

5. Feedback effects should be distinguished from direct controls; a forecaster is not concerned with plans for controlled variables. True forecasts refer not only to variables over which the forecaster has no control but also to variables over which the forecaster has some control or influence. Other things being equal, the more controlled a variable is, the better the chance that it is well-predicted (business short-term anticipations of plant and equipment expen-

ditures would be expected to have a better record than business sales anticipations with the same spans, and they have).

6. For many economic variables, forecast errors appear to be small when compared with the levels of the series concerned but are actually large in terms of
the more meaningful comparisons with the changes to be predicted. Some performance measures such as correlations of the predicted with the actual values
are much more meaningful for change forecasts than for level forecasts. For
aggregates with strong trends and where rates of growth are of particular interest, it is well to define the errors as differences between the predicted and
actual percentage changes (or changes in logarithms).

7. Although knowledge of the decision maker's loss function may not be available or complete, the choice of the measure of average forecast accuracy can
be linked to the assumed form of the loss function. For example, if a quadratic
loss criterion is adopted, the appropriate measure is the root-mean-square
error. This measure, based on the variance of the errors around zero, has the
advantages of mathematical and statistical tractability, and it gives more than
proportionate weights to the large errors, which may be desirable. Nevertheless, other measures, e.g., the mean absolute error, may sometimes be
preferred.

8. Ideally, forecasts should be unbiased, that is, their average errors should
be approximately zero (no systematic under- or overestimation). They should
also be efficient, that is, their errors should not be correlated either with the
forecast values or with each other serially over time. (All this is to be interpreted in terms of the appropriate statistical tests of significance.) The matter
of decomposing the mean-square error into bias, inefficiency, and residual
variance elements is often used. The larger the residual variance component,
given the size of the total measured error, the better the quality of the forecast
is deemed to be. This is because the forecaster should ascertain the correct
model or learn from past errors how to avoid bias and inefficiency, whereas
random errors are largely unavoidable. In practice, however, many economic
forecast series are not long enough or consistent enough to permit successful
measurement of, let alone ex ante correction for, the systematic error components.

9. The standard of perfection (zero errors) is obviously unrealistic, but any other
criterion for evaluating the absolute accuracy of forecasts is arbitrary. It is,
therefore, necessary to measure the relative accuracy of forecasts by comparing summary error measures across sets of authentic economic predictions and
benchmark projections from some objective formulas or models. The extrapolations used as yardsticks range from the simplest models to statistically
sophisticated autoregressive integrated moving-average (ARIMA) models. In
principle, there is an optimal extrapolation for each time series with a known
and stable statistical structure, but the available economic data often do not
satisfy the required conditions. Benchmarks based on objective applications
of other (nonextrapolative) models or methods of forecasting can be used in
many cases.

10. Accuracy is a relative and multidimensional concept, and conclusive discrimination between forecasters is often difficult even where their products are

sufficiently comparable: the differences may not be significant or forecast set X is better in one respect and forecast set Z in another respect. Moreover, even if one source or type of forecast outperforms the others, it does not follow that it alone merits consideration since two or more of the sets may have net predictive values. Many forecasts are products of an informal combination of different elements and techniques. The relative accuracy analysis can help in inferring the structure of such forecasts, that is, the shares of informative content that they have in common with extrapolations or other benchmark models. Formal methods of combining predictors have been proposed, which are optimal under certain restrictive assumptions, and the evaluation of the results suggests that the overall forecasts are frequently superior to each of their components.

A Summary of Evidence

Near the end of each year, forecasters prepare their forecasts of quarterly and annual changes of key economic indicators, such as gross national product (GNP), in dollar and real terms, price indexes, and industrial production. The end-of-year forecasts of annual changes in GNP, have mean absolute errors averaging close to 1 percentage point, only half as large as the errors of several examined extrapolative models. They earn good marks for overall accuracy on other criteria as well, such as correlations with actual changes, which are generally low for the mechanical extrapolations. Moreover, these forecasts have improved during the 1960s and 1970s compared with earlier years, both in terms of absolute errors and, particularly, relative to the extrapolative benchmark models. The annual forecasts for constant-dollar GNP (real growth) and the implicit price deflator (inflation) are weaker. The former suffer from large turning-point errors, the latter from large underestimation errors. For output, overestimates refer primarily to times of low growth, underestimates to times of high growth. Nevertheless, the real GNP forecasts are considerably better than the extrapolations. Forecasts of price change have much in common with projections of the last observed rate of inflation, and so they tend to lag behind the actual rate. The errors of forecasts of real growth are negatively correlated with the errors of forecasts of inflation, which help to make the nominal GNP predictions more accurate.

The favorable record of annual GNP predictions does not apply to the more difficult task of predicting quarterly changes in GNP within the year ahead or beyond. Forecasts for the year as a whole can be satisfactory when based on a good record for the first two quarters; they tend to be more accurate than forecasts with longer spans. An examination of quarterly multiperiod predictions for the first half of the 1970s shows that the errors for real growth and inflation cumulated rapidly beyond the spans of two to four quarters. In previous periods the cumulation was found to be, as a rule, less than proportional to the increase in the span, but in this turbulent period the buildup of errors was much greater than usual. Not surprisingly, the averages and dispersion of errors generally tend to increase steadily with the time span between the base and the target period. Forecasts for one to three quarters ahead are usually better than the various extrapolative models, but the longer forecasts are often worse than the more effective of these models. At the present time, the predictive value of detailed forecasts reaching out further than a few quarters ahead must be heavily discounted.

Forecasts of total GNP tend to have much smaller percentage-change errors than the forecasts of most major GNP expenditure components from the same source. This reflects (1) partial cancellation of errors in predictions of the components; (2) the aptitude of some forecasting methods to deal more effectively with changes in the economy at large than with changes in particular processes or sectors; (3) the fact that many disturbances remain localized so that GNP is smoother than most of its parts. The more volatile a series, the more difficult and less accurate the predictions of its changes is likely to be. Thus, only personal consumption (total and nondurables plus services) and state and local government expenditures are predicted as well as, or better than, total GNP. These components follow a smoother course than GNP. The errors in predicting percentage changes in consuption are far smaller than those in forecasts of gross private domestic investment and net exports, whereas the errors for total government spending are usually of intermediate size. Within aggregate consumption, the errors for durable goods exceed greatly those for either the nondurables or services. Within aggregate investment, the most unsatisfactory predictions are those for residential structures and, particularly, the change in business inventories.

Inflation has been greatly underestimated by most forecasters, who apparently were surprised by its tenacity, acceleration, and coexistence with unemployment in recent years. Overestimates, however, prevailed in the near-term forecasts for 1975 to 1976, a period in which inflation rates temporarily declined.

It is difficult to compare macroeconomic forecasts, if only because the models vary in scale and choice of exogenous variables and the predictions vary in timing (those released late enjoy advantages of additional and more current information). Nevertheless, there have been several independent attempts at comparative assessments of forecasts from well-known private and public sources, and the results agree on two basic points.

1. The rankings of forecasters vary considerably depending on the variables, periods, and spans covered; they vary also, but much less, with the criteria and measurements applied.

2. At least for the predictions of the principal aggregates, the summary measures of accuracy do not show the differences among the forecasters to be both large and systematic.

Not surprisingly, then, the search for a consistently superior forecaster is fruitless and unpromising (and economic forecasting remains competitive).

Different forecasting methods and techniques serve different purposes and are often complementary, which is why they are used in various combinations. Econometric model forecasts with judgmental adjustments are on the average as accurate as the corresponding noneconometric forecasts from professional sources—actually often better, but not systematically so and mostly by slight margins. Without the adjustments, the econometric-model predictions are on the whole considerably worse. Thus, mechanical uses of the existing models cannot be relied upon to produce good forecasts.

Better, richer, and prompter data and better utilization of historical content could certainly contribute to a significant improvement of short-term forecasts, which in turn should help raise the quality of longer-term projections. Progress can also be expected from improvement in survey techniques, econometric estimation methods, time series modeling, input-output analysis, and cyclical indicators. In the final analysis, all remediable deficiencies of the tools and techniques of economic forecasting reflect lacking or wrong information in the relevant areas of knowledge—mainly economics and statistics. Such cognitive shortcomings can in principle be reduced. However, it is clear that there are limits to the potential accuracy of economic (and other social) forecasts, which may be fairly narrowly drawn. Forecasts concern inherently uncertain future events that are not nearly so "knowable" as the data of history and science.

References

Butler, William F., Robert A. Kavesh, and Robert B. Platt (eds.), *Methods and Techniques of Business Forecasting*, Prentice-Hall, Englewood Cliffs, N.J., 1974; Klein. Lawrence R., and Edwin Burmeister (eds.), *Econometric Model Performance*, University of Pennsylvania Press, Philadelphia, 1976; McNees, Stephen S., "The Forecasting Record for the 1970s," *New England Economic Review*, September/October 1979, pp. 33–53; Pindyck, R. S., and D. L. Rubinfeld, *Econometric Models and Economic Forecasts*, McGraw-Hill, New York, 1976; Theil, Henri. *Applied Economic Forecasting*, Rand-McNally, Chicago, 1966; Zarnowitz, Victor (ed.), *The Business Cycle Today*, National Bureau of Economic Research, New York, 1972.

(*See also* Anticipation surveys, business; Anticipation surveys, consumer; Econometrics; Economic forecasts; Economic models; Forecasting methods; Statistical techniques in economics and business. an overview)

Victor Zarnowitz

Administered prices

Administered price is a term of twentieth-century American origin. It was introduced by Gardiner C. Means in a 1933 document entitled *Industrial Prices and Their Relative Insensitivity* (Senate document 13) and is used to refer to a price which is set and kept constant for a period of time and a series of transactions. The term can be applied to prices set by private enterprises or by government and can also refer to wage rates whether set by management or set by contract between labor and management or in some other fashion. The word "administered" implies a degree of pricing power which gives some discretion in setting a price regardless of the precise price which would just clear the market by equating supply and demand. This discretion can arise when there is vigorous competition among a few enterprises. The greatest theoretical importance of administered prices arises in connection with macrotheory and the two problems of involuntary unemployment and simultaneous inflation and stagnation("stagflation").

Administered Pricing and Macrotheory

Classical macrotheory is built on the concept of prices which are set in the market by the equating of supply and demand, with no intervention or independent power to determine price on the part of either buyer or seller. Classical macrotheory based on this assumption is set forth in a set of equations introduced by Léon Walras (1874) which assumed perfect flexibility of price. Adam Smith's "higgling and bargaining" in the marketplace and the auctioning of the organized exchanges in the wheat, the cotton, and the stock markets exemplify such flexible price behavior.

The lack of pricing discretion was fundamental to the macrotheorizing of Adam Smith and his classical and neoclassical followers. Even monopoly theory was fitted into the macrotheory of flexible pricing by the assumption that a monopoly set its price to equate marginal cost and marginal revenue and continuously adjusted its price to changes in demand or cost. These economists were well aware that in practice many prices were set and did not change frequently. But for macroanalysis, the nonclassical behavior of such prices was treated as a matter of frictions. Prior to the Great Depression of the 1930s, no traditional theorist had indicated how an economic system could be expected to operate where some prices were arrived at classically but a substantial proportion were administered by competing firms.

Yet during most of the twentieth century, prices for the bulk of competitive market transactions in the United States and in most other industrial countries have been reached not through bargaining or auction but through private price setting. This is true of most transactions in retail stores where prices are posted and changed from time to time. Likewise, where production is concentrated among a few producers, individual companies are likely to sell at list prices or fixed discounts from list prices with the transaction price often held constant for months at a time and then changed by several percentage points. A change in steel prices is often front-page news.

When the pricing discretion implicit in administered pricing is built into macrotheory, it entails such a radical revision of that theory as to create what is essentially a new macrotheory. It can explain the depth of the Great Depression of the 1930s by the relative inflexibility of administered prices and can explain the possibility of simultaneous recession and inflation as well as inflation in the presence of stagnation by the perverse behavior of administered prices.

Consider involuntary unemployment arising from a deficiency of aggregate demand at an initial level of prices and wage rates. According to traditional theory, this would produce an immediate drop in the price-wage level which would increase the real buying power of money, making the existing money stock redundant. As the redundant money was spent, the extra spending would absorb unemployed workers and idle plant, thus tending to clear all markets. Such was the basis for the traditional view that the free enterprise system contained an automatic corrective which would tend to eliminate excessive unemployment. Frictions could delay the adjustment, but according to the theory full recovery was just around the corner.

The introduction of administered pricing into macrotheory changes the nature of the behavior of the economy according to traditional theory. Where competition is among a few competing sellers, it is seldom that specific markets will clear. The great advantage of buying and selling at administered prices rather than higgling or bargaining over each transaction as in an oriental bazaar or putting products up for auction makes selling at administered prices the most common form of marketing where there is pricing discretion. Then it is only by chance that the amount offered for sale at the administered price is the amount demanded. Where the price is set by the seller, the quantity offered will usually exceed the amount demanded at that price, and no price change will occur unless a substantial discrepancy has developed. On occasion, demand may exceed supply and orders may be taken with delayed deliveries but with no change in price.

This obvious failure of demand and supply to be equated by administered prices is not in itself important. The price might be changed often enough to approximate the flexibility of traditional theory. And traditional economists could avoid the issue of inflexibility by redefining supply to refer to the quantity sold at the price set rather than offered for sale at that price. What is really important for macrotheory is the pricing discretion which is signaled by an administered price and the nontraditional behavior which arises from the exercise of this discretion.

When a competitive enterprise has a significant degree of pricing discretion, it is faced with a wide range of factors in its decision making which do not arise where competition is among the many. It is well-recognized in current microtheory that a price setter must take into account the probable reaction of the few competitors to the price that is set; that a high price can stimulate new entrants who will further divide the market; that, once a price has been set, there can be significant costs in making a change; that advertising, which has no value in a classically competitive market, can be a major factor in pricing; that there can be significant costs and uncertainties in gathering information for pricing policy, thus shifting the emphasis from optimizing to sufficing; that a major goal of big corporations may not be maximum profit but some other goal such as the volume of sales, share in the market, or growth; and that even where profit is the goal, price policy can differ depending on whether the goal is short-run or longer-run profits.

As a result of these and other pricing complexities various simplified pricing formulas have been developed over the years such as markup pricing, full-cost pricing, short-run profit pricing, and long-run target pricing. Most of these are based on standard cost accounting and give little if any attention to marginal costs. Their use reflects a very considerable degree of pricing discretion which is reflected in macro behavior.

Prices in the Great Depression and Recovery

In the Great Depression, the nontraditional behavior of administered prices in the United States took the form of the great inflexibility of prices where competition was among the few. In the 4-year recession, prices behaved in the traditional fashion where competition fitted the classical postulate. For example, farm prices dropped 60 percent, and there was no fall in farm production and employment. If all prices had behaved in this fashion, it is doubtful that there would have been any great recession. But in the concentrated industries, the fall in general demand did not produce a comparable drop in prices. Rather, the primary effect was a drop in production and employment. The index of industrial prices dropped only 25 percent in spite of the inclusion of such classically competitive industries as textiles, leather, and shoes and such classically competitive raw industrial materials as lead, zinc, and scrap steel.

It is easy to see how this inflexibility of administered prices occurred. Once the price of a product had been set, why change it because of a recession? If recovery was just around the corner, recovery would make the adjustment unnecessary. If the price had initially been set low to avoid enticing new entrants to the market, this danger would be dissipated by the recession, eliminating need for a price reduction. Also, with the industry selling at administered prices, a significant price cut might lead to a destructive price war. Likewise, some of the pricing formulas used pointed to no change in price or only small price reductions in the presence of falling demand. It was such considerations which led corporate management to use its pricing discretion to limit price reductions and to adjust to falling demand by curtailing production and employment. Such action can go a long way toward explaining the relative inflexibility of administered prices in the recession and the resultant heavy drop in the employment of workers and machines.

Conversely, in the period of recovery, prices rose classically in the areas where competition was among the many. Where competition was among the few, it was primarily production and employment which rose while prices rose far less. Indeed, in the United States when full employment was first reached in early 1942 under the impetus of monetary and fiscal measures plus growing war demand, both market-dominated prices and administration-dominated prices were back to their predepression levels. Thus, the recovery of price was in the nature of a desirable reflation largely correcting the distortions which developed between market and administered prices during the recession.

This nonclassical behavior of administered prices during depression called for a major revision of the traditional laissez faire policy. It pointed to the need for government intervention to maintain the level of aggregate demand necessary to support full employment in order to avoid the disruptive effect of the depression inflexibility of administered prices. This, in itself, involved a revolution in macro policy.

Administered Prices and Stagflation

Stagflation cannot be explained under traditional theory or by the inflexibility of administered prices. But it can be explained by the perverse behavior of administered prices. Where competition is among the few, there are various conditions which can lead price setters to use their pricing discretion to raise prices when demand falls off. For example, where a price setter uses a full-cost pricing formula that includes fixed costs in arriving at cost per unit, a fall in sales during recession will require that fixed costs be divided over a smaller output so that unit costs increase while the danger of new entrants diminishes. This can often lead to a price increase during recession. If a pricing formula also includes a factor for an aggregate amount of profit regardless of volume—for example, a 10 percent return on capital—the profit goal would also need to be spread over a smaller volume, and the formula would call for a larger price increase during recession. There are other pricing formulas which can have the same kind of inflationary effect in a recession.

Such formulas do not require a recession to produce inflation. If total aggregate demand were stable but some concentrated industries were expanding while some were contracting, those with falling demand and full-cost pricing would tend to raise prices while expanding industries would have no compelling reason to reduce prices. If the net effect were a rise in the average level of prices, this would itself cause a recession unless monetary and fiscal measures expanded nominal aggregate demand, thereby extending the price rise to classically competitive prices.

Finally, where enterprises have a considerable degree of pricing descretion, the expectation of inflation can be a self-fulfilling expectation; this would not be the case if prices in each market were dominated by the many. In a classically competitive market, the net effect of a general expectation of inflation would tend to be self-correcting. For example, the expectation of a rise in wheat prices would lead speculators to buy wheat for a profit, pushing up the price. But when they unloaded, there would be a downward pressure on prices. If the speculators' expectations were wrong, the net effect of their entry and exit from the market would be negligible; and if they were right, the speculators would have made profits which would have otherwise gone to someone else, with the final market-clearing price not significantly altered by the speculation. But where competition is among the few, there is seldom a speculative market. Rather, a price setter who expects general inflation can simply raise prices arbitrarily, and if the expectation is widespread, the few competitors are likely to go along. There would be no speculative purchases to be put back into the market to reverse the rise or to limit further price increases if monetary and fiscal measures are used to validate the initial price increases and to limit unemployment. The source of such self-induced inflation is even less obvious when price setters raise their prices because they expect that the replacement cost of their plant and equipment will rise in the future. A past rise in capital costs presents serious problems of passing through inflation which has been generated elsewhere. But a formula which raises current prices to take care of extra capital costs that have not yet occurred but may develop in the future provides another perfect engine of inflation.

Strong organized labor can also be an initiating source of stagflation if rates of compensation to labor are pushed up too fast. Under some conditions, a wage formula which raised administered wages in proportion to increases in labor productivity and living costs would pass on inflation from other sources but would not initiate inflation. But if the increases in output per worker are accompanied by a worsening of the terms of trade with other countries such as occurred after the oil cartel was formed in 1973, only the increase in productivity after covering the real increase in exports would be available for division between labor and capital. Likewise, part of a nation's productivity gains can be used up in a variety of ways, such as reducing pollution and improving education, that do not allow for either wage or profit increases. A simple wage formula which increased the compensation to labor in proportion to living costs and labor productivity could be inflationary. A wage-setting formula would have to take account of such factors to avoid generating inflation.

Since World War II there have been two periods that have clearly been dominated by stagflation. The first was from 1956 to 1958 when the wholesale price index rose 8 percent in spite of a sharp fall in production and employment. The second was from 1969 to 1972 when the wholesale price index rose 12 percent while unemployment increased sharply. Since 1973, stagflation and the energy crisis have combined to provide rising prices and a relatively low rate of capacity operation. In other periods since World War II, the role of perverse price behavior is less clear.

Revision of Methods Needed

It is clear that while the unemployment engendered by inadequate demand and the downward inflexibility of administered prices can be offset through monetary and fiscal measures, the inflation engendered by the perverse flexibility of administered prices cannot be so controlled. Just as the recession inflexibility of administered prices called for a major revision of macrotheory and of laissez faire policy, the perverse behavior of administered prices calls for a second major revision of macrotheory and a different kind of departure from laissez faire.

In an economy dominated by administered prices, the problem of achieving a high level of employment without serious administrative inflation and with the minimum interference with free enterprise is in some ways like that of traffic on the highways. In the early nineteenth century, traffic on the King's Highway was a matter of free enterprise. The driver of a wagon could drive on the right, the left, or down the middle and pass on either side. But in 1835 Parliament passed an act that set the new rule of the road that drivers keep to the left and pass on the right. It then became in the interest of practically all drivers to abide by the rule. Similarly, the high speed of the modern car has made speed limits an interference with laissez faire, which is in the interests of practically everyone.

In the case of administrative inflation, the first step is to review the rules of the road. Under the traditional rules, so long as there was active competition, the individual enterprise was free to set whatever price it chose in the light of its costs and its competition. But under modern conditions, this rule opens up the opportunity for perverse price behavior where competition is among the few. There is, therefore, great need to review the various methods used in setting administered prices and wage rates to discover which serve to generate administrative inflation and which do not. This is the crucial distinction between a pricing formula that measures overhead cost according to current output or sales, thus producing perverse price behavior, and a target formula that uses a standard rate of operation consistent with longer-range profits. It is also the distinction between raising administered prices because of an expectation of general inflation and waiting until costs actually rise. The same distinction exists between a wage formula which takes account of only labor productivity and inflation and one which also takes account of changes in production costs which do not contribute to the output available for division between capital and labor, such as expenditures in reducing pollution or a worsening of the external terms of trade.

Such a clarification would require the combined talents of business, labor, and consumer leaders either independently or in collaboration with government. The publication of the results and the education of the public as to their significance could contribute to reducing inflationary price behavior. Progressive business and labor leaders would then have rules of the road which they could follow and could urge on other organizations. To some extent, big buyers could insist that sellers adhere to the rules and management could play the same role with respect to wages. Adherence to the rules by big business and labor would be a way to carry out the responsibilities to the public which arise from their economic power. If the new rules of the road were widely accepted, only a minimum of monitoring and enforcement would be needed to keep administrative inflation to an acceptable minimum while monetary and fiscal measures supported the appropriate level of aggregate demand.

References

Means, Gardiner C., *Pricing Power and the Public Interest*, Harper & Row, New York, 1962; Walras, Léon, *Éléments d'economie politique pure*, Lausanne, 1874, William Jaffé (trans.), Allen and Unwin, London, 1954.

(*See also* Classical school; Demand; Employment and unemployment; Government regulation of business; Great Depression; Inflation; Macroeconomics; Monopoly and oligopoly; Price theory; Stagflation; Supply)

Gardiner C. Means

Advertising, economic aspects

Any system or method of attracting attention to and inducing the purchase or sale of goods or services may be defined as advertising. However, the definition in practice is usually restricted to more formal methods of persuasion, i.e., to circumstances in which the advertising message is conveyed along with other information or entertainment in a variety of media.

Classification of Advertising Expenditures

Expenditures on advertising are usually classified in two ways: first, in terms of the size of the area within which the advertiser sells the product, and second, in terms of the medium employed by the advertiser. The first classification essentially divides all advertisers into local and national categories, with retailers as the dominant local advertisers and national manufacturers as the dominant national advertisers.

In the late 1970s, out of a total advertising expenditures level of over $40 billion, approximately 55 percent was spent by national advertisers. The remainder was spent by local advertisers.

The second form of classification categorizes expenditures according to the various media in which the advertising is carried. The major media consist of the print media (newspapers, magazines, business papers), broadcasting (television and radio), outdoor advertising, and direct mail. Several of these media carry both local and national advertising (for example, newspapers, television, and radio). Others carry only national advertising (for example, business papers).

In recent years, newspapers have accounted for 29 percent of all advertising dollars, and direct mail for over 14 percent. The broadcast media, television and radio, have accounted for about 20 percent and 7 percent, respectively, of the total advertising market, and magazines for under 6 percent. The remaining 24 percent of total advertising outlays were spread among outdoor advertising, business papers, and a variety of miscellaneous media (e.g., farm publications).

This distribution changes when the individual media shares are broken into national and local categories, for some media are more concentrated in one category than the other. Newspapers, for example, account for only 8 percent of total national advertising expenditures, but they account for over one-half, 55 percent, of the local advertising total. Television, on the other hand, accounts for 27 percent of national advertising, but for only 12 percent of local advertising. Radio holds only 3 percent of the national advertising market, but as much as 11 percent of local advertising. Magazine advertising, which is essentially national in character, makes up 11 percent of this market, with direct mail, business publications, outdoor advertising, and a residual category of miscellaneous advertising expenditures accounting for 51 percent of the national market. Of local advertising expenditures, outdoor advertising and miscellaneous advertising account for about 22 percent of the market.

Growth of Advertising Expenditures

Advertising expenditures have increased during the past four decades and have roughly paralleled the growth in gross national product and in personal consumption expenditures, although there has been some downward drift in the ratio between advertising and these aggregates over the last two decades. Advertising expenditures have risen from about $2 billion in 1939 to over $40 billion in the late 1970s.

The years immediately following World War II were characterized by very rapid growth in both national and local advertising—10 and 8 percent per year, respectively. The late 1950s and early 1960s were associated with much lower growth rates. The middle and late 1960s saw an increase in advertising growth rates, particularly in local advertising. Over this period, local advertising was again rising at almost 8 percent a year, while national advertising increased between 5 and 6 percent per year. From 1970 to 1975, the growth rates for both categories edged up slightly. Over 1976, 1977, and 1978 an unprecedented boom in advertising pushed both rates up again, national to 16 percent a year, local to 15 percent a year. In 1979, growth in both categories moderated somewhat, national to roughly 9 percent, local to about 11 percent.

Generally, advertising expenditures are cyclically sensitive, that is, they tend to be synchronous with the periodic up-and-down movements of the economy. Historically, most media experience some declines in their dollar volume of expenditures in a year of recession, although in the highly inflationary environment of the 1974–75 recession, the various media witnessed only moderating rates of growth rather than declines. One medium, direct mail, appears to have weathered recessions of the past decade and a half without any corresponding declines, although some moderation in growth was apparent in recession years.

Advertising and Economic Theory

Within the framework of economic theory, advertising occupies a somewhat uncertain place. Some view it as a source of varied information on the diverse range of goods and services available in the marketplace, and in turn, a necessary aid to consumers in their purchase decision making. That function, providing information about the marketplace, should operate in the direction of increasing competition and promoting a more efficient allocation of resources.

On the other hand, the more common view is that advertising serves as a method of increasing monopoly power by increasing industrial concentration and barriers to entry.

Under this latter view, espoused, among others, by N. Kaldor several decades ago, and more recently by J. S. Bain, and W. S. Comanor and T. Wilson, advertising is thought to magnify differences among products with relatively minor differences and to create spurious differentiation among basically similar products, thereby promoting the development of brand loyalties. This process leads to inelastic demand schedules, and producers are then able to raise prices above competitive levels. Barriers to entry are said to exist because of the high advertising costs required to surmount these presumed brand loyalties.

Presumed economies of scale in advertising are also involved in the barriers-to-entry argument. One view is that the psychological response of consumers to various levels of advertising involves increasing returns to scale over some significant range of advertising effort. Such returns to scale would obviously benefit large companies. Accentuating this presumed phenomenon are quantity discounts obtainable from the large-scale purchase of advertising in some media.

In sum, the alternative view holds that advertising erects barriers to entry, augments industrial concentration, and thus leads to unduly high prices and, often, excess profits.

Thus far, empirical studies have failed to establish adequately causality between advertising and industrial concentration. The argument that there are significant economies of scale in advertising has also found little empirical support.

As a consequence, this alternative view has come under increasing attack from economists (e.g., L. G. Telser, Y. Brozen, J. M. Ferguson, J. L. Simon), who conclude that advertising improves rather than disrupts the efficient allocation of resources.

In this view, advertising is seen as enhancing competition and, rather than representing a barrier to entry, permits entrenched firms to be overturned by facilitating rapid buyer exposure to new products or new brands. New products can be introduced more quickly and production can be expanded more rapidly to the point of minimum long-run average cost. Retail margins can be reduced substantially.

The grievance that new product entries of new firms must incur advertising costs far above those of entrenched products of existing firms is viewed as an artifact of current accounting procedures. For, despite the fact that advertising effects persist over time, advertising expenditures are customarily treated as current expenses, rather than capitalized and written off over time as are other capital assets. Were the latter accounting method employed, it appears that the difference in cost for advertising between new and old products would substantially decrease, erasing the appearance of higher initial cost to the new entrant.

References

Pro

Ferguson, James M., *Advertising and Competition: Theory Measurement, Fact,* Ballinger, Cambridge, Mass., 1974; Julian, Simon L., *Issues in the Economics of Advertising,* University of Illinois Press, Urbana, Ill., 1970; Ornstein, Stanley I., *Industrial Concentration and Advertising Intensity,* American Enterprise Institute for Public Policy Research, Washington, D.C., 1977.

Con

Bain, Joe S., *Barriers to New Competition,* Harvard University Press, Cambridge, Mass., 1956; Comanor, W., and T. Wilson, *Advertising and Market Power,* Harvard University Press, Cambridge, Mass., 1974; Kaldor, Nicholas, "The Economic Aspects of Advertising," *Review of Economic Studies,* vol. 18, 1949–1950, pp. 1–27.

(*See also* Economic growth; Economies of scale; Marketing research and Business economics)

David M. Blank

Agricultural economic policy

General agricultural economic policy consists of a body of policies that have been formulated and implemented to influence the economic health, or well-being, of the agricultural sector. In the nineteenth century in the United States such policies were concerned with the distribution of land, tariff protection, and money and credit, and with improving the productive capacity of farmers through education and training. In the twentieth century such policies have been concerned with production control, surplus disposal (both domestic and foreign), market discrimination, demand expansion, price support, income transfers, and commodity stabilization, as well as tariff protection, agricultural credit, education, and training. Finally, economic policy in agriculture in the twentieth century has placed great emphasis on research, technological development, and farm technological advance.

Goals and Policies

The goals of the U.S. general agricultural economic policy in the twentieth century are:

1. A stable, prosperous farming sector
2. A family farm structure of farming
3. An adequate, nutritious supply of food at reasonable prices
4. An efficient agricultural marketing and distribution system, both domestically and internationally, with a minimum of government regulation

Since 1920, farmers, with the assistance of the Federal government, have made a major effort to manage, or control, the supply of their products and as a result push up farm prices in the marketplace. Two techniques have been employed: first, control over the input, land, as a means of controlling output; second, the management of the flow of product to different markets through the use of marketing orders. The use of these supply-management devices in adjusting supplies to demand at prices deemed acceptable by farmers has been moderately successful.

Prices of farm products have been supported directly by government action through the use of two types of programs. First, the government has supported the price of storable commodities through the use of the nonrecourse loan mechanism; in this type of action the government makes a loan—a nonrecourse loan—to a farmer on the farmer's commodity (e.g., wheat) at the price-support level; if the market price falls below the price-support level, the farmer keeps the loan and gives the collateral, wheat in this example, to the government; if the market price stays above the price-support level, the farmer sells the commodity in the open market and pays off the loan from the government. Second, the government enters the market and purchases sufficient commodity to drive its price in the marketplace up to the defined price-support level.

The government has sometimes supported the incomes of farmers directly in several ways. It has paid farmers to remove land from production and to undertake desirable conservation measures. But most importantly, it has made deficiency payments to farmers to increase the return on each unit produced and sold by an amount equal to the difference between the market price and a defined fair price.

The government has undertaken a variety of policy measures to expand the demand for farm products and thus act to support or raise the level of farm prices. Most importantly, the government has taken title to farm commodities acquired through the operation of nonrecourse loan and purchase operations, stored those commodities and thereby held them off the commercial market, and finally disposed of those products through noncommercial channels at home and abroad. At home the government has given those commodities to persons and families living on relief or on welfare, to the Red Cross, and to schools and charitable institutions for their feeding programs. Abroad the government has distributed these surplus commodities to the poor and needy across the less-developed world through Public Law 480. Foreign food aid programs under this law ran at a level of between $1 and $2 billion through much of the 1950s and 1960s.

The federal government has also sought to expand the demand for food through a variety of specialized food programs. It developed and now operates a large food stamp plan to assure the very poor of an adequate supply of food. It has developed and operated special milk programs and lunch programs for school children and food assistance programs for pregnant and nursing mothers and preschool children.

The government has fostered and supported the development of special credit institutions and instruments to assist farmers in the purchase of land, the obtaining of production credit, and the financing of their cooperative purchasing and marketing associations.

The government has protected certain industries—dairy, beef cattle, sheep, and sugar—through the imposition of tariffs, import quotas, and public health measures.

Finally, the government has assisted both farm production units and agribusiness service units to reduce costs of operation through the financial support of a research, development, and extension system that has made possible a rapid rate of technological development in American agriculture since 1920, with the concomitant increases in resource productivity and reductions in unit costs of production.

The specific set of economic policies and programs adopted by and implemented by the federal government in any given year since 1920 has depended upon a host of circumstances: the economic conditions of the time, the critical problems of the time, the basic politico-economic philosophy of the electorate, the political power of special interest groups, the budget situation and goals of the government, the interests and commitments of the President, the leadership skills and economic philosophy of the secretary of agriculture, and so on. From this array of political pressures, economic philosophies and goals, and economic conditions, the specific set of agricultural policies and programs that took shape in a particular year represented a compromise among the many and varied contending interests. The policy results were thus acceptable in a political action sense, but many, if not most, of the contending interests were unhappy with the final result. Farmers typically have been dissatisfied with the levels of price and income support realized in their programs; they have felt that they were deserving of higher levels of support. Urban consumers generally have been of the opinion that the farm programs cost too much, and they result in food prices that are higher than they need to be. Agribusiness leaders often view farm programs as too much, or unneeded, government interference with the workings of the market. The President and advisers often view farm programs as involving unnecessarily high expenditures of governmental funds. But each interest group accepted the policy result because it was known that, in the political process in which policies are forged, it was the best alternative.

Economic and Social Consequences

What have been the economic and social consequences of these policies and programs? It is generally agreed that the policies and programs of the 1930s kept many farmers from losing their farms and assisted many others who had gone broke to get started once again, and that they contributed to an increase in a cash flow into the farming sector that was literally starved for cash. It is also generally agreed that the policies and programs of the 1950s and 1960s held farm prices and incomes higher than they otherwise would have been in a short-run context, and kept the farming sector from going through a serious asset deflation. But many economists argue that if the farming sector had gone through an asset wringing-out process in the 1950s, farm prices and incomes would have been higher in the 1960s than they were. In other words, the policies and programs were beneficial to the farming sector in the short run, but the implications for the long run are questionable. However, farmers, their representatives, and the rest of society opted for protection and support in the short run.

The argument has been developed and is being increasingly accepted that the general agricultural economic policy of the nation has contributed, and continues to contribute, to a changed structure of American farming—a structure in which there are fewer and fewer and larger and larger farms. And the number of farms has declined significantly in recent years—from 5.6 million in 1950 to about 2.7 million in 1977. Commercial agricultural production has been increasingly concentrated in a relatively few large farms; in 1960 some 340,000 farms, each grossing $20,000 or more, accounted for some 51 percent of the total cash receipts from farming; in 1977 some

162,000 farms, each grossing $100,000 or more, accounted for some 53 percent of the total cash receipts from farming.

The argument runs as follows. Where agricultural policies and programs operate (1) to stabilize farm prices over time and reduce economic risk, (2) to increase the cash flow to the larger farmers via government income payments, and (3) to maintain a flow of new and improved production technologies which reduce unit costs of production, the better, more aggressive managers exploit this set of policy circumstances to expand the size of their operations. They are able to do this only by acquiring the productive assets of their less able, less efficient neighbors, which they have been doing for three decades. Thus, the argument goes, the policies and programs pursued by the United States for the past 30 years in the name of helping the small family farmer have in fact operated to destroy that farmer. The larger, more innovative, more aggressive farmers have cannibalized the smaller, less efficient farmers.

Demand for Change in Policy

The ever-widening view by consumers that food should be looked upon as a public good of which all citizens are assured of an adequate and nutritious supply, and the increased fear and apprehension that the world may be entering a prolonged period of short food supplies, have led to growing demand for a change in the direction of the general agricultural economic policy of the nation. For example, consumers are demanding an adequate and secure supply of food. As a result the largest program currently administered in the U.S. Department of Agriculture is the food stamp plan. And the Carter administration initiated a grain reserve program to moderate upswings in food prices as well as downswings in farm prices.

Consumers are also demanding a food supply that is nutritious, healthful, and protected against injurious practices and ingredients. Thus, the government is expanding its programs of research and education in nutrition, and it is placing greater emphasis on its food inspection services and food regulatory services.

Questions are being increasingly asked about the desirability of making large income payments to large farmers. As a result limits have been placed upon the size of payment that any farmer may receive, and the issue is being raised as to whether income payments should be made to farmers at all.

Foreign Trade and Foreign Policies

The role of foreign trade in agricultural products in the national economy is not in itself an issue. The importance of a continued strong foreign demand for many of the products of American agriculture is fully understood and appreciate. Nonetheless, there are policy issues with respect to the agricultural export market that are receiving increased attention. What are the responsibilities of the United States, as a reliable supplier, to its leading and regular foreign national customers? To what extent should fluctuation in export demand be permitted to destabilize the domestic market for food? What should be the commitment of the United States to provide food aid to the less developed world? As the leading supplier of food commodities to the world market, the United States must have more consistent, and acceptable, answers to these policy issues in the future than it has had in the past.

The changing general agricultural economic policy of the United States is not unique or atypical. Every developed nation in the world has a comparable and elaborate set of policies and programs to manage and direct in its food and agricultural sector. This is the case because the farming sector of any country is inherently unstable; unpredictable variations in the weather and the extreme inelasticity of demand for food make it so. In addition, the adequacy and the security of the food supply is viewed by the citizenry of each of these nations to be too important to be left to the market. The national government of each nation feels compelled to undertake policies designed to stabilize the farming sector and to guarantee its population an adequate supply of food.

The specific policies and programs adopted and implemented by each developed country do, however, vary importantly. They vary first in accordance with the position of the country as a food importer or food exporter. The policies and programs of Canada, for example, are concerned first and foremost with developing and retaining export markets. The policies and programs of Japan, on the other hand, are concerned with the acquisition of an adequate domestic supply of food through domestic production subsidies and the location of cheap and assured foreign supplies. No foreign developed country and few underdeveloped countries depend on the market to direct the production and distribution of its food supply. Like the United States, each has an elaborate set of policies and programs to guide and direct the production and distribution of its food supply. No matter how glowingly economists describe the operation of free markets, the citizens of each developed country around the world seem to be saying to their governments, "We want you to take conscious and effective actions to assure farmers of a stable, prosperous agriculture and to assure consumers of an adequate, nutritious food supply at reasonable prices." They are not willing to leave the achievement of these goals to chance.

References

Benedict, Murray R., Farm Policies of the United States, 1790–1950, Twentieth Century Fund, New York, 1953; Cochrane, Willard W., and Mary E. Ryan, American Farm Policy, 1948–1973, University of Minnesota Press, Minneapolis, 1976; Food and Agricultural Policy, American Enterprise Institute for Public Policy Research, Washington, D.C., 1977; Rasmussen, Wayne D., and Gladys L. Baker, Price-Support and Adjustment Programs from 1933 through 1978: A Short History, U.S. Department of Agriculture Information Bulletin 424, 1979.

(See also Agricultural productivity)

Willard W. Cochrane

Agricultural productivity

Productivity is the ratio of output or product to an input or group of inputs. Frequently used productivity measures in agriculture are yield of crops per unit of land, output per animal, or output per worker. Such productivity measures may be for a specific time and place—for example, the corn yield in 1979 in Iowa was 119 bushels per acre; or as an index of change over time—for example, the corn yield in Iowa in 1979 was 2 percent greater than in 1978.

Measuring Agricultural Productivity

The appropriate measure of agricultural productivity depends upon the objective of the measurement. Care must be taken in interpreting yields per unit of land or output per farm worker. A comparison of crop yields across either space or time does not indicate whether the land with the highest yield is more productive than the land with the lower yield. Since it takes more than one input, land, to produce a crop, the output from a particular piece of land will depend upon what other inputs are used with the land. Thus, the yield from land depends upon seed (amount and quality), fertilizer, moisture or rainfall, temperature, land preparation, cultivation, use of herbicides or insecticides, and disease control measures. Thus, differences in yield per unit of land may measure many factors other than the quality of the land.

One important objective of measuring agricultural productivity is to determine if there has been a change in technology or productivity over time. In other words, can the same resources produce more now than in some time past? This seems like a simple question, but the complexities in measuring it are not. The debate between Griliches and Jorgenson on the one side and Denison on the other reveal the major complexities. Stated simply, productivity measurement involves estimating a function such as the following:

$$Y = CAKLFEWT$$

Where Y is a measure of output; C a constant; and A, K, L, F, and E are measures of specific inputs such as labor, land, fertilizer; a group of inputs such as machinery; or current operating expenses. W is included as a measure of conditions over which the producers have no control; in most cases it would be an index of weather. The data are observations over time, generally on an annual basis. T is a measure of time; the size of T is a measure of the annual rate of change in Y per unit of input. In other words, T is a measure of productivity change. If it has a value of 1.5, it means that output per unit of input is increasing at the rate of 1.5 percent annually.

Measurement Problems

There are important measurement problems in productivity analysis. Quality changes in both the outputs and inputs can present major difficulties, and the importance of the difficulties grows as the period covered becomes longer. Outputs, such as beef and poultry, do not remain the same over time; yet such products usually enter the output measure without adjustment for any differences that may occur. Quality change in the inputs have been important for agriculture. Farm tractors today are very different machines from what they were one or two decades ago. Farm managers are better educated today than in the past. The quality of seeds is changing continuously.

When input quality changes are ignored, the change in output attributed to productivity change will be too large. While in many ways the U.S. Department of Agriculture is a leader in producing an annual measure of productivity change in agriculture, the failure to adjust for changes in input quality adversely affects the value of its work. In addition, no consideration is given to the effects of climate or weather upon agricultural output. Consequently, the measure of agricultural productivity that is generally available may be misleading for consideration of year-to-year comparisons since most of the difference in the productivity measure may have been due to differences in weather.

Why does output per unit of measured inputs increase over time? Changes in productivity do not occur at a uniform pace. Evidence indicates that from 1880 to 1930 there was no increase in agricultural productivity in the United States. In the next half-century, output per unit of input more than doubled. The fundamental source of increased productivity was increased knowledge created primarily through research. In effect, knowledge of the fundamental processes of nature has improved over time; the improved knowledge permits the use of available resources more effectively. For example, new crop varieties are made possible by increased understanding of genetics. Since there is much that is unknown about nature, it is reasonable to assume that maximum productivity in agriculture remains far from being realized.

References

Hayami, Yujiro, and Vernon W. Ruttan, *Agricultural Development: An International Perspective,* Johns Hopkins Press, Baltimore, 1971; Economic Research Service, *Changes in Farm Production and Efficiency: Historical Series,* U.S. Department of Agriculture, Statistical Bulletin 561, September 1978; Jorgenson, Dale W., Zvi Griliches, and Edward F. Denison, *The Measurement of Productivity,* Brookings, Washington, D.C., 1972; Loomis, Ralph A., and Glen T. Barton, *Productivity of Agriculture: United States, 1870–1958,* U.S. Department of Agriculture, Technical Bulletin 1238, April 1961.

(*See also* Agricultural economic policy; Agricultural revolution; Productivity)

D. Gale Johnson

Agricultural revolution

The term agricultural revolution is used in economic history with both a wide and a narrow connotation. In its wider sense, it refers to thoroughgoing conversion from one of a sequence of fixed types of agricultural technology to another in the production of the grains, with an associated livestock husbandry. The earliest example of this is the invention of agriculture itself, the so-called neolithic revolution of about 8000 to 3000 B.C. During this time, the art evidently changed from the gathering of rich stands of wild grasses—barley, emmer, and a form of wheat—to the purposeful sowing of seed and some preparation of the soil. By 3000 B.C., conversion from the hoe to the plow with the use of draft cattle had occurred at some sites. The breeding of sheep, goats, and cattle is traceable at least to 5000 B.C., in the Near East. Since wild grasses were cut and milled before their actual cultivation, the making of agricultural tools and equipment—sickles, mortars, and even pottery jars for storage— must have begun before agriculture itself, but these allied arts, together with spinning and weaving, are usually taken as part of the neolithic revolution. The locus of origin for the cereal grasses is usually placed in eastern Anatolia and Lebanon; the development of maize in meso-America and of rice cultivation in China and Southeast Asia are separate and somewhat later phenomena. In their neolithic form, these arts then spread, from the Near East across the Mediterranean lands and by migrations into Central and Northern Europe between 3000 and 1000 B.C., adapting field techniques and genetic materials to the variations in soils and climates.

Boserup's Five-Stage Sequence

Recently, the later stages of development of the grain-livestock technology have been formalized by E. Boserup in a five-stage sequence, the changeover from one stage to another being radical enough to deserve the name "revolution" despite the long periods of time required for diffusion of the new technique. These stages are determined by the type of soil cover when not planted in crops, or by the time between successive plantings of an area in a soil-exhausting crop. They are: (1) forest fallow (20 to 40 years), (2) bush fallow (5 to 10 years), (3) biennial or triennial fallow, (4) continuous cropping, and (5) multicropping. These stages use the land successively more intensively, and therefore involve successively more labor per year per acre in cultivation, but yield larger annual outputs both per farmer-year and per acre encompassed in the whole agrarian system. Boserup's hypothesis, of wide applicability in African and Asian agriculture, and historically in Europe between 1000 B.C. and A.D. 1900, is that the revolutions from one stage to the next are caused by population pressure which gradually forces the conversion to a regime of harder work and higher yields. Boserup further suggests that forms of landholding and social organization undergo corresponding changes from communal or tribal landholdings to village agriculture in settled fields to private property in land.

European Agricultural Revolution

In an earlier and still perhaps most common usage, the term agricultural revolution denotes the conversion of European grain agriculture from the triennial fallow regime of the high Middle Ages and early modern period to one of continuous cultivation (i.e., from stage 3 to 4 in the Boserup sequence). In the classic three-field regime which existed in a wide belt from central England and northern France across to central Russia, and from southern Sweden to Bavaria and Hungary, the standard three-field rotation—wheat (or rye), barley (or oats), fallow—was replaced by varied rotations involving a cover crop (clover, sainfoin, alfalfa) or a root crop (turnips, beets) instead of fallow, or by a multiyear rotation of cereal and grass (convertible husbandry). The earliest forms of continuous cropping occur in the low countries before 1500, and the most widespread and rapid conversions occur in England between 1650 and 1850. Here, the change appears to have been called forth by a growing urban demand for meat and dairy products, since the new crops were feed crops, but the higher stocking levels thus achieved raised fertilizer supplies, and the system increased the depth and fineness of tillage, reduced weeds, and raised yields in the grains. These systems spread on commercial estates in Scandinavian and East German areas in the late eighteenth century and more slowly in the peasant agriculture of western and southern Germany and northern France throughout the nineteenth and early twientieth centuries. Open-field villages with strip farming, many preserving old rotation patterns, persisted in Russia until the collectivization of the 1920s and in Eastern Europe into the 1930s. In all areas, enclosure, consolidation of strips, conversion of commons to private ownership were changes not absolutely necessary to new techniques, but this organizational revolution greatly facilitated the technical changes, allowed for breed improvement in stock, and opened the way for agricultural experimentation and innovation. In Marx's view, these technical and organizational changes were a necessary part of the separation of the peasant from a feudal status in relation to lord and soil and the formation of a wage-labor force in agriculture and industry.

This technical revolution differed from the Boserup model in that it appeared to have been called out by market growth ahead of intense population pressure, and so permitted the rising living standard which gave demand for industrial products in northwestern Europe. Even where it did not or could not occur, the market growth from the sixteenth century onward produced an accompanying organizational revolution which had productivity-raising effects in agriculture and profound social effects on the forms of landholding and the distribution of landed property. As Blum has detailed them (1978), the changes on the Continent between 1750 and 1863 involved virtually everywhere in the old open-field areas:

1. The division and plowing up of the fields formerly held by villages in common
2. The abolition or commutation to money rents of labor services owed by peasants to the lords
3. The emancipation of the peasant from juridicial serfdom and termination of judicial powers of lords.

Slowly, too, the system of divided strips in the fields was replaced by enclosed and consolidated holdings, and the shift from communal and feudal tenures remote from commercial influence to an agriculture of estates and peasant holdings, receptive to innovation and responsive to market pressures, was complete. The continuation of similar changes with modern biochemical techniques and machinery has continued agrarian change in tropical and semitropical countries in recent decades. The so-called green revolution in India-Pakistan and similar rapid rises in grain yields in the Western Hemisphere and Europe have proceeded far faster than the classic agricultural revolution of the eighteenth and nineteenth centuries, and have organizational and social consequences equally revolutionary.

References

Blum, J., The End of the Old Order in Rural Europe, Princeton University Press, Princeton, N.J., 1978; Boserup, E., The Conditions of Agricultural Growth, Aldine, Chicago. 1965; Chambers, J. D., and C. E. Mingay, The Agricultural Revolution, 1750–1880, B. T. Batsford, London, 1966; Grantham, George, "The Diffusion of the New Husbandry to Northern France," Journal of Economic History, vol. 38, June 1978, pp. 311–337; Kerridge, E., The Agricultural Revolution, Kelley, New York, 1968; Parker, W. N., and E. L. Jones (eds.), European Peasants and Their Markets, Princeton University Press, Princeton, N.J., 1975; Reed, Charles A. (ed.) Origins of Agriculture, Aldine, Chicago, 1978.

(See also Agricultural productivity)

William N. Parker

Allocation of resources (see Distribution theory)

Alternative cost (see Opportunity cost)

Anticipation surveys, business

Business anticipation surveys ask participating companies about their plans or expectations of future activity regarding sales, prices, and capital investment, as well as questions regarding past activity. In certain respects these surveys are theoretically similar to surveys made of consumers. Both types of survey began after the end of World War II. The best-known of the business surveys, the Department of Commerce "Survey of New Plant and Equipment Expenditures, and the McGraw-Hill Spring Survey, and Fall Survey of Plans for New Plants and Equipment, were begun in 1945,

1947, and 1953, respectively, while the Survey Research Center at the University of Michigan began its work in the consumer area in 1946 to 1947.

There are, however, major differences between the two types of anticipation survey: consumer and business. Consumer surveys rely on probability sampling to extrapolate conclusions from a relatively small sample of consumers, perhaps 3000 to 4000, to the much larger universe of all consumers.

Business surveys come much closer to being a modified census than a random sample. Fewer than 0.1 percent of the corporations in the United States account for 60.8 percent of all corporate assets and nearly 40 percent of total receipts. Within the manufacturing sector in 1972, 355 companies out of 203,200 submitting active income tax returns accounted for two-thirds of the manufacturing assets and 56.2 percent of receipts. In business surveys, an attempt is made to include as many of these large companies as possible. A more random sampling is made of the medium- and smaller-sized companies to eliminate any systematic large-company bias.

Reliability of Business Surveys

The reliability of business anticipation surveys tends to be a direct function of how many of the largest companies have responded. In general, business surveys are more reliable than consumer surveys in predicting the magnitude of expected change in sales or investment, as opposed to direction alone. (Consumer surveys are primarily useful in predicting turning points in consumer behavior.) The reason is that companies, particularly large companies, plan expenditures and a future year's activity to a much greater extent than do consumers.

For the same reason, surveys of investment plans tend to be more reliable than sales expectations. The capital investment process by its nature requires planning. Prospective rates of return on alternative projects must be evaluated. Once viable options have been selected, the expenditures must be approved and the funds appropriated by a board of directors. This decision-making process itself fixes probable capital investment into the future. In addition, many capital projects have very long time lags between approval of projects, letting of contracts, and completion of the projects. As long as progress on a project is on schedule, the expenditure stream should be predictable within fairly narrow limits. However, there will be some slippage on the "up" side of a capital goods expansion, as delivery times slow, and companies may cut plans or stretch out projects during a recession to conserve their cash flow.

Still, under normal conditions a company will not spend significantly more or less than planned in any given fiscal year. Accordingly, surveys of such plans are good indicators of future investment activity.

Companies also set sales plans. In many cases sales plans probably could more accurately be described as goals or targets rather than point forecasts. There is rarely a penalty to management for exceeding its sales forecast, while major cost overruns on a capital project could put a company in financial jeopardy. Furthermore, many cyclical companies are vulnerable to factors outside of their control, triggering an unexpected contraction in overall economic activity which would make their sales forecast unrealistically high.

Because of the nature of sales planning, surveys of anticipated sales are better indicators of business confidence than predictors of future activity, However, business confidence plays a very important role in capital investment. Thus, if the outlook for sales turns sour, it may mean that planned capital investment is vulnerable to cutbacks.

Although business anticipation surveys focus mainly on the future, they often include a number of questions pertaining to past activity, Provided they are asked regularly, the answers to these questions are often useful in their own right or as a means of determining the probable error in results of the anticipation survey.

Department of Commerce Survey

The best-known and oldest anticipation survey is that conducted by the Department of Commerce and the Securities and Exchange Commission (SEC). Initially, most companies registered and reporting to the SEC (almost all of the large, publically owned companies) were included, as well as a large sample of unregistered manufacturing companies that reported to the Department of Commerce. It is currently conducted solely by the Department of Commerce, and the size of the sample has increased over time to provide more complete coverage in some industries.

The companies surveyed report not only their planned capital investments but also their actual expenditures in the past period, and the carry-over of uncompleted projects. Manufacturers are asked their actual and preferred operating rates and the adequacy of their capacity as well.

Over the nearly 35 years that this survey has been conducted, it has become apparent that there is a systematic bias in the response of certain industries both annually and on a quarterly basis. The Department of Commerce attempts to compensate for this through application of a bias adjustment. This adjustment has been the source of considerable controversy. In recent years, the adjustment has tended to improve the results for individual industries, while producing the opposite result for total expenditures. The adjustment in some periods has been large. For example, adjusted plant and equipment expenditures for 1979 reported in August 1979 were $174.11 billion. Before the bias adjustment, expenditures of $177.19 billion were reported as anticipated by respondents. Inasmuch as more than 7 months of the year had passed at the time the survey was conducted, the discrepancy was quite large. Under normal conditions, such a large adjustment so late in the year would appear highly questionable. In seven of the ten quarters from the beginning of 1977 through mid-1979 for which actual data are available, actual expenditures have exceeded planned expenditures one quarter ahead. The bias adjustment may be partially responsible for this discrepancy. However, since the bias adjustment is reported quarterly only for the annual data, it is not possible to determine from the published data whether or not these discrepancies correlate with the bias adjustment on a quarter-by-quarter basis.

A further problem with the Department of Commerce survey is that companies are far better at anticipating the full year's expenditures than at estimating the quarterly pattern. At the end of each year, two surveys are conducted very close to each other. The November survey reports planned expenditures through the first half of the following year. The December survey reports planned expenditures for the following year as a whole. Since under normal conditions total expenditures for a year should be very close to the seasonally adjusted annual rate at which expenditures were running at the midyear point, it should be possible to extrapolate an estimate of the full year from the rate at which expenditures are planned for the second quarter. Consistently, the December survey is a significantly better estimator of the following year's expenditures than the November survey. Furthermore, simple inter-polation from the fourth quarter of the current year to the annual expectation for the following year often gives a better result for the first half than the reported quarterly plans. Since the samples are similar, the difference appears to reflect, first, the greater ability of companies to predict plans on an annual basis and, secondly, differences in the bias adjustment.

McGraw-Hill Survey

Only slightly less well known than the Department of Commerce survey is the McGraw-Hill spring survey which began in 1947. The fall survey, incidentally, reports planned plant and equipment expenditures and expected sales and prices for one year ahead. In the spring survey, longer-range plans, planned additions to capac-ity and the previous end-of-the-year operating rate are also surveyed. Various other questions are included, some consistently, some only occasionally. The additional information included in this survey often makes it more useful than the Department of Commerce survey.

Numerous criticisms have been leveled against this survey over the years. Unlike the Department of Commerce survey, no attempt is made to adjust for systematic bias. For reasons that are not clear, the spring survey usually overestimates expenditures relative to the fall survey. However, since no adjustments are made to the data, it is possible to evaluate whether the bias is changing over time.

One of the problems with the McGraw-Hill survey is the lack of consistency from one survey to the next. For example, some years the expenditures have been bench-marked to the Department of Commerce expenditures for the previous year; in other years they have not been. In addition, McGraw-Hill surveys fewer firms than the Department of Commerce and tends to have a large-company bias. Hence, its results by industry tend to be better for those industries where a few large firms dominate than those in which many companies each have a relatively small share of market.

Other Surveys

If one's definition of anticipation survey is not restricted to those which predomi-nantly request information about future business activity, many trade associations' membership surveys could also be included among anticipation surveys. Some of these, such as the National Association of Purchasing Management, predominantly focus on current activity: production, orders, employment, prices, and inventories, but occasionally ask questions regarding the companies' views on the outlook for future activity. Others, such as the American Paper Institute's annual capacity survey, focus on a very narrow range of future activity.

All of these surveys can be useful to the business analyst provided they are well-designed. The longer any given survey is maintained without changes in definitions, the more valuable it tends to become.

References

Eisner, Robert, *Factors in Business Investment*, National Bureau of Economic Research, Ballin-ger, Cambridge, Mass., 1978; *Fall Survey of Preliminary Plans for New Plants and Equipment*, McGraw-Hill Publications Company, Economics Department, New York, published annually; *Spring Survey of Plans for New Plants and Equipment*, McGraw-Hill Publications Company, Economics Department, New York, published annually; Ferber, Robert (ed.), *Determinants of Investment Behavior*, Universities-National Bureau Conference Series, no. 19, Columbia University Press, New York, 1967; U.S. Bureau of Economic Analysis, *Survey of New Plant and Equipment Expenditures*, U.S. Department of Commerce, published quarterly.

(*See also* Anticipation surveys, consumer; Business investment in new plants and equipment)

M. Kathryn Eickoff

Anticipation surveys, consumer

Historically, extrapolation or projection of past trends was the most common method of forecasting. Therefore, forecasting was most successful when prevailing trends continued, but it often encountered difficulties or failed in predicting turning points in the business cycle. Toward the end of World War II there arose an urgent need for information anticipating changing trends, that is, for psychological data rather than contractual or legal.

Thus, the Division of Program Surveys in the U.S. Department of Agriculture began toward the end of World War II, under the direction of George Katona, to include questions in sample interview surveys on people's intentions to purchase houses, automobiles, and household appliances. In the year 1946–47 the Survey Research Center of the University of Michigan expanded the collection of survey data to consumer attitudes and expectations. The collection of such data has continued at regular intervals since that time and now belongs among the accepted tools of forecasting.

Surveys of consumer attitudes and of consumer finances were made possible by a rapid development of survey methods, particularly probability sampling, in the 1940s. It became possible to draw relatively small samples (1500 to 3000 households) in an unbiased manner which were representative of all households or all consumers in the country within margins of error that were known in advance.

The Theoretical Basis of Consumer Anticipation Surveys

The following four propositions summarize the theoretical basis of consumer anticipation surveys:

1. In affluent societies, as they developed first in the United States and later in Western Europe and a few other countries, broad groups of consumers are able to make discretionary expenditures beyond purchasing the basic necessities of life. These expenditures are not solely a function of income or ability to buy. Their size and timing depend also on people's willingness to buy, which may change more suddenly and rapidly than income.

2. The most important discretionary expenditures of consumers resemble investment expenditures of business firms. Consumer purchases of one-family houses, automobiles, and other durable goods that are meant to serve for many years are usually bought on credit rather than out of income. They are often bought because of the attraction of and desire for new or better products rather than because of immediate need; they are subject to sudden and rapid fluctuations that have a great impact on general economic trends, especially at the onset of recession or recovery.

3. Attitudes and expectations represent variables intervening between precipitat-

ing circumstances (stimuli) and spending-saving decisions (responses) and are capable of changing the latter substantially. They represent predispositions to action and usually change earlier than actual expenditures.

4. Major changes in attitudes and expectations of masses of people, or of all people in a country, are measurable. Fairly simple questions, asked in interview surveys conducted with representative samples, about past and expected changes in personal-financial well-being, in the general economic outlook, and in market conditions or prices provide measures of consumer sentiment. Through repeated surveys it is possible to determine the presence or absence, and in the first case direction and extent, of changes in optimism or pessimism as well as in confidence or doubt and uncertainty. Changes in these attitudes and expectations indicate changes in people's willingness to make major expenditures.

Index of Consumer Sentiment

After a few years of experience with measuring changes in consumer attitudes and expectations, in 1952 the Survey Research Center constructed an index of consumer sentiment. It is composed of answers to questions about changes in personal-financial well-being (both in the recent past and in the near future), about people's general economic outlook (during the next year and the next 5 years), and an evaluation of market conditions for durable goods (whether it is a good time or a bad time to buy them).

Measures of consumer optimism are directly linked to subsequent changes in the purchase of durable goods and the incurrence of installment debt, which in turn have an impact on general economic trends. The strongest test of the predictive value of consumer attitudes and expectations consists, therefore, of a comparison of the movements of the index of consumer sentiment with turning points in the business cycle. In every instance, including the minirecession of 1966, the index turned down before a recession began. Significantly, the longest and sharpest decline in the index in 1973 preceded the deepest postwar recession of 1974.

Before economic upturns the performance of the index was satisfactory, but the time lag between the change in the attitudinal indicators and in spending or saving was shorter than it was for downturns. In periods of little economic change, attitudes fluctuated little and the index did not perform better than extrapolative forecasts. The importance of attitude measures at these times consisted of the reassurance they provided that major changes were not imminent.

The surveys of consumer sentiment serve not only to answer the question of what will probably happen but also why it will happen. Policymakers, the business community, and the public in general require information about the reasons for probable future developments in order to evaluate the forecasts and proceed intelligently.

Each quarterly or monthly survey of the Survey Research Center consists of about 30 questions, among which only 5 are used to construct the index. The other questions shed light on how consumers feel about various aspects of the economy, such as inflation, unemployment, interest rates, and government policies. The answers to these questions provide some understanding of the factors that influence prevailing trends.

For many years following World War II only the Survey Research Center collected data on changes in consumer sentiment. In later years several American organizations (the Conference Board, Sindlinger, Gallup) made use of questions similar to those asked by the Survey Research Center, and contributed to the dissemination of economic survey data and the prediction of economic trends. Similar surveys were introduced in other countries. Most importantly, in the 1970s the Common Market arranged for periodic surveys of consumer attitudes and expectations in each of its member countries (Belgium, France, West Germany, Holland, Italy and more recently, England).

Problems with Consumer Anticipation Surveys

Although consumer anticipation surveys have a history of 30 years, there remain a number of unsolved problems. For example, on whom should reliance be placed: A sample of all Americans? Only upper-income families who make most of the major purchases? Or lower-income families who suffer most during a recession? Experience indicates that samples of all people have been most reliable, but this generalization may not hold true in the future.

The relation of the impact of ability to buy and of purchasing power (income trends or income trends adjusted for inflation) to that of willingness to buy presents a second problem. In the past the relative power of the two varied under different circumstances.

Studies of the origin of changes in consumer sentiment are likewise not yet concluded. Attempts by econometricians to substitute for the index of consumer sentiment some economic variables that might be assumed to cause change in sentiment— changes in the rate of unemployment or in prices, for instance—were successful at some periods after the fact, but not in predicting how the index would change in the future. Apparently, changes in consumer sentiment depend on a variety of factors, the relative importance of which varies over time. At any given time, however, the origin of change in expectations can be determined.

Significant new problems arose in the 1970s. In the 1950s and 1960s most of the measured economic attitudes had changed in a consistent manner. This was no longer the case in the 1970s. Backward-looking attitudes and forward-looking attitudes diverged to a large extent (for instance, whether people felt better or worse off financially than a year ago and whether they expected to be better or worse off a year hence). Spread of optimism was no longer linked with growing confidence and assurance but rather coexisted with widespread uncertainty and lack of confidence after 1974. Most importantly, some attitudes pointed toward an increased rate of purchases of durable goods at a time when others reflected the probability of a lower rate of purchases. In 1977 and 1978, surveys indicated that a large proportion of Americans expected the prices of houses and automobiles to advance substantially, and therefore thought that it was a good time to buy houses and cars before prices went up further. In those years, however, pessimism about economic trends grew and pointed toward lower purchases and the probability of a recession in the near future.

Changing times may require changes in anticipation surveys. Further developments may be required in methods of conducting these surveys and in evaluating their implications.

References

Katona, George, *Psychological Economics*, Elsevier, New York, 1975, chaps. 5, 6, 7; Strumpel, Burkhard, James N. Morgan, and Ernest Zahn (eds.), *Human Behavior in Economic Affairs*, Elsevier, New York, 1972, chaps. 15, 16, 18.

(*See also* Anticipation surveys, business; Behavioral economics; Consumer theory; Marketing research and business economics; Sampling in economics)

George Katona

Antitrust policy

Opposition to private monopoly became national policy with the Sherman Antitrust Act of 1890. By the 1880s public opinion became so aroused against the new industrial combinations that 13 states passed antitrust laws. Most did so later, but these state laws can be used only against occasional local conspiracies. The Sherman Act itself received all but one vote in the Senate and a 2 to 1 majority in the House. It provided fine or imprisonment for "every contract . . . or conspiracy in restraint of trade" (section 1) and "every person who shall monopolize, or attempt to monopolize . . . commerce among the several States or with foreign nations" (section 2).

Antitrust Policy Shaped by the Courts

Suits have centered on two major areas, price agreements and monopolization. In its 1899 *Addyston Pipe* opinion, the Supreme Court interpreted section 1 to outlaw price agreements whether or not the prices were reasonable. The practical outcome, as in several later cases, was paradoxical: the defendant companies formed a combination. The *Trenton Potteries* opinion of 1927 expanded the Court's views. Agreements on prices (also sometimes on production, market divisions, or boycotts) keep appearing, and beginning in the 1960s some offenders served short jail terms.

Better known and more in tune with the sentiment of 1890 are the attacks on monopolization (simple monopoly is not unlawful), although indictments usually charge violations of both sections. The 1904 *Northern Securities* decision separating two northwestern railroads (again no new competition was created), led President Theodore Roosevelt to order suits against many big combinations of the preceding quarter-century, while President Taft did it for most of the rest. Du Pont was split into three parts; there were more rail dissolutions; and the courts directed changes in the farm machinery and meatpacking industries. The major success was the Supreme Court's 1911 decision that broke up Standard Oil and American Tobacco into many smaller companies because they had "unreasonably" restrained trade and monopolized. This "rule of reason" shocked many people, and antitrust became a 1912 campaign issue. Woodrow Wilson, the victor, signed two supplementary laws in 1914.

Sherman Act cases remained central, however, during the quarter-century of diminished achievement that followed. In 1916 the trial judge ruled that American Can Company, though created to monopolize, had failed and was now an efficient competitor whose breakup would injure the economy. A 4 to 3 Supreme Court majority said much the same thing in its *U.S. Steel* decision of 1920. Policing trade restraints kept the small federal Antitrust Division occupied. For example, it marked the bounds of trade association activities: interchange of statistics and of actual sale prices was legal (*Maple Flooring*, 1925,—though in 1969 the container ruling was to make any price interchange suspect), but not pledges to sell only at announced prices (*Sugar Institute*, 1936). From 1933 to 1935, under the National Recovery Act (NRA), industry Codes of Trade Practices had antitrust exemption. Antitrust resumed in 1936, when most major oil companies were indicted for continuing their NRA-authorized support of prices. In the 1940 *Socony-Vacuum* decision, any concerted action influencing prices was condemned.

Antitrust Expands

President Franklin Roosevelt decided in 1938 that more price competition among big companies would stimulate employment, and the Antitrust Division was greatly enlarged. The three most famous ensuing decisions were *Alcoa* (1945), *American Tobacco* (1946), and *Paramount Pictures* (1948). The Court of Appeals sitting in New York ruled that Alcoa had retained its monopoly partly through efficiencies of size. When the tobacco convictions were affirmed, with emphasis on practices such as price identity in cigarettes and heavy advertising, normal activities of industries with few competitors seemed to stand condemned. The "new" Sherman Act, said commentators, would end the oligopoly pattern of dominant large firms in many industries. But the Alcoa precedent was not pursued until the 1947 *United Shoe Machinery* suit ended in 1968 with a dissolution order of the Supreme Court; the tobacco companies paid fines, but did not change their practices.

The motion picture suits proved less significant for industry restructuring (ending of the producer-exhibitor affiliations with first-run privileges for exhibitor chains) than for the impetus to treble-damage suits, authorized in 1890 but hitherto rare. Independent theaters, citing antitrust convictions as evidence of law violations, had only to prove a loss of profits to collect three times the jury estimate of these. Their suits were followed in the 1960s by actions by power companies, which collected huge sums out of the electrical-equipment price conspiracies uncovered in 1960. Later antitrust convictions have brought swarms of private suits. These lack the deterrent effect originally expected, partly because some actions are not known to be violations until the Antitrust Division so charges, partly because managers hoping to improve their profit showings by evading the law do not worry about stockholder losses years later.

In several areas Sherman Act cases increased competition. They dissolved some patent licensing and pooling arrangements which, even if first intended to resolve conflicting claims, had hamstrung entry and independent actions. The patent right itself received a degree of Sherman Act approval in 1956, when four Supreme Court justices held that E. I. du Pont's cellophane patents had given the firm a lawful monopoly of one flexible packaging material competing with others, whereas only three believed it had thus monopolized a unique product. In 1957 Du Pont was the loser: the Court directed that it sell its controlling 23 percent of General Motors stock ostensibly because this helped it monopolize the fabrics and finishes bought for GM cars, but actually because of concentration of power.

Federal Trade Commission Act

President Wilson's 1914 legislation assumed that trusts gained dominance through unfair and "predatory" competitive practices. There was evidence for this, but advantages of size in technology, marketing, and finance probably were, both previously and since, more important. The Federal Trade Commission Act created this agency to issue "cease and desist" orders against "any unfair method of competition." Courts of Appeals were soon reviewing the definition of unfair, one review finding that unfairness to consumers was lawful unless it hurt competitors. So a 1938 amendment added any "unfair or deceptive act or practice in commerce." The Commission had early treated price agreements as unfair, thus assuming broad antitrust enforcement powers which the Supreme Court confirmed in 1927. It also has primary, though not sole, responsibility to enforce the Clayton Act, the second 1914 statute.

Clayton Act

This act forbade specific practices: exclusive dealing with an anticompetitive effect, interlocking directors between competitors, price discrimination in favor of big buyers (section 2), and purchasing stock in a competitor (section 7). Exclusive dealing, sometimes putting a squeeze on customers and smaller competitors, has been often attacked, with some degree of success. Companies do not use common directors to avoid competition. Sections 2 and 7 were not effective until strengthened.

The Robinson-Patman Act of 1936 is the amended section 2. Hundreds of Commission actions have attacked discounts, or advertising or promotion favors, to big customers. The law sets up defenses: that costs of serving the customer are lower has almost never been proved to the satisfaction of the Commission or Appeals Courts; that the seller would otherwise have lost the customer, because some competitor had first offered the lower price, is often accepted. Excessive discounts are now fewer; so are cost-justified ones. Because of this, and because the law forbids bypassing commodity brokers, most economists favor repeal.

Celler-Kefauver Act

The Celler-Kefauver Act of 1950 amended section 7, forbidding acquisitions, through purchase of either stock or assets, which tend to suppress competition or create a monopoly. After an unbroken series of Antitrust Division or Commission victories, especially *Brown Shoe* (1962), mergers in which the courts saw such a tendency were off limits. Later mergers, numerous indeed, are conglomerates—either pure conglomerates for diversification; market extensions entering a new territory; or product extensions within the company's area, such as chemicals or textiles. Some product extensions, however, suppress "potential" competition since the court feels, as in *Procter & Gamble* (1967), that the acquiring firm might otherwise have built its own plant to compete.

The Commission has continued antitrust work and broadened its consumer protection activities. One crusade of many years was against the base-point method of pricing, in which the price to a buyer is the one quoted at some other point than that of production, plus transport cost from that other point. The Supreme Court's *Cement Institute* decision condemned this pricing method in the cement industry as unfair because it was collusive and as discriminatory in price because sales to more distant customers yielded less profit. Similar orders went out to steel and a number of other industries. The essence of the system, however, price identity to the customer, can be eradicated only by excluding more distant suppliers.

The combination of formal victory with less of a practical gain has accompanied some of the attacks on deceptive advertising and labeling as well. By the time the Commission has painstakingly gathered evidence, issued an order, and beaten a court appeal, the respondent company will have found a new theme or method, perhaps deceptive in some other way. Nevertheless, most of those worried about preserving ethical practices in competition view the Commission's work as indispensable.

Exemptions from Antitrust

Antitrust is a political "sacred cow," even if exemptions have been passed. The Clayton Act gave one to "labor, agricultural, or horticultural organizations ... lawfully carrying out the legitimate objects thereof." In the 1920s the Supreme Court declined to consider restraints such as secondary boycotts to be "lawful" or "legitimate" but in the 1940s it gave unions not conspiring with employers the desired relief. Most other exemptions achieved little. Export trade associations, allowed in 1918, became less and less important. The fair-trade Sherman Act amendment of 1937, reaffirmed in 1952, could not prevent discount-house operations and was repealed in 1975. Publicly supervised rate bureaus in insurance and transportation received exemptions in the 1940s, but Washington was eyeing them suspiciously at the end of the 1970s. These and other industry exemptions were construed narrowly by the courts, which took an ever stronger antitrust line. After 1963 and 1964, when the Supreme Court overruled regulatory bodies which had approved bank and gas pipeline mergers and when the stock exchanges learned they were not exempt, it was clear that only very specific congressional action, which rarely came, could give any exemption. In the 1970s the professions, even the law, were told that their codes violated the Sherman Act, and government bodies engaged in commerce were receiving warnings.

This is no simple policy against trusts; it is an expanding network of court interpretations (about 300 pages a year in the early 1940s, 3000 in the late 1970s) governing business activity. Most companies know they must refrain from actions which their lawyers say will carry an antitrust risk. The policy has costs: huge legal expenses, business confusion as the rules change, banning of some practices which on balance would be useful and productive. But it has accomplishments too. Dominant single firms gave way to oligopolies, and dominance cannot be restored through mergers. Although fewness of competitors, in heavy industry as in local services, deters price cutting because quick retaliation is likely, there is competition in service, research, and new products, and even sometimes in price, while customers benefit from the economies of large-scale production at the cost of a profit margin which year after year is 5 or 6 cents on the dollar. The rule against cartels is especially important; without it a network of agreements might soon tie up many industries. In the competitive American business climate, these would break down as did some early monopolies spared by antitrust, but it is healthier not to try them. Finally, the fairness of competition has been improved to some degree.

Minority Economists' Views on Antitrust

A dissenting minority of economists views much antitrust enforcement as a war on efficiency. Sheer size is theoretically legal, but a company which becomes large stimulates complaints from competitors who are losing out and becomes a challenge to antitrust enforcers, then to treble-damage seekers. The "big cases," against IBM in 1969 and American Telephone in 1974, will be decided in the mid-1980s when the Supreme Court, whether or not influenced by current public opinion, decides either that they were efficient or that enough of their practices were predatory to call for some restructuring. This school of economic thought also dislikes the occasional argument that competitive advantage, usually in marketing or amount of resources available, makes a merger illegal. In summary, it wants antitrust to protect competition and not competitors.

Majority View

An apparent majority of economists specializing in industrial organization has an opposite philosophy: big companies, competing in advertising rather than price, earn socially unnecessary profits; their bureaucratic organization raises costs and prices and reduces innovation; their slowly rising share of industrial sales and assets, even if due to conglomerate mergers as aging owners sell out their small companies, puts too much business and political power into a few hands. Two proposals are made: that the biggest corporations be allowed no acquisitions and that those next in size be allowed no acquisitions whose social value cannot be demonstrated; and that corporate giants, if unable to prove in court or to a public agency that size is required for efficiency, be broken up. Between the schools of economists a battle of statistical studies rages.

Antitrust is an American specialty. Some type of antitrust action has been taken in Great Britain, Canada, and the European Economic Community, but no one nation claims its laws have an impact even approaching that of the United States.

How far does antitrust explain the immense twentieth-century growth in productivity? This has rested on large natural resources, developed with an acquisitive, aggressive, competitive zest throughout U.S. history; antitrust has added to the competitiveness. But Germany made remarkable progress under cartels before both world wars and again, though with more oligopoly replacing monopoly, after 1945. Japan, with its conglomerates, has a similar record. Perhaps consistent application of science to industry, encouragement of enterprise, and above all hard work and willingness to save have outweighed any anticompetitive effect of cartel structures.

References

Bork, Robert H., *The Antitrust Paradox: A Policy at War with Itself*, Basic Books, New York, 1978; Scherer, F. M., *Industrial Market Structure and Economic Performance*, Rand-McNally, Chicago, 1970; Singer, Eugene M., *Antitrust Economics: Selected Legal Cases and Economic Models*, Prentice-Hall, Englewood Cliffs, N. J., 1968; Van Cise, Jerrold G., *The Federal Antitrust Laws*, American Enterprise Institute for Public Policy Research, Washington, D.C., 1975.

(*See also* Cartel; Competition; Concentration of industry; Economies of scale; Mergers; Monopoly and oligopoly; Restraint of trade)

Simon N. Whitney

Arbitrage

Arbitrage refers to purchases in one market and sales in another market that have the effect of maintaining prices of comparable commodities traded in these markets within limits set by the cost of buying the commodity in one market and selling it in another. The effect of arbitrage is to establish limits within which the price of a given commodity traded in a given market must lie. A tendency for the price to move outside of these limits which depend on costs induces arbitrage, forcing prices back into the limits.

Arbitrage occurs among markets in foreign exchange. Between any pair of foreign currencies there is an exchange rate. In a system where individuals may trade foreign currencies, arbitrage ensures that a sequence of transactions starting in one currency and going through several others will result in the same quantity of the starting currency less transaction costs. For instance, trading U.S. dollars for French francs, French francs for Japanes yen, and, finally, trading Japanese yen for U.S. dollars results in a final quantity of U.S. dollars equal to the initial quantity less transactions costs as an outcome of arbitrage.

Arbitrage also occurs across markets in which the same commodity is traded, if an individual can make transactions in all of these markets, or if pairs of markets can be linked by trades of the same individual. For instance, the price of silver in New York cannot differ from the price of silver in Chicago by more than the cost of transporting the given quantity of silver from one market to the other. A tendency for the price of silver to go outside these limits would induce arbitrage operations that would have the effect of lowering the price in the market to which the commodity is shipped and raising its price in the market from which it is shipped until it is no longer possible to obtain a positive net return from such pairs of transactions.

Although the main effect of arbitrage is to bring about a relation among prices of similar commodities according to the cost of converting the commodity from one form to the other, there need not be certainty about the outcome. For example, in the stock market there may be an announcement of a proposed merger between two companies such that Company A will acquire all of the stock of Company B at a given ratio, say, two shares of Company A stock for one share of Company B stock. If the merger is certain to occur, then the price per share of Company B stock will equal twice the price per share of Company A stock as a result of arbitrage. Until the merger is certain, however, the price ratio of shares of stock of the two companies need not be 2 to 1 because of the risk that the merger will not occur. Trades that take the form of selling shares of one company's stock and buying shares of the other company's stock owing to a departure of the current price ratio from that which will prevail when the merger is certain may be called arbitrage even though there is an element of risk involved.

A form of arbitrage occurs when a merchant acquires a stock of a commodity at a given spot price, sells an equal quantity forward, and as a result of these transactions and similar ones, the forward price is brought into a relation with the spot price such that the forward price does not exceed the spot price by more than the cost of storing the commodity until delivery is called for by the terms of the forward contract. Arbitrage establishes price relations among commodities for delivery at different times such that the price for later delivery cannot exceed the price for earlier delivery by more than the marginal cost of storage between the two dates.

References

Einzig, Paul, *A Dynamic Theory of Forward Exchange*, 2d ed., St. Martins Press, New York, 1967; Einzig, Paul, *The Eurodollar System*, 5th ed., St. Martins Press, New York, 1973.

(*See also* Commodity exchanges; Foreign exchange rates)

Lester G. Telser

Austrian economics

The Austrian school of economics is not an academic institution but a way of reasoning, technique of analysis, program of research, and theoretical system distinct from other schools of economic thought. It differs in essential respects from classical economics, from the historical school, and from Marxian, institutional, and mathematical economics. On the other hand, many of the principles of Austrian economics have been incorporated into neoclassical or modern economics.

Although derived from the writings of the recognized founder of the school—Carl Menger's *Principles of Economics* (1871) and *Problems of Economics and Sociology* (1883)—Austrian economics is not a completely uniform system accepted in every detail by all members of the group. Even the second generation—chiefly Eugen von Böhm-Bawerk and Friedrich von Wieser, often regarded as the cofounders of the school—disagreed with one another and with Menger on several issues; variants and deviations have become more conspicuous over time. This makes it difficult to define the school by a set of doctrines shared by all its members. In the 1890s the following four tenets were given as characteristic: marginalism, diminishing marginal utility, costs as foregone utility, and imputation of value to complementary factors. In later years major emphasis was placed on methodological individualism and subjectivism as most typically Austrian. If one speaks, not of Austrian economics as a whole, but instead of an Austrian approach to methodology, an Austrian theory of value, an Austrian theory of capital, an Austrian theory of the trade cycle, and an Austrian theory of economic freedom, one finds the Austrian school united only on the first two aspects, but divided on the rest.

Precursors, Coevals, and Followers

Several of the Austrian tenets regarding value theory had been anticipated by earlier economists. Among the precursors of the notion of utility combined with scarcity had been Galiani (1750), Condillac (1776), Auguste Walras (1831), Lloyd (1834), Dupuit (1844), and especially Gossen (1854). The last three, and perhaps also Galiani, fully understood the law of diminishing marginal utility. Marginalism not applied to utility had been expounded by many writers, most explicitly by von Thünen (1826) and Cournot (1838). The chief difference between the precursors and Menger was that none of the former had built an integrated theoretical system on the fundamental hypotheses in question.

There were, however, contemporaries of Menger who independently built a hypothetical-deductive system on the same fundamental assumptions: William Stanley Jevons (1862 and 1870) and Léon Walras (1873). A major difference between them and Menger was that their exposition employed mathematical notations while Menger's was verbal. This probably explains why for the last decades of the nineteenth century the Viennese had a much larger following than his colleagues in London and Lausanne, and why the Austrian school is generally regarded as nonmathematical.

The writings of Böhm-Bawerk and Wieser contributed greatly to the worldwide spreading of Austrian economics. Austrians of later generations, such as Ludwig von Mises and Friedrich A. von Hayek, lived and taught for many years in England and America and exerted great influence on their audiences.

The Main Tenets of the Austrian School

The following brief propositions may be offered as statements of positions held many, perhaps most, adherents of the Austrian school:

1. *Methodological individualism.* In the explanation of economic pheno

have to go back to the actions (or inaction) of individuals; groups or collectives cannot act except through the actions of individual members.

2. *Methodological subjectivism.* In the explanation of economic phenomena we have to go back to judgments and choices made by individuals on the basis of whatever knowledge they have or believe to have and whatever expectations they entertain regarding external developments and especially the consequences of their own intended actions.

3. *Marginalism.* In all economic decisions, the values, costs, revenues, productivity, etc., are determined by the significance of the last unit, or lot, added to or subtracted from the total.

4. *Tastes and preferences.* Subjective valuations (utility) of goods and services determine the demand for them, so that their market prices are influenced by (actual and potential) consumers; diminishing marginal utility of each good or service consumed affects the allocation of consumers' incomes among various uses.

5. *Opportunity costs* (first called Wieser's law of costs). The cost with which producers or other economic actors calculate reflect the most important of the alternative opportunities that have to be foregone if productive services are employed for one purpose rather than for the (sacrificed) alternatives.

6. *Time structure of consumption and production.* Decisions to save reflect "time preference" regarding consumption in the immediate, distant, or indefinite future, and investments are made in view of larger outputs to be obtained from given inputs by means of processes taking more time.

The last of these propositions states the two basic principles in Böhn-Bawerk's theory of capital. "Perspective undervaluation of the future" (or "impatience" in Irving Fisher's terminology) induces consumers to discount the expected utility of future consumption (or the importance of future needs); hence, saving (nonconsumption of income) and the supply of capital are scarce. "Roundaboutness of production," that is, the use of productive services (labor, land) over longer periods of production (investment), makes these services more productive, which explains the demand for capital. This theory of capital and interest was rejected by Menger and Wieser, but its main ideas were accepted by many other Austrians.

Controversies within the School

Highly controversial were two additional tenets, proposed by the Mises branch of Austrian economists:

7. *Consumer sovereignty.* The influence consumers have, directly, on the effective demand for goods and services and, indirectly, through the prices that result in free competitive markets, on the production plans of producers and investors, is not merely a fact but also an important objective, attainable only by complete avoidance of governmental interference with the markets and of restrictions on the freedom of sellers and buyers to follow their own judgment regarding quantities, qualities, and prices of products and services. (In a way this tenet is an equivalent of Pareto's optimum. The proposition amounts to a value judgment.)

8. *Political individualism.* Only when individuals are given full economic freedom

will it be possible to secure political and moral freedom. Restrictions on economic freedom lead, sooner or later, to an extension of the coercive activities of the state into the political domain, undermining and eventually destroying the essential individual liberties which the capitalistic societies were able to attain in the nineteenth century. (This is less a proposition of economics than of politics.)

These two added tenets were rejected by other Austrian economists. Joseph Schumpeter (1954) protested against "an association between... marginalism and capitalist apologetics." In the United States, nevertheless, the label "Austrian economics" has come to imply a commitment to the libertarian program.

There have been numerous controversies among Austrians. Menger regarded Böhm-Bawerk's theory of capital and interest as a grave error. Böhm-Bawerk and Wieser debated whether total utility (to whom? for what?) was equal to marginal utility (or price) times quantity or to the integral of marginal utility. Related to this was the problematic significance of surplus utility (equivalent to Marshall's consumer surplus). There was an argument as to whether a progressive income tax can be justified by diminishing marginal utility of income. The disagreement on cardinal versus ordinal utility, and on measurability of utility, has continued to this day.

Still unresolved is the question as to what extent Austrian economics is equilibrium economics, though the answer obviously depends on what is meant by equilibrium. (Surely, the equalization of marginal utilities of expenditures on different goods implies equilibrium of the household, and the notion of opportunity cost implies even more comprehensive equilibration.) That Menger rejected certain notions of equilibrium, especially some of the market equilibriums implied in the Walrasian conception of general equilibrium, need not make him an opponent of the use of the idea of equilibrium in the explanation of mere tendencies interpreted as adjustments to change. The Austrians attached great importance to the path toward equilibrium, but did not formulate precise conditions that must be satisfied at a point of equilibrium (least of all in instances when more than two goods are involved). The list of intraschool squabbles could easily be extended.

Austrian Economists

Not every economist born or residing in Austria was a member of the Austrian school, but there is wide agreement about those who qualify. The second generation included, besides Böhm-Bawerk and Wieser, Eugen von Philippovich, Emil Sax, Robert Zuckerandl, Johann von Komorzynski, Robert Meyer, and Richard Schüller. They all started publishing before the turn of the century. Two Viennese economists of the same period, Rudolf Auspitz and Richard Lieben, ought to be mentioned, though they have sometimes been relegated to the mathematical school and regarded as "un-Austrian Austrians." The same designation has been applied to Joseph Schumpeter, though despite his stronger allegiance to Walras, he is usually counted among the third generation of Austrian economists. Most of them had been members of the Böhm-Bawerk seminar and began publishing after 1900. The most important members of this group were Mises, Schumpeter, Hans Mayer, Alfred Amonn, Richard von Strigl, and Leo Schönfeld-Illy. Austrians who began publishing in the 1920s are regarded as the fourth generation. With the exception of Alexander Mahr, virtually all of them had been members of the private seminar which Mises conducted in Vienna from 1922 to 1934. They included Friedrich A. von Hayek, Gottfried Haberler, Fritz Machlup, Oskar Morgenstern, and Paul N. Rosenstein-Rodan; all had left Vienna before 1938, most of them before 1935. A fifth generation of the Austrian school is still active in Vienna; Erich Streissler is its representative.

Non-Austrian Austrian Economists

If Austrian economics is characterized by methods of analysis and fundamental hypotheses employed rather than by national origin or residence of those who profess it, one will recognize many non-Austrian Austrian economists. Indeed, Charles Gide and Charles Rist wrote as early as 1909 that "lately the Austrian school has become more American than Austrian," and mentioned the writers who "cultivate it with passion." Among the adherents of Austrian economics on the European continent were Maffeo Pantaleoni and later Augusto Graziani of Italy; Nicolas Gerard Pierson and G. M. Verrijn-Stuart of the Netherlands; Paul Leroy-Beaulieu, Adolphe Landry, and Gaëtan Pirou of France; Laurits Vilhelm Birck of Denmark; and most important, Knut Wicksell of Sweden. In England the most eminent of the early Austrian economists was Philip Wicksteed. One may add William Smart and William Robert Scott, and, among our contemporaries, Lionel Robbins and John R. Hicks as the most hospitable to the teachings of the Austrian school.

In the United States at least five economists who began publishing in the last decades of the nineteenth century may be mentioned for their "Austrian connection." John Bates Clark developed his theory of marginal productivity independently, but it converges with the work of the Austrians. Irving Fisher was a Walrasian in value theory, an Edgeworthian in refining indifference curve analysis, but a Böhm-Bawerkian in much of his theory of capital and interest. David J. Green contributed to Wieser's law of costs the term "opportunity cost." Herbert J. Davenport, an institutionalist in some respects, taught the Austrian theory of cost and value. Finally, Frank A. Fetter in his value theory was more Austrian than some real Austrian economists and he created the concept of "psychic income."

A few years after Mises moved to the United States in 1940, a Mises seminar started in New York. Among his American students one may single out Israel M. Kirzner for his theory of entrepreneurship and Murray N. Rothbard for his espousal of libertarian anarchism. Finally, Ludwig Lachmann, a native of Germany with degrees from Berlin and London, has become a prolific author of American-Austrian economics.

References

Böhm-Bawerk, Eugen von, *Capital and Interest*, 3 vols., Libertarian Press, South Holland, Ill., 1959, first published as *Kapital und Kapitalzins*, 1884, 1889, and 1912; Hayek, Friedrich A. von, *The Pure Theory of Capital*, Macmillan, London, 1941; Hayek, Friedrich A. von, *Individualism and Economic Order*, University of Chicago Press, Chicago, 1948; Hayek, Friedrich A. von, "Economic Thought, VI: Austrian School," *International Encyclopedia of the Social Sciences*, vol. 4, Macmillan and Free Press, New York, 1968,pp. 458–462; Hicks, John R., and Wilhelm Weber, *Carl Menger and the Austrian School of Economics*, Clarendon Press, Oxford, 1978; Kauder, Emil, *A History of Marginal Utility Theory*: Princeton University Press, Princeton, N.J., 1965; Kirzner, Israel M., *Perception, Opportunity, and Profit: Studies in the Theory of Entrepreneurship*, University of Chicago Press, Chicago, 1979; Menger, Carl: *Principles of Economics*. Free Press, Glencoe, Ill., 1950, first published as *Grundsätze der Volkswirtschaftslehre*, 1871; Menger, Carl, *Problems of Economics and Sociology*, University of Illinois Press, Urbana, 1963, first published as *Untersuchungen über die Methode der Socialwissenschaften und der politischen Okonomie insbesondere*, 1883; Mises, Ludwig von, *The Theory of Money and Credit*,

Yale University Press, New Haven, 1953, first published in German, 1912; Mises, Ludwig von, *Socialism: An Economic and Sociological Analysis,* Jonathan Cape, London, 1969, first published in German, 1922; Mises, Ludwig von, *Human Action: A Treatise on Economics,* Henry Regnery, Chicago, 1966, 1st ed., 1949; Rosenstein-Rodan, Paul N.: "Marginal Utility," *International Economic Papers,* vol. 10, pp. 71–106, first published, with bibliography, as "Grenznutzen," *Handworterbuch der Staatswissenschaften,* vol. 4, 1927; Schumpeter, Joseph A., *The Theory of Economic Development,* Harvard University Press, Cambridge, Mass.,1934, first published in German, 1912; Schumpeter, Joseph A., *History of Economic Analysis,* Oxford University Press, New York, 1954, p. 870; Spadaro, Louis M. (ed.) *New Directions in Austrian Economics,* Sheed, Andrews and McMeel, Kansas City, Mo., 1978; Wieser, Friedrich von, *Natural Value,* Kelley and Millman, New York, 1956, first published as *Der natürliche Wert,* 1889.

(*See also* Economic history and theory; Economics; General equilibrium; German historical school; Institutional economics; Neoclassical economics; Opportunity cost; Utility)

Fritz Machlup

Automatic stabilizers

Automatic stabilizers are fiscal instruments that have been built into the federal budget that automatically produce swings in the budget in response to fluctuations in economic activity. When the unemployment rate rises, outlays for unemployment compensation, welfare, and food stamps all increase automatically. In addition, a contraction in economic activity reduces the yield from nearly all federal taxes.

These automatic responses are beneficial to the economy because they moderate the effect on aftertax (disposable) income caused by fluctuations in pretax income. They therefore stabilize consumer and business outlays and reduce the magnitude of the second- and third-round respending effects that follow the shocks that cause variations in economic activity. For example, a rise in the unemployment rate increases unemployment benefit payments, and this prevents disposable income from declining as much as would otherwise have been the case. This, in turn, helps to sustain consumer spending. Similarly, when economic activity revives, outlays for unemployment compensation decline. Therefore, disposable income rises less rapidly than would otherwise have been the case, and this helps to prevent the expansion from developing into an inflationary boom. Thus, automatic stabilizers dampen fluctuations in economic activity by reducing so-called multiplier effects.

Quantitative Importance of Stabilizers

Quantitatively, the revenue stabilizers are considerably more important than the expenditure stabilizers. Receipts from the personal and corporate tax and from the payroll taxes that finance social insurance all react sharply to changes in economic activity. The personal income tax is highly responsive to changes in personal income because of its progressive rate structure. When personal income declines, taxpayers move into lower brackets, so that taxes fall both because the amount of taxable income declines and because that lower income is taxed at a lower rate. Although the corporate tax is a flat percentage of business income, profits are a highly volatile component of national income, so that the receipts from that tax show wide variations in response to swings in the gross national product (GNP). Social insurance taxes finally, are payroll taxes and since payrolls move up and down as GNP and employ ment move up and down, these taxes too act as significant automatic stabilizers.

The important point is that the stabilizers drive a wedge between pretax and after-tax income with the effect of moderating the effect of fluctuations in pretax income on aftertax income. For the individual household this means a more stable consumption pattern, and for business it means less change in aftertax profit and an improved ability to maintain stable dividend levels and uninterrupted capital spending programs. Put another way, the federal budget becomes the cushion that absorbs the impact of the shocks that frequently impinge on the economy.

The quantitative importance of the stabilizers is often assessed relative to movements in the unemployment rate. For example, in 1975—when the economy was in a serious recession—unemployment averaged 8.5 percent and the budget deficit for the calendar year was $70.6 billion. However, estimates of the quantitative impact of the stabilizers suggested that each percentage point increase in the unemployment rate raised outlays by $4.3 billion and reduced revenues by $12.3 billion, for a total of $16.6 billion increase in the deficit. This meant that the budget would actually have shown a small surplus had full employment—implying unemployment at around 4 percent—prevailed.

Nearly all economists are persuaded of the extreme importance of the stabilizers to the economy. It is largely for this reason that they almost unanimously oppose legal restrictions that would require annual budgetary balance. Recession brings with it an automatic increase in the deficit. If it is necessary to balance the budget, this would require tax increases and/or expenditure reductions that would worsen the recession. Thus, the purpose of the stabilizers would be negated, and the private economy would become the shock absorber that bounces up and down in order to stabilize the federal budget.

Problems with Stabilizers

Sometimes the stabilizers do not work as well as one might wish. Although unemployment compensation benefits usually are stabilizing, the stabilization effect was partly offset in the 1974–75 recession. Unemployment benefits are financed by payroll taxes on employers levied in large part by the states. Under the financial pressures caused by the recession, the states raised their payroll taxes by over 30 percent between 1974 and 1976, a period when the economy was struggling to escape from the recession. Similarly, the personal income tax is geared to nominal (or "money") personal income rather than to "real" income. In 1974, under the impact of the explosion of food and energy prices, real GNP declined, but because of the inflation induced by these supply restrictions, nominal GNP increased. The result was that even though pretax real income was falling, taxpayers were nevertheless boosted into higher tax brackets. Thus, in this instance, an automatic stabilizer presumed to be reliable became a destablilizer which contributed to the severity of the recession.

Finally, automatic stabilizers tend to smooth out fluctuations around a trend, but they do little to raise or lower a trend that may be unsatisfactory. This occurred during the 1950s when excessive reliance on the stabilizers produced a series of moderate cyclical fluctuations that, however, averaged around a trend line that fell farther and farther below the economy's potential as the decade progressed. This also emphasizes the fact that stabilizers prevent aftertax incomes from rising or falling by less than would otherwise be the case. They do not reverse movements, but merely cushion the direction of movement. Thus, the stabilizers are passive shock absorbers, and they cannot be counted upon to lift a chronically weak economy or to reverse an excessively buoyant economy characterized by a predominance of inflationary pressures.

References

Blinder, A. S., and R. N. Solow, "Analytical Foundations of Fiscal Policy," *The Economics of Public Finance*, Brookings, Washington, D.C., 1974; Dernburg T. F., and D. M. McDougall, *Macroeconomics*, 5th ed., McGraw-Hill, New York, 1976, chaps. 5, 18; Lewis, Jr., Wilfred, *Federal Fiscal Policy in the Postwar Recessions*. Brookings, Washington, D.C., 1962; U.S. Committee on the Budget, "Long Range Fiscal Strategy," U.S. Senate, October 1975.

(*See also* Employment and unemployment; Federal budget; Fiscal policy)

Thomas F. Dernburg

Automation

Del S. Harder first applied the word automation, in 1947, to the automatic handling of parts between progressive manufacturing processes in the mass production of auto parts. This type of Detroit automation is now commonplace in metalworking industries.

John Diebold, author of *Automation, the Advent of the Automatic Factory* (1952), used a somewhat different meaning. He concentrated on the advantages of automatic control made possible by servomechanisms, instrumentation, and computers. Automatic controls allow continuous operation in the processing of fluids, gases, and electricity.

The term was soon extended to cover any technological change that results in the transfer of human skills to machines, a higher capital-labor ratio, and greater productivity. Thus, automation becomes simply the continuation of the process of mechanization begun over 200 years ago.

The special term, however, distinguishes new directions in the progress of mechanization, for computers enormously enhance the ability to replace human labor in control, guidance, and decision-making operations. In contrast to heavy power-using machinery that replaces human muscle, computers operate on weak electrical currents and greatly increase labor productivity when used in information-processing tasks in clerical, managerial, service, and professional work. Complex systems problems of economics, science, engineering, and management are subject to multivariate analyses which were hitherto beyond human capability.

Since the first computer was invented in 1946, the state of the art has advanced rapidly. The space, defense, nuclear, census, and other large-scale government programs stimulated research and development and provided assured markets. A $20 billion science-based manufacturing industry employing over 200,000 has emerged. The price of information processing has been reduced from 77 cents per 100,000 multiplications in 1952, to a fraction of a cent in 1977. Transistors and integrated circuits have greatly increased reliability, capacity, and speed, while miniaturization of components has reduced size.

Effect of Automation on Capital Investment

In the future whole plants and factories will probably be operating under computer control systems, with coordination of pace and precision built into the equipment and programs of the organization itself. Chemical processing plants using a network of computers and minimum of monitoring labor are already in operation. In metal-working factories, robots, computer-aided design, and computer-aided manufacturing systems have been installed to produce job lots at nearly mass-production productivity rates. Human intervention in the step-by-step operations is virtually eliminated.

Paperwork in government, insurance, and other large organizations is expected to be greatly changed by computers, word-processing systems, electronic funds transfer, and telecommunications. "In our time," predicts Herbert A. Simon, computer scientist and Nobelist, "computers will be able to perform any cognitive task that a person can perform."

The spread of automation, however, depends on management decisions which must be justified on the basis of economic criteria rather than on superior technical performance. Cost reduction as a result of increased productivity is usually the major objective. Managers also seek improvements in product and service quality, accuracy, and flexibility, but these intangible benefits are more difficult to quantify. On the cost side, the elusive high costs of software—the systems planning, programming, maintenance, training, installation, and debugging of complex hardware—must be taken into account. The investment decision, therefore, entails complex judgments and high risks. According to McGraw-Hill reports, the proportion of industry's capital outlays spent on automation increased gradually from 19 percent in 1967, to 27 percent in 1977. Automation tends to be limited to large enterprises with substantial capital and managerial resources.

Effect of Automation on Employment

At first, automation had many disturbing social overtones. In 1952, Norbert Wiener, pioneer computer scientist, feared that automation would accelerate labor productivity, bring about overproduction, and cause mass labor displacement. In 1966, the National Commission on Technology, Automation, and Economic Progress reviewed the evidence and concluded that productivity was not likely to accelerate more rapidly than "the growth of demand could offset given adequate public policies."

The fear of runaway technology was muted in the 1970s as the productivity growth rate slowed down to about half the 3.2 annual rate of gain of the previous 20 years. The disrupting "stagflation" and the shock of energy price increases limited investment and research in innovative developments. A more rapid diffusion of automation depends on a more favorable climate for capital investment.

The effects of automation on employment have been extensively studied and debated. Over the long run, total demand for labor has expanded as productivity and real incomes have risen, new industries have been created, and hours of work have been shortened. Automation, however, can and does reduce employment of particular groups of workers in particular occupations, industries, or localities. Where the objective is to reduce labor for a given or smaller output, as in the printing and railroad industries, fewer workers in the short run are needed. But the long-run effect may be to increase jobs as the automated firm becomes more competitive in domestic and world markets. Where automation is used to expand capacity to produce new products or services (e.g., integrated circuits, and information retrieval systems), the result may be additional jobs.

The indirect effects of automation are often more serious. Technologically obsolete plants which become less competitive are shut down, with drastic impact on workers and communities. Another indirect impact results from the reduction of job opportunities for unskilled young people and minorities just entering the labor force.

Private and Public Programs

Studies of worker adjustments to automation have generally found that the transition has taken place so far without serious dislocation. Today, there is widespread agreement that the individual worker should not bear the burden of technological progress that benefits society as a whole.

Private programs have been developed to retrain and reassign the work force for new skills of programmer, systems analyst, and maintenance technician. In some unionized organizations, provisions for attrition, advance notice, interplant transfer, seniority, and longer vacations have helped to protect job security. Where displacement has occurred, workers have been helped by severance pay, early retirement, and supplementary unemployment benefits. Adjustments in nonunion firms take place informally, employers preferring maximum flexibility.

Public programs have expanded substantially since the Manpower Development and Training Act of 1963 was enacted to assist those affected by automation. Government policies, codified under the Comprehensive Employment and Training Act of 1978, now concentrate on training and placing the unemployed, the young, the unskilled, women, and minorities who are disadvantaged in a highly developed technological society. In addition to the public employment service and unemployment insurance, programs are evolving to ease the plight of those affected by the shutdown of plants made obsolete by advancing technology.

The framework for public employment programs is the Full Employment and Balanced Growth Act of 1978, which commits the government to adopt policies to minimize unemployment. Under full employment, shifts resulting from the progress of automation can take place with a minimum burden placed on the worker.

Automation advances inexorably, increasing opportunities for material abundance, better working conditions, and greater leisure. But many believe it is not enough to be simply an adaptive society. Economic progress depends not only on automation and other technological changes but also, paradoxically, on expanding the opportunities for active participation and decision by those engaged in automated production.

References

Dertouzos, Michael L., and Joel Moses (eds.), *The Computer Age: A Twenty Year View*, MIT Press, Cambridge, Mass., 1979; Report of the National Commission on Technology, Automation and Economic Progress, *Technology and the American Economy and Appendix*, vols. I, II, 1966; Simons, Herbert A., *The New Science of Management Decision*, rev. ed., Prentice-Hall, Englewood Cliffs, N.J., 1977, U.S. Bureau of Labor Statistics, *Technological Change and Its Labor Impact in Selected Industries*, Bulletins 1817, 1856, 1961, 2005, 1974–1977.

(*See also* Computers in economics; Innovation; Productivity; Research and development; Technology)

Edgar Weinberg

Balance of international payments

The original concept of the balance of international payments was based on the assumption that international transactions involve receipts or payments through transfers of an internationally acceptable medium of exchange. Initially this medium of exchange was gold, but because of the difficulties of moving and storing gold, it was replaced by banking obligations that were convertible into gold.

According to the original concept, the balance of international payments of a country (the home country) equaled the net receipts or payments, or changes in the holdings of such internationally accepted media of exchange by its residents resulting from their transactions with residents of foreign countries. These transactions include current as well as capital transactions. Current transactions consist of international trade in tangible goods as well as services (such as transportation, travel, and wages earned by foreign workers); dividends, interest, and other incomes from investments; and transfer payments (such as pensions and government grants). Capital transactions consist of purchases or sales by domestic residents of assets held abroad and by foreign residents of assets held in the home country. Such assets include direct investments, i.e., equity interests in foreign enterprises and other property located in foreign countries providing a significant influence over their management and loans between the investors and such foreign affiliates; other securities; loans by government; loans by banks and others to unaffiliated foreign residents including trade credits; and bank deposits. Capital transactions under this concept do not include, however, changes in the holdings by domestic residents of internationally accepted media of exchange, since these changes are the counterpart, and the measure, of the balance on the other transactions.

National Currencies in International Transactions

This original concept must be adjusted, however, for the use of national currencies in international transactions. In contracts with foreign residents the currency in which payments are made has to be specified. The currency may be that of one of the partners in the transaction or that of another country, particularly of a major financial center. In the nineteenth century obligations of British banks, in sterling, and in the twentieth century obligations of U.S. banks, in dollars, were widely used as international transactions currencies. Initially, both of these currencies were convertible into gold at fixed rates and indirectly into other currencies that were convertible into gold. However, this convertibility of a currency at fixed rates into gold or into a supranational monetary asset created by an international organization, such as the International Monetary Fund (IMF), at fixed rates may not be a sufficient or even necessary condition for their acceptability as an international medium of exchange. More important can be the situation that the country issuing the currency has a relatively large share in the international trade and financial transactions, and that the risks encountered by foreign residents investing their monetary funds in its currency are minimal. These risks are minimized by the stability of the country's political and financial institutions, by the ability of its capital markets to absorb inflows and outflows of foreign funds with relatively small disturbances, and by the stability of the purchasing power of its currency, at least compared with other currencies.

If domestic residents have to make payments in a currency other than their own, they usually have to purchase it; if they receive a currency other than their own, they usually have to sell it since they use their domestic currency in their domestic operations. The purchases and sales of foreign currencies are made through international exchange markets usually conducted by large banks. If in these international exchange markets the offers to sell the home-country currency exceed the offers to purchase it, the price of the home-country currency in terms of foreign currencies in general or in terms of the currency of the major financial center will decline. If the monetary authority of the home country—usually its central bank—is responsible for maintaining the exchange rate of its currency relative to other currencies (particularly relative to currencies of the financial centers or an internationally created reserve asset), it has to purchase its own currency to absorb the excess of selling offers for its currency and sell foreign currencies to supply the shortfall of selling orders for the foreign currencies. In order to meet these responsibilities the central banks maintain reserves which are an investment in assets that can easily be sold to obtain the currencies used in exchange market operations. Such assets may include gold or drawing rights on accounts held in international organizations, such as the IMF. They may also include obligations, such as government securities, issued by the countries whose currency is widely used as an international medium of exchange. These currencies thus serve also as reserve currencies, and the countries issuing these currencies serve as reserve-currency countries.

The sales or purchases by the central bank of the home country of its own currency (i.e., deposits in its domestic banks) in exchange for foreign currencies (i.e., deposits in foreign banks) in order to maintain the exchange rate of its currency in terms of a reserve currency (such as the dollar) or in terms of a composite of foreign currencies (such as the special drawing rights issued by the IMF) may be considered compensatory to the transactions which result in the gaps between offers to purchase and to sell the home-country currency. The transactions creating the gaps in the exchange market which consist of current as well as of capital transactions are autonomous because they are initiated by those engaged in them to pursue their own economic (or other) aims.

In the case of a reserve-currency country the compensatory transactions include the same transactions that are compensatory for other countries. Thus, they include sales of foreign currency assets held in its reserves, and purchases of foreign currency assets which are added to its reserves. In addition, the compensatory transactions of the reserve-currency also include net purchases or sales of its obligations (such as government securities or banking obligations) through transactions initiated by the monetary agencies of foreign countries in order to stabilize the exchange rate of their respective currencies against the reserve currency. Compensatory transactions of the reserve-currency countries thus affect the size of their own official reserves and of their obligations to foreign monetary agencies. If the foreign monetary agencies sell obligations of the reserve-currency country to each other, the aggregate liabilities of the reserve-currency country to foreign monetary agencies would not change.

The balance of payments of the home country may then be redefined as the balance of the autonomous transactions between its residents and those of foreign countries at stable exchange rates. Alternatively, it may be defined as the balance of the compensatory transactions of its monetary agency and—if the home country is also a reserve-currency country—the compensatory transactions of the official agencies of other countries involving purchases or sales of home-country obligations in order to stabilize the exchange rate of its currency.

Based on this official settlement concept, the home country is deemed to have had a surplus (or a deficit) in its balance of international payments during any given time period if its autonomous transactions during that period resulted in an excess (or shortfall) of offers to purchase its currency compared with the offers to sell it.

The surplus (or deficit) of the home country is matched by purchases (or sales) of foreign currency assets in exchange for domestic currency assets by its monetary authority and/or (if the home country is a reserve-currency country) by net sales (or net purchases) of home-country obligations by the official agencies of other countries.

With the compensatory transactions, the offers to purchase and to sell a country's currency in the international exchange market can be converted into actual sales and purchases of the currency, since purchases and sales must be equal. This applies to any single transaction, as well as the aggregate of all transactions.

Credits and Debits

The concept that all transactions between domestic and foreign residents consist of two sides, credits (indicated by a plus sign) and debits (indicated by a minus sign)—which must be equal over any period of time—is the basis for balance of payments statistics.

The credit side includes all transactions, autonomous as well as compensatory, resulting in purchases of the home-country currency; the debit side includes all transactions resulting in sales of the home-country currency. The credit side includes exports of merchandise, sales of services such as transportation or accommodations to foreign travelers, receipts of royalties, incomes received by domestic residents from their foreign investments, incomes from sales of assets, located within the home country or abroad by domestic residents to foreign residents, and the proceeds from borrowings by domestic residents from foreign residents. The debit side includes imports of merchandise, purchases of services, payments of royalties, incomes paid to foreigners on their investments in the home country, purchases of assets located within the home country or abroad by domestic residents from foreign residents, and the repayments of borrowings by domestic residents from foreign residents.

Balance of payments statistics typically are not limited, however, to transactions involving purchases and sales of the home country's currency. They also include transactions that do not directly affect the exchange markets, such as barter transactions, or transfers of merchandise or services provided as gifts or grants, or transfers for which payments are deferred by means of loans. The credit side of such transactions (e.g., merchandise exports) are shown separately from the debit side (e.g., "gift" or "unilateral transfer," or loans) as if they were separate transactions, affecting the exchange market by equal amounts in opposite directions. With these inclusions, the balance of payments statistics reflect all transfers among countries of physical as well as financial resources.

For example, merchandise exports of the home country may be reflected in its balance of payments statistics in several ways. The value of the export would appear among the credit transactions. If the export is paid by foreigners by checks drawn on a foreign bank, the debit transaction would be an increase in home-country investments abroad. If the exports are paid by checks drawn on a home-country bank in which the foreigner maintains an account, the debit transaction would be a reduction in liabilities of a domestic bank to a foreign resident (the equivalent of the repayment of a loan to a foreigner). If the export is not paid for in the same period but financed through a loan, the debit transaction would be an increase in home-country investments abroad; if the exports are gifts, the debit transaction would be shown as a gift or a unilateral transfer.

Organization of Balance of Payments Statistics

Balance of payments statistics are generally based on records or estimates for different categories of transactions, such as merchandise trade, international travel expenditures, and various types of capital transactions. Many of the capital transactions statistics are based on records of outstanding assets and liabilities at the conclusion of successive periods such as months, quarters, or years. The data appearing in the statistics reflect changes during these periods. These changes reflect not only the balance between capital inflows (sales of assets to foreign residents) and capital outflows (purchases of assets from foreign residents), but they may also reflect various adjustments for changes in valuation, write-offs, etc. In balance of payments statistics of most countries there are also some categories of transactions for which no data or estimates are available. Consequently, the statistics also show an item called "statistical discrepancy," "errors and omissions," or "balancing item." This item equalizes the credits and debits, and its sign is determined by the lower of the two sides of the account. The balance of payments accounts are usually organized by separating major categories of transactions, such as merchandise trade, service transactions including incomes on investments, and gifts or unilateral transfers, which constitute "current transactions," the capital transactions, and the statistical discrepancy.

The balance of payments statistics do not show the balance of the compensatory transactions by the monetary authorities, but changes in their assets and, for reserve-currency countries, changes in their liabilities to foreign official organizations. These changes are affected by both compensatory and noncompensatory transactions. Furthermore, the liability figures of the reserve-currency countries (particularly the United States) do not fully reflect the reserves of other central banks invested in reserve currencies, because large amounts of such reserves are held in banks located in other countries.

The concept of compensatory transactions assumes free exchange markets. When governments impose controls on international transactions of their residents and thus prevent the operation of exchange markets, the retention of foreign currencies by their central banks and the increase in their reserves cannot be considered a compensatory transaction, and the same applies to the rise in liabilities to foreign official agencies by the reserve-currency country in which such reserves are held. The reserve holdings can also be influenced by a country by selling or lending its reserve assets through special inducements to its private banks and regaining these reserve assets by reversing such transactions. Changes in liabilities by the United States to foreign central banks are affected by their earnings from their investments in the United States. Liabilities of the United States to foreign official agencies also include investments by oil-producing countries which did not acquire these investments as a result of compensatory transactions in the exchange markets.

Even when exchange markets are relatively free, compensatory transactions may not necessarily reflect the position (or changes in the position) of a country in the international markets for goods and services, and for capital. In order to avoid losses of reserves, governments (including their central banks) may attempt to restrict the operation of their economies, so that imports are reduced and exports stimulated. They may also tighten the supply of funds in domestic capital markets to increase net capital inflows. Although such policies may for some time improve the balance of the autonomous transactions, the improvement may not be sustainable. A sustainable balance of the autonomous transactions can be achieved only when it is compatible with sustainable economic conditions in the economies of the home country and of its major foreign partners.

For reserve-currency countries there is the additional problem arising from the use of their currencies as a medium of exchange in international transactions and as a denominator of international debt obligations. Such currencies may be held as reserves not only by official agencies of other countries, but also as monetary assets and reserves by private enterprises and persons residing abroad. These holdings may depend on the size of international transactions, the efficiency with which such reserve-currency assets are used, and the use in international transactions of monetary and other liquid assets in other currencies. They are also contingent on the expectation that the exchange rate of the reserve currency with the currencies of other major countries can be maintained in case foreign residents want to convert their holdings of reserve-currency obligations into their own currencies. The greater the increase in foreign private and official holdings of reserve-currency obligations relative to the resources available to the monetary authorities of the reserve-currency country to defend the exchange rate of its currency, and the more the maintenance of the exchange rate of the reserve currency depends on the willingness and ability of other countries to add to their own reserves of reserve-country obligations, the more private residents of other countries may hesitate to add to their holdings of monetary and other liquid obligations denominated in the reserve currency, and the more they may be tempted to liquidate such holdings. A balance of the autonomous

transactions of the reserve-currency country that depends largely on foreign purchases of its monetary and other liquid obligations may, therefore, be more vulnerable than the figures for that balance may suggest.

Other Balance of Payments Measures

To overcome difficulties in measuring the balance of payments, various attempts have
been made to use other combinations of data in the balance of payments statistics.
However, these attempts require considerable qualifications and further adjustments. The "liquidity balance" which was shown in U.S. statistics prior to the suspension of the fixed exchange rate system in March 1973 was computed by omitting
from the balance of the autonomous transactions (derived from changes in the
reserves of domestic monetary agencies and the changes in liabilities to foreign official agencies) changes in private foreign holdings of domestic liquid obligations and
(in later years) also of changes in private domestic holdings of foreign liquid obligations. The measurement of the balance on that basis did not avoid the difficulties
arising from the use of these figures on changes in domestic reserve assets and in
liabilities to foreign official agencies as a substitute for the balance on compensatory
transactions, and was affected by the additional difficulties of defining and measuring
the liabilities which may be used by foreign private residents as liquid investments
of their dollar reserves.

The so-called basic balance used in the statistics of several countries and international organizations is computed by omitting from the autonomous transactions
changes in all short-term assets held abroad by private domestic residents, and in all
short-term liabilities to private foreign residents. The difficulty with this concept is in
the distinction between changes in assets and liabilities which are classified as short-
term on the basis of legal or other nominal criteria from changes in assets and liabilities which are intended to be made by those initiating the transactions for short
periods of time only. Furthermore, the basic balance is not adjusted to eliminate temporary changes in other transactions, including nominally long-term capital transactions, merchandise trade or services transactions, or in government grants and
credits. Neither is it adjusted for cyclical changes. Consequently, the basic balance
as it is customarily computed does not measure the position and changes of the balance after all temporary changes have been eliminated and thus does not indicate its
"basic" position and the longer-term trends of its changes.

Problems with Balance of Payments Analysis

These examples indicate that even under an international monetary system that is
based on the maintenance of fixed exchange rates through transactions by the monetary agencies to compensate for gaps in the autonomous transactions, the analysis of
the balance of payments to determine whether or not it is in surplus or deficit and
the direction it is moving cannot be made on the basis of a standardized combination
of specified items in the balance of payments statistics. An analysis that can be used
as a guide for policies by official agencies and by private business usually requires a
sophisticated review of the data shown in the balance of payments accounts and of
the relationships of these data with those indicating developments in the economies
of the home country and of other major countries.

An analysis based on the distinction between autonomous and compensatory
transactions cannot be made when the initial gaps between offers to purchase and

offers to sell a currency are closed through adjustments, induced by exchange rate changes, of these offers and of the initially intended transactions. The balance of payments statistics show the transactions after the adjustments have taken place and do not permit an estimate of the initial surplus or deficit that contributed to the exchange rate changes. The problem becomes more complicated when official agencies participate in the foreign exchange markets. They may widen or narrow the initial gaps in the exchange markets. Since it cannot be assumed that the official transactions are intended to close these gaps and are sufficient to maintain the existing exchange rates, they cannot be used to measure the balance of international payments.

In view of these problems, it appears preferable to evaluate the international transactions from the point of view of whether their broad pattern is sustainable or whether it is likely to require adjustments, and to diagnose the underlying problems through a careful analysis rather than by the use of standardized combinations of certain items in the balance of payments statistics. The numerical results obtained on the basis of such statistical measures may appear to be precise and easily understood but can be quite misleading. Even if the conclusions derived on the basis of analytical processes may not always provide exact measures of the balance of payments, and may be subject to differences in judgment, they may, nevertheless, be reliable and helpful in the formulation of policies.

References

The Balance of Payments Statistics of the United States, Hearings Before the Subcommittee on Economic Statistics of the Joint Economic Committee, 89th Cong., 1st Sess., May 11, June 8, and June 9, 1965; International Monetary Fund, *Balance of Payments,* Washington, D.C., published annually; Machlup, Fritz, *International Payments, Debts and Gold,* Scribner's, New York, 1964; Report of the Review Committee for Balance of Payments Statistics, *The Balance of Payments Statistics of the United States, A Review and Appraisal,* 1965; Statistical Policy Division, Office of Management and the Budget, "Report of the Advisory Committee on the Presentation of Balance of Payments Statistics," *Statistical Reporter,* June 1976; U.S. Bureau of Economic Analysis, *Survey of Current Business,* U.S. Department of Commerce, published quarterly.

(*See also* Balance of international trade; Exports; Foreign exchange rates; Imports; International economics, an overview; Mercantilism; Net exports in GNP; Value of the dollar)

Walther Lederer

Balance of international trade

The balance of international trade of a country is the difference between its exports and imports. A narrow definition of exports and imports includes only tangible goods. A broader definition would cover products of factors of production in all forms, such as services related to international transportation and travel, insurance, the planning and supervision of construction projects, management assistance, the work performed by migratory workers, and incomes from royalties and from international investments.

Basis for Trade Statistics

The statistics for trade in tangible goods are usually based on documents filed by exporters and importers with customs officials at the time, or shortly after, the goods move across a country's border. The basic documents indicate a classification of the goods (most countries use uniform international coding systems), the values of the goods, and the destination of exports or the country of origin of imports. The trade statistics of most countries show the movements of goods regardless of whether or when payments are received or made. (Some countries whose trade statistics are based on exchange control documents are exceptions.) Payments may be made before or after the goods cross the borders; in the case of gifts or government grants, payments are not required. Shipments across the border may, but do not necessarily, coincide with the transfers of ownership.

The value of exports usually includes transportation costs to the border (or alongside sea and air carriers), but not beyond that point, even if transportation is provided by companies of the exporting country. Most countries value their imports c.i.f., that is, the costs of the goods, and the charges for insurance and freight to bring these goods to their border or port of entry. This valuation improves the comparability of the total or average values of goods which are imported with those which are produced domestically, but there are many other considerations which have to be taken into account in such comparisons. The United States and several other countries value their imports f.a.s., that is, free alongside ship or other carrier, excluding the cost of loading. More rarely the imports are valued f.o.b., that is, free on board the carrier, which includes the cost of loading. In recent years, the United States has also collected and published import data valued on the c.i.f. basis.

Import data incorporated into the compilations of the balance of international payments are based on f.a.s. values. International transportation transactions are estimated separately. This procedure is necessary to avoid showing transportation and insurance payments to the country's own companies as a part of the imports. Import data based on f.a.s. valuations are also required when exports and imports of different countries are compared.

Export and import statistics usually reflect the values indicated in the invoices. There can be exceptions, however, when the valuations of imports are adjusted to conform with customs regulations affecting the computation of import duties. This applies particularly to goods that are believed to be valued below costs of production and may affect shipments from affiliated companies, goods produced abroad by government-owned and -operated enterprises, and goods whose exports are promoted through government subsidies.

In the 1970s, the United States added to the traditional import data based on customs values import statistics based on the original invoice values. These data are used in balance of payments compilations since they are more likely to be consistent with the data for the financial transactions with which the imports are associated.

The geographic breakdown of the export and import data is subject to problems that affect the trade balances with individual countries more than the trade balance with the total of all foreign countries. Particularly in the case of standardized commodities, shipped in bulk, the export documents indicate only the immediate destinations, which are not necessarily the countries where the goods are finally used. Import documents usually show the country of origin, which is the country from which the goods are shipped. When goods are imported from a country where they were assembled from components produced elsewhere, the import statistics are likely to attribute the entire value of such imports to the country where the goods were assembled. In the United States, statistics of international merchandise trade are assembled and published monthly by the Bureau of the Census. These figures are adjusted, mainly for coverage, for use in the compilations of the accounts covering all international transactions, published quarterly by the Bureau of Economic Analysis, U.S. Department of Commerce. Transactions by U.S. defense agencies and their personnel, which include transfers of goods as well as services, are shown separately in these accounts.

A Broader Concept of Balance of Trade

The balance of trade based on the broader concept, which includes the international transfers of the output of factors of production in all forms, is usually higher than the balance of trade in goods alone for the older industrial countries, such as the United States, because their incomes from investments in other countries exceed the incomes they pay on foreign investments in their countries.

The broader concept of the balance of trade, except for minor adjustments, is used in the computation of the gross national product (GNP). Exports are considered purchases by foreign residents which are added to purchases of domestic residents, and imports are deducted to obtain the total output of the economy.

The balance of trade, even with its broader coverage, does not adequately indicate its impact on the domestic economy. Imports of certain commodities are required in domestic production, while some of the exports may reduce domestic purchases. Furthermore, the trade balance does not reflect flows of monetary funds because to a large extent such flows are reversed through capital transactions, which affect domestic investments and consumption expenditures. This particularly applies to the United States because of its role as a reserve-currency country.

The balance of trade in goods and services is used sometimes to evaluate the competitive position of a country in international business and to indicate the strength of its balance of payments in general. A rise in imports relative to exports may reflect, however, a country's ability to attract foreign capital and the need for resources required by the rise in its domestic investments. Only when a country has to borrow abroad, or use its international reserves to finance its net imports of goods and services (and when these conditions are not due to temporary or reversible developments), so that the increase in its foreign debt is not associated with at least an equal increase in its domestic productive assets, can the net imports of goods and services be interpreted as a sign of an economic weakness, and as an indication that adjustments are required in its economy and/or in the exchange rate of its currency.

References

Commodity Trade Statistics, Statistical Office of the United Nations, New York (provides for as many countries as possible data on the distribution of exports and imports by commodity categories); International Monetary Fund, *Direction of Trade,* Washington, D.C., published monthly (provides data for exports of all countries and imports of partner countries); International Monetary Fund, *International Financial Statistics,* Washington, D.C.; published monthly (provides data on total exports and imports of merchandise and of goods and services for as many countries as possible); Organization for Economic Cooperation and Development (OECD), *Trade by Commodities,* Series B, Paris, France; U.S. Bureau of the Census, *Highlights of U.S. Export and Import Trade,* U.S. Department of Commerce (provides data on U.S. exports and imports of merchandise, by country and by major commodity groups).

(*See also* Balance of international payments; Exports; Foreign exchange rates; Imports; International economics, an overview; Mercantilism; Net exports in GNP; Value of the dollar)

Walther Lederer

Balance sheet (see Financial statements)

Bank deposits

Bank deposits are obligations of a bank to pay to the person, firm, or institution that placed funds with the bank. The deposit may be payable immediately, in which case it is known as a demand deposit (checking account), or it may be payable after the passage of a period of time, in which case it is known as a time deposit (passbook or certificate account). Demand deposits are withdrawn from the bank by writing a check—an instrument in writing—naming the person to whom the funds should be transferred, the amount, and the date, and bearing the signature of the person owning the demand deposit account from which the funds are to be transferred. The withdrawal instrument used in connection with demand-deposit accounts—the check—is a negotiable instrument, which may be written to be payable to one person, who may endorse the check over to yet another person, and so on for a series of transfers from person to person.

Time Deposits

Time deposits may be either negotiable or nonnegotiable. Most personal savings accounts and many corporate time deposits are payable only to a named beneficiary. Some deposits, however, are acknowledged by the bank's giving to the depositor a document saying the bank will pay the principal and interest to the bearer, thus granting the right to the depositor to transfer the piece of paper to any person he or she desires. The most common type of negotiable time deposit is also one of the most important for large corporate depositors. It is the negotiable certificate of deposit (CD) account, issued to depositors of $100,000 or more. Most depositors in negotiable CD accounts are corporations, but many well-to-do individuals also use such deposits.

Interest Rates

Under federal law and regulation, banks may pay any rate of interest they wish on negotiable certificates of deposit, but they may not redeem those certificates prior to the stated maturity date. Businesses often have an uncertain cash flow which might require funds earlier than the maturity date of the negotiable certificate, so an active market in negotiable certificates of deposit has sprung up in the U.S. money market, allowing a depositor to sell the certificate at any time.

Assume, as an example, that a bank accepts $1 million at an annual interest rate of 9 percent for 120 days. After 60 days have passed, the depositor decides that he or she wants the money, and sells the certificate of deposit to another person or institution. In the period between the deposit and the time the depositor sold the certificate, however, the market rate of interest for short-term funds fell to 8 percent. The selling price will, therefore, be higher than the amount of money deposited in the first place. If interest rates had risen instead, the selling price would have been lower than the original purchase price. Negotiable certificates of deposit are like any other financial instrument—their price varies inversely with changes in the rate of interest.

While the risk of loss to a depositor because a bank cannot repay the money at maturity (the credit risk) is very slight, there is a distinct market risk caused by fluctuating interest rates if the depositor sells the certificate before maturity. If it is held to maturity, the stated principal and interest will be paid.

NOW Accounts

As of mid-1979, payment of interest on demand deposits was not permitted by federal statutes and regulations. However, payment of interest on demand deposits was coming in through the back door. Federally insured commercial banks, savings and loan associations, cooperative banks, and mutual savings banks in Massachusetts and New Hampshire were first permitted to offer negotiable orders of withdrawal (NOW) accounts on January 1, 1974. Similar institutions throughout New England were given permission to have NOW accounts on February 27, 1976, and in New York State on November 10, 1978.

NOW accounts are saving accounts for which the withdrawal slip is negotiable, and in form, are substantially identical to the familiar check. A depositor using a NOW account earns interest on money in the account until the negotiable withdrawal slips clear through the banking system and are subtracted from the account. While technically not payment of interest on demand deposits, the NOW accounts are clearly the vanguard of a movement toward a system which accomplishes the equivalent of payment of interest on demand balances while still meeting legal requirements.

References

Klein, John J.; *Money and the Economy*, Harcourt, Brace, New York, 1978; Luckett, Daniel G.; *Money and Banking*, McGraw-Hill, New York, 1976.

(*See also* Banking system; Money supply)

William J. Brown

Banking school

This was a group of influential British economists who opposed the rival currency school in the celebrated mid-nineteenth-century bank charter debate over the regulation of the banknote issue. Led by Thomas Tooke, John Fullarton, James Wilson, and J. B. Gilbart, the banking school disapproved of all forms of monetary regulation except the requirement that banks convert notes into coin upon demand. In particular, the banking school rejected the currency school's plan for a 100 percent gold reserve requirement for notes, a plan embodied in the Bank Charter Act of 1844. Unlike the currency school, which feared that inflationary monetary overexpansion would occur unless convertible banknotes were backed 1 for 1 with gold, the banking school argued that the volume of convertible notes is automatically regulated by the needs of trade and, therefore, requires no further limitation. This conclusion stemmed directly from the real bills doctrine and the law of reflux, which together posited guaranteed safeguards to overissue, obviating the need for monetary control.

The real bills doctrine states that the stock of money can never be excessive as long as notes are issued on loans made to finance real transactions in goods and services. Similarly, the law of reflux asserts that overissue is impossible because any excess notes will be returned immediately to the banks for conversion into coin or for repayment of loans. Both doctrines embody the notions of a passive, demand-determined money supply and of reverse causality running from prices to mone˙ rather than vice versa as in the quantity theory. According to the reverse causalit

hypothesis, changes in the level of prices and economic activity induce corresponding shifts in the demand for bank loans which the banks accommodate via variations
in the note issue. In this manner prices determine the money stock, the expansion of
which is the result, not the cause, of price inflation. As for the price level itself, the
banking school attributed its determination to factor costs (wages, interest, rents, etc.),
thus establishing the essentials of a cost-push theory of inflation.

Nonmonetarist Ideas

The concepts of cost inflation, reverse causality, and passive money are the hallmarks
of an extreme nonmonetarist view of the monetary mechanism to which the banking
school adhered. Its list of nonmonetarist ideas included the propositions (1) that international gold movements are absorbed by idle balances and have no effect on the
volume of money in circulation, (2) that an efflux of specie stems from real shocks to
the balance of payments and not from domestic price inflation, (3) that changes in the
stock of money tend to be offset by compensating changes in the stock of money substitutes leaving the total circulation unaltered, and (4) that discretion is preferable to
rules in the conduct of monetary policy.

In its critique of the monetarist doctrines of the currency school, which contended
that monetary overexpansion is the sole or primary cause of domestic inflation and
external specie drains, the banking school argued as follows. First, overissue is
impossible since the stock of notes is determined by the needs of trade and cannot
exceed demand; therefore, no excess supply of money exists to bid up prices. Second,
in any case, causation runs from prices to money rather than vice versa. Third, specie
drains stem from real rather than monetary disturbances to the balance of payments
and occur independently of domestic price level movements.

These arguments severed all but one of the links in the currency school's monetary
transmission mechanism running from money to prices to gold flows and back again
to money. The final link was broken when the banking school asserted that gold flows
come from idle hoards and cannot affect the volume of money in circulation. To
ensure that these hoards would be sufficient to accommodate gold drains, the banking
school recommended that the Bank of England hold larger metallic reserves. As for
the currency school's claim that the entire stock of money and money substitutes can
be controlled through the banknote base, the banking school flatly rejected it. The
banking school asserted the impossibility of controlling the monetary circulation via
the note component alone since limitation of notes would simply induce the public
to use money substitutes (i.e., checking deposits and bills of exchange) instead. More
generally, the banking school questioned the efficacy of attempts to control the stock
of money in a financial system that can produce an endless variety of money substitutes. With regard to the currency school's prescription that discretionary policy be
replaced by a fixed rule, the banking school rejected it on the grounds that rigid rules
would prevent the banking system from responding to the needs of trade and would
hamper the central bank's power to deal with financial crises.

In retrospect, the banking school rightly stressed the importance of checking
deposits as a medium of exchange. But it was wrong in believing that the real bills
doctrine, which tied note issues to loans made for productive purposes, would prevent inflationary money growth. Henry Thornton in 1802 exposed this flaw when he
pointed out that rising prices would require an ever-growing volume of loans just to
finance the same level of real output. In this way inflation would justify the monetary

expansion necessary to sustain it and the real bills criterion would not limit the quantity of money in existence. Furthermore, Thornton, and later Knut Wicksell, convincingly demonstrated that an insatiable demand for loans results when the loan rate of interest is below the expected rate of profit on capital. In such cases the real bills criterion provides no bar to overissue.

Radcliffe Report

Today the term banking school is closely associated with the British *Radcliffe Report* (1959). Indeed, the principal ideas of the banking school, i.e., the notions (1) of a passive, demand-determined money supply, (2) of reverse causation running from economic activity to money, (3) of cost-push inflation, (4) of new money entering idle balances rather than active circulation, (5) of a large and variable volume of money substitutes, (6) of a high degree of substitutability between money and near moneys, (7) of the futility of attempts to control the total stock of money and money substitutes (liquidity) via control of a narrowly defined monetary base, (8) of nonmonetary as opposed to monetary causes of trade balance disequilibrium, and (9) of the desirability of discretion over rules in the conduct of monetary policy, all have exact counterparts in the *Radcliffe Report.*

References

Humphrey, T., "The Quantity Theory of Money: Its Historical Evolution and Role in Policy Debates," *Economic Review,* no. 60, May/June 1974, pp. 2–19; Robbins, L., *Robert Torrens and the Evolution of Classical Economics,* Macmillan, London, 1958, chap. 5; Viner, J., *Studies in the Theory of International Trade,* Kelley, New York, 1965, chap. 5.

(*See also* Currency school)

Thomas M. Humphrey

Banking system

A banking system is an integrated network of comercial banks legally empowered to hold demand and time deposits and to do a general business in all lending areas, such as commercial and industrial lending, real estate lending, consumer installment lending, lending in foreign countries, financing of exports and imports, and other activities. A banking system, as opposed to a system of financial institutions, consists of commercial banks chartered by the state in which they are located, or by the Comptroller of the Currency as national banks, and possessing powers discussed above. Not all institutions bearing the name "bank" are, in fact, banks as the term is used here. In the eastern part of the United States there are many mutual savings banks, which are much more akin to savings and loan associations than to commercial banks.

Three Major Functions

Commercial banks perform three major functions: (1) they lend, (2) they accept time and demand deposits, and (3) they facilitate the transfer of funds in the economy. All three functions require close coordination with other commercial banks in the system. For example, banks often receive requests for loans so large that an individual bank is unable to handle it. A very large loan exposes a bank to the possibility that a large portion of its assets might suddenly become worthless if the economy changes in such a way that the borrower's business is adversely affected, or if the borrower's business deteriorates through mismanagement. Regulations of the federal banking regulatory agencies, however, prevent banks from making very large single loans. In general, federal regulations prohibit lending more than 10 percent of capital and surplus to any one borrower. But, with corporations merging rapidly, the need for very large loans increased tremendously in the 1970s. In order to meet that need, banks often arrange for a lead bank to make the single loan to the customer, with many banks participating in the loan through a formal arrangement, so the risk is shared among them. In the deposit acceptance function, banks often solicit deposits from other banks or from other financial institutions, as well as from the business and household sectors of the economy. Banks with temporary surplus funds place them at interest with other banks, either for a very short term or for a longer period. The most common such transaction involves lending and borrowing of reserves by one bank from another for periods of one night, or for a succession of one-night transactions. These are known as federal funds transactions because the funds borrowed or loaned are on deposit at the Federal Reserve bank of the region.

It is in the third function of the banking system, that of facilitating the transfer of funds from one bank to another and from banks to other financial institutions, where the total integration of the banking system becomes most obvious. The flow of checks from one bank to another and between banks and other financial institutions is enormous and has been increasing substantially each year. In order for the processing to take place through automated machinery at the Federal Reserve banks, each check must be inscribed with numerals printed with special ink capable of being read by magnetic character-recognition equipment.

When checks are presented to a bank by a depositor for collection to his or her account, the bank wants to collect the funds on that check as quickly as possible. To do so, it either arranges to have the check sent by mail, by truck, by airplane, by courier, or by some other means directly to the bank on which the check is drawn, or it sends the check through the check collection procedures of the Federal Reserve System. By far the largest percentage of checks flow through the Federal Reserve's facilities. In order to reduce to a minimum the time required for check collection, the Federal Reserve charters a fleet of private aircraft. Conventional surface transportation facilities such as trucks are also used. Many banks maintain private check collection facilities, usually aircraft, for collecting checks even more quickly than the Federal Reserve does. The incentive for rapid check collection is that the sooner a bank can collect its funds, the sooner it can have those funds credited to the reserves all Federal Reserve members are required to maintain, and the sooner the bank can earn interest on any funds not held as reserves. Banks use great care to see that their funds are invested each night to earn the maximum amount feasible, and that they have their funds wisely placed either in reserves or in interest-earning financial instruments.

Regulators and Charters

Banks are carefully regulated by banking regulatory agencies because bank failures are disruptive to the business of customers and they undermine confidence in the banking system. Regulators strive to avoid bank failures, despite the fact that most small depositor's holdings are covered by federal insurance against loss, because banks hold as liabilities the major component of the money supply in the United States. Business deposits, however, are quite large and usually are not covered by deposit insurance, so bank failures could cause substantial disruption of a local economy and possibly bankruptcy for a firm.

A bank, like any other corporation, needs a charter to begin business. A group of aspiring bankers might choose to request their charter from state banking authorities. Persons wishing to begin a bank, however, also have another route open to them: a federal charter issued by the Comptroller of the Currency in the U.S. Treasury Department.

If a bank is to be chartered by state authorities, it will almost certainly find it necessary to have the bank's deposits insured by the Federal Deposit Insurance Corporation. At the end of 1977 there were 466 noninsured banks out of 14,741 banks in the nation. Noninsured banks were therefore only 3.2 percent of all banks. However, of the 206 new banks opened in 1977, 49 were noninsured, representing 23.8 percent of the total. States with a fair number of noninsured banks are: California, Colorado, Illinois, Massachusetts, New York, and the state of Washington. A number of other states have some noninsured banks, but some states have none.

All banks chartered by the Comptroller of the Currency are required to obtain federal deposit insurance, and they will be required to become members of the Federal Reserve System. For state-chartered banks, membership in the Federal Reserve System is optional, and many choose not to belong. The Federal Reserve requires each member bank to hold with it reserves in the form of idle cash on deposit at the regional Federal Reserve bank. That is costly to member banks because the cash on deposit earns no interest, but membership in the Federal Reserve System allows banks to clear their checks through the system's facilities, so there is an offsetting gain for members. The required reserves are changed from time to time to facilitate monetary policy, or to achieve other goals of the Federal Reserve.

The smooth operation of the U.S. banking system is important for growth and efficiency in the economy, and also because monetary policy is implemented by changing the quantity of money in circulation. Since commercial banks hold demand deposits, the principal component of the money supply, monetary policy affects banks directly and swiftly. With the large and efficient U.S. banking system, the Federal Reserve can change monetary policy without disrupting the banking system, and it does so regularly in an effort to influence the economy.

References

Comptroller of the Currency, *Annual Report*, U.S. Department of the Treasury; Federal Deposit Insurance Company, *Annual Report*, U.S. Department of the Treasury; Klein, John J., *Money and the Economy*, Harcourt, Brace, New York, 1978; Luckett, Dudley G., *Money and Banking*, McGraw-Hill, New York, 1976.

(*See also* Bank deposits; Federal Reserve System; Financial institutions; Money supply)

William J. Brown

Barriers to trade

Barriers to trade are obstacles which prevent goods and services from moving freely between nations on the basis of pure competition and comparative advantage. They are primarily interferences imposed by national governments as part of trade policy in pursuit of such goals as a balanced international payments position, internal economic development, protection for an important (or influential) domestic sector or industry, and/or maintenance of an indigeneous productive capacity in strategic or essential areas.

Tariffs and Quotas

Early in the history of international commerce, the mercantilist period (1500–1750) gave rise to the first strong feelings of national protectionism in commerce which at that time manifested itself in "bullionism"—the practice of government limiting gold exports in order to restrict the financing, and hence the flow, of inbound goods. While the economic advantages of free and unrestricted trade became recognized by the end of the eighteenth century under the influence of Adam Smith's doctrine, nationalistic feelings resurfaced in the nineteenth century in response to wars and economic depressions. In particular, governments favored the use of tariffs (a duty or tax) on imported goods as a way to raise revenues to finance defense spending, to protect their own infant industries, as well as a way to reduce foreign competition in support of flagging domestic industries. Later, as concern focused more on economic development and international financial solvency, the use of quotas also became a common instrument of trade policy. Quotas, which are quantitative restrictions on imports, provide more absolute protection for domestic producers and for the balance of payments than a comparably restrictive tariff; however, quotas do not generate additional tax revenues and can result in higher prices for domestic consumers if a domestic producing monopoly exists.

Other Barriers

While tariff barriers continue to be important in modern-day trade policy, the nontariff barriers have captured most of the attention in the last few decades. In addition to quotas, some of the more prominent nontariff barriers are multiple (discriminatory) exchange rate systems, countervailing duties, orderly marketing agreements (voluntary export quotas), multiple valuation procedures for purposes of levying tariffs on imports, administrative hindrances in processing of import goods, technical standards and specifications ill-suited to foreign goods, and discriminatory government procurement practices. These barriers represent a diverse collection of protectionist devices whose only common denominator may be their amenability to use by governments in much more subtle and elusive ways than tariffs to influency trade patterns. For example, government purchases of goods and services may be explicitly discriminatory as under the Buy American Act of 1933, which gives American producers a fixed percentage advantage in government contract bidding, or covertly discriminatory as in instances where notification of government contract solicitations are not so adequately or expeditiously made available to foreign producers as they are to domestic producers.

Reducing Worldwide Trade Barriers

Over the past 40 years it has been the purpose of international trade negotiations by national governments to reduce the level of all trade barriers on a worldwide basis. This is because it is the accepted view that free trade allocates the world's resources in the most efficient fashion, and hence maximizes world output and income by encouraging individual countries to shift their resources into their most productive uses and to trade with other nations in order to secure the mix of goods and services it most desires in consumption. While national security considerations, pressures from special interest groups, and economic development programs have resulted in resistance to complete removal of such barriers, considerable progress has been made since World War II through the negotiating rounds of the General Agreement on Tariffs and Trade (GATT). Under the original GATT (1947), a "most-favored-nation" principle was adopted, requiring that any bilateral tariff reduction agreements be automatically extended to all other participating nations to the GATT negotiations. This principle was the basis for highly successful reductions in tariffs in subsequent rounds. For example, the series of postwar multilateral trade negotiations under the GATT reduced average tariff levels in the United States to approximately 10 percent by 1967; in contrast, U.S. tariff levels averaged 53 percent *ad valorem*— on a product value basis—after the Smoot-Hawley Tariff of 1930 which marked the pinnacle of tariff protection in the United States. Under the Kennedy Round of GATT negotiations lasting from 1962 to 1967, the largest reductions in tariffs occurred. The most recent round of negotiations, known as the Tokyo Round, lasted from 1974 to 1979. Its greatest contributions to the trade liberalization effort were made in the nontariff areas, by detailing codes of acceptable conduct and by outlining procedures for settlement of disputes and surveillance of codes.

References

Baldwin, Robert E., *The Multilateral Trade Negotiations: Toward Greater Liberalization?*, American Enterprise Institute, Washington, D.C., 1979; Gruberl, Herbert, *International Economics,* Irwin, Homewood, Ill., 1977; Kindleberger, C. P., and P. H. Lindert, *International Economics,* Irwin, Homewood, Ill., 1978.

(*See also* Comparative advantage theory; Competition; International economics, an overview; Protectionism)

Anita M. Benvignati

Bayesian inference

Bayesian inference is a collection of concepts, principles, and procedures which is designed to assist scientific investigators in learning from their data. Such learning is conceived of as changes in beliefs induced by information in new data. In particular, new data may change beliefs about the adequacy of particular hypotheses or models, about the probable values of parameters, and about the values of as yet unconfirmed observations; that is, new data may help in dealing with the problems of confirming hypotheses or models, estimation, and prediction, respectively. In addition, Bayesian inference techniques are useful in designing surveys and experiments, control problems, and other decision problems. These inference and decision problems are solved in a systematic and unified fashion in the Bayesian approach for which axiomatic support has been provided in the works of Burks (1977), DeGroot (1970), deFinetti (1972), Jeffreys (1957, 1967), Raiffa and Schlaifer (1961), Savage (1954), and others.

Use of Numerical Probabilities

In most forms of Bayesian inference, numerical probabilities are employed to represent degrees of belief. For example, the degree of belief that a particular hypothesis accounts for the variation in a given set of data is assumed measurable by a numerical probability in much the same fashion that one states that the probability that it will rain tomorrow in a particular area is 0.75. Similarly, it is assumed that a degree of belief that a parameter's value lies between, say, 0.7 and 1.0 can be represented by a numerical probability in the interval 0 to 1, where 0 and 1 represent complete certainty and intermediate values represent various degrees of uncertainty. While the assumption that degrees of belief can be represented by cardinal probabilities is a strong one, and some have sought to relax it, its use does permit use of the standard inductive calculus to measure changes in degrees of belief, that is, learning in a logically consistent way for statistical problems encountered in quantitative economics.

Bayes' Theorem

Central in Bayesian inference is Bayes' theorem, a noncontroversial theorem from the probability calculus. Let $p(\mathbf{y}, \theta \mid I_0)$ be the joint probability density function (PDF) for an observation vector $\mathbf{y}$ and a parameter vector θ, both considered random, given prior or initial information, denoted by I_0. The joint PDF can be expressed in terms of its marginal and conditional PDFs to obtain Bayes' theorem:

$$p(\mathbf{y}, \theta \mid I_0) = p(\theta \mid I_0)p(\mathbf{y} \mid \theta, I_0) \tag{1}$$
$$= p(\mathbf{y} \mid I_0)p(\theta \mid \mathbf{y}, I_0)$$

or

$$p(\theta \mid D) = p(\theta \mid I_0)p(\mathbf{y} \mid \theta, I_0)/p(\mathbf{y} \mid I_0) \tag{2a}$$

where $D \equiv (\mathbf{y}, I_0)$, the given sample and prior information. $(2a)$ is often expressed as:

$$p(\theta \mid D) \propto p(\theta \mid I_0)p(\mathbf{y} \mid \theta, I_0) \tag{2b}$$

where $\propto$ denotes proportionality and the proportionality constant is the reciprocal of

$$p(\mathbf{y} \mid I_0) = \int_{R_\theta} p(\theta \mid I_0)p(\mathbf{y} \mid \theta, I_0) \, d\theta$$

In $(2b)$, $p(\theta \mid D)$ is the posterior PDF for θ, $p(\theta \mid I_0)$ is the prior or initial PDF for θ, and $p(\mathbf{y} \mid \theta, I_0)$ is the likelihood function. Thus, $(2b)$ states Bayes' theorem as

$$\text{posterior PDF} \propto \text{prior PDF} \times \text{likelihood function} \tag{2c}$$

Our initial beliefs regarding the parameters' values are represented by $p(\theta \mid I_0)$, the prior PDF. By use of (2), the information in the data, incorporated in the likelihood function $p(\mathbf{y} \mid \theta, I_0)$, is combined with the information in the prior PDF to yield the posterior PDF, $p(\theta \mid \mathbf{y}, I_0)$, which generally differs from the prior PDF. This difference is the change in beliefs regarding values of the parameters induced by the information in the data $\mathbf{y}$. Applications of Bayes' theorem in analyses of many models encountered in economics and statistics are provided in Box and Tiao (1973), DeGroot (1970), Fienberg and Zellner (1975), Jeffreys (1967), Leamer (1978), and Zellner (1971).

Applications of Bayes' Theorem

To use Bayes' theorem it is necessary to introduce and formulate a prior PDF, $p(\theta \mid I_0)$, to represent initial beliefs. When there is little prior or initial information about parameters' values, that is, initial information is vague or diffuse, a prior PDF which represents "knowing little," or ignorance, is employed. Various procedures for formulating such prior PDFs have been employed in analyses of many problems. Their use has enabled Bayesian analysts to produce many estimation results which are technically similar to those provided by non-Bayesian methods but which have a completely different interpretation. On the other hand, if some initial information about parameters' values is available from past studies and/or subject matter considerations, a prior PDF can be formulated to represent it and employed in Bayes' theorem.

Thus, prior or initial information is formally introduced by use of prior PDF, a distinctive feature of Bayesian inference. In applied non-Bayesian analyses of data, prior information is extensively employed but usually in an informal manner. Attempts to obtain posterior PDFs without introducing prior PDFs, as in R. A. Fisher's fiducial inference, have not been successful. By use of a prior PDF, it becomes possible to represent and use all information, including prior and sample information, in a logically consistent fashion, a major objective of Bayesian inference. Much controversy has centered on the extent to which prior PDFs adequately represent initial prior information and on the kinds of prior information which should be introduced. If the prior information and the information embodied in the form of the likelihood function taken together are considered to be a hypothesis or model, it is possible to use data, as will be shown, to compute posterior probabilities associated with such models. These posterior probabilities reflect the degree to which the data support or fail to support alternative models.

The posterior PDF, $p(\theta \mid D)$, in (2) can be employed to make posterior probability statements. For example, one can compute the probability that θ lies in a particular region, $Pr(\theta \subset R \mid y, I_0)$ by integrating the posterior PDF over R. Also, if θ is partitioned, $\theta' = (\theta_1', \theta_2')$, the marginal posterior PDF for θ_1 is

$$p(\theta_1 \mid D) = \int_{R_{\theta_2}} p(\theta_1, \theta_2 \mid D) \, d\theta_2$$

$$= \int_{R_{\theta_2}} p(\theta_1 \mid \theta_2, D) p(\theta_2 \mid D) \, d\theta_2$$

(3)

where $D \equiv (\mathbf{y}, I_0)$ and R_{θ_2} is the region for θ_2. The second integral in (3) shows that the integration with respect to θ_2 can be interpreted as an averaging of the conditional posterior PDF for θ_1 given θ_2 with $p(\theta_2 \mid D)$, the marginal posterior PDF for θ_2 serving as the weighting function. The integration in (3) is a convenient way of removing nuisance parameters, that is, parameters which are not of special interest to an investigator.

With regards to point estimation, a measure of central tendency, for example, the modal value or mean of the posterior PDF, $p(\theta \mid D)$, can be employed. If a convex loss function $L(\theta, \hat{\theta})$, where $\hat{\theta} = \hat{\theta}(D)$, is available, the Bayesian point estimate is the value of $\hat{\theta}$ which minimizes expected loss, that is, the solution to the following problem:

$$\min_{\hat{\theta}} EL(\theta, \hat{\theta}) = \min_{\hat{\theta}} \int_{R_\theta} L(\theta, \hat{\theta}) p(\theta \mid D) \, d\theta$$

(4)

The solution to (4), $\hat{\theta}*$, is the Bayesian estimate for θ. It is known that $\hat{\theta}*$ viewed as an estimator is consistent. Also, when average risk

$$\int_{R_\theta} r(\theta) p(\theta \mid I_0) \, d\theta$$

where

$$r(\theta) = \int_{R_y} L(\theta, \hat{\theta}^*)p(\mathbf{y}|\theta) \, d\mathbf{y}$$

is finite, Bayesian estimators are admissible and minimize average risk. For quadratic loss functions, $\hat{\theta}^*$ is the posterior mean vector. In large samples, under general conditions $p(\theta|D)$ approaches a normal form with mean equal to the maximum likelihood estimate and variance-covariance matrix equal to the inverse of the estimated Fisher information matrix.

With respect to prediction, Bayesians employ the predictive PDF to make probability statements about as yet unobserved values of variables and to calculate prediction intervals and point predictions. The predictive PDF for $\mathbf{y}_f$, a vector of as yet unobserved values of a variable, is given by

$$p(\mathbf{y}_f|D) = \int_{R_\theta} p(\mathbf{y}_f|\theta)p(\theta|D) \, d\theta \tag{5}$$

where $p(\mathbf{y}_f|\theta)$ is the PDF for $\mathbf{y}_f$ given θ, and $p(\theta|D)$ is the posterior PDF for θ given by (2). The predictive PDF in (5) can be viewed as an average of the conditional PDF, $p(\mathbf{y}_f|\theta)$, with the posterior PDF for θ, $p(\theta|D)$, serving as the weighting function. Probability statements regarding $\mathbf{y}_f$ or particular elements of $\mathbf{y}_f$ can be made using the predictive PDF in (5). Also, if a convex loss function $L(\mathbf{y}_f, \mathbf{y}_f)$, where $\hat{\mathbf{y}}_f = \hat{\mathbf{y}}_f(D)$ is a point prediction, is available, a Bayesian point prediction is obtained by solving the following problem

$$\min_{\hat{\mathbf{y}}_f} EL(\mathbf{y}_f, \hat{\mathbf{y}}_f) = \min_{\hat{\mathbf{y}}_f} \int_{R_{\mathbf{y},f}} L(\mathbf{y}_f)p(\mathbf{y}_f|D) \, d\mathbf{y}_f \tag{6}$$

The solution to the problem in (6), $\hat{\mathbf{y}}_f^*$, is the Bayesian point prediction, which has similar desirable properties as Bayesian parameter estimates or estimators. In the special case that $L(\mathbf{y}_f, \hat{\mathbf{y}}_f)$ is a quadratic loss function, it is easily shown that the mean of the predictive PDF is the Bayesian point prediction.

In connection with comparing and testing hypotheses, Bayes' theorem is employed to model the transformation of prior or initial probabilities into posterior probabilities associated with alternative hypotheses. If H_1 and H_2 are two mutually exclusive hypotheses with prior or initial probabilities π_1 and π_2, respectively, application of Bayes' theorem yields

$$K = \frac{\pi_1}{\pi_2} \frac{p_1(\mathbf{y}|D_1)}{p_2(\mathbf{y}|D_2)} \tag{7}$$

where K is the posterior odds ratio, π_1/π_2 is the prior odds ratio, $\mathbf{y}$ is a vector of observations, and

$$p_i(\mathbf{y}|D_i) = \int_{R_{\theta,i}} p_i(\mathbf{y}|\theta_i, H_i)p(\theta_i|H_i, I_0) \, d\theta_i, \qquad i = 1, 2$$

is the averaged likelihood function with the prior PDF, $p(\theta_i|H_i, I_0)$ serving as the weighting function. The ratio $p_1(\mathbf{y}|D_1)/p_2(\mathbf{y}|D_2)$ is called the Bayes factor. In the case of two simple hypotheses $\theta_1 = \theta_1^0$ and $\theta_2 = \theta_2^0$, where θ_1^0 and θ_2^0 are given values, the Bayes factor is exactly equal to the likelihood ratio. As (6) indicates, the prior odds ratio π_1/π_2 is modified by the Bayes factor, which reflects the impact of sample and prior information to yield the posterior odds ratio K. If, for example, $\pi_1/\pi_2 = 1$, a value of $K = 3$ would indicate increased support for H_1 relative to H_2. If H_1 and H_2 are mutually exclusive and exhaustive (as would be the case if H_2 is the negation of H_1), $K = P_1/(1 - P_1)$, where P_1 is the posterior probability associated with H_1 and $1 - P_1$ is the posterior probability associated with H_2. The posterior probabilities P_1 and $1 - P_1$ can be employed to choose between hypotheses H_1 and H_2 if losses associated with incorrect decisions are available.

The Bayesian concepts, principles, and procedures have been applied to many statistical problems in a variety of areas. Current research is directed toward formulating broader ranges of prior PDFs and developing computational techniques for using them. Further study is being done on analyses of random-parameter models, time series models, posterior odds ratios for hypotheses relating to parameters of multivariate models, computational problems, and applications.

References

Box, G. E. P., and G. C. Tiao, *Bayesian Inference in Statistical Analyses*, Addison-Wesley, Reading, Mass., 1973; Burks, A. W., *Chance, Cause and Reason: An Inquiry Into the Nature of Scientific Evidence*, University of Chicago Press, Chicago, 1977; de Finetti, B., *Probability, Induction and Statistics: The Art of Guessing*, Wiley, New York, 1972; DeGroot, M. H.: *Optimal Statistical Decisions*, McGraw-Hill, New York, 1970; Fienberg, S. E., and A. Zellner (eds.), *Studies in Bayesian Econometrics and Statistics in Honor of Leonard J. Savage*, North-Holland, Amsterdam, 1975; Jeffreys, H., *Scientific Inference*, 2d ed., University Press, Cambridge, England, 1975; Jeffreys, H., *Theory of Probability*, 3d ed., Oxford University Press, London, 1967; Leamer, E. E., *Specification Searches: Ad Hoc Inference with Nonexperimental Data*, Wiley, New York, 1978; Raiffa, H., and R. Schlaifer, *Applied Statistical Decision Theory*, Graduate School of Business Administration, Harvard University, Boston, 1961; Savage, L. J., *The Foundations of Statistics*, Wiley, New York, 1954; Zellner, A., *An Introduction to Bayesian Inference in Econometrics*, Wiley, New York, 1971.

(*See also* Forecasting methods; Statistical techniques in economics and business, an overview; Time series analysis)

Arnold Zellner

Behavioral economics

The term "behavioral science," rarely used before World War II, became familiar shortly thereafter. Behavioral science has been defined as the study of the behavior of people, and of groups of people, by means of the scientific method of controlled observation or experimentation. In addition to psychology, sociology, and anthropology, economics has frequently been cited as one of the behavioral sciences. Yet the relation of economics to the behavioral sciences is complex, although in the 1950s, 1960s, and 1970s numerous studies of economic behavior were carried out and their theoretical foundation was clarified.

Characteristics

Behavioral economics has three major characteristics. First, its starting point consists of empirical investigations of the behavior of business executives and consumers in one country at one time. Generalizations about economic behavior emerge gradually by comparing behavior observed under different circumstances.

Second, behavioral economics focuses on the study of the process of decision making on spending, saving, investing, and the like, rather than on a statistical analysis of such results of behavior as amounts spent, saved, or invested.

Third, the study of the human factor looms large in behavioral economics, which, therefore, has also been called psychological economics. Behavioral economics analyzes such psychological antecedents of economic activities as the motives, attitudes, and expectations that influence decisions in economic matters.

In all these respects behavioral economics differs greatly from classical economics, which deduces principles of economic behavior from features of human nature assumed to be valid at all times, and also from econometric studies which commonly begin with setting up a general model and then testing derivations from the model with statistical data.

Consumer Behavior Studies

Consumer behavior has been the most common subject of behavioral studies. The interest in consumers stemmed from dissatisfaction with the approach of economic theorists, who had assumed that consumers' expenditures were a function of income and that consumers' income depended on decisions of other sectors of the economy (business and government). With increasing affluence, Americans acquired great latitude in their spending and saving decisions and were in a position to use part of their income to undertake discretionary expenditures. Instead of postulating that these expenditures depended solely on income received and changes in income, behavioral theorists assumed that they were a function both of ability to buy and willingness to buy. Various aspects of market research—for example, studies of brand loyalty or the impact of advertising—also contributed greatly to the analysis of consumer behavior.

Sample Interview Survey   Studies of consumer behavior make use of case studies and of laboratory as well as field experiments. Yet the most important methodological tool of behavioral economics is the sample interview survey. Rapid progress in the development of reliable sampling as well as of interviewing methods in the 1940s represents one of the factors that made behavioral economics possible. Surveys with representative samples of the population, or of such parts of the population as upper-income families or business executives, permit the researcher to collect three kinds of data from the same individuals who fall in a sample and analyze their interrelations. The three kinds of data are (1) economic-financial data, for example, on consumer expenditures as well as on income received, assets accumulated, and debt incurred; (2) demographic data on age, occupation, education, etc.; and (3) psychological data on people's motives, attitudes, expectations, and intentions to buy, as well as on their opinions about economic developments such as inflation, changes in taxes, and government policies, or domestic and international political trends.

The measurement of expectations through questioning representative population samples about expected changes in prices, in incomes, and about expected economic trends has been undertaken for several decades. The direct approach of measurement, in place of substituting past for expected trends, or of assuming what rational expectations ought to be in the judgment of experts, provides information not only about the average expectations of all Americans but also about the expectations of groups of individuals that can be related to their subsequent actions, such as their purchases. Beyond the impact of expectations the new approach makes it possible to study the origin of expectations. The studies indicate that expectations are often formed according to what has happened in the past (e.g., when the expected level of prices increased after prices had advanced). But at certain and often crucial times expectations differ greatly from past trends. An analysis of the circumstances under which expectations are not extrapolative is important.

Key Findings of Behavioral Studies

Extensive and successful use has been made of the measurement of expectations for the purpose of forecasting major expenditures and the course of the entire economy. Surveys on consumer expectations or on business plans and intentions to undertake capital expenditures have contributed greatly to progress in behavioral economics. The following list gives three specific instances:

1. In 1977 to 1979 data were collected about the proportion of Americans who were primarily motivated to purchase one-family houses and automobiles because they expected further substantial increases in house or car prices. Although prices and interest rates had risen sharply prior to the purchase decisions and therefore the classical law of demand would have predicted a reduction in demand, people hastened to buy houses and cars, many buyers motivated by the fear that later they would be priced out of the market. It was possible to collect quantitative data on the extent of advance buying. In this instance expectations proved to be powerful determinants of behavior. (At the same time, however, reductions in the fares for air travel stimulated such travel, fully in accord with traditional economic principles.)

2. Between 1945 and 1970 economic growth was rapid and the standard of living of millions of people improved greatly. Consumer demand for a great variety of goods and services increased almost continuously, and even after large purchases of major consumer goods there was no sign of saturation. Survey research indicated that consumers as a whole increased their aspirations after they had purchased what they had wanted previously, in accordance with well-established psychological principles.

3. The amount of personal saving at a given time was found to be greatly dependent on decisions to undertake major expenditures that were to be paid for while making use of houses or durable goods. Purchases made by incurring mortgage or installment debt result in negative saving and the subsequent gradual repayment of debt in positive saving. In addition to contractual and residual saving, there is also "discretionary saving," primarily by middle-aged upper-income families and holders of substantial assets. Wealth, rather than reducing the propensity to save, was found to have raised the amounts saved because of rising aspirations for reserve funds and the impact of established habits of saving.

Behavioral Economics and Major Economic Problems

Many studies of behavioral economics have been devoted to some major economic problems. Studies conducted on people's response to inflation, and especially to creeping inflation in the 1950s and 1960s, revealed that the typical behavior following an acceleration of price increases was to save more rather than to spend more. Because of rising prices, most people felt they were in a worse position, including those whose incomes had risen more than prices had increased. The latter complained of having been deprived of enjoying what they considered well-deserved fruits of their labor. In addition, saving was stimulated by the uncertainty generated by inflation and the belief that one needed to save more in order to be able to pay for necessities in the future when they would cost more. The standard response to inflation, saving more, was confirmed by statistical and econometric studies made between 1945 and 1970.

At certain times, however, people responded to inflation in a radically different manner—in the second half of 1950 under the impact of military defeat in Korea; in 1973 when food prices skyrocketed; and in 1977 to 1979, especially with regard to one-family houses and automobiles—buying in advance and in excess of needs was stimulated by inflationary expectations.

The notion that in the 1970s the economy operated under different conditions from those that prevailed in the preceding 25 years may be supported by the high rates of inflation and unemployment in the 1970s. Comprehensive support for the assumption of a "new economic era" has been derived from observations on the attitudes and belief systems of the American people. The 1970s have been characterized by (1) widespread distrust rather than confidence in the government, especially in its ability to alleviate economic evils, as well as in big business and experts in general; (2) disorientation and confusion about causes and cures of inflation, unemployment, and economic fluctuations; (3) a process of scaling down aspirations and doubts in continued growth; and (4) extensive uncertainty and volatility of attitudes.

The 1950s and 1960s, however, differed greatly from the 1970s. For instance, people's confidence in the government's ability to improve economic conditions was reflected in earlier times by the widespread notion that "what goes up will come down" because the government would take suitable measures to fight inflation. In the 1970s most Americans believed that prices in general would be higher a year hence and still higher 5 years later, and said that neither the government nor anybody else knew how to deal with inflation. Even though the spread of mistrust in the government could be traced to political developments (Vietnam, Watergate), it had grave economic consequences. The response to inflation in 1978 to 1979—absence of consumer resistance to price increases, anticipatory buying of houses and automobiles, and anticipatory pricing by businesses, with the prices set reflecting both past and expected cost increases—was strongly influencd by the newly developed attitudes.

A change in underlying economic conditions was also apparent in Western Europe in the mid-1970s. For instance, in West Germany where inflation was at a low level, where the currency was strong, and where exports far exceeded imports, the notion that two decades of rapid economic growth had ended resulted in widespread attitudes not dissimilar to those in the United States. In Germany, too, consumer attitudes became influential even though personal saving remained much higher than in the United States (primarily because of an insignificant growth in installment debt), as did the ratio of business investment to GNP.

Importance of Behavioral Studies

Substantial evidence has been accumulated in support of the proposition that the relation between precipitating circumstances and behavior is neither fixed nor unchangeable. Because human beings are capable of learning, they may respond to the same stimuli in a different manner at a later time than they did at an earlier time. Under these circumstances the need for studies of economic attitudes and expectations has gained in importance.

Traditional assumptions about rational behavior, defined as weighing available alternatives and choosing the alternative that maximizes utilities or profits, also had to be revised. Behavioral economists found a common occurrence of habitual behavior—doing what has been done in the past under similar circumstances—occasionally interrupted by genuine decision making. Only in those relatively few instances when the decision really matters do strong motivational forces arise that lead business executives and consumers to proceed in a circumspect manner. Even then the alternatives considered are usually restricted according to people's attitudes and expectations, and many will choose a satisfying course of action, rather than attempt to optimize the outcome.

Is economics a behavioral science? Many economic studies do not belong to the behavioral sciences because they are concerned with resources, markets, or institutions rather than the behavior of people. Behavioral economics supplements traditional economics. Even though this new discipline is still young, many of its procedures, e.g. the direct measurement of expectations, deserve to be incorporated into the mainstream of economics, and many of its findings constitute revisions of traditional assumptions. The need to conduct empirical studies based on hypotheses derived both from economic theory and from psychological and sociological theory has already been demonstrated and must be pursued in the future.

References

Katona, George, *Psychological Analysis of Economic Behavior*, McGraw-Hill, New York, 1951; Katona, George, *Psychological Economics*, Elsevier, New York, 1975; Katona, George, and Burkhard Strumpel: *A New Economic Era*, Elsevier, New York, 1978; Morgan, J. N.: "Psychology and Economics," *American Economic Review*, May 1978, pp. 58–63; Simon, H. A., *Models of Man*, Wiley, New York, 1957; Simon, H. A., "Rationality as Process and Product of Thought," *American Economic Review*, May 1978, pp. 1–17.

(*See also* Advertising, economic aspects; Anticipation surveys, business; Anticipation surveys, consumer; Consumer theory; Consumption function; Expectations; Marketing research and business economics; Propensity to consume or to save and inducement to invest; Sampling in economics)

George Katona

Bond

A bond is a debt instrument, which represents a financial claim that the holder (creditor) has against the issuer (debtor). It is a written promise to pay a certain sum of money (principal) at a definite date in the future or periodically over the course of the loan. In most cases, the issuer promises to pay the holder fixed money amounts (interest) on specified dates while the bond is outstanding.

History

Who issued the first bonds and when that occurred is uncertain. The best evidence suggests that the Republic of Venice floated the first issue (called *prestiti*) in the late twelfth century. But debt as a means of finance predates that event by at least four millennia. Records of contracts describing interest-bearing loans date back to the Sumerian civilization—around 3500 B.C. Hammurabi's code, compiled about 1800 B.C., indicates that mortgages and promissory notes were used to facilitate commerce at that time. But these instruments, and those that Greek, Roman, and medieval money lenders and merchant bankers used were not bonds. They all involved one creditor lending money to one debtor, while a bond issue implies the existence of many creditors, that is, hundreds or today even thousands of bondholders who have lent money to the issuer.

Although Venice floated the first issue nearly eight centuries ago, bonds became a popular debt instrument much more recently. In the eighteenth and nineteenth centuries, nation states developed and many issued bonds to finance their operations—in many cases associated with military endeavors. And the nineteenth century saw the rapid development of the corporate forms of business organization, many of which used bonds to finance their growth. Consequently, today virtually all industrial nations, many publicly held corporations, and most state and local governments have issued bonds.

Federal Debt Obligations

The United States government issues several kinds of debt obligations, which are classified as marketable or nonmarketable. At the end of 1978, over 60 percent of the nearly $800 billion of Treasury securities outstanding were marketable. The remaining obligations were issued directly to individuals, U.S. government agencies, and foreign, state, and local governments. For example, U.S. government agencies held nearly $160 billion of nonmarketable Treasury securities, while individuals held roughly $80 billion of series E and H U.S. savings bonds.

Of the marketable Treasury securities outstanding at the end of 1978, bonds accounted for approximately 12 percent and notes for more than 50 percent. (Treasury bills made up the remaining one-third. Even though they represent a debt obligation of the federal government, they are not classified as bonds because they are short-term, maturing in 1 year or less.) Treasury notes and bonds are virtually the same, except for the length of time from date of issue to maturity: notes mature between 1 and 10 years, while bonds usually mature in more than 10 years.

State and Local Government Debt Obligations

State and local governments, as well as other political subdivisions, such as school districts, water authorities, and so on, issue debt obligations to finance capital investment projects in most cases. The data show that they have borrowed extensively. In 1902, local government debt outstanding totaled under $2 billion and state government debt was about $230 million. By 1979, local government debt had soared to almost $180 billion, and state government obligations outstanding had increased to about $100 billion. Most of this increase in state and local government debt outstanding has occurred since World War II, when the population boom, the movement to the suburbs, and other factors compelled states and municipalities to finance schools, highways, water and sewerage systems, and so forth.

State and local government bonds, which are exempt from federal income taxes, fall into one of two categories: general or limited obligation bonds. The former rest on the "full faith and credit" of the issuer for payment of interest and repayment of principal, which simply means the issuing government's power to tax. The latter, frequently called revenue bonds, depend on revenues gained from whatever asset— e.g., a bridge, tunnel, or turnpike—they financed for payment of interest and repayment of principal. Other things being equal, the risk of default is obviously greater for limited obligation bonds.

Corporate Bonds

Corporations, the third major issuer of bonds in the United States, have recently relied more heavily on debt for expansion because it is a less expensive method of raising funds than equity financing. The chief reason is that interest payments are tax-deductible, while dividend payments are not, making the effective cost of debt capital substantially lower than the cost of equity capital. Although there are no firm figures on the total amount of corporate debt outstanding, or on how rapidly it has grown, the par value of bonds listed on the New York Stock Exchange (NYSE) gives some idea. At the end of 1964, approximately $32 billion of corporate bonds were listed on the NYSE. By the end of 1979, this figure had risen to about $200 billion.

Corporate bonds are classified as secured (mortgage bonds) or unsecured (debentures). In the former case, the corporation executes either a mortgage pledging specific assets as security, or a blanket mortgage, which establishes a lien as security against all the real property owned by the corporation. In the latter case, although specific assets are not pledged, debentures are secured by all the corporation's unpledged assets and the holder is in the same position as any other general creditor. In both cases, the real safety of a corporate bond essentially rests on the corporation's earning ability.

Bonds are issued under indentures, which are agreements between issuers and trustees that govern the bond issue. For example, an indenture would specify the amount of the issue, any assets pledged as security, method of extinguishing the bonds, and so on. The trustee, who may legally be any person, but is usually a commercial bank, has three major responsibilities: (1) the trustee certifies that the bond contract and indenture meet legal requirements; (2) the trustee makes sure the issuer performs the responsibilities set forth in the indenture; and (3) the trustee acts on the bondholders' behalf if the issuer defaults on either interest or principal payments.

Types of Bonds and Means of Redemption

The different kinds of provisions that a bond can include are limited only by the issuer's ingenuity. Some of the more popular features include the following: Some bonds, like U.S. savings bonds, are registered, while others are not. The latter are referred to as bearer or coupon bonds, which refers to the attached coupons that are clipped when interest payments are due. Some corporate bonds contain a call provision, which gives the issuer the right to redeem the bonds prior to maturity. If the corporation exercises this right and calls the bonds, it usually must pay an amount greater than the face value, or principal—the call premium—to the holders. Obviously, a corporation will call bonds only if interest rates have declined enough to at least cover the premium. Convertible debentures are bonds that the holder may convert into the preferred or common stock of the same corporation at the holder's option. The terms of the conversion privilege are specified at the outset of the issue and include the conversion ratio—how many shares of stock the holder will receive for each bond that is converted.

Bonds may be extinguished in three ways. First, they may be redeemed in cash, either at maturity or over the course of the loan. State and local governments frequently issue serial bonds, which provide for the redemption of a portion of the issue each year it is outstanding. And some corporate bonds carry a sinking fund provision, which requires the company to purchase and retire some bonds each year. Second, bonds may be refunded at maturity with a new issue, a technique that the U.S. government uses in its debt management operations. Finally, with convertibles, a debt is extinguished every time holders decide to convert their debentures into stock.

Economic Function of Bonds

Bonds are important to a growing economy because they represent an instrument used to bring savers and investors together. Advanced economies typically have a high degree of specialization. Thus, the people and institutions that save (consume less than their incomes) are usually different from those who desire to invest (produce capital goods that will increase the output of consumer goods and services). To bring these savers and investors together in the financial sense, several financial intermediaries, such as commercial banks, savings and loan associations, and investment banks, have developed. They use various legal instruments, such as common stock, commercial paper, and bonds, to transfer funds from the savers to the investors. Given the number of bond issuers and the amount of this kind of debt outstanding, bonds are one of the more important, if not the most important, instruments boosting investment and, therefore, increasing the U.S. economy's output.

References

Bogen, Julius I. (ed.), *Financial Handbook*, 4th ed., Ronald Press, New York, 1968; Weston, J. Fred, and Eugene F. Brigham, *Managerial Finance*, 4th ed., Dryden Press, Hinsdale, Ill., 1978.

(*See also* Bond rating agencies; Financial instruments; Stock)

Henry C. F. Arnold

Bond rating agencies

Bond rating agencies are private business firms that provide informed judgments on the quality of corporate, municipal, and other bonds to those (including issuers, investors, and regulatory agencies) interested in the merits of particular issues. But, as the rating agencies emphasize, bond ratings are not recommendations to buy. Since the value of ratings depends on agency credibility, the rating agencies are independent organizations—they do not sell bonds and they are not connected with either issuers or investors.

History and Importance

Until the early part of this century, there was little need for rating agencies because most borrowers and lenders had close personal relationships and the creditor could judge the quality of the debt instrument. But, the number of corporations and governments who issue bonds grew so large that it became impossible for most investors to assess the thousands of debt issues outstanding. To fill this need some financial publishing firms began rating bonds. The first such firm was that of John Moody, who published security ratings in his 1909 *Analyses of Railroad Investments*. Moody's has grown since then and today rates the bonds of some 1300 corporations and has outstanding around 15,000 ratings of municipal general obligation and revenue bonds. Standard & Poor's began rating corporate bonds in 1923 and municipal bonds in 1940. Today that firm has roughly 8000 municipal bond ratings outstanding and has rated the issues of approximately 1700 corporations.

Basis for Ratings

The ratings essentially constitute a ranking of bond issues according to the probability of default—the failure of the issuing entity to make interest or sinking fund payments on time or to repay the principal at maturity. To determine the likelihood that a state or local government will default on a general obligation bond issue, the agencies consider many factors. The most important one is the strength of the local economy because economic forces strongly affect the financial health of state and local governments and their ability to meet debt obligations. Questions that must be answered include: What taxes are relied upon for revenues? What local and regional population, employment, and income trends prevail? How vulnerable are the local and regional economies to adverse economic conditions? The rating agency also investigates the form of government involved and how efficiently it operates. It checks how well it has handled past debt obligations and examines accounting procedures and budgetary factors.

When rating revenue bonds, the agency shifts its focus to determining whether the facility financed by the proceeds from the issue will be able to provide enough revenues above operating costs to meet debt service requirements. Finally, many considerations are taken into account when rating corporate bonds, but the key measure is how many times the corporation's gross earnings cover its fixed charges. Since interest payments usually constitute the major part of fixed charges, the higher the "times interest earned," other things being equal, the safer the bond and the higher its rating.

Although the probability of default is the principal criterion used in determining the rating of a given bond issue, the agencies also consider the specific provisions of the obligation and the relative position of the bondholders as creditors if default, reorganization, or any other event covered by bankruptcy and other laws occurs.

Similarity of Rating Categories

Standard & Poor's and Moody's rating categories are quite similar—even to the letter symbols used. For example, a triple-A rating (S & P's, AAA; Moody's, Aaa) signifies the highest-quality bonds, whose issuers have the strongest capacity to meet their obligations. The chance of a triple-A bond defaulting is extremely small. These agencies' other ratings are listed on the next page.

It has been estimated that more than one-half of the bonds rated by all agencies are placed in the same category. Those bonds that are not placed in this category are rarely more than one category apart. Although this might hint at collusion, this is not the case. The analysts at the rating agencies have been trained similarly, avail themselves of the same data, and use similar rating techniques, so it is not surprising that they come up with comparable ratings.

Data compiled in the mid-1970s show that more than 80 percent of all the rated corporate bonds fell in the top three categories, while only 3 percent were rated B or lower. Statistics on municipal bond ratings are sketchy, but one estimate indicates that about two-thirds are rated A or higher.

S & P's	Moody's	Assessment
AA	Aa	The issuers of these bonds have a very strong capacity to meet interest and principal payments when due and their quality is only slightly below a triple-A rating. The two top ratings include bonds that are usually labeled "high-grade."
A	A	Bonds rated A have a strong capacity to pay interest on time and repay principal when due, but are vulnerable to adverse changes in economic conditions. They are regarded as upper-medium-grade obligations.
BBB	Baa	This rating applies to medium-grade bonds that have adequate capacity to meet obligations, so long as economic conditions remain healthy.
BB, B, CCC, and CC	Ba, B, Caa, and Ca	These ratings indicate that, on balance, the bonds are predominantly speculative so far as the issuer's ability to pay interest and principal on time. BB and Ba bonds are the least speculative, while CC and Ca are the least secure. Moody's Ca rating includes bonds that have defaulted.
C	C	S & P's rating is reserved for income bonds on which no interest is being paid. Moody's applies the C rating to the lowest-quality bonds, which have little possibility of attaining investment standing. Most have defaulted.
D		S & P's uses a D rating for bond issues in default.

References

Cohen, Jerome B., Edward D. Zinbarg, and Arthur Zeikel, *Investment Analysis and Portfolio Management*, rev. ed., Dow Jones–Irwin, Homewood, Ill., 1973.

(*See also* Bond)

Henry C. F. Arnold

Break-even analysis

The break-even point represents the volume of sales at which revenues equal expenses; that is, at which profit is zero. Computationally, the break-even volume is arrived at by dividing fixed costs (costs that do not vary with output) by the contribution margin per unit, i.e., selling price minus variable costs (costs that vary directly with output). In certain situations, and especially in the consideration of multiproducts, break-even volume is measured in terms of sales dollars rather than units. This is done by dividing the fixed expenses by the contribution margin ratio (contribution margin divided by selling price). Often, in such computations, the desired profit is added to the fixed costs in the numerator in order to ascertain the sales volume necessary for producing the target profit.

Break-Even Chart

Other than as a rough indicator of the changes in volume which the company might experience before suffering losses or making profit, the break-even point is in itself of little relevance to managerial decision making. More broadly, however, break-even analysis refers to a crude initial evaluation of the impact on profits of small, short-run changes in volume, in fixed costs, and in the per-unit price and variable cost. Typically, this is achieved by use of break-even charts or graphs which represent linear approximations of the economist's curves of total cost and revenue. These linear approximations are drawn up by assuming both a given decision on output and input level and a given selling price. Thus, they are to be considered reasonable only within a narrow range around the given output; outside such a range, different break-even charts would be called for.

The break-even chart allows management to visualize the sensitivity of profit to such contemplated policy changes as would affect the four operating variables (volume, fixed costs, per-unit price, per-unit variable cost), or sensitivity to errors in forecasting these variables. The indicated sensitivity guides management with respect to the degee of care and effort required in analyzing its plans or in refining its forecasts.

Historical Development   The notion of zero profit and the distinctions between fixed and variable costs evolved early in the nineteenth century, but gained momentum only during the century's final quarter. The first known break-even chart (also referred to later as a crossover chart or profit graph) is attributed to a publication by the American engineer Henry Hess in 1903. Further development of break-even concepts and their application to forecasting and cost control throughout the first half of the twentieth century is credited to C. E. Knoeppel, and also to Walter Rautenstrauch, who was the first to actually publicize the term "break-even point chart." But while Knoeppel stressed the functional classification of the sources of the costs and the uses of profits, Rautenstrauch—in what later became the popular version of the chart—highlighted only the fixed-variable-cost distinction.

Usefulness of Break-Even Analysis

Beyond linearity, other simplifying assumptions limit the usefulness of break-even analysis: actual costs incurred (fixed and variable) are substituted for opportunity costs; the environment is depicted as static; that is, factors other than volume affecting revenues and costs, such as demand and technology, are assumed to be insignificant; still more importantly, uncertainty is ignored.

However, some simplistic assumptions are relaxed in certain extensions of break-even analysis: in a multiproduct, multiconstrained production environment, linear programming can be used to identify such product mixes as would allow the firm either to break even or to maximize profits. Moreover, nonlinear revenue and costs including semifixed costs (discontinuous, stepwise cost functions) and semivariable costs (costs which vary with output, but are partly fixed, even if no output is produced) can be introduced into the analysis by using piecewise linear approximations.

Uncertainty has been incorporated into break-even analysis by allowing sales volume, together with prices and costs, to be random variables and then computing the probability of achieving various profit levels and expected profits. Break-even analysis under uncertainty must incorporate a risk measure. Since any production alternative under consideration is only one among many in the portfolio of projects within a firm, and since stockholders possess portfolios of firms, the use of systematic risk (covariance with a market rate of return) has been suggested in lieu of merely variance of profits. However, from the standpoint of understanding and predicting behavior, it is to be recognized that a manager will act so as to maximize expected utility, instead of shareholders' wealth; thus a risk measure pertinent to the manager's personal portfolio rather than systematic risk is likely to be considered appropriate.

Break-even analysis evolved as an attempt to enable management to use the economic model of the firm by processing cost and revenue data compiled by the accountants. The assumptions and approximations required for this purpose drew criticisms of the tool as too simplistic. But apparently it has been judged that, on balance, costs of accumulating data for the use of the more realistic models are in excess of any possible losses from use of the simpler model. Thus, the use of break-even analysis continues.

References

Harris, Clifford, *The Breakeven Handbook: Techniques for Profit Planning and Control*, Prentice-Hall, Englewood Cliffs, N.J., 1978; Meigs, Walter B., Charles E. Johnson, and Robert F. Meigs, *Accounting, The Basis for Business Decisions*, 4th ed., McGraw-Hill, New York, 1977.

(*See also* Financial statements)

Joshua Ronen

Bretton Woods Conference

At Bretton Woods, New Hampshire, 45 nations in the short period between July 1 and July 20, 1944 agreed to a comprehensive arrangement that would govern the world trade and payments system for 28 years.

The economic turmoil between World Wars I and II had left its mark on the incomes and psyches of all nations. The world depression and the accompanying trade warfare, as expressed in bilateral trade agreements, tariffs, and competitive devaluations, all encouraged international economic cooperation after World War II. Nevertheless, history showed that the prospects for cooperation were poor. Interwar attempts at trade and monetary agreements had demonstrated the inability of nations to look beyond their narrow concerns, underlined by the failure of the 1922 Genoa Conference and the World Economic Conference of 1933. If a post-World War II agreement was to be achieved, it would require mutual recognition of benefits, a reasonable international payments system, and the recognition of mutual dependence.

The Agreement

The United States and Britain, aided by the common cause of wartime camaraderie, cleared much of the necessary groundwork in advance of the meeting so that rapid progress was made at the meetings. Discussions at Bretton Woods touched on national and regional problems but no insurmountable roadblocks emerged. Shunted aside were the raised concerns of accumulated war debts and the volatile export earnings of raw material–producing nations. Any reservations or misgivings individual nations held with regard to the prime American and British objectives of employment and exchange rate stability, which were important but limited goals, were insufficient to forestall agreement.

The participating nations agreed upon an international payments system to be administered by the creation of the International Monetary Fund (IMF) and a supporting institution, the International Bank for Reconstruction and Development

(IBRD), whose function was to promote international investment. The IMF was designed to promote international exchange rate stability, multilateral trade, and currency convertibility. With the creation of the IMF, signatory nations had access to consultative groups and monetary resources which would facilitate these objectives.

Under IMF articles, because nations defined their currency in terms of gold, with only the United States pledging convertibility, fixed cross rates were established. All IMF signatory nations were to contribute both gold and currency, and each nation was expected to promote exchange rate stability. Members were then permitted to borrow those currencies necessary to maintain stability in the foreign exchange market. In this fashion currency borrowings and corrective domestic policies would maintain a self-equilibrating international payments system.

If, however, fundamental changes in rates were required to attain balance of payments equilibrium, nations were given some limited autonomy to redefine their currency value. While the conditions necessary for such a change were never precisely indicated, it was believed that national efforts toward cooperation and stability would render gold parity changes incremental in nature. If difficulties arose, nations had access to the resources of the IMF for remedial help.

Whereas the IMF was charged with supporting fixed exchange rates, the IBRD was intended to have a limited role of primarily guaranteeing private short- and long-term loans for investment in the war-torn nations. It was believed that private international investors would be few and hesitant in the immediate postwar period. Moreover, the Bretton Woods conferees had no desire to usurp the role of private investment throughout the free world.

Reasons for Harmony

The success of the Bretton Woods Conference was a historic achievement in the experience of international economic cooperation. For the first time a world agreement explicitly stipulated the rules of an international monetary system as well as the means to execute and maintain its principles. Nations ostensibly relinquished some degree of economic sovereignty to meet the requirements for a global economic resurgence.

The harmony attained at the Bretton Woods Conference reflected national requirements as much as it did national enlightenment. With the United States recognizing the futility of its interwar isolationism, and the British their trade dependency, the two world economic powers sought to restore trade and reduce the possibility for another worldwide depression. At the same time, both nations sought to alleviate the domestic inflation and depression effects exerted through trade channels.

Planning for the world conference began in 1942, with Britain initiating discussions with the United States. The British proposal was drawn from a declining sense of empire. Their postwar trade position was expected to be in deficit, and they believed that returns on prior overseas investments would decline. With anticipated high levels of domestic unemployment, the British favored an expansive international monetary system, one that permitted aggressive domestic monetary and fiscal policy.

The United States, as the emerging world economic and political power, was also wary of a postwar recession. However, the United States was fearful that easy credit in a war-torn world would require it to become an international postwar reconstruction agency.

The British Position

Consistent with their economic situation, the British, led by J. M. Keynes, envisaged an international agency as a lender of fiduciary money. To the British a central monetary agency would permit trade expansion and exchange rate stability through the creation of an internationally acceptable new money. Keynes proposed a clearing union which would issue a created asset, "bancors," to nations requiring loans for balance of payment purposes. These bancors would be used for debt settlements between debtor and creditor nations, which in turn would promote stable rates and forestall restrictive national policies which might endanger world trade.

The British plan was unacceptable to the United States, both for its interpreted inflationary effects and its envisioned impact on the U.S. international economic position. The Americans believed that under the British scheme they would become the continual recipient of bancors and in effect become the world's resource donor. In place of the Keynes proposal, Harry White of the U.S. Treasury proposed a more conservative arrangement. This plan, through the strong bargaining position of the United States, was eventually proposed and accepted at Bretton Woods. (As it turned out the United States did become an early postwar aid agency through the Marshall Plan and other programs, and an international asset was created later through the IMF in the form of special drawing rights.)

The lively discussions that produced the international monetary proposals were absent in the formulation of the IBRD. From its beginning, the IBRD was viewed as secondary to the IMF. The coupling of modest contributions from member states and the natural bankers' conservatism in using borrowed funds limited its initial role both in reconstruction and development.

The Demise of the Bretton Woods Agreement

The Bretton Woods Conference was a remarkable achievement in international cooperation, and it certainly facilitated the eventual expansion of world trade and incomes. But it also indicated that economists, like the military, plan their strategies based on the outcome of the last battle. The participating nations aimed to solve the economic problems of the 1920s and 1930s, but failed to act on the new realities that eventually became clear. The 1940s specter of too-slow growth and resulting unemployment never materialized, and the U.S. dollar, because of its gold convertibility, became the international currency.

The uneven growth of world incomes, divergent monetary and fiscal policies among the rapidly growing industrial nations, and international liquidity constraints caused the demise of the Bretton Woods system in 1973. The organization and goals of the IMF and the IBRD were both too narrowly drawn.

The IMF, despite its initial restrictive tenets, did belatedly create an international asset. And the IBRD, by the 1960s, began to play an aggressive development role. Both international organizations remain productive. The IMF is a lender to nations in need of short-term financing—though in a restricted way—and is a consultative agency and forum for international monetary problems. The IBRD is a leader in development policy.

References

Acheson, A. L. K., J. F. Chant, M. F. J., Prachowny, *Bretton Woods Revisited*, University of Toronto Press, Toronto, 1972; Dormael, Armand Van, *Bretton Woods: Birth of a Monetary Sys-

tem, Holmes & Meier, New York, 1978; Scammell, W. M., *International Monetary Policy*, 2d ed., St. Martins Press, New York, 1967; Yeager, Leland B., *International Monetary Relations: Theory, History, and Policy*, 2d ed., Harper & Row, New York, 1976.

(*See also* Foreign exchange rates: International monetary fund; Smithsonian agreement; Special drawing rights)

Bernard S. Katz

Built-in stabilizers (see Automatic stabilizers)

Bureau of the Census

The Bureau of the Census is a large federal agency with statutory responsibility and mandatory authority for periodic censuses of population and housing and of economic and social institutions. It also makes interim compilations of data on subjects covered by the censuses as well as on other subjects such as foreign trade. Prior to 1902, the Bureau's statistical work was carried out by a series of temporary decennial organizations, and since then by a permanent organization.

Expansion of Census and Uses of Data

A decennial enumeration was prescribed in the Constitution to apportion seats among the several states in the House of Representatives. The official uses of population counts have expanded greatly, currently including the allocation of many billions of dollars each year to states and local governments.

The growth of the nation can be traced in the expansion of inquiries since the census of 1790. Thus, during the nineteenth century, the addition of questions on occupation, literacy, school attendance, and the defective population reflected the increased concern with economic development and social conditions. The evolution of schedule content continued, and in the 1940 and later censuses, in response to the problem of unemployment, detailed inquiries were made to determine labor-force activity as well as income and migration patterns.

The expanding needs for economic data have broadened the scope of the nation's periodic inventories. Thus, censuses of manufactures in 1810 and of agriculture in 1840 reflected interest in measuring economic progress. Another major addition took place in 1930 with the first census of trade and services. The initiation of the housing census in 1940 was an outgrowth of the collapse in real estate prices following the Great Depression of the thirties and concern with living conditions.

The censuses and surveys conducted by the Bureau of the Census have required the collection, tabulation, and publication of primary data on a scale far greater than elsewhere in government or in private industry. One of the important gains from the creation of a permanent office in 1902 was the opportunity thus provided for continuing development of tools and techniques designed to deal with the Bureau's unique problems of data handling. During the first half of the twentieth century, punched-card equipment was built in the Census laboratories for the Bureau's specific needs. In the 1940s the Bureau pioneered in the development of the first Univac, an electronic computer designed for large-scale data processing and moved to the use of more advanced computers and auxiliary equipment as these became available in later years. The improved methods have increased the accuracy and usefulness of the data by sophisticated procedures for editing and for allocation of missing entries and have expanded the amount of area and subject detail.

Scientific Approach

The beginning of a truly scientific approach to census work came shortly before the 1940 census, with the initiation of a research and development program. Sampling was used on a limited basis in the 1940 census, and later its use was extended throughout the Bureau, with significant improvements in cost and timeliness. The scientific approach was further advanced in the mid-1940s, when published evaluations of the accuracy of all censuses and surveys became an accepted part of the Bureau's program. A little later, the measurement of nonsampling errors and emphasis upon overall statistical design made it possible for the Bureau to shift toward self-enumeration of the population on a small scale in 1960 and on a much larger scale in subsequent censuses.

The achievements of the Bureau's research and development program have been associated with at least three major developments in the past 40 years. One was the creation of sampling designs to provide annual or more frequent measures of many of the subjects included in the periodic censuses. The second development was a marked expansion of the statistical services performed by the Bureau for other agencies of government. The Bureau's field organization, as well as its capabilities and experience, have attracted much service work from other agencies. The third development was the extensive use of administrative records to supply mailing lists for the economic censuses and to meet census needs for data from small enterprises.

The information provided by the several censuses and the associated surveys has unique economic and social importance. For example, the Bureau's data are a major source for the national product and income accounts, the balance of payments, and the index of industrial production. In the private sector, the Bureau's data are widely used in the formulation of corporate policies, in selecting sites for business establishments, and in setting marketing plans. By revealing the complex interrelationships among manufacturing establishments, as well as between distributing and manufacturing establishments, census data provide a unique basis for many operating decisions. Equally important are the uses made by governments—federal, state, and local—for legislating and administering social programs, and the extensive uses by a wide variety of research organization.

Problems with Demographics

The demographic censuses have been subject to increasing controversy, in part because of the growing use of the results for federal fund allocation. Hence, there is strong demand for reducing the undercount, particularly of blacks and other minority groups, for whom it is highest. Controversy has also arisen over the inclusion of certain questions, notably on income and some housing characteristics, which have been attacked as invasions of privacy.

The Bureau has experienced considerably fewer problems with its economic censuses (manufactures, agriculture, retail and wholesale trade, services, construction, and transportation). As noted above, these censuses have benefited from the use of administrative records to provide a mailing list with limited information on characteristics. Through this list, kept up to date by the use of federal records, the Bureau has been able to avoid the cost of inquiries from the smaller establishments and to publish annually at modest cost much current information on industrial, trade, and other establishments.

References

Eckler, A. Ross, *The Bureau of the Census*, Praeger, New York, 1972; U.S. Bureau of the Census, *Bureau of the Census Catalog, 1790–1971*, 1974; U.S. Bureau of the Census, *Historical Statistics of the United States, Colonial Times to 1970*, 1975; U.S. Bureau of the Census, *Statistical Abstract of the United States*, published annually; Wright, Carroll Davidson, assisted by William C. Hunt, *The History and Growth of the United States Census*, U.S. Government Printing Office, 1900.

(*See also* Economic statistics; Sampling in economics; Statistical techniques in economics and business, an overview)

A. Ross Eckler

Bureau of Economic Analysis

The Bureau of Economic Analysis (BEA) of the U.S. Department of Commerce, known as the Office of Business Economics prior to January 1, 1972, is the keeper and developer of the nation's economic accounts. These accounts are structured so that various groups of transactors—sectors, industries, and regions—can be identified in ways that highlight meaningful economic relationships. The result is an efficient framework for the presentation and analysis of economic information.

Economic Accounts and Economic Activiity

Economic accounts are the national income and product accounts, summarized by the gross national product (GNP); the wealth accounts, which presently show privately owned reproducible tangible wealth; the input-output accounts, which trace the interrelationships among industries; personal income and related economic series by geographic area; the U.S. balance of payments accounts and associated foreign investment accounts; and measures relating to environmental change and well-being.

Work on national economic accounts is supplemented by the preparation and analysis of other measures of economic activity. The BEA provides information on business investment through quarterly surveys of plant and equipment outlays. A system of economic indicators is maintained to track and to evaluate cyclical movements in aggregate economic activity. Econometric models are developed and operated to forecast short- and long-term changes in economic activity, and to analyze the economic effects of alternative fiscal and monetary policies. While the BEA provides policy-oriented analysis, it does not provide policy advice. This is essential to preserving the BEA's reputation for objectivity and professional integrity.

The bulk of the data underlying the BEA's etimates is obtained from other government agencies such as the Bureau of the Census, Bureau of Labor Statistics, Department of Agriculture, the Internal Revenue Service, and from private sources such as trade associations. Since the data comes from a multitude of sources, almost none of which developed their information to dovetail with the requirements of the national economic accounts, the BEA has to make many adjustments and fill in many gaps to make sure that the estimates are complete and conform to the definitions and timing of transactions called for by the accounts.

Development of Economic Accounts

Work on economic accounts started with balance of payments accounting in 1921, and the first annual report, issued in 1923, provided data for 1919 to 1922. The development of measures of national income, its industrial origin, and its distribution in the form of wages, profits, and other types of payments was called for in a 1932 Senate resolution. The initial report was published in 1934, covering the 1929–32 period. National estimates of monthly personal income first became available in 1938. State-by-state income payments to individuals were first published in 1939 for 1929 to 1937. National estimates of disposable personal income became available in 1942. The first report on the size distribution of income was issued in 1953 for 1944, 1946, 1947, and 1950. Regional personal income estimates were disaggregated further in 1967, when information was published for the standard metropolitan statistical areas, and in 1974, when annual estimates became available for counties.

The measurement of product flows—consumer purchases, investment, imports and exports, and government purchases—became important during World War II as a means of mobilizing economic resources. These measurements resulted in the preparation of the GNP in 1941. GNP by quarters first became available in 1942. Constant-dollar GNP estimates became a regular feature in 1951; GNP originating by industry was introduced in 1962. Beginning in 1965, benchmark revisions of GNP benefited substantially from the input-output work assumed by the BEA in 1959. In the course of constructing the input-output (I/O) table for 1958, which required a complete accounting for all product flows, a new and powerful cross-check was provided that improved the accuracy of the level of GNP estimates.

The BEA has published I/O benchmark tables for 1958, 1963, 1967, and 1972. Annual updates have been published for the years 1968 to 1972.

In the area of wealth, annual estimates of the stock of durable goods owned by consumers in the United States were first published in 1978 for 1925 to 1977. Estimates of the stock of business capital were first published in 1971 for the years 1925 to 1970.

Estimates of spending for pollution abatement and control by consumers, business, and government were made available within the framework of the national income and product accounts in 1975. These estimates resulted from major pioneering research that produced new concepts and called for the collection of new data. Work is under way to develop such measures of economic well-being as the value of household production and nonmarket time, the value of the services of the stock of consumer durable goods, government capital, human capital, and changes in the environment of the workplace.

The national income and product accounts have been viewed increasingly as having a central position in government economic statistics. A systematic analysis of the data underlying all components of the national income and product estimates was completed by the Advisory Committee on GNP Data Improvement, sponsored by the Office of Management and Budget. The committee reviewed the data produced by over 20 federal agencies and made over 150 recommendations to improve the data base.

References

Business Conditions Digest, U.S. Department of Commerce, published monthly. *The Survey of Current Business*, U.S. Department of Commerce, published monthly.

(*See also* Economic statistics; Gross national product; Statistical techniques in economics and business, an overview)

George Jaszi

Bureau of Labor Statistics

The Bureau of Labor Statistics (BLS) is part of the U.S. Department of Labor and serves as the federal government's principal fact-finding agency in the labor economics field. The current monthly, quarterly, and annual statistical series of the BLS are among the best-known and most widely used in the United States.

The consumer price index (CPI) has served for decades as a guide to wage and salary increases in collective bargaining contracts between labor and management. During the 1970s the index was designated by congressional legislation to provide annual increases in social security benefits for the millions of retired beneficiaries, with semiannual increases for federal ex-employees retired on civil service and other benefit programs.

The wholesale price index (renamed producers index) measures the price changes from month to month of raw materials, semimanufactured goods, and finished products in the economy.

The BLS produces comprehensive and wide-ranging statistics on the labor force, employment, and unemployment, which are issued to the public early in every month.

The productivity (output per worker-hour) statistics for the economy are figured on an annual basis. Although productivity recently declined from a long-time trend increase of 3 percent a year to less than 1 percent, for over 30 years the automobile industry and the Auto Workers Union have negotiated annual wage increases of 3 percent based on the national productivity statistics. Other industries are less definite, but they count on productivity improvements to reduce price increases for their products.

The BLS periodically conducts intensive surveys of wages, salaries, and fringe benefits by occupation in many industries. Such data show not only long-term trends for use in economic analyses but are also widely used in collective bargaining for future contracts.

On the subject of industrial relations, the BLS collects and issues periodic data on strikes and lockouts. These are supplemented by detailed descriptions of collective bargaining contacts recently adopted in major industries and occasionally by a long historical record for a specific industry or firm.

During the closing years of World War II, Congress assigned the BLS the task of developing a minimum annual cost-of-living standard for a wage (or salary) earner with a spouse and two children. The result was presented to a congressional committee in 1947 and was subsequently published. Later, this was expanded to include three different levels of family living, which are recalculated from year to year.

Immediately following World War II, the BLS became active in international statistics. When the Marshall Plan was established in 1949, the BLS was assigned responsibility for stimulating productivity studies in European countries for comparison with the United States. In 1958 the Commissioner of Labor Statistics was named by the State Department as head of a new five-member United Nations Committee on Post Adjustments, which was responsible for making cost-of-living salary adjustments in U.N. headquarters cities throughout the world. In addition, the BLS for many years was responsible for training representatives of underdeveloped countries in research and statistics.

Historical Highlights

In June 1884, Congress passed legislation creating a Bureau of Labor. Its chief official, a nonpolitical presidential appointee, is the Commissioner of Labor Statistics, who serves 4 years from the date of appointment. In 1913, a new Department of Labor was created and the Bureau of Labor became the Bureau of Labor Statistics.

World War I generated a national wage problem, so the President assigned the Commissioner the task of developing a cost-of-living index. Surveys of family expenditures were conducted in 1918 to 1919. The war ended, but prices continued to rise, so the index was carried forward to completion in 1921.

When World War II broke out, a relatively low unemployment rate assured ample labor supply during the war years. But with full employment and rising prices, the accuracy of the CPI was questioned by organized labor. The Secretary of Labor reacted vigorously to the attack on the BLS staff. Meanwhile, the President's committee in the White House (labor, management, and public) approved the BLS position but added some additional points to the index to represent some unmeasurable items.

Labor and Business Advisory Committees

When the eightieth Congress took office in 1947, the BLS suffered a drastic budget cut. In the spring of 1948 the House voted another big cut. However, in the meantime the Commissioner had reestablished a Labor Research Advisory Committee, consisting of AFL, CIO, and Railroad Brotherhood representatives. He also proposed that the National Association of Manufacturers and the U.S. Chamber of Commerce appoint a Management Research Advisory Committee.

In May 1948, the president of General Motors and the president of the Auto Workers signed a new type of contract—annual escalation of wages based on a 3 percent annual increase in productivity, plus a quarterly wage adjustment based on the consumer price index.

The effect on the BLS was spectacular. Congress decided not to cut the budget of the bureau whose data had brought industrial peace. Furthermore, the functioning of these two advisory committees has been a major factor in enhancing the status of the BLS as a reputable statistical agency.

The 1961 Unemployment Statistics Issue

In 1961, the Secretary of Labor cited the rising unemployment figures as a basis for new legislation. The *Readers Digest* wrote a highly critical article on the accuracy of the data. The President immediately appointed an Advisory Committee with labor, management, and public members to review the situation and make recommendations for improvement. Also, the Joint Economic Committee (JEC) called a series of hearings at which the Commissioner and the staff answered the criticisms. The JEC's report vindicated the BLS and its methods. A year later the Advisory Committee came out with a comprehensive report which proposed an enlarged monthly sample and other improvements. During 1979, a Presidential Commission analyzed these statistics and recommended further improvements.

References

Clague, Ewan; *The Bureau of Labor Statistics*, Praeger, New York, 1968; *BLS Handbook of Methods*, U.S. Bureau of Labor Statistics Bulletin 1910, 1976; *The Consumer Price Index: Concepts and Contents Over the Years*, U.S. Bureau of Labor Statistics Report 517, 1977; *Productivity and the Economy*, U.S. Bureau of Labor Statistics Bulletin 1926, 1977.

(*See also* Consumer price index; Economic statistics; Employment and unemployment; Producer price index; Statistical techniques in economics and business, an overview)

Ewan Clague

Business anticipations surveys (*see* Anticipations surveys, business)

Business credit

The term credit refers to a deferred exchange, i.e., a transaction in which the contribution of one of the parties is postponed until some time in the future. Definitions of credit are legion. Some writers stress the uses to which credit is put. A distinction is made between business credit and consumer credit. Thus, loans secured to finance consumption are distinguished from loans employed to finance business. Business credit will be considered here.

One way to view business credit would be to portray the combined balance sheet of all business firms, proprietorships, partnerships, and corporations. The sum of all assets in this imaginary balance sheet would have been financed by an ownership interest or net worth comprised of initial sales of stock plus new issues of stock together with earnings that were retained by the businesses after payments of taxes and dividends. The difference between the sum of all assets minus the net worth of these firms would represent the amount of credit extended to these businesses. An alternate but identical way to present this information would be to suggest that the assets of all business firms are financed by equity plus debt. The debt as viewed by the businesses is precisely the same quantity as the credit extended to these businesses by the lenders.

Needs for Business Finance

Before focusing on the sources of business credit, we examine the forces giving rise to a need for business financing and how these needs are met. Total financing needs of business result from increases in the following types of assets.

Increases in short-term assets
Inventories
Net trade credit
Consumer credit
Net miscellaneous financial assets

Plus
Increases in long-term assets
Plant and equipment
Residential construction
Direct foreign investment

Plus
‾‾‾‾
Increases in liquid financial assets

Equal
‾‾‾‾‾
Total financing needs

Inventories   A substantial portion of the cyclical variability in total financing needs arises from the variability of inventory investments.

Net Trade and Consumer Credit   In the ordinary course of events, the business firm buys its supplies and materials on credit from other firms, recording the debt as an account payable. Accounts payable, trade credit, or trade debt are the largest single category of short-term debt, representing about 40 percent of the current liabilities of nonfinancial corporations. Trade credit is both a source of credit for financing purposes and a use of funds to the extent that the firm finances credit sales to customers. As a rule, large corporations extend substantial amounts of trade credit, especially to smaller corporations, single proprietorships, and partnerships. Corporations also extend credit to their retail customers in the form of consumer credit. In its role as a supplier of trade and consumer credit, the nonfinancial corporate sector functions to some extent as a financial institution by channeling funds to other economic sectors. As with inventories, there has been a substantial cyclical component to the increase in this class of financial assets, which in turn has contributed to the cyclicality in total financing demands.

Plant and Equipment, Other Long-Term Assets   For the corporate sector as a whole the largest financing demands arise from investment in new plant and equipment. Expenditures on new capacity are critically dependent upon the current rate of market demand and the expectation of business of the growth in these demands. As capacity utilization rises from the cyclical trough, there is often substantial slack capacity within an industry. Thus, rising demands generate relatively little need for plant and equipment additions. As industry approaches full capacity, however, small increases in market demand can generate relatively large percentage increases in the desired investment in new production capability. This process generates a clear cyclical component in the demand for plant and equipment additions.

Liquid Financial Assets   Corporations have traditionally accumulated and reduced liquid asset holdings. These liquid assets have served as a buffer in the financial process. When in periods of declining economic activity financing demands fell, liquid assets were accumulated. At a later stage when financing demands accelerated, these liquid assets were run down, thereby providing a source of incremental finance.

Sources of Business Finance

Corporations meet some fraction of their financing demands from the cash flow generated by their own operations. These funds are called internal funds or internal cash flow. Internal cash flow is defined as being equal to retained profits after tax plus depreciation. In addition the rundown of liquid assets would augment internal sources. If total financing demands exceed internal funds, then corporations must obtain the remainder from external sources. Thus, externally raised funds are the difference between total financing demand and internal funds.

There has been a clear but somewhat diminished cyclical component in total financing demands over the last five business cycles. In the late 1960s and early 1970s, the flow of internal funds decreased substantially, while investment as measured by total financing demands continued to grow. This increased investment could be financed only with a sharp increase in external funds. Whereas externally raised funds had traditionally been about one-third of internal funds, they increased substantially in the 1970s.

Sources of Externally Raised Funds   New external funds can be raised in financial markets by issuing financial promises, either in the form of increased short-term debt, increased long-term debt, or new equity issues. The principal source of short-term debt for corporations has been the commercial banking system. The principal sources of long-term debt for corporations are corporate bonds and mortgages acquired largely by life insurance companies and pension funds. Corporate bonds, the general long-term debt obligations of corporations, have generally been the dominant source of long-term debt for manufacturing and public utility corporations. Mortgages have been an important source of funds for financing real property such as office buildings, shopping centers, and apartment buildings.

In addition, commercial banks have often made term loans to corporate business. Indeed, more than one-third of all bank loans in recent years have been term loans. Term loans are generally considered to be intermediate-term finance, being longer than 1 year, the arbitrary breakpoint for most definitions of short-term debt, and yet shorter than the typical 15- to 30-year maturities of long-term debt.

The Historical Pattern of New Funds Raised in Financial Markets   In addition to the cyclicality in the total of externally raised funds, there also appears to be a clear cyclicality in the composition of these funds. In the early phases of a business cycle, long-term sources of funds, particularly long-term debt, are the principal sources of new funds. Toward the middle of each cycle, as total new funds are usually accelerating rapidly, the increase in long-term debt declines. In this period, short-term debt becomes the principal source of funds raised in financial markets. And, finally, toward the end of each cycle in the economic recession or slowdown, the increase in short-term debt declines rapidly and long-term debt resumes its role as the principal source of external funds.

Alternative Strategies for Raising New Funds   The clear cyclical pattern of raising new funds is attributable to corporate financial decision making. To a large extent corporate financial managers attempt to match the maturity of their liabilities to the maturity of their assets. Thus, other things being equal, they attempt to fund increases in short-term assets with short-term debts and increases in long-term assets with long-term funds.

But corporate financing decisions do not always follow a policy of relatively passive maturity matching. As interest rates in financial markets fluctuate, aggressive corporate financial managers may attempt to time their long-term debt issues to avoid periods of relatively high long-term interest rates and exploit periods of relatively low long-term rates. The typical cycle of corporate finance in recent years has been a heavy reliance on short-term debt during the peak of an expansion, corporate concern about the financial imbalances thus generated, and a refunding of short-term debt with long-term funds in the subsequent recession.

The Impact of Inflation on Net External Financing Demands   Inflation increases the financial demands of corporations by raising the current nominal cost of any new plant and equipment, inventory, or financial assets investment needed to support physical growth. In addition, inflation leads to higher wage rates, higher unit labor costs, and thus to increased production costs. If prices expand commensurately, then profit margins can be maintained and the dollar value of internal funds can be expanded proportionately. In several recent inflations, corporations have not maintained their profit margins. As a result, operating profits fell sharply, and internal funds were unable to increase with inflation. Further, the pace of inflation in several key investment areas such as inventories and plant and equipment was often faster than the general pace of inflation.

The corporate income tax system compounded these difficulties. When computing income for tax purposes, corporations are allowed to choose depreciation mainly on the basis of historical costs. Thus, income tax payments are based on an overstated level of income. These increased corporate tax payments seriously erode aftertax internal cash flow during inflationary periods. While reported profits grew throughout, the portion of these reported profits that arose from understatement of the replacement costs of inventory and plant and equipment grew to be very large. As more and more of the funds represented by reported profits were necessary to replace existing inventory and plant and equipment, less and less was available to finance new investment in these areas.

Short-Term Debt

While corporations attract funds from a number of financial markets, short-term debt has played a particularly important role among their sources of external funds. Bank loans are by far the largest source of short-term business debt. Finance companies are an important source of supplementary lending, generally to the smaller companies whose working capital needs they finance. United States government agencies also extend short-term credits to business. In addition, the largest corporations also use commercial paper, short-term unsecured promissory notes sold in the open market to fund some of the short-term needs.

Bank Debt   Because bank loans are the dominant source of corporate short-term finance, their cost and availability play a pivotal role in corporate short-term markets. Unlike most external funds that are raised by the sale of securities, bank loans are negotiated privately between a corporation and its banker. While the terms of each bank loan are tailored to the particular needs of a business, these terms have certain common characteristics. In particular, most bank loans are priced by setting their interest rate at some spread above the bank's prime rate, the interest rate reserved for the bank's most creditworthy borrowers. The prime rate itself tends to be an industrywide rate, with most banks quoting the same prime at any given time. Actually, the total cost of bank borrowing is more complex and varies according to several provisions of a loan agreement, particularly the compensating deposit balances that businesses are implicitly required to hold with the bank.

The prime rate in recent years has become much more responsive to open-market interest rates. Indeed, several large money-center banks have explicitly tied their quoted prime rate to open-market rates, specifically to the rates obtained on commercial paper. Thus, the cost of business loans has become more closely related to the market-determined costs of short-term credit in the financial system.

Banks provide different types of loan arrangements for corporations, which for classification purposes can be divided into lines of credit, revolving credit agreements, and term loans. Both lines of credit and revolving credit agreements are generally classified as short-term credit arrangements.

With a line of credit the bank assures its customers that (if called upon) it will provide short-term funds up to some specified limit with the interest rate generally set at some spread over the bank's prime rate and which thus floats with the prime rate. The customer is generally required to keep certain compensating deposit balances with the bank as a part of the line of credit. While these lines of credit do not appear to be legally binding, banks invariably attempt to stand behind the implied commitments barring an altogether unforeseen and unmanageable set of circumstances. The lines of credit are, of course, periodically reviewed to make sure that they appropriately serve both the interests of the borrower as well as the bank.

A revolving credit agreement, on the other hand, is a written contractual agreement to provide short-term funds; it is binding upon the bank. The credit agreement provides the assurance of short-term funds, up to some specified limit, for a specified period of time, at an interest rate generally tied to the prime rate. The customer is often charged a commitment fee for this credit agreement in addition to the compensating deposit balances which are generally required by the agreement.

The bank is essentially guaranteeing to its customers the availability of short-term funds either implicitly or explicitly. Business corporations enter into these agreements to ensure that their expected and, for that matter, unexpected short-term needs can be met. The compensating balance requirements and fees that are involved in the arrangements are the cost of this insurance.

Commercial Paper Market as an Alternative Source of Short-Term Debt   While large banks are the dominant source of short-term business credit, many large corporations also use the commercial paper market to fund some of their short-term needs.

The commercial paper market provides a means for borrowers to obtain short-term funds from money-market investors without the direct services of the commercial banks. Commercial paper refers to short-term, unsecured, promissory notes issued by both financial and nonfinancial corporations. Traditionally, the commercial paper market has been divided into two segments: the directly placed market and the dealer-placed market.

Direct paper is sold directly to money-market investors by the issuing corporation through its own selling organization supplemented by regional banks who may solicit orders. Dealer paper is sold to investors through an investment banking or brokerage house.

The primary requirement for borrowing in the money markets is that the borrower possess an excellent credit standing. Since money-market lending is conducted on an unsecured and impersonal basis, financial strength and viability are necessary to ensure minimal default risk and investor confidence. It is for this reason that only large, financially strong corporations, sometimes referred to as prime credits, have usually been able to issue commercial paper. Credit rating appears to be influential in assessing credit standing and determining whether a corporation would be able to sell commercial paper in the money markets.

While commercial paper notes are sold in a wide range of denominations, the dealer-placed notes of nonfinancial corporate issuers are generally available in denominations from $100,000 to $5 million. The exact times to maturity for commercial paper notes are primarily influenced by the needs of borrowers and the preference of investors, but they generally have quite short maturities—between 35 and 270 days.

Another important aspect of commercial paper financing is the use of backup lines of credit. It is customary for a commercial paper issuer to secure a line of credit at a commercial bank. The backup line provides an additional measure of safety and liquidity to the borrowing corporation in the event that adverse money-market conditions or a temporary cash flow problem threaten the borrower's ability to redeem its notes at maturity. Although the granting of backup lines may facilitate corporate use of commercial paper financing instead of bank debt, commercial bankers are willing to engage in this business for several reasons. First, because of competition among the banks, it is sensible for each individual bank to provide its prime-credit corporate customers with a high level of service including such services as backup lines. Furthermore, granting these backup lines may be viewed as a profitable business, for the bank can earn a return consisting of either compensating balances or commitment fees without normally investing any assets.

Eurodollar Financing   Our domestic financial markets are now augmented by external markets for dollar-denominated loans. Foreign bank lending to U.S. corporations in the Eurodollar market differs from most lending in the domestic market. The borrowers among U.S. corporations are almost always large, well-known corporations which have the alternatives of borrowing in the domestic loan market and possibly the domestic commercial paper market as well as the Eurodollar loan market. Eurodollar loans are usually individually arranged. Banks do not offer Eurodollar lines of credit under which they assure continuous availability of funds up to a predetermined limit. The Eurodollar loan market is a wholesale market, and these lending banks have no legally imposed reserve requirements or deposit insurance fees. For all these reasons, lending costs in the Eurodollar bank loan market tend to be lower than in the U.S. market. Interest rates in the Eurodollar bank loan market float with open-market rates as does the prime rate on U.S. bank loans. The Eurodollar borrowing rate is based on the London interbank offer rate (LIBO), which measures the rate at which banks in the foreign market will lend dollars to each other.

Long-Term Debt

Corporate bonds are the dominant form of long-term corporate debt. Other forms of long-term debt play important supplementary roles. Commercial mortgages, for example, are important to real estate corporations in the financing of office buildings, shopping centers, and other commercial projects. Bank term loans are used as supplementary forms of intermediate-term finance by many companies. Special forms of tax-exempt financing are used to fund some industrial development projects as well as pollution-control equipment. In addition, leasing arrangements are often used as substitutes for long-term financing.

Suppliers of Long-Term Debt   The long-term corporate bond market has a very broad range of institutional suppliers of funds. Life insurance companies hold more than one-third of the outstanding corporate bonds. Private and public pension funds also hold about a third of the outstanding bonds. The remaining third is divided among mutual savings banks, casualty insurance companies, mutual funds, broker dealers, foreign investors, and others, including individuals and endowments of various educational, religious, and charitable institutions.

There are many different types of corporate bonds and many different segments of the corporate bond market. There are long-term and intermediate-term bonds, high-quality and low-quality bonds, utility bonds and industrial bonds, callable bonds, sinking-fund bonds, and many other types of such instruments. Among the more important distinctions is the distinction between privately placed bonds and publicly issued bonds. Privately placed bonds are relatively illiquid and are sold to a small number of purchasers through private negotiations. Typically, the purchasers are large, sophisticated financial institutions. Publicly issued bonds are sold to a large number of purchasers through a public sale or underwriting. They are accompanied by a wider dissemination of investor information and wider access to potential purchasers.

There are important differences in the market for privately placed and publicly issued bonds. Among other things, the suppliers differ, the terms of the debt securities differ, and the purchasers of these securities differ. Typically, life insurance companies supply 90 percent of the private placements. In contrast, pension funds, both private and public, generally dominate the public issue market. Individuals participate almost exclusively in the public issue market. In the public market the terms of the debt instruments reflect prevailing norms and tend to be standardized. They vary relatively little from issue to issue and tend to be inflexible in terms of any special needs of the issuer and/or the investor. Conversely, the terms of a private placement can be extremely flexible. Special provisions are often created to meet particular financing problems that the borrower may encounter. Also, special protections are often included to meet the interests of the lender or lenders. On average, private placements tend to have a shorter lifetime than publicly issued bonds. Private placements are in many ways the long-term equivalent of bank loans. They are privately negotiated, specifically tailored debt financings which are not traded in the financial markets. On the other hand, publicly issued bonds can be compared to the bond-market equivalent of short-term market instruments, namely open-market commercial paper. While the privately negotiated form of financing bank loans has dominated the short-term corporate market, the open-market form of bond financing, public issues, dominates the longer-term bond markets.

References

Higgins, R. C., *Financial Management,* Science Reserach Associates, Chicago, 1977, chaps. 17, 18, 19; Light, J. O., and W. L. White, *The Financial System,* Irwin, Homewood, Ill., 1979, chaps. 2, 15, 16; Van Honna, J. C., *Financial Management and Policy,* 5th ed., Prentice-Hall, Englewood Cliffs, N.J., 1980, chaps. 17, 18, 19, 20; Weston, J. F., and E. F. Brigham, *Essentials of Managerial Finance,* 5th ed., Holt, Rinehart and Winston, New York, 1979, chaps. 8, 9, 10, 18.

(*See also* Banking system; Bond; Capital markets and money markets in U.S.; Consumer credit; Credit, an overview; Debt; Eurodollar market; Financial institutions; Financial instruments; Financial statements; Interest rates; Money markets)

Eli Shapiro

Business cycles

The definition of business cycles that has led to the construction of a widely accepted chronology of cycles in the United States was formulated by Wesley C. Mitchell in 1927. In 1946 Mitchell and Arthur F. Burns revised the definition in certain respects

but left its major import intact, and it has continued to be used by the National
Bureau of Economic Research in establishing business cycle peak and trough dates.
The definition reads as follows:

> *Business cycles are a type of fluctuation found in the aggregate economic activity
> of nations that organize their work mainly in business enterprises: a cycle con-
> sists of expansions occurring at about the same time in many economic activities,
> followed by similarly general recessions, contractions, and revivals which
> merge into the expansion phase of the next cycle; this sequence of changes is
> recurrent but not periodic; in duration business cycles vary from more than one
> year to ten or twelve years; they are not divisible into shorter cycles of similar
> character with amplitudes approximating their own.*

On the basis of this definition the National Bureau has identified business cycle
peaks and troughs by months, quarters, and years in the United States, Great Britain,
France, and Germany. Table 1 gives the U.S. chronology, starting in 1834 on an
annual basis, and in 1854 on a monthly and quarterly basis. Monthly and quarterly
figures on economic activity were less plentiful than annual data in the early 1800s.
During the entire 141-year period from 1834 to 1975 there were 33 cycles, with an
average duration of 51 months. The expansion phases, running from the business
cycle trough to the peak, averaged 32 months. The contraction, or recession, phases
lasted 19 months on average. The shortest contraction, 7 months, occurred in 1918 to
1919; the longest, 65 months, was in 1873 to 1878. The longest recorded expansion,
106 months, ran from 1961 to 1969; the shortest expansion, 10 months, came in 1919
to 1920.

It is fairly evident, over the long stretch of history covered in Table 1, that business
cycles in the United States have become somewhat longer, whether measured from
trough to trough or from peak to peak. Even more clearly, expansions have become
longer relative to contractions. This is true even when one excludes the extraordinarily long expansion from 1961 to 1969. The typical expansion is now something like
3 to 4 years, the typical contraction about 1 year.

Since the definition of business cycles and the corresponding chronology has come
to be widely used over a period of more than half a century, it is important to understand what it says and what it does not say, and why. It is an empirical, or descriptive,
definition, saying nothing about the causes of business cycles. It is designed to enable
one to distinguish certain types of economic fluctuation from others by referring to
their duration, amplitude, and scope. The business cycle is a fluctuation in aggregate
economic activity, although no specific measure of this activity is referred to. It is an
up-and-down movement that lasts longer than a year but may last as long as 10 or 12
years. It is a movement in which a great many types of economic activity participate.
It is a fluctuation that cannot be subdivided into shorter movements of similar size
and scope.

Burns and Mitchell had reasons for each of these aspects of the definition, based
upon their own experience and that of others in trying to identify cycles over long
periods in several countries. Experience in the years since they formulated the definition has largely confirmed their judgment concerning its principal features. The
fact that it has produced a chronology of business cycles that is widely accepted in
the United States is evidence that the definition can be applied objectively and with
relatively little controversy. It is also evidence, of course, that the phenomenon of the

TABLE 1 Business Cycle Expansions and Contractions in the United States: 1834–1975*

Dates of peaks and troughs						Duration in months			
By months		By quarters		By calendar years		Contrac-tion (peak to trough)	Expansion (trough to peak)	Cycle	
								(Trough to trough)	(Peak to peak)
Trough	Peak	Trough	Peak	Trough	Peak				
				1834	1836		24†		
				1838	1839	24†	12†	48†	36†
				1843	1845	48†	24†	60†	72†
				1846	1847	12†	12†	36†	24†
				1848	1853	12†	60†	24†	72†
Dec. 1854	June 1857	4Q 1854	2Q 1857	1855	1856	24†	30†	84†	36†
Dec. 1858	Oct. 1860	4Q 1858	3Q 1860	1858	1860	18	22	48	40
June 1861	Apr. 1865	3Q 1861	1Q 1865	1861	1864	8	46	30	54
Dec. 1867	June 1869	1Q 1868	2Q 1869	1867	1869	32	18	78	50
Dec. 1870	Oct. 1873	4Q 1870	3Q 1873	1870	1873	18	34	36	52
Mar. 1879	Mar. 1882	1Q 1879	1Q 1882	1878	1882	65	36	99	101
May 1885	Mar. 1887	2Q 1885	2Q 1887	1885	1887	38	22	74	60
Apr. 1888	July 1890	1Q 1888	3Q 1890	1888	1890	13	27	35	40
May 1891	Jan. 1893	2Q 1891	1Q 1893	1891	1892	10	20	37	30
June 1894	Dec. 1895	2Q 1894	4Q 1895	1894	1895	17	18	37	35
June 1897	June 1899	2Q 1897	3Q 1899	1896	1899	18	24	36	42
Dec. 1900	Sept. 1902	4Q 1900	4Q 1902	1900	1903	18	21	42	39
Aug. 1904	May 1907	3Q 1904	2Q 1907	1904	1907	23	33	44	56
June 1908	Jan. 1910	2Q 1908	1Q 1910	1908	1910	13	19	46	32
Jan. 1912	Jan. 1913	4Q 1911	1Q 1913	1911	1913	24	12	43	36
Dec. 1914	Aug. 1918	4Q 1914	3Q 1918	1914	1918	23	44	35	67
Mar. 1919	Jan. 1920	1Q 1919	1Q 1920	1919	1920	7	10	51	17
July 1921	May 1923	3Q 1921	2Q 1923	1921	1923	18	22	28	40
July 1924	Oct. 1926	3Q 1924	3Q 1926	1924	1926	14	27	36	41
Nov. 1927	Aug. 1929	4Q 1927	3Q 1929	1927	1929	13	21	40	34
Mar. 1933	May 1937	1Q 1933	2Q 1937	1932	1937	43	50	64	93
June 1938	Feb. 1945	2Q 1938	1Q 1945	1938	1944	13	80	63	93
Oct. 1945	Nov. 1948	4Q 1945	4Q 1948	1946	1948	8	37	88	45
Oct. 1949	July 1953	4Q 1949	2Q 1953	1949	1953	11	45	48	56
May 1954	Aug. 1957	2Q 1954	3Q 1957	1954	1957	10	39	55	49
Apr. 1958	Apr. 1960	2Q 1958	2Q 1960	1958	1960	8	24	47	32
Feb. 1961	Dec. 1969	1Q 1961	4Q 1969	1961	1969	10	106	34	116
Nov. 1970	Nov. 1973	4Q 1970	4Q 1973	1970	1973	11	36	117	47
Mar. 1975		1Q 1975		1975		16		52	
AVERAGES									
5 cycles,	1834–1855					24†	26†	50†	48
16 cycles,	1854–1919					22	27	48	49
6 cycles,	1919–1945					18	35	53	53
6 cycles,	1945–1975					11	48	59	58
33 cycles,	1834–1975					19	32	51	51

SOURCE: National Bureau of Economic Research.
*The quarterly and annual dates are based upon data summed by quarters or by years. Quarterly peaks and troughs are placed in the same quarter as the monthly date if the latter is the mid-month of the quarter. Otherwise, it is placed either in the same quarter or the adjacent quarter. Annual dates may or may not be in the same year as the monthly dates depending on the behavior of the annual totals.
†Based upon calendar-year dates.

business cycle has not changed its character so completely as to make it impossible to apply the concept during the past century.

No single measure of aggregate economic activity is called for in the definition because several such measures appear relevant to the problem, including output, employment, income, and trade, and no single measure is either available for a long period or possesses all the desired attributes. Quarterly figures for gross national product (GNP) became available only in the 1940s in the United States and even later, if at all, in other countries. Since monthly peak and trough dates are desired, quarterly figures are not sufficient in any case. Furthermore, GNP has always been measured in two different ways, which yield different estimates, one from the income side of the accounts and the other from the product or expenditure side. Similarly, there are two different measures of employment, one based upon a survey of households, the other upon a survey of employers. Income and sales can be expressed in current prices or in constant prices, and output can be measured in physical units or in value terms. Virtually all economic statistics are subject to error, and hence are often revised. Use of several measures necessitates an effort to determine what is the consensus among them, but it avoids some of the arbitrariness of deciding upon a single measure that perforce could be used only for a limited time with results that would be subject to revision every time the measure was revised. At any rate the course adopted has been to employ a variety of the measures of activity that were in common use during the period under review. In determining the peak and trough dates of the 1973–75 recession, for example, some 19 monthly and quarterly series were employed.

Since the definition refers not only to aggregate activity but also to widespread movements in many activities, it is necessary to have some measure of the scope of the fluctuations that are being considered. For this purpose diffusion indexes have been constructed. They show how many types of activity within some group, or how many industries within one aggregate, are experiencing expansion or contraction. Such indexes, usually expressed in terms of the percentage of components that are expanding, reach high levels during the upward phase of the business cycle, and low levels during the downward phase (when a majority are contracting rather than expanding).

Table 2 contains a selection of measures of duration, depth, and diffusion of recessions in the United States between 1920 and 1975. It shows that no two measures give the same answer to the question of how long a recession lasts or how deep it is. Even a single measure can be looked at in different ways. The unemployment rate, for example, reached a higher level in the 1973–75 recession than it did in the year 1948–49, but the increase in the rate was somewhat greater in the period 1948–49 than in 1973–75. The decline in employment in the years 1973–75 was modest compared with its decline in the 1948–49, 1953–54, and 1957–58 recessions, but the opposite was true of the decline in real GNP.

If there are uncertainties about identifying business cycles historically, they are far greater when it is done contemporaneously. How soon a peak or a trough can be recognized depends partly upon how rapidly the economy changes. It also depends upon one's ability and willingness to make forecasts, for example, that a decline in the several measures of aggregate activity will last as long and go as deep as in previously recognized recessions, and that the declines will be as widespread. As a result, most turns in the business cycle have been recognized only with a lag.

TABLE 2 Selected Measures of Duration, Depth, and Diffusion of Business Cycle Contractions

Business cycle contraction, from peak (top line) to trough (next line)

	Jan. 1920 July 1921	May 1923 July 1924	Oct. 1926 Nov. 1927	Aug. 1929 Mar. 1933	May 1937 June 1938	Feb. 1945 Oct. 1945	Nov. 1948 Oct. 1949	July 1953 May 1954	Aug. 1957 Apr. 1958	Apr. 1960 Feb. 1961	Dec. 1969 Nov. 1970	Nov. 1973 Mar. 1975
Duration (in months)												
Business cycle chronology	18	14	13	43	13	8	11	10	8	10	11	16
GNP, current dollars	N.A.	6	12	42	9	6	12	12	6	9	N.D.	N.D.
GNP, constant dollars	N.A.	3	3	36	6	N.A.	6	12	6	9	15	15
Industrial production	14	14	8	36	12	27	15	8	14	13	14	9
Nonfarm employment	N.A.	N.A.	N.A.	43	11	22	13	16	14	10	8	6
Depth (percent)*												
GNP, current dollars	N.A.	−4.9	−3.0	−49.6	−16.2	−11.9	−3.4	−1.9	−2.8	−0.4	N.D.	N.D.
GNP, constant dollars	N.A.	−4.1	−2.0	−32.6	−13.2	N.A.	−1.4	−3.3	−3.2	−1.2	−1.1	−5.7
Industrial production	−32.4	−17.9	−7.0	−53.4	−32.4	−38.3	−9.9	−10.0	−14.3	−7.2	−8.1	−14.7
Nonfarm employment	N.A.	N.A.	N.A.	−31.6	−10.8	−10.1	−5.2	−3.4	−4.3	−2.2	−1.6	−2.7
Unemployment rate†												
Maximum	11.9	5.5	4.4	24.9	20.0	4.3	7.9	6.1	7.5	7.1	6.1	9.1
Increase	+10.3	+2.6	+2.4	+21.7	+9.0	+3.4	+4.5	+3.6	+3.8	+2.3	+2.7	+4.2
Diffusion (percent)												
Nonfarm industries, maximum percentage with declining employment‡	97	95	71	100	97	N.A.	90	87	88	82	83	90
	Sept. 1920	Apr. 1924	Nov. 1927	June 1933	Dec. 1937		Feb. 1949	Mar. 1954	Sept. 1957	Aug. 1960	June 1970	Jan. 1975

SOURCE: U.S. Department of Commerce, U.S. Department of Labor, Board of Governors of the Federal Reserve System, National Bureau of Economic Research. For a fuller version of this table, see Solomon Fabricant, "The Recession of 1969–70," in Zarnowitz (1972), pp. 100–110.

Note: N.A. = not available; N.D. = no decline.

*Percentage change from the peak month or quarter in the series to the trough month or quarter, over the intervals shown above. For the unemployment rate, the maximum figure is the highest for any month during the contraction and the increases are from the lowest month to the highest, in percentage points.

†The maximum figure for 1921, 1924, 1928, and 1933 are annual averages (monthly data not available). Increases, in percentage points, are for 1919–21, 1923–24, 1926–28, and 1929–33.

‡Since 1948, based on changes in employment over 6-month spans in 30 nonagricultural industries, centered on the fourth month of the span. Prior to 1948 based on cyclical changes in employment in 41 industries.

TABLE 3 Growth Cycle Chronologies, Eight Countries

Peak or trough	United States	Canada	United Kingdom	West Germany	France	Italy	Japan	Australia
P	7/48							
T	10/49							
P	3/51	2/51	3/51	2/51				5/51
T	7/52	11/51	8/52					9/52
P	3/53	3/53					12/53	
T	8/54	10/54		2/54			6/55	
P	2/57	10/56	12/55	10/55	11/57	10/56	5/57	8/55
T	4/58	8/58	11/58	4/59	10/59	7/59	1/59	2/58
P	2/60	1/60	3/61	2/61				9/60
T	2/61	2/61	2/63					9/61
P	5/62	3/62			2/64	9/63	1/62	
T	10/64	7/63		2/63	6/65	3/65	1/63	
P	6/66	3/66	2/66	5/65	6/66		7/64	4/65
T	10/67	2/68	8/67	8/67	5/68		2/66	4/68
P	3/69	2/69	6/69	5/70	11/69	2/70	6/70	4/70
T	11/70	12/70	2/72	12/71	8/71	8/72	1/72	8/72
P	3/73	2/74	6/73	8/73	7/74	4/74	11/73	1/74
T	3/75	10/75	11/75	5/75	6/75	8/75	3/75	

SOURCE: For the United States, National Bureau of Economic Research, New York; for other countries, Center for International Business Cycle Research, Rutgers University, New Brunswick, N.J.

In recent years a variant concept of the business cycle has come into use, known as the growth cycle. It is usually defined as a trend-adjusted business cycle; that is, the definition cited above is simply applied to data from which the long-term growth has been eliminated. In this respect it represents a return to an older concept, for trend-adjusted business indexes were used considerably in the 1920s. One of the chief results is that cyclical fluctuations appear clearly in data that otherwise are dominated by the growth trend. Chronologies based upon the growth cycle concept have been constructed for the United States and a number of other countries (Table 3). The number of growth cycles during a given period usually exceeds the number of business cycles, because slowdowns that sometimes occur during long business cycle expansions become actual contractions in the trend-adjusted figures. Hence, the average duration of growth cycles is less than that of business cycles. Another difference is that peaks in the growth cycle usually occur several months before the corresponding peaks in the business cycle, because activity usually slows before a business cycle peak is reached. Growth cycle and business cycle troughs tend to be more nearly simultaneous. As a result of these differences, expansions and contractions in growth cycles are more symmetrical, both in duration and amplitude, than they are in business cycles.

References

Bronfenbrenner, Martin, *Is the Business Cycle Obsolete?*, Wiley, New York, 1969; Burns, Arthur F., *The Business Cycle in a Changing World*, National Bureau of Economic Research, New York, 1969; Burns, Arthur F., and Wesley C. Mitchell, *Measuring Business Cycles*, National Bureau of Economic Research, New York, 1946; Fels, Rendigs, and C. Elton Hinshaw, *Forecasting and*

Recognizing Business Cycle Turning Points, National Bureau of Economic Research, New York, 1968; Friedman, Milton, and Anna Schwartz, *A Monetary History of the United States, 1867–1960,* Princeton University Press, Princeton, N.J., 1963; Haberler, Gottfried: *Prosperity and Depression,* League of Nations, Geneva, 1937; Mintz, Ilse, *Dating Postwar Business Cycles: Methods and Their Application to Western Germany, 1950–67,* National Bureau of Economic Research, New York, 1970; Mitchell, Wesley C., *Business Cycles: The Problem and Its Setting,* National Bureau of Economic Research, New York, 1927; Mitchell, Wesley C., *Business Cycles and Their Causes,* University of California Press, Los Angeles, 1941; Moore, Geoffrey H., *Business Cycle Indicators,* Princeton University Press, Princeton, 1961; Moore, Geoffrey H., *Business Cycles, Inflation and Forecasting,* Ballinger, Cambridge, Mass., 1980; Schumpeter, Joseph A., *Business Cycles: A Theoretical, Historical and Statistical Analysis of the Capitalist Process,* McGraw-Hill, New York, 1939; Thorp, Willard L., *Business Annals,* National Bureau of Economic Research, New York, 1926; U.S. Department of Commerce, *Business Conditions Digest,* published monthly; Zarnowitz, Victor (ed.), *The Business Cycle Today,* National Bureau of Economic Research, New York, 1972.

(*See also* Diffusion indexes; Economic growth; Economic statistics; Great Depression; Juglar cycle; Kitchin cycle; Kondratieff cycle; Kuznets cycle; National Bureau of Economic Research)

Geoffrey H. Moore

Business decision making (see Decision making in business)

Business inventory

Business inventory is the supply of various goods kept on hand by a business firm in order to meet needs promptly as they arise and thus assure uninterrupted operation of the business. Business inventory will be considered in three of its aspects. The first is turnover, a countercurrent circulating capital. If turnover of inventories in a business is taken as given—perhaps over a model year—and in a stationary equilibrium, then inventory levels adjust to monetary or fiscal shock in an economy whose members make efficient forecasts of sales and other variables. Such shocks would have to be intense to deflect the course of the economy. Secondly, the microeconomic foundations of business inventory behavior are sketched out. This work reinforces the result just put, especially to the extent that inventory can be expected to be an inelastic function of sales, relative to given expectations of prices and interest rates. Finally, some of the transmission between monetary-fiscal policy and inventory accumulation is taken apart and examined.

Turnover of Inventories

The so-called period of production (associated with Böhm-Bawerk) is one of the most intractable knots in economics. However, if the data can be transformed into turnover statistics, serious perplexities can at least be bypassed. For example, take the ratio of circulating capital to annual sales in some sector of the economy; call the reciprocal of this ratio T. The circulating capital is said to turn over T times a year. Turnover of grocers' stocks will be high; that of jewelers' stocks low.

Perhaps because real interest rates have risen, perhaps because fiscal restraint is expected to curtail final demand, final sales are expected to fall. Consider the impact on gross investment in inventories, neglecting finer points of microanalysis. By choice of measure, initial annual sales are to be unity. Say that final sales are expected to fall by 1 percent; assume, naively, that desired inventories also fall by 1 percent. It would take 365/100T days for inventories to fall by 1 percent at the previous rate of final sales; (3.65)(1/T)(1.01) days will be required at the new, lower rate of final sales. More generally, if the rate of final sales falls by v percent, it will take 3.65(v/T) (1 + v/100) days to accomplish a v percent reduction in inventory. So, if final sales were to fall by 2 percent per year and inventories typically turned over 40 times per year, it would take 0.186 days to accomplish the adjustment. For $T = 0.5$, it would take 14.89 days; indeed, suppliers would experience a bleak fortnight, and their "permanent" sales would fall by 2 percent. But the value of suppliers' shares would not be much affected. Nor, indeed, would production be suspended for 2 weeks; rather, suppliers would produce for stock, and the adjustment would be spread out over many weeks.

The acceleration principle is not important in inventory expenditure simply because replacement demand bulks so large in expenditure on circulating capital. And the inventory cycles of standard theory are generated by the adaptive properties of specified expectations, as Allen (1967) points out.

Next, consider a product governed by a model year; automobiles in the United States supply a quintessential example. Such a product does not fit into conventional inventory theory, whether or not output is placed with dealers on consignment. There are apt to be massive retooling and other start-up costs. And production is likely to be concentrated in the early months of the model year. But effects of monetary-fiscal policy will be fully comprehended by a simple flow model of the business. (The households must be modeled by stock-flow techniques however.) In such an industry, by far the largest part of what is measured as inventory simply is unsold stock that is not to be replaced. Alternatively, the process is not continuous; it starts up again at the beginning of each model year. And, within a model year, one observes not so much inventory control as the time-profile of sales.

Microeconomic Foundations

Discussion is confined to two problems. One concerns inventory principles for a distributor; the other, inventory principles for a manufacturer.

A distributor, *inter alios*, will consider carrying and reordering costs. Following William J. Baumol, we have the following situation:

> A retailer . . . confidently expects to sell . . . Q* units . . . over the next year at a predetermined price, with demand spread evenly over the year. How much inventory should he keep on hand? . . . He can meet his demand by having the entire amount delivered to his warehouse at the beginning of January . . .; alternatively, he can have 50,000 units delivered to him right after the first of the year and [an] equal amount on July 1.[1]

The first approach avoids reordering cost and entails substantial carrying cost; the second reduces carrying cost and entails much more reordering cost. Of course, carrying cost can be negative: inventories can increase in value over their holding periods because of price inflation or enhancement through aging (as with wine, for example). Not surprisingly, real rates of interest will be a better guide than nominal

---

[1]Baumol, 1977, p. 6. Reprinted by permission of Prentice-Hall, Inc., Englewood Cliffs, N.J.

ones. In any event, the problem's solution reduces to an optimality calculation that is especially useful:

$$D = \frac{2a^*Q^*}{k^*}$$

This equation gives the optimal average inventory level $D/2$ (that is, one-half of the regular intake, sales being spread evenly throughout the year; if, for example, 100,000 units were taken in on January 1, average inventory for the year would be 50,000). The variable D is the optimal reorder quantity corresponding to sales volume Q^*, k^* is the unit carrying cost, and a^* is fixed reorder cost. According to Baumol, "inventory should increase only in proportion to the square root of sales." This last result is especially interesting to the general reader. And it confirms the thrust of the analyses of this article: inventory holdings are less sensitive to sales than might be suggested by the literature of economics.

The simplistic model of a manufacturer evokes a number of considerations ably deployed by Schlaifer (1959):

> Two kinds of uncertainty may enter into an inventory problem. . . . (1) there may be uncertainty concerning the quantity which will be demanded during any given time period, (2) there may be uncertainty concerning the lead time which will elapse between the date on which an order is placed and the date on which the new lot of product will actually arrive.

In very simple inventory problems, each decision is taken to be independent of previous decisions and implications for future decisions are neglected; this is just where stochastic and dynamic programming come in (Hadley, 1964):

> Once storage is possible, this is no longer true. The time required to dispose of any number of units depends . . . on the distributions for demand in a whole series of periods. . . . Analysis of costs is extremely complex if the probability distribution for demand is changing with time.

Because of the difficulties of developing these themes directly in this short article, a model for a manufacturer that permits a simple indirect development will be considered. The analytical properties of the model are developed in Dorfman, Samuelson, and Solow (1958).

A producer is to maximize profit from meeting known demands $x_1, x_2, \ldots, x_n$ over periods 1, 2, . . . , n. The amount of stock (inventory) taken into the first period, Y_1^*, is given, as is the amount that must be taken out of the nth period, Y_{n+1}^*. Productions are $y_1, y_2, \ldots, y_n$. The rate of interest over the tth period is r_t. The interest rate used for discounting from the beginning of the first period through the tth period is r_{1t}. Unit carrying costs in the tth period are a_t. The problem is to

$$\text{Maximize} \quad \sum^n \frac{p_t x_t - c_t}{(1 + r_t)^t}$$

subject to

$$\sum^n y_t + Y_1^* = \sum^n x_t + Y_{n+1}^*$$
$$c_t = f(y_t) + (r_t + a_t)Y_t$$
$$Y_{t+1} = Y_t = y_t - x_t$$

The problem's shape facilitates working out the propositions of Baumol and Schlaifer, and it stresses intertemporal dependence of stocks and outputs. Two remarks are useful. First, the solution will be invariant against a scaling up of all nominal prices and costs together with nominal rates of interest. High nominal interest rates should not be confused with high real ones. Secondly, higher real short-term interest rates need not cause a crescendo in the production plan. [The concept of *crescendo and diminuendo* was developed by Hicks (1946, 1965).] If plants are being operated near points of minimum-cost production, discounted incremental costs of producing more later may dwarf interest savings from carrying less stock.

Transmission from Monetary-Fiscal Policy to Inventories

It has been seen that effects of monetary-fiscal policy, as transmitted by real interest rates and aggregate demand, on inventories may be quite slight (see Hawtrey, 1932, 1950). Two classic articles, Tobin (1958) and Baumol (1952), have led to adaptation of inventory theory to the theory of demand for money and indeed have pushed out the frontiers of inventory theory. Without denigrating these contributions, it should be pointed out that the analogy of cash holdings to inventories of physical goods is imperfect. Cash being altogether fungible, there is overwhelming substitutability between cash now at *i* and cash wanted at *j*. And transmission cost is miniscule. Holding costs, now that almost any firm can earn an economic rate of interest on sight deposits, are slight. Furthermore, it now is possible to make virtually automatic substitution of a wide variety of holdings not eligible as means of payment for holdings thus qualifying. Of course, this is not an argument to abandon study of the theory of demand for inventories. It does verge on one to abandon study of the demand for "money."

In particular, it seems unlikely that constriction of aggregate demand would have intensified effects on inventory accumulation. It remains to observe that squeezes on the availability of credit can work powerfully against inventories and other circulating capital: such capital is fungible and quasi-liquid; it is a prime candidate for attempted disposal when forced liquidation transpires. (True, if there is widespread pressure to liquidate, the upshot will intensify illiquidity.) Appreciating this point, Japanese authorities apparently squeeze credit taken by importers quite routinely when correcting balance of payments deficits. And Bagehot (1915) explained how, when menaced by external drains, the Bank of England reduced its discounts, clamping down on the ability of British importers to maintain their stocks. Economic theory being amorphous, these old theories of macroeconomic policy and inventories only recently have risen to the surface of rigorous analysis, and then through a recondite vehicle, so-called catastrophe theory.

References

Allen, R. G. D., *Mathematical Analysis for Economists*, Macmillan, London, 1938; Allen, R. G. D., *Macro-Economic Theory*, Macmillan, London, 1967; Arrow, K. J., S. Karlin, and H. Scarf, *Studies in the Mathematical Theory of Inventory and Production*, Stanford University Press, Stanford, 1958; Bagehot, Walter, *Lombard Street*, John Murray, London, 1915; Baumol, W. J., *Economic Dynamics*, 3d ed., Macmillan, New York, 1970; Baumol, W. J., *Economic Theory and Operations Analysis*, 4th ed., Prentice-Hall, Englewood Cliffs, N.J., 1977; Dorfman, R., P. Samuelson, and R. Solow, *Linear Programming and Economic Analysis*, McGraw-Hill, New York, 1958, chap. 12; Hadley, G., *Nonlinear and Dynamic Programming*, Addison-Wesley, Reading,

Mass., 1964, p. 238; Hadley, G., and T. M. Whitin, *Analysis of Inventory Systems*, Prentice-Hall, Englewood Cliffs, N.J., 1963; Hawtrey, R. G., *The Art of Central Banking*, Longmans, Green, London, 1932; Hawtrey, R. G., *Currency and Credit*, 4th ed., Longmans, Green, London, 1950; Hicks, J. R., *Value and Capital*, 2d ed., Clarendon Press, Oxford, 1946; Hicks, J. R., *Capital and Growth*, Clarendon Press, Oxford, 1965; Hobbs, J. A., *Control over Inventory and Production*, McGraw-Hill, New York, 1973; Leijonhufvud, Axel, *On Keynesian Economics and the Economics of Keynes*, Oxford University Press, London and New York, 1968; Magee, J. F., *Production, Planning and Inventory Control*, McGraw-Hill, New York, 1958; Morse, P. M., *Queues, Inventories and Maintenance*, Wiley, New York, 1958; Scarf, H., et al., *Multistage Inventory Models and Techniques*, Stanford University Press, Stanford, 1963; Schlaifer, R., *Probability and Statistics for Business Decisions*, McGraw-Hill, New York, 1959, p. 237; Tobin, James, "Liquidity Preference as Behavior Towards Risk," *Review of Economic Studies*, vol. 67, 1958, p. 65; Whitin, T. M., *The Theory of Inventory Management*, Princeton University Press, Princeton, N.J., 1957.

(See also Acceleration principle; Change in business inventories in GNP; Economic growth; Economic statistics; Expectations; Interest rates; Stock-flow analysis)

M. L. Burstein

Business investment in new plants and equipment

Business investment in new plants and equipment is a major component of gross private domestic investment. As defined by the Bureau of Economic Analysis (BEA) of the U.S. Department of Commerce, it includes expenditures for plant, machinery, and equipment for which companies maintain depreciation accounts. Purchases of capital goods and maintenance and repair expenditures charged to current account as well as purchases of land, used plant or equipment, and facilities for installation outside of the country are excluded.

Business investment in new plants and equipment, $166 billion at the beginning of 1979, actually amounts to something less than half of total gross private domestic fixed investment in the national income and product accounts. Excluded from business investment in new plants and equipment are investment in residential structures and equipment and in agriculture and by professional persons, real estate operators, and nonprofit institutions. Also excluded are oil-well drilling costs charged to current expense, and net purchases of used capital goods from government, as well as dealers' margins on purchase of used capital goods. Correspondingly, the new plant and equipment totals are not reduced by receipts from the sales of used capital to foreigners or to dealers in scrap material.

Investment Anticipations Surveys

Business investment in new plant and equipment and anticipations of future investment are surveyed four times a year by the BEA. Key questions asked include information as to new structures and additions to existing plants and new machinery and new equipment for the previous quarter, and anticipations of those expenditures for the current quarter, for the subsequent quarter, and for the quarter after that. Expected expenditures for the entire year are solicited during the first quarter, along with information as to actual expenditures for the previous year. Other questions concern the carry-over of projects previously initiated but not yet completed and proportions of expenditures devoted to expansion and to replacement and modernization.

New structures and additions include all nonresidential construction and major alterations, land improvements, and exploratory and development expenditures chargeable to fixed-asset accounts. New machinery and equipment includes "automobiles, trucks, tractors, etc., furniture and fixtures, office machinery, and all other new equipment." Where motor vehicles or other capital is purchased both for personal and business use, only the portion allocated to business is included. Expenditures for all items charged off as current operating expense, including costs of maintenance and repairs, new facilities owned by the federal government but operated under contract by private companies, and plant and equipment furnished by communities and organizations are excluded.

Expenditures are generally reported as payments are made, and on an ownership rather than a use basis. In airlines and railroads where there is an extensive leasing of equipment, however, the total value of the equipment is counted as expenditure at the time it is leased. The BEA survey is of companies, not establishments, with expenditures allocated to industries on the basis of the primary industry of all of each company's production.

Annual surveys of business investment in new plants and equipment are also undertaken by the Department of Economics of the McGraw-Hill Publications Company on an essentially similar conceptual basis. These surveys are done in the spring to indicate anticipated expenditures for the current year as well as in the fall to secure both first anticipations of the next year's expenditures and a final anticipation of the amount of expenditures to be made in the year being completed.

Despite the fact that business investment in new plants and equipment is a lagging indicator, it is closely watched by economic analysts and forecasters as a particularly important and sensitive cyclical indicator as well as for its relation to long-term growth. It is somewhat influenced, particularly in the short run, by liquidity considerations and the availability of internal funds from profits as well as external sources of finance, and in the long run by the relative cost of capital and other inputs to production. Investment in new plants and equipment is also influenced by needs to modernize and, in recent years, by government standards related to environmental protection. A major portion of business investment in new plants and equipment generally involves the replacement of old capital which has worn out or outlived its usefulness; some 60 percent tends to be classified as replacement and modernization as opposed to 40 percent for expansion. Investment in new plant and equipment is thought to "embody" technological change which adds to productivity and lowers costs.

Investment and the Economy

An overwhelming influence on business investment is the general state of the economy and, particularly, the pressure of demand on existing capacity and the rate of growth of output. The substantial business investment related to expansion clearly depends upon the rate at which demand and output are growing and are expected to grow in the future. Even a modest slowing of the rate of growth of final product, as from 4 to 3 percent, might thus in principle generate a reduction in expansion investment of 25 percent; 3 percent growth requires one-fourth less in the way of additional plant and equipment than does 4 percent growth. At the extreme, an actual decline in output in a recession can be devastating to business investment. Thus, from the beginning of 1974 to the third quarter of 1975, while the unemployment rate rose from

5.2 to between $8\frac{1}{2}$ and 9 percent, real, nonresidential business fixed investment fell 17.5 percent. In current dollars, business spending for new plant and equipment fell from $116 billion in the fourth quarter of 1974 to $112 billion in the third quarter of 1975, a drop of 3.5 percent in three quarters. Since prices of plant and equipment, as measured by the nonresidential fixed investment price index, rose 6.3 percent in this period, the real fall in business plant and equipment expenditures was 9.2 percent during the period, which came to a 12.1 percent annual rate of decline.

Inflation, perhaps paradoxically, does not have a generally negative effect on business plant and equipment spending. Indeed, there is some reason to believe that businesses seek to buy more plant and equipment in periods of rising prices in order to make their purchases before costs get higher as well as in the expectation that proceeds to be realized from higher selling prices of the product of new capital will be greater.

Investment Incentives

There have been various efforts on the part of government to increase business plant and equipment spending. These have generally involved acceleration of depreciation for tax purposes and a so-called investment tax credit, now generally at 10 percent, but limited chiefly to equipment. This credit reduces business income taxes by up to 10 percent of equipment expenditures. It is argued by some that accelerated tax depreciation and the equipment tax credit increase business investment by reducing its aftertax cost relative to that of other business expenditures. Just how much this does so, however, is open to doubt. Both responses by business and the results of various econometric studies suggest that these tax incentives to spur business investment may cost more in the way of lost tax revenues to the Treasury than the amount of new plant and equipment expenditures which they induce. They would also seem to be least effective in periods of recession when business investment falls and most likely to stimulate more business investment in booms where investment is already high and the dangers of the stimuli contributing to inflation may be greater.

References

Eisner, Robert, *Factors in Business Investment*, Ballinger, Cambridge, Mass., 1978; Eisner, Robert, and R. H. Strotz, "Determinants of Business Investment," in Commission on Money and Credit, *Impacts of Monetary Policy*, Prentice-Hall, Englewood Cliffs, N.J., 1964, pp. 59–223; Ferber, Robert (ed.), *Determinants of Investment Behavior*, Universities-National Bureau Conference Series, no. 19, Columbia University Press, New York, 1967; Fromm, Gary (ed.), *Tax Incentives and Capital Spending*, Brookings, Washington, D.C., 1971.

(See *also* Anticipation surveys, business; Capital formation; Gross private domestic investment in GNP; Investment function)

Robert Eisner

Cambridge school

Cambridge school is a convenient term for a body of somewhat discordant ideas associated with a number of economists at the University of Cambridge, England, who either worked with John Maynard Keynes or were deeply involved in the Keynesian revolution of the 1930s, such as Nicholas Kaldor, Joan Robinson, and Piero Sraffa. Members of the Cambridge school see themselves as developing Keynes' theories to deal with the long-run problems of growth and income distribution that Keynes himself largely neglected. For that reason, the ideas of the Cambridge school also travel under the name of "post-Keynesian economics" and indeed the American wing of the Cambridge school, led by Sidney Weintraub and Paul Davidson, recently launched a new *Journal of Post-Keynesian Economics* to promote an approach to economic issues similar to, but not identical with, those of British Keynesians.

Antineoclassical Microeconomics

The Cambridge or post-Keynesian economists are more united by what they are against than by what they are for. They are against any and all versions of so-called neoclassical microeconomics—maximizing economic agents, rapid response to price changes, emphasis on competitive equilibrium outcomes, Pareto optimality, and so on—and to what they scathingly refer to as "bastard Keynesianism," namely, the income-expenditure, 45° diagram interpretation of Keynesian macroeconomics familiar to all students of elementary economics around the world. What they are for, however, is more difficult to describe because different members of the school have different views as to how to proceed in constructing the new edifice of post-Keynesian economics.

109

Sraffa's Role

Piero Sraffa's book, *Production of Commodities by Means of Commodities* (1960), is concerned with the classic problem of how relative prices are determined. Sraffa constructs a model of production in which demand plays no role in the determination of prices, and he concentrates his efforts on demonstrating that we cannot determine prices at all unless we start out either with a predetermined wage rate or a predetermined rate of profit. How these are themselves determined is left open to question. This controversial model is seen by some Cambridge economists as forming the basis of a wholly new microeconomics. Other post-Keynesian economists, however, prefer the ideas of Michael Kalecki, a Polish economist, who developed a theory of markup pricing under conditions of oligopoly. Sraffa's book has also attracted much attention from Marxist economists, some of whom are keen to reformulate Marx in the light of Sraffa; these Marxist members of the Cambridge school are frequently known as neo-Ricardians because of the links between some of Sraffa's arguments and those of Ricardo.

Whether favoring Sraffa or not, Cambridge economists are united in believing that the neoclassical model of pricing contains a fatal flaw: it is not possible in general to draw a negatively inclined demand curve for capital as a function of the rate of profit or rate of return on capital because of the phenomenon of "reswitching." Reswitching refers to the possibility that a given technique may be the most profitable one for business firms to adopt at two different rates of profit, while being unprofitable at rates in between these two. If reswitching of techniques is possible, then so is "capital reversing," meaning that the capital-labor ratio in an economy may not necessarily continue to rise indefinitely as the rate of profit falls. Thus, the widespread neoclassical notion that capital intensity is always uniquely related to the rate of return on capital has to be abandoned.

The point at issue has been conceded by all the leading neoclassical economists, who nevertheless continue to deny the empirical importance of capital reversing in actual economies. The Cambridge economists, however, are convinced that capital reversing is a general and indeed common phenomenon in a capitalist economy, and they argue, therefore, that neoclassical economics has to be scrapped as logically inconsistent.

Pro-growth Models Based on Investment

Apart from such problems of microeconomics, the Cambridge school firmly believes that fruitful theorizing in economics will have to take the form of growth models that are squarely based on the Keynesian primacy of investment, itself the product of business confidence or "animal spirits," rather than on prices and the returns to factors of production, while going beyond Keynes in operating with two saving functions, one for capitalists and a different one for workers. Around these central ideas, both Nicholas Kaldor and Joan Robinson have developed distinct growth models, that is, abstract formulations of the steady-state conditions required for an economic system to reproduce itself, unchanged in all essential aspects, "from here to eternity." Both models have the common property that the respective shares of income received by capitalists and workers are determined simultaneously with the rate of profit, the capital-output ratio, and the overall growth rate of the economy. They give rise to such elegant results as the Pasinetti theorem: the equilibrium rate of profit in steady-state growth is uniquely determined by the growth rate of the economy and the saving propensity of capitalists, completely independent of the saving behavior of workers as well as the underlying technology of production. The import of the Pasinetti theorem is unclear; equally unclear is the importance of theorems that flow from certain alternative neoclassical growth models, such as "the golden rule of accumulation," which tells us that consumption per head is only maximized in an economy growing at a steady state when the rate of return on capital is equalized with the growth rate. However, no economy has ever been observed in steady-state growth, and there are deep, inherent reasons why actual growth is unsteady and unbalanced. It cannot be argued, therefore, that growth theory is as yet capable of throwing much light on actual economies growing over time, which no doubt accounts for the failure to resolve the now 20-year-old debate between Cambridge, England, and Cambridge, Massachusetts. The Cambridge school continues to gain adherents, but only time will tell whether it has the capacity to provide an alternative framework, a new paradigm that is as fertile as that furnished by the orthodox mainstream of neoclassical economics.

References

Blaug, M., *The Cambridge Revolution: Success or Failure?*, Institute of Economic Affairs, London, 1975; Harcourt, G. C., *Some Cambridge Controversies in the Theory of Capital*, Cambridge University Press, New York, 1972; Kregel, J. A., *The Reconstruction of Political Economy: An Introduction to Post-Keynesian Economics*, Macmillan, London, 1973; Weintraub, S. (ed.), *Modern Economic Thought*, University of Pennsylvania Press, Philadelphia, 1977.

(*See also* Economic growth; Keynesian economics; Neo-Keynesian economics; Post-Keynesian economics)

Mark Blaug

Cameralism (see Mercantilism)

Capital, a factor of production

In economics, capital is defined as a commodity itself used in the production of other goods and services. It is a human-made input, such as plant or equipment, created to permit increased production in the future. As such, it resembles saving in the sense that it represents current consumption foregone in order to obtain future production and future consumption. Although this definition of capital, in physical terms, differs from the definition of capital normally employed in the financial community, they are not exclusive terms. Firms acquire money capital by selling bonds or stock in order to finance the acquisition of physical capital; thus, part of any potential returns to such an investment is then interest—the return to physical capital. However, by investing this money capital, the investor also bears risk, one of the functions of an entrepreneur, so some of the returns represent profit—the return to an entrepreneur.

Neoclassical Versus Cambridge View

The neoclassical view of capital was first stated by Eugen von Böhm-Bawerk and Knut Wicksell. These economists regarded capital as an accumulated fund that permitted the roundabout use of labor and argued that, as the wage rate rises relative to the interest rate, production techniques would become more roundabout (i.e., more capital-intensive). To this, John Bates Clark added the concept of a real, homogeneous capital stock such that depletion is constantly replaced to leave the stock unchanged. This neoclassical view of capital went unchallenged until the so-called Cambridge criticism was first voiced by Joan Robinson in 1953. It was argued that, if capital is heterogeneous and production is characterized by fixed proportions (i.e., no input substitutability), then there may not exist an invariant relation between capital intensity and the factor-price ratio. While the Cambridge criticism pointed out a definite potential weakness of simple neoclassical theory, it has been argued that its relevance depends on the empirical question of whether or not there exists sufficient substitutability within the system to establish the neoclassical results. As a response to the Cambridge criticism, Robert M. Solow originated the view of a heterogeneous capital aggregate in which the capital inputs are identified by their vintages (i.e., period of manufacture). Each vintage is weighted by a productivity improvement factor reflecting the fact that newer capital (more recent vintages) embody technical improvements and the fact that older capital has decayed. The concept of capital-augmenting technical change has been extended by Charles Kennedy and Carl C. Weizsacker to consider induced innovation and by Kenneth J. Arrow to consider learning by doing.

Problems

There exist several equally troublesome problems concerning capital in the production function of the individual firm—particularly for empirical investigations. One difficulty results from the fact that capital is acquired by the firm as a durable stock; however, the services of capital are employed by the firm as a flow generated by the stock. In order to precisely define a single-period production function in which the other inputs are assumed to enter as flows, it is necessary not only to define an invariant unit of measurement for the capital stock but also a measure of the flow of services generated (or employed) in the period.

An allied difficulty is the determination of the user price of these capital services. Stated simply, the problem is the identification of the cost of using the capital rather than the return to capital. The use of accounting data does not prove satisfactory since such data do not reflect the opportunity cost feature which is to be measured and may well include some return to capital. A measure that appears to be most appropriate would be that suggested by Dale W. Jorgenson and Zvi Griliches. In this, the price of capital services could be measured as the product of the unit acquisition cost of capital and the user cost per unit which consists of the rate of return for all capital in the economy (the opportunity cost), the rate of depreciation of the capital good (the use cost), and the rate of capital gains or losses on the capital good (the return or cost to holding that specific capital good). There is a final problem. The preceding discussion implies that a given stock of capital generates a given flow of services; thus, the price of capital services should be exogenous to the firm. However, the firm can alter both the rate of utilization of its capital stock and the rate of maintenance. Hence, both the flow of services and the rate of depreciation may be variables which can be adjusted by the firm; therefore, the price of capital would, be endogenous.

References

Ferguson, C. E., *The Neoclassical Theory of Production and Distribution*, Cambridge University Press, London, 1975; Harcourt, G. C., *Some Cambridge Controversies in the Theory of Capital*, Cambridge University Press, London, 1972; Harcourt, G. C., and N. F. Laing (eds.), *Capital and Growth*, Penguin, Harmondsworth, 1971.

(*See also* Capital formation; Factors of production)

Charles W. Smithson

Capital formation

Capital formation is the development of means of future production. In classical economics the means of production was divided into three categories: land, labor, and capital. Land comprised all of the endowments of nature, including resources under the ground, water, and air. These shared with labor the characteristics that they did not come out of the process of production itself. They were also thought, somewhat inaccurately, never to be exhausted in production. Capital was distinguished as both produced by the economy and subject to consumption or depreciation in the productive process.

Concepts of Capital

In terms of business enterprises, capital comprises buildings, structures or plants, machinery or equipment, and inventories. Somewhat more broadly, it also includes residential housing, whether rented or owner-occupied; transportation facilities and equipment, including highways and airports, whether owned by private industry or government; and, still more broadly, all physical or tangible producible facilities, whether owned by government, households, nonprofit institutions, or government.

A still wider concept, increasingly used in recent years, embraces human and nonphysical capital as well. Capital would thus include the knowledge produced by research and development expenditures, the skills derived from education and training, improvement in productivity brought on by investment in the health of workers, and increases in the value of land and natural resources such as might be achieved by clearing forests, improving the quality of soil, exploring for minerals, and investing in the preservation and improvement of the water and air of the environment.

Capital formation in any of these forms is characterized by the devotion of current production to the creation of something which is not consumed or enjoyed now but is utilized in future production, either of consumption services or of more capital. Capital formation is less widely perceived to have a price or cost—loss of the opportunity to produce something else for immediate enjoyment. In return, however, capital formation offers a reward of increased future production which can make possible more future consumption.

While capital formation may generally be expected to increase the capacity for future output, it will not necessarily increase on a permanent basis the opportunities for future consumption. For a given technology, more capital is likely to imply greater productive capacity, but, as capital formation proceeds, the return to capital diminishes, as does the return to any factor of production which is used more and more, while the use of other factors does not increase in proportion. This, indeed, is a facet of the law of diminishing returns. Thus, picks and shovels will enable ditchdiggers to dig much more rapidly than with their bare hands. But eventually, when all of the ditchdiggers have picks and shovels to suit every possible need, both for replacement and a variety of possible kinds of soil, additional utensils will only get in the way and will add no more to productive capacity, let alone cover their own costs.

Similarly, investment in human or nonphysical capital is likely to be subject to diminishing marginal returns. At some point, additional education or additional research and development spending or additional investment in health will not offer sufficient benefits to return their costs.

When is Capital Formation Worthwhile?

If we were all indifferent as to the enjoyment of consumption now and consumption in the future, that is, if our marginal rate of time preference were zero, and if we were starting with an economy in stationary equilibrium, that is, with no growth, capital formation would be worthwhile if its net marginal product were positive. This is to say, for example, that it would pay to produce an additional $100 machine if it would add to future output anything more than $100. Since the machine will eventually break down or become obsolete and have no further value, in order to be worth acquiring it must over its lifetime produce enough to cover its depreciation or return its original cost.

In an economy without growth but with a positive rate of time preference (or positive real rate of interest), where for reasons of impending mortality, general uncertainty, or some other factor, people would prefer to have more now even if this means less later, new capital formation should be undertaken only if it can produce more in the way of additional goods and services in the future than what the resources devoted to the production of capital could otherwise produce in the present. Put another way, utilizing the rate of interest and rate of discount which reflects this preference of the present over the future, the present value of expected future returns from additional capital must be at least equal to its cost.

In a growing economy where noncapital inputs, say labor, are growing, net capital formation, that is, a growth in the stock of capital, will be necessary merely to keep factor proportions constant. If all factors of production, including capital, grow at some constant rate, we may presume, technological change aside, that total production, consumption, and capital formation can and will grow at that same rate. Given the positive marginal rate of time preference, we may then also presume a positive marginal net product of capital, such that additional saving or capital formation will raise the rate of output.

But a higher rate of capital formation, implying a higher capital-labor ratio, implies that more capital will be needed in the future merely to meet increased replacement requirements and increased requirements for additional capital to maintain the higher capital-labor ratio as labor services continue to grow.

For example, if the number of workers is growing by 1 million per year and each worker produces with the aid of $10,000 capital, the net capital formation necessary to maintain this ratio is $10 billion, i.e., 1 million times $10,000. If increased capital formation brings us to a ratio of $11,000 per worker, then $11 billion, which equals 1 million times $11,000, will be necessary in the way of net capital formation to provide the additional capital for each additional worker.

Additional capital formation will increase output. But if it does not increase output by enough to meet the requirements both for reproducing itself as it wears out and for providing enough additional capital for the additional workers to maintain the labor force at its higher capital intensity, this higher capital intensity and higher production can be maintained only be reducing consumption.

We are thus left finally with the conclusion that in most economies, including that of the United States, with a positive rate of economic growth and a positive rate of time preference, more capital formation will lead to more future output but will not necessarily lead to more future consumption. To maximize future consumption, we should proceed with capital formation only to the critical point where the diminishing net marginal product of capital has fallen to the marginal investment requirement necessary to maintain the capital-labor ratio. If we proceed to this point, we will be operating according to the "golden rule" and maximizing consumption. If we have less capital formation or more capital formation, we will have less consumption.

Of course, in the real economies of the world, there are many different types of capital, each of which will add to production and more than pay for its cost and more than maintain itself up to that critical point. For those forms of capital where, by these criteria, we do not have enough capital formation, increased capital formation will add to both output and consumption in the long run. Where, however, we already have enough or too much capital formation, the attempt to increase the rate of capital formation will only reduce the possible stream of future consumption and possibly future output as well.

Profit Motive and Capital Formation

In a freely competitive economy where capital is owned by private producers who themselves enjoy the returns from their capital, we may expect that the owners, with appropriate information, will arrive at optimal amounts of capital formation. Government intervention to encourage more capital formation, unless it is merely counterbalancing other government interventions that have held down capital formation, runs the risk of raising capital formation beyond its optimal levels.

Even in the most free enterprise, private-profit-oriented economies, there is much capital, including both government capital and vast amounts of human capital, the formation of which is not determined by their private owners. While we may expect the profit motive to lead business to acquire appropriate amounts of plant, equipment, and inventories, the profit motive does not readily operate to ensure an optimal amount of capital formation in the form of research and development, education, health, and social overhead or government capital generally. And in the case of business capital formation, the general failure of aggregate demand and macroeconomic breakdown associated with depressions and severe recessions brings on enormous reductions in capital formation. It is thus left to government and the political process both to provide a general climate of prosperity in which private-profit-oriented business capital formation can reach its optimum, and to see to it that nonbusiness capital formation also reaches its optimum.

References

Denison, Edward, *Accounting for Economic Growth 1929-1969*, Brookings, Washington, D.C. 1974; Kendrick, John W., *The Formation and Stocks of Total Capital*, National Bureau of Economic Research, New York, 1976; Marx, Karl, *Capital*, Kerr, Chicago, 1906, especially vol. 1, part VIII, "The Accumulation of Capital"; Phelps, Edmund S. (ed.), *The Goal of Economic Growth*, Norton, New York, 1969; Shapiro, Eli, and William L. White (eds.), *Capital for Productivity and Jobs*, Prentice-Hall, Englewood Cliffs, N.J., 1977.

(*See also* Business investment in new plants and equipment; Capital, a factor of production; Economic growth; Gross private domestic investment in GNP; Human capital)

Robert Eisner

Capital gains

The usual meaning given to the term capital gain is implicit in its name—a gain from a sale or exchange of something which is held as part of one's capital or something which is held as an investment. For those who distinguish capital from income the demarcation is clear. Capital is capital. It may rise in value. It may fall in value. But whether it rises or falls, it remains capital. Capital may take many forms: corporate stocks or bonds, government securities, savings accounts, investment real estate, mortgages, loans, and—especially when currencies are falling in value—gold, gems, and art objects when purchased and held as investments rather than for personal use and enjoyment.

Capital versus Income

The distinction between capital gains and income is significant primarily in connection with income taxation. In all countries, capital gains are either not taxed at all or are taxed in a special category at lower rates. In spite of this universal differential tax treatment of capital gains, in one body of theory capital gains are held to be similar to other forms of income and should be taxed as such.

In the United States, one-half of long-term capital gains usually has been included in taxable income, with a maximum tax rate of no more than 25 percent. A succession of changes brought the maximum rate to over 49 percent compared with a top rate of 70 percent for income by the mid-1970s. In 1978, when the administration recommended still higher taxation of capital gains, the Congress, after reviewing the subject, reduced to 40 percent the fraction of long-term gains to be included in taxable income, giving a maximum rate of 28 percent.

Capital ordinarily produces income at varying rates of return and subject to varying degrees of perceived risks. Income takes the form of interest, dividends, rents, royalties interest, and profits that arise from the use of capital instead of from personal activity. In many, perhaps most, investments, the distinction between the capital value and the flow of income is clear. The analogy of the tree and the fruit—the capital value and the annual crop—is often used, though sometimes derided by those who argue that capital appreciation is another form of income.

Net-Accretion Concept of Income

The differential tax treatment is based on the distinction between capital and income. The case for full taxation of capital gains rests on a net-accretion concept of income. According to this theory, income should be measured by all increases in an individual's wealth during a period, whether they represent flows of income as conventionally measured or increases in value. (To continue the analogy with the fruit tree, the year's growth of the tree should be treated for tax purposes in the same way as the year's fruit crop.) As a practical matter, because of problems of annual valuation of property and difficulties in securing funds to pay taxes on nonliquid assets, the advocates of the net-accretion concept usually favor taxation only when gains are realized by sale or exchange. But taxation on realization is regarded as representing postponement of a tax due previously, perhaps subject to an interest charge to make up for the deferment.

Though the net-accretion concept has no counterpart in national income accounting, in trust law, or in traditional management of family finances, it is frequently advocated in public finance literature and has been responsible for frequent changes and continuing controversy in the tax treatment of capital gains. The persistence of the differential tax treatment of capital gains rests on the widespread acceptance of the proposition that capital gains are fundamentally different from income.

Controversial Tax Treatment of Capital Gains

Though the meaning of capital gains is clear in a general sense, in the tax law as well as in both popular and financial usage, quite dissimilar circumstances and transactions have come to be grouped together under this designation. Much of the controversy regarding the appropriate tax treatment of capital gains arises because of the different forms of capital gains which the various protagonists regard as representative or most significant. Two extreme examples illustrate the range of transactions which are or might be considered as capital gains. The owner of a house which has appreciated in price because of inflation is deemed to have a capital gain on the sale of the home even though the rise in price is not enough to keep up with the rise in construction costs or the price of new houses. The gain is simply the difference between the selling price and cost or other tax basis. Few people would consider this nominal gain to be income camparable to wages, rent, interest, or business profits. The Congress has recognized that such gains should not be taxed as income by a relief provision permitting the taxation of the gain to be postponed until the proceeds of the sale are reinvested in another home.

At the other extreme, the owner of a bond who clips and sells a coupon the day before it is due, at a price equal to the face value less one day's interest, would generally be thought of as merely accelerating by one day the receipt of ordinary interest income. Such a sale of a coupon would no more justify a pretense that interest income had been converted into a capital gain than would the sale of a weekly paycheck which was issued and sold at a slight discount a day before it was payable. Congress has amended the law repeatedly to prevent this and other artificially contrived transactions from being used to bring various forms of income within the capital gains definition.

Ownership of corporate stock represents a more complex situation regarding income and capital. Corporate earnings may be paid out as dividends which are regarded and taxed as income under any princple of income taxation. Earnings retained by a corporation, in theory, should lead to and be the basis for a commensurate capital appreciation, which, when realized, may be thought of as a delayed recognition of the stockholders' income that had previously been withheld and invested on their behalf in expansion of the same corporation. In fact, appreciation in the price of corporate stock seldom corresponds to retained earnings. In successful companies, appreciation runs far ahead of retentions; in unsuccessful companies, the price of stock falls in spite of retention of some or all of whatever corporate earnings exist. The theory, nonetheless, has a certain attraction to the extent that appreciation of stock corresponds to retained earnings. (Taxation of such gains as income would involve the same sort of double taxation as is applied to corporate income distributed as dividends.)

Future Revisions of Capital Gains Taxation

Inflation has made necessary the important distinction between nominal and real capital gains. An inflationary increase in the price of an investment—whether it is a home, a farm, a machine, or a share of stock—represents no increase in its real value. To the extent that the price increase arises from inflation, a tax on the proceeds of the sale or exchange of an asset reduces the real value of the proceeds. In this respect, a capital gains tax may be regarded as a capital levy. Relief from reductions of real capital by taxation of this form of capital gains could be provided by adjusting upward the tax basis of property by an appropriate index number reflecting inflation since the date of purchase. Indexing for capital gains taxation is proposed regardless of the extent of general indexing for income taxation.

A more fundamental revision of capital gains taxation would distinguish between those gains which are reinvested and those which, by not being reinvested, are presumably used for consumption. The latter could be taxed in full as ordinary income. Tax-free carry-overs of reinvested gains would prevent a reduction by taxation of existing capital, whether nominal or real. The tax basis or cost of property would be carried forward indefinitely; to the extent that realized gains were not reinvested, they would be immediately taxed.

References

Seltzer, Lawrence H., *The Nature and Tax Treatment of Capital Gains and Losses*, National Bureau of Economic Research, New York, 1951; Tax Advisory Staff, *Federal Income Taxation Treatment of Capital Gains and Losses*, U.S. Treasury Department, 1951.

(*See also* Capital, a factor of production; Taxation, an overview)

Dan Throop Smith

Capital-intensive industry

A capital-intensive industry is generally regarded as one in which the ratio of plant and equipment costs, essentially as measured by depreciation costs, to total costs is higher than the average such ratio for all industries. The capital intensity of an industry can also be inferred from the relationship of its capital input to its labor input. Hence, more capital input than labor input connotes a capital-intensive industry; conversely, more labor input than capital input indicates a labor-intensive industry. Thus, a labor-intensive industry is one that requires a high proportion of labor compared with the other factors employed, especially capital. Intensities of capital or labor input are relative or comparative terms of measurement.

Examples of capital-intensive industries include petroleum, tobacco, chemicals, and primary metals. Examples of labor-intensive industries include textiles, leather products, furniture, and the production of services. Among the latter, for example, the U.S. Postal Service is about 85 percent labor-intensive (1979).

Measurement of Capital Intensity

Ambiguities in the concept of capital and, hence, in the concept of capital-intensive industries exist. In the eighteenth century Adam Smith dichotomized capital into fixed capital and circulating capital, the latter including financial resources and work in process. In 1977 the Conference Board in its Road Maps of Industry series broadened its definition of capital invested to include land and inventory as well as plant and equipment. However, the board did not include financial capital such as treasury bills or cash on hand as capital invested. According to this broadened definition, an industry with a high inventory investment, such as the gold- or diamond-working industry, would also be regarded as a capital-intensive industry.

Another example would be agriculture, in which the costs of land as well as plant and equipment, especially equipment, take the largest share of total costs. Agriculture's capital share has risen, while the farm labor share has fallen. Figures reveal that 24.9 percent of the population were dependent on farming for their livelihood in 1930 compared with only 3.7 percent in 1977.

The Conference Board's research suggests rising capital intensity over time for virtually all industries in the United States, even for those still regarded as labor-intensive. Work by John W. Kendrick and others substantiates this observation.

Capital intensity, therefore, can be measured not only on an industry-by-industry basis but also from one period to another in the same industry. So also can capital intensity or labor intensity be measured from one period to another for the same economy.

Capital and Productive Efficiency

Capital is usually employed as a means of increasing productive efficiency, i.e., productivity improvement, whatever the industry. Using improved or new technology also increases productivity. These factors help to explain the trend of rising capital intensity in the U.S. economy over time. In the steel industry, for example, the process of converting iron into steel has steadily improved over the past 100 years as evidenced by the progressive switch from Bessemer furnaces to open-hearth furnaces to electric and oxygen furnaces. The development of continuous strip-rolling mills turning out flat-rolled sheets is another example of technology leading to rising capital intensity in the steel industry.

Whatever the industry, almost all technological advances tend to lead to substitutions of more efficient capital equipment for less efficient capital equipment. But in a larger sense, these substitutions amount to factor substitution—the replacement of labor by capital with a decline in unit labor costs usually resulting. This phenomenon is especially the case in decreasing-cost industries. Such industries as well as their customers are the beneficiaries of economies resulting from large-scale production. Manufacturing in general is a decreasing-cost industry, depending on the degree of capital intensity.

Given such high intensity, volume is the key to decreasing costs, as in the automobile industry. Assembly-line production, automatic multiple-boring of engine blocks, giant body-stamping equipment, and the like all demand intensive, almost full-time use for the heavy capital investments to pay off. When they do, unit costs tend to fall. Economies of scale also usually apply to automotive supplier industries, such as aluminum, plastics, rubber, glass, battery, head lamp, spark plug, and so on.

Implications of Rising Capital Intensity

The implications of rising capital intensity are many and far-reaching. National economic development or economic growth, for example, is generally held to be a function of capital investment. Hence, countries have been classified as capital-rich and capital-poor—e.g., the United States is said to be capital-rich and Third World countries such as India capital-poor. Indeed, for the most part the entire Third World is capital-poor. Economic development, according to Walt W. Rostow (*The Stages of Economic Growth*, 1960), proceeds through five stages: the traditional society, the preconditions for takeoff, the takeoff, the drive to maturity, and the age of high mass consumption. The takeoff stage is critical because it is in this stage that capital intensity rises and thus economic development becomes virtually assured. In the nineteenth century the United States was in the takeoff stage because of an infusion of private foreign capital, mainly British and French.

Another implication of the historical proclivity to substitute capital for labor and encourage capital intensity is the role of interest rates. The interest rate is, in a sense, the cost of capital. A falling interest rate, with constant or rising labor costs, other things being equal, tends to induce capital investment and intensity—for capital is then the relatively cheaper input and labor the dearer. Conversely, as the interest rate rises, with constant or falling labor costs, the tendency is the other way around— a pull toward a substitution of labor for capital.

References

Ackley, Gardner, *Macroeconomics: Theory and Policy*, 4th ed., Macmillan, New York, 1978, p. 619 ff; Kendrick, John W., *Productivity Trends in the United States*, National Bureau of Economic Research, New York, 1961, especially pp. 85–94; Kuznets, Simon, *Capital in the American Economy*, National Bureau of Economic Research, New York 1961; Layard, P. R. G., and A. A. Walters, *Microeconomic Theory*, McGraw-Hill, New York, 1978, p. 68 ff.

(*See also* Capital, a factor of production; Capital formation; Productivity)

William H. Peterson

Capital markets and money markets

The highly efficient capital and money markets of the United States are largely a product of the twentieth century. America's financial system began its tremendous development around the turn of the century, and it has been the catalyst in the rapid real growth of America since that time.

This article defines the capital and money markets in the United States to include the total sources and uses of credit and equity funds in the American economy. It includes both long-term (capital markets) and short-term (money markets) sources and uses of funds because these two markets merge closely into one another and at many points are interchangeable. The behavior of interest rates can be understood only within the context of the total market for credit. The available data do, however, permit a rough separation of long-term and short-term sectors.

The Principal Sources of Data

As is true of so much basic economic data, much of the knowledge about the U.S. capital and money markets stems from research by the National Bureau of Economic Research (NBER). Morris Copeland's *A Study of Money Flows in the United States*,

(1952) is the seminal study. Simon Kuznets' report, *Capital in the United States, Its Formation and Financing*, (1961), also contributed enormously to our knowledge of the subject. Raymond W. Goldsmith has also done invaluable work on the capital markets; his monumental three-volume report, *A Study of Saving in the United States* (1955), provides a comprehensive account of the growth of our savings and investment markets during the period 1897–1949, an account which he later brought up to date in his NBER studies.

The Federal Reserve Board is today the basic source of statistics on the U.S. capital and money markets through the flow-of-funds accounts which it has maintained for many years as the outgrowth of Copeland's work. The Board staff has over the years developed the flow-of-funds accounts into the financial system's counterpart of the GNP accounts. The two tables provided in this article illustrate the richness of the data supplied by the Federal Reserve. Table 1 shows a summary of total funds raised by various users in the capital and money markets during the period 1970–1979, and Table 2 presents a summary of total funds advanced from various sources. These two tables are supported by a wealth of detail on individual components of credit used and supplied. The data supplied by the Federal Reserve are available annually going back to 1946, and they are currently supplied quarterly on a seasonally adjusted annual rate basis. They are keyed into the national income and product accounts so that the two systems of basic economic statistics can be reconciled.

The flow-of-funds data are net figures; for example, in Table 1 the estimate of $481.5 billion for total funds raised in 1979 is the net increase in outstanding credit for that year, and the individual components are also net figures. For example, the $38.8 billion figure for U.S. government public debt securities in 1979 is the estimate for the net increase in outstanding direct U.S. government issues. Similarly, the total funds advanced in 1979, $481.5 billion, is the net increase in credit extended in that year, and the individual components are also net figures. The distinction between net and gross is an important one. For example, in 1979 the net funds advanced by the life insurance companies amounted to $34.3 billion. Actually, the gross cash flow for investment by life insurance companies (including not only new savings through life insurance but also repayments from past loans and investments) amounts to about $60 billion. Unfortunately, however, the state of the art does not yet permit the flow-of-funds data to be prepared on a gross basis because of unavailability of data from most users and sources. Although better knowledge of gross flows would be very helpful to an understanding of the behavior of the capital and money markets, the current net data are nonetheless most useful and are widely used by analysts of the capital and money markets.

The data are in nominal dollars—that is, they are not corrected for inflation. It would, of course, be possible to portray the flow of funds in real terms, but it can be argued that the financial markets behave in nominal-dollar terms so that there is no great need or advantage to correct them for inflation.

Trends in the Past Decade

Trends in the capital and money markets during the past decade contain some interesting developments. During this period there have been two cyclical declines in general business activity, the first beginning in late 1969 and extending through most of 1970 and the second beginning in late 1973 and extending through the first quarter of 1975. In both recessions total funds raised and total funds advanced declined moderately. However, the predominant behavior during the decade 1970–1979 was the

TABLE 1   Funds Raised in U.S. Credit Markets, 1970–1979

(Billions of dollars)

	1970	1974	1975	1976	1977	1978	1979*
Total funds raised	116.4	230.5	223.5	296.0	392.5	481.7	481.5
Nonfinancial sectors							
U.S. government							
Public debt securities	12.9	12.0	85.8	69.1	57.6	55.1	38.8
Agencies issues and mortgages	−1.0	−0.2	−0.4	−0.1	−0.9	−1.4	1.4
State and local obligations	11.2	16.5	16.1	15.7	23.7	28.3	21.3
Private domestic							
Corporate equities	5.7	4.1	9.9	10.5	2.7	2.6	3.2
Corporate bonds	19.8	19.4	27.2	22.8	21.0	20.1	21.8
Mortgages							
Home	14.4	34.8	39.5	63.7	96.4	104.5	106.1
Multifamily residential	6.9	6.9	†	1.8	7.4	10.2	10.1
Commercial	7.1	15.1	11.0	13.4	18.4	23.3	27.2
Farm	0.8	5.0	4.6	6.1	8.8	10.2	17.2
Consumer credit	5.9	9.9	9.7	25.6	40.6	50.6	42.3
Bank loans N.E.C.‡	6.7	31.7	−12.3	4.0	27.0	37.3	47.1
Open-market paper	2.6	6.6	−2.6	4.9	2.9	5.2	10.9
Other	5.0	13.7	9.0	14.4	19.0	22.2	27.0
Foreign							
Corporate equities	†	−0.2	0.2	0.3	0.4	−0.5	0.9
Bonds	0.9	2.1	6.2	8.6	5.1	4.0	5.0
Bank loans N.E.C.	−0.3	4.7	3.9	6.8	3.1	18.3	2.8
Open-market paper	0.8	7.3	0.3	1.9	2.4	6.6	11.2
U.S. government loans	1.3	1.6	2.8	3.3	3.0	3.9	3.0
Financial sectors							
U.S. government-related							
Sponsored credit agencies	9.1	16.6	2.3	3.3	7.0	23.1	24.6
Mortgage pool securities	0.7	5.8	10.3	15.7	20.5	18.3	27.8
Loans from U.S. government	−0.3	0.7	0.9	−0.4	−1.2	0.0	0.0
Private							
Corporate equities	6.3	0.3	0.6	1.0	0.9	1.7	1.6
Corporate bonds	0.8	2.1	2.9	5.8	10.1	7.5	7.0
Mortgages	0.2	−1.3	2.3	2.1	3.1	0.9	−1.2
Bank loans N.E.C.	1.5	4.6	−3.7	−3.7	−0.3	2.8	−0.5
Open-market paper and risk premiums	12.9	3.8	1.1	2.2	9.6	14.6	18.4
Loans from FHLBs	4.0	6.7	−4.0	−2.0	4.3	12.5	9.2

SOURCE: Flow of Funds, Federal Reserve Board
*Estimated
†Less than $50 million
‡Not elsewhere classified

quantum increase in total funds raised and advanced, from $116.4 billion in 1970 to $481.5 billion in 1979, an increase of 314 percent. This was not only the outcome of the high inflation rate which affected the capital and money markets in this period but it was also the product of real growth in the economy.

The heavy burden which the net increase in U.S. public debt securities has placed on the capital and money markets during the past decade is readily apparent in Table 1, especially in 1975 to 1976. Funds raised in the nonfinancial sectors through the net issuances of corporate equities have been quite low with the exception of 1975 and 1976. Moreover, there has been a remarkably flat pattern in the net issuance of corporate bonds by nonfinancial sectors during the decade, with 1975 being the one year showing a net increase ($27.2 billion) well above the level of other years. This is surprising because with inflation one would have expected the net increase in corporate bonds to have risen substantially. The flatness of the numbers is undoubtedly a function of the weakness of capital spending in the decade. As is apparent, there has been a large increase in funds raised in the commercial and farm mortgage markets during the decade.

The most startling trend in the past decade has been the enormous expansion of net funds raised in the home mortgage market, from $14.4 billion in 1970 to over $106 billion in 1979, nearly an eightfold increase in 10 years. This was the product of the rising tide of inflation in the housing area as well as, on average, strength in housing construction. Government policy favoring housing has also been a big factor. In 1978 the $104.5 billion net increase of home mortgages exceeded the combined net increase of funds raised in the nonfinancial sectors through the issuance of corporate bonds, commercial mortgages, farm mortgages, and state and local government obligations (aggregating $81.9 billion) by $22.6 billion. In 1979 the net increase in home mortgages of $106.1 billion exceeded the same combined total by $18.6 billion. Thus, it can be seen that in this period the single-family home mortgage market has risen to a point in which it commands the lion's share of the long-term capital market.

The huge growth of consumer credit, again importantly a reflection of inflation, is also apparent as is the growth of bank loans NEC (not elsewhere classified in various forms of mortgage credit and consumer credit). Bank loans NEC include business loans by the commercial banks.

As will be noted in Table 1, there have been some significant developments during the past decade in funds raised by the financial sectors of our economy—such as by commercial banks, insurance companies, and savings and loan associations. The most notable increase has been the tremendous rise in net funds raised through mortgage pool securities, mainly by the Government National Mortgage Association and the Federal Home Loan Mortgage Corporation. Similarly, there has been a huge increase in funds raised by government-sponsored credit agencies, including the Federal National Mortgage Association. Much of the funds raised in these ways has gone to finance home ownership.

Table 2 presents a summary of the various components of total funds advanced in U.S. credit markets in 1970 to 1979. While there are traces of cyclical effects on funds advanced, the predominant behavior is the huge increase in the totals, again a function of the sharp inflation and to a lesser extent real growth in output. The rest-of-the-world component has been particularly interesting in the period 1977–1979. The huge increases in 1977 and 1978 reflected in large measure the support of the weak U.S. dollar by foreign central banks, in which U.S. dollars were bought and invested in U.S. Treasury bills and other government obligations. In 1979, when the dollar strengthened, foreign central banks liquidated holdings of U.S. government obligations and sold dollars.

The tremendous increase in funds supplied by the commercial banking system, which helped to spur and validate the inflation, is shown in Table 2. The growth of the savings and loan associations, the life insurance companies, the private uninsured

TABLE 2   Total Funds Advanced in U.S. Credit Markets, 1970–1979

(Billions of dollars)

	1970	1974	1975	1976	1977	1978	1979*
Total funds advanced	116.4	230.5	223.5	296.0	392.5	481.7	481.5
Households	−1.6	36.5	27.1	19.6	30.5	51.8	51.6
Nonfarm noncorporate business	0.5	0.7	0.8	1.2	1.3	1.5	1.9
Corporate business	0.2	7.5	11.8	7.7	−4.3	−2.6	16.4
State and local governments	−0.2	0.2	2.6	7.9	14.0	14.6	15.0
Rest of the world	11.0	11.7	10.8	17.9	42.0	40.1	−5.5
U.S. government	2.8	9.8	15.1	8.9	11.8	20.4	23.0
Financial institutions							
Sponsored credit agencies	9.6	20.8	4.5	4.7	6.3	26.3	29.6
Mortgage pools	1.6	5.8	10.3	15.7	20.5	18.3	27.8
Federal Reserve System	5.0	6.2	8.5	9.8	7.1	7.0	7.7
Commercial banking system	35.1	66.6	29.4	59.7	87.7	128.8	120.6
Savings and loan associations	12.2	18.3	37.4	51.7	63.5	58.6	46.2
Mutual savings banks	4.2	3.3	10.9	12.6	11.5	8.6	5.9
Credit unions	1.4	2.7	5.4	6.6	7.3	8.8	2.2
Life insurance companies	9.0	15.2	18.8	26.6	28.6	32.8	34.3
Private pension funds	6.8	7.9	12.8	10.9	15.6	13.9	23.0
State and local retirement funds	6.3	9.2	11.7	13.1	15.4	18.8	20.5
Other insurance companies	3.9	4.1	6.6	13.4	18.7	18.0	19.1
Finance companies	2.7	5.0	1.4	9.0	18.7	18.3	23.0
Real estate investment trusts	1.9	0.2	−4.8	−3.8	−2.4	−1.0	−0.3
Open-end investment companies	1.7	−0.8	−0.4	−1.4	−1.4	−1.5	−1.6
Money-market funds	0	0.8	0.7	0.6	−0.1	3.2	19.8
Security brokers and dealers	2.4	−1.4	2.2	3.4	0.1	−2.7	1.1

SOURCE: Flow of Funds, Federal Reserve Board
*Estimated

pension funds, and state and local government retirement funds is also notable. There is some cyclical variability in the total funds advanced by the savings institutions (savings and loan associations, mutual savings banks, and credit unions) due to periodic disintermediation of these institutions in times of credit tightness and high interest rates. Regulation Q ceilings on the interest rates payable by the thrift institutions were the force behind disintermediation.

One of the most interesting elements in Table 2 is money-market funds. The tremendous expansion to $19.8 billion in 1979 is a function of the great increase in liquidity preference by investors as inflation and long-term interest rates soared.

As we enter the decade of the eighties there are disturbing trends in the capital and money markets. The double-digit inflation rate, and the fear that it will continue and possibly escalate, has greatly reduced the availability of credit on a long-term, fixed-income basis (bonds and mortgages). The climate of high inflation and high and rising short-term and long-term interest rates threatens to destroy the long-term capital markets as a strong priority is placed by investors on liquid assets. The thrift institutions are especially vulnerable in this climate because they are suffering from an earnings and cash flow standpoint. If U.S. capital and money markets are to survive and to serve the country well, as they have throughout its history, it is imperative that inflation be brought under control and that a reasonably stable price level be restored.

References

Board of Governors of the Federal Reserve System, *The Flow of Funds in the United States,* 1955; Copeland, Morris, *A Study of Money Flows in the United States,* National Bureau of Economic Research, New York, 1952; Goldsmith, Raymond W., *A Study of Saving in the United States,* Princeton University Press, Princeton, N.J., 1955; Kuznets, Simon, *Capital in the United States, Its Formation and Financing,* Princeton University Press, Princeton, N.J., 1961.

(*See also* Banking system; Bond; Business credit; Consumer credit, Credit, an overview; Debt; Debt management; Disintermediation; Federal Reserve policy; Federal Reserve System; Financial institutions; Financial instruments; Flow of funds; Housing economics; Inflation; Interest rates; Monetary policy; Money markets; Mortgage credit; Saving; Stock; Thrift institutions)

James J. O'Leary

Capital stock (see Wealth)

Capitalism

Economic systems are often classified according to whether the factors of production are privately owned, publically owned, or some mixture of the two. If private ownership prevails, the system is considered capitalistic, while if public ownership prevails, the term socialistic or communistic is deemed an appropriate description. The term "mixed economy" is retained for those systems that reveal ownership features of capitalism and socialism, although where capitalism becomes a mixed system and the latter turns into socialism is never clear-cut.

However, classifying economic systems solely on the basis of one criterion fails to capture some very important economic (and political) differences between capitalist economies, especially as they have evolved in the post-World War II period. However important these differences might be, it seems more important to define capitalism in such a way that it can be used to denote a wide variety of real world economies that are distinguishable from a group of other economies that do not share the basic political and cultural as well as the economic institutions that are the essence of capitalism.

The Perfectly Competitive Market System

In order to sharpen the analysis, it is useful to begin with a favorite tool of those economists concerned with the manner in which economic activities are organized under capitalism—the model of the perfectly competitive market system. In this model, the economy is viewed as a system of markets in each of which a homogeneous good is traded. Moreover, in each market buyers and sellers of the good are so numerous that no single buyer or seller can have an influence on the price at which the good is exchanged. (The notion of a market in this model later was extended to include that market for factors of production as well as goods.) Furthermore, this price, or the price mechanism, acts as a signal that provides all the information necessary to distribute output and factors throughout the economy in such a way that an optimal situation results. In other words, given the initial distribution of resource endowments among the population—human skills, ownership of physical and financial capital and land—the resulting production and distribution of that production will be such that no member of the society can be made better off in some material sense without making someone else worse off.

This outline of the perfectly competitive capitalist economy was first popularized by Adam Smith. It was Smith's view that not only could such a decentralized decision-making system effectively organize itself but also it would do so even though each individual acted according to self-interest, for there was an "invisible hand" at work coordinating the decisions of buyers and sellers in such a way as to promote the common good. So powerful and enduring was the influence of Smith's view of capitalism as a system functioning like the perfectly competitive model of the economists' textbooks that it was not until the Great Depression of the 1930s that economists and public officials (outside of Marxist circles) seriously challenged Smith's doctrines.

However, the inability of capitalist economies in so many countries to right themselves during the 1930s soon brought into question Smith's views. This questioning was strengthened by the writings of John Maynard Keynes, whose book, *The General Theory of Employment, Interest and Money*, provided a systematic explanation of why it might be the natural outcome of an unregulated, decentralized market system to periodically break down. His solution suggested a need for direct intervention from time to time by central governments in the form of tax and spending policies to offset destabilizing fluctuations in private spending.

Dominant Market Forms

The invisible-hand parable and the economist's model underlying it was challenged from another direction at about the same time. During the interwar period, economists developed models of capitalist economies that incorporated various forms of market structure other than the perfectly competitive one. For some time economists and public officials had been aware of the existence of monopolies, i.e., the dominance of a single seller in a market, which allowed the monopolist to exert varying degrees of control over prices. But throughout the interwar period, it became increasingly common for economists and others to view the perfectly competitive model as less and less relevant for explaining how real economies operate. Rather than markets being made up of numerous buyers and sellers in which homogenous goods are exchanged (along with an occasional monopoly), it became increasingly clear that the dominant market form under capitalism was not the perfectly competitive one but rather was one of monopoly, oligopoly (a few sellers), or monopolistic competition (many sellers who are likely to be selling similar, but not identical or homogeneous, goods).

Unfortunately, there is widespread acceptance of the fact that almost from its inception, capitalist economies have borne little resemblance to the world of perfect competition. Furthermore, in some countries it appears that over time the economy has moved further from the competitive form; in others the data suggest that this is not the case. In any case, there seems to be little evidence to substantiate a distinct trend toward fewer and bigger firms across industries even up through the post-World War II period.

Separation of Ownership from Control

What has become increasingly clear in the evolution of capitalism is the increased separation of ownership from control of the modern corporation. By common agreement capitalism requires that private ownership of the factors of production be widespread. However, with the rise of the modern corporation, stockholders, while technically the owners of the corporation, have become a group that does little more than rubber-stamp the decisions of management. This trend suggests that while any definition of capitalism requires private ownership of the factors of production, it should also encompass economies where the authority conferred by ownership can and has been delegated to a managerial class.

This conclusion suggests an additional consideration. The separation of ownership from control has led to an increased inclination on the part of government to provide a supervisory role over the private sector, reinforcing the tendency toward government intervention stemming from the Great Depression. But not only has there been an increased tendency toward government intervention and control, the evolution of capitalism also has been marked by a rising trend in government expenditures as a percent of total expenditures in the economy (until very recently) and, to a much lesser extent, outright nationalization of certain industries. In the post-World War II period especially, the production and distribution of output have become less the outcome of the working of markets, and the mixed economy has become the rule rather than the exception.

It is difficult to generalize about the causes and patterns of public ownership, even in the postwar period when nationalization of existing industries and the formation of government-owned or -controlled industries reached a peak. In some cases, nationalization was essentially a "bailing out" of private industry, a situation in which the industry could not maintain solvency and the government was not willing to let the industry "go under." In other cases government-controlled or -owned industries were established deliberately so that they would act as catalysts for other sectors of the economy. However, it would be difficult to conclude that there has been any dramatic shift toward increased public ownership of the factors of production.

Increased Role of Government

One of the outstanding developments under capitalism has been the increased role played by government in determining the composition of output. Government expenditures and tax revenues as a percent of total output have been rising fairly steadily throughout most of the twentieth century, while consumption of nondurable goods and services as a percent of output has declined. The rise of the role of government within the context of a system of predominant private ownership of the factors of production is largely the reflection of the rise of the so-called welfare state. The spread of public education, public medical and dental systems, pension and welfare schemes, and retraining programs along with retirement and unemployment benefit programs has been one of the outstanding features of post-World War II capitalist development. The rise of the welfare state and increase in public ownership indicate a shift in economic decision making in capitalist economies away from the private sector. This trend leads to a final consideration in the definition of capitalism. Capitalism as used here denotes an economic system in which the owners of the factors

of production and those making economic decisions concerning such things as production, savings, and investment are *predominantly* private individuals. While somewhat vague, such a definition allows the analysis to incorporate some important historical developments as part of the definitive features of capitalism, features which
are useful in distinguishing it from other forms of economic organization.

It is important to recognize that the rising importance of the government sector,
especially during the post-World War II period, in determining the composition of
output was accomplished without a decline in private consumption levels. Thus,
while consumption of nondurable goods and services as a percent of total output fell
in capitalist economies during this period, the absolute level of per capita consumption rose. Moreover, this took place at a time when investment by businesses in plant
and equipment in each country as a share of total output was at an all-time historical
high, at least outside North America. The key to this seemingly paradoxical series of
developments lay in the fact that never in the past had so many capitalist economies
grown so rapidly for such sustained periods of time. The one exception was the
United States. Thus, during the postwar period from, say, the early 1950s up through
the early 1970s, in almost every capitalist economy rates of growth of total output
and output per worker were outstanding compared with each country's previous
performance.

Growth and Development

The similarities in the patterns of growth and development of the different economies
are of interest. In every developed capitalist economy, there was an absolute (and
relative) decline in employment in agriculture and an absolute (and relative) increase
in employment in the service or tertiary sector. Measured by the level of per capita
incomes, employment patterns in industry were also similar. From relatively low per
capita incomes (for developed capitalist countries) relative and absolute employment
in industry rose. After higher levels of per capita incomes were realized (those
attained in most economies by the mid-1960s), employment in industry as a share of
total employment began to drop off. In contrast, in absolute terms employment in
industry rose continuously in the majority of the developed capitalist economies until
the early 1970s when stagnation set in.

A simple way of characterizing this process of growth and development in the
postwar period is to envisage a situation of high rates of growth of productivity and
low rates of growth of demand in agriculture interacting to release labor for industry
and the service sector. The high rates of business investment mentioned earlier
enabled the expanded labor force in the nonagricultural sectors to be equipped with
the most productive capital plant and equipment available. This was especially so for
those economies starting from relatively low levels of per capita incomes since they
were in a position to borrow the most advanced technology from the high-income
economies such as the United States which had already developed the technology.
Thus, an outstanding characteristic of the Japanese postwar modernization process
was the widespread purchases of licenses from the United States of process technologies. These required modifications and adaptation to suit the Japanese needs, to be
sure, but it was also obvious that Japanese industrialists were able to skip some of the
research and development stages involved in implementing a technology and thereby
reduce costs of production. They were also in a better position to borrow and install
only the best technologies available. As a result of these and other factors, the period

from the early 1950s to the early 1970s was one in which there was a strong tendency for countries with relatively low levels of per capita income at the beginning of the period to grow relatively rapidly. For all the developed capitalist economies, the same period marked (in terms of its duration and pervasiveness) capitalism's greatest boom in history.

The period since the early 1970s has been termed a period of "stagflation" for capitalism, characterized by stagnation (slow growth, low investment, and high unemployment) together with inflation. Growth rates (and inflation rates) have continued to diverge from one country to the next during the current period, but there has been a general scaling-down of the pace of growth and development in all the developed capitalist economies. The primary factor involved in the collapse of the worldwide postwar boom has been a fear of inflation engendered by an acceleration in the rate of inflation beginning in the late 1960s and lasting into the mid-1970s. The response of governments to inflation in the majority of the capitalist economies has been, to pursue anti-inflationary demand policies coupled at times with some form of incomes policy. This has led to higher rates of unemployment and lower rates of profits and utilization of capital by business. The impact of the latter on business investment has been definitely depressing, hence the decline in growth rates. Whether such recession-induced anti-inflationary policies will work eventually is still a matter of heated discussions among economists. If they do not, it is predictable that various forms of increased government intervention can be expected and on a more permanent basis. And these may be of such a drastic nature that an entirely new concept defining the essential features of capitalism will become appropriate.

References

Eichner, Alfred, and J. A. Kregel, "An Essay on Post-Keynesian Theory: A New Paradigm in Economics," *Journal of Economic Literature*, December 1975; Kalecki, Michael, *Selected Essays on the Dynamics of the Capitalist Economy, 1933–1970*, Cambridge University Press, Cambridge, 1971; Keynes, J. M., *The General Theory of Employment, Interest and Money*, Macmillan, London, 1936; Svennilson, I., *Growth and Stagnation in the European Economy*, Economic Commission for Europe, Geneva, 1954.

(*See also* Comparative economic systems, an overview; Competition; Monopoly and oligopoly; Nationalization of industry)

John Cornwall

Cartel

A cartel is a group of producers in an industry who act together in an attempt to increase combined and individual profit.

If all producers of a good combine, the cartel may seek to imitate the behavior of a unique supplier—a monopolist. Commonly, however, a fringe of smaller producers will operate outside the cartel. The presence of such a fringe will impede the exercise of complete monopoly power by the cartel.

Cartels and Monopoly

A cartel must deal with all the problems which would be faced by a monopolist operating in the same industry. A cartel will attempt to increase profit by raising price. But the cartel confronts the trade-off between higher price and lower sales along the industry demand curve: as the market price rises, group sales will go down as consumers switch to substitute products. The cartel must deal with the other classic problem of monopoly, that of entry: as market price and profit rise, an incentive is created for new firms to come into the market and offer customers a new source of supply. As new firms increase output, total supply will increase and market price will fall, all else equal. The entry of new suppliers will reduce the ability of the cartel to impose a particular price on the market.

For a complete cartel to exercise monopoly power over time, some impediment or barrier to entry must prevent new firms from entering and eroding market power. Important entry barriers may include patent protection, government regulations, control of high-quality deposits of raw materials which are necessary for production, product differentiation (perhaps enhanced by intense advertising), or technical relations of production which require entry at very large scales if operation is to be efficient. Similarly, long-run exercise of market power by a cartel faced with a competitive fringe can occur only if some barrier to mobility prevents firms in the fringe group from expanding output.

If entry is not completely blockaded, a cartel will have two choices: hold price sufficiently below the monopoly price so that entry is not induced, or set price so high that entry does occur and market power is eventually eroded. Greater profit in the immediate future may be traded for eventual loss of market power. If entry occurs slowly, market power may persist for long periods of time.

Loss of sales—as demand falls or as rivals enter and expand output—will occur even when a single firm exercises market power. Other problems, revolving around the use of market power by a group, are characteristic of cartels.

If a cartel is to raise price and increase profit, group output must be restricted. Different members of the cartel are likely to have different views about the best output level for the group. Consensus must somehow be reached. Open, private agreement is illegal under United States antitrust laws (although regulatory agencies frequently act to enforce effectively the same sort of agreement).

Once an output level is agreed upon, the reduction in group output will have to be divided among the members of the cartel. Each one will naturally prefer to reduce its own output as little as possible.

If group output is successfully reduced, there remains the problem of enforcement. Output reduction will increase the market price, and when this occurs, each individual cartel member will have an incentive to cut price slightly and expand its own output at the expense of other members. But if all cartel members do this, the cartel will break down as group output rises and price falls.

Cartels and Success

A cartel is more likely to be successful in an industry for which demand is relatively insensitive to price increases. If demand does not fall very much when price rises, the gains from successful cartelization will be large. The inducement of individual cartel members to reach and maintain an agreement will be correspondingly large.

A cartel is more likely to succeed when entry is difficult. If entry requires access to scarce mineral resources, or a very large initial investment, or a large advertising campaign, it is less likely to occur at any price set by the cartel. This reduces the danger of bringing uncooperative outsiders into the industry.

It will be easier to enforce an agreement if it is easy to discover cheating, and if retaliation can be rapid. If sales and prices are publicly and promptly reported, price cheaters will be subject to quick counteraction. Where sales are small and frequent, the gain from cutting price on any particular sale will be small. The potential loss, if other cartel members respond in kind, so that price falls on all later sales, will be large. Conversely, if sales are large and infrequent, the gain from cutting price to get a particular piece of business may be large. It will be easier to reach and enforce agreements on price when a product is standardized than when each customer receives a slightly different product.

If a cartel is successful, it will create the same adverse effects which accompany any exercise of monopoly power. Price will be raised above the cost of production. Profit will exceed the normal level. Output will be restricted so that less than the optimal amount of the product in question will be available for society.

References

Adelman, M. A., "Oil Import Quota Auctions," *Challenge*, vol. 18, no. 6. January/February 1976, pp. 17–22; Caves, R. E., and M. E. Porter, "From Entry Barriers to Mobility Barriers," *Quarterly Journal of Economics*, vol. 91, no. 2, May 1977, pp. 241–261; Demsetz, H., "Two Systems of Belief About Monopoly," in H. J. Goldschmidt, H. M. Mann, and J. F. Weston (eds.), *Industrial Concentration: The New Learning*, Little, Brown, Boston, 1974, pp. 164–184; Smith, R. A., *Corporations in Crisis*, Doubleday, New York, 1962, chaps. 5, 6.

(*See also* Competition; Concentration of industry; Monopoly and oligopoly)

Stephen Martin

Census Bureau (see Bureau of the Census)

Change in business inventories in GNP

Change in business inventories in the gross national product is part of gross private domestic investment. The change represents the value of the increase or decrease in the physical stock of goods held by the business sector and valued in current period prices. An inventory increase is regarded as investment because it represents production not matched by current consumption, while an inventory decrease is regarded as negative investment because it reflects consumption in excess of current production.

There are three important facets of inventory change: (1) inventory accounting changes; (2) financing such changes; and (3) establishing the proper macroeconomic context.

Inventory Accounting Changes

The two major conceptual accounting problems concern national income and product statistics, and business profits.

Under first-in–first-out (FIFO) accounting, inflation biases calculations of inventory change upward relative to true changes in real holdings. Since stocks moved out through sales will be accounted for at cost (assumed to be lower than market), even 1 for 1 inventory replacement will seem to add to stocks. Under last-in–first-out (LIFO) accounting, this bias is avoided. This point has been understood for a long time and is now taken account of in the inventory valuation adjustment in national income statistics. According to the U.S. Department of Commerce (1954), the adjustment procedure involves six steps, the last four of which are indicated:

> *The estimates of book value of non-LIFO inventories are converted to a constant price basis. . . . The change in these inventories at constant prices is obtained by subtracting beginning from ending inventories at constant prices. . . . The current value of the physical change in inventories is obtained by multiplying the change in inventories at constant prices by the ratio of current prices to the constant price base. . . . The inventory valuation adjustment is obtained by subtracting the change in the book value of inventories from the current value of the physical change in inventories.*

Inventory turnover can be profitable while absorbing more cash than it releases. Thus, a firm's physical working capital might stay the same; it might have to spend cash in order to maintain this position; and the process is said to be profitable.

Accounting logic resolves the conundrum. Acquisition of fresh stock does not comprise cost of goods sold; cost of goods sold is incurred when inventories are run down. The replenishment of stocks comprises an act of investment. In an inflationary regime, nominal borrowings and nominal profits continuously will increase.

A different chain of reasoning supports a relationship between unplanned changes in real inventories and business profits. This approach has faded in analytical literature, but retains some vitality, especially in applied economics. If there is excess demand for goods at a full employment level of output, and if nominal income, excluding inventory profit, is given for the period, the resulting inflationary gap will be expressed as inventory profit.

Financing Changes in Inventories

An observed (or realized) change in inventories, accompanied by a change in the demand for cash, may be accompanied by disturbance in the financial markets. Inventory accumulation, sparked by an increase in demand for cash, well may be accompanied by higher real interest rates before induced contraction of demand develops. Inventory runoff, sparked by a decrease in demand for cash, well may be accompanied by lower interest rates, at least before induced demand has had a chance to start up.

Consider a possibility developed by H. Rose (1957). Effective demand might change while excess demand for cash does not. Then what might be called the dual of the multiplier relation assures that realized (actual) declines in inventories below intended levels finance aggregate planned investment in excess of planned saving. Unintended runoff of inventories can exactly correspond to underlying excess demand. And the unplanned runoff of inventories would equilibrate supply of and demand for finance: planned deficits in excess of planned surpluses on cash flow account can be financed by unexpected net cash inflows from inventory runoff. Similarly, if an economy produces above the rate of effective demand, so that planned saving exceeds planned investment, unplanned inventory accumulation will generate unexpected demand for finance that can precisely absorb the excess of planned saving over planned investment (D. H. Robertson, 1949). Robertson and Rose (1959) go far to resolve the tangled liquidity preference–loanable funds debate.

Empirical work in the real and nominal macroeconomic effects of changes in planned inventory holdings is impeded by the fact that, in the real world, transactions occur in disequilibrium; there is false trading (Hicks, 1965). Specifically, series of changes in interest rates and bank loans (together with commercial paper, etc.) may look out of phase with inventory (dis)investment. For example, open lines of credit may permit firms to bid for goods. They will anticipate taking down loans after contracts are closed. Contracts will not get closed; they will fail to obtain the goods. Prices will rise. They will borrow after all—in order to maintain real cash balances. Significant macroeconomic effects could be generated by changes in demand for inventories—i.e., by changes in demand schedules—without observed accumulation being affected. Indeed, the result could be disinvestment in inventories. Demand pressures generated by increased demand for inventories could cause unplanned runoff, partly because accelerated price inflation might stimulate anticipatory buying. The dual consequence for finance would find credit taken by business falling because firms had tried, and failed, to take more credit in order to finance purchases of new inventories they did not get. Resulting intensification of demand pressure would lead to runoffs that would increase business liquidity.

There are links between the theories of inventory investment and money. The principle of reflux and the real bills doctrine or banking principle were duly reflected in the earlier performance of the Federal Reserve System. And Wicksell's cumulative inflationary process concerns the response of planned inventory investment to disparities of market rates of interest from the natural rate. R. G. Hawtrey (1932, 1938, 1950) also emphasized how (short-term) interest rates can affect inventory investment, albeit in a different way.

Some Real Macroeconomics of Inventory Investment

Inventory investment entered macroeconomic theory through the inventory cycle. The following passage from R. G. D. Allen (1967) summarizes the inventory cycle theory:

> When sales increase, producers respond to reduced inventories by increasing output to cover higher sales and to replenish stocks. Incomes rise and there are further increases in sales—until ... desired stocks are achieved. Output is then cut back and the downswing of lower sales and higher inventories sets in. The oscillation proceeds.

Thus, the theory of inventory change is based on feedback; the impulse imparted to inventories from a shift in final demand can, in ways developed by L. A. Metzler (1941), become converted into a more intense one, fed back from responses to inventory change to demand.

The feedback mechanism just described is controlled by the formation of expectations. The way in which sales experience affects inventory plans will depend upon how such experience affects expectations of future sales. The work of Michael Lovell (1961, 1964) now must be scanned in light of rational expectations theory. The central contrast, shared with the theory of consumption, is between adaptive and rational expectations. Does sales experience generate exponentially declining "knee-jerk" reaction or does it get fed into a process generating unbiased maximum likelihood estimates of future sales? The query has not been definitively resolved empirically.

If, indeed, inventory investment typically hinged on rational estimates of future sales, the feedback channel would be blocked. Unanticipated changes in sales would be attributed either to random shocks or specification error. Let us assume that sales at a given time were known to be influenced by a random shock. Effects of the shock might linger for some time; replacement of inventories unexpectedly runoff would be timed with due attention to incremental costs of more rapid adjustment; the shock would steadily dissipate and might not cause any oscillation.

The theory of inventory investment, and that of the inventory cycle, can, under rational expectations, get drawn into monetary theory through a regress. Along lines explored by R. J. Barro (1978), unexpected sales changes may be induced by unexpected monetary changes. But the effects will be heavily damped, and the ensuing sales reactions will not impinge upon the formation of sales expectations.

References

Abramovitz, M., *Inventories and Business Cycles with Special Reference to Manufacturing Inventories*, National Bureau of Economic Research, New York, 1950; Allen, R. G. D., *Macro-Economic Theory*, Macmillan, London, 1967; Barro, Robert J., "Unanticipated Money, Output, and the Price Level in the United States," *Journal of Political Economy*, vol. 86, 1978, p. 549; Burstein, M. L., *Money*, Schenkman, Cambridge, Mass., 1963; Evans, Michael K., *Macroeconomic Activity*, Harper & Row, New York, 1969; Friedman, Milton, *Essays in Positive Economics*, University of Chicago Press, Chicago, 1953; Hall, Robert E., "Stochastic Implications of the Life Cycle-Permanent Income Hypothesis: Theory and Evidence," *Journal of Political Economy*, vol. 86, 1978 p. 971; Hawtrey, R. G., *The Art of Central Banking*, Longmans, Green, London, 1932; Hawtrey, R. G., *A Century of Bank Rate*, Longmans, Green, London, 1938; Hawtrey, *Currency and Credit*, 4th ed., Longmans, Green, London, 1950; Hicks, J. R., *Value and Capital*, 2d ed., Clarendon Press, Oxford, 1946; Hicks, J. R., *Capital and Growth*, Clarendon Press, Oxford, 1965, pp. 52–54; Keynes, J. M.: *A Treatise on Money*, 2 vols., Macmillan, London, 1930.; Keynes, J. M., *How to Pay for the War*, Macmillan, London, 1940; Klein, Lawrence R., *The Keynesian Revolution*, Macmillan, New York, 1947, chap. 1 and pp. 189–192; Leijonhufvud, Axel, *On Keynesian Economics and the Economics of Keynes*, Oxford University Press, London and New York, 1968; Lovell, Michael, "Manufacturers' Inventories, Sales Expectations and the Accelerator Principle," *Econometrica*, vol. 29, 1961, p. 293; Lovell, Michael, "Determinants of Inventory Investment," in E. F. Denison and L. R. Klein (eds.), *Models of Income Determination*, Princeton University Press for the NBER, Princeton, N.J., 1964; Marget, A. W., *The Theory of Prices*, vol. 1, Prentice-Hall, New York, 1938, pp. 101–140; Metzler, L. A., "The Nature and Stability of Inventory Cycles," *Review of Economic Statistics*, vol. 23, 1941, p. 113; Robertson, D. H., *Banking Policy and the Price Level*, Staples Press, London, 1949; Rose, Hugh, "Liquidity Preference and Loanable Funds," *Review of Economic Studies*, vol. 24, 1959; Scarfe, Brian L., *Cycles, Growth, and Inflation: A Survey of Contemporary Macro-dynamics*, McGraw-Hill, New York, 1977; U.S. Department of Commerce, Office of Business Economics, *National Income: A Supplement to the Survey of Current Business*, 1954, pp. 134–138.

(*See also* Business credit; Business cycles; Business inventory; Economic growth; Economic statistics; Expectations; Gross national product; Gross private domestic investment in GNP; Interest rates; National income accounting)

M. L. Burstein

Channels of marketing

Channels of marketing is a term that designates patterns of relationships among the many agencies that deliver to users the goods and, some would say, services produced by the economy.

A Set of Flows

The nature of these relationships can be illustrated as a set of flows. First, there is a physical flow of goods from places of extraction as raw material; through successive places where they are assembled, assorted, processed, and dispersed; and finally to places where they are used as finished goods. This movement is intermittent, interrupted while goods are processed or held somewhere as a stock to equalize inward and outward flows.

Next, there is a flow of ownership. During their physical flow down the channel, goods must be owned by someone. Title usually passes through a succession of owners. This flow also is intermittent, although ownership itself is continuous. Transfers of title are arranged through successive sales and purchases. These may be negotiated by the sellers and buyers directly or through intermediaries of various types.

Other flows operate on the fringes of marketing. For example, as any item moves through its ownership channel it represents a growing accumulation of capital. This is brought into and dispersed throughout the channel in many forms by many intermediaries. Other highly specialized agencies provide for flows of information and persuasion among channel members through the performance of such services as advertising, selling, and research.

In the academic world, where the abstract concept of the channel flourishes among a small body of thinkers, any or all of these agencies may find themselves counted as belonging to a particular channel. The world of business, however, prefers to think of channel members as including only (1) those who fit into the flow of ownership because they buy and sell the goods passing through them for their own account, and (2) those who participate in negotiating, bargaining, and arranging sale-purchase transactions for others.

Facilitating Agencies

The rest of the marketing agencies, in this view, are either ignored or lumped into a category of so-called facilitating agencies. Many such agencies are very large and much too powerful to be taken as mere appendages to the distribution industry. Examples are agencies concerned with transportation, storage, finance, and insurance.

There is some disagreement as to whether those who sell services, as distinct from goods, should be included in channels. Services cannot be owned and transferred from hand to hand as can a physical possession. Some of them must be performed on the buyer and so cannot be marketed through intermediaries. Often it is difficult to differentiate services and products from each other. About all one can say is that some find it helpful, whereas others do not, to hold that services can, and in fact are, marketed through channels that must be managed.

The Current System of Channels

The presently prevailing system of channels first seriously challenged the one that preceded it about the time of World War I. Under the then established system, the ownership of finished goods flowed down a channel from producers to wholesalers, then to retailers, and, finally, to consumers. Each agency usually was a separate ownership.

Exceptions to the rule existed, some of which were sizable enterprises, but they controlled only a small percentage of domestic marketing. An overwhelming percentage of the system was controlled by a multitude of small retailers and wholesalers that connected producers with consumers through a sequence of market transactions, each negotiated individually by the two parties involved. Horizontally, the arrangement was one of competition between retailers for the trade of consumers and between wholesalers for the trade of retailers. The competing sellers usually operated within small geographic areas.

The principal instrument that broke down the established order of channels was the corporate chain. This type of operation combined under one ownership a group of retail stores and one or more entities that took over the tasks previously performed by wholesalers. Most such chains grew by opening new stores rather than by taking over individual stores already in existence, although mergers of small chains into progressively larger ones in time became fairly common.

A few contractual chains had been set up by retailers late in the nineteenth century, primarily in effort to bypass wholesalers; but their major growth came as a defense against corporate chains in the 1900s. Once in operation, such organizations both set up new stores and absorbed old ones. The contractual systems take a number of forms. One is the retailer-owned cooperative, where retail merchants organize and control the operation. A second is the voluntary chain sponsored and controlled by wholesalers. The third is the franchise system, where otherwise independent retailers accept some degree of central control by manufacturers (as in the marketing of automobiles) or by enterprises that invent standardized operating methods using specialized facilities, and operating in outlets of distinctive design (as in fast-food operations). The franchisors charge fees for their services and require the franchised outlets to conform to specified operating procedures. The contractual chains vary endlessly in scope and detail and raise many difficulties in management.

A definitive history explaining why corporate, contractual, and franchised systems have taken over the bulk of retailing remains to be written. They clearly have been an aspect of much more comprehensive changes in the American way of life. A major factor no doubt has been the devising of increasingly effective ways of managing from a distance. The automobile, the airplane, and the telephone have expanded enormously the geographic area a manager can keep under a watchful eye. In addition, an accompanying revolution using computers to record and analyze data at high speeds facilitates control by numbers rather than by personal inspection.

Even now, there is little evidence that business managers pay much attention to the complete channel as a concept and, more importantly, to the complete channel as an entity to be managed because it competes with other complete channels for the patronage of the users of goods. There is much evidence, however, that they give close attention to segments of the channel. Much of this seems to be little more than a reorganization of the materials normally presented in textbooks concerned with the management of selling and advertising.

A Lack of Adequate Statistics

Statistics covering the field of channels are few and fragmentary. Largest in scope are the censuses of business that began with an experimental census in 11 cities covering operations in 1926. The Bureau of the Census now takes such a census nationally at scheduled intervals. These provide a mass of numbers that are useful and important for many purposes but throw only a dim light on the various flows of the channel.

The principal block to effective empirical research into channels is the difficulty of tracing individual channels through markets. Badly needed are opportunities to observe, measure, analyze, and evaluate the full sequence and assortment of agencies in individual channels extending all the way from extraction to consumption. A few efforts have been made to compile data for at least long segments of such channels. They have been enlightening but of limited value because there are large gaps in the data available. Many agencies do not keep records in forms suitable for this purpose. Perhaps the rapid spread of computerization throughout the economy will change this situation in the not-too-distant future.

In the meantime, lacking adequate statistics to support a comprehensive empirical analysis of channels, some students have turned to instruments derived from the behavioral sciences. In addition to or in place of assuming that would-be managers seek singlemindedly to maximize profits, these students assume that managers try to control segments of channels by using concepts that are primarily sociological in nature, such as power, control, leadership, role, cooperation, and conflict.

International Aspects of Channels

During the years since World War II, interest in international aspects of channels has grown appreciably. Many published reports provide superficial descriptions of the channels through which foreign countries do their own domestic marketing. A few projects have gone more profoundly into the organization and operation of domestic marketing in a number of countries. Such projects have concerned themselves with trying to help exporters from the United States make use of local entities in marketing their wares or with evaluating the social effectiveness of these channels.

References

Mallen, Bruce, Principles of Channel Management, D. C. Heath, Lexington, Mass, 1977; Mallen, Bruce E., (ed.), The Marketing Channel: A Conceptual Viewpoint, Wiley, New York, 1967; Rosenbloom, Bert, Marketing Channels: A Management View, Dryden Press, Hinsdale, Ill., 1978; Stern, Louis W., and Adel El-Ansary, Marketing Channels, Prentice-Hall, Englewood Cliffs, N.J., 1977.

Reavis Cox

Chicago school

The Chicago school refers to the philosophy, policy preferences, concept of the economic system, and methodology associated with the department of economics at the University of Chicago. The principal characteristic of this philosophy is its emphasis on individual freedom as a primary goal, which differs fom the emphasis of many economists on equality in the distribution of income. The dominant role given to individual freedom stems primarily from the work of Frank H. Knight, who was appointed a professor at the University of Chicago in 1928 and was active until the late 1960s. His books of essays, The Ethics of Competition and Other Essays and Freedom and Reform, combine the study of economics with social philosophy.

There are three important policy positions associated with economists of the Chicago school:

1. They believe that the best way to organize economic activity is through competitive markets.
2. They are opposed to most types of government regulation of the economy.
3. They believe that a country's monetary system is of primary importance.

Competitive Markets

To Chicagoans, the teaching of economics is viewed largely as the explanation of how it is possible to organize economic activity through a system of competitive markets. The preference for such a system is based primarily on the predominant role given to freedom as a social goal. As stated by Milton Friedman, (1974) who was a professor of economics at the University of Chicago from 1947 to 1979, competitive markets are viewed as "the only means so far discovered of enabling individuals to coordinate their economic activities without coercion." In addition, competitive markets are believed to be efficient—scarce resources are used to produce those goods and services in greatest demand. A principal difference between Chicagoans and others is that Chicagoans view the market system as basically stable, provided there is an appropriate monetary system, and not necessarily subject to recurring periods of severe recession and inflation. They attribute cycles primarily to large swings in the rate of growth in the money supply. Non-Chicagoans usually insist that cycles are the result of the instability of investment spending and the development of maladjustments in an unplanned economy.

Government Regulations

Chicagoans are critical of most types of governmental regulation of the economy. Their attitude is one of skepticism about the relationship between the intent and the actual effects of such regulation. Economists such as George J. Stigler and Friedman would be inclined to prefer unregulated monopoly, if that were the only alternative, to either government regulation or government ownership and operation. They believe that the rapid growth of government regulation has had undesirable effects on both economic efficiency and individual freedom. Their preference for unregulated monopoly over government ownership and operation is based largely on their evaluation of the experience with nationalized industries, especially in Great Britain.

Monetarist Theory

The insistence that "money matters" is one of the important characteristics of the Chicago school. The principal empirical work supporting this point of view is the study by Milton Friedman and Anna J. Schwartz, *A Monetary History of the United States, 1867–1960*, published in 1963. The monetarist theory of inflation differs from the cost-push theory that attributes inflation primarily to excessively rapid increases in wages or to increases in commodity prices. Chicagoans believe that the acceleration in the rate of inflation in the United States since 1965 would not have occurred if the Federal Reserve System had not permitted the money supply to increase at an excessively rapid rate.

In Friedman's monetarist theory of business cycles, the principal cause of recession is a decline in the rate of expansion in the money supply. He believes that it was the Federal Reserve's tight money policy in 1928 and 1929, designed to combat stock-market speculation, that led to the beginning of the Great Depression. He also believes that the Federal Reserve System could have prevented the sharp decline in the money supply during the Great Depression if it had wanted to do so. One of his most controversial proposals is that the monetary authorities ought to be required to maintain a constant rate of growth of the money supply.

Chicago School and the Economic System

The Chicago concept of the economic system assumes that competition is a major force in the economy. In the early years of the Chicago school, Henry C. Simons believed that labor unions had excessive monopolistic power over wages. In later years, the empirical work of H. Gregg Lewis at the University of Chicago supported the point of view that even union power over wages is significantly restrained by competition. In addition, the widely held belief that the managers of large corporations are very powerful—that they can control consumer demand through advertising, that they do not need to maximize profits because they are not selected by the stockholders, and that they have great control of the prices and kinds of products they produce—is rejected.

The Chicago concept of wage flexibility is also different from the conventional view. Even though Friedman stressed that both wages and prices respond slowly to changes in aggregate demand, Chicagoans usually assume that in the long run wages are sufficiently flexible to equate the demand and the supply of labor. In the conventional view, even during periods of prosperity there is typically a large pool of workers who cannot find jobs. It is believed that this results from the tendency for the growth of the labor force to exceed the growth of aggregate demand and the long-run inflexibility of wages.

Scientific versus Policy Approach

The distinctive characteristics of the methodology of the Chicago school are twofold: Chicagoans insist on the empirical testing of theoretical generalizations, and they use competitive price theory as a tool for analyzing a wide range of concrete problems. The scientific approach of the Chicago school should be distinguished from its policy approach, and the original leaders of the two approaches are different. From the point of view of scientific attitudes, the important early figures in the school include Jacob Viner, Paul H. Douglas, and Henry Schultz. Knight and Simons were the leading early figures in Chicago's policy approach. There is also a difference in the scientific approach of Knight and Simons and that of economists such as Viner, Douglas, and Schultz. Although Knight and Simons emphasized the usefulness of competitive price theory, they did not insist on empirical testing of economic theories. In recent years, the promotion of empirical testing of theoretical generalizations has become one of the principal characteristics of the methodology of the school.

Competitive Price Theory

Economists at Chicago have always insisted on the usefulness of competitive price theory. In the 1930s and 1940s, when the theories of monopolistic competition and oligopoly were predominant at other universities, economists at the University of Chicago continued to stress the theory of perfect competition as the most useful approach to understanding economic activity. As stated by Friedman in his essay entitled "The Methodology of Positive Economics," the test of a good theory is "its ability to predict much from little" rather than the realism of its assumptions. A principal argument given in support of the theory of monopolistic competition is that it is descriptively more accurate than the theory of perfect competition. Also, critics of the Chicago school often reject the results of analyses using competitive price theory because they believe that the theory's assumptions of individual choice and maximizing behavior are unrealistic.

Competitive price theory has been extended by economists influenced by the Chicago school—many are not at the University of Chicago—to a wide range of problems traditionally viewed as outside economics. Ronald H. Coase has applied neoclassical economic analysis to the role of managerial coordination within the firm and the effect of transactions costs on individual bargaining; Gary S. Becker has analyzed human capital, marriage, and family planning using economic tools; Jacob Mincer has done important research on the labor-force participation of married women; and Richard A. Posner has examined legal decisions from the point of their effect on economic efficiency.

Positive Analysis

A major development coming out of the Chicago school has been the extension to governmental activities of the same type of positive analysis used in economics. The positive approach attempts to explain how the political process shapes public policies, and the analysis assumes that public policies reflect the self-interest of those involved. For example, Director's law (named for Aaron Director, a law professor at the University of Chicago) states that economic policies of government are often directed at benefiting the middle class, at the expense of both the very poor and the very rich. This is because the majority often controls political decisions, and it is assumed that the voting behavior of the middle class, which commands a majority of the vote, is based on self-interest. The positive approach to politics has mushroomed into a major field of economics known as public choice. The leaders in this field include James M. Buchanan and Gordon Tullock. The public-choice approach to government is very different from the traditional approach in which the economist assumes that he or she is offering advice to an all-wise and benevolent government.

Differences within the Chicago School

Although some of the attitudes and ideas associated with the Chicago school have continued over the years, there have been significant changes. While Simons stressed the importance of equality as well as freedom, Friedman and Stigler reject most governmental measures intended to reduce inequality. They are skeptical of the effects of egalitarian government programs and believe there is little relationship between the intent of such programs and their actual effects. Also, Friedman's interpretation of business cycles is very different from that of Simons. Simons's explanation of recessions emphasized the decline in business confidence and the fall in the velocity of money rather than the decline in the quantity of money. The countercyclical policies proposed by Simons—stabilization of a price level, fiscal policy, government antimonopoly programs, and reform of the financial structure to differentiate sharply between money and other types of financial assets—have been rejected by Friedman.

The Chicago School and Keynes

There has been some discussion among historians of economic thought of the relationship between the Chicago school and the economics of John Maynard Keynes.

The historical studies of J. Ronnie Davis have shown that during the Great Depression, Chicago economists recommended the use of budget deficits, and they were opposed to cutting money wages as a method of stimulating the economy. These are the same as the basic policies of the Keynesian revolution. Despite this, at Chicago there was not the enthusiasm for Keynes' *General Theory* that there was at other universities. There are some important differences between Keynes and the early Chicagoans. To Keynes, the purpose of fiscal deficits was to increase government expenditures and thus to increase aggregate demand. To the early Chicagoans, the purpose of the fiscal deficit was to increase the money supply, and their solution was called "fiscal inflation." In addition, while Keynes was pessimistic about the long-run prospects for full employment in capitalist economies, the Chicagoans were not.

There has also been some discussion of the relationship between Friedman's monetary theories and policies and those of his predecessors at the University of Chicago. Don Patinkin maintains that Friedman's reformulation of the quantity theory of money is more closely related to the Keynesian theory of liquidity preference than to the quantity theory of money held by the early Chicagoans. Recent historical research by George S. Tavlas has shown that Friedman's views of the causes of the Great Depression and his proposal to increase the money supply in proportion to the increase in output are similar to those of Paul H. Douglas, a professor of economics at the University of Chicago during the early period of the Chicago School.

References

Friedman, Milton, "The Methodology of Positive Economics," *Essays in Positive Economics*, University of Chicago Press, Chicago, 1953; Friedman, Milton, "The Monetary Theory and Policy of Henry Simons," *The Journal of Law and Economics*, vol. 10, October 1967, pp. 1–13; Friedman, Milton, "Schools at Chicago," *The University of Chicago Magazine*, August 1974, pp. 11–16; Miller, H. Laurence, "On the 'Chicago School of Economics,'" *The Journal of Political Economy*, vol. 70, February 1962, pp. 64–69; Samuels, Warren J. (ed.), *The Chicago School of Political Economy*, Michigan State University, East Lansing, Mich., 1976.

(*See also* Business cycles; Competition; Economics; Federal Reserve policy; Federal Reserve System; Government regulation of business; Indexation; Keynesian economics; Monetary policy; Money supply; Monopoly and oligopoly; Permanent income hypothesis; Price theory; Quantity theory of money; Velocity of circulation of money)

Colin D. Campbell

Classical liberalism

Classical liberalism may be defined simply as the social philosophy that recognizes the need for open markets and for decentralized control of the means of production for individual liberty. John Locke, the celebrated philosopher of the so-called glorious revolution, is considered to be the father of classical liberalism, although elements of his teachings can be located in Roman stoic thought as early as the fourth century B.C. In his *Second Treatise on Government* (1690), Locke developed three important notions about the relationship between the individual and government: first, that individuals existed in cooperative social groupings prior to the creation of civil government; second, that individuals enter into political society with certain natural rights that cannot be legitimately traded away in commercial exchange or eliminated by government; and third, that when government is no longer able (or willing) to protect these rights, the members of society are justified in overthrowing their government and replacing it with a more effective one. Of these three notions, the second and third are frequently cited by intellectual historians especially because they formed the antiauthoritarian ideologies of both the American and French Revolutions. Locke's first notion, that society existed prior to government, encouraged a search for the factors promoting order and organization among individuals and in this way served as an important formative influence on social scientific thought in the eighteenth century.

Classical Liberals Are Foes of Socialists

The eighteenth-century British philosophers, Bernard Mandeville, David Hume, Adam Smith, C. L. de Montesquieu, Edmund Burke, John Millar, Adam Ferguson, and later writers such as Sir Henry Maine, Carl Menger, Ludwig von Mises, and Friedrich A. von Hayek, explored the actual social processes by which custom, business law, private property, money and banking institutions, and so on come into existence and are maintained. Frequently, those institutions most useful to humanity evolved as an unintended consequence of self-interested behavior in the market. By way of contrast, those arrangements brought about by government planners often fail to meet their objectives and are chaotic and oppressive to individual liberty. For these reasons, modern classical liberals join company with traditional conservatives (followers of Burke) and warn of the dangers of damaging through government intervention in business the wisdom of the ages as contained in established customs and business practices. Classical liberals are the archfoes of socialists who propose centralized control of the means of production and the substitution of central planning for impersonal market mechanisms.

In the eighteenth and nineteenth centuries, economists explained how markets contain a variety of self-regulating devices that move resources (constantly) toward their most highly valued uses and thereby promote economic development. The role of open markets in eliminating waste and responding rapidly to changing consumer wants left classical liberals opposed to all those monopolization schemes that would restrict entry into markets and limit competition. Classical liberals generally oppose the creation of public utilities, the issuance of licenses and entry requirements into professions, the imposition of restrictions on international trade, immigration quotas, and the use of state power to restrict competition. Still, classical liberals are not advocates of strict laissez faire. They offer a long agenda of duties and responsibilities for the state to perform such as national defense, police protection, regulation of public health and industrial safety, provision of large-scale capital projects such as harbors and dams, patents to encourage innovation, and the creation of a sound and secure currency. As constitutionalists, classical liberals believe the purpose of the law is to provide a framework or rule of law within which individuals may freely associate and interact for their mutual benefit. Law must be designed to create broad incentives for individuals to take one course of action rather than another and be applied to all individuals regardless of race, religion, or personal wealth. At all times the political system must avoid substituting a rule of human beings for the rule of law because discretionary behavior on the political level can open the way toward abuses of state power in the form of political favoritism and corruption.

Fiscal Conservatism

As supporters of representative government, classical liberals wish to make the politicians responsible to the voters in the most obvious and basic ways possible. That is why they favor fiscal conservativism, that is, the creation of a close connection between government projects and the actual economic cost of those projects in the minds of the voters. If every dollar of government money spent in a fiscal year is financed by a dollar of current taxes, the voters would be informed of the economic cost of government programs quickly and dramatically. When, however, the state issues bonds and the banking system uses them as a basis for creating bank money (checking accounts), then the politicians choose to finance their spending by monetizing new debt rather than by raising taxes. Politicians prefer to increase the money supply rather than to raise taxes even when this policy results in severe inflation. That is because the voting population is generally unable to connect their loss of wealth through inflation with the successive bouts of government spending. The voters blame the rise of prices on scapegoats such as foreigners, unions, multinational corporations, or simply private greed, allowing the otherwise unacceptable public projects to escape voter scrutiny. Unexpected inflations produce great anxiety among the civilian population as wealth becomes redistributed in a mysterious manner. This fosters a general distrust for the market economy, which is blamed for the inflation and the economic uncertainty that accompanies it. Discouraged by inflation, many citizens support national economic planning and with it the severe modification of capitalist institutions. With national planning, politicians are better able to pursue costly government projects. Classical liberals view these trends as a threat to prosperity and political liberty.

For this reason classical liberals such as Ludwig von Mises favored the international gold standard. The plan was to remove the size of the various national money supplies from the hands of the politicians. Contemporary classical liberals such as Milton Friedman also want to limit the money-issuing powers of the state but by means of a constitutional amendment limiting by law the rate of growth of the money supply. Classical liberals understand that individual liberty and open-market processes cannot survive during an escalating inflation when the majority of voters demand and willingly elect totalitarian parties that promise stability at the expense of liberty.

References

Baumgarth, William P., "Hayek and Political Order: The Rule of Law," *Journal of Libertarian Studies*, vol. 2, Winter 1978, pp. 11–28; Buchanan, James M., and Richard E. Wagner, *Democracy in Deficit*, Academic Press, New York, 1977; Nozick, Robert, *Anarchy, State and Utopia*, Basic Books, New York, 1974; Rothbard, Murray N., *For a New Liberty*, Macmillan, New York, 1973; Tame, Chris R., "The Revolution of Reason: Peter Gay, The Enlightenment, and the Ambiguities of Classical Liberalism," *Journal of Libertarian Studies*, vol. 1, Summer 1977, pp. 217–228.

(*See also* Austrian economics; Economic history and theory; Economics; Laissez faire)

Laurence S. Moss

Classical school

Ever since Karl Marx referred to all those economists with a less than perfect vision of how the economy operated as belonging to the classical school, it has been usual for historians to speak of the classical school as representing a naive or even primitive understanding of the economic system. This label is commonly attached to the group of predominantly British economists who followed Adam Smith in the search for the laws regulating the production, distribution, and consumption of wealth. The group of classical writers includes David Ricardo (*Principles of Political Economy and Taxation*, 1817), James Mill (*Elements of Political Economy*, 1821), John R. McCulloch (*Principles of Political Economy*, 1825; *An Outline of the Science of Political Economy*, 1836), Robert Torrens (*An Essay on the Production of Wealth*, 1821), Mountifort Longfield (*Lectures on Political Economy*, 1834), John Elliot Cairnes (*Some Leading Principles of Political Economy*, 1874), John Stuart Mill (*Principles of Political Economy*, 1848), and several French writers including Jean Baptiste Say (*A Treatise on Political Economy; or the Production, Distribution, and Consumption of Wealth*, 1821).

It is usual to date the end of the classical school sometime before the publication of Alfred Marshall's *Principles of Economics* (1890)—an event that marks the ascendancy of the Cambridge school of economics, but there is major disagreement on this point. John Maynard Keynes described most of the economic work that predated his *General Theory of Employment, Interest and Money* (1936) as classical because it accepted what he called the erroneous doctrine that the economy naturally tends to a position of full employment of labor and other resources. If we follow Keynes, we would have to include nearly the entire early Cambridge school as part of the classical school.

Smith's Influence

Disagreement about definitions stems from the fact that there was no classical school in the sense of a well-defined group of economists drawing intellectual sustenance from a single great master and acting in combination for a given purpose. In many cases the label classical school has served mostly as a polemical device to make one writer's personal theories seem superior to earlier alternative points of view. This is unfortunate because the period following Adam Smith's *Wealth of Nations* (1776) is bubbling with analytic contributions and suggestive controversies that reappear in different form with every new generation of writers. Institutions change, but the substantive issues of social and political organization retain a permanence that time has difficulty erasing. We need only point to the similarities between the monetary-fiscal debate of recent years and the older nineteenth-century controversy between the currency and banking schools following the Napoleonic Wars.

Still, there is something to be said for grouping these writers together under the heading classical. They shared a great respect for and profound intellectual debt to Smith's *Wealth of Nations*. This is not to say that they revered the work or swore allegiance to every doctrine of the old master—quite the contrary. The classical writers used Smith's writing as a springboard for their own analyses of economic problems. Often a single chapter, paragraph, or even sentence in the *Wealth of Nations* launched an enormously rich and lively secondary literature full of doctrinal innovation.

Consider the impact of Smith's casual remark that the profits of the capitalists represent a deduction from the worker's wages. Karl Marx used the deduction theory of profit to explain the origin of surplus value. Furthermore, Marx declared that one fundamental task of scientific socialism was to explain how this surplus value gets extracted from the working class when the entire market process is based on voluntary exchange. Ricardo molded the deduction theory into his inverse profit-wage theorem. According to Ricardo, a general rise in real wages will lower profits—the two always vary inversely. Government-imposed taxes affect the allocation of resources, but unless these taxes also alter the general rate of wages, they will have no effect on the rate of profit and the distribution of income. Ricardo went on to explain how diminishing returns in agriculture result in a rise in food prices and wages, ultimately lowering profits and propelling the economy toward the stationary state in which both capital accumulation and population growth end.

The Irish economist Mountifort Longfield readily admitted Smith's point that profits represent a deduction from the worker's wage, but he explained with considerable optimism that the worker is not exploited because net wages are considerably greater than what could be earned by working unaided without any capital at all. Longfield went on to develop this idea into a marginal productivity account of how capital goods are priced. Finally, in the famous wage-fund controversy that raged during the latter part of the nineteenth century between W. Thornton, J. S. Mill, and others, the issue was whether or not organized labor could negotiate a larger share of the national income at the expense of the capitalists.

Deductions from the laborer's wage can be arbitrary or necessary; they can result from outmoded institutions or correspond to important psychological determinants of economic action. N. W. Senior implied that the latter was the case in his abstinence theory of profit, which later influenced both J. S. Mill's and Alfred Marshall's thinking about profit and its relationship to wages. Senior insisted that profit was needed to compensate the capitalists for the inconvenience of waiting for repayment of their loans.

This thumbnail sketch of the impact that just one of Adam Smith's remarks has had on generations of writers illustrates in what form a classical school existed in the history of economic thought. Essentially, the classical school consisted of a diverse number of talented writers who developed ideas and corrected alleged errors found in the *Wealth of Nations* and in so doing improved the analytic foundations of the nascent science of economics.

References

Hollander, Samuel, *The Economics of David Ricardo*, University of Toronto Press, Toronto, 1979; Moss, Laurence S., *Mountifort Longfield: Ireland's First Professor of Political Economy*, Green Hill, Ottawa, Ill., 1976; O'Brien, D. P., *The Classical Economists*, Clarendon Press, Oxford, 1975; Schwartz, Pedro, *The New Political Economy of J. S. Mill*, Duke University Press, Durham, N.C., 1972; Sowell, Thomas, *Classical Economics Reconsidered*, Princeton University Press, Princeton, N.J., 1974.

(See also Cambridge school; Economic history and theory; Economics; Laissez faire; Marshallian economics; Neoclassical economics)

Laurence S. Moss

Closed-end investment companies

Investment companies obtain funds from individuals and buy financial assets. Closed-end funds are investment companies whose shares are purchased by investors. Closed-end funds do not redeem their shares at prices that reflect the day-by-day value of their security holdings as do open-end funds. Instead, closed-end fund share prices fluctuate according to supply and demand, often selling at deep discounts from their per-share net asset values.

These funds are called closed-end because the number of shares is not likely to be reduced unless such funds buy in their own shares in the open market. The number of closed-end shares is also more or less fixed in terms of new offerings. Like other corporations, closed-end funds may sell to new or existing stockholders through rights or under prospectus, but closed-end funds do not support sales organizations by paying high commissions, and the same lack of commissions means less support for the shares from brokers—especially since 1970, when the nation's largest broker began to offer open-end shares. As a result, this route to equity capital expansion is restricted if not closed.

The number of closed-end shares can be reduced, however, if closed-end companies purchase their own shares in the open market. The investment companies have an incentive to do so when their shares are selling at a deep discount to the market value of their assets since this would increase net asset value per share—a chief index of management's performance. In practice, however, most closed-end funds have failed to take advantage of this long-run opportunity to attract new investors because, in the short run, such policies reduce the amount of net assets under management, which usually determines fund management's remuneration. This occurs because some assets must be sold to buy in the funds' shares, and only the amount representing the discount can be reinvested.

The opportunity to buy securities at substantial discounts from the current market prices of closed-end funds' underlying assets is an example of an imperfection in modern capital asset pricing and efficient market theory, according to Burton G. Malkiel (1977), who, through regressions, attempts to explain closed-end funds' discounts. Tax liability on unrealized capital gains in closed-end funds, in particular, has not been sufficient to account for the discounts. Malkiel also attempts to measure the impact of other more subjective factors such as past performance in terms of net asset per share and investment policies that permit funds to purchase relatively illiquid foreign and letter stock. He finds that adding these factors to built-in tax liability to explain wide discounts does not add significantly to the power of his equation. Variations in the level of management fees are also found to be insignificant in Malkiel's regressions.

Malkiel (1978) has suggested that the risk of a wider discount can be hedged in part by the purchase of a special kind of closed-end fund, namely, the dual fund. Dual funds allow one class of shareholders to collect all the dividends while an equal number of shareholders receive the value of all assets after income shares have been redeemed at their purchase price. Since dual funds have a fixed expiration date, any widening of the discount between the underlying assets of both income and capital shares will be reduced as liquidation approaches. Moreover, upon redemption, any discount will be eliminated. Malkiel therefore suggests the purchase of equal amounts of income and capital shares of dual funds to create an investment that is equivalent to a closed-end fund with this additional advantage: liquidation (and hence the elimination of the discount) is assured by a certain date.

Malkiel also notes that average discount of selected closed-end dual funds (with matched income and capital shares) appears to decline when the funds' share prices are declining and to rise when funds' shares prices rise. It follows that the risk of such investments is reduced in line with the negative covariance of these funds' discount and their market prices. For this reason the average beta (a measure of market-adjusted risk) on closed-end funds' shares is lower than the average beta on shares held in the same closed-end's portfolio—and dramatically so for pairings of dual fund capital and income share investments. This results in higher returns from the same investment with lower risk. As indicated, this is in apparent conflict with current capital asset pricing theory, which, with restrictive assumptions, is based on the theory of efficient markets.

There are a number of nondiversified (and generally smaller) closed-end funds that did not transform themselves into diversified funds after the passage of the Investment Company Act in 1940. Unlike diversified closed-end funds, these corporations may continue to hold securities of particular issuers (including the U.S. government and other investment companies) in excess of 5 percent of their total assets, and they may hold more than 10 percent of the voting securities of particular issuers. Because of the lack of restrictions on such companies and because they may hold large blocks of individual securities for long-term control purposes, unrealized capital gains (and hence built-in capital gains tax liability) is often substantial. For this reason and others most nondiversified closed-end funds sell at deeper discounts from their net asset value per share than diversified funds.

Dual Funds

In general, original prospectuses for dual fund share offerings promised both classes of shareholders that investments would be made in common stocks providing somewhat below-average current yields, with the expectation that cash dividends for such securities would rise (or commence) after a reasonable period. The inherent conflict of interest between the two classes of shareholders was also addressed in some cases with a promise to include investments affording above-average yields if there was an expectation of capital appreciation within the holding period.

Income Shareholders Income shareholders in most dual funds are entitled to cumulative dividends, whether or not earned, up to some stipulated nominal amount, payable quarterly, with any excess net investment income in any fiscal year being distributed in the form of an extra dividend. In general, such "extras" do not apply against minimum dividend payments in the future, however. Thus, in the event that the minimum dividend is not earned and is in arrears, net investment income distributed in any year is applied first to cover such arrearages.

As a rule, income shares are noncallable prior to the date on which the liquidation of the dual fund is called for, and on that date income shareholders are entitled to receive out of the assets of the dual fund then on hand a specified par value for each of their shares—generally close to or equal to their purchase price—plus accumulated and unpaid dividends through that date. Since income shares have 200 percent of their initial asset coverage, it is generally assumed that there would be sufficient capital to pay off the income shareholders.

Net investment income distributable to income shares is generally interest, dividends, and other income received or accrued less management fees, bank custodian fees, taxes (except federal and foreign capital gains taxes), and all other expenses that might be properly charged against income. On the other hand, capital gains, stock dividends, and distributions designated as return of capital, and also transfer taxes and brokerage commissions, do not enter into the computation of net investment income. Moreover, to the extent that there are dividend arrearages in the income shares at the time of redemption, management fees and other current expenses are generally borne by the capital shareholders.

Capital Shareholders   All net capital gains accrue to the capital shares, but they are also the first to bear capital losses with the fund reinvesting all long-term capital gains. Capital shareholders are entitled to credits for taxes paid by the dual fund on such gains. Therefore: (1) the capital shareholder includes as his or her own long-term capital gain the pro rata share (determined without reference to income shares) of the dual fund's long-term capital gain on which the fund has paid the applicable tax; (2) the capital shareholder will therefore be entitled to a credit on the return or a refund of this tax; (3) the capital shareholder will be allowed to increase the adjusted tax basis of the capital shares by 75 percent of the amount so included in the return.

If short-term capital gains are distributed to the holder of capital shares to entitle the dual fund to tax treatment as a regulated investment company, such distributions will be reportable as ordinary income. Finally, the amount paid upon redemption by the fund for the shares of the capital shareholder will constitute a long-term capital gain (or loss) to the extent that such amount is greater (or less) than the adjusted tax basis for the shares, provided that the holding period is greater than 6 months.

References

Malkiel, Burton G., "The Valuation of Closed-End Investment Company Shares," *Journal of Finance*, June 1977; Malkiel, Burton G., and Paul B. Firstenberg, *Journal of Portfolio Management*, Summer 1978; Pratt, Eugene J., "Myths Associated with Closed End Investment Company Discounts," *Financial Analysts Journal*, July–August, 1966; Snyder Linda, "The Closed End Funds May be Opening Up," *Fortune*, February 1978, p. 137; Stoll, Hans, "Discounts and Premium on Shares of Diversified Closed End Investments Funds," Working Paper 11-73, Rodney L. White Center for Financial Research, University of Pennsylvania, Philadelphia, 1973; Thompson, Rex, "Capital Market Efficiency and the Information Content of Discounts and Premiums of Closed End Shares: An Empirical Analysis," Working Paper 30, Graduate School of Industrial Administration, Carnegie-Mellon University, Pittsburgh, February 1978.

(*See also* Mutual funds)

Arnold X. Moskowitz and George Harben

Cobweb theorem

The cobweb theorem concerns fluctuations over time in the prices and quantities of some competitively produced commodities. The fluctuations take on cyclical patterns with prices and quantities moving up and down in opposite directions. Such fluctuations, which have long been observed, occur in many agricultural products, for example. When prices are high, growers expand their outputs with the result that after a while they drive prices down. The lower prices in turn cause cutbacks in production, which consequently brings a later upswing in prices. Then the cycle begins again. The cobweb theorem is a general explanation of such cycles, in the form of a particular demand-supply-price analysis. The name "cobweb" comes from the appearance of one of the diagrams that can be drawn to illustrate the theorem.

The cobweb analysis applies to competitive markets. Demand is a function simply of price, but supply is a function of the price in the previous period of time. The period can be 1 year, as with annual crops. Or the period can be 2, 3, or more years, as with hogs, beef cattle, fruit trees, etc. The period of time in fact could conceivably be a whole generation. Alfred Marshall (*Principles of Economics*, 1890) said that the supply of labor in an occupation in any one generation "tends to conform to its earnings not in that but in the preceding generation." During the period of time under consideration, producers decide on volumes of output that they can little change once they have made their commitments: crops are sown, animals are bred, trees are planted.

Three simple models illustrate the essentials of the cobweb theorem. In the models, demand is a linear function of price in each period of time. That is, $D = f(p_t)$. Supply, however, is lagged, being a linear function of price in the preceding period. That is, $S = f(p_t - 1)$. In the three models both the demand and supply functions remain constant for several periods. In each model the equilibrium price and quantity are given by the equality of demand and supply, by the intersection of the two curves. The cobweb theorem addresses itself to the kinds of fluctuations of prices and quantities about their equilibriums.

Perpetual Oscillation Model

The model of perpetual oscillation has demand and supply curves the slopes of which, disregarding sign, are equal. If the price is at its equilibrium level, it will stay there indefinitely, under the assumption of constant demand and supply. But suppose that the price in period 1 is above equilibrium. Then in period 1 the producers will, under the lagged-supply assumption, produce and offer for sale a quantity larger than the equilibrium amount. But that same quantity has to sell in period 2 for less than the equilibrium price. Believing that this low price will prevail in period 3, the producers cut back to a smaller quantity in period 3. The smaller quantity sells for a higher price in period 3. This higher price is exactly the same as the price in period 1, owing to the assumed equality of the slopes of the linear demand and supply curves. Then the cycle begins anew. In succeeding periods the price will be high and low and the quantity small and large. Price and quantity oscillate perpetually about equilibrium. The cycles are exactly periodic. Their constant amplitude depends simply on the equal slopes of the linear demand and supply curves. To bring the results of this model close to reality requires only slight modifications of some of the assumptions. Let the demand and supply curves become nonlinear, let them change from one period to the next, and let their slopes be unequal. Then the cycle would no longer be exactly periodic nor would its amplitude be constant. But there would still be a cycle, irregular and untidy, resembling perhaps some of those that have long been observed.

Damped Oscillation Model

In the damped oscillation model of the cobweb theorem, the slope of the demand curve is less than that of the supply curve, that is, the producers' quantity adjustments in response to variations in price are relatively smaller than the buyers' adjustments. Suppose again that the price in period 1 is above equilibrium. Then in period 2 the producers will produce and offer for sale more than the equilibrium quantity. This sells in period 2 for a price below equilibrium. Then in period 3 the producers reduce the quantity they produce. The resulting higher price in period 3 is not as high as was the price in period 1. The cause is the lesser slope of the linear demand curve. But the price in period 3 is still above equilibrium, and so in period 4 the amount produced causes the price to drop, but not to as low a level as in period 2. What happens in this model, then, is that the oscillations about equilibrium are damped, becoming ever smaller. The cycle attenuates, and as eventual equilibrium is reached, the cycle ceases to exist. But when demand and supply are allowed to become nonlinear and to change, the tendency to equilibrium becomes muddied. Thus, there is still a cycle of sorts because the tendency to equilibrium is constantly upset by changes in demand and supply.

Explosive Oscillation Model

The third of the simple cobweb models yields explosive oscillations. This model has a demand curve with a slope greater than that of the supply curve. In their ever-wider divergences from equilibrium, the quantities sold by the producers in successive periods cause ever-wider movements of prices. Prices plunge and soar as quantities shrink and swell. It seems indeed as if this particular demand-supply-price mechanism must fly apart. Yet everything in this model is otherwise normal—the demand curve slopes down, the supply curve slopes up, and the curves intersect. But the mechanism does not break down, because demand and supply do indeed change and because linearity is most unlikely at extreme values of demand and supply functions. The third model, at least, shows the possibility of ever-wider fluctuations.

The critical assumption throughout is the lagged-supply response. Its rigidity makes the models work as they do. Modification of the assumption to allow for differences in the behavior of producers brings formidable complexities. But commodity cycles persist and are real. No matter what sophistication modern producers put into estimating future prices, it seems that the lagged-supply response continues as a pattern of behavior.

Significance of Cobweb Theorem

One theoretical significance of the cobweb theorem is its holding the kernel of a dynamic theory—variables at different points of time are related in a precise way. Another of its larger meanings concerns the functioning of competitive markets. If they are to behave in such a way as to approach the theorists' ideal of efficiency, competitive markets must constantly and everywhere tend to equilibrium. Although efficiency embraces more than equilibrium, equilibrium is its sine qua non. And so the cobweb theorem draws attention to one more of the imperfections of actual competitive markets.

References

Ezekiel, Mordecai, "The Cobweb Theorem," *Quarterly Journal of Economics*, February 1938, reprinted in American Economic Association, *Readings in Business Cycle Theory*, Blakiston, Philadelphia, 1944, chap. 21; Samuelson, Paul A., "Dynamic Process Analysis," in Howard S. Ellis, (ed),, *A Survey of Contemporary Economics*, Blakiston, Philadelphia, 1948, chap. 10.

(See also Competition; Demand; Dynamic analysis; Expectations; General equilibrium; Supply)

Donald S. Watson

Colbertism (see Mercantilism)

Collective bargaining

There are many views regarding collective bargaining depending upon whether one is a trade union member; an employer of labor represented by a trade union; an employer of nonunion workers; a practitioner of collective bargaining such as a labor lawyer, labor relations consultant, union business agent or representative, labor arbitrator or mediator; or a scholar or educator in the field. These varied views are difficult to distill into a neat and precise definition, but there are some common threads interwoven through the various viewpoints and approaches to the subject that make it possible to give some cohesive definition, though imprecise, to collective bargaining.

The term collective bargaining originated in the 1890s in the scholarly works of Sidney and Beatrice Webb, who were members of England's Fabian Society. It was first introduced in the United States at the turn of the century by the Industrial Commission, which was created by an Act of Congress in 1898. Hence, collective bargaining is a relatively new process and thus is rather recent in engaging the interest of economists, historians, and other social scientists. While there is no neat and precise body of principles to render collective bargaining a science, it is an important human endeavor which occupies the interests of economists, historians, political scientists, sociologists, social psychologists, legal scholars, and practitioners from a variety of backgrounds.

Labor Agreement

Collective bargaining is a dynamic process of trade union representation of employees to employers for the fundamental purpose of negotiating wages, hours, and other terms or conditions of employment into a written labor agreement, and for the purpose of establishing a system of industrial jurisprudence to resolve any grievances which may arise thereunder. Thus, collective bargaining provides a representative function to serve the interests and welfare of trade union members. It is a bilateral means toward achieving ends, the latter being generally wages, hours, and other terms or conditions of employment. The labor agreement defines the terms and conditions of the employment contract between the employer and the individual employee. Adopting a political analogy, we may say that collective bargaining can be described by three functions:

1. A legislative function which culminates into a private law, a labor agreement which is enforceable in legal tribunals and the process of labor arbitration

2. An executive function which requires the administration of the employment relationship between employer and employee in accordance with the labor agreement

3. A judicial function wherein third-party neutral labor arbitrators resolve differences regarding conflicting interpretations of specific language of the labor agreement and adjudicate any grievances that may arise thereunder.

Fair Treatment

Collective bargaining provides the means toward affording fair treatment in the processing of employee grievances through the grievance machinery incorporated into the labor agreement without the necessity of incurring the huge time-consuming expense of litigation. Some authorities refer to this procedure as the "absolute law of fair treatment." Collective bargaining also provides a means of equal treatment of equals in that as the employer-union relationship matures, and as experience is gathered in dealing with day-to-day routine matters, a common body of shop law evolves which may or may not be incorporated with the formal labor agreement or may be mutually accepted as common practice binding both employers and employees. A fundamental aim of collective bargaining is to provide a system of relative claims to available work. There are a variety of techniques to achieve this goal, but all have the common characteristic of providing individual job security through a system of recognizing years of service to the employer as a principal means of determining promotability, order of layoff when economic and/or technological conditions necessitate a reduction in force, and a recall to work from layoff status. Very often, however, strict seniority or job tenure is modified or qualified by skill and ability to perform available work and/or other eligibility conditions reflecting one's training and experience.

All of the above refers to the micro aspects of the employer-employee relationship—that between the individual employer and the union which represents employees of that employer. There is, however, another dimension of collective bargaining which is more aggregative and involves the trade union organization as a political institution to achieve economic security and welfare needs of constituents through political action. Such activity transcends collective bargaining in the conventional sense but is still an important raison d'être of the trade union movement. This is true of large national union organizations and is a particularly important function of federations of trade unions. Thus, trade unions and trade union movements engage in activities which go beyond collective bargaining as described above.

Industrial Jurisprudence

In the absence of collective bargaining, the fundamental questions between employers and employees regarding wages, hours, and other terms or conditions of employment are left to the parties themselves functioning within the broad parameters of their relevant labor market. Under the latter circumstances, the employer and employee determine substantive terms of the employment relationship subject to market forces. These market forces provide the important economic function of allocating scarce labor resources through the pricing mechanism; however, in this case, the important dimension of industrial jurisprudence is left to the good offices of the employer. Consequently, any grievances that may arise between the employer and employee are resolved by the employer unilaterally and, of course, without any provision that unresolved matters between the parties may be adjudicated by a third-party neutral.

Under collective bargaining the employer does not have unilateral authority to make ultimate decisions regarding an employee. A system of industrial jurisprudence prevails that provides bargaining members due process in resolving disputes with employers which provides a check on the power of employers. That is, the employee is provided an assurance of equitable treatment and, in fact, has an absolute claim to fair treatment through the grievance procedure negotiated in virtually all labor agreements. The collective bargaining agreement provides for individual job security or job rights based on some form of seniority which undergirds a system of relative claims to available work determined by seniority rights on the job. Thus, it is important to recognize that the collective bargaining agreement transcends the mere determination of the wage and effort bargain by providing for an individual's relative job security and assurance of fair treatment. In this respect, these characteristics of collective bargaining are unique to the United States in that they reflect the constitutional system of governance. If collective bargaining provided for nothing else but relative job security and fair treatment for employees, it would still be a worthy institution to preserve in the absence of alternative means toward these ends.

References

Beal, Edwin F., E. D. Wickersham, and P. K. Kienast, *The Practice of Collective Bargaining*, 5th ed., Irwin, Homewood, Ill., 1976; Davey, Harold W., *Contemporary Collective Bargaining*, 3d ed., Prentice-Hall, Englewood Cliffs, N.J., 1972; Perlman, Selig: "The Principles of Collective Bargaining," in E. Wight Bakke and Clark Kerr, *Unions, Management and the Public*, 2d ed., Harcourt, Brace, New York, 1960; Sturmthal, Adolph (ed.), *Contemporary Collective Bargaining in Seven Countries*, Institute of International Industrial and Labor Relations, Cornell University, Ithaca, N.Y., 1957; Trotta, Maurice, *Collective Bargaining*, Simmons-Boardman, New York, 1962.

(*See also* Labor-management relations; Labor unions)

Sam Barone

Command economy (see Fascism)

Commodity exchange

A commodity exchange is an association of individuals and/or firms which provides a physical marketplace for the open, competitive, and continuous purchase or sale of various commodities (grains, meats, metals, wood, financial instruments), some on a cash basis for immediate or forward delivery, but most in the form of futures contracts which are binding, standardized, transferable agreements to buy (take delivery of) or to sell (make delivery of) a specific amount and grade of commodity at a future date for the price established at the time of the trade agreement.

A commodity exchange is distinctly different from both a securities (stock) exchange and an options exchange. A securities exchange is an organized trading place where brokers and dealers meet for the purchase and sale of securities, especially stocks. An options exchange is the central marketplace for the trading of put and call options which give the holder the right to sell or to purchase a given number of shares of a stock at a specified price during a given time period.

Function and Governance

The exchange itself neither buys nor sells nor sets the prices of the commodities traded, but simply provides a central facility where its members—and the public through the members—can trade cash and especially futures contracts. During the course of established trading hours while traders are actively engaged in the buying and selling of futures contracts either for hedging or speculative purposes, the open, competitive bidding for various commodities is, perhaps, the best example of free-market enterprise which exists today. Through the bids and counterbids of the traders, a realistic price-discovery mechanism is at work. Finalized trading agreements represent, in effect, a commodity's most accurate current price, which in the final analysis reflects a complex combination of such determining influences as supply and demand, weather, crop expectations, and economic and political developments of both national and international dimensions. Besides providing the marketplace where the price-discovery mechanism can take place, the exchange provides for the accurate, quick collection and dissemination of market prices and data about the major factors (supply and demand, weather, etc.) which affect those prices.

The exchange is a self-governing association. Member committees are responsible for policymaking in different areas of exchange business. Admission to an exchange and to trading on its floor is controlled by the members and is given a value through the sale and purchase of "seats" or memberships by a bid and offer process administered by exchange officials. The number of seats is ordinarily kept at a set level.

The integrity of the trades executed on the exchange floor is secured and protected by regulating the requirements for membership. The credibility of prices and the enforcement of the binding obligations of exchange-traded contracts are ensured by requirements of financial and character standards for members. The credibility of prices negotiated on organized, self-regulated exchanges enhances their performance as allocators of an economy's agricultural, financial, and mineral resources over time.

The exchange obliges its members to observe the association's rules and regulations which cover all aspects of exchange business, including floor operations, customer dealings, financial compliance, arbitration of disputes, government obligations, and the detailed procedures governing the proper trading of individual commodities. Those found in noncompliance are subject to penalties, suspension, and/or loss of membership.

In the United States, a commodity futures exchange must receive official designation as an approved market by the Commodity Futures Trading Commission, the independent federal agency with exclusive jurisdiction over all futures trading on exchanges. Futures contracts proposed for exchange trading must also receive prior approval from that agency. A principal requirement for such approval is a statement of the evidence that the contract will provide benefits both to those who take part in the market and to the public as a whole. These benefits generally issue from the fact that the futures contract will offer a convenient opportunity for risk-averse participants to transfer risks which are a burden to them (hedgers) to others (speculators) who are more willing or able to bear the risks.

History of Commodity Futures Trading

The fundamental principles underlying commodity futures trading go back to ancient Greece and Rome where markets already showed a degree of formalization with a fixed time and place for trading, a marketplace, common barter and currency systems, and a practice of contracting for future delivery. Exchanges, however primitive, were organized at crossroads and ports wherever wheat and other agricultural commodities were cultivated, stored, or traded. Most of them were located near bodies of water to take advantage of favorable transportation costs for bulk cargoes.

These practices survived the Dark Ages and reemerged during the Middle Ages in the form of the medieval fair with its preannounced markets at fixed times and places. Most trading at the fairs was for the immediate delivery of the cash (spot) commodity, but contracting for a commodity's future delivery, with standards of quality established by samples, had begun. The chief contribution of the medieval fair was the formalization of trading practices, which—once codified in England—became known as the Law Merchant. The code effectively established standards of trading conduct acceptable to local authorities.

Early commodity exchanges supervised trading in the cash commodity. Each transaction was consummated by the simultaneous transfer of the physical commodity between the traders. The exchanges provided the physical facilities for trading and the rules to govern the arbitration of disputes among traders and merchants. Contracts specifying other than immediate delivery of the commodity took the form of import or export licenses granted by a municipal or national government.

Forward and Future Markets

Forward markets in commodities further developed in conjunction with cash markets when communication and transportation facilities improved to the point that commodities could be accurately described and reliably delivered. Markets for agricultural commodities such as cotton, tobacco, sugar, and wheat flourished in the decades immediately preceding the Civil War, and as they evolved, contracts specifying the delivery of a certain commodity at a certain price, time, and place became more prevalent. But such trading was still limited because traders had to possess essentially coincident desires for a commodity so the contract could acquire a market value.

Dissatisfaction on the part of traders and users of commodities with specific forward contracts led to the development of standard grades for agricultural commodities. Standard grades for commodities accepted by traders and users enabled them to create standard contracts, specifying all the requirements for transferring the physical product (time, location, quality, and quantity) except the price. The price of the standard futures contract was determined on the trading floor of the commodity exchange. By the middle of the nineteenth century, futures contracts were being traded in major cities such as Chicago, New Orleans, New York, Liverpool, London, Berlin, and elsewhere.

While some contemporary commodity exchanges provide markets in cash, forward contracts, and futures contracts, commodity futures contracts enjoy by far the largest volume of business. The volume of futures contracts traded in the last decade on United States exchanges, for example, increased over 450 percent from 13.6 million contracts in 1970 to 76 million in 1979.

Today, futures contracts in the United States are traded in more than 30 commodities, including grains, livestock, metals, tropical foodstuffs, foreign currencies, and financial instruments (mortgage interest rates, commercial paper, U.S. Treasury bonds and notes, etc.).

The officially designated commodity exchanges are: Amex Commodities Exchange, Inc. (an affiliate of the American Stock Exchange); the Chicago Board of Trade; the Chicago Mercantile Exchange; the Coffee, Sugar & Cocoa Exchange (in New York); the Commodity Exchange, Inc. (New York); the MidAmerica Commodity Exchange (Chicago); the Minneapolis Grain Exchange; the New York Cotton Exchange; the Kansas City Board of Trade; the New York Mercantile Exchange; and the New York Futures Exchange (an affiliate of the New York Stock Exchange).

The Futures Contract

A futures contract is a legally binding commitment to deliver or take delivery of a given quantity and quality of a commodity at a price agreed upon in the trading pit or ring of a commodity exchange at the time the contract is executed. The seller has the option to deliver the commodity sometime during the specified future delivery month. Delivery against a futures contract with a commodity of a superior or inferior quality may be made at a premium over or a discount under the agreed-upon price.

Futures contracts are cleared through the clearinghouse division or separate clearing corporation of the commodity exchange. The clearing corporation assumes the responsibility to buyer and seller respectively as a third-party guarantor of the transaction.

Standardization of futures contracts as to grade, size, and delivery makes one futures contract fully identical and interchangeable with other futures contracts of the same delivery month. This interchangeability means that the original seller can offset his or her obligation to deliver the commodity against the contract, once the price risk has ended, by offsetting or liquidating the contract with an equal and opposite purchase of a futures contract. The buyer has the same ability to offset his or her obligation to take delivery of the actual commodity, once the price risk has ended, through an equal and opposite sale of a futures contract.

Standardization of terms and the ability to offset contracts make futures markets extremely beneficial to a variety of users by providing financial protection against price volatility without having to make or take delivery against the futures contracts.

Commercial firms, producers, merchandisers, and processors of commodities recognize the generally parallel pattern in price movements between cash commodities and futures contracts for those commodities. News of crop losses due to bad weather, for example, is quickly reflected in higher cash prices as buyers seek to buy and store the commodity in anticipation of later shortages. At the same time, futures prices are also bid higher as buyers anticipate the impact of the shortages, not only at harvest but through the balance of the marketing year.

On the other hand, news of higher-than-expected supplies results in weakening cash prices as buyers lower their bids in anticipation of easily available supplies. At the same time, buyers in the futures market scale down their bids on the prospects of increased supplies.

Hedging

Observing these parallel price movements, commercial firms realize that while certain economic factors might result in a cash transaction loss, the situation could be turned into a futures market profit if a position were taken equal but opposite to the risk position in the cash market.

A wheat-flour miller, for instance, might be committed to deliver 500 bags of flour to a baker at a fixed price at a time in the future. The miller might not yet have purchased the wheat, lacking the space to store it until it could be processed. A sudden rise in wheat prices could spell a serious loss. The raw material costs would climb while sales income would remain fixed.

The flour miller could have some protection through the use of futures contracts. As a protective measure—to hedge the risk—the miller would buy wheat futures contracts in an amount roughtly equal to the amount of grain needed to make the flour which he had agreed to deliver to the baker. The miller would buy futures contracts in the futures delivery month closest to the time in which the wheat had to be purchased to process the flour. When needed, the wheat would be bought in the cash market, the purchase of wheat futures contracts would be offset with an equal sale, and the flour would be made and delivered to the customer.

Supposing that wheat prices had risen and that the miller had not hedged in futures, in which case the miller would be faced with smaller profits, a break-even situation, or a substantial loss. Although the cash cost of the wheat had risen, wiping out or cutting profits, futures prices also would have responded to the same economic factors. Wheat futures prices would be higher than at the time the contracts were purchased. In selling futures at the later higher price, the flour miller could recover the loss from increased cash costs.

The risk for the producer of the commodities is that the value of those commodities will deteriorate before they can be marketed. The risk for the processor or user of commodities is the reverse—that the supply situation will tighten to a point that rising prices will add to costs and impair profits. The producer or owner of commodities will use a selling or "short" hedge as a protection against declining values. The user of commodities will use a buying or "long" hedge in futures contracts to protect against rising prices.

Speculating

In addition to hedgers, speculators are another group of users of the futures market; they in effect provide liquidity to the markets and make the hedging mechanism possible.

Noting the inherent price volatility in commodities and the tendency to parallel movements in cash and futures prices, the speculator is attracted to the markets by the possibility of gain from the changing prices in commodities. If the speculator were correct in forecasting price movements, a profit could be made by buying and later selling futures contracts or vice versa. Offsetting transactions eliminate the initial obligation to take or make delivery of the actual commodity.

Though the late 1800s were filled with incidents of public outrage against alleged speculative abuses in commodities and securities markets, the self-regulatory efforts of the exchanges went far to correct problems. It soon became apparent that the presence of speculators in the markets had great economic benefit in providing the ready liquidity to absorb the growing commercial hedging activity.

Because speculators are willing to enter the market to take advantage of even small expected changes in price, they bear the price risk which the hedger wants to transfer, and at the same time they provide the necessary liquidity so that even hedging in large volumes may be done with minimal price effects. In a study of a variety of commodities traded on futures markets, economist Roger W. Gray of Stanford concluded that markets with relatively high levels of speculation are most effective for hedging and those with low levels of speculation are least effective for hedging.

Still other academic studies contend that prices for commodities in which there is no futures trading are more erratic than prices for commodities which are traded on futures exchanges. In this very important sense, commodity futures markets contribute to economic stability.

Worldwide Economic Implications

Commodity exchanges in the United States bear marked similarity to exchanges in other countries. Differences in trading techniques, financing of traders and their customers, governance, and commodities are the salient features distinguishing each nation's markets. The function and contribution of these exchanges to the economic viability of a nation's raw material producers, farmers, firms, and investing public are essentially the same.

Commodity exchanges have attained a substantial record for integrity, credibility, and consistency in pricing the storage and consumption of the products traded in their markets. The evolution and enforcement of their self-imposed rules and regulations have created a climate of fair dealing and financial responsibility. The formation of clearinghouses to supervise and guarantee transactions between trader members, firms, farmers, and the investing public is a cardinal example of how the exchanges have fulfilled their public responsibilities to the economy and society. The exchanges have displayed a record of financial responsibility and integrity that is competitive with the behavior of other major economic markets and institutions.

References

Goss, B. A., and B. A. Yamey, *The Economics of Futures Trading: Readings Selected, Edited and Introduced*, Wiley, New York, 1978; Gray, Roger W., "The Futures Market for Maine Potatoes: An Appraisal," *Food Research Institute Studies*, vol. 11, no. 3, 1972, pp. 313–341; Gray, Roger W., and D. J. S. Rutledge, "The Economics of Commodity Futures Markets: A Survey," *Review of Marketing and Agricultural Economics*, vol. 39, no. 4, 1976, pp. 57–108; Hieronymus, Thomas A., *Economics of Futures Trading for Commercial and Personal Profit*, 2d ed., Commodity Research Bureau, New York, 1977; Peck, Anne E. (ed.), *Readings in Future Markets, II: Selected Writings on Futures Markets*, Chicago Board of Trade, Chicago, 1977; Working, Holbrook, *Readings in Futures Markets, I: Selected Writings of Holbrook Working*, Anne E. Peck (compiler), Chicago Board of Trade, Chicago, 1977.

(*See also* Arbitrage; Stock exchange)

Paul D. Johns

Communism

Communism refers to (1) an ideology, (2) a group of political parties, and (3) a proposed economic system. As an ideology or a coherent system of ideas, communism has ancient roots in various proposed utopias. Karl Marx formulated communism as a critique of the existing capitalist economic system and as a vision of a possible future economic system. Marx divided future systems into socialism and communism. Socialism referred to collective ownership of the means of production, but with continued inequality in wages, paid according to the amount of an individual's work. Communism referred to an advanced stage of socialism in which the means of production—including all factories and land—would continue to be collectively owned, but with equal distribution of goods according to need.

A Group of Political Parties

Communism as a group of political parties is a relatively recent development. Marx envisioned one international Communist Party, and for many years, both before and after the Russian Revolution, this situation prevailed. Following World War II, however, when Communist parties achieved independent political power, international solidarity gave way to violent conflicts between different parties, based on their differing interpretations of the Marxist message.

Some Communist parties still follow, to some degree, the views of Joseph Stalin—some those of Leon Trotsky (who opposed Stalin in the twenties). The Chinese Communists follow the teachings of Mao Tse-tung, since his death emphasising the pragmatic aspects of these teachings over the dogmatic. The Yugoslavian Communists follow the views of Josip Tito. The West European Communist parties have their own concepts, designated Eurocommunism (which advocates socialism plus democracy).

Proposed Economic System

Communism as a proposed economic system (collective ownership of the means of production and equality of income distribution) remains an ideal yet to be realized, even though Communist parties rule over one-third of the world's population (and Socialist parties over another one-fourth).

But political parties do not necessarily advocate the economic system from which they take their name. Most Socialist parties advocate mixed capitalism and socialism, with perhaps an all-Socialist economy years later. Most Communist parties advocate immediate socialism, with communism relegated to the far future.

Free Goods and Services: The Goal

Although communism remains unrealized anywhere, many people through the years have dreamed the utopian idea of a system where labor is given freely by all workers, accompanied by freely available goods and services.

Critics of this egalitarian proposal generally argue: (1) workers will get lazy because they can live without working; (2) there will be an infinite demand for each of the free goods and services; and (3) it would be impossible to plan rationally an economy where there are no changing prices in the marketplace to signal changes in the demand for different goods and services.

The second point has a high degree of validity: wants tend to be unlimited, and some rationing process is necessary. But this is not true of all goods and services. For education or health care, for example, there is a finite demand, a saturation point beyond which no further increased supply would be required. It is also obviously true for many basic necessities, such as bread and potatoes.

It is definitely not true for luxuries such as yachts and expensive vacations, for which some form of rationing would be required.

The first point, that workers would get lazy if they could live without working, may have some validity, at least in some societies, but if availability of free goods and services were extended slowly, workers would easily find other things on which to spend their money, so that the incentive to work would not materially decline.

The third point, that rational economic planning requires price signals, has no particular validity. Economic planning can be done rationally, without price data, if certain information is known. Planners would need to know what resources, both of labor and of capital, are available; what technologies exist for combining resources into desirable outputs; and how much of each free good will be desired at a zero price. The data exist on availability of most resources; engineers, even in a capitalist society, must calculate what technologies are possible; and market surveys and questionnaires can give a good estimate of how much of a good will be desired at a zero price.

The issue, therefore, is how difficult this conceptually possible planning would be, and whether the resulting system would be a great improvement in equity and in human behavior over the capitalist system.

Free Goods and Services: The Reality

In the Soviet Union, China, and all other Communist countries, many goods and services are sold on the market to consumers, but there is still a wide range of goods and services freely available at no cost. For example, in the U.S.S.R., all education and medical care are free.

But availability of free goods and services is not limited to the Communist world.

Even in the present United States, some goods and services are available at no cost; for example, primary and secondary education, and even some higher education. In terms of recreation, there are many national, state, and municipal parks where admission is free.

These goods and services are not free in the sense that no labor is required to produce them. They are free in that the federal, state, and local governments give them, free of charge, to anyone who wants them.

Health Care   A major argument in the United States today concerns the extension of free services to the health sector, with some members of Congress advocating a completely free and comprehensive health care system.

The arguments against expansion of free goods and services to include health care are: (1) it will destroy workers' incentive to work, since they will have less use for money; (2) people will have no choice of doctors; and (3) people may seek health care they do not need. [Points (1) and (3) are, of course, very similar to the arguments cited earlier against making any goods and services available without charge.]

The answers to these arguments are: (1) workers will still have many other things to buy, but will be healthier so they can work better; (2) the present situation in which the poor cannot get any doctor will change, and there will be some freedom of choice of doctors within each clinic; and (3) doctors can exclude patients who do not need health care because the government, not the patient, is paying for the service.

The Goal of Income Equality

Any extension of free goods and services automatically means a more nearly equal income distribution since everyone gets these goods and services equally. Anyone in favor of income equality (in terms of real goods and services available to each individual) supports this extension of the free goods sector as one tool of greater equality. Such an extension of free goods and services also implies that a political commitment has been made by the community to ensure that, every person—regardless of money income—be educated and healthy. Finally, it is argued that free education and health care will reduce the spirit of dog-eat-dog commercialism found in all capitalist societies, and foster a spirit of cooperation.

References

Claudin, Fernando, *The Communist Movement*, Monthly Review Press, New York, 1977; Engels, F., *Anti-Duhring, Part III*, International Publishers, New York, 1939; Sherman, Howard, "Economics of Pure Communism," *Soviet Studies*, July 1970, pp. 24–36; Wiles, Peter, *Political Economy of Communism*, Blackwell, Blackwood, N.J., 1964.

(*See also* Comparative economic systems, an overview; Maoism; Marxism; Socialism)

Howard J. Sherman

Comparative advantage theory

Early in the eighteenth century, it became common to teach the doctrine that it pays a country to import those goods which it is unable to produce at all or which it cannot produce at home at a lower absolute cost than the goods are produced abroad. A few writers advanced the still wider rule that it even pays a country to import goods which it can actually produce more cheaply than another country, provided it can pay for them with exports that are still more cheaply produced at home. It was not generally recognized that this meant that freely traded goods are not necessarily produced in countries where their total cost of production is lowest: what governs the profitability of buying at home or abroad is not the absolute, but the relative or comparative advantage of countries in the production of different goods. Furthermore, when all countries specialize in the production of those goods in which they have a comparative advantage, obtaining whatever else they need by foreign trade, the net result is a larger world output than could have been obtained by a universal policy of national self-sufficiency. Thus, the theory of comparative advantage not only accounts for the commodity composition of foreign trade under conditions of free competition between nations but also demonstrates the mutual advantages of such a "territorial division of labor."

Modern textbooks in economics invariably credit David Ricardo not only with the first explicit formulation of the theory of comparative advantage but also with the first attempt to spell out the implications of the theory for trade policies. But recent research has shown that it was James Mill rather than Ricardo who first formulated the theory and, explained its practical meaning in terms of cost ratios, and that it was his son, John Stuart Mill, who completed the theory by taking account of the role of reciprocal demands. It was from John Stuart Mill, and not from Ricardo, that later economists assumed the theory of comparative advantage as the foundation of the pure theory of international trade.

Ricardo's Example of Comparative Advantage

In Ricardian theory, free trade is important primarily as an offset to diminishing returns in agriculture. To Ricardo free trade meant a policy appropriate to an advanced manufacturing nation seeking to import cheap wheaten bread for its workers and raw materials for its industry from backward agrarian countries. The thrust of his famous chapter on foreign trade was to show that the import of luxuries had no influence either on the rate of profit or on the rate of wages at home, and therefore had no influence on the growth path of the economy. But the numerical example of Ricardo's comparative advantage was in terms of England exporting cloth in exchange for the importation of wine, not wheat, from Portugal. The purpose of the example was to show that, although one country had an absolute cost advantage in both products, it paid both countries to specialize in the production of one of them and to import the other. The notion of Portugal having an absolute cost advantage over England in the production of textile clothing must have struck contemporary readers as peculiar; besides, since England at that time produced no wine at all, the example was certainly ill-designed to illustrate the principle of comparative advantage.

Ricardo supposed that Portugal could produce a given quantity of wine with 80 worker-years (all other inputs being ignored) and a given quantity of cloth with 90 worker-years. England, on the other hand, would require as much as 120 worker-years to produce the same amount of wine and as much as 100 worker-years to produce the same amount of cloth. In Portugal, wine will exchange for cloth at the rate of $80/90 = 0.88$; whereas, in England 1 unit of wine will buy $120/100 = 1.2$ units of cloth. It is clearly to Portugal's advantage to export wine to England as long as 1 unit of wine can be traded with England for more than 0.88 unit of cloth; likewise, it is to

England's advantage to export cloth if less than 1.2 units of cloth must be given for 1 unit of wine. Hence, the theory of comparative advantage states the upper and lower limits within which exchange can take place between countries to their mutual benefit. Ricardo assumed that wine would exchange for cloth at a rate of 1:1. Thus, as a result of free trade, Portugal obtains cloth for 80 worker-years which would have cost 90 worker-years to produce at home, and England obtains wine for 100 worker-years which would have cost 120 worker-years to produce domestically. Before trade, it took $80 + 90 + 120 + 100 = 390$ worker-years for Portugal and England each to produce 1 unit of wine and 1 unit of cloth; after trade, these 4 units require only $80 + 80 + 100 + 100 = 360$ worker-years. The "gains of trade" equal 30 worker-years, which are divided between the two countries depending on where the barter terms of trade between wine and cloth will lie between the upper and lower limits, which in turn depends on the pattern of demand in the two countries, an aspect of the problem which Ricardo ignored.

International Implications

Ricardo recognized that the phenomenon of comparative advantage has definite implications for international wage and price differences between countries, although it was Nassau William Senior, not Ricardo, who first stated classical theory of international prices. Given the situation depicted by Ricardo's example, foreign trade is possible only if Portuguese money wages and hence prices in terms of gold are higher than they are in England. If they were the same, Portugal would never import cloth because its consumers would insist on obtaining cloth more cheaply from domestic suppliers. In consequence, England would have to ship gold to Portugal to pay for wine imports, which would raise wages and prices in Portugal to the point where it would become profitable for Portuguese consumers to import English cloth. In general, then, the low-cost country has the higher gold wage and hence the higher money price for similar goods. There is, as Ricardo said, a "natural distribution of specie" among the trading nations of the world that tends not only to balance each country's exports and imports but also results in such relative price levels between countries as to induce each country to produce those goods in which it has a comparative advantage. Although the world no longer uses the gold standard, this result of the classical theory of international prices still holds: a high level of wages and prices in a country may be the result of higher efficiency and by no means prevents that country from competing successfully in international trade.

Despite all the changes in economics since the days of Ricardo and Mill, the theory of comparative advantage still stands today as a pillar of sound economic reasoning about international trade. Both Ricardo and John Stuart Mill explained the pattern of trade in terms of underlying productivity differences between countries but they left these differences themselves unexplained. The modern Heckscer-Ohlin theory of international trade explains these productivity differences themselves in terms of the relative factor endowments of countries and consequently incorporates the principle of comparative advantage of a more fundamental theorem: a country will tend to have a comparative advantage in those goods which use intensively the country's relatively abundant factor of production, and will therefore import goods which use intensively the country's relatively scarcer factor.

References

Blaug, M., *Economic Theory in Retrospect*, 3d ed., Cambridge University Press, New York, 1978, chaps. 4, 6; Thweatt, W. O., "James Mill and the Early Development of Comparative Advantage," *History of Political Economy*, vol. 8, no. 2, Summer 1976, pp. 207–234.

(*See also* Exports; Factors of production; Imports; International economics, an overview)

Mark Blaug

Comparative economic systems, an overview

Comparative economic systems (CES) is a venerable field in the throes of a revolution. The distinguishing characteristic of the field is that it places the economic system and its institutions at the center of the analysis and makes it the variable to be analyzed. In contrast, most other fields in economics generally ignore systemic considerations altogether or presume, on an ad hoc basis, a particular institutional framework.

The focus on the economic system as the variable subject to analysis and the comparison of alternative systems makes CES an important field within economics. As Jan Tinbergen (1954) stated, "the problem of comparing alternative forms of economic life constitutes the problem *par excellence* of economic science; its real *raison d'etre*."

In the past, CES has relied primarily on institutional description. Recently, there has emerged a new comparative economic systems stressing the theory of economic systems and the application of modern econometric techniques to comparative systems analysis, thereby moving the field toward the frontiers of economics.

CES has antecedents as far back as Plato, Thomas More, and the mercantilists. From the mercantilists, it inherited the emphasis on the rules and institutions governing the conduct of economic affairs and, therefore, concern about the role of government in this process. The utopian socialists and economic liberals in the late eighteenth and early nineteenth centuries fought against this key role given to government by the mercantilists. They developed models of economic systems which placed the government in an ancillary role—the liberals by promoting free-market capitalism, the utopians like Proudhon and Fourier by emphasizing decentralized communal organizations. These early contributors to CES were followed by Karl Marx, who hypothesized that class struggle led to a sequence of economic systems (slaveholding, feudal, capitalist, socialist, communist). There have been many definitions of an economic system, all agreeing that it is a socially established mechanism for resolving economic decisions as to what to produce, how to produce, and for whom to produce.

A Changing Field

The field recently has changed drastically in nature, scope, and approach, and this has brought about a dramatic change in the way the field is viewed both by comparative systems specialists (comparativists) and by economists in general. It is significant that the *International Encyclopedia of the Social Sciences*, published in 1968, did not include a survey of the field or even a single index entry dealing with CES although it included several surveys and 21 index entries on comparative methods in political science, law, psychology, and anthropology. The fact that the present encyclopedia, as well as the latest *Encyclopedia Britannica,* each include a major survey of CES represents recognition of the important changes in the field. The field has moved closer to both the mainstream and the frontiers of economics, and has thereby expanded significantly the scope of economics. In this process, CES has become much more analytical and less political and ideological, and a start has been made on important empirical treatments of the subject. This change, which gathered momentum in the past two decades, moved the scholars in the field (under the auspices of the Association of Comparative Economic Studies) to initiate in the mid-1970s the *Journal of Comparative Economics.*

The earliest modern analyses of economic systems are Enrico Barone's analysis of collectivist central planning in the first decade of the twentieth century and the analysis of socialism by Vilfredo Pareto, who viewed various types of socialism as organizations ruled by different elites. These were followed by debates in the 1920s and 1930s between Ludwig von Mises and Friedrich A. von Hayek who questioned the economic rationality of socialism, and Oskar Lange and Abba Lerner who defended it. Lange (1938) gave an excellent example of systems analysis, in which he responded to the criticisms of socialism by developing a carefully constructed model of an economic system combining social ownership of the means of production with a market for inputs and outputs. This so-called socialist controversy was a major event in the history of CES. It raised the theoretical and technical level of discourse, substituting analyses of economic models for descriptions of actual economic systems, and it raised many of the important issues that are still of central concern in CES: centralization and decentralization in decision making and information, the compatibility of various incentive schemes with the decision-making and information structures, the comparisons of the relative efficiencies of different system models, the true nature of price and market systems, and potential combinations of plan and market.

A Shift from the "Isms" Approach

While this important debate was being conducted primarily at the level of models of economic systems, most of the textbooks of that period, indeed until quite recently, concentrated on what might be called the grand "isms" approach—describing capitalism, socialism, communism, fascism, and similar overall social, political, ideological, and economic systems, in imitation of the comparative government approach. This approach was based on the attempt to understand the newly formed Soviet Communist system, and then the Italian Fascist and German National Socialist systems. More recently, emphasis in the professional literature on CES shifted from these general, comprehensive approaches to CES to somewhat narrower, economically based, and more technical approaches. The modern literature utilizes the advances in economic theory, game theory, econometrics, and organization theory to throw light on the functioning of economic systems and on comparisons of their structure and performance. In this approach, the noneconomic components of the earlier approach, such as ideology and political and social systems, are treated in the same light as technology, resource endowment, or level of development, i.e., as crucial exogenous variables influencing the various features of the economic system and its ability to perform its tasks.

A third important approach to CES, which forms a bridge between these two, is that concentrating on property or ownership relations as the most important feature of economic systems. This approach is based on considering ownership as the sole source of decision-making authority, and distinguishes between systems of private, public, or mixed ownership. If ownership is viewed as a mechanism for providing the owner with a bundle of decision-making rights, including the right to obtain income from the owned object, then this approach, if stripped of its ideological content, may be regarded as part of the decision-making approach to systems analysis.

Systems Theory

The decision-making approach to CES, which is being developed jointly by economic theorists and comparativists, views the economic system as composed of three key structures—the decision-making, informational, and incentive (or motivational) structures—and as operating on the economic environment to produce outcomes to be evaluated by norms or weighting functions. This approach forms the emerging paradigm of the new comparative economic systems.

The most complete, rigorous treatment of the new approach to CES is provided by J. M. Montias (1976), while a less technical development of the paradigm is found in E. Neuberger and W. Duffy (1976), a textbook that attempts to provide a coherent decision-making theoretical framework, based on the Koopmans and Montias (1971) view of the place of the economic system in the total analysis of an economy's performance. David Conn (1977) formalized the Neuberger-Duffy framework and wrote an enlightening survey of the literature in CES, distinguishing the contributions of theorists and comparativists in this endeavor. Leonid Hurwicz's Ely lecture (1973) provides the most complete survey of the theoretical literature in which the system is considered as a variable rather than assumed as given. The Conn, Hurwicz, Montias, and Neuberger contributions represent useful introductions to the area of systems theory and summarize effectively the progress in that field.

Within the emerging paradigm of comparative economics, Koopmans and Montias view the outcomes of economic activities as determined by the environment, the economic system, and government policies. Performance is measured by the outcomes, weighted by a norm (in effect, a social welfare or preference function). Probably the most difficult aspect of this approach is the question of what norm to use in evaluating outcomes. Edward Ames (1973) has stressed the importance of the social preference function in the emerging theory of economic systems, and the problems raised by Kenneth Arrow and others in developing nondictatorial functions of this type. Social preference functions, such as A. Bergson's famous social welfare function, are the choice of most CES students, despite the well-known problems associated with these functions. Economic theorists, on the other hand, tend to start from the postulates of new welfare economics. According to Conn (1978):

> A basic distinction of emphasis exists, however, between the two groups of scholars (the comparativists and the theorists) working in this field. The comparativists (Neuberger and Duffy, Koopmans and Montias, etc.) are primarily concerned with the development of a general theory suitable for positive analysis of a variety of economic systems, whereas the theorists (Hurwicz, Mount and Reiter, etc.) have more of a welfare orientation and hence emphasize the possibility of designing systems that satisfy, among other things, welfare criteria, such as the Pareto criterion.

Given the role of the economic system in partially determining the outcomes of economic activity, the new paradigm proceeds to analyze the three component structures of the economic system. Here again, a difference in emphasis has developed, with economic theorists stressing the information structure and, more recently, the incentive structure, while comparativists have stressed the decision-making structure, i.e., the allocation of decision-making authority among economic agents, and the interrelations among the three structures. Two examples of the interrelations are the requirements placed by different decision-making structures on the information structure, and the impact of the incentive structure on the extent to which information that will be transmitted to the agents is filtered or biased. Another difference is the tendency of some theorists to try to provide institution-free models, while actually depending on concepts derived from a particular economic system. Both Janos Kornai (1971), a leading East European contributor to CES and particularly to the disequilibrium approach to systems analysis, and Koopmans and Montias (1971) stress the danger in using system-bound terminology as though it were system-free. They provide primitive or truly system-free terminology for systemic comparisons.

However, we should not exaggerate the differences between these two groups of scholars. Their common agreement on the nature of the economic system and their mutual interaction are much more important. There have been at least three important conferences—in Berkeley in 1967, in Ann Arbor in 1968, and at Wayne State in 1978—bringing together leading theorists and comparativists. Thus, it is no accident that a common view on economic systems is emerging.

Regional and Other Emphases

For the past 40 years or so, work in CES has tended to have a very strong regional concentration, primarily on the Soviet Union, and secondarily on Eastern Europe and China. This regional concentration is confirmed by a survey of the first 12 issues of the *Journal of Comparative Economics*, in which about one-third of all articles dealing with specific countries or regions concentrated on the Soviet Union alone, and 60 percent on these three regions.

The emphasis on the Soviet Union and other centrally planned economies is not at all surprising. The introduction of a centrally planned system in Russia in the late 1920s played a major role in the development of CES as a recognized special field of study within economics, concentrating on the comparison of this new economic system with the existing capitalist market systems. The emergence of the Soviet Union as a major power during and after World War II, and the availability of financial support in the United States for the study of its institutions and performance, combined to encourage a growth of Soviet studies, including the study of Soviet and Soviet-type economics. The same factors spurred the development of Chinese studies about a decade later.

Other interesting results of the survey of 56 articles in the journal's 12 issues include: (1) 36 percent of the articles are explicitly comparative, while the remainder are case studies dealing with specific countries or regions and are only implicitly comparative; (2) slightly more than half of the articles utilize primarily microeconomic approaches, 30 percent macroeconomic, and the remainder combine the two; (3) about 40 percent deal with models of economic systems, while 60 percent deal with real countries or organizations or with a combination of model and reality; (4) about 60 percent of the articles are primarily theoretical in approach, 25 percent econometric, and the remainder institutional.

The changes in emphasis we would expect, in addition to geographical diversification, are a shift toward more explicitly comparative studies, and a greater use of macroeconomic and econometric approaches. A 1978 conference on the transmission of international disturbances and the contribution by Richard Portes (1980) on macroeconomic models of planned economies represent some recent evidence of a shift in interest toward macroeconomics.

Other Important Contributions

The field of CES also encompasses important studies of specific economies, e.g., the pathbreaking work by Abram Bergson (1961) in calculating real national income accounts for the Soviet Union, and the work by Bergson, A. Nove, E. Ames, and others on the Soviet centrally planned economy. There is also the work by Alexander Eckstein, Robert Dernberger, Dwight Perkins, and others on the Chinese economy; theoretical and econometric analyses, particularly contributions to index number theory, by Alexander Gerschenkron and Richard Moorstein; analysis of the Communist international system by Peter Wiles; analysis of the property rights approach to economic systems by E. Furubotn, S. Pejovic, F. Pryor, and others; new econometric models of various countries, such as the econometric model of the Soviet Union by Donald Green; aggregate production analysis by Martin Weitzman, Yasushi Toda, and others; cross-country comparative econometric analyses within the disequilibrium macroeconomic framework by Richard Portes and David Winter (1980); as well as the comparative empirical studies by the Economic Commission for Europe, the Organization for Economic Cooperation and Development (OECD), the Wiener Institut fur Internationale Wirtschaftsvergleiche, and other centers of comparative studies.

A major subfield of CES has dealt with central planning of various types. It includes the work of Lange and Lerner, already mentioned; applications of Leontief's input-output analysis and of linear programming of L. V. Kantorovich, John von Neumann, and George Dantzig; development of French indicative planning; and the voluminous literature on the theory and practice of Soviet-type planning.

In addition, important work has been done on analyzing economic systems in contexts other than national economies. There has been some development of the analysis of international organizations, such as the Common Market or the Council of Mutual Economic Assistance, but much greater emphasis has been placed on analyzing sectors of economies, such as foreign trade, banking, agriculture, energy, etc., and primary economic units, such as enterprises, associations of enterprises, collective farms, communes, etc. Some of the literature on enterprises, such as the output-maximizing firm under central planning by Ames and the worker-managed firm by Benjamin Ward and Jaroslav Vanek, is very close in spirit to the newly developing decision-making approach to economic systems.

The study of CES has retained some of its interdisciplinary commitment, as, for example, in Frederic Pryor's recent study of primitive economies (1977), which tests quantitatively many hypotheses found in the anthropological literature.

Finally, mention must be made of the important work of scholars who are not normally included in the field of CES but whose contributions are important to the progress of the field. A very partial list would include works of the following scholars: Joseph Schumpeter on the framework within which innovation takes place and participants group and regroup themselves in response to changes in the environment and norms; Herbert Simon and Oliver Williamson on organization theory and industrial organization; Jacob Marschak and Roy Radner on the theory of teams; Kenneth Boulding, Janos Horvath, and Martin Pfaff on the grants economy; and finally Ragnar Frisch, Kantorovich, Henri Theil, and Tinbergen on optimal economic policy, based on the application of operations research methods.

The Future

In conclusion, the field of comparative economic systems has come of age and is beginning to achieve its logical position as one of the central fields in economics. The next 10 years should witness further dramatic progress. With continuing cooperation between theorists and comparativists, the emerging paradigm will yield important new results at the theoretical level in analyzing the interaction of the decision-making, information, and incentive structures. This approach will be enriched by the combination of the decision-making approach with developments in industrial organizations, grants economics, evolutionary economics, and other fields. The rapidly developing econometric cross-country comparisons will provide the essential final ingredient—the ability to test hypotheses on the role of the economic system and its structures in determining performance.

References

Ames, Edward, *Soviet Economic Processes*, Irwin, Homewood, Ill., 1965; Ames, Edward, "The Emerging Theory of Comparative Economic Systems," *The American Economist*, Spring 1973, pp. 22–28; Barone, Enrico, "The Ministry of Production in the Collectivist State," *Giornale degli economisti*, 1905, translated in F. A. von Hayek (ed.), *Collectivist Economic Planning*, Routledge, London, 1935; Bergson, Abram, *The Real National Income of Soviet Russia Since 1928*, Harvard University Press, Cambridge, Mass., 1961; Bergson, Abram, *The Economics of Soviet Planning*, Yale University Press, New Haven, 1964; Conn, David, "Toward a Theory of Optimal Economic Systems," *Journal of Comparative Economics*, December 1977, pp. 325–350; Conn, David, "Economic Theory and Comparative Economic Systems: A Partial Literature Survey," *Journal of Comparative Economics*, December 1978, pp. 355–381; Eckstein, Alexander, *Comparison of Economic Systems: Theoretical and Methodological Approaches*, University of California Press, Berkeley, 1971; Hurwicz, Leonid, "The Design of Mechanisms for Resource Allocation," *American Economic Review*, May 1973, pp. 1–30; Koopmans, Tjalling C., and John Michael Montias, "On the Description and Comparison of Economic Systems," in Eckstein, op. cit.; Kornai, Janos, *Anti-Equilibrium: On Economic Systems Theory and the Tasks of Research*, North Holland, Amsterdam, 1971; Lange, Oskar, "On the Economic Theory of Socialism," in B. E. Lippincott (ed), *On the Economic Theory of Socialism*, University of Minnesota Press, Minneapolis, 1938; originally published in *Review of Economic Studies*, Longman Group, Edinburgh, 1936 and 1937; Montias, John Michael, *The Structure of Economic Systems*, Yale University Press, New Haven, 1976; Neuberger, Egon, and William J. Duffy, *Comparative Economic Systems: A Decision-Making Approach*, Allyn & Bacon, Boston, 1976; Pareto, Vilfredo: *Complete Works*, vol. 5: *Les Systèmes Socialistes*, 1902–1903, Librarie Droz, Geneva, 1965; Portes, Richard, "Internal and External Balance in a Centrally Planned Economy," in E. Neuberger and L. D. Tyson (eds), *The Impact of International Economic Disturbances on the Soviet Union and Eastern Europe: Transmission and Response*, Pergamon Press, Elmsford, N.Y. 1980; Portes, Richard, and David Winter: "Disequilibrium Estimates for Consumption Goods Markets in Centrally Planned Economies," *Review of Economic Studies*, vol. 47, 1980, pp. 137–159; Pryor, Frederic, *The Origins of the Economy: A Comparative Study of Distribution in Primitive and Peasant Economies*, Academic Press, New York, 1977; Thornton, Judith (ed.), *Economic Analysis of the Soviet-Type System*, Cambridge University Press, New York, 1976; Tinbergen, Jan., *Centralization and Decentralization in Economic Policy*, North Holland, Amsterdam, 1954, p. 47.

(See also Capitalism; Communism; Fascism; Maoism; Marxism; Mercantilism; Socialism)

Egon Neuberger

Competition

Competition refers to the nature of the conditions under which individuals may exchange property rights. It assumes a definition of property rights that individuals may trade among themselves as well as a description of the trading process. A competitive equilibrium is the outcome of competition. The very existence of a competitive equilibrium depends on the nature of the property rights. These aspects of competition are particularly important in connection with the development of new technology and new products, and with the use of low-cost, large-scale methods of production.

The simplest situation in an analysis of competition is a market where individuals have initial endowments of commodities that they own and that they may trade among themselves. All trades occur at the same time and place. In this market situation the essential characteristics remain valid when trades do not all occur at the same time and place. However, individuals have incomplete knowledge relevant to making their decisions. This complication changes the description of the outcome of competition. Incomplete knowledge is inevitable because the future is unknown. Even so, it is often less costly to take current actions that will have future consequences without knowing what these will be than it is to respond only to momentary events of the present. These advantages of planning and the exposure to hazards that may occur alter the effects of competition. These basic considerations help explain the nature of production and why the quantities of goods offered will change over time in reponse to the expectations and information available to the firms. They also explain why some common notions of competition are inadequate. Among the inadequate notions about competition is the belief that a necessary condition for competition is a lack of power by any firm to affect the prices of its products. This is sometimes put in another form: it is asserted that competition can exist in an industry only if the demand curves facing the individual firms in the industry are infinitely elastic so that changes in the quantities sold by a single firm cannot affect the product price. This condition is not necessary for competition. Nor is it necessary for competition that the number of firms in the industry be so large that each one is of negligibly small size relative to the total market for the commodities produced by firms in the industry. Finally, it is consistent with competition that some or all firms in an industry have obtained very high profits and high rates of return.

Pure Exchange

Assume there is a market where there are individuals, each of whom starts with given inventories of various commodities. Each one would like to make trades that will result in the acquisition of goods preferable to those goods to be exchanged. The theory assumes that for each trader the purpose of trade is to better the trader's position. Hence, the trader would not willingly leave the market with a bundle of goods worth less than the traded goods. The theory also assumes that each trader owns the commodities to be traded, that they can be traded on terms that are mutually acceptable to the parties directly involved in an exchange, and that each trader may accept or reject the terms offered. Underlying the possibility of exchange is the existence of property in the goods. To have competition it is necessary to have voluntary exchange so that no trader is compelled to accept or reject offers without freely given consent. The very notion of exchange implies, therefore, a voluntary agreement among those who are directly involved in the transaction on the terms that each one will voluntarily accept. In pure exchange, although the total quantities of the commodities exchanged among the parties is constant, each one must regard the obtained goods as worth more than the exchanged goods. If the parties can reach an agreement on mutually beneficial terms of exchange, the result is an allocation of the commodities among the individuals that must make at least one of them better off than before, and cannot make anyone worse off than before.

The theory assumes that no individual accepts terms that would leave that individual in a worse position than if no trades at all were made. In the latter case the individual retains the initial endowment of goods and attempts to improve the situation by seeking others in the market with whom mutually beneficial exchanges can be arranged. The process of improvement applies to groups of traders as well as to individuals. Assume that individuals as well as groups of traders are free to reach agreements among themselves on mutually beneficial terms of trade. Assume there are no restrictions on their choice of trading partners with whom they can arrange multilateral exchanges. Further assume that each individual is free to accept or reject offers without the need of gaining the consent of others. The trades that result from these conditions represent a competitive equilibrium.

The existence of a state of competition in pure exchange allows the participants to seek out the best terms that they can obtain from others. It does not require the presence of a very large number of traders nor does it require that each of the individual traders in the market must be of such a small relative size that none can affect the terms of trade. Traders can make tentative agreements with each other subject to the condition that these agreements become binding only if none can obtain better terms from others. The final outcome is a set of exchanges among the traders such that no individual or group of individuals can improve upon these terms. The set of outcomes with these attributes need not be unique. All possible outcomes with these attributes represent the state of competition. The set of all possible trades that can satisfy these conditions is known as the core of a market. Therefore, the set of trades induced by competition in a market is in the core of the market.

Auction Market—Competition in Practice

Actual markets exist that closely appoximate the theoretical model. An auction market in which the buyers and sellers submit sealed bids to the auctioneer is a leading example. The goods go to the highest bidders from the sellers who submit the lowest offers. Nor is this all. There are rules capable of inducing the participants in the market to give their true valuations in the sealed message they submit to the auctioneer. All successful bidders pay the same price per unit and all successful sellers receive the same price per unit. Therefore, the price paid by a successful bidder never exceeds the bid and is just high enough to exclude enough buyers to enable the quantity demanded to equal the quantity offered at the market clearing price. Similarly, the price received by a successful seller may well exceed the minimum that the seller would be willing to accept. With respect to the sellers the price is low enough to enable the quantity offered to equal the quantity demanded. The outcome is an allocation of the goods to those who value them the most. These rules for conducting a sealed-bid auction are equivalent to the equilibrium determined by the intersection of supply and demand curves.

Spatial and Temporal Competition

The simplest theoretical model of competition assumes that all of the trades occur at the same time and place because all of the traders gather at one time in the same place. However, competition also exists even though the traders are not in the same place and do not all trade at the same time.

Trades dispersed in space (that is, over a distance) need not occur at a common price. This is partly because it is costly to ship goods from one place to another so that prices at different points may differ but not by more than the marginal cost of transportation. Also, prices can differ because traders at one point may not know what prices prevail elsewhere. Because it is costly to acquire information about conditions prevailing in other markets, traders have incomplete knowledge. A trader has that stock of knowledge about market conditions that is optimal, taking into account the cost of acquiring information and the cost of maintaining the stock of knowledge. Because of these costs, less than complete information is optimal. Consequently, prices can differ among the markets although there is competition. Instead of a single price, competition induces a distribution of prices among the markets consistent with the cost of acquiring information about market conditions.

Somewhat similar considerations determine the distribution of prices over time as a result of competition. Individuals make current transactions and plan for later transactions on the basis of current conditions and on the basis of what they believe will occur in the future. They differ in the extent of their knowledge about prevailing conditions and in their ability to predict what is likely to happen later. Thus a distribution of prices over time results that is consistent with competition, cost of knowledge, and ignorance of what the future will bring.

Competition and Production

The conditions of production affect the competitive equilibrium. Although the theory must be more elaborate to embrace the consequences of production, the essential features of competition in pure exchange remain valid. Assume firms can buy inputs or can hire the services of factors of production in order to make commodities for sale to other firms or to consuming households. The description of this process involves transactions in related goods, services, and commodities occurring in different places and at different times. The firm will buy some inputs before it knows the terms on which it can sell the goods that will use these inputs. For instance, a firm buys machinery and builds factories which it can use to make commodities for some time. It must expect to obtain enough revenue from the sale of these commodities to cover the cost of the machinery and the factory and receive a return on its capital commensurate with its best alternatives. The firm acts as an intermediary between the suppliers of inputs at an earlier time and the customers for its outputs at a later time. In essence there are transactions among all of these participants although they are separated in space and in time. Hence, the basic forces of competition described in pure exchange remain valid.

In order to complete the analogy with pure exchange, it would be necessary for all of the participants simultaneously to have agreements for a whole sequence of transactions that will not all be finally consummated until a considerable time has elapsed. Although forward transactions of this type happen, it is less costly for individuals not to tie their hands so completely. Even so, some firms suffer the consequence of error and incur losses, while others benefit from good fortune and make profits. Losses and profits are consistent with competition and are the result of incomplete knowledge of the future, differences of ability among those who make decisions, and the necessity as well as the propensity of individuals to act now and expose themselves to the future consequences—success which brings profits and failure which brings losses.

Rates of Return   Some firms may obtain large profits, but this does not invite others to emulate them by entering into the production of similar or closely related commodities. It is the expectation of future profits that is an inducement for investment and not the current profits which are the result of past decisions and good fortune. Past and current profits are not necessarily a reliable predictor of future profits. Therefore, firms in an industry may enjoy high profits and yet new firms may not enter the industry, which is consistent with competition in the industry.

Under competition it can easily happen that firms obtain different rates of return. The explanation closely resembles that given by David Ricardo to explain why the rent on land may differ from one farm to another although all make and sell the same agricultural product at the same price. Land differs in quality. The better-quality land gives a larger output for a given amount of purchased inputs than poorer-quality land. The owner of the better-quality land can obtain a higher return, i.e., a higher rent, because competition among the farmers for the use of the land bids up the rent to the point where all farms will yield the same rate of return to the farmers who till the soil. Similarly, in the case of firms, owners of the more productive resources can obtain a higher return owing to the competition among those who wish to hire their services. A satisfactory explanation of these differences of ability and quality among firms in the same industry does not yet exist. The differences in the returns among the firms that result from the differences in their abilities is easily mistaken for the effects of an absence of competition among the firms. In the case of musicians, artists, novelists, lawyers, surgeons, dancers, actors, sports stars, and so on, it seems plain that the large differences in income result from forces similar to those that explain differences in the rents of land. It is the scarcity of these great abilities and the active demand for those with these abilities that explain the high incomes. All of this is consistent with competition.

Scarcity   Classical economists use the distinction between "natural" and "contrived" scarcity. The supply of a naturally scarce factor is completely inelastic, and its owners receive rents. The supply of a factor that is artificially restricted is not completely inelastic. The owner of this factor receives a monopoly return. The former is consistent with competition while the latter is not. There is, therefore, the question of what can contrive a scarcity.

Legal restrictions are often the source of a contrived scarcity. Thus, the state may confer a patent to an inventor or a copyright to an author. Hence, none may use the patent without paying royalties to its owner, and none may publish a copyrighted item without payment to its owner. The state may control entry into certain occupations and professions. This may result in a contrived scarcity and give a monopoly return to those who can control entry.

Trademarks and brand names enable a firm to identify its products. The state confers property rights to firms by allowing them the exclusive use of this means of identification. Yet this is not a source of contrived scarcity nor a departure from competition. Without these property rights no competitive equilibrium is possible.

Competition and Product Differentiation

Property rights are essential for competition. No one would be willing to produce without the assurance of ownership of the output. No one would be willing to buy without secure property rights to the purchased goods. Competition requires clearly defined property rights so that individuals can decide what to buy and sell, what to make, what offers to make, and what bids to accept. A failure of markets to function is often the result of an inadequate assignment of property rights. Experience leads to remedies and to new forms of property rights so that a competitive equilibrium can occur.

Although a firm can make a product closely resembling one made by another so that customers may regard the two as nearly equivalent, it cannot make a literal copy of another firm's product and claim it is exactly the same as the other's. Therefore, product differentiation is always present. Without this product differentiation, there would be no incentive for a firm to offer something different that customers would find more appealing than the existing alternatives. Competition often occurs by means of offering goods consisting of new attributes or new combinations of attributes on terms that customers will find more attractive than the existing varieties.

Competition among different products is often more important than the simple textbook case of competition among products that are perfect substitutes. Indeed, owing to the ability and desire of firms to identify their products so that customers can easily repeat the purchase of satisfactory items, the concept of perfect substitutes can have no basis in reality. Competition can exist without perfect substitutes. Customers can choose among alternatives composed of different attributes according to which offers the most utility for the price.

It is a consequence of this analysis that it is not necessary for competition that a firm face an infinitely elastic demand for its product at the prevailing market price. A firm can be in a highly competitive environment and face vigorous challenges from resourceful and innovative rivals although changes in its rate of output have a perceptible effect on the price at which it can sell its product.

Incomplete knowledge, the cost of acquiring information, and the existence of property rights explain why sellers of new products struggle for success. The difficulty of success and the ease of failure does not imply the absence of competition. Advertising outlays and promotional expenses are readily understood as means of competition, although some economists view these expenditures as anticompetitive. Plainly, the lower the real costs are of contacting customers in order to inform them about what is available and on what terms, the greater is the vigor of competition.

Competition and the Number and Size of Firms in an Industry

Owing to the costs of coordinating activities or to the economies of large-scale production, the optimal size of firms may be large relative to the total quantity demanded of the product. As a result an industry may have a few large firms. Some assume that this is a structural indicator of a lack of competition in the industry. The argument asserts that there is monopoly with only one firm in an industry and competition with many firms in an industry. With an intermediate number, there is something between monopoly and competition, often described by the terms monopolistic competition, imperfect competition, and oligopoly.

It does not follow as a consequence of the presence of relatively few firms in an industry that competition is absent. Firms may still act independently and the outcome to be consistent with competition although few firms are in the industry. With few firms in an industry, each takes into account the likely repercussions of its actions. To do otherwise would be imprudent, and such a firm could not survive or obtain a return on its capital commensurate with its most attractive alternatives.

The main argument for the belief that collusion is more likely when there are a small number of firms in the industry is the contention going back to Adam Smith that it is easier for a few than for many to agree on a common purpose. Numbers alone do not settle this issue. Other considerations include similarity in the interests of the firms, stability of the underlying supply and demand conditions, and the costs of policing and enforcing collusion. Even if collusive agreements were legally enforceable, which is not true in the United States, it does not follow that competition would be less profitable than collusion and, therefore, dominated by it. The costs of maintaining a collusive agreement may outweigh the gains so that a firm obtains a higher expected net return under competition than by collusion.

There are circumstances such that the least costly way of satisfying the demand requires a single firm to do so. The natural monopoly as described by Alfred Marshall is an example. More general conditions for natural monopoly are now known. These arise when bargains struck independently between groups of buyers and sellers are inconsistent with overall efficiency. In the terminology for the description of pure exchange, the core is empty. An equilibrium can exist only if there are restrictions on individual freedom to make bids and accept offers. Thus, some overall coordination is necessary to give a feasible outcome. An equilibrium cannot exist without some restrictions that are equivalent to an assignment of property rights among the participants in the market. Some industries seem to illustrate these conditions including public utilities, airlines, railroads, and some of the communications industries.

References

Böhm-Bawerk, Eugen von, *Positive Theory of Capital,* G. D. Hencke and H. F. Sennholz (trans.) Libertarian Press, South Holland, Ill., 1959, 1st ed. in German, 1889; Debreu, Gerard, *Theory of Value,* Yale University Press, New Haven, 1959; Edgeworth, Francis Y., *Mathematical Psychics,* Kegan-Paul, London, 1881; Knight, Frank H., *Risk, Uncertainty and Profit,* Houghton Mifflin, Boston, 1921; Telser, Lester G., *Competition, Collusion and Game Theory,* Aldine, Chicago, 1972; Telser, Lester G., *Economic Theory and the Core,* University of Chicago Press, Chicago, 1978.

(*See also* Antitrust policy; Cartel; Concentration of industry; Economic history and theory; Economics; Mergers; Monopoly and oligopoly; Price theory; Scarcity)

Lester G. Telser

Competitive price theory (see Chicago school)

Computers in economics

A great deal of economics concerns quantitative analysis. Since economics is data-intensive, the electronic computer plays a very important role in economics today. In some form or other, computers—slide rule, desktop mechanical calculator, voltage-analog machines, punched-card tabulators—were in use during the flowering of quantitative economics during the 1920s and 1930s. But heavy computational burdens were always a restraining factor. It required research organization and assistants to implement major quantitative studies dealing with economic trends, business cycle classifications, early econometrics, national income accounting, sample surveys, and censuses.

During the late 1940s and especially during the 1950s, electronic computation began to be used in economic research. It had already been used in the natural sciences. The first cases were for data processing of census and sample survey materials. The analysis of economic time series for business cycle studies made early use of the computer, and several centers of econometric research began to use electronic computers for separate phases of their work.

A revolution took place at this time in quantitative economics. Now, the computer is a commonplace tool in both teaching and research. It is absolutely necessary in applied econometrics, but it is widely used in many branches of economics outside formal econometrics. As universities began to relax foreign language requirements for higher degrees, students began to learn new languages—the languages of computer programming. It is possible to take advanced degrees in economics without using the computer, but it is very common for research students to learn elementary computer programming.

The computer has greatly lightened the burden of data-intensive economics. It enables the investigator to accumulate, use, or tap vast data sources. In many respects it is used for primary or source data analysis, and in more respects it is used for secondary data sources. Large data banks are now available that store in computer files long statistical series of thousands and thousands of economic variables. The computer also stores census and survey materials for analytical work. The economist can tap these data files from remote computer terminals all over the world in only seconds. In the computer data files, statistical series are corrected, revised, adjusted, ready for use. Traditional printed delivery of data usually gives only limited amounts of data in this form, and it is necessary to splice or compile many sources for each series. Data are ready to use without such further processing in stored files on the computer. This is of enormous advantage. In its present form, this kind of facility became available only in the 1960s and is under continuous development. It is shared now between private and public sources, but in some countries, the central statistical bureau places the whole array of economic statistics in one set of computer files, available through tape or other distribution, sometimes even for remote-entry withdrawal.

An Experimental Tool

Experimentation in econometrics and other quantitative branches of economics has been greatly opened up by the computer. In searching for regularities in economic life, the economist can experiment with many relationships, almost simultaneously, until one is found that satisfies the theoretical and other criteria. If several statistical series—10, 20, 30, or more—are simultaneously withdrawn from a computer data file, the investigator, in seconds, can obtain estimates of relationships among many combinations of these, as many as the human eye can carefully scrutinize, before going on to the next experimental stage. These can be linear or nonlinear relationships. The sample span can be split into components. Graphical displays and many diagnostic statistics can be obtained. There is enormous flexibility that far surpasses the former methods of examining one single case at a time, each case requiring up to an hour's calculating effort, and with much less accuracy.

Not only is it possible to search experimentally over a wide range of alternative specifications of economic relationships, but it is possible to experiment with different estimation procedures of varying degrees of sophistication or complication.

After the stage of estimation of economic relationships, the investigator will usually be concerned with testing and applications. The computer is an invaluable experimental tool here, too. Most economic relationships are dynamic, meaning that they show motion of the economy, or parts of it, over time. They are also probabilistic because of uncertainty about the true state of the economy, either from the viewpoint of the knowledge of the true relationships or of the external factors affecting the relationships. That the relationships are nonlinear, in most cases, poses numerical problems in obtaining solutions for economic magnitudes, given the initial state of the economy and the external factors affecting the economy. The computer, however, handles these complications in a very direct and manageable way through the technique of simulation. This technique can be used to cut through all these problems and generate time paths of economic variables, given the inputs for initial and external magnitudes. The uncertainty aspect can be handled by computer generation of random numbers and adding them to the economic relationships. This would be called a probabilistic simulation. Otherwise, the result would be called a deterministic situation.

The great advantages of the computer for this type of analysis are:

1. Alternative formulations of economic relationships can be tested in a dynamic mode against historical reality. These are validation experiments.

2. Alternative projections for future possibilities can be examined with a variety of assumptions about input values, which are unknown.

3. Drawings of random numbers for probabilistic simulations and solutions of nonlinear equations can be approximated by the computer.

4. Large-scale systems of economic relationships for many periods in a dynamic simulation can be handled very quickly and economically by computers.

Computers have been found to be indispensable for simulation studies in economics. A wide range of alternatives can be explored; this was never possible in economics before the 1960s. Nowadays many important public policies and private business decisions are investigated by the means of alternative computer simulations. This has become a standard tool for quantitative economics.

The calculations produced by the computer are often meaningful only to the primary investigator, but the computer also has been harnessed for interpretation of findings through programming for informative tabular displays and graphics.

Through appropriate preprogramming, the results of the solution of an economic exercise can be automatically transformed for information display.

Software (programming) packages have been developed that are capable of doing all the following tasks separately or in regular sequence:

1. Assembly of data in a data bank
2. Withdrawal of data for analysis
3. Estimation of relationships from data
4. Simulation testing of relationships against historical data
5. Simulation projections of economic data, given initial values and external input values
6. Display of tables, summary measures, and graphs of results

From beginning to end, it is possible to go through this series of steps entirely within the computer system, automatically and without manual intervention, although for economic understanding it is generally necessary to have human intervention at various stages.

Some Future Tendencies

While the computer has made possible a revolution in economic teaching and research, it has not yet reached the limits of development, and evolutionary process is presently at work. A number of directions being followed at the present time indicate the way of the future.

The fully integrated software packages and the large complicated problems in economics have been dealt with on large powerful computers in centralized installations. A wide network of users has been served by remote terminal connections in a mode called time sharing. A new possibility is the use of mini computers. The size and price of computers have been declining markedly over the past 20 or more years, and it is now possible for the individual researcher to own a modest machine. As computer technology progresses, it will undoubtedly be possible for more and more people to be independent of the large central installation, except possibly for withdrawal of data from large storage files.

More governments will probably make their statistical services available in public files than can readily be accessed by telephone or other simple communication devices. And more and more information will be found in these files. More international statistics will be available, possibly through the efforts of several national bodies to make public information available more broadly through direct satellite communications systems.

At present most economic data are collected at sources—the enterprise, the market, the household, or the individual—and then transferred manually to the computer for processing and storage for potential use. The manual steps of data collection and transfer can potentially be eliminated through direct logging of economic transactions from the point of occurrence to the computer file. This is already done for sales and inventory statistics of large commercial establishments.

References

APL Econometric Planning Language, Program Description/Operations Manual, 3d ed., IBM Form Sh 20-1620, IBM Corporation, Armonk, New York, 1977; Kuh, Edwin, "An Interactive

Econometric Environment: The TROLL System," in F. Schohr and H. D. Plotzeneder (eds.), *Okonometrische Modelle und Systemme*, Oldenbourg, Munich, 1978, pp. 107–123; Norman, Morris, *Software Package for Economic Modelling*, IIASA, no. RR721, Laxenburg, November 1977; Schleicher, Stephen, "Design Principles for Econometric Software," in F. Schohr and H. D. Plotzeneder (eds.), *Okonometrische Modelle und Systeme*, Oldenbourg, Munich, 1978, pp. 63–75.

(*See also* Data banks; Econometrics; Forecasting methods; Operations research; Simulation in business and economics)

Lawrence R. Klein

Concentration of industry

Economists have long recognized that one enterprise can constitute an industry and have called this circumstance a monopoly. Economists have also recognized that many equal-sized enterprises can coexist in an industry, a situation designated as atomistically competitive. Between these extremes, various firm-size distributions are possible. Any distribution in which a few firms account for a significant portion of an industry's output or sales is called concentrated.

The interest in the phenomenon of concentration within industries comes from economic theory which maintains that atomistically competitive or lowly concentrated industries will produce a higher output and charge a lower price than if the same industries were concentrated. Data with which to test this proposition became available for a large number of industries after World War II.

The Bureau of the Census, of the Department of Commerce computes discrete ratios which measure for the Standard Industrial Classification's four- and five-digit codes the percentage of an industry's sales accounted for by the top 4, top 8, top 20, and top 50 companies. These ratios have been published for the years 1947, 1954, 1958, 1963, 1967, and 1972.

Causes and Consequences of Concentration

These data, particularly the top 4 concentration ratio (CR_4), have been extensively employed in empirical studies concerned with measuring the causes and consequences of concentration. The principal findings which emerge from the concentration statistics and their use in various empirical works are:

1. There exists considerable stability over time in the concentration ratios. Most industries do not experience much change in their CR_4 over considerable periods of time.

2. There is a substantial minority of industries which possess CR_4's in excess of 50 percent, the level generally found from empirical study to produce a tendency toward monopolistic pricing behavior.

3. Statistical studies which measure the impact of CR_4 on firm or industry profitability generally find that there is a positive, significant effect, which is particularly pronounced when CR_4 exceeds 50 percent. However, the degree of the impact is relatively small.

4. Other statistical investigations relating CR_4 to various effects find a tendency for CR_4 to influence positively the degree of technological progressiveness, but

only up to moderate ranges; CR_4 has no systematic impact on the rate of inflation; CR_4 seems to contribute to patterns of racial discrimination and to the uneven distribution of income. Beyond these effects, research has not produced enough to warrant any generalizations.

5. There is uncertainty about the causes of the high levels of CR_4 that exist in a substantial fraction of manufacturing industries. It seems to be that economies of scale, either with regard to the individual plant or to the firm operating more than one plant, do not, in general, explain existing levels of high CR_4. Some evidence indicates that as the intensity of advertising increases, measured by the ratio of advertising to sales, CR_4 also increases. And where advertising intensity exceeds 10 percent, there has been a persistent increase in CR_4 over time. These findings apply only to consumer goods industries.

These various relationships are increasingly being subjected to statistical tests with data from other countries. Although other nations draw different industry boundaries and sometimes use a different level for the concentration measure, e.g., share held by the top three firms, certain patterns emerge. The important ones are the similarity in the degrees of concentration among the leading firms across similar industries and that concentration's influence on profitability is similar to that found using the U.S. Census data.

Tentative Quality of Research Results

The research results have a marked tentative quality. There are two reasons for this:

First, CR_4 is not the best measure of firm-size distributions because it is neither linked to any theoretical support concerning the effect of firm-size distributions on the variation in price from competitive to monopolistic behavior nor does it capture a theoretically important characteristic of the firm-size distribution such as whether the top firms have equal or unequal market shares with respect to each other.

Second, interpretations of the findings are in dispute. In particular, the one for which there seems to be consensus—that concentration positively influences profitability—receives its principal challenge on the grounds of cause and effect. The conventional view that the positive relationship reflects a variation in pricing behavior from competitive to monopolistic competes with the view that industries which are highly concentrated earn high profits because the dominant firms are more efficient than their smaller challengers.

This controversy is not likely to be settled in the near future. Economic theory produces too many competing hypotheses for the outcome of any particular empirical experiment to bear a single interpretation. Further, the data, including the widely used CR_4, mismeasure in various ways the theoretical concepts an investigator seeks to measure. Until theory improves to limit the scope for alternative interpretations and better data become available by which to test predicted relationships, the causes of and the consequences of industry concentration will be debated.

References

Hause, John, "The Management of Concentrated Industrial Structure and the Size Distribution of Firms," *Annals of Economic and Social Measurement*, National Bureau of Economic Research, New York, June 1977; Scherer, F. M., *Industrial Market Structure and Economic Performance*, Rand, Chicago, 1980; U.S. Bureau of the Census, *1972 Census of Manufactures: Con-*

centration Ratios in Manufacturing, U.S. Department of Commerce, 1975; Weiss, L. W., "The Concentration-Profits Relationship and Antitrust," in H. J. Goldschmid et al. (eds.) Industrial Concentration: The New Learning, Little, Brown, Boston, 1974.

(See also Competition; Monopoly and oligopoly)

H. Michael Mann

Conference Board, Inc.

The Conference Board is a nonprofit, nonpolitical group of approximately 250 persons who specialize in (1) producing short-term forecasts of the gross national product and its components for the United States and for Canada and its provinces, and (2) the collection, analysis, and reporting of worldwide management practices and policies of interest to the chief executive officer or to the principal officers reporting directly to the chief executive.

In the conduct of its operations, the Conference Board sponsors approximately 50 conferences open to anyone who wishes to attend. It prepares and publishes approximately 35 major research studies and 40 short reports each year, copies of which are available on a subscription or individual order basis to libraries and individuals. In addition, it produces approximately 15 periodicals providing monthly or quarterly information on a variety of specialized topics, such as capital appropriations, mergers and acquisitions, help-wanted advertising, consumer confidence, and the federal budget. The findings in these studies are released to the public through newspapers, magazines, radio, and television.

Financial support for the Conference Board comes from voluntary contributions by over 4000 organizations, primarily larger corporations, but there is significant participation by labor unions, consultants, publishers, colleges, government agencies, and others interested in business and the economy. Approximately 2000 are U.S.-based, 600 are in Canada, and 500 in Latin America, Europe, the Pacific Basin and other areas. Of the 2000 in the United States, over 500 are colleges and universities.

History

The Conference Board originated with a series of informal discussion meetings held during 1915 and attended by a select group of leaders of that day. Originally conceived as a federation of manufacturers' trade associations, it adopted the name National Industrial Conference Board. It immediately became a nonpolitical agency for impartial investigation and discussion drawing support from individual companies as well as trade groups. In December 1924 the National Industrial Conference Board was incorporated as a nonprofit corporation under the membership corporation laws of the State of New York. In September 1970 the name of the organization was changed to the Conference Board, Inc., reflecting both the wide participation by retail, wholesale, financial, and service organizations as well as manufacturers and the expansion of its research and information programs to reflect the needs of business leaders in all parts of the world.

Original Research

The importance of the Conference Board to economics rests in its program of original research and its independent quantitative forecasts of the short-term outlook. The original research work includes regular surveys of business organizations with respect to capital appropriations, capacity utilization, sources of capital, and expectations with respect to costs of capital. In addition, original work is done on the volume of help-wanted advertising, consumer confidence and buying plans, and discretionary income.

Conference Board economic forecasts are developed for the United States, Canada, and major European countries. Each of the forecasts includes quantitative estimates of unemployment as well as changes in price levels. The research on concentration of industry relates to the nature of the underlying statistical information and the problems of attempting to use it in the study or administration of antitrust actions.

The strength of the Conference Board rests in the quality of its professional staff and its access to private information from business organizations. It is free to select the nature and timing of its studies and to execute its self-imposed obligation of full disclosure of methods employed and results obtained.

References

Annual Report, Conference Board, Inc., 1970–1980.

George H. Brown

Conglomerate

In general, a conglomerate is a corporation, formed by many mergers and acquisitions, in which the acquired companies are engaged in activities that may have little or no relation to the activities of the acquiring company. The original acquiring company may itself be engaged in some commercial line, usually manufacturing, or it may be an investment company seeking a controlling interest in nonfinancial firms. Conglomerates of this latter type are known as financial conglomerates.

The Federal Trade Commission classifies three types of conglomerate mergers: (1) product extension mergers: firms which have some degree of functional relationship in either product or distribution; (2) market extension mergers: firms which are in the same product line, but sell in different geographic markets; and (3) unrelated combinations.

A fourth classification is a concentric conglomerate in which a firm combines activities with similar specific management functions such as research, engineering, production, marketing, etc. A specialist counsel is provided by corporate staff, and a carry-over of the general or generic management functions of planning, organizing, directing, controlling, etc., is emphasized.

Three Economic Functions of Financial Conglomerates

In financial conglomerates there appears initially to be no type of carry-over, but a closer analysis reveals three possible economic functions: (1) portfolio effects, (2) financial responsibility, and (3) resource allocations. The portfolio effects refer to investment diversification. However, home-made diversification by individual investors can substitute for corporate or business diversification. In addition, investment companies can achieve diversification more efficiently than conglomerates because of greater flexibility in entering and withdrawing from individual situations.

A second economic function of financial conglomerates is the avoidance of bankruptcy of one of its divisions because of a temporary adverse run of losses. If the long-run prospects for a division are favorable, it will be sustained through a period of losses until demand conditions or managerial performance improves. In this respect a financial conglomerate is clearly distinguished from an investment company, which does not take a controlling position.

A third possible function of financial conglomerates is to redeploy assets. If the potentials for a product line are favorable, but the individuals managing assets in these product market areas are not achieving the potential, those managers may be redeployed. In addition, assets may be redeployed as the potentials in some product market areas become more favorable than others.

Thus, even in the pure financial conglomerate some economic functions may be performed. In addition, multiproduct firms whose activities are related in a concentric way have the potential of achieving economies of scale and lowering cost functions by combining complementary business activities.

Three Categories of Empirical Studies

A critical issue is therefore raised as to the actual performance of conglomerate firms. Empirical studies dealing with conglomerates have been of three categories. The first type of study was concerned with their accounting performance. Some studies in the early 1960s concluded that conglomerate mergers satisfied managers' desires for larger firms but did not increase earnings or market prices. Later studies found that conglomerates as a group raised the return on total assets up to the average for all firms. Other studies indicated that conglomerates acquired more profitable firms than did nonconglomerate acquirers and increased the utilization of latent debt capacity.

The second type of empirical study focused on conglomerate performance within the context of the capital asset pricing model. Studies through 1969 found that conglomerates provided higher ratios of return to systematic risk than did mutual funds. However, other studies through the 1970s found that conglomerates exhibited higher levels of systematic risk, but not significantly different risk-adjusted rates of return or other performance measures.

A third type of empirical study utilized residual analysis to remove market and industry effects, thereby testing for possible gains from mergers. These studies did not distinguish between conglomerate and other types of mergers. It was found that the shareholders of acquired firms as a group gained from merger activity. The shareholders of acquiring firms, however, neither gained nor lost from merger activity.

Influence of Economic Environment

Recent merger activity which has been mainly conglomerate in nature has been greatly influenced by particular characteristics of the economic environment. For nonfinancial corporations as a whole, market values of assets are below 70 percent of the current replacement values of their assets. New investments within a given industry do not present favorable returns. Investments in other industries may be made by purchasing firms at prices below the current replacement values of assets. This has stimulated across-industry merger activity. Because market values of securities are generally low, cash tender offers have been widely used in merger activity. The shareholders of bidding firms as well as target firms gained from successful tender offers. On unsuccessful tender offers, the shareholders of target firms gained because other buyers subsequently purchased the firms after attention was called to their value potentials. However, the shareholders of the bidding firms did not gain from unsuccessful tender offers.

While dramatic examples of conglomerate mergers between large entities can be found, most conglomerate merger activity involved the purchase of a relatively small firm by a larger firm. Market shares acquired in conglomerate mergers typically were below 2 percent of total industry output. Conglomerate merger acquisitions therefore represented mainly toehold acquisitions into new areas of business activity.

Objections to Conglomerate Firms

A number of antitrust issues have been raised with regard to conglomerate firms. One is that conglomerate mergers permit the extension of market power of one firm into other industries where it had not previously participated. However, the specification of what constitutes market power is usually not formulated rigorously. The opposite conclusion seems equally plausible. Conglomerate diversification by the acquisition of firms in other industries may encourage potential competition. The threat of potential entry becomes even more pervasive because the range of potential entrants is increased.

A cross-subsidization criticism argues that in the large conglomerate various types of predatory behavior can occur because activities that are less profitable can be subsidized by the profitable segments of the business. However, this argument lacks plausibility because if some activities are unprofitable, it is better to dispose of them rather than to subsidize them. A related argument is that a "deep pocket" policy may be followed. This refers to the ability of large firms to engage in heavy advertising and product differentiation which smaller firms may not be able to afford. However, this argument can also be extended to other clearly socially desirable forms of competition, such as quality improvements and research and development expenditures.

Another concern with conglomerate firms is the possibility of increased reciprocity. This is the practice of a conglomerate basing its purchasing policy on projected sales rather than on prices and product quality. But with the broadened application in recent years of decentralized management responsibility and accountability, reciprocity would conflict with established management policies. Managers must be free to follow the most economic and efficient policy if they are to be fairly evaluated. The corporate office of a conglomerate firm must promulgate clear criteria based on competitive business and economic practices to guide its sales and purchasing departments. Thus, the conglomerate development is likely to reduce reciprocity rather than to increase it.

Another objection to conglomerate firms is that they result in increased concentration on a large scale. The share of the largest 200 manufacturing firms in 1956 was 53 percent of total manufacturing assets. This share rose to 61 percent in 1977. A portion of this apparent rise is due to the diversification by manufacturing firms into nonmanufacturing activities. The nonmanufacturing activities are then included in the numerator of the 200 largest firms, but excluded from the denominator which measures manufacturing assets alone. This influence can be corrected by relating the assets of the 200 largest nonfinancial corporations to the total of all nonfinancial assets. This ratio has remained stable at slightly under 40 percent during recent decades. Thus, this provides a measure of the aggregate concentration ratio, which is much lower than the more narrowly defined manufacturing assets ratio. Nor has it risen over recent decades.

A number of proposals have been made in recent years to circumscribe and limit conglomerate merger activity. However, merger activity is associated with a high rate of new business formation. Thus, merger activity is a part of a well-functioning market for capital assets. Even conglomerate mergers perform an important role in the long-range planning and internal and external diversification programs of business firms. In addition, a well-functioning market for capital assets performs an important role in directing resources to their highest and most efficient use. To the extent that the merger activity in the late 1970s has resulted from the wide disparity between the market values of assets and their current replacement values, it would be more appropriate for economic policy to focus on the fundamental factors that have caused this substantial divergence between market values and current replacement costs.

References

Mueller, Dennis C., "The Effects of Conglomerate Mergers: A Survey of the Empirical Evidence," *Journal of Banking and Finance*, vol. 1, December 1977, pp. 315–348; Smith, Keith V., and J. Fred Weston, "Further Evaluation of Conglomerate Performance," *Journal of Business Research*, vol. 5, March 1977, pp. 5–14; Weston, J. Fred, "The Nature and Significance of Conglomerate Firms," *St. John's Law Review*, vol. 44, Spring 1970, pp. 66–80; Weston, J. Fred, and Surenda K. Mansinghka, "Tests of the Efficiency Performance of Conglomerate Firms," *Journal of Finance*, vol. 26, September 1971, pp. 919–936.

(*See also* Integration; Mergers)

J. Fred Weston

Consumer anticipation surveys (*see* Anticipations surveys, consumer)

Consumer credit

Consumer credit is defined by the Federal Reserve Board as "short-and intermediate-term credit extended to individuals through regular business channels, usually to finance the purchase of consumer goods and services or to refinance debts incurred for such purposes." Important exclusions from this definition are mortgage financing, although some junior liens are included, and borrowings against the cash value of life insurance policies or generally against savings accounts.

Two Classes of Consumer Credit

There are two main classes of consumer credit: noninstallment credit and installment credit. Noninstallment credit is consumer credit that is scheduled to be repaid in a lump sum and includes single-payment loans; charge accounts, such as 30-day accounts at retailers, some gasoline credit cards, and travel and entertainment cards; and service credit, principally amounts owed to doctors, hospitals, and public utilities. Installment credit represents all consumer credit that is scheduled to be repaid (or with the option of repayment) in two or more installments. Consumer installment credit greatly exceeds noninstallment credit. At the end of 1978, outstanding sums on these two types of consumer credit were $275.6 billion and $64.3 billion, respectively.

Consumer credit for the purchase of goods and services (sales credit) began in Colonial times with the granting of open-book credit. The privilege was generally limited to affluent consumers. Sales credit was made available to farmers on a crop-to-crop basis. Generally, no direct finance charge was levied on sales credit, but the cost of credit was built into the price of the merchandise. The installment purchase of automobiles created an explosion of consumer installment credit in the 1900s. Cash loans were also available to consumers in the 1800s from unregulated lenders who devised various schemes for evading the state usury statutes. Beginning in 1916, states enacted exceptions to the usury laws in order to permit consumers to obtain small amounts (initially, $300) of legal cash credit. Whereas the time-price differential on retail credit was not limited by law in that era, rate ceilings on small cash loans were initially fixed at 42 percent per year. Most states now limit rates on small loans to 36 percent, with lower rate ceilings for large loans.

Recently, the most rapidly growing form of consumer credit has been revolving credit, a form of installment credit. Originating in the late 1930s, revolving credit (open-end credit) has three distinctive features. Typically, it is a plan whereby the creditor (1) permits the consumer to make purchases or obtain loans from time to time, either directly from the creditor or indirectly by means of a credit card; (2) permits the customer to pay amounts owed in full or to make minimum monthly payments; and (3) may compute a periodic finance charge on the outstanding balance. The convenience or low transactions cost involved with this type of credit explains in large part its growing acceptance by consumers.

Economic Function

The basic economic function of consumer credit is to move consumers' consumption of goods and services forward in time. While some have argued that the payment of finance charges represents a nonproductive expenditure, consumers' willingness to pay such charges is evidence that there is a time utility in consumption. A refrigerator today has greater value than a refrigerator 24 months from now.

Consumers use credit for the same reasons that business and government use credit. A large portion of consumer credit is for investment purposes or capital financing. Some of this credit is economically productive in the same sense that business firms use credit for acquiring machinery. Thus, the installment purchase of a washing machine enables consumers to avoid the time and outlays required to travel to the laundromat. Other capital outlays based on credit, such as the credit purchases of a dress or suit, may not substitute for other expenditures, but are justified by the consumer as providing immediate, rather than delayed, satisfaction.

Consumers also use credit to meet emergencies, such as hospital and doctors' bills—just as governments turn to credit to meet the crises of wars and depressions. Finally, in a manner similar to the use of open-book credit by a business, consumers use credit as a matter of convenience to pay for multiple purchases. For example, telephone bills are paid monthly, and many consumers use revolving credit plans as a convenient means of summing small purchases into one or more monthly payments.

Macro and Micro Effects of Consumer Credit

Legislators and economists are concerned with the macro and micro effects of consumer credit. At the macroeconomic level, some have argued that consumer credit is destabilizing and, therefore, should be controlled directly through adjusting minimum down payments and maximum maturities. While such controls are presently used in some other nations, they have been employed in the United States only during World War II and the Korean intervention.

Some have also been concerned about the quality of consumer credit, arguing that when consumers become overextended their inability to repay their debts will depress the economy. Also, deteriorating quality may remove the stimulus provided by consumer credit to the economy. Delinquencies, repossessions, and losses rise during recessions and fall during recoveries, but the cause-and-effect relationship is unclear. Since consumer credit makes up only about 7 percent of net public and private debt, other forms of credit may be more influential over the business cycle.

Concerns about the microeconomic effects of consumer credit upon the family have led to a great quantity and variety of state and federal legislation. Some has been directed at better informing the consumer, such as requirements that finance charges be disclosed in a uniform manner (Truth-in-Lending Act) and that consumers have the access necessary to correct their credit reports if necessary (Fair Credit Reporting Act). Other laws have as their intended effect the protection of consumers: restrictions on levels of finance charges, limits on collection remedies, and bans on discrimination in the granting of credit. Much of the current economic research in the area examines whether the actual effects of these laws and regulations match the intended effects.

References

Durkin, Thomas A., and Gregory E. Elliehausen, *1977 Consumer Credit Survey*, Federal Reserve Board, 1978; Federal Reserve Board, *Consumer Instalment Credit*, 6 vols., 1957; National Commission on Consumer Finance, *Consumer Credit in the United States*, 1972.

A series of working papers and monographs concerning the effects of government regulation of consumer credit and access to a computerized bibliography covering consumer and mortgage credit are available from the Credit Research Center, Purdue University, West Lafayette, Ind.

(*See also* Business credit; Credit, an overview; Debt; Interest rates; Mortgage credit; Selective credit controls)

Robert W. Johnson

Consumer price index

The consumer price index (CPI) is the name typically applied in both the United States and other countries to the statistic that measures the price changes of the vast number of goods and services purchased by households. The broad concept underlying the CPI is that it measures the purchasing power of money with respect to a fixed market basket of consumer goods and services.

The CPI for the United States was first published in 1921 and contained data going back to 1913. Indexes for food and some U.S. cities are available prior to that. The CPI is compiled and released monthly by the Bureau of Labor Statistics (BLS).

Laspeyres Index Formula

The mathematical formula used to calculate the U.S. CPI is basically the Laspeyres index formula. That formula is:

$$I_t = \frac{\Sigma \ p_t q_a}{\Sigma \ p_0 q_a} \times 100$$

where I = index

$\qquad p$ = price

$\qquad q$ = quantity

$\qquad \Sigma$ = the summation of the products of price and quantity for all the items in the index

$\qquad t$ = the time period to which the index refers

$\qquad a$ = the base period to which the quantity weights refer

$\qquad o$ = the base period to which the prices refer

If the base period to which prices refer is identical with that to which the quantity weights refer, the formula is exactly equivalent to a Laspeyres index. In any event, the quantities are fixed in some base period, and changes in the index therefore reflect changes only in the prices consumers must pay for that fixed market basket of goods.

Since it is difficult to measure quantities in a consistent way for use in the above formula, it is recast to permit the index to be calculated without having to determine quantities directly. That reformulation is:

$$I_t = I_{t-1} \left[\frac{\Sigma \, (p_{t-1}q_a)(p_t/p_{t-1})}{\Sigma \, p_{t-1}q_a} \right]$$

The first term in the numerator, or the same term in the denominator, represents the proportion of the consumer's dollar that would be spent on each item in the market basket if the consumer purchased the base quantities. It is called a relative importance and may change from period to period if the price of the item changes relative to all other prices. It is the relative importances that are quantity weights. The relative importances may be used to calculate special indexes for particular time periods from among the component price series comprising the CPI.

Consumer Expenditure Surveys

The relative importance required to calculate the index based upon the formula just derived are usually obtained through a periodic survey called the consumer expenditure survey. Weights currently reflected in the index are those obtained in the consumer expenditure survey for the year 1972–73. This survey obtains information about the various amounts spent on the full spectrum of goods and services purchased by the population of consumers represented in the index. Such surveys may also include questions designed to obtain information on savings and, in some cases, even on assets and liabilities. But the consumer price index measures only prices associated with expenditures on goods and services.

The decision about how frequently weights are to be revised depends both on resource availability and other considerations. The frequency of weight revisions is, however, an important matter because it is generally thought that as base periods become more and more out of date the calculation of the CPI through the use of the Laspeyres formula yields an upward bias.

The population covered by the consumer price index varies from country to country. In the United States, indexes are calculated for two consumer groups, the all-urban consumers and the urban wage earners and clerical workers. The index for the first group was initiated in 1978.

While the base year to which CPI weights currently apply is the year 1972–73, the index is now expressed as 1967 = 100. Thus, 1967 is the reference base as distinct from the weight base. The selection of a reference base is arbitrary—any time period can be selected without affecting the rate of change of the index. Traditionally, however, the reference bases of U.S. government statistics are changed about once every 10 years.

Two Criteria for Price Data

The other major ingredient of a price index is, of course, prices. There are two major criteria which the price data must meet. One is that they are a sample representative of the items purchased by the population group covered by the index and of the outlets in which that group makes those purchases. The second is that every attempt is made to ensure the comparability of what is being priced from one time period to the next. The first criterion is usually met by drawing a probability sample of items from the consumer expenditure survey. However, such a survey rarely gives details on the outlets where these items were purchased. In practice, the data on outlets are usually derived from a separate survey of households sometimes called a point-of-purchase survey, or from retail trade data that are collected for other purposes.

The second criterion is usually met by drawing up a precise specification of the item to be priced and the outlet in which the price is to be collected, and following that item in that store over time. In practice this may be difficult, and other methods must be relied on to compare prices of items for which the specification has changed.

Use of the CPI

CPIs have several important uses. Early in this century, changes in economic conditions required new data related to industrialization, besides those already collected for agricultural and external trade. Industrialization was often accompanied by collective bargaining for setting wages. Thus, in the United States, the need arose for a CPI to be used in labor-management negotiations, especially when inflation accelerated during World War I.

As economic conditions changed, the use and the design of CPIs changed. During the 1930s, CPIs were used to measure real income flows of families. The CPI was being used as a deflator, but during a time of price decline it actually inflated incomes. With the advent of Keynesian economics and government short-run policies to stimulate employment and stabilize prices, the CPI grew in importance as an input for policymaking. In recent years, when worldwide inflation has accelerated, the CPI has become a closely watched statistic and is widely used to compensate for inflation through automatic adjustments to wage contracts, interest payments, and social transfers.

CPI Detail

In the United States, the aggregate CPI and component detail are published monthly. The item detail for the United States includes the major components: food and beverages, housing, apparel and upkeep, transportation, medical care, entertainment, and other goods and services. These are broken down further into a large number of subindexes.

CPIs are also available on a monthly or bimonthly basis for the standard metropolitan statistical areas (SMSAs) in which 28 major cities are located. Bimonthly indexes are also prepared for four regions of the country and for five size classes of cities. Some indexes for selected size classes of cities in particular regions are also prepared.

Currently, the CPI is based on about 125,000 monthly quotations of prices, rents, and property tax rates collected from about 60,000 sources. The sources are located in 85 primary sampling units which are geographical areas.

In the United States and many other countries the statistical agencies make data available on both nonadjusted and seasonally adjusted bases. The former estimates are usually used in the escalation of contracts, the latter by policymakers in assessing the short-run course of inflation.

Conceptual and Measurement Problems

Like all economic statistics, the CPI has conceptual and measurement problems which are potential sources of error. For example, there is considerable disagreement about how owner-occupied housing should be weighted and priced for CPI. The food component is an example of a special problem since some foods are seasonal in nature and are only found in markets during particular months. The medical care component is illustrative of the question of measuring quality change. The question is raised as to whether or not the item to be priced for the medical care component is the cost of cure or the price associated with the different components of that cure, the hospital room, surgeon's fee, etc. The calculation of the weight for new cars vis-à-vis used cars also raises some specific problems.

References

U.S. Department of Labor, *The Consumer Price Index: Concepts and Content Over the Years*, Bureau of Labor Statistics Report 517, 1977.

(*See also* Bureau of Labor Statistics; Cost of living; Economic statistics; Index numbers; Inflation; Price measurement; Statistical techniques in economics and business, an overview; Value of the dollar)

Joel Popkin

Consumer theory

The theory of consumer behavior has evolved over the last several decades from being concerned solely with normative statements about the way in which consumers allocate a given income among a set of purchased goods and services to a theory incorporating concerns about the division of income between saving and spending, the supply of labor services to the market, and the way in which consumers allocate their time generally between market production, home production, and consumption or leisure activities.

Marshallian Demand Analysis

The standard theory of the consumer is represented by Marshallian demand analysis and the Hicks-Slutsky analysis of indifference functions. In Marshall's classical treatment, consumers face a set of prices for various goods and services and hold a set of demand functions for these goods and services. The demand functions picture the amount that consumers are willing to buy at each hypothetical price. Generally, the lower the price of the product the greater the quantity consumers will wish to obtain—the familiar downward-sloping demand curve, based on diminishing marginal utility in the consumption of individual goods and services.

In Marshallian analysis, many other things besides price affect quantity consumed, but these are thought of as shifting the location of the entire demand function. An increase in income, for example, normally means that people would be willing to buy more of the product at each price than previously, hence the entire demand function shifts outward and to the right. A rise in the price of a commodity that is complementary in consumption would shift the demand function inward and to the left—for example, a rise in the price of bacon would mean that people would be less willing to buy eggs at each particular price for eggs, because the demand of eggs depends partly on the price of bacon; and so on.

Marshallian demand theory contains two other aspects of technical interest. The first is the proposition that a unique demand curve, defined as the relation between the amount people are willing to buy of any product and different hypothetical prices for that product, does not really exist in theory, for Marshallian demand curves are based on the underlying assumption that nonprice forces affecting demand are unchanged as the price changes. But one of those factors is real income, and real income must be changing as the price of any single product changes because real income is represented by money income adjusted by an index of price change. Thus, if the price of housing services were to fall, consumer real income would rise because the same money income would be able to buy more total goods and services owing to the fall in the price of housing services. Thus, in Marshallian terms, any movement along a demand curve due to a decline in the price of a product will result in a (miniscule) rise in real income, which would move the demand curve to the right. Hence, a Marshallian demand curve does not actually hold real income constant, but holds it constant only to the extent that real income is affected by factors other than the decline in price of the product under consideration.

The second aspect is the idea of consumers' surplus. In Marshallian analysis, consumers will buy a product up to the point where the marginal utility from purchasing the last dollar's worth is equal to the marginal utility of money income generally. But the total utility from consuming a particular product is obviously not represented by the marginal utility of the last dollar's worth multiplied by the number of dollar-equivalent units acquired: all units but the marginal one must have yielded greater utility, assuming that marginal utility declines with increased quantities consumed. Hence, total consumer utility from purchase of any commodity must be greater than the product of marginal utility times units consumed (which is equivalent to price times quantity consumed). The difference between those two is called consumers' surplus, and for purposes of analyzing social welfare is an important concept.

Indifference Function Analysis

The indifference function analysis developed by Hicks and Slutsky asks how consumers should allocate a fixed budget between various purchasable commodities. The usual strategy is to define one commodity (y) as "all other commodities taken together," the other as a particular commodity (x) under investigation. Thus, if all income were spent on commodity x, nothing of all other commodities y could be acquired, while if no x at all were purchased, an amount of all other commodities y equal to income divided by the price index could be acquired. The line connecting these two opportunity points is called a budget constraint, and under assumptions that consumers cannot affect price by buying more or less, the budget constraint is a straight line. Movements in income would shift the budget line outward, while movements in the prices of either x or y would rotate the budget line around one or the other point.

To go along with the budget line or opportunity locus, functions relating consumer preferences toward purchasing alternative sets of commodities are constructed as follows. Given consumption of any particular amount of commodity x, say quantity a, and an amount of commodity y (all other commodities) equal to b, consumers would be at a certain level of total satisfaction. (The purchase of a and b exhausts consumer income.) If people were to acquire more of commodity x, how much y would have to be taken away to keep total satisfaction at the same level as before? Creating a set of alternative combinations of commodities x and y—points of equal total satisfaction— leads to creation of an indifference function, a locus of points where consumer satisfaction is identical throughout. Other indifference curves can be constructed, involving more of both x and y, or less of both x and y, that in the first illustration, and thus we have a family of indifference curves.

Indifference functions have certain properties. They will generally be convex to the origin, suggesting that consumers would be less and less willing to give up commodity x as they got to hold smaller and smaller amounts of x (and larger and larger amounts of y). Convexity holds so long as the marginal rate of substitution between x and y declines as more x (and thus less y) is consumed. Interestingly enough, the implied marginal utility conditions are a little less stringent than would be true of Marshallian demand analysis, which is based on the assumption of declining marginal utility. Indifference curves are convex to the origin so long as the ratio of marginal utilities (x/y) declines, a condition consistent with decreasing, constant, or increasing marginal utility for any one product. And indifference curves cannot intersect, since otherwise consumers would be both indifferent to sets of commodities and simultaneously hold preferences for equivalent sets of the same commodities—a logical impossibility.

The basic theory underlying both Marshallian demand analysis and indifference function analysis is, of course, exactly the same, and one can easily move from one analysis to the other. Indifference curve construction is such that it is easier to observe certain kinds of relationships in consumer choice theory than with Marshallian demand functions—for example, whether a demand function is of elastic, inelastic, or unitary elasticity can be seen at a glance with indifference curves, but is more complicated to observe with the Marshallian apparatus.

Both the Marshallian and Hicks-Slutsky analyses of consumer behavior are concerned entirely with the way in which consumers allocate income among a set of goods and services purchased in the market. Neither has much in the way of empirically refutable content, except for the proposition that consumers will reduce purchases of normal goods (those whose consumption rises with income) when prices increase.

Although this analytical apparatus technically can be used to examine the allocation of consumer income between spending and saving (more precisely, between current consumption and future consumption), that problem is of little concern to theorists in the Marshallian or Hicks-Slutsky tradition. It was of concern to Fisher, whose interest was in the role of time preference in determining the choice between present and future consumption, but even Fisher was not concerned with cyclical variability in consumer saving and spending patterns. In general, classical consumer theory pays little attention to aggregate movements in consumer spending or saving relative to income, while much modern economics has that flavor.

Observation of data for the U.S. economy since World War II suggests the reason for the modern interest in aggregate consumer spending and saving behavior. Since World War II, consumers appear to have been the driving force behind most business cycle contractions and expansions in the United States, largely reflecting changes in expenditure rates on houses, cars, and other durable or discretionary items. In part, this finding relates to issues of definition: we conventionally treat consumer expenditures on durable goods as current consumption rather than as investment, hence as reducing consumer saving. In contrast, consumer purchases of owner-occupied housing are treated as business investment.

It is now widely recognized that consumer expenditures are highly volatile cyclically, that phenonema which cause consumers to speed up their rates of acquisition of housing, cars, durables, and other large items will generate increased demand for goods and services in the aggregate and are likely to fuel cyclical expansions, and that a collapse of spending on such discretionary items is apt to be associated with periods of economic recession.

Consumption Function

Although there is a voluminous literature analyzing the so-called consumption function, i.e., the relation between consumer income and consumer spending, much of it does not actually address the cyclical characteristics of consumer behavior. A substantial part of the consumption function literature relates to the permanent income theory developed by Friedman, which treats consumption decisions as being based on a longer-run concept of income than receipts during some arbitrary accounting period such as a year. But in the Friedman model, it is consumption (defined as the using up of goods and services, not their acquisition) that is being analyzed, not consumer expenditures. Thus, the permanent income literature says little about the causes of cyclical variation in consumer spending.

The life-cycle model developed by Modigliani, Ando, and Brumberg represents an attempt to deal normatively with the way in which consumers dispose of their income over time, and in that model wealth is assigned a crucial role in consumption decisions. In the life-cycle model, wealth includes not only property (houses, stocks, bonds, savings accounts, etc.) but also the value of future earnings. Thus, consumers visualize themselves as having a stock of initial wealth, a flow of income generated by that wealth over their lifetime, and a target (which may be zero) for their end-of-life wealth. Consumption decisions are made with that whole series of financial flows in mind. Thus, changes in wealth, as reflected by unexpected changes in earnings profiles or unexpected movements in asset prices, would have an impact on consumer spending decisions because they would enhance future earnings from property or labor or both. The theory has empirically testable implications for the age pattern of saving, and for the role of wealth in influencing aggregate consumer spending.

Another approach to cyclical variations in consumer spending and saving behavior relies more on the movement of waves of optimism and pessimism growing out of consumers' perceived improvement or deterioration in present and prospective financial position. One can trace the elements of this back at least to Keynes, who noted that the relation between consumption and income depends on, among other factors, expectations, optimism, and other psychologically related phenomena. Keynes downgraded the empirical importance of such phenomena for consumers, essentially arguing that they tended to cancel out, although psychological factors played a major role in Keynes' investment theory.

In the United States, the canceling-out presumption does not hold up. The work of Katona and his colleagues at the University of Michigan documents the quantitative importance of consumer optimism and pessimism in influencing consumer spending and saving decisions, and in recent years many analyses of cyclical movements in the U.S. economy have relied on measures of changes over time in the way consumers perceive the general economy, their own personal financial prospects, market conditions, etc.

There is little agreement even now among students of consumer spending behavior about the relative importance of factors such as income change, asset holdings, expectations about lifetime income, and psychological factors with labels like "optimism" or "pessimism." The empirical data that might be used to test alternative explanations for the cyclical variability of consumer saving and spending are not sufficiently detailed to allow one to distinguish between competing explanations, and the empirical data at the level of individual households are too dominated by measurement error to permit strong tests of competitive theories.

Consumer Theory on the Supply Side

A second important modern development in consumer theory concerns analysis of the supply side of consumer choices, and of the way in which consumers allocate their time between various types of consumption and production activities. Most of the consumer theory discussed previously focuses on the way in which consumers allocate income among various goods and services, or the way in which they allocate income between spending and saving. But both analyses presume that consumer income is a given and do not recognize that income reflects a choice about participation in the market.

The basic idea underlying the broadening of consumer theory on the supply side is that consumer decisions about how to spend time represent choices, an idea which is especially important in multiperson households where it is possible to have a complex division of labor between market and nonmarket activities. Moreover, focusing on the way in which consumers allocate their time over various activities—market production, home production, and consumption or leisure—forces us to recognize that the real budget constraint facing consumers is not income but time.

Recent developments in consumer theory that focus on the way in which consumers allocate time take the view that households are best thought of as miniature firms providing labor services to the market, purchasing goods and services from the market, providing services to each other within the framework of the household itself, and generally deciding how much time to spend in a set of activities that exhaust the total time budget of 24 hours per day.

The germ of theory in this area is attributable to Becker, who developed the notion of households as firms producing commodities with a combination of goods purchased from the market and their own time. Thus, households produce a commodity called "child quality" which is obtained by acquiring food, clothing, music lessons, schooling, etc., from the market, and combining it with time spent by parents in various activities involving children—feeding, teaching, training, disciplining, playing games, etc. How people choose to spend their time depends on their productivity in various activities open to them—market work, home production of various sorts, etc. How much of market goods they choose to combine with their own time depends on the value of their time and the price of market goods, and in multiperson households, on the relative values of time spent in the market and time spent in home production by the several household members.

This relatively new idea in economic thinking has both advocates and critics, and it is too soon to say how much potential there is in the view of households as miniature firms. The proponents would argue that treating time as the basic currency reflecting choice is bound to provide a much more comprehensive picture of the way in which individuals choose to pursue the maximization of well-being, and that economists' notions of prices and productivity can be applied with appropriate analytical modifications to virtually all decisions made by consumers. The skeptics would argue that economic analysis is best applied to situations in which objective economic actors buy and sell products at defined prices, not to situations where the choice of activities is influenced by personal commitments of a continuing nature, where the commodities produced are often unobservable, frequently perceptual, and rarely measurable, and where there is neither a price at which transactions can take place nor a market where transactors gather together.

References

Ando, Albert, and Franco Modigliani, "The 'Life-Cycle' Hypothesis of Saving," *American Economic Review*, vol. 53, no. 1., part 1, March 1963, pp. 55–84; Becker, Gary S., "A Theory of the Allocation of Time," *Economic Journal*, vol. 75, no. 299, September 1965, pp. 493–517; Hicks, T. R., "A Reconsideration of the Theory of Value: Part I," *Economica*, no. 1, February 1934, pp. 52–76; Fisher, Irving, *The Theory of Interest, as Determined by Impatience to Spend Income and Opportunity to Invest It*, Macmillan, New York, 1930; Friedman, Milton, *A Theory of the Consumption Function*, National Bureau of Economic Research General Series, no. 63, Princeton University Press, Princeton, N.J., 1957; Juster, F. Thomas, *Household Capital Formation and Financing, 1897–1962*, National Bureau of Economic Research General Series, no. 83, Columbia University Press, New York, 1966; Katona, George, *Psychological Analysis of Economic Behavior*, 1st ed., McGraw-Hill, New York, 1951; Keynes, John M., *The General Theory of Employment, Interest and Money*, Harcourt, Brace, New York, 1936; Marshall, Alfred, *Principles of Economics: An Introductory Volume*, 8th ed., Macmillan, London, 1938; Mincer, Jacob, "Labor Supply, Family Income, and Consumption," *American Economic Review*, vol. 50, no. 2, May 1960, pp. 574–583; Slutsky, Eugen, "Sulla Teoria del Bilancia del Consumatore," *Giornali Degli Economisti*, vol. 51, July 1915, pp. 1–26.

(*See also* Anticipation surveys, consumer; Behavioral economics; Consumers' surplus; Consumption function; Demand; Keynesian economics; Marshallian economics; Money illusion; Permanent income hypothesis; Propensity to consume or to save and inducement to invest; Saving; Utility; Wealth)

F. Thomas Juster

Consumerism

Consumerism can be most accurately identified as a label. Initially introduced by journalists as a pejorative to discredit the efforts of consumer activists, the label has now gained stature and credence, growing in acceptance as the consumer movement has gained confidence and matured.

The term carries many definitions. Stephen Greyser and Steven Diamond use it as a synonym for the so-called buyers rights movement. E. Scott Maynes's definition (1973) focuses "on the failures of the market and the widely shared feeling among consumers that they are ill served and need to take corrective action." Other definitions emphasize rights, redress, and advocacy. Most seem to identify consumerism as a response to failures or lacks in the marketplace.

A few recognize consumerism as a growing initiative that complements a well-functioning enterprise system. In a more positive vein, it can be defined as the rising level of public awareness of problems, policies, and issues that affect consumer well-being both in the private market and in the public sector. This definition allows a focus on the consumer interest in market successes as well as failures and includes public policy issues that also affect the flow of goods and services to the ultimate users.

Consumerism is a useful term despite its early rejection by the pioneers in the consumer movement. It allows a recognition of common forces and trends in diverse developments, such as: (1) expanded consumer education courses and programs; (2) consumer institutes and/or new consumer research thrusts in psychology, sociology, economics, and law; (3) recently established consumer offices or agencies at all levels of government; (4) expanded redress systems; (5) the current recognition of consumer affairs as a separate and important function in corporate management; (6) the rekindled interest of trade associations and the growing popularity of the consumer press. The term no longer seems to imply the negative and derogatory aspects associated with its original usage.

History

The roots of consumerism are in the consumer movement, in itself somewhat amorphous and hard to define. However, most consumerists agree that it has been an intermittent development going back to earlier times, with sustained spurts of activity in the period 1890–1906 and again in the 1930s. Current public awareness of consumer activity dates from March 1962, when John F. Kennedy delivered a consumer message to Congress that took cognizance of several facts: that affluence alone had not necessarily generated quality and service in the consumer goods market; that much product information was either inadequate, misleading, or false; that some products were dangerous; and that consumers, furthermore, had rights in these directions including the right to be heard. A new breed of consumer activist emerged as consumerists entered politics, a new outlook by the press appeared that amplified and encouraged what had been a latent discontent on the part of the public; and a sustained period of consumer activism was launched.

Since 1962 consumer organizations have gained membership, and consumer advocacy has grown from an isolated phenomenon to a respected profession. Several former activists now hold responsible positions in government and industry, and consumerism is being accepted as a legitimate development in a market-oriented economy.

Consumerism and Economics

Although the economics profession has held in great reverence the dictum of Adam Smith that "consumption is the sole end purpose of all production," professional economists were seldom found in the vanguard of consumerism or in consumer economics. Those who were in the vanguard generally had associations in the applied fields such as home economics, law, or education and were seldom in the mainstream of the economics profession. Unless the issues were specifically monopoly or price-centered, economists were not likely to be involved in the early consumer research. In recent years, however, consumer economics has become an identifiable subcategory within the economics profession, and many able economists are now associated with established programs of consumer studies in several institutions. These programs may or may not be in the departments of economics; however, the importance of economic understanding in programs of consumer education, consumer studies, consumer behavior, and other related titles is growing. The fact that a section on consumerism is included in the *Encyclopedia of Economics* is also evidence of this development.

Economists will undoubtedly continue to focus their research interests more toward the larger consumption questions or the supply-demand relationships than to the less well-defined consumer issues. What constitutes rational consumer behavior? How much market search is enough? What about information overload? Who pays? How should firms measure consumer satisfaction? These are questions that bridge disciplines, and they are most pertinent in light of the basic economic assumptions of rationality, perfect knowledge, and mobility that prevail in the purely competitive model. The fundamentals of consumer problems and the political realities of consumerism should keep economists interested in the developing field of consumer studies. Furthermore, the basics of the customer-provider relationship, whether in the private or the public sector, should keep consumerists interested in economics for a long time to come.

Consumerism in Other Countries

The past 20 years have seen an increase in the number of product testing, labeling, and certifying programs among the nations of the Western world. In 1960 the International Organization of Consumers Unions with headquarters at the Hague was established, and consumer policy is a growing field in several countries. Northern European countries have long led in the consumer cooperative movement; many foreign testing and labeling programs predate and continue to lead those in the United States. Exchanges of scholars among universities attests to a growing international interest in the consumer field. Thus, consumerism is not just a United States experience—it is a growing force particularly in those industrial countries that enjoy some discretionary income.

Consumer awareness is growing, and this fact must be accommodated within the enterprise system or we can expect more regulatory and legal sanctions in a political attempt to ensure that consumers' rights prevail. Information, safety, and choice are not free goods. Redress systems and avenues of communication between consumers, industry, and government are costly to maintain. However, given the ever-widening gap between those who make production decisions and those who consume final products, standards for disclosure, i.e., prepurchase information and corrective or redress mechanisms, probably offer the most promising solutions to the problems emerging out of a growing consumer awareness.

In the long run consumerism may develop the alert, informed consuming public that is necessary to the continued existence of a market-directed economy. As such a force, consumerism deserves a recognized niche in the field of economics and the serious attention of its practitioners.

References

Aaker, David A., and George S. Day, *Consumerism: Search for the Consumer Interest*, 3d ed., Free Press, New York, 1978; Bymers, Gwen J., "A Response," in Eleanor B. Sheldon (ed.), *Family Economic Behavior: Problems and Prospects*, Lippincott, Philadelphia, 1973, pp. 295–304; Greyser, Stephen A., and Steven L. Diamond, "Business is Adapting to Consumerism," *Harvard Business Review*, September–October 1974, pp. 38–58; Maynes, E. Scott, "Consumerism: Origin and Research Implications," in Sheldon op. cit., pp. 270–294; Sentry Insurance, *Consumerism at the Cross Roads*, A National Opinion Research Survey of Public Activist, Business and Regulator Attitudes Toward the Consumer Movement, 1977.

(*See also* Behavioral economics; Government regulation of business; Monopoly and oligopoly]

Gwen J. Bymers

Consumers' surplus

Consumers' surplus was introduced into economics by Alfred Marshall, although the use of the concept goes back at least to the French economist Dupuit in the first half of the nineteenth century. Current evaluation and use of the concept is subject to much controversy; for example, two Nobel Prize winners in economics disagree fundamentally about the utility of the concept: John Hicks sees great use to be made of the concept as a cornerstone of welfare economics, whereas Paul Samuelson believes that we may discard the concept without loss.

Demand and Demand Curve

The meaning and use of consumers' surplus may be seen from the following example. Suppose that it is agreed that a certain commodity should be produced if the benefits exceed the provision costs. The problem is that the measurement of benefits would seem to be a complicated, difficult, and practically impossible task. Economists, however, thought that they had found a simple way to estimate consumer benefits. The method involves the concepts of demand and a demand curve.

Imagine a household's demand per week for a particular commodity x as a function of the price per unit of that commodity. If all other influences on the demand for a commodity are constant, the relationship between the price of x and the quantity of x demanded per week will be inverse. Specifically let it be as follows:

Price of x	Quantity of x demanded per week
$1.00	0
0.90	1
0.80	2
0.70	3
0.60	4
0.50	5
0.40	6
0.30	7
0.20	8
0.10	9
0	10

If the price is 40 cents per unit, the household purchases 6 units and spends $2.40. Is the household, in fact, prepared to pay more than $2.40 for 6 units? According to the demand schedule, the answer is yes! The household is prepared to pay 90 cents for one unit, 80 cents for the second unit, and so on; thus, it follows that for 6 units the household will pay a maximum of $3.90, i.e., $1.50 more than it actually has to pay. It is this difference between the amount actually paid and the maximum that would be offered that Marshall called consumers' surplus.

We are sometimes concerned with a change that alters the price of a product, that is, not with the total benefits derived from the existence of a particular commodity but with the change in benefits due to a change in the price of a commodity. Equally, the concept of consumers' surplus may be applied to such changes. In terms of a demand curve consumers' surplus may be restated as follows: the benefit derived from the provision of a commodity or service at a particular price is the area under the demand curve at that price (assuming this area is finite), and the change in benefit is the change in the area due to a price change.

If we think of an aggregation of all individual demand curves into the market demand for a product, we have via consumers' surplus a powerful way of estimating consumer benefits from an innovation that will lower the price of a commodity. All that appears to be required is the statistical estimation of demand functions. Suppose for, example, an authority is contemplating building a river bridge that will be free to users; then its estimate of consumer benefit as a measure of the gain to the community in its capacity as a consumer will be the area under the demand curve.

Consumers' surplus, therefore, would appear to be a powerful tool in the evaluation of proposed public projects, and it is indeed regarded by some commentators (E. Mishan, 1977) as a central tool in cost-benefit analysis.

Doubts about Use and Validity of Consumers' Surplus

Other economists are much more doubtful about the use and validity of the concept. The main concern is that once the assumptions under which Marshall originally drew up his measure of consumers' surplus are relaxed, the area under the demand curve may not be an accurate measure of benefits. There are two main reasons for this skepticism.

First, changes in the price of a good will alter real income, the extent of which will depend on expenditure on the good, and this in turn will shift the demand curve. Thus, one of the initial assumptions of the measure of consumers' surplus is violated. By using a method developed by Slutsky whereby the effect of price change is divided into a substitution effect and an income effect, it can be shown that there are several measures of consumers' surplus that will coincide only under very restrictive conditions. For commodities where purchases constitute a percentage of total expenditure this does not pose an important problem empirically.

Secondly, there is the problem of the interrelationships between the demand for different commodities. Suppose the price of x falls and more money is now spent on the commodity: the extra purchases result in an increase in consumers' surplus. But the net benefit will be less because less will be bought of other commodities, and this will alter the sums of consumers' surplus arising from the purchase of them.

Whether or not the concept of consumers' surplus will continue to be used in economic analysis remains to be seen, but it is certain that the issue will be debated in the coming years.

References

Marshall, A., *Principles of Economics*, 9th ed., C. W. Guilleband (ed.), Macmillan, New York, 1961, Book III, chap. 6; Mishan, E., *Elements of Cost-Benefit Analysis*, Allen and Unwin, Winchester, Mass., chaps. 5, 6, 7, 1971.

(*See also* Cost-benefit analysis; Demand; Marshallian economics; Normative economics; Welfare economics)

Bernard A. Corry

Consumption function

The consumption function relates total consumption to the level of income or wealth and perhaps other variables. Consumption functions are sometimes defined for individual households, but their major role is determining total national consumption in a macoreconomic model.

One characteristic of the consumption function, the marginal propensity to consume (MPC), is an important determinant of the stability of the economy in simple models of the multiplier type. The MPC measures the responsiveness of consumption to assumed changes in income and is the ratio of the change in consumption to the change in income, other things being equal. Generally, the smaller the MPC, the more stable is the economy with respect to changes in government spending, investment, net exports, or money.

Introduced by Keynes

The consumption function was introduced by John Maynard Keynes (1936) as a major element in his model of income determination. Although Keynes catalogued many of the factors discussed below, he argued that consumption depends mainly on the total net income of consumers and that the MPC would be less than the ratio of consumption to income (the average propensity to consume, or APC). The latter assertion was justified by reference to the decreased marginal utility of current consumption at higher levels of income.

The simple Keynesian consumption function can be expressed as

$$c = a + by$$

where c is consumption, b the MPC, and y net income. If a is greater than zero, the APC exceeds the MPC (by a/y). In Keynesian analysis, consumption and net income are measured in real (deflated) terms. This consumption function was widely used until the early 1950s when more data and improved statistical techniques demonstrated its inadequacy.

Optimizing Hypothesis

A number of hypotheses were proposed as alternatives to the Keynesian absolute income hypothesis, but only variants of the optimizing hypothesis have withstood the test of time. The optimizing hypothesis states that current consumption will be determined as part of an optimal lifetime allocation of current and future income to current and future consumption and bequests. An increase in current or future income increases the total wealth to be allocated and so generally increases current and future consumption and bequests. Thus, factors which cause a persistent or permanent increase in income would have a much greater effect on wealth and current consumption than a temporary or transitory increase in income. In this way, the optimizing hypothesis suggests that the short-period changes in current net income considered by Keynes should have relatively small effects on consumption; that is, the MPC for transitory variations in income is small.

If income were permanently increased by some factor, then wealth would rise proportionately. The simplest assumption would be that this increase in wealth would be allocated proportionally among current and future consumption and bequests. Whether this in fact happens in the optimizing model depends on whether the ratios of marginal utilities of current and future consumption and bequests are unchanged as their levels are increased proportionally. If this is so, an increase in wealth will result in a proportional increase in current consumption. Keynes' belief that consumption would fall relative to income as wealth increased was based on looking at only the falling marginal utility of current consumption. But the marginal utility of future consumption and bequests also falls as wealth increases, and a rational plan compares the marginal utility of consumption given up now with the marginal utility of future consumption or bequests obtained. No general theoretical statement can be made as to whether current consumption rises more or less than in proportion to wealth. Since the empirical data dating from the 1800s reveal a roughly constant APC for the United States, proportionality of consumption and wealth is widely used as a working hypothesis.

Permanent Income and Life-Cycle Hypotheses

Two forms of the optimizing hypothesis are widely used: the permanent income hypothesis and the life-cycle hypothesis. Although they are equivalent in their most general forms, different simplifying assumptions have been used in empirical work.

The permanent income hypothesis of Milton Friedman (1957) attempts to divide current net income into two components termed permanent income and transitory income. Permanent income is real perpetuity yield from total current wealth. On the assumptions that there is a constant long-term real interest rate and that consumption is proportional to wealth, consumption is a constant fraction of permanent income and permanent income is that interest rate times wealth. Wealth increases over time owing to normal saving from permanent income plus the (positive or negative) windfall effect of transitory income. Transitory fluctuations in income thus have relatively small effects on permanent income and consumption.

The life-cycle hypothesis of Franco Modigliani and Richard Brumberg (1954) has made use of direct estimates of nonhuman wealth and substitutes for human wealth based on variables such as current labor income and this income times the unemployment rate. The life-cycle approach has been most popular in analyzing survey data on individual households in which age, marital status, and other demographic variables play an important role.

It has been usual in applications of the life-cycle approach to assume that bequests are zero. Although all income is consumed over an individual's life, aggregate saving results in a growing economy because youthful savers are richer and more numerous than retired savers. Recent evidence indicates that bequests are a much larger source of aggregate saving in the United States. As with retirement saving, bequests are a source of aggregate saving only in a growing economy so that individuals accumulate to leave a larger estate than they inherit. The assets which are eventually bequeathed serve as a general reserve during life, so precautionary motives as well as concern for heirs explain their size.

The optimizing hypothesis is strictly applicable only to the consumption of service flows: that is, to purchases of nondurable goods and services plus the rental value (not purchases) of durable and semidurable goods and services. This differs from Keynes' consumption concept (consumer expenditures for all goods and services) which is of interest in macroeconomic models. Some analysts have applied permanent income and life-cycle models of consumption of service flows directly to consumer expenditures data. The results can be characterized as inconsistent and misleading. Others (including Friedman, Modigliani, and their associates) have applied the optimizing models to data on consumption flows. Other models are used to explain consumer expenditures on durable goods. Accounting identities are then used to derive implied estimates of total consumer expenditures. Michael Darby (1977–1978) has combined the consumption flows and durable goods models into a single consumer expenditure function. Because consumer durable goods purchases are quite responsive to transitory income, the estimated value of the MPC is substantial—about 0.4 or 0.5. This MPC estimate is rather less than indicated initially by the Keynesian absolute income hypothesis but much greater than would be supposed from the effect on consumption flows alone.

Controversy

A source of some controversy has been the appropriate concept of net income to use. It was once popular to use only cash receipts of households as measured by disposable personal income. Much recent work has shown that undistributed corporate profits (or business saving) seems to be treated by households in large part as income. Other things being equal, higher business saving increases consumer expenditures and reduces personal saving. Also, some increases in income are supposed to be intermediate between temporary and permanent, while others such as temporary tax decrease to be paid for by a future tax increase leave wealth unchanged. Various methods have been proposed to improve wealth estimates by taking account of these differences, but none has been generally accepted. In most aggregate work permanent income or life-cycle measures are used for total wealth.

The major unresolved issue is the empirical importance of the real balance effect. The real balance effect refers to higher levels of real money balances causing higher consumer expenditures for given values of other variables. Some economists have argued that this would occur because money (at least government-issued money) is a component of wealth missed in permanent income and other measures of wealth. Others have explained the real balance effect in terms of substitution from money to consumers' durable goods during the adjustment to an unexpected change in the money supply. Traditional Keynesian economists have been skeptical of both views. This is a topic requiring substantially more empirical research.

In sum, the consumption function has developed from little more than a rule of thumb to a sophisticated empirical model of aggregate consumer expenditures.

References

Darby, Michael R., "The Consumer Expenditure Function," *Exploration in Economic Research*, no. 4, Winter–Spring 1977–1978, pp. 645–674; Friedman, Milton, *A Theory of the Consumption Function*, Princeton University Press, Princeton, N.J., 1957; Keynes, John Maynard, *The General Theory of Employment, Interest, and Money*, Harcourt, Brace, New York, 1936; Modigliani, Franco, and Richard Brumberg, "Utility Analysis and the Consumption Function: An Interpretation of Cross-Section Data," in K. E. Kurihara, *Post-Keynesian Economics*, Rutgers University Press, New Brunswick, N.J., 1954.

(*See also* Consumer theory; Investment function; Microeconomics; Permanent income hypothesis; Propensity to consume or to save and inducement to invest)

Michael R. Darby

Corporate income taxation (*see* Taxation, an overview)

Corporate liquidity (*see* Liquidity, corporate)

Cost-benefit analysis

Cost-benefit analysis is a generic term applied to any systematic, quantitative appraisal of a public project to determine whether, or to what extent, that project is worthwhile. In this context, a "project" may range from conventional public investments in flood control or transportation through social programs in the health or education areas to the passage of public laws or regulations. Essentially, a cost-benefit analysis attempts to determine whether the benefits of a public project justify the costs. Ordinarily, cost-benefit studies are prospective—evaluating proposed projects—although there are also retrospective studies. In all cases, the hallmark of a cost-benefit analysis is the systematic comparison of alternative courses of action. Cost-benefit analyses are considered aids to decision makers rather than directives; whereas, cost-benefit analysis is described as applied welfare economics, and draws much of its theoretical basis from that discipline.

Five Steps in a Cost-Benefit Analysis

There are five steps in the performance of a cost-benefit analysis.

Identification of Effects   First, all the effects of the project are identified. Typically, such effects might include changes in output levels, prices, income distribution, environmental parameters, and social parameters. The effects are identified both for the present and for all relevant future time periods. This involves forecasting trends and events about which little may be known with certainty. The key in this step is estimating as accurately as possible what difference the project will make.

Quantification of Effects   The second step is the development of quantitative estimates, in physical units, of the effects identified in the first step. For example, changes in output of a certain good might be specified as so many tons per year for each year of the project. Some effects, such as contributions of a project to social harmony, democracy, aesthetics, or culture, may be difficult to quantify. Such intangible effects, while meriting description within the cost-benefit study, necessarily remain outside the quantitative aspects of the study.

Monetary Quantification   The third step is the valuation, or monetary quantification, of the effects identified in step 1 and physically quantified in step 2. For example, for an increase in output of so many tons per year of some good, a monetary value for that change in output is developed. The rule governing the determination of monetary values is social willingness to pay, which refers to the valuation of items according to what society, if perfectly informed, would be willing to pay to gain a benefit or avoid a cost. Under certain conditions market prices reflect social willingness to pay, and these prices can be used to accomplish this step of the study. Under other conditions, principally those involving situations in which the real world differs markedly from the model of perfect competition, market prices either do not exist or are not adequate measures of social willingness to pay. Cases involving public goods or externalities typify such situations. In these cases, the monetary values often used are shadow prices, that is, estimated prices of social willingness to pay. Effects amenable to physical quantification, but which are difficult to translate into monetary terms (such as lost lives or cases of cancer), are often called incommensurables.

Aggregation   The fourth step is aggregation of all effects in each time period, and over all time periods. The purpose of aggregation is to reduce costs and benefits over the span of the project to a single number which captures the overall worth of the project. Of the many approaches to aggregation, the three most popular involve the calculation of the project's internal rate of return, benefit-cost ratio, and net present value. Each of these measures has advantages and disadvantages, though there appears to be a developing consensus that net present value is the preferred approach. All reasonable aggregation schemes involve discounting future costs and benefits, that is, placing less weight on an effect the further into the future it is expected to occur. Discounting is accomplished by employing a discount rate, and assigning weights to time periods by the formula

$$w_t = \frac{1}{(1 + d)^t}$$

where t is the index of time periods (usually in years), d is the discount rate, and w_t the weight assigned to all effects in period t. By convention the current time period is designated as $t = 0$, so its weight w_0 equals 1. All future years have weights less than 1, declining from 1, and eventually nearing 0 as t becomes large. For example, the weight for effects expected 20 years from now using a discount rate of 10 percent is roughly 0.15. This means a \$100 benefit 20 years from now would be counted as having the same value as a \$15 benefit this year. Experience has shown that the results of cost-benefit studies tend to be quite sensitive to the discount rate employed. Economists continue to debate the proper choice of a discount rate for cost-benefit studies.

Sensitivity Analysis   The final step is sensitivity analysis, which involves calculations to determine how sensitive the results of the study are to changes in the values of the variables and parameters used in the study, and to changes in the probability of their occurrence. This provides an indication of the validity of any conclusions, and allows (typically through tabular and/or graphic displays) the decision maker to insert chosen parameters, variables, and probability values and to determine how the results of the study would thereby change.

History and Importance

The inception of cost-benefit analysis occurred in 1844 with the publication of an essay, "On the Measurement of the Utility of Public Works," by Jules Dupuit, a French engineer. Dupuit developed the concept of consumers' surplus, an idea which today is a cornerstone of cost-benefit analysis. However, Dupuit's ideas lay dormant until the passage of the U.S. Flood Control Act of 1936, which decreed that flood control projects should pass the test that "the benefits to whomsoever they may accrue are in excess of the estimated costs." This act stimulated work in both the theory and application of cost-benefit analysis, first only in the area of water resources, but by the 1950s in defense analysis, and since the 1960s in virtually all areas of public expenditure. Today, cost-benefit analyses are routinely carried out throughout the federal bureaucracy, and sometimes at the state and local levels as well. Such studies often play a prominent role in the debates over the public projects, but because such project decisions are made in the political arena, it is difficult to establish the degree to which the results of cost-benefit studies actually influence those final decisions. Certainly, there are many examples of public decisions running counter to the results of cost-benefit studies.

International Considerations

Cost-benefit analysis has found acceptance outside the United States, both in advanced and lesser-developed countries. In particular, Great Britain has produced many significant contributions to the field. Under the leadership of international organizations such as the United Nations and the Inter-American Development Bank, cost-benefit analysis is being brought to bear on the development programs of the Third World. In these applications, cost-benefit analysis faces more than its usual complement of difficulties due to the multiple (often conflicting) objectives and chronic disequilibrium conditions of the host countries.

Relation to Other Terms

The field of project appraisal abounds with terms similar in appearance or intent to cost-benefit analysis. Capital-budgeting analysis is the private-sector equivalent of cost-benefit analysis. It is project appraisal from the firm's point of view. Cost-effectiveness analysis is a special case of cost-benefit analysis in which, among the alternatives under consideration, either the cost of each or the benefit of each is the same, and the purpose of the study is to identify the alternative with the greatest effectiveness (benefit) or the least cost. Social impact assessment, economic impact assessment, environmental impact assessment, and technology assessment can all be considered partial cost-benefit analyses in the sense that each typically considers only a subset of the whole range of project effects and typically progresses only through step 2 (and perhaps partially into step 3) of the five steps described above.

Positive and Negative Views

Criticisms of the field are both general and specific. One general criticism is that cost-benefit analysis attempts to reduce everything to the common denominator of money, and that this is simply not possible. Another general criticism is that public project decisions are, and and should be, political decisions, and that economic substitutes for the political process are insidious. Another such criticism is that cost-benefit analysis feigns an objectivity it indeed lacks, and that cost-benefit results are hopelessly biased by the subjective attitudes of those performing the study. Criticisms often revolve around effects allegedly erroneously included or excluded as benefits or costs, as valuation procedures, or as aggregation procedures.

Even proponents of cost-benefit analysis admit some criticisms are justified. They point, however, to the continuing evolution of cost-benefit analysis: over time researchers and practitioners have worked to eliminate glaring deficiencies. For example, while in earlier years the only project effects included in cost-benefit studies were those affecting gross national product, today many studies attempt to treat environmental and social factors, regional factors, and income redistribution factors as well. But the real justification advanced by proponents is summed up by their query, "What is the alternative?" At the very least, a cost-benefit analysis forces assumptions, projections, estimates, and reasoning to be laid open to scrutiny. It is, in this sense, a scientific procedure.

References

Dasgupta, P., A. Sen, and S. Marglin, *UNIDO Guidelines for Project Evaluation*, United Nations, New York, 1972; Harberger, Arnold, ed., *Cost-Benefit and Policy Analysis*, vols. 1–4, Aldine, Chicago, 1972–1975; Little, I. M. D., and J Mirrlees, *Project Appraisal and Planning for Developing Countries*, Basic Books, New York, 1974; Mishan, E. J., *Cost Benefit Analysis*, Praeger, New York, 1976; Sassone, P. G., and W. A. Schaffer, *Cost-Benefit Analysis: A Handbook*, Academic Press, New York, 1978.

(*See also* Consumers' surplus; Normative economics; Utility; Welfare economics)

Peter G. Sassone

Cost of living

The cost of living is a term loosely used to refer to the cost of purchasing a basket of consumer goods at today's prices compared with what the same basket would have cost in some previous or base period. In its general usage, the term is viewed as synonymous with the consumer price index (CPI). However, in a more technical sense, an index of the cost of living is quite different from that of consumer prices. When reference is made to such a cost-of-living index as distinct from a consumer price index, that distinction is generally heralded by the use of the phrase "true cost-of-living index."

A True Cost-of-Living Index

A true cost-of-living index introduces the notion that there may be more than one bundle of goods or market basket that affords the consumer a given level of satisfaction. Thus, a consumer may consider that he or she is equally well off when consuming 6 pounds of beef and 3 pounds of pork as when consuming 3 pounds of beef and 8 pounds of pork. Note that the foregoing example of equivalence is predicated on a 50 percent reduction in beef consumption and a greater than 50 percent increase in pork consumption to achieve equivalence. The inference is that, on balance, consumers prefer beef to pork. But, there are some circumstances—i.e., those in which the consumer gets more than 1 pound of pork for each pound of beef given up—as yielding equivalent satisfaction.

In fact, if the consumer viewed beef and pork as yielding equivalent satisfaction, pound for pound, then one would expect that a 50 percent reduction in beef would be offset by a 50 percent increase in pork if the consumer satisfaction were to remain unchanged. Under those circumstances, beef and pork are not really different products, but are the same product, meat.

If equivalent market baskets exist, then the consumer is free to choose among them. On what will the selection be predicated? The unique market basket that will be selected among all equivalents will be determined, according to economic theory, by relative prices. That is, if the price of beef rises relative to the price of pork, the consumer will pick an equivalent basket from among the equivalent baskets; it will be a basket that contains more pork relative to the basket that would have been selected had the price of beef not risen. In other words, given the consumer's tastes, reflected by the rate at which the consumer is willing to substitute beef for pork, the consumer will select the unique equivalent market basket that yields the greatest possible satisfaction given the relative prices of the items in the market basket and given the consumer's income. In a second time period, relative prices may have changed, leading the consumer to select a different market basket. In order to calculate the change in the true cost of living, it is necessary to calculate the amount of income it would cost to purchase the new market basket compared with the amount of income it would take to purchase the basket of the previous time period. The ratio of the former to the latter will be an index of the true cost of living.

The Equivalent Market Basket Problem

In a consumer price index the same market basket is priced in every time period. For a true cost-of-living index, an equivalent market basket, not necessarily the identical market basket, is priced in every time period. The logical question is whether or not the true cost of living will rise faster or slower than a consumer price index based on a fixed market basket in the base year. The answer is that if consumer tastes and real income are unchanged from one time period to another, then a true cost-of-living index will rise less than an index such as the CPI, calculated by using the Laspeyres formula. However, in the real world, such conditions are rarely met, so it is not really possible to know whether or not a true cost-of-living index would rise faster or slower than a Laspeyres index or than a Paasche index.

There are some studies that suggest that the difference between the Laspeyres index and the true cost-of-living index might be of the order of magnitude of one- to two-tenths of a percentage point a year in terms of rates of change, the true cost-of-living index rising more slowly than the CPI. But such studies are still in the pioneering stage and involve making assumptions about the constancy of consumer tastes and the degree of interaction in the consumption of various products.

Other Differences

Some think that there are other differences between the consumer price index and the true cost-of-living index than merely the notion of equivalent market baskets. However, most of these differences could be relevant to either a CPI or cost-of-living index. For example, some think that taxes and saving and the benefits derived from government purchases belong rightfully in a true cost-of-living index, but not in a consumer price index. However, it is possible to formulate both indexes to answer the question of what level of income is required at today's market prices to maintain the base-period living standard. The present CPI and its true cost-of-living analog described above were intended to answer the question of what level of expenditures is required in today's market prices to maintain the base-period living standard. Thus, both indexes can be framed in terms of either expenditures or income. In fact, both can be framed even more broadly to encompass total wealth rather than income. Such an index would address the issue of what is the change in wealth required to leave an individual equally well off in two price situations. So the main difference between the technical use of the true cost-of-living index and the consumer price index has to do with the fact that the former may include more than one market basket that would yield equivalent satisfaction, whereas the CPI is based on only one market basket.

References

Braithwait, Steven D., "The Substitution Bias of the Laspeyres Price Index: An Analysis Using Estimated Cost-of-Living Indexes," *American Economic Review*, March 1980, pp. 64–77; Konus, A. A., "The Problem of the True Index of the Cost of Living," *Econometrica*, 1939, pp. 10–29.

(*See also* Consumer price index; Index numbers; Price measurement)

Joel Popkin

Council of Economic Advisers

The Council of Economic Advisers (CEA) is a three-member board which advises the President of the United States on national economic policy. Established under the Employment Act of 1946, the Council's primary role is to provide economic analysis and advice to the President and to assist in the development and implementation of national economic policies designed to achieve the government's objectives for employment, output, and price stability. The Council also assists the President in the preparation of the annual economic report, gathers information on economic conditions, appraises the economic programs and activities of the federal government, and makes economic studies at the President's request.

With the enactment of the Full Employment and Balanced Growth Act of 1978—the Humphrey-Hawkins Act—the chartering legislation of the Council was substantially revised for the first time since 1946.

The Council is responsible for advising the President not only on federal fiscal policies but also on regulation and regulation reform, energy policies, and international economic policies.

Advising the President in macroeconomic policy continues to be one of the Council's major responsibilities. The Council develops economic forecasts several times a year with the assistance of an Interagency Forecasting Committee, which includes, in addition to the Council member, representatives from the Office of Management and Budget, and from the Departments of Treasury, Commerce, and Labor. The Chairman of the Council, in turn, presents these forecasts to the Economic Policy Group, which is made up of the President's principal economic advisers. The Council works with members of the Economic Policy Group in the final months of each year to develop and present to the President proposals for the stance and structure of federal fiscal policies during the next year. The Council also monitors the progress and offers advice on when changes in fiscal policy are in order.

Since its inception, the CEA has become increasingly involved in the analysis of microeconomic issues—the development and policy actions that affect individual industries, markets, or sectors of the economy. The Council has taken part in formulating and presenting the administration's policies on agriculture, energy, health insurance, hospital costs, welfare reform, regulatory reform, and international trade.

The Council's three-member board consists of the Chairman and two members. The Chairman is responsible for communicating the CEA's views to the President. The two Council members directly supervise the work of the Council's professional staff, which consists of economists, econometricians, and statisticians.

The annual *Economic Report* is the vehicle through which the CEA informs the public of its work and its views.

(*See also* Joint Economic Committee of Congress)

Douglas Greenwald

Council on Wage and Price Stability

The Council on Wage and Price Stability (CWPS) was created in August 1974 to help fill the void left by the termination of President Nixon's Economic Stabilization Program. The CWPS was instructed by Congress to monitor both private wage and price decisions and public regulatory policy and assess their potential effects on inflation. Although it can be viewed as the successor to the Cost of Living Council which administered the 1971–74 controls program, the CWPS differs significantly from that agency because it is explicitly barred from imposing mandatory wage and price controls.

During its first 4 years, the CWPS was a small, low-profile agency with about 39 staff members. The Council divided its efforts between scrutinizing private-sector wage and price decisions and evaluating the potential inflationary impact of government regulatory actions. In some instances, the Council held public hearings and issued public reports of its findings. On occasion, it requested delays or reductions of private-sector price increases.

On October 24, 1978, President Carter ordered the CWPS to design and administer a voluntary program of wage and price restraint. The Council was also expected to continue monitoring government regulatory activities. The new responsibility pushed the Council into the public eye and necessitated an expansion in staff to about 230 members.

A Voluntary Program of Standards

The standards program represented a new element in an anti-inflation program for the United States. In 1974 the nation had ended an unsatisfactory experiment with a peacetime program of mandatory wage and price controls.

The voluntary effort differed significantly from its immediate predecessor because of the explicit recognition that government intervention in wage and price decisions could not, by itself, permanently reduce inflation. Unlike the Nixon controls, the

Carter administration's voluntary program was accompanied by monetary and fiscal restraint as well as regulatory reform.

The program was intended to reverse a wage-price spiral that fueled inflation in the absence of demand pressures. The standards were viewed as a temporary approach that would terminate once market forces moderated and began to act as a restraining factor on prices.

Initially, the CWPS proposed to monitor directly the price behavior of firms with annual sales of $500 million or more. Later, the Council's efforts were extended to companies with sales of $250 million or more annually. The Council also focused its attention on pay increases granted by firms with 5000 or more employees.

Although participation in the program remained voluntary, the Council subsequently asked these larger firms to submit periodic reports on their price and pay practices. In addition, the Council conducted inquiries into the price practices of smaller businesses when aggregate data indicated unusually high price increases in a specific sector of the economy.

The decision not to monitor directly a larger segment of the economy on a routine basis was predicated on the belief that compliance by the biggest firms would induce smaller businesses to follow the market leaders. In addition, the limited monitoring coverage represented a recognition of the inherent limitations of a small agency.

During the first year of the program, the standards asked that average annual increases in wages and fringe benefits for specified employee groups be held to 7 percent or less. Average price increases for a company's entire product line were to be at least 0.5 percentage point less than the average increases in 1976 and 1977. In addition, the Council provided an alternative profit-margin standard for firms faced with uncontrollable cost increases that made compliance with the deceleration test an economic impossibility.

The CWPS estimated that 100 percent compliance with the standard would have reduced the rate of price increases to 5.75 percent. Realizing that some slippage was inevitable, the Council established an inflation rate target of 6 to 6.5 percent. However, market conditions in food, housing, and energy (sectors largely outside the scope of the standards) caused prices to rise at double that rate despite widespread compliance with the program. Consequently, the CWPS found itself with the anomaly of a wage-price program that functioned much as intended, but failed to stem inflation.

The worsening of inflation meant that the program faced a new challenge in its second year. Rather than attempting to decelerate wage and price increases, the CWPS aimed at preventing advances in food, energy, and housing costs from becoming permanently embedded in the industrial price structure.

One of President Reagan's first official acts was to abolish the CWPS as one step in eliminating government interference in the marketplace.

(*See also* Government regulation of business; Incomes policy; Inflation)

R. Robert Russell

Countervailing power

Economists in both the classical and Marxist traditions in economics are fully agreed on the socially damaging character of unchecked economic power. Countervailing power is the force by which such power is checked. The damage that can be done by the monopoly (or monopsony) in enhancing its profits at the expense of those to whom it sells or from whom it buys is common ground in both traditions. A principal difference lies in the conclusion that is drawn. In the classical/neoclassical tradition monopoly or monopoly power is exceptional, and in the common textbook view of economic policy it can be made more exceptional by well-considered policy. Antitrust action and lower tariffs are other steps to promote competition and are an effective antidote to monopoly and market power. In the Marxist tradition this, of course, is not the case. Capitalist concentration of monopoly power increases along with the attendant exploitation until the inevitable end.

Curbing Economic Power

The concept of countervailing power does not deny the role of competition as a solvent for economic power. It does argue against efforts to dissolve positions of economic power as the principal remedy. It is the curious tendency of much economic instruction that it disguises the everyday reality, and countervailing power is a case in point. Specifically, when sellers and buyers are faced with the practical consequences of monopoly power, they are usually more successful in organizing opposing and neutralizing positions of power than in dissolving the original concentration. The clearest case is the labor market. In theory it is open to the seller of labor to hope that through public policy buyers or employers of labor will be made as numerous and as weak in the market as they are themselves. In practice no one thinks this possible. And in consequence the trade union comes into existence to develop an equalizing or countervailing power. But while the trade union is the outstanding manifestation of countervailing power, it is by no means the only one. Farmers faced with the strong monopolistic or oligopolistic position of the buyers of their products have in all modern countries organized themselves into selling cooperatives. Or they have sought the support of the state in enhancing their bargaining power. And faced with strong sellers of fertilizer, petroleum, and other farm supplies, farmers have similarly organized themselves into buying cooperatives. Such organization has also been the commonplace recourse of consumers. And within the framework of capitalist markets the large mass-market retailers develop and deploy their buying power to negate the market power of manufacturers and other suppliers—the practical deployment of countervailing power. As a device against economic power it is far more effective and much more used than action through the antitrust laws to dissolve such power.

The concept of countervailing power was developed in the volume *American Capitalism: The Concept of Countervailing Power*. On the whole, it has survived the ensuing discussion. However, not all of the argument originally put forward can be sustained. For example, the argument concerning the inevitability of countervailing power or its tendency to an equilibrium in which all or most market power is dissolved no longer seems valid.

Time has revealed another flaw. It was recognized and argued in the initial version that countervailing power did not work well under conditions of excess demand or inflation—that it could dissolve into a coalition against the larger public. But it was not then foreseen that inflation would become a normal circumstance in the modern industrial economy. And to the extent that it has become normal, the role of countervailing power has been reduced. This reduction has not been complete; the rise of consumerism in the sixties and seventies is obviously a powerful manifestation of the phenomenon. But inflation is assuredly inimical to a socially benign deployment of countervailing power.

References

Galbraith, John Kenneth, *American Capitalism: The Concept of Countervailing Power*, Houghton Mifflin, Boston, 1952, rev. ed., 1956.

(*See also* Competition; Monopoly and oligopoly)

John Kenneth Galbraith

Credit, an overview

Credit and its opposite, debt, are transactions in which command over resources is obtained in the present in exchange for a promise to repay in the future, normally with a payment of interest as compensation to the lender. Such transactions were a part of life in the earliest and simplest societies, and they are today more crucial than ever before to the economic process. Credit appears wherever capital is used and savings are required—in economies in which the production process is socialized and centrally directed, where it becomes a major arm of the planning process, as well as in market-oriented, enterprise economies built on the institution of private property. Because its use has been marked by excesses that led to some of the most spectacular crises of commercial history, and because it is recognized as a basic force in inflation, credit is naturally of great interest to economists, businessmen, and consumers alike.

Credit transactions can occur between individuals as simple personal arrangements, as when money is loaned to a friend, but its importance as an economic institution lies in formalized transactions carried out in highly developed financial markets under a carefully formulated contract. The parties involved, the kind of instruments used, and the terms on which credit is extended are enormously varied and in continual evolution. Institutional arrangements vary from country to country; yet, essentials are the same everywhere: a present value transferred by a creditor (investor) to a debtor (borrower), who undertakes to repay in the future on terms specified in a credit agreement, with the debtor promising also to pay interest or other fees as compensation to the creditor.

Based on research that began in the United States at the National Bureau of Economic Research in the 1940s and that was continued by the Board of Governors of the Federal Reserve System, data are estimated quarterly in the flow-of-funds accounts that show the volume of credit raised in U.S. credit markets by all groups of borrowers and the several sources from which it is obtained. The excess (deficiency) of credit extended in any period over repayments on earlier extensions results in an increase (decrease) in the volume of debt outstanding, which is estimated to have accumulated by the end of 1976 in the United States to $3354 billion.

Range of Credit Instruments and Agreements

Having evolved to serve a great variety of borrowers seeking credit for widely different purposes under varying circumstances from creditors with different investment objectives, credit instruments and the agreements underlying them exhibit a wide range of features.

Promise to Repay   The promise to repay, which is found everywhere except in the unusual case of perpetual debt (e.g., British consols), is usually supported by some form of security. This may be only the promise of the debtor, attested by his or her signature or by the signature of a designated "signing official" for a business concern. Although such a credit is typically called unsecured, the borrower's promise to repay allows claims to be entered against his or her income or assets in the event of default. Security may be provided by additional names (cosigners), by a lien on specific assets (home mortgages on real property, railroad equipment, trust receipts, etc.), by an assignment of accounts receivable, or by claims to inventory; alternatively, there may be an assignment of rights to a flow of income, as in revenue bonds used frequently to finance public improvements, or a pledge of the "full faith and credit" of government. In all cases, the purpose of security is to give the lender or investor something of value to fall back on if the loan contract is not fulfilled.

Time to Repay   Credits vary according to the length of time permitted for repayment. Transactions may be entered into to borrow only overnight, which is common between commercial banks, or for a long period, as in bond and mortgage financing. Thirty years is a common term-to-maturity period for long-term corporate, government, and home mortgage financing in U.S. credit markets; consumer installment credit typically requires full repayment within one to five years. In some instances, loans must be repaid in equal amounts in regularly spaced installments, which is typical in consumer installment credit, but repayment is usually at least in part at the discretion of the borrower. Some loan contracts specify that repayment is due only at final maturity, in which case refinancing may be required. In the United States, it was common before 1929 for commercial banks to write mortgages for short periods, often for only a year, and to require no reduction of principal in the interim; at maturity the loan was allowed to remain in a technically defaulted status as long as interest was paid. This practice proved disastrously unwise when personal incomes and property values collapsed in the 1930s, forcing a multitude of loans into default and embarrassing large numbers of banking institutions. In the spate of remedial federal legislation that followed, the Homeowners Loan Corporation was established as a federal agency to purchase defaulted mortgages from lending institutions, and loan insurance was provided by a newly established Federal Housing Administration for home mortgages made by qualified lenders on terms calling for periodic reduction of principal.

Means of Transfer   Debt instruments may be transferable by sale or assignment to other investors (as with negotiable or bearer bonds), or may be nonnegotiable. Trading in negotiable securities constitutes the daily business of bond markets associated with national security exchanges, but may be conducted directly between investors. Since interest on a security is normally fixed at origination, the market value of the instrument varies inversely with subsequent fluctuations in interest rates, which makes bonds a potential vehicle for speculative investment. In addition, markets exist for trading in futures contracts on financial instruments (rights to buy a specified instrument at a specified price at some future date).

Terms of Agreement Although credit instruments normally convey no right of ownership to the creditor, loan agreements in recent years have included in some cases what is colloquially called an "equity kicker," which entitles the creditor under specified conditions to a share of ownership in the borrower's assets, or a right to participate in the borrower's income over and above the interest payments originally contracted for. Older arrangements directed to similar ends involve convertible bonds (exchangeable at the investor's option for common stock) or warrants (rights to purchase common stock at a specified price).

Interest Interest payable on a credit instrument is usually fixed, but because of more frequent and wider fluctuations of interest rates in the 1970s variable rates are now more often used. Usually, interest is paid at regular intervals over the life of the loan, sometimes on presentation of a coupon attached to the credit instrument (giving rise to the expression "coupon clipper"); alternatively, interest may be taken in the form of a face value of the debt at maturity greater than the amount originally advanced.

Transaction Finally, credit may be extended in a single transaction, as when a bond is sold or a loan is made, or the proceeds may be advanced at intervals at the discretion of the debtor under an open credit agreement. Credit cards are the most widely used example of the latter. The amount of open credit extended is subject to limitation, however, if repayment obligations are not respected according to schedule.

Extension of Credit

The determination of whether credit can be extended safely may be casual or highly formal, as when the loan committee of a bank must act on a loan application or when a public offering of bonds is underwritten by an investment banking syndicate. To service these activities, private agencies have been formed that rate bonds, and credit reporting companies are found in most markets to provide information on the credit standing of individuals and businesses. Also, some lending institutions have developed a sophisticated credit scoring system under which various characteristics of the credit and the debtor are used in a statistical formula designed to separate acceptable from nonacceptable risks.

Losses on loans are typically charged against a loan loss reserve, in which crediting to the reserve is counted as a charge against the lending institution's income and thus a cost of the credit-extending process. Along with other features of the credit agreement, the interest rate may vary according to the creditor's judgment of the risk involved.

Credit Regulations

Few areas of enterprise are regulated and supervised by government more closely than the extension of credit. Commercial codes in the legal system of all countries specify the rights and obligations of debtors and creditors; interest rate ceilings are specified in the usury statutes of many states; loans to individuals are commonly subject to limitations as to maximum amount and maximum interest rate in state small-loan legislation; and in the interest of protecting depositors, shareholders, or policyowners, most types of lending or investing institutions are subject to regular examination by state or federal authorities, or both. Where home mortgage loans have been insured or guaranteed by government, as by the Federal Housing Administration or the Veterans Administration, not only the mortgage but the property that secures it, and the purposes for which the credit is advanced, are subject to federal regulation. At times, controls have been imposed directly on specified types of credit, as in the selective control of consumer credit and home mortgage credit during World War II and the Korean conflict.

Under a series of laws, the Federal Reserve Board has issued regulations designed to protect the consumer in credit transactions:

1. The Consumer Credit Protection Act of 1968 (Truth-in-Lending Act) specifies what information must be provided on the cost of borrowing money or buying on credit.

2. The Equal Credit Opportunity Act prohibits discrimination in the extension of credit on grounds of age, race, sex, or marital status, and certain other factors.

3. The Fair Credit Reporting Act establishes procedures for correcting mistakes on an individual's credit record.

4. The Fair Credit Billing Act provides procedures for correcting errors in billing and disputes arising particularly from the use of credit cards.

5. The Community Reinvestment Act is designed to prevent so-called redlining— a practice alleged to involve arbitrary limitations on lending in specified areas of a community.

Fractional Reserve System

Although legislation has been concerned increasingly with the fairness aspect of credit extension, the major public interest in credit arises from the use of a fractional reserve system, as in the United States, in which a commercial bank is required to hold reserves only up to a specified fraction of its deposit liabilities, and from the connection between this process and changes in the nation's money supply. The connection arises because a commercial bank commonly advances loan proceeds by crediting the borrower with a deposit that becomes part of the nation's money supply. Economic studies show a connection between changes in money supply and changes in the level of prices, with monetarists emphasizing the connection more heavily than others. There is, therefore, a keen interest in controlling the credit-extending and related deposit-generating processes in the public interest.

In the U.S. banking system, the instruments of control are in the hands of the Federal Reserve System, which can influence the volume of bank reserves and thus the degree to which deposit volume can be expanded (or contracted) through net credit expansion (or contraction). It was once a widely held view that no harm would be done by credit expansion and deposit creation so long as credits were limited to loans for self-liquidating purposes (e.g., where credit was extended for the accumulation of inventory and repaid from sales receipts as inventory was turned over), but the conventional view currently is that it is the quantity of credit extended, regardless of quality, and the corollary expansion of deposit liabilities and money supply, that is crucial.

References

Board of Governors, *Flow of Funds Accounts*, Federal Reserve System, December, 1976; Dusenberry, James S., *Money and Credit: Impact and Control*, 3d ed., Prentice-Hall, Englewood Cliffs, N.J., 1972; Henning, Charles N., William Piggott, and Robert Haney Scott, *Financial Markets and the Economy*, 2d ed., Prentice-Hall, Englewood Cliffs, N.J., 1978; The Hunt Commission, *The Report of the President's Commission on Financial Structure and Regulation*, December 1971; Young, Ralph A., *Instruments of Monetary Policy in the United States*, International Monetary Fund, Washington, D.C., 1973, chap. 2.

(*See also* Business credit; Consumer credit; Debt; Federal Reserve policy; Federal Reserve System; Interest rates; Monetary policy; Mortgage credit; Selective credit controls)

Raymond J. Saulnier

Credit, business (see Business credit)

Credit, consumer (see Consumer credit)

Credit controls, selective (see Selective credit controls)

Credit, mortgage (see Mortgage credit)

Cross-sectional analysis in business and economics

Cross-sectional analysis is the study of relationships between two or more variables which measure the situations of different households, firms, or geographical entities at the same point in time. It contrasts with time series analysis, which measures the changing situations of a single entity (e.g., a national economy) at successive points in time. Since the 1950s, interest has developed in the possible ways of pooling information from cross-sectional and time series studies.

The statistical technique generally used in cross-sectional studies is least-squares regression analysis. Some of the problems involved are the same as in time series analysis: choosing the form of the function to be fitted, allowing for the biasing effects of errors in the independent variables, and recognizing the probable effects of excluded variables.

If the observations are listed according to some ordering principle, the Durbin-Watson statistic used to test for autocorrelation in time series may also be helpful in cross-sectional studies. For example, if the successive observations in a cross-sectional study refer to geographically contiguous areas, positive autocorrelation in the residuals may disclose systematic effects of climate, large-region food habits, or other omitted variables. Prais and Houthakker (1955) listed households in order of total expenditure and used the Durbin-Watson statistic to determine whether the residuals from linear regressions indicated significant departures from linearity; if so, they proceeded to fit appropriate nonlinear functions.

Random errors in the independent variable of a simple least-squares regression equation bias the regression coefficient toward zero in cross-sectional as well as in time series studies. Friedman created an elaborate economic theory to explain why the regression coefficients of family expenditures upon family income in (ungrouped) cross-sectional data were lower than those obtained from time series of national income and consumption expenditures. However, Houthakker maintained that errors of measurement in the family income data were sufficient to account for the lower cross-sectional coefficients, and that Friedman's economic theory, right or wrong, was logically independent of the statistics on which he based it.

In cross-sectional studies, as in time series studies, it is important to be clear about what is being measured. For example, the gross outputs of different farms in a given year may be strongly influenced by weather. If we regress gross output on gross input, positive deviations may or may not indicate greater managerial efficiency. If we have data on each farm for several successive years, weather effects may be largely eliminated by fitting a regression equation based on several yearly average values of the variables for each farm; the residuals from this equation should give a much clearer indication of differences in efficiency.

History

The earliest type of cross-sectional analysis was the study of household expenditures upon different categories of goods. The first and most famous empirical relationship based on such a study was Engel's law, proposed in 1857: "The poorer a family, the greater the proportion of its total expenditure that must be devoted to food."

Household expenditure studies increased in number and improved in quality from the 1870s on. William F. Ogburn, known primarily as a sociologist, was (in 1916) among the first to fit multiple regression equations to such data, expressing expenditures on each category as a function of family income and family size. Stigler (1954) calculated income elasticities of expenditure from Ogburn's equations.

In the early 1950s, several economists tried grafting cross-sectional estimates of income elasticities into time series regressions of per capita food consumption upon food prices and per capita income. Thus, if the original time series demand function were $q_t = a + bp_t + cy_t + u_t$ and the regression coefficient of q on y in the cross-sectional data were c^*, these economists would compute an adjusted consumption variable $q_t^* = (q_t - c^*y_t)$ and fit the equation $q_t^* = a + bp_t + u_t$ to estimate the net relationship between consumption and price. This procedure was criticized by other economists on the allegation that cross-sectional data should reflect long-run adjustments of family consumption patterns to family incomes, while time series of annual observations should reflect short-run adjustments only. This allegation is probably not true for food, but the possibility that cross-sectional and time series regressions may reflect different types of behavior must be carefully considered in each particular case.

As more time series data for individual firms became publicly available, it became possible to combine cross-sectional and time series data for identical firms. The first major study of this sort was published by Kuh in 1959 using annual data for 73 firms over a period of 17 years. Averaging values of the variables over the 73 firms in each year gave him 17 times series observations, and averaging values of the variables over the 17 years for each firm gave him 73 cross-sectional observations. He fitted equations of the same form to the two sets of observations and obtained substantially different regression coefficients. He also demonstrated more powerful methods based on variance and covariance analysis of all 1241 (73 firms times 17 years) observations.

Maddala (1971) asserted that the use of analysis of covariance techniques in the pooling of cross-sectional and time series data had become a common practice in econometric work.

References

Kuh, Edwin, "The Validity of Cross-Sectionally Estimated Behavior Equations in Time Series Applications," *Econometrica*, vol. 27, 1959, pp. 197–214; Maddala, G. S., "The Use of Variance Components Models in Pooling Cross Section and Time Series Data," *Econometrica*, vol. 39, 1971, pp. 341–358; Nerlove, Marc, "Further Evidence on the Estimation of Dynamic Economic Relations From a Time Series of Cross Sections," *Econometrica*, vol. 39, 1971, pp. 359–382; Prais, S. J., and H. S. Houthakker, *The Analysis of Family Budgets*, Cambridge University Press, Cambridge, 1955, 1971; Stigler, George J., "The Early History of Empirical Studies of Consumer Behavior," *The Journal of Poltical Economy*, vol. 62, 1954, pp. 95–113.

(*See also* Elasticity; Regression analysis in business and economics; Time series analysis)

Karl A. Fox and Tej K. Kaul

Currency school

The currency school refers to a group of influential British economists who wrote about monetary regulation in the middle decades of the nineteenth century. Led by Lord Overstone (Samuel Jones Lloyd), George Warde Norman, and Robert Torrens, the currency school advocated 100 percent gold reserve backing for banknotes to ensure that the volume of notes varied identically with changes in the nation's monetary gold stock. This prescription was derived from the principle of metallic fluctuation, the cornerstone of the school's analysis. According to the metallic principle, a mixed currency of paper and coin should be made to behave exactly as if it were wholly metallic, automatically expanding and contracting dollar for dollar with inflows and outflows of gold. Departure from this rule would permit inflationary overissue of paper, forcing an efflux of specie through the balance of payments, which in turn could endanger the gold reserve, threaten the gold convertibility of the currency, compel the need for sharp contraction, and thereby precipitate financial panics. No such consequences would ensue if the currency conformed to the metallic principle, however. Forced to behave like gold (regarded by the currency school as the stablest of monetary standards), the currency would be spared those sharp fluctuations in quantity that constitute the main source of economic disturbances.

Strict Regulation

Given the desirability of making banknotes behave like gold, by what means was this result to be achieved? Earlier writers, notably David Ricardo, had found the answer in convertibility. If the currency were convertible, they reasoned, any excess issue of notes, which raised British prices relative to foreign prices, would be converted into gold in order to make cheaper purchases abroad. The resulting loss in specie reserves would force banks to contract their note issue, thus eliminating the excess.

A series of monetary crises in the 1820s and 1830s, however, convinced the currency school that mere convertibility was not enough to safeguard the currency. It was an insufficient safeguard because it allowed banks too much discretion in the management of their note issue. Banks could and did continue to issue notes even as gold was flowing out, delaying contraction until the last minute when reserves were almost depleted, and then contracting with a violence that sent shock waves throughout the economy. What was needed, the currency school thought, was a law removing the note issue from the discretion of bankers and placing it under strict regulation. To be effective, this law should require banks to contract their note issues one for one with outflows of gold, thereby putting an early and gradual stop to specie drains.

The currency school scored a triumph when its ideas were enacted into legislation. The famous Bank Charter Act of 1844 embodied its prescription that, except for a small fixed fiduciary issue, notes were to be backed by an identical amount of gold. In modern terminology, the act established a marginal gold reserve requirement of 100 percent to back notes. With notes rigidly tied to gold in this fashion, external gold drains would be accompanied by a domestic reduction of a like amount of notes, as required by the metallic principle.

Banking School's Arguments

The currency school's prescription, however, was not universally endorsed. The rival banking school flatly denied the need for statutory note control, arguing that the note issue was automatically regulated by the needs of trade. Indeed, the banking school rejected the entire analytical framework underlying the act. Comprising the quantity theory of money and the classical price-specie-flow mechanism, that framework postulated a causal chain running from note overissue to domestic inflation to specie drains. By contrast, the banking school contended (1) that overissue is impossible because the supply of notes is demand-determined, (2) that causation runs from prices to money rather than vice versa, and (3) that specie drains stem from nonmonetary shocks to the balance of payments rather than from domestic price inflation. Finally, the banking school asserted the impossibility of controlling the monetary circulation via the note component alone, since limitation of notes would simply induce the public to use checking deposits and bills of exchange instead. In other words, the total circulation is like a balloon; when squeezed at one end, it expands at the other. The currency school, however, rejected this criticism on the grounds that the volume of deposits and bills is rigidly constrained by the volume of notes and therefore can be controlled through notes alone. In short, the total circulation is like an inverted pyramid resting on a banknote base, with variations in the base inducing equiproportional variations in the superstructure of money substitutes. In counting deposits as part of the superstructure, the currency school excluded them from its concept of money. It did so on the grounds that deposits, unlike notes and coin, were not generally acceptable in final payments during financial panics.

Shortcomings of the Currency School

In retrospect, the currency school erred in failing to define deposits as money to be regulated like notes. This failure enabled the Bank of England to exercise discretionary control over a large and growing part of the money stock, contrary to the intentions of the currency school. The school also erred in not recognizing the need for a lender of last resort to avert liquidity panics and domestic cash drains. With regard to cash drains, the currency school refused to distinguish between domestic and foreign ones. As far as policy was concerned, both drains were to be handled the same way, i.e., by monetary contraction. By the end of the century, however, it was widely recognized that the two drains required different treatment, and that the surest way to arrest an internal drain was through a policy of liberal lending. The currency school nevertheless remained opposed to such a policy, fearing it would place too much discretionary power in the hands of the central bank. These shortcomings, it should be noted, in no way invalidated the school's contention that convertibility is an inadequate safeguard against monetary overexpansion and therefore must be reinforced by positive regulation. Nor did they undermine the school's monetary theory of inflation, which was superior to any explanation its critics had to offer.

Currency School and Monetarism

Today the term currency school is closely associated with monetarism. The school's principal conclusions—(1) that rules are preferable to discretion in the conduct of monetary policy, (2) that inflation is largely or solely produced by excessive monetary growth, (3) that monetary shocks are the primary source of economic disturbances, and (4) that the entire stock of money and money substitutes can be governed via control of a narrowly defined base—constitute the core of monetarist doctrine.

References

Humphrey, T., "The Quantity Theory of Money: Its Historical Evolution and Role in Policy Debates," *Economic Review*, no. 60, May/June 1974, pp. 2–19; Robbins, L., *Robert Torrens and the Evolution of Classical Economics*, Macmillan, London, 1958, chap. 5; Viner, J., *Studies in the Theory of International Trade*, Kelley, New York, 1965, chap. 5.

(*See also* Banking school)

Thomas M. Humphrey

Data banks

The primary purpose of data banks is the maintenance and rapid dissemination of information. This involves centralized collection, upkeep, documentation and access facilities for a community of users. While the terms data bank and data base are used almost interchangeably to denote any organized, usually computer-readable collection of data—whether textual, numerical, or both—they should be differentiated. Data bank implies the concept of deposits by the "banker" or administrator and withdrawals by a relatively large number of independent users, in contrast with data base, which is intended primarily as a basis for a particular study, economic model, accounting system, or some other special purpose.

Textual data banks consist of bibliographies, abstracts, indexes, or other reference material. The contents of numerical (or statistical) data banks may be internal company statistics, cross-sectional microdata, macroeconomic time series, or any variation and combination of these. Collections stored for preservation and future use are called data archives. Individual machine-readable volumes (tapes, cassettes, disks, etc.) containing data resulting from a particular survey or enumeration are called data files.

Microdata Banks

The term "microdata" refers to individual reporting units—families, individuals, companies, establishments, etc. Machine-readable microdata banks consist of microdata files which are usually organized in a cross-sectional manner, i.e., they contain a number of items of information (variables) about each unit at one point in time (or over one period of time). A collection of cross-sectional data files, each of which refers to the same unit at successive points in time, is called a longitudinal microdata bank.

Microdata can be generated as the by-product of an administrative process. More often, however, they are the result of a specific sample survey or an entire census enumeration. Advances in computer technology, sophisticated programming, and data organization have made it possible to retrieve and manipulate large masses of microdata for economic or sociological analysis. They are indispensable for analyzing the behavior of individual economic units and the relationships among different variables and activities. Also, by providing the smallest possible building blocks for the aggregation of statistical information, microdata make it possible to compute income distributions and aggregations along different lines.

Until recently, microdata sets often entered the public domain insufficiently documented and unedited for errors, inconsistencies, and unreadable codes. This made their use costly and of dubious value. In the last few years, however, considerable progress has been made toward improving documentation standards and manipulatory software. These developments facilitate editing and documentation of microdata prior to their release and greatly enhance their usefulness.

The proliferation of computer-accessible records and the advances of computer technology have increased the ease with which privacy and confidentiality can be violated. The concept of microdata banks has thus aroused considerable controversy. The very term data bank is often treated in a pejorative fashion, synonymous with dossier, to describe any "collection of information about individuals assembled in one place for easy access by a number of users" (Westin and Baker, 1972). However, in this respect it is information on criminal activities, sources of income, medical records, credit ratings, etc. which is the chief area of concern, and it is the administrative records of justice systems and collection agencies which represent the greatest threats to the citizen's privacy. By contrast, the microdata banks used for economic-statistical analysis are usually well-safeguarded. Not only do they carry no recognizable identification (except with the consent of the individual respondent), but their administrators are also very careful in their analysis of possible disclosure violations. The Census Bureau's 1970 public use sample, for instance, was released in six different versions, each containing somewhat different variables, in order to avoid the possibility of identification through detailed cross-classification.

Time Series Data Banks

Several machine-readable economic time series data banks are available in the United States today. They contain historical time series at all levels of aggregation. Some carry national totals only; others specialize in regional data; and still others carry series for detailed industrial or other classifications. They also vary in accessibility: some are available on magnetic tape only, others through time-sharing systems; some can be used only by purchasers of models, forecasts, or similar services, while others are available independently. Typically, data are collected from published sources; put in standardized computer-readable form; checked for accuracy, consistency, and continuity; and finally disseminated to the users. Some data banks include estimates derived from econometric models.

Time series data banks are also available for foreign data. They are being maintained in the United States as well as abroad. Except for the data bank maintained by the Canadian government and the tape maintained by the Organization for Economic Cooperation and Development (OECD) there is, so far, no systematic access for U.S. users to data banks maintained abroad.

Printed collections of economic time series data have existed for a long time. The *Statistical Abstract* started 100 years ago, the *Survey of Current Business* about 50 years ago. Computer-readable data banks became possible around 1953 when computers were first employed for economic analysis, but such banks were not actually used until the advent of time sharing around 1966. Before that time, the only generally available data bank consisted of a magnetic tape containing macroeconomic time series, put together by the Brookings Institution and updated every year or so. However, program sharing, encouraged by user organizations of large computers, was practiced by economists. The advantages of sharing the cost of maintaining machine-readable time series—particularly those which are updated and revised frequently—were apparently first recognized by a group of New York business economists engaged in short-term forecasting and business conditions analysis. Calling themselves Project Economics, they started operations in 1967 as a cooperative venture, with each participant responsible for a group of time series.

The group soon found that professional statisticians and data handlers were needed to ensure the reliability and integrity of the data, and, since the National Bureau of Economic Research (NBER) was part of Project Economics, it was decided that its staff take over the upkeep and further development of the data bank. Thus, the first time series data bank was maintained under the auspices of the NBER. Subsequently, the number of time series in the bank was greatly increased, as were the number of users and the amount of effort involved. Eventually, it became too large and too service-oriented an activity for an organization specializing in pure research, and thus in 1978 the data bank moved, with its staff and customer base, to Citibank's Economics Department.

Other data collections were started soon after Project Economics by the producers of various large econometric models, with the intention of providing their customers with access to the time series on which their models were based. However, the model builders, academic as well as commercial, soon found that their customers were interested in other series as well; thus these data bases were turned into data banks carrying a wide spectrum of information. In an attempt to provide for all conceivable data needs of actual and prospective customers, some data banks became very large. Whether or not uniformly high quality is attainable in such giant collections is questionable.

Some federal statistical agencies responsible for the compilation of time series also maintain machine-readable data bases and make them available to users. The Bureau of Labor Statistics, for example, now maintains a very sophisticated on-line data base. The Federal Reserve Board issues a monthly tape containing all flow-of-funds data, and the Bureau of Economic Analysis puts out a monthly tape with the data it publishes in *Business Conditions Digest*.

An obvious advantage of time series data banks is that they eliminate duplication of effort. Users do not have to collect data from various publications as they are updated; they do not have to keep track of the numerous revisions; and they need not computerize the data for use in analysis, models, simulations, or other processes.

Disadvantages

One potential disadvantage of data banks is that users have little control over the accuracy of the data. Also, the user is somewhat removed from the data sources, and has to depend on the explanatory information which the data bank provides. Thus, the services offered by a data bank must include accuracy and a thorough documentation with regard to data sources, description of concepts, references to descriptions of concepts, revisions, and so on.

A good data bank not only provides continuously updated documentation, but also supplements these services by a newsletter, which keeps users informed about changes in concepts, new series, and other developments. Since users employ series in regressions or other analyses without the benefit of qualifying footnotes, they must be able to rely implicitly on the continuity and consistency of any series in the bank. When a significant conceptional change or a change in coverage is made by the source agency, it is better for the data bank to carry two series—perhaps with an overlap—than to carry what seems to be a continuous series but is not. Thus, it has become the responsibility of the data-bank manager to provide and disseminate the professional statistical circumspection which was previously supplied by the individual user of printed statistical information.

References

Bisco, Ralph L. (ed.), *Data Bases, Computers, and the Social Sciences*, Wiley-Interscience, New York, 1970; Boschan, Charlotte, "The NBER Time Series Data Bank," *Annals of Economic and Social Measurement*, National Bureau of Economic Research, New York, April 1972; Darrow, Joel W., and James R. Belilove, "The Growth of Databank Sharing," *Harvard Business Review*, November–December 1978, pp. 180–194; Juster, F. Thomas, "Microdata Requirements and Public Policy Designs," *Annals of Economic and Social Measurement*, National Bureau of Economic Research, New York, April 1973; Miller, Arthur R., *Assault on Privacy: Computers, Data Banks, and Dossiers*, University of Michigan Press, Ann Arbor, 1971; Ruggles, Nancy, "The Development of Integrated Data Bases for Social, Economic and Demographic Statistics," *United Nations Studies in Methods*, ser. F, no. 27, United Nations, New York, 1979; Ruggles, Nancy, and Richard Ruggles, "The Strategy of Merging and Matching Microdata Sets," *Annals of Economic and Social Measurement*, National Bureau of Economic Research, New York, April 1974; Sessions, Vivian (ed.), *Directory of Data Bases in Social and Behavioral Sciences*, Science Associates, New York, 1974; Smith, Robert Ellis, *Privacy: How to Protect What's Left of it*, Anchor Press/Doubleday, Garden City, N.Y., 1979; Watts, Harold W., "Micro-economic Data Banks: Problems and Potential," in Nancy Ruggles (ed.), *The Role of the Computer in Economic and Social Research in Latin America*, National Bureau of Economic Research, New York, 1974; Westin, Alan F., and Michael A. Baker, *Databanks in a Free Society: Computers, Record-Keeping and Privacy*, Report of the Project on Computer Databanks of the Computer Science and Engineering Board, National Academy of Sciences, Quadrangle, New York, 1972.

(*See also* Bureau of the Census; Computers in economics; National Bureau of Economic Research; Regression analysis in business and economics; Time series analysis)

Charlotte Boschan

Debt

Debt is created by voluntary contract between a lender and a borrower. The lender transfers a sum of money to the borrower and receives a promise of repayments at some future dates, plus periodic payments of interest.

In order to analyze the various functions of debt, five classes of market participants can be distinguished—households, nonfinancial business enterprises, governments, foreigners, and banks and other related financial institutions. The last of these groups is said to "intermediate" transactions among ultimate borrowers and lenders in the other classes. Bank accounts are loans from other participants; these are pooled and loaned out to ultimate borrowers by the bank.

Motives for Borrowing

One motive for consumers, business, or governments to borrow money is to correct mismatches between receipt of income and spending plans. Consumers, for example, typically wish to maintain a stable standard of living that is geared to total expected lifetime resources. This involves borrowing at younger ages and lending in middle ages to accumulate assets for retirement years. Businesses often borrow to maintain production levels despite temporary declines in sales, and governments borrow to maintain spending levels before large tax receipts become due.

There are other significant motives for borrowing. Consumers often borrow in order to purchase rather than rent durable goods such as houses or cars. This type of transaction can be viewed as socially efficient if a durable good is used and maintained more efficiently by an owner than a renter. The willingness of any consumer to borrow for this or other purposes will depend on the rate of interest charged by the lender.

Businesses may borrow to purchase plant and equipment which provide an expected net income from production activity great enough to pay interest on the debt and leave a margin of profit. Businesses also have the alternative of issuing shares of stock. In general, it is expected that the decision of how much to borrow will be made with the objective of maximizing the value of the enterprise to the present shareholders. The level of interest rates, relevant tax laws, and risk appraisals are major influences on the choice of borrowing versus issuing new shares.

Governments may borrow money as an alternative to collecting taxes in order to pay for purchases of goods and services or to transfer funds to persons eligible for some form of public assistance. Historically, major expansions of public borrowing have occurred during wartime. Only in the last two decades has borrowing by the national government been significant in peacetime.

Effects of Government Borrowing

When governments borrow from foreigners, the debt incurred is known as external debt. Such borrowing allows imports to expand over exports without a devaluation, at least temporarily, or loss of reserves. External debt increases the physical resources available to the domestic economy. Similarly, interest and repayment of external debt will subtract from tangible domestic resources and constitutes a burden on the national economy.

When governments borrow from domestic citizens, the result is internal public debt, which in the short run does not change the nation's productive resources. It is said that we owe it to ourselves. In other words, the government bonds are held as assets by some citizens, while all taxpayers face increased future tax liabilities to pay interest on the debt. Although there is considerable controversy as to the consequences of debt issue by government, the eventual consequences depend on how the government revenue is used, on the economic circumstances when new debt is issued, and on the perceptions of citizens about the future tax liabilities incurred.

If proceeds of government debt issues are used to pay for public assets such as school buildings, bridges, or sanitation plants, then the future contribution of these assets to national productivity may outweigh the interest cost and any losses due to decline in investment in the private sector. If charges to the users of public assets are sufficient to avoid taxes to pay interest on the debt, it would appear that a type of fairness is achieved whereby those future citizens who benefit from a current public expenditure have been indirectly contracted to pay the cost.

When government issues debt, it competes with other borrowers for a limited supply of funds. New loans can be made only by citizens willing (to a degree based on interest rates offered) to forego purchase of goods and services. The resources released by such citizens can be used either for expansion of assets in the private sector or for public purposes. If the initial situation is one of full utilization of resources, government borrowing may cause some reduction in private capital formation. This development would constitute a relative burden on future citizens, which in the case of wartime finance might be seen as a desirable partial shift of the sacrifice toward national defense.

However, if an economy persists with idle productive resources, debt issue is less likely to involve a net sacrifice of capital accumulation. The reason is that government spending, not fully matched by taxes, increases total demand for goods and services, calling forth the utilization of idle resources.

References

Browning, Edgar, and Jacqueline Browning, *Public Finance and the Price System*, Macmillan, New York, 1979, chap. 13; Buchanan, James, *Public Principles of Public Debt*, Irwin, Homewood, Ill., 1958; Fisher, Irving, *The Theory of Interest*, New York, 1930, reprinted by Kelley, New York, 1965; Lerner, Abba, "The Burden of the National Debt," in L. Metzler et al. (eds.), *Income, Employment, and Public Policy: Essays in Honor of Alvin Hansen*, Norton, New York, 1948; Samuelson, Paul, *Economics*, 10th ed., McGraw-Hill, New York, 1976, chap. 6, 19, 30.

(*See also* Business credit; Consumer credit; Credit, an overview; Debt management; Interest rates; Mortgage credit)

Bernard S. Friedman

Debt management

Any borrower who has issued a variety of securities specifying repayment at particular dates of maturity, and who wishes to maintain a permanent total volume of debt, has a management problem. As one loan reaches maturity, the existing lender must be repaid and new lenders found to refinance the debt. Economists have focused attention on debt management by national governments because these activities often constitute an important share of financial transactions and can contribute to the multiple objectives of macroeconomic policy.

In the United States, the Treasury Department has direct responsibility to repay holders of maturing securities and market new securities. The total federal government debt exceeds $600 billion, and in a typical year more than one-third of this amount must be refinanced. This volume of transactions is several multiples of the size of recent annual budget deficits.

Monetizing the Debt

The type of security and terms offered by the Treasury will affect the size of interest payments which have themselves become a significant fraction of total federal outlays. Prior to 1951, a major object of debt management was to hold down interest costs. This objective was pursued with the assistance of the Federal Reserve System, which can increase its holdings of government debt, thereby expanding bank reserves. This process is called monetizing the debt since it stimulates expansion of bank lending and the holding of money balances.

The Treasury can decide how much of its total debt to offer in the form of short-run bills or notes as opposed to longer-term bonds. If the principal objective were to minimize interest cost, the average maturity of federal debt would be generally decreased during a business expansion and increased during a business contraction. During a business contraction, the overall level of interest rates is relatively low and it is attractive to contract on a long-term basis, while the opposite incentive prevails during a business expansion.

Savings to the Treasury from a policy of countercyclical lengthening of average maturity will be at least partially frustrated by intelligent expectations of private lenders and borrowers. Long-term interest rates will typically exceed short-term rates when short-term rates are expected to rise during a forthcoming period of business expansion or acceleration of inflation. Correspondingly, when short-term rates are expected to decline, the term structure of rates is said to be inverted, with longer maturities paying lower interest rates. This anticipatory behavior of market participants reduces the Treasury gain from countercyclical lengthening of debt maturity.

Since 1951, minimizing federal interest cost has not typically been a primary objective of either the Treasury or the Federal Reserve Board. To stabilize the private economy, the government will lean toward encouraging business long-term borrowing during a contraction—this policy involves engaging more in short-term refinancing of public debt. Conversely, lengthening the maturity of public debt during an expansion has been used to compete against business investment.

Mistakes in Debt Management

James Tobin argued that during the 1950s and early 1960s the practice of debt management switched too strongly to competition against business investment and economic growth by lengthening average debt maturity and restricting growth of bank reserves. He argued that monetary expansion and debt management should be designed to encourage low interest rates and business investment and that budget surpluses should be used if necessary to restrain aggregate demand. The political process necessary for fiscal restraint, however, has not appeared to be reliable.

In more recent years, the level of economic activity and the money supply have grown substantially relative to the volume of government debt held by the public. Also, the higher level and variability of inflation have led economists to focus attention on monetary growth and reform of spending programs as primary instruments of macroeconomic policy for stability and growth. The role of debt management in these objectives appears correspondingly weaker.

References

Musgrave, R., and P. Musgrave, *Public Finance in Theory and Practice*, 2d ed., McGraw-Hill, New York, 1976, chap. 28; Ritter, L., and W. Silbert, *Principles of Money, Banking and Financial Markets*, 2d ed., Basic Books, New York, 1977, chaps. 16, 17, 19, 29; Roosa, R., *Federal Reserve Operations in the Money and Government Securities Markets*, Federal Reserve Bank of New York, New York, 1956; Tobin, J., *National Economic Policy*, Yale University Press, New Haven, 1966, chap. 12.

(*See also* Debt; Federal Reserve policy; Fiscal policy; Monetary policy)

Bernard S. Friedman

Decision making in business: a behavioral approach

Behavioral decision theory seeks to explain and predict decisions in business and elsewhere. A decision is a choice, a commitment to action. Decision making is the set of processes culminating in choices; these processes involve environmental stimuli, perceptions, beliefs, thoughts, and actions, as well as the interaction of people, and sometimes computers and other technical systems, in organizational contexts. The domain of behavioral decision theory encompasses firms' choices concerning strategies, prices, budgets, acquisitions and divestitures, scopes of markets, and staffing. It includes choice situations at the interfirm level and intrafirm level as well as at the firm level.

History and Criticism of Behavioral Decision Theory

The term "behavioral" distinguishes this theory from the theory of economic marginalism and emphasizes the importance of human behavior in the collective making of decisions, beyond the behavior described by marginalism. The founders of behavioral decision theory viewed economic marginalism as inadequate both as an explanation and as a means to predict business decisions. They argued that ambiguity in choice situations causes administrators to make decisions different from those predicted by economic marginalism. The concept of ambiguity is delineated below; it includes the notions of cognitive limitations, uncertainty, complexity, and conflict.

Business practitioners have always discussed how decisions are made, but not in terms of a behavioral theory. Rather they articulated what they called management philosophies; these philosophies, however, lacked implications for actions. Groundbreaking work was done by Chester I. Barnard, who published *The Functions of the Executive* in 1936 after his retirement. Barnard incorporated behavioral hypotheses into a theoretical structure describing organizations' decisions. His work, which contrasted the administrative individual with the economic individual, had important impacts within the academic community.

The work of Herbert A. Simon converted this initial interest by the academic community into a well-developed conceptual framework and stimulated extensive research. Simon laid the interdisciplinary conceptual bases for decision making in business. Research has drawn heavily upon his book, *Administrative Behavior,* published in 1947. This work emphasized that administrators operate under conditions which limit and shape their decisions. Simon argued that assumptions attributable to economic marginalism are inappropriate and should be replaced by behavioral assumptions about cognitive and organizational limitations. From these new assumptions, he inferred general patterns which make administrative decisions predictable.

Another important root of behavioral decision theory is the study by R. L. Hall and C. J. Hitch which was published in 1939. They proposed that prices are set by full-cost (markup) rules under certain conditions rather than by marginalism.

The view that behavioral decision theory better predicts business decisions than economic marginalism was widely criticized. Fritz Machlup (1967) argued that the assumptions made within behavioral decision theory can be incorporated within a revised theory of marginalism. He delineated models of firms' decisions which incorporate behavioral constraints.

The resolution of this controversy is not a matter of logical consistency. Each theoretical approach can be generalized until the other approach becomes a special case within the larger framework. Consequently, the issue is one of use: Which approach will scientists and practitioners use to explain and predict business decisions? The issue remains moot.

Major Concepts and Hypotheses

Program is the central concept of behavioral decision theory. A program is a set of activities patterned into sequences. The activities are evoked by stimuli, and alternative sequences depend on consequences of the activities and on additional stimuli. For example, a decrease in inventory (stimulus) can evoke the ordering of material (a program). The program can incorporate simple or complex decision rules. A simple rule may involve the calculation of the amount to reorder assuming a fixed amount is used in a future period; a more complex rule may involve a procedure for estimating the future amount demanded.

Programs can be conceived to fall on a continuum from well-defined, structured decision processes to ill-defined, unstructured ones. A well-defined program is one which occurs in the same form repeatedly so that exact sequences can be specified. An ill-defined program does not occur repeatedly, so only rough rules of thumb (heuristics) govern the sequences of activities.

Behavioral decision theory assumes that, even though the participants may not perceive it, much of their decision behavior is standardized and follows well-defined programs. Thus, business decision making can be modeled and predicted by delineating the programs used by firms. Models have been formulated to describe and predict decision behavior in diverse situations. These models range from ones which portray decision making as highly structured programs to ones in which ambiguity makes choices seem fortuitous.

A landmark model was designed by Richard M. Cyert and James G. March in *A Behavioral Theory of the Firm* (1963). The model categorizes programs according to their associations with goals, expectations, and choices, and hypothesizes how these goals, expectations, and choices are determined. For example, the goals of a firm depend on which coalition controls the firm and on the needs of the participants in this coalition. In addition, operational goals depend upon what sequences of activities are evoked by problems and what people are associated with these sequences. The model does not assume that profit is the only goal of a business firm, or even one of several goals, nor does the model assume that a goal is maximized; rather the decision makers try to surpass some levels of aspiration that depend on past goals, past performances of the firm, and past performances of comparable firms. The levels of aspiration represent an application of Simon's concept of "satisficing"—being satisfied by performances which are good enough.

Other key concepts in Cyert and March's model are the quasi-resolution of conflict, uncertainty avoidance, and organizational learning. The model assumes that goals can conflict, that is, achieving one goal impedes achievement of another. Such conflicts need not be resolved but may persist indefinitely; thus programs can be formulated which make choices despite the conflicting goals. For example, some divisions of a firm can hold goals inconsistent with other divisions. Each division can make choices based on its goals without resolving the inconsistency with the goals of other divisions. Buffers such as inventories ameliorate the goal conflicts. Another kind of buffer is time: the programs guiding activities now may be pursuing goals which conflict with those pursued previously.

The model does not represent uncertainty explicitly, but it assumes that programs avoid confronting the issue of uncertainty. For example, only short-run commitments are made, and these commitments are adjusted on the basis of information feedback about outcomes. Also, participants absorb uncertainty as they process information with the consequence that the information is characterized by greater certainty when it is received by the decision makers.

Finally, a firm is assumed to learn as a consequence of its decisions and the results of those decisions. Consequently, decision rules and programs are modified over time. For example, the search for a better solution begins in the vicinity of the existing solution.

Various computer programs have been written to simulate business decision making. For example, C. Edward Weber designed programs to simulate budgeting. Other processes which were simulated are production scheduling, purchasing, forecasting, pricing, and competitive market responses.

Another model, formulated by March and others in *Ambiguity and Choice in Organizations* (1976), postulates that ambiguities multiply the variety of choice behaviors. Heuristics for a classical approach to strategy formulation have focused on reducing the gaps between an actual situation and a desired situation, whereas this model asserts that ambiguities can prevent these gaps from being specified and eliminated. Ambiguities can invalidate any of four postulates: the cognitions and preferences held by people affect their actions; the actions of individual people affect organizational choices; organizational choices affect environmental activities; and environmental activities affect the cognitions and preferences of individual people.

The possibility that these postulates can be false is incorporated in the "garbage can" model delineated by March and others. The organization provides occasions for making decisions, and occasions can be likened to garbage cans. Figuratively, problems and solutions are tossed into various garbage cans, and participants crawl in and out. Problems, solutions, and participants all flow separately from each other into occasions, and the organizational and social structures direct these flows to occasions. Choices depend on what problems, solutions, and participants are present at the times of decisions. The model provides hypotheses about the nature and interaction of the flows of occasions, problems, solutions, and participants.

Prescriptions for Decision Making

In addition to explaining and predicting choices, behavioral decision theory has sought to improve the effectiveness of choice behavior. Emphasis has been placed on unstructured situations in which the firms formulate strategies. Prescriptions for strategic decision making include those which identify occasions for decisions, those which search for or design possible solutions, and those which select solutions. The prescriptions of each type can operate separately from each other, or they can interact.

Some prescriptions, for example, aim to improve the flows of participants. Bo L. T. Hedberg, Paul C. Nystrom, and William H. Starbuck advocated in 1976 minimal structures ("tents" instead of "palaces") to permit free flows of participants. Participants are to have weak constraints on their abilities to change decision programs. Tents are said to be better than palaces if environments are changing rapidly, because bureaucratic structures prevent participants from perceiving changes.

Other prescriptions attempt to facilitate the design of solutions. On the premise that firms are unresponsive because they are unable to see changes taking place in their environments, these heuristics guide participants toward identifying the assumptions underlying their current strategies and toward creating new assumptions and strategies which can be synthesized by a dialectic process. This approach is presented by Ian I. M. Mitroff and James R. Emshoff (1979).

Still other prescriptions promote playfulness, myths and storytelling, conflict and bargaining, games and judgment. They complement classical prescriptions for strategic decision making.

References

Barnard, Chester I., *The Functions of the Executive*, Harvard University Press, Cambridge, Mass., 1938; Beyer, Janice M., "Ideologies, Values and Decision Making in Organizations," in Paul C. Nystrom and William Starbuck (eds.), *Handbook of Organizational Design*, Oxford University Press, London, 1980; Carter, E. Eugene, "Resource Allocation," in ibid; Cyert, Richard M., and James G. March, *A Behavioral Theory of the Firm*, Prentice-Hall, Englewood Cliffs, N.J., 1963; Hall, R. L., and C. J. Hitch, "Price Theory and Business Behavior," in T. Wilson and P. W. S. Andrews (eds.), *Oxford Studies in the Price Mechanism*, Oxford University Press, Oxford, 1951, pp. 107–138; Hedberg, Bo L. T., Paul C. Nystrom, and William H. Starbuck, "Camping on Seesaws: Prescriptions for a Self-designing Organization," *Administrative Science Quarterly*, vol. No. 21, no. 1, 1976, pp. 41–65; Khandwalla, Pradip N., *The Design of Organizations*, Harcourt, Brace, New York, 1977; MacCrimmon, Kenneth P., and Ronald N. Taylor, "Decision Making and Problem Solving," *Handbook of Industrial and Organizational Psychology*, Rand, Chicago, 1976; Machlup, Fritz, "Theories of the Firm: Marginalist, Behavioral, Managerial," *American Economic Review*, vol. 57, no. 1, 1967, pp. 1–33; March, James G., and Johan P. Olsen, *Ambiguity and Choice in Organizations*, Universitet, Bergen, 1976; March, James G., and Herbert A. Simon, *Organizations*, Wiley, New York, 1958; Mintzberg, Henry, Duru Raisinghani, and André Théorêt, "The Structure of Unstructured Decision Process," *Administrative Science Quarterly*, vol. 21, no. 2, 1976, pp. 246–275; Mitroff, Ian I., and James R. Emshoff, "On Strategic Assumption-Making: A Dialectical Approach to Policy and Planning," *Academy of Management Review*, vol. 4, no. 1, 1979, pp. 1–12; Nystrom, Paul C., Bo L. T. Hedberg, and William Starbuck, "Interacting Processes as Organizational Designs," in Ralph H. Kilmann, Louis Pondy, and Dennis P. Slevin (eds.), *The Management of Organization Design*, vol. I, Elsevier, New York, 1976, pp. 209–230; Simon, Herbert A., *Administrative Behavior*, Free Press, New York, 1947; Weber, C. Edward, "Intraorganizational Decision Processes Influencing the EDP Staff Budget," *Management Science*, vol. 12, no. 4, 1965, pp. B69–B93.

(*See also* Economic models; Firm theory; Simulation in business and economics)

C. Edward Weber

Demand

Demand is a key concept in microeconomics, in which it takes the form of aggregate demand. The demand for any one product or service has a function whose specification depends on the purpose of analysis. In the theory of general equilibrium, the demand for any one commodity is a function of buyers' tastes, their incomes, and the prices of all other commodities. In partial equilibrium theory, where analysis applies to one commodity or industry, the demand for a commodity is a function of buyers' tastes and incomes, the possible prices of the commodity itself, and the prices of the commodity's substitutes and complements. In empirical analyses, the particular facts found relevant for a commodity enter into its demand function, which might include, for example, volumes of advertising.

The classical economists of the late eighteenth and the first half of the nineteenth centuries had little to say about demand, taking it mostly for granted. Current theory rests on foundations laid by Alfred Marshall in his *Principles of Economics* (1890).

Much economic analysis focuses on the relation between prices and quantities demanded, the other variables being provisionally held constant. At the several prices that could prevail in a market during some period of time, different quantities of a product or service would be bought. Demand, then, is considered a list of prices and quantities, with one quantity for each possible price. Demand is the entire list, or demand schedule, as Marshall called it. When the schedule is plotted on a diagram, with price on the vertical axis and quantity on the horizontal axis, demand becomes the demand curve. This curve slopes downward from left to right, signifying that smaller quantities are bought at higher prices and larger quantities are bought at lower prices. The inverse relation between price and quantity is often called the law of demand. The law rests on two foundations. One is the theory of the consumer. With one exception, the logic of that theory shows that the consumer responds to lower prices by buying more. The other foundation is empirical, innumerable studies of demand in actual markets having demonstrated the existence of downward-sloping demand curves. And the law of demand has always reflected the universal experience of traders.

Exceptions to the Law

Exceptions to the law of demand are the curiosa of theorists. The best-known exception is the Giffen effect—a consumer buys more, not less, of a commodity at higher prices when a negative income effect dominates over the substitution effect. Whether the Giffen effect has ever prevailed in real markets is a matter of doubt. Another possible exception is the Veblen effect—some commodities are theoretically wanted solely for their high prices. The higher these prices are, the more the use of such commodities fulfills the requirements of conspicuous consumption, and thus the stronger the demand for them. Impressions from casual observation often suggest what might seem to be exceptions to the law of demand. Higher prices often go along with strong demands and lower prices with weak demands. At work here, however, are the results of changes in demand, not evidences of exceptions to the law of demand.

Changes in Consumer Demand

Changes, i.e., increases or decreases in demand, are changes in the quantities that would be bought at any of the possible prices. Changes in demand are shifts or movements of the entire demand curve. A shift to the right means an increase in demand. It can come from any one or a combination of the following: stronger consumer desire, a rise in consumers' incomes, a rise in the prices of substitutes, a fall in the prices of complements, and sometimes augmented volumes of advertising. Opposite changes in these factors cause a decrease in demand, a leftward shift of the curve. The only exception here applies to so-called inferior goods. They are defined as those goods bought in smaller amounts as consumer incomes go up. The law of demand, though, still holds for inferior goods. But increases in consumer incomes, *ceteris paribus,* cause the downward-sloping demand curves for inferior goods to shift to the left, not to the right.

In a turbulent economy, especially an inflationary one, another influence on changing demands—price expectations—deserves mention. For storable commodities, expectations of future prices can be a powerful force on current demand. When they expect future prices to be higher, buyers increase their current demands, thus tending to make their expectations self-fulfilling. In the modern economy, too, the rapidity of communications makes possible many sudden shifts in the demands for particular things, as fads and fashions spring into being and then fade away. Nevertheless, broad patterns of consumer demand are remarkably stable over long periods of time.

The demands for durable goods can fluctuate widely over time, as consumers' incomes vary and as producers' profit expectations alter with the business cycle. A durable good has both a stock demand and a flow demand. The stock demand is for the amount that consumers or producers want to hold over a period of years. The flow demand in a given year consists of replacement demand, i.e., for purchases to maintain the stock at some level, and of expansion demand, i.e., for purchases to increase the stock. If the stock demand increases, the yearly flow demand will increase relatively much more—it will include a positive expansion demand along with the replacement demand. If, on the other hand, the stock demand diminishes, the yearly flow demand will drop relatively far, because the negative expansion demand has to be subtracted from the replacement demand.

Changes in Producer Demand

The demands of producers for productive services, i.e., for labor, equipment, semifinished and raw materials, etc., have properties like those of consumers' demands. Producers' demands are derived demands, ultimately depending on consumers' demands. In a given context, the quantities demanded by any one producer for any one service are inversely related to price. Again in a given context, additional quantities of a productive service yield diminishing marginal products. With more units being worth less per unit, the producer is willing to pay less for more units. For producers who must accept lower prices if they are going to sell more in a given market, another factor comes into play. Since for them added outputs carry lower selling prices, the marginal products of the corresponding added inputs are thus worth still less per unit (marginal revenue product). The law of demand, then, holds with full force for producers. For them, too, changes in demand come from changes in the prices of related productive services, as well as from changes on the prices of outputs and in technology.

Sellers' Demand

From the points of view of the sellers of products and services, demand needs another perspective. In markets with many sellers of homogeneous products, the demand for the product of any single seller is infinitely large; that is, the individual seller can sell all of the product at the going price. The seller's own demand curve can be visualized as a horizontal line extending indefinitely to the right. The height of the line is the prevailing price. Such sellers, farmers being typical examples, incur no advertising or other promotional expenses. Their business strategies are those of adjusting their outputs to prices they cannot individually control. In markets with few sellers, however, demand appears as a line sloping down to the right. But the demand functions of such sellers are critically interdependent, because in each the most important variable is the prices charged by the other sellers in the same market. Another feature of markets with few sellers is that prices are often stable, except for times of rapid inflation, for months at a time. The so-called kinked demand curve is an effort to explain such constancy of prices. The kink in this demand curve is at the prevailing price. Above that price demand falls off sharply, reflecting the seller's belief that rival sellers would not increase their prices if he or she were to raise prices. Below the prevailing price sales would increase only slightly because the seller thinks that rival sellers would match any price cut he or she might initiate.

Scarcity and Demand

The concept of demand is essential to the understanding of the meaning of shortages or scarcities. They occur when the quantities demanded at some prices exceed the quantities available at the same prices. At the (too low) prices some able and willing buyers cannot buy what they want. Such low prices come from government price controls, and sometimes from lags in market adjustments when demand increases rapidly. Business pricing policies can also cause shortages, as when, for example, a corporation adheres to an unchanging price for months during which the demand curve for its product shifts sharply to the right. The quantities demanded at the unchanged price begin to exceed those the corporation can sell, resulting, for example, in a waiting list for the product. Shortages disappear when prices rise or are raised to levels where the quantities demanded are equal to those available in the market.

References

Chamberlin, Edward, *The Theory of Monopolistic Competition*, Harvard University Press, Cambridge, Mass., 1933; Marshall, Alfred, *Principles of Economics*, 8th ed., Macmillan, London, 1920, Book III; Schultz, Henry, *The Theory and Measurement of Demand*, University of Chicago Press, Chicago, 1938; Stigler, George J., "The Kinky Oligopoly Demand Curve and Rigid Prices," *Journal of Political Economy*, vol. 40, no. 5, October 1947, pp. 432–449; Veblen, Thorstein, *The Theory of the Leisure Class*, Macmillan, New York, 1908.

(*See also* Consumer theory; General equilibrium; Marginal cost; Marginal revenue; Monopoly and oligopoly; Scarcity; Stock-flow analysis; Supply)

Donald S. Watson

Demographics and economics

The population of a nation—its size, growth rate, and age composition—significantly affects its economic fortunes. The fact that population in many of the less-developed nations of the world has been increasing more rapidly than its industrial and agricultural output has created severe social and human problems. In such nations, efforts to reduce the birth rate are an important facet of economic policy since it is a prerequisite for improving living standards.

More generally, abrupt changes in fertility or mortality rates have far-reaching economic implications for a nation. A sharp rise or decline in the level of the nation's births during any particular period will eventually determine the size of its labor force, and hence, most likely, its rate of economic development. Similarly, medical advances almost always increase longevity; thus, in most nations of the world today an increasing proportion of the population consists of relatively older and economically dependent individuals.

When changes in the fertility and mortality rates occur slowly, the consequences are generally moderate, but abrupt shifts have ripple effects that are extensive and often persist over a long time period. The relatively recent large drop in infant mortality in many of the less developed nations of the world has accelerated population growth, making it increasingly difficult to improve living standards.

In the United States, the post-World War II birth boom, followed by a sharp decline in the fertility rate, has had, and will continue to have, an appreciable effect on the population age mix with extensive current and anticipated consequences. In the 1980s a larger proportion of Americans will be of working age and a smaller proportion dependents, a situation which should contribute to improving living standards. But when the birth-boom generation begins to reach the age of retirement early in the next century, retirement and income policies will have to be changed drastically.

Since the end of the postwar baby boom, fertility rates have actually been below that necessary for zero population growth. Thus, a continuation of this trend over a long period of time will result in an aging society with an increasing median age and eventually declining total population by the middle of the twenty-first century.

The economic implications of demographic changes ahead in the United States are enormous. Thus, we can look forward to major shifts in product markets and advertising, in clothing styles, in social and residential facilities, in location and type of housing, in health care facilities, and in personal entertainment.

The economic destiny of a nation is, of course, determined by innumerable forces other than its demographic history. Nevertheless, at any particular moment the size and structure of a country's population can have a significant effect on its economic growth and its general well-being.

References

Cohen, Wilbur J., and Charles F. Westhoff, *Demographic Dynamics in America*, Free Press, New York, 1977; National Bureau of Economic Research, *Demographic and Economic Change in Developed Countries*, A Conference of the Universities-National Bureau Committee for Economic Research, Princeton University Press, Princeton, N.J., 1960.

(*See also* Economic growth; Employment and unemployment; Labor force; Zero population growth)

Fabian Linden

Depletion allowance

Depletion allowance is the deduction from income for the exhaustion of resources ("wasting assets"), such as mineral deposits, oil and gas wells, and timber, in the process of production. For income tax purposes it is the higher of conventional depletion based either on cost recovery or on an alternative percentage depletion allowance calculated as a specified percentage of gross income from the mineral property not to exceed 50 percent of the net income. Percentage depletion is not available for timber.

In addition to depletion allowances, mineral producers can deduct as current expense certain capital outlays for exploration, drilling, and development. The expensing of these capital costs reduces the basis for future cost depletion but not percentage depletion. The result is equivalent to a double tax deduction for capital recovery on the same investment. The structure is designed to encourage the discovery and exploitation of mineral and energy sources essential to the national economy and defense. Percentage depletion has long been a controversial feature of the income tax and a target of intense criticism by the tax reform movement.

The statutory rates of percentage depletion (section 613 of the Internal Revenue Code) range from 5 percent on items such as gravel, peat, and sand to 22 percent on sulfur, uranium, and a list of domestically produced priority items. Seven percentage depletion categories (one open-ended) cover a list of over 100 mineral items. Geothermal deposits were added to the list by energy legislation in 1978. Rates have been based in part on economic priority and in part on the ratio of gross to net income for the product. Rate classification may depend upon location of deposit, type of geologic formation, method of production, quality and use of product, and type of producer. A higher 27.5 percent allowance on oil and gas wells, traditionally the focal point of tax reform opposition, was reduced in 1969, then repealed for large integrated oil companies in 1975. The only percentage depletion for the oil and gas industry is now limited under special rules to: (1) small independent producers and royalty owners, and (2) geopressurized methane gas wells.

Cost Versus Percentage Depletion

Cost depletion consists of a write-off similar to depreciation computed by the production or service unit method: the total unrecovered cost of the mineral property is divided by the total number of future units (tons of coal or barrels of oil) the property is expected to produce. The quotient—unit cost depletion—is multiplied by the number of units produced in any period to determine the cost or "adjusted basis" depletion. The percentage depletion allowance is a flat percentage of the gross income from the property, generally not to exceed 50 percent of net income computed without regard to depletion. Cost depletion depends upon, and is limited to, the unrecovered cost of the property; it ends when the entire cost is written off. Percentage depletion, by contrast, is computed without regard to capital cost, continues as long as there is income from the property, and over time may cumulate to many times the investment. Estimated tax benefits (revenue loss) due to the excess of percentage over cost depletion for both corporate and noncorporate taxpayers are about $1750 million at 1980 levels and $2175 million projected to 1984.

The original income tax legislation provided a "reasonable allowance," limited to 5 percent of gross income, for wasting assets, later changed to cost or 1913 value depletion. An alternative allowance based on discovery value was introduced in 1918. Percentage depletion was adopted for oil and gas in 1926 in lieu of discovery value depletion, which had proved administratively impracticable. It was extended to metals, sulfur, and coal in 1932, then expanded over the years to cover other products. Its purposes were: (1) to provide (like discovery depletion) a more reasonable allowance where the historic cost of a mineral property was low, possibly representing the unpaid efforts of the prospector, and (2) to afford both incentive and internal financing for the continuing replacement of exhausted natural resources.

Numerous technical provisions affect the percentage depletion allowance itself or the overall tax status of mineral income. These include among others:

1. Definition of gross income forming the basis for percentage depletion (involving eligible mineral treatment processes as distinguished from manufacturing operations)

2. Definition of the mineral property and related aggregation rules for applying the percentage of net income limitation

3. Capital gain rules on disposition of mineral properties and royalties
4. Foreign tax credit rules for foreign mineral operation of U.S. corporations
5. The treatment of "carved-out" production payments and the complex "ABC" transactions affecting the parties to the sale and financing of producing properties

Percentage depletion in excess of the unrecovered cost basis is also subject to the minimum tax on tax preferences affecting wealthy individuals and corporations.

Pros and Cons

The percentage depletion system reflects the conflict between equity and economic considerations in tax policy. Equity criticisms dwell upon the contrast between lucrative mineral operations sheltered by artificial capital recovery allowances and taxpayers generally who are limited to cost recovery or pay tax on earnings without adjustment for wasting personal earning capacity. Economic proponents cite the unusual risks of mineral, especially oil and gas, development; the large amounts of capital needed to finance new discoveries; and the desirability of encouraging continuity of operation against resale of productive property to realize earning prospects at capital gains rates. Critics contend that percentage depletion is ineffective in eliciting new sources of supply and leads to overinvestment in favored industries and overexploitation adverse to conservation objectives. The substantive case for percentage depletion has sometimes been obscured by simplistic arguments put forward by the industries affected, while its condemnation by economists and tax reformers reflects some overreaction to these arguments. Critics may be insensitive both to the significance of large potential monetary rewards in aleatory undertakings and to the natural resistance of regional interests—expressed politically in various ways—to having their nonreproducible economic base run through the income tax mill.

The disposition of percentage depletion for petroleum in the midst of a mounting energy crisis—one of the ironies of tax legislative history—seems to reflect public reaction to high oil prices, the image created by oil industry profits, the internationalization of the industry, and persisting national dependence upon foreign oil sources in spite of liberal tax incentives. It does not necessarily portend the future of the percentage depletion structure as a whole, which may be seen to have the incidental merit of automatically adjusting capital recovery allowances for inflation.

References

Byrne, Robert F., and Wilbur A. Steger, "Assessment of the Effectiveness of Federal Tax Incentives for Natural Resources," *Tax Incentives,* Tax Institute of America, D.C. Heath, Lexington, Mass., 1971, pp. 85–103; McDonald, Stephen L., *Federal Tax Treatment of Income from Oil and Gas,* Brookings, Washington, D.C., 1963; *1979 U.S. Master Tax Guide,* Commerce Clearing House, Chicago, 1979, paragraphs 1195–1199, pp. 452–455; Pechman, Joseph A., *Federal Tax Policy,* 3d ed., Brookings, Washington, D.C., 1977, pp. 151–153.

(*See also* Depreciation allowance; Taxation, an overview)

Richard E. Slitor

Depreciation allowance

Depreciation allowance is the deduction from income for the exhaustion, wear and tear, and obsolescence of property used for business or investment purposes. Depreciation is a factor in business and regulatory accounting, in the national income and product accounts, in the appraisal of depreciable property, and in the determination of taxable income. The pervasive impact of taxation on business investment has made the term depreciation allowance virtually synonymous with the income tax deduction. The basic allowance, designed to spread the cost of an asset over its useful life, serves to avoid taxing return of capital rather than income, and liberalized or accelerated allowances provide a stimulus to investment. Depreciation is one of a family of capital consumption or capital recovery allowances which includes amortization, optional expensing of certain capital expenditures, depletion, and others.

Measuring Depreciation

The economic concept of depreciation regards it as a measure of the decline in present discounted value (PDV) of future earnings. There are various engineering and appraisal approaches to measuring depreciation. Both accounting and tax concepts have traditionally treated it as amortization of capital viewed as prepaid costs or as an element of cost reflecting the gradual attrition of productive assets due to physical deterioration and economic obsolescence.

The annual tax allowance is determined by allocating the historic cost (or other basic value) less salvage over the service life or write-off period, by means of a systematic allocation formula. Major methods of allocation include the straight-line method (uniform annual allowance), declining balance and sum-of-the-year–digits methods (decreasing charges), and production or service-unit method (cost spread over life measured in terms of output potential). Annual depreciation used in determining current net income is accumulated in depreciation reserve accounts for the valuation of depreciable assets in the balance sheet and for figuring their adjusted basis, the amount subtracted from proceeds of sales to determine gain or loss.

Timing is essential in tax depreciation. Retarded allowances give taxes priority over capital recovery and raise effective tax rates, while speedier write-offs defer taxable income and lighten burdens on capital formation. Certain investment-linked incentives, such as the former British investment allowance and the American investment tax credit, go beyond acceleration, giving a tax benefit equivalent to capital recovery in excess of 100 percent of cost.

The advantages of acceleration to investors are measurable in various ways: increase in the PDV of the stream of future tax deductions; enhancement of cash flow position; shortening of the "payout" period, reducing both capital at risk and risk of possible loss of tax benefit; increase in internal capital sources; saving of interest on debt financing; and improvement in aftertax rate of return on investment. The value of acceleration varies directly with the applicable rate of tax and interest rates.

History

The basic depreciation allowance structure of the federal income tax laws, contained in section 167 of the Internal Revenue Code, provides a reasonable allowance for depreciation including obsolescence, specifies certain acceptable methods, and allows an optional class life or asset depreciation range (ADR) system. The product of both administrative and legislative actions in 1971, the ADR system is designed both to encourage modernization of industrial capacity and to simplify administration. The ADR system represents one of a series of historic redirections of depreciation policy since the inception of the modern income tax in 1913.

After an initial period of relatively relaxed administration, a more restrictive administrative approach to depreciable lives was prompted by the fiscal stringencies of the Great Depression. This was highlighted by Treasury Decision 4422 (1934) and the famous useful life schedules of the 1942 edition of *Bulletin F*. Substantial rapid amortization programs for certified defense facilities marked the World War II and Korean conflict periods.

The accelerated depreciation methods (declining balance at 200 percent of the straight-line rate, sum-of-the-year digits, and consistent formulas) were adopted in 1954. This departure from primary reliance upon straight-line with only limited use of the 150 percent declining balance method was an early response to the extensive experimentation by the industrial nations of Western Europe and Japan with depreciation incentives. Additional first-year depreciation (20 percent "bonus" depreciation) was added in 1958 for productive equipment in limited amounts to aid small business. Rapid amortization has been provided from time to time for high-priority items in the social sector, such as pollution-control equipment and rehabilitation of rental housing. A guideline life system was introduced by administrative action of the Kennedy administration in 1962 as a companion measure of the investment tax credit. This set aside *Bulletin F* with its multiplicity of asset life schedules and engineering concept of economic life, substituting shorter guideline lives applicable to a smaller number of broad industry classes of productive equipment. Guideline use was subject to monitoring by a controversial reserve ratio test for conformity between tax life and retirement practice of the particular business. Despite liberalization of its transition rules, widespread failures of the reserve ratio test and consequent depreciation cutbacks were imminent when the ADR system intervened in 1971.

The ADR system removed the reserve ratio test and instituted a simplified class life structure built upon the 1962 guidelines. It allows the taxpayer to choose a life within a range of some 20 percent above or below the asset guideline period. The ADR guideline periods are subject to revision by the Internal Revenue Service and thus retain some link with actual service life expectancy on a broad experiential basis.

The inflation of the seventies challenged the adequacy of historic cost-based depreciation. Partly to cope with higher asset replacement costs, proposals for further acceleration were made that further relax or eliminate the link between tax and actual service lives, such as doubling the 20 percent leeway under the ADR system; a 10-5-3 plan allowing business to depreciate buildings in 10 years, equipment in 5 years, and trucks and autos in 3 years; and even current expensing of most machinery and equipment. Conditions of "stagflation" emphasize the role of acceleration as an anti-inflationary, productivity-oriented form of tax reduction; as a pragmatic surrogate for indexation of cost-based allowances; and as relief from tax burdens on "phantom" profits that aggravate upward price pressures due to the artificially high effective tax rates on real profits.

Some critics regard any depreciation in excess of true economic depreciation as a source of tax unneutrality, economic distortions, and resource misallocation. Abstracting from feedback effects, critics argue that acceleration narrows the revenue base and favors more general tax reduction. Doubts as to the cost-effectiveness of its investment stimulus and revenue feedback are underscored by the difficulties of econometric measurement. Comparative benefits per dollar of revenue sacrifice for acceleration and the investment credit are controversial. Fast write-downs of the cost of assets below their economic value, of which expensing is the extreme example, is analytically equivalent, critics assert, to exempting from tax normal returns on investment, a selective retreat from business income taxation.

Acceleration may create book losses. Wastage of deductions may result unless there is flexibility at the taxpayer's option or adequate loss carry-over rules. Differences between tax and book depreciation create other problems, highlighted by the tax rules on "flowthrough" and "normalization" accounting methods for public utilities.

Moderate views give further acceleration priority in future tax reduction but reflect concern lest excessive measures confer widely varying benefits among different sectors of the economy and encourage formation of tax shelters.

Reform of depreciation allowances has historically been interrelated with the treatment of gains on sale of overdepreciated property, since favorable capital gain rates on artificial gains created by fast write-offs permit conversion of ordinary income into capital gains. "Recapture" rules taxing gains reflecting prior depreciation alowances have been adopted to curb this effect. Special depreciation restrictions and recapture rules apply to real estate. Accelerated depreciation on certain types of property is a tax preference item subject to the minimum tax.

References

Hulten, Charles R., and Frank C. Wykoff, "On the Feasibility of Equating Tax to Economic Depreciation," *1978 Compendium of Tax Research,* Office of Tax Analysis, Department of the Treasury, 1978; Musgrave, Richard A., *The Theory of Public Finance,* McGraw-Hill, New York, 1959, pp. 336–346; *1979 Depreciation Guide,* Commerce Clearing House, Chicago, 1979; Terborgh, George W., "Inflation and the Taxation of Business Income," Machinery and Allied Products Institute, Washington, D.C., 1976.

(*See also* Capital gains; Depletion allowance; Taxation, an overview)

Richard E. Slitor

Diffusion indexes

A diffusion index is a time series, usually monthly or quarterly, representing the percentage of items in a given population that are rising over a specified interval. Thus, a diffusion index of 75 means that 75 percent of the items are rising and 25 percent are falling. The index can be as high as 100 and as low as zero. The same information can also be reported in other ways, as explained below.

Use in Economic Analysis

Diffusion indexes are used in economic analysis in several ways. One is to report information that is available only in the form of directions of change. In some surveys of business enterprises, for example, the respondents may be asked only whether production increased during the past month, remained the same, or declined. No information is obtained about the size of the change. The percentage of respondents reporting an increase is a diffusion index. Another type of index is derived from the components of an aggregate, such as total industrial production or total employment. The figures for the individual industries, for example, are used to determine how many industries have experienced an increase in production, and this number is expressed as a percentage of the total number of industries in the aggregate. The daily stock market report on the number of issues that rose or fell in price is an example of this kind of diffusion index. A third type of diffusion index may be constructed from, say, a list of leading indicators that are not commensurate with one another in terms of units but that behave in a simillar way during business cycles. The percentage rising during a given interval shows how widespread the expansion or contraction is among these indicators.

Diffusion indexes of the first type are compiled in many countries from surveys of business executives, purchasing managers, and consumers. Often the questions are directed not only to past changes but also to expected future changes. Since the questions are simple, they can be answered quickly by individuals who are likely to know the answers or to have informed opinions. For the same reason the answers can be tabulated and released promptly.

Calculating Diffusion

The results of these surveys are often reported in the form of net balances, obtained by subtracting the percentage reporting a decline from the percentage reporting an increase. The percentage reporting no change is left out of the calculation, though it does affect the result. The method is arithmetically equivalent, except for a scaling factor, to the alternative method that is commonly used in the two other types of diffusion indexes, which is to divide the no-change group equally between the increases and the declines. If R, U, and F are the percentages rising, unchanged, and falling, respectively, so that $R + U + F = 100$, then the net balance is $R - F$, while the percentage rising plus half the unchanged percentage is $R + \frac{1}{2}U$. It follows that $R - F = (R + \frac{1}{2}U) - 100$.

Diffusion indexes expressed in either of these two ways are influenced by the size of the no-change groups and hence are superior to methods that report simply the percent rising without regard to how the remaining returns are divided between the no-change and the declining groups or to methods that split the no-change group proportionately between the rising and declining groups. Since diffusion indexes are based upon information about changes over time, they are related to rates of change computed over similar intervals. Thus, a diffusion index showing the percentage of industries reporting a rise in employment during the past month will be related to the rise in total employment reported by those industries during the month. The relation will not be precise because the diffusion index ignores the magnitude of the change in each industry, recording only the direction. It answers a different question, namely, how widespread the increases or decreases are among the several industries. It gives information about employment that cannot be inferred directly from the aggregate figure itself. In many instances diffusion indexes are less affected by erratic movements than are rates of change since an occasional large movement in a single component may have a substantial effect upon an aggregate; whereas, in a diffusion index the size of the change doesn't matter.

Diffusion Indexes and the Business Cycle

Studies of business cycles have shown that diffusion indexes act in a characteristic way. As a business cycle expansion gets underway, the number of companies, industries, geographic areas, and types of activity that participate in the expansion increases. Diffusion indexes rise. But after the expansion has been underway for some time, forces develop that prevent further expansion in one industry or another, or one sector or another. Capacity limitations may become a factor here and there, the cost of holding inventories may become burdensome, competition for business may become more intense, the banking system may begin to restrict further credit expansion, etc. The scope of the expansion begins to recede and diffusion indexes decline. Aggregate economic activity—output, employment, income, sales—is still likely to continue to expand for a while, however. As recessionary factors take hold, diffusion indexes continue to drop and begin recording a majority of activities declining. The downswing spreads over more and more sectors for some months, but then prospects start to brighten in some areas. Purchases that had been postponed are found more attractive and new investment projects are revitalized. Hiring picks up. Diffusion indexes reach their lows and start to rise. Soon thereafter the decline in aggregate activity comes to a halt and a new business cycle expansion gets underway.

Historical studies of this process have shown how diffusion indexes undergo cyclical movements corresponding to the business cycle but also leading it in the manner described. They have shown that severe recessions are generally more widespread them mild recessions. Hence, diffusion indexes compiled currently have become one of the tools that analysts use to appraise the state of the business cycle. In Japan, the Economic Planning Agency has constructed a chronology of business cycles based upon diffusion indexes. Diffusion indexes have also been employed to show the extent to which business cycles spread from one country to another.

Diffusion Indexes of Prices and Inflation

Diffusion indexes of prices are of special interest in connection with the study of inflation, since inflation is usually defined as a general rise in prices and since price diffusion indexes measure the degree of generality. As inflation spreads, a larger percentage of prices rise. As it subsides, the percentage of rising prices declines. In 1972, for example, in a survey of business executives conducted by Dun and Bradstreet, the percentage reporting that their selling prices had increased since the year before was about 75 percent. By the spring of 1974, this diffusion index had risen to about 95 percent. Then as a recession developed the proportion reporting price increases fell and reached about 80 percent early in 1975. A similar swing occurred in price diffusion indexes constructed from commodity price quotations.

Diffusion indexes are often used to report expectations. Expected changes in prices, profits, sales, income, and expenditures are regularly reported in this manner. Changes in the climate of opinion can thus be determined and their potential effect on the economy evaluated.

References

Alexander, Sidney S., "Rate of Change Approaches to Forecasting—Diffusion Indexes and First Differences," *The Economic Journal*, June 1958, pp. 288–301; Broida, Arthur L., "Diffusion Indexes," *American Statistician*, June 1955, pp. 7–16; Burns, Arthur F., "New Facts on Business Cycles," *Thirtieth Annual Report*, National Bureau of Economic Research, New York, May 1950, pp. 3–31, reprinted in Geoffrey H. Moore (ed.), *Business Cycle Indicators*, Princeton University Press, Princeton, N.J., 1961, chap. 2; Burns, Arthur F., and Wesley C. Mitchell, *Measuring Business Cycles*, National Bureau of Economic Research, New York, 1946, pp. 66–71, 96–107; Hastay, Millard, "The Dun and Bradstreet Surveys of Businessmen's Expectations," *Proceedings of the Business and Economics Statistics Section*, American Statistical Association, Washington, D.C., 1955, pp. 93–123; Hickman, Bert G., "Diffusion, Acceleration and Business Cycles," *American Economic Review*, September 1959, pp. 535–565; Hultgren, Thor, *Costs,*

Prices, and Profits: Their Cyclical Relations, National Bureau of Economic Research, New York, 1965; Mintz, Ilse, *Cyclical Fluctuations in the Exports of the United States since 1879*, National Bureau of Economic Research, New York, 1967; Moore, Geoffrey H. (ed.), *Business Cycle Indicators*, Princeton University Press, Princeton, N.J., 1961, chaps. 2, 8, 9, 18, 19; Shiskin, Julius, "Business Cycle Indicators: The Known and the Unknown," in John J. Clark (ed.), *The Management of Forecasting*, St. Johns University Press, New York, 1969, pp. 47–88; Strigel, Werner H., *Trade Cycle Indicators Derived from Qualitative Data*, Ifo-Institut fur Wirtschaftsforschung, Munich, 1972; Theil, Henri, "Recent Experiences with the Munich Business Test," *Econometrica*, April 1955, pp. 184–192; U.S. Bureau of Labor Statistics, *Chartbook on Prices, Wages, and Productivity*, published monthly; U.S. Department of Commerce, *Business Conditions Digest*, published monthly; U.S. Department of Commerce, *Handbook of Cyclical Indicators*, May 1977.

(*See also* Business cycles; Economic forecasts; Economic statistics; Forecasting methods; Leading indicator approach to forecasting; Statistical techniques in economics and business, an overview)

Geoffrey H. Moore

Diminishing returns law

The law of diminishing returns is the general notion that the productive process becomes progressively less efficient as it expands. Recognized in the 1760s by Anne Robert Jacques Turgot, who served Louis XVI of France as finance minister, the law of diminishing returns states that adding more of a particular input to a productive process will yield progressively less additional output per unit of input. For instance, if tomatoes are planted by hand on a certain farm, augmenting the number of workers engaged in planting will increase the total output of tomatoes less and less. Indeed, adding more workers might ultimately make this process so inefficient that the harvest might end up being absolutely smaller.

Thomas Malthus provided one of the most famous examples of the law of diminishing returns, though he did not use the term and may not have realized the full significance of his conclusions. In the first edition of his *Essay on the Principle of Population* (1798), he hypothesized that, when population grows according to a geometric progression (2, 4, 8, 16 32, . . .), food production would grow only according to an arithmetic progression (2, 4, 6, 8, 10, . . .). This clearly implies that as population and food production expand, the output per worker will shrink; or, seen another way, the input of additional labor required to achieve constant increments of output will need to rise dramatically.

A precise statement of the law of diminishing returns requires several elaborations. One is that the law becomes operative only if at least one input into the productive process becomes relatively scarce. Both of the above examples assume that the supply of land used in production does not increase, so that as production expands the supply of land becomes scarce relative to the other inputs. In some land-rich countries, this limitation may not apply because more land is available to be brought into production. If all inputs can be augmented in equal proportions (including such intangibles as management skills and transportation facilities), the law of diminishing returns will not operate; some scarcity must develop before it does. Land-rich countries may be subject to the law of diminishing returns if they suffer from relatively limited supplies of labor or capital.

Another elaboration is that the law of diminishing returns may, under certain circumstances, be temporarily replaced by its logical opposite, the law of increasing returns (better known as economies of scale). If the input that is, relatively speaking, scarcest in the production of a certain item can be augmented, output may well rise disproportionately. For example, a large, fully equipped factory may have had to operate inefficiently because of a shortage of workers who could handle the machinery. Breaking this bottleneck, e.g., through immigration or by training more workers, will permit better use of the resources (land and machinery) that are already available, so that the productivity per worker might well increase. But this effect will work only up to a point. When one or another of the inputs becomes relatively scarce, the law of diminishing returns will again come into play.

In sum, the impact of the law of diminishing returns may be disguised or postponed by any development that increases the supply or the productivity of the scarcest input. Increased population, division of labor, better specialization, new invenions or innovations, improved technology, and discovery of new resources all serve, temporarily, to stretch the limits imposed by relative scarcity of one of the inputs into the productive process. As soon as the impact of such a development has played itself out, however, the law of diminishing returns will, without fail, reassert itself.

References

Fellner, William, *Modern Economic Analysis,* McGraw-Hill, New York, 1960, pp. 62–69; Hamberg, Daniel, *Principles of a Growing Economy,* Norton, New York, 1961, pp. 501–511; Watson, Donald S., and Mary A. Holmes, *Price Theory and Its Uses,* 4th ed., Houghton Mifflin, Boston, 1976.

(*See also* Economies of scale)

G. H. Mattersdorff

Discount rate (*see* Federal Reserve policy; Monetary policy)

Discrimination economics

Discrimination is often equated with the unequal economic position typically observed across demographic groups within an economy. In the United States race and sex differences are of prime concern. In other countries ethnic differences are often more relevant.

To whatever group discrimination applies, economists use the same methodology to measure differences in economic strata. Wage and occupation typify indicators of economic well-being, and discrimination is measured indirectly as a residual, the unexplained difference in wage (occupation) if productivity differences are held constant. Whether such a definition is without measurement error is open to question, as is the issue of where within society the causes for discrimination lie.

Causes for Discrimination

Several theories of discrimination exist, each of which may be categorized as either demand- or supply-oriented.

Demand-oriented theories consider the possibility that firms or nonminority workers express preferences regarding workers and coworkers. Such taste patterns result in the relegation of minority workers to the least desirable jobs at the lowest possible wages. When firms themselves discriminate, nonminority white male workers are paid premiums for their services in order to eliminate blacks, women, and others from the firm. When employees discriminate, then employers must pay wage premiums to nonminority employees to induce them to work with the discriminated.

Evidence seems to contradict such an interpretation. Clearly, firms would not be behaving so as to maximize long-run profits because wage premiums reduce profits. Hence, nondiscriminating firms would enter the market at a competitive advantage. Either discriminators would be driven out of business, or two types of firms would emerge—ones comprised solely of minority workers and others comprised solely of majority workers. With the possible exception of the nonprofit sector such a long-run prognosis is inconsistent with data. Consequently, a supply-oriented approach has become an increasingly more realistic theory.

Supply theories indicate that differences in economic position are more a societal phenomenon. Institutions within society, such as marriage, the division of labor within the home, and the educational system, create (or are indicative of) group differences in labor-market expectations and productivity. The value of noting the existence of such supply differences lies in appropriate governmental policy to achieve economic equality.

Supply theory asserts that discrimination takes place not by firms, but in other sectors of the economy chronologically well before an individual even enters the labor market. As such, wage differentials merely reflect differential productivity.

For women, evidence indicates strong sex differences in labor-market aspirations long before entry into the labor market. For example, the average woman in the 30 to 54 age range in 1967 has spent over 10 years out of the labor force. Expectations of intermittent lifetime labor-force participation have led women to take different subjects in school, and to specialize in nonmarket-oriented fields in college. Accordingly, women tend to locate in jobs that require less training than do men. Further, married women with children are willing to forego good jobs to minimize commuting time.

Although this scenario depicts general behavioral tendencies, it should be remembered that not all women follow such labor-force work patterns. Some women work every year after leaving school, and some women achieve high-level jobs. In fact, evidence indicates that those women with the strongest labor-force commitments are the ones most likely to achieve the highest-paying, most prestigious jobs. Those with the most intermittent labor-force participation are most likely to be in relatively menial jobs.

For blacks, there is a history of governmental discrimination, including educational inequality. It is only since the 1954 Supreme Court decision that younger blacks seem to be achieving equal schooling and labor-market success almost equal to that of whites. If demand theories are correct, then current equal employment opportunity (EEO) legislation may be appropriate; but if supply factors are as important as the evidence seems to indicate, then government policies should focus more on society and less on firms.

Measuring Discrimination

The amount of discrimination is ascertained by computing a discrimination coefficient. This measure represents the proportion, for example, of the wage gap between race, sex, or ethnic groups unexplained once productivity differences are controlled statistically. The discrimination coefficient (d) is computed conceptually according to the following formula:

$$d = \frac{\tilde{Y}_F - \overline{Y}_F}{\overline{Y}_M - \overline{Y}_F} \tag{1}$$

where Y = measure of economic success (e.g., earnings)
$\overline{Y}_M$ = mean earnings of group M
$\overline{Y}_F$ = mean earnings of group F
$\tilde{Y}_F$ = earning power of group F if they have M's productivity

Clearly, the denominator $\overline{Y}_M - \overline{Y}_F$ is the mean earnings differential between M and F, and $\tilde{Y}_F - \overline{Y}_F$ is the gap in earnings unexplained by productivity differences. The discrimination coefficient represents the proportion of unexplained earnings differentials.

Implementing this formula is difficult. $\tilde{Y}_F$ is not directly observable, and hence must be estimated by statistical regression analysis. In addition, no direct measures are available for worker productivity so that socioeconomic variables such as education, age, experience, marital status, industry, union membership, and region must be used as proxies in the regression. Essentially this procedure entails using employee data to fit a mathematical function to relate race, sex, and ethic groups to wages while holding constant the socioeconomic variables designed to reflect productivity.

A commonly used regression has the following form:

$$Y = \delta G + \beta X + \epsilon \tag{2}$$

where $Y \equiv$ a measure of economic well-being such as earnings (usually measured in logarithmic form)
$G \equiv$ a dummy variable denoting whether an individual is a member of the particular minority group in question
$X \equiv$ a vector of an individual's socioeconomic characteristics

Studies of discrimination concentrate on estimating the δ coefficient. This coefficient reflects earnings differences among race, sex, or ethnic groups. It represents the earnings gap remaining between any two groups, holding constant the socioeconomic variables chosen to proxy productivity. For example, when Y is measured as the logarithm of earnings and δ is found to be 0.3, then there exists approximately a 30 percent wage premium of one group over another. If the total between group wage differential is, say, 50 percent, then the discrimination coefficient is 0.60 (0.30/0.50), implying that 60 percent of the wage gap remains unexplained by socioeconomic factors.

Current computations for the United States using 1960, 1967, and 1976 data yield economywide male-female discrimination coefficients between 40 and 80 percent. However, this diminishes to about 20 percent and less within narrow occupations. For blacks and whites using 1976 data the discrimination coefficient is about 50 percent.

Potential Biases

Obviously, these measures of discrimination may be over- or underestimated depending on the existence of possible errors embedded within this procedure. Most crucial are the socioeconomic variables chosen as proxies for worker productivity. As an example, take the case of adjusting by marital status in an analysis of sex discrimination. For the average female, being married is associated with lower lifetime labor-force participation, lower human capital investment, and hence lower on-the-job productivity. For males the opposite is true: being married is associated with greater labor-force attachment, more human capital, and higher on-the-job productivity. Thus, assuming that marital status (or other socioeconomic variables) affects males and females in the same way could lead to biases in estimating discrimination. In particular, productivity-adjusted earnings of married women would be overestimated as would be the discrimination coefficient. Since exact measures of worker productivity are not available, the exact choice of socioeconomic variables is crucial. Much criticism of current esimates centers on this issue.

Even the relevance of productivity adjustments themselves can be questioned on philosophical grounds. The motive for adjustment is apparent. It is expected that payment schemes be based on worker productivity. Observing equally productive workers receiving different wages constitutes discrimination. Yet is is quite possible that discriminatory practices have led to differential productivity in the first place. For example, if unequal employment practices have led to blacks receiving inferior education (or women frequently dropping out of the labor force), then the fact that whites obtain more schooling than blacks (or that men have higher job aspirations than women) may be a form of discrimination in itself. Netting out these factors may lead to an underestimation of the discrimination coefficient. Even if firms are not responsible, societal influences may be a factor and should be considered.

Other biases also exist to mar the exact computation of a discrimination coefficient. These include errors typical of most econometric studies. Despite these biases, estimates of intergroup differentials are robust.

References

Becker, Gary S., *The Economics of Discrimination*, 2d ed., University of Chicago Press, Chicago, 1971; Freeman, Richard B., "Black Economic Progress After 1964: Who Has Gained and Why?," National Bureau of Economic Research Working Paper 282, New York, November 1978; Mincer, Jacob, and Solomon Polachek, "Family Investments in Human Capital: Earnings of Women," *Journal of Political Economy*, March/April 1974, pp. 576–1108; Polachek, Solomon, "Potential Biases in Measuring Male-Female Discrimination," *Journal of Human Resources*, Spring 1975, pp. 205–229.

(*See also* Demographics and economics; Employment and unemployment; Labor force)

Solomon Polachek

Diseconomies of scale (*see* Diminishing returns law)

Disintermediation

Financial institutions serve as intermediaries for individuals and nonfinancial corporations that typically channel the bulk of their investible funds into the credit markets. Disintermediation is the term applied to a situation in which the normal flow of funds through financial institutions is disrupted because of sudden switches in the preferences of the nonfinancial sector toward direct investment in financial instruments. For example, instead of augmenting a bank savings account, an individual might buy a U.S. Treasury bill.

The motivation for such switches is economic—more specifically, interest rates in the open market that exceed rates available from financial institutions by an unusual margin. What is meant by "unusual" is open to question, but it will help to recall that in long-term equilibrium, the intermediaries must cover all costs, including a return on capital. Hence, some margin—$1\frac{1}{2}$ or 2 percentage points—in favor of open-market rates over institutional rates represents the normal compensation the market exacts for the financial intermediation service.)

Problem and Results of Disintermediation

Disintermediation is unlikely under conditions of uncontrolled interest rates. If open-market rates rise above institutional rates by more than the normal margin, competitive forces will compel institutions to raise their rates in order to protect their intermediary function. Interest rate controls are a necessary, but not a sufficient, condition of disintermediation.

The United States has experienced four significant episodes of disintermediation in the period 1965-1980. The term was coined in 1966, when the first of these episodes occurred. The others occurred in the years 1969-70, 1973-74, and 1979-80. Each one of these experiences coincided with attempts to curb the upward-ratcheting inflation through monetary policy. Rising short-term interest rates—one major evidence of monetary restraint—occurred in each instance. Increasingly flexible and upwardly adjustable institutional rates during this period proved to be insufficient to prevent the emergence of strong incentives toward disintermediation and its actual occurrence. A combination of regulatory policy and of economic pressures upon financial institutions, including especially past contractual obligations, accounted for those four periods of disintermediation.

The extent of the problem can be gleaned from the following figures. In an average year without disintermediation, such as 1972, financial institutions account for roughly 95 percent of all funds domestically supplied to the credit markets. (The main groups of institutions are commercial banks, savings and loan associations, mutual savings banks, insurance companies and pension funds, investment companies, and various others including credit unions, finance companies, and specialized credit agencies of the federal government.) Thus, the nonfinancial public supplied directly only 5 percent of the total funds raised. In contrast, during heavy disintermediation years such as 1973 and 1974, the directly supplied portions rose to 15 and 20 percent, respectively, with the institutional contribution declining proportionately.

The problem is more acute when particular groups of institutions or specific financial markets are singled out for attention. Thus, the public has customarily deposited a large portion of its savings in thrift institutions (savings and loan associations, mutual savings banks, and credit unions). This practice has been a key factor in the supply of residential mortgage funds, in which the savings and loan and mutual savings industries have specialized. A cut of over 50 percent in the net savings inflows of this group between 1972 and 1974 drastically affected the cost and availability of mortgage credit since the public sought nonmortgage outlets for the diverted funds (primarily short-term and intermediate paper such as Treasury bills and notes).

Although restrictive monetary policy must have an impact somewhere to be worthy of its name, the authorities have been troubled by its uneven impact, especially upon housing, throughout the period 1965–1980. Disintermediation is an integral part of such dislocations. Yet, regulatory policies have been revised only very slowly to cope with the new environment. Not until the late 1970s were persons and entities disposing of $10,000 at a time permitted to obtain interest rates comparable to those of money-market instruments from commercial banks and thrift institutions (say, 10 to 12 percent or even higher). If one had only lesser amounts, yields higher than $5\frac{1}{2}$ percent were obtainable from institutions only by committing the money for fixed periods far in excess of typical money-market maturities, and even then available yields were below market rates.

The reluctance to revise interest rate regulations more drastically relates in part to the financial situation of the institutions primarily affected by disintermediation. Long-term fixed-rate mortgages constitute an "embedded portfolio" that sharply limits the ability to move rates paid upward with the market. State usury laws and contractual life insurance policy loan provisions constitute further obstacles in the way of a quick solution. Yet, by 1980 the majority of academic and congressional opinion was clearly swinging in the direction of a market-oriented solution. Under a law passed in that year, the main interest rate control on institutions (regulation Q) was to be phased out over a 5-year period.

Disintermediation and Credit

There is little, if any, dissent regarding the proposition that disintermediation reallocates credit among ultimate borrowers. Mortgage and, perhaps, other long-term flows are curbed. Those aided are short-term borrowers who can offer what are deemed safe and liquid investments besides a high yield.

There is considerable dissent, however, about the influence of disintermediation upon total credit availability. It can be shown theoretically that potential credit expansion upon any given liquidity base (such as nonborrowed member bank reserves, or the narrowly defined money supply) is directly correlated with the degree of financial intermediation in the economy. Thus, disintermediation should curb total credit expansion.

The difficulty with an empirical demonstration of the point is twofold. In the first place, since disintermediation coincides, virtually by definition, with monetary restraint, the effect of such restraint has to be separated from that of disintermediation. Was total credit curbed by restricting the liquidity base or by the dislocation of credit flows? No satisfactory statistical answer is available.

In the second place, the concept of disintermediation has become somewhat muddled through institutional changes that have occurred since the term was coined. For example, by the late 1970s heavy flows of funds, disintermediated out of traditional thrift institutions, were going into mushrooming money-market funds (MMFs), which then acquired short-term paper of financial and nonfinancial borrowers. The diversion of credit flows continues to be demonstrated by these facts, but whether or not total credit creation has been impaired by disintermediation importantly depends not only upon a study of total credit flows at the time of the rise of the MMFs but also upon whether the term disintermediation should be applied to shifts of funds among intermediaries, which the MMFs surely are.

Disintermediation is a part of inflation pathology. Inflation forces essentially undesired changes in people's financial habits and causes major dislocations in the institutional framework of money and credit.

References

Ritter, Lawrence S., and William L. Silber, *Principles of Money, Banking and Financial Markets*, 2d ed., Basic Books, New York, 1977.

(*See also* Credit, an overview; Federal Reserve policy; Financial institutions; Financial instruments; Housing economics; Inflation; Interest rates; Monetary policy; Mortgage credit; Open-market operations; Thrift institutions)

Francis H. Schott

Disposable personal income

Disposable personal income is the income that persons retain after they have deducted personal taxes—federal and state income taxes, as well as personal property taxes and estate and gift taxes—and fines and fees for such services as education and hospitals. It is the concept closest to what the average person considers take-home pay. It is the amount which individuals can use either to make personal outlays—consumer expenditures for goods and services plus personal interest payments and gifts to foreigners such as relatives abroad—or to save.

Personal income is the amount of current income received by persons from all sources. It is composed of labor income—wages and salaries, propietors' income, rental income of persons, dividends, personal interest income, and the difference between transfer payments and personal contributions for social insurance.

In the national income accounts, the term "persons" includes individuals in their roles not only as consumers or heads of household but also as unincorporated business executives, because household and business accounts of retailers, self-employed professionals, farmers, and other individual enterprises have not successfully been separated. The term also includes nonprofit institutions such as private colleges and hospitals; private trust funds; and private pension, health, and welfare funds.

Disposable personal income is considered by economists to be the single most important determinant of consumption expenditures, since it represents spendable purchasing power that individuals and other persons derive from current income. It is one of the key indicators which retail executives follow closely, and its trend helps to determine whether retailers buy more goods or reduce their inventories.

However, the inclusion of nonmonetary income—such as wages and salaries paid in kind (food, clothing, lodging furnished directly to employees), rental value of owner-occupied homes, food and fuel produced and consumed on farms, and the income of unincorporated businesses and nonprofit institutions—makes it difficult to tell how much disposable income is received and retained by consumers only.

Trend and Importance

Disposable personal income has grown since World War II far more steadily than other measures of economic activity. In the 34 years from 1946 through 1979, consumers spent an average of 94 percent of their disposable income on goods and services and interest payments on their debts, with approximately 6 percent going for their personal savings. During this period the share of disposable income going for consumption and interest payments ranged from 91.5 to 96.7 percent, while the share going for personal savings ranged from 3.3 to 8.5 percent. However, at the beginning of 1980 the consumption rate rose to 97 percent while the savings rate dropped to 3 percent.

At the beginning of 1980 disposable personal income ran at an annual rate of well over \$1.7 trillion, accounting for 84 percent of personal income and 68 percent of GNP.

After disposable personal income is adjusted first for changes in population (per capita disposable personal income) and second for price changes (real disposable personal income per capita), it is frequently used to measure changes in the nation's standard of living. It is also used for international comparisons of standards of living. In the United States, per capita disposable income, measured in current dollars, topped \$7800, annual rate, in the first quarter of 1980. Measured in constant 1972 dollars, it was about \$4500.

The Bureau of Economic Analysis of the U.S. Department of Commerce calculates quarterly data on disposable personal income in current dollars and in real terms and on a per capita basis for the United States, and reports these statistics in the *Survey of Current Business*.

References

Ruggles, Richard, and Nancy Ruggles, *National Income Accounts and Income Analysis*, 2d ed., McGraw-Hill, New York, 1956.

(*See also* Gross national product; National income accounting; Personal consumption expenditures in GNP)

Douglas Greenwald

Distributed lags in economics

In economics, many causes produce effects not all at once but spread over time. A company appropriates funds for a new plant all at once, but those funds are spent gradually as the construction is carried out and the equipment put in place. A consumer's income increases; at first the consumer saves most of the increase but after awhile buys a new car or a bigger house. The value of the dollar falls relative to European currencies, but Americans do not immediately cancel their European vacations or stop buying parts for their European automobiles. Gradually, however, they shift away from European goods.

In each of these cases, a cause—the appropriation, the increase in income, or the change in exchange rates—has effects which appear only with a lag. The effects, when they appear, are usually spread over a period of time. If, for example, all of the spending from the appropriation came exactly 6 months after the appropriation, we would call the lag discrete; but since the spending is spread over a number of months or quarters we say that the lag is distributed. Description of distributed lags forms a major part of the work of explaining quantitatively how the economy works.

If we let x be the time series of observations on the cause and y be the time series of observations on the effect, then one way of expressing a distributed lag between x and y is

$$y_t = \sum_{i=0}^{n} w_i x_{t-i} + z_t \tag{1}$$

where n = number of periods over which the lag extends

z_t = factors other than x which influence y

In the appropriations case, w_i is the fraction of an appropriation spent during the ith period after it was made.

Equation (1) assumes that y is a linear function with fixed weights of x. Although we will be concerned here with only such distributed lags, it should be pointed out that the w_i might be variable. For example, in the appropriations-expenditure lag, the w_i may depend on the backlogs of orders of the equipment suppliers. Or the whole relationship may be nonlinear, as would be the case if a second devaluation speeded up the effects of a first devaluation. However, we will concentrate on how to estimate the w_i of Equation (1).

The approach to the estimation depends upon whether n, the number weights, is finite or infinite.

Finite Lags

The direct way to estimate the w's in (1) is by ordinary least-squares regression. If this method gives satisfactory results, if the successive values of w_i rise and fall in a reasonable pattern, no further analysis is necessary. It will often happen, however, that the pattern of weights which results is irregular, raising the suspicion that it is being influenced by chance correlations. One may then impose linear restrictions on the w's to smooth them out. For example, to impose the requirement that the weights w_1, w_2, and w_3 lie on a straight line, one places on them the restriction

$$w_2 - w_1 = w_3 - w_2 \qquad \text{or} \qquad w_3 - 2w_2 + w_1 = 0$$

With an appropriate regression program, one can specify one's subjective trade-off between closeness of fit of the equation on the one hand and conformity to the restriction on the other. The program will then minimize its user's "displeasure" with misses in the fit and with nonconformity to the restrictions.

Often the requirement that the weights lie on a straight line will seem excessively heavy-handed, and it will seem better to require that they lie on a quadratic, for example,

$$w_4 - 3w_3 + 3w_2 - w_1 = 0$$

or on a cubic by requiring

$$w_5 - 4w_4 + 6w_3 - 4w_2 + w_1 = 0$$

Again, conformity with these restrictions must be balanced against the desire to have the equation fit the data closely.

This approach of imposing restrictions only where they seem necessary is due, basically, to Robert S. Shiller and generalizes the method of Shirley M. Almon, which requires that all the weights lie exactly on a polynomial of some specified degree.

Infinite Lags

Another, altogether different approach stems from the work of L. M. Koyck. Koyck assumed an infinitely long lag ($n = \infty$) with $w_i = a\lambda^i$, thus

$$y_t = a \sum_{i=0}^{\infty} \lambda^i x_{t-i} \tag{2}$$

We may then lag this equation once and multiply both sides of λ to get

$$\lambda y_{t-1} = a \sum_{i=0}^{\infty} \lambda^{(i+1)} x_{t-(i+1)} = a \sum_{i=1}^{\infty} \lambda^i x_{t-i} \tag{3}$$

Subtracting (3) from (2) gives

$$y_t - \lambda y_{t-1} = a\lambda^0 x_{t-0} = ax_t \tag{4}$$

or

$$y_t = \lambda y_{t-1} + ax_t$$

In (4), one just regresses the dependent variable on its own lagged value and on x_t.
The Koyck lag can be written as

$$y_t = \frac{1}{1 - \lambda L} ax_t \tag{5}$$

where L is the lag operator defined by the equations

$$Lx_t = x_{t-1} \qquad \text{and} \qquad Ly_t = y_{t-1}$$

Synthetic division gives

$$\frac{1}{1 - \lambda L} = 1 + \lambda L + \lambda^2 L^2 + \lambda^3 L^3 + \cdots + \lambda^n L^n$$

and this equation applied to (5) gives (2). If we multiply both sides of (5) by $1 - \lambda L$, we get precisely (4).

The Koyck lag in the form (5) can be readily generalized to, say,

$$y_t = \frac{1}{1 - \lambda L - \mu L^2} (ax_t + bx_{t-1}) \tag{6}$$

This equation would be estimated in the form

$$y_t = \lambda y_{t-1} + \mu y_{t-2} + ax_t + bx_{t-1} \tag{7}$$

and the weights w_i calculated by synthetic division. Equation (7) incorporates both moving-average ($ax_t + bx_{t-1}$) and autoregressive ($\lambda y_{t-1} + \mu y_{t-2}$) elements. It illustrates, therefore, what is called the autoregressive moving-average (ARMA) method. Obviously, more terms of each type could be included.

There are two principal difficulties with equations which include autoregressive terms.

1. If there is more than one explanatory variable, all of them must have the same pattern of lag weights.

2. Lagged values of the dependent variable pick up the influence of other omitted variables that affect y_{t-1} in about the same way as they affect y_t. Thus, y_{t-1} becomes not merely a proxy for earlier values of x but also of other variables. Thus, the estimate of the lag becomes very sensitive to errors of specification. The estimates of λ tend to be too high; and the lag, too long.

Neither of these problems arises with the finite lags. For versatility and reliability, finite methods, therefore, are preferable.

References

Almon, Shirley M., "The Distributed Lag Between Capital Appropriations and Expenditures," *Econometrica*, vol. 33, 1965, pp. 178–196; Griliches, Zvi, "Distributed Lags: A Survey," *Econometrica*, vol. 35., 1967, pp. 16–49; Koyck, L. M., *Distributed Lags and Investment Analysis*, North Holland, Amsterdam, 1954; Shiller, Robert J., "A Distributed Lag Estimator Derived from Smoothness Priors," *Econometrica*, vol. 41, 1973, pp. 775–788.

(*See also* Regression analysis in business and economics; Time series analysis)

Clopper Almon, Jr.

Distribution theory

Distribution theory is based on the notion that the optimum allocation of resources is achieved through the workings of the price system in which resources move from less profitable to more profitable uses and from less important to more important uses. A widely accepted definition of economics, which itself points out the importance of distribution theory, is the study of of the allocation of scarce resources among unlimited and competing uses and users.

A basic problem of every economic system is the means of achieving an allocation of resources that will result in maximum efficiency. In order to achieve this goal, resources should be channeled into the production of goods that consumers want most and should be prevented from entering the production of goods that consumers want least. Prices affect our decisions as consumers and producers.

Consumers' Preference

In a free enterprise society, wants are usually ranked by the preference of consumers, whether individuals or businesses. Thus, the power of the consumer in the economy is indicated by consumer sovereignty, for it is consumers' decisions about the quantities and qualities of goods and services purchased in the marketplace which determine what is to be produced and in what proportions. Since the expenditures of consumers are reflected in market prices, prices play a key role in the decisions that actually determine the allocation of resources.

When producers do not appraise correctly consumers' preferences, their prices will fall because they will generate an oversupply of goods. Subsequently, their profits will decline and unless they alter their policy, they will be unable to pay for the resources they buy and use in the production process. Sooner or later the less efficient businesses will gradually lose out both in competition for consumers' demands and in competition for resources needed in production. And, finally, these firms will fail and go into bankruptcy.

Scarcity

Resource allocation becomes a major problem when the economy is operating under conditions of full or nearly full employment. It is then that resources become scarce. But economic resources are not usually scarce right across the resource board. Thus, there are degrees of scarcity with some resources more plentiful than others. When resources are scarce, however, the scarcer they are the higher the price.

Scarce goods are insufficient to satisfy all the wants for them. Thus society faces the choice among the resource range of wants that are to be satisfied. Hence, when resources are devoted to one segment of production, they are unavailable to other segments of the economy. It is then that we have the problem of distributing scarce resources among different uses and users.

It is to society's interest that production techniques be employed which make the greatest use of plentiful resources or make the least use of relatively scarce resources. Resources that are plentiful relative to total demand for them will be lower in price than resource items that are scarce.

Optimum Resource Allocation

A necessary condition for an optimum allocation of resources is that the marginal product of any resource be the same for all its alternative uses. With price competition in all product and resource markets, an optimum allocation is achieved automatically, but monopoly or monopsony leads to different marginal product with different uses and thus to misallocation.

There are other impediments to optimum resource allocation. Among them are ignorance of profitable opportunities, sociological and psychological factors (e.g., lack of factor mobility), and institutional restraints (e.g., labor unions and patents).

References

Bodenhorn, Diran, *Intermediate Price Theory*, McGraw-Hill, New York, 1961, pp. 261–270; Hamberg, Daniel, *Principles of a Growing Economy*, Norton, New York, 1961; Leftwich, Richard H., *The Price System and Resource Allocation*, 6th ed., Dryden Press, Hinsdale, Ill., 1976; Trescott, Paul B., *The Logic of the Price System*, McGraw-Hill, New York, 1970.

(*See also* Demand; General equilibrium; Price theory; Scarcity)

Douglas Greenwald

Division of labor

Division of labor, a key characteristic of a modern industrial economy, is a method of production in which each worker specializes in some phase of the production process. In a chronological division of labor, one worker carries out one step in the production process, another worker performs the next step, a third then adds the next contribution, and so on until the product is finished.

Specialization of function allows each person to use his or her own skills to best advantage. Moreover, division of labor results in the acquisition of appropriate skills which increase efficiency.

Different personal abilities make some persons better qualified for certain types of jobs than others. For example, manual dexterity in electronics industry workers is needed in one stage of producing miniature radios.

Specialization is undertaken because it enhances productive efficiency and results in increased output at lower cost. Devoting one's time to a single operation or occupation eliminates the loss of time in shifting from one job in a factory to another. The simplification of function resulting from specialization within a single production process lends itself to mechanization and the use of labor-saving equipment.

Simple repetitive operations, carried out by workers in a manufacturing plant, can result in economies of large-scale output. In turn, the large-scale output potential justifies the introduction of new and improved technologies.

The advantages of specialization have been recognized since the late eighteenth century, when Adam Smith illustrated the increased productivity of specialization with his classic example of pinmaking. He pointed out that a worker's efficiency is higher if the worker performs only one production operation than if he or she performs many operations.

If division of labor helps to increase productivity in the plant, then it also increases productivity in the industry and in the economy.

Inherent in specialization is the existence of interdependence or the need for the specialized worker to rely on others for the goods and services needed for daily life. Division of labor has also resulted in workers complaining about the monotony of their jobs. A slowdown strike was initiated by workers at a Chevrolet plant in Lordstown, Ohio, in the early 1970s in protest of a speedup in monotonous assembly line operations. As a result of this protest, some automobile manufacturing companies are using work teams which follow the job rather than stand at one position in the monotonous production process of assembling cars.

References

Alchian, Armen A., and William R. Allen, *University Economics*, 3d ed., Wadsworth, New York, 1971; Smith, Adam, *The Wealth of Nations*, Random House, New York, 1937.

(*See also* Productivity)

Lewis Koflowitz

Dumping

Dumping is the practice of selling goods in a foreign country at a price below their domestic selling price, after allowing for differences due to transportation expenses, tariffs, and other cost justifications. Many governments view the activity as an unfair, or at least questionable, competitive practice and frequently expose those engaged in dumping to the imposition of an antidumping duty. This generally unfavorable view of the practice stems from the monopoly precondition which underlies it. Economic theory specifies that in order for a producer to discriminate in the pricing of identical goods between markets (or classes of consumers) some element of monopoly power must be present; otherwise, the producer is merely a price-taker forced to adopt the uniform competitive price determined in the overall marketplace.

When International Dumping Can Occur Successfully

International dumping can occur successfully only when (1) the home and foreign markets are sufficiently separated, as by domestic tariff protection, to prevent arbitrage by foreign buyers in such a way that the cheap dumped goods cannot be resold by foreign buyers in the original market at a price which undercuts the domestic monopoly price; and (2) there exists less competition in the home market than the foreign market (often because the foreign market is not protected from outside producers), making foreign customers more responsive (or foreign demand more elastic) to an individual producer's price changes than domestic customers (or domestic demand). Under these circumstances, the incentive for a producer to engage in international dumping is explained by the broader concept and theory of third-degree price discrimination, of which dumping is really a special case.

Simply stated, the theory is as follows. A producer interested in maximizing profits given these conditions should price goods in different geographical locations so that the marginal revenue received from the last unit of those goods sold is equal in all locations, and at the same time equal to the overall marginal cost of production of those goods. If it is assumed that there is no difference in costs between markets if the revenue the producer receives from selling an additional unit of goods in the foreign market exceeds that received from the last unit sold in the home market, it is more profitable to lower the foreign price in order to sell another unit there and to raise the domestic price in order to sell a unit less at home. The incentive to reprice continues until the marginal revenues from each market are equilibrated to each other as well as to marginal cost of production. Where foreign market demand facing the producer is more responsive to price changes than domestic market demand, and where arbitrage cannot occur, this profit-maximizing formula will ultimately result in a situation where the producer is motivated to price goods in the foreign market more cheaply than at home.

Three Types of Dumping

The use of such price discrimination in the international trade on a regular basis is termed "persistent dumping"; its use to unload unexpected inventory accumulations on foreign markets (usually generated by a slump period in home business conditions) is termed "sporadic dumping"; and its use to drive foreign competitors out of business with the intention of later raising prices in the foreign market (assuming barriers to reentry exist) is termed "predatory dumping." From the point of view of economic welfare, positions taken by economists regarding the practice of sporadic and predatory dumping are generally in agreement. Sporadic dumping is viewed as relatively harmless since it is temporary in nature and roughly equivalent to a bargain sale. Predatory dumping is universally found objectionable because the disruption and losses caused to the foreign producing sector is coupled with ultimately higher (monopoly) prices for foreign customers. However, the situation in the case of persistent dumping is somewhat more ambiguous. While profits of local producers in the market where goods are being dumped stand to diminish (as with predatory dumping), it can be viewed that this economic loss is more than offset by the economic benefit accruing to local consumers due to access to cheaper consumption goods. On the other hand, if there are grounds for regarding the welfare of a country's producers as more important than that of its consumers, the overall effect may be viewed negatively. This subjective question may be decided by purely political consideration such as the relative lobbying power of industry and consumer groups, or possibly by some broader economic policy objective such as income redistribution goals directed to shifting gains to the lower of the two income groups.

History of Dumping

Recognition of the practice of dumping has a long and rich history, beginning with the advent of mass production techniques in the late nineteenth century which nurtured the necessary monopoly preconditions. With further industrialization and expansion of international trade, dumping became of widespread concern to national governments, to the point where most nations today have their own legislation dealing with the practice. In 1967 an International Dumping Code was signed by all nations participating in the Kennedy Round of the General Agreements on Tariffs and Trade (GATT) in an attempt to harmonize policies of individual countries.

The fundamental legislation in effect today in the United States is based on the Anti-dumping Act of 1921, which subjects dumping violators to an antidumping duty constructed to just offset the domestic-foreign price differential. A foreign producer may be judged to be in violation of the U.S. law after a two-stage process of investigation. Charges of dumping made by U.S. producers, or on their behalf, are registered with the U.S. Department of the Treasury, where it is determined if, in fact, foreign goods are being sold at an unfair price in the U.S. market; then, the U.S. International Trade Commission (formerly the U.S. Tariff Commission) decides if the dumping activity is inflicting economic injury on the American industry.

The process itself has been the subject of criticism. First, it is difficult to define what actually constitutes an unfair price or domestic injury. A most recent example which highlights the problem of determining fair market is the Polish golf cart case brought before the Treasury in 1974. The usual benchmark, the home market price, was not available since the price of the item was not determined solely by the free market. In addition, no other producers existed outside of the United States and Poland, making unavailable a third-country price, the regulatory alternative. As a result of this case, Treasury officials in 1975 changed U.S. regulations to allow a constructed price to be used in such cases, calculated by adding up the fair market value of all inputs of production.

A second criticism sometimes made of the U.S. adjudication process is that, because such critical terms can be difficult to define, the process is highly susceptible to political maneuvering. And, thirdly, foreign importers charged with dumping have complained that U.S. procedures are too lengthy and time-consuming, frequently leaving them in awkward positions with goods stalled at the border; this problem has been alleviated to some extent by the U.S. Trade Act of 1974, by which regulations were issued placing limitations on the period of investigation.

References

Kindleberger, Charles, and Peter H. Lindert, *International Economics*, Irwin, Homewood, Ill., 1978; Kreinen, Mordechai E., *International Economics: A Policy Approach*, Harcourt, Brace, New York, 1975; Scherer, Frederick, *Industrial Market Structure and Economic Performances*, Rand-McNally, Chicago, 1979; Viner, Jacob, *Dumping: A Problem in International Trade*, University of Chicago Press, Chicago, 1923.

(*See also* Arbitrage; Competition; General Agreement on Tariffs and Trade; International economics, an overview)

Anita M. Benvignati

Dynamic analysis

Dynamic analysis refers generally to any analysis in which changes that occur only with the passage of time are explicitly and essentially considered. In economics, these changes frequently involve changes in stock variables due to flows in or out over time. Although dynamic analysis is used in both microeconomic and macroeconomic applications, it has been particularly central to the latter because inflation, business cycles, and economic growth are by their nature inherently dynamic.

A dynamic analysis begins with a compact description of the equilibrium of the system being examined. The existence of such an equilibrium is a sine qua non for the analysis. Usually this equilibrium can be characterized by constant proportional growth rates of the variables in the model, in which case a steady-state equilibrium exists. In dynamic models with explicit random or stochastic elements, this steady-state equilibrium may exist only in an expected-value sense. Two variables with the same steady-state growth rates will have an equilibrium ratio and are said to display balanced growth. If two variables have different growth rates, their ratio approaches zero or infinity over time, a fact which may suggest a problem with the model. Occasionally, the steady-state equilibrium is characterized by zero growth rates so that the equilibrium values are unchanged over time—this is termed a stationary state. In some cases, the equilibrium is characterized by repeated oscillations which can be described as trigonometric or by other functions of time.

In Paul Samuelson's classic formulation (1947), essentially all dynamic analysis was termed comparative dynamics. We can now distinguish between comparative dynamics proper and adjustment dynamics. A comparative dynamics analysis would investigate the final effects on the equilibrium of alternative assumed values of initial conditions or on other parameters in the model. If the equilibrium were a stationary state, the analysis would reduce to comparative statics as noted by Samuelson. Adjustment dynamics, on the other hand, studies how and whether the economy converges to equilibrium following a specified permanent or temporary change in the parameters of the model. Stability analysis in comparative statics is, thus, a limited-adjustment dynamics analysis of a stationary state.

Besides the important applications to macroeconomics noted above, dynamic analysis is used to address a number of microeconomic questions. One such question is how price and quantity in a particular industry adjust subsequent to a permanent change in a parameter such as a tax rate. An approach suggested by Alfred Marshall (1920) and formalized by John Hicks (1939) examines a sequence of short periods in which supply curves and demand curves shift over time. Supply curves shift as resources in industries producing complements and substitutes adjust. This reduces the analysis to a sequence of comparative statics problems which converge to a specified long-run equilibrium. Recently, more rigorous tools involving the calculus of variations and optimal control theory have been applied to this and other microeconomic problems, such as the firm's investment plan and the use and pricing of exhaustible resources.

References

Hicks, John R., *Value and Capital*, Oxford University Press, Oxford, 1939; Marshall, Alfred, *Principles of Economics*, 8th ed., Macmillan, London, 1920; Samuelson, Paul A., *Foundations of Economic Analysis*, Harvard University Press, Cambridge, Mass., 1947.

(*See also* Dynamic macroeconomic models; Macroeconomics; Stock-flow analysis)

Michael R. Darby

Dynamic macroeconomic models

Many macroeconomic questions are inherently dynamic because they involve, in an essential way, changes which occur with the passage of time. Business fluctuations—recessions and depressions—result from changes in underlying conditions to which the economy must adjust. We are primarily interested in the dynamic adjustment process itself rather than the final equilibrium. Both economic growth and secular inflation involve changes over time—in one case, in real output and factors of production, and in the other in money supply and the price level. For these problems the techniques of comparative dynamics are the natural tools. Even macroeconomic models (such as the *IS-LM* model) which are formulated as static models are often used for dynamic analysis by applying them to a sequence of short periods.

One of the earliest formal dynamic models was proposed by Irving Fisher (1896) to analyze the relationship between the interest rate and the expected inflation rate. Such a model is inherently dynamic on two counts. First, it involves the rate of inflation which is the growth rate of the price level. Second, the formulation of expectations of the average future inflation rate over the life of the loan is based on the stock of information which accumulates over time. In Fisher's view, an increase in inflation would not be immediately reflected in the expected inflation rate. This would cause a characteristic transitional dynamic adjustment.

Fisher's classic statement of the equation of exchange (1922) was formulated in a static framework which related the level of prices to the levels of money, transactions, and velocity. However, he applied the model to analysis of both inflation and the transitional period consequent upon an (unexpected) change in money. Similarly, although Keynes accepted the static *IS-LM* model as an exposition of the main argument of his *General Theory* (1936), his book was necessarily concerned with dynamic applications, particularly with respect to expectations affecting investment and speculation in the bond market. In practice, dynamic elements have been introduced into Keynesian analyses by allowing for period-to-period changes in such variables as the capital stock and holdings of government bonds due to each period's flows, but incorporation of expectations formation has been generally weak.

Milton Friedman (1971) proposed a dynamic model which integrates secular inflation and economic growth with dynamic analysis of the adjustment to unexpected changes in the growth rate of money. This approach has been refined and extended by Darby (1976, 1979) to incorporate the economy's dynamic adjustment to a variety of macroeconomic shocks. These authors view the macroeconomy as fluctuating because of macroeconomic shocks around a (sometimes changing) steady-state equilibrium.

The methodology of the Friedman-Darby approach is first to analyze the comparative dynamic problem to find out how, if at all, the steady-state equilibrium is affected by a specified macroeconomic shock (unexpected change in a parameter of the model). An adjustment dynamic analysis is then used to describe the trajectory of such variables as real income, the price level, and interest rates as the economy moves from the original to the new steady-state equilibrium. This methodology assures that the changes which occur during the adjustment period will be consistent with a movement from the original to the new steady state. For example, this consistency requires that the long-remarked lag in adjustment of the inflation rate to an unexpected increase in money growth implies a catch-up period in which the inflation rate overshoots its new steady-state level.

The Friedman-Darby approach overlaps with a large class of models called rational-expectations models or classical models. These models generally are distinguished by two elements:

1. An information lag exists so that macroeconomic expectations are formed based on a stock of information which does not include current information.

2. The economy is displaced from steady-state equilibrium only if the actual value of a driving variable (say, money) differs from its expected value.

Note, however, that once the economy is displaced, an adjustment process may be required to return the economy to steady-state equilibrium. Generally, such models imply that monetary or fiscal policy can stabilize the economy only to the extent that policymakers have an identifiable informational advantage compared with the general public.

These examples of dynamic macroeconomic models could be expanded to include almost all modern macroeconomics. Owing to both increasing professional facility with the required analytical tools and increasing professional appreciation of the empirical relevance of steady-state equilibrium, dynamic analysis is now standard operating procedure for macroeconomic research.

References

Darby, Michael R., *Macroeconomics: The Theory of Income Employment, and the Price Level,* McGraw-Hill, New York, 1976; Darby, Michael R., *Intermediate Macroeconomics,* McGraw-Hill, New York, 1979; Fisher, Irving, "Appreciation and Interest," *Publications of the American Economic Association,* vol. 11, no. 4, August 1896; Fisher, Irving, *The Purchasing Power of Money,* 2d ed., Macmillan, New York, 1922; Friedman, Milton, *A Theoretical Framework for Monetary Analysis,* National Bureau of Economic Research Occasional Paper 112, New York, 1971; Keynes, John Maynard, *The General Theory of Employment, Interest, and Money,* Macmillan, London, 1936.

(*See also* Dynamic analysis; Economic models; Macroeconomics)

Michael R. Darby

Econometrics

Econometrics is the branch of economic science that applies the methods of mathematics and statistics to measurement of economic relationships and their implications for economic behavior. It means, literally, measurement (-*metrics*) in economics (*econo-*). Pure measurement issues or problems in economics that do not come under the heading of econometrics are descriptive measures of the economy that serve as raw material for econometrics. Social accounting measurement of national income, wealth, production, and flow of funds are not, in themselves, econometric work, but they are used extensively in econometric work. The same is true of preparation of indexes (prices, wages, interest rates) and other economic statistics. They are all part of the broader subject of quantitative economics, of which econometrics is a branch. Some analytical problems of index construction, depreciation accounting, and wealth measurement may, however, be econometric problems.

The essential feature is that there must be a mathematical formulation of the economics involved and a use of statistical methodology for measurement. The measurement may be hypothetical, in which case it is not actually implemented. Theoretical econometrics usually does not deal with actual measurement, only with what could or should be done in the presence of data. Applied econometrics is concerned with data preparation and use for execution of economic measurement that fits a mathematical specification.

Econometrics must proceed from a mathematical formulation of economic structure. It draws upon statistical inference, which is probability-based. Both inferential and descriptive statistics are used in econometrics.

Examples of Econometric Analysis

Further understanding of the definition of econometrics may be gained from a listing of the more important examples of econometric analysis or practice.

1. Estimation of economic relationships
   Demand functions
   Engel curves
   Production functions
   Cost functions
   Supply functions
   Market clearing (supply-demand balance) functions

2. Estimation of simultaneous systems
   Cobweb models
   Macro models of cycles and of growth
   International trade models
   Input-output models
   Planning models

3. Distribution
   Generation of distribution of income, wealth, enterprise size
   Lorenz curves and concentration measures
   Aggregation of micro relationships

4. Econometric method
   Simultaneous-equation estimation
   Corrections for serial correlation and heteroscedasticity
   Treatment of multicollinearity
   Estimation of distributed lags
   Time series analysis—seasonal and cyclical variations
   Testing economic theory or maintained hypotheses about behavior
   Pooling of cross-sectional and time series data
   Factor analysis and other multivariate methods
   Profit analysis
   Estimation with nonnormal errors

5. Applications
   Model validation
   Forecasting
   Simulation analysis of economic policy and hypothetical scenarios
   Multiplier analysis
   Probabilistic simulation
   Optimal control for stabilization policy

History

Early work in the subject began with attempts to estimate demand and supply functions for basic commodities some 50 to 60 years ago, often for agricultural products. Work on Engel curves showing the relationship between family spending and income started more than 100 years ago. Interest grew during the 1930s in estimating behavioral relationships for enterprises in the area of production cost and supply. Macro models of the economy as a whole were first estimated during the 1930s, and much work was done at an earlier stage on income or other distributions. Input-output analysis also was undertaken on a significant scale during the 1930s. After World War II there was a surge in interest in the theory of estimation of simultaneous-equation systems and its implementation in a series of macro models, first of the United States and then worldwide. Input-output analysis also experienced a burst of activity during this time.

During the 1960s the electronic computer became a pervasive tool of econometrics. It was mainly used in applied investigations but was also used in sampling experiments for understanding of small-sample theory and other intractable problems. It also opened the way for new theoretical developments because it showed that many computational bottlenecks could be broken, and thus it gave freer rein to theorists.

During the 1970s large economic data banks and comprehensive computer software (programming) packages tailored for the subject paved the way for widespread application of econometric methods to public and private decision making.

The Scope of Econometrics

A great deal of effort in econometrics is devoted to the problem of estimating economic relationships. These relationships describe the decision-making behavior, technological limitations, or legal/institutional limitations of the households, enterprises, and public agencies that make up the economy.

Behavioral Decision A typical economic decision is that associated with household demand. Mathematical theorists may express this as

$$X = f(P_x/P, P_r/P, y/P) + e$$

where X = quantity demanded
P_x = price of X
P = general price level
P_r = price of good related to X
y = income of consumers
e = error

This mathematical relationship indicates that demand for a commodity X is a function f of the price of X relative to goods in general, the price of related goods (either substitutes, complements, or both), and real income of consumers. This relationship is probabilistic because it is assumed to have an additive random error, representing omitted factors that may influence demand.

The econometrician would have to specify some of the characteristics of this demand function, i.e., whether it is linear or curvilinear, whether demand varies directly or inversely with own price or related price, whether historical incomes and prices as well as present incomes and prices affect demand.

The econometrics of estimation requires that a sample of data, actual or hypothetical, be defined. Often, the data will consist of aggregate market transactions on volumes purchased and average prices paid. National and related income statistics provide data for y and p. A series of observations at different time points for market aggregates make up the most frequently used samples of data, but sample survey data from individual household reports on purchases and incomes provide microeconomic data sets too. The econometric estimation problem is how best to fit the function f to these data. If the equation were specified to be linear, it would mean estimation of the coefficients in

$$X = a_0 + a_1(P_x/P) + a_2(P_r/P) + a_3(y/P) + e$$

Other (curvilinear) functions define the coefficients differently. Mixtures of mathematical theory of economic behavior and statistical fit to realistic data are used together to choose a best estimate. With present-day computer facilities, this selection process usually involves a great deal of experimental calculation in the search for the best.

Technological Limitation   The output of economic product is obtained by using the input of economic factors of production. The inputs are often classified as fixed capital, labor, energy, and materials. The production function is expressed as

$$X = F(K, L, E, M) + u$$

where X = volume of output
K = amount of capital used in production
L = amount of labor used in production
E = amount of energy used in production
M = amount of materials used in production
u = error

This relation states that output of good X is a function F of inputs of factors. Omitted factors affect output through the additive error u. A distinguishing feature of this relationship is that the variables are measured in physical units. X should be the number of units of output of a homogeneous product. K should measure the number of equipment or other capital units, L the number of labor units, E the number of energy units, and M the number of material units. If there is a single good and single type of each factor, there is no problem in measurement. Natural units exist for some variables—worker-hours for L and Btu's for E—but even these are approximate. Most production processes have multiple outputs and heterogeneous factor inputs. Approximate index measurement is required for preparing data on each of the variables in most studies. This, in itself, is a first-stage econometric problem. Then assembly of data on time variation for an industry or enterprise-to-enterprise variation in a cross-sectional sample is used to fit the function F to data, and selection of the best estimated function follows.

   The specification of F should take account of the technology of the production process and economic restrictions on the function that are associated with the mathematical theory of economic efficiency.

Legal/Institutional Limitations   The economy is restricted not only by the laws of technology and science but also by the laws of human beings, which vary from place to place, depending on politics, culture, social systems, and other noneconomic factors. A striking example of a legal relationship is a taxation statute.

$$T = g(Y_1, Y_2, \ldots, Y_n) + v$$

where T = tax revenues
Y_i = income received in the ith tax bracket
v = error

This relation, simply stated, makes tax collection a function g of incomes. If the tax system is progressive, as it is in most advanced countries, the rate will vary with income, going up, to a maximum, as income rises.

   Tax laws are written for the individual and have many special allowances or exemptions; therefore, this is only an approximate relationship, and allowance for additive error v must be made. In a simplified case, we would have a linear relationship

$$T = r_1Y_1 + r_2Y_2 + \cdots + r_nY_n + v$$

where r_i is the rate applicable to income in the ith tax bracket. Published statutory rates could be used as estimates for r_i if the system is simple, but most complicated legal systems would not admit such a quick and ready estimate. Statistical fitting is then an appropriate procedure for estimating r_i. To use this relationship requires knowledge of the distribution of income among tax classes as well as its aggregate level. This leads to a new dimension of econometrics dealing with income distribution.

Corresponding to income tax relationships, there are other kinds of taxes, related to different variables, subsidies, and welfare payments. There are also institutional relationships for the rules of the banking system, the insurance system, and other supervised parts of the economy.

Distribution Underlying aggregative measures of the economy such as total income, total wealth, and total employment are corresponding distributions. The distribution of income by tax brackets is one particular example. The striking characteristic of many distributions in economics is their skewness. The distributions of income, wealth, and size of firm (by number of employees) are all skew. They tend to show high concentration in the form of a "hump" at low levels and have a long "tail" for higher levels. In other words, the frequency of occurrence is relatively high for low values and relatively low for high values of income, wealth, or size. Many other economic phenomena are also skew. They lack symmetry.

Econometrics is concerned with fitting types of skew distributions of observed frequencies of occurrence. The names of some of the more familiar skew distributions are the Pareto distribution, the logarithmic normal distribution, or members of the Pearson distribution system.

Characteristics of these distributions are called parameters, and their estimates indicate the degree of inequality of the variable being measured, the degree of dispersion, and average size. Many aggregative econometric relationships depend on such measures as additional explicit variables.

A particular field of econometric study is the generation of such distributions. A problem that is posed to econometricians is to describe analytic processes of income or wealth formation that tend to produce particular forms of income or wealth distributions.

Macroeconometric Systems The economic system can be conceptualized as a system of simultaneous equations. This idea was introduced by the French economist L. Walras in the nineteenth century. A complete description can be indicated in mathematical theory but cannot be implemented in practice because it is too complicated and detailed. At an aggregative level, approximations to such systems have been made. At first, the aggregative approximations were relatively small, no more than about 50 equations and frequently less. In the computer age, such systems run into the hundreds or even the thousands. An equation system of 5000 to 10,000 relations may seem to be complicated and detailed, yet it is still an aggregative approximation to the complete Walrasian system.

Econometricians prepare data for macroeconomic systems from the main social accounts—national income, national product, and flow of funds—supplemented by statistics of prices, labor markets, financial markets, and other sources. These data form the sample from which coefficients are estimated in the relationships of macro-econometric models. Such models explain the interrelationships among spending, production, income payments, price formation, wage formation, interest rate formation, public spending, taxation, welfare systems, and foreign commerce.

These aggregative models are regularly reestimated and revised in making ever-better approximations to the Walrasian ideal. They are kept up to date, in readiness, on computer files for repeated use in analyzing the macroeconomy.

A particular system of the economy as a whole is called an input-output system. In one respect it may be looked upon as a detailed representation of the production process, more detailed than production functions, in showing how intermediate inputs of materials and fuels are transformed into outputs. This method extends the production function concept because it simultaneously treats the entire spectrum of inputs and outputs across industrial sectors of the whole economy. Several hundred (or thousands of) sectors are frequently treated simultaneously.

Solutions of Econometric Systems

A macroeconometric system has three kinds of variables: (1) simultaneous dependent (endogenous) variables, (2) simultaneous independent (exogenous) variables, and (3) prior values (lags) of either dependent or independent variables. For any point of time, present or past, the econometrician, having an estimated system, can insert into the equation prior values of the lagged variables and assumed contemporary values of the independent variables and solve the system for contemporary values of the dependent variables. In this solution procedure either zero or some specific a priori values may be assigned to the random error terms for deterministic solution. Random numbers may be drawn for use in probabilistic solutions.

After a solution is obtained for one period, the computed values of the dependent variables can be used as new lagged values for the next period, together with assumed values of the prior and new from the (next period) contemporary independent variables. From these values and the solution procedure, a solution for dependent variables in the next period can be obtained, and so on. This provides a dynamic solution, which is called a simulation. The solution procedure is straightforward if the system is linear. Routine iterative methods of successive approximation can be used to solve nonlinear systems of equations. Either for large linear systems or for nonlinear systems of any size, the electronic computer is the factor that makes this kind of analysis possible.

Input-output equations are linear systems and equate a linear function of each sector's output to final demand for the sector. By solving the linear equation system it is possible to express each output as a linear function of the final demands for all sectors. This standardized linear solution forms the basis for the principal uses of input-output analysis.

Time Series Analysis

An econometric approach to the dynamics of the economy that does not work through complete equation systems is the analysis of the time series patterns of individual variables in single equations. Each single equation relates one dependent variable to its own past history; to other variables, both contemporary and historical; and to errors. These errors may also be distributed through historical time.

Best-fitting, dynamic single equations are thus used to project the unlagged dependent variable for this equation in much the same way that it is done for sets of dependent variables in simultaneous systems. Dynamic properties of these equations in terms of cyclical, trend, and probabilistic properties can be established, given estimated values of the coefficients.

The principal difference between the time series approach and the macroeconometric systems approach lies in the fact that the former is not specified to conform to economic behavior or structure in any restrictive way. It allows the data more scope in determining the outcome of projections for dependent variables. It is not so closely guided by a priori economic analysis as is the methods of macroeconometric model building. Some economies can be introduced, however, by classifying different single-equation relationships according to their perceived or institutional role in the economic process.

The Uses of Econometrics

Originally, econometrics was used to illustrate or demonstrate economic theory. The econometric approach gives empirical content to economic theory. At the same time it can be used to test theory or to validate theory. Many theoretical propositions are qualitative:

- Demand for a good varies inversely with its own price, *ceteris paribus*
- Supply of a good varies directly with its own price, *ceteris paribus*
- Prices adjust to equate supply and demand

It is important to note the *ceteris paribus* condition attached to these statements, requiring that other things remain equal or unchanged. Econometrics, by estimating multivariate relationships, enables one to apply *ceteris paribus* conditions when examining relationships for these qualitative conditions.

Many propositions are more quantitative. Often, in the process of defining economic stability, it is required that certain coefficients lie between -1 and $+1$ or 0 and $+1$. We might examine constancy of returns to scale in production analysis, which requires that some coefficients add to unity or homogeneity of demand relationships, which requires that some coefficients add to zero.

Some relationships might fit the facts better, in a quantitative sense, than others. We might choose the set that agrees more closely, in a quantitative sense, than do others. But in many instances, the econometric method is used simply to lend a quantitative dimension in a descriptive sense. At the present time there is much interest in energy price policy, in which one is required to know, within estimation error, how sensitive energy demand and energy supply are to price changes. In economic stabilization policy, it is important to be able to estimate the employment stimulative effects of a tax reduction, of an easing of credit, or of a combination of both.

Econometrics is used as a decision-making tool by both public and private leaders. Public authorities have to make policy decisions about stabilizing the economy, about improving economic performance, about serving public welfare. All these involve examination of alternatives. It is in this area where the idea of a simulated solution of an estimated econometric equation system is useful. The policymaker can be provided with a wide range of alternative simulation paths, each based on different policy assumptions, and can choose the result that looks best.

The policymaker need not confine the options to those that are generated from econometric systems, but the advantage of this approach is that the computer can generate a number of alternatives quickly. All the alternatives should maintain interrelated consistency for the economy as a whole or that part of it being examined.

That branch of econometrics called optimal control theory aims to produce the best among feasible alternatives. The best is one that optimizes the policymaker's objective function, that is, that maximizes gain or minimizes loss, while observing all the constraints imposed by the estimated economic system.

What has been said about the public policymaker is also true of the private decision maker who may be an executive of an enterprise or a business owner. A private decision maker will consider alternative choices open to the firm and select the one that leads to greatest return, minimum cost, or to some other desired end based on similar criteria. An optimal decision that observes the model's estimated restraints is then the desired one.

The models and the decision process are both subject to great uncertainty. In order to bring out this aspect of the problem, it is possible to make probabilistic simulations for the choice of alternatives. In some cases, formulas for ranges of decisions can be developed for superposition on deterministic solutions of economic systems.

A principal use or particular simulation that underlies practically all decisions is forecasting. General simulations may be based on hypothetical values for independent variables or coefficients. Simulations can be made after the fact, when observed values of independent variables and initial values of lagged variables are available for use. In forecasting, a careful assessment must be made of possible values for these magnitudes. Some are fixed by statute or custom. Some change gradually and can be assigned values with a high degree of accuracy, while some are difficult to assess for the future. Even initial values for lagged variables are not known with much precision at the beginning of a forecast exercise because there are reporting delays. For many months after a forecast has been prepared, there will be a succession of revisions of main economic magnitudes that are used for initial values.

Careful forecasting is, therefore, usually confined to the near future, say up to 3 years, often in quarterly or monthly steps. This is the practical range of plausible assessment to typical independent variables in econometric systems, but there is, nevertheless, a great desire and need to plan ahead for longer periods by both private and public decision makers.

Five-year, ten-year, and quarter-century horizons are becoming increasingly relevant in applied econometrics. Simulated projections into the future for horizons in excess of a few years are not, strictly speaking, forecasts. They usually are based on likely trends for independent variables, sometimes adjusted to produce a balanced growth path for the economy. A balanced path would be one that eliminates large chronic surpluses or deficits in savings, profits, trade account, public budgets, labor force, and similar variables. Methods of optimal policy choice can be used in a formal sense to lay out trends for independent variables. The balanced growth path conveniently serves as a baseline case, and alternative future scenarios are then worked out in terms of deviation from the base case.

An excellent test of a theory is its ability to predict. Predictive testing of macroeconometric models is a highly developed practice. Partial models and microeconometric models can also be subjected to predictive tests, but most systematic analysis of prediction errors has been done for macro models that are closed except for the assumed values of independent variables. They are conditional predictions based on the assumptions for values of independent variables. The testing procedures have been carried out on both a conditional and unconditional basis.

A record of observed values of dependent variables must be established in order to perform predictive tests. This requires the elapse of some years before a sample of cases can be prepared. Some individual period tests or small sample tests were made during the 1950s and 1960s, but systematic testing has been done on a large scale, covering several different models and several time periods during the past 10 years. For comparative purposes, the tests have also been made for judgmental, time series, sample survey, and other forecasts that do not use the econometric method.

Limitations of the Econometric Method

Econometrics is, to a large extent, based on statistical inference, which, in turn, is based on the laws of probability. There will, therefore, be error in econometrics. Theoretical econometrics analyzes properties and implications of error. Applied econometrics is subject to this error. In contrast with applied mathematics in natural sciences, especially those branches based on controlled experimentation, the error component is relatively large in econometrics.

Econometrics is formulated mathematically; it is often based on large-scale computer calculations, which do not necessarily keep the errors small. The widespread and growing use of applied econometrics by decision makers attests to its usefulness in spite of the presence of significant errors. A subject that is based on sampling of human populations, human behavior, and inability to experiment is bound to be imprecise, yet all approaches to analysis of economic problems—econometric or other—must deal with great uncertainties, and the econometric method is found to have an important contribution to make in spite of its deficiencies.

Omission of Variables   The error term in economic relationships stands for lack of information—an information gap about all the factors that may be at work in the economic process or an inability to quantify and include some variables that are strongly suspected of being relevant but not lending themselves to explicit quantification. These may be subjective, psychological, or personal variables that are significant in the aggregate but not included in the measured relationship. They make up the noise component in the noise-to-signal ratio.

Faulty Measurement   There are errors of behavior, or more broadly economic structure, but there are also errors of observation or measurement. Some magnitudes are inherently difficult to measure—income tax evasion, illegal earnings, earnings in kind, inventory changes—and the appropriate variables in economic relationships should consist of two components, the true component and the error component. When this error component is combined with structural or behavioral error, the probability characteristics become considerably more complicated. No matter how the complications are dealt with, there is a significant error component that is due to imprecise measurement.

Misspecification   The various linear, logarithmic, or other curved economic relationships are rarely chosen on the basis of firm knowledge about the form of the relationship. It is generally an empirical choice based on accuracy of fit. There is danger that econometricians may choose an incorrect specification of the relationship that will show up in uses outside the realm of sample experience. Not only the form but the list of relevant variables can be in error. This kind of error is surely present, but it is generally not possible to ascribe a particular amount to it. In computer-based sampling experiments, however, the effects of particular misspecifications can be analyzed. Changing economic structure is a particular form of misspecification and is especially relevant for extrapolation into the future.

Inadequate Sampling   Sampling error is an inherent part of statistical inference in economics. The subject deals with finite samples, which all too often are small. Frequently, in statistical time series analysis of economic relationships, the number of observations is between 50 and 100 (often smaller), while large sample theory of statistics would require more than 200 data points. Not only are errors large in small samples, but their distributions are hard to determine. This is another point where replicated computer sampling experiments have been useful and revealing.

In describing the procedure for simulation and forecasting, it was noted that independent variables had to have assigned values for the whole period of solution. In forecasting applications, this period extends into the future, and there are bound to be errors in choice of these values.

References

Dhrymes, P., *Introductory Econometrics*, Springer-Verlag, New York, 1978; Klein, L. R., *An Introduction to Econometrics*, Prentice-Hall, Englewood Cliffs, N.J., 1962; Kmenta, J., *Elements of Econometrics*, Macmillan, New York, 1971; Theil, H. *Principles of Econometrics*, Wiley, New York, 1971.

(*See also* Economic forecasts; Economic models; Economic statistics; Forecasting methods; Input-output analysis; Statistical techniques in economics and business, an overview; Time series analysis)

Lawrence R. Klein

Economic Analysis Bureau (see Bureau of Economic Analysis)

Economic aspects of advertising (see Advertising, economic aspects)

Economic development, stages theory (see Stages theory of economic development)

Economic forecasting accuracy (see Accuracy of economic forecasting)

Economic forecasts

Time frames for short-, medium-, and long-range forecasts may refer, respectively, to (1) the monthly, quarterly, or, at most, yearly outlook in which, for example, the operations of a firm might be quickly adjusted to meet seasonal or other needs; (2) that period which is sufficiently long that cyclical developments need to be considered, measured as more than 1 and as much as 3 to 5 years; and (3) a time horizon that extends beyond cyclical repercussions to encompass the potential effects of long-run change in the status of the firm or the economy.

Short-Term Forecasting

The short-term forecast normally is concerned with readily adjustable and reversible decisions that might be involved in production, sales, prices, or other such matters. Periodicity in movement during short periods of a day, a week, a month, or a season might be useful to forecast. For example, December retail sales typically represent the high point of the production or merchandising cycle of many consumer products, while construction activity might be lowest in the winter. Since well-explored methods exist for calculating seasonal adjustment factors, such methods increasingly provide a basis of short-term forecasts. In addition, spectral or time series analysis by extrapolation are relatively new developments in seasonal adjustment methods. In brief, the short-term forecast, though sometimes statistically complicated, typically proceeds on the so-called naive forecast assumption that the pattern of the past and recent state of affairs will be repeated, barring exceptional happenings such as strikes or shortages. The complexity in procedure results from a search for that pattern. Since the accuracy of information on current conditions is crucial in short-term forecasts, the increased availability and diffusion of economic statistics on business cycle developments in recent years has brought a new dimension to short-term forecasts—quicker adjustments can be made. Indeed, frequently they are made in anticipation toward actions that would be taken in accordance with medium-term forecasts.

Medium-Term Forecasting

The recent hallmarks of medium-term forecasting involve more elaborate and sophisticated mathematical methods, oriented toward identifying in advance the possible turning points in the business cycle. Among formal methods of forecasting are structural econometric models, which contain empirically derived equations purporting to represent causal relationships established by economic theory; barometric or symptomatic measures that depend upon selected time series that typically lead or lag business cycle turning points; and mathematically elaborated time series models, which extrapolate a variable on the basis of its own past values. This last method reflects the view that causal relationships established by economic theory are considered unknowable or too costly to obtain.

The causally articulated econometric model approach in forecasting beyond 1 year has achieved the widest acceptance since the 1960s, especially because computers have made possible easy manipulation of large numbers of equations. Macroeconomic models owe much to the pioneering work of Jan Tinbergen in the 1930s, and L. R. Klein and A. S. Goldberger in the 1950s. There are, perhaps, nearly a dozen of such large multiequation macroeconomic models now available for commercial use in the United States. In precise or modified form, they have been much used by governments in forecasting such aggregate variables as GNP, prices, unemployment, etc., and in economic policy simulations. Business use also has grown in such microeconomic applications as forecasts of market demand, inventory control, price-cost relations, etc.

Macroeconomic models have experienced mixed success in forecasts of the general economy—the severity of the 1974–75 recession and the high inflation rate of the year 1978–79 were recent failures. In part, such failures can be attributed to the inconstancy in the economic structure that is embodied in the equations, as well as the uncertainty of their causal relationships. For example, the supply of money is considered by some as the principal determinant of overall economic activity and the price level; the so-called Keynesians, however, look to a circular flow of income and expenditures by government, business, and consumers as crucial in the overall economic situation.

Forecasting by reliance on extrapolation of past values of a variable—the so-called Box-Jenkins method—has expanded in use recently. The forecast utilizes a stochastic (probabilistic) value of recent observations and its error of estimate as the basis for future values. Ignoring the search for causal relationships sought by the large-scale econometric models, the method involves reliance on the previous recorded values of a variable plus its calculated error or estimate. Concern centers on past errors of prediction as the most likely basis for a forecast in the succeeding period, and so on. Clearly, this approach is structurally designed to establish a trend or periodicity and to miss turning points in movements. Advocates of this method attribute misses in forecasting turning points to shocks, which also result in the forecasting errors made by other methods.

Another perspective in the typology of forecasting is the distinction between judgmental and so-called scientific (or replicative) methods. However, this distinction becomes blurred because in the scientific method, judgment enters into the selection of variables of the endogenous or determining equations; in the choice of mathematical form; in the forecasted values of the exogenous or predetermined variables; and, finally, in the common use of additive or multiplicative factors, which alters the constant term on the basis of extraneous information in order to account for some missed or unexplained influence that has rendered implausible the forecast of the structural equation.

Cyclical forecasting by barometric or symptomatic means is typified by the so-called indicators approach, originally developed by the National Bureau of Economic Research and subsequently elaborated by the U.S. Department of Commerce. The method depends upon selection of time series that typically lead, coincide, or lag business cycle turning points. Among the 12 component leading indicator series are those for stock prices, new factory orders, the real money supply, etc. The method depends heavily on the dubious accuracy of current business statistics. Critics also note that the advance-notice time of the leaders prior to recessions since 1948 usually has varied from 4 to 11 months (and in one case was 23 months); in addition, a decline in the leaders sometimes signals a slowdown in economic growth rather than recession.

Of some significance in recent years as barometric measures are the several new indexes of consumer and business sentiment—attitudinal surveys. These supplement other such established and much-used older surveys of household and business intentions to spend (e.g., those of the Survey Research Center of the University of Michigan and the U.S. Department of Commerce, as well as the McGraw-Hill Publications Company), which have provided the basis of forecasts of consumer and investment outlays, respectively. The results of such surveys are sometimes incorporated into structural macroeconomic models.

Long-Term Forecasting

Long-term forecasts (sometimes called projections) have been used in planning capital outlays and labor-force requirements, the structure and volume of future markets of goods and services, necessary conditions for overall balanced economic growth as perceived by the government, and so on. In industry, forecasts may be made by a variety of simple or complex methods, from simple extrapolations of growth trends in output or other variables, to elaborately developed so-called Delphi procedures, which statistically process successive judgements about the future made by "experts." Special attention usually is given in long-range forecasts to demographic impacts on specific markets such as housing and those resulting from general aspects of growth in GNP, industrial production, and other major economic variables that comprise the forecasting efforts of the major econometric models.

Both private and government econometric models that have been structured to project GNP and related magnitudes for long-range planning purposes have been developed in recent years. As in simpler approaches, assumptions are made regarding (1) growth of the labor force (with a population already in existence, the participation rate in the work force is the principal unknown); (2) the trend in the work week; and (3) productivity, or output, divided by labor input measured in hours. This calculation yields a supply estimate of GNP at some future date which provides the major planning base for estimation of potential markets. (In some models, a full-employment assumption is made in calculating the projected GNP, though this need not be done.)

A major new methodological development in these econometric procedures is that a demand side of GNP is derived from the incomes that are generated in production, which necessarily equals the calculated value of the supply side. The latter provides a control total within which purchases by consumers, business, and government must reach some reasonable relation to income, by sectors; if not, fiscal or other policy action is introduced to attain a coherent balance of supply and demand under given assumptions of employment, unemployment, and productivity. One major objective of such a model is to test whether a balance can be reached at either economic growth or unemployment rates that are acceptable to policymakers.

Long-range forecasts necessarily involve many assumptions and uncertainties, for example, the state of international relations, international exchange rates of currencies, capital and labor productivity, the effect of environmental and safety requirements on the efficiency of the capital stock, energy composition, technological discoveries, etc. Frequently, these are exogenously determined variables in an econometric model and subject to increasingly arbitrary resolution as time progresses. Economists generally conceive of long-range forecasts as useful in broad outline, but only as approximations which need periodic revision. A minority grant only marginal importance to them or regard them suspiciously as aids to unnecessary planning which is potentially dangerous to concepts of a market economy.

Input-output methods frequently have been used as a final step to convert a macroeconomic model projection of the aggregate economy into the demands for intermediate goods and services that the various industries and sectors would be required to supply at a given level of GNP or final demand. For each industry in an interindustry matrix, inputs of current costs of materials plus value added will equal gross output or sales. These are organized into input-output tables, which, in the U.S. Department of Commerce version, show how the output of 162 industries is allocated among intermediate sales to other industries or to final demand sales (which make up the GNP). The coefficients in an interindustry matrix of purchases and sales represent the value of intermediate inputs or purchases made by each industry from each other, in terms of a share of the industry sales dollar that is required to supply a dollar change in final demand. Thus, the quantity of specific inputs plus value added as a percent of output of each industry is specified and fixed, as of a given time. This had led critics to note that it assumes absence of substitution among inputs, even when relative prices and costs change; constant returns per unit in output and revenues when scale of operations change; fixed technology; etc. Defenders of input-output analysis claim that modifications can be made that resolve these difficulties. The method's grand design appears useful because it enables a conversion of GNP totals and sectors into specific industry supply requirements of materials, output, work force, and other resources in a system of accounts that compels structural logic and internal consistency.

References

Butler, William F., Robert A. Kavesh, and Robert B. Platt, *Methods and Techniques of Business Forecasting*, Prentice-Hall, Englewood Cliffs, N.J., 1974; Klein, Lawrence R., and A. S. Goldberger, *An Econometric Model of the United States., 1929-1952*, North-Holland, Amsterdam, 1955; U.S. Department of Labor, *Employment Projections for the 1980's*, Bureau of Labor Statistics Bulletin 2030, 1979; Zarnowitz, Victor, *An Appraisal of Short-term Economic Forecasts*, National Bureau of Economic Research, New York, 1967.

(*See also* Accuracy of economic forecasts; Anticipation surveys, business; Anticipation surveys, consumer; Business cycles; Economic models; Economic statistics; Forecasting methods; Gross national product; Leading indicator approach to forecasting; Input-output analysis; Seasonal adjustment methods; Seasonal variations in economic time series; Time series analysis)

Herman I. Liebling

Economic growth

Economic growth is a sustained increase, over a significant period, in the quantity of material goods and services produced in an economy. The economy may encompass a nation or some other geographical, political, or social unit, such as a region, a city, or a population group; it may include a group of nations or the world.

Historically, over the period for which quantitative observation has been possible, growth in the absolute amount of goods, and services produced usually has been associated with increases in the average material well-being, i.e., in the quantity produced per person, and with growing population. For that reason the contemporary definitions of economic growth include the concept of rising economic well-being. Thus, according to Simon Kuznets (1973), "Modern economic growth ... reflects a continuing capacity to supply a growing population with an increased volume of commodities and services per capita." More generally, economic growth may be positive or negative for the total production or for production per capita, and the two need not be in the same direction. This more general concept of absolute growth is also well-recognized. "The capacity to sustain rapidly increasing numbers at the same or only slightly lower levels of living, in and of itself, can be viewed as economic growth" (Kuznets, 1966).

Measurement of Economic Growth

Economic growth is measured by comparing the total output of the economy at different times. Because the individual goods and services produced in an economy are not directly comparable with each other, in order to arrive at a measure of their total amount the different outputs are added up in proportion to their value, as reflected in their full cost of production (factor cost) of a given base period. In market economies, the cost of different goods is reflected in their prices. This method of measurement, also called the index numbers method, permits measurement of a total output of different goods and services which is not affected by inflation and other changes in prices of different goods. Hence, it is usually referred to as measurement of the real product of the economy. The most widely known measure of the real output of the economy is the gross national product (GNP), which is a measure of the total volume of goods and services produced in an economy during an accounting period, such as a year. Other related measures of the national output are the gross domestic product (GDP) and national income. Most often, economic growth is measured in terms of the average annual rates of change in real GNP, total or per capita, which have occurred during a period. Thus, for example, the real GNP of the United States grew at a rate of 3.6 percent a year during the period 1948–1978. Because during the same period, the U.S. population grew at a rate of 1.3 percent a year, the real economic growth per capita was 2.3 percent a year.

While it is a useful construct permitting measurement of the total output of the economy, the GNP is subject to limitations. The measured volume of output and its growth vary with the basis used for valuing the individual products. This index number problem is especially serious in comparing radically different economies, as is the case in comparing successive stages of the same economy over a very long time period, or in comparing two economies at different stages of economic development.

In addition to this problem and apart from frequent difficulties in obtaining adequate statistical data that satisfy the criteria of economic measurement, the concept of economic growth and its statistical indicators are subject to certain substantive limitations. First, considerations of economic growth and its measurement are limited to economic production and economic well-being, leaving out many other aspects of human well-being, such as the modern improvements in health care, which have been associated with economic growth. Second, the existing methods of measurement leave out, for the most part, the more narrowly defined economic production, especially production outside the market and government sectors, such as the goods and services produced within the family and household, e.g. home cooking and gardening, and educational and other personal services provided by parents to children. Also, these measures of economic production omit some of the important results of economic growth, such as improvements in working conditions and increases in leisure time, which have occurred as a result of reductions in the work week, paid vacations, and retirement benefits. Some recently developed analytical approaches attempt to fill some of these gaps by broadening the scope of measurement of well-being to include such social indicators as the state of health. At the same time, measurement of household production seeks to define the economic objectives of families and individuals in more fundamental ways than can be indicated by the quantity of goods and services consumed, and to account for the economic production within households.

Theories of Economic Growth

Theories of economic growth have been concerned with the three basic factors and their interactions: population growth, capital formation, and technological change.

Some of the most important interactions between the factors of economic growth, which may enhance or limit it, were identified by the classical economists. Adam Smith saw the realization of the economies of large-scale production as an important source of growing national prosperity. In his view, realization of these economies was made possible by the growth of the markets which permitted progressively more efficient organization of production based on division of labor and the resulting specialization of skills and of methods of production. The principle of diminishing returns, developed by Malthus and Ricardo, identified the limits to economic growth in the limited amount and capacity of land to yield continually increasing produce even with improvements in agricultural techniques and increasing applications of labor and capital in its cultivation.

Later, the neoclassical economists developed theories of industrial production dependent upon available labor and capital and not subject to the limitation of land supply. Within this framework, economic growth was seen primarily as a result of accumulation of sufficient capital to permit use of the economically most efficient combinations of labor and capital. These methods were often thought to involve a deepening of the capital structure and an increase in capital intensity of the economy. Moreover, the available methods of production were often thought to be characterized by increasing returns to scale, a property of the production system which permitted growth in output at rates more rapid than the growth rates of labor and capital inputs.

A radically different theory of the production system and of economic growth was advanced by Joseph A. Schumpeter. This theory made innovations and technological change the prime movers of the economic process, at least in the modern capitalist economies, accounting simultaneously for economic growth and for the business cycle fluctuations. According to this theory, successful innovators are imitated by a large number of firms attempting to profit from the new production technology. As a result, too much is invested and the ensuing losses cause a depression and a sorting out of surviving firms. Eventually, the new superior technology raises the productivity of the economy to a new higher level.

Beginning with the work of John von Neumann in the 1940s, economists developed mathematical theories of economic growth which were used to investigate the formal requirements for stable growth and other dynamic properties of economic systems.

Simon Kuznets developed an approach to the analysis of economic growth over long historical periods which he calls "economic epochs." Each epoch is characterized by a corresponding "epochal innovation," i.e., "a major addition to the stock of human knowledge which provides a potential for sustained economic growth" (Kuznets, 1973). Exact delineation of these epochs is a matter of judgment, but the innovation defining the epoch should operate throughout its period, providing the main stimulus to growth and to structural change during the epoch. In Kuznets' view, the present scientific epoch of modern economic growth is characterized by a feedback relationship between science and applications of science. It began with the industrial revolution, in particular with the steam engine and the early industrial innovations in production of iron and textiles. This epoch succeeded the earlier epoch of geographic discoveries during which the expansion of land available to the Western world provided the main source of sustained economic growth.

Modern Economic Growth

The period of modern economic growth is characterized by rapid growth in population and in per capita production and by much higher rates of capital formation than those that prevailed in earlier epochs. It is also characterized by an increasingly extensive use of science-based technology. Kuznets estimates that over the 100 years since the mid-nineteenth century, the growth rate in output per capita was about 10 times greater than in the earlier long period from the late Middle Ages to the mid-nineteenth century (2.0 versus 0.2 percent per year) and probably 4 to 5 times more rapid for population (1 versus 0.2 to 0.25 percent). Thus, the growth rate in total output accelerated some 40 to 50 times from that of the earlier period.

In addition to the high growth rates, by historical standards, modern economic growth is characterized, according to Kuznets, by a high rate of growth in productivity (i.e., in output relative to labor, capital, and other inputs); by structural shifts in the economy, most significantly from agriculture to industry and then to services; by social and ideological changes, especially urbanization and secularization; and by much increased international economic linkages. This growth experience, however, has been limited to only some regions of the world, and the gaps in the economic product per person between the economically developed and the less-developed countries have persisted.

While by historical standards the rates of economic growth have been very high in the past 100 years in all countries of the developed world, over shorter periods there were large differences in the growth rates among countries. Also, the economic growth rates in the same countries have varied considerably over shorter periods. Among the larger industrial countries, the economic growth rates experienced over the past 100-year period ranged from 2 percent a year for Great Britain and France to nearly 4 percent for the United States and Japan (Kuznets, 1966).

Sources of Economic Growth

There are indications that during the twentieth century the rate of economic growth in the developed countries has accelerated, and that the sources of growth have changed. In the more recent decades, there has been more growth in productivity (increase in output per hour worked), and less growth in labor input (fewer hours worked). The accompanying table gives estimates by Angus Maddison (1979) of the annual growth rates in GDP and in GDP per hour worked, averaged for 16 industrial countries:

Period	GDP, %	GDP per hour, %
1870–1913	2.6	1.7
1913–1950	1.9	1.8
1950–1970	4.9	4.4
1970–1977	3.2	3.8

A number of studies made by American economists in the 1950s established that the rates of economic growth prevailing in the twentieth century were considerably higher than could be explained by the combined growth of labor and capital inputs. Thus, according to estimates by John W. Kendrick, this unexplained residual growth, defined as growth in total factor productivity, continued at an annual rate of 1.7 percent for the private domestic economy in the United States during the period 1900–1950. In the period 1950–1969, this growth rate increased to 2.0 percent a year.

The discovery of this residual growth stimulated interest in technological change as a source of economic growth and gave rise to research on innovations, on the effects of research and development activities, and on interindustry and intenational transfers of technology. It also gave rise to growth accounting, which refers to systematic attempts to assess the contributions made to economic growth during a given period by such different contributing factors as the quantity of the labor and capital inputs, education of the labor force, and others. Edward F. Denison analyzes the annual growth of real national income in the United States during the period 1929–1969 according to the accompanying table, summarized to include only the major estimated effects:

	Percent
National income	3.33
Total factor input	1.81
Labor	1.31
Employment	1.08
Average hours worked	−0.50
Education of workers	0.41
Other	0.32
Capital	0.50
Output per unit of input	1.52
Advances in knowledge and NEC*	0.92
All other	0.60

SOURCE: Denison, 1974, p. 127.
*NEC = not elsewhere classified.

The effects of technological change on economic growth have not yet been successfully isolated, although growth accounting analyses and some recent research results provide indirect indications regarding their possible magnitude.

References

Denison, Edward F., *Accounting for United States Economic Growth, 1929–1969*, Brookings, Washington D.C., 1974; Kendrick, John W., *Productivity Trends in the United States*, Princeton University Press, Princeton, N.J., 1961; Kuznets, Simon, *Modern Economic Growth: Rate, Structure, and Spread*, Yale University Press, New Haven and London, 1966, pp. 63–65; Kuznets, Simon, *Population, Capital, and Growth: Selected Essays*, Norton, New York, 1973, pp. 1, 2 ff.; Maddison, Angus, "Long Run Dynamics of Productivity Growth," *Banca Nazionale del Lavoro Quarterly Review*, no. 128, March 1979, pp. 3–43; Schumpeter, Joseph A., *Business Cycles: A Theoretical, Historical and Statistical Analysis of the Capitalist Process*, McGraw-Hill, New York, 1939; Smith, Adam, *The Wealth of Nations*, London, 1776, reprinted by J. M. Dent, London. 1960; von Neumann, John, "A Model of General Economic Equilibrium", *Review of Economic Studies*, vol. 13, no. 1, 1945–1946, pp. 1–9.

(*See also* Business cycles; Capital formation; Classical school; Demographics and economics; Gross national product; Human capital; Income; Index numbers; Innovation; Kuznets cycle; Productivity; Neoclassical economics; Research and development; Technology)

Nestor E. Terleckyj

Economic history and theory

Two hundred years ago an event occurred in England which irrevocably changed the course of human history—the industrial revolution. It increased output to an extent thought impossible, and this increase has been accelerating ever since. But in this process of economic growth, the disparity between rich and poor has increased, a traditional way of life has been destroyed, and new tensions have been created as expectations have grown even faster than real output. (See Time Table of Economic Events, p 985.)

The Climate for Change

On the eve of the industrial revolution, almost all energy was provided by animate muscle power, as it had been since the dawn of human history, by millions of peasants and serfs tied to the soil, by galley and plantation slaves, by draft animals in the fields and in the mines. In 1776 Watt patented his steam engine improved by a separate condenser, ushering in the substitution of mechanical for animate energy. This energy revolution was complemented by two other fundamental technical innovations. Stronger materials were needed to withstand the new steam power: iron and steel. And the new power was economically efficient only if applied to more complex machines capable of producing a larger output. The demand for mass production was first effective in the cotton textile industry, and the industrial revolution is therefore often identified with a sequence of innovations in spinning and weaving. But its most fundamental aspect remains the shift to inanimate sources of energy. At first the new energy could be transmitted, if at all, only at high cost, and workers had to move to the source of power: the industrial factory, and along with it the British industrial town, "huge and hideous," was born.

The industrial revolution was not planned; the term was coined a century after the event (A. Toynbee, *Lectures on the Industrial Revolution*, 1884). Technical innovations were introduced piecemeal, in response to market stimuli, with each innovation providing the stimulus for other innovations. This unique and cumulative process had three prerequisites:

1. The existence of a market
2. The existence of traders with resources for a market response
3. The existence of an "investment climate" to encourage innovation.

The Market   Most societies with some division of labor have markets where traders can exchange their products. Eighteenth-century Europe had many local markets for trade between country and town, in addition to larger markets for long-distance trade. Market transactions were protected by a legal system, the common law in England and some adaptation of the Roman law on the Continent, both of which defined and recognized the property rights of market traders.

Traders   The commercial revolution, which followed the European discoveries of the New World, supplied a wide variety of new consumer goods for expanding markets. It also provided the relative affluence which permitted capital formation and more effective demand for larger output. It spawned the financial institutions, banks and bourses, to facilitate new enterprise. It accelerated the shift from status to contract which permitted land to be freely traded in a private market, thus encouraing improvements in farm productivity, which in turn made possible larger per capita food production and freed labor for industrial pursuits.

Climate for Investment   To encourage innovation a market must somehow reconcile change and order, must reward innovation without destroying the social stability which makes possible investment for the future. Eighteenth-century England attempted to solve this dilemma by combining strong property protection with a willingness to allow rapid obsolescence through new technology. As Adam Smith put it in *The Wealth of Nations* (1776):

> *In all countries where there is tolerable security, every man of common understanding will endeavor to employ whatever stock he can command, in procuring either present enjoyment or future profit. . . . In those unfortunate countries, indeed, where men are continually afraid of the violence of their superiors, they frequently bury and conceal a great part of their stock, in order to have it always at hand to carry with them to some place of safety.*

Some of these prerequisites were met by other civilizations, yet none produced the unique cumulative interaction of an industrial revolution. Why did such an extraordinary event occur in England toward the end of the eighteenth century? This question will remain among the great controversies in the interpretation of human history. Observations referring to the unique character of medieval and early modern Europe and to the unique position of England within this Western civilization provide some clues as to why the industrial revolution occurred in England.

Character of Europe

Europe closed the medieval period by adopting three unique inventions: ocean navigation, gunpowder, and printing. Ocean navigation, carefully nurtured after eastward expansion had been blocked by Mongol and Turkish conquest, made Europe the center of world trade. Combined with the military advantage of gunpowder, it also assured European political domination of the world for the next five centuries. Within Europe, gunpowder terminated local independence and created the modern nation-state. Printing supported this process through national languages and permitted an unprecedented accumulation of knowledge.

Throughout the medieval period Europe was never a unified political empire. There was a common tradition and acceptance of a universal church, but debates within the church, and struggles between church and secular authorities, prevented any totalitarian control over the whole of Europe at any one time. With the advent of humanism, the Renaissance, and the Reformation, divisive or secular forces further strengthened, with individual loyalties gradually shifting from local community and universal church to the nation-stage. Europe, though maintaining the common tradition, thus developed competing centers of knowledge and power, culminating in the so-called century of genius, followed by the Enlightenment of the eighteenth century.

It is against this background that Europe developed a science of political economy and a spirit of capitalism. In medieval Europe asceticism had been the ideal preparation for the next world. With secularization of life, the virtue of asceticism became saving for investment, capital to increase production in this world. In medieval Europe economic questions had been discussed by religious orders interpreting the

Bible, dealing with the prohibition of usury and the just price in terms of equity. With secularization of life, economic growth became a goal in its own right. As the nation was identified with the royal household, national wealth was identified with "treasure," just as the individual would count economic success in terms of money gained. Again analogous to the individual, treasure is increased by selling more than buying, by a favorable balance of trade, the mercantilist goal of economic policy. Such an approach seems appropriate so long as the total wealth of the world, the aggregate stock of treasure, is thought to be constant, so that one country's gain is inevitably another's loss. Yet as exports increase with greater productivity, the thought gradually emerged that trade may be more than a zero-sum game where gains and losses cancel. With productivity growth, all may gain from trade, and free trade rather than mercantile restrictions will maximize the wealth of nations. This idea was most cogently expressed by Adam Smith, the founder of classical economics, who stressed the apparent errors of the preceding mercantile system.

Intra-European Rivalry   These momentous events took place in a setting of intense national rivalry, exemplified by mercantilist thought, when centers of power repeatedly shifted and offered ready competition to any institutions rigidified after their initial success. The first century after the great discoveries saw the hegemony of Portugal and Spain, with Lisbon becoming the world trade center, and Charles I of Spain (1516–1556) ruling an empire over which the sun never set. But the very extent of this world empire, and the effort to protect it through rigid trade controls, made it vulnerable to the ambitions of rival contenders, the Dutch, the English, and the French. Knowledge flourished at places which offered freedom of inquiry, such as some Italian universities (Galileo), France (Bodin, Pascal, Boisguilbert, Quesnay, Voltaire, Turgot), Holland (Grotius, Descartes, Spinoza, Mandeville), Germany (Pufendorf, Leibnitz, Sonnenfels), and above all England (Mun, Petty, Locke, Newton, Hume, Smith). Similarly, the center of trade shifted to places which could offer both the political stability to protect and the freedom to pursue the rewards of private enterprise, from Lisbon to Antwerp and Amsterdam, and finally to London.

The development of economic thought should be seen in this context. Mercantilism is concerned with policies appropriate for war, or potential war. Treasure assures the liquidity to pay for mercenaries and war supplies. Most important for English mercantilism were the Navigation Acts (1651), assuring a large merchant marine, useful also for piracy and war. As J. B. Colbert, the leading French mercantilist, saw it (1669):

> Commerce is a . . . war of enterprise and industry among all nations. It is carried on by 20,000 ships, and that number cannot be increased. Each nation strives to have its fair share and to get ahead of the others. The Dutch now fight the war with 15,000 to 16,000 ships . . . the English with 3,000 to 4,000 . . . and the French with 500 to 600. The last two countries can increase their commerce only . . . by paring away from the 15,000 to 16,000 Dutch ships.

The transition from mercantilism to the classical economics of Adam Smith presupposed two events:

1. Recognition of global productivity growth which could benefit all nations
2. Acceptance of a peaceful world market not endangered by the continuous

threat of war, a condition ultimately fulfilled by the Pax Britannica established in the Treaties of Utrecht (1713), Paris (1763), and the Act of the Congress of Vienna (1815)

England's Unique Position

Why did England emerge as the final victor of this intra-European rivalry, a victory reinforced by the very fact that England became the locus of the industrial revolution?

An obvious observation refers to the unique geographic position of England, close to but separate from the European Continent; an island always close to the sea that had become the gateway to the world; a small area, yet large enough to provide, in the United Kingdom of 1707, the largest domestic free trade market known up to that time.

The insular position offered great military advantages to England. It made navigational skills, both for coastal and overseas shipping, a distinct necessity. The sea clearly defined national boundaries so that England, after the Hundred Years War, did not get involved in the endless border struggles which exhausted continental resources. Sea warfare provided carry-over benefits for the civilian economy, such as merchant shipping, while land warfare often completely destroyed the food base of the continental powers.

Another stimulus was supplied by the early dependence on coal rather than wood as a source of energy: England thus turned to advantage the potential disaster of forest depletion. Coal could be mined close to the sea; coal shipped from Newcastle to London became proverbial in Tudor England. Coal suitable for low-sulfur coke was found close to iron deposits (near Birmingham, in 1708), giving England an important head start in mining technology as well as iron metallurgy, both essential to the economic efficiency of the steam engine.

Perhaps the most important advantage England derived from the insular position, against the background of prevailing military technology, was the freedom to develop domestic institutions without fear of external attack. After settlement of the Scotch border wars, and the seventeenth-century constitutional struggles, a self-reliant private sector could build on a common national tradition, the "natural" market of Adam Smith, a market assured against both internal oppression and external aggression.

British mercantilism thus exhibits distinct differences from continental thought. In France and Germany mercantilist policy was based on government guidance given to business regulated by the state. English writers, often from the business world rather than government, pleaded for free enterprise rather than regulation, and there was an early emphasis on the self-interest of traders in a competitive market: "Private Vices, Public Benefits" by the "skillful management of the clever Politician," as Bernard Mandeville put it in 1714.

Analysis of Economic Growth

All societies share the economic problems of what to produce, how to produce it, and for whom to produce it. Throughout most of human history, "what" has been determined by physical subsistence needs such as food and shelter, "how" has been determined by tradition, and "for whom" by the customary community status of individuals. Technical experiments are fraught with danger in a subsistence economy subject to the vagaries of nature and prohibitive transportation costs. Yet over the last 10 millennia, urban civilizations have risen in different parts of the world, often with minute division of labor, with markets to exchange products from distant regions of empire, such as the civilizations of the Indus Valley and China in the Far East, Egypt and Mesopotamia in the Near East, or the Maya culture in pre-Columbian America.

Why did none of these civilizations develop an industrial revolution? They all cultivated some form of writing and the arts, some system of faith and logic, and all mastered techniques to assure at least temporary survival of urban settlements. Some of these civilizations made advances later adopted by the West, such as the decimal numbers of India or the compass and gunpowder of China. There are no final answers to the question of the unique industrial rise in the West, but the vast literature of historical interpretation suggests certain observations about order versus change, about values and civilization, and about the cyclicality of the process of economic growth.

Order Versus Change Economic growth presupposes an achieving society eager to apply its resources to economic goals. Where the prevailing values stress contemplation or resignation to a fate imposed by supernatural forces, economic growth is less likely to occur, though these basic values may change once the society feels itself threatened by new events, such as a climatic catastrophe or attack from hostile neighbors. It has been suggested that the agricultural revolution in neolithic times may have been a response to such adversity and population pressures threatening the survival of a primitive economy based exclusively on food gathering. Or the great European discoveries toward the end of medieval times can be seen as a response to losing control of the Mediterranean after the Crusades and the Turkish conquests. Or again, English dependence on coal has been interpreted as a response to the threat of forest depletion.

The success of these adjustments depends on the ability of a society to reconcile change with order, to maintain social stability in the face of changing values and production techniques. A society based on rigid social stratification in its division of labor may find its willingness to change impaired as growth benefits are limited to a small elite, such as in a caste or slave economy. This type of society excludes most of its members from active participation in the market and therefore also lacks incentives for increasing the output of consumer goods. Major technological change appears to require as prerequisites an increase in costs to stimulate input savings, and some affluence to afford the larger output. These prerequisites appear on the surface to be contradictory, but they may reinforce each other. Moreover, they both occurred in eighteenth-century England.

Values and Civilization Closely related to the issue of order versus change is the general problem of values and their diversity in the makeup of civilization. A society feeling threatened by hostile nature or neighbors will be less tolerant of deviation from established customs and taboos than a society secure of its survival. Civilizations of the past have often been totalitarian in the sense that a single-value system has been rigidly enforced, with little opportunity for new ideas or technical experiments. Whenever knowledge needs the sanction of the past, innovation is excluded by definition. The rigidity of such a society may prevent a positive response to challenges from within or without, and the civilization may not survive such challenges.

In the judgment of some scholars, it was the very diversity of medieval Europe which contributed to the rise of the West. As mentioned already, Europe, after the decline of the Roman Empire, was never under unified political control, though the church provided a common tradition and language. The medieval town offered escape from feudal restrictions. The commercial revolution proceeded under intense intercity and international rivalry, though this plurality of institutions and loyalties never destroyed the common tradition of Western civilization. The industrial revolution occurred at the unique moment when political rivalry was temporarily subdued by a Pax Britannica.

The Cyclical Process   The economic growth process is characterized by complex sequences. Short cycles are recognized as a regular feature of the capital goods industries. But there are also much longer historical cycles, interrupting periods of rapid growth with perhaps even longer times of consolidation, when institutions adjust to the requirements of new production techniques, when change and order are reconciled in a complex pattern over time. Historians sometimes refer to still longer Malthusian cycles when population pressures are ultimately accommodated by technological innovation and demographic change.

In medieval Europe a climax of achievement in the thirteenth century was followed by the calamitous fourteenth century when the Black Death reduced whole regions to one-third of their population. Yet only another century later Europe was to begin its domination of the world, with another period of distress in the seventeenth century when the very weakness of the big powers led the Dutch to commercial triumph. It was this same seventeenth century which laid the scientific and institutional foundations, e.g., in the English Civil War, for the acceleration of economic growth in the eighteenth century.

It is therefore not possible to judge history and economic growth in the ephemeral time span of a single generation. As change is painful for the many whose lives are uprooted, periods of growth may also be times of frustration and tension for the contemporaries. The industrial revolution has often been described in the literature as a period of acute distress for the new working class in the towns of England. A century later, at the very moment when the United States became the industrial leader of the world, Americans talked about the great depression of the 1890s. Amid the frustrations of the late twentieth century, it seems important to remember this great difficulty in order for contemporaries to appraise their own position in the long-run course of history, as satisfaction is measured by the gap between reality and ever-rising expectations that also have become the powerful motivation for further economic growth.

History thus has important implications for economic analysis. Decisions—both public and private—depend on the time horizon of the decision maker. Time is scarce to all mortals, but the specific content of time preference will be greatly influenced by our image of the future, our identification with the society of which we are such an ephemeral part, the opportunities and support for long-run saving and investment we visualize. The classical economists saw all this as elements of a rational individual utility function. The rational individual wants to maximize satisfactions in the long run as a good citizen of the community: "The individual decides that certain actions are proper or improper by observing the reactions of others to his behavior," as Adam Smith put it in his *Theory of Moral Sentiments* (1759).

A generation earlier, the Italian philosopher Vico, in his *Scienza Nuova* (1725), speculated that human achievements proceed in a cycle of growth when the individual identifies his or her own satisfactions with the common good, and decay when the very success of the preceding period narrows the scope of individual utility functions. Throughout the period preceding the industrial revolution, capital formation benefited from a tradition of medieval asceticism, yet there also arose the apparently contradictory problem of how capital formation could proceed without corresponding increases in the effective demand for consumer goods. Indeed, the ability of a market economy to resolve this apparent contradiction became a central issue in the later history of economic thought.

Impact of Economic Growth on Economic Thought

In the two centuries since the industrial revolution, human beings have changed the world more thoroughly, and more irrevocably, than throughout the preceding millennia. More people have a longer life and enjoy a higher standard of living than at any time before. Humans can travel around the world at a speed faster than sound, and can destroy all life on this earth many times over.

This unique accomplishment of economic growth has changed the very process of industrialization, and with it the pattern of economic thought. In an analysis of this pattern it is useful to distinguish between the following factors:

1. Problems within each national economy as it has entered the growth process
2. Problems of diffusing industrial technology from England to the rest of the world
3. Changes in economic thought

Problems within National Economies

For whom output is produced has been a central problem for all societies, determining the relative status of their members, their social stratification, and thus the moral basis of a just society. In the words of David Ricardo (*Principles of Economics and Taxation*, 1817): "To determine the laws which regulate this distribution is the principal problem in Political Economy." To Ricardo and the classical economists, this problem of distribution was not primarily a problem of equity, as it had been to earlier moral philosophers, but a problem of economic efficiency: Which distribution of the national income will maximize total output?

The Role of Profits   The classical economists discuss the functional distribution of income to land, capital, and labor, under the names of rent, profits, and wages. At the time of the industrial revolution, these factors of production are identified with three classes of England: the proprietor of the land, the owner of stock or capital necessary for its cultivation, and the workers by whose industry it is cultivated. To assure growth, income should motivate production. Land is a bounty of nature which cannot be increased. A sharp distinction is therefore made between "rent" and the "real cost" of production: wages and profit. Wages must cover the subsistence of the worker, a cost increasing as population presses against the margin of arable land. Profits are a precarious residual, endangered by the rising cost of subsistence and rent. Growth depends on capital formation to counteract diminishing returns on land, and ultimately on profits to motivate capital formation.

In the two centuries following the industrial revolution, this strong protection of profits as the most important share of a growing national income has been under attack. The extension of the franchise to nonproperty owners has led to profound institutional changes, in England as elsewhere. Property rights have been more narrowly circumscribed, workers have gained the right to collective bargaining, progressive taxes have limited capital accumulation, and transfer payments have guaranteed a minimum income to all. Much of this has been based on the apparent inconsistency of democratic ideals with an income distribution which placed on individual workers the main burden of adjustment to the new industrial state. Here again, economists have been concerned with the ultimate impact of income distribution on economic growth.

If all production serves consumption, capital as a factor of production derives its ultimate value from the consumption goods it has helped to produce. Could it be then that underconsumption or oversaving hinders rather than furthers economic growth? The role of consumption in stimulating investment has been discussed for a long time. There has been recognition that the industrial revolution was based, at least in part, on the market demand for cheap textiles. Benjamin Franklin, known for his praise of thrift, could also write (Smyth, 1906):

> I have not yet, indeed, thought of a remedy for luxury. . . . I am not sure that in a great state it is capable of a remedy; nor that the evil is in itself always so great as it is represented. . . . Suppose we include in the definition of luxury all unnecessary expense, and then let us consider whether laws to prevent such expense are possible to be executed in a great country, and whether, if they could be executed, our people generally would be happier, or even richer. . . . Is not the hope of being one day able to purchase and enjoy luxuries, a great spur to labor and industry?

Two generations later, in 1820, at the height of the post-Napoleonic depression, Thomas Malthus, in *Principles of Political Economy*, observed:

> If the conversion of revenue into capital pushed beyond a certain point, must by diminishing the effectual demand for produce, throw the laboring classes out of employment, it is obvious that the adoption of parsimonious habits beyond a certain point may be accompanied by the most distressing effects at first, and by a marked depression of wealth and population afterwards.

Income Distribution   As productivity rapidly increased throughout the nineteenth century, as food shortages gave way to surpluses brought by rail and ship from the distant corners of the world, as unemployment in the capital goods industries occurred at every low point of a business crisis, the idea of a more equal income distribution favoring consumption gained new adherents among reformers and revolutionaries alike. Political reform shaped the income distribution prevalent in most markets today, with capital formation often shifted from the private to the public sector. The private capital market has completely disappeared in those societies which, under Marxian influence, have adopted a planned economy run by a government bureaucracy.

Orthodox market economists stress the automatic market forces which assure just the right expenditures for consumption and investment, in accordance with individual preferences. As Adam Smith put it in *The Wealth of Nations* (1776): "In all countries where there is tolerable security, every man of common understanding will endeavor to employ whatever stock he can command, in procuring either present enjoyment or future profit." Income will always be spent as "supply creates its own demand," later referred to as Say's law, after the French economist Jean-Baptiste Say who promoted the ideas of Adam Smith on the Continent (1803). In a competitive market, productivity growth will be passed on in the form of lower prices that lead to higher real income though money wages may remain stable or even decline in monetary terms. But if prices fall, why should consumers and investors not hoard their money and wait until prices fall even further? Low prices seemed to coincide often with unemployment: from this observation grew the idea that "money does not manage itself" (W. Bagehot, *Lombard Street*, 1873). In response to the Great Depression of the 1930s, Keynes, in *General Theory of Employment, Interest and Money* (1936), added the need for functional public finance through an active fiscal policy.

These ideas have given strong intellectual and political support to an income redistribution favoring poor spenders over rich savers, not only for reasons of equity but also to stabilize the economy through the business cycle. This neoclassical macroeconomic monetary and fiscal policy has evolved against a historically unique background of deflation rather than inflation, concerned with the problem of how to have the money supply keep up with the spectacular and apparently unlimited productivity growth of the nineteenth century. In these circumstances it was easily forgotten that the restrictive international gold standard, and the rules against budget deficits, had been the result of bitter historic struggles against the absolute power of profligate governments. Not in his *General Theory* (1936), but in his *Tract on Monetary Reform* (1923), Keynes himself had warned:

> There is ... an almost unbroken chronicle ... back to the earliest dawn of economic record, of a progressive deterioration in the real value of the successive legal tender which have represented money. Moreover, this ... is not an accident, and has had behind it two great driving forces—the impecuniosity of Governments and the superior political influence of the debtor class.

But productivity growth cannot be taken for granted. Expectations of more leisure and a higher standard of living, shifts to low-productivity service industries, settlement of the frontier and the rising cost of environmental protection, increased transfer payments to a rapidly aging population, international tension and uncertainty, all have combined toward the end of the twentieth century to slow the productivity growth of earlier generations, in the mature as well as the planned economies, at the very time when institutional ingenuity to create additional liquidity, with or without sanction of the central bank, has expanded the world money supply by leaps and bounds. Indexation has further increased inflationary expectations which become self-fulfilling. Since the most important function of money is to offer a stable yardstick for the future, a loss of this function may shorten the time horizon for capital freedom. Gold and other assets not subject to monetary management or control become again the preferred reserves, as they have always been in times of governmental mistrust.

Industrial Diffusion Throughout the World

Throughout history the locus of economic advance has shifted. The agricultural revolution of neolithic times occurred in the fertile crescent of the Near East and diffused from there to other parts of the world where it also may have started independently. The rise of the West moved from the Mediterranean to the shores of the Atlantic, and leadership of the commercial revolution in early modern Europe shifted from Italy and the Iberian Peninsula to the low countries and England where Dutch trade capital helped to finance the industrial revolution. From England industry spread through the world.

This diffusion of industry has taken many forms. In some cases it has meant primarily the adjustment to British demand for more foodstuffs and industrial raw materials. British trade from and to overseas was greatly facilitated by the transportation revolution which followed the steam engine. In other cases this diffusion started a complex sequence of catching up and surpassing, latecomers benefiting from the very fact that they could build on a technology first developed elsewhere. These countries started as customers and suppliers of England, but ended as rivals surpassing the older technology. In all cases industry had to be reconciled with institutions and traditions different from those that had originally spawned the industrial revolution. In this process industry itself changed its character, and each country becoming industrialized provides its own distinct national case history.

In all cases the pace of industrial diffusion is greatly influenced by the mechanism of international finance. Industrialization depends on resource mobility to provide the large investment in new skills, plant, and equipment. Whenever this investment does not come directly from the same persons who save, financial liquidity is needed to bring together savers and investors, a process greatly facilitated by wise governments and financial institutions, such as the Bank of England (1694). The international gold standard of the nineteenth century guaranteed the stability of foreign exchange rates, and the Pax Britannica provided the means to enforce international claims. In these circumstances, there was little difference between domestic and foreign finance, a fact greatly contributing to the rapid diffusion of industry through British capital exports, with the city of London becoming for a century the undisputed center of the world money market.

British leadership was not seriously challenged in the first 100 years following the industrial revolution. But after 1830, it was the railroad, the very creation of British technical ingenuity, which changed the world by building new land empires to defy the Pax Britannica. Though most of the countries drawn into the industrial era before the First World War still shared the Western tradition, the economies showing the highest growth rate, Germany and the United States, also displayed large institutional variations, both from each other and from the British original.

The United States   The United States is a country of European immigrants who brought with them the values of the old country without the institutional restrictions they sought to escape. The same year, 1776, saw the publication of Smith's *Wealth of Nations* and the American Declaration of Independence. The military isolation America enjoyed under nineteenth-century technology offered an ideal setting for individualism in a free market offering ample rewards to those willing to face the uncertainty of an open frontier. America also retained the full protection of property rights in a private business sector well into the twentieth century, until the Great Depression of the 1930s ushered in the New Deal, which finally recognized the problem already inherent in the eighteenth-century philosophy of the Enlightenment: how to reconcile the potential conflict between individual liberties and the demands of a majority-controlled democratic welfare state.

Germany   Germany started nineteenth-century industrial development with a more rigid class structure under a paternalistic government introducing protective labor legislation and social security to ensure that citizens were fit for army service. The government remained the main, and often sole, industrial customer for military and civilian needs, as railroads and public utilities were almost exclusively built by the public sector. Exports played a large role, to "grow out of foreign incomes," as the mercantilists (called cameralists in Germany) had recommended previously. Against this background, German economic interests were polarized: a conservative political coalition supported the expansionist goals of the imperial government, while the Social Democrats (SPD) formed the largest Marxian party in the world, with only scant support given to the free market. Business flourished with active government support, its technological advance assured by a large flow of well-trained scientists and economists who effectively put science in the service of German industry.

Marxism and the Russians   In the *Communist Manifesto* (1848), Karl Marx and Friedrich Engels explained "the history of all hitherto existing society" as "the story of class struggles" and urged "working men of all countries, unite!" Yet the first Working Men's International Association (1864) was rent by internal dissension, and in most of the advanced industrial countries Marxism led to conservative trade unionism rather than revolutionary international solidarity. Against this background V. I. Lenin transformed the idea of domestic class conflict into a struggle between rich and poor nations, exploiting and oppressed countries, a theory of what he called imperialism, the highest stage of capitalism. Marxism in this form suggested the possibility of "catching up and surpassing"; it held the promise of successful revolution for preindustrial countries skipping the stage of "bourgeois capitalism"; it had great appeal to underdeveloped countries eager to acquire Western technology but wanting to retain their non-Western traditions.

Lenin wrote his version of Marxism with his native Russia in mind. Russia was the largest land under one political sovereignty, spanning Asia and Europe, pulled together by the trans-Siberian railway (1891–1903), searching for a mission and identity as world power. The Russian Revolution of 1917, under great hardships imposed on the Russian people, gave this vision reality. Marxism formed an effective link between Russian national tradition and Russia's ambition for world leadership. The Russian twentieth-century experience suggests a few general observations. The more backward a country's economy, the more likely it is that its industrialization will start as a sudden spurt because so much of it is catching up with known technology; and also, the more pronounced may be the stress on producers' goods, with heavy pressure on the levels of living, because domestic consumer demand is less needed as an incentive in an economy controlled by a small political elite enforcing an idealogy suitable for rapid economic growth. By definition, such an economy will rely on the government for the supply of capital through forced savings and a highly coercive network of bureaucratic controls.

Japan's Late Entry   Another latecomer, industrializing with a sudden spurt, is Japan, emerging in the 1860s from a feudal past hardly touched by the West. Direct imitation of Western technology was based upon an ideological upsurge which identified national interest and expansion with conscious modernization and entrepreneurship, upon a social system drawing large forced savings from an efficient agriculture, and upon massive state action to create a strategic infrastructure in transportation and heavy industry. Not unlike the German case, armaments were an early lead sector, followed by a successful export drive, with effective cost controls and technical education giving the country unique advantages in the world market, despite poor natural resource endowments and heavy dependence on raw material imports.

Maoism—A Painful Transition   China illustrates the painful transition to a modern economy of the most populous country in the world, clinging to a traditional culture boasting the longest continuity of any civilization on earth. The Chinese Revolution, leading to the proclamation of the People's Republic of China in 1949, has been the greatest in history, measured either by the number of the people or by the extent of the changes made in the methods of production. China's metamorphosis has been helped by the very tradition it set out to destroy. Chinese governments, struggling throughout the centuries to spread and maintain a unified state and a uniform culture over a vast and diverse subcontinent, have become skilled at imposing centralized military, social, and ideological controls. In the decades immediately preceding the People's Republic, warlordism, followed by 8 years of Japanese invasion and 4 years of civil war, had produced a nationwide craving for central authority, firm leadership, and peace and order. Thus, the new China was less purely a product of Marxism-Leninism than it claimed to be, though here again Marxism served as a useful link between Western technology and non-Western tradition. In a country where order had dominated change since times immemorial, this perennial conflict took peculiar forms. Chairman Mao Tse-tung himself attacked "manifestations of bureaucracy: at the highest level there is very little knowledge," and repeatedly encouraged rebellion against any new order of "bourgeois reaction." From 1949 to 1958, when Russian models dominated, the Communists consolidated their power and started China on the road to industrialization. In 1958 came the Great Leap Forward, and in 1966 the Chinese unleashed the Great Proletarian Cultural Revolution which, for the next 10 years, through countless humiliations and trials, affected the lives of several hundred million people. In 1976, after the death of Mao, the Peking regime embarked on a more moderate course, in an apparent effort to reestablish order along more pragmatic lines, under the slogan of "four modernizations"—rapid development of agriculture, industry, defense, and technology.

Changes in Economic Thought: Policy Issues

The momentous events following the industrial revolution have spawned a huge literature on political economy. In a brief overview, it may be useful to separate two distinct, though overlapping, developments in the literature:

1. Policy issues raised by the rapid changes in industrial technology
2. Later writings articulating more explicitly what had been implicit in earlier economic writings

The Market   The most obvious policy issue refers to the market itself. Adam Smith already had expressed some concern about the tendency of markets to destroy themselves through monopoly. As long as decreasing returns prevail, size will increase costs and thus prevent market monopolization. But as economies of scale become more important with the progress of industry, conflicts between technical efficiency and the maintenance of competition may arise. Marshall, in his *Principles of Eco-*

nomics (1890), hoped that economies of scale could be secured externally, through the market, rather than internally, within the firm. Where competition becomes clearly wasteful, as with some public utilities, prices must be regulated, or the government itself must provide the service.

These topics have been discussed in the extensive literature concerning industrial organization. The theory of monopolistic competition established that all markets lie somewhere between the polar cases of perfect competition or monopoly (E. H. Chamberlin, *Theory of Monopolistic Competition*, 1932). Since perfect competition is not attainable, or even desirable, the policy goal becomes workable competition (John M. Clark, *Preface to Social Economics*, 1937). Joan Robinson (*The Economics of Imperfect Competition*, 1933) introduced the concept of monopsony, markets with a single buyer, important in labor relations. If labor organizes, bilateral monopoly (F. Y. Edgeworth, *Mathematical Psychics*, 1881), or collective bargaining, results. With only a few sellers, characteristic of many industries, oligopoly exists. In all these cases, final price and quantity sold depend on the bargaining skills of the parties who may form market coalitions to improve their bargaining strength. Economic behavior in such situations has been analyzed by a theory of games (von Neumann and Morgenstern, 1944).

Doubts about the welfare implications of such imperfect markets have lent intellectual support to a wide variety of fair trade laws and government regulation of business. Yet there has also been growing concern that the cure might be worse than the disease, and that occasional market failure may be preferable to the inefficiencies of the regulatory process. Among leading economists of this generation, Milton Friedman and his students at the University of Chicago have become associated with the view that less government interference would greatly improve market performance.

Trade   The most important coalition of modern times has been the nation-state, and the theory of games can be used to analyze international relations. To the early political economists, trade meant trade among nations, and the mercantilists were concerned with the proper trade strategy for economic growth. To the classical economists, mercantilist reasoning was in error, for "what is prudence in the conduct of every private family, can scarce be folly in that of a great kingdom": Adam Smith thus pleads for free trade not only at home but also among nations. Such a policy is well-designed for a country to use its resources best within a given world allocation of knowledge, capital, and other resources. But a country eager to develop its resources, to catch up and surpass, may prefer a more aggressive policy to change this resource allocation. Thus, in American history before the Civil War, the South was for free trade, having adjusted its economy to British demand for cotton, while the North, eager to compete with English industry, pursued a high tariff policy. Tariffs may be easily abused, of course, to protect obsolete skills rather than to develop new ones.

To generalize this observation, there are two distinct optimizing strategies. One is to accept a given market in an attempt to win within the given rules of the game; the other is to change these rules and build a new market with more favorable chances to win, through political action and revolution. The classical economists were essentially concerned with peace, with acceptance of the rules, in the sincere belief that free trade would ultimately benefit all. The very rapidity with which British industry was diffused to other countries through free exports of British capital would seem to bear out their expectations.

The Demographic Dilemma   Adam Smith shared the optimism of the Enlightenment, trusting that a benevolent providence and human reason would bring progress and the wealth of nations. The next generation of classical economists, Malthus and Ricardo, shared the disillusionment brought about by poverty in the new industrial towns, by the violence of the French Revolution and the Napoleonic Wars. They emphasized the law of diminishing returns and the limits to growth: reason could adjust to these limits but not repeal them. Unprecedented growth in productivity, brought about by capital formation and the cultivation of virgin land overseas, have stilled these fears for the next 100 years, until they have been revived in the twentieth century by war, shortages of energy, environmental damage, remaining stark poverty in many areas of the world, all reflecting an annual world population growth rate approaching 2 percent, an exponential rate which must lead to an ecological catastrophe if maintained for any length of time.

Demography has, therefore, become a field of major interest for economists. In an age of technical substitutability, specific shortages of food and materials can be overcome by capital and new technology, but there remain absolute limits of living space for an exponentially growing population. Adjustments in the birth rate will ultimately occur, as they have in the past, but this process may be too slow to prevent great hardship. Once population growth is checked, the age structure of the population will change, with far-reaching implications for per capita productivity and the need for large intergenerational transfer payments.

Expansion of the Public Sector   The classical economists saw all economic decision making in the private market, with the public sector limited to enforcing the rules of the game. This separation of *res privata* and *res publica* went back to the Roman law, which had defined the rights and obligations of traders in the markets of the Roman Empire and had been adapted to the commercial needs of early modern Europe. There had always been recognition of public functions other than law enforcement, of course, such as national defense and what is called today social overhead, e.g., ports and lighthouses, where the externalities benefiting others than the immediate traders are obvious and very great.

Over the last century the public sector has greatly expanded everywhere, and in the planned economies of the people's republics it has almost completely replaced the private market. To put it differently, externalities have been defined much more broadly than was ever anticipated by the classical economists. There are many reasons for this development. Perhaps most ominous is the growing importance of national defense in a century which has seen two world wars. Crowding in metropolitan areas has multiplied the need for public services such as roads, airports, environmental protection, and many others. Nonprofit enterprises in education and health care have increased faster than the goods-producing sectors of the economy.

A rationale often given for the growth of the public sector are economies of scale. Big business is supposed to be more efficient, and the public sector takes over because the competitive market breaks down, an argument also important in Marxian ideology. But as Alfred Marshall pointed out in his *Principles of Economics* (1890), economies of scale may be external as well as internal. The commercial revolution was furthered by economies of scale found in the large trade centers of early modern Europe, and the industrial revolution benefited from efficient interaction among mine operators, iron works, machine shops, and textile factories in eighteenth-century

England, without their complete vertical integration. Today, many professional and technical services can be bought in the market without the need of their incorporation into a single form.

Still another reason for public sector expansion is the importance of public finance as a tool of economic policy. Smith's *Wealth of Nations* (Book V) talks of the revenue of the sovereign or commonwealth. Services of government must be financed, and the potential misuse of the taxing power had been a major reason for constitutional limitations on absolute government. The classical economists were anxious for taxes to be neutral, not to change the natural income distribution provided by a free market.

Yet the nineteenth century saw growing dissatisfaction with the workings of the market, accompanied by pressures for reform and a more equal income distribution. Taxes were seized upon to achieve such redistribution, with inheritance taxes, progressive income taxes, and an ever-increasing flow of transfers from taxpayers to beneficiaries presumably less able to pay for themselves, all in the interest of a more equitable wealth distribution which hopefully would also increase productivity through better community morale and more equal career opportunities. Such income transfers account for almost half of the 1981 U.S. budget.

The Great Depression of the 1930s has added still another dimension to the functions of public finance. If and when private expenditures are not sufficient to maintain full employment, public spending should "prime the pump" with a multiplier effect on private consumption or investment. Keynesian functional public finance thus made fiscal policy a macroeconomic tool of economic policy, devoted to the performance of the economy as a whole, especially with regard to aggregate employment and output. There was no need then to finance these expenditures through taxes, as deficit finance would only compensate for the shortfall in the private sector. This apparently painless way to increase public expenditures had obvious political appeal, and the new economics received enthusiastic support. Yet it was easier to increase public expenditures than to decrease them once full employment had been reached. Functional finance thus became a one-way street, offering a politically convenient rationale for expanding the public sector through deficit finance, precisely what parliaments of old had fought so hard to prevent by constitutional limitations on government budgets.

Money Values Trade is awkward without some acceptable medium of exchange, and money is, therefore, as old as trade itself. To be acceptable, money must have a generally recognized value and be able to retain this value. In most civilizations, the precious metals met these conditions: they could be readily stored or transported without spoilage, they could be easily subdivided, their aggregate supply was not likely to be increased, and they therefore could be expected to retain their value over time. For the convenience of those unable to test the fineness and weight of small pieces, it became important to guarantee the metal content of coins, and governments were anxious to secure for themselves the exclusive right of coinage.

Scarcity makes the value of money but also creates problems whenever real output expands. The traditional concern of monetary theory has been to analyze the complex relations between money, real output, and prices. Neoclassical economists used for this purpose the so-called identity of exchange (I. Fisher, *Mathematical Investigations in the Theory of Value and Prices*, 1892):

$$MV = YP$$

where M = money
   V = income velocity of this money
   Y = real output of final goods and services
   P = general price level

If real output Y grows and the money supply M remains constant, there are two possible adjustments: V can accelerate through credit extension and financial instruments, or P can decline. Might the scarcity of money actually retard real income growth, directly or through lower prices? These questions are the essence of all discussions on monetary policy, questions raised by the mercantilists who wanted a favorable balance of trade, not only to have more treasure for the king, but also because they expected more M to stimulate real income growth.

The classical economists thought that more M would raise prices P rather than output Y, the so-called quantity theory of money. They therefore wanted to focus on real rather than monetary analysis, and Ricardo, in his famous pamphlet, *The High Price of Bullion* (1810), ascribed British wartime inflation to the monetary expansion of the Bank of England. Throughout the nineteenth century, most industrial countries followed Ricardo's sound money policy and accepted the rules of the international gold standard. The vast increase in real output that followed the industrial revolution was financed by accidental gold discoveries, especially in California (1848) and Australia (1851); the use of bank notes and checks, based on and freely convertible into gold; and lower prices which de facto put the burden of uncertainty and adjustment to industrialization on debtors and the unemployed. It was a great age for bondholders who financed the expansion of industry throughout the world.

In this process the very definition of money changed. Banknotes and checks became money, redeemable in gold, a right rarely used as long as confidence in the financial system was maintained. In financial panics, holders of these notes asked for redemption, and the result was a drastic decline of the total money supply. It is against this background that Walter Bagehot (*Lombard Street*, 1873) wrote "money does not manage itself," that Knut Wicksell (*Interest and Prices*, 1898) established the dichotomy between natural interest rates, equalizing real saving with investment, and market interest rates which reflect monetary factors and may differ widely from the natural rate. It was in response to the panic of 1907 that the Federal Reserve System was founded in the United States (1913) as a lender of last resort. A year later the international gold standard broke down as countries entered World War I.

The Gold Standard   The international gold standard was designed to encourage free world trade, both in product and factor markets, by having a single world money, with the intended implication that no country could or should have an independent monetary policy. Domestic policy within each country was subject to balance of payments discipline: a country expanding its money supply would raise its own prices and thus lose out in the world market. Yet once countries were eager to establish their own independent macroeconomic policies, after the end of World War I, there could be no return to the rules of the gold standard. This also implied a further breakdown of world trade: to customs barriers were now added foreign exchange controls as new weapons of international trade rivalry.

In order to avoid the dismal experience of the interwar period, a new international monetary system was designed during World War II at Bretton Woods (1944). An International Monetary Fund was to help countries with temporary balance of payments problems so that there was no need for self-defeating foreign exchange controls. The system worked reasonably well as long as the financial strength of the United States supported it. With the decline of the United States dollar the system broke down in the 1970s. The world money supply is now made up of numerous independent paper currencies, none redeemable in gold, their value dependent on the monetary policies pursued within each country. Foreign exchange rates fluctuate against each other roughly in line with their domestic "purchasing-power parity," a term used by the Swedish economist Cassel after World War I in his memo on *World Monetary Problems* (1920). The high price of bullion, to repeat Ricardo's phrase of 1810, reflects the general lack of confidence in managed money.

Changes in Economic Thought: Later Developments

The literature that developed somewhat independently of specific policy issues may be further subdivided between empirical investigations and advances in the logic of pure theory.

Data's Evolution   Science progresses through the empirical testing of working hypotheses, and to economists observed data of past economic behavior serve this purpose. The mercantilists used "political arithmetic" (W. Petty, *Political Arithmetic*, 1678) or statistics for "sound advice on all matters of economic policy and taxation." As their interest was focused on foreign trade, they collected the administrative records of the custom house and arranged the aggregates in a balance of trade, analogous to the balance sheet of a private business firm. This was the beginning of social accounting. As Edward Misselden explained the English balance of trade he had constructed for the year 1622 (*Free Trade*): "We felt it before in sense; but now we know it by science."

In the nineteenth century empirical work focused on price and other microeconomic data to assure more perfect markets. Thomas Tooke, leading proponent of the banking school, compiled his classic *History of Prices* (1838–1857). James E. T. Rogers wrote about the *History of Agriculture and Prices in England* (1866–1902). Clement Juglar traced *Les Crises commerciales et leur retour périodique* (1860). To gain some understanding of movements in the general price level, there was much discussion of index numbers. E. Laspeyres constructed an index to measure aggregate price changes (1864), widely used to the present day. To estimate fluctuations in the money supply, William Newmarch published his *Amount of Bills of Exchange* in 1851. As a guide to the expanding private capital market, stock market information multiplied, especially on railroads with their apparently unsatiable demand for new capital.

The twentieth century saw a revival of interest in macroeconomic data. The mercantilist balance of trade became a balance of payments, with separation of current and capital accounts, to trace the international indebtedness resulting from World War I. The National Bureau of Economic Research, founded in 1920, pioneered empirical work in business cycle (W. C. Mitchell, *Business Cycles*, 1913) and national income analysis (S. Kuznets, *National Income and Its Composition*, 1941). National income and product accounts were constructed in response to the Great Depression of the 1930s and have become, with their concept of gross national product, universally accepted as a guide to Keynesian policies. Input-output tables (W. W. Leontief,

The Structure of American Economy 1941), showing the interindustry gross flows of goods and services, were first applied in World War II to forecast bottlenecks in strategic defense industries. Money-flows accounting (M. A. Copeland, *Moneyflows in the United States*, 1952) became the responsibility of the central bank to pinpoint shifts in the liquidity of the various financial sectors. Throughout this period, there was a move from the use of census data to the statistical inference drawn from scientifically designed small samples.

The most spectacular revolution in economic statistics came with the computer after World War II. What had been before a theoretical exercise in symbolic logic, such as Walrasian general equilibrium analysis, became now operational with the power to store and manipulate a very large number of interdependent variables in systems of simultaneous equations. Input-output tables are just one illustration of the many macro models now widely used for economic forecasting.

Pure Theory: The Neoclassical School   In pure theory, the nineteenth century saw the marginal revolution, the beginning of what now is called the neoclassical school. Implied in classical reasoning was the idea that trade somehow improves and maximizes economic welfare. But as value seemed an objective characteristic located within the good traded, it was hard to see why people should trade at all, or why there was not always a danger that one trader would take advantage of the other in a zero-sum game. Ever since Aristotle, a clumsy distinction was made between value in exchange and value in use. Adam Smith talked about the "propensity to truck, barter, and exchange one thing for another." But why?

The founders of the neoclassical school (W. S. Jevons, *The Theory of Political Economy*, 1871; K. Menger, *Foundations of Political Economy*, 1871; Marshall, 1890) reasoned that subjective use value is in the mind of the user, a psychological relationship between the commodity and its user, which diminishes with the abundance of the good. Trade occurs whenever traders attach different marginal utilities to the good traded, and trade will therefore always be beneficial to all traders, who optimize by spending their money so that they receive equal satisfaction from each dollar spent. Similarly, as Augustin Cournot had already expressed it in 1838, the business firm will expand operations to the point where marginal cost equals marginal revenue. If all traders act this way in a competitive market, all will optimize, and total satisfaction of the community will be maximized. This can be expressed in a general equilibrium system of simultaneous equations for all goods and traders (L. Walras, *Elements of Pure Economics*, 1874).

This neoclassical marginal utility theory can be seen as a culmination, historically and logically, of the eighteenth-century rationalistic and individualistic intellectual movement which created economics as a distinct discipline. Attacks on this world view were made from both the right and the left. From the left, Marx saw the capitalist market as a transitory stage, carrying within itself the seeds of destruction through monopolization of the economy. On the right, romanticism and the German historical school emphasized the importance of unique institutional roots and values for the determination of economic development and growth.

Twentieth-Century Economic Thought

The twentieth century has seen further refinements in neoclassical analysis and the use of mathematics, in particular to express rates of change at the margin (calculus) and to describe simultaneous-equation systems (matrix algebra). Yet there has also been a growing realization that actual markets will never be perfectly competitive, since workers and investors alike need some minimum security, and that market solutions depend on the initial endowment of the market participators, of their natural abilities as well as their legal protection through private property rights. Even more fundamentally, all economic reasoning will depend on the initial choice of parameters: economists have traditionally chosen to treat values, such as individual preference functions, and all other institutional data as either constants or as independent variables, focusing on price and quantity of goods produced as the interdependent variables.

Welfare Maximization   The question then arises in what sense the market can be said to maximize community welfare. A. C. Pigou, in his *Wealth and Welfare* (1912), introduced the concept of "external diseconomies," leading to a discrepancy of private and social cost whenever traditional cost calculations do not include harmful production effects, such as damage to the environment. V. Pareto, in his *Manuale d'economia politica* (1906), rejected cardinal and additive utility functions altogether, defining a Pareto optimum as a position from which it is impossible to improve anyone's welfare without impairing someone else's. As satisfaction often depends on relative ranking in society, the Pareto conditions offer little guidance for social policy. Moreover, once the attainment of "first-best" in a perfectly competitive market is given up, markets as such cannot tell how to choose between second-best, third-best, and so forth (Lipsey and Lancaster, *Theory of Second Best*, 1956). What have economists then to say about welfare maximization?

The classical school, in line with the individualistic utilitarian philosophy of the eighteenth-century Enlightenment, sought to define welfare solely with reference to the individual whose values should not be imposed upon by any totalitarian authority. This was the ethics of a free market society. Yet the moral philosophers of the Enlightenment took it for granted that the rational individual, as a good citizen, would identify with the values of the community, and they therefore did not anticipate any major conflict between individual choice and what twentieth-century economists have come to call a "social welfare function" (Bergson, 1938), at least no conflict that could not ultimately be reconciled by competitive market pressures. But if these pressures do not give any clear guide for welfare optimization, who will determine the criteria for evaluating economic policy decisions?

Just as the scope of orthodox economics was defined by the world view of the individualistic Enlightenment, so has the scope of twentieth-century economics been redefined by the need to understand the political dimensions of a social welfare function. The recent work of economists such as K. Arrow (*Social Choice and Individual Values*, 1951), N. S. Buchanan (*Social Choice, Democracy and Free Markets*, 1954), H. Downs (*An Economic Theory of Democracy*, 1957), Jerome Rothenberg (*Conditions for a Social Welfare Function*, 1953), and G. Tullock (*The Calculus of Consent*, 1962) indicates this new concern of political economy. It also explains why the same optimization techniques of the economist apply to quite different political settings. In a totalitarian society, values are set by a political planning authority, but implementation of the plan can be best achieved with the help of neoclassical tools, such as linear programming and other market simulation models. In a domocratic market society, market rules of the game will reflect the political bargaining of various interest groups, while the market itself will determine the prices optimal with reference to the politically established social welfare function.

Game Theory   Another approach to the same basic problem is offered by game theory (von Neumann and Morgenstern, 1944), an unfortunate name taken from its first application to parlor games. Any interest conflict, except in perfectly competitive markets, calls for some bargaining strategy on the part of all "players" who will attempt to anticipate each other's behavior. Many strategies refer to the coalitions players may form to improve their bargaining strength, a matter of obvious importance in industrial organization, in the labor market, and in international relations. To permit any forecast as to how players will react to different market constellations, there must be some consistent adherence to formal or informal rules of the game, a condition economists have always described by assuming rationality of the players, not meaning perfect foresight—an impossibility—but rather that all players will consistently follow the same rules of behavior, that they all speak the same language, that they all share similar time horizons, similar images of history.

Here again the problem arises as to what the impact of these coalitions will be on community welfare. The problem is greatly complicated by the fact that the most important coalitions may have as their very goal to shape the values of their members and their social welfare function. They are not formed for a fleeting game strategy, but rather to satisfy the emotional needs of individuals who wish to identify their ephemeral selves with a group of more lasting significance: their family, their profession, their church, the nation-state, the world. These coalitions are thus not just means for reaching autonomous ends, their preservation may become an end by itself. In the context of economic growth, these coalitions have greatly extended the time horizon of their members and have become a powerful motivation for saving and capital formation. Indeed, economic growth of the last centuries is hard to separate from the history of the nation-state, the most powerful and most fateful coalition of modern times.

Matrix Algebra   Mathematical reasoning suggests still another insight into economic systems analysis. Mathematicians are familiar with the existence problem of matrix algebra. J. Von Neumann, in cooperation with A. Wald (1934), applied this reasoning to Walrasian general equilibrium analysis. There are many systems of simultaneous equations, of course, for which no solution exists. Indeed, Marx specified such a system and called it capitalism. Orthodox market economists have proceeded with the usually implicit assumption that at least some of the systems equations have enough flexibility to adjust toward solutions acceptable with reference to both, a community social welfare function and economic efficiency.

Economic Uncertainty   Perhaps the most fundamental contrast of twentieth-century economic thought with earlier speculation has been the pervasive recognition of uncertainty. Uncertainty, of course, has always dominated economic life: it is a universal attribute of the human condition, and especially of industrialization which by definition implies continuous change in technology. But a unique feature of the industrial revolution has been its confidence that uncertainty would ultimately be benevolent rather than harmful. In the past, mythology and religion helped human beings to overcome the dread of the unknown: savings were made to forestall future calamity, or to propitiate the supernatural, rather than to provide growth. Only a rare combination of favorable circumstances led humanity to find relief from uncertainty, not in the lost paradise of some distant past, but in the reasoned knowledge of a better future. This confidence in progress was based on the unique political position of Europe as well as on the advance of science, the Newtonian physics (1687) which promised a fuller dominion over nature. Classical and neoclassical economics, in step with the social philosophy of the Enlightenment, are based on this world view which limited uncertainty to shifting production techniques essential to economic growth. Unfavorable uncertainty, such as market anarchy, would be fatal to growth, as Adam Smith repeatedly stressed, but could be expected to diminish further with the rule of reason. This faith in progress was fully shared by Marx whose confidence in the benevolence of scientific socialism was essential to the political appeal of Marxism. Among the founders of neoclassical economics, Jevons was quite explicit about his confidence that statistics would contribute to more perfect markets, and thus to more certainty and better economic systems.

The twentieth century has been a basic reorientation of thought, both in the natural and social sciences. Werner Heisenberg's uncertainty principle has converted the laws of physics into statements about relative probabilities rather than absolute certainties. The revival of intense national rivalry amidst a worldwide depression, two world wars, consumer expectations far outrunning the reality of economic possibilities, rapid industrialization in countries far removed from the Western tradition, an increase of knowledge which has greatly widened the range of choice and which has thus made forecasting more, rather than less, difficult—all have shaken the confidence of earlier generations and led to growing doubts that "the future isn't what it used to be." Keynes in his *Economic Consequences of the Peace* (1919), Pareto in his *Trattato di sociologia generale* (1916), Spengler in his *Untergang des Abendlandes* (1918–1922), Max Weber in his *Aufsätze zur Religionssoziologie* (1904–1920), all wrote in very different ways about these doubts which profoundly shaped the new century, in an effort to give expression to the complex interaction of facts and values, of historical consciousness and society, which ultimately determines how human beings face their uncertain future.

Adam Smith's friend and mentor David Hume suggested at the very height of the Enlightenment (1752) that we must cope with uncertainty or "may be swallowed up in a paralyzing scepticism, and become, like Hamlet, sickled o'er with the pale cast of thought." Economists have followed this advice, even through the uncertainties of the twentieth century. Frank Knight, in his *Risk, Uncertainty, and Profit* (1920), explained profits as the reward for successfully shouldering uncertainty, distinguishing unpredictable uncertainty from predictable risk which can be insured against. Keynes, in his *General Theory of Employment, Interest and Money*, published in 1936 when the last countries of the world gave up their allegiance to the international gold standard, saw uncertainty as the basic problem of private capital investment: government deficit spending was thought to assure greater effective aggregate demand for private goods and thus to create the precondition for more certainty and stable capital formation in the private sector; all the controversies about the efficacy of Keynesian policies concern the validity of this crucial assumption.

More recent economic analysis of decisions under uncertainty is based on the expected utility theorem of von Neumann and Morgenstern (1944), developed again in the context of game theory, or on defining all economic claims with reference to specified states of the world (K. Arrow, *Social Choice and Individual Value*, 1951; G.

Debreu, *Theory of Value,* 1956). This conceptualization suggests how much is implied in the traditional assumption of rational economic behavior. Rational is a shorthand to describe consistency of means and ends, of ultimate goals with the state of the world as visualized by the decision maker. But except in trivial cases, means-end relations constitute such a complex hierarchy that the decision maker usually will not have fully spelled out all the probability judgments involved.

The reference to states of the world is a cogent reminder that rationality is shaped by the continuous interaction between community members' experience and values as they influence each other and the confidence in their own probability judgments. Any great innovator will be considered irrational until success establishes rationality in the hindsight of the innovator's more conservative contemporaries. But this very success will depend on the spirit of the age: there can be no innovation without at least some community acceptance and support. This accounts for the complex ties between ideology and technology, science and industry, not only in the obvious sense of scientific application to production techniques, but in the more subtle sense of a willingness to experiment. It suggests the need of a growth rationality, beyond the mere explosion of consumer expectations, and beyond the mere copy of foreign production techniques.

Closely related to such considerations is the concept of rational expectations (Muth, 1961), first applied to a critique of Keynesian macro models and stabilization policies (Lucas, 1972). Economic expectations have been compared to the working hypotheses of the scientist: both embody imperfect knowledge to be continuously tested and revised by later experience and new visions of the world (L. M. Lachmann, *Capital and Its Structure,* 1956). The rational expectations approach to uncertainty clarifies the traditional assumptions of economic theory and the fundamental issue of why and when market prices can be regarded useful guides to social action (K. Arrow, *The Future and The Present in Economic Life,* 1978; H. A. Simon, *Rational Decision Making in Business Organization,* 1978). It emphasizes the great difficulty of all economic explanation based on extrapolations of the past (J. R. Hicks, *Causality of Economics,* 1979; C. A. Sims, *Macroeconomics and Reality,* 1980; K. F. Wallis, *Econometric Implications of the Rational Expectations Hypothesis,* 1980), and the resultant danger of oversimplified mechanical policy application: functional relations in macro models are not stable over time because rational individuals learn from the past and may change their future behavior. In the 1970s it was learned that Keynesian policies may lead to inflation rather than to economic growth.

References

American Economic Association and Royal Economic Society, *Surveys of Economic Theory,* St. Martins Press, New York and London, 1965-1967; Bergson, Abram, "A Reformulation of Certain Aspects of Welfare Economics," *Quarterly Journal of Economics,* vol. 52, February 1938, p. 310; Blaug, Mark, *Economic Theory in Retrospect,* 3d ed., Cambridge University Press, Cambridge, 1978.; *Cambridge Economic History of Europe,* Cambridge University Press, Cambridge, 1965-1978; Davis, Lance E., Richard A. Easterlin, and William N. Parker (eds.), *American Economic Growth, An Economist's History of the United States,* Harper, New York, 1972; Deane, Phyllis, *The Evolution of Economic Ideas,* Cambridge University Press, Cambridge, 1978; Ekelund, Robert B., and Robert F. Helbert, *A History of Economic Theory and Method,* McGraw-Hill, New York, 1975; Fogel, Robert W., and Stanley L. Engerman (eds.), *The Reinterpretation of Economic History,* Harper, New York, 1971; Fusfeld, Daniel R., *The Age of the Economist,* 3d ed., Scott, Foresman, Glenview, Ill., 1977; Heilbroner, Robert L., *The Worldly Philosophers,* 4th ed., Simon and Schuster, New York, 1972; *International Encyclopedia of the Social Sciences,*

Macmillan, New York, 1968; Koopmans, Tjalling C., *Three Essays on the State of Economic Science,* McGraw-Hill, New York, 1957; Kuhn, William E., *The Evolution of Economic Thought,* 2d ed., South-Western, Cincinnati, 1970; Kuznets, Simon, *Modern Economic Growth,* Yale Unversity Press, New Haven, 1966; Lucas, Robert E., Jr., "Expectations and the Neutrality of Money," *Journal of Economic Theory,* vol. 4, no. 2, April 1972, pp. 103–124; Muth, John F., "Rational Expectations and the Theory of Price Movements," *Econometrica,* vol. 29, no. 3, July 1961, pp. 315–355; Neumann, John von, and Oskar Morgenstern, *Theory of Games and Economic Behavior,* Princeton University Press, Princeton, N.J., 1944; Oser, Jacob, and William C. Blanchfield, *The Evolution of Economic Thought,* 3d ed., Harcourt Brace Jovanovich, New York, 1975; Rostow, Walt W., *The World Economy: History and Prospect,* University of Texas Press, Austin, 1978; Schumpeter, Joseph A., *History of Economic Analysis,* Oxford University Press, New York, 1954; Smyth, Albert H. (ed.), *The Writings of Benjamin Franklin,* vol. IX, Macmillan, London, 1906, p. 243; Spiegel, Henry W., *The Growth of Economic Thought,* Duke University Press, Durham, N.C., 1976; Supple, Barry E., *The Experience of Economic Growth,* Random House, New York, 1963; Weintraub, Sidney, *Modern Economic Thought,* University of Pennsylvania Press, Philadelphia, 1977; Wright, Chester W., *Economic History of the United States,* 2d ed., McGraw-Hill, New York, 1949.

Book reviews and current bibliographies on economic history are published quarterly by *The Economic History Review* for the Economic History Society of England, and by the *Journal of Economic History* for the American History Association. Book reviews and current bibliographies on the history of economic thought are published quarterly by the American Economic Association in *The Journal of Economic Literature* and by the Duke University Press for the History of Economics Society in *History of Political Economy.*

Werner Hochwald

Economic models

A model is an abstract, simplified design of a working system. An economic model is a simplified rendition of economic reality. It could be a diagram, a flowchart, statistical tables, or equation systems. The tendency now in economics is to express models as equation systems. But some economic models are expressed in different ways. They are, however, hardly ever presented in three-dimensional physical form, as are some scientific, engineering, or medical models. There was, at one time, a brief interest in a hydraulic model of an economic system, but its use was short-lived, and mathematical methods appear to be the most widely used form for presentation.

Classification of Economic Models

Some classifications of economic models are

- Theoretical versus applied
- Deterministic versus probabilistic (stochastic)
- Particular versus general
- Micro versus macro
- National versus international
- Supranational versus subnational
- Static versus dynamic
- Mainstream versus monetarist

The contrasts among model types reveal the range of consideration.

Theoretical and Applied Models   A theoretical model is an economist's idea of how people behave or ought to behave. Behavior is worked out according to some principle of optimization or equilibrium, and the implied equation system defines a model.

A system of equations expressing

$$\text{Output} = f\,(\text{factor inputs}) \tag{1}$$

$$\text{Marginal productivity} = \text{real factor rewards} \tag{2}$$

$$\text{Factor supplies} = g\,(\text{real factor rewards}) \tag{3}$$

may be cast in mathematical form to lay the basis for a model of a producing establishment or an industry. If there are several factors, then there will be several relationships in (2) and (3)—one for each input factor. There could also be models with multiple outputs.

This simple model can be developed from economic principles of profit maximization under conditions of free competitive market structure. It is abstract and theoretical, but if functions f and g are specified according to some particular mathematical forms, we can fit the coefficients of such equations to real-world observations and derive or estimate an applied model of the actual economic situation. A numerical version of this model with statistically estimated coefficients would be an applied model.

Equation (1) would be called a technical relationship. It would be governed by the laws of science and engineering. The next two groups in (2) and (3) are behavioral relationships, showing how economic decisions are made. Two other kinds of economic relationships that are used in models are definitional and legal/institutional. If we had defined

$$\text{Profits} = \text{receipts} - \text{cost}$$

in the above system of profit mazimization, we would have had one more equation and one more variable. This relationship is purely one of definition and has no unknown coefficients. If we had introduced a tax or regulatory system, there would have been need for a legal relationship showing how the taxes or regulations were related to the economic variables.

The theoretical system is written as though it were composed of exact relationships. The applied system would be fit to real-world data, and this fit would be only approximate; thus, there would be error, and models are built in economics on the assumption that error follows the laws of probability. Probabilistic or stochastic relationships characterize econometric models, as opposed to those of the deterministic theory of mathematical economics. All numerical models or all applied models are not probabilistic, but those of econometrics are.

Deterministic and Probabilistic Models   In econometric models, the definitional equations are assumed to be exact, that is, without error, but the other relationships are stochastic.

The small economic model in Equations (1) to (3) is only a partial model of a firm or industry. No attention is paid to explanation of demand for the firm's output or to variables from outside the region of operations of the firm. It represents partial analysis and to be used in applied work would have to be based on some assumptions about what is taking place in the rest of the economy.

Micro and Macro Models   Another approach to modeling is to combine the equations from all the different sectors of the economy into one comprehensive and general system. An economywide model is the general type. It can be either a micro or a macro model. A theoretical breakthrough in economic thinking of the nineteenth century was achieved by the French economist Léon Walras, who reasoned that the general economy could be described by a large system of simultaneous equations balancing supplies and demands for all goods and services throughout the economy. His system forms the basis for the model of general equilibrium. It is very large and detailed, covering every conceivable good and service traded in the economy. It is a micro model, as is the model of an individual firm. By contrast, sectors can be aggregated or averaged, and a macro model may be constructed for several combined sectors. A macro model covering behavior, technology, legal relations and accounting identities for

- Agriculture
- All nonagricultural firms
- Households
- Banks
- Public authorities
- Average wages, prices, interest rates

could be expressed as an aggregative model. While the Walrasian micro system would consist of billions and billions of equations, a macro system could have as few as 2 to 20 equations. In a practical sense, however, applied macroeconometric models now have as many as several hundred equations. They are still classified as macro models because a few hundred is small relative to billions and billions.

National and International Models   Most applied models of the economy as a whole are built by using the national income and product accounts of a country. These macro models describe economic activity in the whole nation. In recent years, there has been more and more interest in modeling the world economy through tracing the flows of international trade and payments among countries. An international or supranational model brings together models of several countries or regional groupings of countries, put together in a consistent way to reflect inter country or inter regional trading relationships. For example, the project LINK model of world trade (Waelbroeck, 1976) combines macroeconomic models of some 20 countries and five regions that cover the whole world. Consistency in trade is imposed by making total world exports balance total world imports. International payments flows as well as international goods flows can be related to one another in a similarly consistent way, and supranational models of this type have also been constructed.

Supranational and Subnational Models   Macro models of a nation can be extended in two directions, either toward international economic relationships, as described above, or toward disaggregated regional economic relationships within a nation. Models of individual subregions of a nation have been constructed on a broad scale. These consist of models of states, metropolitan areas, or regional groupings of states. For the most part, individual regional models have been constructed that are open with respect to the nation; that is, national aggregates, determined as output from a national macro model, serve as input into a local regional model. If the region is large enough or strategic enough, it can feed back on national performance and the two models (regional and national) can be solved together in an iterative fashion.

A fresh approach to regional model building is now taking place, in which national totals are built from the regional components. Lack of adequate data has made regional modeling more difficult to develop than national modeling, but this deficiency is gradually being overcome, and regional systems are being put together into a total national design. It is unlikely, however, that regional modeling will displace national modeling. It is more likely that the two approaches will remain complementary, with complete regional systems serving mainly to distribute national aggregates among local components.

Static and Dynamic Models   If a model is not specific about relative dating of its interrelated parts, it is static. A dynamic model, by contrast, interrelates magnitudes at different dates, or it interrelates levels, rates of change, and historical accumulations. A dynamic model shows how the economy evolves through time, both in its short-run patterns of the business cycle and its long-run patterns of growth or decline.

Forecasting models, planning models, and policy simulation models are generally dynamic. They indicate time trajectories for the economy. A well-known static model has, however, been the input-output, or interindustry, model. This model shows how final demand in the economy requires or entices output from all the various industrial sectors through the workings of the matrix of technical coefficients. It also shows how prices of goods from different industrial origins get combined into prices for final goods purchased by households, businesses, governments, and foreigners. The fundamental equations of input-output analysis are written as

$$(I - A)X = F$$

where I = the identity matrix
   A = the technical input-output coefficient matrix
   X = the column vector of industry outputs
   F = the column vector of final demands by sector

This model is static (everything is dated at the same time point). It is not stochastic, but it is generally numerical, and it is open. If it is tied to a macroeconometric model of the economy as a whole, to determine the components of F and prices by industrial sectors, then it can be used to allocate industry output levels and prices of final products. Various dynamic and stochastic extensions have actually been made, and the system is being used on both a regional and supranational level.

Mainstream and Monetarist Models   The mainstream macro model of a national economy builds up the national product accounts by explaining first the main components of total expenditure. These are consumer, business, government, and net foreign expenditures, often by detailed types. It also explains the main components of national income such as wages, interest, rent, dividends, retained corporate earnings, income from self-employment, and transfer payments. There will be groups of equations to explain prices, wage rates, employment, productivity, labor force, unemployment, money markets, and credits markets. As indicated above, a complete input-output sector with interindustry flows of intermediate goods is also integrated into the largest of such national models.

The mainstream model pays a great deal of attention not only to total demand in the economy but also to the technical conditions of supply. At the present time, there is high interest in modeling more detail from the supply side in the form of the energy system, the agricultural system, the regulatory mechanism, labor-force participation, environmental conditions, and the incentive aspects of the tax transfer system.

Doctrinaire models of the financial system, known as monetarist models, create alternative types of structure in which the supply of monetary aggregates determine overall activity and price levels, which are then split into components through equations that are much like those of the mainstream models. The flow-of-funds accounts are now being developed to the point when they can be combined wih national income and input-output accounting systems to enlarge the mainstream model in a direction toward paying more attention to financial markets.

Use of Economic Models

Economic models are used in many ways: to work out theoretical implications of economic analysis, to test economic theories, to make economic forecasts, to plan economic development, to examine alternative economic policies, to simulate alternative scenarios for the economy, and to replay economic history. Much theoretical analysis of economic models is carried out by examining the mathematical properties of solutions to equation systems, both static and dynamic. The long-run or steady-state implications of a solution to a model are used to establish or test long-run properties of economic theory. Such long-run properties might be stability of key ratios, such as savings-income ratio, capital-output ratio, or wage-national income ratio. Also certain key balances should hold for the long run, balances between real interest rate and real growth rate, and between international receipts and payments.

Numerical economic models are generally solved by electronic computation as simulations over time, either historical or future projections. Economic forecasting is the best known and most frequent of such applications of models. Historical values of lagged variables (the initial conditions) and future values of exogenous (external) variables are assembled as model inputs. Also tax coefficients and technological parameters are fixed. The model with these inputs are fed into electronic computers and the solutions of the models over future time constitute the forecast. The procedure is not automatic, in that much judgment of the forecaster usually goes into adjusting the model so that it approximates the observed levels of the economy at the initial stages immediately preceding the forecast. The adjusted model is then extrapolated over the forecast horizon.

Alternative forecasts based on different assumptions about economic policy (taxes, public spending, monetary policy, international trade policy, regulation of industry) or external environmental conditions are often generated. These show the estimated policy impacts over time. In longer-run projections, scenario inputs about economic behavior, policy variables, or changes in external conditions are then compared with a reference simulation. The reference simulation is not necessarily a strict forecast but a model solution that has widely accepted long-run or steady-state characteristics. These scenario investigations may be wanted by policymakers, long-range planners, and private-sector executives. Scholars examine such long-run scenarios for explaining or describing ideas about economic development. Such scenarios can be computed on a forward (prospective) basis or on a historical (retrospective) basis. In one case, models are used to examine what might be and in the other, to examine what might have been.

References

Chenery, H., and P. Clark, *Interindustry Economics*, Wiley, New York, 1959; Klein, L. R., *An Introduction to Econometrics*, Prentice-Hall, Englewood Cliffs, N.J., 1962; Klein, L. R., and E. Burmeister (eds.): *Econometric Model Performance*, University of Pennsylvania Press, Philadelphia, 1976; Klein, L. R., and R. M. Young, *An Introduction to Econometric Forecasting and Forecasting Models*, D. C.Heath, Lexington, Mass., 1980; Waelbroeck, J., *The Models of Project LINK*, North Holland, Amsterdam, 1976.

(*See also* Econometrics; Economic forecasts; Economic statistics; Forecasting methods; Statistical techniques in economics and business, an overview)

Lawrence R. Klein

Economic planning

Economic planning is the process of consciously and systematically organizing economic and technical information into an internally consistent conceptual framework within the context of economic and noneconomic constraints toward the realization of a prescribed goal. The methods available to implement these plans are as varied as the countries themselves in which the techniques of planning have been introduced.

Some form of economic planning is used in every country of the world. The extent to which the methods of planning—organization, implementation, and impact—differ, depends on the political, cultural, social, technological, and institutional profile of the individual countries.

Definition of Planning

According to Jan Tinbergen (1968), "planning should be seen as a manifestation of the ever-growing tendency consciously to organize human activity. In this process there is a continuous search for efficiency in its broadest sense." The planning process is predicated on the realization of a feasible goal or set of goals. Goals may include the maximization of profit for a business enterprise, full employment at relatively stable prices, or, more generally, the desirable economic and social development of a country. With such goals delineated, an economic plan—the blueprint of the economy—is a particularly useful tool to bring these predetermined goals into fruition, since a plan, as W. Arthur Lewis (1968) remarked, "organizes consistent thinking, helps to clarify what we expect, reveals its inconsistencies, and therefore . . . improve[s] the process of making decisions." A plan should not be rigidly adhered to since unforeseen developments and newly acquired information will modify both the stated goals and the methods of achieving them. A plan, as Wassily Leontief (1977) has said, "is not a forecast. The whole idea of planning assumes the possibility of choice between alternative feasible scenarios."

Theory of Planning

In establishing goals for either a business enterprise or a national economy, those responsible for achieving these goals would necessarily concern themselves with phenomena which, directly or indirectly, hasten or impede their realization. For example, a corporate planner for the domestic steel industry, in addition to requiring information on the availability of raw materials for steel and on the projected economic climate for the domestic economy, would no doubt require information regarding such matters as the projected level of world demand for steel, possible changes in pollution abatement standards, or perhaps even new techniques in the production of aluminum. Each of these will, even in the short term, affect the price of steel, the level of steel output, and, consequently, profits.

On the other hand, those vested with the responsibility of monitoring and coordinating the activities of a national economy would naturally concern themselves with all economic, social, political, and technological considerations that might, however indirectly, affect the performance and development of the economy and consequently the realization of the desired goals.

A prerequisite for developing a plan—either for a private firm or on the scale of a national economy—is a body of facts. These facts consist of information available to the firm or nation about the stock of resources—labor, capital, and natural resources—that can be drawn upon during the course of the plan, about the structural or technical relationships which govern the way in which the economic variables interact with each other, and about the social and institutional restrictions imposed on the firm or the economy.

Since the activities of a firm, not to say of a national economy, are affected by both direct and indirect influences, some method must be developed to identify and describe these factors and to incorporate them into one internally consistent theoretical framework. A model is a mathematical representation of the structural relationships that link the producing and consuming sectors of the economy. The model should be capable of incorporating the technical or structural relationships that exist among the various sectors, the predetermined feasible goals as well as the factual data regarding the availability of factors of production and natural resources, and the social and institutional setting. The model should be sufficiently well-specified in terms of its complexity to simulate closely the actual course of the economy. It should also possess the flexibility of incorporating adjustments in the light of political, social, technological, or institutional changes and the availability of new information governing the structural interrelationships of the economy, the factors of production, and the feasibility of achieving the prescribed goals. In this internally consistent, general equilibrium framework, both the direct and indirect effects of changes can be systematically tracked and measured in quantitative terms.

Planning and Economic Policy

The two main methodological planning tools currently employed by both developed and developing nations for the purpose of policy analysis are econometric models and input-output analysis. The former, pioneered by Tinbergen, Ragnar Frisch, and Lawrence Klein, is structured around Keynesian macroeconomic aggregates such as the consumption function, the investment function, a money and labor market, variants on the aggregate production function, and a government and foreign sector. The relationships linking the different variables are estimated by well-known statistical techniques such as regression analysis and hypothesis testing. Since fiscal and monetary policy are the two main instruments available to policymakers to coordinate the economy in the short run, econometric models are heavily weighted toward influencing the demand side of the economy. For example, if tax rates are reduced, by how much will expenditures on durables increase? Or, on the other hand, if the dollar depreciates against foreign currencies, by how much will imports of manufactured goods decrease? If the Federal Reserve Board increases the supply of money, how will residential construction be affected? Since econometric models have the characteristic of internal consistency, both the direct and indirect effects of any single policy measure on the various markets and variables of the system can be quantitatively assessed.

Input-output analysis, developed by Wassily Leontief in the 1930s, describes the structural profile of the economy by representing the various sectors of the economy in terms of their input requirements, i.e., raw materials, labor and capital, per unit of their respective output. By integrating all the producing sectors into one comprehensive, internally consistent framework, it is possible to estimate, in quantitative terms, the direct and indirect requirements that must be produced for any specified bill of demand, that is, level and composition of consumption, investment, and government expenditures and foreign trade.

Since traditional input-output models assume the final demand component as given rather than attempting to explain its level and composition, the main focus of this methodological framework is centered on the production and distribution sides of the economy, or more simply, on the supply side. As a result, the input-output technique is a particularly suitable tool for answering the following policy questions: For a given state of technology, what is the structure of industrial outputs that must be produced and the amounts of primary factors of production that must be provided in order to satisfy any given bill of final demand or any change in that bill of goods? How will the structure of production be affected by changes in technology, or by the changing tastes of consumers? Because of increasing lead time required to install new industrial capacity in the capital-intensive sectors, what level of current investment will be consistent with the projected future levels of final demand? The general equilibrium format of input-output analysis provides detailed and systematic answers, in an internally consistent way, to questions or sets of questions posed from the point of view of policymaking.

Not unexpectedly, the most refined and up-to-date economic modeling combines the use of econometrics with input-output analysis. The estimation of the demand side of the economy using the econometric approach concomitant with the description of the supply side, using the detailed sectorial approach of input-output analysis, has led to unparalleled success in coordinating the short-term management of the developed economies and in providing signals and insights for government planners in the developing nations.

The Scope, Range, and Impact of Economic Planning

In some countries, such as the Soviet Union and Eastern Europe, the economy is managed and coordinated by a highly centralized planning commission, whose plans have strongly emphasized heavy industry at the expense of consumer goods. However, even within the Soviet bloc countries, considerable variation exists in the degree of centralized planning. Particularly in the Yugoslavian economy, prices play a significant role in allocating scarce resources, which is in stark contrast to the methods used to allocate scarce resources to the production sectors in other socialist countries.

In the United States, medium-term economic planning is typically initiated at a decentralized level, the individual firm or corporation. Both econometric models and input-output analysis are progressively being used for investment planning and sales management. Short-term management and coordination of the U.S. economy at large is under the general supervision of the President's Council of Economic Advisers and the Federal Reserve Board.

In some Western European countries, particularly in Scandinavia, both long-term and short-term planning efforts are usually vested in government ministries where continuous discussions among perennial adversaries, such as employees and employers, are negotiated within the framework of the existing economic models. In others, for example, France, the planning effort is "indicative." The role of the planners is to disseminate information to the various agents in the economy to lend consistency to the decisions made in the different sectors of the economy.

Development planning, the main focus of planning activities in the developing countries, involves the very rudimentary stage of coordination and management. Much of these efforts are concentrated around laying the foundation for achieving the general goal of increasing per capita incomes. These efforts include establishing a set of social and economic statistics and in providing the appropriate economic infrastructure, road networks, power facilities, educational institutions, etc., toward the desired goal of industrialization.

With the above definition of economic planning, it would not be difficult to impute a significant part of the increase in per capita income over the past 30 years, particularly in the developed countries, to the process of planning. Advances in the availability, processing, and storage of both economic and noneconomic information in conjunction with a better understanding of the mutual interrelationships of the economy within the wider framework of political, social, institutional, and technological considerations, has made economic planning, in one form or another, an indispensable tool for policymakers in all nations.

References

Almon, C., et al., *1985 Inter-industry Forecast of the American Economy*, D. C. Heath, Lexington, Mass., 1974; Blitzer, C. R., P. B. Clark, and L. Taylor (eds.), *Economy-wide Models and Development Planning*, Oxford University Press, London, 1975; Klein, L. R., "The Supply Side," *American Economic Review*, vol. 68, no. 1, March 1978, pp. 1–8; Leontief, W., and H. Stein, *The Economic System in an Age of Discontinuity: Long-Range Planning or Market Reliance?*, The Charles C. Moskowitz Memorial Lectures, College of Business and Public Administration, New York University Press, New York, 1976; Leontief, W., with A. Carter and P. Petri, *The Future of the World Economy*, A United Nations Study, Oxford University Press, New York, 1977; Lewis, W. A., "Economic Planning, Developmental Planning," in David L. Sills (ed.), *International Encyclopedia of the Social Sciences*, vol. 12, Crowell Collier & Macmillan, New York, 1968, pp. 118–125; Tinbergen, J., "Economic Planning, Western Europe," in Sills, ibid., pp. 102–109.

(*See also* Econometrics; Economic forecasts; Economic models; Economic statistics; Forecasting methods; Input-output analysis; Statistical techniques in economics and business, an overview)

Ira Sohn

Economic rent

Economic rent is the payment made (or attributed) to a productive resource beyond what is necessary to get that resource to perform its function. Most commonly, rent is thought of as compensation "for the use of the original and indestructible powers of the soil," meaning the putting into production of a piece of available unimproved land, that could be used for growing a crop or supporting a building even if it earned nothing as a result. This payment might be considered superfluous because it plays no role in "coaxing" the resource (e.g., the piece of unimproved land) into production. However, the payment is necessary in order to assure the renter who offers the highest payment that the resource will indeed be available to him or her and not to someone else. Thus, rent results from buyers' competing demands that bid up the resource's price even when the price rise does nothing to increase the supply of the resource in question.

The theory of rent is generally associated with David Ricardo, the British stockbroker, economic analyst, and legislator of the early nineteenth century who discussed the phenomenon in his book, *Principles of Political Economy and Taxation.* Adam Smith's treatment of the issue was varied: sometimes he considered rent to be one of the factors helping to determine the price of a commodity; other times he saw rent as being determined by the price that a farmer could charge for a product. Ricardo clarified the matter by showing how a particular parcel of unimproved land might yield its owner a rental income if several potential users bid for it and were willing to pay rent because their only alternative was to farm on other, less productive land. (In this connection, improvements such as fertilizer applied to the land, or a building upon it, or a road for better access count as capital investments that do not give rise to payment of rent.)

One measure of rent is the difference in output between an acre of unimproved top-quality land and an acre of unimproved second-quality land that a farmer might have to cultivate because no more top-quality land is available. When all available top-quality land is in production, its owners can begin to charge their tenants rent up to the difference between the value of its output (per acre) and the value of output (per acre) of the next-best available land. If the landowners miscalculate and demand rent exceeding this difference, farmers will prefer to move to the second-quality land that is less productive but costs no rent, at least until it, too, is fully utilized and the next-best alternative is third-quality land. When only third-rate land is available, the owners of second-rate land can begin to charge rent, and the owners of prime-quality land can raise their rent and so on.

An important aspect of rent is that it is the result of high demand and high price for land (in the aggregate), and that it does not itself push up the price of land or of farm products. As Ricardo stated, "Corn is not high because rent is paid, but a rent is paid because corn is high; and it has been justly observed that no reduction would take place in the price of corn although landlords should forego the whole of their rent. Such a measure would only enable some farmers to live like gentlemen" (Sraffa, 1951).

An individual farmer might consider rent to be a cost that must be paid if the farmer wants to farm on better-than-marginal land; if the rent is not paid, someone else would bid the land. But farmers as a group cannot cite rent as a cost of production: rent arises only when their collective demand for land of a given quality exceeds the supply.

This same principle also pertains to some nonagricultural applications. For example, famous movie actors and professional athletes command very high salaries when competing studios or teams bid high for their services because their appearance assures large ticket sales. Yet the supply of such talent is strictly limited and cannot be increased; less well-known substitutes simply do not command as much attention or bring in as much revenue. This fact gives the individual leading stars extraordinary power to demand high salaries, regardless of the fact that they do not now appear any more often than they did when they were less well known. However, in these and other corresponding cases, and contrary to the example of land, an initial wage or compensation is a cost of production: the top stars or athletes must first be enticed away from their prior occupations to become available to the film or professional sports industries. The salaries that must be offered in order to attract them to the industry in the first place is a cost that the industry must bear. Only the sum that is paid to them in excess of this amount—and it is often substantial—can be thought of as economic rent.

Other similar examples can be cited, especially where natural limitations, administrative regulations, or monopoly elements frustrate any expansion of supply.

References

Blaug, Mark, *Economic Theory in Retrospect*, 3d ed., Cambridge University Press, Cambridge, 1978; Krueger, A. O., "The Political Economy of the Rent-Seeking Society," *American Economic Review*, vol. 64, no. 3, June 1974, pp. 291–303; Lackman, C. L.,"The Classical Base of Modern Rent Theory," *American Journal of Eonomics and Sociology*, vol. 35, no. 3, July 1976, pp. 287–300; Ricardo, David: *On the Principles of Political Economy and Taxation*, in Piero Sraffa, *Ricardo's Works and Correspondence*, vol. I, Cambridge University Press, Cambridge, 1951.

G. H. Mattersdorff

Economic statistics

Economic statistics provide quantitative measures of economic phenomena in the private and public sectors of the economy. The field is composed of two broad categories: (1) collection, classification, and presentation of data; and (2) analysis, interpretation, and projections of future trends.

An overview of macroeconomic statistics in the United States will be presented. Such statistics are the major indicators of overall economic activity at the national level that provide current measures (typically monthly and/or quarterly) of output, employment, prices, and financial markets. The specific series covered are the gross national product, industrial production index, consumer and producer price indexes, labor force and employment, money supply, and corporate profits. The focus is on highlighting the main characteristics and interrelationships of these series, and on their use in economic analysis and forecasting for policymaking.

Macroeconomic data are aggregates of more detailed microeconomic data, which provide greater elaboration of industry structure, product markets, labor-force characteristics, income distributions, geographic composition, etc.

Role of the Federal Government

The federal government is the major supplier of economic statistics. Within the government, the responsibility for compiling particular series of data is diffused among a number of agencies: Bureau of the Census, Bureau of Labor Statistics, Bureau of Economic Analysis, Federal Reserve Board, Federal Trade Commission, Internal Revenue Service, Department of Agriculture, and many others. The overall coordination of these statistical activities on a governmentwide basis is provided by the Office of Federal Statistical Policy and Standards in the U.S. Department of Commerce. (This decentralized organization differs from the centralized organizations of many other countries where the statistical series are compiled by one or two government agencies.)

Because of the importance of having useful and accurate measures of the economy and of social trends, outside review commissions have from time to time been established to evaluate the statistical system and recommend ways for its improvement. While recognizing the generally good quality of data provided by the statistical agencies, the review groups have continually identified the need to have a better coordination of statistical activities throughout the government. These include means of obtaining better planning and priorities for statistical programs, more consistency among individual series, increased use of existing data while protecting the confidentiality of the information, and safeguarding against politicization of the data. In addition to these reviews of the overall statistical system, other audits are made of selected macroeconomic series.

Macroeconomic Data

Macroeconomic data, or measures of economic activity, are monitored closely in the public and private sectors. Their primary use is by the federal government in evaluating and developing fiscal, monetary, and wage-price policies for achieving the employment and anti-inflation goals of the Employment Act of 1946 and Full Employment and Balanced Growth Act of 1978. The major policy users in the government are the Council of Economic Advisers, Federal Reserve Board, Department of the Treasury, Office of Management and Budget, Joint Economic Committee, and Congressional Budget Office.

In the private sector, these data are used by companies for analyzing prospects for their own company markets and investments in an economywide framework. They are also used in labor-management wage negotiations by unions and companies.

Output Measures

Gross National Product   The gross national product (GNP) is the most comprehensive measure of economic activity. It is constructed quarterly from two perspectives. As a measure of demand, the product side provides estimates of final markets: consumer expenditures, private investment, government purchases, and net exports. As a measure of supply, the income side estimates the resources used in production: employee compensation, proprietor's income, corporate profits, net interest, rental income, capital consumption allowances, and indirect business taxes. The difference between these two alternative measures of the GNP is the statistical discrepancy. This is a broad indicator of the net effect of errors and inconsistencies in the data sources and estimating procedures on both sides of the accounts.

The GNP is estimated in both current and constant dollars. The deflated series in constant dollars is the measure of real output, i.e., the physical volume of economic activity. Macroeconomic policy usually focuses on the quarterly movements of of real output, which is heightened during periods of high inflation.

The underlying data or data base for develping the GNP estimates come from a wide range of survey and other information provided primarily by a number of federal agencies. The GNP measures are constructed by the Bureau of Economic Analysis in the U.S. Department of Commerce, and are published in the *Survey of Current Business.*

Industrial Production Index   The industrial production index (IPI) is a monthly measure of the physical volume of output in the manufacturing, mining, and electric and gas utility industries. It is presented in two broad groupings. One is a measure of demand of market categories that distinguish consumer goods, equipment, intermediate products, and materials. The other is a measure of supply by producing industry.

The IPI is constructed from data on actual product output by individual industries, or from industry measures of employee-hours or kilowatthours, adjusted for estimated changes in output per unit of labor and energy input. It is prepared by the Federal Reserve Board and published in the *Federal Reserve Bulletin.*

Comparison of GNP and IPI   These two measures of the nation's output are based on different concepts and underlying data. Comparisons of the two series are made after making the necessary statistical adjustments to place them on as nearly comparable a basis as possible. The series generally show similar cyclical movements, although there are differences in turning points and in amplitude of fluctuations.

Analysts view the two series as complementary measures of output. As a monthly series, the IPI is available on a more timely basis than the quarterly GNP. The GNP, on the other hand, gives more information for analyzing the factors accounting for the output trends. When the two measures give noticeably different gauges of output, analysts tend to be more cautious in appraising the current state of the economy. It also is a signal to the agencies preparing the measures to investigate the causes of the differences in more depth, as well as to apply further checks on their own data sources and estimating methodology.

Price Measures

Consumer Price Indexes   The consumer price indexes (CPIs) are the most widely used indicators of inflation. In addition to their use in formulating macroeconomic policy, they are used for adjusting wage, pension, and other employee benefit levels, as well as for a wide range of cost and price estimation by business and other organizations. The indexes provide measures of the monthly change in prices paid by urban households for a fixed basket of goods and services.

Two CPIs are calculated each month. The most comprehensive one is for all urban consumers, which includes urban wage earners and clerical workers; professional, managerial, and technical workers; the self-employed, short-term workers; the unemployed; retirees; and others not in the labor force. The other CPI is limited to urban wage earners and clerical workers.

Price indexes are developed for food, housing, apparel, transportation, medical care, entertainment, and other goods and services. The relative importance of these categories, or "weights" of the index, is based on periodic surveys of household expenditures (the most recent one for the year 1972–73). Changes in the price indexes provide a guide to changes in living costs, but because the price measures do not reflect changes in the relative amounts and types of goods and services purchased, in a technical sense they do not measure changes in the cost of living.

Actual data on current prices are obtained by direct surveys of business establishments. Considerable attention is given to identifying changes in the availability and quality of the items priced to ensure that they are adequately accounted for in measuring pure price change. The CPIs are compiled by the Bureau of Labor Statistics in the U.S. Department of Labor and are published in the *Monthly Labor Review.*

Producer Price Indexes   The producer price indexes (PPIs) measure the monthly changes in prices received by producers of commodities. They are prepared in three broad categories: (1) stage of processing (finished goods, intermediate materials, and crude materials); (2) commodity groupings (farm products and industrial commodities); and (3) output of selected industries (presently mining and manufacturing).

Among the various PPIs, the finished-goods component in the stage-of-processing series is featured in news releases as the key overall indicator of inflation in primary markets. Most of the monthly data on prices are obtained from surveys of business establishments, and others are taken from trade publications and government agency program data. The aim is to measure actual transaction prices, but list or book prices are used when transaction prices are difficult to collect. The PPIs are compiled by the Bureau of Labor Statistics and published in the *Monthly Labor Review.*

Comparison of CPI, PPI, and GNP Deflator   Because price transactions in the PPI occur early in the production process, they are considered to be harbingers of movements in the CPI. Detailed series from both indexes are used to deflate current dollar expenditures of the GNP, e.g., the CPIs for personal consumption expenditures and the PPIs for equipment and inventory investment.

The implicit GNP deflators provide a third measure of price change. These are derived indirectly by dividing current-dollar expenditures by constant-dollar expenditures for the GNP and its major components. While these differ from the CPIs and PPIs in both coverage and weights, they do provide alternative measures of price change. For example, the CPI for all urban households and the GNP deflator for personal consumption expenditures are conceptually similar (although not identical), and the measured differences indicate the effect that alternative pricing methodologies yield in estimating changes in consumer prices.

Employment Measures

Labor Force   The monthly data on employment and unemployment are the most comprehensive measures of the absorption of the population into the labor force. Employment and unemployment data are provided by demographic characteristics of age, sex, and race. Additional information is available on employment by full-time and part-time workers, industry and occupation, and on unemployment by reason and duration of joblessness.

The labor-force data are obtained from monthly surveys of a sample of households. It counts the number of persons 16 years or older who are working or actively seeking work in the civilian sector (excluding the armed forces). To be counted as unemployed, a person must be actively pursuing employment. Special attention is given in the survey to determine which persons who do not have jobs are actively seeking work. The unemployment rate is calculated as the number unemployed divided by the sum of employed and unemployed persons. These measures are provided by the Bureau of Labor Statistics and are published in *Employment and Earnings* and the *Monthly Labor Review.*

Nonagricultural Employment   The monthly series on employment in nonagricultural establishments are the basic measures of labor inputs in the nonfarm sector of the economy. This provides a count of the number of jobs of all workers on business and government payrolls, and the average weekly hours and earnings of nonsupervisory workers, classified by industry.

The information is obtained from monthly surveys of a sample of employers (business establishments and governments). The survey is conducted as a cooperative program of federal and state governmental statistical agencies. The measures are provided by the Bureau of Labor Statistics and are published in *Employment and Earnings* and the *Monthly Labor Review*.

Comparison of Labor-Force and Employment Series   The labor-force data focus on the utilization of persons of working age who are available for work. Therefore, major attention is given to the unemployment rates as a human gauge of the performance of the economy and as measures of the looseness or tightness of labor markets.

By contrast, the employment series concentrates on the use of labor in the production process. Thus, as a count of jobs, this series includes dual jobholders twice; on the other hand, as a count of persons, the labor-force series counts dual jobholders once. In terms of coverage, the labor-force series is broader because of its inclusion of the self-employed, farm workers, unpaid family workers, and domestic workers in households.

Both series give measures of employment. The two differ because of the conceptual differences noted above and the use of different survey universes—households for the labor force and employer establishments for nonagricultural employment. Generally, figures on the monthly change in employment as reported in the employer establishment series are considered to be more reliable.

Financial Measures

Money Stock   The money-stock figures focus on funds that move through the banking system. These measures have increased in importance over the years as greater attention in economic analysis and monetary policy is given to the effect of the money supply on overall economic activity. They are also closely observed by private investors for indications of future trends in interest rates based on anticipated Federal Reserve Board policy on loosening or tightening the availability of credit.

Four alternative measures of the money stock are prepared on a regular basis. The first is M-1A, which is composed of demand deposits in commercial banks and currency in circulation (the actual definition has further refinements). In the subsequent series of M-1B through M-3, the scope is continually broadened to include additional categories of money in various types of savings and liquid investments in banks and thrift institutions.

The figures for M-1A and M-1B are provided weekly, and those for M-2 and M-3 are available monthly. The estimates are based on daily Treasury Department data on currency in circulation, daily demand-deposit data reported by member banks of the Federal Reserve, call and other reports of banks and thrift institutions. The measures are provided by the Federal Reserve Board and published in the *Federal Reserve Bulletin* (weekly figures are provided in a special release).

Corporate Finances   Industrywide measures of corporation income and balance sheet statements in manufacturing, mining, and trade are provided quarterly. These data focus on domestic activities of U.S. corporations. The information gives an overall view of the economic health of companies in an important segment of the economy and also is a basic data source for the corporate profits component of the GNP.

The information is obtained from a survey of a changing sample of companies. It is compiled by the Federal Trade Commission and published in the *Quarterly Financial Report*.

In addition to the above measures of output, prices, employment, and financial transactions, a number of other current economic statistics are used in macroeconomic analysis. These include such series as retail sales, housing starts, business inventories and orders, plant and equipment expenditures, industrial capacity utilization, bank reserves, flow of funds, consumer credit, interest rates, and international trade and balance of payments.

Analytic Framework

The above macroeconomic series are used predominantly in economic analyses of the performance of and outlook for the economy. Among the most frequent uses are in the construction of econometric forecasting models; studies of changes in productivity and in utilization of resources; and development of leading, coincident, and lagging economic indicators.

Econometric forecasting models   These are typically developed in the GNP framework, including interconnecting equations with measures of employment and inflation. In some cases, they are further linked to financial variables such as the money-stock figures and flow of funds. Policy variables for considering alternative mixes of fiscal, monetary, and wage-price policies also permit mathematical solutions of such models that provide alternative forecasts of the economy. These reflect the potential effect of the policy instruments on output, employment, and inflation. Econometric models are developed by the federal government and private organizations.

Productivity   Productivity is widely defined and measured as output per employee-hour. The numerator of output is based on one of the constant-dollar measures of GNP, and for more detailed industries on the industrial production indexes. The denominator of labor inputs is based on data for the appropriate industry level of employment and hours. Because of the complexity of the production process, these broad measures of productivity are not necessarily indicative of the labor efficiency. Other research in the measurement of productivity includes the contribution of plant and equipment investments, quality of the work force, and measures of actual hours on the job. Ongoing measures of productivity are provided by the Bureau of Labor Statistics.

Utilization of resources   Utilization of resources is measured from various perspectives. One is the comparison of actual GNP to "potential GNP." Potential GNP is an analytic construct developed from calculations of output trends in a fully employed economy. Another is the utilization of the working population from the unemployment rate in the labor-force series. A third is the utilization of industrial capacity, one measure of which is based on a comparison of the Federal Reserve Board industrial production indexes with estimates of industry capacity that are consistent with these indexes. Alternative estimates of industry capacity utilization are available from the federal government and private sources.

Economic Indicators   Leading, coincident, and lagging economic indicators correspond to different stages of the business cycle. They incorporate several of the macroeconomic series either directly or as derivatives. Sensitive statistics on the economy tend to have erratic short-term movements because of random shocks from the real world (e.g., oil price rises, strikes, policy changes). In this complex environment, the indicators are a useful tool for gauging the outlook for future business activity. They verify the present stage of the business cycle, suggest changes in the pace of economic activity in the immediate months ahead, and anticipate turning points at the peak and trough of business cycles. The sensitive indicators are provided by the Bureau of Economic Analysis and published in *Business Conditions Digest.*

Selected Statistical Topics

There are several technical aspects associated with the preparation of eonomic statistics. The more common ones are cited here.

Data Quality   The basic information for economic statistics comes from survey data and administrative reports to governments. Because of the dynamism and complexity of the economy, there is a continuing need to maintain and improve the content, reliability, and timeliness of the data sources. This includes refining concepts, definitions, survey methodology, benchmarking, etc., of existing series, as well as developing new measures. The pressures to improve the quality of the data as well as the development of new measures are balanced against other competing programs in allocating funding in the federal budget for additional resources and for the effect of such resources in adding to the reporting burden on the public.

Seasonality   There is considerable seasonal fluctuation in economic activity during the course of the year, resulting from weather changes, holidays, model-year changes, tax payment dates, etc., that affects different industries at different times of the year and at varying rates. Mathematical statistical procedures are used to remove the parameters of seasonal movements from individual data series in order to prevent seasonal highs and lows during the year from being interpreted as basic changes in the course of the economy. Although the procedures are highly sophisticated, the measurement and adjustment for seasonality continue to be a problem. Therefore, ongoing research is maintained to devise better means of adjusting for seasonal phenomena.

Index Numbers   Index numbers are a convenient method for summarizing many statistical series and easily determining the rate of change in the aggregate over time. The movement of index numbers can be affected by the selection of the base period (typically a year or group of years), which is set equal to 100 because the relative importance of the component items of the index is not constant. Index numbers are also sensitive to whether the relative importance, or weights, of the component items are fixed for one period, or if they are allowed to vary with time.

The differential effects of alternative weighting schemes can be measured (as in the case of the implicit GNP deflators, which are presented on three different weighting schemes). Although the economic significance of the difference is difficult to articulate, the measured variation suggests an upward and lower bound to the index movement. While there is no theoretically perfect conceptual basis for the construction of index numbers, the choice of a particular method is dictated by a judgment on the major use of the series. For example, the consumer price index has fixed weights for the base period because of the determination that users wish to measure price changes of a constant basket of goods and services.

Revisions   In monitoring current economic trends, policymakers need timely statistical measures of the economy. This necessitates the use of information that is reported from relatively small survey samples, incomplete records of survey respondents, errors in tabulations, etc. Such early information is labeled as "preliminary." As later, more complete and reliable information is obtained, the early series are revised. From time to time, the revised data give a somewhat different view of the state of the economy than was initially depicted. In these cases, the preliminary data might have signaled the need for economic policies at variance with the revised data. Sophisticated users of the data are aware of potential revisions in the timely information and attempt to verify recent trends before making policy recommendations. However, the possibility of significant revisions in preliminary data remains an uncertainty in the use of economic statistics.

Descriptions of Statistical Methodologies   In using economic data for analysis, it is important to have a basic understanding of the content and quality of the source information. Users can obtain documentation on the methodology used to construct the series from the agencies that provide the data. Abbreviated descriptions are available in the *Supplement* to the monthly series on *Economic Indicators* published by the Joint Economic Committee of Congress.

Statistical Standards   In order to ensure the accuracy, comparability, and objectivity of economic statistics, it is necessary that they be developed under a wide set of technical and policy standards. For accuracy, the methodology of data collection and processing should include the use of scientifically designed samples or universes of businesses, households, and other entities to be surveyed; checks on the validity of the reported data; and sound techniques for estimating data items from partial or indirect information. For comparability, the capability of relating one series to another depends on the use of uniform definitions and classifications such as those encompassed in the standard industrial classification (SIC), standard metropolitan statistical areas (MSAs), and standard occupational classification (SOC), as well as those which are harmonized with standards adopted by international organizations. For objectivity, the credibility of published data requires that statistical methodologies are documented and made available to the public, and that procedures are followed which safeguard against attempts to compromise the integrity of the data. Other uses of statistical standards include controlling reporting burdens on the public, ensuring the confidentiality of reported data, and establishing professional qualifications and job responsibilities for statisticians.

The Office of Federal Statistical Policy and Standards oversees the government-wide coordination of standards for federal statistics. A number of the standards are published as directives in its *Statistical Policy Handbook*.

Advisory Committees   The development of economic statistics is an evolutionary process that involves continued adaptation for providing the necessary data to analyze current-day economic issues and to refine the technical methodologies used in obtaining the information.

As part of this process, the federal government periodically convenes nongovernmental review groups to take stock of the present status and prescribe future directions for major economic statistical measures. These advisory committees are composed of recognized authorities in the field of economic statistics from universities, businesses, and research organizations. The advice given by these groups has been an important factor in the long-run development of statistical programs in the national economic accounts, prices, employment, and balance of payments.

In the latter part of the 1970s, four reports of this type have been published which promise to have an impact on macroeconomic statistics in the years ahead. The *Gross National Product Data Improvement Project Report* centered on strengthening the data base of the GNP and related measures in the economic accounts. *Counting the Labor Force* focused on developing new conceptual measures and refining existing ones on employment. *The Measurement and Interpretation of Productivity* considered ways of better identifying the extent of productivity change and the factors contributing to productivity improvement. *Improving the Monetary Aggregates* concentrated on strengthening the conceptual and measurement aspects of the money-stock measures.

References

General

Duncan, Joseph W., "Recent Developments in Reorganization of Statistical Policy," *Statistical Reporter*, U.S. Government Printing Office, April 1980; "Improving the Federal Statistical System: The Report of the President's Reorganization Project for the Federal Statistical System," *Statistical Reporter*, U.S. Government Printing Office, May 1980; Malkiel, Burton G., "Problems with the Federal Economic Statistical System and Some Alternatives for Improvement," *The American Statistician*, American Statistical Association, Washington, D.C., August 1978; Morgenstern, Oskar, *On the Accuracy of Economic Observations*, 2d ed., Princeton University Press, Princeton, N.J., 1963; Office of Federal Statistical Policy and Standards, *A Framework for Planning U. S. Federal Statistics for the 1980's*, U.S. Department of Commerce, 1978; Wonnacott, Thomas H., and Ronald J. Wonnacott, *Introductory Statistics for Business and Economics*, 2d ed., Wiley, New York, 1977.

Advisory Committees

The Advisory Committee on Gross National Product Data Improvement, *Gross National Product Data Improvement Project Report*, issued by the Office of Federal Statistical Policy and Standards, U.S. Department of Commerce, 1979; National Commission on Employment and Unemployment Statistics, *Counting the Labor Force*, 1979; Panel to Review Productivity Statistics, Committee on National Statistics, *The Measurement and Interpretation of Productivity*, National Academy of Sciences, Washington, D.C., 1979; Report of the Advisory Committee on Monetary Statistics, *Improving The Monetary Aggregates*, Board of Governors of the Federal Reserve System, June 1976.

Statistical Publications

Available as sales documents from the U.S. Government Printing Office, except for the *Federal Reserve Bulletin* (available from Board of Governors of the Federal Reserve System).

Economic Indicators, Joint Economic Committee of Congress, published monthly; *Federal Reserve Bulletin*, Board of Governors of the Federal Reserve System, published monthly; *Monthly Labor Review*, and *Employment and Earnings*, U.S. Department of Labor, published monthly; *Quarterly Financial Report for Manufacturing, Mining and Trade Corporations*, Federal Trade Commission, published quarterly; *Survey of Current Business*, and *Business Conditions Digest*, U.S. Department of Commerce, published monthly.

[See also Bureau of the Census; Bureau of Economic Analysis; Bureau of Labor Statistics; Consumer price index; Economic forecasts; Employment and unemployment; Federal Reserve System; Federal Trade Commission; Forecasting methods; Gross national product; Index numbers;

Industrial production index; Labor force; Money supply; Potential gross national product; Producer price index; Productivity; Profits measurement; Seasonal adjustment methods; Statistical techniques in economics and business, an overview]

Joseph W. Duncan and Norman Frumkin

Economic systems analysis (see Comparative economic systems, an overview)

Economic theory of interest (see Interest, economic theory of)

Economic theory of profits (see Profits in economic theory)

Economics

The term economics has assimilated so many connotations that it would be misleading to put a rigid meaning upon it by a single crisp definition. To say "economics is what economists do" could be useful if we knew just how to sort out economists from the rest of the world; but do we know? To say "economics is the study of allocation decisions about scarce resources" draws attention to an important focus of economic thinking, but it may imply an overemphasis upon theory and involves explanations as to why economics is not the science of card games or chess. To say "economics is the study of humankind in the ordinary business of life" conveys an edifyingly humanistic tone, but is too diffuse to make clear what is at stake. Most of these definitions, besides, may overstress "study." Whether or not it is studied, an economic aspect of human society is a fact of life: a society has an economics as it has a politics or a demographics.

A definition in the spirit of nineteenth-century economic thought is perhaps still the best: economics deals with aspects of human behavior related to the holding of goods and to flows of goods and services. It is concerned with production, allocation, ownership, valuation and consumption of goods and services, and of claims directly upon goods and services or based upon other layers of claims.

In dealing with these problems, economists have to assemble a mass of facts concerning what happens in the real world, to find ways to organize these facts in descriptive or historical patterns, to explain economic events and processes, to predict, to elucidate harmonies and conflicts of interest, to formulate alternative measures that might be adopted as public or private economic policies, to sort out the probable and possible effects of alternative policy measures, and to shape recommendations. In all these matters allowances must be made for uncertainty which reflects incomplete knowledge, for the freedom of action which exists for private and public decision makers (even though economists must tell people "you are not as free as you think,"), and for the events exogenous to economics which keep generating surprises. These exogenous events incude the vagaries of climate and of such biological parameters as bacteria and viruses, the evolution of pure and applied science, social changes which affect the way people cooperate and compete (for example, the recent sudden changes in human fertility and family organization), as well as the political processes that come to a head in elections and in intergovernmental wars.

Fundamental to economics is the existence of a network of interacting economic quantities. The economist must remember that to think in terms of the "behavior" of such quantities may introduce bias: after all, it is people and not things that behave. But such reminders about the human content of the quantities do not absolve the economist from the need to understand processes of interaction where many quantities are involved. The increasing prominence of mathematical thinking in economics thus relates to essential characteristics of this side of human existence. The concept of a set of simultaneous equations which link a number of variables is more than an analogy: it is an indispensable tool for understanding an important aspect of human relations.

The Evolution of Economics

Economics has evolved through controversy. Economists have never agreed easily or fully with each other, and one of the safer economic forecasts is that they never will. A number of recognizable schools of economic thinking have existed at various times and places, and there generally has been active competition between them as well as a considerable spread of views within each school. True, there is often repression of some schools within a given society. A Marxist view is obligatory for professional economists in Russia, China, and associated countries. In the United States and some other countries, there has been for generations a climate of opinion which has made it difficult for an economist to entertain Marxist views, or to avoid falling into uncritical advocacy of capitalist institutions and opinion slants. In Europe and in Japan, there has been more interplay of Marxist and non-Marxist approaches. And the present generation of economists in the English-speaking countries, while unwilling to abandon its own cultural traditions, is much less scornful of some sides of the Marxist tradition. The degree to which insights have been gained from Marxist analyses of production of commodities by means of commodities is a reminder that correctives are needed to the Western habit of opening the analysis of many questions by setting up models of exchange without production. (At the same time, the actual content of present Marxist views on production as on many other matters rests heavily on insights from the Western economic tradition.)

Widespread and systematic thinking about economics has been a by-product of the industrial revolution (and of its predecessor, the commercial revolution) and does not go much farther back than the seventeenth century. Adam Smith's *Wealth of Nations* (1776) is widely seen as the watershed between the rather inchoate mercantilist thinking and that of the classical school which flourished for about a century. (However, mercantilist thinking still flourishes in many important quarters, along with influential "just price" concepts of ancient origin, which too many economists suppose went out when Adam Smith came in.) The classical school, of which Marx may be considered a member, attempted to avoid problems of interdependence among economic variables by using the labor theory of value to explain pricing and resource endowment to determine production. Concerned largely with international trade, the classical economists put great emphasis on diminishing returns in food production as the work force grew relative to the natural-resource base, and on trade with land-rich economies to mitigate this process.

From the 1870s into the 1930s, the major influence in economic thinking was a neoclassical school, centered in England but powerfully reinforced by parallel tendencies in the Austrian school; and by the work of Irving Fisher and Frank W. Taussig in the United States and of Knut Wicksell in Sweden. Alfred Marshall, the most influential neoclassicist, stressed continuity with the classical thinking of Adam Smith, David Ricardo, and John Stuart Mill; he alsc made it unmistakable that we must deal with the interplay of supply and demand forces ("the two blades of the shears") rather than exaggerate the role of supply. The Austrian school, on the other hand, tended to overdo the reaction against excessive emphasis on supply, stressing the demand side under the banner of marginal utility as the source of value for commodities and services.

The mathematical school (or Lausanne school) also rose to prominence from about 1870. It was led by Léon Walras and his successor Vilfredo Pareto; W. Stanley Jevons in England and Fisher in the United States expressed similar tendencies. In place of the labored arithmetical examples of Ricardo and Marx, it became possible to deal with interdependence problems through the elegance of algebra. The seminal notion that the whole network of economic variables could be tied together in a model of general equilibrium expressed as a set of simultaneous equations took a long time to penetrate economic thinking, but by now is part of the consciousness of every serious economist.

In Germany and in many other countries a historical school contributed a major thread to economic thinking. The idea that historical perspective was essential to an understanding of the process of industrialization and urbanization, and to the spread of modern economic behavior into the new lands of European settlement and also into the countries already populated and with different traditional economies, was, of course, tremendously valuable. In the United States, there developed a powerful institutional school, which like the historical school tended to play down the importance of the theorizing central to the neoclassical and mathematical approaches. The institutionalists stressed the importance of understanding an economy in terms of its patterns of organization (corporations, trade unions, market practices, interest groups and their conflicts, and the impact of government).

The so-called Keynesian revolution led economists to shift emphasis from the traditional microeconomic problems to the macroeconomic problems of unemployment, price level changes, investment, and rates of economic development. In recent years there has been a return to emphasis on microeconomics, which is clearly warranted by the importance of problems of the environment (including externalities where important effects of operations that benefit or harm outsiders fail to enter the incentive structure of private decision makers), by concern with problems of economic structure and of development, and by the very real success of policies influenced by macroeconomics in abating problems of unemployment. Through these shifts, economists have become more and more aware that theoretical models need to be developed in relation to substantive problems, and that simplifying assumptions appropriate for approaching one problem may distort the view of another problem.

As quantitative formalizations penetrated economic thinking, there developed a powerful tendency to amplify and systematize the fact-finding work of the profession, and to coordinate information in such forms as the national accounts, input-output matrices, and flow-of-funds statistics in addition to such smaller constructs as indexes of production and prices. An econometric school developed, which strove to tie together mathematical-economic thinking and numerical evidence for the explanation of economic processes. Models for specific processes developed (starting with demand-supply relations for specific commodities); and beginning with the work of Jan Tinbergen and Lawrence Klein there began to be large models which tried to explain macroeconomic processes in the United States and other economies. A major by-product of econometrics has been the formalization of dynamic models which step outside the framework of static equilibrium and which have largely taken over the domain of business cycle theory.

Economics as a Profession

Economics is among the professions which have undergone a population explosion since World War II. Where economists used to be numbered in the thousands, they are now numbered in the tens of thousands. The academic world of economics has expanded. So has the employment of economists in government and in business. As with so many subjects, there has been in economics a fragmentation of learning. Those engaged in research and writing work in increasingly narrow specialties; the number of professional journals has increased, specialization among journals grows narrower, and there are fewer books and articles that are read by a large proportion of the profession.

The expansion of the field of economics is a worldwide phenomenon. At the opening of the postwar period, the position of the United States was predominant in economics as in so many other fields. This fact reflected in part the fact that the American profession, traditionally very open, had absorbed a number of talented European economists displaced by the war. For example, several of the recent presidents of the American Economic Association began their professional careers in Vienna. In addition, military service displaced study for a longer time in Europe and in Japan than in the United States, and in many countries academic disruption had been extreme during the 1930s. In any event, the American institution of the graduate school had few counterparts in other countries before World War II. There has been a great expansion in the number of centers where good economists can be trained, both in the United States and elsewhere. It is not an accident that most economists in the world have formed the habit of writing and thinking in English, and journals outside the English-speaking countries publish in English a large share of their articles. Despite the linguistic isolationism of the United States, the profession is still able to profit quickly from what goes on elsewhere. Not only the traditional Swedish or Dutch economist but the economist from Japan, Israel, India—or even Hungary or France—communicates effectively. Thus, in a time when the interaction of the U.S. and other economic systems is becoming much more important for Americans to understand, it is becoming harder to be altogether provincial.

Some Weaknesses in Present-Day Economics

The present state of economics leaves much to be desired. To begin with, economics is too isolated from related disciplines. The range of interdependence in social processes does not stop with the processes which the economist can describe in numbers. Proper allowance must somehow be made for the fact that noneconomic processes in society affect the context of economics and the way in which economic policy measures actually take hold on the economy. If the non-Marxist economist is going to reject the view that everything in society is determined by the mode of production, he or she should not adopt the view that everything which impinges on the economy is to be treated as accidental; nor should feedbacks into the economy be ignored which are channeled through noneconomic processes.

Admittedly, the other social sciences which in principle should be coordinated with economics may not be in an ideal state. The economist may also claim that he or she is more able than formerly to evaluate at least the political dimensions of society because so many colleagues are available who have been counselors to policymakers or have themselves been policymakers. But has not the economist an obligation to work harder on collaborations with social scientists and others from related fields, in hopes of creating a situation where better-qualified collaborators will become available?

Within economics itself, many broadening tendencies have faded. Economic history is more and more neglected—particularly the type of history which compares the evolution of different societies, for which "cliometrics"—quantitative history—is no substitute. The institutionalist tradition of understanding economic processes by study of law cases has died out except in the field of industrial organization. The traditional field of public utilities no longer exists in economics departments. The field of labor relations is also disappearing from the economist's interests. This fadeout of institutionalist approaches is partly compensated for by aspects of the fruitful work being done on "human capital," and by Herbert Simon's concern with the functioning of the decision-making groups which fill the place of the economist's "entrepreneur." But something has been lost as well as something gained on this side.

With important exceptions (notably inquiries into business plans for fixed investment), the assembly and synthesis of economic data are being left to specialized government organization, and regarded as too laborious and expensive for individual economic researchers or small institutes. The skill of piecing together the available basic information is becoming rare. Economists who use data tend to become nominalists, to disregard major discrepancies between the labels of economic series and their actual informational content, and to use series for purposes to which their informational content is not adapted.

The mechanism which students of monopolisic competition call product differentiation is, of course, at work in economics itself, and brings forth the expected result of too many varieties with too little actual variety. To offer for publication a product which is clearly distinct from what has gone before and yet does not call for the risk of disregarding fashion and engaging in a creative effort whose fruit may not be marketable, the safest path is to find a problem that grows out of recently fashionable work by some ingenious change in assumptions. A large proportion of the topics chosen for dissertations and articles are artificial and trivial.

Above all, economists are excessively pleased with analyses which prove too much. All too often, we come out with a finding which simply cannot be traced to the explicit informational content of the data going into the analysis; on close inspection, this proves to hinge upon information labeled "simplifying assumptions." A prominent example in the last few years has been the tendency to use models of so-called rational expectations to spread defeatism about prospects of improving the functioning of the economy through governmental stabilization policies. On closer inspection, rational expectations turn out in many cases to be (in the words of one candid model builder) "model-conforming": what economic actors would expect if they believed the economy functioned just like the highly artificial model under study. Economists engaged in such work show remarkably little curiosity as to how economic expectations and plans are actually formulated by the actors. Assumptions of equilibrium are applied much too casually. It might be beneficial to adopt as the official definition of an equilibrium "a situation which could arise even though expected" and to recognize that many actual situations are positions we would never have got into if we had not been aiming at something different.

Professional Journals

While professional journals on the whole address a specialized audience, two journals in particular are of general use.

1. The *American Economic Review* has for years published in its March number the latest presidential address before the American Economic Association. These papers show a series of very distinguished minds writing self-contained accounts of professional concerns about which they feel strongly.

2. The *Journal of Economic Literature* attempts to maintain communication within the economic profession despite tendencies to fragmentation. It reviews a large proportion of the significant books and prints abstracts of numerous articles. Its indexing and classification systems are admirably designed and evolve helpfully over time, and it facilitates search for work done on any special topic one may have in mind. It is also one of the main producers of survey articles which analyze economic events with respect to a series of important topics.

Albert Gailord Hart

Economics of discrimination (see Discrimination economics)

Economies of scale

Given the state of technology in an industry, a systematic relationship will exist between the size or scale of plants and firms operating in that industry and the lowest attainable level of the average cost of production and distribution. With size or scale measured in terms of the designed rate of output of the production facilities employed by the plant or firm, increases in the scale of production normally make possible reductions in average cost, at least to a certain size called the minimum optimal scale. The reductions in average cost made possible by increasing size are called economies of scale.

At Plant and Firm Level

Economies of scale can arise at both the plant level and the firm level. A plant is usually defined as a set of production facilities (buildings, machinery, etc.) at a single location. Increasing the scale of the plant often generates economies of scale by facilitating greater specialization in the use of labor resources, a source of efficiency first described by Adam Smith in 1776 in the *Wealth of Nations* and today exemplified by modern assembly-line methods of manufacture. In larger plants more effective use also may be made of managerial talent and of certain types of large-scale equipment, spreading the costs of these "indivisible" resources over a larger volume of output.

As plant size is expanded, eventually all opportunities for economies of scale are exhausted, and minimum optimal plant scale is reached. Still larger plant sizes are likely also to be optimally efficient, there typically being a range of optimal plant scales. Eventually, however, a point may be reached at which diseconomies of scale set in owing to either (1) rising transportation costs, as more and more output is shipped from a single location to more and more distant customers, or (2) the increasing difficulties of managing plants of ever-larger sizes, or both.

An individual firm can, and frequently does, operate more than one plant in the same industry. In some cases, further economies of scale, beyond those obtainable through the operation of a single plant of minimum optimal scale, may result from multiplant operations. Such economies may arise from more effective use of managerial talent, economies associated with large-scale distribution, or lower prices for purchased inputs. When significant multiplant economies exist, minimum optimal firm size will exceed minimum optimal plant size. Firm sizes larger than minimum optimal scale are likely to be optimally efficient also, at least to a point at which the increasing difficulties of managing and coordinating a large-scale enterprise may lead to the onset of diseconomies of scale.

Real and Pecuniary Economies

In the normative evaluation of economies of scale, an important distinction must be made between real and pecuniary economies. Real economies of scale are cost reductions which reflect genuine improvements in efficiency: fewer inputs are required to produce any given volume of output. Society clearly benefits since scarce resources are used more productively. Pecuniary economies of scale are cost reductions which simply reflect the ability of the larger firm to obtain inputs at lower prices through the exercise of monopsony power. The firm reaps a private benefit at the expense of its resource suppliers, but no improvement in the ratio of physical input to physical output, and hence no social benefit, is implied. For the most part, economies of large-scale plants, which are based on production technologies, are real. To the extent that they exist, some economies of multiplant operations are likely to be purely pecuniary in nature.

Industry Differences

The importance of economies of scale varies widely from industry to industry. In some industries, technological conditions will yield economies of scale extending over a wide range of output size, and only very large firms can be optimally efficient. In other industries, economies of scale can be fully exploited at relatively small scales. In any industry, the relationship between the minimum optimal firm size and the size of the market served by the industry is one of the most important determinants of the competitive structure of the industry and of its degree of seller concentration. In some industries this relationship will be such that the market demand can absorb the output of a large number of efficiently sized producers, and the industry will tend to be characterized by relatively low concentration, with many competing sellers. In other industries, market demand will be sufficient to absorb the output of only a few efficiently sized producers, and the market will tend to be oligopolistic with relatively high concentration, particularly if there is a significant cost disadvantage inherent in operating at suboptimal scales. Finally, at the extreme, economies of scale may be so extensive (or the market may be so small) that there is room for only one efficiently sized producer in the market. Again assuming that there is a significant cost disadvantage from operating at suboptimal scales, a condition of natural monopoly exists, with monopoly all but inevitable.

The actual incidence of economies of scale in particular industries and throughout the economy generally is an empirical question of great importance in the making of public policies toward industry, particularly in the areas of antitrust and regulation. Unfortunately, the research terrain has proved to be difficult, and while the question has been studied extensively by a number of leading economists, reliable estimates of the extent of economies of scale have been produced for only a relatively few industries in the United States, Great Britain, and a few other countries, primarily in the manufacturing sector. The empirical evidence to date, which varies widely in quality, would support several tentative generalizations for the United States. In most U.S. manufacturing industries, minimum optimal plant scales are small relative to the size of the national market, and real multiplant economies appear to be slight. Therefore, high market concentration, where it exists, is rarely a technological imperative. In fact, seller concentration often appears to be substantially higher than efficiency considerations would require. This latter result has apparently been abetted by the absence of any pervasive pattern of diseconomies of large firm size in American industry.

Of course, exceptions to these generalizations exist. A number of important industries can be characterized as natural oligopolies, and a few natural monopolies exist. Further, it must be noted that much additional research is needed, particularly on the nature and extent of multiplant economies of scale.

References

Bain, Joe S., *Barriers to New Competition*, Harvard University Press, Cambridge, Mass., 1956; Robinson, E. A. G., *The Structure of Competitive Industry*, University of Chicago Press, Chicago, 1958, 1st ed., 1931; Scherer, F. M., Alan Beckenstein, Eric Kaufer, and R. Dennis Murphy (with the assistance of Francine Bougeon-Maassen), *The Economics of Multiplant Operation*, Harvard University Press, Cambridge, Mass., 1975; Shepherd, William G., *The Economies of Industrial Organization*, Prentice-Hall, Inc., Englewood Cliffs, N.J., 1979, especially chaps. 11, 12.

(See *also* Advertising, economic aspects; Competition; Concentration of industry; Diminishing returns law; Integration; Mergers)

Brian C. Brush

Elasticity

In general, elasticity is the ratio of the relative change in a dependent variable to the relative change in an independent variable. The relative changes in the variables can be expressed in different ways. Here percentage changes will be used. For example, if the price of a product goes up by 1 percent, and if, other things remaining equal, the quantity bought goes down by 2 percent, the elasticity of that product is -2, that is, $-2/1$. Elasticity here is elasticity of demand, more particularly, price elasticity of demand. In public discussions of gasoline prices and of airline fares, for example, much attention goes to their elasticities.

Price elasticity of demand must always have been implicit in the minds of buyers and sellers. But the name itself and the exact definition are due to Alfred Marshall (*Principles of Economics*, 1890).

Coefficient of Price Elasticity

Price elasticity of demand is defined as

$$e_p = - \frac{\% \text{ change in quantity}}{\% \text{ change in price}}$$

where quantity is a function of price and where other variables (tastes, incomes, and the prices of related goods) are held constant. The coefficient of price elasticity is e_p, whose sign is negative owing to the inverse relation between quantity and price. Because it is a pure number, the coefficient makes it possible to compare the price elasticities of different products and services. Such comparisons can be conceptual or speculative; they can also come from quantitative estimates. Empirical studies of demand usually yield numerical estimates of price-elasticity coefficients.

Discussion of price elasticities usually centers on the absolute values of the coefficients, their negative signs being ignored. The coefficient can range in value from zero to infinity. Where the coefficient is zero, demand is said to be perfectly inelastic. The demand curve is a vertical line, which means that, no matter what the price, buyers would purchase the same quantity of the commodity. If demand for gasoline, for example, were perfectly inelastic, people would buy just as many gallons at $1 million per gallon as they would take if they could get it free. The example illustrates that zero price elasticity can be ruled out. Over some narrow range of possible prices, however, the coefficient can be close to zero. When the coefficient lies between zero and unity, demand is said to be inelastic. A coefficient with an absolute value of 0.1 means that demand is highly price-inelastic, whereas one of 0.9 is slightly inelastic. Empirical studies nearly always find the demands for farm products to be inelastic, sometimes highly so.

When the coefficient is equal to 1, demand has unit elasticity. An occasional empirical result, unit elasticity is often an assumption in applied theoretical work. When the coefficient is greater than unity, demand is said to be elastic. A coefficient of, say, 1.1 is slightly elastic; whereas one of, say, 5 is highly elastic. A coefficient of infinity does not apply to products bought in markets by many thousands of buyers, but it does indeed have meaning for the demand for a seller's product as seen by that seller. For example, demand is infinitely elastic for the output of any one wheat farmer, who could sell all of the farm's output at the prevailing price but who could sell nothing at a higher price.

Another insight into price elasticity of demand comes from looking at the effects of price changes on buyers' expenditures, which, of course, are the same sums of money as the sellers' receipts. A rise in price where demand is inelastic causes buyers to spend more on the smaller quanitity, and thus sellers receive more. This follows from the definition of price elasticity—a price rise with an inelastic demand means that the percentage change in quantity is less than the percentage change in price, and that therefore price multiplied by quantity increases. (The federal government's efforts to raise farm prices for the benefit of farmers have always been predicated on the inelastic demands for farm products.) Conversely, a price decline, when demand is inelastic, means that buyers spend less. Likewise, a price reduction where demand is elastic means that buyers spend more and that sellers receive more; a price increase means that buyers spend less.

Commodities with price-elastic demands are those with several close substitutes, with many uses, and with large positions in buyers' budgets. Substitution over time strongly influences price elasticity. The longer the period of time, the greater is the ease of substitution and thus the more elastic the demand. Price inelasticity characterizes commodities without close substitutes and, above all, commodities on which buyers spend small fractions of their budgets. The coefficient of price elasticity probably varies in size from one range of prices to another, because a good's substitutes depend on how high or how low its price might be. Statistical studies of demand, however, often use for convenience an assumption of constant price elasticity, i.e., no matter what the price, the size of the coefficient is always exactly the same.

The concept of price elasticity plays a prominent role in the theory of the unregulated profit-maximizing monopolist, for whom the optimum price is always in a range of prices where demand is elastic. Where such a monopolist can increase profits by dividing markets and charging different prices in the submarkets, he or she sets the lowest price in the submarket with the most elastic demand.

Coefficient of Income Elasticity

Changes in quantities bought can come from changes in buyers' incomes, as well as from changes in price. When demand is a function of incomes, prices and other variables being held constant, elasticity is income elasticity of demand. It is defined as

$$e_y = \frac{\%\text{ change in quantity}}{\%\text{ change in income}}$$

where e_y is the coefficient of income elasticity. With one exception, the sign of e_y is positive, which is to say that quantities purchased go up and down with incomes. When e_y lies between 0 and 1, income elasticity is said to be low, and when e_y is greater than 1, it is high. Products and services with low income elasticities are those occupying small positions in consumers' budgets. One way to define a necessity is to so name any good with a very low income elasticity. Such a definition is free of value judgments. Products with high income elasticities are those whose purchase takes large parts of consumers' budgets. These include the expensive durable goods. Thus, luxuries have high income elasticities. Although it looms large in family budgets, housing seems to have an income elasticity close to unity. Negative income elasticities apply to so-called inferior goods. For them increases in income cause declines in quantities bought. Just why inferior goods exist at all is explained by the theory of consumer behavior.

Coefficient of Cross Elasticity

Cross elasticity of demand concerns the relations between the quantities bought of one commodity and the prices of another. The demand for commodity A is a function of the price of commodity B. Held equal are tastes, incomes, and commodity A's price. Cross elasticity is defined as

$$e_{AB} = \frac{\%\text{ change in quantity of } A}{\%\text{ change in price of } B}$$

The sign of the coefficient e_{AB} is positive if A and B are substitutes. Thus, for example, a rise in the price of beef causes, other things being equal, an increase in the purchase of chicken. The size of the coefficient shows how close A and B are as substitutes.

Sometimes, in antitrust work, a monopolized product is defined as one whose cross elasticities with its substitutes are low. A negative coefficient signifies that A and B are complements.

The cross-elasticity formula is used as a way of expressing the competitiveness faced by a firm or firms. Thus, the formula can be set up to show the sales of firm C as they are affected by changes in the price charged by its rival, firm D. Many variations on this theme are possible.

Elasticity of Supply and of Substitution

Elasticity of supply is defined as

$$e_s = \frac{\% \text{ change in quantity}}{\% \text{ change in price}}$$

and is therefore symmetrical with price elasticity of demand. The coefficient is generally positive, i.e., larger quantities are sold at higher prices.

A complex concept, the elasticity of substitution is a property of production functions. It is a measure of the ease or difficulty of substituting capital for labor in response to a change in the ratio of the prices of labor and capital. In some production functions the elasticity of substitution is assumed to be unity; many empirical studies have also shown values close to unity. This means that a 1 percent increase in the ratio of the price of labor to the price of capital causes a 1 percent increase in the capital-labor ratio. The elasticity of substitution is also important in analysis of the shares of labor and capital in the national income.

Elasticity of Price Expectations

The elasticity of price expectations is a concept first proposed by J. R. Hicks in 1939. This elasticity is defined as the percentage change in expected future prices divided by the percentage change in current prices. The coefficient can be positive or negative. If it is positive and greater than unity, the elasticity of price expectations is high, meaning that buyers and sellers, seeing current prices go up, will then expect future prices to go up even more. When they act on this belief, they cause the very price increases they foresee. A high elasticity of price expectations, then, is unstabilizing. In contrast, a low elasticity means that increases in current prices are believed to cause smaller relative changes in expected future prices. And if the coefficient is zero or negative, current price increases are regarded as merely temporary. An important question, of course, is how widely shared are similar elasticities of price expectations at any one time.

References

Hirshleifer, Jack, *Price Theory and Applications*, Prentice-Hall, Englewood Cliffs, N.J., 1976, chap. 5; Miller, Roger L., *Intermediate Microeconomics*, McGraw-Hill, New York, 1978, chap. 5; Watson, Donald S., and Mary A. Holman, *Price Theory and Its Uses*, 4th ed., Houghton Mifflin, Boston, 1977, chaps. 3, 4.

(*See also* Competition; Consumer theory; Demand; Isoquant; Monopoly and oligopoly; Production function; Supply)

Donald S. Watson

Employment and unemployment

Prior to the world depression of the 1930s, there was little information about the dimensions and changes in employment and unemployment other than decennial censuses and some fragmentary current statistics from establishment reports and, in European countries, some administrative data from trade union or national unemployment insurance funds. This reflected both the state of the statistical arts and the absence of any great policy demands for such information on a current basis.

The definitions and procedures for current estimates of employment and unemployment were the result of experimental sample surveys in the final part of the 1930s, by the Works Progress Administration (WPA), for introduction into the 1940 census and for initiation of a monthly series on the labor-force status of the population. For the decennial census this meant the abandonment of the old concept of gainful occupation which, since 1820 in the United States, identified persons with an occupation by which they usually earned a living but said nothing as to whether they were employed or unemployed. Needed for the transformation was a current labor-force activity status classification by which the noninstitutional, civilian population (then over 14, now 16, years of age) would be divided into three parts: the employed, the unemployed, and those not in the labor force, i.e., all others, in some specific period of time. How to conduct such a survey has not proved altogether simple; it is still being debated after critical reviews by an interagency committee in 1948 and 1955, a presidential committee in 1962, and a congressionally created commission in 1970.

Activity Status in Time

The decision in 1940 to determine labor-force status as of a single week-rather than a day, a month, or year—has proved satisfactory enough. Some questions arise in counting as unemployed those persons who performed any work at all during the survey week, and in giving work priority over seeking work if the respondent had done both during the survey week. As a counterweight, looking for work is given priority over the status of "with a job but not at work" in the survey week. But in a count of the unemployed, job search could not be so simply limited to a single week, and has not been. Review committees wrestling with this problem have made recommendations to make more specific the time period and what constitutes looking for work.

Why persons should be classified as employed rather than unemployed, or out of the labor force rather than with a job, or looking for one, depends upon some underlying principle governing the survey classification and, in turn, upon the public policy purposes the survey was designed to serve. Some indications of the character and the aims of the new monthly survey in 1940 are implicit in the definitions and procedural rules, which have been little changed in 40 years, and they have been made fairly explicit by the continuing argument for changes in definitions, rules, and purposes. One common ground has been that the survey should provide some useful measures of jobs needed to serve public policy needs. The dispute has centered on how well current concepts and methods do so, whether in fact it is possible to provide an objective, measurable labor-supply type of count of jobholders plus job seekers equal to a full-employment demand for labor during periods of less than full employment.

A Competition-for-Jobs Model

The model that may be discerned in the original set of definitions and operating procedures—and largely to the present time despite some modifications—is one of job attachments and competition of unattached job seekers for available job openings. The jobless count resulting from the 1940 to 1957 definitions can be interpreted as the jobs necessary to be created over and above the number of jobs to which other persons are or believe they are attached. There was nothing surprising about counting as at work those who although looking for work did some work for pay or profit during the survey week, or counting as unemployed those with a job who did not work at all during the survey week but were looking for work. But what gave the labor-force survey its special character was its definitions and treatment of certain groups of inactive workers and of inactive job seekers.

Counted as employed were persons who were on layoff with definite instructions to return to work, within 30 days, or waiting to report to a new job, provided they were not seeking work; while counted as unemployed were persons laid off for an indefinite period even though they were not actively looking for work. Both groups were held to have some job attachment. The so-called discouraged workers, "who would have been looking for work except they believed no work was available in their line of work," were also regarded as having some measure of labor-market attachment in certain circumstances. Thus, the labor force untill 1957 consisted of those with a claim to a job and those without a claim to a job but wanting one (with some excuse if not looking).

The continuing technical problem during the years since 1940 has been how to achieve objectivity of the measurement on a current activity basis, and the political problem, how to ensure that such a labor-market concept of the labor force served the essential needs of employment and social policy.

Controversy and Changes in Labor-Force Measurement

From the very beginning the labor-force surveys have been the center of controversy because of the pronounced effects of the overall estimate of unemployment each month on public opinion, the Congress, and the presidential administration of the day. The common division of opinion is between those who think the figures are too high and exaggerate the need for public concern and action and those who think exactly the opposite. In 1961 media attacks on the scientific objectivity of the Bureau of Labor Statistics (BLS) and the Bureau of the Census led to the establishment of the President's Committee to Appraise Employment and Unemployment Statistics in view of their "vital importance as measures of the economic health and well-being of the nation" and as "guides to public policy in the development of measures designed to strengthen the economy, to improve programs to reemploy the unemployed and to provide assistance to those who remain unemployed."

In quite a changed economic environment 17 years later, in 1978, the Congress authorized the President to appoint a National Commission on Employment and Unemployment Statistics primarily for the reason that with the passage of time the series "may not fully reflect unemployment and employment trends, and may produce incomplete and, therefore, misleading conclusions, thus impairing the validity and utility of this critical economic indicator." Specifically, the Congress was concerned about the adequacy of the available state and local unemployment figures as used to allocate tens of billions of federal funds to the states and localities.

Members of this second public review group differed on matters of principle chiefly on one definitional and procedural question, namely, how to classify and measure discouraged workers, that had not been settled in the intervening years. By a 5 to 4 margin, the Commission in its 1979 report confirmed the essential character of the 1940 concepts as modified in 1957 and once again rejected the urgings of those who favor including as unemployed all persons who say they want work and would be available if a job were offered to them. Nonetheless, immediately thereafter, in the economic crisis at the end of 1979, there were many complaints that the current unemployment figures include too many people who do not need a job, thus giving support, it was felt, to unnecessary and inflationary labor-market measures.

The changes that have taken place since 1940 in the enumeration of the American labor force, in terms of a continuum of attachments to the labor market, may be summarized briefly.

With a Job but Not at Work   Prior to the 1962 Gordon Report the BLS changed the classification of persons on layoff with definite instructions to return to work from employed to unemployed. This breach of the with-a-job/without-a-job dichotomy, as recommended by the 1955 interagency Review of Concepts Subcommittee of the Bureau of the Budget, was justified on the ground that the promised recall to a job was uncertain and at the discretion of the employer; also it reflected a common-sense view of joblessness, especially since most were unemployment compensation recipients. Accordingly, since 1957 all persons on layoff are counted as unemployed, as are persons waiting to report to a new job within 30 days. The one remaining qualification was that these two groups of inactive workers be currently available for work although excused from the requirement of looking.

Able and Willing but Not Looking   How to classify discouraged workers, those not looking because of their belief that no job is available, has proved the most difficult conceptual issue debated by all the official review committees. In the original 1940 continuum of attachment to the labor force, they were regarded as in the labor force and unemployed. The 1955 Review of Concepts Subcommittee tentatively proposed that discouraged workers should be classified as unemployed only if they had looked for work in some way within 2 months. In 1962 the Gordon Committee endorsed this suggestion. Its chief complaints about existing procedures were that there was no direct question on the questionnaire for the interviewer to ask the respondent why he or she was not looking for work, and no time limit (4 weeks? 2 months?) within which either active or inactive job seekers must have tested the market. From 1940 to 1967 a discouraged worker was counted as unemployed only if he or she volunteered the information or, equally likely, if the interviewer knew the local situation well enough to classify the person as unemployed even though not looking.

The Gordon Committee asked the BLS to undertake research to determine whether or not the labor-market attachments of discouraged workers were any stronger than those of other persons currently classified as out of the labor force, and to consider setting an outer time limit for job seeking in any one of a number of ways to be specified in the questionnaire.

Since 1967, as a result, discouraged workers have been counted as unemployed in the official statistics only if upon direct questions they are found to have engaged in some job-seeking activity within the past 4 weeks, such as making inquiries of friends, relatives, or of employment agencies, and are available to work as of the time of the survey. The effect of this is that discouraged workers are enumerated but classified as out of the labor force. The same rule applied also to another category of inactive job seekers, those who would have been looking except for temporary illness. In fact, the same time limitation was made to apply to active and inactive job seekers alike.

This classification of discouraged workers as out of the labor force rather than unemployed, if they had not looked for work during the past 4 weeks, did not put the issue to rest. Professor Stanley Moses and others ("Planning for Full Employment," 1975) made this a central point of attack on American unemployment estimates, claiming that they underestimated the number of jobs needed to be created as an objective of economic policy. On this issue the members of the Commission on Employment and Unemployment Statistics agreed that current procedures for enumerating discouraged workers (as a special group outside the labor force) systematically tend to exclude certain groups such as full-time students and women with household responsibilities. The Commission concurred on certain procedural changes including a 6-month cutoff requirement for testing the labor market, for the better measurement of discouraged workers. The majority, however, refused to shift such discouraged workers back into the unemployed category because of evidence that their subsequent labor-market behavior was not significantly different from that of other persons outside the labor force. Their inclusion as unemployed, further, would not provide a better measure of potential labor supply, or jobs needed, because during expansions of employment the labor force grows by more than the number previously enumerated as discouraged workers.

Employment and Labor-Market Policy

For most of the postwar period, employment policy in the United States emphasized tax and expenditure measures to maintain employment—a derived demand—at or close to full-employment levels. The primary objective was to stabilize the economy at high levels of demand and thus minimize cyclical unemployment. Only within the past decade has monetary policy achieved perhaps a dominant emphasis in macro policy as price stability began to be given at least equal status with high employment in national economic policy.

As early as the beginning of the 1960s, these macro policies began to be supplemented by a new emphasis on labor-market measures. Under the rubric of "active manpower policy," these measures were designed (1) to minimize the volume of frictional unemployment, at any given level of demand, and (2) to reduce so-called structural unemployment which, in the short run at least, cannot be reduced by further expansion of aggregate monetary demand, or only with a great risk of fueling inflation. The policy included selective demand measures as well as traditional employment services and mobility measures to improve the functioning of the labor market, and thus was intended to improve the Phillips curve tradeoff by lowering the volume of unemployment consistent with price stability.

By the recession and recovery of 1974 to 1975 the distinction between macro and selective labor-market demand measures was blurred. In the special circumstances of the time, there was a heavy reliance on unemployment benefit payments—long regarded as a quantitatively significant automatic stabilizer at the macro level—in order to ease the hardship occasioned by the apparent necessity of a deflationary demand policy to combat inflation, and to permit the government to pursue such a policy without a political backlash. More significantly for current policy needs, job-creation projects and selective wage subsidies designed to increase employment and decrease unemployment among workers having little or no influence on wages or prices, i.e., whose unemployment was irrelevant to curbing inflation, began to be viewed as selective demand-management measures—even though, except for Public Service Employment, not quantitatively significant for American employment policy—to "cheat" the Phillips curve.

The particular character of American labor-market policy since 1960 has been determined by a number of special factors—the exaggerated fears of automation, the ensuing aggregate demand–structural unemployment controversy, the civil rights movement, and the war on poverty.

The Manpower Development and Training Act (MDTA) of 1962 was conceived against a background of a not too implausible fear of the displacement effects of the new technology. During the postwar years productivity had been running above the long-term trend. At the time of congressional consideration of the bill, the unemployment rate appeared to be continuing to rise to new highs both in the peaks and troughs of the successive business cycles. Crucial for congressional passage of this legislation designed to retrain experienced workers expected to be displaced by automation was the rise in unemployment among married men, reaching 4.6 percent in the spring of 1961. The new program was barely launched by the Office of Manpower, Automation, and Training when, with the decrease in unemployment of married men and an increase in unemployment of youth, the emphasis shifted away from training of displaced, experienced unemployed workers.

The Economic Opportunity Act of 1964 and amendments to the Manpower Development and Training Act confirmed the change in policy emphasis from retraining of experienced workers to employability training of the disadvantaged, to overcome their personal disabilities for adaptation in the job market. From the beginning of the new orientation there have been objections to the high degree of restriction of employment and training services to the underside of the labor force. In the years after 1973 and the transition from MDTA to CETA—the Comprehensive Training and Employment Act—there have been indications of some broadening tendencies. These appear to be consequences of the decentralization of the program to prime sponsors, and resulting community pressures, as well as recession-induced tendencies favoring services to a wider range of the working population.

International Comparisons of Unemployment

Comparison of employment and unemployment in the United States and other countries has become increasingly feasible since 1962 when the BLS first began to adjust foreign estimates, at the request of the Gordon Committee, to approximate the American current labor-force sample survey estimates. Since that time more countries have begun to publish sample survey data consistent with the definitions recommended by the International Labor Organization Conference of International Statisticians in 1954 fashioned after the U.S. labor-force concepts. Variations permitted within the ILO schemata, such as differences in the age cutoff depending on country differences in compulsory education, or inclusion of career military personnel in the labor force (as now recommended for the United States because of the new competition on the labor market for recruits for an all-volunteer armed forces), may require adjustments for comparability in the country series.

Currently published are quarterly and annual estimates for Germany, Great Britain, France, Italy, and Sweden in Western Europe, and for Japan, Canada, and Australia among the other leading industrial countries, adjusted to approximate the American statistics. The household survey data published by the various European countries are not necessarily the official figures. For purposes of comparability and timeliness of release, the nine member countries of the European Community continue to publish, as offical figures, unemployment estimates and rates derived from administrative data on the insured or registered unemployed.

The adjusted estimates for 1951 to 1961 prepared by the BLS for the Gordon Committee confirmed the commonly held view that joblessness was significantly higher in the United States and Canada than in Europe (other than Italy in that period) or Japan (no comparable data were then available for Australia). Recently published estimates for 1959 to 1978 show roughly the same results through the 1960s but a narrowing of the differential between the unemployment in the United States and in Germany, Great Britain, France, and Australia, possibly also Sweden and Japan, during the 1970s.

Assuming that the adjustments made by the BLS eliminate most of the incomparabilities in the estimates, why is it that the U.S. unemployment rates typically have run noticeably higher than in most other leading industrial countries? And why in more recent years does there appear to be some lessening of this spread?

The more rapid increase in population and labor force than in the European countries is one factor contributing to high U.S. joblessness. The changing proportions of youth in the labor force, however, has had a perverse effect, tending to decrease the U.S.-European differential in the earlier years and to raise it since the mid-1960s, for until then teenagers constituted a larger proportion of the labor force in Europe than in the United States. Similarly, teenage unemployment rates are higher in the United States than in the other countries, because of the much more common phenomenon of students in the labor force, but since 1970 European rates have risen more than in the United States. Much the same can be said in the case of the role of women: participation rates in the earlier years were higher in Europe and Japan and have tended to decline in more recent years relative to the United States. And again, with respect to agricultural and other self-employed or unpaid family workers, the greater proportion of wage earners in the American economy contributes to higher unemployment rates but to a lesser degree as more European workers move from farms to the cities.

The legal regularization of migrant workers from the less industrialized Mediterranean countries made it possible for the principal continental countries to expand or decrease the volume of migrant workers contracyclically, thus reducing unemployment, which is not the case in the United States. During the years of high unemployment since 1974, however, these countries, while restricting fresh inflows, have tended to tolerate larger numbers of migrant workers as the price of maintaining a supply of workers for jobs their own citizens do not want.

Since compositional factors do not seem to have strong explanatory value, one may hypothesize that the explanation for these differences in level, and changes in the direction of the trends observed, is to be found in the traditional security-mindedness of European society together with the constraints on mobility in the labor market, and the gradual erosion of these constraints from the early 1960s on. Labor-market behavior was governed by rules and regulations designed to ensure job security and resistance to economic change, with dismissals only *in extremis*. As a result there was little turnover and, hence, frictional unemployment, and much hoarding and underemployment, during the postwar years of fairly well-sustained full employment.

For these reasons cyclical fluctuations in demand tend to be reflected more fully in variations in employment and unemployment in the United States, especially because of the degree to which American employers resort to temporary layoffs through the unemployment insurance system. This practice is not common in Europe where separation from the payroll is ordinarily reserved for outright dismissal, hence the widespread recession use of government payments to workers on short-time schedules to maintain job connections and, one may suspect, to reduce the official unemployment count.

For years the forces of economic change, particularly new patterns of international trade and modernization of European industrial structures, were leading to widespread reorganizations and to redundancies of workers in declining firms and sectors. Structural unemployment was on the rise as reflected in the upward trend in unemployment in European countries since the beginning of the 1960s. The world crisis of 1973 to 1974 unleashed a backlog of dismissals, the severity of which were mitigated variously by government takeovers and bailouts to save communities, payments to persons on short-time work weeks in supposedly viable situations to avoid dispersal of company work forces, wage subsidies to encourage hiring of youth or special groups, as well as training and relief employment programs.

The immediate post-1975 experience in the United States proved remarkably different from that of other countries. In the United States, unemployment began to decline in the first quarter of 1976 while continuing to rise elsewhere through 1978 except for the beginning of a reversal in Germany and Great Britain. At that time the unemployment rate was lower in the United States than in Canada and Australia, marginally higher than Great Britain and France, but still substantially above that of Germany and Italy in the 3 percent range and Sweden and Japan in the low 2 percent range.

References

Counting the Labor Force, National Commission on Employment and Unemployment Statistics, 1979; "How Much Unemployment?," *Review of Economics and Statistics*, February 1950; *Interim Report of the Review of Concepts Subcommittee to the Committee on Labor Supply, Employment, and Unemployment Statistics*, U.S. Bureau of the Budget, 1955; International Comparisons of Unemployment, U.S. Bureau of Labor Statistics Bulletin 1979, 1978; *Joint Economic Committee Hearings*, "Employment and Unemployment Statistics," 84th Cong., 1st Sess., November 7–8, 1955; "Measuring Employment and Unemployment," President's Committee to Appraise Employment and Unemployment Statistics, 1962; "Planning for Full Employment," *The Annals*, American Academy of Political and Social Science, Philadelphia, March 1975.

(See *also* Economic statistics; Labor force; Phillips curve; Statistical techniques in economics and business, an overview)

Charles D. Stewart

Energy costs

Energy is required as an intermediate good in producing other goods and services. Energy costs, therefore, are the amounts that are paid for the energy used in producing these other goods and services. For example, consumers purchase electricity, natural gas, and a host of petroleum products. But it is the heat, light, cooling, and transportation produced by the energy which are the products desired, not the energy itself.

In addition to direct use of energy to produce other goods and services, substantial amounts are used in producing, converting, and transporting energy supplies. For example, the production of electricity from primary energy forms (especially coal, but also large amounts of petroleum and natural gas) accounted for 22 percent of all U.S. energy consumption in 1978, measured in heat units. So energy costs are incurred at all levels, from primary products of mine, farm, and forest, to household production.

Energy and Economic Activity

Historians and others have pointed to the close relationship between energy use and economic development. The industrial revolution of the eighteenth and nineteenth centuries may be described in terms of an enormous increase in energy consumption, at first in the manufacturing of metals and textiles, later in transportation and chemicals manufacture. A similar, earlier revolution occurred in the neolithic period, when the discovery of agriculture and the domestication of animals led to the conversion of solar energy for human use. A great increase in living standards, paralleling that of the industrial revolution, took place in the neolithic period. Today, we can observe a strong, though far from perfect, correlation between energy consumption per capita and real income per capita across nations. The less-developed nations consume far less energy per person than the wealthier nations.

Until the late 1950s, the United States was a net exporter of energy. But low-cost petroleum, mainly from the Middle East, won an increasing share of the U.S. market so that by 1973, net energy imports represented 17 percent of all energy consumption. Concern about energy costs was heightened by the Arab oil embargo of 1973 to 1974, which reduced the flow of petroleum imports, and by the sharp increases in oil prices which followed the actions of the OPEC (Organization of Petroleum Exporting Countries) cartel.

The Arab embargo created great concern over possible economic disruption from use of the "oil weapon." The 1973–75 recession, which was the worst since World War II, is attributable in large part to the embargo and accompanying oil price hikes. World oil prices, which had been rising since 1970, were quadrupled in 1973 and have been increases several times since then. Net imports of energy, meanwhile, have risen to nearly 25 percent of total consumption by the end of the 1970s. The high prices for imported oil have caused a substantial and persistent deficit in the U.S. balance of payments.

Domestic wholesale energy prices, though partially controlled, have also risen substantially, largely as a result of the OPEC actions. From December 1973 to December 1978, for example, they rose 120 percent. This intensified domestic inflation.

Energy Conservation

A major method of dealing with energy problems, strongly supported by the federal government, is the promotion of energy conservation. (Another method is, of course, the expansion of domestic energy production.) Energy conservation has led to some controversy in both popular and technical discussion. The basic question is whether or not energy use can be constrained to a lower rate of growth in the future than in the past without serious consequences for the economy. That is, does energy conservation mean penury or merely adjustment? One aspect of the discussion has centered on whether energy and capital are complements or substitutes in industrial production. Complementarity suggests that growth in capital equipment will of necessity result in increased energy use, thus implying penury as a consequence of energy conservation. The issue remains undecided; scholarly studies variously have supported either complementarity or substitutability.

Energy Efficiency

A second aspect of energy costs is concerned with the efficiency of energy use in the United States. Many students of energy problems maintain that the United States is an energy waster, consuming large amounts of energy unnecessarily. In this connection, comparisons are made with other nations which have similar levels of income per capita. The United States and Canada generally fare poorly in such comparisons. However, other analysts point out that energy prices are generally lower in the United States and Canada than in other developed nations, both before and after the 1973 developments, partly because of differential government policies and partly because of natural-resource endowments; U.S. and Canadian energy consumption patterns, it is argued, are therefore largely the result of low relative energy prices.

Since 1970, energy consumption (in heat units) per dollar of gross national product (in constant prices) has been declining in the United States; and, since 1973, the rate of decline has accelerated. These developments coincide with changes in relative energy prices, and imply that an adjustment to the new price situation is underway. Recent changes in energy consumption patterns have been in the form of reductions in the relative importance of goods that use large amounts of energy in their production. That is, conservation of energy is taking place, in the short run, in the form of changes in product mix.

References

Cipolla, Carlo M., The Economic History of World Population, Penguin, New York, 1978; Energy Information Administration, Monthly Energy Review, Annual Report to Congress, U.S. Department of Energy; Halvorsen, Robert, "Energy Substitution in U.S. Manufacturing," The Review of Economics and Statistics, vol. 59, no. 4, November 1977, pp. 381–388; Richardson, Harry W., Economic Aspects of the Energy Crisis, Lexington Books, Lexington, Mass., 1975.

(See also Externalities)

John G. Myers

Entrepreneurial ability, a factor of production

Of the factors of production, entrepreneurial ability (or capacity) is the most difficult to define and quantify and, given the rise of the corporate form of organization of firms, is the most difficult to identify as a specific factor. The entrepreneur may be viewed as an individual specific to the firm who has decided to become the residual income recipient rather than entering into some contractual agreement for his or her services (i.e., rental of services). Hence, the entrepreneur uses human capital in combination with other "hired" inputs to produce a product and receives as income the residual (i.e., profit). While it is virtually impossible to define this factor of production explicitly, it is possible to distinguish the factor from labor by enumerating some of the unique functions performed. The entrepreneur (1) collects and organizes the hired inputs into a production process; (2) innovates both in terms of output and the production process; (3) manages the day-to-day operation of the firm; and (4) as the residual claimant, bears the risk associated with the firm.

The concept of the entrepreneur is more closely associated with the owner-managed firm (e.g., a sole proprietorship). In the modern corporation, the hired manager or executive may indeed perform some entrepreneural functions. This input thus incorporates both labor and entrepreneurial ability for which part of the compensation must be viewed as profit rather than as wages. (Indeed, executive compensation plans which include shares of stock or profit sharing may well reflect this feature as well as an attempt on the part of the firm to have this hired input perform more like a classical entrepreneur.) Furthermore, the returns received by the individual shareholders also include profit since the shareholders bear risk (albeit limited)—a function of the entrepreneur. Thus, the workings of the corporate form of organization have had the effect of spreading the functions of the entrepreneur to several inputs, making the identification of entrepreneurial ability as a specific factor of production almost impossible.

Pros and Cons

Alfred Marshall was one of the earliest writers specifically to consider entrepreneurial ability as a factor of production and as the residual income recipient. In this context, he showed that these skills, like the hired factors, capital, labor, and land, represent a cost of production to the firm. That is, without the entrepreneur to collect and organize the hired inputs, production would be impossible; so the return to the factor, profit, must be regarded as a cost of operation in the same way that interest, wages, and rent are considered costs. Indeed, this view has led economists to subdivide profit into normal and economic profits, where normal profit is that amount necessary to keep the entrepreneur involved in the activity and economic profit is any in excess of normal. Hence, normal profit must be viewed as the opportunity cost of the entrepreneur. The concept of the entrepreneur as an innovator was developed primarily by Joseph Schumpeter, while Nicholas Kaldor emphasized the role of the manager and Frank H. Knight stressed the risk-bearing function.

In recent decades, discussion of the entrepreneur as a specific factor of production has diminished. The concept of firm-specific entrepreneurial ability has been presented as a possible explanation for the existence of many firms in a given market in that, since this factor is fixed and firm-specific, diseconomies of scale may be encountered. Other recent literature compares the classical entrepreneur-controlled firm with alternative forms of organization (e.g., cooperatives and stockholder-owner corporations) and attempts to explain the choice of organization on the basis of property rights considerations as well as information and transaction costs. Building on the work of Ludwig von Mises, the Austrian economists have reasserted the crucial role of the entrepreneur in the market process, stressing the view of the entrepreneur as arbitrageur.

References

Alchian, A. A., and H. Demsetz, "Production, Information Costs, and Economic Organization," *American Economic Review*, vol. 58, December 1972, pp. 777–795; Ekelund, R. B., and R. F. Hebert, *A History of Economic Theory and Method*, McGraw-Hill, New York, 1975; Friedman, M., *Price Theory*, Aldine, Chicago, 1976; Kirzner, I. M., *Competition and Entrepreneurship*, University of Chicago Press, Chicago, 1973.

(*See also* Factors of production)

Charles W. Smithson

Environmental costs

The term environmental costs is usually understood to mean environmental pollution-control costs. The shorthand is unfortunate since some have innocently used the expression as a substitute for pollution damages, that is, the costs society suffers because of pollution. Given its more usual interpretation, the word "cost" in the term environmental costs has the same meaning that it has in benefit-cost analysis. Consequently, it ideally should refer to the true opportunity costs of a policy or strategy intended to reduce the level of pollution. Opportunity costs refer to what society foregoes in order to shift resources toward the policy.

Breaking Down Pollution-Control Costs

It is often important to distinguish between pollution-control costs engendered by policy and pollution-control costs that have other origins such as "good will" or profitability. Complete discharge of valuable raw materials is clearly not in the interest of the profit-maximizing firm. Neither is it in the firm's interest to eliminate completely the discharge of raw materials since the costs of control will eventually exceed the value of recovered raw materials. Generally there is an ideal profit-maximizing level of control somewhere between these two extremes. If one is interested in assessing the costs of governmental pollution-control policy, it should be recognized that this policy is usually not necessary to force a rational polluter to eliminate that amount of discharge that would be eliminated in any event in the interests of profitability. Therefore, the costs associated with this amount of discharge should not be considered as costs of pollution-control policy. Only the unprofitable control costs engendered by the policy should be so considered.

Unfortunately, given the standard accounting practices used by firms, in practice it is extremely difficult to separate out the unprofitable control costs from the profitable costs. Often engineering analysis and good judgment must be intelligently integrated with the available cost data. The task is further complicated because the data often represent expenditure information and not cost information. Expenditure data differ from cost data in that they are influenced by the firm's institutional setting. For example, two firms with the identical control costs may generate different expenditure data depending on such factors as whether certain inputs necessary for control, such as land, are already owned by the firm or whether they must be purchased or rented.

Identifying the truly incremental costs of pollution-control policy is also complicated by severe joint-cost problems. While many pollution problems can be attacked at the point where residuals are discharged to the environment (so-called end-of-pipe controls), often it is cheaper to reduce residuals through either process changes, input changes, product-mix changes, or a combination of these strategies in addition to end-of-pipe controls. Thus, facing pollution restrictions, a firm might decide to discontinue the production of one of its products and to produce the remaining products with a different technique requiring new investment and annual outlays for materials. Since capital replacement and material purchases are an ordinary occurrence, it would be a mistake to attribute all these outlays to the pollution-control strategy. However, estimating the portion of the outlays exclusively engendered by the control strategy requires a complex analytical effort.

Most current pollution-control cost estimates are extremely short-run in that they implicitly assume that the polluter faces fixed demands. The longer-run implications of product substitution, declines in investments, effects on innovation, and managerial efficiency (in both the public and private sectors), that conceivably could result from costly environmental regulatory programs, are usually not reflected in the cost figures. However, recent analyses of the effects of regulation on productivity and a growing concern about the administrative burden, on the private sector, of a large number of regulations is stimulating researchers to broaden their concepts of environmental costs to include the longer-run and indirect implications of policy.

References

Cremeans, John E., and Frank W. Segal, "National Expenditures for Pollution Abatement and Control, 1972," *Survey of Current Business*, vol. 55, no. 2, February 1975; Hanke, Steve H., and Ivors Gutmanis, "Estimates of Industrial Waterborne Residuals Control Costs: A Review of Concepts, Methodology, and Empirical Results," in Henry M. Peskin and Eugene P. Seskin (eds.) *Cost Benefit Analysis and Water Pollution Policy*, Urban Institute, Washington, D.C., 1975; U.S. Bureau of the Census, *Pollution Abatement Costs and Expenditures, 1976*, MA-200 (76)-2, 1977.

(*See also* Externalities; Government regulation of business)

Henry M. Peskin

Escalator clause

An escalator clause is a provision of a contract that calls for the adjustment of the contract price or prices to reflect fully, or to some degree, changes in specific prices and costs or in the general rate of inflation. The use of escalator clauses in contracts is predicated on expectations that the purchasing power of the dollar will change. Escalator clauses are generally more widely used when purchasing power is changing markedly and/or when the contract extends over a long period of time—particularly time periods beyond what might be viewed as a period in which future price changes may be known with some degree of certainty.

The types of contracts in which escalator clauses are most frequently found are multiyear wage agreements, long-term leases for both commercial and residential property, alimony agreements, social security and other government-financed retirement programs, and long-term procurement contracts.

The Index Used

The parties who elect to include escalator clauses in their contracts usually rely on one or more of several official U.S. government measures of prices and other costs. Government series are usually selected because of the impartiality with which they are compiled, ease of access, frequency of publication, absence of major revisions, and the likelihood that such indexes, without major alteration, will be published for a long time into the future.

The series actually selected usually bears some relationship to the price that is being escalated. If an escalation index were to be used to adjust a wage contract for future price inflation, then the consumer price index (CPI), representing changes in the purchasing power of the dollar with respect to things bought by consumers, would usually be the series used. The CPI may also be relevant for the escalation of alimony payments and retirement benefits which, like wages, are used to purchase a bundle of consumer goods. For rents and other long-run procurement contracts, there is usually no single index that is appropriate. Users frequently construct their own from various component price index series. For example, a landlord and commercial tenant may select for escalation of their long-term lease the CPI component for residential rent, the CPI for fuel oil and electricity, and a series on wages paid to individuals in the service industry (some of whom may service the commercial building). The three series would be added up using appropriate weights.

A company in a defense industry holding a long-term contract with the federal government for armaments may employ an escalator based on a weighted average of wages paid in the industry and the various materials, such as steel and nonferrous metals, used to produce the armaments. Wage-rate series, like most price series, are published by the Bureau of Labor Statistics and are available in considerable detail on a monthly basis. Series on the prices of commodities manufacturers buy to transform into products produced under long-term contracts are usually obtained from the producer price index (PPI), which contains monthly price indexes for some 3000 industrial commodities.

Escalation Formulas

The contract may call for escalation in an exact step with the index used for escalation. For example, if the CPI rises 10 percent in the first year of a labor contract, wages may be increased by 10 percent. However, sometimes the increase in wages may be based on a formula which calls for translation into a given number of cents of wage increase per percentage points of change in the index being used for escalation. Under these circumstances, the percentage change in wages may not be equal to the percentage change in the price index used for escalation. And sometimes the formula may provide for an increase in wages equal to half the increase in prices or some other fraction. Finally, some contracts provide what are called caps, which limit the amount of escalation vis-à-vis the increase in prices. For example, a provision might be that wages will be raised by three-quarters of the percentage increase in prices up to a limit of 5 percent in any given year.

Importance to the Economy

There are various measures of the dollar volume of transactions in the U.S. economy that are subject to escalation. A recent study of users of the PPI for escalation found that contracts valued at more than $100 billion were escalated by these indexes. Contracts covering at least six million unionized workers are escalated by the CPI.

Escalator clauses provide some kind of insurance that neither party to a contract will benefit unduly as a result of unforeseen inflation. Whether or not such clauses themselves contribute to inflation has been widely and inconclusively debated. It is clear, however, that their use has become increasingly pervasive over the last decade and they are considered an important tool for use in adjusting for inflation.

References

BLS Series for Use in Escalation Clauses, U.S. Department of Labor, Bureau of Labor Statistics, Regional Report 46, Atlanta, Georgia, August 1978; Cunningham, Francis S., "The Use of Price Indexes in Escalator Contracts," Monthly Labor Review, BLS Reprint No. 2424, Bureau of Labor Statistics, August 1963; Escalation and the CPI: Information for Users, U.S. Department of Labor, Bureau of Labor Statistics, Washington, 1978; Escalation and Producer Price Indexes: A Guide for Contracting Parties, Bureau of Labor Statistics, Report 570, September 1979.

(See also Consumer price index; Inflation; Producer price index; Value of the dollar)

Joel Popkin

Estate and gift taxation (see Taxation, an overview)

Eurodollar market

The Eurodollar market is an international telephone and telex network located in the world's major financial centers in which banks bid for and offer dollar balances, typically, but not always, with the aid of specialized brokerage institutions. It is the most important sector of the Eurocurrency market in which banks accept deposits denominated in currencies other than those of the country in which they are located. Thus, Eurodollars are dollar balances held in banks outside the United States by residents and nonresidents of this country. They come into existence when a U.S. or foreign holder of dollar deposits in a U.S. bank instructs the bank to credit the deposits to an account in the United States held by a foreign bank. Similarly, Euro-deutsche mark deposits are deutsche mark–denominated liabilities of banks outside Germany. The intermediaries in the market are the world's major banking institutions. They either redeposit the balances that they accept with other banks, either in dollars or after conversion to third currencies in the foreign exchange market, or they relend them to end users such as multinational corporations, governments, central banks, public corporations, or large institutional investors.

Importance of Eurodollar Market

The emergence of the Eurodollar market in the late 1950s, its gradual rise to prominence in the world's monetary system, and its explosive growth during the last decade is one of the most significant events in recent financial history. By the end of the 1970s the market, together with that for several other Eurocurrencies had reached a gross size of more than $900 billion. Its net size (after deducting interbank deposits) added up to more than $500 billion. The market has become the dominant channel for the international movement of capital. It is the principal depository for the liquid reserves of innumerable commercial banks throughout the world. For many central banks it has become the major investment outlet for their monetary reserves. It serves as an important receptacle for the cash reserves of multinational corporations and for a broad variety of nonbank financial institutions. The market has added immensely to the ability of banks in many countries to reach out for huge amounts of resources outside their own relatively narrow domestic markets and to provide financing for their customers as well as to seek out new customers. Its syndicated loan sector outpaces by a very substantial margin the International Monetary Fund as a source of funds for balance of payments support. As a source of financial aid to less-developed countries, this sector plays a far more important role than the aggregate credit extensions of the World Bank and similar institutions. Eurobanks, as banks active in the Eurocurrency markets are often called, are not only suppliers of short-term funds, but have become increasingly major intermediaries in the international capital formation process.

History

The market emerged in the mid-1950s when several banks in Eastern Europe, because of fear of attachment of their balances in U.S. banks, shifted them to their correspondents in Western Europe. A few banks' banks in London, Rome, and Milan then recognized the potential uses for foreign currency balances and began to solicit them actively from their banking friends. The market in its early stages received considerable support as a result of the British decision to curtail sharply the use of sterling in international trade transactions, a decision which greatly stimulated the demand of European banks for dollar balances for the purpose of financing Western Europe's exports and imports.

By the late fifties, the rudiments of the market had been formed, but its size at the time did not exceed a few billion dollars. Toward the end of the fifties, Federal Reserve Board regulatory restrictions began to exert a stimulatory effect on the market, as money-market rates in the United States rose well above the maximum interest rates that U.S. banks were allowed to pay under the Board's regulation Q. On top of this, banks in Europe desirous of earning a return on their fast-growing short-term dollar balances turned to the Eurodollar market since U.S. banks were not permitted to pay interest on balances maturing in less than 30 days.

During the sixties, expansion was greatly aided by several additional regulatory measures adopted by the U.S. government. The voluntary and mandatory restraints on capital outflows adopted in 1965 in response to the President's balance of payments program forced U.S. banks and their multinational customers to look to the Eurodollar market for covering their overseas financing needs. Their worldwide search for dollar balances to provide financing from offshore locations through overseas branches and affiliates gave the market a very significant lift. Moreover, in 1966 and again in 1968 to 1970, the head offices of U.S. banks became major users of Eurodollars themselves in order to offset large time-deposit losses resulting from the Federal Reserve Board's refusal to lift regulation Q ceilings even though open-market rates in the United States had risen well above these ceilings. Thus, the use of regulation Q as a monetary policy instrument drove the major U.S. banks into the Eurodollar market in order to regain their ability to cover their credit-line commitments to major customers.

Another important stimulus to the expansion of the market emerged in the 1970s when a number of OPEC countries began to accumulate huge balance of payments surpluses, a large part of which found a resting place in the market. Eurodollars became one of the principal investment vehicles for the oil exporters of the Middle East. At the same time, central banks and a number of other depositors offered increasing amounts of funds in the market that represented the counterpart of the large balance of payments deficits of the United States during the early 1970s. The tendency of many central banks, including the Federal Reserve, to inject substantial amounts of funds into their monetary systems to stimulate their economies or to finance budget deficits was another reason for the extensive liquidity in the market. Very often this liquidity did not find outlets in domestic loan markets and was shifted to the Eurodollar market, which then recycled excess funds to countries requiring additional resources to finance their oil and other payments requirments.

Apart from specific supply and demand developments the major cause of the explosive growth of the market has been a number of efficiencies that characterize it. Among them are the great convenience of making uncollateralized deposits over the telephone and telex, the freedom from restrictions often imposed on transactions between domestic banking systems and nonresidents, and the freedom from reserve requirements and concentration on large transactions with major banks at low administrative costs.

Market Problems

The phenomenal surge of outstanding deposit liabilities of Eurobanks has created some disquietude and concern among central banks and supervisory agencies and even among thoughtful market participants. It also has attracted the attention of the academic profession and has led to heated debates among economists on major theoretical and practical issues. Much of this concern has focused on the alleged contribution of the market to world inflationary pressures. In this context, several prominent economists have charged that the Eurodollar market can create credit on a large scale through its own lending operations. By applying the standard textbook treatment of credit and deposit creation, these economists have claimed that Eurobanks, unconstrained by reserve requirements, can as a group create deposits or credit by some multiple of their primary deposit inflows and therefore should be considered an engine of world inflation.

Another common criticism of the Eurodollar market has been that it has become a major source of financing currency speculation and thereby has contributed greatly to exchange rate instability. It has been claimed that the market is a pool of liquidity from which weak currencies, such as the dollar, can be borrowed in large amount to finance hedging and speculation in favor of strong currencies.

Many policymakers and some market observers have been unhappy because borrowers have been accommodated at excessively liberal maturities and at spreads over the cost of funds so low that they leave very little profit considering the risks associated with such loans. Moreover, it has been alleged that the ease and cheapness of these loans have made it easy for borrowing countries to avoid desirable balance of payments and monetary policy adjustments, thereby prolonging the conditions that initially prompted the borrowing country to resort to the market.

These criticisms and allegations reflect a considerable amount of unease among governments and central banks which have come to look upon the huge capital movements associated with the market as a major source of domestic and international monetary instability. As a result, such governments and central banks are actively cooperating in a search for ways and means to bring the markets under some measure of restraint through a variety of controls and surveillance measures, few of which appear to show much promise. The dilemmas for domestic and international monetary policy posed by the market will not easily be resolved.

References

Bell, Geoffrey, *The Eurodollar Market and the International Financial System*, Halsted Press, New York, 1974; Einzig, Paul, *The Euro-Dollar System: Practice and Theory of International Interest Rates*, Macmillan, London, 1973; Klopstock, Fred H., "Money Creation in the Eurodollar Market—A Note on Professor Friedman's Views," *Monthly Review*, Federal Reserve Bank of New York, New York, July 1970; Machlup, Fritz, "The Eurodollar System and Its Control," *International Monetary Problems*, American Enterprise Institute, Washington, D.C., 1972; Prochnow, Herbert (ed.), *The Eurodollar*, Rand-McNally for the University of Wisconsin, Madison, 1970.

(*See also* Financial institutions; Financial instruments; Foreign exchange rates; Interest rates; International economics, an overview)

Fred H. Klopstock

European Economic Community

The purpose of the European Economic Community (EEC) is to promote the harmonious development of economic activities, balanced expansion, increased stability, a rising standard of living, and closer relations among the member countries. Among the primary goals of the EEC are the elimination of customs duties and quotas; the establishment of a common tariff and commercial policy in contrast to other countries; the free movement of persons, services, and capital; and the establishment of a common policy pertaining to agriculture and transport.

History

The EEC was established by the Rome Treaty signed on March 25, 1957, and entered into force in January 1958. The EEC was preceded by the European Coal and Steel Community (ECSC), which became effective in July 1952 and created a common market in coal and steel for Belgium, France, Germany, Italy, Luxembourg, and the Netherlands. The Rome Treaty not only established the EEC but also Euratom, providing for a common European Atomic Energy Community.

The EEC quickly moved toward the accomplishment of its major goals: in December 1961, all quantitative restrictions on industrial goods trade among member countries were abolished; in July 1967, a common agricultural policy was enunciated; in July 1968, a common market was established that provided for the free movement of goods and labor and a common external tariff. Certain provisions for the preferential treatment of other countries, pertaining mainly to Africa, were first laid down in the Yaoundé Convention of 1964 and revised by the Lomé Convention of 1975. In July 1967, the ECSC, Euratom, and the EEC institutions were merged into a single set of governing organizations, which has become known as the European Community.

In January 1973, Denmark, Italy, and the United Kingdom became associated with the EEC, and a system of free trade agreements in industrial commodities was negotiated with the members of the European Free Trade Association (EFTA). The European Monetary Agreement was instituted in March 1979, laying the foundation for increasing financial integration and a system of fixed but adjustable exchange rates, a common unit of account, and the eventual formation of a European Monetary Fund. The first direct elections to the European Parliament were held in June 1979. Greece is scheduled to join the European Communities as a full-fledged member in 1981, and membership negotiations with Portugal and Spain are in progress. Turkey is an associate member.

Organization

The Treaty of Rome established four central institutions for the governance of the EEC: the European Parliament, the Council of Ministers, the Commission, and the Court of Justice. Each one of these institutions has, and continues to play, a unique role in the governance of the European community of nations.

The European Parliament, located in Strasbourg, France, was initially appointed by the legislatures of the constituent countries. In June 1979, the first direct elections to the European Parliament took place. It should be noted that the representation in the European Parliament is along political, not national, lines. That is, the Parliament is essentially a community body and not a body representing the various member nations. The Parliament exercises control over the Commission by its power to question the Commission on points of substance and to force the resignation of the Commission as a whole by a vote of no confidence. The Parliament also has certain financial powers, including the codetermination of the budget.

The Commissioners of the European Community are appointed on proposal by the member governments for 4 years. The Commissioners are solely responsible to the European Community and the Parliament, and not to the various national governments. The Commission is the guardian and executor of the Treaty, being responsible for the implementation of its provisions. The Commission is empowered to draw up regulations to implement the treaty. These regulations have the power of law after being approved by the Council. In general, all community actions have to emanate from the Commission.

The Council represents the various member governments of the communities and has to ratify the actions proposed by the Commission. It is important to note that the Council can act only on proposals put forth by the Commission. It can adopt proposals of the Commission by majority vote, but can amend them only by unanimous consent of all member countries. The Parliament is to be consulted before an important Commission proposal is submitted to the Council for action.

The European Community, acting through the Commission and the Council, can act through the following: the adoption of regulations that have the power of law in every member country; the issuance of directives that call upon member countries for the implementation of certain policies; the adoption of decisions that are binding upon the public or private body addressed; or the promulgation of recommendations that are purely advisory in nature.

The Court of Justice is composed of nine judges, one representing each member country. The Court is responsible for the interpretation of the EEC treaties and the adjudication of any conflicts arising among the member countries in the implementation of the treaties.

Given the broad charter of the EEC, it is evident that the organization has broad responsibilities that transcend narrowly defined national and functional concerns. In the international arena, the EEC represents the member countries in a wide variety of international organizations, in particular those incorporated in the United Nations family. The functional role of the EEC includes the further development and coordination of economic, social, environmental, legislative, and political concerns of the European community of nations.

References

General Report on the Activities of the European Communities, European Economic Community, Brussels and Luxembourg, published annually.

(*See also* International economics, an overview)

H. Robert Heller

Exchange rates (see Foreign exchange rates)

Excise tax (see Taxation, an overview)

Expectations

It is a truism of economic thinking that what people do is influenced not only by events that have occurred in the past but also by expectations regarding events that have yet to occur. In its extreme form truism has the homely characteristics of common sense. If one expected the world to end tomorrow, the relation between one's wealth, current income, and consumption would be dramatically different from what it would be if one expected the world to continue indefinitely. On a less drastic level, if one confidently expected prices to double over the next year, one's willingness to hold assets of various kinds would be different from what it would be if one expected prices to be at the same level a year hence. And if one were a 40-year-old parent with three children approaching college age, one's behavior would be very different from what it would be if one were a nonparent under identical circumstances.

While all economists recognize the crucial importance of expectations about future events in conditioning present behavior, economic analysis generally is not characterized by serious attempts to measure expectations, or to incorporate expectations into empirical work. Rather, most economic analysis tends to incorporate expectational notions into either theory or empirical work by formulations that focus on the stabilities inherent in economic life.

Adaptive Expectations

For example, a widely used method of incorporating expectational phenomena into economic thinking is to treat behavior as adaptive to the difference between expected and realized events. Phillip Cagan's classic analysis of hyperinflation is a good case in point (1956). The problem is to explain behavior under conditions where the rates of increase in prices are extreme. In Cagan's model, buyers expecting certain rates of price increase observed that actual rates of price increase were different, and revised expectations (adapted to past error) by changing the next period's expectations by some proportion of the difference between last period's expected and actual outcomes. Thus, during a period of accelerating inflation, people would continually expect lower rates of price increase than are actually realized, since the adaptive behavior reflected in the model never quite catches up with actual events.

Cobweb Theory

An even earlier version of reaction to differences between expected and actual outcomes, which contained no provision for learning from past errors, is represented by the cobweb theory, devised to explain the relationship between agricultural prices and supply. In this expectational model, farmers had no basis for gauging next year's price except to assume it would be the same as this year's price. Production (planting) decisions for next year's supply were made on the basis of this year's price, extrapolated into next year as a forecast. Thus, if the current price were low because of abundant supply, farmers would restrict production because they expected next year's price to be equally low. But the resulting supply shortage would actually result in high rather than low prices next year. Thus, high prices would be observed next year, and when farmers extrapolated that year's high price to the following year, they would greatly expand production—again expecting the (high) price of that year to continue into the next year. The greatly augmented supply would therefore result in low prices, and so on. Depending on which assumptions are made about the responsiveness of supply and demand functions to price, this model indicates a situation of continually widening swings in both prices and production, with no tendency toward stable equilibrium.

In both the adaptive expectations and cobweb models, the role of expectations is handled by assumptions of extraordinary simplicity. The cobweb model assumes that nobody noticed that high prices one year would be followed by low prices the next year, and that there was no alternative to forecasting next year's price except by the assumption that it would be the same as this year's. Thus, in the cobweb theory, nobody learns from past experience. In the adaptive expectations theory, people learn from experience, but the nature of their learning is sharply circumscribed. For example, one would suppose that the reaction function between previous expectations and previous outcomes would depend on some of the serial properties of that difference. If people underguessed for several years in a row, one might expect them to adjust expectations by more than the difference between last year's expectation and last year's outcome, rather than by some fraction of the difference. More generally, one would like to suppose that the nature of the adaptation to past experience would itself be a variable rather than a constant.

Rational Expectations Theory

The most popular current theory dealing with expectational phenomena is known as the rational expectations theory. Here, it is argued that people make guesses about the future on the basis of the best information available to them at the time that a decision must be made. People are assumed to have enough information about the causes of future events, that is, to have a sufficiently good model of what determines the future, to behave in such a way that only genuinely new information will have an influence on either expectations or behavior. The model does not say that expectations are always accurate—indeed, forecasting errors are to be expected simply because forecasting models are not perfect. But the error embodied in such models is expected to have specific properties—not to be biased in terms of sign, and, of course, not to be predictable.

The proponents of rational expectations theory initially set out to explain why it was difficult to be consistently successful in certain kinds of speculative markets—securities, commodities, etc. In such markets, it may well be true that all existing information has been assimilated into decisions, that a sufficiently large number of people are continually concerned with improving forecasts of relevant variables so that only genuinely new information gives anyone an advantage, and, thus, that the spirit of rational expectations is indeed captured in market behavior. Attempts to extend the domain of rational expectations theory into problems of macroeconomic policy seem to be less successful, or at least are commonly judged to be so by many economists.

These models—adaptive expectations, the cobweb theory, and rational expectations—all have a number of elements in common. They are concerned solely with expected values of relevant variables, that is, with the average or mean expectation, and are not concerned with the fact that expectations are in essence a probability distribution with dispersion (variance) as well as central tendency (mean). All infer the structure of expectations from observed errors models where expectational phenomena are replaced by lagged values of nonexpectational phenomena. And all point to the dubiousness of attempts to obtain direct measures of expectations, on the ground that true expectations are reflected by behavior and not by statements about the future obtained from economic actors.

Direct Measure of Expectational Phenomena

A body of research on expectational phenomena, which stands somewhat outside the mainstream of economics in the United States, takes issue with the propositions inherent in traditional expectational models. Its origins can probably be traced to the Swedish school of economics. An important feature of expectational analysis in this tradition is the importance given to uncertainty, or, alternatively, to the dispersion of expected values, in contrast to concentration on the mean or average expectation.

A given expectation associated with a small variance of possible outcomes will not necessarily lead to the same behavioral response as the same mean expectation associated with a large variance. In the first case, possible outcomes do not differ very much from the mean expected outcome, and the appropriate response may in effect ignore the variance. But when the variance of possible outcomes is large, different forces comes into play which will often lead to different behavioral implications. For example, an entrepreneur facing an expected sales function with a given mean and a large dispersion will design a plant with greater flexibility than if faced with the same mean expected sales and less variance. And consumers, faced with a given mean expected income and a high variance would be apt to take a more conservative stance than if faced with the same expectation but lower variance, simply because the cost of "surprises" is not symmetrical. The work by Albert Hart on business decision making, and by F. Thomas Juster on consumer behavior, explores this area more fully.

A related line of economic thinking, which has its roots more in psychological theory than economic theory, stresses a decision process which comes out of the interplay of past economic events, reactions to those events as forming persistent habits reflected in behavior, and modification of those persistent habits as a consequence of new information or new circumstances. This way of thinking about economic phenomena stresses not so much expectations—thought of as probability statements relating to future events—but rather a set of perceptions about the world that can be usefully described by terms such as attitudes, aspirations, and values.

For example, will a continued increase in real income lead to greater satisfaction with living standards, a feeling of satiation with consumer goods, and thus a higher rate of personal saving? In some theoretical formulations, that consequence would be expected. But writers such as George Katona (1951) point out that the realization of consumption goals is likely to lead to the formulation of more ambitious goals, while failure to reach goals may lead to a downward adjustment of goals rather than increased efforts to attain them.

An important difference between those who deal with expectations by implicit theorizing based on a structure of observed forecasting errors, and those who deal with expectations empirically, lies in the priorities given to measuring expectational phenomena and to the appropriate methods for empirical modeling of behavior. Implicit theorizing, whether it be adaptive expectations, cobweb theory, or rational expectations, infers the structure of expectations from the statistical properties of forecasting errors and places little priority on measuring expectational phenomena directly. Those who see expectations as coming from a complex structure dealing with the interplay of past events, probability distributions of expected outcomes, and perceptions of an attitudinal cast argue that there is no substitute for direct measurement of the expectations held by relevant economic actors like business executives and consumers.

On the side of appropriate models of behavior, the implicit expectations school, as well as many of those who argue for direct measurement of expectational phenomena, see behavioral relationships as sufficiently stable to warrant the use of time series data to gauge future events from the structure of past relationships. Theorists who focus on the way in which psychological perceptions act as a filter in determining the relationship of events, expectations, and aspirations to behavior are apt to believe that time series models will inevitably be misspecified, in that the future cannot be well forecast from knowledge of the particular structure existing in the past.

References

Cagan, Phillip, "The Monetary Dynamics of Hyperinflation," in Milton Friedman (ed), *Studies in the Quantity Theory of Money*, University of Chicago Press, Chicago, 1956, pp. 25-117 (excerpts are reprinted as "The Theory of Hyperinflation," in R. J. Ball and Peter Doyle (eds.), *Inflation: Selected Readings*, Penguin Modern Economics, Penguin, Middlesex, England, 1969, pp. 117-135); Ezekiel, Mordecai, "The Cobweb Theorem," *Quarterly Journal of Economics*, February 1938, pp. 255-280; Hart, Albert G., *Anticipations, Uncertainty, and Dynamic Planning*, Studies in Business Administration, vol. XI, no. 1, University of Chicago Press, Chicago, 1940; Juster, F. Thomas, and L. D. Taylor, "Towards a Theory of Saving Behavior," *American Economic Review*, vol. 65, no. 2, May 1975, pp. 203-209; Katona, George, *Psychological Analysis of Economic Behavior*, 1st ed., McGraw-Hill, New York, 1951; Lindahl, Erik R., *Studies in the Theory of Money and Capital*, Allen and Unwin, London, 1939; Lucas, Robert E., Jr., "Expectations and the Neutrality of Money," *Journal of Economic Theory*, vol. 4, no. 2., April 1972, pp. 103-124; Muth, John F., "Rational Expectations and the Theory of Price Movements," *Econometrica*, vol. 29, no. 3, July 1961, pp. 315-335.

(*See also* Behavioral economics; Cobweb theorem)

F. Thomas Juster

Exports

Exports are, in the conduct of foreign trade, goods taken from one country into another country with the first country the exporter, the second the importer. The U.S. Bureau of the Census publishes monthly data on U.S. exports on two bases: seasonally adjusted and unadjusted. The method for seasonal adjustment was changed in January 1979 and backdated. The analyst of U.S. monthly export data should, therefore, be sure that, in the entire series used, the same seasonal adjustment method has been applied.

Conceptual Differences

In addition to monthly export statistics, the Balance of Payments Division of the U.S. Department of Commerce reports U.S. exports on a quarterly basis. These data are adjusted for various conceptual differences from the monthly series in order to make them comparable with other elements of the U.S. balance of payments. The main adjustments are for military sales, reconciliation with Canadian statistics, private gift parcels, and exports from the Virgin Islands.

In statements of the balance of payments and in national income accounts, the term exports is often used to mean total exports of services as well as goods. The main export services of the United States are military sales, tourist expenditures in the United States, transportation earnings of the United States, and earnings from U.S. investments abroad.

In the U.S. national income accounts the term "net exports" is applied to the overall balance of payments impact on the U.S. gross national product. Like the balance on goods and services it is thus the difference between exports and imports of goods and services, but there are conceptual differences between the balance of payments and national income definitions.

Importance of Export Growth

In the period from 1963 to 1977 the volume of world exports increased an estimated 180 percent compared with an estimated 125 percent rise in world industrial production. Thus, the role of exports has become more important. For the United States moreover, the policy significance of exports has changed greatly. In the period between 1949 and 1971, when the value of the U.S. dollar was fixed under the Bretton Woods system, exports were viewed mainly as an addition to total aggregate demand and thus as a contribution to U.S. economic growth.

With the breakdown of the Bretton Woods system, however merchandise exports came to be regarded as more critical than might have been indicated by their relatively small proportion of total gross national product—about 6.7 percent in 1978. With a floating dollar it was recognized that without rising exports the U.S. trade balance would deteriorate, the dollar would devalue, and prices of imports would rise and influence the overall U.S. price level.

Thus, a growing consciousness has developed in the United States that export growth is critical to stability in the U.S. economy. This consciousness became stronger when the cost of U.S. imports was raised drastically in late 1973 after the major oil-exporting countries adopted a more than fourfold increase in the price of oil.

Reasons for Poor Showing in Exports

However, widespread consciousness of the U.S. need to export has not resulted in sustained trade balance improvement. In fact, the U.S. trade balance (balance of payments basis), after improving to a $9.0 billion surplus in 1975, swung to a record $34.1 billion deficit in 1978. This adverse swing in the trade balance was only partly explained by rising oil imports. A substantial part of the deficit was due to the out-of-phase relationship during 1978 between the United States and other major countries: U.S. economic growth in 1978 was significantly more rapid than in most other developed countries. This difference led to the so-called locomotive theory that world trade might be equilibrated if other countries raised their growth rates in line with those of the United States. The locomotive theory met resistance, however, since it is widely argued that too much stimulus to growth will only exacerbate worldwide inflation.

The poor showing of U.S. exports in 1977 to 1978 may also have been affected initially by U.S. inflation, which in 1978 tended to run ahead of the rest of the world and, therefore, may have undermined the competitive position of some U.S. exports. Inflation in the United States was, however, more than offset by depreciation of the U.S. dollar in 1978. But in the short run the impact of devaluation on exports may be counterproductive because of the so-called J curve. The J curve arises because, when a country devalues, the prices of its exports decline with respect to countries whose currencies have not devalued. The devaluing country expects to gain in export volume because its prices are lower. But, immediately following a devaluation, export volume may not rise rapidly enough to offset the decline in export prices. Thus, the value of exports may decline in the short run.

Aside from the quantifiable effects of incomes and relative prices on exports, there are significant nonquantifiable influences. In spite of their growing importance, exports amount to a smaller percentage of the U.S. gross national product compared with other major countries where this percentage can be as high as 50 percent. Thus, the U.S. manufacturer may emphasize exports in his overall business planning far less than would be done by some major U.S. competitors, notably Japan. And this lack of emphasis may be reflected in unaggressive marketing and product development not adapted to foreign markets.

References

Hein, John, "United States Exports in World Markets," *The Conference Board Information Bulletin,* The Conference Board, New York, December 1978; Junz, H. B., and R. R. Rhomberg, "Price Competitiveness in Export Trade Among Industrial Countries," *American Economic Review,* vol. 63, no. 2 May 1973; pp. 412–418; Kenan, Peter B., *A Model of the U. S. Balance of Payments,* D. C. Heath, Lexington, Mass., 1978; Kindleberger, Charles, and Peter H. Lindert, *International Economics,* 6th ed., Irwin, Homewood, Ill., 1978; Quinn, Melanie R., and James H. Sood, "Cutting Through the Maze of Trade Data Classification," *Columbia Journal of World Business,* Fall 1978, pp. 54–71.

(*See also* Barriers to trade; Comparative advantage theory; Dumping; Foreign exchange rates; General Agreement on Tariffs and Trade; Imports; International economics, an overview; Net exports in GNP; Protectionism)

James L. Burtle

Externalities

Externalities have been a part of economic theory since first discussed by Alfred Marshall, but since about 1960 the term has been expanded and employed more widely in economic analysis. An externality exists when an activity by one or more parties affects, for good or bad, another one or more parties who are not a part of, or are external to, the activity. Expressed another way, externalities result from a failure of private costs (or benefits) to equal social costs (or benefits), and economic inefficiency is the consequence.

Several common examples illustrate the problem. Steel production causes smoke which damages the health and property of those who live near the plant. These nearby residents are external to decisions to produce steel but are damaged by that activity. Each of many fishermen who flock to a superior fishing site reduces the catch of all others there, imposing costs on them. External benefits arise when one homeowner keeps an attractive house and lot and adds to the pleasure of the neighbors.

If these external costs are ignored by the steel producers and the fishermen as they determine their costs and level of output, their steel and fish will be priced below the social cost of production and their output will be inefficiently high. Similarly, if the homeowner considers only his or her own pleasure, home maintenance will be assigned an artificially low price and will be below the socially optimum level.

Pecuniary and Technological Externalities

These examples typify the current emphasis on externalities. However, Marshall's original discussion of external diseconomies dealt with one firm purchasing a resource and bidding up its price for all other users. Was the true marginal cost of the resource, then, only the market price paid by the firm, or should it include the increase in cost paid by all other users? Later analysis showed that the higher payments made by others represented rent to owners of the resource and that the market price paid for the resource was the price that would promote economic efficiency. A similar problem concerned external economies, which were shown to result from the lower prices of a decreasing-cost firm, supplying increasing amounts of some product to firms in another industry. However, no generally accepted proposal evolved for promoting Pareto optimality in this case.

The externalities described by Marshall were later classified as pecuniary, inasmuch as they produced changes in prices of goods and services which were taken into account by other buyers and sellers. The newer externalities, resulting from smoke, congestion, and well-kept lawns, were classified as technological, because they presumably affected the technical patterns of production and consumption by individuals. There was no price mechanism for dealing with these problems, and an extensive literature developed treating them as a form of market failure.

Ronald Coase's seminal article (1960) showed how technological externalities might be treated within accepted economic theory. He pointed out that negative externalities, such as smoke in the air, occur because people are using some asset without paying for it—in this case, air quality. Were the asset owned and competitively priced, as Frank Knight earlier had suggested, a social optimum would be obtained.

Coase also stressed the importance of transactions costs. While there might be social gain from less pollution, the cost of bringing parties together and effecting a trade for greater purity might exceed the gain. Many writers continue to consider such a case a market failure, but others have pointed out that transactions costs, like transportation costs, are real and must be considered if a social optimum is sought.

Perhaps Coase's most important contribution was to point out that externalities are bilateral. When smoke from a mill bothers nearby residents, the mill imposes external costs on them. But if laws are enacted to reduce the output of smoke, the neighbors impose external costs on the nearby mill. If natural forces of wind and gravity prevail, consumers of steel will gain at the expense of the neighbors who would like air of higher quality. If the law allows the neighbors to prevail, they will gain cleaner air at the expense of those who prefer more steel. Economists have recognized that the Pareto optimum level of pollution (or purity) is where the marginal benefit of additional purity is equal to the marginal cost of providing it, and this does not often call for complete elimination of pollution as we usually think of the term.

Policies to Deal with Externalities

Three broad policies have been advanced to deal with externalities.

1. Where transactions costs are high, government, it is argued, may instead regulate those affected by externalities to produce a Pareto optimum. There is strong empirical evidence, however, that these regulations often produce an equally inefficient or worse level of externalities by requiring levels of purity above the optimum.

2. Taxes may be levied on those creating negative externalities and subsidies paid to those creating positive externalities. These sums are more accurately characterized as charges (instead of taxes) for the use of some asset, or payments (instead of subsidies) for providing the services of an asset. Again, there is the practical problem of determining how large the payments should be and who should pay and be paid.

3. Where it is possible to designate the asset that two or more parties are seeking to use in mutually exclusive ways, property rights can be established and the owner would charge the users of the asset. This solution recognizes scarcity and treats the asset like other privately owned scarce assets.

Many other problems may be analyzed as examples of externalities, or spillovers, or neighborhood effects. Congestion, for example, occurs when too many parties try to use some asset, such as a highway. Because the price is below the optimum, each user imposes a cost on other users. Public goods and joint products may be considered a form of positive externalities in that when a good is produced to provide a service to one consumer, others may enjoy it at little or no cost. The problem of the free rider arises from other users seeking to benefit without paying. Even monopoly has been treated as an externality where the transactions costs of consumers bargaining for lower marginal prices exceed the gains they would realize.

References

Coase, R. H., "The Problem of Social Cost," *Journal of Law and Economics*, vol. 3, October 1960, pp. 1–44; Dahlman, Carl J., "The Problem of Externality," *Journal of Law and Economics*, vol. 22, no. 1, April 1979, pp. 141–162; Macaulay, Hugh, and Bruce Yandle, *Environmental Use and the Market*, Lexington Books, Lexington, Mass., 1977, pp. 39–42, pp. 113–122; Mishan, E. J., "The Post-War Literature on Externalities: An Interpretative Essay," *Journal of Economic Literature*, vol. 9, no. 1, March 1971, pp. 1–28.

(*See also* Economic rent; Energy costs; Environmental costs; Government regulation of business; Marginal cost; Scarcity)

Hugh Macaulay

Factor cost

Factor cost refers to the method of valuing product and income in terms of the factors of production rather than the market price. It is used most often in connection with the valuation of net national product and/or national income. With respect to net national product, factor-cost valuation measures what it costs to produce the output of the nation in terms of the payments to the factors of production employed. With respect to national income, factor-cost valuation measures the income which the factors of production are paid for their services. Factor-cost valuation is in contrast to market price valuation which measures output and/or income in terms of the prices paid for goods and services on the market. Thus, gross national income and product at market prices reflect what gross output of the nation is sold for on the market and how the receipts generated from such sales are allocated among all of the costs incurred by producers including nonfactor costs such as capital-consumption allowances and indirect tax payments to the government (e.g., sales and excise taxes).

The rationale behind factor-cost valuation is that it provides a measurement of the factors of production which are used in creating national income and product and, thus, represents a measure of the resources used. The concept of the factors of production has roots in both classical and neoclassical economic literature. The classical economists Adam Smith and David Ricardo held the view that land and labor constituted the factors of production. Karl Marx in *Das Kapital* held that any value in excess of the payments to labor constituted surplus value, in effect that part of value which belonged to labor but was appropriated by the capitalists. Neoclassical economists took the position that, in addition to land and labor, capital was a factor of production. The factor return to capital has generally been considered to include interest and profit and represents payment for the use of capital, risk taking, and entrepreneurship.

Factor-cost valuation has been of primary importance in measuring national income and in analyzing the allocation of resources in the economy. In examining specific industries, factor cost measurements can indicate what resources are used to produce a given output. In those cases where an industry pays substantial excise taxes, the factor costs of production may be considerably less than the market value of the output. Thus, for example, tobacco products sell for much higher prices on the market than indicated by their factor costs, because of the heavy excise taxes which are levied upon them. For this reason, the payments made directly to the factors of production are considered to be more appropriate for showing how the economy's productive resources are allocated to various industries.

Factor Cost Can Be Misleading

As a measure of resource utilization, however, factor-cost valuation can often be misleading. Only under conditions of perfect competition, where producers and consumers have full knowledge and where resources are completely mobile, will factor-cost valuations accurately reflect actual resource utilization. In statistical terms, factor costs are measured by the payments made to the factors of production, but these payments would only be equal to factor costs under conditions of competitive equilibrium. Thus, low factor payments in a given industry may reflect (1) the use of less productive resources, (2) reduced returns due to depressed demand conditions, or (3) reduced returns due to oversupply of resources in the industry. To assume that factor-cost valuation reflects resource utilization is to assume that resources are in fact correctly allocated. For this reason, factor-cost valuation cannot be used to measure the extent to which resources are misallocated.

Although the concepts of national income and net national product at factor cost are still widely used by many countries, gross domestic product and gross national product valued at market prices are the basic economic constructs used in the national income accounts of most countries. In part this fact has been due to increased interest in the expenditure breakdown of final output which is measured in market prices and contains gross capital formation rather than net capital formation. It also reflects an interest on the income side of the account in showing all the charges against gross output including both capital consumption allowances and indirect taxes paid by producers.

References

Ruggles, Richard, and Nancy D. Ruggles, *National Income Accounts and Income Analysis*, 2nd ed., McGraw-Hill, New York, 1956.

(*See also* Gross national product; National income accounting)

Richard Ruggles and Nancy D. Ruggles

Factors of production

Factors of production are those inputs employed in the production of goods and services. The factors are traditionally classified under four broad headings—capital, labor, land, and entrepreneurial ability. The factor returns (or payments) corresponding to these categories are respectively interest, wages, rent, and profit.

Capital

Capital is a commodity itself used in the production of goods and services. Thus, capital must be viewed as a man-made input created to permit production in the future. In this context, capital is similar to saving in the sense that it represents current consumption which has been foregone in order to obtain future production and consumption. While this physical definition of capital clearly diverges from the concept of money capital in the financial markets, it should be noted that firms normally acquire such money capital in order to obtain the physical capital actually used in production. Two features of capital as a factor of production are particularly noteworthy. First, capital is a heterogeneous rather than a homogeneous commodity. This feature was central to the so-called Cambridge criticism of neoclassical capital theory. In order to accommodate this feature, the concept of embodied technical change was developed in order to consider a heterogeneous capital stock consisting of different vintages of capital. Second, capital is acquired by a firm as a durable stock, but it is employed as a flow. That is, the firm actually employs the flow of services generated by the capital stock in the production process, rather than the stock itself. This feature requires that the flow of services be imputed for a given stock of capital and that some user price be calculated for the flow.

Labor

Labor represents the services of human inputs in the production process. However, raw human power is not itself generally employed; rather, the firm requires the ability to apply effort. Hence, labor, like physical capital, represents the flow of services generated by a heterogeneous stock of human capital. The effectiveness of this stock of human capital and, therefore, the effectiveness of the flow of labor services generated are determined by the amounts of education, training, health maintenance, and mobility applied to the basic human input. Thus, the distinction between capital and labor is blurred since both involve the services generated by a stock of capital—one physical, the other human—as well as investment decisions based on potential returns.

Land

Land represents the services of natural, untransformed resources. Included is not only land as commonly defined but also other natural resources, as long as they are in their natural state. Once the resource is extracted or transformed, it consists of both land and capital. For instance, crude oil is land before it is extracted or refined, but once processed, the refined petroleum used in another production process not only incorporates some capital but also possesses characteristics of a capital good, i.e., the petroleum is a commodity used in the production of other goods and services. The distinction between land and capital is—like the distinction between labor and capital—blurred further by the fact that land is also acquired by the firm as a stock but is used as a flow. Indeed, agricultural land is more like physical capital since it can be renewed and, therefore, may be viewed as a commodity produced to be used in the production of other goods and services. The primary distinguishing feature of land as a natural resource is its inherent dynamic nature. Since it is depletable, the rate of usage or extraction in the current period affects the rate of usage or extraction in future periods; that is, extracting and using a larger amount of the resource in the current period increases the cost of extracting and using a specific amount of the resources in a future period. Hence a profit-maximizing firm using or extracting such resources cannot simply maximize profit in the current period but must maximize profit over its time horizon, i.e., maximize present value or net worth of the firm.

Entrepreneurial Ability

Entrepreneurial ability is the most difficult of the factors to define and is even more difficlt to quantify. The entrepreneur may be viewed as an individual specific to the firm who has elected to receive the residual rather than enter into some contractual agreement with the firm for services. Like labor, the entrepreneur employs human capital in combination with other hired factors of production to generate output; however, in contrast to hired labor services, the entrepreneur must function as organizer, innovator, manager, and risk bearer. While the distinction between entrepreneurial ability and capital is blurred by the same stock-flow difficulties encountered in hired labor, the difficulty in distinguishing entrepreneurial ability as a specific factor of production is further compounded by the workings of the modern corporation. The employed manager (executive) clearly performs some of the functions of the entrepreneur; this input may be viewed as both labor and entrepreneurial ability, and compensation must include not only wages but also profit. Furthermore, the stockholders perform the risk-bearing function (albeit limited) of the entrepreneur; thus their returns must also include profit.

Additional Factors of Production

From the preceding discussion, it is clear that these categories of factors of production are not functionally distinct, so that their usefulness may well be limited to exposition since a specific input of interest may possess characteristics of several of these categories. Indeed, this broad categorization is most relevant only in societies like the England of the eighteenth and early nineteenth centuries where the three factors—capital, labor, and land—corresponded to the major social classes. Furthermore, the four categories, including entrepreneurial ability, do not necessarily exhaust the factors of production. For instance, money may well be considered a specific factor of production, as might advertising, distribution, etc. However, the main feature that distinguishes such factors from those previously enumerated is that the latter factors are not essential to the production of physical output. These additional factors might have the effect of reducing transaction costs or allowing the firm entrance to wider markets in order to benefit from economies of scale, but they do not affect the basic production relation. In essence such a distinction represents an application of functional separability. That is, the production relation may be viewed as a function of many inputs; however, the secondary inputs do not affect the primary relations between the basic inputs—capital, labor, land, and entrepreneurial ability—in the basic production process. Thus, these additional factors of production may be viewed as inputs that merely facilitate production rather than as essential inputs.

Production Function

The factors of production are normally considered in the context of a neoclassical production function,

$$Q = Q(X_1, \ldots, X_n)$$

where output Q is a function of the level of usage of the factors of production X_i in a specific time period. In this context there exist several general relations that are important to the consideration of the factors of production. The marginal product of a given factor of production, $MP_i = \Delta Q/\Delta X_i$, is assumed to be positive and, as a result of the law of variable proportions, diminishing (at least over some range of usage). This relation is itself derived from the distinction between fixed and variable factors of production. A factor is defined as fixed if its usage level cannot be changed in the short run. Thus, if more of a variable factor is added to a fixed amount of another, the resulting increases in output must diminish. Factors of production may be classified as either complementary or competitive, since an increase in the usage of one factor either increases or decreases the marginal product of the other factor. Further, the output elasticity of a given factor of production (i.e., the percentage increase in output associated with a given percentage increase in the usage of the particular factor) is given by the ratio of the factor's marginal product to its average product. Then, a given production function can be characterized by increasing, constant, or decreasing returns to scale (i.e., whether a given percentage increases in the usage level of all factors of production will increase output by a larger, equal, or smaller percentage) as the sum of output elasticities for all of the factors of production employed is greater than, equal to, or less than 1.

The rate at which factors of production may be substituted for one another in a production process is given by the marginal rate of technical substitution between a pair of factors, defined as the number of units by which the usage of one factor may be reduced when the usage of the other factor is increased by one unit while holding output constant. Since the marginal rate of technical substitution measures, in a sense, the price of substitution and, for a given output, the prevailing ratio of usage of the factors measures the rate at which the factors have actually been substituted, a final general relation between factors of production is the elasticity of substitution. Defined as the percentage change in the relative usage of the factors corresponding to a given percentage change in the marginal rate of technical substitution, elasticity of substitution measures the degree to which the factors may be substituted for one another (i.e., the relative ease with which inputs may be substituted). If substitution is impossible (i.e., if the factors are required in fixed proportions), the factors are said to be complements, where as if some substitution is possible, they are said to be substitutes. At present, an issue receiving considerable empirical attention is the degree to which factors of production are actually substitutable. (This is particularly true in the instance of the substitution of reproducible factors of production for depletable factors.)

Effect of Technical Progress

Another issue of general interest with respect to the factors of production is the effect of technical progress. Basically, technical progress has the effect of increasing the marginal products of the factors of production; hence for a given level of usage of the factors, technical progress results in increased output. The major questions involved in the consideration of technology concern both the form and the possible neutrality of such technical change. Technical change may be either exogenous or endogenous (i.e., originate either outside of or within the firm) and may be either disembodied or, if the effect of technology enters the production process only through a particular input, embodied in a particular factor (e.g., capital-embodied technology would affect output only through machines produced in a specific period and therefore containing the technology of that period). Technological progress is said to be neutral only if it shifts the production function and thereby increases output in such a manner that the ratios of input usage are left undisturbed. Otherwise technical progress can be factor-using or factor-saving for a particular factor of production depending on whether it increases or decreases the relative usage of the factor.

References

Becker, G. S., *Human Capital*, 2d ed., National Bureau of Economic Research, New York, 1975; Ferguson, C. E., *The Neoclassical Theory of Production and Distribution*, Cambridge University Press, London, 1975; Friedman, M., *Price Theory*, Aldine, Chicago, 1976; Hirshleifer, J., *Price Theory and Applications*, Prentice-Hall, Englewood Cliffs, N. J., 1976.

(*See also* Capital, a factor of production; Entrepreneurial ability, a factor of production; Labor, a factor of production; Land, a factor of production)

Charles W. Smithson

Family budgets

The Bureau of Labor Statistics publishes estimates of the annual costs of purchasing three hypothetical market baskets of goods and services for each of two urban family types—a retired couple and a specific type of four-person family. These estimates are referred to as standard, or family, budgets. The budgets include allowances for food, housing, transportation, clothing, personal care, medical care, and certain other consumption items. Other allowances consist of gifts and contributions, and, for one family type, allowances also include occupational expenses, social security, and personal income taxes. The three hypothetical market baskets were originally constructed to represent different standards of living. The standards are now referred to as lower, intermediate, and higher in order to reflect their relative, as opposed to absolute, nature.

Estimates of the budgets are published for the urban United States, in particular, for 44 selected urban areas. By calculating ratios of the cost of the budgets in particular areas relative to the U.S. urban average cost of the budgets, it is possible to compare the costs among the 44 different areas. Such comparisons are sometimes referred to as interarea living-costs comparisons.

Within the scope of the family budgets program the BLS also publishes equivalence scales which allow for the adjustment of the total consumption cost in the four-person family budgets for various other family sizes and types.

Description of the Manners of Living
Represented by the Family Budget Market Baskets

The market baskets for the three budgets are precisely specified as to the quantities and types of items included. Together with the assumptions regarding the reference family, these market baskets describe a certain manner of living. The following is a brief description of the manner of living for the four-person family at the intermediate-level budget.

The four-person family is well-established, living in an urban area, and headed by a 38-year-old man who is a fully employed worker. The family contains a girl of 8 and a boy of 13 years and a wife who does not work outside the home. The family possesses average inventories of items such as clothing and house furnishings, and the market baskets reflect annual replacement rates for these items.

For the intermediate-level budget, the family lives in either a five-room, one-bath rental unit or a five- to six-room, one- to one-and-a-half-bath home purchased 7 years earlier; 25 percent of the families are assumed to be renters and 75 percent, home-owners. For the renter family, the market basket contains contract rent, fuel and utilities (when not included in the rent), replacement rates for a refrigerator and range, and an insurance policy for household contents. For the homeowner family, the market basket contains principal and interest payments, property taxes and homeowner insurance, fuel and utilities, repairs and maintenance, and replacement rates for a refrigerator and range. If the family owns a car, it will be a 2-year-old used car. This car will be kept for 4 years before being sold and replaced by another 2-year-old car. The market basket contains goods and services associated with maintaining and operating this car for a year, plus an allowance for its eventual replacement.

In some of the larger urban areas, a certain percentage of these families do not own a car, but rather use public transportation. The market basket contains an allowance for a certain number of rides on public transportation. There is an allowance for families who own cars but also take some rides on public transportation.

The family is covered by a basic hospital and surgical insurance policy obtained by the husband at his place of employment, and the family makes a certain number of visits to the doctor and dentist each year.

Methodology Used to Determine Standards of Living

In the 1940s the BLS was directed by a congressional subcommittee to determine "what it costs a worker's family to live in the large cities of the United States." To carry out this mandate, the BLS, with the assistance of a technical advisory committee, undertook the development of a list of goods and services which could be used to determine the dollar level required for the maintenance of health and social well-being, the nurture of children, and participation in community activities. A budget was derived for a "modest but adequate" standard of living for a city worker's family.

The cost of this budget was estimated for spring 1946, summer 1947, autumn 1949, 1950, and 1951. Employing the same methodology as in the mid 1940s, the BLS derived a new list of goods and services for an autumn 1959 interim revision of the budget.

With a few exceptions, the market basket–construction methodology employed in the mid 1940s and in 1959 to establish the budget level intended to represent a "modest but adequate" standard of living was again used in 1966 to derive a budget level for a "moderate" standard of living. In 1967 for the first time the BLS developed lower and higher budgets in response to user needs. These budgets were updated to 1978 for price change only—the market baskets were held constant. The former moderate-level budget became the intermediate budget.

The items and quantities which make up the intermediate budget basket were derived from two sources: (1) expert judgments concerning the requirements for physical health and social well-being and (2) analytical studies of the choices of goods and services made by consumers in successive income intervals.

Expertly determined standards of adequacy were available for the food-at-home and the shelter components of the budget. Nutritionally adequate diets for individuals in different sex-age groups had been developed by the Food and Nutrition Board of the National Research Council and translated into food plans at various cost levels by the U.S. Department of Agriculture. The moderate-cost food plan developed in 1964 is used for the food-at-home component of the intermediate budget.

The shelter component of the budgets is based upon recommendations originally made by the American Public Health Association and the U.S. Public Housing Administration. These recommendations describe sleeping space requirements, essential household equipment (including plumbing), adequate utilities and heat, structural condition, and neighborhood location.

For the other components of consumption—food away from home, household furnishings and operations, transportation, clothing, personal care, medical care, reading, recreation, educational expenses, tobacco, alcohol, miscellaneous consumption expenses, gifts and contributions, and life insurance—no standards had been formulated by experts. For this reason, the budget makers attempted to use data on the actual spending patterns of families as collected in the BLS 1960–61 Survey of Consumer Expenditures together with a statistical procedure known as the quantity-income-elasticity (q-i-e) technique in order to derive quantities of goods and services to represent a standard based on expressed social goals.

It was anticipated that expenditure data would show that as income increased, families would increase spending on a group of related items at an increasing rate; subsequently, expenditures would increase at a decreasing rate. It was expected that if expenditures in relation to income followed such a trend and if initially quantity, not quality, increased, then a quantity-income curve would take the same form, that is, an S shape.

The inflection point of an S-shaped curve was interpreted as the point on the income scale where families stop buying more and more and start buying either items that are better and better or something else less essential to them. Locating this income level would allow the budget makers to select the quantities of the particular group of items purchased at this level and use these quantities in the market baskets that described a standard of living. The purpose of using the q-i-e technique was to locate the inflection point by determining the income level at which elasticity, defined as the percentage change in the quantity purchased divided by the percentage change in income, reached a maximum.

Geographic Comparisons of Costs of Living

Interarea weight variations are incorporated into several major components of the area market baskets for the intermediate standard budgets. The food-at-home component incorporates regional differences in food consumption patterns; the transportation component incorporates different weights assigned to the ownership and usage of automobiles, with lower proportions in large than in small cities; the shelter component incorporates varying quantities and types of fuel associated with climatic differences from place to place; the clothing component also incorporates different climatic requirements resulting in different quantities of selected items in different localities. Furthermore, in nonmetropolitan areas (places with populations of 2500 to 50,000) some components incorporate differences in life style compared with metropolitan areas.

BLS Equivalence Scales

Because of resource constraints, the BLS was able to derive family budgets for only two family types, the four-person family and the retired couple. Because users needed estimates of budget costs for other sizes and types of families, the BLS developed the equivalence scales based on the following assumption: that families spending an equal proportion of income on food have attained an equivalent level of total consumption. The scales were calculated using data on U.S. average food expenditures and income after taxes for various urban family sizes.

The family budget program, reviewed by the BLS staff in the mid-1970s, was reviewed by a committee of experts in the late 1970s and will undergo a revision in the early 1980s.

References

Brady, D., "The Use of Statistical Procedures in the Derivation of Family Budgets," *Social Service Review*, no. 23, June 1949, pp. 141–157; Bureau of Labor Staistics, *Three Standards of Living for an Urban Family of Four Persons, Spring 1967*, Bulletin 1570-5, U.S. Department of Labor, 1969; Bureau of Labor Statistics, "Autumn 1978 Urban Family Budgets and Comparative Indexes for Selected Urban Areas," press release 79-305, U.S. Department of Labor, April 29, 1979; U.S. Department of Health, Education, and Welfare, "Bureau of Labor Statistics Family Budgets Program," Technical Paper *The Measure of Poverty*, April 1976.

(*See also* Cost of living; Standard of living)

Mark Sherwood

Fascism

In a fascist economic setting, the sanctity of private property is maintained, at least *de jure*. The state, however, intrudes at various points and in a variety of ways by the exercise of the prerogatives that might otherwise normally accompany the institution of the private ownership. Control may be formal or informal, but it will be substantive and it will take the form of influencing certain decisions regarding the productive activities of the economy, most generally and commonly the output of industries, especially that of the heavy industrial sectors. Thus, for example, in the classic European cases the Fascist governments spawned a profusion of state agencies, ministries, and bureaus with varying degrees of priority and authority, whose duties were to oversee the mining of this or that mineral or ore, to direct the production of this strategic industry or that vital sector, and so on. Further, the institutional rights of labor were also heavily circumscribed. What it all added up to was a significant intervention into the operation of the economy, and a deliberate departure from the allocative decisions that freely operating and unencumbered markets would otherwise have generated.

Ironically, perhaps, in the areas of social science in which it has enjoyed relatively greater attention than in that of economics, the term fascism exhibits a remarkable lack of conceptual precision or agreement. Indeed, the terminological discussions and differences account for a not insignificant portion of the literature dealing with fascism in these fields. The irony is intensified when it is noted that in economics it is a fairly straightforward matter to define fascism with a solid measure of rigor. Thus if one focuses upon capital resources embodied in productive capacity and then distinguishes between ownership of these resources on the one hand and control of them on the other, each may be further divided into two sectors—private versus public. The set of possible permutations may be arrayed as shown, with fascism being one variant in the category of centralized capitalism.

		Ownership	
		Private	Public
Control	Private	Decentralized capitalism	Decentralized socialism
	Public	Centralized capitalism	Centralized socialism

Of course, in the purest sense each of these systems exists only as an ideal type, and actual economies are structured as some mix of these but a tendency and emphasis will normally emerge with sufficient clarity to permit classification and categorization. Today, for example, few would have real difficulty in determining where, within this typology, to assign the West German economy as opposed to that of East Germany. Similarly, that both of these are substantively differentiable from the German economy of 1935, in terms of these defining relationships, will be readily granted.

Command Economy

The histories of the Fascist European economies between the First and Second World Wars offer copious illustrations of the inefficiencies and waste occasioned by the imperfect efforts of those governments to impose a significant degree of central planning upon their basically capitalistic economies. They also offer, however, some impressive evidence of the ability of such an alliance of private sector and state to move toward a fuller employment of resources, especially labor, and to marshall a society's assets in a drive for higher rates of economic growth and higher levels of development. Some version of a command economy—whatever the particular ideological underpinning—has proven increasingly attractive to economically lesser-developed societies seeking an enhancement of their growth performance. In this context, fascism has an additional appeal, for the typical fascist emphasis upon loyalty to the state (or to some leader-figure representative of the state) can be a device for defusing potential internal tensions and conflicts and uniting the society behind a common effort. Fascism, then, may offer a way, not of removing such antagonisms and struggles as commonly accompany industrialization, but of blunting them; by subsuming particular interests and subordinating them to the common allegiance of nationalism, the nation in effect assumes them out of existence. Fascism may thus offer a command economy alternative to those radical left varieties that typically represent a real threat to the institution of private property. For these reasons economists would be well advised not to dismiss fascism as a currently irrelevant strategy of economic development.

Although students of history, politics, and sociology have generated a rich and fairly continuous literature on the subject, even passing reference to it is less and less likely to be found in the standard textbooks on comparative economic systems. There appear to be two major reasons for the neglect accorded the study of fascism by economists. First, the functioning of the economies of the classic Fascist societies in Europe in the 1920s and 1930s became embroiled in the preparation for, and then the actuality of, military conflict, thus rendering it difficult to distinguish the pristine economic characteristics of fascism. Second, the assumption seems to dominate that fascist economic regimes occupy a category of purely historical interest and curiosity. Thus, both World War II and the temptation to equate fascism exclusively with Nazi Germany have had the combined effect of obscuring the more general dimensions of the subject.

References

Laqueur, Walter (ed.), *Fascism, A Reader's Guide*, University of California Press, Berkeley, 1976; Moore, Barrington, Jr., *The Social Origins of Dictatorship and Demoracy*, Beacon, Boston, 1966; Schweitzer, Arthur, "Plan and Markets: Nazi Style," *Kyklos*, Internationale Zeitschrift fuer Sozialwissenschaften, Basel, vol. 30, 1977; Turner, Henry A., Jr. (ed.), *Reappraisals of Fascism, New Viewpoints*, Franklin Watts, New York, 1975.

(*See also* Capitalism; Communism; Comparative economic systems, an overview; Socialism)

Richard Roehl

Federal budget

Until fiscal year 1922, the executive branch of the federal government had neither a centralized budgeting office nor a unified budget procedure. Each agency prepared its own budget and transmitted it to the Treasury Department, which submitted it to Congress without substantive review.

The Budget and Accounting Act of 1921 established the first centrally prepared federal budget. In this sense, the fiscal year 1923 budget—the first one entirely prepared by the newly created Bureau of the Budget—marked the beginning of the era of the unified federal budget, i.e., a centrally prepared budget covering all important activities of the executive branch, subject to direct presidential scrutiny and congressional review. This new budget became known as the administrative budget; it remained the budget for administrative planning and congressional control, as well as for overall economic analysis, until after World War II. But the administrative budget excluded revenues and expenditures of the federal trust funds, as well as the activities of several so-called government enterprises.

The budget document for fiscal year 1957 contained the first official set of accounts of the so-called consolidated cash statement. Federal receipts from and payments to the public, as included in the consolidated cash budget, covered the activities of the administrative budget, the operations of the trust accounts, and the transactions of several government enterprises which were excluded from the administrative budget. This newly devised consolidated cash budget provided a much more comprehensive measure of cash flows between the federal government and the remainder of the economy. For assessments of the government's financing and net borrowing requirements, the consolidated cash budget superseded the old administrative budget. Its major shortcoming was the failure to differentiate between federal spending on the one hand and federal lending on the other.

Consolidated Cash, Unified, and National Income Accounts Budget

The present unified budget—the successor of the administrative and consolidated cash budgets—made its first appearance in fiscal year 1969. It includes federal-fund activities as well as the trust funds and government enterprises, and spending as well as net lending. Not covered are guaranteed and insured loans, as well as loans made by government-sponsored agencies which are not (or are no longer) government-owned.

Another budget concept that has been used since the early 1960s, mainly for fiscal policy analysis, is the so-called national income accounts budget. It measures federal transactions as recorded in the national income and product accounts (NIA). This NIA budget, prepared by the Office of Economic Analysis of the Department of Commerce, contains the most useful data for measuring the impact of the federal budget on the private economy. The main features of the NIA budget which differentiate it from the unified budget are (1) the exclusion of most lending (except nonrecourse agricultural commodity loans which are recorded in the NIA budget as purchases) and of capital contributions to international financial institutions; (2) the inclusion of the government contributions for employee retirement; (3) the inclusion of some transactions on a gross rather than a net basis; (4) the recording of most budget receipts from the business sector on an accrual basis (i.e., when the tax liability is incurred, rather than when the tax is paid) and of payments by individual taxpayers on a payment basis (i.e., when the tax is paid or withheld, rather than when it is received by the Treasury); (5) the recording of defense expenditures, especially those with long lead time, on a delivery basis; and (6) the exclusion of certain U.S. territories.

Prior to the Budget and Accounting Act of 1921, the budget actually consisted of individual agency budgets, separately prepared, largely independent and uncoordinated. Moreover, the most serious defect of these budgets was the basic budgeting approach: they were item, or line budgets, listing line-by-line expenditures for each individual item purchased (one line per item).

With the greater centralization and coordination of the administrative budget came greater consolidation of expenditures by agency or department, and by major program within each agency. Yet, this was essentially a consolidation along the lines of the organization of the federal bureaucracy, with little or no emphasis on program goals and social priorities.

Functional Classification

The next important advance toward program budgeting came with functional classification of budget expenditures, first introduced in the 1936 budget. Expenditures were grouped by broad functions which, at times, cut across agency or departmental

Federal Budgets by Revenue, Source and Outlay Function

Fiscal years, $ billions, and as a percent of GNP

	$ billions				As a percent of GNP			
	1948	1958	1968	1978	1948	1958	1968	1978
Receipts by Source	$41.8	$79.6	$153.7	$402.0	17.0%	18.0%	18.5%	19.7%
Individual Income taxes	19.3	34.7	68.7	181.0	7.9	7.9	8.3	8.9
Corporation Income taxes	9.6	20.1	28.7	60.0	3.9	4.5	3.5	2.9
Social insurance taxes	4.0	11.2	34.6	123.4	1.6	2.5	4.2	6.0
Excise taxes	7.3	10.6	14.1	18.4	3.0	2.4	1.7	0.9
Estate and gift taxes	1.0	1.4	3.1	5.3	0.4	0.3	0.4	0.2
Custom duties	0.4	0.8	2.0	6.6	0.1	0.2	0.2	0.3
Miscellaneous receipts	0.2	0.8	2.5	7.3	0.1	0.2	0.3	0.4
Outlays by Function	29.8	82.6	178.8	450.8	12.2	18.7	21.5	22.1
National defense	7.8	43.7	78.8	105.2	3.2	9.9	9.5	5.1
International affairs	4.6	3.4	5.3	5.9	1.9	0.8	0.6	0.3
General science, space, and technology	0.0	0.1	5.5	4.7	0.0	0.0	0.7	0.2
Energy	0.3	0.3	1.0	5.9	0.1	0.1	0.1	0.3
Natural resources and environment	0.8	1.4	3.0	10.9	0.3	0.3	0.4	0.5
Agriculture	0.1	2.4	4.5	7.7	0.0	0.5	0.5	0.4
Commerce and housing credit	0.3	0.9	4.3	3.3	0.1	0.2	0.5	0.2
Transportation	0.8	2.3	6.3	15.4	0.3	0.5	0.8	0.8
Community and regional development	0.1	0.2	1.3	11.0	0.0	0.0	0.2	0.5
Education, training, employment and social services	0.2	0.6	7.6	26.5	0.1	0.1	0.9	1.3
Health	0.2	0.5	9.7	43.7	0.1	0.1	1.2	2.1
Income security	2.9	15.2	33.7	146.2	1.2	3.4	4.1	7.2
Veterans' benefits	6.5	5.4	6.9	19.0	2.7	1.2	0.8	0.9
Justice	0.2	0.3	0.7	3.8	0.1	0.1	0.1	0.2
General government	1.0	0.5	1.6	3.8	0.4	0.1	0.2	0.2
General purpose fiscal assistance	0.0	0.1	0.3	9.6	0.0	0.0	0.0	0.5
Interest	5.1	6.9	13.8	44.0	2.1	1.6	1.7	2.2
Undistributed offsetting receipts	-1.0	-1.9	-5.5	-15.8	-0.4	-0.4	-0.7	-0.8

SOURCE: Department of the Treasury, Office of Management and Budget, The Conference Board.

lines. The names and details of these functions have changed somewhat over the years, but the essential functional grouping has remained relatively stable and has included from the outset such broad categories as national defense, international affairs and finance, agriculture, natural resources, community development and housing, veterans benefits and services, and several others.

This functional classification has been revised and refined repeatedly; it has been retained in the unified budget. The most recent functional classification consists of 18 separate functions, listed in the accompanying table. Budget revenues are comprised of five major tax receipts, custom duties, and several miscellaneous revenue sources. Budget revenues by source are shown in the table for 10-year intervals since fiscal year 1948. The chronological divisions of the table indicate shifts in the relative importance of some major functions and revenue sources. The primary human resources functions—education, training, employment, and social services; health; and income security—have grown very rapidly, particularly since the mid-1960s. Correspondingly, among the federal revenue sources, social insurance tax receipts have increased most rapidly; in fiscal year 1968, they surpassed the corporation income tax receipts and became the second largest source of revenue—after the individual income taxes.

Expenditure projections in the federal budget are prepared and monitored by the Office of Management and Budget (formerly the U.S. Bureau of the Budget); whereas, revenue estimates and changes in the tax system are prepared and monitored by the Treasury Department. From fiscal years 1921–1930, the federal budget was in surplus every single year; since then, budget deficits have been the norm. There was not a single budget surplus during fiscal years 1932–1946 or during the 1970s; during the intervening 23 years, the federal budget was in surplus only eight times: fiscal years 1947, 1948, 1949, 1951, 1956, 1957, 1960, and 1969.

From fiscal years 1921–76, the fiscal year for the federal budget covered the period from July 1 (of the preceding calendar year) through June 30. The Congressional Budget Act of 1974 changed the timing of the fiscal year—effective with fiscal year 1977—to October 1 through September 30. The purpose of this shift was to give Congress more time to review and reshape the budget and to pass all necessary budget legislation prior to the start of the fiscal year. This shift was accomplished by means of a transition quarter in July to September 1976; but the goal—passage of all budget legislation before the start of the fiscal year—has remained elusive.

References

U.S. Office of Management and Budget, *The Budget of the United States Government*, published annually on a fiscal-year basis.

(*See also* Federal budget process; Fiscal policy; Government expenditures in GNP)

Michael E. Levy

Federal budget process

The Constitution of the United States stipulates: "All bills for raising revenue shall originate in the House of Representatives; but the Senate may propose or concur with amendments as on other bills" (article 1, section 7). Until the post-Civil War period, under this mandate control over both federal revenue raising and federal revenue spending was vested in the House Ways and Means Committee. (Later the Senate Finance Committee served in a parallel capacity for the Senate.) But the press of work became too great for a single committee and, in 1867, while responsibility for raising revenues and for approving federal borrowing remained with the Ways and Means and Finance Committees, new appropriations committees were established in both houses to act on expenditures. Within two decades, further fragmentation of the congressional budget process occurred when legislative committees assumed sole authority over eight of the thirteen appropriations bills.

Increase of Executive Budget Control

In an attempt to streamline and reform budget procedures, Congress passed the Budget and Accounting Act in 1921. This act established the Bureau of the Budget—originally placed in the Treasury Department but moved to the executive office of the President in 1939. The President, with the assistance of the Bureau of the Budget, was required to submit a coordinated fiscal plan to Congress, thus supplanting the previous practice of having the Treasury submit each agency's individual budget requests.

To offset the new executive power, Congress restored full authority over appropriations to the two appropriations committees. The various legislative committees, however, soon circumvented this new centralization by such devices as backdoor spending. The act also established the General Accounting Office (GAO) for the purpose of monitoring and auditing government spending on behalf of Congress.

In 1970, to enhance and centralize executive budget control further, President Nixon replaced the Bureau of the Budget with the Office of Management and Budget (OMB) and enlarged its responsibilities.

Under the congressional procedures, each bill or budget proposal was processed piecemeal on its own merits, based largely on administration proposals. There was no review of the budget as a whole. Taxes and revenue measures were handled separately by the House Ways and Means Committee and the Senate Finance Committee. No procedure existed for an overall review by the Congress of total budget outlays or of the balance (or shortfalls) between total outlays and total receipts. Moreover, even after budget legislation had been passed by Congress, the President was able to modify—and, at times, frustrate—the will of Congress by impoundment of funds appropriated by Congress.

This budgetary conflict between Congress and the administration came to a head in the closing days of the Ninety-second Congress. After $1\frac{1}{2}$ years of hearings and debates, Congress enacted the Congressional Budget and Impoundment Control Act of 1974 (Public Law 93-344), which was signed by the President on July 12, 1974. This act determines the timing, rules, and procedures of the present federal budget process. The act consists of two distinct parts: the Congressional Budget Act of 1974 and the Impoundment Control Act of 1974.

Congressional Budget Act of 1974

This act contains provisions for the following major areas of budget development and enactment.

Separate House and Senate Budget Committees In order to give Congress a better perspective of budget totals and fiscal policy requirements, the Congressional Budget Act established separate House and Senate Budget Committees to study and recommend changes in the President's budget. Each committee is supported in this task by its own professional staff.

The act established a 23-member House Budget Committee, subsequently expanded to a total of 25 members. Under the provisions of the act, five seats are assigned to members of the Ways and Means Committee and five to members of the Appropriations Committee; the remaining thirteen seats are occupied by one member from each of the 11 legislative committees, by one member from the majority leadership, and by one member from the minority leadership. Members of the House Budget Committee serve for a full Congress (i.e., a 2-year period); but the act assures a reasonable amount of membership rotation by prohibiting any member from serving on the House Budget Committee for more than 4 years in a 10-year period.

The act also established a 15-member Senate Budget Committee, to be selected by normal Senate committee selection procedures. No rotation is required; however, since 1976, any member holding seats on two other major committees had to drop one.

Congressional Budget Office   The act established a joint Congressional Budget Office (CBO) within Congress to provide experts and computer facilities needed to digest and analyze the information and data accompanying the President's budget. The Congressional Budget Office is run by a director, appointed for a 4-year term by the Speaker of the House and the President *pro tempore* of the Senate.

Fiscal-Year Revision   The act moved the start of the fiscal year from July 1 to October 1 (effective October 1, 1976) and set a stringent timetable. To give Congress an earlier start in reviewing and reshaping the budget, the act requires the executive branch (beginning in 1975) to submit a current services budget by November 10 for the new fiscal year starting the following October 1. Based on the programs and funding levels in effect for the ongoing fiscal year, this current services budget should project the spending required to maintain these programs throughout the following fiscal year at existing commitment levels—or at commitment levels specified by the existing legislation. Thus, the current services budget projects spending requirements under existing legislation and based on current economic assumptions, but prior to any program expansions or new initiatives. The Joint Economic Committee was asked to review and assess the current services budget and report to Congress by December 31. In 1978, this provision was eliminated. Instead, the executive branch now provides current services estimates with each new budget when it is introduced (including 5-year projections).

As under past law, the President continues to submit the new budget to Congress in late January or early February. In addition to the traditional budget totals and breakdowns, however, the budget document now includes a list of existing tax expenditures—estimates of revenues lost to the Treasury through preferential tax treatment—as well as any proposed changes in tax expenditures. According to the act, the budget must also contain estimates of expenditures for programs for which funds are appropriated a year in advance. Five-year budget projections of all federal spending under existing programs must also be included.

Tentative Congressional Budget   After reviewing the President's budget proposals—and considering the advice of the Congressional Budget Office and other committees—the House and Senate Budget Committees draw up a concurrent resolution outlining a tentative congressional budget.

Under the conference report timetable, congressional committees have until March 15 to report their budget recommendations to the Budget Committees. The Congressional Budget Office report is due on April 1. By April 15, the Budget Committees must report concurrent resolutions to the House and Senate floors, and Congress has to clear the initial budget resolution by May 15. (As in all cases, Congress can "stop the clock" when it needs more time, and has done so, for example, in 1979.)

This first budget resolution sets target totals for appropriations, outlays, taxes, the budget surplus or deficit, and the federal debt. Within these overall targets, the resolution breaks down appropriations and outlays by the functional categories used in the President's budget document, as well as by classifications used by the appropriations subcommittees for the 13 appropriations bills. The resolution includes any recommended changes in tax revenues and in the level of the federal debt ceiling. It can also instruct Congress to withhold appropriations bills and bills creating federal entitlement programs from the President until Congress has completed its final budget reconciliation in September. Individual appropriation bills, upon passage by the Congress, may be sent to the President to be signed (or vetoed) as previously. Under this procedure, however, such appropriations remain preliminary, subject to approval or modification by the final congressional reconciliation bill.

Deadline for Authorization of Bills   To clear the way for prompt action on appropriations before the new fiscal year begins, the act requires that all bills authorizing appropriations be reported by May 15, the deadline for enactment of the first budget resolution. (This requirement can be waived by majority vote in both the House and the Senate.) There are two exemptions from the May 15 deadline for reporting authorizing legislation: (1) social security legislation and (2) entitlement legislation.

Starting with the programs for the fiscal year 1977 budget, the administration has had to submit requests for authorizing legislation no later than May 15 of the calendar year preceding the start of the budget year for which new authorization is requested (i.e., $15\frac{1}{2}$ months in advance). This gives congressional committees at least a full year to study the requests.

Procedure   The basic appropriations process proceeds within the appropriations committees and the various subcommittees as in the past, but is subject to the guidelines from the first budget resolution. The appropriations committees subdivide their allocations among the 13 subcommittees that handle appropriations for different departments and agencies.

The actual appropriations process follows the customary congressional procedure for each of the 13 regular appropriations bills, which usually includes the following steps: House subcommittee and full committee action; Senate floor action; House-Senate conference reconciliation; final House and Senate approval.

All appropriations bills have to be cleared by the middle of September—no later than the seventh day after Labor Day. (That deadline can be waived, however, for any appropriations bill consideration of which was delayed because Congress had not acted promptly on necessary authorizing legislation.)

Final Budget Resolution   By September 15, Congress must adopt a second, and final, budget resolution that may either affirm or revise the budget targets set by the initial resolution. If separate congressional decisions taken during the appropriations process do not fit the final budget resolution totals, the resolution must provide for a final reconciliation by changing either one or more of the following: (1) appropriations (both those recommended for the upcoming fiscal year and those carried over from previous fiscal years) and/or entitlements; (2) revenues; and (3) the public debt. The final resolution directs the committees that have jurisdiction over these matters to report the necessary legislative changes. The budget committees then combine these changes and report them to the floor in the form of a reconciliation bill.

If Congress has withheld all appropriations and entitlement bills from the President until passage of the final reconciliation bill, this bill becomes the final budget legislation subject to presidential signature (or veto). If, on the other hand, each individual appropriations bill has been signed by the President upon passage by the Congress (the common procedure), the final reconciliation bill—upon signature by the President—supersedes all the previously passed individual bills.

Backdoor Spending

For many years backdoor spending has been the Achilles' heel of all spending control programs because it evades the scrutiny of the regular appropriations process. Backdoor or mandatory spending is the approval of budget authority by routes other than the regular appropriations process. It may take four different forms:

1. Borrowing authority, i.e., authority for a federal agency to borrow from the public for programs such as student loan guarantees, the rural electrification program, and public housing.

2. Contract authority, i.e., authorization to enter into contracts not entailing present appropriations but involving obligation of federal funds for payment at a later date (sewage treatment plants, for example).

3. Permanent appropriations, whereby basic legislation makes funds available for several years, or for an indefinite period of time (e.g., the revenue sharing program and social security). No further appropriation is needed to authorize annual spending.

4. Mandatory spending which results from payment levels established in basic legislation—such as public assistance, veterans' benefits, and interest on the public debt—that become a binding obligation of the government to be funded by annual appropriations.

Congressional Budget

The Act specifies that all existing backdoor or mandatory spending programs shall continue to remain outside the appropriations process. Moreover, the act also exempts all future backdoor spending arising from (1) the Social Security Act; (2) trust funds that receive 90 percent or more of their financing from earmarked taxes rather than from general revenue; (3) general revenue sharing funds; (4) insured and guaranteed loans; (5) outlays by federal government corporations or independent public corporations; and (6) outlays from earmarked gifts to the government. In fiscal year 1980, combined backdoor spending from all these programs was estimated at $408.7 billion, or 75.2 percent of total federal spending.

The act requires new review procedures by the appropriations committees only in the limited case of newly initiated backdoor spending programs that do not qualify for any of the six exemptions listed above. These new procedures tend to arrest further erosion of spending control, but their applicability is extremely limited. Thus, backdoor spending continues to add a heavy burden to the reconciliation process of the budget committees, as the uncontrolled elements of federal spending have to be incorporated into the budget totals.

Impoundment Control Act of 1974

Under practices and procedures existing before the Impoundment Control Act of 1974, the executive branch had been in a much better position than Congress to exercise centralized control over budget spending. Presidents have claimed the right to impound funds—not to spend funds appropriated by the Congress—since the time of Jefferson. This practice became more widespread after the Dawes Memorandum of 1921. Charles Dawes, the first Director of the Bureau of the Budget, stated that appropriations from the Congress "were to be treated as ceilings on expenditures rather than as directives to spend the full amount." The passage of the Employment Act of 1946 broadened the President's responsibility for economic policy and led postwar Presidents to use impoundment as an anti-inflationary tool.

Presidents have used impoundment for two basic purposes: (1) efficient financial administration and (2) countercyclical economic policy. Examples of the former include impoundment pending changes of approved plans and specifications between the government and the contractor completion of feasibility or cost studies for a government project or establishment of the organization necessary to manage the obligated funds. Impoundments for reasons of efficient financial administration have been far less controversial with Congress than countercyclical impoundments.

The impounding of funds by the executive branch has been debated and contested ever since the Dawes Memorandum, because it tends to frustrate and override the explicit intention of the legislative branch. In extreme cases, it is liable to affect the fundamental balance between the responsibilities of the President and those of the Congress.

The Impoundment Control Act of 1974 represents an attempt to institutionalize an accommodation between the Congress and the President. The act prescribes two procedures by which Congress can overrule Presidential impoundments and force the release of funds. If an impoundment merely defers spending, Congress can force the President to release the funds if either the House or the Senate passes a resolution calling for such a release. There is no time limit for such congressional action.

If an impoundment represents a permanent rescission, the termination of a program, or a cut in total spending for fiscal policy reasons, the act requires that the President release the impounded funds after 45 days, unless both the House and Senate pass a rescission bill within that 45-day period.

To remove language in existing law that had been cited as justification for past Presidential impoundments, the act repealed a clause in the Anti-Deficiency Act of 1950. This allowed the President to withhold funds from obligation because of other developments, as well as in order to save money, to take account of changing requirements, or to improve efficiency.

To keep Congress informed on impoundment actions, the act requires the President to report deferrals or to request rescissions. If the Comptroller General finds that an impoundment has been made without being reported to Congress, the Comptroller General can then report the impoundment for congressional consideration and action. If a President refuses to comply with a congressional action that overrules an impoundment, the Comptroller General can ask the court to issue an order requiring the release of the funds.

Execution, Control, and Audit

Once the money is appropriated and the new fiscal year gets under way, the Office of Management and Budget immediately reviews each agency's spending requests on a quarter-by-quarter basis and provides quarterly allotments. Each agency, in turn, has its own budget office with authority to make allotments of funds to subdivisions within the agency. Appropriation warrants for each agency are drawn with approval of the Treasury Department and the General Accounting Office. Disbursing officers, acting for the Treasury, then proceed to issue checks to pay approved bills.

Reporting of the actual expenditures and receipts is done by the Treasury, through its Bureau of Accounts, in the Daily and Monthly Treasury Statements. In addition, the Office of Management and Budget publishes a Midyear Review of the Budget which contains changes and revisions in recent revenue and expenditure trends or goals, reflecting congressional action as well as changes in economic activity.

When the budget for the following fiscal year is submitted in January, it contains further revisions in the estimates of receipts and expenditures of the current budget. Final (actual) figures are published shortly after the beginning of the next fiscal year.

The final step in the budget process is that of independent auditing on behalf of the Congress. This is done by the Comptroller General through the General Accounting Office. This auditing function proceeds on a continuing year-round basis.

References

Steiner, Peter O., "Public Expenditure Budgeting," *The Economics of Public Finance, Studies of Government Finance*, Brookings, Washington, 1974; Weidenbaum, Murray, L., "Federal Budgeting: The Choice of Government Programs," *Congress and the Federal Budget*, American Enterprise Institute for Public Policy Research, Washington, D.C., 1965.

(*See also* Federal budget; Government expenditures in GNP)

Michael E. Levy

Federal-funds rate (*see* Federal Reserve policy; Monetary policy)

Federal Reserve policy

The Federal Reserve System exercises an important, although indirect, influence over broad trends in prices, output, and exchange rates. The Federal Reserve does this largely through its ability to control both the money supply and bank credit and through the general influence it exerts over interest rates, credit flows, and other developments in the financial sector of the economy. Other more specific powers allow the Federal Reserve to control maximum interest rates payable on certain deposits offered at member banks and to determine the proportion of stock purchases which may be financed with credit. On certain occasions the Federal Reserve has been given temporary power to exercise direct control over consumer credit and also credit for residential and nonresidential construction. The manner in which the Federal Reserve has exercised its powers has evolved over time, as have its policy objectives.

How the Federal Reserve System Influences the Economy

The Federal Reserve implements its policy primarily with three tools, all of which operate through the volume of reserves that member banks hold at their Federal Reserve banks. These tools are (1) open-market operations, which affect the volume of reserves; (2) the discount rate, which affects the cost of reserves; and (3) reserve requirements, which determine the percentage of deposit liabilities that member banks must hold as reserves, either at Reserve banks or in their vaults as cash.

Reserve requirements have been greater for demand deposits, which are withdrawable on demand, than for either time deposits, which have a specific maturity, or savings deposits, which may require notice of withdrawal. Also, for demand deposits, requirements rise—to a limit—with the volume of deposits a particular bank holds. It is the responsibility of individual member banks to maintain, on a weekly basis, average reserves adequate to meet these requirements.

In doing this—through portfolio adjustments—banks strive to maintain a minimum of reserves in excess of requirements because reserves earn no interest. This effort requires constant attention, however, since the ownership of reserves among the System's member banks changes continually as checks which are drawn on one bank and deposited into another often are cleared by a transfer of reserves from one member bank to another. Also, currency withdrawn from one bank may be redeposited in another.

Through its major policy tool, open-market operations, the Federal Reserve causes member banks to adjust their supply of deposits and loans by creating or extinguishing the reserves available to support them. It does this by purchasing or selling U.S. government and agency securities from dealers in the market for these instruments. For example, when the System purchases securities, it pays for them by crediting the reserves of member banks in which dealers maintain accounts; likewise, member-bank reserves are debited when the Federal Reserve sells securities.

Open-market operations can have an important influence on financial conditions. For example, by increasing the volume of member-bank reserves, open-market purchases result in downward pressure on the federal-funds rate, the yield which banks earn on reserves sold in the federal funds (largely interbank) market. Banks may also use redundant reserves for other purposes. For example, they may reduce their reliance on the more expensive types of liabilities, particularly by lowering interest rates offered on large time deposits or on other sources of funds. Finally, banks may acquire additional assets, such as loans. Since long-term rates tend to move with short-term rates, the cost of all sources of credit tends to decline when the supply of reserves is increased. At the same time, additional reserves support an acceleration in the growth of money and credit.

When the Federal Reserve wishes to reduce liquidity, on the other hand, it typically sells securities out of its portfolio. In response, member banks generally attempt to replenish reserve holdings as their excess reserves begin to fall below desired levels. Consequently, interest rates and the cost of credit come under upward pressure, and the growth of money and credit slows.

Changes in the cost and availability of money and credit exert a powerful influence-albeit with a lag—over broad trends in aggregate demand and hence over the pace of economic activity, the cost and utilization of resources, and the balance of payments. The length of this lag is somewhat variable since it depends on how quickly a change in policy is perceived; whether it is judged to be permanent; how rapidly expenditure can be adjusted to changes in credit conditions; and on other factors, such as fiscal policy, which are simultaneously affecting the economy.

Occasionally, the Federal Reserve acts to affect the supply of credit and deposits by changing—within statutory limits—the required percentage of deposits which member banks must hold as reserves. A reduction in these requirements, with no change in the quantity of reserves, leaves member banks with additional reserves available to purchase assets and to support an expansion of deposits. An increase in reserve requirements, on the other hand, forces member banks to seek additional reserves, reducing the amount of credit and deposits they supply to the economy. Unless they are offset by open-market operations, changes in reserve requirements typically produce large effects on the supply of both credit and bank deposits. Thus, this second tool of monetary policy is used relatively infrequently to affect general credit conditions. However, the Board of Governors has employed this instrument to influence member banks' reliance on specific types of deposits, and also to affect the maturity structure of their liabilities.

The third tool of monetary policy relates to the provision for member banks to borrow directly from the Federal Reserve System. These loans usually take the form of a direct advance to the borrowing bank, secured by certain eligible assets—today, typically U.S. government and agency securities. The interest cost of these loans is called the discount rate.

Today, only a small portion of the reserves held by member banks is borrowed from the System. Most member-bank borrowing arises from unexpected deposit and reserve outflows, and the funds are typically borrowed for adjustment purposes for no more than several days. The availability of this credit allows the Federal Reserve to draw reserves from the banking system through open-market sales when it is deemed appropriate for macroeconomic policy purposes without fear that individual member banks may find it excessively difficult to maintain adequate reserves.

The discount facility also enables certain member banks to make up seasonal reserve deficiencies without having to reduce loan portfolios or make other adjustments. The availability of this credit frees these members—typically smaller, rural banks lacking reliable access to national money markets—from having to hold unnecessarily large portfolios of liquid assets, such as Treasury bills, which could be sold to meet seasonal loan demands. As a result, these banks are able to use a larger share of funds they attract to meet the reasonable credit needs of their communities on a year-round basis. Because of the nature of seasonal borrowing needs, this credit is often outstanding at any particular member bank for as long as several months.

Member banks' access to the System's credit is not automatic; the System controls the volume of its loans through administrative procedures—by evaluating the appropriateness of loan requests—and through adjustment of the discount rate. Occasionally, the discount rate is changed to provide a highly visible signal of the direction in which the Federal Reserve intends interest rates to move. More typically, however, movements in the discount rate reflect adjustments which prevent it from getting out of alignment with market rates.

Making Policy

Formulating and implementing policy are ongoing tasks. Apart from infrequent changes in reserve requirements and the occasional changes in the discount rate that are designed to initiate, rather than adapt to, changes in short-term interest rates—actions which are the responsibility of the Board of Governors—monetary policy is implemented by changing the quantity of member bank reserves through open-market operations. These are the responsibility of the Federal Open Market Committee (FOMC). To formulate monetary policy, the FOMC meets regularly—in recent years approximately monthly. It evaluates a vast array of information dealing with recent and projected trends in the ultimate goals of policy—real economic activity, employment and price developments, and the soundness of the dollar—as well as in major financial variables such as growth in monetary aggregates, credit flows, and interest rates. The effects of recent and prospective developments in fiscal policy are also evaluated and taken into account.

During the meeting, each FOMC member presents his or her views about prospects for the economy. A vote is then taken to determine the FOMC's monetary policy decision. Often, the views expressed coalesce into a consensus; however, sometimes disagreements remain unresolved at the end of the meeting and the vote is not unanimous. Based on the decisions reached at the meeting a directive is issued setting policy until the subsequent FOMC meeting.

The directive—which also summarizes in a very general way recent economic developments and the general goals of current monetary policy—provides specific near-term objectives which the FOMC has chosen to achieve its longer-run economic goals. It is issued to the Federal Reserve Bank of New York where a senior officer—the manager of the System open-market account—oversees open-market operations.

Since about 1972 the directive has generally incorporated 2-month growth rate ranges of tolerance for several definitions of the monetary aggregates (currency plus various deposit liabilities of commercial banks and other financial intermediaries). The manager is generally instructed to vary the federal-funds rate in an interval which is believed to be consistent with the monetary-aggregate target ranges. If the federal-funds rate has moved to the directive's upper or lower limits and the monetary aggregates remain outside their ranges, the manager informs the head of the Board of Governors who decides whether further instructions from the Committee are needed. The directive, along with a text summarizing the meeting of the FOMC from which it emerged, is made public shortly after the Committee's subsequent meeting.

Other Policy Instruments

The Federal Reserve's powers allow it to control the stock of money, although, in the short run, not with precision, as well as to influence the cost and availability of credit generally. The Federal Reserve also has more specific powers. One is the authority to establish maximum interest rates that member banks may pay on time and savings deposits. Originally established to promote the safety and soundness of member banks, interest rate ceilings, under the Board of Governors' regulation Q, have since come to be used for other purposes. First, they have kept yields on savings deposits and smaller time deposits offered by member banks somewhat below rates available on similar deposits offered by institutions specializing in mortgage credit, namely savings and loan associations and mutual savings banks. Congress first provided this advantage to lenders of long-term mortgages in September 1966 in the belief that it was necessary to sustain their viability and to channel credit toward the housing industry. The rising interest rates characterizing many recent periods have made it difficult for these financial intermediaries to attract deposits without experiencing earnings pressures, because the average return on their mortgage portfolio changes only sluggishly.

The authority to impose rate ceilings has also been used in the past to control the yields on large denomination time deposits which member banks sell to corporations and other large investors. Maximum rates on deposits offered at insured nonmember banks and thrift institutions have been controlled by other regulatory agencies working in coordination with the Federal Reserve.

Currently, the Federal Reserve has direct control over only a single category of credit, that used for the purchase of stocks. The Board of Governors is empowered to determine the percentages of security purchases which may not be purchased on credit. These are called margin requirements. Separate requirements are set for stocks and convertible bonds, and they may be raised to discourage what appears to be excessive speculative demands for credit. The requirements have generally varied between 50 and 80 percent and have not changed frequently.

To counter disorderly conditions in foreign exchange markets and to contribute to the stability of the dollar, the Federal Reserve has from time to time operated in those markets. Before the early part of 1973, central banks—including the Federal Reserve—bought and sold foreign currencies (and gold until 1934) in order to keep their currencies' values relative to one another (or gold) within the fairly narrow bounds established by the international monetary regimes of the times. Since 1973, many countries have been allowing their currencies to fluctuate more or less freely; operations in foreign exchange markets have nevertheless continued with a view to countering disorder in exchange markets. In 1978, the volume of gross sales and purchases by the Federal Reserve totaled $10.6 billion.

History of Policy

Early Policy   World War I began soon after the Federal Reserve System was established, and the primary goal of early monetary policy very soon became support of the Treasury's mushrooming debt-financing requirements deriving from war-related expenditures and from loans to allied nations. The Federal Reserve cooperated with this effort by urging member banks to lend funds to customers for purposes of purchasing government bonds. The System's officials were aware of the limitations imposed on monetary policy by the decision to support government war financing, and particularly by their complaisance regarding the Treasury's desire to maintain a low discount rate in order to minimize the cost of the government's debt.

By early 1920, with an economic boom in progress and wholesale prices at about twice their level of 1914, the Treasury withdrew its resistance to an increase in interest rates. The discount rate was increased immediately at most Reserve banks. The boom peaked in mid-1920 and was followed by a sharp decline in economic activity and by falling prices. A recovery began in late 1921.

In formulating policy in the early 1920s, the Federal Reserve was free of Treasury financing constraints for the first time. The discount mechanism was the tool that was most employed in these early years. The Federal Reserve Act called for each Reserve bank to propose the discount rate which was to be effective in its district and for the Board of Governors to approve these rates. During these years various Reserve banks often posted different rates, reflecting regional economic differences as well as differences in policy judgments.

Moreover, there were different opinions as to the proper formulation of discount policy. An influential view at that time suggested that the central bank supply credit to accommodate the demand for it, provided that the credit supplied was used for productive purposes.

Although this view—known as the real bills doctrine—had an important impact on prevailing thought, there was also an opposing position that the total quantity of credit—and its cost—were more relevant measures of policy, that there were limits to the economy's productive capacity, and that it was not practical or meaningful to attempt to distinguish between productive and unproductive loans. Moreover, one could not determine how a bank would use advances once it got them. Indeed, the total volume of member-bank borrowing came to play a role in guiding policy after it was observed to rise when policy was restrictive and decline when policy was aimed toward ease. In 1923 the Board's annual report set forth policy guidelines that included the importance of influencing both the quantity and the cost of credit as well as influencing the kinds of credit making up the total.

Gold began to flow into the country in the early twenties, reflecting, in part, repayment of foreign loans made to finance World War I. This inflow increased reserves of member banks which responded by reducing their indebtedness to Federal Reserve banks. The Reserve banks, in order to offset the consequent decline in their interest-bearing assets and to bolster earnings, purchased other assets, primarily U.S. government securities, on the open market. The observed impact of these purchases led the Board to set up the Open Market Investment Committee to coordinate the execution of such purchases. The Committee, composed of the presidents of the Federal Reserve banks, was under the Board's supervision and also was responsible for supervising foreign exchange transactions. Although the Board in 1923 laid down the principle that open-market operations were to be governed chiefly with regard to their effects on credit conditions, the Reserve banks still had the right to carry out the Committee's decisions or not, as they saw fit. This procedure was maintained until the present system was established in 1935.

Open-market purchases in the middle part of the decade were influenced by developments abroad. European countries had abandoned the gold standard during World War I, and there was a desire within the System to help them reestablish it on the grounds that greater economic stability worldwide would result. Partly for this reason, the System at times undertook large open-market purchases designed to check the flow of gold into the United States by keeping interest rates low and adding to the supply of credit. England returned to the gold standard in 1925.

During the second half of the 1920s the view developed that interest rates were too low, and some within the System thought that credit should be restrained by raising discount rates. Nevertheless, in 1927 the System reduced the discount rate and expanded its open-market purchases in order to help France regain the gold standard. These actions helped to create the conditions in which lending at all commercial banks picked up in 1927. Discount rates were subsequently raised during the first half of 1928 as fears of too-rapid credit growth arose, but they then remained unchanged at most Reserve banks even as loan growth further accelerated in 1928. In early 1929, the System issued a statement to member banks telling them not to make speculative loans based on Federal Reserve credit, and in early August of that year the Federal Reserve Bank of New York raised its discount rate a full percent. But by this time, the stage had been set for the stock-market collapse in October 1929.

In the following months the discount rate was reduced substantially, and open-market purchases began promptly. Total member-bank reserves remained largely unchanged, however, as member banks began to repay loans to Reserve banks. As interest rates began to reach very low levels, opposition to further open-market purchases developed within the System, and excess reserves at member banks did not rise very appreciably for several years.

By the fall of 1931, a serious financial crisis had developed, stemming in part from the deepening depression and in part from a decision by Britain to go off the gold standard once again. Gold began to leave the country as fear developed that the dollar too would be devalued. In response, many Federal Reserve banks raised their discount rates in October. Bond prices fell sharply, currency was withdrawn from banks, bank failures increased, and credit became scarce. The decisions to raise discount rates were consistent both with the classic central bank response to a gold outflow—which, however, typically reflected relatively high inflation or relatively low interest rates in the country suffering the outflow—and with the technical requirement to back Federal Reserve notes with gold.

A substantial impediment to monetary ease was removed with legislation in early 1932 which eliminated the technical barrier to continued open-market purchases by allowing Reserve banks to use government securities as well as their holdings of discounted paper and gold to back their currency notes outstanding. From the end of February through mid-July 1932, open-market purchases totaled over $1 billion. Nevertheless, excess reserves rose only modestly owing to continued gold outflows and repayment of loans to Federal Reserve banks.

By March 1933 the banking system had collapsed. It had succumbed to the cumulative effects of the steady decline in economic activity, currency runs by depositors who feared for the loss of their savings, and closings by supervisory authorities of banks whose assets had depreciated. Almost 4000 banks closed their doors. Rural banks and nonmember banks who lacked access to Federal Reserve credit fared worst.

The debacle coincided with President Roosevelt's inauguration. His recovery program included substantial federal spending financed with debt issuance, some of which the Federal Reserve purchased. As a result, excess reserves rose rapidly and by the end of 1933 stood at almost $800 million, over 10 times the level of 3 years earlier, and by 1935 they had reached $3 billion.

The volume of excess reserves by then exceeded in value the Federal Reserve's portfolio of securities, and a consensus developed within the System that its ability to restrict credit—should the need arise—had been seriously eroded. However, there was concern over how excess reserves could be reduced without jeopardizing the recovery which had slowly begun. The Banking Act of 1935, which established the FOMC, also provided for statutory limits within which the Board of Governors could set reserve requirements. In the period between August 1936 and May 1937, the Board took full advantage of this provision and raised reserve requirements to twice the values initially set by the Federal Reserve Act. This action, which reduced excess reserves to about one-half of the System's security portfolio, also may have deprived banks—which had experienced massive deposit withdrawals—of desired liquidity, and it has been cited as possibly having contributed to the recession of 1937.

Gold imports continued unabated, however, and following the earlier cut excess reserves continued to rise, approaching $7 billion by the end of 1940. In these circumstances, the discount window fell into disuse and further open-market purchases generally were believed to be superfluous. In 1939, policy shifted to supporting the bond market to prevent it from being destabilized by the outbreak of war in Europe. The System began to operate from time to time in the long end of the market, and swaps between bills and bonds were employed to limit fluctuations in bond prices.

World War II and Pegging   As the necessity to finance expenditures for World War II became apparent, the System made the success of Treasury financing its primary goal. The Reserve banks established, as they had during World War I, a system of preferential discount rates to encourage the purchase of government debt. More importantly, the Federal Reserve conducted its open-market operations so that interest rates—both long- and short-term—were maintained at their early 1942 levels throughout the war and into the postwar period.

Short rates were extremely low—less than $\frac{1}{2}$ percent on Treasury bills—reflecting the high excess reserves and limited demand for credit in the immediate prewar years. Since longer-term rates were considerably higher—$2\frac{1}{2}$ percent on government bonds—a substantial demand for bonds developed once it became clear that they had become as liquid as shorter-term instruments. Moreover, the Treasury and debtors generally were able to borrow sizable quantities of funds without causing any increase in market rates of interest since the Federal Reserve was compelled to supply credit automatically to meet demand as long as rates were being pegged. The stock of loans and investments at commercial banks more than tripled over the period of pegging.

When the war ended, the economy grew rapidly and inflation accelerated, partly because of the high level of liquidity which had accumulated under the pegging regime and partly because of the cessation of wartime controls on spending and prices. However, the Treasury's need to sell debt did not end with the war; therefore, the administration continued to resist further suggestions from the System that rates be allowed to rise.

When a recession developed in 1948 to 1949, the Federal Reserve found that its commitment to pegging bond prices precluded an active policy of resistance, although reserve requirements were reduced. The advent of the Korean war brought a reemergence of inflationary pressures. By this time the Federal Reserve had become, in the words of its Chairman, "an engine of inflation." The discount rate was raised by $\frac{1}{4}$ percent in August 1950 and short rates rose somewhat. However, the Federal Reserve maintained a policy of pegging long-term rates as the difficult confrontation with the administration continued.

Finally in March of 1951 an agreement—known as the Accord—was reached between the Treasury and the Federal Reserve System. It established a schedule for the cessation of pegging and ended a protracted period of fundamental disagreement by restoring to the Federal Reserve the freedom to conduct independent monetary policy.

Selective Credit Controls   Partly reflecting an awareness that the ability to exercise monetary restraint had been abandoned by the decision to support bond prices, and partly reflecting the need to facilitate the transfer of resources to defense-related projects, authority was granted to the Reserve, even before the United States entered World War II, for the direct control of consumer credit. This authority—coming from an executive order of the President—allowed the Federal Reserve to establish legal maxima regarding (1) the percentages of various consumer expenditures which could be financed with credit and (2) terms to maturity of this debt.

When controls were lifted in late 1947, expenditures financed by consumer credit grew rapidly. The rate of inflation accelerated and within a year Congress gave President Truman temporary authority—expiring in mid-1949—to direct the Federal Reserve to reestablish controls. Shortly after controls were again imposed in September 1948, consumer expenditures weakened—perhaps reflecting in part earlier anticipatory purchases—and by early 1949 a general business slowdown became apparent. Controls were eased in the spring to the point where they ceased to be effectively binding, and they expired on schedule several months later.

In September of the following year, as the economy began to feel demands related to the Korean war, the Defense Production Act revived, on the recommendation of the President and of the Board of Governors, the Board's authority to reinstate consumer credit controls and gave it, for the first time, similar controls over the use of credit for construction. Consumer credit controls expired in the spring of 1952, and construction credit controls expired the following September.

Monetary Policy Since the Accord   After the Accord, the System found itself with the authority and willingness to exert independent and effective monetary policy for the first time since the mid-1930s. Reserve requirements, which had been raised and maintained at high levels during the period of pegging, were systematically reduced in the decade that followed. In order to encourage a revival of free market for government securities the System supplied a greater share of member-bank reserves through discounting, and the FOMC announced that it would not seek to achieve any particular pattern of market yields and would, so far as possible, confine its open-market operations to the short end of the market. Indeed, with rare exceptions, all open-market operations during the years 1953–1960 were limited to short-term bills. It was believed that this procedure—which came to be known as "bills only" or "bills preferably"—would minimize market disruptions due to Federal Reserve operations, since the market for bills was much more active than that for bonds. Nevertheless, it was expected that the impact of open-market operations in the short end of the market would be transmitted to the longer end as relative rates were kept in alignment by market participants.

To implement policy in the post-Accord period, members of the FOMC needed operating guides and were compelled to become more analytical in their statements about how policy should be carried out. Typically, they focused on short-term interest rates and on the member-bank levels of excess and borrowed reserves which they believed would be appropriate for policy. Eventually, policy recommendations came to be expressed in terms of excess reserves, net of borrowed reserves, or free reserves.

The first post-Accord recession occurred in the year 1953–54. The Federal Reserve resisted this development vigorously, on conjunction with parallel adjustments to fiscal policy, and the ensuing economic recovery was strong enough to be accompanied by a troubling increase in prices. The Federal Reserve moved strongly to counter this inflation, maintaining free reserves in the 1956–57 period well below their recession levels. Business activity turned down again in 1957 to 1958; the tenor of the Federal Reserve's response was altered by experience, however, and the downturn was resisted more cautiously and on a more modest scale than had been its predecessor. By the time the recovery began, inflation had abated significantly.

When the economy turned down again, in 1960, international considerations had introduced a new dimension to policy deliberations. The 1957–58 recession had coincided with a period of rising interest rates at foreign money centers; as U.S. monetary policy moved toward putting some downward pressure on interest rates, short-term funds seeking maximum yields began to move out of the United States. This increased the supply of dollars that was already swollen by a large U.S. balance of payments deficit, and it put further upward pressure on the value of the currencies into which the funds were invested. To resist changes in their exchange rates the central banks of these countries proceeded to sell their currencies for dollars. Earlier in the postwar period, foreign official institutions had generally been willing to place the proceeds of these sales in dollar-denominated assets, such as Treasury bills. However, as fear grew that the United States would devalue its currency, foreign official institutions began to sell their dollar holdings to the Treasury in exchange for gold.

Thus, the accumulated effects of balance of payments deficit and its most obvious manifestation, the gold outflow, presented a strong case for higher interest rates; the developing recession of 1960 to 1961, however, argued for ease. To attempt to cope with this, the Federal Reserve and the Treasury embarked upon a joint attempt to stimulate the economy while at the same time trying to minimize the downward movement of short-term rates. To finance the federal deficit, the Treasury put unusual emphasis on the issue of bills; the Federal Reserve, meanwhile, tended to sell bills and purchase bonds. Thus, the Federal Reserve's policy of deliberately limiting open-market operations to the short end of the market had come to an end.

Swap arrangements were made with foreign central banks in order to stem the gold outflow. These allowed the Federal Reserve to obtain foreign currencies from foreign central banks. The dollars which the foreign central banks received through the swap were covered against exchange risk, so that drawing on the swaps by the United States meant substitution in foreign central-bank portfolios of covered for uncovered dollars. These measures reduced the downward pressure on the dollar and reduced or postponed purchases of gold by foreign governments.

By the early 1960s, some within the System had begun to question the use of free reserves and interest rates as operating or intermediate objectives of monetary policy. It was observed, for example, that interest rates by their nature were procyclical, so that using them to gauge monetary policy made it appear to be countercyclical whether it was or not. Similarly, since the level of excess reserves which banks preferred to hold tended to respond to the interest earnings foregone, this measure too displayed a natural cyclical movement which detracted from its use as a measure of the thrust of monetary policy.

Interest subsequently began to focus on credit aggregates and monetary aggregates as intermediate objectives of policy. By the mid-1960s the directive to the manager of the open-market account, which previously had been couched strictly in terms of money-market and interest rate objectives, came to include a proviso clause which directed the manager to modify his money-market objectives if bank credit growth deviated sufficiently from expectations.

In response to a concern with the strength of bank credit growth in the mid- and late 1960s, interest rates were allowed to rise to very high levels. Moreover, the Board of Governors placed effective ceiling rates on very large time deposits, limiting the ability of large banks to attract funds in this form. The imposition of these measures restricted the growth of bank credit. It also promoted a rechanneling of financial flows. To some degree, particularly in the second episode, the affected banks were able to secure funds from other sources, such as the Eurodollar market, and often used innovative techniques. Nevertheless, some credit flows that would have been intermediated through the banking system went elsewhere, typically to the commercial paper market. In 1973 all interest rate ceilings on large deposits were suspended.

The decade spanning the mid-1960s to the mid-1970s was also a period in which the Board used changes in reserve requirements to achieve bank credit and other objectives. To slow bank credit expansion in the late-1960s, the Board imposed or raised reserve requirements on those specific liability items that banks were actively using to acquire substantial volumes of loanable funds. In addition to large-denomination time deposits, these included proceeds of commercial paper issued by bank holding companies provided to subsidiary banks, loans sold to parent holding companies, and the issuance of U.S. dollar deposits at foreign branches (Eurodollar deposits).

In the early 1970s the Board used reserve requirements to influence the relative cost to member banks of various kinds of deposits in order to promote a lengthening in the average maturity of their liabilities. On several occasions the Board has adjusted reserve requirements to affect the relative cost of Eurodollar deposits—in order to influence the market for the dollar.

Recent Monetary Policy

Monetary policy in the 1970s has been characterized by the use of monetary aggregates as intermediate objectives of policy. The choice of monetary aggregates (particularly the narrow definition of currency plus demand deposits, or M-1) was based upon considerable research indicating that narrowly defined money had been somewhat more closely related to variables which the Federal Reserve could directly influence, such as interest rates, and to ultimate objectives, such as national income and prices, than to either more inclusive measures of liquidity or measures of bank credit. This outcome seems to reflect the fact that M-1 includes the only widely used media of exchange, whereas the composition of the broader aggregates is more heterogeneous, including time and savings deposits in addition to M-1, while bank credit is but one of several alternative forms of credit.

Research also indicated that an understanding of the behavior of intermediate targets was crucial if the likelihood of policy errors was to be minimized. For example, the following of a policy which emphasizes the control of money provides a type of automatic protection against a temporary failure to recognize and react to an undesirable movement in economic activity. Thus, if economic activity rises, the economy's need for media of exchange typically also increases and M-1 tends to accelerate. If the Federal Reserve acts to resist this acceleration by cutting back on the reserves it provides to member banks, interest rates will tend to rise and the excessive strength in the economy will automatically encounter resistance. By contrast, a policy which instead relied on interest rates as an intermediate objective was in greater danger of underestimating the need for restraint or expansion and thus more likely to contribute to undesired deviations of income from its preferred path.

On the other hand, it was clear that a policy which focused on monetary aggregates was vulnerable to error if the public's demand for money unpredictably shifted independently of changes in the pace of economic activity. Resistance to such shifts by the Federal Reserve would produce changes in interest rates and credit conditions which would tend to deflect income from its preferred course.

By the early 1970s experience had suggested that, on balance, the likelihood of policy error is lower if money is given more emphasis than interest rates. In addition to the professional research alluded to above, this conclusion was based on two other considerations: first, an assessment of the outcome of earlier policies which had relied more heavily upon interest rates and money-market conditions than upon monetary aggregates as intermediate objectives; second, the recognition that interest rates are influenced by expectational factors, particularly the expected rate of inflation, which can make their movements hard to interpret.

In recent years, however, monetary policy has been complicated by the growing use of computer-assisted cash management techniques and a series of financial innovations and regulatory decisions which have spawned a variety of new interest-bearing deposits which can be used to effect transactions. These developments have changed familiar relationships between the monetary aggregates as intermediate objectives of policy and such final targets as the pace of economic activity. These shifts have served to reemphasize the Federal Reserve's often-stated view that there exists no single formula or operating target on which it can rely to work effectively in all circumstances.

References

Anderson, Clay J., *A Half Century of Federal Reserve Policymaking, 1914–1964*, The Federal Reserve Bank of Philadelphia, Philadelphia, 1965; Board of Governors of the Federal Reserve System, *Open Market Policies and Operating Procedures—Staff Studies*, 1971; Prochnow, Herbert V. (ed.), *The Federal Reserve System*, Harper, New York, 1960; Wallich, Henry C., and Peter M. Kier, "The Role of Operating Guides in U.S. Monetary Policy: A Historical Review," *Kredit und Kapital*, Vol I, Duncker and Humblot, Berlin, 1978, pp. 30–52.

(*See also* Bank deposits; Banking system; Business credit; Chicago school; Consumer credit; Credit, an overview; Economic statistics; Eurodollar market; Federal Reserve System; Gold standard; Great Depression; Inflation; Interest rates; Keynesian economics; Monetary policy; Money supply; Mortgage credit; Open-market operations; Selective credit controls; Thrift institutions; Velocity of circulation of money)

Henry C. Wallich and Thomas F. Brady

Federal Reserve System

On December 23, 1913, President Woodrow Wilson signed the Federal Reserve Act, and the Federal Reserve System became the nation's central bank. The System began to operate about a year later. The Federal Reserve was established chiefly in response to financial crises and economic disruptions arising from periodic imbalance in the supply of money and credit which had begun to develop during the latter half of the nineteenth century. The System's designers gave it the ability to influence the supply of money and credit and to act as a lender of last resort to the banking system.

In addition to its responsibilities toward monetary policy, the Federal Reserve System performs several other functions. It acts as a fiscal agent for the Treasury, issuing and redeeming Treasury bonds. In close cooperation and consultation with the Treasury, and often in cooperation with other central banks, the Federal Reserve operates in foreign exchange markets to correct disorders which may occur in the market for the dollar. The System also provides the economy with coin and currency. The Federal Reserve exercises a regulatory and supervisory role, primarily with respect to state-chartered member banks, member banks with foreign branches, and bank holding companies. In recent years the Federal Reserve has been given the responsibility of prescribing and enforcing regulations to implement several pieces of consumer credit legislation, including controls. Federal Reserve Banks provide various services to their member banks, notably access to the System's check-clearing and fund-transfer facilities.

By design, the Federal Reserve System enjoys substantial independence from the executive and legislative branches of government. Congress provided this independence in order to protect the conduct of monetary policy from political pressures. Membership in the Federal Reserve System is obligatory for federally chartered (national) banks and optional for banks receiving their charters from state governments. As a condition of membership, member banks must purchase shares in the Reserve bank of their district equal to 3 percent of their capital (with an additional 3 percent subject to call) and bearing a statutorily determined interest rate of 6 percent; however, member-bank influence over the Reserve's operations is quite limited. All member banks are required to maintain a percentage of their deposit liabilities as noninterest bearing reserves. This requirement entails the major cost of membership. There are, however, no fees associated with services the System provides member banks. As of December 1978, 5591 of the nation's 14,730 commercial banks—holding about 71 percent of domestic deposits at all commercial banks—were members of the Federal Reserve System.

The organization of the Federal Reserve System is fairly detailed, reflecting both the inherent complexities of central banking and the intent of the System's designers to ensure that it be both well-insulated from political influence and somewhat decentralized. In accordance with provisions of the Federal Reserve Act, the United States is divided into 12 Federal Reserve Districts, each served by a Federal Reserve bank. At the end of 1978, these banks had 22,438 full-time employees, including officers. At the center of the Federal Reserve System is its Board of Governors, located in Washington, D.C., with a staff, at the end of 1978, of 1474. Expenses of the entire System in that year amounted to $652 million, of which $60 million was accounted for by printing, issuing, and redeeming Federal Reserve notes.

Structure and Organization

The Federal Reserve System is headed by its Board of Governors. The Board is composed of seven members, including its presiding officer appointed by the President and subject to confirmation by the Senate. Members' terms are for 14 years, and once a member has completed a full term, reappointment is not possible. Continuity of membership on the Board is provided for by the structuring of terms so that one expires every second year; this feature also tends to limit the influence a particular President may have on the Board's composition. The President designates two members of the Board to act as its chair and vice-chair, each for renewable terms of 4 years, also subject to Senate confirmation.

The Board may take several types of monetary policy actions. The Board determines—within statutory limits—the percentages of demand, time, and savings deposits which member banks must hold as reserves. It must review and approve the level of the discount rates—the rates of interest charged on loans the System makes to member banks—at each of the 12 Federal Reserve banks. Generally, discount rates are the same at each bank. Also, the seven-member Board constitutes a majority of the 12 members of the Federal Open Market Committee. The Board is empowered to determine maximum interest rates which member banks may pay on savings and time deposits. These ceilings are determined after consultation with other agencies— the Federal Deposit Insurance Corporation, the Federal Home Loan Bank Board, and the National Credit Union Administration Board—which determine interest rate ceilings on deposits offered by federally insured financial institutions competing with member banks. The Board is responsible for setting margin requirements on credit extended by brokers, banks, or others for the purpose of purchasing or carrying stocks. This provides the Board's only influence over a particular type of credit. The Board also has regulatory, supervisory, and administrative duties.

The Federal Open Market Committee (FOMC) is the most important policymaking body in the Federal Reserve System. Its decisions determine the quantity of reserves that the System supplies to member banks. Reserves are created whenever the System purchases government securities on the open market, paying with its own liabilities in the form of currency or deposits. Reserves are withdrawn whenever the System sells securities on the open market. These actions—called open-market operations—largely determine the quantity of deposits which member banks can offer and, thus, the money supply. They strongly influence the cost and availability of credit, interest rates, and financial developments generally. The FOMC also operates in foreign currencies—which it may borrow from other central banks—to purchase or sell dollars in foreign exchange markets when such transactions are judged necessary to counter disorderly conditions in these markets. Foreign exchange operations are always done in consultation with, and often on behalf of, the Department of the Treasury.

The membership of the FOMC includes, in addition to the seven members of the Board of Governors, five presidents of Federal Reserve banks. By tradition, the head of the FOMC is the head of the Board of Governors and the vice chair is the president of the Federal Reserve Bank of New York, a permanent member of the FOMC. The four remaining positions are shared by the 11 other Reserve bank presidents, using a procedure of rotation. All Reserve bank presidents participate in FOMC meetings which are held approximately once a month.

The Federal Reserve banks operate under boards of nine directors, three of whom are appointed by the Board of Governors; the rest are elected by the member banks of each district. The directors of each Reserve bank select its president and first vice president, subject to the approval of the Board of Governors. The Reserve banks determine conditions under which loans are made to member banks (in accordance with general instructions from the Board of Governors) and establish discount rates fortnightly subject to review and determination by the Board. The Reserve banks provide most of the System's services to member banks.

The directors of each Federal Reserve bank also have the responsibility of annually electing a district member, usually a banker, to the Federal Advisory Council, which was created to allow responsible observers from outside the System an opportunity to provide advice and policy recommendations. The Federal Reserve Act requires that the Council participate at least four times a year in discussions with the Board of Governors.

Supervisory and Regulatory Responsibilities

The Federal Reserve's supervisory and regulatory activities are the responsibility of the Board of Governors. The Board supervises the admission of state banks seeking membership and is jointly responsible with the various states for periodic examinations and the enforcement of regulations pertaining to state member banks. Rulings must also be made on branching applications and requests for certain changes in capital structure. The bulk of this work has been delegated by the Board of Governors to the Federal Reserve banks.

Congress has given the Board of Governors, along with the other banking agencies, the responsibility of administering the Bank Merger Act and the Bank Holding Company Act. In accordance with the Bank Merger Act, the Board must act on bank mergers when the surviving bank would be a state member. In exercising this authority, the Board takes into account such factors as the effect the merger would have on competition, public convenience, and the quality of bank management.

The Bank Holding Company Act requires all bank holding companies—organizations which substantially control, through ownership or other means, the management of one or more banks—to register with the Federal Reserve. Bank holding companies have been formed to allow a single management to control one or more banks as well as companies engaged in certain nonbank activities. This type of organization—particularly the one-bank holding company-expanded rapidly in the late 1960s. The aim of this act is to maintain the separation between banking and commerce and to prevent the development of monopoly in banking.

The Board of Governors is responsible for certain foreign activities of member banks and bank holding companies, and it charters and regulates Edge Act corporations, domestic subsidiaries of U.S. banks licensed to do an international banking business. Member banks wishing to establish foreign branches must seek approval from the Board. These branches and other foreign activities of member banks are regulated by the Board. The Board also authorizes overseas investments by member banks, Edge Act corporations, and bank holding companies.

The Board of Governors has been assigned supervisory and regulatory responsibilities by several pieces of legislation included in the Consumer Credit Protection Act. For three of these—the Truth-in-Lending Act of 1968, the Equal Credit Opportunity Act of 1974, and the Electronic Funds Transfer Act of 1978—the Board has been directed to prescribe regulations to carry out the purpose of the acts and to enforce them at state member banks. The Truth-in-Lending Act was based on the premise that "competition among the various financial institutions . . . would be strengthened by the informed use of credit." Accordingly, this act requires creditors to furnish borrowers with certain basic information—in a uniform manner—regarding the cost of the credit they are seeking. The act also contains stipulations regarding disclosure in the advertising of credit terms.

An amendment to the act prohibits the unsolicited issuance of credit cards, and places at $50 a cardholder's maximum liability for the unauthorized use of stolen or lost cards.

The Equal Credit Opportunity Act proscribes credit discrimination on the basis of an applicant's "race, color, religion, national origin, sex, marital status or age (provided the applicant has the capacity to contract)." At the Board's suggestion, this act directed that the Board establish a Consumer Advisory Council to furnish it with advice and to be available for consultation regarding the Board's responsibilities under the Consumer Credit Protection Act.

Congress's purpose in establishing the Electronic Funds Transfer Act was "to provide a basic framework establishing the rights, liabilities, and responsibilities of participants in electronic fund transfer systems." The act deals primarily with individual consumer rights.

The Board is also responsible for enforcing at state member banks the Fair Credit Reporting Act of 1970 and the Fair Debt Collection Practices Act of 1978. These pieces of legislation deal, respectively, with procedures for rectifying mistakes made regarding a person's credit record and with practices used to collect debt incurred for personal, family, or household purposes when the collector is acting for another person or under another name. The Board has also been directed to prescribe regulations necessary to carry out the Home Mortgage Disclosure Act. The purpose of this act is to make information publicly available regarding lending patterns of depositary institutions to aid in determining whether they are meeting their "obligations to serve the housing needs of the communities and the neighborhoods in which they are located."

With several other financial supervisory agencies, the Federal Reserve was given the responsibility for writing regulations to implement the Community Reinvestment Act of 1977. The purpose of this act is to encourage financial institutions to meet the "credit needs of their local community or communities." The act requires the supervisory agencies to take into consideration compliance with this act when acting on applications dealing with branching, merging, establishing bank holding companies, and so on. The Federal Reserve enforces the act with respect to state member banks, and follows its guidelines when reviewing applications for membership in the System.

Services Provided by the System to Its Member Banks

Most of the services which the Federal Reserve offers its member banks are provided by the 12 district banks and their branches. These banks clear checks presented to their member banks for payment. Member banks also have access to a Federal Reserve communications system which transfers funds from one member bank to another on a same-day basis by adjusting reserves of the transferring and receiving banks. Finally, member banks may trade marketable U.S. government securities using the Federal Reserve communication system in conjunction with a computer-recorded transfer-of-ownership system jointly operated with the Treasury. The securities themselves do not move and often remain at the Federal Reserve Banks in safe-keeping facilities which are also offered to member banks.

Coin and currency are provided to member banks by their district Reserve Banks; payment is effected through a reduction in reserves member banks maintain on deposit at Reserve Banks. Typically, nonmember banks replenish net currency losses through the services of a larger member bank. The System—through the Federal Reserve Bank of New York—also provides storage and safekeeping for gold and U.S. government securities held by foreign central banks.

Independence

The Federal Reserve, like some other central banks, enjoys a degree of independence within the government. This status reflects a recognition that the conduct of monetary policy relies substantially on judgment and that it is susceptible to political influences. Congress designed the Federal Reserve System to incorporate an element of formal executive and legislative control, but limited this influence to the appointment and confirmation of the members of the Board of Governors. However, generally close contact between members of the Federal Reserve Board and important members of the executive and legislative branches ensures a forum through which viewpoints can be exchanged. Moreover, an appointment to the Board must be made at least every 2 years and, in practice, these appointments are made much more frequently since Board members, for a variety of reasons, frequently do not serve full 14-year terms.

The System must employ its independence with the recognition that Congress has the power to amend the status of the Federal Reserve Act in any way it sees fit. Moreover, the Board and the FOMC are required by the Full Employment and Balanced Growth Act of 1978 to state "objectives and plans ... with respect to the ranges of growth or diminution of the monetary and credit aggregates for the calendar year during which the report is transmitted." These objectives and plans—transmitted to Congress twice yearly—must also be related to "the short-term goals set forth in the most recent Economic Report of the President."

An important part of the Federal Reserve System's independence is its immunity from potential influence via the appropriations process. The System's portfolio of securities provides the bulk of its income, and earnings in excess of expenses, which include both dividends paid to member banks and losses, if any, on sales of government securities and on foreign exchange transactions, are remitted periodically to the Treasury. In 1978, earnings amounted to $7.7 billion. They are included in the national income accounts as part of corporate profits, of which in 1978 they accounted for 3.8 percent before and 6.5 percent after taxes.

History

Almost all nations have central banks, and among developed countries that of the United States is one of the more recently established. The central banks of Sweden and England, for example, were each founded in the seventeenth century. Central banking services in the United States prior to the Federal Reserve were provided from time to time by other institutions. The First and Second Banks of the United States, large private institutions chartered and partly owned by the federal government, were able to exert some deliberate influence on the supply of credit. In the period from 1863 to 1914, the Treasury exerted a certain amount of control over credit by moving its silver and gold holdings between its own vaults and the banking system. This control was generally inadequate, however. Indeed, the Federal Reserve System was established in the wake of a series of financial crises often precipitated by credit demands related to needs for agricultural credit at rural banks. As these smaller banks drew on the reserves they held at larger city banks, credit pressures developed in money centers. When the banking system's reserves proved to be inadequate to meet these demands, the ensuing credit shortages sometimes led to financial panics. These periodic and difficult episodes made it clear that the lack of a central bank was a serious gap in the economic structure of the United States.

The Federal Reserve Act was drafted by Representative Carter Glass and Senator Robert Owen, with the active participation of President Woodrow Wilson. The Federal Reserve Board created by the original act included the Secretary of the Treasury and the Comptroller of the Currency as ex officio members. One of the Board's earliest tasks was to determine the exact number of Federal Reserve districts (the act called for between eight and twelve), to denote their boundaries, and to locate and establish the district banks. The Board also determined that, as a condition for membership, banks would have to clear checks at par, and a system of check clearing was developed.

The Federal Reserve System's earliest actions affecting credit were primarily limited to making loans to member banks through the discounting of commercial and agricultural paper. Much of this activity took place at the discretion of individual Reserve banks. After World War I, the Reserve banks began to engage in uncoordinated open-market purchases, largely with a view toward increasing earnings by expanding their portfolios of interest-bearing assets. As it became clear that these operations had an effect on member-bank reserves, the Board set up a nonstatutory committee to coordinate these operations among Reserve banks.

In the 1930s several pieces of legislation were enacted which added to the strength and flexibility of the Federal Reserve System while simultaneously promoting a concentration of its powers in Washington. Legislation which was passed in early 1932 allowed the System to add government securities acquired through open-market operations to other assets—gold and discounted paper—which it could use to back its liabilities. This eliminated a serious limitation of the System's ability to resist the weakening economy by adding to member-bank reserves through purchases of government securities on the open market.

The Banking Act of 1935 made several important changes. The Federal Open Market Committee was established as a statutory body to determine the System's policy with respect to open-market operations. The Board of Governors was given the authority to adjust the percentages of deposits which member banks must hold as reserves up to a maximum of twice the original percentages. The System's role as a lender of last resort was enhanced by giving it the ability to make loans to member banks secured to the satisfaction of the Federal Reserve banks, operating under rules and regulations prescribed by the Board of Governors. Earlier in the 1930s banks needing credit often could not obtain it because the paper in their portfolios was not eligible to be discounted. Moreover, the Reserve banks were given the authority (previously unclear) to refuse to discount paper for a member bank, thereby establishing the principle that access to Federal Reserve credit was a privilege—rather than a right—of member banks.

The composition of the Board of Governors was amended in 1935 to remove the Secretary of the Treasury and the Comptroller of the Currency. Appointive membership was increased to seven and terms were lengthened from 10 to 14 years. Under a provision of the Securities Exchange Act of 1934, the Board was given the power to impose margin requirements on credit extended by banks, brokers, and dealers for the purpose of purchasing or carrying stock.

During World War II, the task of financing government expenditures seriously compromised the System's ability to achieve any other objectives of monetary policy. In recognition of this, the Board was authorized in the fall of 1941 to establish consumer credit controls. Congress rescinded this authority in November 1947. It was subsequently reinstated in 1948 to 1949 and again during the Korean war period, when controls on credit for residential and nonresidential construction were also established.

With the end of the Second World War, the Federal Reserve began to limit its efforts to maintain short-term interest rates. However, it remained committed to maintaining the price of long-term bonds until March 1951, when an agreement—known as the Accord—was reached between the Federal Reserve and the Treasury.

Since the Accord, the supervisory activities and responsibilities of the Federal Reserve System have been broadened considerably by a series of legislative actions—notably the Bank Holding Company Act of 1956 and the several pieces of consumer credit legislation passed between 1968 and 1978.

In recent years, the System has faced an acceleration of withdrawals by state member banks. This development is largely due to the high nominal interest rates which have accompanied high rates of inflation. On the one hand, high interest rates have added significantly to the earnings which member banks forgo owing to reserve requirements. On the other, high rates have strongly encouraged bank depositors to find methods of reducing their holdings of demand deposits, which earn no explicit interest. These developments have had an adverse impact on member-bank profits and have placed member banks at a competitive disadvantage. By the end of 1978, member banks held 71 percent of total commercial-bank deposits, down from about 80 percent in 1970.

The growing importance of foreign banks in the United States has also affected the Federal Reserve. The International Banking Act of 1978 authorized the Federal Reserve to impose reserve requirements and deposit interest rate ceilings on U.S. branches and agencies of foreign banks, and to prescribe for these institutions terms of access to Federal Reserve credit and its other services, while subjecting them to federal regulation through one of the federal bank regulatory agencies. As of this writing, the Board of Governors has announced proposals to implement these provisions.

References

Board of Governors of the Federal Reserve System, *The Federal Reserve System—Purposes and Functions*, 1974; Johnson, Roger T., *Historical Beginnings: The Federal Reserve System*, The Federal Reserve Bank of Boston, Boston, 1977; Prochnow, Herbert V. (ed.) *The Federal Reserve System*, Harper, New York, 1960.

(*See also* Banking system; Federal Reserve policy; Monetary policy; Open-market operations)

Henry C. Wallich and Thomas F. Brady

Federal Trade Commission

The Federal Trade Commission (FTC) is a U.S. government agency, created by the Federal Trade Commission Act of 1914, which lays down a general prohibition against use in commerce of unfair methods of competition and unfair or deceptive acts or practices. Since the creation of the Federal Trade Commission, its duties have been further defined and enlarged in 14 different acts of Congress. For administrative purposes, the FTC became an independent administrative agency in 1951.

Activities

Its activities, which center on attempting to create an atmosphere of competition and healthful business climate, are summarized in the following list:

1. The FTC attempts to promote free and fair competition in interstate commerce through the prevention of general trade restraints, such as price-fixing.

2. The FTC works continually to prevent dissemination of false or deceptive advertisements. In recent years, the FTC has taken this aspect of its work much more seriously, and on several occasions it has asked advertisers to run additional advertising correcting their alleged errors in earlier advertising.

3. The FTC works to prevent both discrimination in price and arrangements which lessen competition or tend toward monopoly.

4. The agency regulates packaging and labeling, and takes an active role in ensuring that sellers do not deceptively package their products and that they make their labels informative.

5. The Commission protects trademarks held by U.S. business firms.

6. In an effort to promote U.S. exports, the FTC is responsible for licensing and supervising associations of American exporters.

7. The FTC works in conjunction with financial regulatory agencies of the U.S. government to assure both truth in lending for consumer creditors and fairness in consumer reporting activities, such as those undertaken by credit bureaus.

8. The FTC gathers and publishes statistical information relating to business, such as annual reports on mergers and quarterly financial data for manufacturing industries, mining, and trade by size of company.

The FTC also has watchdog and enforcement activities. They include the following:

1. The FTC fosters voluntary observance of statutes and regulations by publishing guidelines, trade regulation rules, and advisory opinions as to what industry may do under laws administered by the FTC. The emphasis is always on voluntary compliance first, with stronger measures taken only when the FTC judges that a violation is chronic or willful.

2. In the event that voluntary compliance is not forthcoming or that the FTC and a business firm do not view a situation in the same way, formal litigation may be initiated by the FTC to force compliance through the courts.

Continuing Heavy Legal Casework Load

Legal cases may originate from a consumer or competitor, by congressional initiative, or at the request of any governmental agency, including the FTC itself. If the case is not dismissed or settled informally, the first hearing is held before an administrative law judge of the FTC.

If dissatisfied with the hearing before the administrative law judge, complainants or defendants can appeal to:

1. The Commission
2. The U.S. Court of Appeals
3. The Supreme Court

In the event that a decision against the defendant is sustained or modified, a cease-and-desist order is issued. All firms against which cease-and-desist orders are filed must file reports with the FTC proving compliance. Failure to comply can lead the firm into civil and/or contempt proceedings.

References

Annual Report to Congress, Federal Trade Commission.

(*See also* Competition)

William J. Brown

Financial institutions

Financial institutions are private or governmental organizations which serve the purpose of accumulating funds from savers and chaneling them to individuals, households, or businesses needing credit. In that role, financial institutions perform the vital function of facilitating the flow of savings from those business and household units with surplus funds to businesses and households with insufficient funds to accomplish the purchasing they wish. The smooth flow of funds from savers to investors is essential to the growth of the economy and to the welfare of individuals. Financial institutions are intermediaries providing savers with the type of financial asset they wish and investors with the type of financial assistance they need to buy goods and services.

Only a small portion of the borrowing that takes place in this country is financed by direct negotiation between the saver and the borrower. In some cases, household members may borrow from friends or relatives, but such activities are a very small part of total credit transactions. Financial institutions are concerned with the flows of funds from savings into investment that occur between unrelated parties.

Classification

Financial institutions may be classified according to the following categories:

1. Deposit-type institutions—bank
2. Deposit-type institutions—nonbank
3. Contractual savings institutions
4. Investment-type institutions
5. Personal and business finance companies
6. Government and quasi-government agencies
7. Miscellaneous lenders

Deposit-Type Financial Institutions—Bank Commercial banks are now, and have been for decades, the most important element in our financial system. Banks hold the widest variety of assets of any financial institution, and they issue the widest variety of financial liabilities. Since banks hold demand deposits (checking account funds) they hold the major portion of the narrowly defined money supply, M-1. Through their actions, banks can influence the size of the money supply, and they are therefore, carefully observed and regulated. But regulation of banks refers only to their actions concerning safety of deposits and concerning their activities which affect national economic policy. Their profits are not regulated.

Most of the effect of monetary policy on banks is carried out through Federal Reserve open-market operations (purchases and sales of U.S. government securities).

Sales of securities to the private sector of the economy drain funds out of banks as purchasers write checks payable to the Treasurer of the United States. Purchases, on the other hand, provide funds to the banks.

Deposit-Type Financial Institutions—Nonbank   These consist of savings and loan associations, mutual savings banks (in states where they exist), and credit unions. Savings and loan associations trace their ancestry to building and loan associations, begun in the middle of the nineteenth century, which were designed so that a group of prospective homeowners could pool their funds and gradually finance the purchase of homes. As time went on, savers and borrowers became distinct groups, and the associations grew, enabling more rapid purchase by prospective homeowners and the payment of interest to savers who had surplus funds. Most savings and loan associations are of the mutual type, with depositors owning a share of the association and voting for directors, although stock associations are permitted in some states.

As might be expected from their heritage, savings and loan associations invest very heavily in mortgage loans, although recent legislation has permitted them to make some installment loans for equipment in homes. One of the problems faced by savings and loan associations is that the interest rates they charge are fixed for the life of the loan, while the rates paid for savings may vary with market interest rates. In practice, interest rates on savings have been at or near the legal ceilings, but depositors have tended to switch from short-term, low-interest deposits to higher-interest-earning, long-term deposits, thus raising the effective cost of funds to the institution.

Contractual Savings Institutions   These institutions are primarily life insurance companies and pension funds. They are characterized by defined obligations for future payments, given that certain prescribed conditions occur in the future, such as retirement or death. Since their liabilities are predictable, they are able to invest in longer-term securities than can deposit-type financial intermediaries. In the past, bonds and common stocks have been the favorite investment vehicles for these types of intermediaries, but in the 1970s contractual savings institutions have moved aggressively to investments in real estate, commercial loans, mortgage loans, and a broad range of other investments.

Insurance companies are regulated by state insurance commissioners, and pension-funds administrators are regulated through both federal and state statutes and regulations. The federal influence upon pension-funds administrators is primarily through the Employee Retirement Income Security Act, which requires both reporting and procedures incident to the administration of a pension fund, as well as disclosure of information to covered employees.

Because of the longer-term nature of the investments undertaken by pension funds and insurance companies, these institutions tend to finance new construction and investment in durable equipment, which builds long-term productive ability in the economy. Commercial banks often finance construction projects while they are under construction, and the bank is paid off by the permanent loan from an insurance company or pension fund.

Investment-Type Institutions   These include mutual funds and trusts. Mutual funds own securities and issue shares of stock whose value is dependent upon the value of the securities owned by the mutual fund. Until the late 1970s most mutual funds were devoted to either common stock holdings, a mixture of common stock and bonds, or all bonds. However, in recent years it has become possible for mutual funds to hold tax-exempt securities and to pass on the tax exemption to their shareholders, and other mutual funds have been formed to hold short-term money-market securities. Such securities yield high rates of interest at times and offer investors good liquidity.

Trusts include both personal trusts and trusts used as investment vehicles, much like limited partnerships. It is common for a family to establish a trust to protect the principal and to provide beneficiary with the income from the body of the trust. However, it is also possible to use trusts as commercial investment vehicles. Many shopping centers and other types of investments use the trust form, with investors owning beneficial interests in the trust. For all practical purposes, such beneficial interests have all the characteristics of common stock to the investor.

Personal and Business Finance Companies   These companies finance large purchases by households, such as refrigerators, autos, washing machines, and vacations. Business finance companies assist firms in purchases of durable equipment, other companies, inventories, and similar items. Unlike banks, the personal and business finance companies raise funds by selling common stock and notes payable to persons or institutions in the private sector of the economy. Banks are frequently lenders to finance companies even though the two types of institutions compete in the marketplace for personal and business loans.

Interest rates on personal loans are often higher than for business or other types of loans. However, the personal lending field is one in which competition is high, and entry into the business may be obtained without great difficulty. A single default in a group of loans means that the lender must charge significantly more for all loans to recoup the loss due to default, and such defaults are encountered at times in the personal or business lending fields. There is little evidence that lending to either households or businesses is unusually profitable.

Government and Quasi-Government Agencies   These agencies have become important in lending to the private sector, particularly in the housing fields. Such institutions as the Government National Mortgage Association (GNMA), referred to as Ginny Mae, or the Federal National Mortgage Association (FNMA), referred to as Fanny Mae, channel funds to housing primarily through purchases of mortgages from private-sector lenders. Such purchases provide funds for the lenders to make additional mortgages. Federal agencies also provide guarantees for lenders which enable lenders to make loans to persons who would not otherwise qualify.

In order to keep the federal direct debt as low as possible, most agencies involved in providing funds to the private sector have been established as independent agencies or government corporations which issue debt in their own right and not as part of the public debt; that is, a government agency might issue debt instruments and use the funds to purchase mortgages in the open market, but the debt instruments would not count as part of the public debt.

Miscellaneous Lenders   Included in this category are pawnshops, wealthy individuals, and illegal lenders.

Relative Importance of Various Financial Institutions

The deposit-type financial institutions dominate. Their assets constitute more than 50 percent of all assets held by financial institutions. Next in importance are life insurance companies, followed by pension funds. The growth of private pension funds has been enormous, and many insurance companies provide financial counsel and, in some cases, life insurance to private pension funds. The assets held by private pension funds have been growing rapidly as a percent of total financial institution assets, while those held by life insurance companies have been declining.

References

Henning, Charles N., William Pigot, and Robert H. Scott, *Financial Markets and the Economy*, Prentice-Hall, Englewood Cliffs, N.J., 1978; Polakoff, M., et al., *Financial Institutions and Markets*, 2d ed., Houghton Mifflin, Boston 1980.

(*See also* Banking system; Capital markets and money markets; Interest rates; Money markets; Mutual funds; Thrift institutions)

William J. Brown

Financial instruments

The term financial instruments covers a wide variety of different types of instruments concerned with money. Most frequently thought of are those financial instruments which indicate an obligation of one party to another. A share of common stock, for example, is sold to an investor and conveys to that investor participation in the earnings of the corporation. If the corporation prospers, the shareholder expects to prosper also either through dividends paid or through appreciated value of the security. If things do not go well for the corporation issuing the stock, however, the shareholder can do no more than vote for new officers and directors. With shares of stock, the obligation of the issuing concern is to work diligently and well on the shareholder's behalf.

In the case of bonds issued by corporations, however, the obligation is one of debt. If the corporation fails to pay either interest or principal, the bondholder has specific remedies, spelled out in the indenture. The indenture describes exactly what steps the trustee shall take to protect the interests of the bondholders in each and every circumstance that may arise. Bonds are generally secured by a physical asset which is owned by the corporation and which may be seized and sold to satisfy the claims of bondholders. Debentures, on the other hand, are usually unsecured promises by a corporation to pay, and if interest or principal is not paid, the debenture holders are general claimants against the corporation rather than preferred claimants (as bondholders are).

Capital Markets

Common stock, bonds, and debentures are all associated with the capital markets. Long-term capital is also provided in some instances by beneficial interest in trusts, and the beneficial interests may be transferred from one person to another much like stock certificates. Partnership interests also provide long-term investments, but partnership interests are typically not evidenced by a piece of paper which is readily transferable in the marketplace, and, therefore, partnership interests are not normally considered financial instruments.

The federal government issues many securities, either through the direct obligation of the Treasury or through various governmental agencies and corporations. The long-term securities of the federal government are notes and bonds, with maturities typically ranging from 2 to as long as 30 years. Since those securities are risk-free, they are highly regarded by investors.

Money Markets

The money markets use an array of financial instruments, and those instruments change as the needs of financial institutions change, and as regulations affecting them are modified. Some of the more familiar forms of financial instruments used in connection with short-term obligations are as follows.

U.S. Treasury Bills   These are obligations of the U.S. government with original maturities of less than one year. They are regarded as the soundest form of short-term investment because the government has the power to repay without credit risk. In addition, there is a large secondary market for Treasury securities, so holders of bills can sell them easily if they wish their money before maturity. There is, of course, a market risk associated with sales prior to maturity. The price of bills may be higher or lower than the original purchaser paid, depending upon the changes that have occurred in market interest rates. Since the term to maturity is always very short for Treasury bills, however, the market risk is small.

Treasury bills are issued in 3-, 6-, 9-, and 12-month maturites at auctions held on a weekly basis by the Federal Reserve banks as fiscal agents for the Treasury. Lenders to the government submit bids on either a competitive or a noncompetitive basis. The competitive bids specify the price the purchaser is willing to pay; the noncompetitive bids state that the purchaser will accept the average yield at the particular auction. Noncompetitive bids are usually limited to specified amounts, such as $100,000 or less.

Repurchase Agreements   These agreements are a method of secured financing in which a borrower sells U.S. government securities to a lender for a short period of time, usually one day, and at the time of sale agrees to repurchase the securities at a stated price, so the lender knows the exact interest to be earned and is in a secured position in the event of default by the borrower. The securities are usually held by a bank trust department as trustee or by the Federal Reserve bank of the region because U.S. government securities are in bearer form and thus must be kept under safekeeping. Nevertheless, the securities would pass to the lender in the event of default. Repurchase agreements are widely used by U.S. government bond dealers to finance their inventories of securities at as low a cost as possible, and such lending is popular with both banks and nonfinancial firms because the loan is fully secured.

Commercial Paper   Commercial paper consists of unsecured promissory notes by nonfinancial firms. Commercial paper is the oldest of the money-market instruments and is unique to the U.S. financial system. Canada is the only other country with a commercial paper market, developed by Canadian manufacturers on the U.S. model, but the Canadian market is still very small. Commercial paper of less well known firms is often sold through commercial paper dealers, while paper of the very well known firms is normally sold directly by them to purchasers. For example, General Motors Acceptance Corporation regularly sells large amounts of commercial paper directly to short-term investors and uses the money to finance purchases of new automobiles.

Negotiable Certificates of Deposit   These are evidences of money on deposit at interest in a commercial bank in amounts in excess of $100,000. Negotiable certificates are payable to the bearer and may be sold by an individual if the funds are desired before the maturity of the instrument. There is, therefore, a market risk associated with selling negotiable certificates, but the credit risk associated with the issuer is generally thought to be quite small. Prior to 1960 certificates were issued in nonnegotiable form, and many banks still issue nonnegotiable certificates. However, large corporate purchasers of the certificates needed a way of obtaining their money prior to maturity because of uncertain cash flows and changes in financial opportunities. The issuing banks were forbidden by statute from redeeming certificates prior to their maturity, so a secondary market was developed by a Wall Street house, and other financial houses soon joined in, providing an active nationwide secondary market.

There are many other financial instruments used in the money markets, such as bankers acceptances, but the general nature of such instruments and the variety available are illustrated by the aforementioned examples.

The Common Check

It is important to note that a financial instrument is not necessarily a negotiable instrument as the term is used in the legal profession. Certificates of deposit are negotiable instruments, as are common checks, written by a member of a household or by a commercial firm. Checks are unlike the money-market or capital-market instruments mentioned above in that checks are for the transfer of funds, rather than for the investment of surplus funds at interest. For an instrument in writing to qualify as a negotiable instrument, it should have the following attributes:

1. Be in writing
2. Be signed by the maker or drawer
3. Have a certain promise or order
4. Be unconditional
5. Pay a certain sum of money
6. Except as authorized by the uniform commercial code, contain the full promise and no other promise to pay
7. Be payable on demand or at a definite time
8. Be payable either to the order of a named person or firm, or to bearer

References

Conley, Robert N., and William J. Robert, *Fundamentals of Business Law*, Prentice-Hall, Englewood Cliffs, N.J., 1974; Henning, Charles N., William Piggott, and Robert Haney Scott, *Financial Markets and the Economy*, Prentice-Hall, Englewood Cliffs, N.J., 1978; *Money Market Instruments*, 4th ed., Federal Reserve Bank of Richmond, Richmond, 1977; Smith, Len Young, and G. Gale Roberson, *American Business Law*, vol. 1, 2d ed., West Publishing Co., St. Paul, Minn., 1971.

(*See also* Bond; Capital markets and money markets; Money markets; Stock)

William J. Brown

Financial statements

Financial statements are the principal means of communicating accounting information to those outside of an enterprise. The financial statements most frequently provided are (1) the balance sheet, or statement of financial position; (2) the income or earning statement; and (3) the statement of changes in financial position, or statement of sources and applications of funds. Information can also be communicated voluntarily by means of financial reporting other than formal financial statements, in order to satisfy disclosure requirements by authoritative pronouncements or to comply with regulatory rules, or by custom. Corporate annual reports, prospectuses, and annual reports filed with the Securities and Exchange Commission are common examples of reports that include financial statements; other financial information; and nonfinancial information in such forms as news releases, management forecasts, and other descriptions of plans or expectations, as well as descriptions of the enterprise's social or environmental impact.

Financial statements are often audited by independent accountants in order to enhance confidence in their reliability. Some financial information reported outside of the financial statements is audited or reviewed, but not by independent accountants.

The Balance Sheet

The balance sheet depicts assets owned or controlled by the company on a given date together with the liabilities and owners' equities in the company at that date. Assets are objects, claims, and other rights owned by and having value to an organization. They derive value either because they can be exchanged for cash or goods and services in the future or because they can be used by the organization to increase the amount of cash or other assets at its disposal in the future.

In a balance sheet, four major kinds of assets are listed. Under current assets are included cash, accounts receivables, and inventories. Cash is the amount the company has in its cash registers and in its bank accounts. Accounts receivables are the claims the company has against its customers, quantified into the amount of cash the company expects to receive from these customers. These two items represent monetary assets: claims on specified amounts. The third item under current assets, inventories, is a nonmonetary asset representing physical items the company intends to sell or consume in operations. These three items are classified as current assets because they are reasonably expected to be realized in cash or sold or consumed during the normal operating cycle of the business or within 1 year, whichever is longer. They are listed in decreasing order of their convertibility into cash. A fourth item, plant and equipment, is also a nonmonetary asset and is classified as a noncurrent asset because it is expected to produce benefits not only in the next year but for many years to come. Both nonmonetary assets with some exceptions are quantified at the cost of their acquisition or creation. In the case of plant and equipment, a net value is used based on depreciation charges that are designed to reflect wear and tear and obsolescence. Examples of assets not mentioned include intangible assets such as goodwill, short- and long-term investments, prepaid expenses, etc.

Thus, some of the assets (such as cash and accounts receivable) are quantified at values approximating their worth to the company—others, such as inventories and plant and equipment, are quantified at a cost which can deviate from their original economic value. The sum of the quantifications of the four kinds of assets represents neither the cost nor the value of the company's assets.

Liabilities are obligations of the organization to transfer economic resources to other entities in the future as a result of past transactions or events affecting the enterprise. Under liabilities, the item "accounts payable" measures the amounts due to entities that have not yet been paid for goods and services they supplied to the company prior to the date of statement. Accounts payable are listed under current liabilities since they come due for payment within the next year. Bonds payable, classified as a long-term liability, is the amount lent to the company for relatively long periods of time in return for an agreement to pay specified amounts at specified future dates. Stockholders' equity reflects the amounts invested by stockholders in the company. They are entitled to the residual remaining after legally fixed obligations are met, and as a consequence they bear the residual risk inherent in the operations of the business.

Income Statement

The income statement purports to measure the amount of income the company has been able to generate during a specified period. Economic income is often defined as the amount the owners could take out of the business and leave it as well off by the end of the period as at the beginning. Accounting income is different in that it is quantified as the difference between the total revenue and the total expense, where revenues of the period are the resources received by the business as a result of providing products or services to outsiders, and expenses are the resources consumed by the company in the creation of revenue during that period. The income statement reflects revenues arising from the delivery of merchandise to customers in exchange for monetary assets—cash and customers' promises to pay cash or to provide services in the future. Since the value of these resources received can be determined easily, revenues are measured by their value. But revenues are not recorded before these resources are received and the service giving rise to them is performed. Measurement of the value of resources consumed in the creation of revenue is much more difficult, and, therefore, accountants measure expenses by the cost of the resources consumed in the process of generating the revenue. Four kinds of expenses are as follows:

1. *Cost of goods sold.* Resources given up or scheduled to be given up in the near future to buy or manufacture the product sold during the year.

2. *Wages and salaries expense.* Resources given up or scheduled to be given up for the services provided by the employees during the year.

3. *Other operating expenses including depreciation.* Resources given up or scheduled to be given up for other goods and services used up in the operation of the business during the year, plus the estimate of that portion of cost of plant and equipment reflecting resources used during the period.

4. *Interest.* The cost of using borrowed money during the period.

The difference between total revenue and total expenses is defined as income. The company received assets (mostly cash and receivables) in exchange for other assets (such as inventory) and services (such as employees' time). Income is thus a quantification of the excess of the value of the assets received over the cost of assets and services used up. If the company gives up more than it gets, it has a net loss.

The balance sheet and income statement are prepared on the basis of accounting records which record the effect of events or transactions on at least two kinds of assets, liabilities, and stockholders' equity. For each transaction, the sum of the asset changes must equal the sum of the changes in liabilities and the stockholders' equity. This rule is reflected by the double-entry system, which also guarantees that the balance sheet and the income sheet readily show that net income for the period equals the increment in net assets (assets less liabilities).

Historical Perspective

The history of financial statements dates from the beginnings of commerce and finance and from the first evidence of accounting concepts. The first stage of this development occurred during the Babylonian era, extending from roughly 3000 to 1000 B.C. The development of accounting can be traced, albeit tenuously, to the priests and scribes of the temple corporations. The second stage is the classical stage (from 1000 B.C. to A.D. 500), marked by the contributions of the Phoenicians, Greeks, and Romans in the city-states bordering on the Mediterranean Sea. The third stage covers medieval times, roughly from A.D. 1000 to 1400. This stage begins in Norman England and continues into Western Europe. The mercantile period marks the fourth stage, extending from 1400 to about 1800—the beginning of the industrial revolution. This is the beginning of the capitalistic, laissez faire economy during which clerical records and books of accounts were common. The end of this period marks the beginning of professional accountancy as known today. The last 150 years marks a rapid growth of national economies, the development of the business corporation, and the formation of business schools coincident with the systematic study of economics and accountancy.

With the advent of continuing enterprises, with successions of various ventures, and with the emergence of the joint stock companies, periodic evaluations had to be made to permit the transfer of stock. This marked the beginning of the trend that led to annual reports (balance sheets and income statements) known to us today. The earliest steps in this direction were taken by the East India Company, chartered by Elizabeth I in the year 1600. Its charter of 1657 provided for valuation of the stock at the end of the first 7 years and every 3 years thereafter.

Objectives of Financial Statements

The process of preparing financial statements evolved as a means of monitoring the actions and their consequences of agents held accountable to principals. The recent recognized role for accounting is that of informativeness. Noting that managers of companies, more informed than outsiders, may not have the incentives for voluntary reporting of all facts pertinent to the valuation of a company's stock, and given that information contained in annual reports is similar to a public good in that nonpurchasers of the information cannot be excluded, groups of economic interests brought about the creation of the professional regulatory mechanism that determines the objectives of financial statements. These objectives have been stated as the communication of information useful to present and potential investors and creditors when making investment and credit decisions. In order to guide utility-maximizing individuals to invest so that resources in the economy are efficiently allocated, the objectives of financial statements stipulate that financial reporting should provide information to help investors, creditors, and others assess the amounts, timing, and uncertainty of prospective net cash inflows to the enterprise. The content of a balance sheet and income statement that best accomplishes this objective is now being debated by the profession. It is recognized that in order to help predict cash flows, measures other than historical cost quantifications, on which present financial statements are based, must be considered. Already, supplementary disclosures of the impacts of general (e.g., changing value of the dollar) and specific price changes on principal financial statement items are required.

References

Littleton, A. C., *Accounting Evolution to 1900*, American Institute of Certified Public Accountants, New York, 1933; Ronen, J., "The Dual Role of Accounting: A Financial Economic Perspective," in James L. Bicksler (ed.), *Handbook of Financial Economics*, North-Holland, Amsterdam, 1979; Shillinglaw, G., J. J. Gordon, and J. Ronen, *Accounting: A Management Approach*, Irwin, Homewood, Ill., 1979.

See also Securities and Exchange Commission)

Joshua Ronen

Firm theory

The firm is the fundamental unit of organization of production in a market economy. Firms have been described by Ronald Coase (1952) as "islands of conscious coordination floating in a sea of market relations like lumps in buttermilk." Business proprietorships, partnerships, and corporations are firms, and in much modern literature cooperatives, nonprofit agencies such as universities and hospitals, and some government agencies are treated as firms. A group of firms producing the same product constitutes an industry.

Maximization of Profit

Since the firm is an "island of conscious coordination," it is usually assumed that the coordination is directed toward some definite goal or goals. The goal most commonly assumed is maximization of profit. On this assumption, if costs and revenues are determined by a few controllable variables such as output, inventories, advertising expenditure, and so on, then the theory of the firm is no more than an exercise in calculus. For example, let revenue be a function of output, $R(q)$, and cost be a function of output, $C(q)$. Then the firm will choose output so as to

$$\max \Pi = R(q) - C(q)$$

for which the first order necessary condition is

$$\frac{d\Pi}{dq} = \frac{dR}{dq} - \frac{dC}{dq} = 0$$

The latter equation is implicitly the firm's supply function. However, some recent literature allows for goals other than profit and for multiple goals. Among the suggested goals are gross revenue, revenue growth, and managerial perquisites. If there are multiple goals, then the firm may be thought of as maximizing a utility function with profit, revenue, revenue growth, and so on as its independent variables.

Maximizing Something Other Than Profits

In assuming that the firm may maximize something other than profit, we gain a great deal of theoretical flexibility. There is for example a large literature which treats worker cooperatives as firms, assuming that the cooperative maximizes the average net revenue product of labor. Similarly, it is hardly plausible that not-for-profit hospitals maximize profits, but the hospitals may maximize a utility function which has the incomes and prestige of the associated physicians among its independent variables.

The firm's cost function is customarily derived from a given production function in the theory of the firm. The production function would be written

$$q = f(x_1, x_2, \ldots, x_n)$$

where q is the quantity of output and x_i is the quantity of input i. A "well-behaved" production function has the property that

$$\frac{\partial^2 f}{\partial x_i^2} < 0$$

for each i. This property is an expression of the law of diminishing returns. The production function represents the technology available to the firm, which is assumed to be given. This technology may also be expressed by the cost function

$$C = g(q, w_1, \ldots, w_n)$$

where w_i is the price of input i. Function g is derived from f by minimizing

$$\sum_{i=1}^{n} w_i x_i$$

subject to the foregoing equation.

The firm's revenue function is derived from the conditions of demand, if these are determinate. Under perfect competition, the output price is parametrically given to the firm, and thus revenue is proportionate to output. In monopoly, price declines with increasing output, so that revenues increase less than proportionately with output. This implies that the profit-maximizing monopoly will sell less than the socially efficient output. This in turn implies allocative inefficiency. In oligopoly, however, the firm's revenue function may not be determinate since the revenues earned by a firm depend not only on its own output but also on the output of its rivals. If its rivals' policies are not known, then the firm's own revenue function is not determinate. This problem remains unresolved in the theory of oligopoly.

Satisficing

In assuming that the firm maximizes something, we attribute to the firm's decision maker a kind of perfect rationality and an inexhaustible fund of information. Critics such as Herbert Simon find this construct implausible and propose to replace maximization with satisficing, also known as bounded rationality. The satisficing decision maker does not aim at a maximum, but only at a satisfactory level of profits (revenue, growth, etc.). If these levels are attained, the satisficer feels no need to do anything further. Unfortunately, the theory of bounded rationality does not give clear answers to many of the questions which economists ask of the theory of the firm. It does not, for example, yield well-defined supply functions. Thus most economic theorists continue to rely on theories which assume that the firm maximizes something.

Some studies indicate that the allocative inefficiency due to monopoly is quantitatively minor but that many firms do not routinely attain maximum production with the resources they use. This is sometimes called X inefficiency. If monopoly status protects X inefficiency, then the losses due to monopoly could be much greater than these studies suggest.

A fundamental problem in the theory of the firm is this: Why are there firms? In other words, why do we not find all individual activities coordinated by market relationships? Why do we instead find some of these activities coordinated by nonmarket relationships within firms? This question, raised by Coase, remains a focus of lively controversy.

References

Coase, R., "The Nature of the Firm," *Economica*, vol. 12, no. 16, November 1937, pp. 386–405, reprinted in G. Stigler and K. Boulding (eds.), *Readings in Price Theory*, Irwin, Homewood, Ill., 1952, pp. 331–351; McCain, R. A., *Markets, Decisions and Organizations*, Prentice-Hall, Englewood Cliffs, N.J., 1980, chaps. 5 to 8, 17; Simon, H., "Rationality as a Process and as a Product of Thought," *American Economic Review*, vol. 68, no. 2, May 1968, pp. 1–16; Vanek, J., *The General Theory of Labor-Managed Market Economics*, Cornell University Press, Ithaca, N.Y., 1970.

(*See also* Competition; Decision making in business: a behavioral approach; Monopoly and oligopoly; Production function)

Roger A. McCain

Fiscal policy

Fiscal policy refers to the use of government spending and taxing power to achieve macroeconomic objectives. An outgrowth of Keynesian economics, modern fiscal policy has been a relatively recent development in government policy. It has received systematic attention only since World War II. Thus, Franklin Roosevelt, during his first presidential campaign at the depth of the Great Depression, pledged to balance the federal budget if elected; he still attempted to contain and reduce the recession-induced budget deficit as late as during the 1937–38 recession. Only since the end of World War II has a passive, or accommodating countercyclical, fiscal policy become generally accepted practice in the United States. Such a policy relies mainly on built-in characteristics of federal expenditure programs and the tax system to cushion economic declines through enlarged budget deficits. In fact, no postwar President or Congress has ever attempted to curtail spending or to raise taxes during a recession in order to reduce a budget deficit caused by the built-in stabilizers of the economy.

An active, or discretionary, fiscal policy introduces changes in spending programs or in the tax structure in order to counteract recession or inflation, or in order to stimulate economic growth. The systematic application of discretionary countercyclical fiscal policy is of even more recent origin; it dates back to the New Economic Policy of the Kennedy-Johnson administrations, that is, the first half of the 1960s. The practice of active fiscal policy has been short-lived and erratic; it was not applied (for political reasons) during the crucial early inflationary phase of the Vietnam war. Moreover, the concept of an active, or discretionary, fiscal policy as such is not yet generally accepted; it was challenged in the early 1970s, when the Nixon administration reverted to a strictly passive fiscal policy stance.

Passive Fiscal Policy: The Built-in Stabilizers

The economic and fiscal structure of all modern industrialized nations provides a large degree of passive fiscal stabilizers. Built-in fiscal stabilizers are defined as those government expenditures and receipts which without any explicit policy decision or action move the government budget toward a larger deficit (or a smaller surplus) during an economic contraction. Many of these built-in stabilizers also tend to move the budget toward a smaller deficit (or a larger surplus) during inflationary periods, but their operation is not strictly symmetrical with the increased-deficit moves. (The main reasons for this lack of symmetry are the cost-of-living escalators that have become a part of many social-expenditure programs of the federal government.)

In the United States, during recessions or even during growth recessions (i.e., periods of sluggish real growth well below the economy's potential), federal government spending is boosted countercyclically by enlarged payments for unemployment benefits, various welfare programs (e.g., food stamps), and accelerated early retirement under Social Security provisions. Government receipts are reduced (or at least held down well below their high-employment level) mainly because of the interaction between declines or slower gains in personal income and the progressive rate structure of the individual income tax and because of eroding corporate profits and reduced employment and consumption (which affect payroll and excise taxes). Social security and excise taxes are also held down by higher unemployment and sluggish consumer spending. The resulting enlargement in the budget deficit (or reduction in the surplus) cushions, but does not arrest or reverse, the decline of the private sector's income during recessions, and it tends to restrain the pace of the subsequent recovery.

It is important to distinguish the effects of these accommodating fiscal responses of the built-in stabilizers from the effects of discretionary fiscal policy actions. The former reflect and mitigate changes in economic activity, whereas the latter initiate or trigger such changes.

Discretionary Fiscal Policy

An active, or discretionary, fiscal policy requires legislative changes in budget programs for macroeconomic purposes. Discretionary countercyclical fiscal policy specifically requires program changes designed to stimulate the economy during recessions or periods of sluggish growth or to restrain the economy during inflationary periods. Stimulation may take the form of increased spending—through enlargement of existing programs or through introduction of new ones—or of tax reductions. Restraint, in turn, requires either curtailment of spending programs or increases in taxes (or a mixture of both).

In static Keynesian analysis, attainment or retention of full-employment output requires that ex ante full-employment saving equal ex ante full-employment investment. If the government budget is measured in terms of the national income accounts rather than in terms of the traditional unified presidential and congressional budget, then the full-employment budget surplus represents full-employment saving of the federal government. Static countercyclical fiscal policy requires that the federal government's full-employment saving (S_g^*) be adjusted so as to balance any discrepancy, at full employment, between ex ante saving both of the private sector (S_p) and of state and local governments (S_{sl}) on the one hand, and investment (I) on the other. Thus, an expanded static Keynesian equilibrium condition can be stated as follows (where starred symbols denote full-employment values):

$$S_p^* + S_{sl}^* + S_g^* = I^*$$

By rearranging the terms of this expanded equilibrium condition, we can bring into sharper focus the role of discretionary countercyclical fiscal policy.

$$S_g^* = I^* - (S_p^* + S_{sl}^*)$$

hence

$$S_g^* < 0 \quad \text{for} \quad I^* < S_p^* + S_{sl}^*$$

and

$$S_g^* > 0 \quad \text{for} \quad I^* > S_p^* + S_{sl}^*$$

This formulation highlights the fact that the strength of investment and saving in the nonfederal sector (private, state, and local) determines whether it is appropriate for the federal government to propose a budget that would generate a surplus or a deficit if the economy were operating at the full-employment level.

It is clear from this policy prescription that it would be desirable to formulate fiscal policy decisions on the basis of explicit estimates of full-employment investment and saving in the nonfederal sector. Unfortunately, few such estimates have been developed as a guide to fiscal policy, and there are serious estimating and reliability problems. Moreover, shifts in the saving or investment functions in the private sector are hard to detect as they occur; yet, such shifts are disruptions that require changes in economic policy. As a practical matter, policymakers rely mainly on general economic indicators—such as the unemployment rate, the real-growth rate of GNP, and the inflation rate—and on economic forecasts in order to assess the need for either greater fiscal stimulation or more fiscal restraint.

Limitations of Fiscal Policy

In recent years, with most industrialized countries suffering simultaneously from too much unemployment and from excessive inflation, the static neo-Keynesian countercyclical fiscal policy described here has become inadequate. (High unemployment would call for fiscal stimulation, whereas high inflation rates would require fiscal restraint.) Experimentation with new policy tools has come to supplement traditional countercyclical policies. At the macroeconomic level, new policy approaches include various forms of incomes policies, such as voluntary or mandatory wage and price restraints. At a less aggregate level, increased emphasis is being placed on selective employment and training programs as a means for improving the so-called unemployment-inflation trade-off. Most forms of incomes policies have been effective, at best, in restraining inflation during relatively brief periods of time. Such policies are most promising when designed to deescalate inflationary expectations during periods when the economy is not afflicted by excess demand. Increased emphasis on selective employment and training programs in the United States is of very recent origin but has been gaining support since the mid-1970s.

Measures of Fiscal Policy

In order to compare the fiscal impact of different federal budgets over time—or of alternate budgets for a given year—it is necessary to utilize a measure (or a series of measures) of fiscal impact. Estimated or observed budget surpluses or deficits cannot properly serve this purpose since they reflect a mixture of both discretionary fiscal policy and economic feedbacks through the built-in stabilizers. Specifically, a large and growing budget deficit during a recession may reflect mainly the negative feedback from a weak economy, or a combination of negative feedback and discretionary policies of fiscal stimulation. Similarly, a large and rising budget surplus during a period of high employment with inflation may merely reflect the positive feedback of the inflation (which, in the short run, tends to raise government revenues faster than it does government expenditures), or may reflect a combination of positive feedback and discretionary policies of fiscal restraint.

Consequently, the full-employment budget surplus (at times also referred to as the high-employment surplus) has been used in the United States since the early 1960s as a simplified measure of fiscal policy designed to isolate discretionary fiscal policy from the effects of passive budget feedback and changes in economic activity. The full-employment surplus is estimated by computing both receipts and expenditures of a given budget program that could be expected to materialize if the economy were to operate at full-employment output (GNP) consistent with price stability. For comparisons over time, this full-employment budget surplus is best expressed as a percentage of GNP. Generally, the higher the full-employment budget surplus, the more restrictive the federal budget. Thus, the full-employment budget surplus serves as a useful shorthand guide for the design and assessment of fiscal policy.

Unfortunately, estimates of the full-employment surplus are beset with difficulties that become particularly severe during inflationary periods. First, the concept of full employment has to be defined; then observable revenues and expenditures have to be adjusted to that level which would have materialized at this hypothetical full-employment level.

During the first half of the 1960s, full employment was defined pragmatically in terms of a 4 percent unemployment rate. Since then, the labor-force mix has changed drastically. There is now a much higher proportion of women, teenagers, and young adults in the labor force. Since these groups traditionally have above-average unemployment rates, the current equivalent unemployment rate (i.e., the rate adjusted for changes in labor-force mix) that corresponds to the 4 percent full-employment rate of the 1960s would be in the range of $4\frac{3}{4}$ to 5 percent.

When unemployment is far above the so-called full-employment rate (whichever way defined), estimates of the full-employment gap—i.e., the difference between the actual and the would-be full-employment budget numbers—become more and more tenuous. This problem is particularly severe for estimates of the revenue gap. For example, during the years 1975 to 1977, the unemployment rate remained above 7 percent with but a few brief exceptions. This meant that estimates of full-employment revenue gaps made during these years could not be tested and might have been far off the mark.

But a far more serious deficiency of the full-employment surplus as a measure of fiscal impact arises from the effects of inflation on the budget. In contrast to other feedbacks from the economy into the budget (i.e., the more traditional built-in stabilizers), the current measures of the full-employment surplus do not include any means for neutralizing in the calculation the effects from inflation. Specifically, in the short run, inflation tends to inflate many federal government expenditures approximately in line with the overall inflation rate, and some more slowly, whereas revenues are inflated at a faster rate. This inflation leverage of federal revenues is due mainly to the progressive nature of the personal income tax. (Taxpayers are shifted into higher marginal tax brackets.) Thus, in the short run, the feedback from inflation into the federal budget causes the deficit (actual as well as full-employment) to decline, or the surplus to increase, as the case may be.

One other summary measure of fiscal policy has been developed in recent years that avoids many specific estimating problems—and most of the inflation-induced distortions—that impair the reliability of the full-employment surplus. This measure, termed fiscal thrust, consists of increases in discretionary budget expenditures plus any discretionary tax reductions (or minus any tax increases)—where discretionary tax changes are defined as changes in tax receipts due to changes in the tax base or the tax rate. All these changes are valued at the prevailing GNP level (rather than at a hypothetical full-employment level). Fiscal thrust measures the initial, autonomous expansionary impact of the federal budget to which a traditional Keynesian multiplier may be applied in order to assess the full ultimate effect on the economy. Fiscal thrust excludes all feedback effects on the revenue side, whether caused by cyclical fluctuations or by economic growth and inflation.

A potentially superior way of assessing the fiscal impact of the federal budget is through econometric simulations. Discretionary spending and tax components may be introduced directly into the econometric models, so as to trigger dynamic and steady-state multipliers. Thus, if the fiscal sector of current econometric models were adequately developed and reliable, the time path of the economic effects of each fiscal policy action—such as an income tax reduction or a social security tax increase—could be traced by introducing into the model its impact value (as estimated for the purpose of measuring fiscal thrust) and running an econometric simulation. Unfortunately, most currently used econometric models—even the most elaborate ones—have a relatively simple and underdeveloped fiscal sector, and simulations with alternate models yield, at times, mutually inconsistent results. Moreover, the amount of time and real resources required for such simulations is still very high.

References

Blinder, A. S., and R. N. Solow, "Analytical Foundations of Fiscal Policy," *The Economics of Public Finance*, Brookings, Washington, D.C., 1974; Dernburg, T. F., and D. M. McDougall, *Macroeconomics*, 5th ed., McGraw-Hill, New York, 1976, chaps. 5, 18; Lewis, Wilfred, *Federal Fiscal Policy in the Postwar Recessions*, Brookings, Washington, D.C., 1962; "Long Range Fiscal Strategy," Committee on the Budget, U.S. Senate, October 1975.

(*See also* Automatic stabilizers, Employment and unemployment; Federal budget; Incomes policy; Phillips curve)

Michael E. Levy

Fixed annuity (see **Variable annuity**)

Flow of funds

The flow of funds is the term used to describe accounting systems which trace transactions involving the transfer of money between sectors in an economy. It is a set of social accounts for the economy that shows money inflows and money outflows by transaction groups.

Since the expenditures of one economic unit are the receipts of others, and every financial liability is someone else's asset, the system is used to give an overall picture of financial relationships between the various sectors of the economy. This approach throws light on the process of economic expansion and contraction.

The transactions are delineated in statements of sources and uses of funds. Conceptually, a complete flow-of-funds system covers nonfinancial items of current income and expenditure as well as financial transactions, i.e., transfers involving changes in balance sheet items. The uses of funds, that is, current spending, investment, and changes in financial assets, are totaled on the one side, while the sources of funds, that is, current income, saving, and changes in liabilities, are totaled on the other, and the totals must be in balance. A generalized and basic accounting framework for a complete system of money flows is as follows:

Uses of funds		Sources of funds
Current expenditures Change in net worth (saving)		Current receipts
Change in real assets (investment) Change in financial assets (lending) Change in money (hoarding)		Change in net worth (saving) Change in liabilities (borrowing)
Total	=	Total

Such an ambitious system of money flows, however, has never been fully implemented. Instead, attention has focused on the saving and investment and borrowing and lending aspects. Most of the flow-of-funds systems used in the United States, including the flow-of-funds accounts developed and regularly published by the Federal Reserve, concentrate on tracing the channels whereby different types of saving move into different types of investment through lending and borrowing transactions. In other words, currently a flow-of-funds system covers who borrows from whom for what purpose, or the flows of funds through the credit markets.

A flow is distinguishable from a stock in that a stock represents an accumulated amount at a specified point in time; whereas, a flow represents the change over a specified period. The flow-of-funds systems currently used cover net changes in each type of outstanding asset and liability, that is, the amounts borrowed or acquired less the amounts redeemed or sold over a period. Statistics on gross flows, or the amounts borrowed, are available for securities and mortgages, but the lack of availability both of statistics on gross amounts of loans issued and of complete data on amounts acquired has prevented the construction of a complete flow-of-funds system on a gross basis.

Flows of funds are basically related to, and dependent upon, the various types of income and product transactions in the gross national product accounts. However, some financial transactions are not directly traceable to current output, as in transfers of existing assets which include capital gains or losses (for example, borrowing through a mortgage to purchase an existing home). Furthermore, in the present state of development of the statistics, it is not possible to trace many other relationships between current expenditures and borrowing transactions directly. Nevertheless, in forecasting flows of funds, a GNP forecast is either explicitly or implicitly employed in providing the parameters for the projections of the various flows.

Elements of a Flow-of-Funds Account

In a system of flow-of-funds accounts, a summary table is built up from statements of sources and uses of funds for each sector. The broad sectors are business, government, foreign, and household, but the sectors are usually disaggregated further into groups—for example, corporate, noncorporate, and farm business in the business sector and U.S. government, federal agencies, and state and local governments in the government sector. In addition, the financial intermediaries, i.e., banks, nonbank thrift institutions, etc., are important factors in lending (and in some cases in borrowing) transactions and must be covered.

The individual items of the sources and uses of funds for each sector are derived from compilations of balance sheet items, which usually cover separately types of credit instruments, e.g., mortgages; corporate, municipal, and government securities; and loans. The uses of funds of an individual sector include loans through the credit instruments, as well as changes in holdings of cash, real estate, other physical assets, and miscellaneous assets; whereas the sources include borrowing through credit instruments, as well as changes in deposits received, reserves, and other liabilities, in addition to changes in the current surplus. Thus, the sources and uses of funds of an individual sector should balance, except for statistical discrepancies.

In summarizing the flows of funds through the credit markets, only the portions of the sources and uses of funds covering borrowing and lending through credit instruments are included. Cash and deposits, real estate, other physical assets, and miscellaneous assets, on the uses side, and deposits, reserves, and other liabilities, on the sources side, are omitted. For the financial intermediaries, the savings of the public, which flow into their omitted liability items of insurance and pension reserves, and deposits or shares, are represented in the summary by their purchases of credit instruments (or lending). Thus, the uses of funds of financial intermediaries become sources of funds to the credit markets as a whole.

It is usual in a flow-of-funds summary to show the net changes in credit instruments that are outstanding in varying degrees of disaggregation lined up on the uses side, as funds raised (or borrowing), and the net changes in the holdings of these credit instruments by the various institutional groups on the sources side, as supplies of funds (or lending). Alternatively, the funds raised can be shown according to borrowing sectors, or groups within those sectors. However, in view of the fact that the financial markets are compartmentalized into separate markets which deal with particular types of credit instruments, the alternative classification is not as useful for financial analysis as it is for economic analysis.

Although the flow of funds is regarded as the financial counterpart to the GNP, there is no one established total for funds raised similar to total output in the GNP accounts. It is a problem to relate money-flow estimates to gross national product estimates largely because of the way social accountants distinguish between final and nonfinal product expenditures by business in the GNP.

In practice, not all flow-of-funds summaries contain the same detail. A generalized framework for the composition of a flow-of-funds summary is as follows:

Funds raised	Funds supplied
Mortgages	Financial intermediaries
Corporate bonds	Life insurance companies
Corporate stocks	Other insurance companies
U.S. government securities	Private pension funds
Federal agency securities	State and local retirement funds
State and local government securities	Savings and loan associations
Short-term credit:	Mutual savings banks
Business credit	Credit unions
Consumer credit	Money-market funds
Security credit	Investment funds
Foreign loans	Banking system
Other loans	Business
Total short-term credit	Government
	Foreign
	Households (residual)
Total =	Total

Uses of Flow of Funds

In economic and financial analysis, the funds raised are often referred to as demands for funds and the funds supplied as supplies of funds. Initially, when the flow-of-funds concept was first being implemented after World War II, financial analysts hoped that projections could be made to compare projected demands against projected supplies to provide an indication of the degree of pressures on the financial markets and interest rate movements, as could be obtained from a supply and demand schedule in the loanable-funds theory. Under that theory, schedules are constructed which show anticipated demands plotted against anticipated supplies. These intersect at the price (or interest rate) at which the markets would be cleared. However, at that time the lack of availability of such statistics for past periods, as well as for the future, precluded the construction of an ex ante system, and an ex post system had to be settled upon, that is, one with projections of the magnitudes of demands that would actually be financed rather than of the magnitudes that would be desired.

It soon became apparent, however, that flow-of-funds projections could be utilized in measuring the weight of demands for funds in affecting interest rate movements, at least to some degree. This could be accomplished through analysis of movements in the household, or residual, sector. A complete total could be summed up for the funds raised but, on the supply side, statistics were not available for noninstitutional investors, e.g., the household sector (which includes nonprofit associations, trust funds, and some other groups). Thus, the household sector had to be calculated as a residual in order to meet the constraint that supply equal demand. Since residual investors need to be enticed by high or rising interest rates to bypass the savings institutions and purchase credit-market instruments directly, the volume of such purchases proved to be indicative of interest rate trends. It must be noted, however, that although the residual analysis is a useful tool for forecasting interest rates—and probably indicates major trends—it has never been considered a major key since it is subject to all the errors in the projections from which it is derived. Furthermore, interest rate movements are not solely dependent upon the supply and demand for funds; other factors, such as inflation premiums and international developments, which might require arbitrary government action to raise or lower interest rates, often intervene. In fact, many interest rate forecasters do not employ the flow-of-funds method at all but rely instead upon judgment or regression or other econometric analysis.

The flow of funds has been used extensively in the United States for forecasting both pressures in the credit markets in general and in particular markets and the effects of such pressures upon interest rates. It has also been of value both in studying the interdependence of the financial markets and the real economy and in assessing the impacts of shifts in monetary and fiscal policy. Elsewhere, notably in Canada, Japan, and the United Kingdom, where the availability of current financial data is less comprehensive than in the United States, flow-of-funds systems have been constructed and analyzed but have not been highly developed as forecasting tools.

Critics of the use of projections of flows of funds for interest rate forecasting have pointed out that the margin of error in the forecasts of credit flows has been wide and that this lack of ability to forecast accurately diminishes their usefulness. Nevertheless, more and more financial institutions are regularly producing flow-of-funds forecasts as an aid in assessing prospective financial developments. Other critics point out that there is an inherent problem with basing interest rate forecasts on projections of credit flows which themselves are necessarily based in part on assumptions regarding interest rates. This objection, however, is equally true of projections of economic activity, which necessarily depend upon assumptions regarding interest rates. Yet, it is undoubtedly more desirable to have well-thought-out economic and financial forecasts than to operate with implicit assumptions.

References

Board of Governors, Federal Reserve System, *Introduction to Flow of Funds*, 1975; Copeland, Morris, A., *A Study of Money Flows in the United States*, National Bureau of Economic Research, New York, 1952; Massaro, Vincent G., *A Guide to Forecasting Interest Rates*, The Conference Board, New York, 1973; National Bureau of Economic Research, *The Flow of Funds Approach to Social Accounting*, Princeton University Press, Princeton, N.J., 1962; Taylor, Stephen P., "Uses of Flow-of-Funds Accounts in the Federal Reserve System," *Journal of Finance*, May 1963, pp. 249-258.

See also Business credit; Capital markets and money markets; Consumer credit; Credit, an overview; Financial institutions; Financial instruments; Gross national product; Interest rates; Money markets; Mortgage credit)

Sally S. Ronk

Forecasting methods

Economic decisions by consumers, business, and government necessarily involve implicit or explicit forecasts of economic developments. These forecasts may take the form of a specified or formally quantified model or may simply be unspecified or informal hunches and guesses. Frequently, the belief that recent experience will be repeated is considered as useful as any formal forecast. At the extreme, the new rational expectations viewpoint assumes that economic decision makers anticipate the eventual results of even drastic changes in public economic policy and thereby render those policies ineffective.

Development of Scientific Models

It is clear that formal or quantitatively explicit forecasts increasingly have been developed and used as the basis for decision making. Both the need for more information in mobilization planning during World War II and, subsequently, the requirements of economic stabilization spurred the development of large information systems in the framework of the national income and product totals and sectors (which later were supplemented by the financially oriented Federal Reserve System's flow-of-funds accounts). Information systems were further necessitated by the increased diversity of production, distribution, consumption, and other business and consumer statistics bearing on studies of the business cycle. In addition, national information systems became manageable and less costly through the use of high-speed electronic computers. This trend was supported by progress in the theory of statistics and its econometric applications, particularly in the field of statistical inference, i.e., establishing probabilistic or valid mathematical generalizations from sample phenomena by using associated measures of forecasting error, tests of statistical significance, etc.

As a result, forecasting increasingly has been performed by means of so-called scientific econometric models of the economy—scientific in the sense of being replicative by independent practioners, in contrast with so-called judgmental models.

However, this distinction is only broadly valid. While scientific models consist of replicable single or multicquation systems which provide coefficients of weights to variables that purport to explain economic behavior, these systems in practice are modified by judgment in at least three ways:

1. Important variables (such as federal expenditures in GNP forecasting models) typically are entered as exogenous to the system in the form of a judgment of their future values rather than determined by an endogenous behavioral equation.

2. A so-called additive or multiplicative factor is used, consisting of a judgmental or mechanical adjustment to the constant term of the individual behavioral equation. This is a typical step in large-scale econometric model forecasting

when apparently absurd results have been generated because of misspecification of causal factors, data revisions, or special circumstances (e.g., strikes or other shocks).

3. Following solution of the multiequation model, the overall results may be considered unrealistic, requiring either further modification of the "add" factors in the structurally based endogenous equations or changes in the magnitude of the exogenous variables.

Finally, judgment has entered into the selection of each of the independent variables affecting the forecasted variable, the time-lag structure, etc., in a manner that does not easily meet the replicability stipulation.

Judgmental Approach

Setting aside those which represent mere guesses or hunches, forecasts using judgmental approaches, nevertheless, may retain the systematic development and the constraints (if not replicability) that are considered virtues in so-called scientific procedures. The typical judgmental approach views the fixed coefficients in equations of econometric models with suspicion, based on experience, concerning the accuracy of the recent statistics, and it recognizes the frequent superiority of business or consumer anticipations surveys over behavioral equations in forecasting business investment, retail sales, etc. Procedurally, GNP judgmental forecasts, for example, might sum up sectoral demand by government, business, consumers, and net exports by first correcting current figures of these variables for seeming implausibilities and possible revisions of the data. In the second step, relating to the nonconsumer sectors, important but not sole reliance might be placed on anticipations surveys reported by business for fixed capital expenditures; on housing starts and permits as a basis of estimates of outlays on residential construction; and on official budget projections for federal, state, and local government purchases. Since they are volatile, especially at turning points or in reaction to external shocks, forecasts of business inventory change and net exports of goods and services typically are subject to much manipulation and adjustment of historical relationships for recent events in arriving at a forecast. To obtain the final component of GNP, one might apply a "multiplier" to the sum of nonconsumer outlays in order to forecast consumer expenditures, in part or in the aggregate.

To meet consistency requirements of scientific work, however, one can seek the theoretical and statistical equality between values for national product and income. Furthermore, constraints are obtained by inspection for reasonableness of those measures which make consistent the two sides of the accounts, measures such as the personal saving rate, the profit rate, the income, and the real growth implied in the forecasts of employment, of wage and salary payments, of productivity costs, and of unit labor costs. Indeed, such tests in judgmental approaches appeared valid and dependable enough in making the GNP forecasts which foreshadowed U.S. economic policy in the 1960s. Finally, there are few, if any, so-called judgmental forecasts worthy of notice that do not involve some degree of sophisticated statistical analysis at some stage of development; nor are they nonreplicable in principle, though lengthy oral or written explanations might be necessary.

Typology of Methods

Other than the somewhat arbitrary distinction made between judgmental and scientific approaches, forecasts may be separated into (1) those which do not rely at all upon economic theory and instead extrapolate, by simple or sophisticated means, the past values of the variable, and (2) those which seek causal relationships among economic variables as posited by economic theory and are expressed empirically by a single or multiple regression model or by indexes of time series for selected economic indicators which lead, coincide, or lag business cycle turning points.

Extrapolative Methods   Advocacy of this approach proceeds on the premise that causal relationships affecting a variable are too complicated to discern, possibly unknowable, or are too costly to be pursued. For many years, the older methods of time series forecasting involved simple deterministic procedures, such as unweighted or weighted moving averages of the historical values of the variable; simple or logarithmic functions relating the movement of the variable against time; and the autoregressive model in which linear or compounded rates of growth of a variable over time are related to those registered by its earlier values. Deterministic methods may be criticized because they generate forecasts that depend heavily on the selection of years that are used as base data; on the degree of the polynomial, which in the extreme can be such that the slope registers a passthrough of every data point; and on the assumption of a systematic evolution in the data.

While remaining an extrapolative method, a newer time series forecasting method has been developed by Box and Jenkins which relates a variable to its own past values and to a weighted sum of current and lagged random disturbances. The distinctive nature of this approach is the treatment of the observed values as having been generated by a stochastic process—i.e., that the observed values represent random drawings from a probability distribution. Accordingly, a model based on these values contains structural elements or coefficients which make allowances for errors of observations that normally are inherent in sample data.

A so-called ARIMA (autoregressive integrated moving-average) method combines (1) an autoregressive model in which the current value of a variable is a function of both a weighted sum of its past values and a random disturbance term; and (2) values derived from a moving-average model in which the current value is a function of a weighted sum of current and lagged random disturbances. (In this procedure a "stationary" condition initially is sought in order to attain the required conditions of a stochastic time series, frequently described as a "random walk" in which errors fall into probabilistic ranges. Because most economic data contain seasonal, cyclical, and secular trends, which make values nonrandom, time series are "differenced" successively to attain stationariness.)

Representing essentially an extrapolation of trends or changes, time series models appear to be most useful in short-term forecasting when causal factors which might offset the historical pattern are ineffective. Over long-term periods, forecast values necessarily converge to the stationary mean. Moreover, the ARIMA method predisposes toward "misses" in turning points. Also, inconsistency of forecasts may develop among such connected variables as nominal GNP, real GNP, and prices since each series would be extrapolated on its own. Practitioners rebut such criticism, saying that structurally oriented multivariate models also miss turning points. One study by Charles Nelson in 1972 showed that time series methodology performed in superior fashion more often than a major structural macroeconomic model in forecasting 9 of 14 series for one quarter ahead. A later study by Stephen McNees indicated decreased accuracy of ARIMA methods over longer time periods.

Econometric Structural Models   These embody a set of mathematical functions fitted to empirically derived data which purport to reflect causal relationships developed by economic theory. Typically, the equation system or model contains a selection of series that are either (1) exogenous to the system, i.e., predetermined outside the model, perhaps by assumption; or (2) endogenous, or determined by a mathematically fitted behavioral or structural relationship to other variables. The latter are likely to be stochastic. Given the predetermined exogenous and lagged endogenous values, such a system can be solved if a structural equation exists for each endogenous variable.

The validity of an econometric model in part rests on proper identification of the major determinants of the variable as tested by credibility in economic theory with respect to size and sign of the coefficients, absence of serial correlation (a condition where errors of observation in time series are random and carry an expected value of zero), freedom from multicollinearity among the independent variables, etc. In a multiequation model, there are additional problems which reflect the unevenness in goodness of fit of the several equations. As a result, the composite error of estimate of the entire system is uncertain; indeed, the errors in the several equations may be related.

Tests of statistical significance (the null hypothesis, goodness of fit, and the Durbin-Watson statistic) may identify some sources of forecasting error. However, the main source of forecasting error in large-scale econometric models is centered in incorrect specification. Economic theory contains areas of controversy and uncertainty, so that the guidance of theory may result in omission of relevant variables or use of irrelevant variables (as well as in incorrect choice of functional form).

Typically, this source of error is not evident in the data for the sample period upon which a model is developed, though it has been clearly reflected in the very mixed forecasting performance registered by the several models that have been examined in various studies. Moreover, advocates of the extrapolative univariate time series approach argue that the requirement of forecasting exogenous variables in structural models means merely transforming rather than solving the forecasting problem.

Nevertheless, the capability of structural models in processing, organizing, and integrating the several available extensive sets of national information systems makes them attractive in imparting clarity and coherence in dealing with the huge volume of data now available—even where the equations and forecasts themselves frequently are viewed with skepticism by users.

Business Indicators   Forecasting by the simpler means of business cycle indicators has been less extensively used in recent years. Inherently, this approach does not generate specific solutions to such forecasting problems as quantifying the impact of changes in fiscal or monetary policy, the effect of variations in investment plans on the economy, etc. Instead, this system involves studies of leads and lags among hundreds of economic indicators in relationship to business cycle turning points.

A selection of these series has been grouped into indexes of leading, coincident, and lagging indicators, which singly or in combination purport to foreshadow the turning points—but not the potential magnitude of change. The system of symptomatic leads and lags initially was developed by the National Bureau of Economic Research and has been revised and promulgated by the U.S. Department of Commerce and published in *Business Conditions Digest.*

The approach depends heavily on the sometimes dubious accuracy in its latest reading of component series, as well as on an absence of structural shifts or shocks such as strikes which might affect lead or lag times. With respect to accuracy in forecasting, the leading indicators since 1945 have predicted many more upper turning points in the business cycle than in fact were realized because they signaled only retardation in growth rather than actual downturns.

With respect to the several approaches treated earlier, econometric models appear to be growing in use. The initial forecasting success of the econometric models during the 1960s was followed by a mixed performance in the 1970s as these methods failed to predict, first, the deep recession in 1974 to 1975 and, then, accelerated inflation in 1977 to 1979. Moreover, a central controversy—still unresolved—has emerged with respect to their superiority over the time series approaches. The results of these several methods differ markedly depending upon length of the forecasting period, presence of cyclical factors, shocks, etc. As a final observation of the still unresolved issue of successful performance, it is interesting that the consensus GNP forecasts of 50 to 60 practitioners collected by the American Statistical Association–National Bureau of Economic Research, which contain a great variety of methods, registered no greater error than those provided by the several major econometric model commercial services.

References

Box, G. E. P., and G. M. Jenkins, *Time Series Analysis,* Holden-Day, San Francisco, 1970; Butler, William F., Robert A. Kavesh, and Robert B. Platt, *Methods and Techniques of Business Forecasting,* Prentice-Hall, Englewood Cliffs, N.J., 1974; Granger, C. W. J., and Paul Newbold, *Forecasting Time Series,* Academic Press, New York, 1977; McNees, Stephen K., "A Critique of Alternative Methods of Comparing Macroeconomic Models," in J. Ramsey and J. Kmenta (eds.), *Methodology of Macroeconomic Models,* North-Holland, Amsterdam, 1980; Nelson, Charles R., *Applied Time Series Analysis for Managerial Forecasting,* Holden-Day, San Francisco, 1973; Pyndyck, Robert S., and Daniel L. Rubinfeld, *Econometric Models and Economic Forecasts,* McGraw-Hill, New York, 1976; Vaccara, Beatrice N., and Victor Zarnowitz, "How Good are the Leading Indicators," *1977 Proceedings,* Business and Economics Section, part 1, American Statistical Association, Washington, D.C., 1977.

(*See also* Accuracy of economic forecasts; Anticipation surveys, business; Anticipation surveys, consumer; Business cycles; Computers in economics; Data banks; Decision making in business: A behavioral approach; Econometrics; Economic models; Economic statistics; Expectations; Gross national product; Index numbers; Leading Indicator approach to forecasting; Random walk hypothesis; Regression analysis in business and economics; Seasonal variations in economic time series; Secular trend; Statistical techniques in economics and business, an overview; Time series analysis)

Herman I. Liebling

Foreign direct investment

Foreign direct investment describes the acquisition of managerial control by a citizen, i.e., corporation, of a home nation over a corporation of some other host nation.

Corporations that widely engage in foreign direct investment are called multinational companies, multinational enterprises, or transnational corporations. The term foreign direct investment is something of a misnomer: when foreign direct investment takes place, investment in the economic sense may or may not occur. If, for example, a U.S. company acquires ownership of an ongoing British firm, foreign direct investment is deemed to have taken place; however, no net creation of productive capital, and hence no economic investment, has occurred. By contrast, if the same U.S. company creates de novo a subsidiary in Great Britain, building new plant and equipment, then both foreign direct investment and economic investment have taken place.

Numerous economic analyses of foreign direct investment have begun with the assumption that real capital is exported from the home to the host nation, but this assumption is not necessarily true. Thus, foreign direct investment is not a special case of the international transfer problem, which has been a favorite subject of economists since John Maynard Keynes' early treatment of it. Indeed, even when economic investment results from foreign direct investment, capital may not be transferred from the home nation to the host nation. Rather, the multinational corporation may acquire real capital from local (or third-nation) sources and may utilize local (or third-nation) sources of financing. The multinational firm may thus act as an agent for transforming host-nation savings into host-nation investment.

Exactly why foreign direct investment should take place at all has been the subject of considerable inquiry in recent years, the point having been made that in a world characterized by perfect markets for goods and factors of production, foreign direct investment would not occur. This argument suggests that imperfections in these markets must account for foreign direct investment, and theories based on imperfections in foreign exchange markets, financial markets, and markets for technology have been advanced.

Theories based on imperfections in financial markets derive from modern portfolio and capital asset pricing theories, which maintain that holding a diversified portfolio of financial securities rather than one or a few securities carries real benefits and that an internationally diversified portfolio is more beneficial than one containing securities of one nation only. Such theories assert that significant barriers to international portfolio diversification exist at the level of the individual investor, and therefore that the multinational firm serves as a financial intermediary which enables investors to obtain the benefits of such diversification.

The Harry G. Johnson–Stephen P. Magee theory of technology-market imperfection is based on the premise that in order to internalize the benefits arising from the development of a new technology, a private firm must hold a monopoly or quasi monopoly over the commercial use of that technology. Magee asserts that the patent system alone does not provide the innovating firm with sufficient market protection to enable it profitably to develop new technologies. Such firms thus extend their horizontal market power to ensure a captive market for new technologies, the extension including the penetration of foreign markets. Magee claims that this explains why multinational firms most often operate in industries characterized by high levels of investment in research and development.

The hypotheses that have gained the widest acceptance are those that John Dunning (1979) has collectively called the eclectic theory of the multinational firm. The eclectic theory is based on imperfections in markets for real goods and factors of production. The pioneering work of this approach was the 1959 doctoral thesis of Stephen Hymer (1976). Hymer noted that multinational firms tend to be larger in absolute size than most other firms and tend to operate in industries characterized by high seller concentration and high levels of investment in research and development. These findings have been confirmed by numerous researchers. Raymond Vernon (1971) in particular noted that the 187 international firms appearing on the *Fortune* 500 list were larger in terms of sales than the remaining 313, tended to spend more on research and development and advertising as a percent of sales, and were concentrated in a relatively few industries. Hymer hypothesized that firms became international if they possessed intangible assets—chiefly superior knowledge or technology and internal scale economies—that gave them real market advantages over local rivals. Thus, Hymer claimed that dominant market positions were the result of superior technologies rather than that the development of new technologies necessitated market dominance, as claimed by Magee.

Important extensions to the Hymer hypothesis include those of Vernon (1966), who asserted that foreign markets for products embodying new or superior technologies would be served first via exportation from a home-nation firm, and only later via local production in the host nation, after local rivals had become capable of generating substitutable products. This assertion is the basis of Vernon's "product life cycle" hypothesis of international trade and investment. Richard Caves (1971) and others have noted that the intangible assets of the multinational firm might include marketing and other managerial skills. Peter Buckley and Mark Casson (1976) have suggested that internalization of information flows accounts for the scale economies possessed by multinational firms. F. T. Knickerbocker (1974), E. B. Flowers (1976), and Edward M. Graham (1978) have all introduced hypotheses suggesting that rivalry among major firms in oligopolistic industries may account for certain of their investment activities.

References

Buckley, Peter, J., and Mark C. Casson, *The Future of the Multinational Enterprise*, Macmillan, London, 1976; Caves, Richard E., "International Corporations: The Industrial Economics of Foreign Investment," *Economica*, vol. 38, no. 149, 1971, pp. 1–27; Dunning, John H., "Explaining Changing Patterns of International Production; in Defense of the Eclectic Approach," *Oxford Bulletin of Economics and Statistics*, vol. 41, no. 4, November 1979, pp. 269–285; Flowers, E. B., "Oligopolistic Reaction in European and Canadian Direct Investment in the United States," *Journal of International Business Studies*, vol. 7, no. 2, Fall–Winter, 1976, pp. 43–55; Graham, Edward M., "Transatlantic Investment by Multinational Firms: A Rivalistic Phenomenon?", *Journal of Post-Keynesian Economics*, vol. 1, no. 1, Fall 1978, pp. 82–99; Horst, Thomas O., "Firm and Industry Determinants of the Decision to Invest Abroad: An Empirical Study," *Review of Economics and Statistics*, vol. 54, no. 3, August 1972, pp. 258–266; Hymer, Stephen H., *The International Operations of National Firms: A Study of Direct Foreign Investment*, M.I.T. Press, Cambridge, Mass., 1976; Johnson, Harry, G., "The Efficiency and Welfare Implications of the International Corporation," in C. P. Kindleberger (ed.), *The International Corporation*, M.I.T. Press, Cambridge, Mass., 1970; Keynes, John Maynard, "Foreign Investment and the National Advantage," *The Nation and Athenaeum*, vol. 35, London, 1924; Kindleberger, Charles P., *American Business Abroad*, Yale University Press, New Haven, Conn., 1969; Knickerbocker, F. T., *Oligopolistic Reaction and Multinational Enterprise*, Harvard University Press, Cambridge, Mass., 1974; Magee, Stephen P., "Technology and the Appropriability Theory of the Multinational Enterprise," in J. Bhagwati (ed.), *The New International Economic Order: The North-South Debate*, M.I.T. Press, Cambridge, Mass., 1977; Vernon, Raymond, "International Investment and International Trade in the Product Cycle," *Quarterly Journal of Economics*, vol. 80, no. 2, May 1966, pp. 190–207; Vernon, Raymond, *Sovereignty at Bay*, Basic Books, New York, 1971.

(*See also* International economics, an overview; Monopoly and oligopoly; Multinational corporation)

Edward M. Graham

Foreign exchange management

Foreign exchange management is that branch of company financial management that arises when businesses carry out transactions and calculate profits and losses in foreign as well as domestic currencies. Foreign exchange management has become of critical significance to most major companies as international trade and investment have become vastly more important over the past 25 years. Moreover, exchange rates in relation to the dollar, which for most countries seldom changed in value between 1949 and 1971, have become much more volatile since August 1971 when the United States stopped converting dollars into gold.

In the United States the importance of volatile exchange rates in company financial management was brought into even sharper focus in 1975 when the Financial Accounting Standards Board (FASB) issued Bulletin 8, which set out specific standards for reporting foreign exchange gains or losses. Prior to FASB-8, companies had used a number of different methods for reporting foreign exchange gains or losses, and in some cases it was possible to set up reserves for foreign exchange losses over a relatively long period ahead. FASB-8 disallowed reserving systems and required companies to report all foreign exchange gains or losses during the same reporting period in which the exchange rate change occurred.

International companies were thus facing large overseas operations, floating exchange rates, and foreign exchange losses that would immediately affect their profit and loss statements. Three issues in dealing with these problems have become of paramount importance for foreign exchange management: (1) forecasts of exchange rates, (2) strategies for foreign exchange management given an exchange rate forecast, and (3) possibilities for reforming accounting rules in order to better represent foreign exchange gains or losses as a result of exchange rate changes.

Exchange Rate Forecasting

As exchange rate fluctuations have become a challenge to management, at least 20 consulting organizations in the United States alone have developed techniques for analyzing the foreign exchange market and are supplying forecasts of the outlook for major exchange rates. But in spite of the wide range of foreign exchange forecasts, companies have tended to rely strongly on the advice of foreign exchange traders in the major banks for advice on the outlook for exchange rates. This advice has the advantage of reflecting the latest international money-market information that is likely to be available only to bank traders. Many foreign exchange traders would readily admit, however, that they have no special expertise in forecasting exchange rates beyond a short horizon, possibly of 2 weeks' duration. Thus, corporate money managers have tried to supplement advice from traders with longer-term forecasts extending ahead for at least a year.

Particularly in cases where exchange rates are fixed temporarily by action of central banks to support the foreign exchange market, a political approach has sometimes been advised for determining when and by how much an exchange rate is likely to change. It has been argued that if enough is known about the background and monetary predilections of finance ministers, of directors of central banks, and sometimes of heads of governments, it can be determined whether or not they will devalue or revalue the currency. Certainly, political elements are an important ingredient in any evaluation of an exchange rate outlook. But the difficulties in a purely political approach should not be understated. High government officials are almost certain to be disingenuous in their statements on exchange rate policy. Even in cases where heads of governments are determined to maintain a fixed exchange rate, this resolve may be vitiated by market forces. A country holding to a fixed exchange rate may face inescapable devaluation as it runs out of foreign exchange reserves or unavoidable revaluation as an avalanche of foreign currency enters the country, destabilizing its own money supply and price levels.

At the opposite extreme from the political approach to exchange rate forecasting are the efficient-market theorists and chartists who believe all foreseeable political and economic events have been discounted in current exchange rates. The efficient-market theorists believe that the discounting of future events has been carried to the point where no effective forecasting is possible and that foreign exchange management thus becomes of decidedly limited value. The chartists believe that any identifiable economic tendencies affecting an exchange rate have been discounted. Nevertheless, they hold that trends persist in the data relating to exchange rates and that effective forecasting depends on identifying these trends and their turning points. (Momentum and filter-rule analyses are forecasting approaches that are usually more mathematically rigorous than the chartist approach, but are similar to charting in that political or economic variables have no explicit role in the forecast.)

Because a chart indicates basic trends, the foreign exchange analyst avoids the dissipation of time in random day-to-day events. But the bias of charts is to indicate that what is going up will continue to rise and vice versa. Thus, at an early stage in the development of exchange rate forecasting, as with longer-established areas of business forecasting, analysts began looking for lead indicators of exchange rate changes.

The most famous lead-indicator approach to exchange rate forecasting is called purchasing power parity. This is the theory that exchange rates tend to equalize world prices so that if prices in a country rise above world price levels, the exchange rate will tend to fall. Conversely, if price levels rise more slowly than in the rest of the world, the exchange rate will tend to rise. A variation of this theory is the use of money supplies instead of prices as the lead indicator. This approach is based on the theory that with a lag, prices tend to move in line with money supplies.

Purchasing power parity and money-supply data as lead indicators for exchange rate movements seem to be workable over long periods—5 years or more—but are less effective for the short run. For shorter periods, changes in a country's balance of payments—for example, the bulge in U.S. oil imports in 1977 to 1978—can adversely affect a country's exchange rate to a greater extent than would be indicated by purchasing power parity. Lead indicators based on a country's trade account are the reserves-imports ratio and the reserves-money supply ratio. The first of these indicators if it declines to a low level—for example, if a country can finance only 2 or 3 months of imports out of its reserves—may mean that it is dissipating reserves and may be forced to devalue. The second indicator, if it rises to a level exceeding about 10 percent on an annualized basis, may indicate that the country's reserve buildup, converted into local currency, is creating such a rise in the money supply that the central bank will be forced to revalue in order to control inflationary pressures. (The use of either of these indicators implicitly assumes that there has been some control over the exchange rate by the central bank, which may be forced into action by too great an inflow or outflow of foreign exchange.)

Lead indicators, while sometimes useful, are often considered insufficient for an adequate exchange rate forecast. It is sometimes argued that the exchange rate outlook should be analyzed comprehensively in terms of all inflows and outflows of foreign exchange to and from a country instead of in terms of a lead indicator. This analysis should include inflows and outflows of foreign exchange for transportation, tourists, immigrant remittances, profit remittances, foreign aid, foreign investment, and all other important items in a country's balance of payments.

There is, however, a serious practical difficulty with comprehensive balance of payments analysis as a vehicle for exchange rate forecasting. This approach is simply too expensive to attempt to apply unless the foreign exchange manager has more resources than are usually available. Suppose currency forecasts are required for 10 countries. The balance of payments of each country involves 10 items, thus resulting in a total of 100 forecasts. And each of the balance of payments items may be as difficult to forecast as the exchange rate itself.

In view of both the inadequacy of single lead indicators for exchange rate forecasting and the complexity of balance of payments analysis, the more recent attempts to forecast exchange rates have turned to computer-based econometric models that it is hoped will sort out the significant from the insignificant elements affecting exchange rates. Track records are not yet long enough to judge the success of these methods (or the claim of efficient-market theorists that sustained effective forecasting is not really possible). However, some differences among econometric forecasts are worth noting. It seems possible to classify these differences in line with four contrasting methods of exchange rate forecasting: (1) trade-weighted and bilateral forecasts, (2) partial and general equilibrium models, (3) general and unique specifications for forecasts, and (4) trade- and monetarist-oriented models.

Trade-Weighted and Bilateral Forecasts Econometric models of exchange rate determination differ as to what type of exchange rate is being considered. The exchange rate ordinarily quoted in U.S. newspapers is, of course, the bilateral rate, e.g., 2.5 DM = $1. But this exchange rate with respect to the dollar is not the whole story for the deutsche mark because it also fluctuates in relation to the British pound, the French franc, and all other currencies. If, for example, the deutsche mark and pound both gain 10 percent against the dollar, the deutsche mark would not change in relation to the pound. This would be a different situation compared with the deutsche mark rising 10 percent against both the dollar and the pound. One way of expressing the overall change in the value of an exchange rate is to take a weighted average of all of its percentage changes in relation to each other exchange rate. Weights are usually based on the relative amount of trade with each country.

Some forecasts of exchange rates begin by forecasting a trade-weighted exchange rate and then work backward to a bilateral rate. Other exchange rate forecasts go directly to bilateral exchange rates, usually in relation to the dollar. Bilateral exchange rates may miss important relationships to third countries of the currency being considered. Trade-weighted exchange rates, on the other hand, create special forecasting difficulties because each exchange rate depends on elements affecting every other exchange rate.

Equilibrium Models   General equilibrium models are complete systems for forecasting not simply exchange rates but most of the important macro variables in the world economy. The general equilibrium model might forecast GNP, the price level, and trade and interest rates, as well as exchange rates. Most of the variables affecting an exchange rate would be forecast in a general equilibrium model.

In a partial equilibrium model, on the other hand, only the exchange rate is forecast—usually in a single-equation model. Other variables in the equation are judgmentally forecast or are lagged variables for which past values are already known. Thus, partial equilibrium models have the disadvantage of possible guesswork involving the inputs into the model. And the output cannot be of better quality than the inputs. General equilibrium models, on the other hand, have the advantage that major variables on the model are forecast without guesswork. General equilbrium models are, however, expensive to construct. Moreover, a mistake that would be easily identified in a partial equilibrium model may not be recognized readily in one of many equations of general equilbrium and, therefore, may vitiate the results of the whole model.

Specifications   When a number of exchange rates are forecast, one approach is to attempt a unique specification, i.e., to consider each country as a special case and to work with a series of experiments with a wide number of possibly relevant independent variables until an equation is found that fits past data and thus appears to provide a basis for a successful exchange rate forecast. The same process is repeated for each currency. Another approach is to use a general specification, deciding at the outset what independent variables are likely to be significant, and then applying this general specification to all forecasts (though for each currency there will, of course, be differences in the estimated coefficients in the forecasting equations).

The use of unique specifications has the advantage that special characteristics peculiar to each currency are taken into account. All currencies are not forced into the same mold. On the other hand, there is a danger in not using a general specification that simply by chance as a result of repeated trials an "explanation" will be found for past exchange rate movements for each country. These explanations built up without theory may not work into the future.

Trade and Monetary Theories   Finally, exchange rate forecasting methods differ with respect to the economic theory used as a basis for formulating models of exchange rate fluctuations. Until about 10 years ago most standard exchange rate analysis focused mainly on the trade and current account balances with relatively little attention to capital accounts. More recently, however, this focus has been reversed in the so-called monetary theory of the balance of payments: exchange rate adjustment is considered mainly a monetary process in which separate consideration of movements in trade and current accounts is not of crucial importance. Today, proponents of both theories are found in the competition among exchange rate forecasters. Some more eclectic forecasting groups combine elements of both theories.

Foreign Exchange Management Strategies

Once a forecast of the exchange rate outlook is completed, the foreign exchange forecast must be applied to protect the company from foreign exchange losses. Potential foreign exchange losses depend on a company's exposure, that is, on its vulnerability to foreign exchange losses. Broadly, there are two kinds of exposure: commercial and translation. Commercial exposure arises when a company has an obligation to make or receive a payment in foreign currency, for example, on receipt of imported goods or for goods that the company has exported. In either case losses can arise. In the first case, with imports there would be losses from an appreciation in the exchange rate in relation to the dollar, thus raising the company's payment for its imported goods. In the second case, if there were a devaluation of the foreign currency, the company would lose on the payment for its exports. In some instances the company can avoid commercial losses by quoting prices in dollars, but this is not always acceptable to foreign customers or sources of supply. When billing in dollars is not possible, companies often use the forward foreign exchange market in order to avoid foreign exchange risk. This is a market in which currencies are sold forward at specific dates ahead. Forward rates may be higher or lower than current rates, commonly known as spot rates. In the language of foreign exchange trading, forward rates above spot rates are at a premium and forward rates below spot rates are at a discount. Premiums and discounts in foreign exchange contracts are of major concern to the foreign exchange manager because they represent the cost of being covered against foreign exchange losses. The decision to hedge or not to hedge a foreign exchange exposure depends on the foreign exchange manager's assessment of whether or not the cost of a contract is worth it compared with the risk of losses from an exchange rate revaluation or devaluation.

Aside from the forward market, possibilities for hedging also arise, for the case of devaluation risk, in the borrowing of weak currencies with the possibility of repayment after a devaluation takes place. To head off a revaluation threat the company may extend loans in the suspect currency. For larger multinational companies with subsidiaries operating in most countries and with a network of transactions among the subsidiaries, the exact hedging strategy may become complex, possibly even requiring the use of the computer as discussed by G. Lieberman (1978).

Foreign Exchange Accounting

Aside from commercial exposure, companies face translation exposure. This arises because, in addition to risks of losses on commercial transactions, international companies already have assets and liabilities abroad. In the simple case, a company might have cash abroad in the form of a bank deposit and would lose from currency depreciation. Or it might have a short-term debt abroad and would lose from appreciation; i.e., after the value of the currency rises, it will cost more in dollars to repay the local currency debt. Translation exposure becomes complicated, however, because in the accounts of most companies there is a wide range of assets and liabilities, and in different accounting systems there are very different rules as to which elements in the balance sheets are considered exposed to losses. For many years, considerable leeway was permitted in company practices regarding translation exposure. In 1975, however, FASB Bulletin 8 set up standard rules for translation exposure accounting in the United States. The FASB-8 rules provided that cash (including bank deposits and short-term money-market investments) be considered exposed. Also there is general agreement that accounts payable and short-term debt are exposed. With respect to other balance sheet items, however, the FASB-8 rules are controversial and may be modified in the future.

In practice, for the majority of cases, under FASB-8 rules inventory is not considered exposed. This rule is criticized as illogical because a devaluation will result in inventory being sold for less in terms of dollars.

The other controversial feature of FASB-8 is its treatment of long-term debt as exposed and of fixed assets as not exposed. Again, it is argued that there is an inconsistency in the translation treatment of the two sides of the balance sheet. In some accounting practices abroad, symmetry of exposure on both sides of the balance sheet is maintained by considering fixed assets as exposed.

Another objection to FASB-8 is that amortization and other types of reserving for foreign exchange gains and losses are not permitted. This rule is in line with the widespread suspicion among accountants that too much reserving allows companies to avoid showing losses.

In the opinion of many international accountants it now seems probable that FASB-8 will be modified, and in March 1979 the Financial Accounting Standards Board appointed a committee to recommend changes in Bulletin 8. As long as exchange rates are volatile, however, international financial management is likely to remain one of the most serious challenges facing international business.

References

Eiteman, David K., and Arthur I. Stonehill, *Multinational Business Finance*, 2d ed., Addison-Wesley, Reading, Mass., 1978; George, Abraham M., *Foreign Exchange Management and the Multinational Corporation*, Praeger, New York, 1978; Jacque, Laurent L., *Management of Foreign Exchange Risk*, D.C. Heath, Lexington, Mass., 1978; Lieberman, Gail, "A Systems Approach to Foreign Exchange Risk Management," *Financial Executive*, Financial Executives Institute, New York, December 1978; Rodriguez, Rita and E. Eugene Carter, *International Financial Management*, 2d ed., Prentice-Hall, Englewood Cliffs, N.J., 1979.

(*See also* Foreign exchange rates; International economics, an overview)

James L. Burtle

Foreign exchange rates

Foreign exchange rates are market quotations of the prices of foreign currencies in terms of domestic currency, or, equivalently, the reciprocal, foreign currency prices of the domestic currency. As such, they represent rates of exchange of one currency for another which are used for most of the myriad transactions crossing national boundaries, whether foreign trade, tourism, international investment, or short-term money flows between countries. These exchange rates may either be set by governments, as in the pegged exchange rate system, or be set by a combination of market forces and government policies, as in the floating exchange rate system.

Exchange rates may be quoted either for spot, or immediate (i.e., 2-day) delivery of one currency against another, or at various forward delivery dates, such as 1 month, 3 months, etc. The difference between spot and forward quotations generally reflects the difference between the costs of borrowing the two currencies for the relevant time period.

Since each country has trade and investment relationships with a number of other countries, no single foreign exchange rate can adequately measure the purchasing power of the domestic currency over foreign currencies in general. The concept of effective exchange rate has been developed to measure the weighted average price of foreign currencies in terms of domestic currency. Various weighting schemes have been devised, including import weights to reflect purchasing power over imports, bilateral trade weights to reflect the importance of trade relations with individual foreign countries, global trade weights to reflect the importance of different currencies in world trade, and elasticity-weighted trade shares to reflect differing degrees of competitiveness of a country vis-à-vis different foreign countries. Further discussion of the exchange rate will refer to the effective exchange rate concept.

Microeconomic Role

For an economy that is relatively open to foreign trade and investment, the exchange rate has important effects on relative prices. Changes in the price of foreign exchange affect the domestic price of imports, the profitability of producing import substitutes, the profitability of exports, and the domestic price of exportable goods. For large countries producing differentiated export products such as manufactured goods over whose price they have significant influence, changes in the exchange rate frequently lead to changes in the terms of trade, the ratio of the price of exports to the price of imports. For a smaller country whose trade prices may be determined in world markets, changes in the exchange rate have significant effects on the prices of traded goods relative to the prices of goods which are not traded abroad because of high transportation costs or other barriers. By changing relative costs of production in different countries, changes in exchange rates have significant effects on the profitability of investing in different countries. Since different groups of producers are likely to be involved in producing exportable goods, import substitutes, or nontraded goods, changes in the relative prices of these different types of commodities have major effects on the distribution of income among these groups and among consumers, as well as upon the allocation of resources among different sectors of the economy and among different countries.

Macroeconomic Role

The exchange rate is also important as a macroeconomic variable, influencing domestic inflation, unemployment, and the balance of payments. Changes in the price of foreign exchange affect domestic inflation both directly, through the prices of traded goods and their substitutes, and indirectly, through the income adjustment mechanism and the monetary adjustment mechanism. For example, if a change in the level of the exchange rate generates a substantial surplus of exports over imports of goods and services, that surplus represents additional foreign demand for domestic goods and services over and above domestic demand for foreign goods and services. That foreign demand represents a source of income generation in the export sector which spills over in a Keynesian multiplier process to the rest of the economy, raising prices and production in both the export sector and elsewhere, depending on conditions of capacity utilization in the different sectors of the economy. This Keynesian income adjustment mechanism reaches equilibrium when the excess of domestic saving over domestic investment matches the net accumulation of foreign assets or net foreign investment represented by the export surplus. The same process works in reverse for a deficit in which imports of goods and services exceed exports.

The classical monetary adjustment mechanism becomes operative under floating rates when private investment abroad (or foreign borrowing) is unable to finance the export surplus (or deficit) at given prices, incomes, interest rates, and exchange rates. If the surplus on current account payments for goods, services, and unilateral transfers exceeds private capital outflow or lending abroad at the current exchange rate, the monetary authorities have three choices: (1) adopting expansionary domestic macroeconomic policy; (2) changing the exchange rate either by changing the pegged exchange rate or by allowing the price of foreign currencies to float downward; (3) keeping the exchange rate unchanged by selling domestic currency and buying foreign currency to hold up the price of foreign currency. In the latter case, the country's foreign exchange reserves rise along with its domestic money supply as the central bank creates additional money to pay for the foreign currency. The expansion in the domestic money supply will normally lead to a reduction in domestic interest rates and expansion in domestic spending, prices, and production. This monetary adjustment process may be cut short by a monetary policy designed to prevent the rise in the money supply. This is called sterilization of the reserve movement.

Changes in foreign exchange rates, together with changes in domestic macroeconomic policy, direct controls over various components of the balace of payments, income adjustments, and monetary flows represent the various possible mechanisms through which international payments imbalances are resolved. The process involves a mixture of adjustment policies, which seek to alter the existing surpluses and deficits, and financing, which seeks to provide both capital flows and monetary flows to enable their continuation.

Determinants

Various partial theories of exchange rate determination have been developed over the years, which may in combination provide an adequate, if impure, explanation of the many factors affecting market-determined, or floating, exchange rates. The purchasing power–parity, or monetary, theory, observing that the exchange rate is the relative price of different currencies, focuses on the relative purchasing power of the different currencies in terms of goods and services. The theory implies that exchange rates move to offset relative inflation rates in different countries, after allowing for shifts in the relative importance of traded and nontraded goods. (The qualification is required because the theory rests on equality of traded-goods prices, while the prices of nontraded goods can differ significantly between countries.) Most evidence suggests that the theory is correct only as a long-run approximation of reality, except under conditions of hyperinflation, since traded goods do not flow instantaneously from one market to another to equalize prices.

The interest rate–parity theory concentrates on capital flows and the factors determining the relationship between spot and forward exchange rates. Comparison of the return from short-term assets held in one currency with the return from assets in another currency covered against the risk of a change in the exchange rate shows that arbitrage will equate the domestic interest rate to the foreign interest rate plus the forward premium on the foreign currency.

The formula is

$$R_d = R_f + \frac{y - x}{x}$$

where R_d and R_f are the domestic and foreign short-term interest rates in percent per period, y is the forward price of foreign currency for delivery at the end of the period, x is the spot price, and $(y - x)/x$ is the forward premium on foreign currency, in percent per period (Levich, 1979). The evidence suggests that this theory is usually valid except when capital controls, the risk of possible future capital controls, or other types of market uncertainty become important. Such factors are often significant in comparisons between domestic financial markets in different countries but are usually absent in comparisons between Eurocurrency-market interest rates.

The efficient-market theory postulates that the forward exchange rate is an unbiased predictor of the expected future spot exchange rate. Tests of this theory suggest that it may be valid in some average sense but that changes in exchange rates are not predicted very well by forward rates, indicating the presence of substantial risk in speculation on changes in exchange rates.

The asset-market theory of exchange rates integrates the various other theories into a complete theory which can be cast in terms of flows in the balance of payments (Branson, 1979). According to this approach, the exchange rate is determined in the short run by equality of supply and demand for assets denominated in different currencies. The demands for these assets depend upon the relative interest rates, forward premiums, and expectations of changes in exchange rates emphasized by the interest rate–parity and efficient-market theories. Changes in the supplies of these assets to private wealth holders in different countries depend on surpluses and deficits in the current account of the balance of payments, together with central bank intervention in the exchange markets. These surpluses and deficits, on the other hand, depend upon deviations of exchange rates from purchasing power parity in different countries as well as upon other factors such as changes in tastes, technologies, and fluctuations in aggregate demand in different countries.

Historical Background

Elements of the basic theory of foreign exchange rates were developed by David Hume (1752), David Ricardo (1811), and earlier writers. Hume's analysis focused on the mechanism by which excessive money creation under the gold standard (or a pegged exchange rate) leads to domestic inflation, a balance of payments deficit, and an outflow of money. Ricardo, writing about the gold value of the pound sterling under the floating rate conditions prevailing during the Napoleonic Wars, emphasized the importance of excessive money creation and domestic inflation in determining the fall in the gold value of the pound. Cassel (1922) formulated the purchasing power–parity doctrine in its modern form to help explain the movements of exchange rates in the period following World War I. The interest rate–parity theory was developed by Keynes (1923), and the modern asset-market and efficient-market theories are developments of recent writers.

Controversial Issues

Both the theory of foreign exchange rates and exchange rate policies have generated debate. Theoretical debates have frequently questioned the validity or the sufficiency of one or another of the theories. More frequently, practical economists and policy-oriented analysts have argued that exchange rates are determined by flows in the balance of payments, attributable to a myriad of causes, without recognizing the overall pattern of causation and influence suggested by the asset-market theory.

The efficiency of the forward exchange market is hotly debated, for efficiency together with interest rate parity implies that capital markets are essentially risk-free and that assets denominated in different currencies are perfect substitutes. Such a finding would imply that floating exchange rates could operate relatively free of central bank intervention to smooth out fluctuations in exchange rates.

The debate over pegged versus floating exchange rates involves a choice either for individual countries or for the international monetary system as a whole. The Bretton Woods system, established in 1944 on the basis of pegged rates among all countries, broke down in 1971 and was replaced with a mixed system of floating and pegging in 1973, formalized by the second amendment to the charter of the International Monetary Fund, effective in 1978. The proponents of pegged rates argue that pegging reduces the short-run variability of exchange rates and hence the riskiness of international trade and investment. At the same time the maintenance of a constant exchange rate requires that domestic inflation match foreign inflation to avoid excessive balance of payments surpluses or deficits, thus implying a certain discipline over domestic monetary and fiscal policies.

The proponents of floating rates note that the failure of such discipline leads to occasional large changes in exchange rates which rectify departures from purchasing power parity and introduce additional risk into foreign trade and investment, as well as induce speculation against the central bank. On the other hand, they argue that floating rates provide domestic economic policy with additional freedom by eliminating the Hume mechanism through which money flows in or out of the economy.

References

Branson, W. H., "Exchange Rate Dynamics and Monetary Policy," in A. Lindbeck (ed.), *Inflation and Unemployment in Open Economies*, North-Holland, Amsterdam, 1979, pp. 189–224; Cassel, G., *Money and Foreign Exchange After 1914*, Macmillan, London, 1922. Hume, D., "Of the Balance of Trade," in *Political Discourses*, Fleming, Edinburgh, 1752, reprinted in E. Rotwein (ed.), *David Hume: Writings on Economics*, University of Wisconsin Press, Madison, 1955; Keynes, J. M., *A Tract on Monetary Reform*, Macmillan, London, 1923; Levich, R. M., "On the Efficiency of Markets for Foreign Exchange," in R. Dornbusch and J. A. Frenkel (eds.), *International Economic Policy: Theory and Evidence*, Johns Hopkins University Press, Baltimore, 1979; Officer, L. H., "The Purchasing-Power-Parity Theory of Exchange Rates: A Review Article," *IMF Staff Papers*, vol. 23, no. 1, March 1976, pp. 1–60; Ricardo, D., *The High Price of Bullion*, 4th ed., J. Murray, London, 1811.

(*See also* Balance of international payments; Balance of international trade; Exports; Imports; International economics, an overview; Liquidity, international; Value of the dollar)

Stanley W. Black

Free enterprise system (see Capitalism)

Fringe benefits

The term fringe benefits is used synonymously with employee benefits. Although "fringes" are decorative outer edges, implying relative unimportance, estimates of fringe benefits for 1977 place costs to U.S. companies at $310 billion, an average of $4700 per worker, or 36.7 percent of employee compensation. Comparable figures for 1971 and 1929 are $140 billion and $1.5 billion, respectively. A definition as nonwage (nonsalary) benefits is common, but involves a contradiction with payroll figures of the U.S. Department of Labor which include in wages and salaries pay for time not worked although the worker is able to work, and pay for sick leave. Social insurance costs are included in fringe benefits. Perquisites is a term frequently applied to fringe benefits instituted for limited numbers of managerial employees; it is more rarely used to apply to all fringe benefits other than those mandated by social insurance laws. Some fringe benefits involve rights of employees, without requiring any monetary outlay.

Prior to the 1930s there was probably an upward trend in fringe benefits, though with many irregularities due to such factors as early diminution of payment in kind and a later increase and subsequent decline of company towns. In specific sectors of the economy, the railroad industry for example, an early relatively high level of fringe benefits was reached. Since the 1930s, governmental action and labor union pressure in negotiations have been dominant, sometimes interrelated, influences in the upward trend in value and in relative importance of fringe benefits. Employer initiative stemming from such reasons as personnel policy, social responsibility, competition, and personal gains of management from fringe benefits has also been important. Inflation has been a big factor in the rising cost of fringe benefits.

In addition to federal and/or state legislation mandating Old Age, Survivors, Disability and Health Insurance (OASDHI), unemployment insurance, and worker's compensation, tax laws and rulings encourage employer expenditures for fringe benefits because of their classification as tax-deductible business expenses or investment tax credits. In addition, there are numerous state laws and some federal laws that, while not mandating fringe benefits, determine some of their provisions if they are initiated. Examples of relevant federal legislation are the Taft-Hartley Act, the Employment Retirement Income Security Act (ERISA), the Equal Employment Opportunity Act, the Civil Rights Act of 1974, the Health Maintenance Organization (HMO) Act, and the Age Discrimination in Employment Act. Federal laws that free employee wages contributed for fringe benefits from taxation include section 403(b) of the Internal Revenue Code (for employees of government or nonprofit institutions) and ERISA, providing for individual retirement arrangements (IRAs).

Fringe Benefit Categories

Because the same fringe benefit may be used in alternative ways, there is some difficulty in a clear-cut categorization. One group of fringe benefits includes pay for time a worker does not work though able to work. As a rule, these periods interrupt the normal worktime sequence, and the employee is expected to return to work. Examples are paid meal periods; paid rest or smoking breaks; vacations of an ordinary nature; individualized leave in connection with birthdays, elections, births, deaths, attendance at meetings, etc.; extended vacations; sabbatical leaves; and those parts of the guaranteed annual wage and call-in time that are not offset by wages for time worked. In those few industries having extended vacations, the practice has sometimes arisen of offering the choice of extra compensation instead of the extended vacation. Business interruption insurance may cover payroll.

Another category of fringe benefits includes pay or other benefits for time not worked because of physical condition (including pregnancy), or pay because of the existence of a specific physical condition. Examples are sick leave days, worker's compensation, short-term disability plans, long-term disability under OASDHI, long-term disability (not under OASDHI), disability income and waiver-of-premium provisions of life insurance, disability income and pension accumulation provisions of pension plans, travel-accident insurance, and disability income provisions of unemployment compensation in a limited number of jurisdictions. Under schedule disabilities of worker's compensation laws, the dismemberment part of accidental-death-and-dismemberment insurance, and similar provisions of travel-accident policies, payment may be made to the employee, dependent on the incurrence of specific injuries but independent of actual work time lost. Frequently, offset provisions are included for the purpose of preventing duplication of benefits. Because of this, long-term disability income (not under OASDHI) is sometimes referred to as a phantom benefit. At times unused sick leave days may be taken in cash, either periodically or on separation from employment.

Unemployment compensation is provided for under federal and state laws. In addition, supplementary unemployment benefits (SUB) are established by firms in a minority of industries. The payment of such supplementary benefits is likely to be dependent on the status of funds that are established for this purpose. As already mentioned, the cash equivalent of unused sick leave may be available, as may accumulated vacation time, profit sharing proceeds, deferred compensation, or an early pension. Termination or separation pay is another fringe benefit, and where this is available, it is likely to vary with length of service. Often provision for payment of life and health insurance premiums is made for limited periods of unemployment. Placement services are sometimes established on an ad hoc basis, but this is mostly a fringe benefit of middle and upper management.

Health expense benefits almost invariably include surgical costs as well as a fairly complete range of other services utilized during hospitalization for limited periods of time (usually up to one year). Insurance of the employee's family is usual. Coverage may be extended to nursing homes. Otherwise, out-of-hospital medical expenses are included in major medical insurance, as is long-term hospitalization. HMOs, which under certain circumstances must be offered as alternatives to health insurance plans, stress preventive care. Otherwise, physical examinations are not likely to be covered, except under managerial perquisites. Some companies pay for health screening. Dental insurance may be an independent plan or may be included in major medical insurance. Prescription-drug coverage by itself is rare, as is vision care, although the former is frequently found in other health insurances. Medicare payments may be made for employees in the appropriate age category as well as for retirees.

Coverage of death benefits is found in OASDHI, life insurance, worker's compensation, accidental death and disability, travel-accident insurance, and pension plans or other retirement arrangements.

Retirement benefits are generally approached through pension plans, and these cover most employees under OASDHI, with many coming under public and private plans in addition. Retirement benefits are also created through profit sharing, deferred compensation, stock bonus plans, employer contributions to IRAs, paid-up whole life insurance, savings plans, employee stock ownership plans (ESOPs), tax reduction act stock ownership plans (TRASOPs), stock-appreciation rights, and phantom stock and salary-continuation plans. Life and health insurance may be continued for retirees.

Prepaid legal expense and group automobile and homeowner's insurances are relatively new. Other fringe benefits include free or reduced-price meals; merchandise discounts; use of automobiles, airplanes, and yachts; club and professional society memberships; parking; educational expense support; professional society meeting expenses; low- or no-interest loans; airline and railroad passes; financial and tax counseling; child care centers; housing; and expense accounts. Some fringe benefits are products of the times, examples being kidnap and ransom insurance and the provision of vans for transportation to work. "Costless" fringe benefits include some maternity and almost all paternity leave.

Fringe Benefits in Other Countries

Throughout the free world, fringe benefits follow multivaried patterns. They are usually underdeveloped in underdeveloped countries. Social insurance laws may be somewhat disregarded, as in some countries in middle-belt Africa. There, as in underdeveloped countries elsewhere, the best fringe benefit systems are found in multinational companies. In many of the more highly industrialized countries, there is greater inflexibility in health and pension benefits than in the United States. Some examples of significant differences are unfunded private pension obligations (West Germany), very large termination benefits (Mexico, Belgium), the contracting out of social insurance (England), low retirement age (Japan).

References

Greenough, William C., and Francis P. King, *Pension Plans and Public Policy,* Columbia University Press, New York, 1976; Mehr, Robert I., and Bob A. Hedges, *Risk Management: Concepts and Applications,* Irwin, Homewood, Ill. 1974.

(*See also* Collective bargaining; Labor-management relations)

Theodore Bakerman

Game theory, economic applications

Game theory is the mathematical analysis of principles of decision making in situations involving two or more players with (at least partly) conflicting interests. Its central problem was formulated by John von Neumann (1928) as follows: "n players S_1, $S_2, \ldots, S_n$ are playing a given game of strategy, G. How must one of the participants play in order to achieve a most advantageous result?"

A game of strategy, said von Neumann, consists of a series of events each of which may have a finite number of distinct results; the results of some events are determined by chance and of others by the free decisions of the players; for each event it is known which player is to make the decision and how much the player knows about the results of the earlier events at the time the decision is made; when the outcome of all events is known, the payments the players S_1, S_2, $\ldots$, S_n must make to each other are calculated according to a fixed rule. Von Neumann asserted that almost any event in daily life could be viewed as a game of strategy and that the principal concern of classical economics was as follows: "How is the absolutely selfish 'homo economicus' going to act under given external circumstances?"

Mathematicians and Game Theory

Von Neumann was a mathematical genius whose work has had a lasting impact on several fields of pure and applied mathematics and on quantum physics. His 1928 paper "On the Theory of Games of Strategy" was published in German in a mathematical journal and went virtually unnoticed by economists. His interest in doing a major work on game theory was kindled by the economist Oskar Morgenstern, who arrived in 1938 at Princeton University where von Neumann was a professor. The result of their collaboration was the classic *Theory of Games and Economic Behavior* (1944). Economic motivation is presented in Chapter 1 in a series of sections on the mathematical method in economics, the problem of rational behavior, the notion of utility, and the structure of game theory—solutions and standards of behavior. Four sections of Chapter 11 deal with the economic interpretation of general nonzero-sum games for cases of one, two, and three players and "the general market"; the rest of the book is heavily mathematical, and there is no attempt to relate the results to economic as distinct from other possible contexts.

Until the late 1950s the work of developing and extending game theory was done almost exclusively by mathematicians. Several of the concepts that proved to be of greatest importance for economists were the Nash bargaining equilibrium in 1950, the Shapley value in 1953, and the core by D. B. Gillies in 1953. In 1956 Harsanyi pointed out that a solution to the bargaining problem proposed by the economist Zeuthen in 1930 was mathematically equivalent to Nash's, and in 1959 Shubik demonstrated that the core of an n-person game was equivalent to the contract curve derived by the economist Edgeworth in 1881. Other economists noted that Nash's solution of the bargaining problem includes as a special case the duopoly model published by Cournot in 1838.

Economists and Game Theory

During the 1960s, an increasing number of economists became interested in reformulating problems of market structure and competition in game-theoretic terms, and by the late 1970s, this was one of the most active and prestigious fields of economic research. As of 1979, nearly all publications in this tradition were directed toward clarifying economic theory; Telser (1978) was one of the few who tried to check game-theoretic models of oligopoly against market data.

The difficulties of applying game theory in real-life situations are suggested by Shubik's contrasting list of the major assumptions used (1) in game-theoretic models and (2) in behavioral models such as business management games that are intended to approximate the actual working environments of corporation executives:

Game theory	Behavioral theories
Rules of the game	Laws and customs of society
External symmetry	Personal detail
No social conditioning	Socialization assumed
No role playing	Role playing
Fixed, well-defined payoffs	Difficult to define and may change
Perfect intelligence	Limited intelligence
No learning	Learning
No coding problems	Coding problems
Primarily static	Primarily dynamic

SOURCE: Shubik (1975).

Shubik saw game theory as "a useful bench mark and a fundamentally important methodological approach to the study of situations involving potential conflict" and devoted nearly half of his book to an elucidation of game theory even though his primary concerns were describing and improving behavioral games of the business management type. In real life, executives might use a game theory model with its well-defined rules and outcomes as a checklist for identifying those key aspects of a situation which depend on personalities, communication patterns, and loyalties specific to the situation.

In a similar spirit Johansen (1977) devotes about 40 pages of his practically oriented book on macroeconomic planning to a discussion of game theory. His conceptual model includes what he calls the Central Authority and also a number of the larger noncentral decision makers whose preferences may be in conflict among themselves and also with those of the Central Authority. These larger decision makers are keenly aware of the interdependencies involved and may be viewed as engaging in a sophisticated game of strategy; the situation cannot be resolved by using classical methods of maximization (e.g., by regarding the Central Authority as an autonomous decision maker selecting an optimal point on its own preference function). Johansen does not attempt to operationalize such a model but puts it forward for its conceptual value.

Core Theory

As of 1979, Telser has done more than anyone else to adapt the theory of the core of a game to economic applications. In his 1978 book, *Economic Theory and the Core*, he applies core theory to the analysis of externalities, public goods, and free riders; to specification of sufficient conditions for natural monopoly or natural monopsony; to certain problems in the theories of location and storage; and to empirical studies of storage and of price distributions. He also shows that the core is empty, i.e., no competitive equilibrium exists, for an industry in which all plants have identical U-shaped average cost curves and rising marginal costs—thus upsetting the familiar example of industry equilibrium that has appeared in most economics textbooks since 1930. In an earlier work Telser also applies core theory to the Cournot-Nash model of duopoly and to clarification of the conditions under which collusion can be expected to dominate competition in an industry (in the absence of legal restraints).

Harsanyi noted that the theory of games had not found extensive applications in the sciences of social behavior up to that time—mainly because the von Neumann and Morgenstern approach did not yield determinate solutions for two-person, non-zero-sum games or for n-person games. Harsanyi proposed a general theory of rational behavior in game situations which "by means of a few additional and more powerful rationality postulates" would provide determinate solutions for both of these game classes: "Only a theory providing determinate solutions can suggest reasonably specific *empirically testable hypotheses* about social behavior and can attempt to *explain* and to *predict* . . . the outcome of social interaction in various real-life social situations" (Harsanyi, 1977). Harsanyi reformulated many of the classificatory game theory models in such a way as to facilitate social science (including economic) applications.

The theory of the core of an n-person game as n becomes very large (in a certain sense, even infinite) has led to an impressive reformulation of general equilibrium theory. Aumann, Debreu, Vind, and Hildenbrand have been among the major contributors to this development. The core of a pure-exchange economy is the set of all allocations that do not exceed the sum of the endowments initially held by the n households participating in the economy and that cannot be improved upon by any coalition (set of households), including the coalition of all n households. Any allocation in the core is Pareto-efficient in the sense that there is no way of making every household better off. Aumann and Shapley (1974) make the assumption that the households form a continuum (i.e., the resources of each household constitute an infinitesimal piece of the entire economy) and show that, under the further assumption that utility may be transferred (i.e., side payments made) between households, there is a unique point in the core of the economy, and this point coincides with the Shapley value. They define the notion of competitive equilibrium for such an economy and show that this equilibrium yields a unique payoff (and, hence, a unique system of relative prices) which also coincides with the Shapley value and, therefore, with the unique core point.

References

Aumann, R. J., and L. S. Shapley, *Values of Non-atomic Games*, Princeton University Press, Princeton, 1974; Friedman, J. W., *Oligopoly and the Theory of Games*, North-Holland, Amsterdam, 1977; Harsanyi, John C., *Rational Behavior and Bargaining Equilibrium in Games and Social Situations*, Cambridge University Press, Cambridge, 1977, p. 4; Johansen, Leif, *Lectures on Macroeconomic Planning*, part 1: *General Aspects*, North-Holland, Amsterdam, 1977; Shubik, Martin, *Games for Society, Business and War: Towards a Theory of Gaming*, Elsevier, New York, 1975, table, p. 158; Telser, Lester G., *Economic Theory and the Core*, University of Chicago Press, Chicago, 1978; von Neumann, John, and Oskar Morgenstern, *Theory of Games and Economic Behavior*, 3d ed., Wiley, New York, 1953, 1st ed., originally published by Princeton University Press, Princeton, N.J., 1944.

(*See also* Competition; General equilibrium; Statistical techniques in economics and business, an overview)

Karl A. Fox and Ted K. Kaul

General Agreement on Tariffs and Trade

Since the nineteenth century, the dominant view of economists, at least those of the developed world, has been that an open, nondiscriminatory trading system among nations would maximize global economic welfare. It was not until 1948, however, that a major group of nations not linked by strong common cultural or imperial ties undertook to enter into a formal agreement to establish such a system. The agreement, the General Agreement on Tariffs and Trade (GATT), was initially signed by only 22 nations, but by 1979 this number had grown to almost 100. Seven multilateral tariff negotiations have been held since 1948, the results of which have been to extend the 1948 agreement.

Three factors doubtlessly motivated nations to enter into the 1948 agreement. The first was the belief among many national leaders that the events leading to the Second World War were triggered by the Great Depression of the 1930s, which in turn was believed to have been prolonged and deepened by the very high tariffs enacted by virtually all of the major trading nations during the early 1930s. Liberalization of the international economic system was widely perceived as a way to avoid recurrence of a similar calamity, and in this spirit a thorough reform of the international monetary system as well was undertaken during the 1940s. The second factor was the leadership role of the United States. The United States actually began the 1930s tariff escalation with the passage of the Smoot-Hawley Act of 1930, but in 1934 legislation was passed to enable the President to negotiate mutual reduction of tariffs on a bilateral basis. By the late 1930s, U.S. economic leaders became convinced that vastly reduced tariffs would be in the nation's best interest if these could be regulated multilaterally. The third factor was the need to rebuild Europe following World War II. The belief of many European leaders was that an open international economic system was prerequisite to this rebuilding.

In the years immediately following World War II, U.S. leaders saw the GATT as only one part of a more wide-ranging program to create an open international economy. This program was to have been embodied in an International Trade Organization (ITO). Preparatory meetings for the creation of the ITO were held from the fall of 1946 through early 1948. As part of this work program, the GATT itself was drafted in Geneva, Switzerland, from April to October 1947 and was to have been part of the

ITO charter. The charter itself was scheduled to be completed at the Havana Conference of 1948. By the time a draft charter was worked out, however, the spirit of international cooperation that had prevailed in the U.S. Congress during the immediate aftermath of the Second World War had waned, and by early 1950 it became clear that Congress would not accept the ITO. A somewhat more modest proposal for an Organization for Trade Cooperation was rejected by Congress in 1955, and thus the GATT became by default the central agreement.

Because it was seen originally as part of a wider-ranging agreement, the GATT came into effect on January 1, 1948, by means of a temporary "Protocol of Provisional Application," which established an administrative organization to implement the agreed upon articles. Had the ITO come into being, this protocol would have expired, and the administrative organization would have been absorbed into the secretariat of ITO. However, because this did not come to pass, the GATT administrative organization evolved into a permanent secretariat, now headquartered in Geneva, Switzerland.

A Series of Agreements

As a legal document, the GATT is not a single agreement but rather a series of agreements. The key to the document lies in article II, which makes national obligations with regard to tariff schedules an integral part of the GATT and its treaty obligations. The general negotiations produced a series of agreements by participating nations to limit tariffs on specific items to negotiated amounts, and the focus of most of the succeeding multilateral tariff negotiations has been on further tariff reductions.

Much of the remainder of the GATT is designed to prevent evasion of the tariff obligations of article II by the use of nontariff barriers. Article III outlines a national treatment obligation whereby member nations must not submit imports to more restrictive standards with respect to taxation or regulation than domestically produced goods. Article VII regulates customs valuation procedures, article VIII regulates import and export fees, article IX regulates required marks of origin, article X provides for transparency of trade regulations, and article XI, with exceptions, prohibits import quotas. Article XVI puts some restraint on export subsidies by governments.

Article I of the GATT is the celebrated most favored nation (MFN) clause under which each member nation must give treatment to other member nations' imports and exports that is at least as favorable as that applied to the most favored nation.

As a step toward liberalization of international trade, the GATT is a major step forward, but even so it is riddled with exceptions. Principal exceptions are embodied in articles XII to XIV, allowing a nation to restrict imports under a balance of payments crisis; articles XX and XXI, allowing exceptions for purposes of implementing health and safety regulations and for national security; article XIX (the escape clause article), allowing temporary restraints on imports which cause serious or material injury to domestic producers; article XXIV, allowing customs-union member states to deviate from article I with respect to trade from other member states; and article XXV, allowing signatory nations collectively, by a two-thirds majority, to grant waivers or exceptions to other articles in exceptional circumstances.

Modifying Codes

Agreements reached in the most recent Multilateral Tariff Negotiation, concluded in Geneva in 1979, to a large degree focus on limiting or clarifying some of these exceptions and on eliminating nontariff barriers to trade. These agreements are embodied in a series of codes which modify or interpret the application of specific articles of the GATT. The principal codes are as follows:

1. Subsidies/countervailing measures, pertaining to articles VI, XVI, and XXIII, both limit the extent to which governments can subsidize exports and standardize procedures under which governments can impose countervailing duties (or other measures) on imports subsidized by exporting nations.

2. The antidumping code, pertaining to article VI, standardizes determination of dumping practices (exporting to a foreign market at a price below that charged in a domestic market) and establishes uniform remedies to be used against dumping nations by importing nations.

3. Customs valuation, pertaining to article VII, defines standard procedures for valuing imports for customs duty purposes.

4. The government procurement code obligates a signatory government generally not to discriminate unreasonably against foreign sources of supply when procuring goods or services for its own use.

5. The technical barriers to trade code disallows governments to use technical standards or certification requirements to discriminate unreasonably against imports of foreign-made goods.

6. Import licensing procedures simplify and standardize import licensing procedures.

7. The code for trade in civil aircraft virtually removes any tariff or nontariff barriers to international trade in civilian aircraft.

Two additional codes, the international dairy agreement and the bovine meat arrangement, attempt to ease trade restrictions pertaining to dairy and meat products.

References

Baldwin, R. E., "The Multilateral Trade Negotiations: Toward Greater Liberalization?," unpublished manuscript. June 1979; Brown, W. A., *The United States and Restoration of World Trade*, Brookings, Washington, D.C., 1950; Curzon, Gerard, and Victoria Curzon, "The Management of Trade Relations in the GATT," in S. Shonfeld (ed.), *International Economic Relations in the Western World 1959–1971*, Oxford University Press, London, 1976; Dam, K., *The GATT: Law and International Economic Cooperation*, University of Chicago Press, Chicago, 1970; Diebold, William, "The End of the I.T.O.," *Essays in International Finance*, no. 16, Princeton University Press, Princeton, 1952; Evans, J. W., "The General Agreement on Tariffs and Trade," *International Organization*, University of Wisconsin Press, Madison, January 1968; General Agreement on Tariffs and Trade, *Basic Instruments and Selected Documents*, Geneva, 1969, revised periodically; Jackson, J. H., *World Trade and the Law of GATT*, Bobbs-Merrill, Indianapolis, 1969; Jackson, J. H., *Legal Problems of International Economic Relations*, West, St. Paul, Minn., 1977, chaps. 7–12; U.S. Senate Committee on Finance and U.S. House of Representatives Committee on Ways and Means, *Multilateral Trade Negotiations: International Codes Agreed to in Geneva, Switzerland, April 12, 1979*, 1979.

(*See also* Barriers to trade; Dumping; Exports; Imports; International economics, an overview; Protectionism)

Edward M. Graham

General equilibrium

General equilibrium analysis deals with the basic issues of economics: value, distribution, and welfare; however, it is the branch of economics that is the most technical and least accessible to the nonprofessional. Even a definition of general economic equilibrium is not easy to formulate. The concept economic equilibrium suggests that market forces are in balance, while general equilibrium analysis is distinguished from partial economic equilibrium analysis by the requirement that the price of every good is free to vary and that all markets must clear. In partial equilibrium analysis the prices of several commodities are held fixed relative to one another and spillovers between markets are largely ignored. General equilibrium analysis emphasizes relations among markets: a technological advance in the process of steel production typically changes not only the price of steel, but in general equilibrium changes also wages in the steel industry, the price of aluminum, the demand for machines that make aluminum, the number of plants devoted to steel production, and so on.

Most general equilibrium theory refers to markets in which there is perfect competition and private ownership. Among the requirements of perfect competition is the assumption that consumers and firms act as if the amount that they buy or sell on each market does not affect the price in that market; private ownership means that all of the land, labor, and capital in the economy is owned by consumers. Consider an economy in which there is perfect competition, private ownership, and a large number of consumers and firms. Equilibrium is described as follows. For every list of commodity prices, each firm has a production plan that maximizes profit among the plans that are technologically possible for the firm; similarly, each consumer has a consumption plan that is preferred among the plans that the consumer can afford given a certain level of wealth. The economic system (described by consumers, firms, and the distribution of ownership) is in equilibrium if firm plans and consumer plans are consistent. In the absence of equilibrium, either demand exceeds supply or supply exceeds demand on some markets, and prices must change to ration buyers or sellers. If demand exceeds supply in a market, there will be a tendency for prices to increase and ration buyers; similarly, if supply exceeds demand, prices will tend to fall. Equilibrium requires that the forces which bring about changes in prices are in balance; that is, equilibrium requires the equality between the demand and supply for each commodity.

History

Adam Smith's *The Wealth of Nations* (1776) is concerned with general equilibrium analysis. His insight that social equilibrium is determined by, yet different from, the action of individual agents is perhaps the single most distinctive characteristic of the general equilibrium point of view. Léon Walras, in his *Elements of Pure Economics* (1874) developed and studied an abstract model of general equilibrium that has most of the features of the general equilibrium models we study today, and F. Y. Edgeworth (1881) and V. Pareto (1909) provided the first rigorous formulations of the welfare notion that is now referred to as Pareto efficiency. The fact that under rather general conditions equilibria are Pareto-efficient gives precise meaning to Smith's celebrated claim that individuals acting in their own self-interest unintentionally promote the social good.

Modern general equilibrium theory is a technical subject; however, its central themes remain at the heart of economic analysis. Abraham Wald (1936) was the first to prove a general theorem concerning the existence of equilibrium prices for an economy; his results were subsequently generalized by K. J. Arrow and G. Debreu (1954), L. W. McKenzie (1954), and Debreu (1959). Arrow (1951) used set theory to expose the precise relation between equilibrium and Pareto efficiency, and his formulation has been the basis for all subsequent analysis. More recently, the relation between competitive equilibrium and various game theory notions of equilibrium (in particular the core and Nash equilibrium) have been an important area of investigation. Shubik (1959), Scarf (1962), Debreu and Scarf (1963), Aumann (1964), and Hildenbrand (1974) studied the relation between the core and competitive equilibrium and generalized Edgeworth's analysis of the contract curve. Negishi (1961) generalized Cournot's partial equilibrium analysis of oligopoly (1838) to the case of general equilibrium and proved a theorem on the existence of an equilibrium with imperfect competition.

Equilibrium in an Edgeworth Box Economy

For exposition we begin with a highly simplified model in which the only consumers are Amy (A) and Bill (B) and there are two commodities. Suppose that there are X_1 units of the first good, X_2 units of the second, and that initially wealth is specified as follows: Amy is endowed with e_1^A units of first good and Bill holds the rest ($e_1^B = X_1 - e_1^A$), Amy holds e_2^A units of the second good and Bill holds the rest ($e_2^B = X_2 - e_2^B$). The accompanying figure describes an Edgeworth box with horizontal dimension X_1 and vertical dimension X_2. Each point x in the box indicates an allocation of the total commodity amounts between Amy and Bill as follows: x_1^A and x_1^B represent the division of X_1; similarly x_2^A and x_2^B represent the division of X_2. Observe that the initial wealth point is an allocation of X_1 and X_2, and that it is indicated in the box. In the figure the preferences of consumers are summarized by the use of indifference curves. Amy's indifference curves are indicated by a solid line and Bill's indifference curves are indicated by a dashed line. Amy improves her position by moving to an indifference curve that is above (and to the right of) the one she is on; Bill improves his position by moving to an indifference curve that is below (and to the left of) the one he is on.

With the aid of the Edgeworth box diagram we can give a geometric representation of general equilibrium, at least for the case of two consumers and two commodities. First, we imagine that perfect competition prevails, so that each consumer believes that the amount being offered to buy or sell does not affect price. (Later, when we generalize the analysis to include many consumers, this assumption will appear more natural.) Now, consider the price list ($\hat{P}_1$, $\hat{P}_2$). At these prices the sale of each unit of the first commodity will raise $\hat{P}_1$ dollars and allow the consumer to buy $\hat{P}_1/\hat{P}_2$ units of the second commodity. The collection of commodity pairs made possible by such purchases is indicated in the figure by the line $\hat{P}\hat{P}$. The most preferred bundle available to Amy is indicated by ($\hat{x}_1^A$, $\hat{x}_2^A$). Similarly, at prices ($\hat{P}_1$, $\hat{P}_2$), the most preferred bundle available to Bill is ($\hat{x}_1^B$, $\hat{x}_2^B$). The important point to note is that $\hat{x}_2^A + \hat{x}_2^B > X_2$, and $\hat{x}_1^A + \hat{x}_1^B < X_1$. The price list ($\hat{P}_1$, $\hat{P}_2$) is not an equilibrium price list since the independent actions of consumers do not balance. We might expect that the price of the second commodity will rise to ration the demand for that commodity. On the other hand, suppose that PP represents the commodity pairs that each consumer can attain via purchase and sales when the price list is (P_1, P_2). With these prices Amy and Bill have (x_1^A, x_2^A) and (x_1^B, x_2^B) as most preferred choices, and these choices balance the commodity supplies since $x_1^A + x_1^B = X_1$ and $x_2^A + x_2^B = X_2$. Observe that after each consumer executes the most preferred choice, the consumer is better off than he or she was at the initial endowment. Furthermore, the gains from trade are exhausted, since at the competitive allocation x, it is not possible to improve Amy's position without harming Bill. (Similarly it is not possible to improve Bill's position without harming Amy.) To see this, note that there are no points above the indifference curve aa

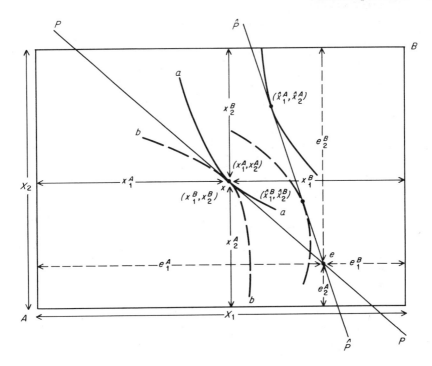

that are also on (or southwest of) the indifference curve *bb*. Such an allocation is referred to as Pareto-efficient.

The discussion that follows is substantially more technical and is devoted to two of the major themes of general equilibrium analysis. First, under what general conditions is there always at least one equilibrium price for an economy? This question is addressed in the literature on the existence of competitive equilibrium. Second, are equilibria necessarily Pareto-efficient?

The Existence of Equilibrium Prices

It is known that the existence of equilibrium prices for an arbitrary economy is closely related to a classical result in mathematical analysis called the Brouwer fixed-point theorem. This theorem states that for every continuous function g defined on a convex, closed, and bounded subset S of l-dimensional euclidean space and taking values in S, there exists a point $x \in S$ such that $g(x) = x$. However, for the case of just two commodities and pure exchange, the existence of equilibrium can be established by a completely elementary argument. Using the same notation as for the Edgeworth box case, we note that for each price list $P = (P_1, P_2)$, each consumer who prefers more to less makes a consumption plan $(x_1 (P), x_2 (P))$ such that $P_1 x_1(P) + P_2 x_2(P) = P_1 e_1 + P_2 e_2$: income equals expenditure. If we index consumers by i, then for each i,

$$P_1 x_1^i(P) + P_2 x_2^i(P) = P_1 e_1^i + P_2 e_2^i$$

and summing over i, we conclude

$$P_1 \sum_i [x_1^i(P) - e_1^i] + P_2 \sum_i [x_2^i(P) - e_2^i] = 0$$

This equality is called Walras's law. Now fix the price of the second commodity at unity, so that P_1 indicates the price of commodity 1 relative to commodity 2, and assume that for a high enough price for commodity 1, say $\hat{P}_1$, every consumer chooses no more X_1 than held initially, and for a low enough price for commodity one, say $\check{P}_1$, every consumer chooses at least as much X_1 as held initially. Since $x_1^i(\hat{P}_1, 1) \leq e_1^i$ for all i and $x_1^i(\check{P}_1, 1) \geq e_1^i$ for all i, we have

$$\Sigma\, x_1^i(\hat{P}_1,\, 1) \leq \Sigma\, e_1^i \quad\text{and}\quad \Sigma\, x_1^i(\check{P}_1,\, 1) \geq \Sigma\, e_1^i$$

Provided that demand changes continuously with price, there will exist $\hat{P}_1 \geq \overline{P}_1 \geq \check{P}_1$ such that

$$\Sigma\, x_1^i(\overline{P}_1,\, 1) = \Sigma\, e_1^i$$

that is, at $(\overline{P}_1, 1)$ demand is equal to supply in the market for commodity 1. But from Walras's law,

$$\overline{P}_1[\Sigma\, x_1^i(\overline{P}_1,\, 1) - \Sigma\, e_1^i] + 1[\Sigma\, x_2^i(\overline{P}_1,\, 1) - \Sigma\, e_2^i] = 0$$

and so

$$\Sigma\, x_2^i(\overline{P},\, 1) = \Sigma\, e_2^i$$

Thus, the price list $(\overline{P}_1, 1)$ leads to the equality of demand and supply in both markets.

One can establish the existence of equilibrium prices for economies with an arbitrary but finite number of commodities, say l, by confining attention to price vectors in

$$\mathcal{P} = \{P = (P_1, P_2, \cdots, P_l) : P_h \geq 0 \text{ for all } h \text{ and } \Sigma\, P_h = 1\}$$

and considering the function g from $\mathcal{P}$ to $\mathcal{P}$ defined by

$$(g(P))_h = \frac{P_h + (f(P))_h}{1 + \displaystyle\sum_k (f(P))_k} \qquad h = 1, 2, \cdots, l$$

where $(y)_h$ denotes the hth coordinate of the vector y, and

$$(f(P))_h = \max\left[0, \sum_i (x_h^i(P) - e_h^i) \right]$$

If each consumer demand function x^i is continuous on $\mathcal{P}$, then the function g will be continuous. By the Brouwer fixed-point theorem g must have at least one fixed point, and if $\overline{P}$ is a fixed point of g that is not on the boundary of $\mathcal{P}$, then $\overline{P}$ is an equilibrium price vector. The proof follows from Walras's law:

$$\sum_h P_h \left[\sum_i (x_h^i(P) - e_h^i) \right] = 0$$

The Pareto Efficiency of Competitive Equilibrium

Provided that there are no externalities in consumption or production, and provided that consumers prefer more of each commodity to less, every competitive equilibrium allocation is Pareto-efficient. This means that in a competitive equilibrium it is not possible to improve any welfare without making some other consumer worse off. The argument is somewhat simplified if there is a single firm, and it goes like this. In an equilibrium the firm and consumers are content with their plans and supply equals demand. Let P be the equilibrium price list. Since each consumer chooses a most preferred consumption plan consistent with the value of his or her resource endowment and the income received from the firms, the consumer must be assigned a bundle with a higher value at price P in order to be better off. In fact, since each consumer prefers more of each commodity to less, if a consumer is to be kept at least as well off as in the competitive equilibrium, then he or she must be assigned a plan of value (at prices P) at least as great as the sum of the value of the resource endowment and the income received from the firm. If there are no externalities, then any distribution that makes one consumer better off and keeps every other consumer at least as well off must have a value at prices P that exceeds the total value of resource endowments plus the total of profits received from the firm. But since the resource endowment of the economy is fixed, this distribution can only be provided if the firm chooses a production plan that yields a greater profit at prices P than the original equilibrium plan. But such a plan is not possible because, in the equilibrium plan, the firm is at a profit maximum. This means that the resources of the economy cannot be used to make some consumer better off and keep every other consumer at least as well off.

References

Arrow, K. J., "An Extension of the Basic Theorems of Classical Welfare Economics," in J. Neyman (ed.), *Proceedings of the Second Berkeley Symposium on Mathematical Statistics and Probability*, University of California Press, Berkeley, 1951, pp. 507–532; Arrow, K. J., "Economic Equilibrium," in *International Encyclopedia of the Social Sciences*, vol. 4, Macmillan, Free Press, New York, 1968, pp. 376–386; Arrow, K. J., and Gerard Debreu, "Existence of an Equilibrium for a Competitive Economy," *Econometrica*, vol. 26, 1954, pp. 265–290; Arrow, K. J., and F. H. Hahn, *General Competitive Analysis*, Holden Day, San Francisco, 1971; Aumann, R. J., "Markets with a Continuum of Traders," *Econometrica*, vol. 32, 1964, pp. 39–50; Cournot, A. A., *Researches Into the Mathematical Principles of the Theory of Wealth*, Kelley, New York, 1960, First published in French, 1838; Debreu, G., *Theory of Value: An Axiomatic Analysis of Economic Equilibrium*, Wiley, New York, 1959; Debreu, G., and H. Scarf, "A Limit Theorem on the Core of an Economy," *International Economic Review*, vol. 4, 1963, pp. 235–246; Edgeworth, F. Y., *Mathematical Psychics: An Essay on the Application of Mathematics to the Moral Sciences*, Kelley, New York, 1953, first published in 1881; Hildenbrand, W., *Core and Equilibria of a Large Economy*, Princeton University Press, Princeton, N. J., 1974; Hildenbrand, W., and A. Kirman, *Introduction to Equilibrium Analysis*, North-Holland, Amsterdam, 1976; Koopmans, T. C., *Three Essays on the State of Economic Science*, McGraw-Hill, New York, 1957; McKenzie, L. W., "On Equilibrium in Graham's Model of World Trade and Other Competitive Systems," *Econometrica*, vol. 22, 1954, pp. 147–161; Negishi, T., "On the Formation of Prices," *International Economic Review*, vol. 2, 1961, pp. 122–126; Pareto, V., *Manuel d'Économie Politique*, Girard & Briere, Paris, 1909; Scarf, H., "An Analysis of Markets with a Large Number of Participants," *Recent Advances in Game Theory*, Princeton University Press, Princeton, N.J., 1962; Shubik, M., "Edgeworth Market Games," in A. W. Tucker and R. D. Luce (eds.), *Contributions to the Theory of Games*, vol. IV, Princeton University Press, Princeton, N.J., 1959; Wald, A., "On Some Systems of Equations of Mathematical Economics," *Econometrica*, vol. 19, 1951, pp. 368–403, first published in German in *Zeitschrift für Nationalökonomie*, vol. 7, 1936; Walras, L., *Elements of Pure Economics*, William Jaffé trans., Allen & Unwin, London, 1954, first published in France as *Éléments d'Économie Politique Pure*, 1874–1877.

(*See also* Competition; Decision making in business: A behavioral approach; Demand; Distribution theory; Factors of production; Game theory, economic applications; Laissez faire; Microeconomics; Monopoly and oligopoly; Normative economics; Price theory; Supply; Welfare economics)

Hugo Sonnenschein

German historical school

The German historical school is so named because of its belief that only through detailed attention to historical development could economic analysis make real progress. It thus came to criticize classical economic theory for its "cosmopolitanism" and its "perpetualism"—that is, for its claim that economics was founded on natural laws valid in all places at all times. This perspective led these economists to embrace empiricism and induction and to eschew abstraction and deduction. Their approach urged emphasis on the analysis of economic change and a focus on economic process rather than on presumed equilibrium states. Finally, they embraced interventionism, and while they did not all agree about what constituted correct policy, they appear to have agreed that economists qua economists had a role to play in its pursuit.

As is often true, this school was by no means without antecedents. Among many, the two mentioned most often are August Comte and Friedrich List. Adam Müller is also frequently mentioned.

The school was launched by the publication in 1843 of Wilhelm Roscher's *Grundriss zu Vorlesungen über die Staatswirthschaft nach geschichtlicher Methode (Outline of Lectures on Political Economy, following the Historical Method)*. The period of its greatest influence is generally conceded to have ended in 1883 with the publication of Carl Menger's *Untersuchungen über die Methode der Sozialwissenschaften under der politischen Oekonomie insbesondere*. The movement continued to be extremely influential for many years thereafter, particularly in Germany, but it no longer went unchallenged.

Older versus Younger School

It is customary to break the German historical school into an "older" and a "younger" historical school (the older versus younger categorization appears to have begun with Charles Gide and Charles Rist). Where this is done, the undisputed major figures of the older German historical school are its founder, Wilhelm Roscher, Bruno Hildebrand, and Karl Knies. Joseph Schumpeter is one, however, who argues that this group did not constitute a true school because there was at least as much distinguishing them from each other as there was holding them together. Though his is perhaps a minority view, he concurs with the majority view that Gustav Schmoller, the leader of what is customarily referred to as the younger historical school, did indeed found a school. Lesser figures in the younger school include Lujo Brentano, Karl Bucher, Adolf Held, and George Friedrich Knapp. Schumpeter argues that there is a "youngest" German historical school with a claim to recognition as well, including Arthur Spiethoff, Werner Sombart, and Max Weber. Ultimately, the school influenced economic thought in a number of countries, with adherents (successors) in England, including John K. Ingram and Cliffe Leslie, and in the United States, the group known as the American institutionalists.

The School's Emphasis

Roscher in his *Grundriss* established the school's historical emphasis and suggested a procedural approach to economics, all of which he ultimately elaborated in his *System der Volkswirtschaft*. Today it is generally the view that he promised more in the direction of reconstituting economic analysis than he was able to deliver.

Hildebrand's *Die Nationalökonomie der Gegenwart und Zunkunft (Political Econ-*

omy of the Present and Future) represented a more decisive break with the classical tradition than did Roscher's work. His emphasis was on the need to recognize that economies are not static entities but evolving institutions.

Knies's major contribution was his *Die politische Ökonomie vom Standpunkte der geschichtlichen Methode (Political Economy from the Standpoint of the Historical Method)*. He went further than the other two in denying the existence of natural laws in economics and is remembered for his espousal of the importance of statistics.

It was Gustav Schmoller who developed and crystallized the ideas of the older historical school. He argued that the older historical school had not gone far enough in denouncing the assumptions and methods of classical economics and had indeed at times slipped back into their ways, and he attempted to synthesize the argument of the historical school.

The work of Schmoller and his associates embroiled them in two controversies. Because of their espousal of social reform as a natural outgrowth of the historical approach, a journalist nicknamed them "Kathedersozialisten"—literally socialists of the chair, or more generally, academic or professorial socialists—academics who also taught socialism from the classroom. They chose to take it as a compliment and to brand their opposition reactionary.

Even more famous was the *Methodenstreit*, the controversy over method that began when Schmoller wrote an unfavorable review of Carl Menger's *Untersuchungen*. Menger was attacking the German historical school's rejection of the *weltanschauung* of classical economics. The issues were ultimately overdrawn on both sides but can be summarized as (1) empirically based induction versus abstract deduction, (2) emphasis on process or evolution versus acceptance of statistics in economic analysis, and (3) a broad multifaceted setting from which to pursue economics versus a narrowly defined economics with all the rest either held constant or defined out of consideration.

Influence of Historical School

Both Schumpeter and Wesley Clair Mitchell argue that by the time Schmoller had written his *Outline* at the turn of the century he realized that he had gone too far, and they argue that denying the extremes of theory is a more modest, and thus preferable, departure from the mainstream than denying the need altogether for theory. Even though the *Methodenstreit* ultimately died out, it remains a direct antecedent of the institutionalist debate in the United States. It involved, therefore, issues that are still in contention.

Schumpeter regarded as a "myth" the idea that economics had ever passed through any period when it eschewed concern with history. He nonetheless concluded that at best the German historical school had made a positive contribution in directing the attention of economists to the need for grounding study of the emerging economy on the historical analysis of all the societal forces surrounding it.

As such, the German historical school influenced economics and economists in ways not always explicitly recognized. As noted already, they are linear antecedents of the American institutionalists (John R. Commons, Thorstein Veblen, Wesley Clair Mitchell, etc.). They had at least one other influence. The German historical school founded in 1872 the *Verein für Sozialpolitik (The Union for Social Politics)*, a model for the group which founded the American Economics Association in 1885.

References

Works by Major Members
of the German Historical School:

Hildebrand, Bruno, *Die Nationalökonomie der Gegenwart und Zunkunft*, Literarisches Anstalt, Frankfurt-am-Main, 1848; Knies, Karl, *Die politische Ökonomie vom geschichtlichen Methode*, Braunschweig, 1853; Roscher, Wilhelm G. F., *Grundriss zu Vorlesungen über die Staatswirtschaft, nach geschichtlicher Methode*, Dietrich, Gottingen, Germany, 1843; Schmoller, Gustav F., *Grundriss der allgemeinen Volkswirtschaftslehre*, Duncker and Humbolt, Leipzig, vol. 1, 1900, vol. 2, 1904.

Works about the German Historical School:

Dorfman, Joseph, in *Institutional Economics: Veblen, Commons and Mitchell Reconsidered*, University of California Press, Berkeley and Los Angeles, 1963; Gide, Charles and Charles Rist, *A History of Economic Doctrines*, 7th ed., vol. IV, D. C. Heath, New York, 1947, chap. 1; Mitchell, Wesley Clair, *Types of Economic Theory*, vol. 2, Kelley, New York, 1969, chap. 19; Roll, Eric, *A History of Economic Thought*, 4th ed., Faber and Faber, London, 1973, chap. 7; Schumpeter, Joseph A., *History of Economic Analysis*, Oxford University Press, New York, 1954, chap. 4; Spiegel, Henry William, *The Growth of Economic Thought*, Prentice-Hall, Englewood Cliffs, N.J., 1971.

(*See also* Economic history and theory; Economics; Institutional economics)

Philip A. Klein

Gino coefficient (see Lorenz curve)

Gold standard

In the decades before 1914, the gold standard was a type of monetary system with the following characteristics: the national monetary unit was defined in terms of a given quantity of gold; the central bank or treasury stood ready to buy and sell gold at the resulting fixed price in terms of the national currency; gold was freely coined and gold coin formed a significant part of the circulating medium; and gold could be freely exported and imported. The exchange rate between any two countries adhering to such arrangements was determined by the gold content of their respective monetary units and could vary from this parity only within a narrow band (the "gold points") reflecting the cost of shipping gold from the one country to the other. Private arbitrage shipments of gold, which became profitable when either of these limits was reached, prevented the band from being breached.

Gold-Exchange Standard

Arrangements of this kind—sometimes called the gold-coin standard—were not the only variant of the pre-1914 gold standard. A number of countries adopted or drifted into various forms of what has been called a gold-exchange standard, the distinguishing feature of which was that the monetary authorities of the countries concerned held a substantial part or even the bulk of their reserves in the form of claims on currencies that were redeemable in gold, and they stood ready to buy or sell these currencies at fixed prices in terms of their own. Such official purchases or sales served to supplement, and in some cases virtually to substitute for, private gold arbitraging as a means of keeping exchange rates within narrow margins of parity. The holding of foreign exchange reserves enabled the authorities to economize on gold and to earn interest on these reserves without any significant risk of being unable to convert them into gold when needed. Gold coin tended to circulate to only a limited extent if at all in gold-exchange-standard countries, either because the authorities did not freely redeem their notes in gold or because of the public's preferences.

The overriding objective of economic policy under the pre-1914 gold standard was to maintain the redeemability (convertibility) of the national currency directly or indirectly into gold at the legal parity, i.e., to keep exchange rates fixed against other gold-standard currencies. Drains on a country's gold and/or foreign exchange reserves usually led to increases in central-bank discount rates or to other official actions designed to check the loss of reserves. Increased interest rates tended, in the short run, to stem the drain by attracting capital from abroad. In the longer run they did so, according to the traditional view, by improving the country's trade balance through their further effect on the money supply, prices, and economic activity. While controversy still prevails as to exactly how the pre-1914 gold standard worked, the fact remains that from about 1880 to 1914 exchange rates among gold-standard countries remained fixed without support of payments or import controls, with virtually no countries being forced off the gold standard once adopted, with a minimum of international cooperation, and with a relatively small stock of international reserves. On the other hand, this remarkable fixity of exchange rates may in some cases have been achieved at the cost of internal economic activity.

During World War I most countries suspended the redeemability of their currencies into gold (de facto or de jure), withdrew gold coins from circulation, and concentrated gold holdings in official reserves. The currencies of most belligerent countries did not, however, depreciate by much in terms of gold and the dollar because of official pegging operations supported by gold sales, foreign borrowing, liquidation of assets abroad, and imposition of some import and exchange controls. At the end of the war the United States was virtually the only country on a full gold standard.

Return to Gold

A dominant objective of economic policymakers after the war was to return to the gold standard at an early date. This was a laborious process that was not generally completed until 1927 because of the widespread economic dislocations that followed the war. In some cases the return to gold involved stabilization of the currency at the prewar parity, the most notable example being that of Great Britain in 1925. In other cases, such as that of France, Italy, and Belgium, currencies were repegged to gold at only a fraction of their prewar parities. In those countries where hyperinflation had occurred in the early postwar years, notably in Germany, the stabilization process necessitated the introduction of completely new currencies.

The international gold standard that was restored in the mid-1920s differed in several respects from that of the pre-1914 period. Apart from in the United States, the gold-coin standard had virtually disappeared, and gold holdings remained predominantly in official hands. Several countries, including Great Britain, adopted a so-called gold-bullion standard under which the currency was redeemable in gold but only in the form of bars of a minimum weight. This in effect made gold available only for purposes of settling international balances. The great majority of countries, partly in view of a prevailing belief in an actual or impending world shortage of gold, adopted varieties of the gold-exchange standard. The structure of exchange rates adopted seems to have been less appropriate to underlying price-cost levels and economic conditions than it was before 1914. For example, the British pound was believed to have been overvalued and the French franc undervalued. Finally, monetary authorities appear to have been less ready than before the war to gear their policies to the state of the balance of payments and to changes in their reserve holdings in view of their increased concern with internal economic stability.

The Breakdown of the Gold Standard

The restored international gold standard, which for the most part was a gold-exchange standard, broke down in 1930 to 1932 under the impact of the world depression, the virtual cessation of international lending, the massive liquidation by central banks of their foreign exchange holdings, and the large-scale flights of capital from individual countries. Great Britain abandoned the gold standard in September 1931, and the pound floated under official management until the outbreak of World War II. The United States suspended the gold standard in March 1933 at which time the redemption of dollars into gold and the export of gold were prohibited and all gold coin and gold certificates were called in from circulation. On January 31, 1934, the United States returned to a modified gold standard, with the dollar price of gold being raised to $35 per fine ounce. At that repegged price the United States Treasury stood ready to buy and sell gold but only for legitimate monetary purposes, which in practice meant for international settlement. The prohibition on the holding of gold by private United States residents was continued. The currencies of the so-called gold bloc countries—France, Belgium, Switzerland, and the Netherlands—remained tied to gold at their existing parities until 1935 to 1936, when they were devalued. Of these countries only Belgium continued thereafter to buy and sell gold at a fixed price until 1939.

The international monetary system which was set up at Bretton Woods, N.H., after World War II and which functioned until the early 1970s had some similarities to gold-exchange-standard arrangements. The United States bought and sold gold at $35 per fine ounce in its dealings with foreign monetary authorities, while the latter bought and sold dollars against their own currencies at prices that remained fixed for considerable periods. But an essential difference was that countries were authorized under the Bretton Woods agreement to alter their exchange rates under specified circumstances, and from time to time many of them, including leading ones, did so. The fixity of exchange rates, a hallmark of the gold standard, could no longer be taken for granted. Since March 1973, currencies generally have been floating (including the dollar, no longer tied to gold), and even gold itself is no longer being used as an international means of settlement and is being phased out of the international monetary system.

References

Bloomfield, Arthur I., *Monetary Policy under the International Gold Standard: 1880-1914*, Federal Reserve Bank of New York, New York, 1959; Brown, William Adams, *The International Gold Standard Reinterpreted, 1914-1934*, 2 vols., National Bureau of Economic Research, New York, 1940; McCloskey, Donald N., and J. Richard Zecker, "How the Gold Standard Worked, 1880-1913," in J. A. Frenkel and H. G. Johnson (eds.), *The Monetary Approach to the Balance of Payments*, University of Toronto Press, Toronto, 1976; Nurkse, Ragnar, *International Currency Experience*, League of Nations, Princeton, N.J., 1944.

(*See also* International economics, an overview; International Monetary Fund)

Arthur I. Bloomfield

Government expenditures in GNP

Government purchases of goods and services, as measured in the gross national product (GNP), are made up of both the net expenditures on goods and services by the three levels of government—federal, state, and local—and the gross investment of government enterprises. Government plays an important part in our economy. It acts as an employer, customer, and entrepreneur. In the GNP government purchases of goods and services consist of two major categories: (1) federal and (2) state and local. Government expenditures on goods and services include (1) all the government payroll expenditures for its employees, such as teachers, economists, statisticians, lawyers, fire fighters, and police officers, and (2) the goods it buys from the private sector, such as computers, autos, paper, and airplanes.

Some economists argue that government expenditures for goods and services should be broken down in similar fashion to private product, that is, into a current consumption category and a net investment category (increases in equipment, buildings, and inventories).

Federal Purchases

Federal government purchases of goods and services in the national income accounts differ from government expenditures in the federal budget. The former does not include transfer payments to persons, such as welfare payments and old age pension payments from the government. These transfer payments are not included in the government component of the GNP because, in effect, they are not payments for current productive services. In addition to transfer payments, net interest paid, subsidies less current surplus of government enterprises, and wage accruals less disbursements are not included in government spending in the GNP, but these items are included in the federal budget.

At the federal level, government purchases include those for national defense—Department of Defense military functions, military assistance to other nations, development and control of atomic energy, and stockpiling of strategic materials—and for nondefense functions such as purchases of agricultural commodities under price-support programs, outlays for space research and technology, and investment of government enterprises such as the Tennessee Valley Authority and the U.S. Postal Service.

State and Local Purchases

State and local government purchases of goods and services such as for education, roads and highways, and hospitals are credited to these levels of government in the GNP regardless of who actually pays for them. Thus federal grants-in-aid for education are counted as purchases of goods and services by state and local governments.

State and local governments account for nearly two-thirds (64 percent) of the total government expenditures on goods and services. The manifold government units involved include 50 states and more than 100,000 jurisdictions. Despite the fact that several big cities, such as New York, Newark, and Cleveland, were very close to bankruptcy in the late 1970s, state and local governments, overall, have been running sizable surpluses while the federal government has been running sizable deficits.

Government purchases of goods and services are directly determined by government decision. These expenditures, especially those of the federal government, differ significantly from the expenditures of the private sector, which are autonomous in nature.

Between 1947 and 1980, total government spending on goods and services as measured in the GNP grew nearly 2000 percent in dollar terms and 270 percent in real terms. For the same time period, federal government purchases of goods and services increased by 1400 percent in dollar terms and 180 percent in real terms, while state and local purchases rose nearly 2600 percent in dollar terms and 354 percent in real terms.

References

Ruggles, Richard and Nancy Ruggles, *National Income Accounts and Income Analysis*, 2d ed., McGraw-Hill, New York, 1956.

(*See also* Federal budget; Federal budget process; Fiscal policy; Gross national product; National income accounting)

Douglas Greenwald

Government regulation of business

Apart from public utility regulation, the concept of government regulation of business means the legal setting or maintenance of conditions required for a private enterprise system to function fairly, safely, and efficiently. Implementation of this concept usually involves creation of a public authority—a commission or agency— to establish rules of conduct for the businesses in a given industry or for all industry.

The Regulatory Agencies

Regulatory agencies have been largely introduced in three waves: pre-World War I, the 1930s, and the 1960s to 1970s.

First of the regulatory commissions was the Interstate Commerce Commission (ICC), which was established in 1887 to supervise competition in the railroad industry. Regulation of pipelines, inland waterways, and trucking has since been added to the ICC's authority. Similarly, the Pure Food and Drug Act of 1906 created the forerunner agency to today's Food and Drug Administration. In like manner the Meat Inspection Act of 1907 provided for federal meat inspectors operating under the U.S. Department of Agriculture. And in 1914 Congress established the Federal Trade Commission (FTC) to prevent unfair competition and false and deceptive advertising.

The 1930s witnessed the birth of still other regulatory bodies, including the Federal Power Commission (FPC) in 1930, the Federal Deposit Insurance Corporation (FDIC) in 1933, the Securities and Exchange Commission (SEC) in 1934, the National Labor Relations Board (NLRB) in 1935, and the Civil Aeronautics Board (CAB) in 1938.

The 1960s to 1970s saw the birth of other regulatory agencies such as the Equal Employment Opportunity Commission (EEOC) in 1965, the Environmental Protection Agency (EPA) in 1970, the Occupational Safety and Health Administration (OSHA) also in 1970, the Consumer Product Safety Commission (CPSA) in 1972, and the Council on Wage and Price Stability (COWPS) in 1974.

Regulatory Reform and Costs

The rising economic impact of regulation has given rise to calls for regulatory reform and even deregulation. In 1978, Barry Bosworth of the Brookings Institution, then director of the Council on Wage and Price Stability, said in a memo that while proposed regulations might be beneficial, "they do imply a significant increase in the impact of regulation on the measured rate of price inflation." In a 1979 speech on regulatory reform President Carter stated: "We must cut the inflationary costs which private industry bears as a result of government regulations." An ad hoc Federal Paperwork Commission during the 1970s counted 4400 different federal forms in the federal inventory, outside of banking and tax forms. A 1978 law sponsored by Senator Edward M. Kennedy has brought about substantial deregulation of the airline industry and calls for the extinction of the Civil Aeronautics Board by 1985.

Estimates of total regulatory costs, direct and indirect, vary widely. A 1979 White House report on regulatory reform noted estimates ranging from a high of $150 billion to a low of $25 billion. Murray L. Weidenbaum, director of Washington University's Center for the Study of American Business, held that regulatory costs for the American economy in 1979 totaled $102.7 billion, the greatest proportion of which was in compliance costs to U.S. industry.

Pros and Cons

Proponents of regulation hold that industry cannot function in a legal vacuum. Private property rights have to be defined and provision made for redress against breaches of them. Proponents also hold that business competition is not self-regulating and, hence, requires antitrust statutes and other rules of fair play. They point to the pioneering work in the 1930s by economists Edward H. Chamberlin of Harvard University and Joan Robinson of Cambridge University who held that modern industrial competition is monopolistic or imperfect. Proponents argue that the state must proscribe monopolies, unfair competition, and the marketing of such things as dangerous drugs or unsafe playground equipment.

Proponents of deregulation concede that an orderly society and economy need proper rules and regulations for business behavior, including prohibition of fraud and force in business dealings. But they also argue that excessive regulation has added to inflationary pressures and has jeopardized American competitiveness in world markets. They argue that in many instances regulatory agencies, however well-intentioned, have imposed costs on industry that surpass any benefits to society, including clean air and water. According to Yale Brozen of the University of Chicago, for example, the initial $4 billion annual cost of auto-emission controls buys about $5 billion in antipollution benefits each year. But if the auto-emission standards planned for 1985 stay in effect, society will then be getting but $6 billion in benefits for an annual outlay of $11 billion.

A frequently proposed type of law to meet the regulatory problem is the so-called sunset statute. Such a law provides for a periodic congressional review of regulatory bodies. Those not satisfying cost-benefit standards would then be closed down, probably in stages.

References

Brozen, Yale, "Regulatory Excess," paper for National Association of Manufacturers, Washington, D.C., Mar. 29, 1979; Chamberlin, Edward H., *The Theory of Monopolistic Competition*, Harvard University Press, Cambridge, Mass., 1933; Clark, J. M., *Social Control of Business*, McGraw-Hill, New York, 1939; Pegrum, Dudley F., *Public Regulation of Business*, Irwin, Homewood, Ill., 1959; Peterson, Mary Bennett, *The Regulated Consumer*, Green Hill, Ottawa, Ill., 1971; Robinson, Joan, *The Economics of Imperfect Competition*, Macmillan, New York, 1933.

(See also Cost-benefit analysis; Council on Wage and Price Stability; Environmental costs; Externalities; Federal Trade Commission; Securities and Exchange Commission)

William H. Peterson

Grants economics

Grants economics identifies the size and traces the leverage of grant elements as they interface with exchange elements in different economic processes. A simple definition of a grant is an unmatched transaction where the net worth of one party—the grantor—dimishes while the net worth of the other party—the grantee—increases. Any transaction deviating from the norm of exchanging equal values contains certain grant elements. Beyond the clearly visible explicit grant—gift, aid, and unilateral transfer—there exists a vast network of implicit grants in the private as well as public sectors of the economy. The visible explicit grants are only the tip of the iceberg, while the larger, amorphous bulk of implicit grants remains hidden and, therefore, often escapes attention.

It is a conventional view that goods, services, and factors of production move from one party to another at a matching price (quid pro quo). Yet there exists a broad assortment of subventions (subsidies, bounties, favoritism) on the one side, and a broad assortment of tributes (underpayments, extortions, dispossessions) on the other side. However, because these cases do not fit the neat abstractions of dominant theories, they are usually relegated to gray areas (assumed away) and the analysis continues *ceteris paribus*. Unfortunately, by ignoring or downgrading production and distribution processes which do not fit the neoclassical pattern, one narrows the scope of economic policy analysis unnecessarily.

Since mixed-type transactions are predominant, analysis must start with an identification of the exchange and grant elements. The measurement of an explicit grant is simple: the grant equivalent equals the market value. The size of implicit grants is more elusive because such grants arise when the system of market prices is superseded. Thus, the grant elements embodied in trade protection will surface if one contrasts the world market price with the domestic price after the imposition of a tariff. Implicit grants accrue to the domestic producer and government at the expense of the domestic consumer and foreign producer. When the United States government purchased a bushel of wheat at $2.50 while the world market price stayed around $1.00, a grant equivalent of $1.50 was extended. Likewise, grant impact statements can be calculated about regulation Q in banking, the stipulation of routes-cum-fares for trucks. Monopoly power also creates implicit grants. Whether it is the stereotypic restraint of trade, or restrictive admission into the ranks of labor unions, a common characteristic of all such practices is that the visible hand of powerful special interest groups preempts free-market solutions. Intrafirm subsidization is intriguing, particularly with multinational corporations. Other cases abound.

Studies utilizing the notion of grants economics have led to a variety of conceptual explorations as well as empirical works. In the field of finance, for example, loans are classified on a continuous scale since they contain both a grant equivalent and an exchange equivalent. Generally, lower rates of interest, longer maturity times and moratorium periods, and higher market rates of discount (opportunity costs) will result in greater grant elements. The grant may be altered by certain trading stipulations supplementing these concessionary terms: for instance, reducing it for the recipient of foreign aid because of tying purchases in the donor country, or enhancing it for the home owner in the United States because interest payments are deductible for income tax purposes. Grant ratio is the expression of the grant equivalent as a proportion of the face value of the loan ($g = GE/FV$). This ratio provides a standard for comparison as well as a base for deriving the sensitivity of the grant ratio with respect to contract terms and the trade-offs between them.

History of Grant Economics

The history of grant as an economic-social-political organizer is perhaps older than recorded history itself. It is not unlikely that various unmatched transfers had preceded exchange transactions as communities practiced reciprocal granting. As exchange became common, the terms of trade favored the stronger party, thereby transferring tribute to priests and kings and artists. Such was the dominant social characteristic through the feudal age. In modern times institutionalized transfers have provided a big push toward economic development, as illustrated by the enclosure movement in eighteenth-century England and collectivization in the twentieth-century Soviet Union. Nowadays, when traditional welfare roles—care for the poor, disabled, and elderly—are shifting from the family to the public sector, and as government undertakes to deliver an increasing bundle of public goods—education, health, recreation, transportation, research—the share of the grants economy grows.

The history of grant economics as a formalized concept began with the works of Kenneth Boulding, who subsequently formed, together with Martin Pfaff and Janos Horvath, the Association for the Study of the Grants Economy (ASGE) in 1968. The association is an instrument to explore a neglected area in economics and the social sciences. It holds conferences, organizes joint programs, and facilitates publications. Among the notable contributors are Abram Bergson, Evsey Domar, Wassily Leontief, Abba Lerner, James Morgan, Mancur Olson, Tibor Scitovsky, Robert Solo, Jan Tinbergen, William Vickrey, and Burton Weisbrod.

A Theory of Reciprocity

Much of the initial work in grants economics has dealt with the issues of the urbanized economy, and income distribution and redistribution as these affect efficiency and equity, the tax-expenditure structure, externalities in the environment, and intra-family and intergenerational granting. The international economy is a major field of inquiry. The inflation-unemployment dilemma is explained in part through institutional rigidities which generate implicit grants to those who restrain potential supply. A recurrent theme is that grants economics is a major instrument by which people hope to change the world for the better. In the macroeconomy a grant dollar spent tends to generate more production and income than an exchange dollar because the granting often stipulates complementary exchange transactions. As a network of policy instruments, the grants economy represents the heart of political economy, because routinely it is by pulling the levers of positive and negative subventions that the political system intervenes smoothly in the economic system.

On philosophical grounds, grants economics extends beyond neoclassical exchange economics, public choice, and radical economics in important respects, such as perceiving the motivation of economic actors and assessing the significance of distribution norms. To explain individual behavior, institutional dynamics, and normative policies, it is no longer necessary to regard unselfishness as an aberration of rationality. Grant economics provides a theory of transfers by affirming the interdependence of utility functions among individuals that integrate into economic science such agents as love, altruism, hate, and fear. Thus, utility interdependence considers (1) the utility derived from the contemplation of another person's welfare and (2) the utility derived from giving because it conforms to the individual's norms. Hence benevolent behavior: the individual's increased utility due to more consumption is outweighed by the individual's decreased utility due to the perception of another's miserable state. This leads from the Pareto optimum to the Boulding optimum, bringing within the scope of economic analysis a humanly flair assumed away routinely in the name of value-free science. Now economics can tackle the axiom that whether life on earth is hell or heaven depends largely on the attitude of one human being toward others.

Grants economics has been accused of charting vague boundaries. But its boundaries are vague precisely because it is a link between all the disciplines of the social sciences. Providing a theory of reciprocity, it links economics, psychology, sociology, anthropology, and political science. Stretching over several disciplines, it points to the enormous economic importance of the family, an institution neglected in exchange economics. It is an important part of economics itself, where the grants structure profoundly affects the dynamics of the price system. Notwithstanding its versatility, the grants economy is subject to perverse effects. Just as the theory of market failures acknowledges that exchange economy cannot achieve certain types of economic ends, the pathologies of the grants economy call for diagnosis. It is a political irony that far from remedying all distortions brought about by the market process, regulations and subventions have often exacerbated the problem. Indeed, grants economics could make a unique contribution to the regulatory reform through sorting out good grants from bad grants, i.e., those which achieve socially desirable goals from those with perverse effects.

Applied to specific cases (e.g., the export-import bank), grants economics has provided impact statements toward refinement in policymaking. It has been suggested that the United States Congress may require grant impact statements for every legislative and regulatory act, estimating who gains, who loses, and who stays unaffected. Likewise, the facilities of national account statistics might improve by including certain measures of grant elements.

References

Boulding, Kenneth E., *The Economy of Love and Fear: A Preface to Grants Economics*, Wadsworth, Belmont, Calif., 1973; Boulding, Kenneth E., Martin Pfaff, and Janos Horvath, "Grants Economics: A Simple Introduction," *The American Economist*, vol. 16, no. 1, 1972, pp. 19–35; Horvath, Janos, *Chinese Technology Transfer to the Third World: A Grants Economy Analysis*, Praeger, New York, 1976; Pfaff, Martin (ed.), *Grants and Exchange*, North-Holland, Amsterdam, 1976; Pfaff, Martin (ed.), *Association for the Study of the Grants Economy Tenth Anniversary Brochure*, INIFES, Augsburg-Leitershofen, 1978.

(See also Normative economics; Welfare economics)

Janos Horvath

Great Depression

The Great Depression was the longest and most severe period of economic depression ever experienced by the United States. It began with a collapse of prices on the New York Stock Exchange (NYSE) in October 1929, and did not end until the United States entered World War II in late 1941. At its worst point—in early 1933—the American economy seemed on the verge of total collapse. National income had declined by almost one-half in a little over 3 years; capital investment had dropped to the point where net investment was negative; one out of three people in the labor force was out of work; and on March 6, 1933, President Franklin Roosevelt was forced to declare a bank holiday to forestall a complete collapse of the banking system.

Recovery from the depths of this economic decline was excruciatingly slow. After a period of mild economic expansion between 1933 and 1936, recovery was interrupted by a new and very severe downturn in 1937 and 1938. In 1941, 12 years after the initial shock of the stock-market crash, more than 10 percent of the labor force was still unemployed, and per capita income had not yet regained the level of 1929. The most protracted period of economic stagnation in American history was finally ended by the war mobilization efforts in 1942. While there is no question that it was the wartime spending which brought the economy out of the Great Depression, economic historians are much less certain what caused the contraction to be so severe. Obviously, no single event or factor was responsible for the decline. There are, however, several factors which seem to play a prominent role in most explanations of the period.

The Collapse of Asset Prices

The stock-market crash which began on October 24, 1929, was not confined to a single day; the decline in asset prices was a process of continual erosion for almost 3 years. By late 1932 stock prices on the NYSE had fallen to only 20 percent of their values in late 1929, and the prices of other assets had similarly declined. This enormous fall in the value of assets not only wiped out countless individual fortunes and savings, it also placed serious pressures on the stability of financial institutions, particularly banks. Financial intermediaries which held assets in their portfolios were badly squeezed by the fall in prices, and in many cases the collapse forced them into insolvency. In addition to these direct effects from the stock-market crash, some economic historians have viewed the decline in stock prices as a highly visible index of economic activity which not only mirrored public attitudes about the economy but also contributed to the falling level of confidence and pessimistic expectations of the American people as well.

Bank Failures and the Decline in the Supply of Money

In 1929 there were about 25,000 banks in the United States. In 1933 there were only 14,000. The failure of so many banks, together with the reduced level of money and credit provided by those banks which remained open, created a powerful pressure for reduced economic activity. Indeed, in the view of some economists, the decline in the money supply, which fell by about 20 percent between 1929 and 1933, by itself accounted for the severity of the Great Depression. According to this monetarist interpretation, had the monetary authorities been willing to meet the public's increasing demands for cash at the outset of the contraction, the banking panics which took place between 1930 and 1933 would not have occurred, and most of the difficulties which followed the collapse of the monetary system could have been avoided.

The Decline in Spending

While the decline in money and credit clearly was a major factor contributing to the crisis in 1933, many economists feel that the monetarist explanation is incomplete. In particular, they insist that monetary factors alone can not explain the failure of the economy to recover quickly after the crisis of 1933 passed. There had been other financial panics in American history which had not produced the prolonged period of economic stagnation which characterized the 1930s. These economists stress the impact which financial losses and the loss of confidence had on the behavior of consumers and investors in the economy. The so-called spending thesis analyzes the Great Depression in terms of the enormous fall in both consumption and investment expenditures between 1929 and 1933 and in terms of the failure of these expenditures to recover after 1933. In this view, the interrelationship of income, consumption, and investment, together with the pessimistic expectations following the financial collapse, acted to discourage spending and thus to hinder the recovery of income. Not until government spending increased dramatically following the 1937–38 slump did aggregate spending return to a level sufficient to restore employment to a full-employment level.

Structural Weaknesses in the American Economy

Both the spending thesis and the monetarist thesis acknowledge the importance of serious flaws in the institutional framework of the American economy which contributed to the problems of 1929 to 1941. Most obvious was the inability of the financial sector to adjust to the decline in asset values, a failure which was transmitted to other sectors of the economy as well. The extent to which personal income and wealth were concentrated in the hands of a small fraction of the population may have magnified the effects of the stock-market crash on spending. Even more significant was the absence of any institutional arrangements to cushion the effect that loss of income due to unemployment had on aggregate spending. In short, the institutional framework of the United States in 1929 was simply not equipped to deal with such a dramatic shift in expectations and the level of economic activity. Once the momentum of the decline had built up, there were no institutional arrangements which might stem the tide of activity.

The Great Depression had a profound effect on the economic history of the United States. That impact is evident in at least three broad changes which took place in the 1930s.

Institutional Reform

The New Deal of Franklin Roosevelt introduced major changes in the structure of the American economy. Banking legislation in 1933 and 1935 provided federally backed insurance for deposits in banks (the Federal Deposit Insurance Corporation) and created the Securities and Exchange Commission to monitor activity in the stock market. Both steps are credited with increasing the stability of the financial sector. The Agricultural Adjustment Act (AAA), passed in 1933, committed the government to the active support of farm incomes and laid the groundwork for the program of farm price supports which continues to the present. In 1935 social security and unemployment insurance were introduced, laying the foundation upon which the system of old age and health insurance programs which emerged 30 years later could be constructed. The Wagner Act, which guaranteed labor's right to organize and bargain collectively, was enacted in 1935. The rapid expansion of union activity which followed passage of this law brought about substantial changes in the labor market. All these acts, together with other measures passed in the New Deal era, represented a reaction to the insecurity brought on by the experience of the Great Depression.

Economic Philosophy in the United States

The experience of the Great Depression shattered Americans' faith in their laissez faire economic philosophy. The inability of the economic system to stem the economic decline after 1929 produced increasing pressures for action by the government—pressures which undoubtedly contributed to Roosevelt's election in 1932. Roosevelt responded with a variety of programs intended to promote recovery. These included: programs for income maintenance (the AAA, and social security and unemployment insurance); government-sponsored price and wage codes designed to limit the harmful effects of cutthroat competition (the National Recovery Administration); and, finally, programs of public works to provide jobs for the unemployed (the Works Projects Administration, the Tennessee Valley Authority). This last approach—public works—increasingly became the mainstay of the government's effort to reduce unemployment.

Whether or not these programs actually had an impact in promoting economic recovery (most economic historians claim their impact was minimal), they unquestionably had the effect of increasing government's role in the economy. The notion that government should play an active role in maintaining economic stability was a major tenet of New Deal thinking, and that commitment was reaffirmed after World War II with the passage of the Employment Act of 1946.

A New Economics

One of the things which inhibited government actions in the early years of the Great Depression was the absence of useful suggestions by economists. Contemporary economic doctrines in 1929 insisted that the market was self-correcting. But as the economic situation continued to worsen without signs of recovery, economists began to question their theories. By 1939 a growing number of American economists—including a number of advisers to the Roosevelt administration—were espousing a new approach to economic policy based on the ideas of the British economist John Maynard Keynes. The proponents of the new economics argued that the corrective tendencies in the marketplace were not strong enough to ensure full employment, and they advocated government spending as the best means of maintaining a level of spending sufficient to ensure full employment. Eventually, these arguments not only provided the basis for countercyclical economic policy but also created a powerful impetus for the expansion of the government sector in the years following World War II. Economists such as Harvard University's Alvin Hansen looked at the performance of the American economy during the 1930s and concluded that without continual government intervention the United States would stagnate. Fears of a return to the economic pattern of the 1930s prompted widespread support for government spending programs as a protection against economic stagnation in the postwar years.

The Great Depression marked, in a sense, the coming of age of the United States as a mature industrial economy. The events of the 1930s demonstrated the need for changes in the economic structure. The New Deal introduced some of those changes in response to the pressures at the time and began a process of economic reform which was to continue for the next 40 years. Finally, the experience of the Great Depression serves as a continual reminder of the potential instability of our market economy, a memory which spurs a continued search for economic stability.

References

Chandler, Lester V., *American's Greatest Depression, 1929–41*, Harper and Row, New York, 1970; Friedman, Milton, and Anna Schwartz. *A Monetary History of the United States, 1867–1960*, Princeton University Press, Princeton, 1963, chaps. 7–9; Galbraith, John K., *The Great Crash*, Houghton Mifflin, New York, 1955; Temin, Peter, *Did Monetary Forces Cause the Great Depression?*, Norton, New York, 1976.

(*See also* Business cycles; Chicago school; Economic history and theory; Federal Reserve policy; Fiscal policy; Keynesian economics; Monetary policy; Stagnation thesis)

Roger L. Ransom

Gresham's law

Gresham's law, an empirical generalization relating to the circulation of coins in a multiple-media monetary system, is conventionally stated as "bad money drives out good." Attributed, inappropriately, to Sir Thomas Gresham, who as adviser to Queen Elizabeth I in 1558 observed that lighter-weight, worn or clipped coins freely circulated as money; whereas, newly minted or full-weight coins were driven from circulation (hoarded, melted into bullion, or exported), the principle was previously well known, having received cogent exposition by many writers as early as Aristophanes.

Gresham's Law: Virtues of Brevity and Paradox

The paradox consists in the contrast offered between money and an ordinary consumer good. Competition should dictate that where various qualities of a good are available at the same price, the best should be preferred and survive, and the inferior cast into oblivion. For currency, the opposite appears to prevail.

The paradox is resolved by a more careful statement of the law. It may be noted that in a free market and in accordance with normal self-interest, a product will tend to be allocated to its most valuable use. Gresham's law in refined form is a corollary: whenever a coin is worth appreciably more in a nonmonetary use (as bullion or as money elsewhere, for example), it will flow into such use. Thus, where coins of various weights circulate at parity, by convention or as legal tender, the buyer has a motive to offer, and cannot be compelled to offer more than, the most debased currency available. As a consumer, a person is a buyer; as a user of money, that person acts as a seller.

Explanations by Gresham's Law

Gresham's law explains the difficulty of maintaining a uniform and high-quality system of coinage with full-valued coins—the problem that Elizabeth I and her predecessors confronted. It explains the driving out of metallic coins by paper issues, as occurred with the continentals in America after 1778, the assignats of France during the revolution, and the greenbacks of the United States after 1861.

It explains the failure to maintain the joint circulation of full-bodied gold and silver coins in bimetallic systems in the United States and abroad. Generally when the mint ratio, the ratio of weights at which silver and gold are freely coined at the mint, is at variance with relative commodity values in the market (or in other systems), the metal that is overvalued at the mint will dominate, with the undervalued metal driven to other uses. Thus, in the United States, a bimetallic system that overvalued silver at a ratio of 15:1 in 1792 established a de facto silver standard. The change in the mint ratio to 16:1 in 1834, together with the cheapening of gold commodity values by new discoveries, led to a de facto gold standard thereafter.

The latest example of application of these forces was the disappearance of silver subsidiary coinage from circulation in the United States in the early 1970s. Once the price of silver exceeded or was expected to exceed $1.29 an ounce, silver coins were worth more as bullion than as money and disappeared from circulation. Indeed, even silver certificates, representing rights to silver dollars, also rose in price above their monetary value, disappeared from circulation, and had to be replaced by Federal Reserve notes.

As monetary systems have come to rely increasingly or exclusively on purely token forms of circulating media, Gresham's law, a generalization relating primarily to the commodity aspects of money, has become less relevant.

References

Harrod, Roy, *Money*, Macmillan, St. Martin's Press, London, 1969, chap. 1; Hawtrey, R. G., *Currency and Credit*, Longmans, Green, London, 1919, chap. 11; Whittlesey, Charles R., Arthur M. Freedman, and Edward S. Herman, *Money and Banking, Analysis and Policy*, Macmillan, New York, 1968, chap. 2, appendix.

(See also Gold standard)

Arthur M. Freedman

Gross national product

The national income and product accounts provide a systematic, internally consistent, and theoretically unified set of measures which show the production, distribution, and use of newly produced goods and services during a specified time period, typically a quarter or a year. While the aggregates are most frequently used as measures of national output and income, sector and activity subtotals are also developed on the basis of accounting principles, which assist in the analysis of economic processes and transactions involving the separate differentiation of current consumer outlays and income.

George Jaszi, in the fiftieth anniversary issue of the *Survey of Current Business* (1971), "The Economic Accounts of the United States: Retrospect and Prospect," noted:

> *Gross national product should not be interpreted primarily as an economic barometer but rather as the center of a tableau, the magnitudes are presented within the framework of a disciplined accounting system in which the various economic flows are shown in relation to each other. The structure and classification of the system has been designed to provide a realistic description of the important features of the economy and hence tends to meet the requirements of practical economic analysis and of policy formulation and execution.*

A nation's output may be measured alternatively as the summation of the value of final products (receipts from sales plus the value of change in inventory) and as the summation of costs incurred in producing that output (counting profits as a factor of production cost). Output measured from the receipts or expenditure side is the gross national product, defined specifically as the market value of newly produced final goods and services supplied by the residents of the country before deduction of capital consumption allowances. Final products are those newly produced goods and services which are not resold in the accounting period. The value of intermediate products (purchases and sales of unfinished goods) is netted out because their contribution to output will be included in the value of final products.

The value of gross national income (GNI) is tantamount to the market value of gross national product (GNP), since it represents the sum of rewards to the factors of production (including profits), plus nonfactor changes (e.g., indirect taxes) which affect market prices. Where foreign transactions are important, as in many European countries, gross domestic product (GDP) is the more frequently cited measure because, unlike the GNP, it excludes output produced abroad to which residents have a claim. When deflated by price indexes for change in purchasing power, constant-dollar GNP provides a measure of real output in the economy. A national income total is identified when only returns to the factors of production are considered. The latter essentially represents the value added to purchased intermediate products.

Not all transactions in the economy are covered in the GNP accounts, one notable example being financial transactions involving the transfer of ownership of existing assets—thereby excluding capital gains or losses. Moreover, as noted earlier, transactions representing sales and purchases of intermediate products are excluded because they are consumed in the process of production of final output. However, one exception to this last exclusion rule in the GNP measure is the capital consumption charge; consequently, net national product is the more valid measure of output. This has become especially true in the 1970s with the improvement of previously poor estimates of depreciation.

By imputation, the value of some nonmarketed final products and services is added to the GNP to achieve an improved measure of output. Amounting to less than 10 percent of GNP, imputations include wages and salaries in kind, food and fuel consumed on the farms, housing services generated by owner-occupied dwellings, etc. On the other hand, because of measurement problems, the principle of measuring unpaid economic output is not applied to services of homemakers, other non-market household labor, and rental value of nonhousing durable goods.

The uses of the GNP accounts have increased over the years, especially since having been expanded to show the income and product of major industry groups, more detail on transactions of the several sectors by functions, and integration of these accounts with input-output tables (which show the flows of intermediate as well as final products among industries). Future developments will encompass integration of national income with balance sheet accounts in order to relate income and wealth.

The development of the mass, integrated information system that is inherent in the national accounts has provided business and government with the means for more sophisticated analysis of current economic conditions, projections of economic prospects, and testing by econometric models of economic hypotheses, e.g., the effects of changes in fiscal policy on total GNP. Private and public planning goals often are cast in the framework of the national accounts—the former, frequently in shares of projected national sales of particular products, and the latter, centering on issues of total and major industry employment and unemployment and on inflation prospects. The GNP deflator is often considered the most comprehensive measure available of price change for the economy as a whole.

History

While the nineteenth century witnessed significant advances in the United States and abroad in the development of such national product and income concepts as value added, factor cost, and final expenditures, progress accelerated following the particular theoretical analysis of economic processes of consumption, saving, and investment provided by J. M. Keynes in 1936. The need for data on civilian and military output shares in U.S. mobilization efforts of World War II provided the inducement to build upon work pursued at the National Bureau of Economic Research and the U.S. Department of Commerce in the 1920s and 1930s. In the post-World War II period, the United Nations Statistical Office developed a standard system of national accounts that was recommended for use by member nations. Estimates in simple or complex detail are now available for nearly all countries.

Current Criticism

The GNP has been criticized as a measure of changes in welfare. Satisfaction of consumer wants may not be equivalent to welfare progress. Critics argue that many GNP expenditures are worthless, harmful, or unethical if the criteria of welfare are scientific standards or ethical behavior. For example, outlays for cigarette smoking have been cited as deleterious to health in several respects, though contributing to GNP growth. Other GNP expenditures not only reduce welfare—e.g., those that increase environmental pollution—but, in fact, necessitate outlays for control that should be counted as offsets to GNP. On the other hand, there are nonmarket activities which increase welfare, such as social work or work by unpaid volunteers.

References

Kuznets, Simon, *National Income: A Summary of Findings*, National Bureau of Economic Research, Arno, New York, 1975; Ruggles, Richard, and Nancy D. Ruggles, *National Income Accounts and Income Analysis*, 2d ed., McGraw-Hill, New York, 1956; Schultze, C. L., *National Income Analysis*, 3d ed., Prentice-Hall, Englewood Cliffs, N.J., 1971.

(*See also* Bureau of Economic Analysis; Disposable personal income; Economic forecasts; Economic statistics; Factor cost; Flow of funds; Forecasting methods; Government expenditures in GNP; Gross private domestic investment in GNP; Input-output analysis; National income accounting; Net exports in GNP; Personal consumption expenditures in GNP; Potential gross national product; Statistical techniques in economics and business, an overview)

Herman I. Liebling

Gross national product potential (see Potential gross national product)

Gross private domestic investment in GNP

Gross private domestic investment (GPDI) is the most comprehensive measure of private investment. It is composed of fixed investment—both nonresidential and residential—the additions to and replacement of private capital brought about through acquisitions by business and nonprofit institutions of durable equipment and structures for business and residential purposes, and the change in business inventories—inventory investment.

Gross private domestic investment represents all private capital formation without any deduction for the portion of the stock of capital used up in the course of producing the current period's output. It is gross, not net, because there is no satisfactory technique for directly estimating actual wear and tear, obsolescence, and destruction and accidental losses of physical capital that occur through the economy during a given time period. There is no direct estimate of the volume of capital consumption or the portion of gross investment that should be counted as replacement.

There is, however, an indirect measure of capital consumption allowances. In distributing its revenues, American business makes an accounting provision for capital replacement. In effect it allocates a portion of gross revenues to depreciation reserves. Thus, on the income side of the U.S. national accounts appears a total for depreciation. These business depreciation charges are measures of the gross-net difference in private domestic investment.

Business depreciation charges are based upon a variety of formulas that often have little relationship to the actual length of life of the assets. During periods of rapid inflation, serious understatements are made of the present replacement cost of current capital consumption because business depreciation accounting is tied, in large part, to outmoded valuations of assets.

Economists traditionally have regarded the durability of most investment goods as a partial explanation of the wide variability in investment expenditures. In the national income and product accounts, purchases of capital goods are defined as those nonhousehold purchases of goods which are not bought for resale and are of a minimum specified durability.

The basic purpose of fixed investment is to increase the capacity to produce goods and services for future consumption. An increase in inventory is regarded as investment because it represents production not matched by current consumption. A decrease in inventory is regarded as disinvestment because it reflects consumption in excess of current production.

Residential construction outlays are, by definition, part of gross private domestic investment, but new housing outlays seem to be similar to consumer expenditures for automobiles and dissimilar to outlays for capital goods. New houses, like automobiles, are bought by households, and they are purchased by particular households only infrequently. Another similarity is the substantial used market for these items. On the other hand, capital goods are bought by businesses, and new purchases of plant and/or equipment are made every year for either modernization, replacement, or expansion. The market for used capital goods is relatively small.

Capital expenditures, inventory investment, and residential construction outlays are the volatile sectors of the economy. The recessions during the post-World War II period have been accounted for by declines in one or more of these three key sectors of the economy.

During the decade of the 1970s, U.S. gross private domestic investment averaged about 15 percent of GNP in nominal terms and about 13 percent in real terms. These figures are significantly lower than comparable estimates for Japan and West Germany.

References

Kuznets, Simon, *National Income: A Summary of Findings*, National Bureau of Economic Research, Arno, New York, 1975; Ruggles, Richard, and Nancy D. Ruggles, *National Income Accounts and Income Analysis*, 2d ed., McGraw-Hill, New York, 1956; Schultze, C. L., *National Income Analysis*, 3d ed., Prentice-Hall, Englewood Cliffs, N.J., 1971.

(*See also* Business investment in new plants and equipment; Capital formation; Change in business inventories in GNP; Depreciation allowance; Gross national product; Housing economics)

Douglas Greenwald

Guaranteed income (see Negative income tax)

Housing economics

The housing industry is one of the most important and volatile sectors of the American economy. Over the years, the fluctuations in the housing sector have been much more pronounced than the fluctuations in the gross national product (GNP). Because of the magnitude of the industry—about 5 percent of GNP and 30 percent of fixed investment—and the large number of industries which are either directly or indirectly dependent on new home construction, movements in the housing industry tend to foreshadow movements in the overall economy.

In many ways, housing is different from most other goods. Housing is generally immobile, with most units being tied to a particular parcel of land until they are removed by demolition or other means. In 1980, there were 80 million units in the occupied housing stock, of which roughly two-thirds were owner-occupied. The purchase of a unit is usually the largest single expenditure an individual or family ever makes. Besides paying for the actual unit, households also must continually make additional expenditures for property taxes, insurance, and upkeep (utilities, trash collection, etc.).

Perhaps the most significant difference between housing and most other goods is that it tends to appreciate rather than depreciate in value. This factor is especially important in the inflationary economy in which we now live. During the 1950s, when record numbers of single-family units were constructed, the annual inflation rate averaged less than 2.5 percent; hence, home purchasers were mostly concerned with buying shelter. However, in periods of double-digit inflation, the purchase of a house provides not only a place to live but also, in most cases, an excellent investment. People with mortgages can watch inflation make their houses more valuable, and they can pay back their loans with less valuable dollars than they borrowed. They can deduct both the interest and property tax payments from their income tax, and they do not have to pay taxes on the appreciated value of their units unless they move into lower-priced units and realize capital gains. And homeowners who are at least 55 years old are now permitted a one-time, tax-free profit on capital gains of up to $100,000 on a home sale.

Characteristics of the Housing Industry

Housing is one of the most localized industries and has among the fewest large producers of any major sector of the economy. The top 400 firms control only 25 percent of the total housing market. According to a survey conducted by the National Association of Home Builders in 1976, about two-thirds of all single-family home builders constructed fewer than 25 units per year, while only 8 percent built over 100 units per year. The vast majority of builders run their own businesses. The survey found that selling single-family homes was the primary operation for 59 percent of the builders, custom home building for 27 percent, multifamily rental units for 4 percent, and land development for 3 percent. The average number of construction workers on a builder's payroll was 13, and the average number of all other workers was 6.

Despite the large number of small producers in the industry and the absence of any producers who dominate the national market, the housing industry is not a good model for perfect competition. There is no uniformly organized housing exchange resembling the stock exchange or the commodity markets. Housing units have little uniformity, varying in size, structure, amenities, and the land on which they are located. The sales price or rental cost of a unit depends in large measure upon the bargaining powers of the buyer and seller or the lessor and lessee. There is no set product with a set price. Appraising the value of a unit is extremely difficult, especially during inflationary periods when real estate values fluctuate rapidly. At any given time in any given market, there are usually few units on the market, a fact which tends to limit competition.

Demand and Supply

Housing demand is a function of the price of housing relative to real disposable income (or weekly earnings), the price of other goods, mortgage market conditions (interest rates, down-payment requirements, and amortization periods), government efforts to stimulate demand through subsidy programs, and household formation rates. The household formation rate is influenced by demographic trends and the general state of the economy. Young and individual households are the two most sensitive to economic conditions; for instance, a young person who might prefer to live alone might from economic necessity stay with his or her parents, get married, find roommates, etc. A larger percentage of family households vis-à-vis individual households usually results in a greater demand for family-oriented units such as single-family houses vis-à-vis individual-oriented units such as rental apartments. Thus, the household formation rate influences both the number and the types of units constructed.

Housing supply is sensitive to market conditions and the cost of production. These factors determine the profitability of housing development and construction. Builders also react to the cost and availability of both short-term and long-term financing and to the inventory of competitive units on the market. Construction costs relative to housing prices determine the profitability of housing development and construction to the builder and are directly related to the supply of starts. Home sales, vacancy rates, and the inventory of unsold units indicate market conditions and potential profitability. For example, a large inventory of unsold units and high vacancy rates are indications of a slack market and cast doubt upon the potential profitability of construction.

Cost Components of Housing

Mortgage credit is the lifeblood of the housing industry. Builders need to borrow funds for purchasing land, labor, materials, and other components of building a home, and consumers need to borrow funds for the purchase of the finished product. If the funds dry up, the process grinds to a halt. The supply of mortgage funds is a function of the portfolio choices of individuals and institutions, and is reflected in the supply of savings funds; the actions of savings and loan associations; the actions of the Federal National Mortgage Association, the Government National Mortgage Association, the Federal Home Loan Mortgage Corporation, and the Federal Home Loan Bank Board; as well as in the actions of other mortgage-creating institutions.

Construction financing is one of the most rapidly rising component costs of a house. The construction financing rate is generally tied to the prime rate. Builders usually borrow at a rate 2 to 3 percent or more above the prime rate. Between 1977 and 1979, builders saw the prime rate jump from 6.25 percent to 15.75 percent, a jump which meant that construction financing rates went from roughly 8 or 9 percent to 17 percent or more. The high rates not only drive up the eventual sales price of the house, but also can create serious cash flow problems for builders. Any delays in the construction process caused by inclement weather, government red tape, or lack of availability of certain building materials can compound the problem.

In addition to financing, land is the other most rapidly rising component of the cost of housing units. Many metropolitan areas are experiencing shortages of developable lots both in their cities and in their nearby suburbs. As gasoline prices continue to rise, these lots either in or near the central cities (where most of the jobs usually are) become more desirable, and the greater demand drives the price up. The lot-scarcity problem has been exacerbated in numerous jurisdictions by restrictive land-use ordinances.

With the price of land for housing escalating rapidly, there is increased pressure on farmers to sell their land for potential residential use. The trend has been strongest in the Pacific states, as one would expect from the statistics on the westward movement of the population. Likewise, the decline in importance of the Northeast in new residential construction is reflected in the declining volume of farmland sold for residential use.

The hard costs, which consist of the labor and material components, comprise slightly less than half of the final total sales price of the typical single-family house. Since World War II, the hard-cost share of the sales price has grown less quickly than other components. Of the hard cost, about $2 is spent on materials for every $1 that is spent on labor.

Labor costs have been rising less quickly than material costs, even though wage rates have increased significantly in many areas. The major reason for this slower increase is that improved construction techniques have made labor more productive. The construction process has become more standardized and mechanized and is employing a greater number of industrialized methods. Enormous improvements in the tool industry have likewise increased productivity. And because of rapidly rising construction labor costs, builders have been pressured to use more parts produced in shops or factories and fewer produced by on-site labor.

Problems for the Housing Industry in the 1980s

One of the biggest construction labor problems is caused by the cyclicality of the industry. From 1971 through 1973, there were more than 2 million total housing starts per year. Between 1973 and 1975, the starts rate plummeted 43 percent to 1.17 million units. In 1977 and 1978, the starts level was once again averaging more than 2 million per year. The people who work in the construction trades must support themselves during the slumps, and if they cannot find construction work, they find a different kind of work. When the building market picks up again, the construction workers who found work in a different field may not return, and new workers must be found. There are problems not only with the availability of labor but also with the quality of the work performed because the newcomers may lack the skill and experience of those who left. Unless the housing cycles are smoothed out, this problem will continue.

Building material producers experience similar problems because of housing cycles. Demand for their products is heavily dependent on the amount of construction activity at any given time. If the housing market is slumping, material plants may have to operate at far less than peak capacity and lay off workers. If the slump is particularly severe, some plants may even have to shut down entirely. When demand for the product starts to increase again, shortages of certain materials may develop. It is very difficult for many industries to speed up or slow down their production schedules based on the vagaries of the building cycles.

One of the biggest economic issues facing the home-building industry involves the price and availability of building materials. Most building materials either are energy-intensive to produce or are themselves composed of scarce natural resources so that the ability to control prices is limited. During the 1970s, the producer price index for all construction materials rose at roughly the same rate as the index for all commodities in the economy—approximately 128 percent. However, some of the most important building materials, especially lumber, rose far more quickly than the average.

Lumber and wood products account for about 15 percent of the sales price of a house, and the share has been rising rapidly. While the index for all building materials was rising 128 percent in the seventies, the softwood lumber index was increasing 211 percent. Lumber prices are extremely sensitive to fluctuations in the building industry. As the level of housing activity increases during the 1980s to accommodate the record levels of demand, lumber prices are expected to rise even more rapidly, with possible shortages arising. As a result, builders may start trying to substitute other products for lumber. They may start using more masonry walls, particle board, and foam board, and it is even possible that steel and aluminum studs will become competitively priced.

Builders can make other adjustments to adapt to rising energy prices. Asphalt paving materials are rising in price because they are made with a petroleum base, so there will probably be a movement away from their use. Furnaces and mechanical equipment in general will become smaller as new houses get tighter and more fuel-efficient. A greater emphasis can be placed on designing houses that save energy by using a greater amount of insulation or by adopting passive solar techniques. Many of the articles that have been written on housing affordability concentrate solely on price versus income calculations and ignore the crucial consideration of whether the buyer can afford the upkeep on the unit.

The affordability crunch hits the first-time home buyer harder than any other group. Even with housing prices rising more quickly than personal income in the late 1970s, there were still record levels of sales. One explanation may be that the majority of home buyers are already homeowners and have built up equity from the rapid rise in existing home values. They may not utilize all of their equity in buying another home, but a lender will take the total equity into account when a loan application is evaluated. However, nonowners without equity will have trouble both in saving up for a down payment and in qualifying to make the monthly payments.

Despite the difficulty for many of buying a unit, there are mitigating forces at work in the housing industry working against an expansion of the rental market. The rental stock will grow during the 1980s, but it will play a declining role in the total housing inventory, growing only about half as quickly as the owner-occupied sector. The problems in the rental market stem from both the supply and the demand side. The shifting age distribution of the population during the 1980s will tend to favor home ownership as all the baby-boom children move up through the ranks. This will be the most important factor affecting demand for rental units. Also, there is a growing desire by many traditional renters to try to hedge against inflation; this, along with an increasing shortage of rental apartments, will encourage many would-be renters to opt for ownership. In some cities, the rental vacancy rate already has dropped below 1 percent; normally, a 5 to 6 percent rate is considered necessary to allow for the normal flow of people in and out of units.

On the supply side many builders, especially in the Northeast and North Central regions of the United States, are deciding not to build rental apartments because of their uncertain profitability. Builders, like other business executives, consider the rates of return and the risks involved in a construction project compared with other investment opportunities. Currently, the environment for building and operating rental properties is very uncertain, with the risks overshadowing the purely economic considerations. Besides having to borrow a large sum of money and having to cope with proliferating amounts of government red tape while building projects, builders who complete units must worry about rent-control laws and increasingly militant tenant associations while managing them. With ownership units, builders simply borrow money, build the units, sell them, and go on to build something else. Because of the problems with operating rental units, many apartments have been converted into condominiums, which is partially responsible for the shortage of rental units in some areas.

All in all, the biggest economic question facing the American housing market during the 1980s will be whether or not the nation can muster the resources to produce enough reasonably priced units to satisfy the unprecedented levels of demand. More cluster developments and zero-lot-line units may have to be produced in order to adapt to problems with obtaining usable lots. New types of building products and new construction materials may have to be substituted for currently used products and materials. Work-force training programs may have to be expanded in order to accommodate the increased demand for construction labor. Different forms of financing may have to be adopted on a wide scale in order to produce enough money for the building and buying of all the needed units—such a movement is already under way with the introduction of variable-rate mortgages, graduated-payment mortgages, and other alternative mortgage instruments. The American people must adapt their lifestyles to the changing energy situation. The housing industry is constantly evolving, and the speed with which it responds to these challenges will in large measure depend on the degree of economic exigency.

References

Klaman, Saul B., *The Postwar Residential Mortgage Market*, Princeton University Press, Princeton, N.J., 1961; Newcomb, Robinson, "Housing and Other Construction," in William F. Butler, Robert A. Kavesh, and Robert B. Platt (eds.), *Methods and Techniques of Business Forecasting*, Prentice-Hall, Englewood Cliffs, N.J., 1974; Sumichrast, Michael, and Maury Seldin, *Housing Markets: The Complete Guide to Analysis and Strategy for Builders, Lenders and Other Investors*, Dow Jones–Irwin, Homewood, Ill., 1977.

(*See also* Demographics and economics; Disintermediation; Federal Reserve policy; Federal Reserve System; Financial institutions; Financial instruments; Interest rates; Monetary policy; Real estate investment trusts; Thrift institutions)

William C. Young

Human capital

Human capital is the stock of economically productive human capabilities. These capabilities are formed or produced by combining innate abilities with investments in human beings. Examples of such investments include expenditures on education, on-the-job training, and health and nutrition. Such expenditures increase future productive capacity at the expense of current consumption. Since most capital stock deteriorates or depreciates with the passage of time, with intense use, or with lack of use, the stock of capital increases in a period only when gross investment exceeds such depreciation (or, alternatively, if net investment is positive).

The amount of output of an economic entity depends upon the state of knowledge (or technology) for converting inputs into economic products, upon the efficiency with which such inputs are combined, and upon the service flows of such inputs. This abstraction is useful for considering the production of a nation, a farm, a firm, or a family. Before about 1960 most economists focused on a triumvirate of primary inputs: human labor, natural resources, and the stock of physical capital (primarily plant and equipment). The production of other purchased inputs was dependent ultimately on this same trinity. Of course, it was realized that these primary factors varied in quality in the real world. Joseph Schumpeter, for example, in the early part of this century emphasized that some humans have unusual entrepreneurial qualities that result in their taking leadership positions by introducing economic innovations, applying better technology, opening up new markets, developing new products, making more efficient use of inputs, and locating new sources of inputs. Hypotheses were proposed that explained the difference in capabilities of humans with regard to entrepreneurship and other economic characteristics as due to familial and social conditions and to genetic endowments. But for many purposes qualitative differences among inputs, human or otherwise, simply were ignored. Even when qualitative differences were recognized, no theories were widely accepted that provided an economic structure for decisions related to investment in humans.

Human Capital School and Model

About 1960 Theodore Schultz, Gary Becker, and Jacob Mincer provided such a structure by introducing explicitly the notion that people invested in themselves in order to increase their stock of human capital. They emphasized the analogy between investment in physical capital and investment in human capital. Both involve forgoing current consumption in order to increase expected future production and earnings possibilities and, thereby, future consumption possibilities. For example, individuals may pay tuition and forgo current earnings while studying in college in part to increase their expected future earnings. Of course, there also may be other returns to education such as becoming a more knowledgeable or cultured person. But what the human capital school emphasizes is that purely economic returns relative to economic costs may be a major factor in determining such human capital investments.

The human capital model has had substantial impact on the economics profession. It has provided a more satisfactory framework for identifying the causes of macro, or national, growth. It has permitted the incorporation of diversities of human capabilities into formal models that still are sufficiently simple to be manageable. It has tied together investment in financial, physical, and human capital. It has improved the framework for analyzing the implications of private and social decisions relating to such areas as education, health, and nutrition, training programs, unemployment, income maintenance, family planning, the distribution of earnings, and women and youth labor-force participation. It has spawned a large number of empirical efforts to measure the returns on various investments in humans, particularly in education. It also has provoked broader theoretical and empirical considerations regarding the role of time in consumption and production, the role of family background in investments in humans, and the nature of intrafamilial consumption, production, and investment decisions.

Controversies

Despite such a major impact on economic thought—or perhaps because of that impact—a number of controversies about the human capital model currently exist on empirical and theoretical levels.

One important issue revolves around the assumption that "perfect" information exists about alternatives both at a given point of time and in future time periods. Users of the human capital model, for example, analyze fertility determinants under the assumption that choices are made on the basis of good knowledge concerning contraceptive options. Yet for some populations for which these models have been applied—particularly in the less-developed countries—there is considerable evidence that numerous individuals are not aware of modern contraceptive options. The estimations of the returns on education provide another example. They are made under the assumption that individuals have a good estimate of the expected returns on the investment in terms of later earnings. But this implies that individuals deciding about going to college in the 1920s, to provide a specific illustration, had good expectations of the impact of the Great Depression, the Second World War, the postwar decolonialization, the electronic revolution, etc.

A second issue is related to whether individual or family preferences enter into human capital investment decisions. This is important because such preferences are not directly observable. Most human capital studies focus exclusively on investment decisions without dealing with the role of such preferences. Recent work, however, suggests that for some problems preferences may be quite important. For example, parental preferences regarding the distribution of expected earnings among their children may enter into human capital investment decisions involving these children. In other words, parents may not try to maximize the monetary rate of return on such investments.

A third issue is related to the empirical importance of the human capital model. In fact, observed variations in human capital investments such as education account for only a small part of variations in actual earnings among individuals. Moreover, recent studies suggest that the magnitude of such returns reported in many such studies may be biased upward because of a failure to allow for family background and related ability and motivation. The actual value of such returns, moreover, has important policy implications since it indicates the extent to which human capital investments such as in education can be used to change the income distribution or to alleviate poverty.

A fourth issue is whether or not human capital investments, particularly in education or in training, actually increase productivity. An alternative explanation is that the attainment of such education is merely a means by which a capable individual signals his or her capabilities to potential employers.

References

Becker, Gary S., *Human Capital: A Theoretical and Empirical Analysis, with Special Reference to Education*, National Bureau of Economic Research General Series, no. 80, Columbia University Press, New York, 1964; Mincer, Jacob, "Investment in Human Capital and Personal Income Distribution," *Journal of Political Economy*, vol. 66, no. 4, August 1958, pp. 281–302; Schultz, Theodore W., "Education and Economic Growth," in N. B. Henry (ed.), *Social Forces Influencing American Education*, University of Chicago Press, Chicago, 1961.

(*See also* Factors of production; Productivity)

Jere R. Behrman and Paul J. Taubman

Implicit price deflator

The implicit price deflator is the price index that is usually associated with the gross national product (GNP) and its components. Such a deflator could, however, be constructed to deflate other economic time series.

The reason the price index for gross national product is called an implicit price deflator relates to the way in which it is constructed. Price indexes based on the Laspeyres formula are used to deflate in the greatest detail possible the various spending series that comprise gross national product. When these spending series are divided by the Laspeyres indexes, the result is a spending in constant dollars. These constant-dollar spending series are then added up to form gross national product in constant dollars. When that total is divided into gross national product in current dollars, an implicit measure is obtained of the price index that will exactly reconcile the current and constant-dollar GNP figures. Since this index is implicitly derived as the quotient obtained by dividing the current-dollar figure by the constant-dollar figure, it is termed an implicit price index.

The formula for the implicit deflator is

$$\frac{\Sigma \, p_1 q_1}{\Sigma \, p_0 q_1}$$

where p_1 = price in the current period
q_1 = quantity in the current period
p_0 = price in the base period

It can be seen that multiplying the implicit price deflator times the Laspeyres index of output yields a measure that is the total revenue or gross national product in current dollars

$$\frac{\Sigma \ p_1 q_1}{\Sigma \ p_0 q_1} \times \frac{\Sigma \ p_0 q_1}{\Sigma \ p_0 q_0} = \frac{\Sigma \ p_1 q_1}{\Sigma \ p_0 q_0}$$

The implicit price deflator, thus, is the only price measure which exactly reconciles a fixed-weight quantity index with a total value series.

The implicit price index, however, is not itself a fixed-weight index of prices. Thus, its movements do not reflect price change alone. Indeed, they are a composite of changes in prices and changes in quantity when measured between periods other than the base period.

Comparison of the implicit price deflator with its base always yields a measure of pure price change for that time period based on fixed, current-period weights. In this respect, the implicit price deflator is a Paasche index, distinct from the other, more widely used measure of price change, a Laspeyres price index. The latter has base-period weights; the former, current-period weights.

Problems and Alternatives

Because the implicit price deflator is not a measure of pure price change and is affected by changes in the composition of gross national product in constant dollars or by changes in the quantity weights, it has not been a totally satisfactory measure of pure price change for use and analysis of the gross national product. As a result, the Bureau of Economic Analysis (BEA), which is responsible for the estimation and publication of the national income and product accounts, has developed two other price series which more exactly approach measures of pure price change. One is a fixed-weight price index in which the deflators for the various components of gross national product are added up using base-period weights. Another measure developed by the BEA for analysis of prices associated with gross national product is the so-called Chain index, which is a base-period index, but one in which the base weights change from quarter to quarter. Thus, between any two quarters, it is a measure of pure price change. But for more than the period between those quarters, it is a mixture of price change and weight or quantity change.

The implicit deflator for gross national product has been available quarterly since 1946 from the Bureau of Economic Analysis. In addition, the BEA publishes annual estimates going back to 1929. Annual estimates prior to that have been developed by various scholars.

References

Department of Economics and Social Affairs, *Guidelines on Principles of a System of Price and Quantity Statistics*, Statistical Papers, ser. M, no. 59, United Nations, New York, 1977.

(*See also* Consumer price index; Cost of living; Economic statistics; Gross national product; Index numbers; Statistical techniques in economics and business, an overview)

Joel Popkin

Imports

Imports are defined as goods taken into one country from another country in the conduct of foreign trade, with the first country being the importer, the second the exporter. In practice, imports are more complicated than this simple definition implies. The monthly data published by the U.S. Bureau of the Census on U.S. imports appear in four different series: imports c.i.f seasonally adjusted, imports c.i.f. not seasonally adjusted, imports f.a.s. seasonally adjusted, imports f.a.s. not seasonally adjusted. Imports c.i.f. (cost, insurance, and freight) include shipping costs from the country of origin to the United States; imports f.a.s. (free along side) exclude shipping costs from the country of origin, though shipping charges within the country of origin are included, as, for example, the shipping of goods from a factory to the port.

One problem with analyzing import statistics is that, although import data on both a c.i.f. and an f.a.s. basis are published regularly, the U.S. financial press usually reports the f.a.s. figure. In most foreign countries, on the other hand, imports are usually reported in the press on a c.i.f. basis. Since January 1979, the bases for the seasonal adjustment of U.S. imports have been changed. Thus, the analyst should make sure that trade data with a consistent seasonal adjustment are used.

On a quarterly basis the Balance of Payments Division of the U.S. Department of Commerce also reports United States f.a.s. imports. These figures are, however, adjusted for various conceptual differences from the monthly series in order to make them comparable with other elements of the U.S. balance of payments. The main adjustments to a balance of payments basis—which, for example, raised 1977 f.a.s. imports on a balance of payments basis by about $4 billion over the monthly series— are imports of the Virgin Islands from foreign countries, nonmonetary gold imports, imports of U.S. military agencies, and reconciliations with Canadian export data.

In balance of payment and national income statistics, especially for foreign countries, the term imports may be confusing because it may include imports of services as well as imports of merchandise. In the broad definition, in addition to merchandise, imports include travel, transportation, military expenditures abroad, license and royalty payments, and earnings on foreign investment in the United States.

Significance of Imports Growth

Since the early postwar years, imports have grown in significance to the U.S. economy. Between 1950 and 1978 U.S. imports grew from $9.1 to $176 billion. As a percentage of U.S. gross national product, imports were 8.2 percent in 1978 compared with 3.1 percent in 1950. In the world economy the volume of total imports increased an estimated 180 percent during 1963 to 1977, compared with a 125 percent estimated rise in the same period for world industrial production. This rapid growth in world imports is in marked contrast with the prewar decade when world trade stagnated as import restrictions were widely applied, often in retaliation to restrictions in other countries.

In the early postwar years, the growth of world trade seemed almost automatic as incomes in most developed countries grew rapidly, technologies were transferred internationally, and tariff barriers were gradually broken down—in part because of more travel and better communication. World trade appeared to be able to solve its own problems with a minimum of interference from governments, all of which seemed to be its beneficiaries.

In the early 1970s, however, this image of world trade changed. The U.S. trade balance began to deteriorate, and in 1971 the United States moved into a trade deficit which was certainly a contribution to the devaluations of the dollar in December 1971 and February 1973. Moreover, in late 1973 U.S. imports received another shock in the more than fourfold rise in oil prices.

The surge in U.S. imports and the dollar devaluation brought into sharper focus two issues that were of minor importance in the 1950s and early 1960s. These were (1) unemployment attributed to competition from U.S. imports, and (2) the impact of U.S. import prices on the U.S. price level generally.

Imports and Unemployment

In the earlier postwar period with rapid growth in the U.S. economy there was less of a tendency for imports to displace employed workers. In the late 1960s, however, the overvaluation of the dollar made the United States less competitive and made U.S. employment more vulnerable to imports. As a result, the position of U.S. labor organizations switched from a view generally favorable to free trade to one favoring trade restrictions to prevent massive unemployment in industries competing with imports. In 1972 many U.S. labor organizations supported the Burke-Hartke bill that provided for regulation of U.S. imports. The Burke-Hartke bill did not pass, but a consciousness developed that there is a trade-off between unemployment arising from imports and the favorable effect of lower prices for consumers due to imports. In order to limit political pressures for controls on imports, the U.S. government has negotiated so-called orderly marketing agreements limiting imports from major exporting countries, particularly of consumer goods. On the other hand, the so-called Tokyo Round of trade negotiations was concluded in 1979 with significant reductions in tariffs and other trade restrictions.

Imports and the Price Level

The other aspect of U.S. imports that is now being reexamined is their effect on the U.S. price level. In the 1950s and early 1960s, U.S. imports tended to restrain U.S. inflation because prices of imports tended to be lower than prices of domestically produced goods. This effect was reversed, however, after 1971 when depreciation of the U.S. dollar raised the price of imports.

It is sometimes argued that devaluation does not have much effect on the U.S. price level because imports in 1978 were only about 8 percent of gross national product. This argument ignores, however, the fact that a much larger proportion of U.S. goods are internationally traded and, therefore, tend to move in line with the price of imports. Thus, if the U.S. dollar depreciates against the Japanese yen, the price of Japanese car imports may rise and exert an upward pull on the price of all U.S. autos. Moreover, with world tastes and production methods becoming more cosmopolitan, the percentage of goods with domestic prices affected by international trade is certainly rising.

Thus, imports have moved from a relatively passive part of the U.S. economy, mainly of interest to specialists, to a vital influence on the two key economic problems of employment and inflation.

References

Ahluwalia, Isher J., and Ernesto Hernandez-Cata, "An Econometric Model of U.S. Merchandise Imports under Fixed and Fluctuating Exchange Rates 1959–1973," *Staff Papers*, International Monetary Fund, Washington, D.C., November 1975; Joy, James, and J. D. Stolen, "The Change in the U.S. Import Demand Function from the 1950s to the 1960s", *Review of Economics and Statistics*, vol. LVII, no. 1, February 1975, pp. 109–111; Khan, Mohsin S., and Knud Z. Ross, "Cyclical and Secular Income Elasticities of Demand for Imports," *Review of Economics and Statistics*, vol. LVII, no. 3, August 1975, pp. 357–361.

(*See also* Barriers to trade; Comparative advantage theory; Dumping; Exports; Foreign exchange rates; General Agreement on Tariffs and Trade; International economics, an overview; Net exports in GNP; Protectionism)

James L. Burtle

Income

Income is most familiar to people as the amount of money received from participating in the labor market, that is, earnings from paid employment. Most would recognize that items such as interest payments on savings accounts or dividends from stocks also represent income. And it would be generally agreed that earnings from self-employment, e.g., the receipts of doctors and lawyers less their expenses of doing business, represent income.

Economists attach a special significance to income payments that arise from current participation in the production process: these payments—whether they are wages and salaries associated with some number of hours worked; interest associated with the use of money; or dividends, rents, profits, etc.—are defined in such a way as to add up to the total income of society, i.e., to the national income. This total is then redistributed among the members of society by various voluntary and involuntary transfer and tax programs, which result in a new distribution of spendable or disposable income. Thus, social security payments are an important source of disposable income but are not part of production-related national income since recipients are not being paid for current participation in production.

Concepts

Among economists the most widely accepted analytical definition of income associated with the production process is that it represents the yield from wealth. Defining income in that way underlines the importance of relating the income concept to a corresponding wealth concept. The common sense of that idea is most easily established with reference to conventional financial assets. All would agree that the interest return on a $1000 savings account represents the income from that asset: that is, if an individual received a $60 annual payment from holding a $1000 savings account, that $60 represents income. Note that income has a clear time reference—the $60 is an annual rate of flow, while the asset that yields income—the savings account—does not, being a stock existing at a point in time.

But what about a slightly more complicated case, still within the realm of financial assets: What is the income of the owner of a share of common stock that sells at $100 and pays $5 annually in dividends? Certainly the $5 per share represents income and can be thought of as the dividend return from the shareholder's ownership of a part of the corporation. Over the course of any given time period such as a year, however, several other things might happen that could affect what we think of as the income from owning a share of stock: for example, the corporation typically earns more (after paying all expenses) than it actually pays out to the shareholders in dividend—that is, the corporation is likely to have retained earnings. And the price of the stock is likely to change, for any number of reasons.

Here, economists would be likely to say that income of the shareholder is clearly different from the $5 per share paid on stock valued at $100 since the retention of earnings by the corporation presumably has made the corporation more valuable, hence likely to earn more in the future, hence likely to pay more dividends in the future, etc. A common view would be that the income of the shareholder consists of a proportionate share of the corporation's total earnings, not just the earnings paid out as dividends. Thus, undistributed profit per share might well be added to dividends per share to provide a more accurate measure of the income associated with ownership of stock.

Finally, what about a still more complex case—a self-employed business executive whose gross receipts are $100,000 per year and whose out-of-pocket expenses are $70,000 per year? Is the income from owning that business the remaining $30,000? If so, how would one characterize the asset that has yielded the $30,000 income?

Economists are apt to suggest that part of the $30,000 isn't really income at all, on the reasonable assumption that the true costs of conducting business are not represented in toto by the $70,000 out-of-pocket expenses, but should include depreciation of the company's assets as well. That is, the $30,000 differential between gross receipts and out-of-pocket expenses would be income only if the ability of the business to generate future income were to remain the same. But if the company's assets were depreciating because they were being used up in producing goods and services, some provision for replacing those assets would be needed, and that is commonly labeled depreciation.

As to the nature of the asset that has yielded the income of $30,000 (less depreciation allowance) from the business, most would say that the income comes from two sources: part represents a return on the capital assets invested in the business (equipment, inventories, working capital), and part represents a return on another kind of asset—the human skills of the business executive. It has become customary in recent decades to refer to the latter as the stock of human capital owned by the person who owns and manages the business.

It is now easier to see how one should view the wage and salary payments received by members of the population engaged in paid employment. These payments represent income, and they can be thought of as a return on knowledge, experience, and skills, i.e., on human capital assets. The difficulty with this idea may be seen by considering the income of medical interns or advanced graduate students: the former may be paid $10,000 to $15,000 a year during the 2 or 3 years they are polishing the skills of their trade, while the latter are likely to have an income of less than that while working as teaching or research assistants. Such people are apt to have about 20 years of formal schooling and can easily look forward to a future income of several times the amount paid while interning or teaching/assisting. Are the incomes of such people represented by what they are currently being paid?

Most economists would answer no to that question and argue that medical interns and teaching assistants are actually earning a much higher income than the nominal amount of money wages being paid to them because they are investing heavily in training designed to enhance future income. While there is usually no observable counterpart to the true income being earned by medical interns or teaching assistants, conceptually it would be represented by the amount that people with that level of training could earn if they were employed in a job that contained no training component, and hence no enhancement of skills and of future income.

Thus, the idea that only wage and salary payments are income does not hold up, unless the individuals receiving those wage and salary payments are in the situation of just maintaining their stock of skills at a steady level—neither adding to them nor allowing them to deteriorate. Otherwise, earnings may be higher or lower than actual income, when the latter is defined as the return on the human capital skills represented by ability, schooling, training, and experience.

For example, health insurance paid for by an employer on behalf of an employee is clearly part of the employee's income—it simply constitutes services-in-kind in lieu of direct cash payments. Similarly, free or subsidized meals provided by employers, free or subsidized parking, payments into a pension fund, etc., all constitute part of employee income. The only issue that arises in these cases is one of quantification: Since the employee may have no choice about the nature of the various benefits received in the form of free or subsidized goods and services, some fringe benefits may be worth less to the employee than they cost the employer. However, if the market for employment is sufficiently flexible, employees should be able to find employment opportunities that offer a set of fringe benefits that match their preference.

In a similar vein, owner-occupied housing, as well as personal automobiles and other durables, clearly yield income to their owners in the form of a flow of services. To understand that notion one might consider the nature of income that takes the form of net receipts to the owner of a rental housing property or to the owner of an automobile leasing business—such receipts, after expenses, would represent income. Why should it matter whether the assets are owned by those who are in the business of providing such services or by those whose main occupation is something else but who happen to provide those services for themselves by virtue of ownership?

As in the discussion of fringe benefits, there is an empirical question of the appropriate measurement of income from such owned assets. Conventional practice in the United States is to impute income to homeowners by using valuations obtained from the rental value of comparable properties. At present, conventional U.S. practice does not make a similar imputation for automobiles or other durable assets owned by consumers.

Other questions do not have neat conceptual or empirical answers. For example, should tax payments be counted as part of the income of the taxpayer? Conventional practice in the United States is to treat income taxes and all social security taxes as part of employee income whether paid by employees or employers, but not to treat other taxes, e.g., sales taxes, in that way. Treating tax payments as part of income has some justification—people pay taxes and get in return certain services (national defense, public administration, subsidized schooling, etc.). While it is hard to argue that the distribution of such public services matches the distribution of tax payments, it is equally hard to think of any sensible alternative imputation to individuals or households of the services provided by government and paid for by taxes. One view is that taxes, and the public services provided by them, reflect the political preferences of the population as a whole and that people must typically get about as much services from government as they pay in taxes or else the tax-expenditure system would be changed to correspond to what people want.

How far should one stretch the concept of income to cover unpaid work of various sorts? The question is important because over the last several decades many services formerly provided without compensation by household members for each other are now provided in the market by paid employees. And the reverse is also true—services formerly provided for pay in the market are now provided without pay by members of households for each other.

In the first category are activities such as child care and care of the elderly, which in earlier decades were almost exclusively provided within families or extended families, without compensation. Child care centers and institutional facilities for the elderly now abound in the United States, and the measure of earned income is affected in consequence. In the second category are activities such as domestic housework and entertainment. In earlier decades many millions of domestic workers were paid by households to cook, clean, etc., but in recent years the number of people employed in this activity has dwindled markedly. And in previous decades people were more apt than now to seek entertainment in movies, theaters, and similar establishments, whereas now television viewing in the home has significantly reduced the size of the paid entertainment market.

A little reflection suggests that the appropriate measurement of income flows associated with nonmarket activities is a complex problem, at both the analytical and the empirical levels. The most important factor to realize is that meaningful measures of income flows, and particularly of changes in income flows over time, depend crucially on the maintenance of consistency in the activities associated with the generation of income. For example, if the location of care for children and the elderly were to shift from within households to the market, the national income as conventionally measured would be much larger simply because of a transition in the location of activities. But the increase in income would be largely, if not entirely, illusory: it is not even clear that the quality of service provided to young and old would be better in commercial establishments than in households, although theoretically efficiency would be enhanced and thus fewer resources would be needed for the same product.

Income and Output

To an individual, income is a comparatively well-defined and easily understood concept, subject to the qualifications discussed previously. What may not be so easily recognized is that an appropriate definition of income has the property of making the total income of all members of society exactly equal to the total amount of output produced within that society. This identity between two different concepts—income and output—is achieved by defining one particular type of income flow as a residual that can be obtained only if one knows the amount of output.

To illustrate: The value of steel output is measured by the quantity of steel produced over some time period, multiplied by the average price of steel products. But all the contributors to this production process are paid income for their participation—workers in steel mills receive wages, suppliers of raw materials receive prices multiplied by quantities for their contribution, bondholders receive interest, stockholders receive dividends, owners of land on which steel facilities are located receive rent, etc. And there is a residual income receiver—the owners of the steel company—who receive the amount (positive or negative) that remains after all other payments, including dividends, have been made. This profits residual is simply the difference between the total value of steel output produced over some accounting period and the total amount of the income payments made to various factors of production. Since profits are also an income flow, it must, therefore, be definitionally true that the total value of steel output is equal to the total amount of income payments received by those involved in the steel industry.

One of the payments listed above does not represent income in the same sense as the others—the payments to suppliers of materials are not really income, but constitute receipts for the sale of goods from one firm to another. While that is true, exactly the same argument can be used to distribute the total value of materials purchased by the steel industry into payments to various inputs plus a profits residual. That is, suppliers of iron ore also pay wages to workers and managers, dividends to stockholders, interest to bondholders, etc., and they also would have a residual profit to balance the books, so to speak. Thus, all production of goods and services gives rise to an associated flow of income to participants in the production process, and that accounting identity gives rise to the double-entry-bookkeeping nature of our national income and product accounting system. Thus, economists speak interchangeably of the national income or the national product, knowing that the two are identically defined.

Real Income and Money Income

In an era when inflation rates of 8 to 12 percent are commonplace, everyone is familiar with the difference between money income and real income. Money income reflects the nominal value of income flows to individuals, households, or society as a whole. Real income reflects the adjustment of these money-income flows to account for the fact that a given amount of money income will not buy as many goods and services in one period as in another because the average price of goods and services has changed (in the 1970s, for example, it rose significantly). Thus, real income is simply money income deflated by the appropriate price index. At the level of individuals, the money income of the person or household would be deflated by a price index reflecting the particular bundle of goods and services purchased by that person or household.

Put another way, the concept of real income represents command over resources—that is, the degree to which a given flow of money income is able to translate into a flow of consumable products such as food, clothing, utilities, housing services, vacations, haircuts, insurance coverage, etc. Hence we adjust the flow of money income in different periods of time by the degree to which a particular common bundle of consumable goods and services varies in price from one period to the next, i.e., by an overall index of price change. Another way to view the same phenomenon is to recognize that money-income flows are measured in nominal units (dollars, francs, pounds, etc.); the notion of real income takes account of the fact that the yardstick itself (dollars, francs, pounds, etc.) can shrink or grow depending on whether one can acquire more (or less) goods and services for any given amount of dollars, francs, pounds, etc.

References

Becker, Gary S., *Human Capital: A Theoretical and Empirical Analysis with Special Reference to Education*, National Bureau of Economic Research General Series, no. 80, Columbia University Press, New York, 1964; Jaszi, George, "The Conceptual Basis of the Accounts: A Reexamination," in Studies in Income and Wealth, vol. 22, *A Critique of the United States Income and Product Accounts*, National Bureau of Economic Research, Princeton University Press, Princeton, N.J., 1958, pp. 13–145; Juster, F. Thomas, "A Framework for the Measurement of Economic and Social Performance," in Milton Moss (ed.), *The Measurement of Economic and Social Performance*, National Bureau of Economic Research Conference on the Measurement of Economic and Social Performance, Columbia University Press, New York, 1973, pp. 25–109; Kuznets, Simon S., *National Income and Its Composition, 1919-1938*, vols. I, II, National Bureau of Economic Research General Series, no. 40, Arno, New York, 1941; Kuznets, Simon S., and Milton Friedman, *Income from Independent Professional Practice*, National Bureau of Economic Research General Series, no. 45, Arno, New York, 1954; Samuelson, P. A., "The Evaluation of 'Social Income' Capital Formation and Wealth," in F. A. Lutz and D. C. Hague (eds.), *The Theory of Capital: Proceedings of a Conference*, St. Martin's, New York, 1961; Schultz, T. W., "Investment in Human Capital," *American Economic Review*, vol. 51, no. 1, March 1961, pp. 1-17; U.S. Office of Business Economics, *National Income: A Supplement to the Survey of Current Business*, U.S. Department of Commerce, 1954.

(*See also* Disposable personal income; Gross national product; Income distribution; Money illusion; National income accounting)

F. Thomas Juster

Income distribution

What are the principles which determine how the annual output of goods and services are distributed among the population? Are these principles fair? Do they promote efficiency? What do they imply about how the degree of inequality will change in the course of economic growth or in response either to the establishment of trade union or monopoly power or to different government policies? Will there be more or less poverty in the future? Many economists would say, along with David Ricardo, that distributional issues such as these are the central questions of all of economics.

The process out of which the income distribution emerges is dominated by the interaction between governments and markets. A government influences market allocations of material and human resources through its taxes (particularly corporate income taxes, property taxes, excise taxes, and capital gains and inheritance taxes), through its transfers (subsidies to selected industries, and to education and health, as well as payments through the social security and welfare systems), and through its regulatory policies (particularly the Federal Reserve System). Once the market has allocated resources and established resource prices, government taxes and transfers once again alter the income distribution (particularly through personal income taxes and transfers to those without marketable resources).

The Role of Markets

After nearly a century of intense debate, the main lines of what is now the orthodox distribution theory describing the role of markets were set down by Alfred Marshall near the close of the nineteenth century. Orthodox theory takes as its central question: What determines the prices at a point in time of each of the factors of production—labor, capital, entrepreneurship, and land? That is, what determines the wage rate, the interest rate, the profit rate, and the rental rate of land? The key contribution of Marshall and his contemporaries (particularly J. B. Clark) was to shift the question to prices in the present and away from shares in the future. Ricardo was intrigued by the question: What happens to the share of income going to landlords in the course of economic growth? Marx was interested primarily in the share of income decades in the future going to capital. Shifting the question away from shares brought income distribution under the general theory of price—i.e., the determination of the trading ratio at which supply and demand are equilibrated. Of course, once the price and equilibrium quantities determined by supply and demand are known, it is a small additional step to reckoning shares.

As orthodox economists see it, the key attribute which characterizes factor prices in equilibrium is that each factor is paid according to its contribution to the value of output. To see how this works, consider what would happen were this not the case. Employed workers whose productivity exceeded or could exceed their wage would find themselves being bid for and find their wages raised. Workers who did not produce what they cost would be fired. From such homely examples powerful implications follow. First, many would take the resulting distribution of income to be equitable—each is paid according to how diligently and effectively he or she contributes to meeting the desires of everyone else as expressed in the market. Furthermore, this distribution supports efficiency—each factor is bid into its highest and best use.

From the beginning, the idea that a market economy, capitalist or socialist, generates a fair but unequal income distribution has been controversial. Both critics and enthusiasts for markets have raised objections. Market advocates point to the impediments which make for less-than-perfect factor markets: trade unions, monopolistic resource sellers, monopsonistic buyers, race and sex discrimination, central bank control of interest rates, distortionary taxes on income from capital, and so on. Also, nearly all market advocates admit to the difficulties of calculating the productivity of a factor at the margin.

Nonbelievers come in many forms. At present, the most outspoken critics are followers of Joan Robinson or John Rawls.

The Robinsonians, or post-Keynesians, start from the difficulty of calculating marginal products. Going further than the orthodox critics they believe that orthodox theory is not consistent. The theory is alleged to be wrong at its foundations. They contend that the outputs of factors of production working jointly cannot be partitioned among those separate factors, even analytically —that it cannot even be presumed that as more of one factor is added to, its productivity necessarily declines. In the market, these theorists continue, this ambiguity results in a conflict over shares among powerful coalitions (landlords, laborers, capitalists), with the bargaining power at the moment and the political skills of the contestants determining the outcome. In the hands of the post-Keynesians, then, distribution theory returns to the determinants of shares. It is not surprising that they have redirected attention to Ricardo's work.

John Rawls and his followers have taken a different line of attack. Rawls simply rejects the ethical postulates of the orthodox view. Allocating the output of an economy to those who produce it in accordance to their contribution to output violates Rawls's view of justice—such rules of the game are simply not fair. It is not fair, he argues, that those born smarter or stronger than others should receive a larger share of output, even if they have contributed more to that output, unless it can be shown that such rules benefit those who are least productive. If such benefit cannot be so shown, and Rawls clearly doubts that it can, then other rules need to be devised. Devising alternative fair rules constitutes one frontier of the theory of income distribution.

The critics have been politically effective. No government now simply accepts the distribution of income as generated by markets. On the contrary, all governments now actively seek to affect income distribution.

The Role of Governments

Whether governments can alter the distribution of income in the long run has been debated by economists since John Stuart Mill. Around the turn of this century, V. Pareto was putting forth empirical support for his law—a law which held that inequality was roughly the same in all countries. Contemporary studies find that, by most measures, inequality tends to remain the same in any one country over remarkably long periods. Inequality does, however, differ from country to country. Inequality also appears to respond to economic development (increasing at first and then decreasing), and governments, it appears, can have some influence over inequality. While it is technically difficult for governments to significantly alter the distribution of incomes, the major difficulties appear to be political. In most developed countries, tax systems tend to be proportional, rather than progressive, for example, and that approach appears to be primarily a political decision. Similarly, transfer systems tend to benefit large segments of the population, not just the poor. If taxes were progressive and transfers were target-efficient, inequality would be less, but reducing inequality is not generally the most important economic objective of Western governments.

References

Atkinson, A. B., *The Economics of Inequality*, Clarendon, Oxford, 1975; Bronfrenbrenner, M., *Income Distribution Theory*, Aldine, Chicago, 1971; Weintraub, S. (ed.), *Income Inequality*, The Annals of the American Academy of Political and Social Science, vol. 409, Philadelphia, September 1973.

(*See also* Factors of production; Income; Lorenz curve; Negative income tax; Poverty; Social security programs; Taxation, an overview)

Eugene Smolensky

Income statement (see **Financial statements**)

Incomes policy

An incomes policy is a policy aimed at reducing inflation by restraining the growth and by influencing the relative shares of nominal incomes, such as wages and profits. Incomes policies are typically used as a supplement to traditional monetary and fiscal policies. The term incomes policy refers to a varied group of policy actions through which the government attempts to slow the growth of nominal income—hence its name—by directly influencing wages and prices. It can have many forms, and it can be comprehensive or selective in its application. It is generally recognized that incomes policies cannot serve as a substitute for fiscal and monetary restraint.

Types of Incomes Policies

The mildest form of government wage and price restraint is the public monitoring of wage-price decisions. The monitoring agency obtains information—either after the fact or through voluntary or mandatory prenotification—and analyzes it. The agency's ability to restrain inflationary behavior is rooted in (1) its ability to rally public opinion and (2) the offending parties' sensitivity to adverse public reaction. A well-established strategy for rallying public opinion is public exhortation ("jawboning") by the President. Available evidence indicates that this type of incomes policy has had little impact on wage and price movements.

A second type of incomes policy is voluntary wage-price guidelines. It is similar to public monitoring except that a general standard for wage and/or price movements is established. The general wage standard is usually a function of overall, longer-term movements in labor productivity, movements in consumer prices, or a combination of the two. For example, the guide for noninflationary wage behavior may stipulate that the allowable rate of increase in industry wage rates be equal to the trend rate of overall productivity growth, possibly adjusted to take into account some proportion of the increase in overall prices above a certain rate. There is no consensus about the effect of the guidelines in restraining inflation. Advocates of such guidelines argue that they are more effective in restraining wage and price inflation than public monitoring alone because they stiffen the resistance of firms to excessive wage increases and permit a more persuasive case to be made to the public. Critics argue that they may exacerbate inflation by placing a floor below all wage increases.

A third type of incomes policy offers incentives—in the form of tax cuts, social programs, etc.—to parties that maintain their wage and price increases below a predetermined standard. A principal issue in the design of such a program is the determination of the size and nature of the incentives and the standard. The standard is typically some combination of the longer-term productivity growth trend and the current rate of inflation. A further issue is how a tax reduction or spending increase is to be financed. Government deficits, if they are not properly coordinated with other policies, can be a source of inflation; therefore, the plan could be self-defeating. A necessary ingredient to these programs is a desire on the part of both management and labor to move from bilateral determination of wages and prices to a tripartite process that includes public representation.

Examples of this type of incomes policy include the Okun plan (1977), the Dutch Central Agreement of 1973, and the Construction Industry Stabilization Committee (CISC) (1971). While the Okun plan has yet to be tried, incentive-based social contracts to restrain wage and price increases have had widespread use in Europe. The European experience suggests that incentive-based social contracts work best in the short run under conditions of excess supply. The CISC, which operated during a period of excess supply of union labor, was able to achieve notable success in constraining construction wage increases. Moreover, the desire to move to a tripartite relationship was the motivating force in the formation of the CISC and was essential to its operation. Some adverse impact on resource allocation is inevitable in a program that applies a fixed incentive schedule on a widespread basis. The distortion from the market solution should be kept moderate, however, by the voluntary nature of these programs. Individual firms and workers, or their representatives, are still making wage-price decisions.

A fourth type of incomes policy imposes penalties—principally tax surcharges—on parties that increase wages and prices by more than a predetermined standard. Such programs vary in the determination of the standard, the size and nature of the penalty, and the coverage. Western democracies have experimented little with the penalty approach, confining their attention to incentive-based systems for inducing wage-price restraint. Three examples of proposed penalty-based programs are the tax-based incomes policy (TIP) of Henry Wallich, Sidney Weintraub, and L. Seidman, the wage-increase permits (WIP) of Abba Lerner, and final-offer bargaining.

The tax-based incomes policy would restrain wage and price increases by imposing a progressive tax surcharge on firms that had granted wage increases greater than a predetermined standard. The government guideline would reflect nationwide productivity gains plus some proportion of the current inflation rate. Firms would be free to give larger increases; if such increases were granted, however, the firm would have to pay a surcharge on its corporate income tax equal to some multiple of that portion of the wage increase which was over the guideline. A variation of the basic TIP concept attempts to combine penalties and incentives for wage restraint into a single program. Progressive rebates on the payroll tax for wage increases below the standard are added to the TIP program; the rebate would rise inversely to the average wage increase relative to the norm.

The wage-increase-permit plan is another variant of the TIP concept. Rather than use the tax system for imposing penalties, however, the wage-increase-permit plan uses the market system. The plan would penalize firms willing to increase their wage rates above a predetermined standard by requiring them to purchase, on the open market, permits issued by the government authorizing such increases. This plan also incorporates incentives for wage restraint; that is, income may be derived from selling of the permits by firms that raise wages less than the standard.

Final-offer bargaining is a variation of compulsory arbitration, except that it penalizes extreme positions taken in negotiations. The arbitrator does not determine a settlement but, rather, selects the most reasonable of the two final positions submitted by both parties if the negotiating process has reached an impasse. All three of these penalty-based programs rely, in part, on market forces and avoid explicit regulation of prices, on the assumption that over the long run prices reflect a constant percentage markup over unit costs. Therefore, these types of plans tend to minimize the disequilibrium conditions and consequent distortions that are characteristic of some other incomes policies.

A final type of incomes policy is mandatory controls. Mandatory controls are fundamentally different from the plans described so far in that the wage and/or price decision is imposed on the parties with fines or imprisonment as the penalty for not complying. As with the other, less stringent programs, the various approaches to mandatory controls differ in the determination of the appropriate wage-price change, in the penalties imposed, and in the program coverage. In general, some degree of distortion in the structure of wages and prices occurs with mandatory controls because they tend to freeze relative prices and wages and, as a result, immobilize the market mechanism. As conditions change, shortages and surpluses are created, and the controls typically break down. Breakdowns tend to occur proportionately earlier when less effective fiscal and monetary restraint have been used.

History of Incomes Policy

The use of incomes policies spans almost all recorded history. In Egypt, Babylon, Sumeria, China, India, Greece, and Rome various forms of regulations over the economy were tried; in general, they were not successful. One of the best-known examples in the ancient world is the comprehensive wage-price program set up by the Edict of Diocletian. In the Middle Ages, prices were widely prescribed by guilds and governments. In colonial times, unsuccessful attempts were made to control prices directly. During the nineteenth century, however, the principle of free trade prevailed and prices were allowed to fluctuate with the market.

United States Experience in the Twentieth Century

In most wartime periods, including the Revolutionary War, mandatory controls have been employed partly to allocate resources to the war effort. During World War I selective controls were imposed on prices and wages, although no formal statute was enacted. During World War II a comprehensive mandatory controls program, which initially froze prices and wages, was put into effect by the major nations. The freeze was followed by tight regulations on margins, prices, and wages, particularly in the United States, United Kingdom, Canada, Australia, and Germany. During the Korean conflict United States prices and wages were partially controlled, first by a general wage-price freeze and then by mandatory controls on prices for selected items. The controls period ended in 1953.

No explicit incomes policy existed in the United States between the Korean war period and the early 1960s. Then, in 1962 the Kennedy administration established guideposts for noninflationary wage and price behavior. The guideposts involved voluntary standards for wage and price increases and thus were less formal than those used during the war periods. A more aggressive incomes policy was initiated in March 1971 when the Construction Industry Stabilization Committee, a tripartite group, was established to reduce the rapid wage inflation in the construction industry.

In an attempt to bring down the inflation rate for the economy as a whole, the Nixon administration imposed mandatory wage and price controls in August 1971 for the first time in a peacetime period. The controls, which began as a comprehensive 90-day freeze on all wages, prices, and profits, were followed by several phases of selective wage-price controls that remained in effect until April of 1974; they were part of what was referred to as the New Economic Policy. In the last phase, which began early in 1973, the controls became largely voluntary in nature. Shortly after the end of the formal controls the Nixon administration turned to the mildest form of incomes policy, organizing the Council on Wage and Price Stability (CWPS) to monitor and analyze inflationary problems in specific sectors of the economy.

A more active incomes policy was not initiated again until the voluntary anti-inflation program of the Carter administration starting in 1977. At first the program consisted only of public exhortation and budget recommendations. When this effort failed to slow the pace of inflation, however, the program was formally strengthened in October 1978 with voluntary wage and price standards, regulatory reform, and changes in federal budgetary policy.

Foreign Experience

The use of incomes policy has been more prevalent in Europe than in the United States. Since World War II most European countries have experimented with various types of programs. During much of the postwar period, the United Kingdom has tried many different incomes policies including a wage freeze in 1948 to 1950, a voluntary compliance policy in 1961, a pay freeze and controls in 1966 to 1969, pay controls in 1972 to 1974, and in 1975 to 1978 the pay norms known as the "social contract." (Canada employed a similar program between 1975 and 1978.) The common pattern with British programs has been initial success in holding back wages followed by a release of pent-up wage pressures.

In the Netherlands incomes policies have generally involved extensive government intervention. The Dutch Central Agreement of 1973, which was signed by the central organizations of employers and trade unions, established a target cost-of-living increase for 1973. The incentives which were offered in exchange for this agreement were far-reaching. To name a few, the government agreed to leave unchanged the lowest rate of the value-added tax, contain the costs arising from the implementation of the Social Relief Work Act, show restraint in raising public-sector prices and tariffs, and encourage investment and employment in less-developed regions. Denmark initiated a partial freeze on wages, prices, profit margins, and dividends in 1962 to control inflation. In 1968 and 1970 it depended on wage norms and price freezes. Austria also has set up wage and price agreements. Israel has a history of extensive wage and price controls. Incentive-based social contracts to restrain price and wage increases were set up by the Irish National Agreement in 1970 and Finland's Stabilization Agreement in 1968.

France relied on price control as a method of indirect wage control and as an anti-inflation device in the postwar period. In addition, it offered incentives for wage restraint in the late 1960s. A 3-month freeze on prices and wages was implemented in 1977, coupled with a ceiling on wage and price increases. In contrast to France, the West German incomes policy has relied since the early 1960s solely on wage guidelines. The guidelines were set up by the Council of Economic Experts beginning in 1965 to keep wage growth consistent with the growth of the economy. Sweden, on the other hand, has had no formal incomes policy except at the end of the 1960s, when a price freeze was initiated prior to the 1970 elections. Instead, the parties to the centralized system of collective bargaining have taken responsibility for containing wage movements. In Italy no systematic attempt has been made to develop an incomes policy, although an emergency freeze on wages was imposed from 1946 to 1947.

Australia had wage indexation from 1921 to 1953. The indexing of wages was renewed in 1975 and continues today. There was, however, no active government policy of controls for the three decades up to 1973. In 1973, the Prices Justification Tribunal was established to administer voluntary price controls. In April 1977, the Australian government imposed a freeze on prices and wages. The freeze was voluntary in nature and gained very little support. It was abandoned, just 41 days after its inception, as a failure.

The Soviet economy has operated with total wage and price controls for more than 50 years. Its planned economy has not permitted any form of market price structure since the 1920s.

Importance of Incomes Policy in Economics

The search for a means to reconcile full employment and reasonable price stability has preoccupied economists and policymakers of most advanced industrial countries for many years. In attempts to solve the problem of inflation, most of these nations have experimented with various forms of incomes policies. Incomes policies represent a direct attack on wages and prices and thus can improve the trade-off between inflation and unemployment and break inflation expectations, at least in the short run. They are used as a supplement to monetary and fiscal policies in achieving price stability and full employment. Incomes policies include guideposts, guidelines, standards or norms, and mandatory controls. It is generally recognized that incomes policies cannot serve as a substitute for fiscal and monetary restraint.

Positive and Negative Views of Incomes Policy

Views on the effectiveness of incomes policies are mixed. On the positive side, it is maintained that they reduce the pace of inflation. In addition, incomes policies may improve the inflation-unemployment trade-off that results from the use of standard monetary and fiscal policies, and they may stiffen the resistance of firms to excessive wage increases. Restrictive monetary and fiscal policies could slow the pace of inflation, but could also produce substantial unemployment. Moreover, incomes policies are purported to dampen inflation expectations. This will be reflected in interest rates, wage contracts, and other economic decisions, and thus will influence inflation and overall economic activity. Incomes policies are important in handling the problems associated with allocation and capacity constraints during wartime. They help to allocate materials and encourage production for the war effort while restraining aggregate demand through selective controls on wages, prices, credit, and profits. In addition, they provide a means to redistribute income other than through the tax system. The latter has been a goal of some European policies but does not apply to the experience of the United States.

On the negative side, there are, however, many problems associated with incomes policies which in the past have led to their demise. In general, it appears that incomes policies reduce the pace of inflation only temporarily, generally early in the program; after a period of time support wanes. As conditions change, shortages and surpluses are created and administrative problems and costs become more complex.

A principal issue in the design of incomes policies is the determination of the standards and the coverage of the program and, for some programs, the incentives and/or penalties. There does not appear to be any fair set of standards that is both specific for and applicable to many situations. If the rules are specific, they lack flexibility and may cause distortions and inequities; if they are too general, they may be difficult to apply. In addition, they usually do not distinguish between inflationary and non-inflationary wage increases. It has also been suggested that the rules may set a floor below all wage increases.

The amount of coverage is another problem in designing an incomes policy. It is not clear what type of income and how much of the economy should be covered. If all incomes, including profits, interest income, and rents, and all sectors of the economy are covered, the program is difficult to set up and is subject to avoidance and inefficiencies. Incomes policies, in most cases, require costly administration and enforcement that generally increase over time. These costs are borne by the private sector and are reflected as well in increased federal budget expenditures. The costs to the private sector, although difficult to measure, have been estimated to be significant. The budget costs of incomes policies depend on the size and administration of the program.

Most importantly, incomes policies—particularly mandatory controls—may distort product and labor markets because the norm has only a tenuous relation to the behavior of market forces. On the one hand, incomes policies can lead to misallocations of resources since demand for the output of a given industry probably will not be consistent with a given program's pricing practice. In addition, experience suggests that some forms of incomes policies result in inefficiencies in production by causing or exacerbating shortages of products which in turn eventually result in higher prices than otherwise would have occurred. That is, incomes policies may delay increases in supplies because firms are not induced by higher profitability to expand supply. Moreover, by inhibiting relative price movements incomes policies make it difficult to detect signals indicating relative scarcity, thereby preventing the market from efficiently allocating resources. Price adjustments to supply and demand conditions are delayed, but eventually prices will find their equilibrium. The adjustment may be evidenced in a price bulge after the program is disbanded. On the other hand, policy-induced distortions may create inequities. Inequities occur when the policy is not applied evenhandedly, for example, between labor and management or among different sectors of the economy. They also are likely to occur as a consequence of the obstacles to adjustment created by the program. The view also exists that under such policies wages are more tightly controlled than are prices or profits. Incomes policies also may undermine the philosophy of the free market in that they may cause dislocations in capital formation and investment because they negate the profit motive.

In addition, incomes policies may encourage overly expansive monetary and fiscal policies. If they temporarily suppress inflationary signals, demand policies may be more expansive than otherwise would have occurred. Moreover, they do not counter demand-pull inflation mainly because business and labor will not cooperate when labor markets are tight; as a result, production bottlenecks may occur unless relative prices are allowed to rise where necessary. Furthermore, the effect of an incomes policy is weakened in periods with large exogenous price shocks—for example, for food and energy—that emphasize the limitations of, and erode the real wages implicit in, the policy. Price shocks may set off a wage-price spiral and generally are insensitive to control by aggregate demand measures. In such periods, incomes policies may provoke a number of labor union strikes for pay increases in excess of the government-established standard. Incomes policies in general cover up the real causes of inflation and mask the need for structural reform. Finally, voluntary controls may revive the fear of direct controls.

Based upon these positive and negative views of incomes policy, there appear to be several necessary conditions for enhancing the success of the policies in restraining increases in prices and wages. First, in order for incomes policies to be viable, they must command widespread respect and assent among both decision makers and the public. Second, they are generally more successful in periods of substantial unused capacity in the economy and operate more efficiently in the short run. Third, they are more effective in controlling inflation when there is an absence of major exogenous shocks in commodity prices and when they are coordinated with other economic policies.

References

Galbraith, John Kenneth, *A Theory of Price Control*, Harvard University Press, Cambridge, Mass., 1952; Mills, Daniel Quinn, *Government, Labor and Inflation: Wage Stabilization in the United States*, University of Chicago Press, Chicago, 1975; Okun, A. M., "The Great Stagflation Swamp," *Challenge*, vol. 20, November/December 1977, pp. 6–13; Stein, Herbert, "Price-Fixing as Seen by a Price-Fixer: Part II," in William Fellner (project director), *Contemporary Economic Problems*, American Enterprise Institute, Washington, D.C., 1978; Ulman, L., and R. J. Flanagan, *Wage Restraint: A Study of Incomes Policies in Western Europe*, University of California Press, Berkeley, 1971; Wallich, H. C., and S. Weintraub, "A Tax-Based Incomes Policy," *Journal of Economic Issues*, vol. 45, June 1971, pp. 1–19.

(*See also* Council on Wage and Price Stability; Federal Reserve policy; Fiscal policy; Indexation; Inflation; Monetary policy)

Henry C. Wallich and Rosemary Rainey

Increasing costs (*See* Diminishing returns law)

Increasing returns law (*See* Economies of scale)

Index numbers

Two different approaches can be distinguished in the study of index numbers: the statistical, which deals with their construction, and the purely economic, which deals with the theoretical foundations of the indexes.

An index number is a statistical measure of the percentage change observed in a single or composite variable. The comparisons may be chronological, geographical, or categorical. The majority of index numbers have been constructed to provide a dimensionless measure of the time path of economic phenomena such as prices, production, wages, imports, and exports. The price and production indexes, which are time series, have been in use longer than other indexes and are the best known.

Those with greatest influence on policymaking are the consumer price index (CPI); the producer price index (PPI), formerly the wholesale price index (WPI); and the implicit price deflator (IPD) for the gross national product.

The most familiar index is probably the consumer price index, which measures price changes of a constant market basket of goods and services over time. The constant basket is periodically revised to ensure that it is representative of the actual spending habits of the population to which it relates. The CPI is widely applied and it serves various purposes. Because the CPI measures price changes at the final level of consumer demand, it is often used as an index of inflation and serves as an economic indicator to evaluate the success or failure of economic policies. A second use of the CPI is as a deflator of other economic series. A third use of the CPI is as an escalator of various forms of income in order to maintain the purchasing power of the income recipients. In this use, the CPI is considered as a cost-of-living index although, technically, it is not a true cost-of-living index. In effect, it does not reflect the various substitutions that consumers tend to make in order to maintain their standard of living in the face of changing market conditions.

The PPI measures price changes of goods sold at the primary market level. The prices are basically those charged by manufacturers or wholesalers to retailers or to other distributors. Another important member of the family of price indexes is the IPD, which acquired relevance as an outcome of the development and implementation of the system of national accounts. Several types of the PPI can be obtained by performing an appropriate sectoral disaggregation of the IPD.

Another type of index of wide application in economics is that of the change in production over time. The index of industrial production is perhaps the best known and it measures changes in the physical volume of output in manufacturing, mining and utilities. The two major subgroups of manufacturers are durables and nondurables.

In international trade, in addition to the import and export price and volume indexes there is the terms of trade (TT). It purports to measure the relative change in the price system of the goods being exported by a country with respect to the price system of the goods being imported. This index is used in the assessment of imported or exported inflation, and it was extensively discussed in the post-World War II debates between developing and developed nations.

Construction of an Index Number

Elementary Indexes The first step in the construction of an index number is to define its purpose. The purpose of the index determines (1) the variables to be included, (2) the sources of the data, (3) the collection of the data, and (4) the formula for calculating the index.

If the index is intended to measure, say, price, production, or sales changes affecting a single variable, it can be directly defined and measured as the ratio of the observed prices, physical volumes of production, or dollar values of sales at the different periods of time. These ratios are called price relatives, quantity relatives, or value relatives and are elementary indexes. In general, the elementary index or relative of a single variable X at time t, with the base period 0, is $I_{t/o}(X) = X_t/X_o$. From the definition of a relative the important property of circularity is deduced. This property means that the change in X can be measured between any two different dates and not only between the base and the current periods. Circularity implies the time-reversal property, which means that if the order of the dates to be compared is changed, the new index is the reciprocal of the old index; and the linkage property, which means that the index $I_{t/o}(X)$ can be obtained by the successive multiplication of relatives that measure the change between two consecutive dates.

Composite Indexes   An index that measures the total change of a set of variables is called a composite index. The fundamental problem of a composite index is to find the appropriate formula to measure the average movement of the relatives. If the relatives are not scattered, the composite index is easy to measure and has a concrete meaning, whereas if the relatives are highly scattered, then no composite index provides a good representation. The most widely applied formulas for constructing a composite index were proposed by the German economists, E. Laspeyres in 1864 and H. Paasche in 1874.

The Laspeyres composite index is a weighted arithmetic average of elementary indexes, where the weights are constant and they measure the relative importance of each component at the base period 0. That is,

$$L_{t/o}(X) = \sum_{i=1}^{n} w_{io} I_{t/o}(X_i) \tag{1}$$

where X is the variable that results from the composition of n other variables, and X_i and w_{io} are the weights given to the component variables at the base period 0. The sum of the weights w_{io} is equal to 1.

The Paasche composite index is a weighted harmonic average of elementary indexes, where the weights are constant and they measure the relative importance of each component at the current period t. That is,

$$\frac{1}{P_{t/o}(X)} = \sum_{i=1}^{n} \frac{w_{it}}{I_{t/o}(X_i)} = \sum_{i=1}^{n} w_{it} I_{o/t}(X_i) \tag{2}$$

where
$$\sum_i w_{it} = 1$$

In 1899, A. L. Bowley proposed to combine the Laspeyres and Paasche indexes to obtain a new index that I. Fisher (1927) called "ideal" because it fulfilled certain properties. The ideal index is the geometric mean of the Laspeyres and Paasche indexes. In symbols,

$$I_{t/o}(X) = \sqrt{L_{t/o}(X)\, P_{t/o}(X)} \tag{3}$$

If the set of weights w_{io} and w_{it} are equal, then the Laspeyres index, which is an arithmetic average, is larger than the Paasche index, which is a harmonic average. The Laspeyres index will be smaller than the Paasche index if the relative weights w_i of the various components tend to decrease for those components with high elementary indexes and tend to increase for those components with low elementary indexes. None of the three indexes, Laspeyres, Paasche, or Fisher's ideal index, fulfills the circularity property. The ideal index, however, fulfills the time-reversal property discussed above.

Value and Price Indexes

The composite value index for a set of n commodities is, by definition,

$$I_{t/o}(V) = \frac{\sum_{i=1}^{n} p_{it}q_{it}}{\sum_{i=1}^{n} p_{io}q_{io}} \tag{4}$$

The composite price indexes using the Laspeyres and Paasche formulas are, respectively,

$$L_{t/o}(P) = \frac{\sum_{i} p_{it}q_{io}}{\sum_{i} p_{io}q_{io}} \tag{5}$$

$$P_{t/o}(P) = \frac{\sum_{i} p_{it}q_{it}}{\sum_{i} p_{io}q_{it}} \tag{6}$$

Formulas (5) and (6) are related to (4) as follows: The two price indexes are equivalent to the total value index if the quantities of this latter are held constant. In the Laspeyres formula the constant quantities correspond to the base period 0; and in the Paasche formula, to the current period t. Similar kinds of equivalence are observed for quantity indexes where the prices are kept constant and the quantities vary.

The composite price indexes shown in (5) and (6) are constructed by computing aggregate values, and, as such, they show the relative change in the total value (total expenditure) of a given set of commodities that results from differences in prices between the current and the base periods. By introducing a simple transformation, formulas (5) and (6) can be equivalently expressed as weighted averages of price relatives, where the weights are value or expenditure weights. In effect,

$$L_{t/o}(P) = \frac{\sum_{i} p_{io}q_{io}\,(p_{it}/p_{io})}{\sum_{i} p_{io}q_{io}} \tag{7}$$

$$P_{t/o}(P) = \frac{\sum_{i} p_{it}q_{it}}{\sum_{i} p_{it}q_{it}\,(p_{io}/p_{it})} \tag{8}$$

Price indexes constructed as weighted averages of elementary indexes are valuable for analyzing the impact of the price change of a single item or a subgroup of items on the global price movement.

The discrepancy between the Laspeyres and Paasche price indexes was calculated by the statistician L. V. Bortkiewicz in 1924. The formula for the discrepancy between the two price indexes is:

$$P_{t/o}(P) - L_{t/o}(P) = \text{cov}\,\frac{I_{t/o}(p_i),\,I_{t/o}(q_i)}{L_{t/o}(Q)} \tag{9}$$

The discrepancy is the weighted covariance between the price and quantity relatives. The Paasche index is: (1) smaller than the Laspeyres index if, on average, price and quantity vary in opposite directions; (2) greater than the Laspeyres index if, on average, price and quantity vary in the same direction; and (3) equal to the Laspeyres index if there is no correlation between price and quantity.

Constant-Utility Price Index

The constant-utility price index can be considered the true cost-of-living index but is still an abstract concept of economic theory. The elements involved cannot be obtained from only price and quantity data, and, thus, the index cannot be estimated in practice. The Laspeyres and Paasche indexes are used as rough approximations instead.

The constant-utility price index is a measure of the change in prices of a set of commodities that produce constant utility or satisfaction to an individual consumer assumed to be a utility maximizer. The members of the set do not need to be identical, but their utility to the consumer must always be the same. The constant-utility price index is, thus, strictly confined to an individual consumer with a fixed preference map. The preference map comprises two sets of intersecting functions —one made of convex indifference surfaces, and the other made of Engel curves. The indifference surfaces correspond to a given level of utility, and points on a given surface show the various combinations of goods and services that provide constant utility or satisfaction to the consumer. The Engel curves cut across the indifference surfaces and show how purchases change as the consumer's income increases at constant market prices. The assumption is made that the consumer always balances his or her budget, given income and the market prices. For this the consumer chooses the quantities and set of commodities that maximize utility. The constant-utility price index is then the quotient of two budgets or expenditures at optimal level for different market prices but that give a constant utility.

References

Allen, R. G. D., *Index Numbers in Theory and Practice*, Aldine, Chicago, 1975; Eichorn, W., R. Henn, O. Opitz, and R. W. Shephard (eds.), *Theory and Applications of Economic Indices*, Physica-Verlag-Würsburg, Germany, 1978; Fisher, F. W., and K. Shell, *The Economic Theory of Price Indices*, Academic Press, New York, 1972; Fisher, Irving: *The Making of Index Numbers*, Houghton Mifflin, Boston, 1927; Frisch, Ragnar: "Annual Survey of General Economic Theory: The Problem of Index Numbers," *Econometrica*, vol. 4, 1936, pp. 1–38.

(*See also* Consumer price index; Economic statistics; Forecasting methods; Implicit price deflator; Industrial production index; Inflation; Leading indicator approach to forecasting; Producer price index; Seasonal adjustment methods; Statistical techniques in economics and business, an overview; Time series analysis)

Estela Bee Dagum and Camilo Dagum

Indexation

Indexation is the tying of deferred payments to the value of an index, usually a price index. Cost-of-living adjustment (COLA) clauses in labor contracts, the linkage of interest and/or principal payments to the price level (indexed bonds), and the automatic adjustment of tax brackets for inflation are important examples of indexation. Of lesser importance are payments linked to the exchange rate, or the price of a particular commodity (for instance, gold or wheat).

Indexation makes it possible to use long-term contracts even when there is considerable uncertainty about the future price level, and, thus, the value of money. In practice, indexation has been most widespread in countries experiencing high rates of inflation, e.g., in Finland (until 1968), Israel, Brazil, and Argentina; however, there are few nonsocialist countries where there is no indexation of any sort. A. Braun (1976), H. Giersch (1974), and S. Page and S. Trollope (1974), provide details on the types and extent of indexation prevalent in recent years.

Index clauses have been used for centuries. Willard Fisher (1913) traced them back as far as 1747, when the Massachusetts Colony specified that interest and principal, and later wage, payments were to be based on the value of an index of corn, beef, wool, and leather prices.

Indexation in Practice

Wages Indexation of wages is common, though less so in the United States than elsewhere. In the late seventies in the United States, about 60 percent of workers covered by major union contracts had escalator clauses, but such workers constitute only about 10 percent of the work force. In some countries, such as Israel and Belgium, coverage by index clauses applies to almost all workers. Escalator clauses do not typically increase wages 1 percent for each 1 percent increase in the price index. The adjustment may be partial, or may have a cap, or upper bound. Adjustments to wages may be made at prespecified time intervals (monthly, quarterly, etc.) or when the price index has increased by some definite percentage since the base period (threshold agreements). Wage indexation tends to stabilize the real wage within the life of a contract; real-wage flexibility over longer periods need not be significantly affected by indexation, since real wages can be renegotiated at contract time.

Financial Instruments Indexation of financial instruments is less widespread than wage indexation. More or less comprehensive capital-market indexation has been used in Israel, Brazil, and Finland in the postwar period. Linked instruments have included savings deposits, long-term government bonds, and mortgages. Bonds linked to the price of the firm's own output (e.g., third-class railway tickets) were issued in France and Israel in the 1950s. The United Kingdom has since 1974 made indexed savings bonds available in small quantities to wage earners and pensioners.

It is noteworthy that no indexed bonds have been issued by private firms in the most developed capital markets in recent times, despite high rates of inflation, considerable public and professional discussion, and continuing innovation in the capital markets. Some of this innovation, such as the floating rate note, deals with problems caused by high and varying inflation by a means other than indexation. Reasons for the absence of privately issued index bonds remain unclear (Fischer, 1975, 1977a).

Social Security and Pensions   Social security payments and government pensions are indexed in many countries, including, since 1972, the United States. The linkage in the United States is to the consumer price index. Social security benefits are adjusted by legislative action. Private pensions are not generally indexed, in part because there is no financial instrument available to pension funds that will generate a safe real rate of return.

The Tax System   Indexation of tax brackets has been implemented in Canada and elsewhere, and bills to this end have been unsuccessfully introduced in the U.S. Congress. Indexation of the taxation of capital and profits is more difficult, both administratively and politically (Aaron, 1976). The essential notion would be to tax real interest and real capital gains. Political difficulties would arise in applying the same principle to the deductions for interest payments, since mortgage borrowers would lose most of their interest deduction. A similar issue arises in the case of the corporate income tax, where the question is whether only real interest payments would be deductible or, equivalently, whether corporations would be required to treat capital gains resulting from the fall in the real value of outstanding bonds, as income. In the case of depreciation allowances, indexation to the general price level would be simple.

A separate tax and indexation issue concerns the possible tax treatments of indexed bonds under the present tax system. The question is whether or not the indexed component of the payment on an indexed bond would be taxed at all, and if so, whether at the income tax rate or the capital gains rate. Presumably corporations would be treated symmetrically, that is, if the individual gets to treat the indexed portion as a capital gain, the corporation does not get to deduct it as an interest payment.

Other   Indexation is used in life insurance contracts, in rental agreements, and in long-term construction or manufacturing contracts. In the latter cases, payments are usually tied to specific components of the producer price index, and an attempt is made to match the type of product, or the costs of inputs for that product.

Theoretical Issues

Indexation has been supported by such distinguished economists as A. Marshall, S. Jevons, J. M., Keynes M. Friedman, and J. Tobin. Their arguments have generally been based on the efficiency of indexation as a means of removing inflation risk from long-term contracts, or on the distributional equity of doing so.

The major theoretical issue in the case of wage indexation concerns its effects on the stability of the economy. Over the lifetime of the labor contract, indexed wages tend to be problematic in real terms. Thus, any policies or adjustments relying on the flexibility of real wages will be hampered by wage indexation. Devaluation is the most important example. In some cases, governments have sought and obtained the suspension of indexation at the time of a devaluation. Policies that do not require real-wage flexibility could be helped by indexation. Gray (1976) and Fischer (1977b) have shown that indexed wages tend to stabilize the economy in the face of nominal disturbances, defined as those that in the presence of fully flexible prices would affect only equilibrium absolute prices. Similarly, indexation exacerbates the effects of real disturbances, which require a change in the real wage as part of the economic adjustment to them.

In 1974, the most recent occasion on which there was full discussion of the merits of indexing, the argument was that wage indexation would permit a more rapid deceleration of inflation with less unemployment by making nominal wages more responsive to policy-induced reductions in the price level (Friedman, 1974). By the same token, inflation would accelerate more rapidly, with less real output effect, as a result of expansionary aggregate demand policy. Fellner (1975) argues that index-ation is of little help in reducing the inflation rate, since the rate of price increase first has to be reduced in order to get the beneficial effects of the indexation.

Another important issue concerns the index to which wages and other contracts should be linked. Devaluation, and similarly the imposition of excise taxes to reduce aggregate demand, would be partly self-defeating if wages rose automatically in response to price increases resulting from such policy changes. Accordingly, the appropriate index to which to tie wages, from the viewpoint of the stability of the economy, would exclude imported goods and indirect taxes.

Other objections to wage indexation are based on the argument that indexation both increases the instability of the economy and increases the average rate of infla-tion by making more inflation necessary to achieve the same adjustment of real claims.

In the case of capital indexation, the major issues concern the effects of such indexation on total savings and on portfolio allocations. It has also been argued that indexation makes it possible to maintain the operation of the capital markets under inflationary conditions, and that stabilization policy could be improved by govern-ment issue of an indexed bond.

The effect of the availability of indexed instruments on total savings is theoreti-cally and empirically indeterminate. The availability of a safe asset would be likely to reduce the extent of portfolio shifts to real assets such as housing and gold in the presence of uncertain inflation. Of course, if the rate of inflation were certain, nom-inal interest rate adjustment could completely compensate for inflation.

Governments are well-placed to issue indexed bonds since their nominal reve-nues can be expected to increase with the price level. Private firms' willingness to issue indexed bonds would depend on the correlation of their earnings with the aggregate price level. Blinder (1977) has suggested that firms would be willing to tie interest payments to the price of their own outputs, and that a mutual fund of such bonds would provide a close approximation to an indexed bond. The willingness of firms to issue such bonds would depend on whether changes in their output prices are chiefly the result of demand or cost shifts, and on the tax treatment of such bonds.

In the absence of indexation, long-term lending and borrowing would tend to dry up as uncertainty about the inflation rate increased, and bond transactions would be concentrated at the short end of the maturity spectrum. It has often been suggested that the introduction of indexed bonds would adversely affect the equity markets, but there is no theoretical reason to think this. Little evidence can be brought on the point. Tobin (1963) suggests that government issue of an indexed bond would make it easier for the monetary authority to affect the rate of investment by providing it with control over the supply of an asset which is a close substitute for capital. One benefit of the introduction of government indexed bonds would be that the real interest rate would become a known number rather than, as at present, one that has to be (imperfectly) estimated.

Policy Issues

The main policy issues are concerned with whether or not the government should issue indexed bonds and index the tax system. The policy issue for wage indexation is whether or not it should be encouraged, in part by the government's indexing the wages of its own employees. This depends on the primary source of disturbances to the economy.

The most common argument against government support for indexation is that indexation would indicate that the government has given up the fight against inflation. This argument becomes less persuasive after a decade of inflation at more than 7 percent. Similarly, it is argued that indexation reduces the incentive to avoid inflation by making it easier to live with it.

Advocates of indexation of the tax system argue that government should not benefit from inflation by obtaining increased real revenues automatically as the reward for inflating; however, tax brackets have in practice been adjusted since the 1950s in such a way as to keep real brackets unchanged (Aaron, 1976). It is clear that the more serious inflation-induced distortions in the tax system arise on the side of capital income, and that tax reform in this area is a major undertaking.

Indexation of U.S. savings bonds has received wide support from American economists, at least on the grounds that current sales campaigns, to persuade the small saver to invest in a supposedly safe asset at a supposedly positive interest rate, are distasteful. At the same time, it should be recognized that social security is equivalent to the provision of indexed bonds in limited quantities to American workers. Few of the objections to government issue of a marketable indexed bond, such as its adverse effects on the ability of corporations to raise funds, would apply to a small experimental issue.

Continuation of inflation at high rates would likely lead in the United States to the continuing piecemeal introduction of indexation as inflation-induced distortions become more obvious and the prospect of their disappearance through the ending of inflation becomes less likely. But international experience shows that indexation arrangements are, at best, clumsy instruments for dealing with inflation.

References

Aaron, Henry J. (ed.), *Inflation and the Income Tax*, Brookings, Washington, D.C., 1976; Blinder, Alan S., "Indexing the Economy Through Financial Intermediation," in Karl Brunner and Allan Meltzer (eds.), *Stabilization of the Domestic and International Economy*, Carnegie-Rochester Conference Series on Public Policy, Vol. 5, North-Holland, Amsterdam, 1977; Braun, Anne R., "Indexation of Wages and Salaries in Developed Countries," *IMF Staff Papers*, International Monetary Fund, Washington, D.C., March 1976, pp. 226–271; Fellner, William, "The Controversial Issue of Comprehensive Indexation," in Herbert Giersch et al., *Essays on Inflation and Indexation*, American Enterprise Institute, Washington, D.C., 1974; Fischer, Stanley, "The Demand for Index Bonds," *Journal of Political Economy*, June 1975, pp. 509–534; Fischer, Stanley, "On the Non-Existence of Privately Issued Index Bonds in the United States Capital Market," in E. Lundberg (ed.), *Inflation Theory and Anti-Inflation Policy*, Macmillan, New York, 1977; Fischer, Stanley, "Wage Indexation and Macroeconomic Stability," in Brunner and Meltzer, op. cit.; Fisher, Irving, *Stabilizing the Dollar*, Macmillan, New York, 1920; Fisher, Willard, "The Tabular Standard in Massachusetts History," *Quarterly Journal of Economics*, May 1913, pp. 417–454; Friedman, Milton, "Monetary Correction," in Giersch, op. cit.; Giersch, Herbert, "Index Clauses and the Fight Against Inflation," in Giersch, op cit.; Gray, JoAnna, "Wage

Indexation: A Macroeconomic Approach," *Journal of Monetary Economics*, April 1976, pp. 221–235; Page, S. A. B., and Sandra Trollope, "An International Survey of Indexing and Its Effects," *National Institute Economic Review*, no. 70, 1974, pp. 46–60; Tobin, James, "An Essay on the Principles of Debt Management," in Commission on Money and Credit, *Fiscal and Debt Management Policies*, Prentice-Hall, Englewood Cliffs, N.J., 1963.

(*See also* Escalator clause; Incomes policy; Inflation)

Stanley Fischer

Indicator approach to forecasting (see **Leading indicator approach to forecasting**)

Individual income taxation (see **Taxation, an overview**)

Inducement to invest (see **Propensity to consume or to save and inducement to invest**)

Industrial concentration (see **Concentration of industry**)

Industrial production index

The industrial production index (IPI) is a comprehensive monthly measure of the physical quantity of goods produced at manufacturing, mining, and electric and gas utility plants. Two-thirds of their output is represented by (1) the highly cyclical products used as business equipment, durable consumer goods, and construction supplies, and (2) steel, textiles, and other industrial materials which are subject to large fluctuations in business inventories and foreign trade. The remaining one-third of the IPI is composed of nondurable consumer goods, defense and space products, and business supplies.

Comparative uses

The National Bureau of Economic Research has cited the IPI as the closest single measure of the U.S. business cycle, and it is one of the four components of the Bureau's composite index of cyclical coincident indicators. The greatest historical differences in U.S. cyclical behavior developed in the 1973–74 period when total employment continued to rise and the IPI was maintained until the autumn of 1974, while currently deflated economic series were reduced in late 1973, reflecting partly a probable overstatement of the price indexes following the end of federal price controls.

Combined output of the industrial sector in the United States amounts to a third or more of total gross national product (GNP), compiled by the U.S. Department of Commerce, and for a much larger portion of fluctuations in the total because of generally more stable output in the sectors of the economy which are not represented by industrial production—agriculture, construction, distribution, and services. This was illustrated from the third quarter of 1974 to the first quarter of 1975 when there were decreases of 14 percent in the IPI and 4 percent in constant-dollar GNP. Over longer-run periods the growth in industrial production has also been greater than in GNP, but not in the accompanying employment numbers reflecting usually smaller labor productivity growth recorded in the rest of the economy.

Media and other public interest in economic affairs is usually confined to changes in the broadest total measures having political implications. On the other hand, analysts should be concerned with all of the informational aspects of economic measures. Thus, they would also want to compare quarterly industrial production movements with nonfarm goods output which is the closest published GNP component and to examine the other more detailed available data on differences in scope and changes in inventories, foreign trade, and price indexes affecting the alternative measures.

Industrial production data relate only to the industrial plant level—except for the utility series which include distribution—and they include potential exports. In order to derive changes in domestic new supplies of goods, exports are subtracted and imports added to the IPI. The broader current GNP data are based on final purchases—including imports—of consumers, business firms, and government agencies which are deflated and adjusted for changes in inventories. Thus, GNP goods represent distribution outlays as well as industrial and farm production, and exports need to be added and imports subtracted. Since there are many fewer industrial producers than final purchasers, and since changes in price indexes and in inventories involve additional measurement problems, the currently published changes for the IPI have been subject to smaller revisions than those for GNP goods.

Construction of the IPI

The primary IPI structure is based on establishment reports grouped in accordance with the standard industrial classification, e.g., textile mill products and transportation equipment. These groups are most appropriate for comparison with data on employment and dollar shipments by type of industry and for indicated changes in industrial productivity and unit labor costs. About 30 industry groupings have been published since 1947, a few of which have been published since 1919.

In addition, all industrial production series are classified by primary type of market use. These groupings are given precedence in publication and review, and are the basis for determining changes in the seasonally adjusted total IPI. Fifty-seven market groups are published currently, some dating back to 1939. Such major groups of products as consumer goods and business equipment are also combined with gross value weights for more appropriate comparisons with final sales of those products. Additional market groups are published for monthly comparisons with construction activity, defense expenditures, and energy supplies and use. Such comparisons by stage of processing or sale may indicate production imbalances reflecting excessive changes in inventories; the broadest of these over major cyclical time intervals has been the accumulated differences in movements between the total materials and products groups. In addition, historical changes in industrial production materials in relationship to plant capacity data, when adjusted for foreign trade flows, provide the most adequate measures of U.S. industrial capacity utilization—except in wartime.

Compilation

The IPI was originated by the staff of the Federal Reserve Board in the early 1920s, and with various improvements in scope and compilation has continued to be published by the Federal Reserve. Most foreign industrial countries compile similar indexes patterned on a United Nations study (1950).

Summary monthly industrial production data are initially estimated for publication about the fifteenth of the following month. Preliminary detailed figures are published a month later and accompanied by monthly indexes of electric power use by 134 groupings of industrial plants on the basis of reports to the Federal Reserve System. A computer program for industrial production provides 4 months' printed figures for about 7000 lines of aggregates and indexes within an hour for editing and interpretation.

Industrial production data are regularly published as index numbers (i.e., percentages) of production in a recent comparison year (at this writing, 1967) as 100. The resulting figures since 1967 are based on 235 individual series which are combined with Census-reported value-added dollar weights totaling $304 billion in 1967. The resulting figures can also be expressed in constant-dollar value-added amounts or, when gross dollar weights are employed for combining final and intermediate products, in gross value terms. In addition, the IPI weight structure can be reprogrammed with alternative data to provide special-purpose, seasonally adjusted monthly indicators of resource requirements, such as steel tonnage, or of resource output, such as energy in British thermal units.

Nearly half of the industrial production series are compiled from available monthly physical product data, such as tons of coal and steel and the number of autos assembled and kilowatthours of electricity generated as reported by various government and trade agencies. These product data are converted to daily averages for monthly compilation purposes.

The remaining series are derived from extrapolations of historical relationships based on two types of monthly input data. The first type is industrial electric power use—these series represent one-third of total industrial production and do not include the heaviest power users such as the aluminum and paper industries; the remaining one-fifth of total industrial production is based on production worker-hours (U.S. Department of Labor). The monthly extrapolations are generally small, smoothly changing factors subject to current review based on related data and subsequent adjustments to data from the Census Bureau's Annual Survey of Manufactures and the quinquennial Censuses of Manufactures and Minerals.

Revisions

The Census data are the basis for periodic, detailed revisions of all manufacturing and mining series and groups, where necessary, to the levels of comprehensive measures, extending back to 1919. The Censuses are also the principal source for the weight data used to combine the individual series, while the annual value and output data available for the utility series are sufficiently comprehensive.

The detailed IPI weight data have been periodically updated (from 1919 to 1923, 1937, 1939, 1947, 1954, 1958, 1963, and 1967) and the resulting aggregates linked at each revision to provide continuous series. This procedure yields more appropriate value relationships over long periods, but it means that any regrouping of series before 1967 must use the matching weight-base data and be relinked.

For the recent period the 1967 value-added data are shown as proportions of total industrial production in the initial columns of the monthly release. These proportions can be multiplied by the indexes to calculate aggregates to determine the contribution of changes in any series or group to changes in any larger group or total industrial production.

Seasonal adjustments for individual series are calculated by use of the Census X-11 method. The published seasonally adjusted total IPI results allow for cyclical-change problems affecting the computer-method results and also permit flexible current review of the summary market and industry results. Finally, it may be noted that the amount of revision in the total IPI has averaged 0.2 percent between the original estimate and the third monthly published figure over the past 5 years.

References

Board of Governors, Federal Reserve System, *Industrial Production*, 1971; Board of Governors, Federal Reserve System, *Industrial Production*, 1976; *Index Numbers of Industrial Production*, Statistical Office of the United Nations, New York, 1950.

(*See also* Business cycles; Economic statistics; Gross national product; Index numbers; Statistical techniques in economics, an overview)

Clayton Gehman

Industrial revolution

Arnold Toynbee in the 1880s broadly defined the essence of industrial revolution as the substitution of capitalist competition for the medieval regulations which had previously controlled the production and distribution of wealth. Although the concept may apply to a particular industry or to a particular branch of the economic activity of society (agriculture, mining, commerce, manufacturing, etc.), its widest application is associated with a national economy. A definition of industrial revolution must identify its temporal as well as social and economic characteristics.

Definitions since the time of Toynbee have stressed particular forms of productive organization, industrial revolution often being associated with the adoption of the factory system. To the contemporary economic historian the concept of industrial revolution is more complicated but is synonymous with a series of related developments. One is the application of science and empirical knowledge to the production of commodities for the market. Associated with this is the invention and adoption of new and improved machinery, the discovery and adoption of new sources of power, transport innovations, the use of large-scale production (factories), and increased division of labor. This enlargement of the typical unit of production means that the household is no longer the primary economic unit for productive purposes, and there is a need for a large pool of mobile labor resources. The migration of labor from rural areas to urban areas is symptomatic of this development.

In addition, the revolution is associated with increased capital accumulation. Savings and investment increase as a proportion of national income; innovative financial institutions arise to facilitate the mobilization of capital; and industrial profits, most of which are reinvested, increase. New social and occupational classes emerge and are defined by their relationship to or ownership of the means of production. The revolution is associated with major demographic changes. The birth rate increases and, as the revolution progresses, the death rate decreases. The result is rapid population growth, which provides both a source of labor and a mass market for the products of the expanding industries. Social and political institutions which are inimical to continued growth weaken or disappear and are replaced by institutions which foster or accept growth and development (rationalism, economic individualism, laissez faire, or, in more recent times, aggressive state planning). The result of these changed conditions is a rapid and sustained increase in the rate of growth of total and per capita output.

It is apparent from the preceding definition that an industrial revolution is a complicated process that may take a considerable amount of time to develop. It is seldom possible to identify a particular year, or even decade, as a nation's industrial revolution. The antecedents of an industrial revolution may take place decades or even centuries before the revolution is underway. The period of rapid growth is the culmination of the process of industrialization.

The First Industrial Revolution

The first industrial revolution reached fruition in England in the last quarter of the eighteenth and the first decades of the nineteenth centuries. Although it was not inevitable that an industrial revolution should occur first in England, that nation exhibited a number of characteristics that tended to favor industrialization. These included a highly developed agricultural sector, an aggressive and sophisticated commercial class, an environment relatively (but far from totally) free from government regulation, an adequate transportation system (turnpikes, improved rivers, and canals), and a class of entrepreneurs willing to take risks in the search for profits.

It was the wave of technical innovations, beginning in the 1760s, that signaled the advent of the factory system in England and which marks the traditional boundary of the industrial revolution. In its early phases the most spectacular advances were made in the textile, iron, and power-machine industries. In the textile industry the major breakthroughs were in spinning and weaving: Kay's flying shuttle (invented in the 1730s, but not adopted until the 1760s), Hargreaves's spinning jenny (1764), Arkwright's water frame (1769), Crompton's mule (1779), and Cartwright's power loom (1785). These inventions increased the supply of cloth, lowered its price, and increased output per unit of labor input by as much as 200-fold in the industry. In the iron industry the major breakthroughs were in smelting with coke, developed by Abraham Darby of Coalbrookdale (1709), but not adopted until much later, and the puddling process discovered by Henry Cort (1784). This led to roughly a 30-fold increase in the output of iron between 1760 and 1800. Perhaps the most spectacular of all inventions was James Watt's steam engine (1765). By adding a separate condenser to the Newcomen atmospheric engine, Watt increased the efficiency of the engine by a factor of 4. This freed the engine from having to be located near a source of fuel and made it a potential source of mechanical power for all industries. Although these innovations together were crucial in mechanizing industry and concentrating it in factories, many other discoveries were made which contributed to the industrial revolution in England. More production, which necessitated greater use of raw materials and mechanical power, was the result of industrial change.

The effects of the industrial revolution in England were profound and widespread. Growth involved an expansion of the flow of goods and services as well as a change in its composition. A process that leads to such expansion as well as to a lowering of the amount of human effort needed to produce a unit of output should lead to a corresponding rise in the standard of living of the average member of society. Whereas there is little doubt that the long-term benefits in terms of material living standards have been substantial, there is considerable controversy regarding the immediate effects of the industrial revolution on the worker. The pessimistic school of thought derives from the writings of Karl Marx, Friedrich Engels, the Fabian socialists, Toynbee, and, more recently, E. J. Hobsbawm. The pessimists argue that although the industrial revolution witnessed a great increase in the output of goods and services, the ownership of these commodities was not evenly spread and that the majority of society, the working poor, saw a marked deterioration in their standard of living for at least a generation or two. The industrial revolution ushered in a world of stannic mills, squalid cities, and social discontent.

The optimists draw upon J. R. McCulloch, T. Tooke, J. Clapham, and, more recently, R. M. Hartwell. They argue that although the revolution created hardship for some individuals, the majority of the working population benefited from falling prices, rising real wages, increased opportunities, and, ultimately, a more humane social order. Unfortunately, the aggregate data of the early nineteenth century are too fragmentary to lead to an unequivocal answer regarding the impact on the standard of living. What is clear is that after the middle of the nineteenth century the commoner fared much better than in the previous century: there was more regular employment for all members of the family; the composition of the labor force shifted toward more highly specialized, hence more highly skilled, occupations; and more and better consumer goods were available for purchase.

The Spread of the Industrial Revolution

The change from a preindustrial to an industrial economy began much earlier in some nations than in others, and the pace of industrialization has varied considerably. Even though the industrial development of Europe and the United States can be described in terms of a general pattern based on the English experience, that development was fundamentally different from the English experience. However, the industrial revolution in England affected the course of all subsequent transformations. The first nations to benefit from the English experience were France, Germany, Belgium, and the United States.

France was in a particularly good position to emulate England. France had a population larger than England and, thus, had a potentially large labor pool and larger home market than England, a traditional rival. France was also a wealthy country, with a flourishing overseas trade, a sophisticated scientific community, and a government which was willing to foster the expansion of the manufacturing sector. France had disadvantages, however, such as internal customs barriers, an inadequate transportation sector, and inadequate coal resources, each hampering progress toward industrialization. Political considerations played a large role in France's drive toward industrialization. By the 1830s, French government and financial officials, aware of increasing economic and military weakness relative to England, attempted to duplicate the innovations which had made England prosper. Between 1830 and 1870 France increased its per capita production to the level that existed in England and joined the industrialized world.

Germany had peculiar political disadvantages which delayed the process of industrialization, but with the establishment of the Zollverein in 1834, the transformation began. Coal and pig iron production accelerated, the railroad was laid in the 1840s, and the textile industry was mechanized. The rate of increase of production per capita approached and then surpassed that of England by the turn of the twentieth century.

The magnitude of the initial financial capital necessary for the industrial concerns of France and Germany in the 1840s to 1870s was much larger than it had been for English firms decades earlier (many of which were financed through retained earnings). In order to be competitive, these concerns had to be larger than the optimal size of a generation earlier. This meant that the mobilization of capital was a serious bottleneck in these nations, but large financial institutions grew up to address these problems (the Kreditbanken and Crédit Mobilier), which made the experience of industrialization fundamentally different in France and Germany than it had been in England.

The United States joined the ranks of the industrialized nations about the same time as France and Germany. The lack of factory endowments had postponed American industrialization for some time. The relative dearth of labor encouraged the substitution of capital for labor, but the absolute size of the population prevented the widespread adoption of the factory system until well into the nineteenth century. Industrialization came to the United States coincidentally with expansion to the West. The key phases of the process were the mechanization of textile production in the Northeast after 1815 and the more far-reaching process of developing an infrastructure, especially the laying of the railroad in the 1840s and 1850s.

By the turn of the twentieth century, a number of countries, including Sweden, Norway, Denmark, Holland, Japan, Russia, Italy, Canada, and Australia had begun the process of industrialization. Russia presents an interesting case. Still an agrarian country in the 1860s, with no railroads, banks, and little manufacturing, Russia doubled industrial output by the 1880s, largely as a result of the aid of the Russian state. During the last decade of the nineteenth century, the growth of Russian industry outstripped nearly all of the industrialized countries (although in terms of per capita income Russia was hampered by a primitive agricultural sector). More rapid growth was a common phenomenon for countries that came relatively late to industrialization. Continued technological progress in the developed countries laid the basis for a more rapid rise in productivity and output per capita in the latecomers, because the latecomers could immediately adopt the most advanced techniques. According to Alexander Gerschenkron, this was one of the advantages of backwardness.

From the standpoint of the 1980s, the world contains an array of nations at very different stages of industrial development and economic growth. As the nations that have passed through an industrial revolution continue to expand, the gap between the industrialized and nonindustrialized world continues to widen. The nonindustrialized nations contain the majority of the world's population. Over 60 percent of the people in the world live in countries in which per capita income is less than 10 percent of that of the industrialized world. Some nations have been more successful than others in responding to the challenge of the industrialized world. W. W. Rostow has argued that the beginnings of an industrial revolution can be seen in countries such as Brazil, Mexico, Argentina, China, Taiwan, and South Korea. Rates of growth in these countries are currently higher than those in the developed countries, but the question remains whether or not these rates can be maintained into the future.

In sum, industrialization is synonymous with modern economic growth. It entails a sometimes lengthy but predictable sequence of events. There is a change in the content of national product away from agriculture, and a change in the organization of production. An industrial revolution implies the mechanization of manufacturing processes and the concentration of those processes in a factory. It implies the construction of new systems of transportation and the growth of cities. Fundamentally, it means the accumulation of capital on an unprecedented scale, and eventually, a significant increase in the standard of living of a nation.

References

Crafts, N. F. R., "Industrial Revolution in England and France: Some Thoughts on the Question, 'Why Was England First,'" *Economic History Review*, vol. 20, August 1977, pp. 429–441; Landes, David, *The Unbound Prometheus*, Cambridge University Press, Cambridge, 1969; Rostow, W. W., *The World Economy*, University of Texas Press, Austin, 1978; Toynbee, Arnold, *Lectures on the Industrial Revolution of the Eighteenth Century in England* (1884), in *Toynbee's Industrial Revolution*, Kelley, New York, 1969.

(*See also* Economic history and theory; Innovation; Productivity; Stages theory of economic development; Technology)

William J. Hausman

Inflation

Inflation means generally rising money prices of goods and services. To understand what inflation is and is not, consider the above definition in detail:

Goods and services—This refers not to stocks or bonds or other financial assets, but to the tangible and intangible commodities economic agents produce and sell to one another. These are commodities to be consumed or held for future use: e.g., food, haircuts, shelter, houses, health care, schooling, cars, tractors, machine tools.

Money prices—This refers to amounts of money, dollars and cents in the United States, per commodity unit, e.g., per pound of butter, gallon of gasoline, haircut, bus trip, kilowatthour, or diesel engine. In contrast, imagine the barter prices at which one commodity trades for another: e.g., 3 gallons of gas for 1 hour of labor, two bus fares for 1 pound of butter, one haircut for 100 kilowatthours. From the money prices for any two commodities can be calculated their implicit barter price, their relative price in economists' language. Inflation does not refer to movements of relative prices, but to movements of absolute prices, i.e., money prices.

Rising—This does not mean "high." By some measures, money prices in the United States were twice as high at the end of 1978 as in 1967. Thus, in the interim the annual average inflation rate was 5.8 percent. (If a dollar deposited in 1967 earned this rate, compounded continuously, it would have doubled after 12 years.) If by some miracle prices had ceased to rise and were the same at the end of 1979 as 12 months earlier, the inflation rate would have been zero for the year 1979. But a dollar would still have bought only half as much and could have been obtained by selling only half as much, as in 1967.

Generally—Inflation refers to pervasive, widespread increases of money prices. A rising price for a single commodity, even beef or oil, is not per se inflation, any more than declining prices of pocket calculators or digital time pieces represent deflation.

Measurement of Inflation

To measure inflation over a month or a year or decade, it is necessary to average the diverse changes in thousands and thousands of specific prices. This is not easy, and it is bound to be arbitrary. If prices all moved together in proportion, there would be no ambiguity about the direction and amount of change in the price level. But they do not; relative prices are always changing. In practice, statisticians, usually in government agencies, calculate price indexes. In these indexes commodities are weighted by their importance in consumer budgets, or in the gross national product (GNP), or in other aggregates. Indexes with weights differing in concept or in base data give different results.

Averaging and weighting are not the only problems. Products change in design and quality, for better or worse. A truck, a computer, a pair of skis, a subway ride, are not the same as a year ago, let alone 10 years ago. Wholly new products are introduced; others vanish from the scene. According to the U.S. consumer price index, prices were 365 percent higher in 1978 than in 1940. But television was not available then at any price, and new 1940 Ford cars are not available now. The physician may do more or less for the patient in an hour than formerly, but statisticians cannot measure units of health and can only enter in the index the rise in the fee per visit.

Though the measurement of inflation is inevitably imprecise, the standard price index numbers capture the big changes. For example, the years 1974 to 1978, when the GNP price index increased on average 6.8 percent per year, were very different from 1965 to 1969, when it rose 1.8 percent per year.

Money and Inflation

Inflation is by definition a monetary phenomenon, a decline in the commodity value of the monetary unit of account, the dollar in the United States. Deflation too is monetary, a rise in the commodity value and commodity cost of a unit of money. (From 1929 to 1933, for example, prices fell at, on average, 6.7 percent per year.)

To understand inflation and deflation, therefore, it is necessary to review the role of money in economic life. An economy where goods and services are always bartered directly for each other would be spared inflation or deflation. It would also be terribly inefficient. Perhaps the village cobbler can trade shoes for the farmer's eggs, and even promise shoes tomorrow for eggs today. But imagine the difficulties if steel plants had to pay their workers in steel ingots, or else trade the ingots for eggs and shoes and other goods more to their employees' tastes. Without money, much time and effort would be spent seeking and executing mutually advantageous trades, and much capital would be tied up in inventories. To escape these inefficiencies the people of even primitive societies have agreed among themselves on a common trading commodity, a money.

The money of a society serves as a commonly accepted medium of exchange and as a unit of account and calculation. Goods and services can be traded for money rather than directly for other goods and services. The cobbler can sell shoes for money and use the money later to buy eggs, as well as leather, nails, and the services of an apprentice. The steel plant can sell ingots for money and pay employees in money, and the workers can find and buy what they individually want. Prices can be quoted and values calculated in units of money. Imagine the difficulty of keeping track of barter prices for all possible pairs of commodities.

These are money's functions. But what is money? It is whatever the society collectively fixes upon, by convention and tradition and in modern nations by law. The substances chosen have differed widely, including cattle, land, rocks, silver, gold, and engraved paper. Some, so-called fiat moneys, have had no value except that conveyed by their status as money. Others have been commodities with intrinsic value in consumption (such as cigarettes among prisoners of war) or production. Even commodity moneys have had, thanks to their monetary designation, more value in terms of other goods and services than they would have had on their own. Some things make more convenient moneys than others, but the vast advantages of money to the society are gained by agreeing on a common medium of exchange and account, whatever it is. In this respect, money is a social institution comparable to language. In both cases, the immense contribution to social cooperation and communication depends on the general currency of whatever medium is chosen.

Money is also a store of value, in which individuals can save and hold wealth for future use. Otherwise, it would be useless as a medium of exchange. The farmer parts with eggs for the cobbler's money only because the farmer expects the money will later be acceptable payment for shoes or seed or fence wire, tomorrow or next week or next year. Everyone who accepts fiat money—or commodity money such as cigarettes or silver in excess of consumption needs—is counting on its future acceptability to others.

But money is not, of course, the only store of value available to savers and wealth owners, or even the principal form of wealth. Even in primitive societies land, livestock, and other commodities are more important vehicles of wealth. This remains true in modern economies, where ultimate ownership of real properties is often indirect, expressed through a network of financial claims.

In a modern national economy, many assets and debts are denominated in the monetary unit of account. Some of these are media of exchange, but most are not. In the United States, for example, the basic physical manifestation of the dollar is the fiat issue of currency—paper bills and coin—by the federal government. The federal government also has outstanding obligations to pay specified amounts of these dollars, some on demand (notably the deposits of commercial banks in Federal Reserve banks), some on stated future dates (Treasury bills, notes, and bonds). Currency and demand deposits do not bear interest; time obligations do. In addition, nonfederal debtors have issued an immense volume and variety of dollar-denominated obligations, some payable on demand, others at future dates. The debtors include banks, savings institutions, state and local governments, business firms, individuals (homeowners, car buyers, department store customers, students, etc.), and foreigners. Most of these IOUs bear interest, but demand obligations (e.g., bank checking accounts) generally do not.

In addition to currency itself, some promises to pay currency on demand are generally or frequently acceptable instruments of payment. These include not only checkable deposits in banks and savings institutions but also the obligations of credit card and travelers' check companies and of some mutual funds.

When inflation or deflation alters the value of the dollar, it affects the real values of all dollar-denominated obligations, whether private or public, whether demand or time, whether media of payment or not. For this reason, both the causes and consequences of changing values of the dollar qua unit of account extend far beyond government issues of basic dollar currency and beyond the dollar means of payment supplied by banks.

Throughout history, the value of monetary stores of value has been variable and unpredictable. Considering the nature of money, this is not surprising. The notion that price stability or predictability is natural and normal, while inflation and deflation are pathological aberrations, is an abstraction with little realistic foundation.

People save for future consumption, for their old age, or for their children. But whatever form of wealth they accumulate, they can never be sure what value it will have when they or their heirs need it. Since they cannot store precisely the commodities they will want to consume, they are always dependent on what other people will be prepared to pay for their assets. This is true of land, houses, personal skills (human capital), machines and tools, and common stocks. It is certainly true of money, the value of which depends not on its intrinsic utility in consumption or production, but always on what others expect its value will be to them. Investors are always speculating about the relative values of goods and titles to them, on the one hand, and money and titles to money, on the other. Fluctuations in the value of money are costs societies have to pay for the efficiency that monetary institutions contribute in trade and division of labor. The problem is to keep the fluctuations from being so violent that they negate those positive contributions.

Anticipated and Unanticipated Inflation

In a hypothetical pure case of anticipated inflation everyone correctly foresees the future path of the money price of every commodity. In deciding how many dollars to borrow or lend, for how long, and at what interest rates, everyone can correctly calculate the depreciation of the dollar vis-à-vis the commodities consumed and produced. Lenders expecting more inflation demand more interest in compensation, and borrowers likewise are able and willing to pay it when they expect to repay their debts in depreciated currency. As Irving Fisher observed 60 years ago, in these circumstances market interest rates would adjust point for point of expected inflation, leaving unchanged all real interest rates (those implicit in the expected future amount of each commodity purchasable directly or indirectly by a unit of the commodity today). The path of the real economy—relative prices, physical quantities—would be independent of the rate of inflation anticipated. The inflation would make no difference and would do no one either harm or good.

This abstraction contains a valuable practical lesson. The more thoroughly adjusted an economy becomes to an ongoing inflation, the less consequential is the inflation.

However, there are a number of economic institutions that adjust slowly, if at all, to changes in actual and expected inflation rates. One crucial rigidity is the zero nominal interest rate on base money, currency and its equivalents. Legal or conventional interest limitations often apply to demand and savings deposits and to loans and mortgages, though these rate ceilings can be and have been changed at intervals. Their ceilings prevent the Fisher adjustment of nominal interest rates to expected inflation. With higher inflation, the real rate of return from holding currency becomes lower (more negative). As owners of wealth seek to substitute other assets of money, the reduction of real rates spreads to them. Since it modifies the structure and level of real rates of return, expected inflation is not neutral. One effect of higher expected inflation is to induce economies in cash management; holding periods are shorter, money turns over faster, more costs are incurred, and more resources are diverted in order to avoid losses on depreciating assets uncompensated by interest. Against these social costs are possible gains from greater capital formation. In some circumstances, it may not be possible to get real interest rates low enough to encourage a socially desirable degree of accumulation of productive capital unless the attractiveness of holding monetary assets is diminished by expectations of inflation.

Unanticipated inflation is different. People have made monetary commitments on the basis of price expectations that in the event turn out wrong. Examples of such commitments are loans of a few weeks, wage contracts of 1 to 3 years, life and retirement insurance contracts, 30-year mortgages, and long-term bonds and leases. The economy is always carrying heavy baggage of contracts made at various dates in the past, with various expectations about prices today and in the future. Deviations of inflation rates from past expectation will bring capital gains to some, capital losses to others. As every history student knows, unexpected inflation is good for debtors, who borrowed at low rates, and bad for their creditors. By the same token, farmer-debtors revolted against the deflations of 1879 to 1896 and 1926 to 1933; it wasn't possible to pay off 6 percent loans when grain prices were steadily declining. Pensioners and civil servants enjoyed the deflations but suffered from wartime and postwar inflations.

Redistributions of this kind are painful disappointments and often cruel disasters for the losers. But several points should be remembered:

1. There are winners as well as losers. The nation as a whole does not lose except as its foreign debts become unexpectedly onerous or its foreign loans yield disappointing real returns.

2. Gains and losses occur whenever events fail to confirm the expectations held when contracts and commitments were made, not from inflation per se. The culprit could be deflation, or any deviation of actual prices up or down from previously expected paths. For example, in the 1970s many companies incurred debts at double-digit interest rates premised on the continuation of inflation at 8 to 12 percent per year. Many householders assumed mortgages at rates they expect to pay from inflation in their wages and in real estate values. If the inflation were dramatically curbed in the 1980s, these debtors would be in trouble.

3. Inflation and deflation are by no means the sole sources of unexpected income redistributions. Most capital losses and gains are related to mistakes and surprises that afflict forecasts of relative prices and of real economic phenomena. Consider, for example, current or imminent retirees who in the 1960s and 1970s sought protection from inflation by investing in common stocks rather than fixed-dollar securities. Consider enterprises that built glass office buildings or bought gas-guzzling cars just as the Organization of Petroleum Exporting Countries (OPEC) was raising prices. Consider young people who committed themselves to teaching careers in the 1960s and 1970s and later found education to be a declining industry.

Inflation and the Quantity of Money

As media of exchange, currency circulates from hand to hand and checking balances from account to account. At any instant of time, however, every dollar of money in circulation is in someone's hands or someone's account. At the end of any business day, it is possible in principle, though not in practice, to account for the entire stock by a census of the amounts held by everybody. At the end of the next business day, the census would find quite a different distribution even though the total stock was virtually unchanged.

How big a stock does it take to handle the business of the nation? The answer clearly depends on, among other things, prices. If all prices were halved, would it not be possible to execute the same trades with a money stock half as large? If all prices were doubled, would it not take a circulating stock twice as large to make the same real transactions? Affirmative answers are plausible, and they are the kernel of an ancient and important doctrine. Although it is commonly known as the quantity theory of money, a more descriptive label is the quantity of money theory of prices.

The doctrine goes back at least to David Hume, and in its modern form of monetarism its leading protagonist is Milton Friedman. In its starkest form, the proposition is that prices are proportional to the quantity of money. Suppose, for example, the stock of money in dollars were doubled. Having more than needed to handle transactions at prevailing prices, households and businesses would try to get rid of excess money holdings by buying more goods and services. But the excess money would not be extinguished, merely transferred to other households and businesses, which would act in the same manner. In the process the money prices of goods and services would be bid up until they are high enough so that the stock of money would no longer be excessive. That occurs when prices have doubled. In summary, there is a certain amount of purchasing power that the society needs and wants to hold in the form of money. Whatever the nominal, or dollar, stock of money, prices will adjust until the purchasing power of this stock is the needed and desired amount. By extension, the quantity theory says that the rate of inflation depends on the rate of increase in the nominal money stock.

History provides at least some rough confirmations. As Hume observed, European inflation in the sixteenth and seventeenth centuries was associated with the discovery, importation, and monetization of gold from the New World. In the late nineteenth century, a gold shortage produced deflation in Europe and North America, reversed at the turn of the century when new technology and discovery flooded the world with South African gold. History is full of inflations resulting from undisciplined issues of fiat moneys, e.g., Continentals by the rebellious American colonies, Civil War greenbacks, German marks in the 1923 hyperinflation, the currencies of almost every Latin American country again and again.

Nevertheless, the quantity theory is an incomplete explanation of inflation in advanced capitalist democracies in the late twentieth century. The sources of inflation are more complex and diverse, and the cures less obvious and sure than the theory suggests.

A popular capsule explanation of inflation is "too much money chasing too few goods." Now money chasing or "money on the wing" in the words of the English monetary economist D. H. Robertson is not the same as what Robertson called "money at rest." The stock of money enumerated in the hypothetical census above is at rest in its holders' pockets, vaults, and accounts at the end of the business day. Money is chasing or on the wing when it circulates during the day, moving from one holder to another as goods are bought and sold and other transactions are consummated. Irving Fisher expressed the relationship of circulation to stock in the concept of velocity, or turnover, the average number of times a dollar is transferred within a period. (This can be measured for checking accounts by calculating the ratio of the aggregate dollar value of checks drawn to average balances in the accounts debited. The ratio averaged 12 per month for the United States as a whole in 1978, and 45 for New York banks alone.) But the bulk of these transactions are not for purchases of the final goods and services counted in the GNP, whose prices are those relevant for inflation. A more restrictive concept, GNP velocity, tells the average number of times a dollar of money stock buys GNP goods and services during a year. (This figure was 5.9 in 1978, for the so-called narrow money-stock concept M-1, consisting of publicly held currency and demand deposits.)

The Equation of Exchange   Fisher provided a framework for analysis, the equation of exchange. For the purpose at hand it can be written $MV = PQ = Y$, where M is the stock of money, V its GNP velocity per year, P the GNP price index, Q the real (constant-price) GNP per year, and Y the dollar GNP per year. The equation is actually an identity, since V can be estimated only by dividing GNP in dollars per year (PQ) by M. In this framework the quantity theory holds if V and Q are constants, independent of M and P. Then P must move proportionately to M. However, both theoretical reasoning and empirical evidence cast doubt on the two premises of the quantity theory, at least during short-run cyclical fluctuation in economic activity.

The equation of exchange may also be written in terms of year-to-year rates of growth; the following is a close approximation:

$$\left(\begin{matrix}\% \text{ growth} \\ \text{of } M\end{matrix}\right) + \left(\begin{matrix}\% \text{ growth} \\ \text{of } V\end{matrix}\right) = \left(\begin{matrix}\% \text{ growth} \\ \text{of } P\end{matrix}\right) + \left(\begin{matrix}\% \text{ growth} \\ \text{of } Q\end{matrix}\right) = \left(\begin{matrix}\% \text{ growth of} \\ \text{dollar GNP}\end{matrix}\right) \quad (1)$$

$$\frac{\Delta M}{M} + \frac{\Delta V}{V} = \frac{\Delta P}{P} + \frac{\Delta Q}{Q} = \frac{\Delta Y}{Y}$$

As an illustration of Equation (1) consider 1978 relative to 1977. Dollar GNP Y rose 12 percent from $1900 billion to $2128 billion. But the real volume of goods and services produced, Q, increased only 4.4 percent. The difference was the inflation rate, 7.6 percent. On the left-hand side of the equation, the money stock grew 7.3 percent, from $335 billion average in 1977 to $360 billion in 1978. Velocity rose by 4 percent from 5.7 to 5.9.

If the changes in velocity $\Delta V/V$ and in real output $\Delta Q/Q$ are constants, independent of the other terms in Equation (1), the inflation $\Delta P/P$ and money growth $\Delta P/P$ must vary together point for point. In this dynamic form, the quantity theory does not require that velocity V and output Q be unchanging—they may have nonzero trends and vary unsystematically around them. The trend of output Q is constrained by trends of labor force and productivity, which change slowly and gradually. In the United States since the Second World War, these trends have yielded average growth of real GNP of 3 to 4 percent per annum. As a result, the average inflation rate has been three or four points less than the average growth of Y, dollar spending on GNP. In cyclical short runs, there are considerable deviations from the trend; year-to-year values of $\Delta Q/Q$ vary from -2 to 8 percent. During business cycles, fluctuations in Y and in $\Delta Y/Y$ are generally registered in output Q and $\Delta Q/Q$, at least as much as in prices P and $\Delta P/P$.

Velocity V is not a mechanical property of · ₁ney, but the outcome of the decisions and behaviors of millions of individuals. A way to interpret velocity is to notice that its reciprocal $1/V$ is roughly the average length of time an individual holds a dollar between transactions. (In this context the relevant measure of velocity refers to all transactions, not just to GNP purchases and sales. The figures given above imply holding times of $2\frac{1}{2}$ days for the United States; and of $\frac{2}{3}$ day for New York City.) But holding periods are economic decisions. In between necessary transactions, funds can be taken out of cash and placed in interest-bearing assets. The incentive is the interest earned. Against the interest gains must be set the inconveniences, costs, and risks of keeping cash balances low by making frequent conversions into and out of other assets. The incentive becomes relatively stronger when interest rates are high. The downward trend of velocity in recent decades of rising interest and inflation rates, and the procyclical movements of both velocity and interest rates, are empirical confirmations. Inflation itself heightens the incentive to economize cash holdings and shorten holding periods, to acquire either real assets rising in price or financial assets with interest rates reflecting the inflation. Interest rates also reflect monetary policies. In business cycle short runs, active restriction of monetary growth will, other things being equal, be associated with tight credit markets and high interest rates, and thus with high velocity of money. On these systematic effects are superimposed more volatile changes in liquidity preferences and expectations, as well as innovations in financial markets, institutions, and technology.

The following sections discuss some sources of inflation in the late twentieth century in industrial societies with democratic and capitalist institutions. Monetary factors are always important, though in some instances their role is accommodative rather than initiative. In any event, it is always necessary to ask why monetary expansion is occurring, given that modern governments and central banks have the capacity to prevent it. The answer may be that the government finds printing money and consequent inflation the expedient way of mobilizing resources for war or other government purposes. Or the answer may be that the government regards the economic consequences of severe anti-inflationary monetary policies, with their political and social by-products, as the greater evil.

Excess-Demand Inflation

In the classic inflation drama, government is principal actor and villain. It needs more goods and a larger work force, typically for war. The economy is already operating close to its normal capacity. If government is to buy more, private citizens will have to buy less. Higher taxes are the straightforward way to achieve this shift, but government cannot or will not levy them. Instead, the sovereign simply prints the money needed, or at least enough new money so that the rest can be borrowed cheaply. New government demands accumulate in addition to diminished private demands, and the economy cannot supply both. In terms of the equation of exchange, the higher growth of dollar spending induces little extra GNP and spills into higher inflation. The government gets what it wants. The price rise squeezes out private citizens caught by surprise, especially those dependent on fixed-dollar incomes and assets. Thus, inflation earns its reputation as the cruelest tax.

The drama has played many times throughout history, in the United States as elsewhere. The most recent performance, subdued compared with most previous wartime inflations, accompanied the Vietnam war. In 1966 President Johnson, against his economists' advice, chose not to ask Congress for higher taxes to pay for his escalation of the conflict. By 1968, defense spending had increased more than 50 percent and had thrown the budget into a $12 billion deficit at a time when unemployment was well below the official 4 percent target. The economy was overheated for most of 4 years, and the inflation rate rose from 2 percent per year to 5 percent. Comparing 1968 with 1965, money-supply growth had accelerated from 4.7 to 8.1 percent, and GNP velocity increased from 4.1 to 4.5 percent.

Excess demand need not be so striking as in wartime, and it need not be government spending that initiates the acceleration of dollar GNP. A dollar chasing goods is a dollar, whoever the spender. A boom in business investment or housing construction or purchases of consumers' durable goods could outrun the economy's productive capacity. Worldwide private speculative stockpiling of materials was a significant inflationary factor in 1973, as it had been in 1950 at the outset of the Korean war. (Thereafter, President Truman kept Korean war procurement noninflationary by insisting on a stiff dose of taxation to pay for it.)

Easy monetary and credit policies may be the source of excess demand. Business investment, homebuilding, purchases of cars and appliances, and inventory building may be overstimulated by opportunities to borrow at interest rates low relative to anticipated returns in dollars or in use. One symptom of such policies will be high rates of monetary growth $\Delta M/M$. The period 1972–73 is a widely cited example. Monetary growth in 1972 was 9.1 percent. Dollar GNP rose 10.1 percent, real GNP 5.7 percent. The inflation rate accelerated in the following year to 6 percent, the highest year-over-year rate since 1948.

Inflation without Excess Demand: "Stagflation"

Excess demand is not the only inflation story. Simultaneous inflation and excess supply afflicted the world economy through much of the 1970s. The symptoms of excess supply are abnormally high unemployment of labor and underutilization of productive capacity. In the United States in 1975, for example, unemployment averaged 8.5 percent of the labor force, compared with an average of 5.4 percent over the previous 5 years. Industry was operating at 74 percent of capacity, compared with 83 percent on average from 1970 to 1974. Inflation, at 9.7 percent according to the GNP price index, could scarcely be attributed to contemporaneous excess demand.

The lesson of stagflation, and of earlier experience as well, is that inflation has a life of its own, in several senses.

1. Historical patterns of wage and price increase have a strong momentum during periods of excess supply. They respond slowly and erratically to economic circumstances reflected in monetary spending, unemployment, excess capacity, and GNP growth.

2. A modern economy appears to have an inflationary bias. Inflation rates rise more easily and more quickly in response to excess demand than they fall in response to excess supply.

3. Accidents may occur; events not connected with the state of the economy or with monetary and fiscal policies can change price levels as well as relative prices, and affect inflation rates at least temporarily. Recent examples are union wage push (1970–1971), world food shortages (1973), good harvests (1976), and, of course, OPEC (1973).

The inertial inflation continues because it is self-consistent and because it becomes habitual and expected. Workers, unionized or unorganized, look at the wage gains of their peers and seek to do as well or better. They seek to catch and overtake the cost of living too, and cost-of-living adjustment (COLA) clauses help. Employers pay the pattern wage increase in their labor markets and industries, knowing they will not jeopardize their competitive position by doing so. Industrial pricing is strongly cost-based. If hourly labor costs are rising 9 percent per year, and productivity is increasing 2 percent, the average industry will raise prices 7 percent, and this will be reflected in the workers' cost of living. The same real outcomes would occur if wage inflation was 4 percent and prices were rising 2 percent, as in the early 1960s. Only if dollar wage rates rise, on average, no faster than labor productivity can there be stability in price levels. But a higher pattern, once built in, is very stubborn.

The pattern can change, for better or worse. Wage inflation is not wholly insensitive to economic conditions. Econometric estimates are that the difference between a 7 percent unemployment year and a 6 percent unemployment year is a quarter to half a percentage point of inflation. Even on the more optimistic estimate, it would take 6 years of the higher unemployment rate to wring three points from the inflation rate. It is this dismal calculus that leads the governments here and abroad to seek more direct solutions—wage and price controls or less drastic and less mandatory interventions in private wage bargains and price decisions.

The inflationary bias is that wages and prices respond faster to demand pressure than to excess supply. Expanding firms and industries in tight labor markets are ready to bid above pattern for the labor they need; their existing employees are delighted. But it's not so easy for employers in less prosperous industries and regions to pay less than the prevailing pattern. Queues of job seekers at the factory gate, willing to work for less than those inside, seldom force rapid wage reduction. Existing employees, even if not under union contract, have considerable collective power; wage patterns give way only when the financial plight of the employer is a credible threat to their jobs. Minimum wages and unemployment insurance benefits limit downward movements of wages. Similarly, industrial firms raise prices when demand for their products is strong but are reluctant to compete by price-cutting when demand is slack.

Inflexibility and inflationary bias appear to be developments of our twentieth-century amalgam of industrial capitalism and social democracy. In nineteenth-century Britain and the United States prices and money wages moved freely down and up. Periods of deflation were not prosperities, especially for farmers in debt, but output growth continued. As late as 1919, a sharp postwar inflation of commodity prices in the United States pulled money wages up; but both promptly fell just as sharply, and the setback to output and employment was small and short-lived. In the 1920s and 1930s, however, deflation of wages and nonagricultural prices occurred very slowly in both countries in spite of prolonged mass unemployment and idle capacity. The deflations that did occur did not seem to ameliorate the situation.

These observations led John Maynard Keynes to challenge the orthodox economic view that flexibility of wages and prices would restore full-employment equilibrium after monetary or nonmonetary disturbances. His challenge is still relevant, though it may be a pattern of inflationary increase of wages and prices, not just their level, that resists competitive pressure.

The modern economy does not behave like a world of atomistic competition among small shops, farms, and unorganized workers. True, there is still a "flex-price" sector as well as a "fix-price" sector. Not all sellers can set their own prices. In agriculture and mineral extraction, in which there are numerous producers of identical commodities, prices are determined in impersonal auction markets. But the flexible price sector has declined relative to the economy. In any case farmers and other competitive producers have obtained government-supported price floors making their prices, too, less flexible down than up.

In these circumstances large increases in individual prices become sources of inflation for the whole economy. Food prices rise because of bad weather. Oil prices rise because of OPEC. Hospital prices rise because of medicare. Such events require changes of relative prices: scarcer goods naturally become more expensive. In a world of flexible prices, this could happen without inflating economywide price indexes. Dollar prices of other goods would fall enough to balance the increases in food, energy, medical care. In our world that does not happen. Instead, as in the years 1973–74 and 1978–79, large upward adjustments of prices of important commodities bring double-digit inflation.

The Unemployment-Inflation Trade-off

In a striking empirical study published in 1958, A. W. Phillips showed that in the United Kingdom from 1861 to 1957 unemployment among trade union members was negatively correlated with rates of increase in money wages. The relationship was curvilinear: the rate of wage inflation appeared to be much more sensitive to variation in the unemployment rate when unemployment was low than when it was high. This shape embodies the asymmetries that lead to inflationary bias. Phillips curves fit for other countries and to modern statistics told the same story. Moreover, a Phillips curve relationship appeared to describe price inflation as well as wage inflation, as could be expected if prices are essentially marked-up labor costs.

Macroeconomic theorists warmly embraced the Phillips curve, for several reasons. Keynesian economics contained no theory of inflation except for an economy operating at full employment with excess demand. According to the model of Keynes' *General Theory*, there should be no continuing inflation when the economy is operating below its full-employment capacity. For that situation, which he regarded as usual in peacetime, Keynes provided a theory of the price level (it would move upward as employment and output increased) but not a theory of inflation (the price level should be stable or may be declining if employment and output are stable). But there were plenty of cases, especially after the Second World War, when inflation kept going although employment and other measures of utilization were stable or declining. The concept of full employment itself was troublesome in peacetime. Did the occurrence of inflation mean the economy was fully employed, even though employment did not look full according to unemployment rates and other statistics? The Phillips curve appeared to solve, or to finesse, these problems by making the inflation rate, rather than the price level, an increasing function of employment and capacity utilization, and by making fullness of employment a matter of degree rather than a yes-or-no condition.

Elevated from an empirical scatter diagram to a functional macroeconomic relationship, the Phillips curve also implied that monetary and fiscal policymakers faced a usable trade-off, by which lower unemployment rates could be obtained at the cost of higher inflation rates and vice versa. Whether any government explicitly made policy on this basis is doubtful, but the notion of trade-off certainly has been indirectly influential.

In 1967 and 1968, Edmund Phelps and Milton Friedman independently raised serious theoretical questions about the Phillips curve and the reliability of the Phillips trade-off as a basis for policy. They argued that rational workers, unions, and firms will take account of inflation and expected inflation in setting wages and prices, so that only deviations from the expected trend will be related to unemployment rates. Thus, the eventual inflation effects of a reduction in unemployment would be much greater than the initial impact. Events after 1966—inflation rates increasing while unemployment rates were low, but stable—supported these arguments.

According to Phelps and Friedman, there is in principle only one unemployment rate—Friedman's natural rate—at which wages and prices will continue on their anticipated path, whatever inflation rate that may imply. (Thus, full employment reappears in new guise, but with considerable residual mystery as to why it involves so much unemployment.) If unemployment is held by policy below the natural rate, inflation will be ever accelerating. Symmetrically, if unemployment is held above the natural rate, inflation will decelerate and eventually there will be ever-faster deflation. The latter implication may seem empirically doubtful, but the theory does not exclude the possibility that downward adjustments are slower than upward adjustments.

A common synthesis is to combine a short-run Phillips curve with the natural rate. Even though there may be no long-run trade-off, the short-run relationship tells how hard or easy it is to diminish the prevailing inertial inflation by running the economy for a time with unemployment higher than natural. Once this has been done, once price expectations have been revised downward or eliminated, the economy can return to the natural rate without re-igniting the previous inflation.

But how can policymakers know what the natural rate is? The new classical macroeconomists, Robert Lucas, Thomas Sargent, and others, say they cannot and should not try. These theorists take the old Phelps-Friedman argument a long step farther. They regard the economy—labor markets included—as always in equilibrium, with neither excess supply nor excess demand. Prices and wages adjust to clear markets, subject to the expectations that the actors form with the information they have. In this sense, the economy is always at its natural rate, but this rate itself varies. Future policies are an important dimension of economic expectations. So the predictability or capriciousness of policymakers is crucial for the stability or volatility of the economy. The recommendation is that the makers of monetary policy simply announce and stick to noninflationary rates of monetary growth. Workers and employers will then expect zero inflation and behave accordingly. The economy will then gravitate quickly to its correct-information natural rate of unemployment. To put it another way, whatever rate it moves to will be that natural rate.

Monetary Accommodation

Inertial inflation and increases in important specific prices confront central banks and governments with cruelly difficult choices. Shall they accommodate these price movements or not? That is, shall they permit a growth of monetary spending Y sufficient to sustain normal increases of output and employment at the rising prices? If they do so, they are doing nothing to arrest the inflation itself, and indeed they are in a sense ratifying the behavior and the institutions that bias the economy toward inflation. (With accommodation, incidentally, $\Delta M/M$ and $\Delta P/P$ may be positively correlated, as quantity theory suggests, but the causation runs in reverse, from prices to money stock.) If they do not accommodate, then as in 1974 to 1975 they will depress output and employment, while the counterinflationary effects are uncertain and slow at best.

The makers of monetary and fiscal policy in democracies are always seeking politically acceptable compromises. Their natural bent is to lean against the evil wind of the day, to fight inflation when it is the most vivid popular complaint and to combat recession and unemployment when they become the uppermost concerns. Business cycles due to stop-go alternation of policies are the result. Some economic observers believe that a resolute irreversible commitment of nonaccommodation would melt the rock of inertial inflation much faster than previous experience under counter-cyclical and semiaccommodative policies would suggest. Others believe that nonaccommodative policies will eliminate inflation only at great and prolonged cost in lost output and employment, and quite possibly not at all. They are reconciled either to living with inflation, possibly accelerating inflation, or to limiting wage and price increases directly by more or less formal controls.

Inflation as Symptom

Inflation is, as emphasized above, a monetary phenomenon. But inflation may also be the symptom of some real economic, social, and political difficulties. The monetary authorities may choose accommodation in the belief that inflation is one of the less painful manifestations of the underlying disease.

It is an economic burden on a society to fight a war, and usually to lose one. Inflation is probably not the most orderly or just way to distribute the burden. But doing it differently would not avoid the basic social cost, the diversion or loss of productive resources. After the First World War, the victorious Allies imposed punitive reparations on the German people. The German government mistakenly tried to pay the victors by printing marks and selling them in the foreign exchange markets for the francs and pounds they were required to deliver. As the mark depreciated in the exchange markets they had to print more and more, and the result was the most famous hyperinflation of history. As disastrous as the inflation was, the original burden on the German economy, which had to be shouldered one way or another, was still the reparations. In the 1970s the OPEC cartel inflicted a heavy social loss on oil-importing countries, whose residents had to work harder and longer to import a barrel of oil. This is the true and unavoidable cost. The OPEC price boosts also inflated U.S. price indexes, but that is a symptom rather than the cause of losses of real income. Even if sufficient wage reductions were absorbed to keep the price indexes from rising, U.S. citizens still would be losing to OPEC.

A more disquieting possibility is that inflation is the symptom of deep-rooted social and economic contradiction and conflict, between major economic groups persistently claiming pieces of pie that together exceed the whole pie. Inflation is the way that their claims, so far as they are expressed in nominal terms, are temporarily reconciled. But it will continue and indeed accelerate so long as the basic conflicts of real claims and real power continue.

There are a number of possible scenarios of conflict inflation in the 1970s. A common story is that a combination of misfortunes—OPEC, long-run energy shortage, environmental dangers and costs—has sharply lowered the paths of potential output, real wages, and real returns on capital investment. But it has not lowered the standards of real-income progress to which employed workers are accustomed, or the profit rates that managers and shareowners expect. The relative price shocks of the mid-1970s are the source of serious and lasting conflict, not simply of a temporary bulge of inflation statistics.

References

Cambridge Economic Handbook, originally published by Cambridge University Press, Cambridge, 1922; Fisher, Irving, *The Purchasing Power of Money*, rev. ed., Macmillan, New York, 1926; Friedman, Milton, and Anna Schwartz, *A Monetary History of the United States*, National Bureau of Economic Research, Princeton University Press, Princeton, N.J., 1963; Friedman, Milton, "The Role of Monetary Policy," *American Economic Review*, vol. 58, no. 1, March 1968, pp. 1–17; Hume, David, "Of Money," in T. H. Green and T. H. Grose (eds.), *Essays, Moral, Political, and Literary*, vol. I, 1977, Longman, New York and London, 1912; Keynes, John Maynard, *The General Theory of Employment, Interest, and Money*, Macmillan, London and New

York, 1936; Lucas, Robert, and Thomas Sargent, "After Keynesian Macroeconomics," *After the Phillips Curve*, Federal Reserve Bank of Boston Conference Series, no. 19, Federal Reserve Bank of Boston, Boston, 1978, pp. 49–83; Phelps, Edmund S., "Phillips Curves, Inflation Expectations, and Optimal Employment over Time," *Economica*, vol. 34, August 1967, pp. 254–281; Phillips, A. W., "The Relation Between Unemployment and the Rate of Change of Money Wage Rates in the United Kingdom, 1861–1957," *Economica*, vol. 25, November 1958, pp. 283–99; Robertson, Dennis A., *Money*, 4th ed., University of Chicago Press, Chicago, 1959.

(*See also* Administered prices; Bank deposits; Consumer price index; Employment and unemployment; Federal Reserve policy; Fiscal policy; Incomes policy; Index numbers; Interest rates; Keynesian economics; Labor unions; Monetary policy; Money illusion; Money supply; Neoclassical economics; Phillips curve; Price theory; Quantity theory of money; Stagflation; Value of the dollar; Velocity of circulation of money)

James Tobin

Infrastructure

Infrastructure refers to those economic activities which enhance, directly or indirectly, output levels or efficiency in production. Essential elements are systems of transportation, power generation, communications and banking, educational and health facilities, and a well-ordered government and political structure.

The term infrastructure was introduced in the early 1950s by the North Atlantic Treaty Organization (NATO) in its studies on war mobilization. Studies of infrastructure have since become part of the literature on economic development. Economists differentiate infrastructure from the more traditional uses of private capital accumulation for plant and equipment. However, once established, it is viewed as facilitating increases in private investment. It thus represents a necessary, although not sufficient, condition for development.

Development economists sometimes use the term "social overhead capital" as a synonym for infrastructure. Social overhead capital, or economic investment whose output provides services for more than one industry, is further divided into economic overhead capital and social capital. Economic overhead capital refers to the necessary capital accumulation for roads, power transmission systems, telecommunications, etc.; social capital is investment in such services as education, health, police, fire, etc.

A common feature of economic infrastructure is its high initial fixed cost and its relatively low variable costs of operation. As its benefits accrue to numerous diverse groups, its value is often difficult to measure precisely. With high fixed and declining marginal costs, and with the difficulties of pricing and capturing its pecuniary reward, the infrastructure does not conform to normal market investment analysis. Thus, infrastructure development financed by private capital tends to be regulated by government agencies. Frequently, even in some developed countries, government financing has been relied on to create the infrastructure. This mixture of private and public financing—although usually with public control in either case—is in part responsible for the broad definition of infrastructure.

While there is diversity in views of the infrastructure concept, there is unanimity in views of its necessity. For economic development infrastructure is viewed as providing the outputs and services necessary to generate higher levels of national output by linking and subsidizing its diverse users.

Problems of Size, Timing, and Pricing

The necessity of a growing infrastructure has been argued from both the demand and supply perspective. From either point of view infrastructure generates incentives for further private investment. Both forms also base this argument on infrastructure's externalities and its large capital requirement.

As an example, it is often argued that development is slowed owing to the limited size of local markets. If disparate small markets can be linked through investments in transportation and communication networks, the extended market will provide incentives for further private industrial investment and output. Since no group of investors can either carry out or reap the full advantages of the extensive infrastructure project, it is left to the government.

On the supply side, infrastructure development can reduce costs in two ways. By charging only incremental costs, infrastructure investment can subsidize existing industries and their customers and generate incentives for new firms. An example of this form of externalities is power generation.

Social capital can also generate private externalities. For example, the establishment of an educational system not only adds to the general welfare of a nation but also reduces the expense burden of an industry to train its own work force.

The debate about infrastructure centers not on its role, but rather on its timing in a nation's development. As large power plants and even road networks in less-developed nations often operate with excess capacity, critics argue that smaller, privately operated investments would have chosen plants of a more appropriate size.

The pricing of infrastructure's output has also come under question. Based on infrastructure marginal-cost pricing, total revenues rarely cover total costs (resulting in the subsidization advantage). As taxes make up the revenue shortfall it is not clear, under welfare economics, whether the disincentive and resource reallocation effects of taxation offset the projects' subsidization benefits. Lastly, social capital investments may be too extensive and premature, generalizing negative externalities. For example, an extensive array of social services available in the major cities of low-income nations has attracted the uneducated and unskilled to urban areas. The resulting overcrowding and substandard housing conditions have posed additional development problems.

Owing to the ownership and general welfare implications of infrastructure investment, economists of the socialist nations have become interested in the subject. However, infrastructure's definition and problems of size, timing, and pricing appear to be no less real to this group than to the more market-oriented development economists.

References

Fiedorowicz, K., "Planning of the Economic Infrastructure," *Eastern European Economics*, vol. 16, no. 1, Fall 1977, pp. 48–73; Hagen, Everett E., *The Economics of Development*, rev. ed., Irwin, Homewood, Ill., 1975; Hirschman, Albert O., *The Strategy of Economic Development*, Yale University Press, New Haven, Conn., 1958; Kindleberger, Charles P., and Bruce Herrick, *Economic Development*, 3d ed., McGraw-Hill, New York, 1977.

(*See also* Stages theory of economic development)

Bernard S. Katz

Innovation

Innovation is a pragmatic concept. It refers to the infusion of something new into real-world activities; hence, it excludes abstractions such as new theories or concepts. Innovations may come about as a result of such new theories or concepts, as a result of new inventions, or simply as a result of new ways of implementing previously known principles. The concept is value-free, but under the assumption of rationality, innovations are commonly taken to be oriented toward progress and, therefore, an improvement, at least in the innovator's own evaluation.

In economics, innovation means one of three things:

1. The implementation of changes in production, i.e., changes in the production function

2. The introduction of new types of commodities in the market, i.e., the appearance of new supply functions

3. Procedural changes introduced into markets or the economy as a whole, i.e., social reform

Of these, the first is the most important and can also be translated to apply to the process of consumption via the technology of the consumption concept.

In economics, innovation is not necessarily viewed as wholly beneficial, primarily because of frequent inherent conflicts between the interests of the innovator and that of the market or society as a whole. For example, the introduction of a new piece of improved machinery may upgrade productivity, but it may also bring about technological unemployment (at least in the short run), and it may, in addition, cause environmental pollution.

The concept of innovation is not among the most commonly found subjects in the history of economic thought, particularly prior to the 1950s and 1960s, but where it does appear, it tends to occupy a place of fundamental importance. The one name in the history of economic thought most closely associated with the analysis of innovation belongs to the Austrian, later American, economist, Joseph A. Schumpeter. In his theories of economic development, business cycles, and, more generally, the course of and the outlook for the capitalist process the concept of innovation assumes a position of central importance.

In brief, Schumpeter starts his analysis by postulating a static economy, characterized by a given, undisturbed circular flow of economic activity. From time to time, the circular flow is disrupted by an innovation, undertaken by a profit-seeking entrepreneur. Successful innovations will then be imitated by others until the innovation becomes absorbed into a new circular flow pattern. This, according to Schumpeter, is the essence of economic development. It also leads to cyclical fluctuations in economic activity.

In his outlook, however, Schumpeter predicted the demise of capitalism partly because he foresaw the disappearance of investment opportunities, caused in no small measure by the anticipated decline in the innovative entrepreneurial spirit. Socialism would then ensue, according to Schumpeter.

In his analysis of the capitalism-to-socialism process, Schumpeter incorporated a number of concepts advanced earlier by Karl Marx, particularly on subjects of innovation and technology, yet Schumpeter was anything but a Marxist. He foresaw the demise of capitalism but he did not advocate it.

After the death of Schumpeter in 1950, the subject of innovation, along with more general aspects of technological change and research and development, moved into the limelight in the economics profession. This surge of interest is attributable to the Sputnik-inspired international space race and to important defense-related innovations made during the period. The literature of the late 1950s and early 1960s was predominantly empirical in character, but it produced at least two important conceptual propositions, one in contradiction to Schumpeter, the other focusing on a phenomenon neglected by Schumpeter.

The first of these propositions challenged Schumpeter's assertion that innovators tend to be the large, monopolistic firms. Findings of the 1950s and the 1960s have shown that considerable innovative activity can be attributed to firms not meeting these criteria. The second proposition was more important. In Schumpeter's treatment, the knowledge foundation of innovation was not a factor. What mattered was entrepreneurship, and given the presence of entrepreneurship, there was no dearth of new know-how or of inventions required for the innovation process.

During the 1950s and the 1960s when economists first recognized the economic importance of research and development, innovation became a link in the newly postulated chain of progress: research and development–invention–innovation–economic growth and development. In other words, innovation and the inventions required were taken out of the conceptual class of freely available or spontaneously forthcoming phenomena and were incorporated into the class of regular, planned economic activity. Inasmuch as basic research constitutes an important part of the gamut of progress, and inasmuch as governmental promotion of basic research is a prerequisite, a link between government patronage and innovation was established, a link that would have appeared alien to Schumpeter.

Other questions concerning innovation during the 1950s and the 1960s centered on the link between innovation and the profit incentive; on the character of capital-saving, labor-saving, and neutral innovation; on the diffusion of innovations in industry; and on the relationship between innovation and economic growth, both on the micro- and the macroscale. Empirical measures of innovation consist of direct counts (of named innovations); and counts of patents, licenses, and copyrights.

References

Mansfield, Edwin, *The Economics of Technological Change*, Norton, New York, 1968; Nelson, Richard R., Merton J. Peck, Edward D. Kalachek, *Technology, Economic Growth and Public Policy*, Brookings, Washington, D.C., 1967; Schumpeter, Joseph A., *Business Cycles*, McGraw-Hill, New York and London, 1939; Schumpeter, Joseph A., *Capitalism, Socialism, and Democracy*, Harper, New York, 1950.

(*See also* Economic growth; Research and development; Technology)

Theodore Suranyi-Unger, Jr.

Input-output analysis

Input-output analysis is the study of the exchanges of goods and services among industries. It describes the inputs necessary to produce the outputs of the various sectors of the economy. Input-output starts from the accompanying intersectorial flow table. To use this table to study questions such as how automobile imports affect employment in various industries, or how oil price increases influence other prices, or what widespread use of electric automobiles would do to other industries, one uses basic mathematical methods.

Input-Output Accounting

Input-output analysis usually begins from an intersectorial flow table showing who bought how much of each industry's products in a particular year. A hypothetical intersectorial flow is shown in Table 1. The economy is divided into a number of producing sectors, listed down the left side of the table. In the simple example shown here, only four sectors are distinguished. (In practice, published tables range from about 30 to over 400 sectors, with tables having 40 to 100 sectors being the most common.)

Across the top of the table are listed these same sectors, but they are listed as purchasers. The cells of the table then show the sales from the seller sector on the left to the buyer sector at the top. Thus, in the table, agriculture sold $76 billion of products to industry. This sale from one producing sector to another is called an intermediate flow. Further to the right, beyond the first double line, are the sales to final demands—personal consumption, investment, exports, and government. Imports appear as a negative column. Thus, although the $76 billion shown for purchases of industry from agriculture includes imported products, the sum across the "Agriculture" row will—because of the negative entry in the import column—give exactly the domestic production of agriculture.

Below the first double line in Table 1 appear the factor payments by industry. Only three have been shown: labor income (wages, salaries, supplements), capital income (profits, interest, and depreciation), and indirect taxes (property, excise, and sales taxes), but actual tables often show much more detail.

The sum of the "Total" row, $1221 billion, is also the sum of the "Total final demand" column and is the gross national product (GNP). The entries in the "Total" row under the "Intermediate" columns show the gross outputs of the sectors; the entries under the "GNP components" columns show the values for the components in the product side of the usual, aggregate national income and products account (NIPA). The entries in the "Total" column show, in the rows for producing industries, the gross outputs of these industries (matching exactly the outputs shown in the "Total" row), while in the value-added rows, the total factor payments appear, as in the income side of the NIPA. Thus, the input-output table may be viewed as an expansion of the NIPA, and, is in fact, a valuable tool in establishing accurate NIPA.

Within this general framework, there are numerous variations. Some of the most important are in the following matters:

Sectors: Sectors may be defined by commodity, by establishment, or by company groupings.

Pricing: Flows may be priced in producer prices or in purchaser prices. The meaning of the entries in the "Trade and transportation" row depend on the pricing used. In producer price tables, they show margins on the goods received by the sector named at top; in purchaser price tables, they show the margins on goods shipped by that sector.

Imports: Sometimes imports are completely separated from domestic output, and two tables are given. Often imports are shown as a positive row instead of as a negative column, but this practice causes problems in working with the tables.

TABLE 1 Illustrative Input-Output Table

(Billions of dollars)

Sellers \ Buyers	Intermediate sales: Agriculture	Industry	Trade and transportation	Services	Total intermediate	GNP components: Personal consumption	Fixed investment	Change in inventory	Exports	Imports	Government	Final demand	Total
1. Agriculture	...	76	...	4	80	20	0	−3	10	−8	1	20	100
2. Industry	8	150	30	45	233	313	110	12	50	−48	30	467	700
3. Trade and transportation	1	15	3	5	24	249	10	...	2	−5	20	276	300
4. Services	2	50	10	20	82	276	5	...	30	−33	40	318	400
5. Total intermediate (= 1 + 2 + 3 + 4)	11	291	43	74	...	858	125	9	92	−94	91	1081	
6. Labor income	66	260	170	200		...	...	...	...	...	140	140	
7. Capital income	20	130	70	106		...	...	...	...	...			
8. Indirect taxes	3	19	17	20		...	...	...	...	...			
9. Total value added (6 + 7 + 8)	89	409	257	326	1081	...	...	...	...	...	140	140	1221
10. Total (5 + 9)	100	700	300	400	...	858	125	9	92	−94	231	140	1221

Basic Mathematics of Input-Output

An input-output flow table of this sort may be used to answer many questions about how changes in one part of the economy will affect other parts; it may also be used in economic forecasting to achieve consistency between forecasts of final demands and forecasts of industry outputs and factor incomes, or consistency among forecasts of various industries. For these uses, one needs to define the input-output coefficient,

$$a_{ij} = x_{ij}/q_j$$

where x_{ij} = flow from industry i to industry j
q_j = output of industry j

The requirement that the output of sector i should be equal to the sum of intermediate plus final demands (f_i) for this sector may be written

$$q_i = \sum_j a_{ij} + f_i$$

There is one such equation for each sector. The equations can be solved with changed values of the f's or a_{ij}'s to study the effects of these changes on the outputs of all industries. In matrix form, these equations may be written

$$q = Aq + f$$

or

$$q = (I - A)^{-1}f$$

The matrix A is often called the direct-requirements matrix and $(I - A)^{-1}$ is then called the total-requirements matrix because the element of it in the ith row and jth column shows how much sector i will be required to produce in order for sector j to deliver one unit of output to final demand.

Input-output relations also apply to prices, for the value of one unit of output of a good is the sum of material costs and value added per unit of product; thus

$$p_j = \sum_i a_{ij}p_i + v_j$$

where p_j is the price of product j and v_j is the value added per unit of output of this product. By thinking of p and v as row vectors, these equations may be written

$$p = pA + v$$

or

$$p = v(I - A)^{-1}$$

where $(I - A)^{-1}$ is the same total-requirements matrix which appeared above.

History of Input-Output Tables

Input-output was introduced by Wassily W. Leontief in 1936. A large, 450-sector table was undertaken to describe the United States in the year 1947, but the work was never published in full detail. An 82-sector table for 1958, prepared by the Department of Commerce and published in 1965, launched the regular preparation of input-output tables as a part of the NIPA in the United States. Tables with 360 to 450 sectors have been published for 1963, 1967, and 1972, each with a lag of 6 or 7 years between the reference date and the appearance of the table.

Other countries began preparing tables regularly during the 1960s. Annual tables are available for France, Norway, West Germany, the Netherlands, and the United

Kingdom, with as little as 2 years between the reference year and the publication date. Tables have been made for over 120 countries, including all of the major developed countries, most socialist countries, and many less-developed countries. Tables have also been made for a number of states and cities.

Applications

A typical early application of input-output analysis was to change a part of the final demand vector—for example, by replacing a portion of defense spending by an equal volume of foreign aid or consumption expenditure—and to calculate the consequent changes in the output and employment in various industries. The price equations were used, first in Israel and then in several socialist countries, to calculate factor-cost prices. A uniform rate of return was assigned to capital in all industries and all subsidies were eliminated (in the calculations). Foreign currency for importing was assumed to be "made" by exports, and the corresponding value of the foreign currency in terms of the factor-cost prices was calculated. Such prices could be used to obtain better measures of true social costs of various projects than could be derived from actual selling prices.

Since the 1960s, input-output analysis has played an increasing role in econometric forecasting models where it connects the product side of the model with the income side. That is, it connects the expenditures on final demand categories, such as consumption or investment by product bought with labor and capital income, in the industries that contributed to making the products. Models using input-output analysis in this way are now operating in several developed economies, and efforts are being made to link them together.

In the late 1970s much interest centered on making the input-output coefficients sensitive to prices. The question of price-induced substitution among energy sources has generated particularly lively debate. Many other applications will be found described in the proceedings of the International Conferences on Input-Output Techniques which have taken place about once every 4 years since the early 1950s.

References

Brody, A., and A. P. Carter (eds.), *Input-Output Techniques*, North-Holland, Amsterdam, 1972; Leontief, Wassily W., *The Structure of American Economy*, 1st ed. (1919–1929), Harvard University Press, Cambridge, 1941; 2d ed. (1919–1939), Oxford University Press, New York, 1951; Polenske, K. R., and J. V. Skolka (eds.), *Advances in Input-Output Analysis*, Ballinger, Cambridge, Mass., 1976.

(*See also* Economic forecasts; Economic models; Economic planning; Forecasting methods; Macroeconomics; Microeconomics; National income accounting; Statistical techniques in economics and business, an overview)

Clopper Almon, Jr.

Institutional economics

Institutional economics is the term most commonly used to denote the school in American economic thought associated with Thorstein Veblen, John R. Commons, and Wesley Clair Mitchell. The name has served to underline the emphasis which this group placed on looking at the economic decision-making process against the entire cultural and social context within which it operates. It has often been described as a movement of dissent against the assumptions and perspective of classical and neoclassical economic theory. In this it reflects its antecedents in the German historical school, most particularly Gustav Schmoller, as well as the utopian socialists and others. Contemporary institutionalists argue that institutionalism is more than mere dissent.

The essence of institutionalism lies in a view of economics as evolving entities which both shape and express the emergent choices of society concerning the uses to which resources shall be put. The view of this interactive process by which societal values are formed and through which resource decisions are made is institutionalism's most distinctive feature, and it is what ultimately distinguishes it from other schools of economic thought. Institutionalism stresses process and evolution rather than statics or equilibrium. The natural condition for participants in economic decision making is conflict rather than harmony. Moreover, institutionalists believe that political economy subsumes markets and prices but transcends exclusive focus on them because the real focus must be on analysis of the process by which modern societies express emerging societal values as they are reflected in the entire resource-allocation process. As such, institutionalists believe that the emphasis must be on how values are formed, not on how prices are formed, and on how the valuational system changes through time. Therefore, institutionalists are concerned with economic progress and ideas of progress, how they are formed and change, rather than merely on economic growth. Because these questions involve the entire institutional structure of society over time, the name "institutionalism" has stuck, although evolutionary economics is perhaps more appropriate. It also explains why institutionalists have had perhaps their greatest impact in the field of development economics.

The Three Founders

Veblen devoted himself to critical examination of the American capitalist system and bequeathed to institutionalism his concern with the cultural milieu within which economic decisions are made. He began with a distinction between industrial values and pecuniary values which in one form or another is found in the thinking of most institutionalists. The industrial values derive preeminently from the technological process, and nowhere did this process make itself more prominent than through the impact of industrialization on successive capitalist economies. It was this aspect of evolving economies which most interested Commons. He focused on the impact of industrialization on economies previously analyzed preeminently by classical economists through the assumptions of Smithian competitive economics. He argued that the inherent conflict in society, expressing itself in labor-management disputes in the industrializing United States during the last quarter of the nineteenth century and the first quarter of the twentieth century, required a new perspective in economic theory, one which Commons called the economics of collective action. A larger role for the public sector was an inevitable concomitance.

Mitchell looked at these same emergent phenomena and concluded that a primary requirement of economic analysis was for a far more profound knowledge of the facts of economic development than economic theorists had previously demanded. His use of statistics in economic analysis led to the founding of the National Bureau of Economic Research and permanently influenced the character of economic research in the United States. His main concern was with the instability evidenced by evolving economies and led to his path-breaking work in business cycle measurement and analysis.

Neoinstitutionalists

In the wake of the three founders there were a number of economists who qualified as institutional economists. Prominent among them were Richard Ely, J. M. Clark, Rexford Guy Tugwell, and Gardiner Means. Other institutionalists included Walton Hamilton, Robert F. Hoxie, Selig Perlman, A. B. Wolfe, Morris Copeland, and Edwin F. Witte. In 1972 Allan Gruchy suggested the term "neoinstitutionalists" for the second generation of institutionalists, a term he applied to John Kenneth Galbraith, Clarence Ayres, Gunnar Myrdal, and Gerhard Colm. If this group represents the most prominent of institutionalists who wrote in the past 20 or 25 years, they are followed today by a number of economists whose work appears regularly in the Association for Evolutionary Economics' *Journal of Economic Issues*, which is dedicated both to clarifying and advancing institutionalists' views.

Present Influence of Institutionalism

There is disagreement about the present influence of institutionalism. There are those who regard institutionalism as essentially the dissent expressed by the founding trio, and, as such, a movement which is dead. Paul Samuelson has taken this view, arguing that institutionalism "withered away" 40 years ago. On the other hand, one could argue that many institutionalist views and concerns have found their way into mainstream economic thinking. Current interest in economic development invariably focuses on the institutional structure within which economic decisions are made in precisely the manner that institutionalists have always insisted is essential to economic analysis. Current concern with the quality of life, with the costs of growth to the environment, and with the ultimate direction which economic activity is thrusting the modern world reflects the interest in economic progress, which has long been an institutionalist hallmark, rather than in mere growth.

References

Breit, William, and William Culbertson, Jr., (eds.), *Science and Ceremony: The Institutional Economics of C. E. Ayres.*, University of Texas Press, Austin, 1976; Commons, John R., *Institutional Economics: Its Place in Political Economy*, 2 vols., University of Wisconsin Press, Madison, 1959; Dorfman, Joseph, et al., *Institutional Economics: Veblen, Commons and Mitchell Reconsidered*, University of California Press, Berkeley, 1963; Gruchy, Allan G., *Contemporary Economic Thought*, Macmillan, New York, 1972; Mitchell, Wesley Clair, *Business Cycles, The Problems and Its Setting*, National Bureau of Economic Research, New York, 1927; Veblen, Thorstein, *The Theory of the Leisure Class: An Economic Study of Institutions*, rev. ed., New American Library, New York, 1953.

(*See also* Economic history and theory; Economics; German historical school; Neoclassical economics)

Philip A. Klein

Integration

A company may increase in size by expanding its capacity to produce a given product (e.g., automobiles), which is known as horizontal integration, or by undertaking to produce the raw materials required to make its main product (e.g., glass or steel to make automobiles) or to market its products to ultimate consumers (e.g., retail sales agencies for automobiles), which is known as vertical integration.

Horizontal Integration

Management usually seeks to expand horizontally in order to obtain the economies of large-scale production. By increasing its size, a company can:

1. Reduce the cost of purchased materials because of the larger volume or because of its improved ability to schedule purchases and thus to make more effective use of inventories
2. Afford to buy more efficient equipment
3. Make better use of by-products
4. Create a broader base on which to conduct and to finance research and development
5. Afford to hire more experienced management
6. Lower unit costs
7. Develop a more efficient sales force and undertake more extensive advertising
8. Obtain capital at lower costs
9. Develop a stronger market position

Historically, a company has sought to achieve these goals either by internal expansion (investment in new plant and equipment) or by the acquisition of other companies (mergers). After the passage of the Celler-Kefauver Act in 1950, the Supreme Court imposed stringent restrictions on horizontal mergers. In testing the legality of such mergers, it gave major weight to the effects on the structure of an industry rather than to the economies to be derived by the combined company. The key question became what percentage of the market would the combined company control.

Even though banking is a highly concentrated local industry, in the *Philadelphia Bank* case (1963) the Court held that the merged company would hold 30 percent of the geographic market and hence was anticompetitive. With a few exceptions, the largest bank in a city usually accounts for much more than 30 percent of the market.

In the *Von's Grocery* case (1966) a combined share of 7.5 percent of the grocery sales in Los Angeles was held to be excessive against a background of a declining number of companies in that market.

Even though an acquired company added only a small percentage to the market share controlled by a large company, the merger has been disapproved in some decisions. For example, the Aluminum Company of America, with 27.8 percent of the combined market for aluminum and copper conductor wire and cable, was not permitted to acquire Rome Cable Corporation, which accounted for 1.3 percent of that market.

However, in 1974 a merger of coal producers was approved although it resulted in modest increases in the market share of the two largest firms in two geographical markets (from 45 to 49 percent and from 44 to 53 percent). This merger took place against a background of a substantial drop in the number of coal producers. The Court pointed out that market shares alone do not determine market power.

Similarly, in two bank cases decided soon thereafter, the Court followed the same approach as in the *General Dynamics* case by holding that market shares are not of overriding significance.

The U.S. Department of Justice has established guidelines as to the horizontal mergers it would challenge. Thus, if the four largest firms had 75 percent of the market, the government indicated it would challenge a merger when the shares were as follows:

Market shares, %	
Acquiring company	Acquired company
4	4 or more
10	2
15 or more	1

SOURCE: Wilcox and Shepherd (1975).

Against this background, the ability of any company, which has a large share of any given product or geographic market, to grow through mergers was severely limited. One result was the shift to large conglomerate mergers in the 1960s, companies acquiring another company which operates in an unrelated line of business—for example, the acquisition of Marcor (retailing and containers) by Mobil (petroleum). Firms that have followed this merger route include International Telephone and Telegraph, Litton, Gulf and Western, and Loews.

This does not mean that a company that expands by investment in plant and equipment rather than through merger may not have an antitrust problem. If it becomes too big in a given product market, it may be attacked under the monopolization provision (section 2) of the Sherman Antitrust Act. The classic decision (1945) held that Alcoa had a monopoly of aluminum because it accounted for 90 percent of total ingot production.

Although Alcoa grew through internal expansion rather than by merger, the Court held: "It was not inevitable that it [Alcoa] should always anticipate increases in the demand for ingot and be prepared to supply them. Nothing compelled it to keep doubling and redoubling its capacity before others entered the field." It will be noted that the Court was concerned solely with market share rather than with the efficiency of the company.

Vertical Integration

The production process embraces all stages from raw materials to semifinished goods to finished goods, through wholesaling to the sale of the final product at retail. Vertical integration develops when a company operates in more than one stage in the production process. Thus, when a steel mill also produces coal and iron ore, two of its basic raw materials, it is integrating backward. When Avon Products produces cosmetics and then retails them from door to door, it is integrating forward. Relatively few large companies confine their activities to only one stage of production. Such specialization is characteristic of smaller companies (e.g., the many small companies that supply parts for General Motors).

The major objectives of integrating backward are to reduce or to control raw materials costs or to assure the certainty of supplies of such materials. One can attain efficiencies—better flow of materials, parts, and components—from lower to higher stages of production. A company integrates forward to wholesale and/or retail to control the distribution of its products and to be able to profit from its brand name. Vertical integration also increases the size of a company and thus enables it to obtain the advantages of lower-cost financing, to spread overhead costs, and to hire better-trained managers and executives.

Vertical integration also has been subject to the antitrust laws. The anticompetitive effects alleged to develop from vertical mergers are as follows:

1. *Foreclose markets to rivals.* Under section 7 of the Clayton Act (1914), suit was successfully brought against Du Pont, which controlled 23 percent of General Motors (GM). In 1957 the Court ruled that because of its stock ownership, Du Pont had a preferred position in supplying GM with synthetic lacquers and fabrics. Parenthetically, it should be noted that Du Pont acquired its interest by supplying the funds that GM required to remain a viable enterprise. Nevertheless, the Court found that because of its position, Du Pont was able to foreclose the large GM market from other sellers of those products.

   Similarly, in overturning the Brown Shoe–Kinney merger in 1962 the Court found that other shoe manufacturers would be foreclosed from sales through the Kinney retail stores.

2. When a company producing raw materials is acquired, it is claimed that the acquiring company will be able to supply all of its needs in times of shortage at the expense of its competitors. Thus, when Bethlehem Steel Corporation sought to merge with Youngstown Sheet & Tube Company in 1958, the merger was ruled to be anticompetitive by a federal court for a variety of reasons including the probability that it would prevent nonintegrated competitors from obtaining raw materials in times of shortage (e.g., nail wire).

3. There is also concern that a major supplier of raw materials that integrates forward will be able to squeeze independent fabricators by its pricing policy. Thus, if the integrated concern increases raw material prices and maintains finished goods prices unchanged, the independent will find itself in a profits squeeze. In the Alcoa case cited earlier, the Court specifically prohibited such pricing. This pricing problem must be kept in mind in any industry in which there is a large number of independent fabricators in addition to large vertically integrated companies.

References

Bork, Robert H., *The Antitrust Paradox*, Basic Books, New York, 1978, chaps. 10, 11; Phillips, Almarin (ed.), *Perspectives on Antitrust Policy*, Princeton University Press, Princeton, N.J., 1965, chaps. 2, 7, 8; Posner, Richard A., *Antitrust Law: An Economic Perspective*, University of Chicago Press, Chicago, 1976, chaps. 6, 8; Scherer, Frederic M., *Industrial Market Structure and Economic Performance*, Rand-McNally, Chicago, 1971, chap. 20; *United States v. Aluminum Co. of America et al.*, 148 F. 2d 416 (1945); Weston, J. Fred, and Sam Peltzman (eds.), *Public Policy Toward Mergers*, Goodyear, Pacific Palisades, Calif., 1969, chaps. 3, 10, 11, 12; Wilcox, Clair, and William G. Shepherd, *Public Policies Toward Business*, 5th ed., Irwin, Homewood, Il., 1975, chap. 8, table, p. 241.

(*See also* Concentration of industry; Conglomerate; Mergers)

Jules Backman

Interest, economic theory of

The concept of interest embraces theories of time preference, marginal productivity, liquidity preference, and loanable funds. However, these apparently diverse views of interest can be grouped into two broad classes: real and monetary. Real theories of interest are long-run theories in which interest is the return for real abstinence and the yield on real capital. Monetary theories of interest are short-run theories in which the monetary (also called the nominal) rate of interest is the cost of borrowing money and selling securities, and the yield on lending money and purchasing securities. Expressed differently, the real rate of interest is determined by the demand for and supply of real savings, whereas the monetary rate of interest is determined by the demand for and supply of money (or, alternatively, the demand for and supply of securities). The modern link between real and monetary theories of interest is that the monetary rate of interest should approximately equal the real rate plus (or minus) the expected rate of inflation (or deflation).

Real Theories of Interest

Real theories of interest have a long doctrinal history, first appearing in the writings of Richard Cantillon and David Hume in the eighteenth century. But they were developed principally by Eugen von Böhm-Bawerk and Knut Wicksell in the nineteenth century and by Irving Fisher in the early twentieth century. Real theories held sway until the Keynesian revolution of the mid-1930s. They were then overshadowed by monetary theories as monetary authorities manipulated their national money stocks and nominal interest rates as part of an effort to stabilize employment at high levels. More recently, real theories have provided the base for contemporary theory as the high inflation rates of the 1970s and the reemergence of neoclassical monetary economics resulted in empirical studies of the impact of money and inflation on interest.

The two parts to real theories of interest are the act of saving and the use of saving. The act of saving is the abstinence from consumption, and real resources are released for use in the production of new plant and equipment. Interest is a reward for the act of saving and the provision of real capital. Theoretically, there is some interest rate which is just equal to the rate at which each saver is willing to substitute future for current consumption. Generally, the higher the rate of interest, the greater the saving and the willingness to sacrifice present consumption.

Just as savers have a choice of consuming present or future goods, producers have a choice of producing present or future consumable goods. When producers divert current resources from the production of present to future goods, new real capital is added to their resources with a resultant net gain in their ability to produce future consumables. The ratio of this net gain to the new capital that generated it is called the yield on capital (or, alternatively, the marginal product of capital). Given diminishing returns, and other things remaining the same, the greater the amount of real capital, the lower its yield. Firms must compare this yield from new capital with the interest cost of obtaining the funds needed to acquire the real resources devoted to producing the new capital. Since the yield on capital decreases as more capital is acquired, it follows that the amount of capital demanded can only expand as the interest cost of funds decreases.

The real rate of interest is set when the yield on capital is just equal to the rate at which the saver abstains and substitutes future for current consumption. This real rate is ultimately determined by the time preferences of individuals for present and future goods and by underlying real productivity forces such as technology, the availability of raw material resources, and the stock of capital. Productivity forces change slowly over time and, thus, the real rate of interest also changes slowly.

Monetary Theories of Interest

Monetary theories of interest, like real theories, have a long doctrinal history dating from the mercantilists and John Locke in the seventeenth century, who regarded interest as the "price of the hire of money." Early nineteenth-century classical economists and the neoclassical economists of the late nineteeth and early twentieth centuries held principally to real theories of interest, but recognized that money-stock changes may have a temporary effect upon market interest rates. They reasoned that in high-employment economies, an increase in the stock of money would temporarily depress market rates below the real rate of interest and, given the relatively fixed rate of production, the price level would rise, leading to a decrease in the real supply of money and thereby causing the market rate to return to the original real level.

As noted earlier, high-unemployment levels of the 1930s and expansive monetary policies of the post-World War II period caused most economists to utilize monetary theories of interest. J. M. Keynes (1936) developed the principal monetary theory, the liquidity preference approach. The logic of this theory was that an expansive monetary policy would cause the market rate of interest to decrease and, if the demand for goods were responsive to interest rate variation, the demand for investment goods would rise. In turn, firms, given their excess capacity, would increase production and hire more workers with little price change. Given continued monetary expansion and excess productive capacity, the market rate could be below the long-run real rate of interest for extended periods.

Contemporary Interest Theory

The extended inflation of the 1970s caused economists to reassess their theory of interest. They have built upon the neoclassical analysis developed by Irving Fisher (1930). Leading proponents of the new view are Milton Friedman and Eugene F. Fama (1975). Extensive empirical research has been conducted by William E. Gibson (1972), Fama, and Maurice D. Levi and John H. Makin (1979). The contemporary view argues that the nominal (market) rate of interest is equal to the real rate plus the expected inflation rate.

The new theory presents the following model. Assume a high-employment economy in a dynamic equilibrium where the nominal and real rates of interest are equal. The growth rate of money is just equal to the long-run real growth rate of output, and prices are constant. Now postulate an increase in the growth rate of money. Initially the market rate of interest will decline, investment demand will expand, and incomes will rise. Individual firms will at first believe that the rise in demand is unique to them; they will use their resources more intensively and bring some idle resources into production. As demand, incomes, and production increase, the demand for money will rise and the market rate of interest will begin to increase. Additionally, prices and wages will also rise, thereby reducing the real stock of money, causing the nominal interest rate to rise still further and the rate of production to return to its original growth rate. Unlike the neoclassical model, the contemporary model assumes that the nominal interest rate will not stop rising once it returns to its original level. It will stop rising only if the growth rate of money is reduced to its original level and prices stop rising. So long as the growth rate of money is greater than the growth rate of output, there is excess demand for goods and people will expect inflation to be maintained. Savers will insist on receiving a nominal interest rate on savings at least equal to the real rate plus the expected inflation rate, so that there is no deterioration in their real return. Borrowers similarly will be willing to pay the real rate plus the rate of inflation since they know that the higher prices will enable them to pay a nominal rate above the real rate. Thus, the contemporary theory of interest unites the real and monetary theories with a price expectation effect.

References

Fama, Eugene F., "Short-Term Interest Rates as Predictors of Inflation," *American Economic Review*, vol. 65, no. 3, June 1975, pp. 269–282; Fisher, Irving, *The Theory of Interest*, Macmillan, New York, 1930, reprinted by Kelley, New York, 1965; Gibson, William E., "Interest Rates and Inflationary Expectations: New Evidence," *American Economic Review*, vol. 62, no. 5, December 1972, pp. 854–865; Gordon, Robert J. (ed.), *Milton Friedman's Monetary Framework*, University of Chicago Press, Chicago, 1974; Keynes, John M., *The General Theory of Employment, Interest, and Money*, Harcourt Brace Jovanovich, New York, 1936; Levi, Maurice D., and John H. Makin, "Fisher, Phillips, Friedman and the Measured Impact of Inflation on Interest," *Journal of Finance*, vol. 34, no. 1, March 1979, pp. 35–53.

(*See also* Classical school; Interest rates; Keynesian economics; Mercantilism; Propensity to consume or to save and inducement to invest)

John J. Klein

Interest rates

Interest is the price paid for the use of money over time. It is usually expressed as a rate charged or earned per period, hence interest rate. In turn, interest rates are typically expressed as a percentage of a principal (initial amount) borrowed or loaned. Thus, in the formulation

$$S = P(1 + it)$$

a sum S (such as $110) will result from a principal P ($100) if the interest rate i is 10 percent (0.10) for one time period t.

There are innumerable refinements and practical applications of interest calculations, the most important of which is compound interest (meaning interest on interest). In the formula

$$S = P(1 + i)^n$$

S is the sum to which a principle P will accumulate at interest rate i if the interest is compounded for n periods. This equation, which is usually solved using logarithms, shows that any given principal and interest rate will result in larger sums the more frequent and prolonged the compounding is.

This formula is the foundation of virtually all calculations involving the mathematics of finance. Thus, it is helpful in personal finance if one seeks to determine the true interest rate one has to pay on a discount loan (one in which the loan value at maturity is the principal and one receives only a discounted sum, the proceeds, at the outset); or if one obtains an installment loan, requiring periodic repayments, but where the interest rate is stated as a percentage of the original principal.

The formula is also basic to present-value calculations in which one seeks to determine, for example, which price (principal) should be paid for a series of future payments (e.g., a pension or annuity). Similarly, the formula is needed to calculate periodic payments such as one makes in repaying (amortizing) a mortgage loan within a given period at a stated interest rate.

The most important application of the basic interest formula is asset pricing, an application of present-value calculation. The market prices of interest-bearing securities and interest rates themselves are directly and inversely correlated, as shown in the formula

$$PV = \frac{1}{(1 + i)^n}$$

where PV stands for present value, i for the interest rate, and n for the relevant period.

Assume a security has been sold at a par value of 100 and bears a prevailing interest rate of 4 percent per annum. Assume further that the general interest rate level subsequently rises to 8 percent. Then, the security initially traded at 100 will inevitably decline in price to below par. (In order to determine by how much, the simple formula must be expanded to allow for periodicity of interest and capital repayments.)

This is so, of course, not because of the mere existence of mathematical equivalencies of the prices of securities at a single defined interest rate, but rather because supply and demand force interest-paying securities of similar characteristics into line with each other. Thus, a potential investor in long-term bonds of a given company who could obtain 8 percent on a new issue of that company may actually prefer to purchase a seasoned (outstanding) bond of that company. However, if the coupon rate (the originally stated interest rate) of the outstanding bond is indeed only 4 percent, its price must be adjusted so that the yield (the actual interest rate) becomes a close equivalent of the current rate before the investor will seriously consider buying the seasoned bond.

Similarly, and again because of the pervasive nature of the basic interrelation between prices and yields of interest-bearing securities, prices and yields of all types of such securities tend to show fairly close parallel movement. The process bringing about this parallelism is known as portfolio adjustment.

History of Interest Rates

Interest has been a subject of intense study and dispute virtually throughout recorded economic history. In the Roman era and in the early phase of industrialization during the eighteenth century, interest was viewed objectively as one among many prices. For much of the Middle Ages and throughout the history of the Islamic world, however, interest has in effect been a term of opprobrium. A charge for the use of money was often considered unjust per se and hence to be forbidden by law. Thus, official interest rate regulations are as old and traditional as interest itself.

The United States began as a capital-poor country with abundant investment opportunities. Hence, high interest rates for imported European capital were readily acceptable. By the 1830s, however, a pronounced split between the Eastern (lending) and the Western frontier (borrowing) interests began to develop, partly because the beginnings of central banking in the United States (especially the Second Bank of the United States) were interpreted by borrowers as inimical to easy money. The hostility to lenders and to interest reached a peak in the 1870s with the Populist movement. Many state usury laws, fixing maximum permitted rates of interest on a variety of transactions, date from this period. More generally, government influence upon, if not outright control of, interest rates has been generally considered a legitimate governmental function in the United States.

With the establishment of the Federal Reserve System in 1913 a federal influence upon money and capital markets became more systematic and accepted. The Federal Reserve itself and most economists, however, largely neglected the potential influence of interest rates on aggregate economic activity. During the Great Depression of the 1930s, the ineffectiveness of even very low interest rates in stimulating borrower demand led to a downgrading of interest rate studies.

During World War II and the early postwar period, short-term interest rates were held rigidly stable by Federal Reserve action—first as a part of price controls, later to help prevent a much-feared postwar depression. This spell was broken with the March 1951 Accord between the U.S. Treasury and the Federal Reserve under which short-term interest rates once again became flexible. (The U.S. government in effect conceded that the inflationary consequences of the Korean war were being aggravated by the public's ability to convert interest-bearing securities into cash—monetization of debt—at Federal Reserve-guaranteed prices.)

This Accord may be said to mark the beginning of recent interest rate history and theory. The Federal Reserve became expert at manipulating the federal funds and Treasury bill rates for monetary policy purposes. A variety of new fixed-yield instruments developed in the financial markets as pockets of potential investor and borrower attraction were explored. Theoreticians were busy updating and refining interest rate theories with the firm conviction that interest rates were indeed a vital determinant of aggregate economic performance. Meanwhile, the general interest rate level showed a modest updrift in 1951 to 1965 under the influence mainly of the gradual absorption of excess liquidity from World War II and the early postwar years.

Since the mid 1960s, interest rates have been dominated by the influence of incipient, and eventually actual, large-scale inflation. The general interest rate level rose to historic peaks in the 1970s. New interest rate-denominated securities proliferated, partly because of the broadening of international money-market activity. Interest rate regulation, both as an instrument of general economic policy and as a specific-market tool, were used intensively. At the same time, new doubts about the efficacy of interest rate policy arose—first as a consequence of intellectual gains for a theory emphasizing the quantitiy rather than the price of money as an explanation for variations in economic activity; and, second, because the inflation itself came to be viewed as a determinant rather than as a fallout of interest rates.

Variety and Term Structure of Interest Rates

In highly developed financial markets, hundreds of interest rates are quoted (and the corresponding securities traded) at any one time. In terms of their respective yields, the most important characteristics of such trading instruments are their relative liquidity and risk. Liquidity refers to the breadth of a security's market. Roughly, the larger the trading volume per trading period relative to the total outstanding, the more liquid is the security. However, the amount of price change induced by marginal shifts in supply and demand is another relevant and not necessarily coincident measure of liquidity. Risk, of course, refers to the degree of uncertainty attached to the borrower's compliance with all terms and conditions of the security, most importantly, timely payment of interest and repayment of principal.

Liquidity and risk are closely, although by no means perfectly, correlated with the maturity of a security. Financial markets make major distinctions between short-term securities (usually up to 1 year in original maturity); medium-term or intermediate securities (usually 1 to 5 years in original maturity, but frequently up to 10 years); and long-term securities (with original maturity of up to 25 years, or longer).

Yield Curves

Interest rates for securities of comparable quality usually rise (slope upward) along a yield curve as the maturity lengthens, reflecting lesser liquidity and greater risk for the longer maturities. Thus, short-term interest rates on corporate securities (prime commercial paper, 4 to 6 months) have been below long-term rates (AAA corporate bonds) far more frequently and for longer periods than the opposite case, although occasional instances of higher short-term rates than long-term rates have occurred.

An upward-sloping yield curve is often equated with a normal-term structure of interest rates. An inverted yield curve (short rates above long rates) calls for special explanations beyond liquidity and risk. One explanation for such occurrences during the 1970s is the impact of sudden and severe Federal Reserve restraint on the availability of short-term credit at the peak of an economic boom. The demand for such credit is far less elastic than that for long-term credit—long-term borrowing can be postponed more easily than short-term borrowing. In addition, it is expected that short-term rates will again fall below long-term rates so that a succession of short-term borrowings will eventually average less in cost than a single long-term borrowing at the time of the "credit crunch."

Variety of Interest Rates

The federal funds rate is the shortest of all broadly based rates. It is the rate for one-day trades among commercial banks of reserve balances at Federal Reserve banks. The rate is highly sensitive to Federal Reserve operations aimed at lowering or raising the general level of short-term rates. Treasury bill rates (short-term borrowing of the U.S. Treasury), large certificate of deposit rates (short-term borrowing by banks) as well as commercial paper rates (corporate indebtedness) are sensitive to the federal funds rate. There are also close links between U.S. short-term rates and those in foreign money centers, especially Eurodollars (offshore balances denominated in U.S. dollars).

Among long-term rates, one frequently quoted key rate is the AA-rated new utility bond rate (referring to 20- to 25-year obligations of public utilities with a high credit rating at the time of issue). Mortgage rates (loans secured by real estate) fall into two main classes—residential and commercial. In the wake of extensive U.S. government efforts to make residential mortgages more liquid (i.e., give mortgages some of the characteristics of uniform merchandise as are U.S. government securities), mortgage rates have averaged close to corporate bond rates in the late 1960s and in the 1970s, while they were typically above bond rates in earlier decades.

Interest futures are a development of the late 1970s when the Chicago Board of Trade began to permit trading in Treasury bills for delivery as much as 18 months ahead, followed by forward trading in government-backed mortgage packages. By buying Treasury bills forward, it is possible to assure oneself of an interest rate certain on funds not received until a later date. A speculator can, of course, attempt to make a profit by outguessing the course of interest rates. (For example, let us say one contracted to buy Treasury bills at a future date at a price yielding 8 percent. If the price of the bills rose at any time up to and including the delivery date to a yield equivalent of, say, 7 percent, one could profitably sell that contract.) More extensive futures trading (i.e., additional instruments) appears likely in the 1980s.

Interest Rate Theory and Forecasting

The rationale for the level of and changes in interest rates has been a scholarly subject for roughly two centuries. With the development of large-scale computer models of the economy and of econometric examination of interrelationships between numerous variables it has become possible to attempt structured interest rate forecasting.

Interest rate theorizing begins by declaring one particular interest rate (or the general interest rate level) to be the dependent variable on the left-hand side of an equation (or series of equations), followed by a search for that set of explanatory variables on the right-hand side of the equation(s) that logically and functionally best explains the dependent variable by accepted statistical standards.

As in all analytical economic reasoning, two divergent tendencies compete in the mind of the interest rate theorist. The first tendency is to be comprehensive with respect to both interest rates and their explanation. This correctly assumes that everything depends on everything else. This tendency would lead one to a dynamic general equilibrium model in which the entire spectrum of interest rates would be endogenous—i.e., it would both help to explain and be explained by the evolution of and changes in the entire economy. The other tendency is to focus on one interest rate or set of rates (i.e., first long rates then short rates, or vice versa) and to settle for explanatory variables that are simply assumed to be independent of interest rates. This occurs either because the theorist is struck by the need to explain an unusual phenomenon in a particular segment of the money and capital markets, or simply because partial equilibrium analysis is a more achievable goal. The approaches overlap, especially in the case of interest rates, because of the undeniable interrelationships of all rates.

The real-rate-plus-inflation theory of long-term interest rates, formulated by Irving Fisher in the early twentieth century, is an illustration of partial equilibrium analysis. Fisher broke down observed bond rates into a real component—a reward to the answer for consumption forgone—and an inflation component, which would compensate the investor for the expected depreciation in the purchasing power of currency of principal repayments and of interest during the term of the bond. Drawing on nineteenth-century predecessors, Fisher held that the real rate was fairly constant: it depends on the combination of the capital stock (on the demand side) and on savings habits (on the supply side). The inflation component, however, was highly variable, depending on actual inflation experience.

Renewed attention has been paid to Fisher's theory along with mounting inflation and rising interest rates since the late 1960s. The theory has proved sturdy under extensive empirical testing and has an intuitively convincing logical foundation. One serious weakness is that inflationary expectations are not easily measured directly. (A distributed lag or a more simple averaging of past actual inflation experience, used by Fisher and others, is only a substitute for actual expectations.) Yet the theory is the most satisfactory explanation for the strong, general upward trend of interest rates in the late 1970s, and it has become clear that short-term rates as well as long-term rates react to inflation. However, short-term rates have wider swings than long-term rates and rise less predictably with inflation.

The liquidity preference theory of interest, formulated by John Maynard Keynes, focuses heavily on short-term interest rates. (Striving for generality, Keynes added a "marginal efficiency of capital" theory of long-term rates, but apart from exploring and emphasizing investment incentives—the demand side of the real interest rate—the explanation does not vary much from Fisher's theory and earlier theories.) Keynes held that the public's liquidity preference (the demand for money or near-cash equivalents) would vary inversely with interest rates at any particular time, but that liquidity preference would shift with general economic conditions. On the supply side of the determinants of short-term rates, Keynes referred to banking policy (roughly equivalent in today's terms to monetary policy, central bank policy, or, in the United States, Federal Reserve policy).

In a famous example of applied interest rate theory which reflects the experience of the Great Depression, Keynes postulated a "liquidity trap"—a condition in which no realistically possible additional supply of funds could drive interest rates down sufficiently to stimulate additional credit demand. (Note that liquidity here refers to the general economy, not to the liquidity of a particular security as previously discussed.) Hence, Keynes downgraded the role of interest rates and of money in the business cycle, which was his main focus.

The loanable funds theory of interest rates, the origin of which is usually associated with the Swedish economist Knut Wicksell, is self-explanatory—one seeks to identify the proximate causes of interest rate variations by analyzing the supply and demand of credit. Wicksell was searching for a natural rate of interest (a concept that bears a resemblance to Fisher's real rate), around which market rates would fluctuate according to a cyclical demand and supply factor.

An important modern-day offspring of this theory is flow-of-funds analysis. This exercise originated at the Board of Governors of the Federal Reserve System during the late 1940s to early 1950s when it was felt that financial flows could and should be fitted into a comprehensive and internally consistent framework as a supplement to the (conceptually similar) national income and product accounts. Flow-of-funds analysis is hardly an interest rate theory per se since an ex post identity of the supply and demand of funds amounts to accounting rather than analysis. In practice, however, flow-of-funds exercises have been attempted increasingly on an ex ante basis.

In reconciling credit supplies and demands, interest rate predictions are a fallout—quite typically including reasoned opinions about relative interest rates (short-term versus long-term, bonds versus mortgages, etc.), over and above a general interest rate forecast. One key element of the iterative process required to produce ex ante equality between supplies and demand is to judge how much total credit and liquidity the central bank will permit or encourage. Thus, there is a clear link with monetary theory and policy.

Recent interest rate theorizing has aimed at synthesizing older thoughts in the light of modern institutional circumstances and enhanced measurement capabilities. According to one leading study by Martin Feldstein and Otto Eckstein (1970), the fundamental determinants of the long-term corporate bond rate are liquidity, debt, inflation, and expectations. Liquidity (used again in its general sense) refers to monetary policy—how much liquidity does the Federal Reserve inject into the economy? Debt refers to the amount of government debt the market is being asked to absorb relative to corporate demands. Inflation represents the discount on future purchasing power of principal and interest and is estimated on the basis of the experience of recent years. Expectations, finally, refers to the customary continuity of the financial markets—interest rates of immediately preceding periods influence those of the current period.

It is worthy of special note that the relative explanatory power of each preceding theory (that of Keynes, of Fisher, and flow-of-funds analysis) can now be tested. Thus, for 1954 to 1969 the Feldstein-Eckstein formula suggests that liquidity was the most important explanatory factor in the rise of long-term rates over that period but that inflation was rapidly gaining in relative importance toward the end of the period.

Interest rate forecasting remains in a fairly primitive state despite immense statistical work. The key problem is that for any very short period ahead extraneous factors can upset the average past relationships which are the basis of all forecasting equations. In addition, for longer periods ahead the coefficients of the independent variables may change substantially depending on actual experience with these explanatory variables in the meantime—i.e., the accuracy of the interest rate forecast depends on a correct forecast of the independent variables that determine the predicted result for the dependent variable. For example, any forecast of short-term interest rates depends on a current appraisal of the likely course of monetary policy (liquidity), which is known not to be mathematically predictable. Yet, monetary policy functions within reliably known parameters—toward real economic growth, against inflation and disorderly financial markets. Hence, the forecaster is driven back to an attempt to integrate interest rates with a full-fledged model of the economy as a whole, which complicates the statistical task and multiplies the potential errors.

References

Feldstein, Martin S., and Otto Eckstein, "The Fundamental Determinants of the Interest Rate," *Review of Economics and Statistics*, vol. 52, November 1970, pp. 363–375; Homer, Sidney, *A History of Interest Rates*, 2d ed., Rutgers University Press, New Brunswick, N.J., 1977; Hunt, Lacy H., *Dynamics of Forecasting Financial Cycles*, Contemporary Studies in Economic and Financial Analysis, vol. 1, New York University, JAI Press, Greenwich, Conn., 1976; Levi, Maurice D., and John H. Makin, "Fisher, Phillips, Friedman and the Measured Impact of Inflation on Interest," *Journal of Finance*, vol. 34, no. 1, March 1979, pp. 35–53.

(*See also* Business credit; Consumer credit; Credit, an overview; Debt; Disintermediation; Interest, economic theory of; Keynesian economics; Mortgage credit; Propensity to consume or to save and inducement to invest; Yield curve)

Frances H. Schott

Interindustry analysis (see Input-output analysis)

International Bank for Reconstruction and Development (see World Bank)

International economics, an overview

International economics adds a global dimension to traditional domestic economic analysis concerning how individuals, families, and organizations balance their expanding needs and wants against the limited resources available to satisfy them.

The peoples of the nations of the world continually seek to maximize their welfare by a wide variety of interactions and exchanges across boundaries. Differences in aspirations; human, natural, and capital resources; technology; culture; social and political systems; and other factors are always apparent and lay the foundation for mutually advantageous economic relationships.

How Nations Are Classified

Nations are commonly classified into groups that indicate their economic strengths and weaknesses as well as their stage of development.

Industrial or developed nations are those which have achieved substantial manufacturing and service capability in addition to advanced techniques in agriculture and raw material extraction.

Developing nations are usually those whose production sector is dominated by agriculture and mineral resources and are in the process of building up industrial capacity. Typically, these sectors not only serve home markets but also produce for exports. The objective is to try to earn funds from selling abroad in order to have buying power available for future purchases of foreign goods and services. Also, the aim can be to reduce dependence upon foreigners, i.e., to pursue import substitution policies. To achieve a reasonable balance between international payments and revenues is a constant challenge.

Much attention in international economic and political affairs understandably focuses on the welfare gap between the developed and developing nations. Comparisons are frequently made among countries concerning such measures of economic progress and competitive strength as cultivated land area, population, per capita income and wealth, unit labor costs, prices, external debt, and monetary reserves.

The leading Western, free (non-Communist) industrial nations are sometimes referred to as the First World. The Second World comprises the Socialist-Communist nations. The Third World covers the remaining developing countries. There is increasing reference to the resource-poor nations in the Third World group as the Fourth World.

Most of the trade of the world occurs between the industrialized countries. The remaining nations strive to strengthen their economies by trade, barter, aid, and concessions from the major developed nations. The petroleum-rich countries, particularly the Organization of Petroleum Exporting Countries (OPEC), control much of the world's immediately available energy resources which the industrial nations need in order to keep their economies functioning.

The emerging countries with resources and expanding industrial capability, e.g., Brazil, Korea, Mexico, and Taiwan, are more and more called the new industrial countries (NICs).

The generalization is often made that most of the richer nations are located in the Northern Hemisphere and the poorer nations in the Southern Hemisphere. This gives rise to the expression "North/South" in reference to many international problems, confrontations, and dialogues.

International Economic Theory

International economic theorists have developed three important theoretical conclusions:

1. The theory of comparative advantage states that mutually advantageous trade will always be possible because trade patterns will be based on relative prices rather than absolute prices. That is, no one country can have a comparative advantage in all commodities. As initially formulated, the theory of comparative advantage is based on labor-cost differentials. Later researchers have shown that both supply and demand factors play a role in determining the relative prices of commodities that form the basis for mutually advantageous exchange.

2. The Heckscher-Ohlin theory states that a country will tend to export the commodity that uses relatively more of the factor of production that is relatively most abundant in that country. The theory assumes that countries have different quantities of the various factors of production such as land, labor, and capital, but identical production functions.

3. The factor-price equalization theory states that under absolutely free international trade, not only the prices of the traded products but also the prices of the factors of production (inputs) such as land, labor, and capital will be equalized among countries.

Official International Organizations

Many official international bodies have been formed through the years to facilitate trade and to solve pressing problems, for example: (1) to provide a means for discussing and addressing grievances among nations, e.g., United Nations; (2) to formulate rules and procedures for commercial and other interactions between countries, e.g., Organization for Economic Cooperation and Development (OECD), United Nations Commission for Trade and Development (UNCTAD), European Economic Community (EEC); (3) to supervise and monitor global monetary and related affairs, e.g., International Monetary Fund (IMF); (4) to assist in planning and financing development projects, e.g., International Bank for Reconstruction and Development (World Bank); and (5) to offer direct aid, e.g., as offered by various regional development banks around the world.

Few nations are willing to give up much of their sovereignty and accede to direction in their economic affairs from the outside unless they see offsetting gains or they have no other choice. The poorer nations generally look to international organizations for direct assistance and also tend to seek redistribution of global wealth and technology from the economically stronger nations.

Ideological differences among nations are always evident in economic policies and actions and affect participation in world organizations and agreements. Basic disagreements are most evident in the extent to which market forces are encouraged and permitted to operate. The Socialist-Communist nations usually try to isolate themselves from economic markets and seek to control their markets by regulatory edict. The Western industrial nations vary in the permitted freedom of markets, but the degree of freedom is substantially greater than what prevails in the Socialist-Communist nations.

Developing nations with natural resources or commodities to sell usually strive for international agreements—sometimes in the form of cartels such as OPEC—which will reduce price fluctuations (mainly on the down side) and ensure steadily increasing demand and revenues for their goods. Because price stabilization is difficult to achieve in the real dynamic markets of the world, is very expensive in recessionary periods, and is inflationary, many developed countries are reluctant to join in rigid commodity agreements.

Population in many respects determines and foreshadows the world's and each nation's needs and demands for goods, services, and jobs. The more than 4 billion people already living on the earth and the prevailing excess rate of births over deaths indicate that international economic and related questions merit high-priority attention throughout the world if future tensions and conflicts are to be minimized. For developing nations—in particular, for those with large and growing populations—the problem of unemployment poses a constant threat to social and political stability.

Many nations achieve recognized comparative advantages, i.e., relative superiority in cost, quality, and service for certain goods, which can benefit many or all nations if such advantages are widely made available. Such advantages, however, can be lost to other competing nations over time. When this happens, or where no comparative advantage exists, demands on domestic governments frequently arise for protection against job losses and sales and profit reductions from foreign-made goods and services. Dumping occurs when one nation's products are sold in another's market below cost or the prices which prevail at home.

Protectionism and Free Trade

Protectionism takes many forms. Tariffs or taxes are levied on imports, and nontariff rules in the form of quotas, quality and labeling standards, and similar restrictions tend to keep foreign nations' goods and services out of domestic markets. Subsidies to domestic firms similarly provide disadvantages to foreign competitors although foreign consumers get cheaper goods as a result.

The absence of protectionism is termed free trade, wherein goods and services flow across international boundaries on the primary basis of comparative advantage. Free trade is commonly under attack from protectionists.

The United States as well as most countries offer in their laws certain trade preferences favoring some nation's goods and services for economic, political, and social reasons. The best-known U.S. preference is the so-called most-favored nation status. Any nation so qualified by the Congress is permitted to pay only the lowest level of U.S. tariffs. Nonqualifying nations face stiffer barriers against their goods when they seek to export into the U.S. market. Some element of international prestige is associated with the most-favored nation title.

Tariff and nontariff barriers are the subject of continuing global debate and confrontation. National leaders have constituents who fear foreign inroads into their markets and/or demand special terms and conditions favoring their products over others. Periodically, the principal nations join in detailed and lengthy negotiations to reduce trade barriers. These are mainly under the aegis of the General Agreement on Tariffs and Trade (GATT). The overriding objective is to try to keep trade as free and open as possible so as to encourage greater world growth, employment, income, and investment. History records many instances where growing protectionism has led to international trade wars and eventually has caused political wars among belligerents.

Few nations can survive for long in economic isolation from the rest of the world simply because political geographical boundaries do not coincide with the natural resources, skills, and other essentials for the betterment of human welfare. World trade and financial flows reflect sharp variances in needs and advantages among individual countries. At any given time some nations will show surpluses in trade and payments balances, while others will experience corresponding deficits.

Balance of trade refers to the relationship of imports to exports of goods and services. Balance of payments is a more comprehensive measure which is defined variously to include financial investment flows of different maturities and purposes. Official or government-to-government payments and receipts also influence importantly changes in economic relationships among countries.

Aggregate surpluses and deficits must balance for the world as a whole. Chronic surpluses or deficits in any single country or region will cause economic and political repercussions and tensions. Surpluses often must be invested outside the nation, while deficits constitute international accounts payable which must be paid from reserves or financed by borrowing or financial aid from international bodies or foreign government grants.

Since the sharp petroleum price increases beginning in the early 1970s, trade and payments balances across the world have changed appreciably. Several major oil-producing countries have accumulated substantial surpluses, and some large petroleum-importing nations have registered substantial deficits.

Foreign Investment and Transnational Corporations

Investment in one country by individuals and organizations from another is an important aspect of international economics. Investment may be for portfolio, (i.e., in the form of securities) or direct capital (i.e., productive facilities). Colonialism and imperialism have often been described in terms of powerful nations exploiting the human and natural resources of weaker, less-developed countries. While some exploitation charges still remain, most developing as well as developed nations now substantially control the types, scopes, and ownership terms of investments made by foreigners.

In present times most foreign investors become active after political agreements between their own government and that of the nation in which investments are planned.

Much of the global private investment is now made by transnational corporations (TNCs), also widely referred to as multinational corporations (MNCs). Technical distinctions in classifying such global corporations are sometimes made to reflect whether multinational investments and operations are made exclusively by an executive group from one nation or by a combination of different national investment leaders, or by varying degrees of joint public and private ownership. Clearly, these transnational organizations play a major role in world trade and investments because of their demonstrated management skills, technology, financial resources, and related advantages.

MNCs, nevertheless, must confront frequently governmental and other critics who contend that such far-flung companies are able to minimize or avoid national regulation by virtue of their ability to shift new (and at times old) investments from one country to another. Some governments have adopted exacting rules which MNCs must follow in their countries, the most common of which requires a majority or significant minority of domestic as opposed to foreign ownership.

Developing nations in particular face some dilemma in formulating policies covering investments by foreigners. They usually have an urgent need for foreign investment assistance, but domestic political considerations often dictate severe tax and other laws, including nationalization laws, which discourage new foreign investment. Many developing nations have been successful, however, in providing attractive tax and other incentives to foreign investors for sufficient time periods to ensure a satisfactory return on the original investment.

One of the crucial dimensions of foreign investments is technology transfer, not only at the outset of an investment but also subsequently to ensure that the facilities remain competitive. The question of whether or not such technology transfer is a matter of international right of developing countries and what price, if any, is to be paid for it, is a source of intensive international debate.

Taxes clearly have an appreciable impact on international flows of funds, trade, and investment. Tax treaties exist between many, but by no means all, nations. Accordingly, the final payment or return to an international seller or investor can be sharply affected by the nature and level of taxes, the extent to which reciprocal tax offsets are permitted between nations, and the prospect of changes in taxes.

International Banking and Financial System

London, New York, Singapore, Tokyo, and many other global cities constitute important financial centers which, linked by close communications, enable nations and the overall world economy to function around the clock to serve people.

The massive shifting of funds for oil payments and the subsequent investment of oil revenues, for example, have involved a great deal of financial recycling through the complex, far-flung, and effective international monetary, financial, and banking system. Commercial banks have carried a very large proportion of these recycling operations and also play a role in helping some countries meet their balance of payments adjustment problems.

The global money system is now dominated by the United States dollar. The German mark, Japanese yen, and Swiss franc are also key currencies. A number of other money units play important roles in specific local markets. The physical transfer of actual paper money, coins, gold and silver bullion, and travelers' checks among nations is small compared with the massive volume of credit, deposits, and investment funds moving daily across boundaries.

Each national currency necessarily has a value for international exchange purposes. A host of developments, including economic and political news and confidence, will influence the value of a currency. Through time, economic performance, reserves, and the relative rate of inflation seem to be among the most important determinants of value.

Economic theory can again provide some perspective. The purchasing power–parity theory on exchange rate determination states that changes in exchange rates will tend to reflect the changes in the relative price levels in the different countries. That is, a rise in the price level of a country will tend to be offset by a fall of the exchange rate so that the price of the country's export and import commodities will remain the same in world markets. The theory is supported by much empirical evidence in the long run, but has not proved to be a highly reliable guide for short-term fluctuations.

An elaborate global system of foreign exchange trading provides the mechanism by which individual currency values are continually determined for transaction purposes. Ordinarily, governments will intervene through purchases or sales in foreign exchange markets to seek to stabilize the value of their currency.

A fixed exchange policy prevails when a currency is linked to some monetary standard and its value remains unchanged within narrow limits except for a major shift in underlying conditions. Whenever a change in value is made, it occurs by official government action and may be either a devaluation, i.e., loss in value, or revaluation, i.e., gain in value.

A floating exchange policy means in principle that the value of a currency will fluctuate with changing market conditions. A "free" float indicates little or no government intervention, while a "dirty" float describes the situation in which significant government intervention occurs from time to time but considerable variation in the value of the currency nevertheless persists. A "crawling peg" refers to a system of fairly regular or automatic adjustments in the exchange rate of a country.

A translation gain or loss occurs from currency value changes being applied to accounting statements of assets and liabilities of business firms.

International Reserves and Monetary Supervision

Financial reserves of each nation are a measure of strength used by international leaders and investors in judging risks. Hard currencies are usually in strong demand and backed by substantial reserves and general economic strength, while soft currencies lack these attributes.

All major international lenders and investors as well as official institutions use various types of risk measures for the countries of the world. Transfer risk concerns the prospect for being able to repatriate collected funds from the borrowing country. Credit risk pertains to the ability of the borrower to fulfill the repayment terms of the original loan agreement.

Financial reserves usually include U.S. dollars, other key currencies, special drawing rights (SDRs) issued by the IMF, and gold. In recent years the official IMF policy has been to deemphasize gold as too inflexible a reserve for dynamic global monetary and economic purposes, but the use of gold persists. SDRs are based on a basket of currencies and are made available to IMF members by allocation from time to time to provide additional liquidity for the international monetary system. SDRs, however, are restricted exclusively to government-to-government use.

The IMF offers financial assistance to member nations who confront balance of payments difficulties. Its economic and currency surveillance and conditions vary directly with the progress and prospects for improved economic and financial stability of the country applying for support.

The central, or government policy-level, banks—e.g., Federal Reserve in the United States, Deutsche Bundesbank in West Germany, Bank of Japan, and Bank of England—are primarily responsible for the overall direction and function of domestic monetary policy and operations, and they supervise related international activities as well. The central banks of the leading Western nations generally work closely to improve the global monetary system, and to conduct varying degrees of coordinated currency-support actions in times of severe exchange or other financial problems.

The IMF serves in many respects as a lender of last resort to central banks.

The international financial system lacks full participation by most of the Socialist-Communist nations. Traditionally, these nonmarket countries have been reluctant to join the IMF because of the requirements to disclose reserve and other important economic and financial information, to meet reserve quotas, to pay proportionate costs, and to lose sovereignty.

The Socialist-Communist nations, nevertheless, are steadily becoming more involved in world trade and finance in order to achieve their economic growth and welfare goals.

Personal Involvement in International Economics

Many individuals become directly involved in international economics as tourists. They quickly learn differences in currencies, prices, economic standards, laws, and a host of other matters. Most important, they sense differences in relative values in the goods and services available. Herein lies their introduction to the need for further exchanges which are essential to improve human welfare on a global scale.

The widely acknowledged growing interdependence among nations virtually assures that international economics will receive increasing attention in all countries. The challenge facing the peoples of the world will be to keep the global economic, social, financial, and political systems operative through all periods of growth, recession, inflation, currency fluctuations, shortages, and surpluses.

References

Heller, H. Robert, *International Trade Theory and Empirical Evidence*, 2d ed., Prentice-Hall, Englewood Cliffs, N.J., 1978; *International Economic Report of the President*, transmitted to the Congress, January 1977; Kubarich, Roger M., *Foreign Exchange Markets in the United States*, Federal Reserve Bank of New York, New York, 1978; *Tariffs, Quotas, and Trade: The Politics of Protectionism*, Institute for Contemporary Studies, San Francisco, Calif., 1979.

(*See also* Balance of international payments; Balance of international trade; Barriers to trade; Bretton Woods Conference; Cartel; Comparative advantage theory; Dumping; Eurodollar market; European Economic Community; Exports; Foreign direct investment; Foreign exchange rates; General Agreement on Tariffs and Trade; Imports; Infrastructure; International Monetary Fund; Liquidity, international; Multinational corporation; Organization for Economic Cooperation and Development; Protectionism; Smithsonian Agreement; Special drawing rights; Stages theory of economic development; Subsidies; Technology; Value of the dollar; World Bank)

Walter E. Hoadley

International liquidity (see Liquidity, international)

International Monetary Fund

The purpose of the International Monetary Fund (IMF) is to promote international monetary cooperation through a permanent institution which provides the machinery for consultation and collaboration on international monetary problems. Specifically, the function of the IMF is to promote orderly and stable foreign currency exchange markets, to facilitate international trade, and to contribute to balance of payments adjustment. To further these objectives, the IMF makes financial resources available to its member countries in times of balance of payments difficulties.

History

The IMF's charter embodied in the Articles of Agreement was agreed upon at the International Monetary and Financial Conference held at Bretton Woods, New

Hampshire, in July 1944. In December 1945 the required number of countries had ratified the agreements, and in March 1946 the first meeting of the Board of Governors was held. But it was not until March 1, 1947, that the IMF commenced operations at its headquarters in Washington, D.C.

Other milestones in the history of the IMF include: May 1948, first drawing by a member country; January 1962, adoption of the general agreements to borrow (GAB), which constituted an important supplement to the IMF's financial resources; February 1963, establishment of the compensatory financing facility, designed to assist countries that experience a temporary shortfall in export earnings; June 1969, inception of the buffer stock facility that can be used to finance commodity stockpiles; July 1969, adoption of the first ammendment to the Articles of Agreement, providing for the allocation of special drawing rights (SDR) to member countries, with the first allocation of SDRs made on January 1, 1970; September 1974, implementation of the extended fund facility, designed to assist countries with medium-term assistance to overcome structural balance of payments problems; April 1975, establishment of an oil facility to help oil-importing countries to finance the increase in petroleum prices; February 1976, establishment of the trust fund, funded by revenues from gold sales, to aid developing countries with low-interest assistance; April 1978, adoption of the second amendment to the articles providing for liberalized exchange arrangements, the legalization of floating exchange rates, steps designed to eliminate the role of gold in the international monetary system, and enunciation of the goal to make the SDR the central international monetary reserve asset.

Structure

As of September 1979 the IMF was composed of 138 member countries, each of which is represented by a governor on its Board of Governors. Most of the governors are ministers of finance, presidents of the country's central bank, or persons of similar rank. Virtually, all day-to-day functions are delegated to the Executive Board, which is responsible for conducting the business of the IMF and is made up of 21 representatives of the member countries. The Executive Board is presided over by the managing director, who is also chief of staff of the IMF. The managing director is elected for a 5-year term.

Operations

The IMF's rules and procedures are determined by the Executive Board and carried out by the staff. The voting power of each member country is determined by its quota, which is based on a complex formula that takes account of the country's size and its general importance in world trade and finance. In addition, each member country's quota determines the amount of financial resources it has to make available to the IMF (subscription) and its access (drawing rights) to the Fund's facilities.

Each member country is required to make available to the IMF an amount of funds equal to its quota. Prior to the second amendment in 1978, 25 percent of the quota had to be paid in gold or foreign exchange, while the rest could be paid in the member country's own currency. Since thant time, the rules on gold and foreign exchange contributions have been liberalized.

In turn, IMF member countries may utilize the Fund's resources if they find themselves in balance of payments difficulties. Technically, a member country will use its own currency to purchase other currencies (or SDRs) held by the IMF. Drawings will be granted as a matter of course so long as they do not exceed 25 percent of the member's quota. However, drawings are usually limited to 200 percent of a country's quota, but under special circumstances countries may be permitted to draw up to 480 percent of quota. Drawings made under the so-called credit tranches are subject to conditionality, i.e., the imposition of certain performance criteria by the Fund. Repayments to the IMF are normally to be made within 3 to 5 years, but under the extended facility the country may have up to 8 years to repurchase the foreign currencies advanced.

The IMF will charge a country for the use of its financial resources an interest rate of up to approximately 7 percent, while it pays to creditor countries at a rate determined on market interest rates in the largest countries.

Much of the IMF's work is centered around annual consultations with each member country (under article IV of the Articles of Agreement) to ensure that its national policies are directed toward the goals of fostering economic growth, price stability, orderly financial conditions, and the avoidance of unfair exchange manipulations. To ensure compliance with these basic tenets, the Fund is empowered to exercise firm surveillance over the exchange rate policies of member countries. The precise meaning of the surveillance function is still evolving and will, to a large extent, be instrumental in determining the future role of the IMF in the international monetary system.

References

Crockett, Andrew D., and H. Robert Heller, "The Changing Role of the International Monetary Fund," *Kredit und Kapital,* vol. 11, no. 3, Duncker and Humblot, Berlin, 1978; de Vries, M. G., (ed.), *The International Monetary Fund,* 1966–1971, vols. I, II, International Monetary Fund, Washington, D.C., 1976; Horsefield, T. K. (ed.), *The International Monetary Fund 1945–1965,* vols. I, II, International Monetary Fund, Washington, D.C., 1969.

(*See also* Bretton Woods Conference; Foreign exchange rates; Gold standard; Smithsonian Agreement; Special drawing rights)

H. Robert Heller

International payments balance (see Balance of international payments)

International trade balance (see Balance of international trade)

Investment function

An investment function is the relation between the acquisition of capital and a set of explanatory variables. Capital is defined as buildings, equipment and inventories, and sometimes intangibles, such as knowledge and technique, which are both outputs of the productive process and inputs to future production.

In private-enterprise economies such as the United States, investment is characterized as gross private domestic investment, that is, residential housing construction and business acquisition of new industrial plants of, machinery and equipment, and of additional inventory. Most work on estimating investment functions in recent years has been on a disaggregative rather than an aggregative basis. Thus, estimates of investment functions have been made separately for plant or structures, for equipment, for inventory investment, and for residential housing construction; or for various sectors of the economy, such as manufacturing, utilities, railroads, and commerce. There have also been attempts to estimate investment functions for individual firms.

In the classical economic tradition and in its Marxian branch there is the notion that business profits are entirely or partly accumulated as capital investment. Thus, investment becomes a function of profits. The more profits there are, the more investment there is.

Since capital accumulation appeared to contribute to greater productivity and economic growth, this view of the investment function seemed to many an appropriate justification both for a profits system and for having a large share of national income going to profits.

To Marx, the profits-investment relation held the seeds of serious contradiction. As profits and the competitive striving for growth and lower costs brought on more and more capital accumulation or investment, the economy became periodically and increasingly plagued by crises of excessive capital and a falling rate of profit and underconsumption which left insufficient demand for products of additional capital.

Keynes' Ideas

These ideas about profits and investment were developed by John Maynard Keynes in *The General Theory of Employment, Interest and Money* (1936). Keynes emphasized that, whatever the contribution of investment to economic growth, it was an essential component of the total effective demand which determined the rate of output and, hence, of employment in the economy. And to Keynes, there was no assurance that the total aggregate effective demand coming from consumption and investment would be sufficient to stimulate enough production to use all of the labor services that would be supplied at full employment. Hence, an insufficiency of investment demand, as well as of consumption demand, was viewed in the Keynesian system as a prime cause of both cyclical and chronic underemployment. The investment function projected by Keynes, borrowing from the American economist Irving Fisher, made investment depend upon its marginal efficiency or gross profitability. This depended upon the expected returns from investment and its cost or supply price. And the profitability or marginal efficiency in turn must be related to the financial cost of investment or the rate of interest. Thus, firms would invest in additional plant, equipment, or inventories only as long as the rate of return on each unit of investment exceeded the rate of interest, or only as long as the present discounted value of expected future returns, that is, the demand price of capital goods exceeded, or was at least equal to, the supply price or cost.

Development of Investment Functions

It is important to note the essential difference between indicating that investment depends upon profits and asserting that investment depends upon its expected profitability. That investment is determined by and may be explained by profits has simple and long-standing appeal. Yet this view may be considered a negation of the rational underpinning of the profit system in the United States. If enterprises repeatedly reinvest their profits without regard to the investment's profitability, the conditions for optimal, long-run utilization of resources are defied. Profits earned in the past should not automatically be reinvested. Presumably they are not if a profits system is functioning efficiently.

Acceptance of the notion that investment depends upon its expected profitability opens the way to systematic construction of investment functions, but leaves open serious problems in their specific estimation. A key word here is "expected." Expected profitability relates to expected returns or expected cost savings, which in turn will depend upon how additional capital will contribute to output: the role of capital in the production function. Expected profitability will also depend upon current and expected prices of capital goods and other possible inputs to production. And it will depend upon the demand for the product of capital: quantities; prices; and slopes, or elasticities, of demand curves.

Since investment is the acquisition of additional capital and the amount or rate of investment is the rate of speed at which additional capital is acquired, or, in mathematical terms, the derivative of capital with respect to time, investment will also depend upon the capacity in the capital goods industries and the relative costs of acquiring capital more or less rapidly. Both because the expectations which determine investment may be formed gradually and because the costs of investing all at once—building a new factory in an hour—are prohibitive, responses of investment to its determinants are distributed over time.

In principle, the past is irrelevant and the only current data relevant to investment decisions are the amounts and capabilities of the already existing capital stock and the prices of capital goods and their associated current financial costs. In practice, we use a variety of past and present proxy variables for the generally absent information for the essential expectations of the future.

Investment may be viewed as the acquisition of capital for replacement, including modernization, and for expansion. The rate of investment will then depend upon the rate at which existing capital is replaced and the expectation of increases in future demand. It will also depend upon the desired capital-output or capital-labor ratios, which will in turn relate to technological factors, that is, the production function, and relative prices of capital and labor.

A meaningful price of capital would involve the initial cost or supply price of the capital goods being purchased, the expected rate of depreciation or wearing out or replacement requirements of the capital to be acquired, the interest or financial cost of the funds invested in the capital, and any expected capital loss due to changing prices of capital goods. These elements, along with relevant tax parameters, have been incorporated by Dale W. Jorgenson (1963) into a "rental price of capital" which plays a key role in a neoclassical investment function widely estimated in recent years. The lower the rental price of capital, the greater the capital stock that firms would find optimal or desire in order to produce any given rate of output or to increase output by any given amount. The greater the expected output, the greater will be the demand for capital; moveover, the greater the increases in expected output, the greater will be investment.

This leads finally to a general formulation of an investment function in which the rate of investment depends upon past changes in demand, sales, or output, which presumably generate changed expectations of future demand, sales, and output, and also depends upon past changes in the rental price of capital, which generate changes in the desired and effected capital-output ratio. We thus have a distributed-lag function in which investment is related positively to past, current, and, to the extent they are known, expected future changes in sales or output and changes in the rental price of capital.

Controversy Continues

Many empirical or econometric studies attempted to estimate some or all of the parameters of investment functions in these terms. Results have varied and controversy continues as to relative importance of different variables as well as to the lags in response.

There has been fairly widespread agreement that changes in demand are critically related to investment. In accordance with sophisticated modern versions of the acceleration principle, the rate of investment is found to depend upon the acceleration of the rate of output or general demand. Thus, past growth in sales or output generates investment. Faster growth generates more investment; slower growth a decline in investment. Empirical studies confirm clearly that investment is related to past changes in sales or output. The lags in response can be substantial, however, with some investment related to changes in sales of the previous few quarters but significant amounts related to changes of the previous year or two or even, in some studies, to changes dating as far back as 7 years. And since it is ultimately expected future demand which is important, the lags or the relative magnitude of effects due to past changes apparently depend upon the varying relation between past changes and expectations of the future.

In Jorgenson's original neoclassical formulation, the rental price of capital was assumed to have a powerful effect (stemming from certain stipulations as to the production function, perfect competition, and, implicitly, expectations). On the basis of this assumption particularly powerful effects were predicted for changes in tax parameters, such as accelerated depreciation for tax purposes and the investment tax credit, as well as changes in interest rates that might be induced by monetary policies.

Considerable further work (by Eisner and others) has cast doubt on the magnitude of such substitution effects induced by changes in the rental price of capital and the monetary and tax policies that would bring them about. These relate in part to the fact that reductions in the price of capital will bring on more investment only as existing capital gradually requires replacement. And numerical estimates have raised doubt as to the underlying elasticity of substitution of capital and, hence, of the response of investment to changes in the price of capital, at least in the short run.

Application of the acceleration principle, relating investment to changes in the rate of output and to the pressure of demand on capacity, has been complicated by the implication of notions of permanent income for investment. This suggests that changes in demand which are deemed essentially transitory will have little or no effect upon investment, and only to the extent that such changes are viewed as permanent will investment be affected.

While investment functions discussed here have most direct relevance to investment by business firms, similar considerations may be present for all economic units, including households, nonprofit institutions, and governments, to the extent they are attempting to decide upon optimal rates of investment in all kinds of capital. Ultimately, investment is viewed as a function of its expected profitability or contributions to value and net worth, dependent in turn upon expected or projected demand or output, relative prices of capital and other inputs, rates of discount, or future expected returns, which are likely to be increased by higher perceptions of risk, and costs of adjustment and of obtaining information.

References

Ackley, Gardner, *Macroeconomics: Theory and Policy*, Macmillan, New York, 1978, especially pp. 607–667; Eisner, Robert, and R. H. Strotz, "Determinants of Business Investment," in Commission on Money and Credit, *Impacts of Monetary Policy*, Prentice-Hall, Englewood Cliffs, N.J., 1964, pp. 59–223; Jorgenson, D. W., "Capital Theory and Investment Behavior," *American Economic Review*, vol. 53, no. 2, May 1963, pp. 247–259, reprinted in L. R. Klein and R. A. Gordon (eds.), *Readings in Business Cycles*, Irwin, Homewood, Ill., 1965, pp. 366–378; Keynes, John Maynard, *The General Theory of Employment, Interest and Money*, Harcourt Brace Jovanovich, New York, 1936, especially pp. 135–164.

(*See also* Business investment in new plants and equipment; Capital, a factor of production; Capital formation; Gross private domestic investment in GNP; Propensity to consume or to save and inducement to invest)

Robert Eisner

IS-LM model

The *IS-LM* model is a standard representation of the Keynesian system in a form which is particularly suitable for comparative static analysis. Two curves (the *IS* and *LM* curves) are obtained whose intersection determines the equilibrium income and interest rate in the economy. The apparatus is particularly useful as a means of examining the effects of changes in underlying conditions which shift one or the other of the curves, but not both.

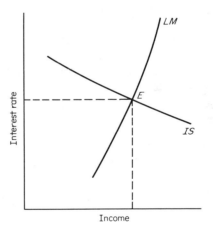

The *IS* curve is the graph of the equation which defines all combinations of income and interest rate for which the goods market is in equilibrium. This equation is obtained by substitution of the goods-market equations to obtain a single equation in income and interest rate, taking as given certain conditions such as the levels of government expenditures, taxes, the capital stock, and the state of expectations. Similarly, the money demand and supply equations are solved to obtain a single equation in income and the interest rate, in which certain conditions as the nominal quantity of money or base money and the price level are taken as given. The equilibrium income and interest rate are determined as shown in the accompanying figure by the intersection of the (normally) downward-sloping *IS* curve and (normally) upward-sloping *LM* curve. This equilibrium is the only combination of income and the interest rate for which the goods market and the money market can be simultaneously in equilibrium.

A change in the underlying conditions will shift the *IS* or *LM* curve, or both, and so change the equilibrium combination of income and the interest rate. Standard results, for example, are that an increase in government expenditures (or any other factor which increases aggregate expenditures at the original equilibrium income and interest rate) will shift the *IS* curve to the right and, therefore, incease both income and the interest rate. Also, an increase in the nominal supply of money (or any other factor which would create an excess of supply of money at the original equilibrium income and interest rate) will shift the *LM* curve to the right and so increase income but reduce interest rates. Just as with supply and demand analysis, ambiguity may arise when a problem implies simultaneous shifts in both curves.

The *IS-LM* model was first proposed by John Hicks (1937) as an exposition of the central argument of John Maynard Keynes' *General Theory* (1936). It was widely popularized by Alvin Hansen (1953) and refined by Don Patinkin (1956). In the 1960s and at least early 1970s, it was the standard tool of most macroeconomic analysis. A lengthy presentation can be found in T. F. Dernburg and D. M. McDougall (1976), and a compact presentation can be found in M. R. Darby (1979).

In recent years, the *IS-LM* model has lost much of its dominance as a tool of macroeconomic analysis. In part, this reflects the increased importance of problems and conditions which involve simultaneous shifts in both the *IS* and *LM* curves. More significant has been new interest in dynamic problems of how the economy adjusts over time to a change in underlying conditions. The *IS-LM* model can be used in a sequential short-period analysis which takes account of shifts in *IS* and *LM* curves due to changes in capital stock, expectations, price level, and money supply, but such analysis is awkward and confusing compared to explicit dynamic macroeconomic models. Nonetheless, the *IS-LM* model remains an important tool for the analysis of problems involving the impact effect of changes in underlying conditions in the goods market.

References

Darby, Michael R., *Intermediate Macroeconomics*, McGraw-Hill, New York, 1979; Dernburg, Thomas F., and Duncan M. McDougall, *Macroeconomics*, 5th ed., McGraw-Hill, New York, 1976; Hansen, Alvin H., *A Guide to Keynes*, McGraw-Hill, New York, 1953; Hicks, John R., "Mr. Keynes and the 'Classics': A Suggested Interpretation," *Econometrica*, vol. 5, April 1937, pp. 147–159; Keynes, John Maynard, *The General Theory of Employment, Interest, and Money*, Macmillan, London, 1936; Patinkin, Don, *Money, Interest, and Prices*, Harper & Row, New York, 1956.

(*See also* Keynesian economics; Static analysis)

Michael R. Darby

Isoquant

An isoquant is the locus of all labor-capital quantities that generate a particular output level.

Let production be governed by the one-output, two-output production function

$$q = f(L, K)$$

where q is quantity of output, and L and K are respective quantities of labor and capital input. This function is assumed to be continuous with continuous first- and second-order partial derivatives. Let $q = 100$. The implicit form for the corresponding isoquant is $f(L, K) = 100$.

Families of Isoquants

Three curves from a family of isoquants are pictured in the accompanying figure, in which labor and capital are measured on the axes. Each isoquant has a label specifying the output level to which it corresponds. Since each point in the labor-capital diagram corresponds to some output, each point lies on some isoquant. Since labor and capital increments normally result in output increments, isoquants farther from the origin correspond to higher output levels. Isoquants normally are negatively sloped as pictured in the figure, since an increment in the quantity of one input with output constant normally implies a decrement in the quantity of the other.

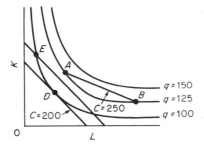

The Rate of Technical Substitution

The slope of an isoquant gives the rate at which one input may be substituted for the other while output is maintained at a constant level. This rate of technical substitution (RTS) is sometimes called the marginal rate of substitution. Differentiating the production function totally,

$$dq = f_L \, dL + f_K \, dK$$

where f_L and f_K are the partial derivatives of the production function and are called the marginal products of labor and capital, respectively; and dq, dL, and dK are differentials, i.e., changes for the output and input quantities. Let $dq = 0$ to reflect the constant output along an isoquant so that

$$\text{RTS} = -\frac{dK}{dL} = \frac{f_L}{f_K}$$

By this definition the RTS is the negative of the slope of an isoquant and is measured by the ratio of the marginal products of the inputs. It is positive and the isoquant negatively sloped as long as the marginal products of the inputs are positive.

The RTS, which gives quantity of capital per unit of labor, normally is assumed to decrease as the quantity of labor increases relative to the quantity of capital, i.e., as one moves from left to right along an isoquant. A decreasing RTS, which means that $-d^2K/dL^2$ and $d^2K/dL^2 > 0$, corresponds to isoquants with the convex shape pictured in the figure. Consider the line segment connecting points A and B, both of which are on the isoquant for $q = 125$. Convexity means that all points on that line segment between A and B are on isoquants with $q > 125$.

Cost Minimization

The production cost, denoted by C, corresponding to a point in the figure is given by $C = wL + rK$ where w and r are fixed unit prices for labor and capital respectively. An isocost line is the locus of all input combinations with a specified cost level. The straight lines in the figure with levels $C = 200$ and $C = 250$ provide examples. If the firm desires to produce 100 units of output, it can produce at any point on the appropriate isoquant. Point E entails a production cost of 250, but is not efficient because other points on the isoquant have lower cost. Point D gives the minimum cost (200) for the production of 100 units. No point on the isoquant lies on a lower isocost line.

The minimum cost of producing an output quantity under usual assumptions is given by a tangency, such as D, between an isoquant and an isocost line. A cost function gives minimum production cost as a function of output, and can be constructed from the locus of the mimimum-cost tangency points corresponding to different output levels.

Homogeneous Production Functions

A production function is homogeneous of degree k if

$$qt^k = f(tL, tK)$$

The first-order partial derivatives for a function homogeneous of degree k are homogeneous of degree $k - 1$. Consequently,

$$\text{RTS} = \frac{f_L(L, K)}{f_K(L, K)} = \frac{t^{k-1}f_L(tL, tK)}{t^{k-1}f_K(tL, tK)} = \frac{f_L(tL, tK)}{f_K(tL, tK)}$$

The RTS is unchanged if the quantities of labor and capital are unchanged by the same proportion. This means that one isoquant is sufficient to represent the entire family of isoquants. Other isoquants in the family can be obtained by integration since their slopes (i.e., their RTSs) are known at each point.

Production functions for which the RTS depends only upon the labor-capital ratio are called homothetic. This class includes all homogeneous production functions as well as some production functions that are not homogeneous.

The Elasticity of Substitution

As one moves from left to right along a convex isoquant, both the RTS and capital-labor ratio decline. The elasticity of substitution, denoted by

$$\sigma = \frac{d \ln (K/L)}{d \ln (f_L/f_K)} = \frac{d (K/L)}{d (f_L/f_K)} \frac{f_L/f_K}{K/L}$$

where ln denotes the natural logarithm. If the capital-labor ratio declines proportionately more than the RTS, σ is greater than 1. If it declines proportionately less than the RTS, σ is less than 1. If they decline in the same proportion, σ equals 1. The degree of substitution between the inputs increases as σ increases.

In general, the elasticity of substitution varies as one moves along a given isoquant. A production function with a constant elasticity of substitution (CES), is given by

$$q = A[\alpha L^{-\rho} + (1 - \alpha)K^{-\rho}]^{-k/\rho} \qquad \text{for } \begin{array}{l} A > 0 \\ < \alpha < 1 \end{array}$$

where $\rho = (1 - \sigma)/\sigma$ reflects the constant elasticity of substitution. The CES production function is homogeneous and of degree k. As σ approaches zero, the isoquants approach right angles with no substitution possible. As σ approaches ∞, the isoquants approach straight lines (similar to the isocost lines) with perfect substitution possible.

References

Frisch, Ragnar, *Theory of Production*, Rand-McNally, Chicago, 1965; Henderson, James M., and Richard E. Quandt, *Microeconomic Theory: A Mathematical Approach*, 3d ed., McGraw-Hill, New York, 1980, chaps. 4, 5; Hirschleifer, Jack, *Price Theory and Applications*, 2d ed., Prentice-Hall, Englewood Cliffs, N.J., 1980, chap. 9; Varian, Hal R., *Microeconomic Analysis*, Norton, New York, 1978, chap. 1.

(*See also* Elasticity; Production function)

James M. Henderson

Joint Economic Committee of Congress

The Joint Economic Committee (JEC) consists of 20 members of Congress equally divided between the House of Representatives and the Senate, each house's delegation on the committee divided between Democrats and Republicans in proportion to their ratios in the chamber. The committee elects a chair and vice chair with these offices rotating between the House and the Senate with each Congress (every 2 years).

An Economic Advisory Service

The JEC (originally called the Joint Committee on the Economic Report) was set up by authority contained in section 5 of the Employment Act of 1946 (79th Cong., Pub. L. 304, 60 Stat. 23) with the following admonitions: "(1) to make a continuing study of matters relating to the Economic Report; (2) to study means of coordinating programs in order to further the policy of this Act; and (3) as a guide to the several committees of the Congress dealing with legislation relating to the Economic Report, not later than March 1, of each year ... to file a report ... containing its findings, and recommendations. . . ."

It was intended that the JEC, divorced from legislative duties, might function as an economic advisory service to the Congress, thus putting that body on a par with the executive branch, which had always had its economic advisers and researchers. Furthermore, the Committee was given wide investigative authority, covering the entire range of economic policy, past, present, and future, whereas committees of Congress commonly have restricted areas of purview. The committee began as soon as practical to recruit an essentially nonpartisan professional staff.

There were no precedents for its operations; the JEC was both biparty and bicameral in character, and so it started somewhat slowly and tentatively. Over the first decade of its existence the JEC steadily grew in influence and reputation. The JEC pioneered the use by expert witnesses of compendiums of papers which it published before hearings were held. This enabled the committee to concentrate on the most disputed points during the public hearings. It also pioneered the use of panels of expert witnesses, thus maximizing the divergence of view and the possibility of bringing out new ideas for public policy design.

Impact on Policy

The JEC also undertook to explore areas of possible policy significance long before they became the subject of ʻwidespread concern. Thus, in 1949 the JEC explored at length the proportions, characteristics, and policy problems connected with what in the 1960s became the war on poverty. Similarly, the JEC was instrumental in making studies of potential GNP (real output of the nation at persistent high-employment conditions) and of the problems and prospects faced by the nation in the long run. These efforts contrasted with the short-term horizons then typical of most policy debates, especially in Congress. Among these studies prepared by the staff were : "Sustaining Economic Forces Ahead" (December 1952), "Potential Economic Growth in the United States During the Next Decade" (October 1954), and "The Potential Economic Growth in the United States" (January 1960).

The committee also led the way on a number of policy debates, notably the need for tax increases and expenditure restraint to control inflation at the time of the Korean war. It also conducted the large-scale investigation of the economy in 1959 to 1960 under the title "Study of Employment, Growth, and Price Levels," which many observers have labeled the basis for much of the economic program of the Kennedy administration.

Some observers of the JEC believe that its major contribution has been to educate both the Congress and the public concerning economic issues and analysis. In turn some are convinced that the Committee has in fact educated many economists and given them both motivation and opportunity to work on major policy issues in the public sector.

Future of JEC

On the other hand, the committee has engaged in so many investigations and hearings on so many widely varying subjects that it can be accused of straying from its fundamental task of promoting full employment and price stability. In fact, the question has been raised as to whether or not the JEC has become of so little use that it might be eliminated. The congressional budget structure erected in the 1970s, including the massive Congressional Budget Office, has created the impression in some circles that the JEC's job has been eliminated and that either the committee should be abolished or it should be given new tasks to perform. It has been charged that the members have too often used the JEC to generate publicity, have allowed staff quality to deteriorate, have introduced too much partisanship and patronage into staff, and have duplicated work now done elsewhere in government, including Congress.

But the JEC is no different from the Council of Economic Advisers (CEA) in the executive branch. Both institutions have long since spread their functions and operations over such a large territory as to obscure their more fundamental roles of solving the problems of attaining continuing full employment with a reasonably stable price level.

The arguments over the roles of these institutions boil down to questions of whether or not the nation's officials can exercise the restraint needed to keep these institutions confined to their proper roles and out of the daily operating problems of such fights as those over wage-price administration, and whether or not the search for ways to stabilize an economy while keeping it in part consistent with freedom for the individual is a task worthy of special institutions' efforts. If the answer to these questions is yes, then certainly there will always be a strong role for the JEC as well as for its counterpart in the executive branch, the CEA.

The task before the JEC and the nation is to coordinate economic and other policies in order to promote full employment and a stable price level. This is a multifaceted job that puts severe strains on the members and staff. For example, the experience of the 1970s with regard to inflation and employment might have been different if the economic consequences of policies abroad on oil prices and availability had been foreseen. Or if the inflationary consequences of budget and monetary policies during the late 1960s and early 1970s had been called strongly to public attention and more stabilizing policies advocated, the experience of the late 1970s and expectation for the 1980s might have been altered significantly. The JEC's role will continue to be coordination and long-range economic research and planning around such issues.

(*See also* Council of Economic Advisers)

James W. Knowles

Joint venture

A business venture is an undertaking involving some element of risk or uncertainty of outcome. A joint venture is such an undertaking conducted by two or more partners who share the risks. The partners may be individuals, corporations, governments, or some combination of these three.

Although almost any joint-stock corporation fits this description, the term joint venture is usually limited to certain special cases as illustrated by the following examples:

1. Two large international oil companies jointly form a subsidiary to explore for oil in a region where the chances of finding commercial deposits are less than certain.

2. A multinational firm establishes a subsidiary with local partners in a developing nation to manufacture and sell in that market. The market is protected by prohibitive tariffs and governmentally granted licenses to manufacture, which are reserved for firms with some local ownership.

3. A firm holding a governmentally granted monopoly in a national market wishes to exploit a patented technology held by another firm. These two firms agree to form a jointly held subsidiary to appropriate mutually a rent from the market using the first firm's monopoly rights and the second firm's technology.

4. A large manufacturing firm based in a Western nation forms a joint venture with a state-owned enterprise within the Soviet Union. The Western firm seeks to sell within the Soviet Union but is unable to do so unless in partnership with the state, while the state seeks the Western firm's managerial expertise.

5. Two firms wish to develop a new technology but face uncertain costs of development and prospects for success. They agree to proceed by creating a joint research and development subsidiary.

All of these examples involve some element of imperfect competition. Except for the first and last cases, this imperfect competition results from governmental action, so that the joint ventures of examples 2, 3, and 4 represent efforts either to overcome governmental obstacles to doing business or to exploit governmentally created and controlled monopolies. Examples 1 and 5, however, involve no governmental intervention. Example 1, typical of numerous arrangements in the natural resource industries, is justified by participating firms as being necessary to diffuse risk. Modern portfolio theory holds, however, that joint ventures among established firms are unnecessary for reasons of risk spreading at the level of the firm, given that individual shareholders can minimize risk via portfolio diversification. (An exception is the case where the individual firm faces the substantial probability of bankruptcy.) Such joint ventures are interpreted by some economists as devices for mutual appropriation of rents by firms operating in oligopolistic industries.

Joint ventures may be economically justified if the partner firms possess complementary capabilities. Such might be the case in example 5, for instance, if the two firms each possessed specialized research personnel not possessed by the other. Complementarities are present in examples 2, 3, and 4, but in each of these cases they have more to do with political than with economic considerations.

References

Bivens, K., and E. B. Lovell, *Joint Ventures with Foreign Partners*, National Industrial Conference Board, New York, 1966; Friedmann, W. G., and G. Kalanoff (eds.), *Joint International Business Ventures*, Columbia University Press, New York, 1961; Hilton, D. H. W. van, *Joint Ventures*, Kluwer, Deventor, The Netherlands, 1968; Pogue, G. A., and K. Lall, "Corporate Finance: An Overview," in Stewart C. Myers, (ed.), *Modern Developments in Financial Management*, Praeger, New York, 1976, see also article by J. S. R. Shad in same volume; Scherer, F. M., "Research and Development Resource Allocation Under Rivalry," *Quarterly Journal of Economics*, vol. 81, no. 3, August 1967, pp. 359–394; Stopford, J. M., and L. T. Wells, *Managing the Multinational Enterprise*, Basic Books, New York, 1972, chaps. 9, 10; Vernon, Raymond, "Foreign Enterprise and Developing Nations in the Raw Materials Industries," *American Economic Review*, vol. 60, no. 2, May 1970, pp. 122–126.

(*See also* Competition; Monopoly and oligopoly)

Edward M. Graham

Juglar cycle

Business cycles are classified according to their average duration, for example, the length of time from one peak in business activity to the succeeding peak, or from trough to trough. Joseph A. Schumpeter's schema involved three classes: the Kondratieff cycles or "long waves" of 54-year average duration, the Kitchin cycles of 40-month average duration, and intermediate between these two were the Juglar cycles of between 9 and 11 years' duration. The Juglar cycle comes closest to what generally is meant by the term "business cycle," and is often referred to as the "major cycle."

As Schumpeter read the historical statistics of business activity, there were six Juglar cycles superimposed on each Kondratieff cycle, and three Kitchin cycles superimposed on each Juglar cycle. Whenever all three cycles were in the same phase, that phase was exceptionally intense. This was one of the explanations for the severity of the depression in the 1930s. While Schumpeter saw no particular reason for the three cycles having the rigid relation of 6 to 1 and 3 to 1, he was impressed with the empirical fact. Others were even more impressed. In particular, two authors, E. R. Dewey and E. F. Dakin, wrote a book presumptuously called *Cycles: The Science of Prediction* in which their forecasting method was based on what they regarded as fundamental rhythms of the economy. The approach fell into disfavor when their predictions did not materialize. Nevertheless, attempts at forecasting cycles on the basis of the presumed inherent rhythmic nature of business continue.

Clement Juglar was a doctor in France who became so fascinated by the study of business cycles that he gave up his medical practice in favor of economics and statistics. What apparently intrigued him most was the idea of periodicity in economic affairs, and he is credited with being the first to speak of business cycles. Prior to Juglar, economists were overwhelmingly concerned with the crisis, i.e., the turning point when economic expansion and prosperity turned into a downswing or depression. Such crises were sometimes dramatic, traumatic events and sometimes barely perceptible. Economists of the time were in fair agreement about the causes of such crises—such random or exogenous forces as wars, droughts, gold flows, credit, and money growth. Juglar changed the emphasis of the study of business fluctuations by his assertion that the sole cause of the crisis was the prosperity phase that preceded it, and that depression always followed the crisis. The excesses and the resulting maladjustments born in the prosperity phase make the crisis and the depression inevitable.

Juglar divided the cycles into three phases: prosperity, crisis, and liquidation. The major emphasis was placed on price level behavior, which had as its root cause the actions of the money, credit, and financial system. The real system of investment, output, and real demand were slighted; and the nominal variables—price levels, interest rates, bank reserves, and borrowing—were analyzed over the three stages of the cycle.

Business Cycle Theories

Explanations of the Juglar cycles have become the standard business cycle theories. These theories have been classified in a number of ways. But the classification which has been accepted most widely is that developed by Gottfried Haberler in his work entitled *Prosperity and Depression*.

Purely Monetary Theory   Fluctuations in money circulation, the money stock (M) times its velocity of circulation (V), directly determine fluctuations in nominal national income (Py), where P is the price level and y is the quantity of real goods and services produced and sold during some specified time period. The theory as expounded by Ralph G. Hawtrey between 1913 and 1937 was within the context of the gold standard, and fluctuations in the money supply came about by flows of gold into and out of the banking system of a country, and by the reaction to those flows by bankers and the public. Short-term interest rate variations were important in transmitting the effect of changing money stocks to the economic system. The purely monetary theory has been revived in a nongold standard or managed money regime by modern monetarists.

Monetary Overinvestment Theories   Most closely associated with the name of F. A. Hayek, the monetary overinvestment theory of the business cycles depends on the distinction between the natural and the money, or market, rate of interest. The natural rate of interest is the rate of interest at which voluntary savings by households would be equal to the amount of investment planned by business units. The market rate of interest is the rate of interest set by market forces which on the supply side include bank expansion of the money stock and "dishoarding" of funds (increase in velocity) as well as saving, and on the demand side includes hoarding (decrease in velocity) as well as investment demand.

The expansion phase of the business cycle could be initiated by banks acquiring new reserves which they use to make loans and expand the money stock, lowering the market rate below the natural rate. When this happens, savings would be less than investment. The price level rises forcing consumers to save more than they intend to save, and there is reason for business firms to wish to invest in larger amounts. The expansion comes to an end when the money stock stops growing, as it must when the banks run out of excess or surplus reserves. The market rate of interest rises, forcing a reduction in investment spending, and the boom collapses. In the process capital goods have become excessive relative to the demand for goods and services at the consumer level, hence the term "overinvestment," and the recession/depression is a period of readjustment involving the elimination of the redundant capital. Workers have to move from the heavy goods industries to consumer goods production, banks retrench by building up their liquidity again, prices fall, and the market rate rises above the natural rate.

Nonmonetary Overinvestment Theories   Nonmonetary overinvestment theories of the business cycle do not see the role of money as crucial to the explanation of the cycle. It is a passive feature. Instead, fluctuations in the demand for real capital goods and the corresponding supply adjustments vary over the cycle. The expansion begins by an increase in the demand for durable goods at a time following a depression period during which capital was allowed to depreciate without replacement, and at a time when liquid funds were being built up in banks and other economic units. The demand increase can also come about by innovations which require investment in capital goods. During the expansion phase, this liquidity decreases as it moves into fixed capital, and the process stops when the investment opportunities have been exhausted or when the quantitiy of savings is inadequate to continue the investment boom. The capital stock has grown to a size which cannot be justified on the basis of total demand; thus a large part of it is excessive, leaving the need for a depression period to eliminate this redundancy.

The major names attached to the nonmonetary school are Karl Marx, Arthur Spiethoff, Mikhail Tugan-Baranowski, and Krut Wicksell.

Underconsumption Theories   According to underconsumption theories, households do not increase their spending on consumption at as rapid a rate as their income rises during the upswing of the business cycle. This causes difficulties because their incomes are rising as technology improves and as productive capacity grows. Thus, the demand for total output is less than the willingness of firms to produce. This leaves unused capacity and a decline in the demand for investment just when savings are increasing.

Explanations of this circumstance vary with the writers. John A. Hobson said it was because consumption skills are less well-developed than production skills. It takes longer for people to learn how to increase their consumption when their income increases, whereas most of the energy of society goes into learning how to produce more, faster. Most underconsumption theorists also believe that the distribution of income contributes to the problem. During business expansions, wage-income growth lags behind property-income growth, and since workers consume a larger proportion of their income than do profit recipients, their argument is that consumption will not rise as fast as national income.

Psychological Theories   While all business cycle theories incorporate psychological aspects of human behavior, those theories which emphasize this element are called psychological theories. Much of the underlying economic analysis is the same or similar to other more purely economic explanations. Since most economic decision making involves the future, and since the future is fraught with uncertainty, optimism and pessimism may play an important role. Since the business community is closely interrelated, waves of optimism and pessimism may pervade that community and exaggerate the economic swings. A. C. Pigou and John Maynard Keynes, in particular, laid heavy stress on psychological factors in their analyses of business fluctuations.

Modern Business Cycle Theories

Recent work on major, or Juglar, cycles has taken on a decidedly mathematical tinge. Since cycles can occur only where the adjustment of economic activity to change takes time, most of the modern theories are based on time lags. The lags are in the time required to adjust production to changes in demand, or in the time consumption or investment activity react to changes in incomes, prices, interest rates, and so on. The acceleration principle is at the heart of most of these mathematical models.

Most contemporary business cycle theorists have abandoned the rigid classification of cycles into those of different time spans. The National Bureau of Economic Research, for example, deals only with one aggregate cycle in any period of time. Some are short and some are long, but they are not superimposed on one another.

References

Clark, John J., and Morris Cohen (eds.), *Business Fluctuations, Growth, and Economic Stabilization, A Reader,* Random House, New York, 1963; Dauten, Carl, and Lloyd Valentine, *Business Cycles and Forecasting,* 5th ed., South-Western, Cincinnati, 1978; Dewey, E. R., and E. F. Dakin, *Cycles: The Science of Prediction,* Holt, Rinehart and Winston, New York, 1947; Haberler, Gottfried, *Prosperity and Depression,* 3d ed., League of Nations, Geneva, 1941; Hansen, Alvin, *Business Cycles and National Income,* Norton, New York, 1951; Schumpeter, Joseph A., *Business Cycles,* vol. I, McGraw-Hill, New York, 1939.

(*See also* Business cycles; Kitchin cycle; Kondratieff cycle; Kuznets cycle)

Lloyd M. Valentine

Keynes' effect (see **Real balance effect theory**)

Keynesian economics

Keynesian economics is a body of economic theory and related policy associated with the English economist John Maynard Keynes. Keynes wrote many books, but the phrase Keynesian economics refers especially to *The General Theory of Employment, Interest and Money* (1936). The ideas and analytical techniques of the *General Theory* stimulated what was called the new economics and more generally the Keynesian revolution. Keynes challenged the fundamental tenets of classical and neoclassical economics stemming from Adam Smith, David Ricardo, John Stuart Mill, Alfred Marshall, and A. C. Pigou. Classical and neoclassical economists hold that a private enterprise economy based on a market system is normally in equilibrium only at full employment. If it departs temporarily from full employment, forces are set in motion to restore equilibrium at full employment. Classical and neoclassical economics allows for voluntary unemployment, by the idle rich and the lazy poor, and for frictional unemployment arising from circumstances such as changing jobs, but it does not allow for involuntary unemployment by those wage earners willing and able to work and actively seeking employment. This self-adjusting system was associated with a policy of laissez faire in a general way.

In contrast, Keynes' general theory of employment postulates that a capitalist economy may be in equilibrium at less than full employment and that the classical/neoclassical economics is a special case in this more general theory. Moreover, Keynes called the characteristics of the classical/neoclassical special case misleading and its teaching disastrous if applied to the real world. Keynes did not accept the automatic, self-adjusting nature of capitalism and believed that under laissez faire chronic, large-scale unemployment is likely to occur. In this sense, his general theory repudiates the theoretical foundations of laissez faire capitalism. He recommended positive fiscal and monetary policies as a means to alleviate unemployment.

Theory of Effective Demand

Keynesian economics is primarily a theory of effective demand, the volume of which is determined by two factors, the propensity to consume and the inducement to invest. The propensity to consume expresses a functional relation between amounts of consumption at varying levels of national income. As income changes, consumption changes in the same direction but by less than the change in income. If national income increases, for example, consumption will increase but by less than the increase in income. The ratio of the increment in consumption to the increment in income is called the marginal propensity to consume and is one of the central concepts in Keynes' theory.

The inducement of business executives to invest is determined by their expectations concerning probable future profits on capital assets, on the one hand, and the rate of interest at which they can borrow for investment, on the other hand. The functional relation between the expected rates of profit and the amounts of current investment is called the schedule of the marginal efficiency of capital, or, more simply, the investment demand schedule. Investment in any period is carried to the point at which the marginal efficiency of capital expressed as a rate of discount on expected future earnings is equal to the rate of interest. Current investment in durable capital assets is the focal point of Keynes' analysis, and because expectations about the return on long-term investments are highly uncertain, investment in durable capital assets is subject to sudden and wide fluctuations. Confidence in expectations is precarious because knowledge about the future is highly uncertain.

Among the complex relations that determine national income and employment, investment is the strategic factor. Low levels of investment are associated with low levels of employment, and fluctuations in investment are associated with wide fluctuations in employment and national income. If investment does not increase, employment cannot increase, given the propensity to consume. There is nothing automatic about increases in investment as there is about increases in consumption (as income rises).

In Keynes' theory of effective demand, investment is strategic because it disburses purchasing power that will be spent for consumer goods without adding to the volume of consumer goods currently coming into the market. The amount of consumer goods a business finds profitable to produce depends on the amount of investment goods being produced. The demand for consumer goods derives from two sources: from the incomes of those employed in producing consumer goods and from the incomes of those employed in producing investment goods.

For example, if a national output of 100 consists of 80 in consumption goods and 20 in investment goods, the 80 in demand needed to clear the 80 in consumption output is 64 + 16: 64 is four-fifths of the income of 80 received by those producing consumer goods; 16 is four-fifths of 20 received by those producing investment goods. The ratio of income derived from the consumer sector to income derived from the investment secton is 4:1 (80:20). This ratio remains constant within a relatively small range of fluctuations in income. So if investment falls by 1, from 20 to 19, consumption will fall by 4, from 80 to 76. Total effective demand is now 76 + 19 = 95. A reduction of 1 in investment has resulted in a fall of 4 in consumption and a total fall of 5 in income. If investment were to rise by 1, from 20 to 21, consumption would rise by 4, from 80 to 84, and income from 100 to 105. This relation is called the investment multiplier, which in this example is 5. It expresses the quantitative relation between changes in income resulting from changes in investment.

Keynes' theory emphasizes demand rather than supply. Current investment is not important in the theory of effective demand because presumably it adds to future productive capacity. Investment is primarily important as a means of disbursing purchasing power into the economy. Any activity which disburses income without simultaneously bringing consumption goods to the market can perform the function of investment as a component of effective demand. For example, government expenditures paid out of loans affect the demand for consumer goods in the same way as private investment.

Compensatory Fiscal Policy

Compensatory fiscal policy is the program most closely associated with Keynesian economics. If the amount of effective demand generated by the private sector is insufficient for full employment, the deficiency can be compensated for by increased expenditure in the public sector. In order for public expenditure to have its desired effect, to increase employment and national income, it must be financed in a manner that will not reduce private spending. Public expenditure paid for out of taxation is not desirable for this purpose because it will reduce disposable (aftertax) income and, hence, will reduce private consumption. Consequently, the increase in public spending should be in the form of loan expenditures. Moreover, expenditure by loans from banks is preferable to loans from private individuals because borrowing from banks is less likely to reduce existing spending in the private sector. The resulting deficit in the governmental budget is necessary in order to avoid substituting public for private spending.

In Keynesian policy governmental deficits are desirable only when spending in the private sector is insufficient to generate demand for the desired level of employment. If demand in the private sector is brisk, there is no need for government deficits, and government spending should be paid for entirely out of current taxes.

Keynesian Influence on the U.S. Economy

Keynesian economics had some influence on the New Deal of Franklin D. Roosevelt. Although Roosevelt criticized President Hoover for failing to balance the federal budget, by his second term (1937–1941) Roosevelt embraced deficit spending as a necessary condition for prosperity. After several years of economic expansion from 1933 to 1937, the American economy went into a tailspin early in 1937 just as the cash budget came into balance for the first time since 1929. At the urging of Federal Reserve Board Chairman Marriner Eccles, Roosevelt recommended the resumption of large loan expenditures designed to increase aggregate demand for goods and services. Eccles, a Utah banker, independently had arrived at Keynesian principles of loan expenditures as a means to prosperity from deep depression. Eccles and other Keynesians recommended that the federal budget should be balanced only at a high level of national income. Attempts to balance the budget at low levels of national income would only make the depression worse. They gave priority to a balanced economy over a balanced budget.

Keynes showed the versatility of his general theory of effective demand by applying to wartime inflation the same framework of analysis he had worked out primarily as a guide to escape from peacetime depression. Wartime inflation arises primarily from excessive demand, whereas peacetime depression is caused primarily by deficient demand. Pointing out that taxation and voluntary saving would be insufficient to prevent inflation during World War II, Keynes devised an anti-inflationary plan under which additional, nontax deductions would be made from incomes during the war and some payments would be deferred until after the war. This was a plan for involuntary or forced saving during wartime. The purpose of the extra wartime withholding of income was to reduce the demand for consumption at a time when only limited supplies of consumption goods were available. While Keynes did not oppose all direct price controls and administrative rationing in wartime, his plan had the advantage of giving maximum freedom of choice to consumers in spending their incomes left over after taxes and deferred compensation. Repayment after the war would have the advantage of offsetting a deficiency of demand in the postwar period, which was anticipated by Keynes and others.

In the United States under the Employment Act of 1946, macroeconomic policies of a Keynesian type became the chief instrument for maintaining and stimulating high-level employment. During the 1950s, when filling war-induced backlogs of demand provided a buoyant economy, automatic stabilizers such as progressive taxation and unemployment compensation were sufficient to limit economic downturns to mild recessions. Under progressive income tax rates personal disposable income does not fall as rapidly as national income and helps to offset the decline in aggregate demand in a downturn. With unemployment compensation, workers who lose their jobs continue to receive income for a substantial period while they are unemployed, and this blunts the fall in demand that would otherwise occur.

Although built-in stabilizers moderate business recessions, they also weaken economic recoveries. Beginning in the 1960s, fiscal drag and full-employment surplus were Keynesian-type concepts used to analyze and explain fiscal policy. Progressive income taxes act as a brake, or a fiscal drag, on economic expansion and may prevent full recovery. The longest unbroken economic expansion in American history occurred between 1961 and 1968, for a period of more than 100 months. In order to sustain the expansion and avoid a possible break in it arising from fiscal drag, major reductions were made in income tax rates in 1964 when the economy was still operating far short of full employment. The amount of purchasing power extracted from the economy by a large budgetary surplus that would exist at full employment might abort the realization of full employment. Discretionary fiscal policy in the form of the big tax cut of 1964 helped to prolong the expansion to a record length. Keynesian economics achieved its greatest influence during the Kennedy-Johnson administrations. During that period members of the President's Council of Economic Advisers were Keynesians almost without exception.

Criticism of Keynesian Economics

During the 1970s Keynesian economics came under increasing criticism because of "stagflation," the simultaneous existence of stagnation (high unemployment) and persistent inflation. The coexistence of recession and inflation presented an apparent dilemma in terms of remedies along Keynesian lines. If demand were stimulated in order to reduce unemployment, inflation would accelerate; and if demand were deliberately constricted to combat inflation, unemployment would rise.

During his first term as President, Richard Nixon tried without success to curb inflation by deliberately inducing a mild recession. During the election year 1972 the Nixon administration imposed mandatory price and wage controls as an anti-inflationary policy. Shortly after the election these controls were relaxed and prices spurted upward. The U.S. consumer price index reached the double-digit level for only the second time after World War II during the recession year 1974. A substantial part of this inflation resulted from the quadrupling of oil prices by the Organization of Petroleum Exporting Countries (OPEC) and a sharp rise in world grain prices. In the midst of this inflation came the great recession of 1974 to 1975, the worst economic decline in the American economy since the Great Depression of the 1930s. Although inflation slowed down in 1976, it began to rise again in 1977 and continued at high levels throughout the remainder of the 1970s. In 1979 the consumer price index rose 13.3 percent while unemployment hovered around 6 percent.

Keynesian theory and policy are designed to deal with inflation caused by excess general demand but not with inflation resulting from increases in individual commodities such as petroleum and food. Untangling cost-push inflation from general-demand inflation is not easily accomplished. Thus, Keynesian economics did not seem to provide satisfactory answers to the perplexing problems of the inflation-ridden, semistagnant 1970s.

A frequent criticism of Keynesian economics is that its application to policy has led to inflation. Observations on this important criticism are limited to three points:

1. Increases in effective demand may at first increase employment, but beyond a critical point will lead to a sharp rise in prices. The critical point is known as the full-employment rate of unemployment. It was fixed at 4 percent by President Johnson's Council of Economic Advisers. The appropriate rate will vary with circumstances, but if set too low it will contribute to inflationary wage and price increases.

2. If Keynesian policies are credited with eliminating major depressions in the post-World War II period, they may be blamed for contributing to inflation in the sense that in pre-Keynesian times depressions were a market-oriented form of price control. For example, between 1929 and 1933 commodity prices fell by approximately 20 percent in the United States. Secular inflation may be part of the price paid for eliminating major depressions.

3. The flexibility required for successful fiscal policy may not be politically feasible, or may work with such long political lags as to render otherwise sound fiscal policy ineffectual. Presumably, to increase tax rates is politically more difficult than to lower tax rates, and to decrease governmental expenditures is politically more difficult than to raise them. These political conditions impart an inflationary bias to fiscal policies of a Keynesian type, although this might seem as much a weakness of political democracy as of Keynesian economics.

The monetarist school became the chief critics of Keynesian fiscal policies. Monetarist policy requires only a steady and modest increase in the quantity of money. Little else is needed by way of government intervention into the private economy. Monetarists asserted that fiscal policy cannot influence the rate of output or employment except in a negative way. They favored major cutbacks in government expenditures and called for a balanced budget. Keynesians viewed monetary policy as a necessary complement to fiscal policy. When employment expands in response to fiscal expansionary measures or for other reasons, an increase in the money supply is needed to finance the additional transactions demand.

The Keynesian framework provides a mechanism for testing the conditions under which purely monetary policy might be effective. An increase in the quantity of money would need to lower the rate of interest by a sufficient amount to stimulate an increase in investment. Whether an increase in the quantity of money would have little or much effect on the rate of interest depends on the shape of the liquidity-preference curve. Keynes felt that beyond a certain point, increases in the quantity of money would not have much effect on the rate of interest because the demand for money becomes highly elastic at low levels of interest. If, however, the rate of interest could be lowered by increasing the quantity of money, its effect depends in turn on the shape of the investment demand schedule. If this schedule is inelastic, that is, relatively unresponsive to changes in the rate of interest, then monetary policy would not have much effect on investment and employment. On the other hand, if the investment demand schedule is elastic, relatively small changes in the rate of interest would increase investment by relatively large amounts. If investment can be increased through monetary policy, the effect on income depends on the size of the investment multiplier. During the Great Depression when Keynes wrote the *General Theory*, he felt that monetary policy would have little effect either on the interest rate directly or on investment and employment indirectly. A main reason for this pessimism about monetary policy was that any changes in the rate of interest would be insignificant in relation to wide fluctuations in the marginal efficiency of capital.

Keynes was more hopeful about monetary policy in economic conditions other than a deep depression. During his early career he had championed monetary policy, but in later years, he believed that monetary policy remained important primarily as a complement to fiscal policy.

A leading criticism at a purely theoretical level is that Keynes failed to demonstrate that the economic system can be in equilibrium at less than full employment. If Keynes' theory is dependent on special assumptions such as inflexible wages and prices, it may be viewed as a special and not as a general theory. A. C. Pigou and others argued that if wages and prices are completely flexible in a downward direction, the real value of certain types of existing wealth will increase with a fall in the price level, and this in turn will increase consumption demand and hence reduce unemployment. Pigou acknowledged that this wealth effect has no practical significance for policy because wages and prices cannot be made perfectly flexible. Keynes' answer to Pigou's purely theoretical point was that in a monetary economy, such as Keynes was analyzing, the assumptions of complete flexibility of wages and prices is not consistent with the essential properties of money, as discussed by Keynes in Chapter 17 of the *General Theory*. It is the properties of money, in a monetary economy, that cause wages and prices to be sticky. If wages and prices happen to be inflexible because of institutional reasons such as strong labor unions and minimum-wage laws, that is incidental and does not have any bearing on Keynes' basic theory.

Keynesian economics originated as a response to a deeply felt need at a time when traditional economics, resting on the premise that the economy tends always toward full employment, had very little to offer by way of explaining the Great Depression. Keynes' seminal ideas made him the most influential economist of the twentieth century in both economic theory and economic policy. With passing decades Keynesian economics required modifications in order to remain relevant to changing economic and historical conditions.

References

Hicks, John R., *The Crisis in Keynesian Economics*, Blackwell, Oxford, 1974; Keynes, John Maynard, *The General Theory of Employment, Interest and Money*, Harcourt Brace Jovanovich, New York, 1936; Morgan, Brian, *Monetarists and Keynesians*, Wiley, New York, 1978; Wonnacott, Paul, *Macroeconomics*, Irwin, Homewood, Ill., 1974.

(*See also* Automatic stabilizers; Business cycles; Capitalism; Classical school; Consumption function; Economics; Employment and unemployment; Expectations; Fiscal policy; General equilibrium; Inflation; Interest rates; Investment function; Laissez faire; Macroeconomics; Marshallian economics; Multiplier; Neoclassical economics; Neo-Keynesian economics; Post-Keynesian economics; Propensity to consume or to save and inducement to invest; Real balance effect theory)

Dudley Dillard

Kitchin cycle

Joseph Kitchin, a British statistician, developed the notion that business fluctuations could be divided into two categories: major cycles and minor cycles. Writing in 1923 he described major cycles as "so-called trade cycles, which are merely aggregates usually of two, and less seldom of three minor cycles," and minor cycles as "averaging 3½ years (40 months in length)."

In honor of Kitchin's work on the minor cycles, Joseph Schumpeter named the 40-month cycle the Kitchin cycle, which then became an element in Schumpeter's three-cycle schema of the Kondratieff cycle (54-year average duration), the Juglar cycle (9- to 10-year average duration), and the Kitchin cycle (40-month averate duration).

The data Kitchin used were of commodity prices, bank clearings, and interest rates in Great Britain and in the United States from 1890 to 1922. While the length of the various cycles over that time span varied somewhat, the dispersion was surprisingly small. W. L. Crum published his study with much the same results in the same issue of the *Review of Economic Statistics*.

Kitchin offered very little in the way of theoretical explanation of the observed phenomenon, stating simply: "These minor cycles are apparently the result of a rhythmical movement due to psychological causes, though, through prices of vegetable foods, they may be influenced by excess or deficiency in crops which fall out of tune with the normal cycles."

Improvement of Methodology

Since Kitchin's time, the 40-month cycle has gained considerable credence since the post-World War II cycles have generally been of that approximate duration. The statistical methodology used by Kitchin was crude, and significant improvements have been made since Kitchin's time. Furthermore, the data he used were limited. The National Bureau of Economic Research and the Department of Commerce's Bureau of Economic Analysis have constructed hundreds of significant economic time series with which to measure and evaluate the phases of business cycles. Consequently, the level of business cycle research has improved considerably.

While many factors contribute to the explanation of business cycles, and while each historical cycle contains its own peculiar features, modern theorists place great stress on inventory investment as the major explanation of minor cycles. Examination of the empirical evidence of the postwar cycles lends strong support for this emphasis. Moses Abramowitz, (1948) in particular, has conducted a highly detailed study of the behavior of inventories in the prewar period and concluded that inventory variations conformed well with the cyclical phases in general economic activity. It is also clear that in the postwar period inventory buildup characterized the expansion phases, and inventory liquidation took place during every recession. In the 1953–54 recession, the decrease in inventories accounted for about 50 percent of the decline in GNP; and in the 1949, 1960–61, 1967, 1969–70, 1974–75 recessions, the inventory reduction was as great as or greater than the decrease in GNP. Fluctuations in inventory, according to Abramowitz's prewar study and according to Carl Dauten's postwar analysis, lag behind general business activity by several months.

In order to understand the significance of inventory behavior to general economic conditions, it is necessary to relate inventories to sales and production. Short-run, such as weekly, fluctuations in sales can be met by merchants or manufacturers by the opposite or inverse movement of inventories without changing production rates. For example, if sales increase in one week and in that week production remains the same, inventories would fall by the amount of the sales increase. Thus, inventories can change, either because of a change in sales which could be anticipated or unexpected, or because of a change in the production rate which is usually, but not always, a conscious decision of the firm's management.

When the demand for goods and services increases in a more or less continuous fashion, as would be the case when the business cycle begins its expansion phase, firms will find their inventories being depleted and will react to this by increasing output or increasing orders from their suppliers. They might also increase prices in order to slow down unit sales. The important aspect of the increased production generated by the increased sales is that production will increase by a larger percentage than the percentage increase in sales. The reason for this magnification is that output will have to increase to make up for the past loss of inventories, but it will also have to increase the absolute level of inventories to service the higher level of sales. The increased output will be further accentuated when managers take the growth in sales to be indicative of even greater growth in the near future, or if inflation is anticipated, or if higher interest rates are expected in the near future.

Once inventories have reached the level desired by the firms involved, even a decrease in the rate of increase in sales can precipitate a reduction in the output of the commodities and a decrease in demand will generate a magnified reduction in output, bringing on what is referred to as an inventory recession. The downswing will continue until the redundant inventory has been eliminated, at which point any increase in primary demand can set off the recovery phase described in the preceding paragraphs.

Investment in fixed capital also varies with business fluctuations in almost as convincing fashion as do inventories, and this type of investment also plays a key role in business cycle theories. The other series which exhibit close conformity to the cycle are consumer durable goods sales and residential construction.

References

Abramowitz, Moses, *The Role of Inventories in Business Cycles,* occasional paper 26, National Bureau of Economic Research, New York 1948; Crum, W. L., "Cycles of Rates on Commercial Paper," *Review of Economic Statistics,* vol. 5, no. 1, January 1923, pp. 17–27; Dauten, Carl, and Lloyd Valentine, *Business Cycles and Forecasting,* 5th ed., South-Western, Cincinnati, 1978; Kitchin, Joseph, "Cycles and Trends in Economic Factors," *Review of Economic Statistics,* vol.

5, no. 1, January 1923, pp. 10–16; Metzler, Lloyd A., "The Nature and Stability of Inventory Cycles," *Review of Economics and Statistics*, vol. 23, no. 3, August 1941, pp. 113–129; Schumpeter, Joseph A., *Business Cycles*, vol. 1, McGraw-Hill, New York, 1939.

(*See also* Business cycles; Change in business's inventories in GNP; Juglar cycle; Kondratieff cycle; Kuznets cycle)

Lloyd M. Valentine

Kondratieff cycle

The longest business cycle found in economic experience is called the Kondratieff cycle. The name was assigned by Joseph A. Schumpeter in his two-volume study, *Business Cycles*, in recognition of the contributions of the Russian economist Nikolai D. Kondratieff. Kondratieff himself referred to the cycles as "long waves."

The Statistical Evidence

Kondratieff analyzed a number of economic time series for France, England, the United States, Germany, and the world. In most of these series he concluded that a long cycle was evident. On the other hand, in a few series, namely French cotton consumption, U.S. wool and sugar production, and several others, the long-wave pattern was not established. Statistical analysis of the data led Kondratieff to conclude that there existed a cycle of an average duration of approximately 54 years.

Establishing historical dates for the various phases of cycles is a major preoccupation of business cycle analysts. Kondratieff contented himself with interval estimates of the turning points, and produced the following table:

Wave	Duration
First long wave	1. The rise lasted from the end of the 1780s or beginning of the 1790s until 1810–1817. 2. The decline lasted from 1810–1817 until 1844–1851.
Second long wave	1. The rise lasted from 1844–1851 until 1870–1875. 2. The decline lasted from 1870–1875 until 1890–1896.
Third long wave	1. The rise lasted from 1890–1896 until 1915–1920. 2. The decline probably begins in the years 1914–1920.

These cycles of general economic activity showed what Kondratieff felt was a high degree of parallelism in the capitalist economies of Europe and in the United States with the exception of such unusual events as the American Civil War and the Napoleonic Wars. This correspondence in behavior was true of price level indexes in the different countries, in interest rate series, in wages, in foreign trade, and in production and consumption data.

Explanations of the Evidence on the Kondratieff Cycle

Kondratieff was very careful not to claim to have discovered the causes of the long waves, though he did say, "We are also of the opinion that the long waves arise out of causes which are inherent in the essence of the capitalistic economy." He does, nevertheless, observe certain empirical characteristics of the cycle he studied which point toward theoretical explanations developed by other economists.

1. He noted that the long waves and the shorter cycles were interrelated in some way since during the expansion phase of the long waves, the years of prosperity in the intermediate cycles (Juglar, or 10- year average) were longer and depression years shorter; and during the contraction phase of the long cycle, depression years were longer and prosperity periods were shorter.

   Schumpeter extended this analysis to form his basic three-cycle schema in which six Juglar cycles were contained in each Kondratieff cycle, and the shorter cycles (Kitchin) fluctuated about the Juglar cycle.

2. Agriculture suffers most severely during the depression phase of the long waves. Kondratieff's findings are in line with those of most other investigators. W. S. Jevons and H. L. Moore, in particular, made agricultural cycles the basis of their business cycle theories.

3. Important inventions or discoveries are made during the downswing of the long waves, but their application and introduction into the economic system occur in the early stages of the upswing. Kondratieff denied that scientific or technical discoveries were random or accidental events. They happen in large part because of the pressure of necessity generated by the hard times of the depression when the need to find cost-cutting techniques, new products, new markets, or new raw material sources becomes intense. However, the discoveries, inventions, or new ways of producing things will not be applied until the conditions are right—when interest rates, wages, material costs, etc. are low, and when the existing capital stock has been depreciated or inventory stock depleted. These conditions arise when the depression has gone on for some time, and so the stage is set for recovery.

   Schumpeter made the distinction between inventions or discoveries and innovations (the application of the inventions or discoveries) the heart of his explanation of business cycles. Cycles of different lengths were the result of innovations requiring different lengths of time for their absorption into the economy. According to Schumpeter's historical analysis, the first Kondratieff wave was associated with a group of important innovations of the industrial revolution, specifically canals and road building, cotton textiles, coal and iron development and mining, and the steam engine, which played an important role in all of the other developments. The second long wave was produced by railroad construction and steel. The third cycle took place during the years of the exploitation of the opportunities in the electric power, automobile, and chemical industries.

4. Wars and revolutions take place during expansion phases of the long waves. According to Kondratieff, "They originate from real, especially economic, circumstances." Marxist economists stress the interrelationship between wars and revolutions, and economic conditions.

5. The opening up of new countries and the development of lagging economies seemed to Kondratieff to take place mainly in periods when the needs of the advanced economies for new sources of raw materials and new markets for their output was greatest, that is, during expansion periods.

6. The discovery of gold, increased production of gold in old mines, and the resulting increase in the gold and money stock also occur mainly in the early stages of economic expansion. These are not random events but are caused by a favorable economic climate—when the general price level is low and, therefore, the value of gold high; when costs of production of gold (mainly wages) are low; and when banks and bank borrowers have the incentive to expand the supply of currency and demand deposits.

Evaluation

The hypothesis of the existence of the Kondratieff cycle has not fared well in the judgment of most economists. The criticisms are mainly statistical. First, $2\frac{1}{2}$ cycles are not enough to establish such a hypothesis. Furthermore, students who have used different techniques of trend and short-run cycle elimination do not find the same pattern that Kondratieff found. Another point often made is that the only strong support of Kondratieff's position is found in the price level series and in interest rates, whereas the real series such as production and consumption data seem not to exhibit the long-wave conformity.

Interest in the Kondratieff waves has diminished in recent years, and more recent analysis of intermediate cycles has centered on the cycles of 15- to 20-year average duration developed by Simon Kuznets. A few articles appeared in the late 1970s using the Kondratieff cycle to suggest the possibility of the approach of a long-term downswing (1979).

References

Dauten, Carl, and Lloyd Valentine, *Business Cycles and Forecasting,* 5th ed., South-Western, Cincinnati, 1978; Garvy, George, "Kondratieff's Theory of Long Cycles," *Review of Economic Statistics,* vol. 25, no. 6, November 1943, pp. 203–220, reprinted in Alvin H. Hansen and Richard V. Clemence, *Readings in Business Cycles and National Income,* Norton, New York, 1953, pp. 438– 466; Hansen, Alvin H., *Business Cycles and National Income,* Norton, New York, 1951. Kondratieff, Nikolai D., "The Long Waves in Economic Life," *Review of Economic Statistics,* vol. 17, no. 6, November 1935, pp. 105–115, reprinted in *Readings in Business Cycle Theory,* American Economic Association, Blakiston, Philadelphia, 1944, pp. 20–42; Schumpeter, Joseph A., *Business Cycles,* vol. I., McGraw-Hill, New York, 1939.

(*See also* Business cycles; Juglar cycle; Kitchin cycle; Kuznets cycle)

Lloyd M. Valentine

Kuznets cycle

The term Kuznets cycle is customarily used to denote secular swings in economic growth rates exhibiting a duration of approximately 15 to 20 or more years. They are named for Simon S. Kuznets, who made extensive studies, particularly of American economic development, and found evidence of such long swings in many economic activities, but most particularly in the building construction industry. In his early work Kuznets dated long swings for the period prior to World War I. Generally, he dated peaks in 1873, 1892, and 1913, and troughs in 1878 and 1896, although there was some variation from one measure of economic activity to another. In addition to studying building construction, Kuznets analyzed population changes, capital formation, income, gross national product (GNP), and other factors.

Cycles in Growth Rates

The distinctive feature of Kuznets cycles is that they are cycles in growth rates rather than in the absolute expansion and contraction of the level of activity. The name was first attributed to this phenomenon by P. J. O'Leary and W. Arthur Lewis (1955). Kuznets was not, of course, alone in his interest in growth rate fluctuations. Others included most notably Arthur F. Burns, Moses Abramowitz, Brinley Thomas, and A. F. Cairncross.

O'Leary and Lewis summarize a great deal of statistical evidence covering a number of countries in addition to the United States. They conclude that there is evidence supporting the notion of long swings in economic activity, notably in the United States, Germany, and France, where they date three such cycles prior to the First World War, and in the United Kingdom, where they find evidence of a fourth, although in series other than production.

Even though the term Kuznets cycle is primarily associated with the U.S. construction industry, it is by no means confined either to that measure of economic activity or to the United States, but is regarded as a phenomenon visible in growth rates in most major industrial economies in the 40 years prior to World War I. Kuznets and others have also argued that these growth rate swings can be found for the 1920s and 1930s, with Kuznets placing a later peak in 1921 and a trough in 1931. The latter statistics are based on his analysis of both total and per capita income.

Cause of Long Swings

The question of what the cause or causes of long swings might be is unclear. Kuznets (1930) concluded, "While the causes of such fluctuations in the rate of secular growth are still obscure and their recurrence not too widely known, sufficient study has been made to affirm their existence." His emphasis on the high visibility of long swings in building construction has led others, notably Brinley Thomas (1973), to argue that demographic factors, including particularly immigration waves to the United States, are undoubtedly central in explaining the long swings. Thomas argues that building cycles in Britain and the United States were inversely related in the 70 years prior to World War I, and that the explanation for them in both countries lies in immigration waves. United States building increased after a wave of immigrants arrived; British building would fall after a wave of emigration. Thomas broadened his argument ultimately to relate long swings to what he termed "population-sensitive capital formation." Whether long swings can or cannot be adequately explained by demographic factors is still debatable, even for the pre-World War I period. O'Leary and Lewis (1955) conclude for roughly the same period analyzed by Thomas that the United States, Britain, Germany, and France were "remarkably independent of each other."

Is the Kuznets Cycle a Valid Concept?

Whether or not long swings, assuming their existence is granted for the earlier period, continue in the post-World War II period is again a debatable proposition. The Kuznets technique for examining instability by looking at deviations from the trend has been adapted to what are called growth cycles today—short cycles in growth rates visible in many market-oriented economies. Moses Abramowitz (1956) has argued that even though much of his own work supports the notion of long swings for the earlier period (i.e., 1840–1914), it cannot remain a valid concept in the post-World War I world because there have been historical and institutional changes which preclude its reemergence. Thomas is not so sure that the Kuznets cycle is dead but argues that certain forces which affected Kuznets cycles earlier are clearly either radically changed or have disappeared. These include immigration waves to the United States, an increase in governmental knowledge about the appropriate application of stabilization policies to avoid severe depressions, and the increase in the absolute and relative size of all levels of government.

Finally, a remaining anomaly is that while Kuznets cycles have always been called "long swings," the term was never meant to apply to the longest recurring pattern economists have considered—the 40- to 60-year cycle typically called the Kondratieff cycle. R. A. Gordon (1961) was, therefore, more accurate when he called Kuznets cycles "intermediate swings." Whether or not the 16- to 22-year growth rate cycle remains a viable concept, economists are increasingly finding that examining cyclical activity in trend-adjusted forms is a rich field for promising research.

References

Abramowitz, Moses, *Resource and Output Trends in the United States Since 1870*, occasional paper 52, National Bureau of Economic Research, New York, 1956; Gordon, R. A., *Business Fluctuations*, 2d ed., Harper & Row, New York, 1961; Kuznets, Simon S., *Secular Movements in Production and Prices*, Houghton Mifflin, Boston, 1930; Lewis, W. A., and P. J. O'Leary, "Secular Swings in Production and Trade, 1870–1913," *The Manchester School of Economics and Social Studies*, vol. 23, May 1955, pp. 113–152; Thomas, Brinley, *Migration and Economic Growth*, 2d ed., Cambridge University Press, Cambridge, 1973.

(*See also* Business cycles; Juglar cycle; Kitchin cycle; Kondratieff cycle)

Philip A. Klein

Labor, a factor of production

As a factor of production, labor is normally defined as the services of human inputs in the production process, receiving compensation in the form of wages (or salaries) based upon labor's marginal productivity. This simple definition is, however, somewhat misleading for two reasons.

First, a worker does not, in general, supply raw, human-generated power but rather the ability to apply effort. Both a ditchdigger and a corporate executive supply labor, but the quantities of labor services they supply and the compensation they receive differ greatly. As Gary S. Becker (1975) has shown, the quantity of labor services supplied is itself determined by the stock of abilities the individual has acquired. Hence, labor might be more appropriately viewed as the flow of services generated by a given stock of human capital. The effectiveness of this stock of human capital is itself determined by the amounts of education, training, health maintenance, and mobility applied to the basic human input. Thus, the distinction between capital and labor is blurred since both involve the services generated from a given stock as well as an investment decision based on anticipated returns. It should be noted, however, that this capital theoretical view of labor can be carried only so far. One important distinction is that physical capital can be transferred (sold), while human capital is very difficult to transfer.

A second difficulty with the simple definition of labor is that it tends to imply that labor is a factor which is entirely variable (i.e., the amount of labor employed can be changed in the short run). However, as first pointed out by Walter Oi (1962), labor may be better viewed as a fixed or quasi-fixed input. To the extent that there exist costs to the firm in addition to direct wage expenditures (e.g., training costs), the cost of releasing and rehiring workers is increased; thus, the labor input may well behave more like a fixed input.

Maximizing Decisions

The amount of labor actually used in the production process is determined on the basis of maximizing decisions by both the individual labor supplier and the firm. The individual first determines the level of investment to make in human capital on the basis of the maximization of lifetime returns (essentially the same as the firm's capital investment decision) and then determines the level of flow of services from that stock the individual will provide to the market based on a utility-maximizing choice between income and leisure. The firm determines the amount of labor that it will employ based on a profit-maximizing decision considering the marginal productivity of the labor and the level of necessary firm-specific investment in the labor.

Historically, labor has occupied a dominant position in discussions of the factors of production, and its importance in the production process may well have been over-emphasized. Indeed, the medieval economists and, much later, John Locke considered labor to be the sole source of value (i.e., the only productive input). In English classical economics, this labor theory of value continued to dominate. Adam Smith stressed the importance of the labor input in the production process, particularly in primitive societies, as well as the effects of division of labor on economic progress. David Ricardo, while not maintaining a strict, uncompromising labor theory of value, stressed more than Smith the importance of labor in production. Thomas Malthus (responsible for the "iron law of wages") was the first to discuss the importance of the other factors of production. The labor theory of value reached its culmination with Karl Marx, who attributed all value to labor. Indeed, Marx viewed capital as nothing more than the stored-up productive power of labor. The current view of labor as a factor of production comes from the neoclassical (or marginalist) economists. The work of Alfred Marshall and John Bates Clark altered the view of the factors of production by considering the marginal supply and demand functions for factors. This led to the marginal productivity approach to the valuation of labor and formed the basis for the analyses of more recent writers.

References

Becker, G. S., *Human Capital*, 2d ed., National Bureau of Economic Research, New York, 1975; Ekelund, R. B., and R. F. Hebert, *A History of Economic Theory and Method*, McGraw-Hill, New York, 1975; Oi, W., "Labor as a Quasi-Fixed Factor," *Journal of Political Economy*, vol. 70, December 1962, pp. 538–555.

(*See also* Factors of production; Human capital; Labor theory of value)

Charles W. Smithson

Labor force

Labor force has no meaning of its own; it is simply the sum of employment and unemployment in world censuses and current household surveys. As is evident, however, from controversy in the United States since 1940, the question of how employment and unemployment are defined depends upon some concept of the labor force.

In historical perspective the labor force, or work force, is that portion of the whole population engaged in activities considered essential to and carried on within the authoritative work organization of a society. In primitive societies the work force may be hardly distinguishable from total population, and the needs for information as to its changing size and composition may go little beyond what may be readily perceived by the political authorities. In more advanced societies during most of the past two centuries, the work force has been conceived as consisting of persons usually engaged in a gainful occupation, for pay or profit, in the organized market activities of the economy. Needs for information by the political and economic authorities have changed and grown over the years and, in the United States in the late 1930s, new sampling techniques began to be used for the timely measurement of the information wanted for public policy purposes.

For more than a century the work-force concept used in Western industrial countries for statistical measurement in decennial censuses in order to obtain information about labor supply and human resources was that of gainful occupation. This provided the basis for periodic estimates of the number of persons with a gainful occupation at which they usually worked for pay or profit in the market-oriented sectors of the economy, with varying detail as to age, sex, geographic location, and industrial attachment. Presumably this served fairly well the limited needs for data for social and economic policy purposes as conceived originally by Jefferson and others who played a role in introducing the concept into the 1820 Census. The first effort to collect information on how many of the gainful workers were employed or unemployed was in 1880 with the growing public concern over the conflict between capital and labor, and continued fitfully through the 1930 Census with little useful or reliable information for employment policy purposes.

Gainful-Worker, Labor-Force, and Labor-Supply Concepts

The labor-force concept introduced in the United States in 1940 and subsequently adopted as a model, with some variation, for census and current estimates by international organizations and other countries, and the earlier gainful-worker concept, may be compared as approximations to measures of labor supply. Both concepts covered only persons attached to the market economy and thus excluded workers within the home, volunteer workers, and, in principle at least, persons engaged in illicit activities. This is also the practice in national product or income measurements. But the gainful-worker count as an approximation of labor supply was particularly deficient in leaving out new, or inexperienced, workers and persons with no usual occupation by which they earned a living. Nor did it distinguish between those with gainful occupations who were actively at work and those who were retired or not at work for reasons such as unemployment.

The current census or household sample surveys surmounted these latter shortcomings (although creating new ones) by the simple device of classifying persons according to their activity in a one-week period along a continuum of degree of attachment to the labor market—from employed, to with a job but not at work, to actively seeking work, to wanting a job but not actively seeking, to out of the labor force.

While the new labor-force concept was not intended as the basis for obtaining a full measure of the labor supply under conditions of less than full-employment demand for labor, it was expected to provide some kind of measure of jobs needed for public policy purposes in recession. That the current labor-force estimates, i.e., the employed plus the unemployed, fail to include all persons who might reasonably be regarded as part of the available supply is shown by the considerably larger numbers enumerated in the labor force at some time during the calendar year (as in the special annual surveys each April). Wartime expansion of the labor force in 1941 to 1945 demonstrated its expansibility under conditions of extremely high demand for labor.

For proponents of full employment as the overriding objective of economic policy, the present labor-force concept, only marginally modified since 1940, is deemed deficient because it does not provide an estimate of persons who want or would seek work if remuneration and other conditions were to their liking. This view gains considerable credence from the fact the labor force rises considerably above its secular trend path in periods of so-called full-employment levels of demand. A determination of that level is the source of unsettled dispute as to the natural rate of unemployment or the level of unemployment consistent with stable prices.

In practice, whatever the level of demand for labor, the objective of current labor-force measurement in the United States, as reemphasized and made more explicit by various definitional and procedural changes recommended by three official review committees since 1955, is to provide a classification of persons in and outside the labor force during a restricted period of time by as objective and measurable indicia of labor-market behavior and attachment as possible.

On the recommendation of the International Labor Organization (ILO) and the United Nations, the labor-force concept has displaced the gainful-worker approach, for national statistics on work attachments of the population, in all country censuses since those of 1970. What the figures mean in the various countries may not be the same for reasons of cultural differences. As used in a large number of developing countries in the Third World for economic planning, the labor-force estimates provide ambiguous data with respect to available labor supply because, for example, of the relative importance of the nonmarket subsistence sectors, whose workers may not in fact be available for work in the modern sectors. Large differences in participation rates of women in the developing countries more likely reflects the influence of cultural factors upon reporting of labor-force activity of women than actual differences. Generally, however, participation rates of women tend to decline in the early stages of economic development with the contraction of opportunities for self-employment and unpaid family work in agriculture.

Since men of working age are ordinarily expected to be gainfully employed and in the labor force, the question that has received most attention since the 1930s has related to the changing labor-force participation rates of women. This appeared first in the form of the additional or secondary worker controversy in the depression years, whether the joblessness of the male head of the household resulted in job seeking by the spouse or other member of the family. Since then, with unemployment insurance and other income supports, the development of chief interest has been the strong secular rise in labor-force participation of women, which has more than offset a substantial decline in participation rates of men. Lower demand in recession tends to arrest only temporarily the upward movement in participation rates of women while accelerating the long-run decline in participation rates of men, and vice versa in periods of higher demand.

The rising participation of women in the labor market has been evident also in Canada, Australia, Great Britain, and Sweden but not in Germany, France, Italy, and Japan where, while the decline in rates for men has been equally marked, rates for women have declined or, in France, remained largely unchanged.

The decline in labor-force participation rates of men have been explained readily in terms of two factors—longer education and earlier retirement—shortening working life. The generally lower rates for black males and higher rates for black women are also easily explained. The extraordinary rise in participation of women in the United States—from 37.7 percent of women over 16 in 1960 to 48.4 percent in 1977, one of the significant social developments of our times—has been more difficult to explain by empirical studies than by intuition.

In the case of married women there is found to be an inverse relation between their work propensities and spouses' income. How, then, can the rise in participation rates in the past 20 years be explained? There has been a considerable loosening up of this statistical relationship since 1960 or before as evidenced by studies for more recent years. The desire for work outside the home appears to be an exogenous variable outside the constraints of conventional economic analysis. The kind of jobs offered by the changing structure of demand for women workers may not help to explain the phenomenon in terms of job satisfactions, yet the historic rise in service employment may help to explain the increased availability of jobs for women and hence the relative rise in women's wages to men's on an opportunity wage basis. As in recovery upswings in demand, the greater availability of jobs draws additional women into the labor force. Even the persistent wage differential between men and women may contribute to the explanation, as evidenced by the marked hiring differential in favor of women in recent years, the employment of women rising by more than 80 percent in the last 20 years compared with 30 percent for men.

Toward a Postindustrial Labor Force

For broad trends in occupational and industrial structure, the census data on gainful workers and more recently on labor force have provided the basis for speculation about the future nature of the labor force in American society, as well as that of other industrialized countries. The most important factor from the time of the American Revolution to World War I was the transformation from an agricultural to an industrial society. As late as 1870 more than one-half of those gainfully employed were in farming, while in 1920 almost three-quarters were engaged in nonfarm activities. In 1920 more than one-half were still employed in goods-producing industries including agriculture. By the 1970s more than two-thirds were engaged in the so-called service industries.

These changes in occupational and industrial structures have been interpreted variously as the rise in discretionary consumption in an affluent society and as the emergence of a knowledge society and postindustrial economy. In no inconsiderable part, however, the growing service activities were in support of goods production. For the service-expenditure component of personal consumption expenditures in the national income accounts has moved only erratically from the 1929 level of 40 percent to 46 percent during the 1970s. As part of total GNP, personal service expenditures have only gradually regained the 1929 level of 29 percent.

The seeds of the heralded postindustrial society are to be found not in the large occupational or industrial classifications but in such employments as research and development activities in industry, schools, and government. What the relative increase in white-collar occupations and service employment appear to signify is the bureaucratization of the production process as corporate planning and the internalization of transactions, and government interventions, diminish the role of the market.

References

Bell, Daniel, *The Coming of Post-Industrial Society: A Venture in Social Forecasting*, Basic Books, New York, 1973; Jaffe, A. J., and Charles D. Stewart, *Manpower Resources and Utilization: Principles of Working Force Analysis*, Wiley, New York, 1951; Moy, Joyanna, "Recent Labor Market Trends in Nine Industrial Nations," *Monthly Labor Review*, U.S. Government Printing Office, Washington, D.C., May 1979; Standing, Guy, *Labor Force Participation and Development*, International Labor Office, Geneva, 1978.

(*See also* Demographics and economics; Employment and unemployment)

Charles D. Stewart

Labor-intensive industry (see Capital-intensive industry)

Labor Statistics Bureau (see Bureau of Labor Statistics)

Labor-management relations

Often the term labor-management relations is used interchangeably with the terms "labor relations" or "industrial relations," which are regarded as synonymous by practitioners and scholars alike. The field of labor-management relations is relatively new having more or less developed in the 1930s during the Great Depression. The labor-management relations function developed as a result of the legitimation of the trade union as a social institution during the New Deal era of President Franklin D. Roosevelt. The growth of trade unionism and labor relations during the period 1930–1945 is directly related to labor laws which were designed to balance the relative bargaining powers of employers and employee representatives engaged in collective bargaining of labor agreements.

The first significant federal labor law was the Railway Labor Act of 1926, which applies only to the railway and airline industry. Then in 1932, the Federal Anti-Injunction Act, commonly referred to as the Norris-LaGuardia Act after its congressional sponsors, was passed to restrict severely the use of court injunctions in labor disputes now broadly defined beyond the immediate employer-employee relationship. But the real landmark legislative act in the field of labor-management relations is the National Labor Relations Act passed in 1935, commonly called the Wagner Act after the late Senator Robert Wagner of New York. These federal labor laws, girded by the judiciary, played an important part in the legitimation and growth of trade unions and collective bargaining in the United States. Accompanying this growth naturally was the development of the field of labor-management relations.

Although, theoretically, trade unionism and collective bargaining are not necessarily required for the field of labor-management relations, prior to the origin of strong labor unions there was little activity in the field of labor-management relations, which needed the important ingredient of strong employee representatives standing in a complementary relationship with management to evolve into a legitimate field of practice and study. It is generally recognized that trade unionism and collective bargaining are the cornerstones and modus operandi of labor relations in America.

Labor-management relations is an important and pervasive field in search of a theoretical construct. According to John T. Dunlop of Harvard University, a former Secretary of Labor, in a landmark treatise on industrial relations systems (1958), "Facts have outrun ideas. Integrating theory has lagged behind expanding experience. The many worlds of industrial relations have been changing more rapidly than the ideas to interpret, to explain, and to relate to them."

There is little debate regarding the conclusion that the great number of facts arising from the real-world practice of labor-management relations has more or less overwhelmed scholars in the field, somehow preventing the development of a neat body of theoretical principles to form a common body of knowledge to assist in the study and development of the field. Scholarship in the field emanates from a variety of disciplinary backgrounds which in itself inhibits a common body of principles. Among these disciplines are economics, industrial sociology, management, psychology, labor law, history, group dynamics, game theory, and social psychology. Although each of these disciplines has made significant contributions to the study of labor-management relations, no single individual is capable of mastering all of these disciplines as they apply to the field. Thus, the difficulty of developing an integrated theoretical construct embracing the various social and behavioral sciences involved is due to the complexity of the field. Notwithstanding this current situation, countless scholars from many fields of study are engaged in working toward the goal of finding common threads which make up the field of labor-management relations from which ultimately will come the theoretical underpinnings that are currently lacking.

Three Contexts

The day-today workings of the industrial relations system are carried out by what Dunlop calls "actors" to refer to participants or parties to industrial relations activity. There are three sets of actors: (1) managers and their hierarchial superiors, (2) workers and trade union representatives, and (3) regulatory rule makers representing some form of government. An understanding of the behaviors of the three sets of actors, and, therefore, the industrial relations system, requires a recognition of what Dunlop refers to as the three contexts: (1) the market context; (2) the context of technology at the workplace; and (3) the context of power relations of the enveloping society, as reflected in the workplace.

The market context is fundamental to the understanding of an efficient pricing and allocation system of the work force in the various private and public sectors to meet the demands of consumers and citizens. It is the market context which dictates the broad parameters within which the actors must devise acceptable work rules and compensation packages. The relative value of the services or products in the marketplace influences the nature of technology in providing a particular service or product by establishing, at a given time, the feasibility of various levels of capital investment. And it is this capital investment which determines the productivity, and, hence, the value of workers performing the services. In other words, the relative worth of labor producing a given product or service ultimately depends on the value placed upon that product or service by those who demand such products or services in the marketplace. Obviously, if the workplace technology is such to render labor highly productive and efficient, one should expect high rates of pay and generous fringe benefits.

Over time these contexts are dynamic and change with improvements in ways of doing things, such as new discoveries or inventions of better and more efficient methods of production. Ordinarily, the more capital-intensive the method of production the more productive will be the labor producing a given product. Thus, labor receives higher rewards in modern capital-intensive industries compared with early nineteenth-century handicraft industries because output per worker-hour or labor productivity is higher under modern conditions compared with the more primitive labor-intensive methods of production of the preindustrial era.

The third context, that of power relations, is critically important because it is in large part the result of the dynamic interactive forces involving the three actors. The actors interact with the goal of establishing substantive rules to govern their relationship in the day-to-day operations. It is the third actors, the regulatory rule makers in the legislative, judicial, and executive branches of government, who establish the legal environment that governs the behaviors of the other two actors: employers and employee representatives. The rule makers protect the interests and equities of all concerned, not the least of which is the public interest, by providing rules for peaceful pursuit of industrial relations activities and resolutions of disputes between employers and employees. The goal is to avoid or minimize job actions such as work stoppages or employee lockouts which could jeopardize the peace and tranquility of the public.

Labor-Management Relations
in the Public Sector

In the United States the principal laws which govern labor-management relations are: the Railway Labor Act of 1926, the National Labor Relations Act of 1935 (amended by the Labor-Management Relations Act of 1947), and the Labor-Management Reporting and Disclosure Act of 1959. These are laws enacted by the federal government to regulate employer-employee relations in industries involved in interstate commerce over which the U.S. Constitution provides jurisdictional authority and regulatory responsibility to the federal government. More recently, in January 1962, President John F. Kennedy issued Executive Order (EO) No. 10988, which for the first time granted collective bargaining rights to federal employees and which has significantly altered the nature of labor-management relations in federal employment. President Richard M. Nixon reaffirmed the basic principles of EO 10988 in the superseding Executive Order No. 11491, issued on October 29, 1969, and subsequently amended in May 1975 by EO 11838 promulgated by President Gerald Ford.

The above executive orders, or presidential actions, accompanied by parallel counterpart legislative and executive actions on the part of state and local governmental authorities, have significantly influenced the nature of labor-management relations in the public sector. Labor-management activity in the public sector is no longer set apart from the mainstream of labor relations in the United States as a separate and distinct segment with totally different rules and regulations. Indeed, there are cetain nominal differences governing labor-management relations in the public sector (e.g., the denial of the right to strike or the prohibition of compulsory union membership in the federal sector), but the overall characteristics of public-sector labor relations in the United States are essentially identical with those in the private sector. While there is no market context in the strictest use of that term in the public sector, the various levels of government are empowered to go into the market place for worker and other required resources to provide services demanded by citizens. Government must compete in the marketplace with private bidders for these resources. Thus, governmental or public employers are affected by market forces which establish the underlying conditions for the setting of wages, benefits, and other conditions of employment. Labor relations activity in the public sector is subject to essentially the same market and technological forces found in the private sector. These forces ensure efficient utilization of scarce resources in providing public services.

America versus Western Europe

Labor relations in the public sector in America differ significantly from its counter-part in Western European countries fundamentally because labor relations and the institution of collective bargaining are so vastly different in other parts of the world compared with in the United States. Contrasted with labor unions in the United States, trade unionism and political parties are closely allied in many European coun-tries. Windmuller (1974) states:

> For almost a century now, the relationship between trade unions and political parties has been an integral element of the political systems of Western Euro-pean countries. . . . Virtually all trade unions and their confederations pursue some of their key objectives through long-established links with political parties, and most political parties take into account the claims of trade unions when for-mulating their programs and objectives, even if they lack formal links to unions. There is hardly any alternative. . . . Therefore, political parties aspiring or cling-ing to power can no more afford to disregard the vital concerns of major trade union groups than trade unions can afford to abstain from participation in the political process.[1]

This is not to suggest that labor organizations are not politically active in the United States. But there is no alliance between organized labor and the political par-ties in the United States, a situation which is quite different from the links which prevail between labor and labor parties in Europe and other parts of the world. Broadly speaking, however, labor relations systems abroad and in the United States are comparable in that mechanisms are put into place to govern the relationships between employers and employees and union-management groups.

Decisions have to be made regarding substantive issues in the employer-employee relationship regardless of the nature of the employer, public or private, and irre-spective of the country of domicile. While it is correct that day-to-day labor-manage-ment relations are more governed by a collective bargaining agreement in the United States compared with Western Europe, processes must be devised to determine such things as rates of pay, eligibility conditions for benefits, and individual job rights or security; and systems are developed to resolve individual and collective employer-employee differences. These mechanisms and/or processes are inherent in virtually all labor relations systems. Some are perhaps more formal (i.e., legislative) than oth-ers, but nevertheless subsystems (procedures or conventions) are devised to establish a network of rules to assist in the making of unavoidable decisions in the workplace.

[1]Reprinted by permission of *Industrial and Labor Relations Review*.

The Labor Agreement

In America, the labor relations function has developed as a result of the evolution of the labor union as a social institution and the acceptance of collective bargaining as the principal modus operandi in labor relations. Free collective bargaining, resulting in a written labor agreement or contract is the cornerstone of labor relations policy. It has long been axiomatic in organized labor circles: "No contract, no work!" Hence, the contract or labor agreement is a vital part of labor-management relations since it constitutes the essence of the agreed-upon rights and privileges, duties, and responsibilities of the parties to the agreement. That is, the labor agreement is the governing document which sets forth the respective interests of employers and employees in substantive provisions in accordance with the prevailing system of jurisprudence. Collective bargaining, however, is more than negotiating a labor agreement. Contract negotiations are but a part of the collective bargaining process. It is the day-to-day administration of the terms and conditions of the labor agreement, which the late Walter Reuther referred to as the "living document," that concerns the bulk of the activities of labor relations practitioners. The labor relations system in the United States, in both private and public sectors, is centered around the labor agreement which governs the relationship between parties. Beyond the determination of wages, benefits, and other conditions of employment, the labor agreement provides for the preservation of individual and union security, management prerogatives, and a host of other concerns.

Perhaps the most important provision of the labor agreement is that which establishes the steps of the formal grievance procedure to adjudicate employee complaints pertaining to managerial actions which allegedly violate the labor agreement. This system of due process provides for the resolution of employee grievances in a fair and equitable manner. If a particular grievance cannot be resolved between the employer and employee representatives at increasingly higher levels of authority, the matter is then heard by a third-party, neutral labor arbitrator for final dispensation. This system of private arbitration is unique to the United States and reflects the American system of jurisprudence. The parties to an unresolved dispute mutually determine who the neutral arbitrator shall be to conduct a formal hearing to adjudicate the matter, and the arbitrator's decision is final and binding on the parties. This unique characteristic of the labor relations system in the United States, labor arbitration conducted by private citizens, is a milestone in the movement toward industrial harmony that originated from practices developed during World War II to avoid work stoppages. The system of private labor arbitration and the practice of reducing to a written labor agreement the results of negotiating terms and conditions of employment between employers and representatives of their employees are landmark contributions to labor-management relations in the United States.

Labor-management relations systems are dynamic and evolve within the three contextual influences indicated. While it may be difficult, if not impossible, to predict precisely future developments in labor-management relations, Dunlop's theoretical construct allows for analysis of the major currents and influences of a given industrial relations system.

References

Beal, E. F., E. D. Wickershap, and P. K. Kienast, *The Practice of Collective Bargaining*, 5th ed., Irwin, Homewood, Ill., 1976; Brent, Alan E., and T. Zane Reaves, *Collective Bargaining in the*

Public Sector, Benjamin/Cummings, Menlo Park, Calif., 1978; Dunlop, John T., *Industrial Relations Systems*, Holt, Rinehart and Winston, New York, 1958, p. vi; Nesbitt, Murray B., *Labor Relations in the Federal Government Service*, The Bureau of National Affairs, Washington, D.C., 1976; Spero, Sterling D., *Government as Employer*, Southern Illinois University Press, Carbondale, Ill., 1972; Sloane, Arthur R., and Fred Witney, *Labor Relations*, 3d ed., Prentice-Hall, Englewood Cliffs, N.J., 1977; Windmuller, John P. (ed.), "European Labor and Politics: A Symposium," (1), *Industrial and Labor Relations Review*, vol. 28, no. 1, October 1974, p. 3; Windmuller, John P. (ed.), "European Labor and Politics: A Symposium," II, *Industrial and Labor Relations Review*, vol. 28, no. 2, January 1976.

(*See also* Collective bargaining; Government regulation of business; Labor unions)

Sam Barone

Labor theory of value

The labor theory of value is a doctrine developed by the English classical economists, chiefly Adam Smith, David Ricardo, and John Stuart Mill, but having older roots in the seventeenth-century political philosophy of John Locke and before that in Greek and Roman ideas of market exchange. It was subsequently adopted by Karl Marx, who gave it the notoriety that it has since acquired.

Three Distinct Theories

The labor theory of value is in fact three distinct theories: it is a theory of relative prices, that is, an explanation of how the exchange ratios between goods are determined in a regime where independent producers compete with each other to maximize their own advantage—the labor theory of relative value; it is also a theory of welfare economics, that is, a statement to the effect that an individual or a society is better off as a result of an economic change—the labor theory of absolute value; finally, it is, in its Marxist version, a theory of the nature of profit as a type of income, asserting in effect that profit is unpaid labor appropriated by capitalists as a consequence of the institution of private property—the labor theory of surplus value. In Smith, the labor theory of relative value is relegated to precapitalist times and attention is focused instead on the labor theory of absolute value. In Ricardo, it is the labor theory of relative value that is in the foreground, but there is also a labor theory of absolute value, different from and opposed to that of Smith. In Marx, we have all three versions; in particular, the labor theory of surplus value is turned into a special case of the labor theory of relative value.

Outside the Marxist camp, the labor theory of value in any of its meanings disappeared from economics around 1870. But the recent experience of central economic planning in the Soviet Union, which is said to be based on material balances and calculations of the labor requirements of production, and the emergence of Leontief's technique of input-output analysis, revived an interest in the now discredited labor theory of value. Modern mathematical economists have rigorously developed the implications of nonsubstitution theorems in which relative prices are entirely determined by labor inputs independent of the pattern of final demand; in short, they have worked out the necessary and sufficient conditions to render the labor theory of relative value a true explanation of prices. The object of this exercise, however, is to explore fully the analytical properties of certain economic models.

No one any longer believes that the labor theory of relative value throws much light on actual pricing problems, and even the Soviet planners make no serious use of the theory. As a species of welfare economics, the labor theory of absolute value is nowadays regarded as a method of making gross comparisons of welfare, as when Soviet living standards are compared with American ones by asking how many hours of work would be required in each of the two countries to buy specific articles of consumption at going wages and prices. Such comparisons assume that the disutility of labor, the irksomeness of an hour of physical effort, is the same in the two countries, an assumption which Smith defended in the *Wealth of Nations*.

Marxian Interpretation

The validity of the labor theory of surplus value remains a matter of controversy even among Marxist economists: the structure of Marx's argument involves a gross manipulation of arithmetic averages and total—the so-called transformation problem—that fails to carry conviction. These technical difficulties are sometimes evaded by the argument that Marx meant only to express the ethical doctrine that property income ought to accrue to workers and not to capitalists. The labor theory of surplus value, according to this interpretation, is a theory of natural rights rather than a positive theory of profits. But Marx clearly believed that he had demonstrated that total output, and hence the proportion retained as profits, is entirely created either by living labor or by "dead" labor invested in machines. The more the complexities of this theory are understood, the more difficult it is to give credence to the theory.

Misinterpretations and Confusion

One of the features that makes the labor theory of value so difficult to understand is that its advocates consistently misunderstood the intentions of their predecessors: Ricardo misinterpreted Smith's meaning, and Marx in turn misinterpreted Ricardo's meaning. Ricardo was convinced that Smith tried to formulate a labor theory of relative value and that he became confused between the concept of the labor "commanded" by a commodity and the labor "embodied" in a commodity. The labor-commanded theory cannot possibly be a theory of relative value, and to suggest that Smith could have confused such different phenomena as the labor price and the labor cost of a commodity is simply absurd. Smith did not try to formulate a labor theory of relative value but rather a labor theory of absolute value.

Ricardo was the first economist in the history of economic thought to insist on the labor theory of relative value: he believed that commodities exchange in ratios that are approximately equal to the ratios of labor required to produce them. Ricardo was aware that these ratios were only approximately equal because commodities cannot exchange exactly in proportion to relative labor costs when they are produced in time periods of unequal length, or with machines of unequal durability, or simply by different ratios of fixed to working capital. Marx recognized that the labor theory of relative value can never account completely for the relative prices of reproducible commodities, not to mention the prices of nonreproducible commodities. Marx dealt with the problem posed by Ricardo by focusing attention on a "typical" commodity produced by a ratio of capital to labor that is an average for the economy as a whole, and both his theory of relative prices and his theory of profits is true only of this typical commodity.

References

Gordon, D. F., "Value, Labor Theory of," in D. L. Sills (ed.), *International Encyclopaedia of the Social Sciences*, vol. 16, Free Press, New York, 1968, pp. 279–283; Blaug, M., *Economic Theory in Retrospect*, 3d ed., Cambridge University Press, New York, 1978, chaps. 2, 4, 6, 7.

(*See also* Classical school; Labor, a factor of production; Normative economics; Welfare economics)

Mark Blaug

Labor unions

Labor unions are organizations of employees established to bargain with employers concerning wages, hours, and conditions of employment. Unions are democratic institutions whose central purpose is improving the economic conditions of their members.

Categories, Importance, and Functions

Workers are organized in unions on either an industrial, craft, or professional basis. In an industrial union workers of an employer generally will be affiliated with similar locals of other employers in a like industry, thus forming a national union. The craft or professional group will have representatives of various employers in a local union which is similarly affiliated with like workers in a national union. In the United States there are 210 unions and associations representing 22,800,000 workers. In 1978 this number accounted for 22 percent of the total labor force and 33 percent of non-supervisory wage and salary employees in nonfarm establishments in the United States.

There is a general confederation of unions called the American Federation of Labor–Congress of Industrial Organizations or, more commonly, the AFL-CIO. There are 106 national and international unions affiliated with the AFL-CIO. The AFL-CIO deals primarily with issues of public policy, international relations with foreign trade unions, and coordination of activities between unions in support of their common goals and objectives.

National and local unions engage in direct collective bargaining activities with specific employers concerning the detailed contracts that set forth wages and conditions of employment. Contracts may cover numerous employers in an industry nationwide, such as the United Steelworkers' contracts with 10 basic steel companies. Some contracts may be with one employer nationwide, such as the United Auto Workers' contract with General Motors. Some contracts may cover just one plant or group of plants or stores of a multiplant corporation, such as the United Food and Commercial Workers' contract with Safeway stores in Houston. Electricians may have one contract with all the electrical contractors in an area. More than one union may have contracts with a single employer with each contract representing certain crafts, as is frequently the case in the railroad industry or the printing industry. Some public employees may be organized on a craft or professional basis, such as fire fighters or teachers; while others may be organized on an overall industrial basis, such as the American Federation of State, County, and Municipal Employees, or the American Federation of Government Employees.

At the state and local levels, AFL-CIO state and local central bodies also exist to deal with common state and local concerns. Such state and local AFL-CIO bodies represent the local unions in local or state public policy matters.

Generally, it is believed that unions tend to raise the wages of their members. Studies by Ashenfelder (1978) and Lewis (1963) indicate that unions tend to lead to a 10 percent differential in favor of such workers. However, some economists dispute the ability of unions to raise the wages of workers above general market equilibrium levels.

There is a general agreement, however, that unions bring a new system of jurisprudence to the workplace that provides a means of governing on-the-job relationships, resolving individual grievances, and providing due process in disciplinary and discharge cases. The union contract restricts the employer's ability to take unilateral personnel actions. It generally assures equal treatment of all workers according to the specific provisions of the contract.

Collective Bargaining

Unions achieve their wage and working conditions improvements through bargaining collectively with employers. When the collective bargaining process does not result in a mutually agreed contract, workers may strike in order to try to enforce their demands concerning wage and conditions of employment. Major strikes provide frequent headlines in the newspapers; however, on the average, strikes occur in less than 3 percent of all negotiations, and 97 percent of the negotiations lead to settlements without disruption of working relationships. In very few instances, employers may lock out employees in a negotiating dispute. Most contracts contain a no-strike provision for the term of the contract, with unresolved differences as to contract interpretation being adjudicated by private arbitrators.

The basic rights of the employee to organize into unions and to engage in collective bargaining is guaranteed in the Labor-Management Relations Act. That law gives the National Labor Relations Board authority to conduct secret-ballot elections to determine workers' desires regarding unionization and provides a mechanism for certifying unions selected by a majority. That law also obligates employers and unions to bargain collectively in good faith. It also provides help to the parties in bargaining through the mediative efforts of the Federal Mediation and Conciliation Service. The internal democratic structure and financial responsibility of unions are spelled out in the Labor-Management Reporting and Disclosure Act.

Legislation similar to the Labor-Management Relations Act exists for employees in the railroad and airline industries under the Railroad Labor Act. Special legislation or executive orders govern federal and postal labor relations, and separate state laws govern union recognition or collective bargaining for state and local government employees.

History

Unions trace their history to the earliest days of the nation. Unions of carpenters and shoemakers were organized shortly after the Revolution. Initially, the courts and the laws tried to restrict the rights of workers to form and join unions. However, in spite of repeated prosecution unions grew and expanded in the nineteenth century. The organization of unions was plagued by strong employer opposition, and many strikes were the result of employer refusal to recognize or bargain with unions.

The first national unions were founded in the 1850s representing workers in the printing industry (International Typographical Workers Union), the machinists (International Association of Machinists) and molders (International Molders and Allied Workers Union). Many unions use the title "international" in their name, indicating their representation of workers in the United States and Canada. They usually do not represent workers in other countries.

The American Federation of Labor traces its history to 1881. At the founding convention a number of existing national unions joined together in a confederation of national unions. While there were earlier confederations, these failed to flourish for any prolonged period. The AFL was the turning point in continuity for a labor federation in the United States. In 1937 the Congress of Industrial Organizations split off from the AFL, and the CIO was founded as a separate organization. Its special emphasis was to organize workers on an industrial basis. The two separate union federations merged to form the AFL-CIO in 1955.

Unions exist in most democratic societies as a basis for providing workers with a means of representation and to provide them a voice in determining their wages and working conditions. These free unions have formed various international confederations such as the International Federation of Free Trade Union and the International Federation of Christian Trade Union. In Soviet societies, unions are established to provide a framework for encouraging worker productivity. Marxist theory had postulated that unions were to become a fulcrum for the overthrow of the bourgeois state. However, Marxist theory never held that unions could actually negotiate with employers concerning wages and working conditions. Some of the unions in Western society trace their antecedents to medieval guilds, and unions are considered an important economic and political element in most Western societies.

Since the 1930s when Congress enacted a number of basic labor laws, unions have flourished in the United States. The Norris-La Follette Act of 1932, made employer antiunion actions illegal, such as the blacklisting of union workers or the requirement that workers pledge not to join a union (yellow-dog contracts). The Wagner Act of 1935 set up the machinery for certifying unions as bargaining agents for workers and set forth a national policy that encouraged collective bargaining as a means of giving workers a voice in their work environment.

References

Ashenfelder, Orley, "Union Relative Wage Effects: New Evidence and a Survey of their Implications for Wage Inflation," in Richard Stone and William Peterson (eds.), *Econometric Contributions to Public Policy*, Macmillan, London, 1978, pp. 31–63; Bok, Derek, C., and John T. Dunlop, *Labor and the American Community*, Simon & Schuster, New York, 1970; Brooks, Thomas R., *Toil and Trouble: A History of American Labor*, rev. ed., Dell, New York, 1972; Lewis, H. Gregg, *Unionism and Relative Wages in the United States*, University of Chicago Press, Chicago, 1963; Marshall, F. Ray, et al., *Labor Economics: Wages, Employment and Trade Unionism*, rev. ed., Irwin, Homewood, Ill., 1976; Mills, Daniel Quin, *Labor-Management Relations*, McGraw-Hill, New York, 1978.

(*See also* Collective bargaining; Labor-management relations)

Rudy Oswald

Laissez faire

The French expression, "laissez faire, laissez passer," means, "Let events go ahead and happen as they might." To pursue a policy of laissez faire means that the government chooses not to intervene and instead allows ordinary market forces to work themselves out. The term is attributed to a legendary conversation between a merchant and the French Minister of Finance Colbert. Colbert, a supporter of mercantilist remedies for business problems, asked the merchant what the state might do to help the business community, whereupon the merchant quickly replied, "Laissez-nous faire!"

Nonintervention and Free Trade

The term is still used to refer to the policy of nonintervention. Writing in *Newsweek* (13 August 1979), Paul Samuelson described a "hard-boiled consistent advocate of laissez faire" as one who, when asked whether the state should subsidize companies that have fallen on bad times, would reply, "Let the losers bite the dust. Ours is a profit-and-loss system. If they can't shape up to the market, let them go through the wringers of bankruptcy. The system will be better for it. Liquidations and closedowns are the healthy catharsis of an effective economic system." And the weeding and pruning that occurs in the market has been hailed by many economists such as Alfred Marshall, Herbert Spencer, Armen Alchian, and Jack Hirshleifer as a process analogous to natural selection in nature. This process makes organizations and institutions better adapted to the needs of the community.

Historians sometimes use the term laissez faire to describe the economic policy of removing tariffs and other barriers to international trade. But this connection between free trade and laissez faire is somewhat misleading. Most supporters of free international trade did not consider themselves laissez faire economists. The leading members of the classical school largely supported free international trade but went out of their way to explain why the noninterference principle or laissez faire rule was not without exceptions. Even John Bright, the most hardboiled of the Manchester school of free trade liberals, was a supporter of the child labor laws that restricted employment among children. John Stuart Mill (*Principles of Political Economy*, 1848) summed up the attitude of the classical school when he wrote that "laissez faire, in short, should be the general practice: every departure from it, unless required by some great good, is a certain evil." Historically, nearly every economist of authority had a rather detailed list of great goods for which departures from the laissez faire principle were permissible. Political items on the agenda for state reform included public sanitation; public education; antitrust legislation; public utility regulation; construction of bridges, harbors, and roads; demand management; national defense; central banking; and the creation of a patent reward system.

In the history of economic thought there have been few thinkers who have considered themselves pure laissez faire economists. It was only among the early French liberal economists of the first part of the nineteenth century that something of a reverence for the widespread application of the laissez faire principle flourished. The Paris group, which consisted of Jean Baptiste Say, Charles Comte, Gustav Molinari, Charles Dunoyer, and Frederick Bastiat, recognized that economic activity is founded on voluntary exchange and that voluntary exchange benefits both contracting parties. Political activity requires taxes, and taxes are obtained by involuntary exchange.

Therefore, it seemed to follow that the way to promote a harmony of interests in society (and increase in social welfare) was to minimize if not eliminate the role of the state in economic life and encourage private provision of all goods and services. In the United States, French liberal thinking had some impact on the private property anarchist movement that still flourishes among libertarian economists in the United States and England of which the leading American authority is Murray N. Rothbard. In Europe French liberal thought influenced the writings of some members of the Austrian school of economics, especially Ludwig von Mises (*Human Action*, 1949).

A Paradox

The paradox of the laissez faire position is that what exists in the real world at any moment in time is the outcome of laws and rules founded on numerous earlier state interventions. The existing distribution of property rights titles is the consequence of all that has happened before. Either this existing distribution is just or unjust. If it is unjust, then political action may be needed to remedy it. And so we have the laissez faire economist advocating coercion to rectify previous coercions. Exactly who is to administer the new round of coercions? A revolutionary tribunal? If the distribution is declared just, then the laissez faire economist becomes the friend of reactionary interests in society and a political conservative. It appears that we must distinguish between laissez faire as an attitude or general rule and laissez faire as a consistent social philosophy. In its former form it has many proponents; in its latter form it is accepted by only a handful of thinkers.

References

Francis, Mark, "Herbert Spencer and the Myth of Laissez-Faire," *Journal of the History of Ideas*, vol. 39, April/June 1978, pp. 317–328; Kittrell, Edward R., "Laissez Faire in English Classical Economics," *Journal of the History of Ideas*, vol. 27, October/December 1966, pp. 610–620; Liggio, Leonard P., "Charles Dunoyer and French Classical Liberalism," *Journal of Libertarian Studies*, vol. 1, Summer 1977, pp. 153–178; Moss, Laurence S., "Private Property Anarchism: An American Variant," in G. Tullock (ed.), *Further Exploration in the Theory of Anarchy*, University Publications, Blackburg, Va., 1974; Rothbard, Murray N., *Power and Market*, Institute for Humane Studies, Menlo Park, Calif., 1970; Samuelson, Paul A., "Judging Corporate Handouts," *Newsweek*, August 13, 1979, pp. 58.

(*See also* Austrian economics; Barriers to trade; Classical school; Manchester school)

Laurence S. Moss

Land, a factor of production

To an economist, the factor of production, land, is defined as the productive power of natural, untransformed resources, receiving rent as its factor payment. As an illustration, that which is commonly referred to as land would be land in an economic context only if it exists in its natural state. The amount of land contained in such a plot and the rent it would command would be determined by its location, topography, fertility, and so on. To the extent that the plot is developed, it would represent a combination of land and capital; thus, the factor payment would be comprised of both rent and interest. It follows then that land might be better defined to be simply natural resources. However, both the natural resources coal and petroleum are land so long as they are in their natural state; but when they are extracted and used in another production process, they not only include some capital but also take on the characteristics of capital (i.e., commodities produced to be used in the production of other goods and services).

Distinction between Land and Capital

The distinction which has historically been made between land and capital is in terms of their supply curves. It has been argued that the amount of land (or natural resources) is fixed by nature; thus, the supply curve for land is vertical, while the supply curve for capital has the traditional upward slope. It should be noted that, in this context, rent would clearly be a residual payment determined only by demand. Such was the view held by the English classical economists including Adam Smith and David Ricardo. Indeed, this view of land led Henry George to advocate taxing away all rent, since it is a residual payment and the same amount of land would be available regardless of the level of rent.

The limitation of this view of land is most clear in the case of extractive resources (i.e., minerals, coal, natural gas, etc.). At a particular point in time, there exists a given supply of these resources—normally referred to as reserves. However, if over time the price of the resources rises or technology advances, known deposits not previously included may be counted as reserves. The point is that while there exists some fixed amount of a resource in the earth's crust, the relevant supply is based on the amount obtainable and this amount is not independent of the factor payment, at least in the long run.

Thus, the distinction between land and capital is blurred by the fact that, when land is used in the production process, it includes some capital and has some of the characteristics of a capital good. The distinction is further blurred by the fact that land, like capital, is acquired as a stock; but the firm actually employs the flow of services generated by this stock in the production process. Indeed, since it can be renewed, agricultural land is almost indistinguishable from capital.

Land as Exhaustible Natural Resource

The primary feature that differentiates land, except agricultural land, as a natural resource from the other factors of production is the fact that it is exhaustible (depletable). This feature is most evident in the case of the extractive resources, and most of the economic analyses have been concentrated on these resources rather than on agricultural land. Since the resource is depletable, it follows that, in contrast to the traditional methodologies for consideration of the other factors of production, analysis of the extractive resources must be dynamic in nature. That is, the rate of extraction or use of the resource in any one period affects the rate of extraction or use in future periods. Additional extraction and use in the current period increases the cost of extracting a particular quantity of the resource in a future period. Hence, a profit-maximizing firm extracting or using this factor of production cannot simply maximize profit in a single period but rather must maximize profit over its time horizon (i.e., maximize the present value or net worth of the firm). The theoretical analysis of these extractive resources has a long tradition beginning in 1914 with Lewis C. Gray, who, while using a static analysis, discussed the fact that the owner of a resource might maximize profits by postponing extraction and pointed to the dynamic nature of the resource. Also using a static model, Donald Carlisle showed that firms must decide not only the optimal rate of extraction of the resource but also the total amount of the deposit to be extracted. The dynamic nature of the resource was first explicitly incorporated by Harold Hotelling, who focused on the optimal rate of extraction of a resource. Building on this foundation, recent writers have considered such issues as the effects of taxation, enforced conservation, monopoly power, and recycling, as well as the optimal rates of consumption of the resource.

References

Anders, G. W., P. Gramm, S. C. Maurice, and C. W. Smithson, *The Economics of Mineral Extraction*, Praeger, New York, 1979; Ekelund, R. B., and R. F. Hebert, *A History of Economic Theory and Method*, McGraw-Hill, New York, 1975; Peterson, F. M., and Anthony C. Fisher, "The Exploitation of Extractive Resources: A Survey," *Economic Journal*, vol. 87, December 1977, pp. 681–721.

(*See also* Economic rent; Factors of production)

Charles W. Smithson

Law of diminishing returns (see Diminishing returns law)

Leading indicator approach to forecasting

The economic system can be viewed as thousands of economic processes called indicators. Some of these processes reach highs (peaks) and lows (troughs) before the general economy reaches those states and, thus, are called leading indicators. Those that represent the general economy are called coinciding indicators because their timing at peaks and troughs of the business cycle tends to coincide with the timing of the general economy. There are also lagging indicators, whose timing at peaks and troughs tend to be later than that of the general economy. These three timing phases—leading, coinciding, and lagging—are incorporated into what has long been known as the indicator approach to economic analysis and forecasting.

Leading Indicators

Leading indicators decline before the general economy at peaks; they recover sooner at troughs. The Commerce Department's Bureau of Economic Analysis (BEA) each month publishes 300 economic indicators in its magazine *Business Conditions Digest* (generally referred to as BCD). Of these, 65 indicators are classified as leading the general economy during the business cycle.

In addition to publishing 65 leading indicators, the BEA also publishes the so-called leading indicator composite that is made up of 12 leading indicators. It is a popular index for sensing the state of the general economy in the next few months. The 12, including their average prerecession lead times in months, are: housing permits, 12.8; liquid assets, 12.3; money supply, 12.0; stock market, 11.0; average workweek, 10.8; sensitive prices, 10.8; business formation, 10.5; layoff rate, 9.8; plant/equipment orders, 8.3; inventories, 7.8; vendor performance, 7.5; and new consumer orders, 6.0. Average post war prerecession lead for the 12 as a composite is 10 months, and the 12 individual lead times range from 6 to 12.8 months (standard deviation: 2.12 months). These 12 leading indicators by no means peak and trough at the same time.

Rather, they spread across a wide timing spectrum of their own. (It should be noted that those leading indicators used at troughs are not necessarily the same as those for peaks.)

Recent Revisions

The leading indicators are reevaluated and updated every few years. They developed a serious weakness during the 1974–75 recession when it was discovered that indicators that included inflation actually kept the composite index rising, even after the recession began. In effect, they prevented the composite from leading the recession. This problem, however, was overcome by including only deflated indicators among the 12 leaders in the great revision that followed the 1974–75 recession. The leading indicator composite prior to the revision had an average lead before recessions of about 5 months. The newly revised composite adopted by the BEA in 1976 had a lead time of 10 months—twice as long as the earlier composite. Such a dramatic change in lead time is significant. If government policymakers initiate an economic policy that impacts on the coinciding indicators 6 to 12 months later, it is desirable to test the impact of the policies on the leading indicators before they impact on the coinciders. Needless to say, a leading indicator with a 10-month lead time would be better for this purpose than one with only a 5-month lead.

Policy versus Traditional Indicators

If there is cause and effect in the economic system, then it would follow that various economic processes peak and trough at different times. In the early postwar years, the indicator approach was criticized for not being causal. It was regarded by some as an omen system. These criticisms have subsided partly because the leading indicators used today include many that are considered causal. These are generally indicators that are closely related to federal government economic policies, which most economists regard as being causal in nature. Their effect is to trigger later leading indicators to peak or trough, these in turn signaling that the government policies are or are not working. So, in effect, there are today two types of leading indicators—those that are policy-related and those that are of the more traditional kind. The policy indicators tend to have longer leads than do the latter.

The policy-type leading indicators tend to lead the general economy by the longest amount of time—1 to 2 years—and emanate from both monetary and fiscal policy. They include such things as money supply, interest rates, and taxes. But there are other long leaders that are closely affected by these, such as housing starts, housing permits, liquid assets, and new businesses—all indicators that are critically dependent upon federal government economic policies.

Leading indicators with a medium length of lead—6 to 12 months—are much more likely to correspond to the behavior of factory operations than to government policy. These relate to orders, profits, and employment. These have been called "smokestack" indicators and serve the very valuable purpose of confirming whether or not the longer-lead policy indicators are working.

The shortest leads—of 1 to 6 months—are highly influenced by inventories. Although inventories represent sensitive leading characteristics, they pose serious problems as leading indicators. For one thing, inventory statistics are not easy for the reporting company to report correctly. In addition, they have a serious problem of being reported late. These problems cause inventories to lose their already rather short leads. Though they are important leading indicators, it is difficult to benefit from their leads, given their dual defects of lateness and shortness of lead.

Indicator Approach versus Econometric Approach

The indicator approach is often contrasted with the econometric approach in analyzing and forecasting the macroeconomy. Actually, the two approaches are quite compatible. The timing considerations that are so important to the indicator approach are equally important in econometrics, but they are treated differently. In econometrics, timing differences are handled by means of regression lags. For example, it is no surprise that housing starts are a leading indicator of furniture sales. We cannot put furniture into the foundation of a house under construction. It is several months before a new house is sufficiently completed to begin moving in the furniture. Consequently, it is logical to conclude that an important part of furniture sales is a function of new houses for which construction began several months prior to sale of the furniture. One of the great contributions of econometrics is the ease with which it can incorporate lead or lag timing relationships within the model through its principal tool—regression. Still, econometrics is weak in graphic portrayal. Graphics, on the other hand, is one of the special advantages of the indicator approach. Indeed, since so many users of both the econometric and the indicator approaches are required to justify their forecasts by both visual and verbal methods, the indicator approach represents a solid addition to econometrics.

One of the most serious challenges to indicator economics is the fact that the leading indicators have reasonably stable mean lead times, but suffer badly with respect to their standard deviations around their means. This statistical defect forces indicator economists to use large numbers of leading indicators since one or even several leaders are simply not statistically reliable. BCD's 65 leading indicators published every month help economists avoid concentrating on too few views of economic performance. The 65 indicators also enable economists to segment economic performance by process. These performance sectors include employment, production, consumption, capital investment, inventories, prices, costs, profits, money, and credit—a sufficient number of processes to allow considerable research and monitoring into special areas of the economy.

Five-Phase Timing Model

The most recent innovation in the indicator approach—again made possible by the large number of indicators available to the public through the BCD—is to expand the system from the traditional three-phase to a five-phase timing model. In the new system, the customary three timing phases—leading, coinciding, and lagging indicators—are included as the middle of the system. But there is a new beginning and a new ending that more closely parallel a total beginning-to-end economic structure. The new beginning is a sector reserved for federal government policy and related indicators. These are considered to be first-cause indicators, which are followed by the leaders, coinciders, and laggers. At the end of the system are the final-effect indicators—prices. This new system, beginning with the causal policies and ending with prices, conforms well to modern economic theory. It is well-documented that monetary policy impacts on production (i.e., coinciding indicators) 6 to 12 months after being initiated. It is also well-documented that policy tends to impact on prices (final effects) 18 to 24 months after initiation. The five-phase indicator system conforms closely to this economic reality.

References

McLaughlin, Robert L., "A New Five-Phase Economic Forecasting System," *Business Economics*, National Association of Business Economists, Cleveland, September 1975; McLaughlin, Robert L., "Never, Never—Repeat—Never Forecast Recession," *Business Economics*, National Association of Business Economists, Cleveland, May 1980; Moore, Geoffrey, H., and Julius Shiskin, *Indications of Business Expansions and Contractions*, National Bureau of Economic Research, New York, 1967; Moore, Geoffrey H., *Business Cycles, Inflation and Forecasting*, National Bureau of Economic Research, Cambridge, Mass., 1980; Shiskin, Julius, *Signals of Recession and Recovery: An Experiment with Monthly Reporting*, National Bureau of Economic Research, New York, 1961; U.S. Department of Commerce, *Business Conditions Digest*, published monthly; U.S. Department of Commerce, *Handbook of Cyclical Indicators*, 1977; Vaccara, Beatrice N., and Victor Zarnowitz, "How Good Are the Leading Indicators?" *1977 Proceedings of the Business and Economics Section of the American Statistical Association*, American Statistical Association, Washington, D.C., 1978, part 1, pp. 41–50.

(See also Econometrics; Economic models; Economic statistics; Forecasting methods; Statistical techniques in economics and business, an overview)

Robert L. McLaughlin

Liberalism

In the seventeenth century, liberalism emerged as the radical philosophy that attacked authoritarianism and paternalism in the political sphere by defending the rights of the individual against the commands of monarchs and other rulers. John Locke and others questioned claims to political authority based on birth, social status, privilege, and divine right. Political authority either derived from the consent of the governed, or else was illegitimate. The later eighteenth-century liberals added the notion of the rule of law, the idea that government in its legislative capacity had to enact general rules that apply to all citizens equally. The substitution of rule of humans for the rule of law created a capricious, uncertain, and sometimes cruel community life. This early variety of liberalism—often termed classical liberalism—stimulated the development of the social sciences by insisting that what holds society together and promotes a bustling and orderly commercial economy is the mutual interplay of the passions and interests of ordinary citizens in the market. A basic principle of liberal thought is that the individual is the best and most accurate judge of his or her own interests and can be relied upon to pursue those interests with great dedication and creativity. The mighty arm of the state with its web of regulations and bureaucratic agents often does more harm than good when trying to substitute coercive methods of organization for impersonal market processes that spring out of self-interested individual action. The philosopher and American revolutionary, Thomas Paine, capsulized the radical side of classical liberalism when he wrote that "society is created by our wants, government by our wickedness."

Classical Liberalism

Classical liberals are not anarchists and at the very least recommend a minimal state: a state that protects lives, defines property rights, and enforces contracts allowing individual self-interest free reign in the market. A great many classical liberals (such as Adam Smith and the later classical school of economists) went somewhat further and requested that the state build and maintain certain public works (bridges, canals, highways, harbors, and so on), maintain standing armies, provide basic education, promote innovation, and intervene in the market on a limited scale for specific purposes (such as the enactment and enforcement of child labor laws).

Generally, the classical liberal believes in the general rule of laissez faire and wants to preserve self-regulating market processes as much as possible. The classical liberal is confident that with the enactment of strict constitutional safeguards and the elimination of monopoly and the never-ending varieties of special-interest legislation, peace and material progress are within the reach of all societies and all social classes. The leading works of classical liberalism include: Adam Smith (*Wealth of Nations*, 1776), Herbert Spencer (*The Man Versus the State*, 1892), Friedrich A. Hayek (*Constitution of Liberty*, 1960), Ludwig von Mises (*Liberalism: A Socio-Economic Exposition*, 1962), and Milton Friedman (*Capitalism and Freedom*, 1962).

Reform Liberalism

By the end of the nineteenth century, this brand of liberalism—antiauthoritarian in its politics and promarket in its economics—lost ground. A new style of liberalism competed with classical liberalism and became the dominant form by the first half of this century. Stemming from the work of Jeremy Bentham (*The Principles of Morals and Legislation*, 1848), John Stuart Mill (*Principles of Political Economy with Some Social Applications*, 1848), T. H. Green (*Lectures on the Principles of Political Obligation*, 1895), Alfred Marshall (*Principles of Economics*, 1890), John Dewey (*Liberalism and Social Action*, 1935), and John Maynard Keynes (*Essays in Persuasion*, 1931), reform liberalism continued to speak of individual freedom and liberty but (paradoxically) advocated an expansion of the state in the marketplace. Whereas the classical liberals defined freedom negatively to mean the absence of coercion or force in human relationships, the reform liberal spoke instead of positive freedom. More specifically, individuals are free when they start out on an equal footing in the marketplace. Reform liberals support progressive taxation, taxes on inheritance, capital gains (windfall) taxes, state-supported higher education, compulsory public health projects, and a variety of leveling measures to promote their notions of distributive justice in the marketplace. In the area of economic policy reform, liberals advocate demand-management policies to keep the economy out of recession and are willing to regulate industries if the allocation of resources can be improved. The idea is to spread the means of social advancement more evenly in the marketplace regardless of birth, social status, privilege, and inherited family income. Unlike the classical liberal, the reform liberal is not overly concerned with the dangers of a powerful state turning into tyranny. The reform liberal is confident that, as long as democratic forms of government are maintained, the political system will attract and select reasonable leaders to manage power in a humane and responsible manner.

Reform liberals are criticized by classical liberals for often being more concerned with the manner in which political decisions are made than with the decisions themselves. For example, if a majority of voters in a less-developed country (e.g., Nigeria) support a bill that prohibits a minority (e.g., Indians) from owning retail businesses in that country, a consistent reform liberal might support this policy on the grounds that it is a democratically enacted law promoting the greatest good for the greatest number and sparking economic development—something that will redound to the benefit of future generations of Nigerians. The classical liberal would object to using the law as an instrument of social reform precisely because it involves one group (the majority of Nigerians) coercing another group (the Indians) for the hypothesized advantage of individuals who are not yet born. Some classical liberals would even reassert the natural rights of the individual against the tyranny of majority.

Reform liberalism merges into socialism when it utilizes the state and its coercive machinery to impose a national plan on the alleged chaos of the marketplace. When reform liberalism becomes socialism as it did in the writings of G. B. Shaw, Beatrice and Sidney Webb, and other Fabian writers at the turn of the century, a doctrinal position emerges that is diametrically opposed to that of classical liberalism. The idea of limiting the state and encouraging decentralized markets for the means of production is abandoned completely.

The use of the term liberalism to refer to these fundamentally different policy models is apt to confuse students of intellectual history. Both liberalisms share the same fundamental goal of promoting individual self-development; they differ only on the means to be employed. This difference, however, remains a major one and is the source of many rich controversies in political and social philosophy.

References

Hayek, Friedrich A., *Law, Legislation and Liberty*, 3 vols., University of Chicago Press, Chicago, 1973; Nozick, Robert, *Anarchy, State and Utopia*, Basic Books, New York, 1974; Rawls, John, *A Theory of Justice*, Harvard University Press, Cambridge, Mass., 1971; Wolff, Robert Paul, *Understanding Rawls: A Reconstruction and Critique of "A Theory of Justice,"* Princeton University Press, Princeton, N.J., 1977.

(*See also* Classical liberalism; Classical school; Laissez faire; Reform liberalism; Socialism)

Laurence S. Moss

Linear programming

Linear programming is a mathematical technique of optimizing (maximizing or minimizing) linear objective functions, subject to restraints in the form of linear inequalities. The aim is to find an optimum schedule for management decision problems. It is designed to select from alternative courses of action the one most likely to achieve a desired goal, such as the manufacture of a product or group of products at the lowest possible cost.

It is convenient to classify mathematical programming problems as (1) linear and (2) nonlinear (in which the objective function or at least one of the constraint functions is nonlinear). For linear programming, programming refers to planning or scheduling of the various activities of the organization, not to programming when preparing a set of instructions for an electronic computer.

Solutions to complex mathematical programming problems have been facilitated by the development and wide-scale use of electronic computers. Linear programming is widely used to solve everyday decision problems. In business it has been employed in a variety of problems ranging from the selection of ingredients appropriate to producing the cheapest cattle feed of a given nutritional value to the determination of profitable sites for plant location.

History

François Quesnay, a French economist, attempted in his *Tableau économique* (1758)—a crude example of a linear programming model—to interrelate the role of the landlord, the artisan, and the peasant. It was not until 1823 that Jean Baptiste Joseph Fourier, a French mathematician, appeared to see the potential of linear programming. Until the 1930s there was little interest shown in linear programming. But in the late 1930s Leonid Kantorovich, a Russian mathematician, recognized that some scheduling problems had mathematical structures.

During World War II, linear programming developed considerably and the use of scientific planning techniques became very important.

But no significant linear programming work was carried out before 1947. However, in that year a team of economists and mathematicians began work under the auspices of the U.S. Air Force, using the structure of the Leontief input-output model developed in 1936 for air force applications. Later the first linear programming model of the U.S. economy was put together with the goal of maximizing an objective function, economic growth. Prior to 1947, general objectives were never cited as goals of these programs largely because of the impossibility of performing all the necessary computations to maximize (minimize) an objective function under restraint.

References

Baumol, W. J., *Economic Theory and Operations Analysis,* Prentice-Hall, Englewood Cliffs, N.J., 1961; Dantzig, George, *Linear Programming and Extensions,* Princeton University Press, Princeton, N.J., 1963; Dorfman, R., P. Samuelson, and R. Solow, *Linear Programming and Economic Analysis,* McGraw-Hill, New York, 1958; Ford, Lester, and D. R. Fulkerson, *Flows in Networks,* Princeton University Press, Princeton, N.J., 1962; Hadley, George, *Linear Programming,* Iowa State University Press, Ames, Iowa, 1962.

(*See also* Economic models; Game theory, economic applications; Input-output analysis; Operations research; Physiocrats; Simulation in business and economics)

Douglas Greenwald

Liquidity, corporate

Corporate liquidity is a measure of a firm's ability to meet its maturing cash obligations. It is important to management because of (1) a significant risk-return trade-off, (2) the terms and conditions of additional financing, and (3) the risks of insolvency and bankruptcy cost. The risk-return trade-off arises because the investment in current assets may yield less than the firm's cost of funds. In addition, short-term debt may be less costly than long-term debt or equity funds, which push the firm toward use of short-term debt.

But if liquidity pressures develop in that a firm has difficulty meeting its maturing obligations, new financing may be available only under very unfavorable loan agreement restrictions and at relatively high interest costs. In the extreme, the insolvency of the firm may lead to bankruptcy and liquidation. The result may be relatively large drains due to bankruptcy costs. Bankruptcy costs may be high because of the need to liquidate assets under pressure at distress prices below their economic values. In addition, the administrative costs of bankruptcy which include fees to lawyers, trustees, referees, receivers, liquidators, etc., average 20 percent of the book value of assets. Thus because of bankruptcy costs, liquidity management can affect the value of the firm.

Corporate Liquidity Measures

While most assets have a degree of liquidity, the most liquid of assets are cash and marketable securities. Corporate liquidity measures reflect the amounts of these two types of assets held by firms. Liquidity is a measure of the ability to convert these liquid assets into money values. Two dimensions are involved: (1) the time necessary to convert an asset into money, and (2) the risk of a difference or loss between the asset's stated value and the amount of money realized for the asset.

Variations in the liquidity positions of firms arise in part because short-term interest rates fluctuate more widely than longer-term interest rates. During business expansions, firms build up their inventories which are typically financed with short-term debt. This is because the sharp rise in interest rates during an expansion makes the firm unwilling to become locked into long-term debt at high rates. These influences reverse during a recession. Firms then seek to replace short-term obligations with longer-term debt and equity issues.

A number of measures of exposure have been developed to evaluate a firm's liquidity position as it reacts to different money-market conditions. Some key liquidity ratios and reference levels are listed in the accompanying table.

Ratios	Reference levels
1. Current assets to current liabilities	1.75–2.00 times
2. Cash plus marketable securities to current liabilities	25 percent
3. Cash plus marketable securities to net revenues	5 percent
4. Current liabilities to net revenues	18–20 percent
5. Net income plus depreciation to the change in gross total assets.	1–1.1 times
6. Short-term, interest-bearing debt to long-term debt	25 percent
7. Stockholders' equity to total assets	50–55 percent

While these ratios may in practice fluctuate from the given reference levels, in response to changes in money- and capital-market conditions, wide disparities are to be avoided. If the ratios deteriorate greatly, the risks of insolvency are increased. If the ratios are too strong, some losses in potential returns are incurred.

Four Major Liquidity Management Policies

Corporate liquidity management is employed to maximize revenues while holding risks of insolvency to desired levels. Major liquidity management policies include: (1) effective cash mobilization, (2) cash flow forecasting, (3) identification of needs for protective liquidity, and (4) productive use of liquid assets.

Cash mobilization aims at the reduction of funds tied up in the process of receiving and collecting checks and in the routines of the transfer of bank balances to the points where they will be most useful. In the management of cash the firm seeks to accelerate collections and to handle disbursements so that maximum cash is available. Collections can be accelerated by means of concentration banking, a lockbox system, and the use of telegraphic transfers. Disbursements can be handled to give maximum transfer flexibility and optimal timing of payments.

Given the total level of liquid assets, composed of cash and marketable securities, the firm must determine the optimal division between these two assets. The optimal level of cash is the greater of (1) the compensating balance requirement of the firm's commercial bank and (2) the optimal level of cash determined by an appropriate cash inventory model. The cash balance models show that cash depends upon the predictability of future cash flows, the volatility of future cash flows, the fixed cost of security transactions, and the carrying costs of holding cash—the interest income on marketable securities.

Most well-run firms have increased their emphasis on cash flow forecasting in recent years. An analysis of past patterns of receipts and expenditures along with a consideration of prospective future patterns has enabled useful cash flow forecasts to be made. Improved cash flow forecasting has led to improved liquidity management. With a firmer knowledge of future cash flow patterns, the availability of funds for investment in marketable securities is more accurately measured. When future needs for cash are more clearly measured, additional time is provided for exploring alternative methods of meeting these future requirements.

Another area for effective liquidity management is defining the needs for liquidity reserves that may develop. This requires identification of contingencies such as the possibility of a strike, a decline in business, a major investment program, etc. Such analysis should include an assessment of the probabilities of the occurrence of such events over a period into the future, including an assessment of the likely amount of cash requirements needed for each contingency.

A final area of liquidity management involves an aggressive approach to the most productive use of money assets. This represents an analysis of the alternative marketable securities in which the firm can invest. These securities can be evaluated in relation to their (1) default risk, (2) marketability, (3) maturity, and (4) taxability. Taking the cash flow pattern of the firm into account, a marketable securities portfolio can be formulated and modified over time consistent with the key characteristics of the securities employed. The categories of investments likely to be included in the marketable securities portfolio include: Treasury securities, government agency securities, bankers' acceptances, commercial paper, repurchase agreements, and certificates of deposit.

Although diversification of the marketable securities portfolio is desirable, there is less opportunity for such diversification than there is with a portfolio of common stocks. This is because of the high degree of correlation in the price movements of money-market instruments over time. Hence, diversification, defined as the reduction of the dispersion of possible returns from a portfolio relative to its expected return, is less possible in using short-term financial instruments. The objective of the marketable securities portfolio is to seek to maximize overall returns, subject to maintaining sufficient liquidity to meet forecasted cash requirements.

References

Searby, Frederick W., "Cash Management: Helping Meet the Capital Crisis," in J. Fred Weston and Maurice Goudzwaard (eds.), *The Treasurer's Handbook*, Dow Jones–Irwin, Homewood, Ill., 1976, chap. 20; Weston, J. Fred, and E. F. Brigham, *Managerial Finance*, 6th ed., part 2, "Working Capital Management," Dryden Press, Hinsdale, Ill., 1978, chaps. 6–8.

(*See also* Business credit; Financial statements)

J. Fred Weston

Liquidity, international

International liquidity comprises the financial assets that governments hold as a reserve to meet international contingencies such as a balance of payments deficit. The term may be used to refer to the reserves of an individual country or to the sum of reserves of all countries.

The financial assets that make up international liquidity include gold, foreign currencies (of which the dollar is the most widely held reserve currency), and claims on the International Monetary Fund (especially special drawing rights). The International Monetary Fund compiles and publishes monthly data on the amount and composition of countries' reserves.

International Liquidity and the International Monetary System

Changes that have occurred in recent years in the international monetary system have brought with them corresponding changes in the role of international liquidity. From the end of World War II until early 1973, under the Bretton Woods system, most countries maintained exchange rates within a narrow margin around a par value agreed upon with the International Monetary Fund. Such par values were altered only rarely in the case of the industrial countries. Under that system the overall balance of payments positions of countries were reflected in their reserve holdings. A country in deficit reduced and a country in surplus increased its reserves, in both instances as a means of maintaining the established exchange rate. Usually these reserve changes took the form, initially, of decreases or increases of holdings of dollars. A country in deficit whose dollar holdings were low might have sold gold to the United States or might have exchanged its claims on the International Monetary Fund for dollars. A country gaining reserves in the form of dollars had the option, if it did not wish to hold the dollars, to convert them into gold at the U.S. Treasury or to acquire claims on the International Monetary Fund.

Countries differed, and still do, in their preferences as to the composition of their reserves. Some held mostly dollars, and a few European countries held a large proportion in the form of gold. The United States, as the only country that stood ready to convert its currency into gold for monetary authorities, held almost all of its reserves in gold.

Under the Bretton Woods system, the sources of growth of international liquidity were new gold production over and above private uses of gold, deficits in the U.S. balance of payments, and, beginning in 1970, the distribution of special drawing rights (SDRs) by the International Monetary Fund. In most years since 1950, capital outflows from the United States exceeded the U.S. surplus on current account. As foreign monetary authorities purchased these excess dollars, their reserves increased. The role of the United States under that system has been likened to that of a bank, which lends and in the process creates money.

Since March 1973, the exchange rate system has been less uniform. Some countries have floating exchange rates; others peg their rates to a particular currency; and still others, notably in Europe, endeavor to maintain a fixed exchange rate relationship with a group of their close trading partners.

In these circumstances, purchases or sales of foreign exchange by governments are less obligatory than in the past. Governments now have the option of letting the exchange rate rise or fall rather than intervening in the foreign exchange market with a consequent increase or decrease in reserves. As a result, changes in reserves are less significant as a measure of balance of payments positions.

Other Changes

Another change in recent years is that the character of international liquidity is less homogeneous. After the quadrupling of oil prices in late 1973, a number of oil-exporting countries have accumulated substantial reserves. In the case of some of these countries, the acquisition of foreign currencies, in counterpart of large balance of payments surpluses, is more in the nature of a long-term investment, to be used in the next century when oil supplies run out, than a liquid asset available to finance a payments deficit or to prevent a downward movement of the exchange rate.

The measurement of international liquidity is also less uniform than in the past. As the market price of gold has risen, some countries have revalued their gold reserves, whereas others continue to carry gold on the books of the central bank or treasury at the equivalent of the price at the time of the February 1973 devaluation of the dollar. The International Monetary Fund now reports countries' gold holdings in million of ounces. Transactions in gold among governments have virtually ceased.

Meanwhile, although the dollar continues to be the most important reserve currency, there has been a tendency for other currencies—notably the German mark, the Swiss franc, and the Japanese yen—to be held as reserves. This tendency toward diversification has been resisted by the governments of Germany, Switzerland, and Japan. The potential for instability in a world with several reserve currencies has led to proposals for a so-called substitution account in the International Monetary Fund. Such an account would accept dollars and issue an SDR asset to governments. Supporters of this proposal point out that it would, in the words of the revised Articles of Agreement of the International Monetary Fund, "be consistent with the objectives of promoting better international surveillance of international liquidity and making the Special Drawing Right the principal reserve asset in the international monetary system" (article VIII, section 7).

References

International Reserves: Needs and Availability, International Monetary Fund, Washington, D.C., 1970; Mundell, Robert A., and Jacques J. Polak (eds.), The New International Monetary System, Columbia University Press, New York, 1977; Solomon, Robert, The International Monetary System, 1945–1976: An Insider's View, Harper & Row, New York, 1977; Williamson, John, "International Liquidity: A Survey," Economic Journal, vol. 83, no. 331, September 1973, pp. 685–746.

(See also Balance of international payments; Balance of international trade; Bretton Woods Conference; Foreign exchange rates; International economics, an overview; International Monetary Fund; Smithsonian Agreement; Special drawing rights)

Robert Solomon

Liquidity preference (see Interest rates)

Location theory

Location theory is a set of propositions that yields a systematic exposition and explanation of the spatial organization of economic activities including both business firms and households. Although its origins can be traced to nineteenth-century Germany, location theory today is regarded as a subdivision of the newer discipline called regional economics or regional science. It is also intimately related to the areas of rural and urban land use.

Neoclassical economic theory as developed by the Anglo-American school of economists neglected almost entirely the spatial aspects of economic activity. For example, the theory of perfect competition, which serves as the keystone of microeconomic theory, implicitly assumes an infinitely large number of producers all marketing an identical product at the same price at one unique point in space, a set of circumstances seldom, if ever, realized in the real world. The only exception to the above generalization was the theory of international trade, which investigated the effects of international commodity exchange on the economies of various countries with differing resource endowments, with or without transportation costs being taken explicitly into account.

German Contribution to Location Theory

The first contribution to location theory was made by the Prussian landowner, Johann Heinrich von Thünen, in the early 1840s. Assuming the existence of an isolated urban community and the allocation of rural land in such a manner as to minimize transportation costs, and given the demands and transportation technology of the day, von Thünen derived the optimal pattern of rural land use. Unfortunately, von Thünen's ingenious contribution attracted no attention outside Germany and had little impact within that country for over 50 years.

Shortly after the turn of the century, another German economist, Alfred Weber (1909), adopted a partial equilibrium approach to the locational decisions of the individual business firm, basing his analysis on the assumption of cost minimization. He was also the first to provide an extensive analysis of the economies of agglomeration, which include both economies of scale and external economies brought about by the clustering of activities at a particular location. However, the crowning achievement of the German economists was made by August Lösch (1944), who derived the first general equilibrium solution to the location of market-oriented industries.

Assuming the existence of an infinite flat plane with ubiquitous natural resources, an identical linear transportation cost function for movement in all directions, a uniform distribution of rural population, the production of one manufactured product (beer), and identical linear demand curves for all individuals, Lösch demonstrated the existence of a general equilibrium solution. The properties of this solution include:

1. A system of identical hexagonal market areas covering the entire plane
2. One monopolistically competitive business firm located at the center of each market area in a state of long-run equilibrium with no monopoly profits
3. Maximization of aggregate output (sales) and minimization of aggregate transportation costs

In addition, by assuming linear demand curves for more specialized products, Lösch was able to derive a hierarchy of ever-larger hexagonal market areas corresponding to the system postulated by central place theory and developed by geographers on the basis of empirical observation. He also demonstrated how to fit the various market areas together in order to minimize aggregate transportation costs of the entire system.

Three Major Directions

During the past two decades the work of Lösch has been generalized in three major directions. First, more attention has been paid to pricing. Since any general equilibrium solution implies a set of prices, the latter can be logically determined once the spatial pattern of demand, the cost curves of the suppliers, transportation costs, and the market structure are known. Second, Jan Tinbergen and H. C. Bos (1962), two economists of the Netherlands, have developed a hierarchical general equilibrium model based on cost minimization rather than profit maximization. Assuming the existence of a uniformly distributed agricultural population with a given fixed level of labor productivity and a number of industrial activities, they located the industries in a hierarchy of centers. They have also succeeded in determining all inputs, outputs, trade flows, and income levels throughout the system. Third, M. J. Webber (1972) has stressed the influence of uncertainty on locational behavior and applied game theory to a wide variety of locational phenomena. The results indicate that uncertainty can significantly modify the results that would be attained in a world of perfect knowledge. Specifically, uncertainty often encourages greater agglomeration of activities as decision makers attempt to avoid possible losses associated with more dispersed (riskier) locations.

Rapid development of the previously neglected theory of residential location has occurred in the last 20 years. The models proposed almost always assume the household chooses a place to live by maximizing a utility function subject to one or more constraints. Land rents and the cost of the journey to work are the most common variables appearing in the constraints.

Pros and Cons

Location theory is important because it provides a more realistic description of economic activity in dispersed markets than the traditional spaceless price theory. Therefore, it advances the economist's theoretical understanding and supplies some additional analytical concepts helpful in real-world application. By using location theory, both the business executive and the urban or regional planner increase their ability to understand and restructure the spatial configuration of economic activity. As the world energy shortage becomes more severe, location theory can provide guidance to adjusting to this problem over the long run in a transportation cost–minimizing manner. In developing countries, it yields insights on how to attain a more efficient spatial allocation of economic activity and population. Socialist countries use location theory in planning the development of new industries, towns, and cities.

On the other hand, location theory cannot be regarded as an unqualified success. It has proved much more effective in explaining the location of tertiary (wholesaling, retailing, and service) industries than the various types of manufacturing. Furthermore, location theorists have experienced difficulty in predicting new long-run regional trends, such as the movement of industry from the snow belt to the sun belt or the reverse migration currently taking place from metropolitan areas to small towns and the countryside.

Location theory has been based largely on static equilibrium analysis. Major advances will be possible only if location theorists can break out of this mold by fully incorporating the time dimension into their work. Accomplishment of this task would result in the integration of location theory with the theory of regional growth and development, yielding a much more powerful engine of analysis than is currently available.

References

Capozza, Dennis R., and Robert Van Order, "Pricing under Spatial Competition and Spatial Monopoly," *Econometrica*, vol. 45, no. 6, September 1977, pp. 1329-1338; Greenhut, Melvin L., and H. Ohta, *Theory of Spatial Pricing and Market Areas*, Duke University Press, Durham, N.C., 1975; Lösch, August, *Die rümliche Ordnung der Wirtschaft*, G. Fischer Verlag, Jena, 1944, William H. Woglom (trans.), *The Economics of Location*, Yale University Press, New Haven, Conn., 1954; Mitchell, Wesley Clair, Wilford I. King, Frederick R. Macauley, and Oswald W. Knauth, *Income in the United States: Its Amount and Distribution, 1909-1919*, vol. 1, summary, Harcourt, Brace, New York, 1921; Paelinck, Jean H. P., and Peter Nijkamp, *Operational Theory and Method in Regional Economics*, Lexington Books, Lexington, Mass., 1975; Thünen, Johann H. von, *Der Isolierte Staat in Beziehung auf Landwirtschaft und Nationalökonomie*, Rostock, 1842, C. M. Wartenberg (trans.), *Von Thünen's Isolated State*, Pergamon, Oxford, 1966; Tinbergen, Jan, and Hendricus C. Bos, *Mathematical Models of Economic Growth*, McGraw- Hill, New York, 1962; Webber, Michael J., *Impact of Uncertainty on Location*, MIT Press, Cambridge, Mass., 1972; Weber, Alfred, *Über den Standort der Industrien*, Tübingen, 1909, Carl J. Friedrich (trans.), *Theory of the Location of Industries*, University of Chicago Press, Chicago, 1929.

(*See also* Regional economics; Urban economics)

John H. Niedercorn

Long-run forecasts (see Economic forecasts)

Long-term interest rates (see Interest rates)

Lorenz curve

The Lorenz curve is a graphic device which presents a vivid picture of the extent of inequality in the size distribution of wealth or income and its components. (Occasionally, the curve is used to represent other distributions as well). The curve (see the accompanying figure) consists of a unit square, a diagonal to that square, and at least one true curve which passes through the endpoints of the diagonal. The horizontals of the square represent the cumulative share of population units and run from 0 to 100 percent. The verticals represent cumulative shares of income (or wealth), starting with the poorest, and likewise range from 0 to 100 percent. Perfect equality is, therefore, represented by the diagonal. At point z, for example, the bottom 30 percent of the population receives 30 percent of income. The closer the curved line is to the diagonal, the smaller is the degree of inequality.

Gini Coefficient

One summary measure of the degree of inequality is the ratio of the shaded area in the figure to the entire area under the line of perfect equality $(A/A + B)$. This measure is called the Gini coefficient (or concentration ratio) after its inventor, the Italian statistician and demographer Corrodo Gini. For developed countries the Gini coefficient tends to be around 0.400. While the Lorenz curve is not controversial (except perhaps for the fact that it implies that perfect equality is desirable), the Gini coefficient has been much criticized. Trying to capture a whole curve with one summary statistic can, of course, be misleading. Further, the Gini coefficient has been characterized as insensitive, difficult to calculate accurately, and devoid of normative content. However, the measure remains the most widely used summary statistic for describing inequality. It is reasonable to conjecture that the measure's continued popularity rests on the vivid representation that the Lorenz curve gives to it.

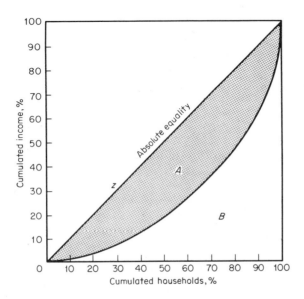

Wilford King's Work

The Lorenz curve is named after its American inventor (there are coincident European inventors), Max Otto Lorenz. Lorenz spent all of his professional life as a government statistician unconcerned with distributional issues. It fell to Wilford King, who followed Lorenz at the University of Wisconsin, to promote use of the diagram. One oddity in this history is that Lorenz drew his curve with income on the horizontal axes and recipients on the vertical. It was not until 1921 that (in collaboration with Wesley Clair Mitchell and others) King drew what he already referred to as the well-known Lorenz curve. Between 1905 and 1921, the curve was drawn by King and others in every conceivable variant.

Widespread familiarity with the curve was deferred until the publication of the textbooks that first appeared after World War II. Prewar texts (including one coauthored by Lorenz) devoted little space to income or wealth inequality among persons and none to the Lorenz curve. Until the war there simply were not sufficient current data to make a chapter on inequality, or presentation of the Lorenz curve, interesting.

References

Bronfenbrenner, M., *Income Distribution Theory*, Aldine, Chicago, 1971, chap. 3; Lorenz, M. O., "Methods of Measuring the Concentration of Wealth," *Journal of the American Statistical Association*, vol. 9, no. 70, June 1905, pp. 209–219; Mitchell, Wesley Clair, Wilford I. King, Frederick R. Macauley, and Oswald W. Knauth, *Income in the United States: Its Amount and Distribution, 1909–1919*, Harcourt, Brace, New York, 1921; Sen, A. K., *On Economic Inequality*, Norton, New York, 1973, chap. 2.

(*See also* Income distribution; Poverty)

Eugene Smolensky

Macroeconomics

The word "macro" means large, and macroeconomics means economics in the large. The macroeconomist's concerns are with such global issues as total production, total employment and unemployment, the overall level and rate of change of prices, the rate of economic growth, and so on. The questions asked by the macroeconomist deal with broad aggregates—what determines the spending of all consumers as opposed to the determinants of the spending decisions of single households; what determines the capital spending of all firms combined rather than the decision to build a new plant of a single firm; what determines the overall level of unemployment in the economy as opposed to why some particular individual is unemployed. Macroeconomics measures overall economic activity; it analyzes the determinants of such activity by the use of macroeconomic theory; it forecasts future economic activity; and it attempts to formulate policy responses designed to reconcile forecasts with target values of production, employment, and prices.

The macroeconomist has several major concerns. First, the macroeconomist must find ways of aggregating the economic activities of individual firms into meaningful totals. To this end such concepts as gross national product (GNP), national income, personal income, and personal disposable income have been developed. The macroeconomist also requires ways of adding disparate elements in order to arrive at the total level of production for the economy, which has been done by valuing different products at their market prices and adding these values together to reach the overall totals.

Macroeconomic analysis attempts to explain how the levels of the principal macroeconomic variables—the unemployment rate, the growth of real output, and the rate of price inflation—are determined at any moment, and it has attempted, through the development of theories of the business cycle and of economic growth, to explain the dynamics of how these aggregates move over time.

Macroeconomics and Policy Issues

The macroeconomist is involved with policy issues that are of vital importance to all citizens. The main goals of macro policy are the maintenance of high levels of employment, satisfactory growth of production, and reasonable price stability. Considerable effort must, therefore, be expended to determine what goals are feasible. Twenty years ago it was believed that unemployment could be reduced to 4 percent of the labor force without creating labor shortages and wage inflation. Today, a 5.5 percent natural unemployment rate is considered an achievement. During the 1950s and the 1960s output per worker-hour (i.e., productivity) grew at a rate of about 3 percent a year. Added to labor-force growth adjusted for a trend toward shorter hours, this implied growth of potential output of about 4 percent a year. But productivity growth slumped after 1968 and more so after 1973, so that potential output now grows much more slowly. Finally, only 10 years ago a 5 percent rate of price inflation would have been considered intolerable. Today, a return to such a rate would produce an enormous sense of accomplishment and relief.

Tools of Macro Policy

The principal tools of macropolicy are monetary and fiscal policy. Monetary policy in the United States is largely under the control of the Board of Governors of the Federal Reserve System. The Federal Reserve controls the supply of money and credit in a number of ways. The most important of the Federal Reserve's instruments is its ability to buy and sell government securities on the open market. Credit tightening, for example, can be accomplished by a sale of government securities to private persons. These persons draw down their bank balances when they purchase the securities. This takes money out of the private economy, leaves less to be lent, and tends to drive up interest rates. The result is less borrowing and spending on goods and services by the private sector of the economy. The Federal Reserve is also empowered to lend funds to private banks, and by varying the rediscount rate which it charges the banks, it can either encourage or discourage bank borrowing. Third, the Federal Reserve can vary reserve requirements, that is, it can vary the fraction of the deposits in member banks that the banks are permitted to lend.

The other principal tool of macropolicy is fiscal policy. This means use of the federal budget to achieve a stable and growing economy. To stimulate the economy, government expenditures may be raised directly or taxes may be reduced, thereby enabling individuals and firms to increase their spending. The opposite set of policies could be employed if aggregate demand is excessive since higher taxes and less government spending would reduce total spending and help slow inflation.

The principal vehicle of fiscal policy is the federal budget. It is planned annually by the administration and is subject to review by congressional budget committees. Tax changes must be legislated by the Congress, and the tax system is administered by the Internal Revenue Service under the general supervision of the Secretary of the Treasury.

A Coherent Macroeconomic Plan

Such a plan for the economy should have the following essential ingredients. First, those responsible for fiscal and monetary policy should agree on a set of feasible targets and objectives for the coming year. Their second need is for a detailed and careful forecast of economic activity, based on the assumption that policy will remain unchanged. (Many macroeconomists specialize in producing such forecasts.) The third step is to compare the forecast with the targets and to agree on the magnitude and mix of the policy changes that would be needed to alter the forecast so that its outcome coincides with the established targets. If the actual outcome then turns out to coincide with the targets, the policy based on this anlysis would certainly be judged to have been successful.

Of course, implementing such a plan is not easy, and macroeconomic analysis and forecasting, as well as the development of a coordinated approach to monetary and fiscal planning, are still a long way from being entirely satisfactory.

Changing Concerns of Macro Policy

During the deeply depressed 1930s emphasis was on restoring full employment by using fiscal and monetary policy to increase aggregate demand in the economy. During the 1950s policy was primarily concerned with the control of inflation, and tight money and tight budgets were the order of the day. This then gave way in the early 1960s to renewed emphasis on high employment and rapid growth.

Stagflation

During the 1970s the United States experienced a new and puzzling phenomenon called "stagflation"—i.e., a situation in which both unemployment and inflation were either simultaneously too high by accepted standards, and/or both were rising at the same time. At the end of the decade, stagflation had created a difficult dilemma for macroeconomic policy: monetary-fiscal policies that lower unemployment raise the demand for goods and services and, therefore, are undertaken at the risk of more inflation. Conversely, restrictive policies designed to stop inflation run the risk of slowing the economy, causing higher levels of unemployment.

As stagflation is studied, it is becoming clear that much of the difficulty in understanding the problem and in dealing with it results from the fact that during the 40 years prior to the 1970s it was believed that macroeconomic policy consisted almost exclusively in the management of total demand. However, the world food shortages of the early 1970s and especially the rapidly rising energy costs indicate that the supply side is also extremely important, and that supply restrictions play an important role in generating and perpetuating stagflation. For example, when the Organization of Petroleum Exporting Countries (OPEC) raised the price of oil in 1974 this directly raised the price level in the U.S. economy. At the same time the higher energy prices lowered the amount of real income that consumers had left to spend on other things so that production and employment fell. The supply restriction was, therefore, a major source of the 1974–75 stagflation.

References

Dernburg, T. F., and D. M. McDougall, Macroeconomics, 5th ed., McGraw-Hill, New York, 1976; Dernburg, T. F., and J. Dernburg, Macroeconomic Analysis, Addison-Wesley, Reading, Mass., 1968; Evans, M. K., Macroeconomic Analysis, Harper & Row, New York, 1969; Gordon, R. J., Macroeconomic Activity, Harper & Row, New York, 1969.

(See also Dynamic macroeconomic models; Economics; Microeconomics)

Thomas F. Dernburg

Malthusian theory of population

Thomas Robert Malthus was best known as a demographer, but like many of his contemporaries he studied and wrote in several fields. He was a clergyman, demographer, economist, and a professor of history and political economy in the East-India College, Hertfordshire.

The basic concept of his social theory is that population tends to increase more rapidly than the food supply. Population tends to increase geometrically, whereas food—the means of subsistence—tends to increase only arithmetically according to the most widely recognized formulation. "The ultimate check to population," Malthus wrote (1817a), "appears then to be a want of food arising necessarily from the different ratios according to which population and food increase. But this ultimate check is never the immediate check, except in cases of actual famine."

The immediate checks were classified, according to Malthus under two general headings— "the preventive, and the positive checks." The former consist of conscious and deliberate limitations on sexual activity either by late marriage or by abstinence. Few people, Malthus felt, would follow such preventive checks. Voluntary—premeditated—birth control was immoral and a vice, which, with all the other vices, was not to be tolerated.

The positive checks are those which really check population growth, i.e., disasters of one form or another—war, pestilence, famine, etc.—and vice. In the 1817 edition, exactly half of the total pages in the four volumes are devoted to discussion of these positive checks.

Malthus summarized his beliefs as follows: "The tendency in population fully to keep pace with the means of subsistence must in general prevent the increase of these means from having a great and permanent effect in improving the condition of the poor" (1817b). Further, he stated, "Natural and moral evil seems to be the instruments employed by the Deity . . . if we multiply too fast, we die miserably of poverty and contagious diseases" (1817c).

Petty's Earlier Analysis

Why was such a pessimistic outlook accepted by so many in his time? Many of his contemporaries, including William Godwin, held contrary opinions, but Malthus outshouted them all. Further, Malthus said little that William Petty had not written about 150 years earlier, yet Petty is unknown outside the academic field.

Analysis of the historical situation in England around 1800, in comparison with the situation at the time of Petty around 1650, provides clues regarding Malthus's excellent public relations. To begin, Malthus's theories were accepted so wholeheartedly because they fitted in with what the country's leaders wanted to hear, namely, that it is impossible for the masses to improve their level of living. Any efforts to improve their lives—by increasing wages, for example—would simply result in their having more children and thus continuing to live as poorly as ever. What Malthus and so many of the political leaders failed to understand clearly was that the industrial revolution was already underway and that science and technology would increase production—both food and nonfood—so greatly as to be able to support a much larger population at a much higher level of living. Some other writers at that time recognized the growth of industry and its implication, but such recognition meant that wages could be increased and the plight of the poor alleviated. This thought was not welcomed by England's leaders.

Petty had written about the multiplication of humanity—*Mankind and Political Arithmetic*—in the middle of the seventeenth century. At that time the world seemed to be empty of people. The vast Western Hemisphere was still unpopulated by Europeans (the Native American population was disregarded) and even Great Britain was still not fully populated. Hence, Petty could only speculate about population growth and calculated that it might take 2000 years to fully populate the world. Nobody worried about what might happen 2000 years hence.

By the time Malthus wrote, however, far more data on population growth were available. The U.S. Census of 1790 together with earlier colonial censuses indicated that the Western Hemisphere was filling rapidly. The English Census of 1801 showed that population was increasing more rapidly than had been thought. Petty's "2000 years hence" had already arrived, or shortly would. And, if a lowered birth rate via voluntary birth control was inadmissable, then Malthus had to be correct, in the opinion of England's rulers.

When large-scale economic growth became evident later in the nineteenth century, Malthus's theory lost prestige. With the discovery of the economically underdeveloped countries following World War II, the ideas of population growth and those of Malthus (not Petty) were revived; today, however, birth control is permitted as a check on population growth.

References

Malthus, Thomas R., *An Essay on Population*, J. Johnson, London, 1798, Murray, London, 1817: (a) Book I, chap. 2, p. 17, (b) Book III, chap. 13, p. 11, (c) Book IV, chap. 1, p. 65.

(*See also* Industrial revolution; Zero population growth)

A. J. Jaffe

Manchester school

The English classical economists were free traders, which in the circumstances of their times meant that they were unalterably opposed to the British system of agricultural protection enshrined in the so-called corn laws. Throughout the period of the industrial revolution in the first half of the nineteenth century, there were annual motions in Parliament in favor of free trade and a more or less continuous agitation against the corn laws. The free trade movement took on new force, however, with the formation of the Anti-Corn Law League in 1838, under the leadership of Richard Cobden and John Bright, two self-educated Manchester businessmen who pioneered the use of the mass rally as an instrument of political persuasion. As a result of their efforts, aided by a severe harvest failure in Great Britain and the imminent threat of a famine in Ireland, the corn laws were at last repealed by the Tory government in 1846.

In the protracted parliamentary debate that led up to repeal, Disraeli, the opposition Whig leader, spoke contemptuously of the movement for repeal as the Manchester school, referring no doubt to the fact that the campaign against the corn laws had its center among the cotton manufacturers in and around Manchester. The label stuck and was soon applied as a term of abuse not only to free traders but to all followers of the laissez faire principle of government. For Cobden and Bright, the unilateral repeal of the corn laws was only a first step toward a worldwide system of free trade, which would eventually banish colonies, diplomatic jockeying, and wars, ushering in a new era of international peace. Such aspirations were linked in their minds with a hostility to factory legislation and trade unionism at home because they thought that least government is always best government. It was this compound of interconnected ideas that came to be described by the term Manchester school, and the label was then employed indiscriminately to caricature the ideas of the English school of classical political economy. Thus, it was enough for any nineteenth-century German protectionist and interventionist to refer to "Smithianismus" and "Manchesterertum" to convey to their readers a whole series of repugnant ideas made up of free trade, laissez faire, anti-imperialism, pacifism, and political individualism.

The case for free trade, however, as stated by Smith, Ricardo, and John Stuart Mill, was hedged by a number of qualifications which called for gradual and partial repeal of the corn laws rather than the total and immediate abandonment of agricultural protection advocated by Cobden and Bright. The leading British economists of the 1830s and 1840s held themselves aloof from the popular debate on free trade and indeed disavowed the vulgar propaganda of the Anti-Corn Law League. And although the agitation for repeal drew on the general free trade position of the classical economists, the campaign which finally secured the repeal of the corn laws in 1846 based itself, more often than not, on arguments directly contrary to the spirit and even the letter of the works of Smith and Ricardo.

Moreover, in the great controversies of the time regarding the legitimate role of government, the English classical economists generally adopted a pragmatic attitude toward government intervention, which allowed frequent exceptions to the general rule of laissez faire. They sanctioned public control over the issue of money; they endorsed factory legislation, albeit haltingly; and they supported state assistance for emigration. Despite individual differences over such questions as state aid to paupers, the legal rights of trade unions, and public control of elementary education, none of the classical economists can be characterized as die-hard enemies of all forms of state intervention. In short, there never was a Manchester school of economists, although there certainly was a Manchester school of business executives and politicians.

References

Crampp, W. D., *The Manchester School of Economics*, Stanford University Press, Stanford, 1960; Blaug, M., *Ricardian Economics*, Greenwood, Westport, Conn., 1973, chap. 10; O'Brien, D. P., *The Classical Economists*, Clarendon, Oxford, 1975, chap. 10.

(*See also* Classical school; Laissez faire)

Mark Blaug

Maoism

Mao Zedong (Mao Tse-tung) thought, Maoism's label in China, is the application of Marxism-Leninism to the Chinese Revolution and to the contemporary international scene. It is a macro-social model for revolutionary modernization which embodies both Marxist principles and analysis and their Chinese solidification with rational instruments for action. It is based on the long experience of Mao and the Chinese Communist Party (CCP) in the struggle for power since 1921.

Linking of Theory and Practice

Mao's model for transforming China into a unified socialist nation moving toward communism links certain Chinese traditions and institutions with selectively adapted Marxist and other Western ideas, institutions, and techniques. This adaptation requires the linking of theory and practice in a continuous class struggle to create the conditions essential for communism: elimination of the three gaps between (1) mental and manual labor, (2) town and country side, and (3) worker and peasant; and the resolution of persisting "contradictions among the people and the enemy." Mao's road follows the usual Marxist route of modifying the economic base and super structure (changing productive forces and relations of production as well as the institutions, ideas, consciousness, etc., that support the foundation), and also takes new interpretive byways (e.g., the progressive role given the peasant in the revolutionary dynamics and exploitation of nationalistic and patriotic values and sentiments). The Chinese struggle with the Soviet Union is placed in the context of a three-part division of the world: two superpowers, the developed countries, and the Third World.

Mao's strategy for revolutionary modernization includes prominent egalitarian, populist, and voluntarist elements. It is postulated on the optimistic notion that since China is "poor and blank," it can more easily shape itself into a new kind of powerful, modern industrial society through collectivist institutions and modes in which group interest subsumes and finally fulfills individual interest. Humanity is considered more significant than machines in this process. Unlike previous avenues to modernity, China's is to be "built on the worst" rather than on elites: the masses working together are to raise material levels. The peasant is given a principal place along with the proletariat. Mass actions, mass movements, mass decision making are to be carried out in a constant class struggle against bourgeois ideas, values, and behaviors. The Cultural Revolution, begun in 1966, was an all-encompassing mass movement to raise popular consciousness in the pursuit of Maoist goals through class struggle against the CCP and other mass organization strongholds of Mao's movement.

Mao's Developmental Model

In its economic aspects, Maoism evolved into a clearly definable developmental model by 1966, after a rejection of the Soviet model in the middle 1950s. China's factor-endowment mix of an extreme dearth of capital, scarce arable land, and abundant labor (mainly unskilled) and the ideological commitments of the CCP yielded a Nurksian-like balanced growth strategy—called "walking on two legs"—requiring simultaneous utilization of traditional indigenous (labor-intensive) and modern (capital-intensive) production techniques self-reliantly developed with minimum dependence on foreign economic involvement. Agriculture was given the highest priority and, through the commune (set up in 1958), was provided with supporting (seasonally labor-absorbing) small-scale industrial and service activities. Heavy industry and other sectors were to grow in tandem with agriculture and to economize in the use of scarce capital resources by developing along both modern and traditional lines.

The translation of labor into land and capital was to be achieved through a planning system in which salient macroeconomic decisions were centralized (key outputs, labor and capital allocation, etc.) and in which tactical implementation was decentralized, with less important products planned at provincial and lower levels. New capital was allocated through state budget revenue sharing with advanced capital accumulators, such as Shanghai, feeding capital to backward ones, such as Tibet. Labor was to be tightly controlled and allocated by a system of placement through local labor bureaus rather than using wages as market allocators.

The administration, motivation, and training of labor relied more heavily on social than on material incentives. In work organizations, which were to be ends in themselves, the usual Soviet-type graded wage and income scales (eight grades and work points) were used. Emphasis, however, was placed on intrinsic motivation—e.g., worker management, physical labor for managers, worker-technician-supervisor task groups—and the negative bureaucratic outcomes of division of labor were to be countervailed by nurturing generalized as well as specialized work functions in an effort to foster more desirable relations of production—covering social relations as well as working conditions and production facilities. Education and training were to be open to the entire community in a two-way flow, e.g., drawing on peasants and workers as teachers as well as learners, and more opportunities were to be opened up to the children of workers and peasants to enter schools at all levels. Admission to higher-education institutions after 2 years of work in the countryside or in the army was based on meeting academic and social (political) standards.

Model for Revolutionary Modernization

This model's implementation was opposed by some high CCP officials such as Liu Shaoqi and Deng Xiaoping. With their purge in the Cultural Revolution, Mao's policies were more fully executed, but after his death in 1976 the model was subjected to considerable modification. The differences between Mao and his adversaries revolved around productive forces versus working conditions, with Mao insisting that the latter be changed before waiting for the former to mature. Liu, for example, favored mechanizing agriculture before collectivization, but Mao pressed for collectivization before extensive mechanization was feasible.

Maoism as a broad model for revolutionary modernization has considerable currency in developing countries, competing with the Soviet model. Mao's prescription for development under socialism and for supporting national liberation movements unquestionably has raised widespread interest as well as controversy over the correct developmental policies for revolutionary developing countries. For economists, the Maoist model provokes a wide range of questions germane to growth theory, labor allocation, industrial organization, planning, and numerous other key economic issues.

References

Eckstein, Alexander, *China's Economic Revolution*, Cambridge University Press, New York, 1977; Gurley, John G., *China's Economy and the Maoist Strategy*, Monthly Review Press, New York, 1976; Nurkse, Ragnar, *Problems of Capital Formation in Underdeveloped Countries*, Blackwell, Oxford, 1953; Schram, Stuart R., *The Political Thought of Mao Tse-tung*, Praeger, New York, 1970; Schurmann, Franz, *Ideology and Organization in Communist China*, University of California Press, Berkeley, 1968; Tse-tung, Mao, *A Critique of Soviet Economics*, Monthly Review Press, New York, 1977.

(*See also* Communism; Comparative economic systems, an overview; Economic history and theory; Marxism; Socialism)

Charles Hoffmann

Marginal cost

Marginal cost is the increment in total cost incurred by a producer as the result of a unit increase in quantity produced. This concept is used in the theory of the firm in conjunction with marginal revenue to help determine the profit-maximizing level of output; it is used in welfare economics to evaluate the consequences of the market structures of reality and their deviation from the standard of perfect competition. Recently, it has been used to judge the conduct of firms with market power in relation to antitrust statutes, the Sherman Act in particular.

Clearly, a profit-maximizing firm has an incentive to reduce its output if marginal cost exceeds marginal revenue ($MC > MR$). By doing so it is saving in total cost more than it loses in revenue. Similarly, if $MC < MR$, the firm can increase its profits by expanding output, since by so doing it obtains more in additional revenue than the added cost of the incremental output. Thus the firm can maximize profit only if it selects an output level at which $MC = MR$.

Similarly, marginal cost can be used to judge whether an output level is socially optimal. For convenience, let us use q^* to denote the profit-maximizing level of output, let MC^* be the marginal cost of producing a small increment of output if the firm is already producing q^*, and let p^* be the maximum price at which q^* can be sold. If p^* exceeds MC^*, then productive social resources are wasted. The reason is that MC^* is the social cost of attracting from other uses the additional resources needed to produce a contemplated increment in output, while p^* reflects consumers' willingness to pay for that added output. Therefore, if p^* is greater than MC^*, a cost-benefit test shows at once that society would be better off if resources were diverted from other uses into the production of the commodity in question. The reverse is true if p^* is less than MC^*. Thus, marginal cost plays a key role in testing whether the economy's resources are allocated efficiently.

Algebraic and Geometric Analysis of Marginal Cost

For a firm that produces only one product—the fictitious single-product firm—the geometry and mathematics of various costs is particularly simple. Let q_0 be the initial level of output and TC_0 the associated total cost. Let q_1 denote some higher level of output and TC_1 the associated total cost. We can then define the increments $\Delta TC = TC_1 - TC_0$ and $\Delta q = q_1 - q_0$. Forming the ratio $\Delta TC/\Delta q$ we obtain an (approximate) measure of the marginal cost. (The smaller we make the increment in output Δq, the smaller is the degree of imprecision.) To evaluate the marginal cost properly at a point such as q_0, calculus techniques are needed.

Figure 1 illustrates the mathematical analysis. On the horizontal axis we plot total output per unit of time and on the vertical axis the total cost. It follows from the

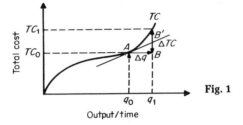

Fig. 1

diagram that when the increase in output becomes very small, the ratio $\Delta TC/\Delta q$ becomes approximately equal to the ratio $B'B/\Delta q$, which is the slope of the tangent to the total cost curve at point q_0. The slope of that tangent is the true marginal cost at q_0.

For a single-product firm we can easily illustrate the relationships between the marginal cost and the average cost AC, which is equal to the total cost divided by the associated level of output; that is, $AC = TC/q$. As indicated in Figure 2, $MC = AC$ at that level of output, denoted by q_0, at which the average-cost curve reaches its lowest point. This geometric relationship can be summarized compactly by the formula $MC = AC(1 + e)$ where $e = (\Delta AC/\Delta q)(q/AC)$ is the (approximate) elasticity of the average-cost curve. We see that if AC is constant, as it will be if there are constant returns to scale, MC will equal AC; if AC is rising so that $\Delta AC/\Delta q$ is positive, MC will be higher than AC. Other cases can be worked out using similar reasoning.

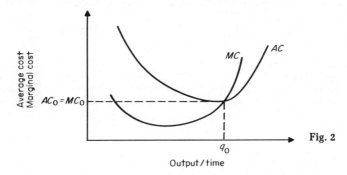

Fig. 2

For a multiproduct firm the above analysis does not hold because of the presence of common cost—costs that cannot be allocated on any rational criterion among the various products. For example, there is no rule which correctly allocates the costs of the railroad track among various types of freight carried by the railroad. Consequently, one cannot form the expression $AC = TC/q$ for each type of freight. Fortunately, at least in theory, it is possible to calculate the marginal costs for each separate type of freight, and this is the main piece of information needed for optimal decisions relating to multicommodity production.

Short-Run versus Long-Run Marginal Cost

The marginal cost of producing additional output depends critically on whether the entrepreneur anticipates that the additional demand that elicits this output will persist for a long or only for a short period of time. If the latter, it is perhaps best to expand production using overtime labor and employing the existing capital stock more intensively. But if the rise in demand is expected to endure, the entrepreneur may decide to purchase additional capital equipment and employ more full-time labor. In general, it is less costly to produce additional output when the quantities of all inputs—labor, capital, land, etc.—can be properly adjusted to new demand conditions. Consequently, the long-run marginal cost (LRMC), with all inputs fully adjusted to additional outputs must be lower than the short-run marginal cost (SRMC), which is calculated for the case where some input quantities are fixed by earlier decisions. Similarly, if output is contracted, the marginal saving in cost from reducing output by one unit is larger when all inputs can be orderly released than it is when some inputs are fixed at their old levels. Figure 3 illustrates those relations on the assumption that the firm initially expects to produce indefinitely q_0 units of output per unit of time and where q_1 and q_2 are some other possible level of output which may or may not prevail for a long period of time. The arrows from A to B indicate that over time the maginal cost will fall toward its long-run value equal to MC_1. This process of adjustment will be the faster the more certain is the entrepreneur that q_1 will be sold for a long period of time. It will be also the faster the cheaper it is to adjust the necessary inputs quickly to their most desired levels.

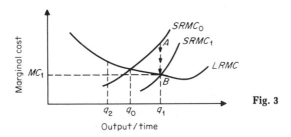

Fig. 3

Social and Private Marginal Cost

It is entirely possible that, from the standpoint of society, the cost of adding one more unit of output will not correspond to the cost incurred by the entrepreneur. This divergence between social and private marginal cost may occur for various reasons. Perhaps the most important is the presence of external benefits or costs. For example, when one whose occupation is fishing decides to spend more time catching more fish, then labor must increase and more fuel must be used for the boat. This constitutes private marginal cost. However, disregarded is the fact that such decisions as depleting the stock of fish affect others who fish, who now must spend more time—and additional resources—to catch the same quantity of fish as they did before. This additional expenditure must be included in the calculation of the social marginal cost which, therefore, exceeds private marginal cost. The opposite case arises when a farmer spends additional resources on pest control, and thereby reduces the number of pests in the field of neighboring farmers who now can use smaller quantities of resources to keep pests at their previous level. The preceding analysis explains in part why the government taxes firms emitting pollutants and subsidizes such activities as research and development.

A discrepancy between social and private marginal costs can also arise because some of the productive inputs purchased by firms are not sold at prices equal to their marginal costs. For example, if steel were monopolized so that the price of steel exceeded its marginal cost, users of steel would be induced to economize on the use of steel and to use other inputs, to a greater degree than they otherwise would. This socially unwarranted substitution is induced by the difference between private above social marginal cost. It also explains in part why there are incentives for vertical mergers.

Estimation of Marginal Cost

Two basic methods are used to estimate marginal cost empirically. The first is to look at historical cost data and relate annual changes in costs to annual changes in outputs.

In doing this, special care must be taken to separate out all those influences such as inflation that can cause costs to change even when there is no change in quantities produced. Indeed, it can be said that for this reason raw accounting data cannot yield correct estimates of marginal cost. In practice, statistical estimation of marginal cost requires careful sophisticated techniques.

The second basic method is engineering analysis. This entails the design of the best production arrangements for two different levels of output. The cost difference, when divided by the change in output, yields an estimate of marginal cost. For a large firm this procedure may involve complex and large-scale computer simulation. The disadvantage of engineering estimates is that they are based on hypothetical situations, whereas historical estimates are based firmly on actual (past) experience. This disadvantage becomes an advantage if technological progress, for example, is rapid so that the past becomes a poor indicator of future costs. It is also clear that the marginal cost of a new product line cannot be estimated directly from historical data.

References

Baumol, William J., *Economic Theory and Operations Research*, 4th ed., Prentice-Hall, Englewood Cliffs, N.J., 1977; Machlup, Fritz, *The Economics of Sellers' Competition*, Johns Hopkins Press, Baltimore, 1952.

(*See also* Competition; Firm theory; Marginal revenue; Microeconomics; Normative economics; Welfare economics)

Janusz A. Ordover

Marginal revenue

Marginal revenue is the (positive or negative) increment in total revenue obtained by a seller (firm, group, cartel) through a unit increase in the quantity sold. This concept is used chiefly in the theory of the firm for the determination of the output and selling price at which profit is maximized; that is, the quantity for which the excess of marginal revenue over marginal cost is zero or, in the case of incomplete divisibility, above zero by the smallest possible amount.

The concept is much older than its name. It was used in mathematical form by Augustin Cournot in 1838. Around 1930 almost a dozen economists developed it simultaneously in verbal, geometric, and algebraic analyses. The clearest expositions, including the term marginal revenue, were by Joan Robinson and Edward H. Chamberlin.

The four concepts, total revenue (TR), average revenue (AR), marginal revenue (MR), and price elasticity of demand (ν), are logically interrelated. With infinitely elastic demand ($\nu = \infty$), TR increases proportionately with q, the quantity sold; AR, or TR/q, remains constant; and $MR = AR$. This is the definition of pure (or perfect) competition, implying the seller's belief that larger quantities of output could be sold at an unchanged price, so that MR equals p, or price obtained. In a range in which demand has an elasticity greater than 1 (neglecting the minus sign), that is, if the percentage increase in q exceeds the percentage reduction in p, TR increases, though less than proportionately with q; AR, or TR/q, declines; and MR declines even faster and is definitely below the price (provided that price discrimination is excluded). In a range in which ν is exactly unity, TR remains constant, as q increases at the same proportion as p is reduced; AR ($= p$) in that range has the shape of a rectangular hyperbola; MR is zero (which is obvious, with TR constant). In a range of ν below unity, TR declines when q increases; AR declines even faster; and MR is negative.

Without subsidies or other special incentives, no firm that prefers higher to lower profits would ever set its price so low, or offer so large a quantity for sale, that marginal revenue is negative. If production cost is positive, nothing outside the range of sales in which price elasticity is above unity, and marginal revenue therefore above zero, is relevant for decisions about price charged or quantity offered. These decisions are dominated by the consideration that any price reduction and output increase can change total revenue by a positive sales gain (the increment in q times the lower price) and a negative price loss (the price reduction times the smaller quantity that could be sold at the higher price).

Algebraic Argument

It is customary to use infinitesimal calculus (differential coefficients) and point elasticities of demand. Since quantities of product are not always perfectly divisible and prices cannot be varied but by finite magnitudes, it is preferable to calculate with first differences and arc elasticities of demand.

Denoting the higher price as p_1 and the smaller quantity saleable at that price as q_1; and the lower price as p_2 and the larger quantity saleable as q_2, marginal revenue will be the difference between $p_2 q_2$ and $p_1 q_1$, or the same as the difference between the (positive) sales gain $p_2(q_2 - q_1)$, and the (negative) price loss, $q_1(p_2 - p_1)$. Thus, MR is equal to $p_2(q_2 - q_1)$ minus $q_1(p_1 - p_2)$ [or plus $q_1(p_2 - p_1)$, which is negative because $p_2 < p_1$]. If arc elasticity of demand is written as $(q_2 - q_1)/q_1 \div (p_2 - p_1)/p_2$, or $p_2(q_2 - q_1)/q_1(p_2 - p_1)$, one recognizes that it is equal to the ratio of the sales gain to the price loss.

Conforming with the original definition of marginal revenue as the revenue change resulting from an increase in quantity by just 1 unit, and thus making $(q_2 - q_1)$ equal to 1, the above expressions become even simpler. Marginal revenue, expressed as the excess of the sales gain over the price loss, becomes $p_2 + q_1(p_2 - p_1)$. Arc elasticity of demand becomes $p_2/q_2(p_2 - p_1)$. Hence,

$$ MR = p_2 + p_2 \frac{1}{\nu} \quad \text{or} \quad MR = p_2 \left(1 + \frac{1}{\nu} \right) $$

which of course is less than p_2, since ν is negative.

Geometric Representation

The usual geometric representation is through continuous curves, analogous to infinitesimally small variations in price and quantity and to point elasticities. Thus, if DD' is the demand curve, its point elasticity at R, that is, at price OP ($= QR$) and quantity OQ ($= PR$), is equal to the ratio OP/PY, where Y is the intercept of the tangent through R with the ordinate. Marginal revenue for quantity OQ can be found by deducting a stretch equal to PY from the price or average revenue, QR. Thus, we obtain QS as marginal revenue corresponding to the average revenue QR (Figure 1). If we constructed the complete marginal-revenue curve, it would satisfy the condition that for each point the area bordered by the curve and the two axes (the integral of the marginal revenues of all additional units of the quantity sold) would be equal

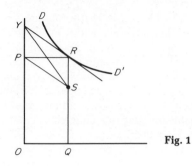

Fig. 1

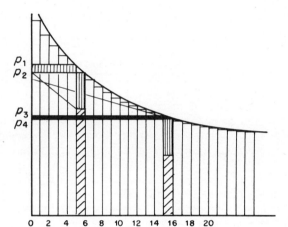

Fig. 2

Total sales	Sales gain	Price loss	Marginal revenue
$5p_1$			
$6p_2$	$1p_2$	$5(p_1 - p_2)$	$p_2 - 5(p_1 - p_2)$
$15p_3$			
$16p_4$	$1p_4$	$15(p_3 - p_4)$	$p_4 - 15(p_3 - p_4)$

to the rectangle inscribed between the demand curve and the axes (average revenue times quantity).

It is more instructive to draw stepped curves, corresponding to finite differences of price and quantity, and arc elasticities between consecutive points. In Figure 2, marginal revenue is shown for the sixth and the sixteenth units. The price losses being deducted from the sales gains, marginal revenue is represented by the light-shaded lower parts of these gains.

The geometric relationship between elasticity of demand and marginal revenue is most clearly seen in the sets of graphs combined in Figure 3. In order to show larger areas, we make the quantity change in larger lumps. Elasticity of demand is represented by the ratio of the sales gain to the price loss, marginal revenue by the difference between sales gain and price loss.

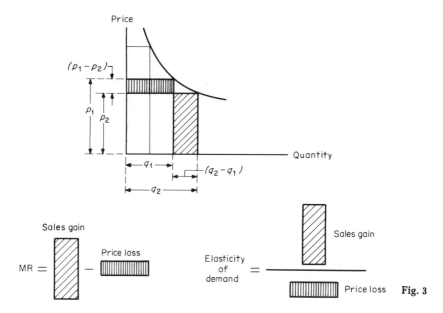

Fig. 3

Theoretical and Practical Uses

The theory of the firm as a part of the theory of prices and allocations deals with imaginary decision makers. Marginal revenue in this theory is calculated or constructed from average revenue, which in turn is calculated from total revenue. Since in reality firms can rarely know total revenues or, still less, average revenues to be obtained for different quantities of particular products, one might think that it would be hopeless for them to calculate marginal revenues. Yet, in actual practice things are quite different: incremental revenues and incremental costs are much easier to take into account than totals or averages. A decision maker in reality does not draw curves or calculates averages, either of recorded data of the past or of expected data of the future. As the decision maker considers accepting or rejecting particular orders, or making adjustments in production plans, he or she thinks exclusively in terms of what incremental revenues and incremental costs are likely to be involved. The practically important question is always what difference it would make to the firm's net revenue if this or that change were made. This incremental thinking corresponds to the marginal calculus which the theorist applies to the abstract hypothetical decisions of the imaginary firms in the constructed models.

References

Chamberlin, Edward Hastings, *The Theory of Monopolistic Competition,* Harvard University Press, Cambridge, Mass., 1933, 5th ed., 1946; Cournot, Augustin, *Researches into the Mathematical Principles of the Theory of Wealth,* Paris, 1838, Macmillan, New York, 1897, 1927; Machlup, Fritz, *The Economics of Sellers' Competition,* Johns Hopkins Press, Baltimore, 1952; Robinson, Joan, *The Economics of Imperfect Competition,* Macmillan, London, 1933.

(*See also* Elasticity; Firm theory; Marginal cost; Microeconomics)

Fritz Machlup

Marketing channels (see Channels of marketing)

Marketing research and business economics

Marketing research is analogous to production research, involving the search for more efficient means of marketing goods and services and the development of new and better methods of marketing. Thus, marketing research encompasses such diverse aspects of a business operation as the distribution network, sales effectiveness, the efficiency of advertising and other promotional methods, finding new markets for products, developing products that satisfy consumer wants, and product strategy. It is in the latter respect especially that marketing research activities are likely to overlap with those of a business economics department, since questions of pricing strategy can be answered only after reliable information is obtained on price elasticities and the nature of the demand curve for a product.

History

Marketing research had its beginnings largely in the United States, initially through the attempts in 1879 of an advertising agency, N. W. Ayer & Son, to use survey methods to obtain information on grain production to prepare an advertising schedule for a client. Scattered reports of the use of advertising appear in the literature on business history during the early part of this century, mostly in connection with the use by advertising agencies of survey methods to estimate the impact of advertising. The first formal marketing research operation was launched by the Curtis Publishing Company in 1911, again dealing primarily with readership, and obtaining information about markets for the publications of that firm.

Books on marketing research only began to appear in the 1920s and 1930s. The first national organization in the field, the American Marketing Association, was established in 1933 by the merger of two smaller groups.

The use of marketing research by industry on a wide scale did not really begin until the 1940s, and it accelerated with the end of World War II. The growth of sample survey methodology lent considerable impetus to the development of marketing research, since the bulk of marketing analysis is based on the collection and analysis of survey data. The enormous expansion of marketing research in the years since World War II is reflected in the fact that spending for this type of research in the private sector in the United States had exceeded $1 billion by 1977. Of this, approximately half was spent internally, that is, by the marketing research departments of business firms, while the other half was spent to purchase marketing research from others, mostly from marketing research firms and other suppliers of commercial research.

Diversity of Marketing Research in Private Sector

The major focus of marketing research in the private sector is the measurement of market potentials, market share analysis, and the determination of market characteristics. At the same time, marketing research departments engage very heavily in research relating to the development of new products and to monitoring how well their competitors are doing. Advertising research is also of major importance, especially studies of the effectiveness of advertising and of how best to get a message across to customers.

In addition, the work of many marketing research departments overlaps with that of business economics departments, which are also heavily engaged in forecasting; marketing research, however, usually focuses on forecasting brand shares and prospects for individual products, whereas business economics is more concerned with prospects for the industry and for the entire economy.

More recently, marketing research departments also have become involved with studies relating to corporate social responsibility, particularly with the modification of the marketing strategy of the firm to take into account legal constraints and consumer interests.

The type of activities undertaken by a marketing research department in one company may be carried out by a different department in another company. For example, pricing studies are as likely to be carried out by a business economics unit or some other department as by a marketing research department. In addition, some types of research, especially that relating to advertising, is frequently done on the outside, usually by the advertising agency that handles the accounts for that company. In fact, a key area such as advertising research may be studied partly by the marketing research department of the company and partly by the research department of the advertising agency of that company.

Marketing research is carried out in both big firms and small firms. In smaller firms, the organization of the marketing research function is more informal, with people frequently conducting research as a part of their other activities or with only one person assigned to the task for the entire firm. In the larger firms, a separate department, and sometimes even several departments, is frequently set up to carry out marketing research. For example, some of the major corporations have a marketing research operation attached to the corporate headquarters as well as separate marketing research operations for each of the major product lines.

A large part of the marketing research needs of business is met not within the firm but by the subcontracting of work to specialized marketing research firms and by studies by the research departments of advertising agencies. Virtually all the major advertising agencies maintain research departments that will provide their clients with information not only on the effectiveness of advertising but also on how a product is used by consumers relative to competitors.

The marketing research industry contains a wide diversity of marketing and management consulting firms that range from small interviewing services operating from a private home to multimillion-dollar companies that will engage in almost any type of marketing research study. Some of these firms, such as A. C. Nielsen Company and Market Facts, maintain continuous national consumer panels, and offer for sale a wide variety of market indicators ranging from readership of particular magazines and the size of television audiences to the market share of particular products and information on the characteristics of the purchaser.

One function of marketing research in the private sector is to ascertain how the firm is doing relative to its competitors. A little-discussed facet of this activity is intercompany espionage. As in chemical and engineering research, this may involve "planting" employees of one company with another to report on the plans and market strategy of the other company. In addition, espionage in marketing research not infrequently involves ascertaining when and how a market test of a new product will take place and then making arrangements to "rig" the test by, say, arranging for spuriously high purchases of the new product and thereby tricking the company to invest millions in a product that is slated to fail.

Marketing Research in Nonprofit and Public Sectors

In the nonprofit sector, marketing research is being used increasingly to study consumer reaction to different social innovations, such as birth-control devices in different countries, religious practices, and different health innovations such as health maintenance organizations.

Various activities of governments, especially national governments, also involve marketing research. Although no numerical estimates have been made of the extent of this research, it includes a wide variety of activities. For example, the U.S. Department of Agriculture studies methods of distribution of farm products as well as the living styles and spending habits of rural families. Regulatory agencies such as the Federal Trade Commission and the Food and Drug Administration study consumer attitudes toward, and knowledge of, products under their jurisdiction. As part of the military recruitment programs, the Department of Defense engages in a significant amount of advertising research. In addition, much of the research in the social sciences funded by the National Science Foundation and the U.S. Department of Health and Human Services relates to marketing research, as do many of the data collection operations of the U.S. Bureau of the Census.

References

Ferber, Robert, *Handbook of Marketing Research*, McGraw-Hill, New York, 1974; Myers, John G., William F. Massy, and Stephen E. Greyser, *Marketing Research and Knowledge Development: An Assessment for Marketing Management*, Prentice-Hall, Englewood Cliffs, N.J., 1980; Twedt, D. W., *1978 Survey of Marketing Research*, American Marketing Association, Chicago, 1978.

(*See also* Advertising, economic aspects; Sampling in economics)

Robert Ferber

Marshallian economics

Marshallian economics takes its name from Alfred Marshall, who was professor of economics at Cambridge University in England from 1884 to 1908 and who is generally regarded as the founder of the Cambridge school of economics. The term neoclassical is often used to describe Marshall's economics. His famous *Principles of Economics*, first published in 1890 and running to its eighth edition by 1920, is sometimes regarded as the *locus classicus* of neoclassical economics and is also usually regarded as one of the greatest works ever written in the field of economics.

A Method of Analysis

Marshallian economics is not just a set of theories or hypotheses to explain the working of a market, capitalistic system; it is much more a method of analysis or a framework within which to operate.

As Marshall realized and continually emphasized, an economic system is one of perpetual change and evolution. Businesses are born, grow, and decay; demand and supply conditions for commodities alter; population changes affect labor supply as do migration movements, education, and changing social morals. In other words, economic systems are complex structures of interrelated factors, all of which are subject to change. This is what makes economics such a difficult subject and often makes those studying it despair of achieving any rigorous, useful results. How should such complexities be handled? Simplification is clearly necessary—this, after all, is the essential ingredient of scientific inquiry—but oversimplification must be avoided.

There are two simplifications that are the hallmark of Marshallian economics and which remain basic ingredients of contemporary economics. One concerns the breaking down of complex interrelationships, the other the handling of time. Marshallian economics is also frequently referred to as partial equilibrium analysis and often contrasted with general equilibrium theory. What does this contrast imply? Let us consider the demand for a commodity. It is possible to conceive of the demand for, say, beefsteak depending upon all relative prices in the system because ultimately all commodities compete for limited consumer income. This assumption—a feature of general equilibrium—also implies that all markets are interrelated. Marshall accepted that this was an appropriate theoretical specification but went on to argue that empirically the demand for beefsteak, for example, would be dominated by one of two variables—the price of beefsteak compared with the price of other meats, and consumer income. Thus, an increase in the demand for beefsteak was assumed to have its major impact in the market for beefsteak and closely related markets (mutton, pork, chicken) so that the analysis is only partial. It does not consider all possible interrelated objects. Secondly, Marshallian economics takes these major influences on demand one by one, *ceteris paribus*; that is to say, we look at the effect of a fall in the price of beefsteak given initially the price of pork, mutton, and chicken, and given consumer income. Allowance for changes in some of these conditions is then made. Strictly, once again, in a general equilibrium sense it is arguable that a change in demand for a commodity will affect all markets and (relative) prices.

Time, of course, is a continuous variable—it does not stop and start but goes on and on inexorably. To make it amenable to inquiry, Marshall broke time down into a series of planning periods, which were associated with the degree of fixity of the factors under control. Let us take an example used by Marshall: Suppose that there is a sudden, unexpected increase in the demand for fish. Marshall considered the supply response in three planning stages. In the immediate period price will simply rise as the extra demand at the quayside faces an unchanged catch—notice here that the assumption is that price adjusts instantaneously to the market clearing price (we return to this crucial assumption later). If the increased demand continues, more trawlers will put to sea or fish more frequently, extra deckhands will be recruited, etc., so that in the short period (partial adaptation period) the supply of fish for market can be increased although at rising average and marginal cost.

If the rise in demand is now regarded as permanent by the fishing industry, increase in fleet size will occur, accompanied, via a rise in relative earnings, by a rise in the labor force. Thus, supply will permanently adjust by full adaptation to the change. In this case it is possible that the extension may occur without any rise in average or marginal cost.

This analysis of time leads us into a central aspect of the theoretical structure of Marshallian economics. This concerns what Marshall called the theory of value, which is now called the theory of relative price determination. The basic argument is that relative prices and changes in them are determined by the demand and supply conditions in different markets and the changes in these conditions. These are the so-called laws of demand and supply so often referred to in economic discussions. As was implicit in the fishing example it is clear that the shorter the planning horizon over which a change in underlying conditions is allowed to have effect, the greater will be the influence of demand conditions.

Thus, returning to our fish-market example, we see that in the very short period with a given stock or catch it is the strength of demand that determines price. As we move into the partial adaptation period, supply factors also play their part in price determination, and in the full adaptation period (or long period) supply factors may come to dominate price formation.

We have then a vision of an economic system in which changing demand and supply conditions in the various commodity, factor, and financial markets are continuously altering the set of relative prices. Decision makers—business executives, householders, suppliers of labor—adjust their behavior accordingly. What principles do they use in making these adjustments to their market behavior? In answering this question, we arrive at another central theoretical idea of Marshallian economics— the principle of substitution. It works as follows: Decision makers—business executives, householders, workers—are assumed to be individual welfare maximizers; that is, they take actions and respond to changes in economic circumstances that will, in their subjective judgment, maximize the welfare of the unit that they represent. Of what does this welfare consist? It is assumed that for business units it consists of expected long-run profits (i.e., the assumption of attempted profit maximization); for households and supplies of labor, attempted utility maximization.

Any change in relative prices will make existing plans nonoptimal and hence will encourage substitution. For example, a business executive faced with a rise in the relative price of a factor of production will attempt to lower the proportion of that factor being used. A household will respond to a rise in the price of potatoes by buying more rice or spaghetti. Suppliers of labor will respond to a rise in overtime hourly wage rates by adjusting the division of household time between work and leisure, etc.

The central importance of the principle of substitution is clear; it is the mechanism by which an economy adjusts to changes in its underlying economic structure, and the signaling system for this mechanism to operate is the system of relative prices. Notice that adjustment in the Marshallian system depends crucially on a system of price flexibility that conveys information about the ever-changing economic environment. A major criticism—and one that can now be seen as the center of much of Keynes' criticisms—is that the real world is not one of price flexibility, and hence the burden of adjustment to changing circumstances normally falls on output and employment.

This last point brings us to the monetary and macroaspects of Marshallian economics. The stereotypical picture mentioned at the beginning of this article would have it that the monetary aspects are adequately described by the assumption of full employment and the quantity theory of prices. It is a fact that in his *Principles*, Marshall made these two assumptions and concentrated on relative price determination. But in his writings on monetary economics there are other important developments, foremost among these is the analysis of the demand for money as a stable function of real income or wealth. The prototype of important later work associated especially with Milton Friedman is to be found here.

References

Blaug, M., *Economic Theory in Retrospect*, 3d ed., Cambridge University Press, Cambridge, 1978, chaps. 9, 10; Marshall, A., *Principles of Economics*, 9th ed., C. W. Guilleband (ed.), Macmillan, New York, 1961.

(*See also* Cambridge school; Chicago school; Consumers' surplus; Demand; Economics; General equilibrium; Marginal cost; Marginal revenue; Neoclassical economics; Normative economics; Quantity theory of money; Welfare economics)

Bernard A. Corry

Marxism

Marxism is a unified social science, representing a particular viewpoint of the combined disciplines of philosophy, history, economics, sociology, and political science. Marxists believe that the non-Marxist disciplines are each too narrow and do not recognize many of the most important problems that lie within several disciplines at once. Moreover, society is viewed as one unified organism, having political, economic, and other aspects. Marxism originated with Karl Marx, who drew on three sources: (1) German philosophy, especially Kant and Hegel; (2) British classical economics, especially Adam Smith and David Ricardo; and (3) French revolutionary thought. Marxism is the official dogma in the Soviet Union, China, Eastern Europe, Indochina, and Cuba, though each of these have somewhat differing interpretations of it. Marxism is also a body of thought accepted in a nondogmatic form by many social scientists around the world.

Four Main Aspects of Marxist Philosophy

First, Marxist philosophy is materialist, devoid of all religious superstition, and it embraces science as a problem solver, based on facts of experience. Yet materialism is not simple empiricism, for Marxists believe that every so-called fact is only found, interpreted, and integrated within some theoretical and ethical framework—there is no such thing as a fact aside from theory and value judgments. Second, it is determinist in that science can discover regularities of natural and social behavior, which determine what will happen in any given situation. Marxism thus rejects the doctrine of free will, though it also rejects any notion that history is predetermined by God or any other force above human beings. Third, it is humanist, in the sense that nothing is higher than humanity, and all decisions should be made on the basis of the needs of the majority of humanity, recognizing that the majority of humanity is the oppressed working class. Fourth, it is dialectic, in the sense that it instructs the social scientist to ask questions (1) about conflicts within society, (2) among opposed groups interrelated with all other groups, and (3) as to the form of change, both gradually within a society and by possible revolution from one social form to another. These dialectical methods of approach are only questions to be asked; they are not dogmas or answers of any sort.

Social Superstructure

The historical approach of Marxism is also materialist in that it does not accept any notion of ideas arising in a vacuum. All ideas emerge from some social environment. Marxism calls the entire range of ideas plus the entire range of social and political institutions (including law, government, and the family) a social superstructure. This superstructure is determined by the economic base of society, which includes technology, material capital, and human relations among classes in the productive process. Marxism is completely opposed to economic determinism. Economic determinism sees that the superstructure is determined by the economic base, but it denies that the base is also determined by the superstructure. Marxism insists that the superstructure of ideas and sociopolitical institutions fully determines the economic base. Revolutions occur, for example, in the form of new ideas and new political institutions brought about through sociopolitical strife—and these new political institutions help create or support new economic institutions. On the other hand, revolutions occur only when fixed human relationships among classes in production conflict with the rapidly widening possibilities presented by new technological forces of production. For example, a slave-owning society cannot take advantage of advanced industrial technology and will resist the spread of industry. When this occurred in the United States, it led—through ideological, theological, social, and political conflict—to the revolution known as the Civil War, which ended slavery.

In sociology, Marxism explains the form of sexual and family relations as well as the form of racial relations as parts of the superstructure determined by, but reacting upon, the economic base. For example, a slave society will have very different racial and sexual relations from a capitalist society, each being appropriate to and supportive of its economic base. In political science, Marxism explains the behavior of government on the basis of the needs of society and the needs of the ruling class of society. The Egyptian government under the pharaohs arose partly to control the Nile and partly because of the need for armed forces (and priests and ideology) to support slavery. Of course, a particular form of government, like particular forms of racial and sexual relations, then act upon and determine the economic base.

Surplus Value

Early primitive peoples had classless societies, according to Marxist anthropology. Since then, societies have been divided into a ruling class (which rules and exploits) and a working class (slaves, serfs, or free workers). The value of every commodity in capitalism is determined by the labor time in it. But the worker is paid only an equivalent of the value of the goods necessary to his or her average consumption. The difference produced by the worker above the value of the wage is the surplus value, which is the source of all profits, rent, and interest. The system causes poverty not only by paying low wages, but by the periodic economic depressions and unemployment which are characteristic of capitalism and only capitalism. Capitalism is also the basic cause of imperialist attempts to dominate and exploit other countries.

Marxists see a future of classless, strifeless society. In its early stage of socialism, there is cooperative or collective ownership, but there are still differential wages according to work done. In the latter stage of communism, there will be collective ownership and collective use according to need.

References

Marx, Karl, *Das Capital,* 3 vols., International Publishers, New York, vol. 1 first published in 1867; Mehring, Franz, *Karl Marx: The Story of His Life,* University of Michigan Press, Ann Arbor, Mich., 1962; Sherman, Howard J., *Radical Political Economy,* Basic Books, New York, 1972; Sweezy, Paul, *Theory of Capitalist Development,* Monthly Review Press, New York, 1958.

(*See also* Capitalism; Communism; Comparative economic systems, an overview; Economic history and theory; Labor theory of value; Maoism; Socialism)

Howard J. Sherman

Mass production (see Economies of scale)

Medicare program

Medicare is a nationwide health insurance program for the aged and for certain disabled persons. The official name of the medicare program is Health Insurance of the Aged and Disabled. Health insurance protection under medicare is available to the aged and disabled without regard to their means and assets. The program is a part, although not a major part, of the nation's income maintenance system.

The medicare program became effective on July 1, 1966, following long years of legislative debate, culminating in the passage of the King-Anderson bill, an amendment to title XVIII of the Social Security Act, included in the Social Security Amendments of 1965. The turning point in passage of this legislation occurred when President Lyndon B. Johnson decided that a health insurance program for the aged was an essential part of his war-on-poverty program.

The legislation was passed over the objections of the health professions and those of the private insurance companies. Originally, the medicare program had been conceived solely as a tax-financed hospital insurance program. However, to meet the medical profession's opposition to passage of the program, on the grounds that it covered only hospital costs, a second part of the program, financed by beneficiary contributions and general revenues, was developed to cover other medical costs. Thus, the medicare program consists of two parts, the hospital insurance, or part A, program, and the supplementary medical insurance, or part B, program.

Who Is Covered by Medicare

In 1979 about 27 million persons were covered by medicare. This included persons over age 65 and certain other individuals as described below.

The vast majority of persons reaching age 65 are automatically entitled to protection without any premium costs under the part A program. Others, aged 65 and older, who are ineligible for automatic coverage because they have not paid sufficient social security taxes, may elect to purchase this coverage voluntarily by paying its full actuarial cost, but they are also required to purchase part B coverage. Premium-free coverage is provided for disabled persons under age 65 after 30 months of disability. This applies to disabled workers under age 65; disabled widows and dependent disabled widowers, ages 50 to 65; beneficiaries 18 years old or older who are disabled prior to age 22; and disabled railroad retirement system members. Persons under 65 with chronic kidney disease are entitled to benefits for kidney transplants or for renal dialysis if they are currently insured under social security, or if they are dependents of insured persons.

All persons 65 and over can enroll voluntarily in the part B program. Disabled persons under age 65 who are covered under part A are also eligible to enroll in part B. Part of the cost of this coverage is derived from the premiums paid by enrollees; the remaining cost is paid through general revenues. (All but four states have entered agreements to pay the part B premiums for their welfare recipients.)

What Medicare Provides

Part A   The following reasonable costs for hospital care are covered:

1. *In-hospital services.* In-hospital services are covered for up to 90 days during each period of confinement. (There are special limits for treatment in mental hospitals.) The patient pays only an initial deductible amount ($160 in 1979) for the first 60 days of confinement. For the next 30 days of confinement the patient must pay a coinsurance amount per day. (In 1979, this coinsurance amount was $40.) There is an additional "lifetime reserve" of 60 hospital days for longer than 90-day hospital stays, which also require the payment of coinsurance ($80 per day in 1979). The deductible and coinsurance amounts are changed each January 1 to keep pace with the inflation in hospital costs.

2. *Skilled nursing facility care.* The patient receives full coverage of all services for the first 20 days of needed care and/or rehabilitation services. After that period, 80 additional days of coverage are available, but there is a daily coinsurance amount ($20 in 1979), which is also redetermined annually. However, benefits are not payable unless the skilled nursing facility confinement was preceded by at least a 3-day hospital confinement.

3. *Home health care.* Up to 100 days of medically necessary home health visits by nurses or other health workers are permitted if they occur in the 12-month period following at least a 3-day hospital stay, or following a discharge from a skilled nursing facility.

Part B   Medicare pays 80 percent (except for radiological and pathological services rendered in a hospital, and home health care services, which are payable at 100 percent) of the reasonable charges for covered services after an initial $60 annual deductible. The services covered include physician services, out-patient hospital service, x-rays and laboratory tests, kidney dialysis, radiation treatments, medical supplies and equipment, ambulance services, and numerous other services and supplies. In addition, up to 100 medically necessary visits a year of home health services are covered without the prior hospitalization requirement.

Excluded from coverage under part B are routine medical checkups, drugs, dental care, eyeglasses or eye examinations, hearing aids, immunization, private-duty nursing, and several other services. Out-patient treatment of mental illness is limited to a payment under the medicare program of $250 in a year.

How Much Do Beneficiaries Receive

According to the January 1979 Social Security Bulletin, the health care costs of persons 65 and over amounted to $41 billion in fiscal year 1977. Of this, the medicare program paid $18 billion, or 44 percent of the total. Medicaid and other public programs paid another 23 percent, while private insurance added 6 percent, leaving about 27 percent, or about $11 billion, for the elderly to pay out of pocket.

The $11 billion out-of-pocket payments by beneficiaries was divided approximately as follows (in billions of dollars):

Hospital care	$0.9
Physician care	1.8
Drugs and sundries	2.4
Nursing home	4.6
Dental service	1.0
Eyeglasses and appliances	0.3

The Administration of Medicare

Medicare comes under the overall direction of the Secretary of Health and Human Services. Within this agency, the medicare program has been placed in the Medical Bureau of the Health Care Financing Administration (HCFA), which is generally responsible for its policy and for its administrative control. Much of the administration of the program is through contract with intermediaries or carriers, which are Blue Cross–Blue Shield plans, or commercial insurance companies. State agencies are responsible for checking participating institutions and providers against the program's standards.

Under part A, each institution can elect its fiscal intermediary, and the institution is reimbursed directly by that intermediary without any need for the patient to submit any claims for institutional service. (Some providers choose to deal directly with HCFA for their reimbursement.)

Under part B, either the patient or the physician submits the claim to HCFA's specifically designated carrier for that geographical area. Physicians' fees are reimbursed for reasonable charges according to an annual guideline set up by the Social Security Administration. This guideline, to be used by carriers, is determined by examining the particular physician's customary charges for given services, which must fall within the prevailing charges in a particular community, and which must not be more than the carrier would customarily cover for its own insureds. The carriers examine the claims, determine the amounts due, and make the payments.

The intermediaries, under part A, and carriers, under part B, are reimbursed by HCFA for their payments for services to medicare beneficiaries, and for their administrative costs.

The Financing of Medicare

The financing of part A of the medicare program is derived almost entirely from payroll taxes paid by all workers covered under the United States social security program. This includes contributions by employers, employees, and the self-employed. The tax rates, which have been determined in advance, are illustrated in the accompanying table.

Persons insured under part B's supplementary medical insurance program pay premiums amounting to somewhat less than one-third the costs of benefits and program administration. The balance is paid for by general revenues. The part B premium rates are revised annually each July 1 to reflect increases in program costs. For example, the monthly premium rate in the period July 1979 to June 1980 is $8.70 per individual.

Hospital Insurance Tax Rates for Employers, Employees, and the Self-Employed

Calendar year	Tax rate, %	Earnings subject to tax
1979	1.05	$22,900
1980	1.05	25,900
1981	1.30	29,700
1982–1984	1.30	Automatically adjusted
1985	1.35	Automatically adjusted
1986 and later	1.45	Automatically adjusted

The monies for part A and part B of the medicare program are deposited in separate trust funds. In fiscal year 1979, the total cost of the program was about $30 billion, with about $21 billion charged to the part A trust fund, and about $9 billion charged to the part B trust fund.

The status of the part A trust fund and the part B trust fund differ. According to the most probable assumptions projected by the social security actuaries, as stated in the 1979 annual report of the board of trustees of the Federal Hospital Insurance Trust Fund, the part A trust fund will become insolvent by 1989 unless the payroll tax is increased by at least 1 percent.

The trustees report that the part B trust fund is sound, pointing out that the general revenues and part B premiums remitted by beneficiaries can be adjusted upward annually for inflation and for other cost increases.

It may be pointed out that the overall inflation in health care costs can, in part, be attributed to the medicare program itself. This can be demonstrated through examination of the medical care component of the consumer price index before and after 1966 (when medicare was first implemented). A sharp acceleration in the trend line occurred. At that time, the margin between it and the rate of general price increases rose sharply as well.

Another impact of medicare has been the development of new health services resources to meet the increased demand. A prime example of this impact has been the mushrooming development of the nursing-home industry.

Medicare Issues

Expansion of Coverage   To better meet the elderly population's out-of-pocket expenses, many proposals have been developed to expand medicare's coverage. These include an effort to improve the physicians' reimbursement mechanism to increase the proportion of physicians' fees paid for by the medicare program. Under medicare, when physicians' services are used, all patients are faced with paying deductibles and coinsurance out of pocket. However, some patients are faced also with paying additional out-of-pocket amounts, depending on whether or not their physicians accept assignments. When a physician accepts an assignment, that phy-

sician agrees to abide by the medicare program's determination, based on a complicated percentile process, of what constitutes a reasonable and customary fee, in
which case the patient pays only the deductible and coinsurance. However, when
the physician does not accept an assignment, the patient is liable for any amounts
which exceed what medicare allows, thus potentially adding significantly to the out-
of-pocket costs. Solving this problem requires either increasing the number of assignments accepted by physicians, or raising the level of physician reimbursement.

Other proposals for reducing out-of-pocket expenses are the addition of coverage
for drugs, dental care, eyeglasses, and hearing aids, and the expansion of existing
coverage for mental disorders, nursing-home care, home care, and long-term care, as
well as the addtion of coverage for catastrophic care.

A proposal has been made to extend eligibility to disabled persons at an earlier
time, that is, after 6 months of disability, rather than the present 30 months. There
are also proposals to extend coverage to social security recipients at age 62, and to
spouses of medicare beneficiaries.

All such coverage expansions are needed most by the nation's population below
the poverty level.

Financing   In order to meet part A's projected insolvency, and to finance any
adopted expansions of coverage, the alternatives for raising more funds are either to
increase payroll taxes or to use more general revenues. Another possibility for meeting some of the needed financing could be through cost savings rather than through
a raising of revenues. Such cost savings may be achieved through effective health
care cost-containment measures, (that is, through a reduction in the costs of providing
health services to the elderly without a lessening in the quality of care), or through
a reduction in the costs of program administration.

Potentially effective cost-containment measures include placing limits on hospital
reimbursements, or changing the method from a retrospective approach to a prospective approach and developing stronger controls on utilization and resources of
health care services.

Since program administrative costs represent only about 3 percent of total program
costs, there is only a relatively small potential for savings there.

Health Maintenance Organizations   Another approach for providing services to
medicare beneficiaries is through health maintenance organizations (HMOs). HMOs
are able to waive deductibles and coinsurance and provide expanded coverage
which meets the out-of-pocket needs of beneficiaries at no extra cost to the beneficiaries, and at little or no additional cost above what medicare currently costs.

In order to accomplish this, however, changes in the medicare program's method
of reimbursing HMOs would have to be legislated. Although presently HMOs do not
exist in all geographic areas, and do not have sufficient capacity overall to enroll all
medicare beneficiaries, there already is sufficient capacity and geographical spread
to make substantial inroads into solving the out-of-pocket problems of the most
needy.

Medigap Insurance Policies   Supplementary private insurance plans called medigap policies have been purchased by many medicare beneficiaries. These policies
usually are very complicated and difficult for the elderly to understand. In some cases

they appear to promise more coverage than actually exists. These and other problems presently are being investigated by State insurance departments and by the Federal Trade Commission.

National Health Insurance   Rather than addressing the coverage expansion and financing issues directly, it has been suggested that a comprehensive national health insurance program be the solution to the problems of medicare. While such a program could solve the program's financial problems, and at the same time provide more comprehensive coverage to all citizens, a national health insurance system could not be implemented for many years, and thus support for this solution is not very great.

Others   Other issues presently being considered, which affect the total population as well as the elderly, are quality of care, a shortage of health services in rural and inner-city areas, and the high costs of medical services.

Studies of Medicare Issues

These medicare issues and others are being reviewed currently by the Advisory Council on Social Security and by the National Commission on Social Security. It is unknown at this time whether it will be possible to make any of the needed changes in the medicare program. Taxpayer resistance is the key inhibiting factor. Thus, any liberalizations probably would have to be financed through program savings, including the greater usage of health maintenance organizations to provide services to medicare beneficiaries.

Other Nations

Most other industrialized nations have developed universal national health insurance systems which provide health care for the aged in much the same manner as they provide care for the balance of the population. Therefore, comparisons with the medicare program are not appropriate, except to indicate that most of the systems, like medicare, began as financing systems. Gradually the systems became concerned with health facilities and human resources. In some countries of Western Europe, health care now is provided for citizens by the government. There are some countries, such as Germany and the Netherlands, where there is still a dominant role played by voluntary institutions and personnel.

References

Blanpain, Jan, *National Health Insurance and Health Resources*, Harvard University Press, Cambridge, Mass., 1978; Hoffman, Richard H., *Medicare Issues and Problems*, National Commission on Social Security, Washington, D.C., December 1979; Pauly, Mark V., *Medical Care at Public Expense*, Praeger, New York, 1971; Skidmore, Max J., *Medicare*, University of Alabama Press, University, Ala., 1970; U.S. Department of Health, Education and Welfare, Social Security Administration, *Social Security Handbook*, 6th ed., July 1978.

(*See also* Social security programs)

Richard Hoffman

Medium-run forecasts (see Economic forecasts)

Mercantilism

Mercantilism was an economic policy pursued by almost all of the trading nations in the late sixteenth, seventeenth, and early eighteenth centuries, which aimed at increasing a nation's wealth and power by encouraging the export of goods in return for gold.

Mercantilists deemed commercialization and industrialization as key objectives. They developed the balance of payments concept primarily because they considered it in the national interest to overbalance imports with exports and thus to acquire "treasure" (precious metals). Thomas Mun, a director of the East India Trading Company and one of the best-known seventeenth-century English mercantilist authors, explained the significance of the balance of payments in *England's Treasure by Foreign Trade*.

The Mercantilist Program

As part of the mercantilist program, individual governments promoted large investments in export industries; built high tariff walls to restrict imports, which could be produced domestically; restricted exports of domestic raw materials, which could be used by the domestic industry; interfered with the emigration of skilled workers; encouraged immigration of skilled workers; and, in several cases, prohibited sales of precious metals to foreigners.

Since one country's gold gain almost always resulted in a gold loss to one of its trading partners, not all nations could succeed at the same time. This resulted in sharpened trade rivalries. When successful, mercantilist policies generally resulted in full employment of a country's resources and led to rapid economic growth.

Mercantilism, Cameralism, and Colbertism

In England, the mercantilist writers were largely merchants and their writings were usually in the form of pamphlets. The German-Austrian brand of mercantilism, called cameralism, was different because the writers, for the most part, were government advisers, public administrators, and teachers, and their treatises were in book form. They stressed domestic industrialization rather than commercial expansion. Their aim was to foster home industry and a self-sufficient economy. The German-Austrian cameralists, such as von Hornigk, argued for the protection and subsidization of specific industries, and suggested that the aim of infant industry protection and subsidization was to bridge an initial period for industries that later would be profitable without further protection.

The French type of mercantilism (Colbertism) was more rigorous than the English brand, and was administered with the aid of a trained civil service staff under Jean Baptiste Colbert. France used strict government control and regulations to bring about national economic unification and industrial growth, but as one of the more rigorously mercantilistic nations, it did not fare too well.

Adam Smith accused mercantilists of not being able to distinguish between wealth and what they called treasure, pointing out that the accumulation of treasure is merely instrumental to the acquisition of wealth (consumable and usable goods).

References

Fellner, William, *Modern Economic Analysis*, McGraw-Hill, New York, 1960; Heckscher, Eli, *Mercantilism*, Macmillan, New York, 1955; Mun, Thomas, *England's Treasure by Foreign Trade*, Doubleday, Garden City, N.Y., 1953; Smith, Adam, *The Wealth of Nations*, Random House, New York, 1937.

(*See also* Balance of international payments; Balance of international trade; Economic history and theory; Economics)

Douglas Greenwald

Mergers

A merger occurs when one firm absorbs another and the latter loses its corporate identity. Mergers have raised important issues with respect to the evolution of the industrial structure in developed countries. The United States has had four distinct merger waves. The horizontal movement—merging firms in the same industry—at the turn of the century resulted in high concentration in many industries. Of 92 mergers studied by Moody, 78 percent resulted in market shares of 50 percent or more of the industry's output. In many industries a few firms accounted for a very high percentage of industry sales (oligopoly). Some attribute the high concentration in the United States to the early merger movement.

Others argue as follows:

1. Industries were typically not atomistic before the merger movement—concentration was already substantial.
2. The merger activity represented the transformation of regional firms into national firms implemented by the completion of the transcontinental railroad system in the late 1800s.
3. Concentration also developed in industries where firms disappeared by bankruptcy rather than merger.
4. High concentration developed in other developed countries in which merger activity was not important until after World War I.

Merger Activity Since 1920

The second major movement during the 1920s represented vertical integration—merging firms in the same industry but in different stages of operation, mining, manufacturing, or distribution. A reason suggested is that the development of national advertising, promotion, and selling media stimulated firms to integrate vertically to achieve economies of scale in rounding out their product lines for efficient distribution systems.

During the period 1940–1947, some 2500 firms were absorbed in mergers. However, the initiative usually came from the acquired firm which was typically small. Concentration was little affected. Tax considerations appeared to play a role in the mergers.

The Celler-Kefauver Act of 1950 amended the Clayton Act of 1914 to close the asset purchase loophole and granted additional power to make illegal those mergers that had a tendency to increase concentration. The relative importance of horizontal and vertical mergers thereafter declined in relation to conglomerate mergers, or mergers of unrelated firms. The conglomerate merger movement peaked in 1968 and 1969 when the total amount involved in large mergers for the 2 years combined was $56 billion. A more threatening antitrust climate toward conglomerate mergers and change in accounting treatment as well as tax treatment of mergers resulted in a substantial decline in conglomerate mergers by 1970. The conglomerate merger movement of the 1960s is said to have increased the share of the top 200 manufacturing firms from 53 percent of total manufacturing assets in 1956 to 61 percent in 1977.

Another increase in merger activity begun in 1977 was associated with special economic developments. New laws were proposed to prohibit any of the largest 200 manufacturing companies to acquire any other firm with total assets over $350 million.

Three Basic Issues

There are three basic issues with respect to the motives and effects of mergers: market power, efficiency, and managerial motives. The early mergers resulted in increased concentration in individual industries. However, the same degree of concentration might have occurred without mergers. Some firms might have grown faster, and some firms might have declined and some even disappeared. Furthermore, the concentration ratio in individual markets and for nonfinancial corporations as a whole has not greatly changed since the 1920s, remaining at an average level of about 40 percent. However, it is argued that without mergers, concentration in individual markets and in the economy as a whole would have declined. This is doubtful because mergers may simply represent the most efficient method by which the market for capital assets rearranges the relative growth rates of individual firms.

What is the efficiency rationale for mergers? For horizontal mergers, typically the basis is to further implement economies of scale in production or distribution. Sometimes important complementaries may be involved such as matching a strong research-oriented firm to a firm with a strong sales organization. The rationale for vertical mergers is a more efficient management of information through planning and control systems than could be performed by the external market. In addition, when specialized assets are involved, there is no economic basis for solving the problem of expropriation, in which either the owner or the user of the specialized assets may extract advantages of its special position at the expense of the other.

The conglomerate merger movement expanded in the 1950s and 1960s as important changes in managerial technology took place. Long-range planning and progress in the development of effective information-management systems in companies occurred. This increased the ability of the top corporate executives to manage divisions in unrelated product or technological areas. Since conglomerate diversification often was an attempt to avoid unfavorable longer-range developments in a firm's traditional product-market areas, it is difficult to evaluate their degree of success. The relevant comparison would be the unfavorable developments that might have occurred if the firm had not broadened activities beyond its traditional areas.

Mid-1970 Merger Activity

At the beginning of the 1970s nonfinancial corporations, on average, had market values that were below 70 percent of their current replacement values. This had several implications. To attempt to enter a new industry de novo would require fixed assets at investment-cost levels substantially above the historical costs of existing firms. Thus, it was more feasible to attempt entry into a new industry by buying an existing firm, often below current replacement costs even when a substantial premium was paid over existing market values. Current investment by existing firms in new capacity had to be made at high replacement costs and often did not promise favorable returns. This generally depressed the total level of investment activity. The unfavorable prospects for investment projects were ascribed to a rise in the risk element in the discount or capitalization factor due to increased uncertainties in the general economic climate. Despite unfavorable tax consequences, purchase of other firms at above their market values was by cash-tender offers, and, to a lesser degree, by exchange of securities as was characteristic of earlier merger movements, particularly the conglomerate merger movement of the 1960s.

One view of the merger activity of the 1970s is that it represented an expression of corporate control by managers. This view holds that lack of evidence in support of the monopoly or efficiency theories of mergers leaves the managerial theory as the remaining plausible explanation. The managerial theory holds that managers gain in salaries and prerequisites when the firm is larger. Thus, managers seek size for its own sake since it will benefit them in the form of higher compensation. It is argued that managers will actually accept projects that promise less than the firm's cost of capital because of the personal benefits that will come to them since the firm is larger even if less profitable. Neither general theory nor empirical evidence, however, provides support for this managerial explanation.

Are Mergers Successful?

The most rigorous of empirical studies of merger success are those performed in financial economics. These use a market model to test for performance that differs from the risk-return trade-offs set by general market relationships. These studies demonstrate that shareholders of acquired firms experience positive and statistically significant gains from mergers. The data are consistent with the finding that the acquired firms have not been performing up to their potential or that the performance of the acquired firms has been improved. The shareholders of acquiring firms have positive returns also, but they are not statistically significant. This result is consistent with a competitive market in acquisitions of companies, which causes potential gains for acquiring firms to be competed away into premiums or gains to the shareholders of acquired firms.

References

Beckenstein, Alan R., "Merger Activity and Merger Theories: An Empirical Investigation," *Antitrust Bulletin*, Spring 1979, pp. 105–128; Ellert, James C., "Mergers, Antitrust Law Enforcement and Stockholder Returns," *Journal of Finance*, vol. 31, May 1976, pp. 715–732; Gershon, Mankelker, "Risk and Return: The Case of Merging Firms," *Journal of Financial Economics*, vol. 1, 1974, pp. 303–335; Weston, J. Fred, *The Role of Mergers in the Growth of Large Firms*, University of California Press, Berkeley, 1953.

(*See also* Concentration of industry; Conglomerate; Integration)

J. Fred Weston

Microeconomics

The word "Micro" means small, and microeconomics means economics in the small. The optimizing behavior of individual units such as households and firms provides the foundation for microeconomics. Microeconomists may investigate individual markets or even the economy as a whole, but their analyses are derived from the aggregation of the behavior of individual units. Microeconomic theory is used extensively in many areas of applied economics. For example, it is used in industrial organization, labor economics, international trade, cost-benefit analysis, and many other economic subfields. The tools and analyses of microeconomics provide a common ground, and even a language, for economists interested in a wide range of problems.

At one time there was a sharp distinction in both methodology and subject matter between microeconomics and macroeconomics, i.e., economics in the large. The macroeconomist focuses upon topics such as total output, total employment and unemployment, the level and rate of change of the price level, and the rate of overall economic growth. The methodological distinction became somewhat blurred during the 1970s as more and more macroeconomic analyses were built upon microeconomic foundations. Nonetheless, major distinctions remain between the two major branches of economics. For example, the microeconomist is interested in the determination of individual prices and relative prices (i.e., exchange ratios between goods), whereas the macroeconomist is interested more in the general price level and its change over time.

Optimization plays a key role in microeconomics. The consumer is assumed to maximize utility or satisfaction subject to the constraints imposed by income or income earning power. The producer is assumed to maximize profit or minimize cost subject to the technological constraints under which the firm operates. Optimization of social welfare sometimes is the criterion for the determination of public policy. Opportunity cost is an important concept in microeconomics. Many courses of action are valued in terms of what is sacrificed so that they might be undertaken. For example, the opportunity cost of a public project is the value of the additional goods that the private sector would have produced with the resources used for the public project.

Theory of the Consumer

The individual consumer or household is assumed to possess a utility function which specifies the satisfaction which is gained from the consumption of alternative bundles of goods. The consumer's income or income earning power determines which bundles are available to the consumer. The consumer then selects a bundle that gives the highest possible level of utility. With few exceptions, the consumer is treated as a price taker—that is, the consumer is free to choose whatever quantities income allows but has no influence over prevailing market prices. In order to maximize utility the consumer purchases goods so that the subjective rate of substitution for each pair of goods as indicated by the consumer's utility function equals the objective rate of substitution given by the ratio of their market prices. This basic utility-maximization analysis has been modified and expanded in many different ways.

Theory of the Producer

The individual producer or firm is assumed to possess a production function, which specifies the quantity of output produced as a function of the quantities of the inputs used in production. The producer's revenue equals the quantity of output produced and sold times its price, and the cost to the producer equals the sum of the quantities of inputs purchased and used times their prices. Profit is the difference between revenue and cost. The producer is assumed to maximize profits subject to the technology given by the production function. Profit maximization requires that the producer use each factor to a point at which its marginal contribution to revenue equals its marginal contribution to cost. Under pure competition, the producer is a price taker who may sell at the going market price whatever has been produced. Under monopoly (one seller) the producer recognizes that price declines as sales are expanded, and under monopsony (one buyer) the producer recognizes that the price paid for an input increases as purchases are increased.

A producer's cost function gives production cost as a function of output level on the assumption that the producer combines inputs to minimize production cost. Profit maximization using revenue and cost functions requires that the producer equate the decrement in revenue from producing one less unit (called marginal revenue) to the corresponding decrement in cost (called marginal cost). Under pure competition, marginal revenue equals price. Consequently, the producer equates marginal cost of production to the going market price.

Price Determination in One Market

Microeconomic theory is sometimes called price theory since price determination occupies a major position. Consider first price determination for a single consumers' good in a market for which all buyers and sellers are price takers. Consumers are the buyers, and producers are the sellers. A demand function for each consumer expresses quantity purchased as a function of commodity prices and income. These are constructed from the conditions for utility maximization subject to income constraints. An aggregate demand function is obtained by summing the demand functions for all the individual consumers. It gives the aggregate quantity of the good under consideration that will be purchased at each possible set of prices and income.

A supply function for an individual producer expresses quantity produced and supplied as a function of output and input prices. These are constructed from the conditions for profit maximization. An aggregate supply function is obtained by summing the supply functions of all the individual producers.

Assume now that the prices for all goods and inputs and inputs other than the one under investigation are at predetermined levels. The price of that good is the only variable determining its aggregate demand and supply. An equilibrium price is one at which quantity demanded equals quantity supplied. The market is said to be cleared. In graphic analyses a downward-sloping demand curve and upward-sloping supply curve are plotted in a price-quantity diagram. Equilibrium price and quantity are given by their intersection. The supply and demand analysis is easily extended to producers' goods markets in which producers are both buyers and sellers, and to labor markets in which consumers are sellers and producers are buyers.

General Equilibrium

The determination of equilibrium for a single market is designated as partial equilibrium because the prices in all other markets are held at predetermined levels. If one is interested in the price system as a whole, there is no assurance that consistent results will be achieved through the determination of equilibrium prices taking one market at a time. Prices and quantities for all goods are determined simultaneously in a general equilibrium, sometimes called multimarket equilibrium, analysis.

General equilibrium is often determined by solving a system of simultaneous equations, one for each market, with market prices as variables. Relative prices, i.e., exchange ratios between goods, are determined in a general equilibrium analysis. It is common to set the price of some legal commodity (cash crop) equal to 1. Let the price of a bushel of wheat equal 1. Now, the price of a barrel of oil, for example, is expressed in terms of the number of bushels of wheat for which a barrel will exchange. Money prices are normally within the domain of the macroeconomist.

Welfare Economics

The object of welfare economics is the evaluation of alternative allocations of economic resources. Positive microeconomics shows how resources would be allocated if underlying assumptions were realized; normative, or welfare, economics asks how resources should be allocated. The tools of microeconomics are used extensively in welfare economics. For example, a social optimum may require that the price of each good equal its social marginal cost. In some analyses the conditions for social optimum are determined by maximizing the utility of one person assuming that the utility level of all other members of society are at predetermined levels.

References

Henderson, James M., and Richard E. Quandt, *Microeconomic Theory: A Mathematical Approach*, 3d ed., McGraw-Hill, New York, 1980; Hirschleifer, Jack, *Price Theory and Applications*, 2d ed., Prentice-Hall, Englewood Cliffs, N.J., 1980; Mansfield, Edwin, *Microeconomics: Theory and Applications*, 2d ed., Norton, New York, 1975; Varian, Hal R., *Microeconomic Analysis*, Norton, New York, 1978.

(*See also* Competition; Consumer theory; General equilibrium; Macroeconomics; Marginal cost; Marginal revenue; Normative economics; Opportunity cost; Price theory; Production function; Utility; Welfare economics)

James M. Henderson

Models, economic (see Economic models)

Monetarism (see Monetary policy)

Monetarist theory (see Chicago school)

Monetary overinvestment theory of the business cycle (see Juglar cycle)

Monetary policy

Unlike other private institutions, commercial banks create money through extending loans and making investments. To do so, banks need reserves which are provided primarily by the central bank, the banker's banker. The essence of monetary policy is to control the release of reserves in a manner which stimulates bank lending and investing in support of consumer and business spending in order to foster economic growth without contributing to inflationary pressures. Monetary policy has the capacity to exert an enormous impact on the level of employment, the volume of output, and the rate of inflation and serves as a major policy tool for influencing economic activity.

Basically, two conditions are required for banks to create money. One is the widespread acceptance of what might be called bank money. At one time, bank money consisted largely, if not exclusively, of paper currency. However, in time, banks were restricted in issuing their own currency and were able to maintain their money-creation role through the introduction and then the widespread adoption of the use of checks (demand deposits) as a means of payment. The other necessary condition is the ability of banks to function either by operating experience or regulatory requirement with reserve balances being maintained at only a fraction of their deposit liabilities; that is, under a fractional reserve system. (If banks held reserves equal to 100 percent of their deposit liabilities, banks could not create money, and they would serve solely as intermediaries between depositors and borrowers.)

The Discount Rate

The instrument of monetary policy at the time the Federal Reserve System was established by Congress in 1913 (and until changes were introduced or legislated in later years) was the discount rate: the rate charged banks for borrowing reserves from their Reserve banks. Fundamentally, the discount window was open to satisfy all of the banks' seasonal demands for reserves. However, the rate was (and still is) changed for cyclical purposes. A rise in the discount rate is intended to discourage bank borrowing at the window and, thus, restrain credit expansion. Conversely, a decline is intended to make reserves more readily available and presumably to increase the demand for bank credit. Only to the extent that changes in the discount rate influence banks to increase or to cut back on their borrowing of reserves can the Federal Reserve affect the availability of credit .

From the beginning, the board of directors of each Reserve bank has been required to set periodically the discount rate for their individual Reserve bank subject to the review and determination of the Federal Reserve's Board of Governors. The Board of Governors' role, in turn, entailed mainly this review process and the coordination in general of Federal Reserve activities.

In time, the Reserve banks began to coordinate their policies on an informal basis. This cooperative effort grew out of the Reserve banks' accidental discovery of a new instrument of monetary policy—open-market operations. The Reserve System covers its operating expenses primarily through earnings generated from the loans it makes to banks and on its investments in securities. It does not receive any appropriations from Congress. (In fact, for some years now, the Federal Reserve has been transferring to the Treasury nearly all of its accumulated earnings surplus.) In its very early years, however, most of its income came from interest earned on loans to banks. During the recession of the early twenties, bank needs for reserves ebbed as loans and deposits fell off. With the resulting decline in borrowings at the discount window, the Reserve banks' earnings contracted. To generate replacement income, the individual Reserve banks began to purchase government securities. It soon became apparent that such purchases were self-defeating. The reserves created by these operations led to increased repayments of discount-window borrowings. Moreover, since the market for government securities was, and still is, concentrated in New York City, the New York Reserve Bank (the major bank in the System) bore the brunt of the decline in discount-window borrowings. In these circumstances, largely at the urging of the New York Reserve Bank, the Reserve banks began to coordinate their open-market operations on an informal basis.

Open-Market Operations

The Federal Reserve soon recognized that its open-market operations were a powerful policy tool to influence the availability of reserves and, in turn, bank-credit activities. Unlike the discount window through which it had to rely on changes in the discount rate to influence the demand for reserves, the Federal Reserve was now aware that it could actively intervene to affect reserve availability. Open-market purchases add to reserves and stimulate bank credit and deposit creation; open-market sales reduce reserves outstanding and tend to restrict bank credit and deposit creation.

Through this new policy instrument, the Reserve banks moved toward becoming a more unified system. At first, with no legislative requirement or guidance, the individual Reserve banks were still free to ignore the open-market policy recommendations of the majority. The Banking Act of 1935 centralized the Federal Reserve's authority in the seven-member Board of Governors and provided for a uniform monetary policy with each Reserve bank required to participate in the System's open-market operations. More specifically, the Act established the Federal Open Market Committee (FOMC), which was given the basic responsibility for determining monetary policy for the entire System.

In further recognition of monetary policy's potential, the Banking Act of 1935 authorized the Federal Reserve to vary bank reserve requirements—the percentage of a bank's deposit liabilities which must be held in an eligible reserve balance. Such funds were considered to be a source of liquidity in the event of a cash squeeze, say, from heavy deposit withdrawals. Eventually, it became apparent that owing to the penalties which would be incurred if a bank's reserve balances were drawn below its required reserves, these funds would not be used unless the bank was ready to close its doors permanently. As part of this recognition, it was perceived that in view of the large volume of deposits outstanding, a small fractional change in the reserve-requirement percentage could have a substantial impact on the ability of banks to expand reserves. (With a 10 percent reserve requirement, for example, banks can extend loans and investment—deposits—10 times the available free reserves, while a 25 percent reserve requirement reduces the expansion potential to a factor of 4.) Accordingly, the act gave the Federal Reserve the authority to vary reserve requirements within a prescribed range. Moreover, as part of the shift to concentrate authority in Washington, the Board was given sole jurisdictional responsibility for setting reserve requirements.

With these changes, the roles of the Reserve banks' boards of directors were effectively neutralized. These boards do not have any influence on monetary policy. They do retain an advisory position with respect to establishing the discount rate. However, with the Board of Governors' authority to review and to approve each Reserve bank's discount rate, the power to effect rate changes lies with the seven Board members in Washington. Furthermore, the Reserve bank boards of directors are not privy to any of the policy decisions of the FOMC or the Board of Governors until they are released to the general public.

An Independent Agency

The Federal Reserve System occupies a special position within the federal government. Congress has established the Federal Reserve as an independent agency. Neither the President nor the Congress has a direct control over or influence on monetary policy. Their only involvement, other than through the laws enacted to govern the Federal Reserve, is indirectly through the appointment and approval of the Board of Governors' members. This does not mean that the central bank can insulate itself from the national government and completely ignore the policies being pursued by the administration in power. For policy to succeed, there has to be a spirit of cooperation between the two. The Federal Reserve's particular niche or responsibilities has been best described as follows: "It is independent within, but not independent from the federal government."

The FOMC is by far the most important body within the Federal Reserve System with regard to setting monetary policy. It convenes now 10 times a year to review economic, credit, and monetary developments and to determine the policy which is best suited to achieve its basic objectives. At the conclusion of each meeting, a directive is issued to the individual responsible for executing the FOMC's policy, the manager of the System Open Market Account who is located at the New York Reserve Bank. These directives instruct the manager with regard to the open-market policies which should be followed until the next meeting is held. In effect, the directive guides the manager in determining the amount of reserves which should be released (or absorbed) through purchases (or sales) of government securities.

Target Rate for Federal Funds Rate

An important element in the directive is the target range specified for the federal funds rate. Federal funds represent reserve deposits held at the Reserve banks or potential claims on such balances. These balances typically are purchased by banks short of reserves and are sold mainly by banks with an excess of such funds. However, the amount of bank reserves outstanding is subject to wide fluctuations through payment flows and currency movements over which the Federal Reserve has no control. The federal funds rate quickly reflects the impact of such changes on reserve availability and generally provides the FOMC manager with a good indication of the need to add or to drain reserves in order to keep the federal funds rate within the target range specified in the directive. If reserves are short, banks will bid up the federal funds rate and, to keep the rate on target, the manager enters the market and provides reserves. Conversely, if reserves are plentiful, the federal funds rate tends to decline and, in this situation, the manager steps in to absorb reserves to restore the rate to the target level.

The targeting of the federal funds rate is an initial objective of monetary policy, and it serves two purposes. One is to provide a signaling device for offsetting the seasonal flows in bank reserves which are not controllable by the Federal Reserve. These flows frequently can cumulate, within a period as short as a few days or a week, to an amount which represents a substantial portion of total reserves outstanding. It is generally agreed that the Federal Reserve (particularly through open-market operations) should offset these swings. Otherwise, for example, at such times as

Christmas when there is a large seasonal drain of reserves, there would be extreme tightness in the money market. (In fact, one of the objectives in establishing the Federal Reserve was to eliminate the seasonal money squeezes which were a frequent problem prior to 1913.) However, it is most difficult to predict with satisfactory accuracy changes in the supply of or need for reserves. The seasonal influences on reserve availability are not stable. Also, such random factors as weather and labor strikes can interrupt payment flows and affect reserves outstanding. With the bidding or offering of federal funds changing quickly in response to these flows, the manager is provided with a sensitive barometer for measuring the need to take appropriate offsetting action.

Bank Credit and Money Supply

The other function served by the FOMC's federal funds target is to create money-market conditions which are considered to be conducive to achieving what might be called the Federal Reserve's intermediate monetary policy objectives—the behavior of bank credit and the money supply. The federal funds rate is the key rate in the money market. It has an important influence on the cost of funds to banks and other borrowers in the money market and, in turn, tends to affect rate levels in much of the credit and securities market. For example, in increasing its target level for the weekly funds rate and eventually tightening upon bank reserve positions sufficiently to maintain this new, higher funds rate target, the Federal Reserve can depress monetary growth in two ways. The higher funds rate level, in stimulating increases in other short-term interest rates, causes the public to manage money balances more tightly relative to spending needs. At the same time, the eventual curtailment of bank reserve growth by the Federal Reserve to maintain its higher funds rate target, serves to limit bank credit and deposit expansion.

The links between changes in money-market conditions (which the Federal Reserve can control very closely) and changes in bank credit and money supply (upon which the Federal Reserve has only an indirect affect), however, are somewhat loose. Many factors beyond those under the Federal Reserve's direct control also influence the public's willingness to borrow and to hold cash balances. Frustrations in being able to achieve satisfactory control over bank credit and the money supply has led the Federal Reserve to change its operating targets over time.

Prior to the mid-sixties, the directives typically instructed the FOMC manager in a general (nonquantitative) way with regard to the degree of reserve expansion and the tone of the money market. As criticism developed that this tactic was not successful in achieving adequate control over bank credit and the money supply and that the Federal Reserve was not paying adequate attention in the policy directives to its intermediate goals, the FOMC in 1966 adopted the so-called proviso clause. (The critics, however, failed to recognize or consider that the FOMC at each meeting did review bank-credit and money-supply developments and that the behavior of these aggregates influences the FOMC's decisions.) This clause required the manager to make appropriate adjustments in the money-market targets whenever bank-credit growth deviated significantly from acceptable rates. However, no explicit target rates of growth were specified.

A more significant change was made in the meeting held on February 15, 1972. At that session, the FOMC decided that "it was desirable to increase somewhat the relative emphasis placed on reserves while continuing to take appropriate account of money market conditions. Committee members believed that doing so would enhance their ability to achieve desired intermediate monetary objectives." For the first time, the FOMC adopted a quantitative goal. At this time, their target measure used was a reserve aggregate RPD (reserves against private deposits). In early 1974, the FOMC added the behavior of the narrow and broadly defined money supply (M-1 and M-2) to the directive, and over time these aggregates began to receive greater attention in the committee's deliberations and greater emphasis in the directive itself. (In March 1976 RPD was dropped.) Moreover, in March 1975, Congress passed Concurrent Resolution 133, which stated that the Federal Reserve should "maintain long-run growth of the monetary and credit aggregates commensurate with the economy's long-run potential to increase production." In November 1977, the substance of this resolution was added to the Federal Reserve Act. In turn, this provision was superseded by the requirements of the Full Employment and Balanced Growth Act of 1978 (the Humphrey-Hawkins Act).

As required by the Humprey-Hawkins Act, the FOMC twice a year (in February and July) reports to Congress in general terms its broad policy objectives. At the same time, it sets out quantitatively the target ranges for three monetary aggregates (M-1, M-2, and M-3) and for bank credit over a 1-year period which it believes will further its stated economic objectives. The FOMC at each of its 10 meetings during the year prescribes target ranges for federal funds along with acceptable growth rates for M-1 and M-2 over 2-month periods. These growth rates are set so as to be consistent with the 1-year targets given to Congress. If the money supply begins to grow at a rate faster than the one specified in the directive, the manager is required to raise the federal funds target or at least to consult with representatives of the FOMC to see whether any responding action should be taken. Conversely, if the money supply starts to fall below the directive's specification, the manager is instructed to consider lowering the federal funds target.

This shift in Federal Reserve tactics affects primarily the central bank's operations with respect to domestic considerations. Monetary policy, however, may be influenced as well by international monetary developments. In fact, the directive for some time has instructed the manager to give due regard to the exchange value of the dollar. If U.S. prices are rising faster than abroad or U.S. interest rates are narrowing in comparison with those in other industrialized countries, pressures develop on the value of the dollar in the exchange markets. Such weakening adds to the cost of imported goods and contributes to the inflationary spiral. (However, at the same time, U.S. goods become cheaper and eventually exports should increase.) To minimize problems for the dollar, the Federal Reserve tends to edge to a tighter monetary posture than it would otherwise be maintaining. A difficult dilemma is created in such situations if domestic developments (such as rising unemployment) call for an easier policy.

A policy dilemma also rises for the Federal Reserve when disorderly markets in government securities arise. The Federal Reserve, despite long-standing concerns over central banks becoming engines of inflation for their national governments, considers the federal government to be a necessitous borrower and thus in the past has stepped in to provide support in a deeply eroding market. Such moves blunt efforts to control the growth of the money supply and often soon lead to a reversal of a tight money policy. Since the FOMC has shifted to including a quantitative target for the monetary aggregates in its directive, a disorderly government securities market has not arisen, and it remains to be seen what the Federal Reserve's reactions would be in such an event under the new policy emphasis.

Criticism of Federal Reserve Policy

Monetary economists, who in the past have been the Federal Reserve's most vocal critics, had some influence on the shift in the emphasis of monetary policy, but they are still far from satisfied. These critics believe that the money supply is the primary determinant of the rate of change in nominal economic activity. They point out that in a given time period, total spending or total income has to equal the average money supply multiplied by velocity (the number of times the money supply turns over during the period). (This is represented in the famous equation $MV = PT$ where M is the money supply, V is velocity, P is the average price level, and T is the number of transactions.) They maintain that V over time is relatively constant. The monetarists also assert that the Federal Reserve through its management of the supply of reserves can control very closely the growth in the money supply. For these reasons, they argue, by the Federal Reserve providing just enough reserves to lead to an expansion in the money supply needed to support a desired rate of growth in the economy, inflation could be minimized. Moreover, some contend that since forecasting changes in economic activity is so difficult, the Federal Reserve should limit its policy operations solely to providing the same amount of reserves year to year, and that such a fixed addition to the reserve base would by itself contribute to stable rates of economic growth.

The events of the past few decades suggest that there are adequate grounds for criticizing Federal Reserve policy. In terms of monetary policy's ultimate objective—a steady, sustainable rate of economic growth with low rates of unemployment and of inflation—the record has not been favorable. Wide swings in output and employment have persisted, and the underlying rate of inflation appears to be accelerating. Just the same, it is questionable whether the policies prescribed by the monetarists would have provided a better chance for success.

With regard to the Federal Reserve's efforts to stem the inflationary spiral, it is clear that it has sufficient policy clout to cut off completely any growth in the money supply that is contributing to a price explosion. The fact that, as a rule, it does not do so, even in the face of strong inflationary pressures, reflects the difficult dilemma faced by the monetary authorities. There is an obvious concern that too severe or too precipitous a shutoff in the supply of reserves would lead to a serious rise in unemployment and decline in economic activity—that is, the cure would be worse than the disease. Also, as the economy approaches the peak of a business cycle, the Federal Reserve seems to become increasingly concerned as to how far it can increase pressure on bank reserves and the availability of bank credit without precipitating a severe money panic and the accompanying severe financial distortions. The Federal Reserve so far has preferred to move at a steady pace and to follow an eclectic, nondoctrinaire approach to monetary policy. It seems to be willing to accept some inflation in order to avoid the huge social costs which result from rising unemployment and declining business profits and investment.

As part of its considerations, the majority at the Federal Reserve may feel that monetary policy is ineffective in controlling inflation stemming from shortages in supplies of goods or declining productivity. (The majority undoubtedly has greater confidence that in a demand-induced inflation fueled by easy credit availability, monetary policy can be more effective in dampening inflationary pressures.) While the Federal Reserve does make an effort to restrict credit in the former circumstances, it is apparent that there is a sense of frustration with regard to the extent monetary policy can contribute to a deceleration of inflationary pressures which are supply-induced. The Federal Reserve must also feel a sense of frustration from the fact that in the absence of a complete cutback in the growth of reserves and rigid controls over the movement of funds, the public is sufficiently innovative and resourceful to blunt at least part of the effect of a Federal Reserve effort to stem the growth in the money supply. Such moves by the public are achieved through more efficient use of the available money stock and are reflected in sharp cyclical increases in velocity, contrary to the monetarists' assertion of stability in this item.

Money-Supply Problems

The Federal Reserve's ability or willingness to follow the monetarist's policies is further complicated by a serious problem which has arisen in defining and in measuring the money supply. For a number of reasons, there has been a marked increase in recent years in the facilities allowing the public to minimize its money balances. There are difficult issues to be resolved in determining which of these new forms of money truly belong in the money supply and those which represent solely stores of value. Without clear guidance as to where the dividing line should be drawn, it is, of course, difficult to have any confidence as to which measure of the money supply the Federal Reserve should be aiming to control. Apart from this problem, the Federal Reserve has serious difficulties in measuring the money supply no matter how it is defined. These result partly from technical issues, such as correcting the data for double-counting of deposits which arise from particular funds being included in more than one deposit account when a check is issued and is in the process of collection—so-called float. They also stem from needed data not being readily available to the Federal Reserve. While the Federal Reserve has been trying to correct each of these prblems, there appears to be little hope that it will meet with much success at an early date.

Practical Monetarism

Underlying these considerations is the fact that many in the Federal Reserve are influenced not to follow a strict monetarist approach owing to serious reservations with regard to the validity of important elements in the monetarists' claims. The monetarists assert that the causality is directly from money to prices and income. (The monetarists also claim that there are long lags between changes in the money supply and their effect on the economy. This is another reason, they assert, for the Federal Reserve to adopt a policy of having reserves grow at a fixed rate.) The opposite view is that the relationship is more complex. The money equation ($MV = PT$), it is contended, is only an identity and does not provide a clear indication of the direction of causality. A rise in prices or income can just as well lead to a rise in the money stock or velocity as a growth in the latter could serve to raise income or to put pressure on prices. There is a complex interaction between the two sides of the equation which cannot be readily delineated. Nonmonetary factors not subject to Federal Reserve control or influence also have an important impact on the level of activity and behavior of prices.

The emergence of practical monetarism—the setting of quantitative targets for the monetary aggregates as intermediate monetary policy goals—suggests that there is an ambivalence on the part of the monetary authorities. They seem to have embraced monetarism without at the same time accepting the rigidities and precepts of monetarism. One senior Federal Reserve official has asserted that practical monetarism gives the central bank and public a better guide to monetary policy than any other approach and provides a needed discipline to the Federal Reserve's short-term activities, particularly in periods of rampant inflation. He has pointed out that inflation cannot proceed without an accommodating monetary growth and that inflation cannot be stopped unless excessive monetary growth is eliminated. He added that the battle against inflation can be assisted by reducing expectations of further price increases and that the setting of money-supply targets can serve this purpose. He also stated that the Federal Reserve has to establish in its anti-inflation efforts a degree of credibility that the targets are meaningful and that there will be prompt responses to excess money growth.

There is much to be said in support of the practical monetarism tactic. In no way can a steep or even a moderate rate of inflation be stopped if monetary policy allows bank-credit and money-supply growth to fully accommodate price excesses. By the same token, monetary policy alone cannot effectively dampen inflationary excesses. Many nonmonetary factors embedded in the economic structure contribute heavily to the behavior of prices. For this reason, the fight against inflation requires, along with a tight money policy, restraint through the federal government's fiscal operations sufficient to help curtail excessive demand pressures on the economy. Further, an effective anti-inflation policy requires longer-term efforts at breaking rigidities and imperfections on the supply side, including productivity-enhancing measures and vigorous moves to combat monopolistic pricing practices.

References

Board of Governors, Federal Reserve System, *Open Market Policies and Operating Procedures—Staff Studies*, 1971; Board of Governors, Federal Reserve System, *The Federal Reserve System, Purposes and Functions*, 6th ed., 1974; Federal Reserve Bank of New York, *Monetary Aggregates and Monetary Policy*, New York, 1974; Friedman, Milton, and Anna Schwartz, *A Monetary History of the United States*, Princeton University Press, Princeton, N.J., 1963.

(*See also* Chicago school; Economic statistics; Federal Reserve policy; Federal Reserve System; Forecasting methods; Inflation; Interest rates; Money supply; Open-market operations; Velocity of circulation of money)

Irving M. Auerbach

Monetary theories of interest (see Economic theory of interest)

Money illusion

Money illusion refers to the choice one makes to alter the demand for, or supply of, any goods or services involved in response to certain changes in the circumstances arising when all the real factors governing demand or supply (such as real income, relative prices, interest rates, and real wealth including real cash balances) remain unchanged.

Suppose, for example, that a worker who was unwilling to accept a new job at the previous wage rate suddenly faces an offer of a higher wage rate. Suppose also that the price level in the meantime has risen, but by more than the wage rate, and that, despite the higher prices now prevailing, the worker's real wealth consisting of bonds and money balances otherwise remains unaltered. Under these circumstances, if the worker, paying no attention to what has happened to the price level, looked at the higher nominal wage rate and decided to accept the job offer, then a problem of money illusion would arise. This would arise since the worker decides to go to work at a lower real wage rate, despite the fact that the nominal wage rate offered has also risen to a higher level.

Let us look at the problem of money illusion from the demand side. Consider a junior business executive who earns $24,000 a year and who has been spending $800 a month on groceries. The junior executive is then given a salary increase of 20 percent. Suppose that the salary increase is awarded by the employer to help the executive partially recover the 22 pecent loss of real income that has resulted from price increases in the past. Assume all other factors affecting consumption demand have increased in their nominal values so that their real values remain fixed. This executive, feeling richer as a result of the salary increase, decides to raise the grocery bill to $1000 a month, a 25 percent increase. More is now spent on groceries in real terms than before at a time when real salary earnings have actually declined. Such an executive can also be considered as suffering from money illusion.

As these two hypothetical cases illustrate, money illusion reflects the irrational choices one makes, choices that would not be made if one thought in terms of real values instead of being blinded by changing nominal values.

Money Illusion and Zero-Degree Homogeneity

Historically, it appears that money illusion was made an issue in formal economics for the first time in 1928 by Irving Fisher. To him, it simply meant "the failure to perceive that the dollar, or any other unit of money expands or shrinks in value." In other words, money illusion was considered present when an individual looked at the nominal dollars only, without relating them to the price level which might change and affect the purchasing power of those dollars. Since the time of Fisher, however, the meaning of money illusion has undergone some changes. Many economists (including W. Leontief, G. Haberler, J. Marschak, P. Samuelson, J. Tinbergen) treated the term synonymously with the zero-degree homogeneity displayed by the commodity demand functions of the classical system. The demands for commodities in this system were assumed to be functions of relative prices only and were determined in the real sector, independent of the monetary sector, which presumably determined the absolute (money) prices. Because the demands for commodities remained invariant with respect to changes in the money prices, these economists took the zero-degree homogeneity as reflecting the absence of money illusion—a conclusion consistent with money as a veil, but not money as an asset to hold.

According to Don Patinkin, (1965) such homogeneity in the commodity demand functions implies that real value of cash balances can never affect these demands within the classical system. For an illustration, suppose there exists an economy with commodities and outside money only, in which an individual were confronted with a proportionate increase in all money prices. What would then be its effects on the amounts of commodities demanded? There would be no change in relative prices, and, as a result, there would be no substitution effect. For the same reason, neither would there be any nonmonetary wealth effect. But the resulting decline in the real value of the individual's fixed initial money balances would generate a wealth effect. In other words, the decline in real wealth would lead the individual to decrease the amounts of commodities demanded. Thus, the zero-degree homogeneity, or the absence of money illusion, in the classical system would specifically deny that there would be any real balance effect.

For a more appropriate definition of money illusion under the circumstances, therefore, money holdings, too, would have to be increased by the same proportion as money prices, so that the individual's real cash balances would remain unchanged. When this is done, the demand function would become homogeneous of zero degree once again, but this time in absolute prices and nominal income as well as nominal money holdings. Under these circumstances, an illusion-free individual, when confronted in the market by new money prices, all of which had increased in the same proportion, would have no reason for changing the amount demanded of any commodity.

If, in the interest of greater realism, an additional asset in the form of bonds were to be taken into consideration, the notion of money illusion would have to be expanded to allow for this addition. That an individual is free of money illusion in this case would mean that the amount demanded, or supplied, of any real goods or services remains invariant when some changes occur in the circumstances the individual faces without affecting relative prices, the rate of interest, the time stream of real income, and the real wealth including the real values of initial bond and money holdings.

Limitation and Usefulness

One major objection that can be raised against the concept of money illusion, as this term is usually treated in the current literature, is the underlying assumption which states that each new price level is expected to be permanent. In reality, prices can and do change, giving rise to all sorts of complications. When prices rise not once but repeatedly, how should expectations be revised and which price level should be taken as new and permanent? What if the price level were then to fall? What would happen to price expectations if prices rose and fell freely, displaying no obvious trend? The price behavior may be marked by short-run fluctuations coupled with a long-run trend or vice versa. Under these and other circumstances, taking any new price changes as permanent is a naive assumption.

In spite of this limitation, money illusion as a formal economic concept can be a useful one, having a pervasive effect with respect not only to the commodity functions but also to the demand for money and demand for bond functions and to the supply of labor functions. Empirical studies, providing direct and indirect evidence of money illusion, tend to confirm the a priori judgment. In particular, money illusion has been shown to be a significant factor in the aggregate consumption function. Furthermore, the search for the microeconomic foundations for money illusion, based upon utility maximization subject to a budget constraint, has yielded meaningful results which tend to reinforce the logical plausibility of the pervasiveness of money illusion in a money-using economy.

References

Branson, W. H., and A. K. Klevorick, "Money Illusion and the Aggregate Consumption Function," *American Economic Review*, vol. 59, no. 6, December 1969, pp. 832–849; Clower, R. W., and J. G. Riley, "The Foundations of Money Illusion in a Neoclassical Micro-Monetary Model: Comment," *American Economic Review*, vol. 66, no. 1 March 1976, pp. 184–185 (see also Dusansky and Kalman's "Reply" in ibid, pp. 192–195); Crouch, Robert L., *Macroeconomics*, Harcourt Brace Jovanovich, New York, 1972; Dusansky, R., and P. J. Kalman, "The Foundations of Money Illusion in a Neoclassical Micro-Monetary Model," *American Economic Review*, vol. 64, no. 1, March 1974, pp. 115–122; Fisher, Irving, *The Money Illusion*, Adelphi, New York, 1928; Patinkin, Don, *Money, Interest, and Prices*, Harper & Row, New York, 1965.

(*See also* Inflation; Value of the dollar)

Joong-Koon Lee

Money markets

The money market consists of a set of institutions and arrrangements through which the supply of and demand for short-term funds are brought together. It is a market for usually standardized, short-term financial assets which are close substitutes for money. Financial assets maturing in 1 year or less customarily are considered short-term, and money-market instruments are close substitutes for money, or near-money, because they are financial assets with minimum money and cedit risk. Money risk is minimal since the short-term nature of money-market instruments limits the volatility of their prices as interest rates change. Thus, money-market instruments are subject to far less money risk than are long-term securities such as corporate bonds, which are traded in the capital market. Credit, or default, risk of money-market instruments is also minimal since the principal desire of investors in money-market paper is to acquire financial assets which quickly can be converted into money without the risk of undue losses. Consequently, only prime-quality borrowers such as government and government agencies, large commercial banks and other financial institutions, and highest-rated nonfinancial corporations have ready access to the money market as a source of funds.

The major money markets in the world have no central trading place similar to the stock and commodities exchanges. Trading takes place entirely by telephone or telex. Yet money markets are centered in major cities such as New York, London, Paris, and Tokyo, where most of the dealers, who buy securities for their own position and sell from their inventories, are located and where the final reconciliation of transactions takes place. The dealers, who form the nucleus of the money market, are in constant touch with each other and with major borrowers and investors throughout the nation and abroad. They engage in arbitrage to take advantage of temporary and small price differentials, which serves to keep prices of the different money-market instruments virtually uniform among the various dealers; and since dealers themselves must finance their positions, or inventories, of financial assets, they are constantly looking for excess money balances at the lowest possible interest cost to them. Thus, they help to even out interest rate differentials for similar securities among various geographical areas. Through the borrowing and lending of temporarily idle cash balances by both financial and nonfinancial, domestic and foreign entities, the money market is the locus of marginal adjustments between the demand for and supply of funds throughout the nation. In this sense, the money market is a national market; and it is not only a low-risk but also a high-information financial market.

Major Participants

Among the major participants in the money market, in addition to the dealers, are the large commercial banks, sometimes referred to as the money-market banks. They are lenders to the market, holding part of their reserves in short-term securities which can be sold quickly for cash and with little risk of capital loss; they are also borrowers in the market, selling short-term notes (in New York and London these notes are called negotiable time certificates of deposit) to raise additional funds for lending. Moreover, some banks are large-scale dealers in money-market instruments. The central bank, such as the Federal Reserve System and the Bank of England, is nearly always heavily engaged in the money market, both on behalf of the government and in its capacity of conducting monetary policy. For example, the Federal Reserve System is the largest single holder of short-term United States government debt and is responsible for maintaining an orderly money market in which funds are shifted smoothly without major upset in interest rates. In order to accomplish this, and also to pursue specific monetary policy goals, the Federal Reserve conducts open-market operations through the money market, buying and selling short-term government securities and engaging in repurchase agreements and matched sale-purchase transactions (the Federal Reserve sells securities to the dealers and concurrently makes a commitment to repurchase the securities at a future date) with dealers in government securities.

In some money markets, foreign governments, central banks, and non official foreign entities are significant net lenders. For example, the American money market is a reserve center in which foreigners hold their external reserves and working balances in the form of short-term financial assets such as U.S. Treasury bills, bankers' acceptances, negotiable time certificates of deposit, and commercial paper. To them, as well as to other investors in the money market, risklessness and liquidity are of prime importance; at the same time, they earn some income on their surplus funds.

Types of Money-Market Paper

In most major money markets, the stock-in-trade is dominated by government obligations. For example, U.S. Treasury securities with maturities of less than one year amounted to more than 50 percent of all money-market paper in th 1970s. Also, transactions in short-term Treasury obligations, most notably in Treasury bills, far exceed the volume of turnover in any other segments of the financial market, making the market for short-term government obligations more efficient than any other financial market in the United States. However, the rate of growth of private money-market instruments surpassed even that of short-term government obligations in the 1970s. The most important private instruments actively traded in the American money market are negotiable time certificates of deposit issued by large banks in denominations of $100,000 or more, with typical maturities ranging from 60 to 120 days; and commercial paper issued by leading finance companies, bank holding companies, non-financial corporations, and public utilities, with usual maturities ranging from 30 to 270 days.

Other important money-market instruments are bankers' acceptances, which are bills endorsed by a major bank and are used to finance trade between the United

States and the rest of the world as well as trade among foreign countries; federal agency securities issued by institutions such as the Federal National Mortgage Association and the Federal Home Loan System; federal funds or bank excess reserves which are borrowed, usually for 1 day only, by banks faced with temporary reserve deficiency; and brokers' loans or loans made by banks to brokers and dealers for purchasing and carrying securities.

The money markets centered in New York and London are by far the largest markets as measured by volume of turnover, variety of instruments actively traded, and number of participants. Both are extremely efficient markets in which transaction costs are very low and relatively small price or yield changes bring forth a large volume of orders to buy or to sell. The wide range of money-market instruments with different risk-return characteristics facilitates quick and low-cost adjustment by lenders to changes in their liquid-asset preferences and by borrowers to changes in their short-term debt preferences.

References

Board of Governors, Federal Reserve System, *Federal Reserve Bulletin,* (published monthly; First Boston Corporation, *Handbook of Securities of the United States Government and Federal Agencies and Related Money Market Instruments,* 29th ed., New York, 1980; Joint Treasury-Federal Reserve Study of the U.S. Government Securities Market, *Report,* Board of Governors of the Federal Reserve System, 1969, *Staff Studies,* part 1, 1970, part 2, 1971, part 3, 1973; Polakoff, M., et al., *Financial Institutions and Markets,* 2d ed., Houghton Mifflin, Boston, 1980; Stigum, M. L., *The Money Market: Myth, Reality, and Practice,* Dow Jones–Irwin, Homewood, Ill., 1978.

(*See also* Capital markets and money markets; Federal Reserve System; Financial institutions; Financial instruments; Flow of funds; Interest rates)

Holger L. Engberg

Money supply

Money is essential to the operation of any economy, as a medium of exchange and as a store of value, or temporary abode of purchasing power. In primitive economies, some widely used and generally acceptable commodity, such as salt, tobacco, furs, feathers, shells, copper, iron, gold, or silver, emerged by common practice as a convenient medium of exchange, thus permitting greater specialization in production and trade than would have been possible in a pure barter system. In modern economies, money, or the money supply, is some combination of coin issued by governments, paper currency or notes issued by governments or banks, and bank deposits.

The crucial role of the money supply in the economy makes the following issues important to households, businesses, and government policymakers: (1) effects of changes in the money supply, such as price inflation, recessions, and fluctuations in interest rates and exchange rates; (2) monetary policy, or how money supply should be made to behave; (3) how the money supply is created and controlled; and (4) what should be included in the definition of the money supply used for monetary policy and as a variable in private and public economic forecasting. In 1980, ideas on all of these issues were changing rapidly because of new findings in monetary research, worldwide inflation and economic instability, and technological innovations in financial institutions and markets.

Effects of Changes in Money Supply

Experience and research in many countries since the mid-1960s have greatly increased emphasis on the role of changes in money supply in explanations of inflation and economic instability and in public policies designed to counter them. This increased emphasis on behavior of the money supply is, in part, a revival of a classical tradition in monetary theory that was widely accepted before the Great Depression caused it to be virtually eclipsed by the income-expenditure theory of John Maynard Keynes. New scientific tools, such as econometrics and computers, and the availability of greatly improved monetary and economic data have added many new elements in an emerging consensus on effects of money-supply changes.

There is a growing recognition that major long-run changes in inflation rates do not occur without major changes in growth rates of the money supply in the same direction. The great worldwide price explosion of 1974 to 1975 was preceded by very large increases in growth rates of the money supplies of all the major industrial countries extending over almost a decade. The reduction in inflation to much lower rates in all major industrial countries, including the United States, by 1976, was preceded by reductions in money-supply growth rates which began in 1973. This experience, and the subsequent reacceleration of inflation in the United States since 1976, powerfully influenced the thinking of economists and policymakers on the role of money in inflation. Although it is generally argued that real shocks, such as crop failures or restrictions on oil supplies, can increase inflation rates for periods of a year or more, the underlying trend rate of inflation is now attributed by many economists to the trend rate of growth of the money supply.

Sudden changes in the growth rate of the money supply are now believed by many economists to be a major cause of business fluctuations, perhaps the major cause. Although there is disagreement on the channels of transmission through which money-supply changes influence incomes, output, employment, and prices, both Keynesian and monetarist economists agree that a sudden, large reduction in the growth rate of the money supply of a country will result in reductions in the growth rates of total spending and real output, or a recession, within a year.

Recognition of the effects of money-supply changes on inflation and economic activity has greatly changed the general view of how money supply influences interest rates. Although Irving Fisher demonstrated as early as 1896 that inflation expectations were the principal determinant of changes in market interest rates (nominal rates), the more general view among economists and people in financial markets before the mid-1960s was that a government or central bank could reduce interest rates by increasing the money supply, or could raise interest rates by reducing the money supply. By 1980, however, economists and market practitioners alike agreed that the so-called liquidity effect of a change in money supply on interest rates is soon more than offset by effects of changes in income and inflation expectations in the opposite direction. The painful experience of investors with inflation since the mid-1960s has convinced them that an increase in the growth rate of the money supply will mean higher interest rates in the future, as Fisher would have predicted, not lower interest rates.

Experience and research since the mid-1960s have also demonstrated that the effects of money-supply changes are not restricted to the country in which they occur. When money-growth rates and inflation began to accelerate in the United States in the early 1960s, this country had increasing balance of payments deficits. Central banks and governments of other countries were obliged by the Bretton Woods Agreement to buy up dollars flowing out of the United States, in order to keep their exchange rates within agreed parity limits. By issuing more of their own currencies in exchange for dollars, these countries thus increased their domestic money supplies and, in effect, imported inflation from the United States.

Under the floating rate system which replaced the Bretton Woods adjustable-parity system in 1973, international effects of changes in growth rates of money supply appear principally, but not entirely, in exchange rate changes. When a country such as the United States increases the rate of growth of its money supply in relation to rates of growth of money supplies of other countries, the exchange rate of its currency in terms of the other currencies will tend to fall, in response to actual or expected exchanges in relative inflation rates. The resulting changes in exchange rates impose internal adjustment costs on the other countries, by changing the relative prices and rates of production of domestic and internationally traded goods and services. These costs can be substantial in countries such as Germany, Japan, and Switzerland, in which a large part of gross national product enters into international trade. Therefore, money-supply changes originating in a large country transmit inflationary or recessionary impulses to other countries through a fixed-exchange rate system, or impose other significant costs through changing exchange rates in a floating rate system.

Monetary Policy

The question of whether or not growth of the money supply should be governed by rules or by monetary authorities exercising discretionary powers has been debated probably since it was first discovered that money does not manage itself. Use of a commodity standard such as the gold standard to determine the money supply automatically was finally discontinued in the 1960s and probably will never by resumed. An alternative procedure would be to make a government-controlled money behave as though it were a commodity-based money, that is, to grow at a steady rate. That idea has been advocated for years by Clark Warburton, Milton Friedman, and others as the most effective way to achieve a reasonable degree of stability in economic activity and the price level.

Discretionary use of money-supply changes to offset changes in inflation rates, and thus to combat business cycles, was advocated by Irving Fisher and other monetary economists before the Great Depression. After the rise of income-expenditure theories in the 1930s, changes in growth rates of the money supply were not believed to have more than minor, slow effects on economic activity. However, policymakers after World War II attempted to supplement fiscal policies with changes in money-supply growth rates as contracyclical instruments and in pursuit of full employment. These policies proved to have an inflationary bias.

By 1980, recognition of the disturbing and often perverse effects of discretionary changes in growth rates of the money supply on economic activity, inflation rates, interest rates, and exchange rates was leading more economists and even some policymakers to advocate reducing the variability of money-supply growth rates. Although no monetary authority in the world has specifically renounced its discretionary powers over rates of monetary expansion, some have begun to behave almost as though they had, by announcing target money growth rates in advance.

The new theories of rational expectations, which were developed in the 1970s, have provided an impressive rationale for the use of a steady-money growth rule rather than discretionary changes in money growth rates. Economists of this school argue that workers and managers of business firms learn to anticipate changes in fiscal and monetary policies. If they beieve, for example, that a restrictive monetary policy intended to combat inflation will be followed by an expansionary policy, they will not reduce rates of increase in wages and prices. This explains the persistence of high inflation rates during recessions that developed after the mid-1960s.

Control of the Money Supply

With recognition of the importance of money-supply changes has come increasing interest in how money supply is created and how it should be controlled. It is now generally recognized that the money supply is jointly determined by decisions by the government or central bank, commercial banks, and the public. The government and central bank control the supply of monetary base, or high-powered money, which consists of paper currency and coin issued by the government and liabilities of the central bank to commercial banks. The money supply held by the public is some multiple of the monetary base so that an increase in the monetary base provided by the government and the central bank will cause the money supply to increase by more than the increase in the base. In early 1980, in the United States, for example, a $1 increase in monetary base would result in an increase of about $2.40 in narrowly defined money supply, M-1A (demand deposits and currency).

The multiplier determining the size of the money supply per unit of monetary base is not constant. Decisions of the banks regarding the quantity of reserves they want to hold in the form of currency or in deposits at the central bank, in relation to their deposits, and decisions of the public regarding the shares of their money holdings they want to keep in currency and in bank deposits change the multiplier and, thus, change the quantity of money supply associated with any given quantity of monetary base. Although such a change in the multiplier can produce unanticipated changes in the money supply over short periods, a substantial body of research indicates that these changes can be predicted well enough to be offset by changes in the monetary base so that the monetary authorities should be able to keep growth of the money supply within a tolerable range of error around a desired growth path, if they decide to try.

In actual practice, until the early 1970s, growth of the money supply in most countries was essentially an incidental result of central bank actions in pursuit of other objectives, such as to stabilize interest rates or foreign exchange rates, or to facilitate the financing of government budget deficits. By 1980, however, the central banks and governments of many countries, including the United States, the United Kingdom, West Germany, Italy, Japan, Spain, and Switzerland, were attempting to achieve more precise control over their money supplies through reducing emphasis on operations designed to stabilize interest rates or exchange rates and increasing emphasis on direct control of the monetary base or other monetary aggregates. On October 6, 1979, for example, the Federal Reserve System of the United States announced that it had changed open-market operating procedures to place more emphasis on controlling bank reserves directly in order to provide more assurance of attaining basic money-supply objectives.

How Money Supply Should Be Defined

The final issue of concern in considering the nature and behavior of the money supply is the one of how money should be defined and measured for conducting monetary policy and for analytical purposes. Interest in this problem has increased greatly in recent years as innovations in financial markets and in governmental regulation of financial institutions have increased the number and variety of financial assets available to households and business firms for possible use as money or substitutes for money. Some economists fear that failure to make adequate allowance for new forms of money or money substitutes in conventional measures of the money supply could impair the effectiveness of monetary policy. The U.S. Federal Reserve System responded to this concern in early 1980 with a comprehensive redefinition of the monetary aggregates it publishes.

The lack of any general agreement among economists and policymakers on criteria for deciding what should be included in the money supply makes the problem of defining and measuring the money supply difficult. At one extreme are those economists who emphasize the transactions function of money. They generally prefer a narrow definition which includes currency in the hands of the public and those deposits at banks that are actively used for carrying out transactions. Disagreements within this group generally concern questions of whether or not a particular liability of a bank or other financial institution is used in transactions. The Federal Reserve's new definitions have added certain balances at nonbank financial intermediaries, such as savings institutions and credit unions, to their earlier definitions, which had confined demand-deposit money to deposits at commercial banks.

At the other extreme are those economists who emphasize liquidity, or the ease with which a particular financial asset can be converted into something which can be used for making payments. They prefer a broader definition which includes time deposits at a wide variety of financial institutions, shares in money-market mutual funds, and other financial assets. They are afraid that the supplies of some of these items might increase when the monetary authorities are restricting growth of more narrowly defined aggregates and, thus, might frustrate achievement of the policy objectives.

Another criterion on which economists and policymakers differ is the closeness of the relationship between a particular monetary aggregate and the ultimate objectives of policy, such as national income and prices. Economists who emphasize this criterion would not rely on a priori characteristics of money in deciding on a definition of money. They would instead use empirical testing of the various proposed measures to find the ones which would yield the most reliable predictions of incomes and prices when used as a policy instrument or forecasting tool.

The degree of controllability by the central bank or government is another major issue in the selection of a money-supply definition. Some economists argue that the proper monetary aggregate for policy purposes would be the one that can be most reliably predicted from changes in variables under direct central bank control, such as a central bank's own portfolio of assets or monetary base. They would settle the issue by empirical testing. This would permit the monetary authorities to set monetary policy targets in terms of variables over which they have the greatest degree of control.

Conclusions

The disagreements among economists and policymakers regarding effects of money-supply changes, monetary policy, how the money supply should be controlled, and the proper definition of the money supply should not be viewed as evidence that efforts to control the money supply are futile. The money supply is too important to be left uncontrolled. The debates are instead essential contributions to improvement in society's prospects for controlling inflation and achieving stability in international exchange rates and higher long-run rates of growth in real income and employment.

References

Bank of England, "Monetary Base Control," *Bank of England Quarterly Bulletin*, vol. 19, no. 2, June 1979, pp. 149–159; Board of Governors, Federal Reserve System, "A Proposal for Redefining the Monetary Aggregates," *Federal Reserve Bulletin*, January 1979, pp. 13–42; Board of Governors, Federal Reserve System, "The New Federal Reserve Technical Procedures for Controlling Money," January 30, 1980; Burger, Albert E., *The Money Supply Process*, Wadsworth, Belmont, Calif., 1971; Cagan, Phillip, "Financial Developments and the Erosion of Monetary Controls," in William Fellner (ed.), *Contemporary Economic Problems 1979*, American Enterprise Institute for Public Policy Research, Washington, D.C., 1979, pp. 151–177; Federal Reserve Bank of Minneapolis, "Rational Expectations—Fresh Ideas That Challenge Some Established Views on Policy Making," *1977 Annual Report*, Minneapolis, pp. 1–13; Friedman, Milton, and Rose Friedman, *Free to Choose*, Harcourt Brace Jovanovich, New York, 1980, chap. 9, pp. 248–283; Friedman, Milton, and Anna J. Schwartz, *Monetary Statistics of the United States: Estimates, Sources, Methods*, National Bureau of Economic Research, Columbia University Press, New York, 1970, part 1, pp. 89–197; Johnson, Harry G., *Essays in Monetary Economics*, 2d ed., Allen and Unwin, London, 1969; Poole, William, *Money and the Economy: A Monetarist View*, Addison-Wesley, Reading, Mass., 1978; Tatom, John A., "Money Stock Control Under Alternative Definitions of Money," *Review*, Federal Reserve Bank of St. Louis, St. Louis, November 1979, pp. 3–9; Warburton, Clark, "Rules and Implements for Monetary Policy," *Journal of Finance*, vol. 8, no. 1, March 1953, pp. 1–21.

(*See also* Bank deposits; Bretton Woods Conference; Federal Reserve policy; Federal Reserve System; Foreign exchange rates; Inflation; Interest rates; Monetary policy; Open-market operations; Smithsonian Agreement)

A. James Meigs

Monopoly and oligopoly

Monopoly is a market structure with only a single seller of a commodity or service dealing with a large number of buyers. When a single seller faces a single buyer, that situation is known as bilateral monopoly.

The most important features of market structure are those which influence the nature of competition and price determination. The key element in this segment of market organization is the degree of seller concentration, or the number and size distributions of the sellers. There is monopoly when there is only one seller in an industry, and there is competition when there are many sellers in an industry. In cases of an intermediate number of sellers, that is, something between monopoly and competition, there can be two sellers (duopoly), a few sellers (oligopoly), or many sellers (atomistic competition). The sellers may be relatively equal in size or unequal, with a few large firms and many small firms.

Monopoly versus Competition

Pure monopoly is a theoretical market structure where there is only one seller of a commodity or service, where entry into the industry is closed to potential competitors, and where the seller has complete control over the quantity of goods offered for sale and the price at which goods are sold. Pure monopoly is one of two limiting cases used in the analysis of market structure. The other is pure competition, a situation in which there are many sellers who can influence neither the total quantity of a commodity or service offered for sale nor its selling price. Hence, monopoly is the exact antithesis of competition. It is generally agreed that neither of these two limiting cases is to be found among existing market structures.

The monopolist establishes market position by ability to control absolutely the supply of a product or service offered for sale and the related ability to set price. Theoretically, profit maximization is the primary objective, and it is often possible to achieve this by restricting output and the quantity of goods offered for sale. Levels of output are held below the quantity that would be produced in a competitive situation. Hence, monopoly is of interest to economic policymakers because it may impede the most efficient possible allocation of a nation's economic resources.

Monopolies held by individuals or organizations may begin by the granting of a patent or a copyright, by the possession of a superior skill or talent, or by the ownership of strategic capital. The huge capital investment necessary to organize a firm in some industries raises an almost insurmountable barrier to entry in these monopolistic fields and, thus, provides established corporations in these industries with potential monopoly power.

The use of such monopoly power may lead to the development of substitute products, to an attempt at entry into monopolistic fields by new firms (if profits are high enough), or to public prosecution or regulation. The antitrust policy of the federal government has prevented the domination of an industry by one firm or even a few firms. Thus, the trend during the last half-century or so in the United States has been away from monopolies in many basic industries and toward oligopolies.

Oligopolies

An oligopoly exists when a few sellers of a commodity or service deal with a large number of buyers. When a few sellers face a few buyers, that situation is known as bilateral oligopoly. In the case of oligopoly a small number of companies supplies the major portion of an industry's output. In effect the industry is composed of a few large firms which account for a significant share of the total production. Thus, the action of the individual firms have an appreciable effect on their competitors.

However, it does not follow as a consequence of the presence of relatively few firms in an industry that competition is absent. Although there are few firms in an industry, they may still act independently and the outcome of their actions is consistent with competition. With few firms in an industry, each takes into account the likely repercussions of its actions. For example, each seller knows that if he or she lowers prices, the few competitors will immediately follow suit and lower their prices, leaving the seller with roughly the same share of the total market but lower profits. On the other hand, the seller may be reluctant to raise prices because competitors might not follow this lead. One feature of markets with few sellers is that prices are often stable, except during periods of very rapid inflation. Also, prices of oligopolistic industries generally fluctuate less widely than in more competitive industries.

Other Monopolies

Aside from private monopolies, there are public monopolies. One example of a public monopoly in the United States is the nonprofit postal service. There are also the "natural" monopolies, like public utilities, whose prices are regulated by government agencies.

Although the precise definition of monopoly—a market structure with only a single seller of a commodity or service—cannot be applied directly to a labor union because a union is not a seller of services, labor unions have monopolistic characteristics. For example, when a union concludes a wage settlement which sets wage rates at a level higher than that acceptable to unorganized workers, the union clearly contributes to monopolistic wage results. In effect, the price of labor (wages) is set without regard to the available supply of labor.

References

Edwards, Corwin D., *Maintaining Competition*, McGraw-Hill, New York, 1949; Hamburg, Daniel, *Principles of a Growing Economy*, Norton, New York, 1961, pp. 518–557; Kahn, Alfred, E., *The Economics of Legislation: Principles and Institutions*, Wiley, New York, 1970–1971; Robinson, Joan, *Economics of Imperfect Competition*, St. Martin's, London, 1969.

(*See also* Competition; Monopsony and oligopsony; Price theory)

Edward G. Mayers

Monopsony and oligopsony

Monopsony is a market structure with only a single buyer of a commodity or service dealing with a large number of sellers. In order to distinguish between monopolistic buying conditions and monopolistic selling conditions economists call the former monopsony.

The most important characteristics of market structure are those which influence the nature of competition and price determination. The key element in this segment of market organization is the degree of buyer concentration, or the number and size distribution of the buyers. There is monopsony when there is only one buyer of a product and competition when many firms buy a commodity or service. Most monopsonistic buyers are faced with some degree of competition for the available supply of a product. Duopsony is when there are only two buyers facing a large number of sellers. Oligopsony is when there are a few buyers facing a large number of sellers. The buyers may be relatively equal in size or unequal, with a few large firms and many small ones.

Monopsony implies the existence of a single buyer or a group of colluding buyers for a particular product or service where the sellers of that product have absolutely no other customers. Thus, the buyer has absolute control over the price of the product. The price is established by the buyer's bid.

In the case of a monopsonist who is also a monopolist, both buying price and the quantity bought are lower than they would be in a competitive situation.

Monopsonistic elements can arise in the market for a homogeneous product in which a large number of competitive sellers offer their goods for sale to a few large buyers. Thus, no seller can influence prices, but the price may be determined by the monopsonistic buyer.

Monopsony power—the individual buyer's ability to influence the purchase price of a commodity or service by controlling the quantity bought—is as incompatible with perfect competition as is monopoly power. Perfect competition is a situation where the number of competing buyers and sellers is so numerous that no one of them can affect the market—influence either the price of the item bought or the item sold—but all of them are governed by forces stemming from the market itself.

Monopsony is rare, but it occurs, for example, in the demand for labor in a company town. A single textile mill in a small southern town may be a monopsonist in the buying of its labor, but when it comes to the buying of cotton, one of its raw materials, it competes against all the hundreds of cotton textile manufacturers throughout the nation.

Oligopsony

Oligopsony exists when a few buyers of a commodity or service deal with a large number of sellers. When a few buyers face a few sellers, that situation is known as bilateral oligopsony.

The high degree of buyer concentration results in a significant amount of interdependence among the few buyers since the purchasing patterns of any one firm can affect all the others.

An oligopsonistic situation can lead to tacit collusion among the buyers to depress their buying prices generally at the expense of the sellers who supply them. It is also possible for a single large buyer, even without collusion, to exercise strong buying power in order to negotiate lower prices.

The main grounds for the notion that collusion is more likely when there are a small number of firms in the industry is Adam Smith's contention that it is easier for a few than for many to agree on a common purpose. But numbers alone do not settle this issue. Other considerations, such as similarity in the interests of the firms, stability of the underlying supply and demand conditions, and the cost of policing and enforcing collusion, are important.

An oligopsonistic market may face either an atomistic competitive market or one with a significant degree of seller concentration. Markets for leaf tobacco, fluid milk, and crude petroleum are examples of concentrated buying from a large number of small sellers, while markets for sheet steel, rails, and primary copper represent cases of concentrated buying from a concentration of sellers.

References

Edwards, Corwin D., *Maintaining Competition*, McGraw-Hill, New York, 1949; Hamburg, Daniel, *Principles of a Growing Economy*, Norton, New York, 1961, pp. 543-551.

(*See also* Competition; Monopoly and oligopoly)

Edward G. Mayers

Mortgage credit

Debt financing of real estate activity represents the single most important type of credit transaction in the nation's financial system. At the heart of the real estate financing process is the mortgage loan. This instrument links lender and borrower in a contract which typically provides for (1) designation of the property as security for payment of the loan; (2) a specified payment schedule and interest rate; (3) the term over which loan payments are to be made by the borrower; (4) penalties, if any, for partial and full prepayment of the loan; and (5) the circumstances under which the borrower fails to satisfy the contractual obligations of the mortgage loan, and is subject to loss of the property.

Home Mortgages

Financing the purchase of a home represents the most significant use of mortgage credit. As of June 30, 1979, home mortgage debt totaled $800 billion or nearly two-thirds of the total amount of mortgage loans outstanding in the United States. The dominant type of home mortgage is a level-payment, fixed-interest rate instrument, that is, the interest rate is unchanged and identical, and periodic payments are made over the entire term of the loan. Each mortgage payment is distributed between interest and reduction of the outstanding debt. Over the life of the loan, the interest portion of the mortgage payment declines while the share going into principal rises. The rate at which these proportions change depends upon the interest rate and maturity of the mortgage.

In recent years, progress has been achieved in developing alternatives to this type of mortgage instrument. Such efforts have emerged in response to the high-interest rate, inflationary periods of the 1960s and 1970s, which have widened fluctuations in the supply of, and reduced borrower access to, home mortgage credit.

Three types of alternative mortgage investments have attracted growing attention from lenders and borrowers alike: (1) variable-rate mortgages (VRMs); (2) graduated-payment mortgages (GPMs); and (3) reverse-annuity mortgages (RAMs). So far, variable-rate loans have exerted the most significant impact on mortgage markets, although overall activity is still far below the volume of level-payment, fixed-rate mortgage lending. VRMs provide for periodic adjustments in the interest rate, according to changes in a specified financial market indicator or lender cost of funds measure. Until recently, statutory and regulatory restrictions have limited VRM lending to relatively few areas, mainly in California and the New England states. However, effective July 1, 1979, federal savings and loan associations received authorization to offer variable-rate mortgages on a nationwide basis, a development which can be expected to enhance the future role of these instruments in real estate markets.

The graduated-payment mortgage carries a fixed rate and maturity, with monthly payments starting lower in the early years of the loan and subsequently increasing to higher levels. The development of the GPM has reflected the growing needs of moderate- and middle-income borrowers with rising income potential, who have found themselves unable to afford the higher initial payment schedules of level-payment mortgages. Efforts to stimulate acceptance of this type of mortgage were initiated by the federal government through the Department of Housing and Urban Development's insured GPM program. Under this program, qualified borrowers can choose from five alternative graduated-payment schedules which provide for beginning monthly payments ranging from 9 to 25 percent below payments on level-payment loans.

Reverse-annuity mortgages, the third major type of alternative mortgage instrument considered potentially significant, has yet to make measurable inroads in real estate finance markets. The basic objective of the RAM is to enable elderly home-owners to utilize the equity built up in their homes without having to dispose of their properties. This is achieved by taking out a loan secured by a portion of the under-lying property value, the proceeds of which are used to purchase one or more annuity contracts. Because of their complexity, and numerous accounting, legal, tax, and reg-ulatory problems, widespread adoption of the reverse-annuity mortgage appears to be some years away. Nonetheless, the concept is considered a highly promising approach in the continuing search for more flexible mortgage instruments.

Income Property Mortgages

In addition to financing the purchase and construction of homes, large amounts of mortgage credit are also provided for the construction of apartments and a wide variety of commercial and agricultural facilities. By mid-1979, one-tenth of total mort-gage debt outstanding was secured by residential structures with more than four dwelling units, 18 percent by commercial properties, and 7 percent by farms.

The extension of mortgage credit on apartment and business properties differs in a number of fundamental ways from the financing of owner-occupied homes. Financing arrangements are significantly more complex and varied because of (1) the lengthy period of time required for planning and construction; (2) the large number of firms and individuals involved in the mortgage financing negotiations; (3) the lender's need to analyze extensively the borrower's present and future financial capacity to develop and manage the property successfully; and (4) the lack of a highly developed secondary market for income property mortgages which are highly differ-entiated as to loan, property, and borrower characteristics.

Sources of Mortgage Financing

In their efforts to obtain mortgage credit, borrowers have access to several kinds of lenders: (1) savings and loan associations; (2) mutual savings banks; (3) commercial banks; (4) life insurance companies; (5) federal governmental entities; and (6) indi-viduals, mortgage companies, and a miscellaneous group of sources largely consisting of real estate investment trusts, pension funds, and credit unions. About 72 percent of all mortgage credit in one form or another is held by savings institutions, commer-cial banks, and life insurance companies.

All types of real estate credit are generally available from these sources. However, their relative significance in specific mortgage-market sectors varies considerably owing to differences in geographic location, statutory and regulatory limitations, and management investment policies. The two major types of thrift institutions—mutual savings banks and savings and loan associations—devote the dominant share of their mortgage funds to loans secured by residential properties. More than four-fifths of their mortgage portfolios are accounted for by one- to four-family and multifamily loans, with virtually the entire remainder in commercial, industrial, and other kinds of nonresidential loans. Commercial banks and life insurance companies, on the other hand, have historically placed greater investment emphasis on nonresidential and farm mortgages. About two-thirds of life insurance company and two-fifths of commercial bank holdings are in these mortgage categories.

Governmental Influence on Mortgage Credit

While the actual financing of real estate transactions in the United States is dominated by private financial institutions, the pattern and volume of mortgage-market activity has been profoundly influenced by governmental authorities. The federal government, in particular, has played a major role in the mortgage-credit process through the exercise of a wide variety of supervisory, insurance, tax, monetary, and debt-management policy functions.

One of the most important examples of this influence are federal mortgage insurance programs. Two major federal agencies, in particular, the Federal Housing Administration (FHA) and Veterans Administration (VA), offer lending institutions protection against financial loss on specified types of mortgage loans, largely on residential structures. These insurance programs helped to revolutionize real estate financing arrangements following their establishment in the wake of the Great Depression of the 1930s and World War II by (1) reducing lender risk; (2) helping to upgrade housing standards and conditions; and (3) facilitating lender use of low-down-payment, long-term fixed-payment mortgages and improved underwriting procedures. The result has been an increased and broadened supply of residential mortgage credit available to borrowers.

FHA-VA programs have also provided a significant impetus to the development of a secondary mortgage market. Largely because of their standardized characteristics, federally underwritten mortgages began to be traded on a national basis. Such a development represented a breakthrough in efforts to reduce the illiquidity of mortgage loans—a major reason many investors avoided mortgage loans in favor of more readily marketable securities investments.

In the late 1970s, insurance of new home mortgages by FHA decreased drastically, partly in response to a combination of strong competition from private mortgage insurance companies, growing administrative problems in FHA, and increased FHA emphasis on special assistance programs designed to provide adequate housing for low-income groups. On the other hand, the existence of federally underwritten mortgages has led to creation of the highly successful GNMA—a marketable, mortgage-related security collateralized by pools of FHA and VA mortgages and guaranteed as to timely payment of principal and interest by the Government National Mortgage Association, a federal mortgage agency.

Moreover, conventional mortgage-backed securities have also begun to proliferate—a development which, along with the introduction of GNMAs, promises to strengthen the nation's mortgage finance structure further. Three other federally related mortgage agencies of particular significance are the Federal National Mortgage Association, the Federal Home Loan Mortgage Corporation and the Federal Home Loan Bank Board. These agencies have been instrumental in standardizing many conventional mortgage provisions and stimulating the growth of private mortgage insurance companies, resulting in a rapidly expanded volume of trading in conventional mortgages.

The general availability of mortgage funds has fluctuated widely in response to changes in Federal Reserve credit policy—shifts which have generally reflected efforts to maintain noninflationary economic growth. During periods of restrictive credit policy, rising mortgage rates and drastically reduced supplies of residential mortgage credit—especially from thrift institutions who were subject until the late 1970s to fixed ceiling rates on all types of savings and time deposits—typically culminated in sharply reduced housing transactions. When a policy of credit ease was pursued, mortgage credit became readily available, sometimes too much so, fueling strong and occasionally unhealthy expansions in residential building activity.

Since mid-1978, the destabilizing effects of federal monetary actions on housing have been blunted by the introduction of more interest rate-sensitive deposits at mortgage lending institutions. Dominating this trend has been the 6-month money-market certificates of deposit—short-term time-deposit instruments whose rates fluctuate with short-term Treasury bill yields. This has enabled financial institutions to compete for individuals' funds and initially maintain mortgage lending during periods of high interest rates. The longer-run impact of these new short-term accounts, however, remains uncertain because their high cost has also intensified earnings pressures at thrift institutions and has helped increase mortgage interest rates to record highs.

References

Klaman, Saul B., *The Postwar Residential Mortgage Market*, Princeton University Press, Princeton, N.J., 1961.

(*See also* Business credit; Consumer credit; Credit, an overview; Housing economics; Real estate investment trusts; Selective credit controls; Thrift institutions)

Saul B. Klaman and Jack Rubinson

Multinational corporation

The definition of a multinational corporation (MNC), or, alternatively, multinational enterprise or transnational corporation, is subject to some debate (Aharoni, 1971). Some consensus seems to exist that a multinational is a firm which exercises managerial control over operations in more than one national market. Exactly what constitutes managerial control, however, is an issue over which there also is debate, involving political and legal as well as economic issues. There would be little argument that a corporation headquartered in one nation holds managerial control over foreign branch operations or majority or wholly owned subsidiaries. It is, however, argued that effective managerial control can be exercised by the corporation over subsidiaries in which it has but a minority interest, or even over foreign firms in which it holds no equity but operates via a management contract or some other contractual device.

If one assumes that the issue of managerial control can be resolved, the above definition of a multinational corporation would include any firm which controlled operation in a nation other than that which constituted the firm's principal market, even if these operations were very small relative to its domestic operations. Most scholars, however, consider a multinational corporation to be a large firm for which nondomestic operations account for some significant portion of total firm revenues. In a study published in 1971, for example, Raymond Vernon used multiple criteria to distinguish between the multinational and nonmultinational of the 500 largest U.S.

industrial firms. Of these firms 187 were deemed to be multinational on the basis of the criteria, and these had substantially greater average sales and numbers of employees than the nonmultinational remainder. A number of studies have suggested that the worldwide total of firms which are multinational by criteria such as those used by Vernon is on the order of 400 to 500 (United Nations, 1978).

Economic and Political Consequences

A question which has sparked heated debate is: What are the economic and political consequences of the existence of multinational corporations? Serious proponents can be found for any number of points of view on this question. For example, those who speak for developing nations—those which belong to the so-called group of 77—have espoused the common view that the presence of subsidiaries of multinational firms in their domestic markets can have insidious effects on local economies. [A review of the arguments is contained in Sauvant and Hasenpflug (1977) and in Hellman (1977).] The group of 77 seeks the creation of a mandatory code of conduct for multinational firms which would prohibit these firms from engaging in specific practices believed to be injurious to developing nations' economies.

Proponents can also be found of the view that multinational corporations act against the interests of home nations (those nations in which the firms are headquartered). [For a review of the major arguments, see Gilpin (1974) and Musgrave (1975).] These proponents include many leaders of the organized labor union movement in the United States, who have pressed for legislation to restrict the international activities of U.S.-based firms. Trade union leaders argue that overseas activities of multinational firms serve to transfer technology and increase profits of these firms at the expense of job opportunities and income for American labor. [The views of U.S. labor are summarized in Goldfinger (1974).]

The view also exists that the multinational corporation serves to generate net economic benefits for home and host nation alike. The benefits derive from these corporations' abilities to transfer resources quickly across international boundaries, including tangible resources such as physical and financial capital and intangible ones such as technology and managerial expertise. This view, which is analogous to the neoclassical gains-from-trade argument, is probably held by a majority of economists who subscribe to neoclassical views. Such economists would note, however, that as is the case with the gains from trade, the benefits from MNC activities may not be evenly distributed throughout society, and, indeed, some elements of society may suffer net reductions in welfare as a consequence of these activities (Weston, Wells, et al. (1977).

References

Aharoni, Yair, "On the Definition of Multinational Corporations," *Quarterly Review of Economics and Business*, vol. 11, no. 3, Autumn 1971, pp. 27–38; Gilpin, Robert, *U.S. Power and the Multinational Corporation*, Basic Books, New York, 1974; Goldfinger, Nathan, "A Labor View of Foreign Investment and Trade Issues," in R. E. Baldwin and J. D. Richardson (eds.), *International Trade and Finance*, Little, Brown, Boston, 1974; Hellman, Ranier, *Transnational Control of Multinational Corporations*, Praeger, New York, 1977; Musgrave, Peggy B., *Direct Investment Abroad and the Multinationals: Effects on the United States Economy*, U.S. Senate Subcommittee on Foreign Relations, 1975; Sauvant, K. P., and H. Hasenpflug (eds.), *The New International Economic Order: Confrontation or Cooperation between North and South*, Westview, Boulder, Colo., 1977; United Nations Economic and Social Council, Commission on Transnational Corporations, *Transnational Corporations in World Development: A Re-exami-*

nation, New York, 1978; Vernon, Raymond, *Sovereignty at Bay*, Basic Books, New York, 1971; Weston, J. F., L. T. Wells, R. G. Hawkins, T. Horst, R. Vernon, and R. N. Cooper, *The Case for Multinational Corporations*, Praeger, New York, 1977.

(*See also* Foreign direct investment; Integration)

Edward M. Graham

Multiplier

The multiplier deals with the magnified impact, or chain reaction, on income of increases in public spending or private capital investment. R. F. Kahn (1931) pointed out, in his pioneering study, that the case for public works as a recovery measure usually includes reference to the "beneficial repercussions that will result from the expenditure of the newly-employed men's wages." The nature and extent of these repercussions had not, however, been analyzed at that time.

The Multiplier in Practice

Kahn showed that the successive spendings would most likely form a converging series and that the size of the ultimate expansion would depend on the leakages which occur at each round of spending. If, for example, people spend two-thirds of any addition to their incomes on home-produced consumer goods—the rest being saved or otherwise immobilized the total increase in income from an additional x dollars spent on public works would be

$$x + \tfrac{2}{3}x = \tfrac{2}{3} \cdot \tfrac{2}{3}x \cdot \cdots$$

This is, of course, a geometric series the sum of which is $x/(1 - \tfrac{2}{3})$.

J. M. Clark (1934) realized independently that the successive spendings out of an increase in income would form a converging series with a finite sum, but he did not develop this insight into a full-fledged theory of the multiplier. J. M. Keynes, on the other hand, employed the multiplier as a key element in his *General Theory*.

Three Offsets to the Multiplier

For the multiplier to take effect the initial increase in spending must be net. There are three possible types of offset to increased public works (or other) spending. First, if the government raises taxes, the increased spending of those employed on the public works will be offset, to a greater or lesser extent, by the decreased spending of the taxpayers. The amount of the offset, Kahn noted, "would depend on the extent to which the increased taxes are paid at the expense of consumption rather than of saving." Later development of this point led to the balanced-budget multiplier theorem in accordance with which an equal increase in spending and in taxes will increase income by exactly the amount of the increased spending. This holds only if the tax increase is designed in such a way as to yield an amount of additional revenue at the new higher level of income equal to the increased government expenditure. Otherwise, the multiplier will not be equal to 1.

If, instead of raising taxes, the government borrows the money, there may be an unfavorable impact on private investment. As incomes expand, consumers and business concerns will normally want to increase their money holdings. Unless the economy is in a state of extreme liquidity, this will raise interest rates, thus crowding out some private investment. The banking system can obviate this danger by increasing the money supply by the appropriate amount. It should be noted that even in a continuing program of government spending and borrowing the quantity of money would not go on increasing indefinitely. Once the demand for increased money holdings created by the higher level of income had been satisfied, the government could finance its spending by borrowing the increased saving generated by the larger income without exerting upward pressure on interest rates.

The third type of offset is less direct. Specific businesses might find their interests adversely affected or business in general might suffer a loss of confidence. Repercussions of either type might be favorable as well as unfavorable.

Impact on Money versus Real Income

Finally, the multiplier might operate to increase money income but not, or not to the same extent, real income. What happens will depend on the elasticity of supply and the behavior of wages as employment increases. In the 1930s discussion of the multiplier was usually based on the assumption that the large amount of unemployment and excess capacity would ensure an elastic supply and that unemployed workers would be willing to accept jobs at constant or slightly reduced real wages.

References

Ackley, Gardner, *Macroeconomics: Theory and Policy*, Macmillan, New York, 1978; Clark, J. M., *Strategic Factors in Business Cycles*, National Bureau of Economic Research, New York, 1934; Kahn, R. F., "The Relation of Home Investment to Unemployment," *Economic Journal*, vol. 41, June 1931, pp. 173–198; Keynes, J. M., *The General Theory of Money, Interest and Employment*, Harcourt Brace Jovanovich, New York, 1936.

(*See also* Keynesian economics; Propensity to consume or to save and inducement to invest)

Alan Sweezy

Mutual funds

A mutual fund is one type of a broad set of savings vehicles known as investment companies. The business of these companies is to invest in securities such as stocks, bonds, and short-term money instruments.

A mutual fund is an open-end investment company, which means that investors who want to own shares in it buy those shares directly from the company, thereby adding to its assets, while those investors who no longer want to participate may redeem their shares from the company, thereby withdrawing assets. (Some investment companies, known as closed-end companies, do not continuously offer new shares or redeem shares when stockholders no longer want to own them; they trade in the equity market, as the shares of any corporation are traded.) All new shares are purchased, and old shares are redeemed at the fund's net asset value per share on the date of the transaction. The net asset value per share is the difference between the total assets and any liabilities owing, divided by the number of shares outstanding. Many funds, in addition, add a sales charge or load to the purchase price, most of which goes to the salesperson. A few funds also make a small charge when shares are redeemed.

Size and History

Investment companies originated in Europe during the nineteenth century and were well-established in the United States by 1900. By 1955, about 2 million investors were participating in some 125 funds with total assets of $8 billion. From 1960 to 1970, however, the number of funds grew from 160 to 360, the number of shareholders surged from 5 to nearly 11 million, and assets expanded from $17 to nearly $50 billion. More than 6 percent of the total market value of shares listed on the New York Stock Exchange in 1970 was held by mutual funds, up from less than 2 percent 20 years earlier.

After 1970, and more particularly after 1973, growth slowed and then went into reverse. By 1978, the number of shareholders had shrunk to about 8 million, and assets to about $45 billion. Net redemptions of equity mutual funds were virtually continuous after 1972 and drained more than $6 billion from their assets during 1973 to 1978.

The industry has, however, been innovative in developing new vehicles to attract the savings of investors. Bond funds became increasingly popular after 1970, but the big new feature since 1973 has been the money-market funds that enable small investors to participate in the market for short-term financial instruments that are denied to them on their own by minimum-size limitations set by government regulators or by excessively high transaction costs. By mid-1979, some $30 billion was committed to money-market funds.

Advantages and Disadvantages

Since investment companies pool the savings of a large number of investors, they provide each investor with an opportunity to share the advantages that accrue to all large investors: broad diversification and economies of scale that bring down the cost of professional management of the assets, transaction costs, and custodian fees. An individual with even as much as $1 million to invest would find it expensive and difficult to duplicate all of these advantages. Furthermore, government regulations protect the investor through full disclosure of fund assets, performance records, management personnel, investment objectives, and operating costs, as well as providing for outside directors to select and supervise the professional management group. Tax regulations for mutual funds make all dividends, interest, and capital gains tax-free to the fund so long as they are substantially distributed directly to shareholders.

Mutual funds have been designed to serve both broad and highly specialized objectives. While some funds aim to protect capital or to provide a total portfolio for their shareholders, most purport to achieve narrower objectives, such as growth, income, or aggressive high-risk investing. Some concentrate in discrete areas of the capital markets such as bonds, convertible securities, options, money-market instruments, or foreign stock markets, or in common stocks of companies in special fields such as energy, raw materials, or new technology.

The mutual fund industry has been criticized on two interrelated counts: (1) Since the fee paid the managers is directly related to the size of the assets in the fund, this may lead to investment practices that may be adverse to the best interest of the stockholder; and (2) the performance record does not justify the costs paid by the stockholder in management fees and brokerage commissions.

The open-end feature does indeed raise some questions about conflicts of interest between the investment adviser and the stockholder. For example, in order to sustain sales of new shares at the highest possible level, will the managers strive for short-term performance and take high risks to achieve a spectacular track record under conditions where the stockholder may be more interested in long-term and less-aggressive investment strategies? Will the managers execute more transactions than are necessary in order to encourage or repay brokers who recommend their shares? Will the aggressive sale of new shares result in unmanageably rapid growth in assets under management or make the fund so large that it can no longer achieve its original objectives? Are some funds so big that they are excessively diversified and, therefore, destined for nothing better than average performance? On the other hand, when stockholders are redeeming more old shares than buying new, will the performance of the fund be blunted by the necessity to carry extra cash reserves to meet these net redemptions?

In addition, careful studies have raised serious questions about the ability of most equity mutual funds to provide better performance than an investor could achieve simply by selecting the portfolio at random or by investing in a fund that precisely duplicates a leading market index such as the Standard & Poor's 500 stock index or the Dow Jones industrial average. While some funds have turned in sparkling performances for limited periods of time, they have done so only by taking large risks that should, indeed, have produced larger-than-average returns. A few funds have shown good results after adjustment for risk, but the data also indicate that past performance is an unreliable guide to what an investment manager may achieve in the future.

Although many of these criticisms are valid, as far as they go, they may also be overstatements of fact, unfair, or incomplete. Stockholders who believe that the investment managers are manipulating the fund for their own purposes can readily recognize such behavior from the reports published by the fund and can promptly redeem their shares. Aside from government regulation, pressures from outside directors, and the risk of lawsuits for failures of fiduciary responsibilities, the mere threat of large-scale redemptions by disgruntled stockholders is a major constraint against self-dealing by investment managers.

The question of performance record is more difficult to resolve. The real issue is whether an individual investor could do better on his or her own, particularly since opportunities for proper diversification and for continuous professional supervision are much more limited for a single investor than for the pooled funds of many. Professionally managed funds may not "beat the market" under all conditions, but they may still "beat the individual investor" at the same game.

Of course, an investor can invest in the market through a mutual fund designed to duplicate one of the leading market indexes. One such fund exists at this writing, with a very low management fee, but it has less than $25 million in assets, indicating that this is not what investors seek. The market as a whole may be too broad an area to be appropriate, particularly for the investor who is planning to turn only partial assets over to professional managers for supervision.

References

Friend, Irwin, Marshall Blume, and Jean Crockett, *Mutual Funds and Other Institutional Investors, A New Perspective,* McGraw-Hill, New York, 1970; Jensen, Michael J., "The Performance of Mutual Funds in the Period 1945–64," *Journal of Finance,* May 1968, pp. 389–416; *Mutual*

Fund Fact Book, published annually by the Investment Company Institute, Washington, D.C.; Smith, Keith V., "Is fund growth related to fund performance?" *The Journal of Portfolio Management,* vol. 4, no. 3, Spring 1978, pp. 49–55; Treynor, Jack L., "How to Rate Management of Investment Funds," *Harvard Business Review,* January–February 1965, pp. 63–75.

(*See also* Closed-end investment companies; Financial institutions)

Peter L. Bernstein

National Bureau of Economic Research

The National Bureau of Economic Research (NBER) is a private, nonprofit, nonpartisan research organization dedicated to improving the understanding of the U.S. economy. With offices in Cambridge, Massachusetts, New York City, and Palo Alto, California, and working arrangements with top economists at universities across the country, the NBER undertakes scientific studies, based on empirical observation, on varied topics of economic interest.

The NBER makes no policy recommendations; instead, it seeks to make objective analyses available to those who are in a position to make policy decisions. In order to ensure its independence and objectivity, the NBER is governed by a board of directors which represents many diverse interests: business, universities, labor, and certain professional organizations (including the American Economic Association, the Committee for Economic Development, and the American Statistical Association). All official Bureau publications must be approved by the board.

Major Areas of Research

The research of the Bureau falls into several major areas: economic fluctuations; business taxation and finance; financial markets and monetary economics; labor markets; and international trade, finance, and investment. Additional programs and special projects, deal with private pensions and social insurance, historical development of the American economy, health and family economics, law and economics, and productivity and technological change. Within these broad categories, specific topics of particular relevance are explored. Studies, made at the end of the 1970s for example, considered youth unemployment, the changing roles of debt and equity finance, capital formation, and inflation.

The NBER was organized in 1920 in response to a growing demand within the government and the academic sector for objective determination of the facts bearing upon economic problems and their impartial interpretation. The founding economists included N. I. Stone, Edwin Gay, John Commons and Wesley Mitchell.

The Bureau's original executive committee chose national income and its distribution as the first NBER research topic—the second topic was business cycles. Within the next few years, a Planning Conference was established, out of which came ideas for the Conference on Research in Income and Wealth and the Universities-National Bureau Committee.

The Conference on Income and Wealth was organized in 1936 by the NBER in cooperation with universities, government agencies, and other research institutions. Designed to improve the conceptual base of governmental economic statistics, the group reports on methodology, data, and research findings in income and wealth, consumption, saving, and other related areas.

The Universities-National Bureau Committee was originally established so that academic economists and their NBER counterparts could confer periodically on topics of common interest. Conference topics during the latter part of the 1970s included youth unemployment, social security, taxation and fiscal policy, rational expectations and monetary policy, and international macroeconomics.

Over the last 60 years, the NBER has pioneered in the development of widely used measures of national income, capital formation, business cycles, and business and economic indicators. Perhaps the Bureau is best known for its business cycle research: when the U.S. Department of Commerce began publishing its *Business Conditions Digest* in 1961, it acquired its historical data from the NBER. The Bureau continues to assist the government in its analysis of economic fluctuations.

NBER research has also made fundamental contributions to the development of economics as an empirical science. Simon Kuznets won the 1971 Nobel Prize for his NBER work on national income accounting, capital accumulation, and economic growth. In 1976, Milton Friedman was awarded the Nobel Prize for work done at the Bureau on monetary economics and household consumption behavior.

(*See also* Business cycles; National income accounting)

                                                                      Martin Feldstein

National income (*see* Gross national product)

National income accounting

The national income accounts provide information about the operation of the economic system in terms of specific activities such as production, consumption, and capital formation; they show the transactions taking place between enterprises, households, government, and the rest of the world. A simplified example of a set of national income accounts for the United States for the years 1976–78 is given in Tables 1 through 5.

National Income and Product Account

Table 1 shows the national income and product account for the United States. On the right-hand side of the account, the disposition of the gross output of the economy (gross national product) is shown in terms of the purchases made for private con-

TABLE 1 U.S. National Income and Product Account

(Billions of dollars)

		1976	1977	1978
N1	Payments to individuals (P6)	1321	1471	1656
	Compensation of employees	1037	1153	1301
	Proprietor income	89	100	113
	Rental income	23	23	23
	Interest	126	141	159
	Dividends	38	44	49
	Business transfers	8	10	11
N2	Payments to Government (G6)	243	268	297
	Corporate profits tax	64	72	84
	Indirect taxes	151	165	178
	Interest	23	26	30
	Surplus of government enterprises	5	5	5
N3	Retained income (S3)	203	222	243
	Undistributed profits	54	58	69
	Inventory valuation and capital consumption adjustments	−29	−31	−43
	Capital consumption allowances	178	195	217
N4	Less: Adjustments	67	75	90
	Subsidies	6	8	9
	Government interest (G3)	40	43	49
	Consumer interest (P4)	25	29	34
	Statistical discrepancy (S6)	−4	−5	−2
	Gross national income	1700	1887	2108

		1976	1977	1978
N5	Consumer expenditures on goods and services (P2)	1090	1207	1340
	Durable goods	157	178	198
	Nondurable goods	443	479	527
	Services	491	549	616
N6	Government expenditures on goods and services (G1)	360	394	434
	Federal	130	145	154
	National defense	87	94	100
	Other	43	51	54
	State and local	230	249	280
N7	Gross domestic investment (S1)	243	298	346
	Fixed	233	282	330
	Nonresidential	165	190	223
	Structures	57	64	78
	Producers' durables	107	127	145
	Residential structures	68	92	107
	Change in inventories	10	16	16
N8	Exports (F1)	163	176	205
N9	Less: Imports (F2)	156	187	217
	Gross national product	1700	1887	2108

Note: Detail may not add to totals due to rounding errors.
SOURCE: *Survey of Current Business*, vol. 59, no. 7, July 1979.

sumption (consumer expenditures), public consumption (government expenditures), and capital formation (gross domestic investment), and the net sales made abroad (exports less imports).

The left-hand side of the account shows how the funds which are generated by productive activity in the economy are distributed to individuals for their role in the production process and to governments for taxes or other payments, or are retained by producers. The compensation of employees includes the wages, salaries and fringe benefits paid by employers. Proprietor income includes the income of the self-employed and the net income of unincorporated business. Payments of property income such as rental income, dividends, and interest include not only payments made to individuals but also the payments which are made to nonprofit institutions such as churches and charitable and educational institutions. The tax payments made to government include direct taxes such as the corporate tax, and indirect taxes such as sales, excise, and property taxes and customs duties. The government may also receive property income either from interest or from the surpluses generated by government enterprises.

Not all the gross income which is generated by productive activity is paid out by producers, however; some is retained as undistributed profits. In addition to undistributed profits, producers charge depreciation to allow for the using up of their capital goods, and these funds are retained for replacement of capital goods. The reported undistributed profits and depreciation may in periods of rising prices reflect the effect of price changes since businesses use original costs rather than replacement costs in their bookkeeping. For this reason, the national income accounts include inventory and capital consumption adjustments to correct the overstatement of profits arising from price changes.

Finally, some additional adjustment items are required to bring the left-hand side of the national income and product account into balance with the right-hand side, for certain types of payments are made to producers which provide them with income which they in turn distribute to individuals or to government or retain, but which are not considered to be part of the gross national product and so are not included on the right-hand side of the account. These include subsidies and government and consumer debt interest. If the government pays a subsidy to a producer, this will not appear as a sale of a good or service on the right-hand side of the account, but it will provide the producer with income which can be distributed or retained. The total of the left-hand side of the national income and product account will exceed the total on the right-hand side by the amount of the subsidy, and introducing the subsidy as an adjustment will bring the two sides of the account into balance.

Similarly, it is generally agreed by national accountants that government interest and consumer interest do not constitute productive activity, and they should be treated like subsidies. Even after all the conceptual adjustments are made, however, one should not expect the two sides of the accounts to show an exact statistical balance since the estimates for various items are based on different and often conflicting statistical sources. For this reason, a statistical discrepancy item is introduced to bring the two sides of the account into balance.

Personal Income Account

Table 2 shows the personal income account, which provides information about the income received by individuals and nonprofit organizations, and its use. The pay-

TABLE 2 U.S. Personal Income Account

(Billions of dollars)

		1976	1977	1978
P1	Payments to government (G7)	322	365	420
	Federal income tax	141	162	188
	State and local income tax	27	31	35
	Social security taxes	125	140	164
	Estate and gift taxes	8	9	5
	Other personal taxes	5	5	7
	Other personal nontaxes	16	18	21
P2	Consumer expenditures on goods and services (N5)	1090	1207	1340
	Durable goods	157	178	198
	Nondurable goods	443	479	527
	Services	491	549	616
P3	Transfers to abroad (F4)	1	1	1
P4	Interest paid by consumers (N4)	25	29	34
P5	Personal Saving (S4)	68	67	77
	Personal outlays and saving	1505	1670	1872

		1976	1977	1978
P6	Payments from producers (N1)	1321	1471	1656
	Compensation of employees	1037	1153	1301
	Proprietor income	89	100	113
	Rental income	23	23	23
	Interest	126	141	159
	Dividends	38	44	49
	Business transfers	8	10	11
P7	Transfer payments from government (G2)	185	199	215
	Federal	158	169	182
	Social insurance benefits	121	132	
	Military and veterans	21	21	
	Other	16	16	
	State and local	27	30	33
	Social insurance benefits	11	12	
	Direct relief	13	13	
	Other	4	4	
	Personal income	1505	1670	1872

Note: Detail may not add to totals due to rounding errors.
SOURCE: Survey of Current Business, vol. 59, no. 7, July 1979.

ments from producers are shown on the right-hand side of the personal income account; they correspond exactly to the same set of transactions as shown on the left-hand side of the national income and product account in Table 1. In addition to these payments by producers, however, individuals and nonprofit institutions may receive transfer payments made by the government. These include social security benefits, veterans' pensions, welfare relief, and grants made to nonprofit institutions. Total personal income is thus the sum of the income received from producers and transfer payments received from the government.

The disposition of personal income is shown on the left-hand side of the account broken down into (1) payments to the government, (2) consumer expenditures, (3) transfers to abroad, (4) interest paid by consumers, and (5) personal saving. The payments made to government include all of the taxes which individuals pay such as income taxes, social security taxes, estate and gift taxes, and other tax and nontax payments such as motor vehicle licenses, fees, and fines.

Consumer expenditures are identical to the consumer expenditure item appearing on the right-hand side of the national income and product account; this item includes the expenditures of nonprofit institutions as well as those of individuals. Transfers abroad represent the net transfers which individuals and nonprofit institutions make to the rest of the world; this would include remittances, gifts, and private relief. Interest paid by consumers is not considered to be a purchase of a service, but corresponds to the same item shown as an adjustment in the left-hand side of the national income and product account. Finally, personal saving is residually determined as the difference between personal income and the total of personal outlays. It represents the amount of personal income which is not spent.

Government Account

The government account (Table 3) presents the consolidated receipts and outlays of federal, state, and local government. On the right-hand side of the account, the payments received from producers and individuals are shown; these are, of course, the same items as are shown on the left-hand side of the national income and product account and the personal income account. In similar manner, most of the items appearing as outlays of government on the right-hand side of the government account appear as receipts by producers and individuals. As already noted, government interest and subsidies appear as adjustments in the national income and product account since they are not considered to be payments for services. Government may also make payments abroad, including both interest and transfer payments. Finally the government surplus, like personal saving, is determined residually and is the difference between government receipts and outlays. When outlays exceed receipts, the surplus will be negative, indicating that the government is running a deficit.

Foreign Trade Account

The foreign trade account (Table 4) shows the current account transactions between the various sectors of the U.S. economy and the rest of the world. The sales of goods and services by U.S. producers to the rest of the world are shown on the left-hand side of the account as exports. The right-hand side of the account shows the payments to abroad to purchase imports and the payments abroad made by government and individuals. Net foreign investment in this account is residually determined as the difference between total receipts from abroad and total payments made to abroad.

TABLE 3 Government Account

(Billions of dollars)

		1976	1977	1978
G1	Government expenditures on goods and services (N6)	360	394	434
	Federal	130	145	154
	National defense	87	94	100
	Other	43	51	54
	State and local	230	249	280
G2	Transfer payments to individuals (P7)	185	199	215
	Federal	158	169	182
	Social insurance benefits	121	132	
	Military and veterans	21	21	
	Other	16	16	
	State and local	27	30	33
	Social insurance benefits	11	12	
	Direct relief	13	13	
	Other	4	4	
G3	Payments to producers (N4)	46	51	58
	Subsidies	6	8	9
	Interest	40	43	49
G4	Payments to abroad (F3)	8	8	13
	Interest	5	5	9
	Transfers	3	3	4
G5	Surplus (S5)	−33	−18	−2
	Federal	−54	−48	−30
	State and local	21	29	28
	Total outlays and surplus	565	633	717

		1976	1977	1978
G6	Payments from producers (N2)	243	268	297
	Corporate profits tax	64	72	84
	Indirect taxes	151	165	178
	Federal excise and duties	21	23	26
	State excise and sales	58	64	71
	Property	58	62	64
	Other	14	16	17
	Interest paid to government	23	26	30
	Surplus of government enterprises	5	5	5
G7	Payments from individuals (P1)	322	365	420
	Federal income tax	141	162	188
	State and local income tax	27	31	35
	Social security tax	125	140	164
	Estate and gift taxes	8	9	5
	Other personal taxes	5	5	7
	Other personal nontaxes	16	18	21
	Total revenue	565	633	717

Note: Detail may not add to totals due to rounding errors.
SOURCE: *Survey of Current Business*, vol. 59, no. 7, July 1979.

TABLE 4 U.S. Foreign Trade Account

(Billions of dollars)

		1976	1977	1978			1976	1977	1978
F1	Exports (N10)	163	176	205	F2	Imports (N9)	156	187	217
					F3	Payments to abroad from government (G4)	8	8	13
					F4	Transfers to abroad from individuals (P3)	1	1	1
					F5	Net foreign investment (S2)	−1	−21	−25
	Total receipts from abroad	163	176	205		Total payments and net foreign investment	163	176	205

TABLE 5 Gross Saving and Investment Account

(Billions of dollars)

		1976	1977	1978			1976	1977	1978
S1	Gross domestic investment (N7)	243	298	346	S3	Retained income (N3)	203	222	243
	Fixed	233	282	330		Undistributed profits	54	58	69
	Nonresidential	165	190	223		Inventory valuation adjustment	−29	−31	−43
	Structures	57	64	78		Capital consumption allowances	178	195	217
	Producers' durables	107	127	145	S4	Personal saving (P5)	68	67	77
	Residential structures	68	92	107	S5	Government surplus (G5)	−33	−18	−2
	Change in inventories	10	16	16	S6	Statistical discrepancy (N4)	4	5	2
S2	Net Foreign Investment (F6)	−1	−21	−25					
	Gross investment	242	277	321		Gross saving	242	277	321

Note: Detail may not add to totals due to rounding errors.
SOURCE: Survey of Current Business, vol. 59, no. 7, July 1979.

Gross Saving and Investment Account

Finally, the gross saving and investment account (Table 5) shows gross domestic investment and net foreign investment on the left-hand side of the account, and all of the saving items (i.e., retained income, personal saving, and government surplus) and the statistical discrepancy on the right-hand side. The system of accounts is fully articulated in that transactions appear in two different accounts, and every account is balanced either by a residual saving entry or by a statistical discrepancy.

The national income accounts record the transactions which take place in the economy and thus reflect the current prices which exist in any given period. As a consequence the year-to-year change will be the result of both the price and the quantity changes. In order to measure the real change in output occurring over time, the current-price transactions data are deflated to yield constant-price data. Generally speaking, it is the final sales of the gross national product (right-hand side of Table 1) which are most often shown in constant dollars.

History

National income accounting has been an evolutionary development resulting from early attempts to measure the income of the nation by such men as William Petty and Gregory King in the late seventeenth century. The worldwide development of national income measurement has been chronicled by Paul Studenski. In the United States, the National Bureau of Economic Research pioneered the estimation of national income in the 1920s and 1930s under the leadership of Wesley Clair Mitchell, Simon Kuznets, and other scholars. Since the mid-1930s, the Department of Commerce has published statistics on national income, and since 1947, full sets of national income accounts have been presented annually. The United Nations published an annual Yearbook of National Accounts Statistics, containing data for over 100 countries.

Uses and Limitations

Almost all countries of the world currently prepare some form of national income accounts on their economies. Centrally planned economies prepare estimates of net material product, which differs from national income because it excludes the value of nonmaterial services such as public administration and defense, personal and professional services, and similar activities. Where foreign transactions are important, as in many European countries, gross domestic product (GDP) is more frequently used than GNP because, unlike the GNP, GDP excludes output produced abroad to which residents have a claim.

These national accounts are used as the basis for countries' fiscal and monetary policy and provide information on the rate of growth, the degree of inflation, and the interrelations among households, government, and foreign trade. The national income accounts have become as important to countries as business accounts have become to enterprises.

It is sometimes argued that national income statistics are misleading and deficient since they do not adequately measure the welfare of a nation. On the one hand, it is pointed out that such things as environmental pollution, the effects of crime, and other disamenities are not deducted from output. On the other hand, nonmarket activities, increase in leisure, advance in medical knowledge, and the introduction of superior products are not included in the measurement of output. These arguments are, of course, valid and point out the limitations of national income accounting statistics. These statistics should not be used to measure welfare, a use for which they are not intended. Nevertheless, they have been found to be very useful in providing valuable information about the operation of the economic system.

References

Kuznets, Simon, *National Income: A Summary of Findings*, National Bureau of Economic Research, Arno, New York, 1975; Ruggles, Richard, and Nancy D. Ruggles, *National Income Accounts and Income Analysis*, 2d ed., McGraw-Hill, New York, 1956; Schultze, C. L., *National Income Analysis*, 3d ed., Prentice-Hall, Englewood Cliffs, N.J., 1971.

(*See also* Change in business's inventories in GNP; Disposable personal income; Factor cost; Government expenditures in GNP; Gross national product; Gross private domestic investment in GNP; Implicit price deflator; Net exports in GNP; Personal consumption expenditures in GNP; Potential gross national product)

Richard Ruggles and Nancy D. Ruggles

Nationalization of industry

National, or public, ownership of enterprises engaged in commercial activity is widespread throughout many nations of the world. Within the Communist nations, virtually all ownership of the means of production is vested in the state. Among the democracies of Western Europe, the state typically owns most enterprises engaged in public utilities and transportation, and in several of these nations, publicly owned firms participate actively in other sectors. Among developing nations, there is growing sentiment that the government should own and control enterprises engaged in the production of exportable natural resources (Seidman, 1975). Even in the free-market-oriented United States, state-owned enterprises operate public utilities in some areas of the nation and most mass transit operations are under public ownership.

Natural Monopoly Industries

In many of the industrialized non-Communist nations, state ownership of enterprises is largely limited to industries characterized by natural monopoly. These include electric power generation and distribution, telecommunications, railroads, airlines, broadcasting, postal services, and mass transit services. Although in some nations such as the United States many of these industries do not generally fall under public ownership, private firms operating in these sectors are heavily regulated by the state. State ownership or regulation of natural monopolies is justified as a means to prevent private firms from engaging in monopolistic pricing or other socially nondesirable modes of behavior.

Extensive nationalization of nonnatural monopoly industries, in industrial nations has often resulted from the actions of a political movement which ascribes economic benefit to public ownership of the means of production. In Great Britain, for example, the Labor Party has adhered to a philosophy of democratic socialism, and has sought nationalization of certain industries because it believes this would increase economic efficiency and improve the distribution of income (Robson, 1960). In the Communist countries, of course, private ownership of business enterprises has been viewed as the root of all social and economic evil, and thus public ownership is all-pervasive.

Noneconomic Considerations

Justification of nationalization of industry, however, is not always based on economic considerations. Italy has a long record, for example, of rescuing bankrupt private firms by placing them under state ownership and control. This occurred even under the Fascist government of the 1930s. Firms thus nationalized have included many for which, arguably, liquidation would have been an economically more sound alternative. In Italy (and elsewhere), publicly owned but economically unviable enterprises can be sustained only by subsidization, which raises serious questions pertaining to economic efficiency.

In a number of developing nations, nationalization efforts have been specifically targeted toward foreign-owned firms. Although such nationalization might be justified on economic grounds, expropriation of foreign firms often represents a political response by a government to nationalistic or xenophobic sentiments within a nation. This is especially likely to be the case where foreign firms play a major or dominant role in the economy of the nation (Moran, 1975). Efforts to establish associations between the socioeconomic characteristics of a nation and the propensity of the nation to expropriate targeted foreign firms (as opposed to broad efforts to nationalize whole industries or sectors irrespective of ownership) have largely been inconclusive (Kobrin, 1979). This probably underscores the noneconomic nature of many expropriatory actions. Some evidence exists to suggest, however, that expropriation is more likely to take place in industries characterized by mature technologies than in younger industries (Kobrin, 1980).

It should be noted that nationalistic sentiments with respect to foreign-owned firms can be as strong in advanced industrialized nations as in developing ones. For example, in Canada sentiments against U.S. ownership of much of Canadian industry appear to be rising, even though it is not at all clear that the economic performance of U.S.-owned firms in Canada has been unsatisfactory.

Economic Efficiency

The presence of nationalized firms in mixed economies such as those of most of the Western industrial nations raises a number of issues pertaining to economic efficiency. Under neoclassical economic thinking, efficiency is maximized if numerous enterprises openly compete for sales of output and procurement of factor inputs in unregulated markets (unregulated here implies both no state regulation and no collusion among enterprises or sellers of factor inputs) and if each enterprise strives to maximize profits. In a state-owned enterprise, however, individual managers may feel less bound to maximize profit than would managers in a private firm, especially if the (state-owned) enterprise receives a government subsidy or is subject to evaluation of performance by national authorities on criteria other than economic ones. Such a relaxation on the part of managers doubtlessly would reduce efficiency, particularly in cases where the firm was subject to little or no competition.

Defenders of state ownership of industry maintain, however, that nationalized firms can confer upon the community external benefits that private firms would not take into account and which justify behavior other than profit maximization. It is not difficult to conceive of such externalities (abatement of pollution, for example), but it is difficult to quantify a trade-off between these and the efficiency losses that might result from non-profit-maximizing behavior. The case probably can be made that where such externalities exist, the firm should be compensated for the cost of bearing them but otherwise ought to strive to maximize profits (see papers by Arrow and Raiffa in Vernon and Aharoni, 1980).

Even if it were to be determined that the state-owned enterprise should strive to maximize profits and not be the recipient of direct government subsidies, some shielding from the competitive rigors of the market is nonetheless likely to ensue from the mere fact of state ownership. This is especially true in capital markets. In these markets, it is likely to be perceived that the creditworthiness of the nationalized firm is implicitly guaranteed by the state. Thus, the riskiness of the state-owned firm would be perceived by the market as less than that of an otherwise identical private firm, which would reduce capital costs to the former firm. This would result in some distortion in the allocation of resources. It is possible also that state-owned firms may pay higher than market wages or grant extraordinary employment security to employees although this is certainly not always the case. Despite this possibility, Wiseman (1963) suggests that there is little evidence in British experience to suppose that relations between labor and employer are better in state-owned enterprises than in privately owned ones.

Whatever the trade-offs between loss of economic efficiency and external gains that might ensue from nationalization of industry, it is clear that in the late 1970s public sentiment in many Western nations turned away from advocacy of public ownership. In Great Britain and Sweden, for example, social democratic parties were voted out of office in 1979 and replaced by conservative governments committed to denationalization of industry. It is believed that one reason a leftist coalition failed to win power in the general election in France in 1978 was public opposition to the coalition's stated aim to nationalize a greater portion of French industry. Public sentiment can, of course, rapidly alter course, but as of 1980, public disenchantment with the benefits of national ownership of industry was high, at least in most Western nations.

References

Cicchetti, C. J., and J. L. Jurewitz (eds.), *Studies in Electric Utility Regulation*, Ballinger, Cambridge, Mass., 1975; Coase, R. H., "The Problem of Social Cost," *Journal of Law and Economics*, vol. 3, 1960, pp. 1–44; Friedmann, Wolfgang, (ed.), *Public and Private Enterprise in Mixed Economies*, Columbia University Press, New York, 1974; Furubotn, E. G., and S. Pejovich, *The Economics of Property Rights*, Ballinger, Cambridge, Mass., 1974; Gunnerman, Jon P., *The Nation-State and Transnational Corporations in Conflict with Special Reference to Latin America*, Praeger, New York, 1975; Hanson, Albert H. (ed.), *Nationalization: A Book of Readings*, Macmillan, London, 1963; Head, John G., *Public Goods and Public Welfare*, University of North Carolina Press, Durham, N.C., 1974; Kobrin, Stephen J., "Political Factors Underlying the Propensity to Expropriate Foreign Enterprises," MIT Sloan School of Management, Cambridge, Mass., 1979 (mimeograph); Kobrin, Stephen J., "Foreign Enterprise and Forced Divestment in LDC's," *International Organization*, vol. 34, 1980, pp. 65–88; Leff, Nathaniel H., "Multinational Corporations in a Hostile World," *Wharton Magazine*, vol. 2, 1978, pp. 21–29; Moran, Theodore H., "Transnational Strategies of Protection and Defense by Multinational Corporations: Spreading the Risk and Raising the Cost for Nationalization in National Resources," *International Organization*, vol. 27, 1973, pp. 273–288; Moran, Theodore H., *Multinational Corporations and the Politics of Dependence: Copper in Chile*, Princeton University Press, Princeton, N.J., 1979; Robson, William A., *Nationalized Industry and Public Ownership*, University of Toronto Press, Toronto, 1960; Seidman, Ann (ed.), *Natural Resources and National Welfare: The Case of Copper*, Praeger, New York and London, 1975; Shepard, William G., "Cross Subsidiary and Allocation in Public Firms," *Oxford Economic Papers,* New Series, vol. 16, 1964, pp. 132–160; Vernon, Raymond, and Yair Aharoni (eds.), *State-Owned Enterprise in the Western Economics,* St. Martin's, New York, 1980; Weekly, J. K., "Expropriation of U.S. Multinational Investments," *MSU Business Topics,* vol. 25, 1977, pp. 27–36; Wiseman, Jack, "Guidelines for Public Enterprise: A British Experiment," *Southern Economic Journal,* vol. 30, 1963, pp. 39–48.

(*See also* Communism; Fascism; Marxism; Multinational corporation; Socialism)

Edward M. Graham

Negative income tax

The negative income tax is a program for a guaranteed minimum income that has received considerable attention from economists in the United States in the last two decades. It would operate through the federal income tax system and would provide income maintenance payments based solely on low income, in contrast to existing programs that use such criteria as age or family composition, sometimes in combination with need, in the determination of eligibility.

The three essential characteristics that may vary among negative income tax proposals are (1) the amount of the income guarantee, which varies with family size; (2) the rate at which existing family income is reduced (or taxed) when it exceeds zero; and (3) the break-even level of income at which eligibility for a grant disappears. Proponents generally favor taxing existing income at a rate less than 100 percent, in order to preserve incentives to work. In fact, with a tax rate of less than 100 percent, the family always benefits from more earnings, as the accompanying table (illustrating a negative income tax with a guarantee of $5000 a year for a family of four and a tax rate of 50 percent) indicates:

Earnings	Grant	Total family income
0	$5,000	$ 5,000
$ 2,000	4,000	6,000
4,000	3,000	7,000
6,000	2,000	8,000
8,000	1,000	9,000
10,000	0	10,000

With a 50 percent tax rate, the break-even point will always be twice the guaranteed income. Thus, such a plan designed to eliminate the poverty gap—that is, the extent to which the family's income falls below the federally determined poverty line—would be very costly. With a poverty line of $6700 for a nonfarm family of four (in 1979), the break-even point would be $13,400 and would bring almost half of all families into the program. Partly for this reason, and partly because of concern over work incentives, most serious proposals have advocated a guaranteed income below the poverty line, or in some cases a higher tax rate.

History

Rhys Williams (1943) of Great Britain is credited with having first proposed a guaranteed minimum income, with a plan of the social dividend type—differing from the negative income tax in providing for a standard government allowance for all families, and then taxing preallowance income so that the tax would be less than the allowance for poor families and more than the allowance for nonpoor families. The first proposal to receive much attention in the United States was made by Milton Friedman (1962), who called for a negative income tax that would replace all existing income maintenance programs, including social security. Although support for the negative income tax grew among economists in the 1960s, the majority favored replacing existing public assistance programs, but not social insurance, by the negative income tax.

In January 1968, the President appointed a Commission on Income Maintenance Programs to study income maintenance policies. However, by the time the Commission issued its report (in the fall of 1969) calling for a "universal income supplement" plan of a negative income tax type, a new President had been elected and had sent a proposal for a family assistance program to Congress. The proposal, calling for a federally guaranteed minimum income for families with children, and for the aged, disabled, and blind, passed the House but was defeated in the Senate Finance Committee. Subsequent major welfare reform proposals have failed to get congressional approval. Congress did, however, enact the Supplementary Security Income Program, providing a guaranteed minimum income for the aged, disabled, and blind, in 1972, and also provided for a modest tax credit for low earners in 1974.

Pros and Cons

Proponents of a negative income tax argue that existing income maintenance programs fail to reach many poor people. Moreover, the major existing public assistance program, Aid to Families with Dependent Children (AFDC), is administered in a punitive manner in many states and has other serious weaknesses as follows:

1. The financial burden is inequitable, falling heavily on large cities with high welfare recipient rates.
2. AFDC fails to help the working poor and may encourage family splitting because, with certain exceptions, aid is available only if one parent is incapacitated or absent from the home.
3. Earnings are taxed too heavily, resulting in disincentives to work.
4. Wide variations in payment levels among states are alleged to induce poor families to migrate to states with comparatively high payments.

Opponents object to expanding the scope and cost of welfare payments. Some economists are skeptical on the grounds that (1) family splitting might be encouraged, (2) income tax provisions would have to be extensively revised to provide for a smooth transition between negative and positive tax payments, (3) the combination of cash payments plus food stamps plus housing subsidies would seriously impair work incentives unless all but cash payments were abolished. There are other, more technical objections as well.

Meanwhile, the negative income tax has been the subject of the most extensive social science experiments ever conducted, under federal financing but carried out by nonpublic research groups. The earlier experiments (in New Jersey and elsewhere) focused primarily on the impact on work incentives and indicated a very slight tendency for work effort to be reduced as a result of income maintenance. Later experiments in Seattle and Denver showed more significant negative effects on work incentives, along with a greater tendency for couples in the experimental group than for those in the control group to split up (Spiegelman and Yaeger, 1979).

The negative income tax has received less attention abroad than in this country, probably because all other industrial countries have family allowance systems, most of which operate somewhat like social dividend plans except that payments are made only on behalf of children. In Great Britain, however, the Conservative government proposed a credit income tax plan in 1972.

Prospects appear more favorable for limited welfare reform than for a comprehensive guaranteed minimum income plan. The issues involved will, however, continue to be of interest to economists for both their welfare and macroeconomic implications. Meanwhile, the social experiments have provided a wealth of data illuminating theories of economic motivation.

References

Friedman, Milton, *Capitalism and Freedom,* University of Chicago Press, Chicago, 1962; Masters, Stanley, and Irwin Garfinkel, *Estimating the Labor Supply Effects of Income-Maintenance Alternatives,* Academic Press, New York, 1977; Report of the President's Commission on Income Maintenance Programs, *Poverty Amid Plenty,* 1969; Spiegelman, Robert G., and K. W. Yaeger, *An Overview of the Seattle and Denver Income Maintenance Experiments,* Stanford Research Institute, Menlo Park, Calif., 1979, (unpublished paper); Williams, Rhys, *Something to Look Forward to,* MacDonald, London, 1943.

(*See also* Poverty; Social security programs)

Margaret S. Gordon

Neighborhood effects (*see* Externalities)

Neoclassical economics

The most remarkable feature of neoclassical economics is that it reduces many broad categories of market phenomena to considerations of individual choice and, in this way, suggests that the science of economics can be firmly grounded on the basic individual act of subjectively choosing among alternatives.

Neoclassical economics began with the so-called marginalist revolution in value theory that emerged toward the end of the nineteenth century. Strictly speaking, neoclassical economics is not a school of thought (in the sense of a well-defined group of economists following a single great master) but more a loose amalgam of subschools of thought each centering around such acknowledged masters as Alfred Marshall in England, Léon Walras in France, and Carl Menger in Austria. What these subschools have in common is the importance they attach to explaining the coordinating features of market processes in terms of plans and subjective evaluations carried out by individuals in the market subject to the constraints of technological knowledge, social custom and practice, and scarcity of resources.

The Subschools

In England, Marshall's appointment to the chair of political economy at Cambridge University in 1885 marked the start of the Cambridge school—a variant of neoclassical economics that stressed continuity with the past achievements of the classical school, especially the economics of David Ricardo and John Stuart Mill. In 1890 Marshall published his *Principles of Economics*, which demonstrated how the forces that determine the normal prices of commodities can be explained by means of supply and demand in the context of firms struggling to survive within industries. Marshall's disciples included A. C. Pigou, D. H. Robertson, Ralph Hawtrey, and to some extent the controversial John Maynard Keynes. (During the 1930s, Keynes turned against his old master by explaining how subjective evaluations can lead to discoordinating market processes and the unemployment of labor and disuse of capital.)

In France, Walras founded the general equilibrium school with the publication of his *Elements of Pure Economics* (1874). This school would eventually take root in Lausanne, Switzerland, through the contributions of Vilfredo Pareto, especially in his *Cours d'économie politique* (1896–1897). Some of Walras's teachings reached England by way of A. L. Bowley's *Mathematical Groundwork of Economics* (1924). Like Marshall, Walras and his followers were concerned with a supply and demand account of market pricing, but Walras went somewhat beyond Marshall and investigated the mathematical conditions under which all markets could be in equilibrium simultaneously.

In Austria, Carl Menger founded the Austrian school with the publication of his *Principles of Economics* (1871). Subsequent professors at the University of Vienna such as Friedrich von Wieser, Eugen von Böhm-Bawerk, and later Ludwig von Mises and Friedrich A. von Hayek, focused on the essential problems of economic organization by starting with Menger's insights about the importance of economizing action in shaping economic institutions in the market. Among Austrians, the important task of economic reasoning is to disaggregate economic phenomena so that the events can be made intelligible in terms of basic market forces of supply and demand operating through the decisions of individuals.

Demand versus Supply

The basic theme of marginalist economics, as emphasized by William Stanley Jevons in his *Theory of Political Economy* (1871), is that an individual's estimation of worth of any object or service depends on the least most important use that would go unsatisfied should that individual have to give up that unit. Jevons, Marshall, and Walras each recognized the link between the amount of supply in an individual's possession and the intensity of the subjective benefit experienced, but it was the Austrian school and later the economists at the London School of Economics during the 1930s, who carefully developed the full implications of the idea that every choice necessarily involves a forgone opportunity. From this the neoclassical school defined rationality in the market as involving a constant comparison and substitutions of bundles of commodities (and services) until one (affordable) bundle is found where the satisfaction received from the marginal dollar spent on all lines of expenditure is equal. A rise in price encourages substitution away from the more expensive commodity in favor of its alternatives. The principle of substitution (as defined by Marshall) implies that at higher prices the rate of individual demand never increases—called the first law of demand. The second law of demand is simply that the substitution effect is greater the longer the time the market has to adjust. The notion of substitution is potentially one of the most radical of all ideas in the social sciences and has been used to criticize much of current social thought based around the misleading notion that national "needs" exist in some fixed unalterable form.

On the supply side of the market, producers are viewed as constantly trying to discover ways of substituting one bundle of resources for another in an effort to find the cheapest way of producing any amount of supply and thereby to survive in the market. Marshall developed the model of firms and industries in which unexpected shifts in demand caused firms to adjust their output gradually, first in the short run by exploiting their capacity more intensively and second in the long run by altering their capacity altogether. As time went by, Marshall hypothesized, firms become more pliable in both their size and organization, and the character of equilibrium between supply and demand becomes more firmly grounded. Marshall also allowed for learning and discovery of new forms of economic organization to encourage economies of scale. The first law of supply is that the increase in quantity will be greater the greater the increase in price; and the second law of supply is that for any given price rise, the increase in the quantity supplied will be greater the longer the time the market is permitted to adjust.

Marginal Productivity and Economic Efficiency

Neoclassical economists estimate the worth of one resource when used in conjunction with several others by looking at the marginal productivity. A resource's marginal productivity is found by varying that factor's amount, holding other factors constant, and observing what happens to output. The more output is diminished by the removal of one unit of a factor, the greater is that factor's marginal product. It remained for Phillip Wicksteed to show in 1898 that, in the absence of economies or disceconomies of scale, when each factor is paid the equivalent of its marginal product, the joint product of all the factors will be paid out without anything left over. Later neoclassical writers such as Paul Douglas in the 1920s and Robert Solow in the 1960s used this theory of factor pricing to measure the contributions of labor, capital, and innovation to the growth of American per capita income. Douglas's startling finding (*Theory of Wages*, 1934)—that the relative share of the national dividend received by the workers has remained fairly constant over time—served as a serious blow to the then-popular Marxist claim that as capitalism developed the working class got a smaller share of a growing pie.

Neoclassical economics bases a great deal of its policy analysis around a particular notion of economic efficiency. If it can be shown that policy A achieves a certain objective with fewer scarce resources than policy B, then policy A is preferred to policy B and it is described as more efficient. When comparing the combined value of resources, one must compare the opportunity costs incurred by the resource owners themselves in making marginal units of supply available—what is termed marginal cost—with the value provided to the consumers when the resources are applied in their present applications. By assuming that market prices are (rough) indexes of value and, therefore, an acceptable basis for policy analysis, neoclassical economists evaluate programs in terms of their measured costs and benefits. Policies generating greater benefits than costs are said to be economically efficient.

In the 1940s neoclassical policy analysis reached a plateau with the articulation of the compensation principle derived from a pattern of reasoning first expressed by Pareto. The claim is made that particular forms of government intervention are justified if those who gain wealth by the intervention gain at least enough to compensate the losers of wealth, even if no actual attempt to compensate is made. By this criterion many politically popular government policies cannot be justified. Tariffs and other barriers to free international trade, for example, impose more harm on buyers than the limited benefits they convey to local suppliers. But the losers are spread out and diffused while the gainers are few in number and lobby for trade barriers on foreign products. So these uneconomic policies remain politically popular.

Criticism of Neoclassical Economics

In the 1970s neoclassical economics came under attack for a variety of reasons. Reform liberals contend that the aforementioned efficiency criterion ignores considerations of equity because market prices already imply a particular underlying distribution of wealth which the neoclassical writers take as given. A complete policy analysis must start with an analysis of who ought to own wealth and for what purposes. Another group of critics, the neo-Ricardian school, claims that neoclassical economics has betrayed the mission of the older classical school because of their insistence on the supply and demand model. According to Piero Sraffa and his disciples, relative demand or utility plays virtually no role in defining relative commodity prices in long-run equilibrium and, therefore, plays little part in determining the social distribution of wealth. Here the technological conditions that surround the production of certain types of goods, especially those consumed by the working class, affect the distribution of income, and, therefore, the task of economic theory is to explain how surplus value is extracted from the working class and used by others. According to the Sraffa group, neoclassical economics represents an aberration from the more profound analysis allegedly offered by David Ricardo and further developed by Karl Marx. The Sraffa–neo-Ricardian school is quite content to do away with individual valuation in the marketplace and concentrate instead on the objective or technological conditions of long-run equilibrium. The attempt is to show that the distribution of income after some basic subsistence allotment to the workers is politically determined and therefore plays no part in the reproduction of annual output within the framework of capitalist social institutions.

Among neoclassical writers, the modern Austrian school adherents such as Israel Kirzner, Murray N. Rothbard, and Ludwig Lachmann are less concerned with the details of equilibrium positions such as described at length in Paul Samuelson's *Foundations of Economic Analysis* (1948) and more concerned with the process by which markets adjust or fail to adjust to change. Modern Austrians challenge attempts to measure opportunity costs by claiming that it is illegitimate to assume that market prices are equilibrium prices. They therefore reject the methodological basis of cost-benefit analysis.

In summary, the neoclassical school offers a remarkably diverse body of concepts to explain the operation of the market in terms of the twin forces of supply and demand. In terms of its admittedly limited concept of economic efficiency (estimated in econometric studies by assuming that market prices are indexes of costs and benefits), neoclassical economics offers a basis for criticizing the most wasteful of government policies by showing that less expensive alternatives exist.

References

Becker, Gary S., *Economic Theory*, Knopf, Chicago, 1971; Buchanan, James, *Cost and Choice*, Markham, Chicago, 1969; Dobb, Maurice, *Theories of Value and Distribution Since Adam*

Smith: Ideology and Economic Theory, Cambridge University Press, Cambridge, 1973; Ferguson, C. E., *The Neoclassical Theory of Production and Distribution*, Cambridge University Press, Cambridge, 1971; Moss, Laurence S., and John M. Virgo (eds.), "Carl Menger and Austrian Economics," *Atlantic Economic Journal*, vol. 6, no. 3, September 1978, pp. 1–69.

(*See also* Austrian economics; Cambridge school; Classical school; Cost benefit analysis; Marshallian economics; Opportunity cost)

Laurence S. Moss

Neo-Keynesian economics

Neo-Keynesian economics refers to the doctrines of a small but influential group of post-Keynesians centered at Cambridge University in England with many supporters around the world. They accept the basic ideas of John Maynard (Lord) Keynes, especially his *General Theory of Employment, Interest and Money* (1936). The main contributors to neo-Keynesian economics have been Joan Robinson, Nicholas Kaldor, Luigi Pasinetti, and Piero Sraffa, all associated with Cambridge University. Also important in neo-Keynesian economics is the work of the Polish economist, Michel Kalecki, who independently worked out a general theory of employment similar to that of Keynes. The neo-Keynesians also have much in common with the great classical economist David Ricardo and of the socialist Karl Marx. Their work is sometimes called neo-Ricardian and/or neo-Marxian. The *Cambridge Journal of Economics*, established at Cambridge University in 1977, has been an outlet for neoKeynesian publications. In the United States, the *Journal of Post Keynesian Economics*, begun in 1978, has served as an outlet for similar ideas.

Neo-Keynesians, and post-Keynesians generally, distinguish sharply between their interpretation of Keynes and that of the orthodox Keynesians (Samuelson, Tobin, Hicks) and label the orthodox interpretation "illegitimate." Neo-Keynesians profess to have an answer to problems of "stagflation," the simultaneous occurrence of rising unemployment and inflation, which is a paradox in terms of orthodox Keynesianism and has led to its discrediting among many economists, policymakers, and a large segment of the general public. During the 1970s, when the influence of orthodox Keynesians seemed to wane, the neo-Keynesian theory had an appeal to those who disagreed with ideas of monetarism as well as mainstream neoclassical economists. The affinity of neo-Keynesianism for some of Marx's ideas suggest leftist overtones. Neo-Keynesians generally favor, in addition to fiscal policy, an incomes policy to curb price inflation but are not properly viewed as socialists.

Investment, Expectations, and Growth

Investment, or capital formation, is central in Keynes' theory of employment, but he confined his analysis to the short period in which investment is the strategic factor for disbursing purchasing power into the economy as a means of augmenting effective demand and thereby increasing employment. The neo-Keynesian theory of growth takes account of the long-term consequences of capital formation in adding to productive capacity in future periods. Building on earlier work by Roy Harrod, Joan Robinson and Nicholas Kaldor analyzed the conditions necessary for sustained growth. Some level of current investment will be sufficient to sustain full employment and keep the economy growing, perhaps at a steady rate. However, Robinson's theory suggests strongly that the conditions necessary for steady growth at high employment are highly improbable under decentralized market capitalism.

A basic consideration is the relation between initial expectations (forecasts) of business entrepreneurs and subsequent realized results of economic activity. Uncertainty about the future was, perhaps, the point of greatest emphasis in Keynes' pessimistic view toward maintaining sufficient private investment to achieve sustained high-level employment. When expectations turn out to be incorrect, business executives adapt either by altering the level of their output or by changing prices, or some combination of the two. In Keynes' analysis, adjustments are made primarily in output but Robinson and Kaldor give attention to price adjustments as well as to output adjustments. Whereas Keynes assumed competition, the neo-Keynesians take account of strong monopoly elements in product markets. Kalecki's concept of degree of monopoly, a measure of market power to fix prices, is integrated into the neo-Keynesian theory of growth.

Fiscal policy may be used to facilitate steady growth, but the neo-Keynesians assume that the quantity of money accommodates the real needs of the economy and money is not a strategic factor in policy, as it is in monetarism. Neo-Keynesianism stands as an alternative to the neoclassical synthesis, which integrates Keynes' short-run theory with neoclassical long-run theory.

Distribution Theory

Although Keynes recognized "arbitrary and inequitable distribution of wealth and income" as one of the two outstanding faults of contemporary capitalism—the other fault being massive unemployment—he was never much concerned about the theory of distribution. The neo-Keynesians, on the contrary, develop a theory of income distribution that is, perhaps, the most revolutionary part of their entire theory. They divide Keynes' consumption function into two parts, the propensity to consume out of wages and the propensity to consume out of profits. In the simplest neo-Keynesian models, workers are assumed to spend all their wages on current consumption. Capitalists' decisions to invest and to consume will determine their profits. Capitalists can increase their share of national income by investing more or by consuming more. This rather startling conclusion is stated in a basic proposition by Kalecki (1968): "Workers spend what they earn and capitalists earn what they spend." Thus, in neo-Keynesian economics investment is strategic in determining the distribution of income between wages and profits as well as in determining the level of national income to be distributed.

In neo-Keynesian distribution theory Kalecki's degree of monopoly replaces the unrealistic assumption of perfect competition in neoclassical economics and directly affects income distribution: an increase in the degree of monopoly will increase the relative share of total national income going to profits at the expense of wages.

This neo-Keynesian macroeconomic theory of income distribution contrasts with the neoclassical microeconomic theory of income distribution. The latter is based on the view that income distribution is essentially a matter of applying a general theory of pricing to the factors of production (labor and capital) according to marginal productivity principles. Based on hints by Sraffa, Joan Robinson during the 1950s challenged the meaningfulness of the neoclassical production function, especially the meaning of capital as a homogeneous entity capable of quantification and measurement. Moreover, the neoclassical theory ascertains the value of capital by using the interest rate to discount (capitalize) future returns and then, in a circular manner, uses the value of capital to determine the interest rate as the marginal productivity of capital.

Reswitching

In an ensuing controversy between Cambridge, England, and Cambridge, Massachusetts, Paul Samuelson of MIT acknowledged logical error in what is called the reswitching problem. Contrary to the neoclassical theory of capital and interest, Samuelson conceded that a technique of production that may be optimal (cost the least) at a low rate of interest, may cease to be optimal at an intermediate interest rate, but may again become optimal at a high rate of interest. Luigi Pasinetti, one of the neo-Keynesians, demonstrated that such reswitching of production techniques is logically possible. Although the practical significance of reswitching was not conceded by the neoclassical economists, the neo-Keynesians interpreted the reswitching possibility to justify their view that marginal productivity theory is not very meaningful, except as an apology for the receipt of (large) incomes by owners of capital. Neo-Keynesian macroeconomic theory of distribution emphasizes the struggle between wage earners and capitalists over the relative shares of national income going to wages and profits. This resembles the well-known view of Marx and of Ricardo for whom it was axiomatic that when wages rise, profits fall, and vice versa.

A Second Revolution

The neo-Keynesians lay claim to a second revolution in economic theory, and if their claim is correct, the thrust of this revolution is even more devastating to mainstream, neoclassical economic theory than the first, or Keynesian, revolution. Keynes, after all, accepted the validity of neoclassical theory under conditions of full employment. Not so with the neo-Keynesians. Marginal productivity is the citadel of neoclassical economics. It addresses itself to the efficient allocation of resources through rational pricing based on marginal productivity and treats income shares as just a special case of marginal productivity theory. Acceptance of the large claims of the neo-Keynesians would demolish the neoclassical citadel.

In neo-Keynesian methodology, in the words of Joan Robinson, the static neoclassical concept of equilibrium would be replaced by history as an irreversible process in time to open vistas of a much more realistic and dynamic economic analysis. Just what is meant by combining economic theory with history is not entirely clear, but the idea is central to an unorthodox methodology that would bring economics closer to Marx than to Ricardo. Ideology also plays a role in the differences between neo-Keynesian and neoclassical economics and is basic to the neo-Keynesian claim of a new paradigm for economic theory. Even if the claims of the neo-Keynesians are exaggerated and if neoclassical theory is basically sound, neoclassical theory nevertheless will have been strengthened by the necessity of responding to the challenge to its foundations by the neo-Keynesians.

References

Blaug, Mark, *The Cambridge Revolution: Success or Failure?* The Institute of Economic Affairs, London, 1975; Harcourt Brace Jovanovich, Geoffrey C., *Some Cambridge Controversies in the Theory of Capital,* Cambridge University Press, Cambridge, 1972; Harcourt Brace Jovanovich, Geoffrey C., and N. F. Laing (eds.), *Capital and Growth, Selected Readings,* Penguin, Harmondsworth, Middlesex, England, 1971; Kalecki, Michael, *Theory of Economic Dynamics,* Modern

Reader, New York, 1968; Keynes, John Maynard, *The General Theory of Employment, Interest and Money*, Harcourt Brace Jovanovich, New York, 1936; Robinson, Joan, *The Accumulation of Capital*, 3d ed., Macmillan, St. Martin's, New York, 1969; Sraffa, Piero, *Production of Commodities by Means of Commodities, Prelude to a Critique of Economic Theory*, Cambridge University Press, Cambridge, 1960.

(*See also* Cambridge school; Capital, a factor of production; Capital formation; Capitalism; Factors of production; Income distribution; Keynesian economics; Neoclassical economics; Post-Keynesian economics; Stagflation)

Dudley Dillard

Net exports in GNP

The foreign sector in the U.S. national income and product accounts consists of two areas: (1) net exports in the gross national product (GNP) account, and (2) net foreign investment in the gross saving and investment account.

Net exports in GNP is something of a misnomer because it really consists of the difference between exports and imports, both defined to include service payments as well as merchandise payments. Major service payments are for transportation, profit and interest remittances, and tourism and military expenditures overseas. There are further complications because net exports in the national income accounts is defined differently from the balance on goods and services in the U.S. balance of payments. The first important difference is that the balance of payments includes payments of interest on U.S. government securities held by foreigners. Because these payments are not for goods and services, they are excluded from the category of net exports which is, of course, a component of GNP.

Another major difference between the balance on goods and services in the balance of payments account and net exports is retained earnings of U.S. businesses abroad and of foreign businesses in the United States. In this context retained earnings refer to earnings that are not remitted out of the country. Prior to 1980 retained earnings were included in the balance of payments but were excluded from net exports. However, since the national income accounts were revised in 1980, retained earnings are included in net exports.

In the gross saving and investment account net foreign investment is added to gross private domestic investment in order to obtain the gross investment figure that by definition is equal to gross saving. Net foreign investment is equal to net exports minus net transfer payments to foreigners with some technical adjustments. Transfer payments are one-way payments mainly for gifts and pensions abroad and for foreign aid. In the U.S. balance of payments, the current account balance, after some statistical and conceptual adjustments, corresponds to net exports in the national income and product accounts.

Current versus Constant Prices

Thus far the foreign sector has been discussed in terms of national accounts at current prices. In the calculation of gross national product in real terms, however, net exports is presented on a deflated basis with exports and imports deflated separately into constant dollars. In the United States and in foreign countries this presentation of net exports on a deflated basis can create conceptual and practical distortions because imports may exceed exports in current prices, but exports may exceed imports in real terms. In 1978, for example, in the gross national product account net exports were $12.0 billion negative, but in 1972 dollars net exports were $8.4 billion positive. This paradox arises because imports in current dollars were running ahead of exports mainly because of the heavy imports of petroleum which had a more than fourfold price rise since the end of 1973. Valued at 1972 prices, however, the oil price rises since 1973 were not taken into account and exports were running ahead of imports.

The paradox of net exports in current and constant dollars moving in opposite directions is unresolved. But it is clear that for some countries it tends to distort overall national accounts even more than in the United States. In Saudi Arabia, for example, gross national product—mainly in oil revenue—has more than doubled in current riyals since 1973, but it has fallen or shown only minimal gains in constant 1972 riyals because the OPEC (Organization of Petroleum Exporting Countries) cartel has restricted oil production.

In the language of international trade theory (rather than national income theory) this paradox of national income moving in one direction in current dollars and in the opposite direction in constant dollars is a case of the terms of trade moving against a country. In other words, there is a loss to the country that pays more for its imports or earns less from its exports. Thus, a country has an exchange gain or an exchange loss. Until recently, however, at least for developed countries the impact of the terms of trade on national income accounts was—particularly in the United States—considered to be limited and was the subject of a relatively small number of somewhat technical papers. Also, as stressed by W. S. Salant (1978), with changing terms of trade real output (real GNP) in standard national accounts will not be affected directly, but real disposable income will certainly change as prices of imports for consumers rise disproportionately. One element in the 1974–75 recession was the decline in real disposable income relative to overall real GNP because of the disproportionate rise in the price of oil imports. In subsequent rounds of spending, real GNP was, of course, affected by the lower level of real disposable income.

Thus, as a result of the continuing oil crisis, the net exports item has become a critical ambiguity in national account statistics.

References

Courbis, Raymond, "Comment on Y. Kurabayashi's System of National Accounts," *Review of Income and Wealth*, ser. 18, no. 2, June 1972, pp. 247–250; Kurabayashi, Y., "The Impact of Changes in Terms of Trade on a System of National Accounts," *Review of Income and Wealth*, ser. 17, no. 3, September 1971, pp. 285–297; Salant, Walter S., "Trade Balances in Constant Prices When Terms of Trade Change," in Jacob S. Dreyer (ed.), *Breadth and Depth in Economics*, Heath, Lexington, Mass., 1978; U.S. Department of Commerce, *Survey of Current Business*.

(*See also* Balance of international payments; Balance of international trade; Exports; Gross national product; Imports; National income accounting)

James L. Burtle

Net investment (see Capital formation)

Nonmonetary overinvestment theory of the business cycle (see Juglar cycle)

Normative economics

In economics as in all social sciences a clear line has been drawn between the positive and normative, that is, between the study of how things are in fact and how they ought to be. Positive economics is independent of any value judgment, while normative economics concerns itself with how our economic lives ought to be arranged; what goods and services ought to be produced; how the production of such desired goods and services should be organized, and by whom; how ownership of productive factors such as land, labor, capital, or material inputs should be distributed; and how income and, therefore, the consumption of goods and services should be distributed among members of the larger society including other nations of the world as well as unborn future generations. In other words, normative economics looks at the utilization of resources, their organization into productive activities, and the distribution of their benefits among people presently existing and yet to be born, and asks, "Are some arrangements better than others?" and "Is there a best arrangement?." In order to approach such questions criteria are needed for what is good or best. Such criteria depend on the political, philosophical, and theological perspective of the appraiser. Within the mainstream of the Western liberal tradition a few principles of appraisal have acquired near-universal allegiance as being helpful, though not necessarily decisive, for judgment of an economic system.

Three Principles of Appraisal

The first of these principles is that an economy is to be judged by the outcomes it produces, that is, specifically by the bundles of goods and services (of all types privately or publicly produced and privately or publicly consumed) it effectively assigns to individuals at the various points in time throughout their lives. (A contrasting view might be that outcomes are not the primary object to be appraised but rather that the processes of transition from one state to another are primary.) Thus, modern economists would ask, "Is this particular assignment of goods and services good; can it be improved upon within the resource limitations available?"

The second basic principle is that for appraising the assignment of goods to people, the individual is the only judge of how the goods and services affect the individual's well-being—the so-called doctrine of consumer sovereignty. (The principle has limits; it would seem to break down if applied to children and the senile, and many believe the effects of some activities on the welfares of some people should be ignored. For example, even though person A is offended by person B's private religious practices, the effect should be ignored.)

The third principle of normative economics is that judgments of the overall or social goodness of economic outcomes depend solely on the corresponding set of individual evaluations of individual welfares and not, for example, on an organic concept of society or the state.

The Pareto Criterion

Given that economic states of the world are to be appraised on the basis of individuals' self-evaluations of their own outcome positions and on nothing else, a widely accepted criterion for judging alternative states is the so-called Pareto-improvement criterion. This criterion proposes that one situation (call it X) is Pareto-preferred or superior to another (call it Y) if no one is worse off at X than at Y and if at least one person is better off at X than at Y. If both X and Y were economically feasible states then the Pareto-improvement criterion would judge that the configuration of resources, production, and distribution of goods at X was superior to that at Y.

In the accompanying figure the curve PP indicates the limit on economically feasible welfare outcomes between two individuals. All points to the northeast of X are Pareto-superior to X, including points S, T, and all points in between them on the PP curve. Point W is Pareto-superior to X but economically infeasible. The Pareto criterion will judge any point below the PP curve to be inferior to some point or points on the curve; similarly, it will judge any point on the curve to be superior to some points beneath it. It will not, however, compare points on the curve—S versus T, for instance—nor will it compare any points such as X and R or X and V. In short, the Pareto criterion does not imply any judgments as to the desirability of absolute redistribution (relative distribution possibly, since A at point Y might be said to be relatively much better off relative to B than at point X).

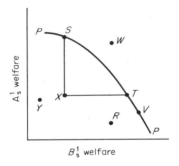

Within its limitations, nevertheless, the Pareto criterion yields very strong corollaries in support of a properly governed, decentralized, capitalistic, competitive, and price-regulated economy. Moreover, the Pareto principle allows for unambiguous normative evaluation of some alternative redistributions. For example, a redistribution which moves the economy from X to V is better than one which moves from X to R. Thus, a redistribution program which does not disturb the decentralized, price-regulated character of decisions regarding production, consumption, saving, investment, etc. is preferable to one that does.

The Pareto criterion, however, is incomplete in two respects. First, it does not allow comparisons between social states when one or more persons gain at the expense of others; and second, it does not identify the best or optimal, social state among those available (the entire curve PP in the figure). In order to allow for the first shortcoming, many believe that a criterion of potential Pareto improvement is satisfactory. This roughly is the criterion that one state V is preferable to another X if the people who benefit from the change could compensate the people who lose from the change so that all groups would end up as net beneficiaries. The potential Pareto criterion is implicit in all benefit-cost analysis, but it is not universally accepted because (aside from some technical difficulties associated with it) it requires only the potential for compensation, not that actual compensation be made. Thus, the potential Pareto criterion could recommend a move from X to V, even though A would be utterly impoverished, simply because B could more than compensate A for that loss.

The Best Social Welfare Function

At best, even if the potential Pareto criterion is accepted, our norms for evaluating alternative economic states would be incomplete. We still would have no basis for judging movements along the curve *PP* where some people gain, others lose, and no compensation could redistribute gains so that all benefit. Within the realm of individualistic normative criteria several formulas for weighting or counting individual welfares so as to arrive at a social welfare function have been proposed. Among these are the Benthamite-utilitarian function, and those attributed to Bergson, Nash, Arrow, and Rawls. All attempt to identify the best alternative social state out of a given environment, e.g., the best of the set contained by *PP* in the diagram.

Thus, modern normative economics has become concerned with how different axioms and assumptions lead to different rules for choice of outcomes. Three examples may elucidate the character of the logical connections which preoccupy modern normative economics. As a first example, Nash (1950) proposed that social welfare is best represented as the product of individual utilities. His proposal depends crucially on the assumption that the welfare level of each individual in a completely autarkic, noncooperative economy is highly relevant to the division of welfare when individuals cooperate. As a second case, Arrow's (1970) concept of a social welfare function crucially involves the assumption that no possible set of circumstances should produce a dictator (i.e., an individual whose preferences govern social choice irrespective of others' preferences). And lastly, there is Rawls's (1971) notion that the best economic organization and distribution of goods is that which would be unanimously endorsed by a society of individuals if a vote were taken before anyone knew what his or her place in the economic order would be.

References

Arrow, Kenneth J., *Social Choice and Individual Values*, 2d ed., Yale University Press, New Haven, Conn., 1970; Boulding, Kenneth E., "Welfare Economics," in Bernard F. Haley (ed.), *Survey of Contemporary Economic Theory*, vol. II, Irwin, Homewood, Ill., 1952; Nash, J. F. "The Bargaining Problem," *Econometrica* vol. xviii, no. 2, 1950, pp. 155–162; Pigou, Arthur C., *The Economics of Welfare*, Macmillan, New York, 1932; Rawls, John, *Theory of Justice*, Harvard University Press, Cambridge, Mass., 1971.

(*See also* Capitalism; Communism; Comparative economic systems, an overview; Marxism; Socialism; Utility; Welfare economics)

Martin C. McGuire

Open-end investment company (see **Mutual fund**)

Open-market operations

In the U.S. economy of the post-World War II decades, open-market operations have been the chief instrument of Federal Reserve monetary policy. The term refers to central bank purchases and sales of government securities in the national money market for the immediate purpose of affecting the availability and cost of bank reserves, but with the broader aim of affecting the availability and cost of money and credit in the economy.

Complementing open-market operations in the United States are two other major instruments of policy: the discount mechanism and changes in member bank reserve requirements. Of the three, open-market operations are the most flexible. Lending through the discount window—originally conceived as the heart of Federal Reserve policy—is at the initiative of the member banks, making it difficult for the System to gauge the amount of reserve provision associated with any given discount rate. As presently conceived, lending through the discount window serves mainly to provide funds on a temporary basis to member banks experiencing unexpected reserve shortages, and as a safety valve for the financial system in times of monetary stress. Compared to open-market operations, changes in reserve requirements are a blunt instrument, for even small adjustments can have large effects on reserve needs. They also affect bank profitability since holdings of required reserves represent nonearning assets. Reserve requirement changes have typically been used to influence the banks' asset-liability structure.

Market in Government Securities

The cornerstone of central bank, open-market operations in the United States is the broad and active market in U.S. government securities which permits the Federal

Reserve to operate readily on a substantial scale without causing wide changes in market prices. An additional underpinning could be said to be the system of reserve requirements under which member banks of the Federal Reserve System must hold reserves with the central bank. It has been argued that, theoretically, Federal Reserve open-market operations could be effective even if reserve requirements were set at zero, as long as some major group of banks found it desirable to hold balances—perhaps for clearing account purposes—at the central bank, since the Federal Reserve could make those balances easier or harder to obtain. However, others believe that central bank control of the money supply in its various forms would be significantly impaired in the absence of reserve requirements.

The absence of such a comparable market for government securities in most other countries limits the ability of their central banks to engage in open-market operations. Thus, while open-market operations are not unique to the U.S. economy, they are more highly developed and are relied on more substantially in the United States than in almost any other country. A major exception is in the United Kingdom, where open-market operations, as in the United States, currently serve as the principal monetary policy tool.

The Federal Open Market Committee

Federal Reserve open-market operations are carried out in the United States by the trading desk at the Federal Reserve Bank of New York, under the policy guidance of the Federal Open Market Committee (FOMC). The Committee is comprised of the seven members of the Board of Governors of the Federal Reserve System, and five of the twelve regional Reserve bank presidents. (However, all twelve presidents participate in the FOMC meetings which are usually held monthly in Washington, D.C.) The head of the Board of Governors also chairs the FOMC. The New York Reserve Bank president is always a voting member of the Committee and traditionally serves as its vice chair, while the other four voting Reserve bank presidents are drawn on a rotating basis, for 1-year terms, from among the other eleven Reserve bank presidents.

Open-market operations are directed by the Manager for Domestic Operations of the System Open Market Account, a senior officer of the New York Reserve Bank. Operations are conducted mainly in U.S. Treasury securities, and to a lesser degree in the securities of federally sponsored agencies (such as the Federal Home Loan Banks), and in bankers' acceptances. Central bank purchases of securities add to bank reserves, thus accommodating or encouraging the expansion of money and credit, while sales of securities extinguish bank reserves and inhibit the growth of money and credit.

The Federal Reserve conducts its operations with primary dealers in government securities (about 35 in 1979). Some are the dealer departments of major banks, while others include diversified securities firms and relatively small firms specializing in government and closely related securities. The Federal Reserve also conducts operations directly with official foreign accounts—foreign central banks which arrange investment activities through the Federal Reserve. This is done when the transactions meet the reserve objectives of the Federal Reserve as well as the investment needs of the foreign account. Transactions with dealers are conducted on a competitive, best-price basis among the dealers.

The form of operations depends on the duration and size of needs to add or absorb reserves. Relatively permanent reserve needs, consistent with growth of money and credit in an expanding economy, may be met through outright Federal Reserve purchases of Treasury and federal agency securities of varying maturity—from bills maturing within a year to notes and bonds of as much as 30 years' maturity. Outright sales are less frequent and smaller than purchases since the long-term trend of Federal Reserve holdings has been upward. On occasion the Federal Reserve may also redeem some of its maturing holdings of Treasury or agency securities, although more typically the maturing holdings are exchanged for new issues offered by the Treasury or agency. Redemptions of maturing securities, like sales, absorb reserves.

When the perceived need for reserves is temporary, or very large, the Federal Reserve may purchase securities under a repurchase agreement—buying the securities for delivery the day the trade is arranged, and committing to sell the same securities back to the dealer 1 to 15 days later at the original price plus interest. If there is a need to drain reserves on a temporary basis, especially if the need is large, the trading desk may arrange matched sale-purchase transactions, in which the System sells securities on the day the trade is arranged and commits to repurchase them at a later date—usually 1 to 7 days later.

Temporary needs to add or absorb reserves result from technical factors which affect the supply of reserves—e.g., the volume of Federal Reserve float or the amount of currency in circulation—and from seasonal variation in the demand for money and credit. The bulk of open-market operations on a day-to-day basis is undertaken to offset the impact of these factors on the availability of reserves.

Monetary Growth Objectives

The theory and conduct of Federal Reserve open-market operations have evolved over time in response to changes in the economy and in economic and public opinion. In recent decades there has been increasing attention to achievement of monetary growth objectives. Thus, in the early post-World War II years, policymakers gave little explicit attention to money and credit growth as such. Open-market policy during the 1950s was directed at ease or restraint, as deemed appropriate in the prevailing economic circumstances. Under a policy of ease, the Federal Reserve bought government securities vigorously, thus providing the banking system with relatively ample reserve availability in order to stimulate the economy by reducing interest rates and inducing banks to invest and lend more readily. At other times, there was a policy of restraint, designed to curtail the availability of reserves through slowing down central bank purchases, or even making net sales of securities, thus tending to raise interest rates and inducing banks to curtail the availability of credit to their customers.

Beginning in the mid-1960s, increasing emphasis was placed on growth of money and bank credit. At first, this emphasis was expressed in the form of subsidiary instructions, or proviso clauses, in the directives of the FOMC to the System account manager. A typical proviso clause directed the manager to alter somewhat the thrust of contemplated operations during the month between FOMC meetings if bank credit did not appear to be growing as expected. By the early 1970s, the proviso clause had given way to committee directives calling for moderate, faster, or slower growth in money and bank credit, with side constraints placing limits on changes in the federal funds rate. The federal funds rate is the overnight interest rate on interbank transactions in reserves; this rate became in practice the immediate focus of Federal

Reserve open-market operations and the key rate affecting other money-market rates, and to lesser degree other interest rates in the economy.

Starting in 1972, the FOMC adopted target rates of growth for key measures of money (monetary aggregates) and bank credit extending initially some two quarters ahead. At the same time, the FOMC typically specified tolerance ranges for growth in monetary aggregates for a 2-month period ending with the month following the Committee's meeting; achievement of growth within these ranges was deemed to be consistent with achieving the Committee's longer-term growth objectives. As the month between FOMC meetings proceeded, the trading desk was expected to modify its federal funds objective in response to incoming information on the monetary aggregates, raising the funds rate within its allowable range if 2-month growth in the aggregates was coming in toward the high side of the 2-month ranges, and lowering the funds rate if monetary growth was running low in relation to the 2-month ranges. On occasion, the FOMC would modify the funds rate range set for the month between FOMC meetings, perhaps to provide greater leeway to the desk if monetary growth was turning out exceptionally strong or weak relative to the 2-month tolerance ranges.

To encourage a higher federal funds rate, the trading desk would tend to provide reserves less readily to the banking system, holding off the purchase of securities until the bank demands for funds had pushed the rate above levels that had previously brought official intervention; or, the desk could sell securities when funds were trading at a level previously deemed acceptable. To encourage a lower funds rate, the desk would provide reserves more readily by purchasing securities when funds were trading at levels considered acceptable earlier, while refraining from selling securities even though the funds rate had declined to levels that previously induced official intervention to drain reserves.

Through the 1970s, the procedures described above became increasingly well-established, with quantitative objectives adopted by the FOMC for longer periods into the future. Thus, beginning in 1975, the directives came to include annual objectives for monetary growth as well as 2-month ranges of tolerance for monetary growth that guided the desk's choice of a particular funds rate objective within the Committee's funds rate range. The Committee's attention to money and credit growth intensified as inflation became a more serious problem.

New Approach to Open-Market Operations

In October 1979, in order to provide greater assurance of achieving its monetary growth objectives for the year, the FOMC modified its approach to open-market operations. Greater emphasis was placed on supplying the volume of reserves deemed appropriate to support the monetary growth sought by the Committee for 1979, while less emphasis was placed on the federal funds rate. The Committee still set broad limits for the funds rate, but was prepared to see substantially greater day-to-day and week-to-week variation than before. Reserve objectives were to be achieved by constructing growth paths for total reserves, the monetary base (total reserves plus currency outside member banks), and nonborrowed reserves (total reserves less borrowings from the Federal Reserve discount window). Techniques for operating under the modified approach are still being refined and are subject to subsequent modification.

In early experience with the new approach, the trading desk focused on achievement of path levels of nonborrowed reserves. To the extent that the banking system's demand for total reserves exceeded the path for nonborrowed reserves, the banks would have to borrow additional reserves at the discount window. But for any particular bank, the discount window is only a temporary source of reserves. Banks that seek to borrow too frequently are counseled to make other adjustments which might include restrictions on loans and investments, or resort to other sources of funding which would place still other banks under reserve adjustment pressure. Generally, excessive borrowing could also lead to an increase in the discount rate. In this manner, excessive monetary growth would in time encourage banks to adjust their policies for asset and liability management, leading in turn to slower growth in money and credit.

Correspondingly, if there were unduly weak growth in money and credit, a policy of supplying the nonborrowed reserves consistent with desired growth in aggregates would lead to a decline in borrowing from the Federal Reserve. This would mean a more abundant and less costly availability of bank reserves that would be expected to encourage credit formation and the desired growth in monetary aggregates.

References

Board of Governors, The Federal Reserve System: Purposes and Functions, Federal Reserve System, September 1974; Chandler, Lester V., and Stephen M. Goldfeld, The Economics of Money and Banking, 7th ed., Harper & Row, New York, 1977, pp. 179–284, 521–609; Meek, Paul, Open Market Operations, Federal Reserve Bank of New York, New York, June 1978; Sternlight, Peter D., Fred J. Levin, Ann-Marie Meulendyke, and Christopher J. McCurdy, "Monetary Policy and Open Market Operations in 1979," Federal Reserve Bank of New York Quarterly Review, Summer 1980, pp. 50–64; Wallich, Henry C., and Peter M. Keir, "The Role of Operating Guidelines in U.S. Monetary Policy: A Historical Review," Federal Reserve Bulletin, September 1979, pp. 679–691.

(See also Banking system; Credit, an overview; Federal Reserve policy; Federal Reserve System; Interest rates; Monetary policy; Money supply)

Peter D. Sternlight and Fred J. Levin

Operations research

Operations research, also called operational research (OR), has both a general and a more specific technical meaning. The historical and more general definition is that OR is the application of scientific analysis to the decision-making process, with problems typically arising in the areas of military planning, industrial management, economic analysis, and the determination of public policy. In a technical sense, OR refers to a number of mathematical modeling techniques, including optimization and simulation methods, which find frequent application in the study of rational decision making.

History

Although operations research first appeared as an organized discipline during World War II, much of the pioneering work had been already completed by then. In the late 1800s, the time and motion studies of Frederick Taylor introduced scientific analysis into factory management. The Danish mathematician A. K. Erlang studied the problems of traffic congestion in telephone networks in his 1909 publication, The Theory of Probability and Telephone Conversations. This work initiated the use of so-called queueing models which have applications to a far broader range of problems. In that same era, F. W. Lanchester brought the tools of mathematical analysis to bear upon problems of military planning, demonstrating the principle of concentration, or n-square law, and establishing other relations which have had a profound influence upon the conduct of modern wars.

During World War II, civilian scientists in several allied countries were organized into groups which were ultimately to become the first operations research teams. These individuals sought to employ scientific analysis in the study of military planning and policy. After the conclusion of the war and as the world emerged into the nuclear era, defense planners observed that scientific programming techniques would be required to coordinate more rapidly the energies of an entire nation in the event of any future war.

Under the auspices of the U.S. Air Force, a team of economists and mathematicians called Project SCOOP (Scientific Computation of Optimal Programs) began intensive work in June 1947 on the modeling of the military structure and the economy. During this period G. B. Dantzig developed the simplex method for computing optimal solutions to linear programs.

By 1950, linear programming and the other tools of operations research began to make their way into industrial applications as business executives became aware of their potential and the growing capabilities of electronic data processing made large-scale mathematical modeling feasible. W. Cooper, A. Charnes, and others used linear programming techniques to solve problems of petroleum refinery scheduling, achieving the first major success of OR in business. Fruitful applications in the food processing, iron and steel, transportation, and power generation industries followed quickly. By the end of the decade, OR applications in the private sector had grown too numerous and diverse to catalog. During the 1960s, operations research matured into a recognized and independent discipline; OR departments and degree programs became common in major universities, and most of the larger corporations included at least one OR team within their organizations. Continuing research resulted in new and productive applications for government and industry. Further growth was experienced in the following decade, with much research being done in energy and economic modeling following the advent of the energy crisis.

General Methodology

The basic methodology employed in the OR study varies little. The first step is the formulation of the problem. Here, the operations researcher studies the problem at hand and attempts to identify the overall objectives of the system and any constraints that limit the range of actions which can be taken.

The next step is the construction of a mathematical model of the system under study. The intrinsic structure of the problem is modeled by mathematical relationships, and the objectives are explicitly represented by a function of the model's variables and parameters. Simplification and approximation of the practical problem is almost always necessary to obtain a computationally tractable model.

Following the construction of the model, a solution must be derived. While algorithms exist for the solution of many of the most commonly used models, the amount of computational effort required can often be significantly reduced by exploiting any special structure present in the problem. Also, problems are occasionally encountered in practice or can be artificially generated for which no efficient solution techniques are known. (These problems are called NP-complete in the technical vernacular.) However, there are heuristic algorithms for many of these problems which return good solutions most of the time and even best solutions all of the time for practical cases.

Once a solution has been obtained, the OR study must now be reviewed and tested. One simple, but revealing, technique is to vary the input to the model and observe whether the changes in output seem plausible. This test will frequently uncover errors or omissions in the initial formulation. When applicable, a more systematic approach is the use of a retrospective test. This involves using historical data to reconstruct the past and then determining how well the model would have performed if it had been employed at that time.

Frequently, the solution obtained from the tested model will be used in an environment where the input data are not precisely known. In this case, a sensitivity analysis is conducted to identify the range of input parameter values over which the given solution remains valid. This type of analysis will frequently identify parameters which should be estimated with particular care, and some extreme circumstances may lead the analyst to select a solution which is slightly suboptimal but robust in its response to variations in the parameters. Also, when the solution is to be applied repeatedly, sensitivity analysis can be used to determine acceptable ranges over which parameters may be allowed to vary before the model must be used to determine a different solution for the new conditions.

General Classification of OR Models

The most frequently used models in operations research studies may be classified by their structures and areas of application into several categories.

1. *Mathematical programming.* Programming in this context means planning or scheduling, not the preparation of instructions for a computer. A mathematical program is composed of an objective function which is to be maximized or minimized over values of the decision variables which satisfy a set of auxiliary constraint inequalities. Linear programs are characterized by objective functions and constraints which are linear in an algebraic sense. Linear programs with special structures may be solved even when they have very large numbers of variables and constraints. Nonlinear programs have algebraic nonlinearities in their objectives or constraints. Computationally, the presence of such nonlinearities makes the solution of problems of even moderate size difficult except in a few special cases. Integer programs are those in which some or all of the decision variables must have only integer values. In general, integer programs fall into the category of hard (NP-complete) problems for which no efficient algorithm is known, and hence most solutions are found by heuristic methods that do not guarantee optimality.

2. *Game theory.* Many competitive and cooperative situations which are encountered in practice can be modeled abstractly as games. Games are generally specified by a set of players, a set of actions which are available to each player, and a set of rewards or payoffs determined by the actions which the players choose to take.

3. *Inventory theory.* A wide range of problems may be modeled abstractly in terms of the acquisition, storage, and disposal of stock. Models in this field may

be grouped into those that deal with deterministic demands and those that deal with stochastic (probabilistic) demands, and those in which there exist convex costs (diseconomies of scale) and those in which there exist concave costs (economies of scale).

4. *Reliability theory.* Since component failures tend to occur at random times, these models are principally statistical in nature. The models may be further subdivided into those which, given a set of data, seek to estimate a parameter (such as the mean or variance) of the distribution of a component's life, those which estimate the life of a system given the reliabilities of the system's components, and those optimization models which treat policies for the repair and replacement of components.

5. *Queueing theory.* As its name would indicate, queueing theoretical models are applicable to situations in which customers periodically arrive at a configuration of servers, where they wait in line until they actually have access to a server for some length of time. In general, customers are assumed to arrive for service at random times and the service time they require is again assumed to be randomly distributed. The queues in a bank or at a gas station may be modeled in this manner, as can demands upon a telephone network or a central processing unit in a time-sharing computer system.

6. *Dynamic programming.* Models in this category are useful in selecting optimal policies over time, where the reward obtained at any given time generally depends upon the decision maker's past actions and the operation of some chance mechanism. Such models are useful, for example, in analyzing situations in which it might be desirable to incur temporary losses in view of possible long-run gains.

7. *Simulation.* Simulation models are fundamentally different from the models within the preceding classes since simulations are primarily useful for comparing proposed programs of action rather than constructing a particular optimal solution. Because no optimization procedure is invoked, simulation models can be made with a very detailed structure. However, no guarantee can be given that even the best of the proposed programs will approximate the actual optimal solution to within any given degree of accuracy. For example, in assigning 200 people to 200 jobs, a comprehensive simulation certain to find the best matching is impractical since it would require even the most advanced computers millions of years to examine each possible combination.

Probable Future of Operations Research

As technology advances and the issues and choices faced by individual and institutional decision makers become more complex, operations research and its allied disciplines will have a continuing and increasingly important role in the analysis of problems and the determination of the optimal solutions. Advances in mathematical techniques and the growing capabilities of electronic data-processing equipment seem to indicate that the field will be capable of handling these greater responsibilities.

References

Churchman, C. West, et al., *Introduction to Operations Research*, Wiley, New York, 1957; Dantzig, George B., *Linear Programming and Extensions*, Princeton University Press, Princeton, N.J., 1963; Hillier, F. S., and G. J. Lieberman, *Introduction to Operations Research*, 3d ed., Holden-Day, San Francisco, 1980; *International Abstracts in Operations Research*, 1961; Wagner, H., *Principles of Operations Research*, 2d ed., Prentice-Hall, Englewood Cliffs, N.J., 1975.

(*See also* Business inventory; Game theory, economic applications; Linear programming; Simulation in business and economics; Stock-flow analysis)

Brian E. Leverich

Opportunity cost

The concept of opportunity cost was introduced by the neoclassicists of the nineteenth century. Opportunity costs are also called user costs or alternative costs. The opportunity cost of producing some good or service (or of otherwise satisfying some economic want) is the real economic cost associated with the production process. Opportunity costs consider what must be forgone in real terms in order to produce a unit of output of some good or service.

For example, the opportunity cost of using labor, raw materials, and other resources to produce a unit of product X is the number of units of the next-best alternative product that must be sacrificed in order to produce that unit of X. Thus, the real economic cost to society of producing some product, such as a ship, is the value of the other items which cannot be produced, such as additional automobiles and appliances, because of the steel and other resources which have been used up in the construction of the ship.

Opportunity costs are an important concept because the supply of the factors of production is limited in any economy. Given this limited supply, it is important that these resources be used in a manner which produces the maximum amount of output that is consistent with consumers' desires, as measured by their willingness to pay for various goods and services.

The best use of any resource is the one which offers the highest return given a level of risk. Thus, the opportunity cost of an investment in American Telephone and Telegraph (AT&T) bonds that promises to yield 10 percent per annum is not the rate of return that could be earned by investing a similar amount in Allegheny Airlines bonds, since these are not assets of equal risk. Rather, the opportunity cost of investing in AT&T bonds might be measured by the returns available in other, similarly low-risk bonds, such as those offered by General Motors.

In many cases, the measurement of the opportunity cost of using a resource such as labor, machinery, buildings, or raw materials is quite simple and is consistent with the accounting definitions of cost. For example, most items which a firm purchases have an opportunity cost equal to the cost of the item. Thus, if a firm buys 100 gallons of fuel oil for $75, the firm has to forgo its claims to whatever else the $75 will buy. In the case of rented or hired factors, such as rented buildings or labor services, the opportunity cost is normally equal to the dollar cost of the rental, considering all explicit costs, such as retirement benefits and other benefits which are normally paid in addition to wages.

There are, however, some instances where these dollar charges may not fully measure the economic cost of the resource being used. When certain commodities are rationed and their prices are fixed, as during wars or as in the 1970s with respect to oil and natural gas, the firm may place a value on a resource which is higher than its price. In normal circumstances, however, market-determined prices of input factors are a good estimate for the opportunity cost of an input.

Two Cases

The following two examples illustrate some special cases of the use of the opportunity cost concept. First, consider a farmer who has decided to plant oats this year. The farmer expects to be able to sell the crop for $60,000. The land could also be used to grow soybeans, which the farmer could sell for $70,000. The opportunity cost of growing oats to the exclusion of soybeans is the difference between the value of the oat crop and the value of the soybean crop, or $10,000. Using the opportunity cost concept, this farmer should choose to grow soybeans rather than oats.

The opportunity cost of capital supplied by the owners of a firm is the rate of return those funds could have earned in the next-best alternative investment of equal risk. Consider the case of a consultant who earns $30,000 per year working for a large consulting firm. The consultant decides to take a life savings of $100,000 and open a new consulting firm. The new firm shows accounting net profits of $35,000 per year. Using the opportunity cost concept, however, there are no real profits earned because the opportunity cost of the consultant's time was $30,000 per year and the opportunity cost of the money invested in the firm would be measured by the return available in some equally risky venture. Assuming a conservative measure of this capital cost to be 15 percent or $15,000 per year, the new firm actually had economic losses of $10,000 per year, rather than the reported profits of $35,000.

References

Lipsey, Richard G., and Peter O. Steiner, *Economics*, 4th ed., Harper & Row, New York, 1975; McGuigan, James R., and R. Charles Moyer, *Managerial Economics*, 2d ed., West, St. Paul, Minn., 1979; Mansfield, Edwin, *Microeconomics: Theory and Applications*, 2d ed., Norton, New York, 1975.

(*See also* Neoclassical economics)

R. Charles Moyer

Organization for Economic Cooperation and Development

The Organization for Economic Cooperation and Development (OECD) is an international organization of 24 industrialized nations. Its basic purpose is twofold: (1) to contribute through cooperative efforts to economic growth, employment, financial stability, and a rising living standard in member countries; and (2) to promote economic development of all nations and trade among them by assisting countries in their efforts to achieve these goals.

History

The OECD was formed on December 14, 1960, as a successor organization to the Organization for European Economic Cooperation (OEEC), whose main purpose was to coordinate the post-World War II economic recovery of Europe and to administer aid provided by the United States through the Marshall Plan. The OECD commenced operations on September 30, 1961, at its headquarters in Paris. In addition to the 18 European members of the OEEC, the United States and Canada were among the original member countries. Since then, Australia, Finland, Japan, and New Zealand have joined the organization, bringing the total to 24 member countries. Yugoslavia is a special-status associated country.

Structure

The Council is the central organ of the organization. The Council may meet on the ministerial level or as a group of permanent representatives (ambassadors) of the 24 member countries. Meetings at the ministerial level are usually held once a year, and the chair rotates among the member countries. The Council meets regularly at the ambassadorial level. These meetings are presided over by the Secretary General of the OECD, who is appointed by the Council for a 5-year term.

An executive committee composed of 14 members assists the Council in its work. In addition, there are numerous committees and semiautonomous agencies that carry on the work of the organization. An indication of the multitude of topics covered by the OECD is given by the various committees, which cover economic policy, energy, development assistance, technical cooperation, trade, international investment, multinational enterprises, insurance, financial markets, consumer affairs, tourism, sea transport, work force, education, environment, science, industry, agriculture, and other areas of concern. Many of these committees have further subcommittees or working parties, so that the total number of committees surpasses 200.

There are also several semiautonomous agencies that operate within the OECD framework. Among the most important agencies are: the International Energy Agency created in 1974 to assist in the implementation of energy policies; the Nuclear Energy Agency, which was established in 1958 to promote the use of nuclear power for peaceful purposes; the Development Center, which has responsibilities in areas of research, liaison, information exchange, and expert assistance related to development problems; the Road Research Program; the Educational Research and Innovation Center; and the Interfutures Project, which is a long-range study and analysis group.

The various committees and agencies of the OECD are served by an international Secretariat, which is headed by the Secretary General. In turn, the Secretariat is composed of various directorates that are organized along functional lines.

Operations

The OECD performs a wide variety of functions and tasks. Among them are the collection and dissemination of statistical information on the member countries, the conduct of basic research and policy studies, and formal policy actions taken by the Council.

The Secretariat maintains extensive data banks and publishes relevant statistical information on the member countries. It also engages in regular economic forecasting exercises and publishes its findings. Frequently, groups of experts are called upon to provide further advice and assistance.

On a more formal level, the OECD Council may adopt decisions which are binding upon member countries or recommendations for their voluntary consideration and possible implementation.

In sum, the OECD serves as an international clearinghouse for a wide variety of governmental activities that have to be coordinated in today's interdependent world.

References

OECD: History, Aims, Structure, Organization for Economic Cooperation and Development, Paris, 1971.

(*See also* International economics, an overview.)

H. Robert Heller

Payroll taxes (see **Taxation, an overview)**

Pension funds

A pension fund is a plan established and maintained by an employer to provide for systematic benefit payments to employees after their retirement. Thus, pension fund assets are actually a pool of capital set aside for the purpose of meeting future liability payments. Pension funds are an important factor in income distribution and in the saving and investment function. They currently account for a significant share of personal savings, and they are clearly one of the largest sources of investment capital.

Daniel M. Holland (1966) said, "A pension plan has fiscal counterparts that may be compared roughly to a bath tub with its drain and faucets both open. The faucets represent fund inflows—that is, contributions by employers and to a lesser degree, as a general rule, by employees—and fund earnings; the drain represents fund outflows, i.e., benefit payments. The change in the level of water in the bath tub represents the net difference between the two flows."

Pension funds represent the largest and fastest- growing segment of institutional capital. Assets of private and state and local pension funds at the beginning of 1980 were estimated at close to $400 billion, on a book-value basis, compared with $196 billion at the end of 1970 and $72 billion at the end of 1960.

Private Pension Funds

There are about 1.1 million pension plans in private industry. Until 1974 private pension plans were quite diverse, but federal legislation in the late 1970s has resulted in plans with similar general features. Very few pension plans are indexed to the consumer price index to take care of the inflation that occurs after a worker retires, and most of these indexed plans have a limit on the amount of increase, usually 3 or 6 percent.

There are two major types of private pensions funds, the noninsured and the insured. Under insured pension plans, pension obligations are funded by premium payments made by the sponsoring company to a life insurance company. In turn, the life insurance company guarantees that it will make specified annuity payments in the future. Life insurance companies attempt to maximize their return on investment of the premiums, but various state laws governing life insurance company activities constrain their investment latitude. During the late 1960s and the 1970s, pension plans that allow life insurance companies greater investment latitude were developed and have grown rapidly. These so-called deposit administration plans are similar in nature to the noninsured type of pension plan, but they are managed by life insurance companies. For smaller companies and for programs in which relatively few employees are covered, conventional insured plans tend to predominate.

In the case of noninsured pension plans, company contributions are generally paid into a trust fund at a bank or a trust company. The trustee holds and invests the accumulated funds. In turn, the trustee makes benefit payments to the plan's participants based on the specific provisions of the program.

The importance of pension funds to the economy, the size of the asset commitments, the number of employees covered by the plans, and the cost to stockholders of providing pension benefits makes it essential that investment of pension fund assets be managed by highly competent professionals.

A trustee may be given either wide investment latitude, or limited latitude in investing the assets, with fixed maximum percentages of assets to go for common stocks, for a specific industry or company, for foreign securities, or for private placements. The trustee may need approval of a designated cotrustee before investments can be made, or the trustee may act solely as a custodial agent and invest only at the direction of the company.

Over the years, the use of conventional insured plans have declined relative to the noninsured plans because the latter permits use of different investment manager relationships as well as imposing fewer portfolio restraints. In effect, the burden of meeting benefit obligations has shifted from the life insurance company to the sponsoring company.

State and Local Government Pension Plans

These plans generally are established and maintained under complex laws which dictate, in large part, the administrative and investment policy. Most public pension plans require considerable employee contributions as well as employer contributions.

Public pension funds have traditionally invested in bonds—tax-exempt but low-yielding—issued by the sponsoring government agency. The trustees of these plans are usually elected or appointed public officials, not professional fund managers. Moreover, they are limited in their investment decisions because of state laws regulating the handling of public funds. Since public pension plans are public, they are open to examination by political partisans. Obviously this situation is not conducive to aggressive investment management. It has been suggested that, from an actuarial viewpoint, many state and local pension plans are technically bankrupt.

With the United States entering an era when fewer and fewer young workers will be forced to support a growing population of retired workers, actuaries and other pension experts indicate that enormous stresses are building up not only in public employee systems but in pay-as-you-go social security and pension funds for workers in the private sector as well.

History

Prior to World War II, pension plans were largely limited to the public sector and executives in private industry. In 1946, the United Mine Workers and the coal industry settled for a $100-per-month pension benefit to be paid in addition to social security payments. In 1949 a steel industry fact-finding commission strongly endorsed a pension welfare benefit program as opposed to direct wage increases at that time. In that same year the United Auto Workers and Ford negotiated a $100-per- month noncontributory (by employees) plan. Since then noncontributory pension plans have grown significantly.

Favorable tax regulation has provided significant employer incentive for establishment and maintenance of employee pension plans. Company contributions are considered tax-exempt from federal corporate income tax liability. In addition, pension fund investment earnings—both income and capital gains—are also exempt from federal corporate income tax liability.

In 1974 Congress passed the Employees' Retirement Income Security Act (ERISA), which provided protection for the pensions of workers in private industry. The act was aimed at safeguarding the pension rights of more than 23 million workers covered by private pension plans.

Minimum funding standards were set requiring pension managers to put aside enough funds to ensure payments of workers' pensions. Also, rules were established determining proper management of pension funds.

All employees 25 years old or older and with 1 year of work experience in the company would have to be enrolled in the plan. However, the employer could select one of three alternative investing formulas that would guarantee an employee at least part of the pension whether or not the employee continued working for the same company until retirement.

A federally run pension plan termination insurance corporation was also established. Its function is to protect workers' benefits in the event that their companies go bankrupt. Employees are also allowed to transfer pension fund credits from one employer to another.

Another important innovation of ERISA was the provision permitting an individual not covered by a company pension plan to establish his or her own retirement plan that would qualify for special tax treatment.

References

Holland, Daniel M., *Private Pension Funds*, occasional paper no. 97, National Bureau of Economic Research, Columbia University Press, New York, 1966; Murray, Roger F., *Economic Aspects of Pensions: A Summary Report*, National Bureau of Economic Research, New York, 1968; Tucker, Richard J., *State and Local Pension Funds*, Securities Industry Association, Washington, D.C., 1972.

(*See also* Financial institutions; Financial instruments; Saving)

Edward G. Mayers

Permanent income hypothesis

The permanent income hypothesis relates total consumption to the income flow which would be obtained if current human and nonhuman wealth were converted to a real (constant-dollar) perpetuity. This income stream is termed permanent income. It is applied both to individual households and to the aggregate economy. In its strictest form, consumption is a constant fraction of permanent income. Thus consumption rises proportionally with wealth and permanent income; or the elasticity of consumption with respect to permanent income or wealth is 1.

The permanent income hypothesis differs sharply from the earlier Keynesian absolute income hypothesis of the consumption function, which related consumption to current measured income. The permanent income and life-cycle hypotheses of the consumption function are equivalent in their full theoretical formulations, but in practice differ in the particular empirical approximations used for statistical estimation and testing.

The permanent income hypothesis has been the principal means by which macroeconomists have reconciled low marginal propensities to spend current income with a secularly constant and high average propensity to spend income. The marginal propensity to consume (MPC) is the ratio of the change in consumption to the change in current income. The average propensity to consume (APC) is the ratio of consumption to current income. Early Keynesian economists had explained consumption as a linear function of current income. When this function was estimated using the 1930s' data, a MPC of about 0.7 was obtained. Compared with the observed APC of 0.9, this suggested that the ratio of consumption to income would fall as income rose over time. The secular stagnation thesis asserted that investment opportunities would be insufficient to fill the growing gap between income and consumption so that a steadily deepening depression would occur, offsetting growth in government expenditure. When the post-World War II data became available, it was soon obvious that in fact consumption rose in proportion to income.

Friedman's Early Work

Milton Friedman (1957) showed that the concept of permanent income, which he had developed previously (Friedman and Kuznets, 1945) to explain household consumption, also could explain aggregate consumption. Friedman first applied the microeconomic analysis of Irving Fisher and John Hicks to observe that pure consumption of service flows (not expenditures) is related to a household's wealth, the real interest rate, and other factors which can be neglected when averaging over all households. For the type of utility functions which imply the observed constant secular average propensity to consume, pure consumption will equal the product of real wealth and a function of the real interest rate. Finally, if the real interest rate on perpetuities is a constant, as in the neoclassical growth model, pure consumption equals a constant times permanent income. Short-run fluctuations of current income around permanent income will affect pure consumption only in proportion to the small change which they induce in wealth and permanent income. Over time pure consumption will grow in proportion to permanent income. Thus, we observe a small MPC defined for current income and a high, secularly constant APC.

The permanent income hypothesis thus gave the theoretical basis for rejecting the secular stagnation thesis, a concept already suffering by comparison with the facts.

In addition, the low estimated marginal propensities to spend current income implied smaller values for Keynesian multipliers than previously supposed so that the economy's apparent stability was enhanced.

Recent Empirical Work

Empirical work following Friedman's lead initially met with mixed success as summarized by Thomas Mayer (1972). Conflicting estimates of the effect of current income on permanent income and hence consumption were reported. Michael Darby (1974) showed that the conflicting estimates could be reconciled by noting that Friedman's permanent income hypothesis referred to pure consumption and not to consumer expenditures. Indeed, under Friedman's hypothesis, fluctuations in current income around permanent income should affect expenditures on durable and semidurable goods over and above the effect on consumption. A statistical bias was introduced which varied according to whether the analyst used data closer to pure consumption or consumer expenditures and to whether annual or quarterly observations were used. Darby also showed that a particular estimator of permanent income proposed by Friedman is the one implied by the permanent income hypothesis.

Recent empirical work aimed at explaining consumer expenditures (such as Darby, 1977–78) has found both permanent and transitory (current minus permanent) income important, as well as other factors which influence household investment in durable and semidurable consumer goods such as automobiles, refrigerators, and clothing. Friedman's earlier implications for the secular stagnation hypothesis and Keynesian multipliers ultimately have proved correct. In addition, the more refined permanent income models of consumer expenditures have enhanced understanding of the macroeconomy while virtually eliminating shifts in the consumption function as a potential source of macroeconomic disturbances.

References

Darby, Michael R., "The Consumer Expenditure Function," *Explorations in Economic Research*, vol. 4, National Bureau of Economic Research, New York, Winter–Spring 1977–1978, pp. 645–674; Darby, Michael R., "The Permanent Income Theory of Consumption—A Restatement," *Quarterly Journal of Economics*, vol. 88, May 1974, pp. 228–250; Friedman, Milton, and Simon Kuznets, *Income from Independent Professional Practice*, National Bureau of Economic Research, New York, 1945; Friedman, Milton, *A Theory of the Consumption Function*, Princeton University Press, Princeton, N.J. 1957; Mayer, Thomas, *Permanent Income, Wealth, and Consumption*, University of California Press, Los Angeles, 1972.

(See also Chicago school; Consumer theory; Consumption function; Income; Propensity to consume or to save and inducement to invest)

Michael R. Darby

Personal consumption expenditures in GNP

Personal consumption expenditures (PCE) reflect the market value of goods—durable and nondurable—and services purchased by persons—individuals and nonprofit institutions—or acquired by them as income in kind. For example, the rental value of owner-occupied dwellings is included but not the purchase of dwellings. In the national income accounts, consumer purchases of owner-occupied housing are treated as business investment, while consumer expenditures on durable goods are treated as current consumption rather than investment and, thus, saving is reduced.

In the national income accounts, the term "persons" includes individuals in their roles not only as consumers or households but also as unincorporated business executives because household and business accounts of retailers, self-employed professionals, farmers, and other individual enterprises have not successfully been separated. The term also includes nonprofit institutions such as private colleges and hospitals; private trust funds; and private pension, health, and welfare funds.

Purchases are recorded at cost to consumers, including excise or sales taxes, and in full at the time of the purchase, whether made with cash or credit. The nonprofit institutions included are those rendering services principally to individuals.

Durable goods in the consumer category are items with a normal life expectancy of 3 years or more. The most common examples of consumer durable goods are automobiles, furniture, household appliances, television sets, and mobile homes. Because of their longevity, consumer expenditures on durable goods are generally postponable. Thus, durable goods purchases are the most volatile component of PCE, with swings of more than 10 percent from peak to trough in a cycle.

Nondurable goods are items which generally last for a relatively short time (less than 3 years). The most common examples of nondurables are food, beverages, clothing, shoes, and gasoline. Consumer nondurable goods are generally purchased when needed, and spending for these items grows less rapidly than income.

Services are intangible items such as medical and legal services; haircuts and other personal care; railway, bus, and air transportation; and the use of housing.

Since World War II, consumers seem to have been the driving force behind most business cycle expansion and contractions, largely reflecting their spending patterns. The factors which cause consumers to step up their rate of spending for autos, other durables, and other high-priced items generate increased demand for goods and services in the aggregate and are likely to fuel cyclical expansions. On the other hand, contractions in spending for discretionary items are likely to be associated with periods of general economic recession.

Consumer Theory

Consumer theory generally focuses on the way consumers allocate income among various goods and services (Marshallian demand analysis and Hicks-Slutsky analysis of indifference functions), and the way in which they allocate income between spending and saving (Keynes' propensity to consume or to save, Friedman's permanent income hypothesis, and Ando-Modigliani's life-cycle model).

Katona (1977) has demonstrated that psychological factors such as optimism and pessimism about the current and short-run economic situation are important in determining the direction of consumer spending. Becker (1977) has suggested that households are miniature firms and that the real budget restraint facing consumers is not income but time.

The significant relationship between consumer income and consumer spending is called the consumption function. In economic literature various theories are offered to explain this relationship. As mentioned above, there are Keynes' propensity to consume, Friedman's permanent income hypothesis, and Ando-Modigliani's life-cycle theory. Keynes' notion was that as income increases, consumption increases but at a decreasing rate. Friedman (1957) treats consumption decisions as being based on a longer- run conception of income rather than just a single year's income. Ando and

Modigliani (1963) offer the theory that consumption decisions are based on the whole series of financial flows, including current wealth, the value of future earnings, and a target (which may be zero) for the value of assets at the end of life.

References

Ando, Albert, and Franco Modigliani, "The Life Cycle Hypothesis of Saving: Aggregate Implications and Tests," *American Economic Review*, vol. 53, no. 1, part 1, March 1963, pp. 55–84; Becker, Gary, *The Economic Approach to Human Behavior*, University of Chicago Press, Chicago, 1977; Friedman, Milton, *The Theory of the Consumption Function*, Princeton University Press, Princeton, N.J., 1957; Katona, George, *The Powerful Consumer; Psychological Studies of the American Economy*, Greenwood, Westport, Conn., 1977; Ruggles, Richard, and Nancy Ruggles, *National Income Accounts and Income Analysis*, 2d ed., McGraw-Hill, New York, 1956.

(*See also* Anticipation surveys, consumer; Behavioral economics; Consumer theory; Consumption function; Disposable personal income; Gross national product; Income; National income accounting; Permanent income hypothesis; Propensity to consume or to save and inducement to invest; Saving; Wealth)

Douglas Greenwald

Personal income taxation (see Taxation, an overview)

Phillips curve

Phillips curve analysis poses the economic issues of the existence and stability of an inverse relationship between unemployment and inflation in the United States (and other advanced capitalistic countries) and, if this should be validated, the choice by policymakers of a socially acceptable combination between the two parameters.

While Irving Fisher in a mostly forgotten 1926 work had made an early contribution to the relationship between prices and unemployment, the modern debate was initiated in a study by A. W. Phillips showing a stable, nonlinear inverse relationship between the change in the wage rate and the unemployment rate during 1861 to 1957 in the United Kingdom. This was subsequently extended and refined in 1960 by Richard G. Lipsey, who independently also found a stable negative relationship between wage inflation and the demand for labor (as well as making an allowance for frictional unemployment); and by Bent Hansen, who described frictional unemployment as a feature of a labor market with incomplete information by job seekers of job vacancies in order to explain how wage inflation could vary with the same unemployment rate. The transformation to a trade-off between price (rather than wage) inflation and unemployment rates was made later in several ways by other economists, frequently by means of an assumption of constant markup pricing on unit labor costs by firms, resulting in an inflation rate which registers the differential between the change in money wages and in labor productivity.

Keynesian Theory

Keynesian theory had viewed inflation as a condition arising only when demand was in excess of full-employment output (while, in the monetarist approach, the impact of increased demand via money-supply growth could result in higher prices much sooner). Implicitly, Keynesian theory assumed that prices would be inflexible downward if circumstances of high unemployment and large supplies prevailed, and would be stable and in equilibrium at the point of full employment. (Graphically, this would be represented by the mirror-image L-shaped graph, with price change on the ordinate and real gross national product, GNP, on the abscissa of a set of axes.)

This perspective of the onset of inflation beginning at full employment appeared increasingly at odds with actual price and unemployment developments in the 1950s and 1960s. While it was rare that the general level of prices declined significantly when unemployment was high in this period, prices of many commodities whose raw materials costs are large (raw industrial products, agricultural products, etc.) or which are subject to import competition were sensitive to demand changes. As demand and employment eased, inflation rates sometimes were reversed or, more frequently, slowed. Moreover, it was argued that product and factor markets need not be in the presumed equilibrium state at full employment—indeed, this might be rare and perhaps unrealizable in the real world since it would express an unusual situation of balance in supply and demand in all markets. Long before that point, premature inflation would ensue because production bottlenecks would have been registered in some sectors. This would be particularly evident in labor markets, where immobilities in supply among regions and occupations, lack of information of job vacancies, union or racial discrimination, etc., generate shortages of skilled workers long before full employment is reached. Finally, the market power of labor unions and big business might more easily be exerted during periods of rising demand (which provide a cost-push inflation explanation of the trade-off between inflation and unemployment rates).

The emergence of inflation long before full employment was reached appeared clearly evident in the data for the 1950s and 1960s in the major industrialized countries. Accordingly, a policy dilemma was posed to the authorities, who were confronted by probable inflation if stimulative macroeconomic measures were used to reduce unemployment. On a graph where price change is marked on the ordinate and the unemployment rate on the abscissa, the policy choice in the 1960s for the United States resembled a round L. On such a graph, an inflation rate of 3½ percent was related to a so-called full-employment unemployment rate of 4 percent.

However, the terms of trade-off, to the advantage of inflation, appeared to worsen at the turn of the decade. Moreover, the apparent stability of the Phillips curve was shattered by data for the 1970s when inflation and unemployment rates increased simultaneously—the former doubling in the United States, Germany, and Japan during 1970 to 1974 relative to 1965 to 1969. Supporters of Phillips curve analyses argued that this represented merely a worsening of the trade-off—a rightward shift of the curve. This shift was ascribed to a changed composition of the labor force toward greater representation of women and teenagers (who are employed at jobs at less-than-average productivity and are more frequently unemployed); more aggressive union behavior; sharply rising energy costs; greater disincentives to work resulting from government income maintenance programs. The range of choices remained, but the cost of inflation was higher at given unemployment rates. Another view in support of an underlying Phillips curve was that the data of the 1970s did not fit into the curve only because of special externally influenced factors such as the oil and agricultural supply shortages and devaluation of the dollar.

Monetarist Analysis

In contrast, the very existence of a stable Phillips curve in the long run was questioned by Milton Friedman, Edmond Phelps, and others in the late 1960s and 1970s.

Ideologically connected with the classical analysis that real wages determine the demand for and supply of labor, Friedman and Phelps assign a critical role to anticipated and unanticipated rates of inflation. At a given anticipated rate of inflation, unemployment will cling to a so-called natural or equilibrium rate. The latter rate is considered equivalent to sustainable full employment, after allowance for frictional and structural involuntary unemployment plus voluntary unemployment (that induced by unemployment compensation, welfare payments, two-income households, etc.). This rate has been judged to be in the range of $5\frac{1}{2}$ to $6\frac{1}{2}$ percent in the late 1970s, in contrast with 4 to 5 percent assumed as full employment in U.S. government reports.

The natural rate of unemployment in a state of equilibrium emerges whenever inflation is completely anticipated. Under that condition, contractual arrangements presumably will have been adjusted to the inflation rate, relative prices in product and factor markets would remain unchanged, and output would remain unaffected. However, should prices rise at an unanticipated rate, say, because of excess stimulation through expansionary monetary or fiscal policy, this will become evident sooner to employers than to workers, whose wages in any event tend to change more slowly owing to contractual arrangements and other immobilities. Employment increases because real wages have declined, temporarily unbeknownst to the workers. It is this misperception by workers that draws them into employment and reduces unemployment below the natural rate. Conversely, when money wages decline, the misperception of a decline in real wages leads workers to leave jobs and seek others which pay more—in the process raising unemployment above the natural rate. In this sense, a short-term Phillips curve does provide a trade-off between inflation and a lowered unemployment rate.

The long-run results are different. As misperceptions concerning unanticipated inflation are dissipated, workers will require higher money wages to restore their previous real income, which reduces profits, lowers employment, and raises unemployment to the natural rate. But, while the real economy has reverted to its natural level, its output is sold at high prices. Indeed, in the so-called accelerationist view, only additional bouts of inflation—always containing some element of temporary misperception of the inflation rate—would succeed in keeping unemployment below the natural rate. Accordingly, stimulative macroeconomic policy by the authorities in the long run would remain a "no-win" game because workers' real wages eventually adjust to inflation. Over time, the Phillips curve is vertical.

In the Friedman-Phelps view, adaptive expectations represent the time interval of lessening misperceptions between the expected and the actual inflation rates and provide the basis for the accelerationist theory. (The latter may be conceived graphically as a layered series of negatively sloped, short-run Phillips curves, depicting successively higher and worse trade-offs as long as excess demand prevails; and a vertical, long-run curve positioned at the natural unemployment rate.)

In the new rational expectations approach, past rates of inflation that affect adaptive expectations represent only part of the information necessary to make a more or less accurate inflation prediction. Because of spreading sophistication and knowledge of the economic system, in a model sense, economic agents may now make decisions rationally, eliminating any gap between actual and expected inflation. Since the role of money growth in creating inflation is well understood by rationally acting economic agents, there are no lags or surprises concerning actual and anticipated rates of inflation and bargains are made accordingly; therefore, no impact on real economic variables results from shifts in economic policy. While the adaptive model implies that lags may influence the course of the real economy for a short period of time, the rational expectations approach concedes such changes in neither the short nor the long run, except through a random mechanism, making economic policy essentially useless.

Evaluation of the major issues of difference between so-called liberal Keynesian and conservative monetarist analyses centers on the magnitude of the natural rate of unemployment and the costs of departure from it. With respect to the natural rate, changes in the demography of the labor force due to higher proportions of women and youths and expanded income maintenance programs appear to have raised the noninflationary unemployment rate to the neighborhood of 6 percent—and even higher rates are conceivable in view of supply-side or external influences such as rising costs of energy and raw materials and the declining value of the dollar. Efforts to lower unemployment rates by stimulative demand policies appear to have commanded an increasingly heavier inflation cost, to have embedded expectations of accelerating inflation into market processes, and to be self-defeating in the long run. As part of a disinflation program, conservatives propose micro measures which improve the functioning of labor markets by reducing the mismatch of job vacancies and the unemployed, facilitating competition in product and labor markets, lessening disincentives to work and to invest, etc. On the macro level, a sufficiently long cooling-off period in the economy is considered necessary to break inflationary expectations. By contrast, liberals dispute significant disinflation effects of high unemployment, citing studies which show flat trade-offs when unemployment rises above the natural rate; deploring the social costs of unemployment; and recommending government price and wage controls in demand management of inflation.

References

Friedman, Milton, "The Role of Monetary Policy," *American Economic Review*, vol. 58, no. 1, March 1968, pp. 1–17; Lipsey, Richard G., "The Relation between Unemployment and the Rate of Change of Money Wage Rates in the United Kingdom, 1862–1957: A Further Analysis," *Economica*, vol. 27, February 1960, pp. 1–31; Okun, Arthur, "Efficient Disinflationary Policies," *American Economic Review*, vol. 68, no. 2, May 1978, pp. 348–352; Phelps, Edmund S., *Inflation Policy and Unemployment Theory: The Cost Benefit Approach to Monetary Planning*, Norton, New York, 1972; Phillips, A. W., "Relationships between Unemployment and the Rate of Change in Money Wage Rates in the United Kingdom, 1862–1957," *Economica*, vol. 25, November 1958, pp. 283–299.

(*See also* Chicago school; Employment and unemployment; Federal Reserve policy; Fiscal policy; Incomes policy; Inflation; Keynesian economics; Labor force; Monetary policy; Money illusion; Post-Keynesian economics)

Herman I. Liebling

Physiocrats

The physiocrats were a group of *economistes* (as they were called in French, the first ones to bear that label) who reacted against the views of the mercantilists and asserted instead that productivity of land is the major force behind economic prosperity. The group was headed by François Quesnay; physician to King Louis XV and Mme. Pompadour, who took a short, but intense interest in economic doctrine. The physiocrats' thinking exerted a powerful influence on leading citizens like Robert Turgot, who was Louis XVI's Minister of Finance; Pierre Samuel du Pont de Nemours, the French industrialist who later came to the United States; and, on the other side of the English Channel, Adam Smith, the well-known professor of moral philosophy at Glasgow College in Scotland.

Fundamental to physiocratic doctrine is a strong belief in a natural order transcending legislative and administrative decisions, a conviction that ran exactly counter to mercantilist views prevalent throughout Europe earlier in the eighteenth century. The mercantilists had played down the role of agriculture and had stressed the contribution of processing, manufacturing, and service industries in raising the value of a nation's exports. They had, through a system of taxes, tariffs, and direct controls, taken steps to discourage and even limit imports. And they had glorified the resulting accumulation of precious metals as the hallmark of a nation's prosperity and power.

Physiocrats, by contrast, considered these policies damaging to the public interest. They believed that only the agricultural sector produces new wealth—the so-called *produit net* that is left over after all of a farmer's costs have been met. This *produit net* could be claimed by landlords as rent and be spent by them in the economy at large. Or it could be taxed by the government—at least in part—without affecting farmers' incentives to produce as much and as efficiently as possible. The physiocrats were single taxers; they proposed dismantling the complex system of taxes and regulations that the mercantilists had installed in an effort to regulate the economy and channel it toward export industry and commerce. According to the physiocrats, this effort not only placed too heavy a burden on agriculture but it also interfered with the self-serving incentive of individual businesses to maximize their own profits and, in the process, buttress the collective welfare of the nation. In their view, expanding the network of trade required commercial cooperation rather than exploitation, especially with respect to agriculture. "Laissez faire, laissez passer," a slogan much used by the physiocrats, signifies their antiregulation, antitariff philosophy.

Hoping to document agriculture's contribution, Quesnay devised the famous *Tableau Économique*, which attempted to trace specifically the flow of production and wealth through a nation's economy. Though not clear in many ways, it was much admired at the time of publication. Even today, it is lauded as the first schematic presentation of how goods and payments move in a circular flow, or how national income and output interact and balance out. From another point of view, the *Tableau* can be pictured as a rudimentary input-output table that attempts to show how the productive class, i.e., the agricultural sector, supplies other producers (the physiocrats called the other producers "sterile"), permits them to subsist and to make capital investments, and thus supports the economy as a whole.

Adam Smith, who visited France repeatedly in order to learn more from his friend Quesnay later wrote that physiocracy represents a reaction to the excesses of mercantilism. The doctrine retains some support to this day, especially in farm communities, among environmentalists, and in resource-oriented economies. But its singleminded emphasis on primary production as the only source of income and wealth has reduced its status to that of a curiosity in the history of economic analysis.

References

Blaug, Mark, *Economic Theory in Retrospect*, 3d ed., Cambridge University Press, Cambridge, 1978; Fellner, William, *Modern Economic Analysis*, McGraw-Hill, New York, 1960, pp. 40–48.

(*See also* Input-output analysis; Laissez faire; Mercantilism)

G. H. Mattersdorff

Pigou effect (see Real balance effect theory)

Planning, economic (see Economic planning)

Population theory (see Malthusian theory of population)

Portfolio management theories

Ever since people first began assembling more goods than they could consume in a reasonable period of time, portfolios have been managed. Having goods in excess of consumption needs corresponded to wealth, and this gave rise to concerns over how that wealth should be deployed. Sometimes it was primarily enjoyed, as when beautiful objects were bought for the home; sometimes it was invested with the intention of earning returns to enhance the amount of wealth. And there is a fine line between the enjoyment use and pure investment use because the durable object of enjoyment can change in value and produce a return in addition to being useful.

Approaches to portfolio management have varied with the times and development of markets. Organized markets for financial claims are recent in origin relative to the period over which wealth has been managed. In earlier centuries assets were primarily divided among precious metals, real estate, deposits with the bankers of the times, and, in earlier centuries, livestock. In places where securities markets do not exist or where securities values have been eradicated by war or changes of government, precious metals, real estate, and bank deposits remain today the favored means of holding wealth.

Balancing Risk and Reward

The principal precepts of portfolio management have been with us for some time and have been highly developed in the past 30 years. Balancing risk and reward remains the principal issue in portfolio management. Some investors have virtually no appetite for risk. For them cash or virtually riskless, highly liquid short-term securities of unshakable governments make up the universe in which they choose to invest. For others, some amount of risk may be acceptable in exchange for commensurate returns. Risk refers to the possibility that the planned values of principal and return cannot be obtained when needed. Because different investors need to use their wealth at different times, it follows that different assets have different risks for different holders. An asset which is virtually riskless in the eyes of a short-term investor may be seen as highly risky for a long-term investor.

The reason for such disparities is that there are two kinds of risks in investing. The first is that one may not be able to sell an asset for as much as had been planned when the funds are needed. This could be a particular problem if the investor needs the funds earlier than had been anticipated when the investment was made. Default on a fixed-income obligation or the sharp reduction of the earnings prospects of a company with publicly traded stock are the most notable instances of this, but market deterioration for any reason can change the terms on which investments can be cashed in. This is the primary risk facing an investor with a short time horizon and is the one with which most portfolio managers are concerned.

For the longer-term investor, a second risk—reinvestment risk— is equally important. An investor with a long-term financial target needs to be concerned not only with the value of the principal but also with the terms on which the returns on that principal can be reinvested before the funds are needed. If investments have yields before the end of the planning period, the terms on which those can be reinvested can have a large impact on the final values of the investments. In terms of either present value or final value, the power of compounding yields is large. For instance, an investor with a 30-year time horizon derives 92.46 percent of the present value of a 9 percent bond from the coupon stream received prior to maturity. If these coupons cannot be reinvested at 9 percent during the life of the bond, some of its value will not materialize. On a less precise basis, the same considerations apply to the dividend income from other investments. This concern would, of course, be negligible for an investor who planned to use the funds in a few weeks or months.

Investment strategies must be tailored to meet the needs and objectives of the investor. Strategies focus primarily either on dealing with reinvestment risk or with principal risk. In the former case, assets are selected with long-term maturities, with as little of the return of the investment coming early in the planning period as possible. By minimizing and delaying the yield on investments, an investor similarly minimizes and delays the changes of having returns impacted by changed market conditions during the time of the investment.

In practice, most investors have shorter or undetermined time horizons and accordingly are more concerned about principal risk. Each investor has an individual set of tastes for risks. These can be thought of as a set of utility frontiers relating the amount of risk one is willing to accept to the return available from taking such risk. The utility frontiers are then compared to a schedule of combinations of risk and return available in the market, and the investor then determines where he or she will be on the market schedule. This is the analytical approach used to consider market risk (discussed in more detail subsequently), but it applies to taking on any kind of risk, of which there are several.

Controlling Risk

The essence of portfolio management is the changing of one's appetite for risks in different environments and controlling risk at any point in time. Handsome returns can be had by taking on greater risk at certain times and avoiding risks at others. Assessing when to do each is the contribution of the portfolio manager. The most straightforward way of reducing risk for a given level of return is through diversification. On both intuitive and mathematical grounds, it is possible to reduce the overall level of risk associated with a portfolio by dividing it among several investments, even if each has the same level of risk as the starting asset, as long as the risks are independent.

Beyond numbers of investments, one can reduce various types of risks by combining assets which are impacted in opposite directions by the risks in question. For instance, many companies, and thus their equities, are negatively impacted by recessions. Their earnings and stock prices fall prior to and in the early stages of recessions. A portfolio which included only stocks of such companies would, therefore, contain a major element of business cycle risk. Conversely, this portfolio would benefit from periods of strong economic activity. Such a portfolio would be an appropriate holding for someone who found this risk acceptable because the investor would hold the view that the economy would be strong indefinitely and he or she would never be forced to sell during a recession. An investor who viewed a recession as likely or simply chose not to take a business cycle risk would seek to avoid such assets.

There is a wide variety of other risks an investor might wish to protect against. There is the risk that inflation will undermine the value of assets. Protecting against this possibility would dictate avoiding assets whose returns are fixed in nominal terms and favoring those which allow a participation in the appreciation of assets or enhancement of earnings that inflation provides. Examples here might be common stocks or real estate. Conversely, if one felt that inflation was likely to decelerate and market values incorporated an expectation of high inflation, the opposite strategy would be appropriate. Inflation risk could also be eliminated by balancing assets which are helped by inflation with some which are adversely affected by inflation.

Investors who are comfortable investing in various national markets typically try to reduce political risk. This can also be a factor for assets whose values are impacted by the domestic policies of a national government or by state and local government actions. Weather risk can haunt a portfolio the fortunes of which are too closely tied to certain agricultural sectors. Geographic risk can impact a portfolio if its holdings are heavily concentrated in a region which is, for instance, depressed more than a national economy.

Portfolio management involves assessing all these risks and balancing them against returns available from various assets. It also means changing appetites for particular risks in response to changing prospects for markets. If a portfolio manager believes that the economy will strengthen, that manager will tend to reallocate holdings to assets which will do well during business cycle expansions. However, there is then additional risk that the portfolio will be hurt by a recession, so that the manager reallocates only up to the point where the return justifies this added risk. With other investors making similar calculations, this period of opportunity may not be particularly long.

Market Risk

Portfolio managers vary in their approaches by varying the types of risk that they attempt to control, and there are many different kinds of risk. Additionally, an investor can only profitably react to a changing outlook for any type of risk up to the point where the market as a whole evaluates the risks the same way. At that point the risk-return trade-off will have adjusted to reflect the revised outlook. Partly as a result of this realization, in the late 1970s the various risks have been combined in the concept of market risk. This notion implicitly says that asset markets are impacted by a wide variety of factors, and these forces are fully reflected in current market prices and returns. By concentrating on only one of the many risks affecting markets, one is open to being unfavorably impacted by another. The new approach leads to strategies defined in terms of whether the portfolio has greater or less risk than the market. In practice, this technique is applied primarily to assets which are traded on organized exchanges where values and returns can be easily monitored. Using this approach, an aggressive manager would hold securities which historically move more than proportionately with the market. A more cautious management strategy would hold assets which move with or less than proportionately with the market. The first manager would do better than the market in up markets and worse than the market in down markets. The second would do the same or worse than the market in good times, but better (lose less) in down markets. This concept also helps quantify how to manage investment timing. If one were confident that markets would advance, assets of the first category would be added to a portfolio while those of the second would be preferred in declining markets.

The proportion of a typical market move that an asset makes, on average, has been given a shorthand symbol, the Greek letter β which is a measure of systematic risk with the market. The return on an asset with a β of 1.2 will, on average, move 20 percent more than the market in each direction, so that it is 20 percent riskier. The β of a portfolio including such an asset can be reduced by including other assets which systematically move in the opposite direction (a negative β) or move by less than the market (a β between 0 and 1). If an entire portfolio had a β greater than 1, it would normally offer a return in excess of the market.

Such considerations open up nearly endless vistas of calculating, measuring, comparing, and the like. Historical comparisons of behavior of prices and yields of specific securities with diversified market indexes produces β estimates. (The relevant estimates are those of the future—the upcoming relationship between security returns and market returns, but these cannot be known ex ante, only estimated.) This particular management approach lends itself easily to quantitative evaluation of portfolio management strategies after the fact. There are two general ways of measuring performance. The first focuses on the total return of the portfolio in dollars and cents. This is by far the most popular method in that dollars are what can be spent or invested in the next period. Low β's, for instance, never paid any bills. Actual return is an easily understood discipline which is generally applicable to all assets whether or not they are traded on organized exchanges.

The second measurement approach refines the first by saying that return can always (on average) be enhanced by taking on more risk, so that return should be adjusted for risk borne. This is done by comparing a portfolio return and risk with the return offered by the market for the same level of risk. For these purposes risk is measured by the historic standard deviation of the total return of a security, a portfolio, or the market. It is necessarily a backward-looking measure. For example, if a portfolio had a higher level of risk than the market but produced a return which was not only higher than the market but also higher than the return produced, on average, by assets or portfolios with that higher level of risk, the management strategy would have been judged a success in that it did better than the market relationship between risk and return would have implied. The margin by which this return is higher than the risk-adjusted market return (called the market line) is a measure of how well the management process worked on a risk-adjusted basis. It too has a Greek-letter designation, α. It measures excellence by measuring how well a manager chooses among assets with the same level of risk. Because it is a margin of return not offered by the initial systematic risk-reward trade-off in the market, it is called the nonsystematic return.

This approach enables one to evaluate whether or not a realized rate of return in excess of the average of all stocks in an advancing market was worth the excess risk required to produce it. It also enables one to be satisfied with a return less than the market if it was produced with assets less risky than the market (e.g., with heavy holdings of cash equivalents) but producing a return greater than that yielded by other assets with limited risk. One can make similar calculations and comparisons on a risk-adjusted basis in deteriorating markets.

Whether one uses this highly developed quantitative technique or more intuitive ones, all these approaches manage the risk-return trade-off. Whether the risk is a market move or some specific brand of risk, management involves changing appetites for risks over time in response to judgments of their magnitudes and the returns offered by taking them.

References

Blume, Marshall E., "On the Assessment of Risk," *Journal of Finance,* vol. 26, no. 1, March 1971, pp. 1–10; Cohen, Jerome B., Edward D. Zinbarg, and Arthur Zeikel, *Investment Analysis and Portfolio Management,* rev. ed., Dow Jones–Irwin, Homewood, Ill., 1973; Friend, Irwin, and Marshall E. Blume, "Measurement of Portfolio Performance Under Uncertainty," *American Economic Review,* vol. 60, no. 4, September 1970, pp. 561– 575; Jensen, Michael C. (ed.), *Studies in the Theory of Capital Markets,* Praeger, New York, 1972; Mlynarczyk, Francis A., "Beta, Alpha—or Omega?," *Institutional Investor,* vol. 6, no. 7, July 1972, pp. 93–99.

(*See also* Random walk hypothesis)

William E. Gibson

Post-Keynesian economics

Modern macroeconomic theory has developed along four or five different analytical, philosophical, and political lines. Table 1 classifies the various shades of analytical views into five relatively homogeneous schools of thought. As listed from right to left in Table 1 these schools are as follows:

1. *The monetarist-neoclassical school.* This is a narrow, almost monolithic view of the economic system whose major base is the University of Chicago, and whose writings almost always bear the imprimatur of Milton Friedman.

2. *The neoclassical-synthesis Keynesian school.* A much broader spectrum of views is represented in this school than in the previous school. Models range from the neoclassical capital theories of Samuelson and Solow to the portfolio and general equilibrium views of Patinkin, Hicks, and Tobin. A majority of the economics establishment dominate this school.

3. *Keynes' school.* This school is an exceedingly small group of economists who have attempted to develop Keynes' original views on employment, growth, and money, e.g., Harrod, Shackle, Weintraub, Minsky, and Davidson.

4. *Neo-Keynesian school.* The members of this small but important group centered in Cambridge, England, have attempted to graft aspects of Keynes' real-sector analysis onto the growth and distribution theories of Ricardo, Marx, and Kalecki. The leaders of this school are Robinson, Kaldor, Pasinetti, and Sraffa.

5. *The socialist-radical school.* The members of this residual category span a vast spectrum of views from left-of-center liberals such as Galbraith through Marxists and the new radical economists. Despite the diversity in this school, the members share two common characteristics, namely: (1) their ideas are typically dismissed as nonscientific by the majority (groups to the right of center) of the economics establishment and, therefore, unworthy of significant serious discussion in the learned professional literature; and (2) the members of this school advocate socialization of those productive sectors of the economy whose

TABLE 1 Political Economy Schools of Thought

	Socialist-radical	Neo-Keynesian	Keynes	Neoclassical-synthesis Keynesian	Monetarist-neoclassical
Politics	Extreme left	Left of center	Center	Right of center	Extreme right
Money	Real forces emphasized—money merely a tool for existing power structure	Real forces emphasized; money assumed to accommodate	Money and real forces intimately related	Money matters along with everything else	Only money matters
Wage rate and income distribution	Wage-rate basis of value. Income distribution the most important economic question	Money wage is the linchpin of the price level. Income distribution very important	Money-wage rate fundamental; income distribution question of less importance	Wage rate one of many prices. Income distribution is the resultant of all the demand and supply equations in a general equilibrium system. Income distribution a matter of equity, not of scientific inquiry.	
Capital theory	Surplus generated by reserve army	Surplus needed over wages	Scarcity theory (quasi rents)	Marginal productivity theory and well-behaved production functions	
Employment theory	Any level of employment possible. Assumes growth in employment overtime. Full employment creates crisis for capitalism	Growth with any level of employment possible, although growth at full employment emphasized	Any level of employment possible; full employment desirable	Full employment assumed; unemployment is a disequilibrium situation	Full employment assumed in long run; no explicit short-run theory of employment
Inflation	Primarily due to money wage changes, but can also be due to profit margin changes	Due to money wage or profit margin changes	Due to changes in money wages, productivity, and/or profit margins	In long run primarily a monetary phenomenon being related to money supply via portfolio decisions. In short run may be related to Phillips curve	Primarily a monetary phenomenon in the sense of being related to the supply of money via portfolio decisions
Government role	Socialize the capitalist sector	Laissez faire except for macroeconomic controls over incomes	Laissez faire except for macroeconomic controls over money, investment decisions, and the earnings system	Laissez faire except for externalities and some ad hoc macro controls	Laissez faire

faults are perceived as noncorrectable by either normal market processes or overall macroeconomic policies.

The members of the radical-socialist school do not claim descent from Keynes. Furthermore, they usually have little to say about monetary theory. Nevertheless, they have raised fundamental questions about the objectives and the path of economic growth in capitalist economies—embarrassing inquiries which are studiously avoided by those schools to the right of center in Table 1.

Table 1 attempts to associate the various schools with different positions in the political spectrum from extreme right to extreme left. The position taken on various key economic issues by the different schools of thought tends to vary monotonically with their position in the political spectrum. Obviously, the five columns are not fixed; views of individuals in any one school may, on certain issues, overlap with the views of those in schools of close proximity.

Post-Keynesian economists are an amalgam of those primarily from the Keynesian and neo-Keynesian schools, but also include some of the right-leaning members of the socialist-radical group such as Galbraith. Moreover, certain left-leaning members of the neoclassical Keynesian school have exhibited considerable sympathy for some post-Keynesian analysis (e.g., Hicks since the mid-1960s).

There are a number of distinguishing features which separate post-Keynesians from monetarists, neoclassical Keynesians, and many socialist-radical economists. The foremost distinguishing feature is that post-Keynesians reject the notion that any general equilibrium system (Walrasian or otherwise) is the basic logical structure for the comprehension of real-world economies. Of course, post-Keynesians recognize that all theories represent abstractions and simplifications of reality. The problem is to develop a framework of the real world so that a comprehensive realistic analysis can be undertaken. All post-Keynesians are united in the view that any logical system which defines equilibrium as uniquely synonymous with the simultaneous clearing of all markets and the prereconciliation of the plans of all economic agents in a world of uncertainty cannot provide a realistic guide to solving real-world problems.

Post-Keynesian Models

Post-Keynesian models are based on five concepts, each of which is considered in turn.

The Economic System as a Sequential Process   This concept is based on the notion that the economic system is a process moving irreversibly through calendar time (i.e., the economy is a process in history). Time is a real-world device which prevents everything from happening at once. The production of commodities takes time, and the consumption of capital goods and consumer durables takes time. In a post-Keynesian world, time is an asymmetric variable and the economy is moving irreversibly and unidirectionally (forward) through time. The past may be knowledge but the future is unknown—yet, economic decisions taken in the present will require actions which can not be completed until some future date. In such a world, economic decision makers are continuously involved in sequential decisions and action which are colored not only by their expectations of the unknowable future but also by the inherited stocks (which embody correct previous guesses as well as past errors) which they possess. Consequently, decisions rarely are made on a clean slate.

In a neoclassical world, on the other hand, all decisions involve the present, all future dates are taken at a single instant in time, and errors are, by assumption, impossible. Thus, neoclassical economics explicitly denies the old maxim, "To err is human."

Sir John Hicks, who provided much of the impetus for modern neoclassical (general equilibrium) theory and who is the progenitor of the *IS-LM* equilibrium model (a standard representation of the Keynesian system suitable for comparative static analysis, the macro framework for the neoclassical school) recognized a decade ago that his framework was a "potted version" of Keynes' theory (Hicks, 1967). More recently, under the prodding of some post-Keynesians who have stressed where mainstream economics has gone wrong, Hicks has recanted on the usefulness of the *IS-LM* framework. Hicks now states that unlike general equilibrium concepts which "signal that time, in some respects at least, has been put on one side," Keynes' monetary framework was an "in [calendar] time" approach where the recognition of an uncertain future (and not just a probabilistic one) shaped economic behavior.

Marshall, in the preface to the first edition of his *Principles* (1890), stated that the "element of time is the centre of the chief difficulty of almost every economic problem." Keynes (1936), in his analytical framework, clearly recognized that money matters only when we wish to analyze the "problems of the real world in which our previous expectations are liable to disappointment and expectations concerning the future affect what we do today." Keynes' revolution is in the Marshallian tradition of emphasizing time at the center of economic problems, while the general equilibrium *IS-LM* approach emasculates the concept of time as a historical process.

The Role of Expectations in an Uncertain World   Neoclassical theorists assume that uncertainty can be represented via probability statements in an economic world that is in a state of statistical control; hence, all future variables can be reduced to actuarial certainty equivalents in the present instant of time. Moreover, in an equilibrium world, all expectations must be realized by events, so that expectations become certainty equivalents. Post-Keynesians, on the other hand, emphasize the difference between uncertainty and risks and deal with the expectations of economic decision makers in a world where there are what Shackle has called "crucial experiments," i.e., in a world that is not in a state of statistical control and, hence, one in which the mathematical laws of probability do not apply. In such a world decision makers recognize that errors and disappointments are part of the human condition. This perception affects the feasible options considered, and often, economic agents in a Keynesian world will take actions that would be considered irrational in a neoclassical world, e.g., the holding of money for liquidity motives.

The Role of Economic Institutions in the Economic System   In the neoclassical world of general equilibrium there are no significant economic institutions—not even commodity or financial markets. In a post-Keynesian world, on the other hand, economic institutions are influential and prominent in determining output, employment, and the money price level. These institutions include the banking and monetary systems; time-oriented markets for goods, factors of production, and financial assets; the institution of money contracts for spot and forward transactions; and especially the money-wage contract as a necessary condition for liquidity over time for a market-oriented, monetary production economy.

Money only matters in a world where there are multitudinous linked forward contracts in money terms. In such an economy it is necessary that there be some continuity as to what will be the thing which by delivery settles the resulting obligations. The existence of market institutions which permit (and encourage) contracting for future payment creates the need for money and liquidity. This essential aspect affects the performance of all real-world, market-oriented monetary economies where the activity of production requires the passage of calendar time.

In a market-oriented economy most production transactions along the nonintegrated chain of firms involve forward contracts. For example, the hiring of factor inputs (especially labor) and the purchase of materials for the production of goods will normally require forward contracting if the production process is to be efficiently planned. The financing of such forward production-cost commitments (i.e., taking a position in working capital goods) requires entrepreneurs to have money available to discharge these liabilities at one or more future dates before the product is sold, delivered, and payment received, and before the position is liquidated. Since orthodox neoclassical theory neglects the concept of contracting over calendar time in organized markets for future delivery and payments, this ubiquitous liquidity problem of entrepreneurs in capitalist economies is ignored by mainstream economists.

For a decentralized market economy moving irreversibly through calendar time (where the future is uncertain), forward contracting for inputs to the production process is essential to efficient production plans. Moreover, in such an economy when slavery is illegal, the money-wage contract is the most ubiquitous forward contract of all; and since labor hiring and payment proceeds in time delivery of newly produced goods, it is the money wage relative to productivity which is the foundation upon which the price level of the new good rests.

As Arrow and Hahn (1971), have noted:

> The terms in which contracts are made matter. In particular, if money is the good in terms of which contracts are made, then the prices of goods in terms of money are of special significance. This is not the case if we consider an economy without a past and without a future. Keynes wrote that "the importance of money essentially flows from it being a link between the present and future" to which we add that it is important also because it is a link between the past and the present. If a serious monetary theory comes to be written, the fact that contracts are indeed made in terms of money will be of considerable importance.[1]

Furthermore, Arrow and Hahn conclude that in "a world with a past as well as a future and in which contracts are made in terms of money, no (general) equilibrium may exist."

If Arrow and Hahn are correct, it follows that a "serious monetary theory" must be based on a money-wage contract view of the economy. It is the stickiness of money wages and prices (i.e., the absence of rapid movements) guaranteed via the law of contracts which permits capitalist economies to engage in time-consuming production processes and provides a basis for a sticky price level of producible goods. This view was the focal point of Keynes' revolutionary ideas on the workings of a monetary economy.

The existence of money contracts for forward delivery and payment is fundamental to the concepts of liquidity and money. In such a setting, changes in money-wage rates—Keynes' wage unit—determine changes in the costs of production and the price level associated with the production of goods that profit-oriented entrepreneurs

[1]Reprinted by permission of Holden-Day Inc.

are willing to undertake. The view that inflation (i.e., a rising money price level of newly produced goods) is a monetary phenomena is logical only in an economy where time-oriented money contracts (especially labor hire) are basic to the organization of production activities.

The Relevance of Distribution of Income and Power   The distribution of income is a basic aspect of post-Keynesian theory; it is virtually ignored in logically consistent neoclassical models. When neoclassical economists have attempted to explain macroeconomic income distribution phenomena, their logic has been proved faulty. In fact, in a general equilibrium neoclassical world, problems of income distribution over time (e.g., due to unanticipated inflation) cannot arise because the future is logically predictable at least in an actuarial sense, and, hence, inflation cannot be analyzed in a general equilibrium model despite neoclassical economists' statements about the desirability of indexing to avoid unanticipated inflation. Since the logic of neoclassical theory does not permit an analysis of income distribution and inflation, it is no wonder that incomes policy discussions are an anathema to logically consistent members of the neoclassical schools.

The Concept of Capital in an Economic System   The distinction between neoclassical and Keynes' views hinges on two factors: (1) whether capital is malleable or nonmalleable (and, therefore, embodies past errors and wears out slowly over calendar time), and (2) whether or not there is an important difference between real and financial capital. Keynes and his followers emphasize the nonmalleability aspect of real capital as well as the difference between financial and real capital and the markets for each. Neoclassical theory is obtuse about the distinction in the latter case, while it requires malleability in the former case.

The object of neoclassical modeling is an idealized state, i.e., the long-run equilibrium solution, whereas Keynes believed that from the outset economists should model the actual state of the real world. As Keynes noted (1936): "But his long run is a misleading guide to current affairs. In the long run we are all dead. Economists set themselves too easy, too useless a task if in tempestuous seasons they can only tell us that when the storm is long past the ocean is flat again."

Model of the Real World

For members of the post-Keynesian schools the forementioned five concepts are fundamental characteristics of the world we inhabit—the real world; the idealized state of the neoclassical model can not exist—even as an ideal—in a calendar-time setting. Accordingly, post-Keynesian economists have attacked neoclassical analysis as irrelevant for the macroeconomic problems of twentieth-century monetary economies. Keynes and his followers believe that a model of the real world requires a completely different specification of the aggregate demand and supply functions of money, goods, and labor than the ones involved in a neoclassical general equilibrium framework. Consequently, Keynes and his followers are logically led to significantly different policy actions compared with the neoclassical schools in attempting to resolve the major economic problems of today.

References

Arrow, K. S., and F. H. Hahn, *General Competitive Analysis*, Holden-Day, San Francisco, 1971, pp. 356–357, 361; Davidson, P., *Money and The Real World*, 2d ed., Halsted, New York, 1978; Eichner, A. S., *The Megacorp and Oligopoly*, Cambridge University Press, Cambridge, 1976;

Harrod, R. F., *Money*, Macmillan, New York, 1979; Hicks, J. R., *Critical Essays in Monetary Theory*, Oxford University Press, Oxford, 1967; Kaldor, N., *Essays on Value and Distribution*, Free Press, New York, 1960; Keynes, J. M., *The General Theory of Employment, Interest and Money*, Harcourt Brace Jovanovich, New York, 1936; Kregel, J. A., *The Reconstruction of Political Economy*, Halsted, New York, 1973; Marshall, A., *Principles of Economics*, 1st ed., Macmillan, London, 1890; Minsky, H. P., *John Maynard Keynes*, Columbia University Press, New York, 1975; Pasinetti, L. L., *Growth and Income Distribution*, Cambridge University Press, New York, 1974; Robinson, J., *The Accumulation of Capital*, Macmillan, New York, 1956; Roncoglia, A., *Sraffa and the Theory of Prices*, Welsy, New York, 1978; Weintraub, S., *An Approach to The Theory of Income Distribution*, Chilton, Philadelphia, 1958; Weintraub, S., and P. Davidson (eds.), *The Journal of Post Keynesian Economics*, published quarterly.

(*See also* Cambridge school; Expectations; Income distribution; *IS-LM* model; Keynesian economics; Laissez faire; Macroeconomics; Marxism; Neoclassical economics; Neo-Keynesian economics; Propensity to consume or to save and inducement to invest)

Paul Davidson

Potential gross national product

Potential gross national product (GNP) is a supply concept, a measure of how much the economy could and would produce under hypothetical conditions of reasonably full utilization of labor and capital. As that definition indicates, some benchmark of reasonably full utilization must be specified in order to derive estimates of potential GNP. When the actual utilization of workers and machines falls short of that benchmark, then presumably actual GNP (in constant prices) is lower than potential GNP. The gap between potential and actual GNP is, thus, a measure of the output that could be produced, but, in fact, is not produced as a result of recession or slack. Although potential GNP is not directly observed, the accuracy of any time series estimating it can be appraised empirically. For example, a successful methodology should produce estimates of the gap that are close to zero at times when actual utilization is close to the benchmark. More generally, the gap estimates should bear a systematic relationship to the magnitude of idle resources.

The Uses of the Concept

A numerical time series of potential GNP has important uses for economists pursuing various types of analysis. First, it provides one guide to the formulation of fiscal and monetary policy and one indicator of the success of those stabilization policies. In light of the requirements of the Employment Act of 1946, fiscal and monetary policies must be formulated with at least an approximate underlying target for employment or unemployment that would represent the fulfillment of the act's goal of maximum employment. In turn, any employment or unemployment target must be linked to a target for real GNP, since monetary and fiscal policies influence employment mainly through the indirect route of stimulating or restraining aggregate demand and hence production. Second, the estimation of potential GNP may be a useful way to specify the relationship between output and employment in econometric forecasting. In particular, it may provide a bridge from a forecast of real GNP to a prediction of employment and unemployment.

Third, and more generally, the potential GNP estimates may help macroeconomists in distinguishing secular and cyclical phenomena. The economist often needs to know whether corporate profits, business fixed investment, automobile sales, or any other variable that is cyclically sensitive should be characterized as weak or strong, taking into account the weakness or strength of the overall economy. For example, in a period of recession or slack, corporate profits must be expected to be lower than they would be in a period of prosperity. The size of the gap between potential and actual GNP in a recession year may help to illuminate whether the observed level of profits reflects an unusual or only a typical shortfall. Indeed, time series have been constructed for many economic variables on a cyclically adjusted basis, showing how they would be expected to behave if actual GNP matched potential GNP with no cyclical fluctuations.

The estimation of the full-employment or high-employment federal budget is an important example of the cyclical adjustment approach. High-employment tax revenues reflect a hypothetical estimate of the tax bills that would be generated if actual GNP matched potential and, thus, corporate and personal incomes were consistent with the attainment of potential. Similarly, government expenditures that are sensitive to the cycle (for example, unemployment insurance benefits) are recalculated as they would emerge if potential GNP were realized. Automatic stabilizers that widen or narrow the actual federal deficit do not alter the high-employment calculation. The difference between the high-employment figure and actual imbalance of the federal budget helps to distinguish the extent to which the strength or weakness of the economy influences the budget and the extent to which the budget stimulates or restrains the economy.

The Estimation of Potential GNP

A technique for estimating potential GNP developed by Arthur M. Okun in 1961 and published in 1962 attracted wide attention. It was preceded by other studies, including an important one in 1960 by James W. Knowles of the Joint Economic Committee. Okun's approach developed a simplified shortcut and was given official sanction by the Council of Economic Advisers under the chairmanship of Walter Heller. The resulting estimates of potential GNP and the implied gaps became a standard tool in the kit of the Council of Economic Advisers, even gaining bipartisan acceptance during the Nixon and Ford administrations. The use of these estimates stimulated a number of articles in professional journals that offered refinements or amendments to the procedures.

The basic procedure in Okun's study was a "leap from unemployment to output," as it was described at the time. First, the benchmark of reasonably full utilization adopted for calculating potential GNP was an unemployment rate of 4 percent. That was an assumption rather than a conclusion; as stated then, "there seems to be more agreement that a 4 percent unemployment rate is a reasonable target under existing labor market conditions than on any of the analytical steps needed to justify such a conclusion." Second and more important, it used the unemployment rate as a proxy for the various ways in which idle resources hold down output. The influences of idle resources on production can be logically separated into two categories: those that affect total hours worked by labor, and those that affect output per hour worked. The effects of slack on hours of employment, in turn, travel along three routes: (1) shifting people from employment to unemployment, (2) holding down participation in the labor force, and (3) lowering average weekly hours per person employed. Postwar evidence established clearly that a weak economy depressed productivity on balance; a substantial portion of labor input behaves like an overhead cost over the cycle. The evidence also made clear that a slack labor market discouraged people from hunting for jobs; the resulting number of discouraged job seekers disappear from the labor-force statistics. Their disappearance is reflected in depressed rates of participation in the measured labor force. Also, the same forces that raise unemployment also lower overtime and increase part-time work, thus reducing the average workweek.

The data for the fifties and early sixties suggested that these combined effects could be summarized adequately by an approximation that each extra point of unemployment is associated with a 3 percent shortfall of real GNP. The shortcut approximation of a 3 to 1 marginal relationship between output and the unemployment rate yielded the following formula for estimating potential GNP: $P = A[1 + 0.03(U - 4)]$, where P is potential GNP, A is actual GNP, and U is the actual unemployment rate. The time series of potential GNP derived directly from that formula was then smoothed to eliminate random variation. The smoothed estimate of potential GNP displayed an annual growth trend of approximately 3.5 percent in the late fifties and early sixties. The trend growth gradually increased to 4 percent later in the sixties. Those calculations of potential GNP and the gap fared remarkably well throughout the sixties and into the early seventies—so well that the 3 to 1 rule of thumb was labeled Okun's law by some enthusiasts.

The Recent Problems of Estimation

As with many other economic concepts and relationships that were successful and reasonably stable in previous decades, potential GNP has encountered problems during the mid- and late-seventies. Indeed, there are three problem areas: (1) the benchmark for reasonably full utilization, (2) the trend growth of productivity and hence of potential, and (3) the cyclical linkage between unemployment and output.

The Benchmark for Utilization   It became clear in the early seventies that any reasonable target for the unemployment rate had to exceed 4 percent. One important reason, highlighted by George Perry, was the shift in the demographic composition of the labor force toward age-sex groups that have traditionally experienced above-average job turnover and especially high unemployment rates. Perry and others who followed him recalculated potential GNP to allow for a gradual upward drift of the overall unemployment rate in light of the changing demographic weights. Other economists sought to estimate a benchmark unemployment rate consistent with non-inflationary behavior. But these efforts to infer the balance point of resource utilization from the data on inflation have yielded unstable results, perhaps because actual inflation has been strongly influenced by oil prices and by adaptations to past inflation. The uncertainty about a benchmark unemployment rate stimulated interest in an earlier approach developed by Edward Denison that focused on the share of non-labor income (as a deviation from its trend) rather than on the unemployment rate as a benchmark for potential performance.

The problems in this area have not been resolved, yet the magnitudes subject to controversy are not enormous. For example, most economists would agree that actual GNP in 1978 (with an unemployment rate of 6.0 percent) deviated from potential GNP by no more than 1 or 2 percentage points (upward or downward).

Even more significantly, many uses of estimates of potential GNP do not depend on an accurate benchmark for resource utilization—so long as the measure is reasonably consistent over time. By analogy, industrial operating or capacity utilization rates are constructed with a benchmark of 100 percent utilization that is clearly arbitrary and generally unattainable in the aggregate. Similarly, a time series of potential GNP geared even to a 4 percent unemployment rate can be used to compare the severity of recessions and to estimate the appropriate cyclical adjustments to corporate profits and other variables, even though it represents an arbitrary and indeed undesirable situation under present circumstances.

The Secular Trend   The growth of potential GNP has clearly been slower in the mid- and late-seventies than it was a decade earlier. The annual trend rate of growth appears currently to be less than $3\frac{1}{2}$ percent and may not be much above 3 percent. That slowdown in turn reflects a pronounced slowdown in the growth of productivity, which has been the subject of intensive professional research. It is generally agreed that a depressed rate of business fixed investment (especially during 1975 to 1977) has contributed to the slowdown. The substitution of capital and labor for energy (in response to the increased relative price of energy inputs) is also widely cited as an adverse influence on productivity. Many other possible contributing factors have been mentioned, including an increased use of resources for health, environmental protection, and safety; sociological developments affecting the attitudes of workers and management; and a lag in research and development.

The Cyclical Link between Unemployment and Output   During the seventies, fluctuations in the unemployment rate have displayed a less stable relationship with the growth of real GNP than in previous decades. Moreover, the typical relationship may have changed somewhat. Since 1970, the 3 to 1 relationship tends to overstate the incremental output associated with a decline in the unemployment rate. For that period, the incremental ratio appears to have been between 2.3 and 2.5 on the average, with considerable variation from year to year.

Reflecting these developments, the Council of Economic Advisers revised downward the estimates of potential GNP in 1977 and 1979. These were the first retrospective revisions in the estimates since they were first advanced by the Council in 1962. As that fact suggests, the measurement of potential GNP is subject to a significant range of uncertainty at present. But so is any other technique for making cyclical adjustments and for distinguishing trend and cycle. Potential GNP continues to be a valuable analytical tool with many important applications.

References

Denison, Edward F., *The Sources of Economic Growth in the United States and the Alternatives Before Us*, Committee for Economic Development, New York, 1962; *Economic Report of the President, January 1962*, 1962; *Economic Report of the President, January 1977*, 1977; *Economic Report of the President, January 1979*, 1979; Knowles, James W., *The Potential Economic Growth of the United States*, U.S. Joint Economic Committee Study Paper 20, 1960; Okun, Arthur M., "Potential GNP: Its Measurement and Significance," in American Statistical Association, *Proceedings of the Business and Economic Statistics Section*, Washington, D.C., 1962, pp. 98–104, reprinted in Okun, Arthur M., *The Political Economy of Prosperity*, Brookings, Washington, D.C., 1970, pp. 132–145; Perry, George L., "Changing Labor Markets and Inflation," *Brookings Papers on Economic Activity*, no. 3, 1970, pp. 411–441; Perry, George L., "Labor Force Structure, Potential Output, and Productivity," *Brookings Papers on Economic Activity*, no. 3, 1971, pp. 533–578.

(*See also* Economic statistics; Employment and unemployment; Federal Reserve policy; Fiscal policy; Gross national product; Monetary policy; National income accounting)

Arthur M. Okun

Poverty

Poverty is a condition of material deprivation, usually defined as a lack of money income relative to some poverty threshold. In most contexts, the poverty threshold, or index of material deprivation, is specified in relationship to the income or goods available to other members of society. Therefore, the poverty threshold in an under-developed country will be very different from that found in an industrial country such as the United States.

The application of modern economic analysis to the causes and cures of poverty is a relatively new phenomenon. During the years after World War II poverty was largely ignored by both professional economists and policymakers. Having survived the Great Depression and having experienced a substantial growth in real incomes, Americans tended to think that affluence was widely shared. Most social legislation during and after the Depression assumed that poverty would be limited to a small group of people with little attachment to the labor force—retired, disabled, and wid-owed persons. These people would be cared for by the income support system estab-lished by the Social Security Act of 1935.

In 1962 Michael Harrington wrote *The Other America,* describing conditions of severe material deprivation in Appalachia. His book brought wide public attention to poverty. Beginning about the same time, the growing resistance of urban blacks to de jure discrimination gained wide media coverage. The combination of these factors led Presidents Kennedy and then Johnson to treat poverty as a public policy problem. In 1964, Johnson declared "war" on poverty.

Measuring Poverty

Defining the scope of poverty proved to be difficult. After much discussion, the pov-erty threshold was defined in terms of the Department of Agriculture's minimum food budget. The cost of the minimum food budget necessary to sustain a family during temporary emergencies was multiplied by 3 to reflect the assumption that food com-prised one-third of the total budget. These poverty lines were later criticized as being unrealistic since the food budget used was never meant to sustain people over long periods of time. However, these poverty lines, which vary by family size and farm-nonfarm residence, became the basis for tabulating poverty statistics.

These poverty lines, which are still used for counting the poor for official govern-ment purposes, are adjusted only for increases in the cost of living. Therefore, during periods of economic growth the difference between the poverty lines and real median income increases. For this reason the official poverty lines are said to reflect an absolute definition of poverty—the same minimal food basket is used in every year. A relative definition of poverty would set the poverty lines as a percentage of what other families are spending, for example, at one-half of median family income. These poverty lines would then increase with both inflation and economic growth.

In 1965 there were 33 million poor families by the official definition. They com-prised 17.3 percent of the U.S. population. While most of the poor were white (67 percent) and most were nonfarm residents (87 percent), the incidence of poverty was higher among blacks (47 percent) and farm dwellers (34 percent).

Under the Johnson administration the Office of Economic Opportunity (OEO) was established to coordinate and administer a variety of programs to eliminate the root causes of poverty. Education, training, and increased participation in local decision making became the cornerstones of the effort. The assumptions behind the programs launched during this period were that if people had skills, they could earn their way out of poverty, and that if they had access to political power, public institutions would work in their behalf. These micro policies, accompanied by expansionary monetary and fiscal policy, would eliminate material deprivation.

The substantial economic growth of the 1960s and early 1970s was indeed accompanied by a drop in absolute poverty. By 1973 the incidence of poverty had reached a value of 11.1 percent, although the ensuing recession and sluggish recovery raised poverty rates again, to 11.6 percent in 1977. If the value of government programs offering goods and services (in-kind transfers), such as food stamps and medicare, is counted as income, the incidence of poverty is reduced to about 6 percent. When one uses a relative definition, the picture which emerges is one of a slight increase in poverty—the incomes of those at the bottom of the income distribution were increasing at a slightly slower rate than median family incomes.

Since demographic groups differed in their 1965 levels of poverty and in their rates of poverty reduction, we find substantial variation in absolute poverty by demographic groups in 1977. The elderly and farm dwellers experienced the largest drop, reaching levels of 14 percent and 13 percent by 1977. The lowest poverty rates in 1977 were experienced by groups, such as nonaged males, who had started with relatively low rates. There, however, remained groups with high incidences. For instance 31 percent of all blacks and 33 percent of all female-headed households remained poor.

Transfer Payments

At first the decline in absolute poverty was attributed directly to economic growth trickling down to the poor in the form of higher earnings. This view was undermined by evidence that payments by the government (transfers) had grown substantially over the same period.

Such transfers were never considered a solution to the root causes of poverty, but, in fact, increased social insurance and income-tested payments (the so-called welfare explosion) became the principal factor leading to a reduction in poverty. Expenditures on social security increased more than threefold between 1965 and 1974. Although expenditures on Aid to Families with Dependent Children (AFDC) were only 7.5 percent of the expenditures on social security, they grew fourfold. Several new programs, such as food stamps and medicare, were also instituted, leading to further poverty reduction if in-kind transfers are counted in determining poverty status.

Shifts in Public Policy

The recognition of the key role played by rapidly increasing transfers led to two important shifts in public policy. First, several major welfare reform proposals were developed by the Nixon, Ford, and Carter administrations. The general thrust of the early reforms was to take the often conflicting programs which had developed over the last 25 years and to replace them under a fairly comprehensive negative income tax. It was believed that a reorganized welfare system would eliminate many of the perverse work disincentives in the existing programs.

Economists recognized that there are two sources of work disincentives in any transfer program. First, the recipient may use the transfer payment to buy leisure by working less. The work disincentive from this source varies directly with the size of the transfer. Another source of work disincentive is caused by varying the benefits according to the amount of other income available to the recipient. Under most programs benefits are reduced as a welfare recipient earns more income. The work disincentive from this source varies directly with the rate at which benefits are reduced as earnings increase (the benefit reduction rate).

Policy analysts pointed out that work disincentives in existing programs could be reduced by offering lower payments or reducing the benefit reduction rate. The latter solution, however, has the consequence of letting people with fairly high earnings continue to receive transfer payments. There is an inherent conflict between work incentives, adequate payments to recipients, and targeting the program to low-income people. The conflict between these goals required a political decision which was not forthcoming.

Major welfare reform proposals were submitted by three Presidents. Congressional conservatives shunned the high budgetary costs and the reliance on work incentives rather than work requirements in these proposals. They also objected strongly to the consequence of keeping benefit reduction rates reasonably low—lower-middle-income people would have been eligible under some proposals. Liberals would not back programs which offered less-than-poverty-line incomes to those who could not work and reduced payments below the amounts available under some existing programs. A political stalemate ensued.

The second public policy response to the lack of improvement in labor-market incomes of the poor was to institute programs aimed at increasing the demand for low-income people. In the 1970s tax credits for businesses which hired welfare mothers, teenagers, the handicapped, and the low-skilled were instituted. Public jobs under the government's major public employment program, the Comprehensive Employment and Training Act, were more tightly targeted toward low-income people. The view that the requirement to work must be accompanied by the availability of a job became more readily accepted as the economy adjusted to high unemployment rates after the 1975 recession.

Root Causes of Poverty Remain Unresolved

While public policy shifted sharply toward a demand-side strategy in the mid-1970s, the academic debate over the root causes of poverty remained unresolved. Those subscribing to the view that poverty was caused by inadequacies of labor supply pointed to the work disincentives in the transfer programs. As long as public assistance offered some reasonable income floor, poverty was the preferred alternative for those who valued leisure highly. According to this view, the expansion in the welfare system had caused the decline in earnings. Those who stressed labor demand as critical argued that if work were available, almost all transfer recipients would prefer work to welfare. According to this view, the existing transfer system was simply not generous enough to those who could work to induce the kind of supply shifts necessary to explain the lack of improvement in earnings. The explanation of the deterioration in earnings clearly lies between these two extremes. Current research is trying to narrow the range of disagreement.

A brief review of the history of poverty policy indicates that there is no longer a political or professional consensus about what causes poverty. There is a loss of belief that the simple solutions to poverty offered during the 1960s—economic growth and a negative income tax—will work in the future. There is a growing tendency to focus on the differences among various segments of the poverty population. Roughly 68 percent of all poor household heads are not expected to work—disabled, aged, women with children. For these people work disincentives are not an issue. A program with high benefits and high benefit reduction rates would be appropriate. The 11 percent of the poor who work full time are in need of job opportunities. The key area of disagreement lies with the appropriate programs for the remaining 21 percent of the poor who are either single or male-headed households.

References

Browning, Edgar, *Redistribution and the Welfare System*, American Enterprise Institute, Washington, D.C., 1975; Danziger, Sheldon, and Robert Plotnick, *Has the War on Income Poverty Been Won?*, Academic Press, New York, 1980; Harrington, Michael, *The Other America*, Penguin, Baltimore, 1964; Haveman, Robert, *A Decade of Federal Antipoverty Programs*, Academic Press, New York, 1977.

(*See also* Family budgets; Income distribution; Negative income tax; Social security programs; Standard of living)

Peter T. Gottschalk

Price-earnings ratio

The price-earnings ratio is the relationship between the current market price of a corporation's common stock and that company's per-share earnings. The ratio indicates how much investors are willing to pay for $1 of earnings in a given corporation.

As published in the stock-market columns of major newspapers, it is computed by dividing the latest annual earnings per share into the closing price of the stock on the last day the market was open. (This means that in some cases, the ratios are badly out of date.) For instance, suppose XYZ Corporation's latest income statement (for the first quarter of the year) showed annual earnings of $4 per share. If the price of XYZ's common stock closed at $40 a share on June 30, its price-earnings ratio would be 10:1.

Evaluation of Stocks and Bonds

Securities analysts and others interested in determining the intrinsic value of a common stock have found the price-earnings ratio a useful tool. Evaluating other kinds of securities is relatively easy compared with evaluating common stock. For example, to determine the value of a bond, the analyst calculates the present value of the interest receipts and the principal, discounted at the appropriate interest rate—that is, the rate that accounts for the degree of risk involved. If bond A is riskier than bond B, a higher rate would be used for bond A and, therefore, its present value would be lower. In other words, bond B is worth more than bond A. When evaluating a preferred stock, the analyst expects the dividend to be paid indefinitely and, thus, treats it as a perpetual annuity, whose present value is found by dividing the amount of the annuity (annual dividend, in the case of preferred stock) by the appropriate interest rate.

Although the same method—discounting future receipts—would also apply to the evaluation of common stocks, two serious difficulties complicate the procedure. First, while the analyst knows what the dollar receipts will be for bonds and preferred stocks, the analyst does not know with certainty what they will be for common stocks. Consequently, the analyst must forecast future earnings, dividends, and stock prices—clearly not an easy task. Second, unlike the fixed receipts expected on bonds and preferred stocks, a common stock's earnings, dividends, and price are expected to grow, obviating the use of formulas and tables for the present value of annuity.

In order to overcome these difficulties and determine a common stock's value, academicians set up various models based on different growth rate assumptions, while practicing securities analysts use the price-earnings ratio. Analysts estimate the earnings per share for the coming year and apply the appropriate price-earnings multiple to find the stock's value. For example: When evaluating ABC Corporation's common stock, an analyst first forecasts that earnings per share will be $5 next year. Then the analyst determines current price-earnings ratios for companies with similar growth prospects and risk as ABC Corporation. If these ratios are around 10:1, the analyst then applies a 10-times multiple to ABC's earnings per share (10 × 5) and estimates the stock's value at $50 per share. If there are any special circumstances applicable to ABC Corporation, the analyst modifies the price-earnings multiple to account for them.

Use of Price-Earnings Multiples

The use of price-earnings multiples allows those evaluating common stocks to take into consideration companies with different growth prospects and varying degrees of risk. The greater the growth rate expected, other things remaining equal, the higher the price-earnings multiple used; the riskier the company, other things remaining equal, the lower the multiple applied.

At any given time, the stock market shows a wide range of price-earnings ratios, reflecting the disparate growth potentials of different industries and the companies within them. And as the projected growth rate of a company changes, or its risk increases or decreases, investors respond by changing the price-earnings multiple they apply to earnings. Aside from the shifting fortunes of individual companies, the general level of price-earnings ratios changes dramatically over time, mirroring investors' overall views of common stocks as an investment. For example, from 1947 to 1954, the price-earnings ratio for the Dow Jones Industrial average remained below or around 10:1. But during the last half of the 1950s, through the booming 1960s and into the early 1970s, the price-earnings ratio rarely dipped below 15:1 and in most of the years was near 20:1, reaching its high of 22.9:1 in 1961. Since 1972, however, the price-earnings ratio slipped below 10:1 in almost every year. The key influences are economic, financial, and political changes; and how these factors affect investors' attitudes determines the overall level of price-earnings ratios.

References

Cohen, Jerome B., Edward D. Zinbarg, and Arthur Zeikel, *Investment Analysis and Portfolio Management*, rev. ed., Dow Jones–Irwin, Homewood, Ill., 1973; Graham, B., *Security Analysis*, 4th ed., McGraw-Hill, New York, 1962.

(*See also* Bond; Stock; Stock exchange; Stock price averages and indexes)

Henry C. F. Arnold

Price measurement

Among the many economic statistics, prices are one of the most difficult to measure. There are six major issues which pervasively affect the ability to measure price levels and price changes.

Quality Change

The first issue concerns the problem that arises when the quality of an item being priced changes. Quality change has two aspects: definition and measurement. There are several approaches to defining quality change. One, based on neoclassical theory, is that it is equal to the long-run marginal cost (equals marginal revenue) of making the change. The second is the change in the product's ability to produce satisfaction if it is a consumer's good, and to produce output if it is a producer's good. A third method of defining quality change for a producer's good is a change in its ability to produce net revenue. The second and third definitions may be consistent with the first. The appropriate definition of quality change ultimately adopted in price measurement frequently depends on the uses to which the price data are being put.

The second aspect of accounting for quality change is how to make the adjustment. A frequently used method is to link in the new quality item for the old one. This requires that price observations on both qualities be collected for an overlapping time period. Its use assumes that the existing market price differential between the old and new qualities measures the quality difference. The second method is the so-called direct-comparison method. Here the items are compared and if deemed to be similar enough, the change is regarded simply as a price change and no adjustment for quality is made. A third method, if the concept is appropriate, is to obtain from sellers estimates of the cost of making the changes associated with the quality change. These resulting figures are then used to account for the difference between the price of the old and new quality in the same time period. If, for example, those costs do not fully account for an increase in price, then only part of the observed price difference is due to quality change. The remainder is treated as a price change.

New Products

Related to quality change is the issue of dealing with new products. It may in fact be quite difficult to establish the difference between a new product and a change in the quality of an existing product. For example, television sets and antibiotics were new products when first marketed. One problem associated with new products is to determine what product they replace or to determine, if they have not fully replaced an existing product, what share of the market basket represented by an index the new product has taken. Such determination is related to solving the most difficult problem with respect to products—when to begin to price them for official price measures. Frequently, new products appear on the market at a very high price, but, as they gain acceptance and are mass-produced, the price falls. Meanwhile, the importance of the new product in terms of total purchases by either consumers or producers has increased.

Transaction Prices

A third issue pertaining to price measurement is that of collecting the actual prices as opposed to list prices at which transactions take place. Frequently, items are sold at standard discounts, and, depending upon business conditions, those discounts may change. Such changes may go undetected when price data are collected. It is usually assumed that producer price indexes (PPIs) suffer from this problem more than consumer price indexes (CPIs) since, especially in the United States, prices of merchandise purchased by consumers are not usually subject to bargaining.

Pricing of Infrequently Purchased, Custom-Made Goods

A fourth problem is how to price infrequently purchased, custom-made goods. Ships and aircraft are ready examples. In such cases, the usual practice has been to represent the price of such items by a weighted average of the cost of the materials and labor used to produce them, both adjusted for changes in productivity. In the 1970s there was a growing tendency to use a more direct method of pricing which involves working with the actual contract prices and making judgments with respect to what represents quality change, what represents a new product, etc.

Contract versus Spot Prices

The fifth issue relates to whether contract or spot prices are appropriate. Frequently, this decision depends on the use to which the price data are to be put. For example, if the prices are to be compiled into an index for use as a deflator of output (to estimate constant-dollar output), a weighted average of the two kinds of prices should be used, since some output is being sold under contract and some at the spot price. If the prices are being used in an index designed to be an early-warning indicator of inflation, the spot price may be more appropriate.

Related to this problem is that of whether the price obtained should relate to orders or shipments. Again, the considerations are similar. Prices of orders, which would include prices at which new contracts are entered into, would be a better gauge of current price change than prices of shipments, which may include goods being delivered at prices previously agreed to.

Methodology of Measuring Prices and Price Changes

A sixth issue relates to the two methods used to measure prices and price changes. The first and more widely used is the so-called specification basis for pricing. This requires the drawing up of a precise description of the item to be priced and an endeavor to price the same item for different time periods. Specification pricing is viewed as an important vehicle for recognizing, if not measuring, quality change and in signaling the appearance of new products in markets.

However, pricing by tightly drawn specification may present some difficulties. Producers or distributors may not carry the precise specification of the item that is selected, or if they do, they may not have it in stock each time prices are collected for the index. This has led some statistical agencies responsible for publishing price indexes to use a looser specification which increases the frequency with which a price may be found for the item. This means that different specifications of the same item may be priced in different stores. Looser specification is characterized by the ability to collect prices for exactly the same thing for two consecutive time periods, and thus not having to collect prices for the same thing in every single outlet. In this case the purpose of the CPI is not to measure the level of prices, which would require one precise specification for each item, but rather their rate of change.

The other method employed to measure prices is the so-called unit-value approach, in which total shipments or orders are divided by some quantity indicator. This method is most frequently used in areas where products are homogeneous. For example, a measure of the prices charged by refineries for gasoline may be derived by dividing the total value of shipments of refineries by the total number of barrels shipped. The method works best when the product is uniform and can be useful in detecting changes in actual transactions prices since, if both shipments and barrels can be properly measured, discounts that might otherwise go unreported will be reflected in the dollar shipment figure.

On the other hand, unit values are plagued with the so-called product-mix problem. If the refinery ships two grades of gasoline, and the mix of its shipments changes between those two grades in a particular time period, and the price of each grade is different, the resulting price measure can be different from that of the preceding period without any change of prices having taken place.

Other Problems

Obviously, there are other problems with price measurement. One is how to treat seasonal items which disappear from markets at certain times or are extremely scarce. The treatment of taxes and the pricing of insurance are others. So, too, is the problem of pricing assets such as houses for consumer price indexes, although that problem is presently one which must be solved at the conceptual level before measurement problems can be addressed.

The problems associated with the measurement of prices over time also pertain to price measurement across space. The product problem, or the problem of quality change through time, is analogous to not being able to find the same product for pricing in two different places either because it is in short supply in one of the two, or because consumers do not demand it. Thus, if one were trying to compare clothing prices in two different locations of the United States, a problem would arise in trying to price winter coats in both Boston and Miami.

References

National Bureau of Economic Research, *The Price Statistics of the Federal Government: Review, Appraisal and Recommendations,* NBER General Series, no. 13, Washington, D.C., 1961; Ruggles, Richard, *The Wholesale Price Index: Review and Evaluation,* Council on Wage and Price Stability Report, June 1977; Triplett, Jack E., "The Measurement of Inflation: A Survey of Research on the Accuracy of Price Indexes," in Paul H. Earl (ed.), *Analysis of Inflation,* Lexington Books, Lexington, Mass., 1975.

(*See also* Consumer price index; Index numbers; Producer price index)

Joel Popkin

Price theory

Price theory, or, as it is often called, microeconomic theory, is concerned with how the price system handles the problem of allocating scarce resources in market economies. Price theory deals with how relative prices are determined, not with how the general price level is determined. The latter task requires a separate theory such as the quantity theory of the demand for money.

Price theory can be divided into five subcategories: (1) the theory of demand and consumer behavior, (2) the theory of the business firm, (3) the theory of market organization, (4) the theory of distribution, and (5) the theory of general equilibrium and welfare economics.

Theory of Demand and Consumer Behavior

In the standard modern approach to demand theory, the consumer's preferences are represented by a utility function defined as a function of the quantities of the goods and services that constitute the individual's consumption bundle. The major theoretical value of the utility function lies in the information it provides about the individual's willingness to trade one good for another in the consumption bundle, which is measured by what is called the marginal rate of substitution. The marginal rate of substitution of X for Y is the amount of good Y that would have to be added to the individual's consumption bundle to exactly compensate for the utility lost by the removal of one unit of X from the consumption bundle.

The simplest form of the theory of demand assumes that the consumer has a given income and faces a given set of prices of goods and services. The consumer then chooses a consumption bundle so as to maximize utility subject to the constraint that the total expenditure on the goods and services purchased does not exceed income. The consumer's decision may be stated as a formal mathematical problem. Let x_1, $\cdots$, x_n represent the quantities of goods 1 to n; let p_1, $\cdots$, p_n represent the prices of these n goods; and let M represent income. The consumer's utility function is $U(x_1$, $\cdots$, $x_n)$. The consumer's choice of a consumption bundle is given by the solution of

$$\max_{x_1, \cdots, x_n} U(x_1, \ldots, x_n) \tag{1}$$

subject to

$$M \geqslant p_1 x_1 + p_2 x_2 + \cdots + p_n x_n \tag{2}$$

where Equation (2) is the income or budget constraint, and where the quantities x_1, x_2, $\cdots$, x_n are understood to be nonnegative. [In this formulation M is often treated as money income (dollars) and price is measured as dollars per unit of the good. Note, however, that the only purpose served by money in this model is to be a unit of account. Actually, any commodity can be used as the unit of account or numéraire.]

The solution to this constrained maximization problem depends on the values of p_1, $\cdots$, p_n and M. As prices and income are varied, the utility-maximizing quantities of the goods will change. The relationship between the quantity demanded of a good and prices and income is known as a demand function. Given some fairly weak conditions on the utility function, it can be shown that the demand function will exhibit an inverse relationship between the quantity demanded of a good and the price of a good when prices of other goods and income are held constant. That is, as the price of a good increases, the quantity demanded of that good will decrease. This inverse relationship between the quantity demanded of a good and its price is known as the law of demand. The market demand curve is obtained by aggregating the demand curves of the individuals in the market.

There are several extensions of this basic model. One important extension makes income endogenous by treating leisure time as a good and allowing the individual to sell time at a given market wage rate. Another extension is to introduce multiple time periods along with interest rates so that investment, savings, and life-cycle consumption patterns may be analyzed. The model has also been modified to deal with consumer choice in the presence of risk thereby allowing extensions to capital theory, the demand for insurance, inventory planning, and other stochastic models.

Theory of the Business Firm

In standard microeconomic theory, the firm is modeled as an economic unit that employs inputs such as capital and labor and uses these inputs to produce a good or service which is sold to consumers or, in some cases, to other producers. The technological process by which the firm transforms inputs into outputs is represented analytically by a production function.

One production function which is used widely in both theoretical and empirical work has the form

$$Q = AK^\alpha L^\beta$$

where Q is output, K is the capital input, and L is the labor input. The parameters α, β, and A are technologically determined. This functional form is usually referred to as a Cobb-Douglas or log-linear production function.

The production function typically allows for the substitution of inputs so that there are many input combinations that will produce a given output. In the simplest case, the firm faces a given set of prices for the inputs and a given production function and then chooses that combination of inputs which produces the desired output at the lowest total cost. The problem is analytically similar to the consumer maximization problem discussed previously. Indeed, the mathematical dual of the problem faced by the firm is to maximize output for a given level of cost just as the consumer maximizes utility for a given budget. The critical difference is that the firm's desired level of output is not determined until output price is considered.

Thus, for a given output and given input prices, it is possible to determine the input combination which produces that output at lowest total cost. The resulting association between output and the cost of producing that output is called the total-cost function. For each level of output the total-cost function shows what the cost of producing that output will be when the inputs are chosen in an optimal manner.

In order to go from the theory of cost to the theory of supply, some additional assumptions are needed. If the firm chooses output levels to maximize profit and if the firm is a price taker in the output market, then the amount the firm will supply at any given output price can be determined using the total-cost function. The resulting association between output price and the quantity supplied by the firm is known as the supply schedule (sometimes called supply curve or supply function) for the firm. In the simplest case, the industry supply schedule can be determined by simply adding the quantities supplied by the firms in the industry for each output price. This simple means of deriving the industry supply schedule is complicated by two considerations: (1) the presence of externalities, and (2) entry and exit of firms from the industry.

Externalities arise when the combined activities of all firms in the industry affect input prices or technology. If the industry uses a specialized input, it is possible that the price of that input will be bid up as firms try to purchase more of it. Thus, from the viewpoint of any individual firm, total cost is affected by both its level of output and the industry level of output. In this case, the industry supply schedule cannot be found by a simple horizontal addition of the supply schedules of the firms in the industry because these firms' supply schedules shift as industry output changes. Similarly, there may be external effects that change the production functions of the individual firms.

Entry and exit of firms will also affect the industry supply schedule in an obvious manner. The problem of entry and exit of firms is often handled by distinguishing between short-run and long-run industry supply schedules. The short-run supply schedules refer to the output decisions of existing firms, while the long-run supply schedules allow for changes in supply because firms have entered or left the industry. This distinction between short-run and long-run supply is also used to account for the fact that during short time intervals it is not feasible for the firm to fully adjust its inputs.

Market Organization

In both the theory of the firm and the theory of demand, price is treated as exogenously given to the economic agents involved. By linking these two sides of the market, both price and quantity can be determined endogenously. The mechanism for doing this is usually described in terms of supply and demand curves such as those shown in the accompanying figure. The curve labeled DD in the figure is the demand curve from the theory of consumer behavior. The supply curve, labeled SS, comes from the theory of the firm. Even though the previous analysis treats price as the independent variable, it is conventional in economics to represent price on the vertical axis in graphs of demand and supply curves.

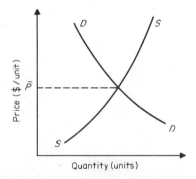

The DD and SS curves represent aggregates across consumers and firms, respectively. The equilibrium price is the price at which DD and SS intersect. It is denoted by $\overline{P}$ in this figure. This is the market clearing price in that at this price, the quantity supplied is equal to the quantity demanded. At prices above $\overline{P}$, the quantity supplied exceeds demand—there is a glut which tends to drive prices down. At prices below $\overline{P}$, the quantity demanded exceeds the quantity supplied—there is a shortage which tends to drive prices up. When price is equal to $\overline{P}$, quantity supplied equals quantity demanded and the market is cleared. Supply and demand analysis is a powerful tool for analyzing the effects of taxes, changes in income and wages, crop failures, and other phenomena relating to the quantity produced and sold of a good and the price at which this exchange takes place.

This model of supply and demand is generally associated with perfect competition, which assumes that the buyers and sellers act as price takers, that the good is homogeneous across sellers, that there are no government regulations or other artificial prohibitions which prevent exit and entry to the industry, and that both sellers and buyers have complete information about price and other relevant variables. There are other forms of market organization in which the sellers or buyers may act as price makers. This is true of pure monopoly where there is only one seller. The single seller directly faces the market demand curve and explicitly recognizes that an increase in output will result in a decrease in price and vice versa. In this case, there is no longer a supply curve in the sense described previously because the price responsiveness (usually measured by price elasticity, roughly defined as the percentage change in quantity demanded arising from a 1 percent change in price) and location of the demand curve will affect the firm's output decision. Thus, the firm determines price and quantity simultaneously in pure monopoly. Economists have developed models of many other forms of market organization including duopoly, oligopoly, and monopolistic competition.

Buyers may also act as price makers rather than price takers. This is the case, for example, when there is a single buyer facing a large number of price-taking sellers— a situation known as monopsony. When a single buyer faces a single seller, the result is an indeterminate situation known as bilateral monopoly.

Theory of Distribution

In addition to the question of what is produced and sold, economists are interested in knowing what determines the prices and income of the factors of production such as capital and labor. The answer is usually developed in terms of the theory of marginal productivity. The marginal product of a productive factor is the additional output that is produced if one more unit of the factor is employed, while holding the employment of all other factors constant. According to the law of diminishing returns, or more precisely the law of variable proportions, the marginal product of a factor ultimately declines as more of the factor is used. If the firm is assumed to maximize profit and is a price taker in both the input market and the output market, then in equilibrium the quantity employed of a productive factor will be such that marginal product multiplied by output price will equal the price of the factor. By using this kind of analysis, including extensions to the case of several inputs, a factor demand function can be derived. Aggregating these factor demand functions across firms with appropriate adjustment for external effects leads to a market demand function for the productive factor. This factor demand function can be combined with a factor supply function to determine the price and quantity employed of the productive factor.

This theory is a simple comparative static theory. In the case of long-lived productive factors such as capital it is sometimes more appropriate to develop a dynamic model which explicitly takes into account the intertemporal nature of the capital accumulation or investment decision.

Other extensions of the theory of distribution involve analysis of noncompetitive markets for inputs and outputs.

General Equilibrium and Welfare Economics

Many problems in price theory are analyzed using partial equilibrium techniques. In other words, the analysis typically concentrates on a single market and ignores the interactions between the market being studied and other markets. This often proves to be a fruitful approach, and economists have used partial equilibrium analysis in the study of a wide variety of practical and theoretical problems. Nonetheless, it is sometimes important to broaden the scope of the analysis in order to understand how equilibrium is achieved in all markets simultaneously. General equilibrium analysis deals with this question. General equilibrium analysis embodies many of the techniques of partial equilibrium analysis but introduces new concepts to deal with the interdependencies among the markets.

Much of price theory is descriptive or positive, but many economists are interested in price theory as a normative device for evaluating economic efficiency and welfare. The welfare criterion most often used for normative evaluations is that of Pareto optimality. If an economic equilibrium has the property that no reallocation of resources can make one or more of the economic agents better off without making one or more other agents worse off, then that equilibrium is said to be Pareto-optimal. Pareto optimality uses the utility functions of the individual economic agents as the yardstick for the terms "better off" and "worse off." Thus, all agents would benefit (or at least not lose) by moving from a non-Pareto-optimal equilibrium to one that is Pareto-optimal. The conditions of Pareto optimality are achieved by a competitive equilibrium but may be violated by the presence of monopoly, taxes, pollution, and other externalities that drive a wedge between private and social costs, or between private and social benefits. The effects of these externalities may be partially or fully self-canceling when they are present simultaneously.

Historical Development of Price Theory

These five categories constitute what is known as neoclassical price theory and are the result of about 200 years of intellectual evolution. Although scholars have been concerned with the issues of economic organization from the time of Aristotle, the modern theory of price began to emerge as a system of scientific principles only with the work of François Quesnay and Adam Smith. Major contributors to the development of modern price theory include the nineteenth-century writers Thomas Malthus, David Ricardo, Jean Baptiste Say, Nassau William Senior, and John Stuart Mill. The early development of utility theory, which played a major role in the unification of price theory, can be found in the work of Hermann Heinrich Gossen, Carl Menger, and Léon Walras. Further development of utility theory and of general equilibrium theory occurred in the latter nineteenth and early twentieth centuries in the work of Walras, Vilfredo Pareto, Francis Ysidro Edgeworth, Eugeny Slutsky, Knut Wicksell, and Irving Fisher. The neoclassical partial equilibrium theory which synthesized much of the earlier work was one of the important accomplishments of Alfred Marshall.

Although the general structure of price theory has changed little in the last 50 years, there have been numerous refinements and extensions of this basic framework. Beginning with the work of Henry L. Moore, economists undertook statistical and empirical measurement of such phenomena as demand and supply schedules. The interest in empirical research grew rapidly, especially after the appearance of high-speed digital computers in the 1950s, and by the 1960s had developed to the point where special statistical and econometric techniques had been devised for dealing with propositions and hypotheses from the theory of price.

The number of important theoretical contributions during the past half-century is too large to consider in detail. However, brief mention of some of this work helps convey a general picture of how economic theory has been developing. The *Foundations of Economic Analysis*, by Paul Samuelson (1948), and the *Theory of Value*, by Gerard Debreu (1959), together provide a comprehensive mathematical statement of the formal structure of price theory. Debreu and Arrow (1964) also showed how state-preference analysis could be used to extend price theory and general equilibrium theory to situations involving risk. The work of George Stigler (1968) opened important new frontiers in industrial organization, the economics of information, and the positive theory of government regulation. Gary Becker (1976) has shown how the principles of price theory extend to many areas such as discrimination, marriage, and criminal behavior that traditionally have not been thought of as part of the domain of economic analysis. Finally, there has been a growing body of research that treats principles of price theory as the basis of all of economic theory, including the macroeconomic issues of inflation, unemployment, and the business cycle (Phelps et al., 1970).

References

Becker, Gary S., *Economic Theory*, Knopf, New York, 1971; Becker, Gary S., *The Economic Approach to Human Behavior*, University of Chicago Press, Chicago, 1976; Debreu, Gerard, *Theory of Value*, Yale University Press, New Haven, Conn., 1959; Debreu, Gerard, and Kenneth Arrow, "The Role of Securities in the Optimal Allocation of Risk Bearing," *Review of Economic Studies*, vol. 51, April 1961, pp. 91–96; Friedman, Milton, *Price Theory*, Aldine, Chicago, 1976; Gould, John P., and C. E. Ferguson, *Microeconomic Theory*, 5th ed., Irwin, Homewood, Ill., 1980; Neumann, John von, and Oskar Morgenstern, *Theory of Games and Economic Behavior*, 3d ed., Princeton University Press, Princeton, N.J., 1953, reprinted by Wiley, New York, 1964; Phelps, E., et al., *Microeconomic Foundations of Employment and Inflation Theory*, Norton, New York, 1970; Samuelson, Paul, *Foundations of Economic Analysis*, Harvard University Press, Cambridge, Mass., 1948; Stigler, George J., "The Development of Utility Theory," *Journal of Political Economy*, vol. 58, August and October 1950, pp. 307–327, 373–396; Stigler, George J., *The Theory of Price*, 3d ed., Macmillan, New York, 1966; Stigler, George J., *The Organization of Industry*, Irwin, Homewood, Ill., 1968.

(*See also* Behavioral economics; Competition; Demand; Diminishing returns law; Firm theory; General equilibrium; Microeconomics; Monopoly and oligopoly; Normative economics; Supply; Utility; Welfare economics)

John P. Gould

Producer price index

Producer price index is the generic name applied to indexes of prices charged by producers. As such, they exclude excise taxes, freight insurance, and other costs involved in transferring commodities to purchasers. The term producer price index is in juxtaposition to an index of purchaser prices such as the consumer price index. In the United States the producer price index (PPI) and its component indexes cover manufacturing, mining, electric and gas utilities, and agriculture. In principle, the indexes could be expanded to include all sectors of the economy. Current work on such indexes for the transportation sector reflects the course of expansion in the development of the PPI.

History

The PPI is the oldest price series published by the U.S. government. It first appeared in 1902 with back data provided to 1890. At its inception, the PPI, which until 1978 was called the wholesale price index (WPI), included detailed price series for about 250 commodities produced in the agricultural, mining, and manufacturing sectors of the economy. The number of individual series has grown steadily over the years and in 1979 totaled 3000.

The indexes are calculated using the Laspeyres formula. The indexes are published monthly, and selected series are seasonally adjusted.

The various component indexes are added together to form several major aggregate indexes. Until 1978, all of the items for which price series existed were added up into an aggregate of all commodities for the WPI. Two major subcomponents were farm products and processed foods and feeds, and industrial commodities. The latter subcomponent represented about 75 percent of the total.

It became increasingly clear that the aggregation of all of the commodities to a single total produced an index which was not as useful as it could be. The problem was that the industrial commodities component, for example, contained the price of iron ore, the price of steel, and the price of cars, each weighted by total shipments of those commodities. If the price of iron ore rose and triggered an increase in the price of steel and the price of autos, the addition of those three increases amounted to an overstatement of the rise in producer prices if, for example, one wanted to compare it with the behavior of consumer prices. In the late 1960s, work began at the Bureau of Labor Statistics (BLS) on the development and analysis of prices in the so-called stage-of-process format. The WPI was aggregated into separate indexes for crude, intermediate, and finished goods. The relationships among those three components and of the components with the consumer price index became the subject of analysis, and models were built encompassing those indexes. By studying prices by stage of process, the analyst was able to detect early warnings of inflation at early stages of production, which might in turn be passed on to final users such as consumers.

Although stage-of-process indexes had been calculated from the WPI since the turn of the century (the BLS reports that such calculations were made at the request of students of price indexes), the use of these indexes was not widely understood. As a result, they were not part of the major components of the WPI which received wide publication. In 1978 the BLS renamed the wholesale price index the producer price index and began to emphasize three major components of that index: finished goods; intermediate materials, supplies, and components; and crude materials for further processing. These three indexes are now the most widely analyzed components of the producer price index.

Prior to the renaming of the index as the producer price index and the emphasis on disaggregation by stage of process, another need developed for producer prices. Analysts were interested in studying the behavior of constant-dollar output by industry. One way of doing so was to calculate the value of output in current dollars and to deflate that series by an appropriate index. But industries and products are not necessarily synonymous. Some industries produce as secondary products commodities that are primary products in other industries, and the value of production for an industry could include both its primary production and that part of its production which was largely produced in another industry. Therefore, the deflation of such value aggregates requires that special indexes be developed that take into account the composition of primary and secondary products in the value of an industry's output. Such series, referred to as industry-sector price indexes, first appeared in 1963.

Thus, the PPI is capable of configuration into an infinite number of indexes depending on the purpose of analysis. The old wholesale price index and its industrial commodities aggregate, the stage-of-process indexes, and the industry-sector price indexes provide three examples of the diversity with which aggregates can be formed from a basic set of producer prices.

Calculation of the Indexes

The component indexes of the PPI are added together using value-of-shipments weights from the various industrial censuses. Current weights are based on 1972 data. Producer prices in the manufacturing sector are weighted by shipments collected in the quinquennial Census of Manufactures. Similarly, mining and agricultural censuses are used to develop weights for those index components.

The stage-of-process index structure requires that those weights be further refined. For example, the price of refined petroleum products would be weighted for the industrial commodities component of the old wholesale price index by the total value of shipments of petroleum products. In the stage-of-process framework that weight must be split depending on the uses to which refined petroleum products are put. Such products going to chemical manufacturers for further manufacture would be classified in the stage-of-process index for intermediate materials, supplies, and components. Most gasoline going to final users would be classified in the finished goods index. The process of splitting shipment weights by stage-of-process is usually accomplished through the use of an input-output table.

The industry-sector price indexes provide yet another example of how value of shipment weights must be modified. The value of the output of steel mill products may not be all produced in the steel industry. On the other hand, some steel mills may produce some products, such as chemicals, that are produced primarily in another industry. Therefore, the value of the weight represented by total shipments of steel mill products must be distributed between the steel industry, which produces such products as primary products, and other industries, which may produce them as secondary products.

The value-of-shipments weights used currently in the PPI are generally those of 1972. The allocation of these weights for the stage-of-process components is based on the 1963 input-output table. Thus the weight base is generally that of 1972.

The reference base is currently 1967 = 100. The selection of a reference base is arbitrary. Any time period can be selected to equal 100 without affecting the rate of change of the index except by 0.1 percent from time to time due to rounding. Traditionally, however, the reference base of U.S. government statistics is changed about once every 10 years.

Problems

Many of the problems involved in price measurement apply to producer price indexes. Since the quality of many goods produced in the agriculture, mining, and manufacturing sectors changes, there is always the problem of making appropriate adjustment for quality change. Tightly developed specifications are used to collect prices for the index in order to facilitate the adjustment of such prices for quality change.

The problem of obtaining true transaction prices is one which is assumed to affect the producer price index more than other indexes. The reason is that in the United States most prices for consumer commodities are fixed and indicated by a price tag. In the manufacturing and other sectors of the economy, prices may have a greater tendency to be negotiable even though list prices are published. A major study of this problem in the PPI was carried out in the 1960s. It offered no conclusive evidence that systematic error owing to the list-transaction price problem was introduced into the larger aggregates of the index.

Another problem of price measurement that arises in connection with discussion and interpretation of the PPI is whether the prices collected should be of new orders or of shipments. For purposes of measuring industry output in constant dollars the shipment price is usually the one desired. On the other hand, for analyzing and forecasting inflation, the order price is a more desirable one to obtain. The current producer price index is a combination of the two.

References

Early, John F., "Improving the Measurement of Producer Price Change," *Monthly Labor Review*, April 1978, pp. 7–18; U.S. Department of Labor, "Wholesale Prices," *Handbook of Methods*, Bureau of Labor Statistics Bulletin 1910, 1976.

(*See also* Consumer price index; Escalator clause; Implicit price deflator; Index numbers; Price measurement)

Joel Popkin

Production function

Let n inputs be utilized in a production process which yields m output. The engineer describes the process in terms of variables such as pressure, density, and horsepower. The economist describes the production process in terms of a production function through which the quantities of outputs produced are functionally dependent upon the quantities of inputs used. The economist's production function incorporates the engineering technology; however, its inputs and outputs usually are quantities which are bought and sold in the marketplace. It also incorporates a degree of optimization. Given values for all of the inputs and values for all but one of the outputs, the production function specifies the maximum attainable value for the remaining output. Similarly, given values for all of the outputs and all but one of the inputs, it specifies the minimum permissible value for the remaining input.

Most production functions are defined for a single output. The number of inputs depends upon the purpose for which the production function is used and the level of aggregation employed. Economywide production functions relate a nation's total output to its aggregate labor and capital inputs. On an establishment level a specific output, such as motorcycles, may be related to an array of inputs such as handlebars, tires, wheels, leather, etc., as well as direct labor and capital inputs.

Some Properties of Production Functions

A wide variety of mathematical formats are used for production functions. These include continuous functions, discontinuous functions, and systems of functions with rules explaining which is applicable for particular circumstances. Most of the major properties of production functions can be illustrated by the following one-output, two-input function

$$q = f(L, K)$$

which is continuous with continuous first- and second-order partial derivatives, and where q denotes the quantity of output secured, and L and K denote the respective quantities of labor and capital used. The function is limited to nonnegative output and input levels. In some cases the input domain may exclude some nonnegative values.

The average product of labor is q/L, and, similarly, the average product of capital is q/K. The marginal product of labor is the rate at which the quantity of output increases per unit increase in the input of labor with the input of capital unchanged as given by the partial derivative of L with respect to q: $\partial q/\partial L \equiv f_L$ for short. A possible graph for the average and marginal products of labor is shown in the accompanying figure. These shapes are often assumed by economists, although many other shapes are possible. The positions of the curves depend upon the value of the fixed quantity of capital.

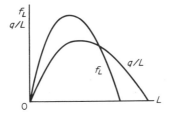

The marginal and average products of labor first increase and then decline as the quantity of labor is expanded relative to the fixed quantity of capital for the case shown in the figure. The value of f_L eventually becomes zero and may even become negative. Similar curves may be constructed for f_K and q/K assuming a variable quantity of capital and a fixed quantity of labor. An isoquant gives the loci of all input values which yield a fixed output level.

Returns to Scale and Homogeneous Production Functions

Let both inputs increase (or decrease) by the same proportionate amount. For convenience, limit attention to input increases. The production function exhibits decreasing returns to scale if output increases by a smaller proportion. There are constant returns to scale if output increases by the same proportion, and increasing returns to scale if it changes by a greater proportion. In general, a particular production function may exhibit decreasing, constant, and increasing returns to scale depending upon the initial labor and capital quantities and their proportionate change.

A production function is homogeneous of degree k if

$$qt^k = f(tL, tk)$$

for nonnegative values of t. If input quantities are changed by the proportion t, output is changed by the proportion t^k for all input values with the domain of the production function. If $k = 1$, there are constant returns to scale with output changing by the same proportion as the inputs. Such production functions are said to be linearly homogeneous. Thus, if $k < 1$ ($k > 1$), there are decreasing (increasing) returns to scale throughout.

Assume that a production function is homogeneous of degree 1, and let $t = 1/L$ so that

$$q/L = f(1, K/L) = F(K/L)$$

In this form output per worker is expressed as a function of the capital-labor ratio. This form of production function is used in most economic growth models.

The Cobb-Douglas production function is given by

$$q = AL^\alpha K^{1-\alpha}$$

where $A > 0$ and $0 < \alpha < 1$. It is homogeneous of degree 1, and is used extensively in both theoretical and empirical analyses. The parameter α is the share of total output going to labor if labor is paid the value of its marginal product. Similarly, $1 - \alpha$ is capital's share. The constant-elasticity-of-substitution production function provides a generalization of the Cobb-Douglas function.

Multiple Outputs

A production function with two outputs and two inputs may be written in implicit form as

$$F(q_1, q_2, L, K) = 0$$

where q_1 and q_2 are the quantities of two outputs. This function gives maximum-output (maximum-input) levels when the other three arguments are at fixed levels. It is assumed to be continuous with continuous first- and second-order partial derivatives. Its properties are similar to those of the one-output functions if one of the outputs is held constant.

Consider a situation in which the quantities of labor and capital are given, and it is desired to consider the trade-offs between the two outputs. A transformation function (or transformation curve) is constructed by selecting a level for one of the outputs and determining the maximum level for the other from the production function. Given the definition of the production function, the same result is achieved regardless of which of the outputs is assumed to be fixed. The rate of product substitution (i.e., the slope of a transformation curve) is given by:

$$-\partial q_2/\partial q_1 = \frac{\partial F/\partial q_1}{\partial F/\partial q_2}$$

The preceding minus sign transforms the rate into a positive number since $\partial q_2/\partial q_1$ is inherently negative; i.e., an increase in the level of one output reduces the maximum attainable level for the other.

A transformation curve also can be constructed from distinct production functions for the two outputs. In this case an explicit optimization procedure is used to maximize one of the output levels given fixed values for the other output, labor, and capital.

Linear Production Functions

Linear, sometimes called fixed-coefficient, production functions are frequently used. It is assumed that a_L and a_K units of labor and capital, respectively, are required to produce one unit of output. The linear production function is given by

$$q = \min{(L/a_L, K/a_K)}$$

Direct substitution between the two factors is not possible. Each of the factors may be limiting.

For example, let 2 units of labor $(a_L = 2)$, and 5 units of capital $(a_K = 5)$ be required for the production of 1 unit of output. Given $L = 20$ and $K = 40$, it follows that $q = 8$; 4 units of labor must go unused. There is enough labor for 10 units, but the available quantity of capital limits production to 8 units. In this situation, the marginal product of labor is zero since labor increments will not result in output increments. The marginal product of capital is 0.2 since this is the amount by which output will increase for each additional unit of capital employed. If $L = 20$ and $K = 50$, $q = 10$, and marginal products of both factors are zero.

Substitution between labor and capital is sometimes achieved by allowing the simultaneous use of several distinct linear processes for the production of a particular good.

References

Frisch, Ragnar, *Theory of Production*, Rand-McNally, Chicago, 1965; Henderson, James M., and Richard E. Quandt, *Microeconomic Theory: A Mathematical Approach*, 3d ed., McGraw-Hill, New York, 1980, chaps 4, 5; Hirschleifer, Jack, *Price Theory and Applications*, 2d ed.; Prentice-Hall, Englewood Cliffs, N.J., 1980, chap. 9; Varian, Hal R., *Microeconomic Analysis*, Norton, New York, 1978, chap. 1.

(*See also* Firm theory; Isoquant)

James M. Henderson

Productivity

Productivity denotes the relationship between output and one or all associated inputs, in real terms. In neoclassical economics, the concepts of marginal and average productivity are an important part of value and distribution theory under the assumption of static equilibrium conditions. In dynamic economic analysis, the concepts and measures of average and total productivity ratios, which reflect the impacts of cost-reducing technological and organizational changes, are an important variable helping to explain changes in economic aggregates and structure, and in costs and prices.

Static Productivity Concepts

Marginal productivity of the factors of production is an important theoretical concept. It refers to the increase in output associated with a given increase in a factor input, if the quantity of other inputs and technology are held constant. It is hypothesized that beyond some point (the optimal combination of inputs), the marginal productivity of a factor declines—i.e., output increases less than proportionately to the input. Conversely, marginal costs (input cost per incremental unit of output) rise as marginal productivity falls since productivity and unit costs are the opposite sides of the same coin.

The average total unit-cost curve of the firm can also be interpreted as the inverse of a total productivity curve (output per unit of all inputs, or real-cost elements). Unit costs decline as output rises up to the point of the most efficient rate of utilization of a fixed plant; thereafter they rise—so total productivity rises up to that point, then falls.

There is also a long-run productivity concept in neoclassical theory, associated with Alfred Marshall's notions of increasing, constant, and diminishing returns in different industries. If output increases faster than inputs (including overhead factors) as the scale of production increases, the increasing return (decreasing unit cost) reflects the operation of economies of scale, not technological innovation since static conditions of constant technological knowledge are still assumed. Diminishing returns presumably characterize extractive industries as increasing output necessitates resort to poorer lands or to more intensive use of existing land. In other industries, productivity and unit costs remain essentially flat as the scale of operations and number of plants increases.

Finally, there is the notion of the production function. Under static conditions, a given volume of output can be produced with different combinations of the factors, as depicted by a production isoquant. The actual combination of inputs depends on their relative prices, which determine the least-cost combination.

In comparative statics, if cost-reducing technological change is assumed, this is depicted by shifts of productivity curves upward, downward shifts of marginal and unit-cost curves, and a shift to the left of production isoquants. Actually, the notions of average and marginal productivity under hypothetical static assumptions are difficult, if not impossible, to implement statistically. This is not true of productivity concepts under more realistic dynamic conditions.

Dynamic Productivity Concepts

In contrast to the static concepts, there is a family of average productivity ratios relating output to one or more inputs over time which reflect the effects of cost-reducing innovations in the ways and means of production and other dynamic forces. The precise meaning of the average productivity ratios depends on the concepts and methods used to measure outputs and inputs, discussed subsequently. Productivity can be measured for the business economy, industries, firms, and organizational units for which separate records are kept.

The ratios of output to individual inputs, or classes of inputs, are called partial productivity ratios. The most common of these is the familiar output-per-labor-hour measure, which is particularly important since labor is the dominant cost of production in the economy, and the major part of value added in most industries. The partial productivity measures reflect factor substitutions as well as changes in productive efficiency. Thus, output-labor ratios reflect increases in capital and other nonhuman inputs per labor hour, as well as cost-reducing technological innovations.

Only if output is related to all associated inputs is the net saving in real costs per unit of output measured, and thus the increase in productive efficiency. Such measures are called total productivity ratios. When gross output is measured, the associated inputs are not only the factors of production—human (labor) and nonhuman (human-made capital goods and land or other natural resources) but they also include the purchased intermediate products—the materials, supplies, energy, and other services consumed in the production process. A variant of the total productivity measure is total factor productivity, in which net output of the intermediate product purchases is measured, and the resulting real value added is related to the factor inputs above. Since the sum of value added by industry equals national product, total factor productivity estimates by industry have the advantage of consistency with national measures. But since managements of firms are interested in the least-cost combination of all inputs, and in conserving over time in the use of intermediate goods and services as well as of factor services, total productivity measures are of interest for establishments, companies, and industries. At the national level, the total and total factor productivity measures are identical, for in consolidating production accounts of all industries, interindustry sales and purchases of intermediate products wash out, and the value of the final products that compose gross national product (GNP) equals the gross factor costs of production, plus indirect business taxes less subsidies since GNP is measured at market prices.

It is clear that the concept of productivity is rooted in the notion of the production function, that the volume of output depends on the volume of inputs used in production and on the state of the art (technology). As technology advances, reflected in shifts in the production function as discussed previously, more outputs can be produced with the same inputs. To use the simple Cobb-Douglas production function, devised in the mid-1920s:

$$Q = AK^\alpha L^\beta$$

In this formulation, A is the technology scalar that constrains the amount of output Q that can be obtained from given quantities of labor L and capital K. The exponents α and β relate to the marginal products of the factors, or, if index numbers are used to fit the function, the percentage shares of gross income. If the production function is linear and homogeneous, of degree 1, there are no scale economies and α and β sum to 1.0. If cost-reducing technological changes occur through time, this is reflected in shifts in the scalar A. The rate of change in the scalar could be measured by a time trend $(1 + r)$, in the place of A. Or, more flexibly, the period-to-period rates of change in the productivity scalar can be computed as the difference between the rates of change in output and a weighted average of the rates of change in the inputs:

$$\Delta A/A = \Delta Q/Q - \alpha \, \Delta K/K - \beta \, \Delta L/L$$

This is why total factor productivity has sometimes been called a residual—that part of the change in output that cannot be explained by the change of input.

Another way to measure the productivity scalar is as the ratio of output to a weighted average of inputs, as discussed at the outset:

$$\frac{Q}{K^\alpha L^\beta}$$

As a practical matter, total input has been measured as an arithmetic rather than a geometric mean of the component inputs. The difference is small unless the rates of change of the inputs differ substantially. Also, instead of the weights coming from the exponents of a statistically fitted production function, factor shares in national income are used.

Since the Cobb-Douglas function was formulated, various other types of production functions have been developed. But the type of function assumed as background for total productivity measures affects chiefly the system of weights, and it has been demonstrated that weighting differences have relatively little impact on the movement of productivity, at least over intermediate time periods.

Measurement

Gross output is measured as a weighted quantity aggregate

$$\sum_{i=1}^{n} Q_x P_o,$$

with units of each of the n goods and services produced in the given period x weighted by base-period prices P_o, or unit costs. Actually, for production and productivity analysis, in contrast to welfare analysis, unit-factor-cost weights are preferable to market prices in measuring relative resource costs since they are not distorted by indirect business taxes less subsidies. But as a practical matter, market prices are generally used as weights or as deflators of current values. Instead of directly weighting quantities, one ideally can obtain the same results by deflation of values by Paasche-type price indexes. This method is preferred if value and price data are more plentiful than detailed quantity data. The same methodology is used to estimate intermediate inputs as to estimate outputs, whether the real intermediate costs are deducted from gross output to obtain real value added, or are treated as an input. After all, the intermediate inputs are the outputs of the supplying industries. Special problems of measuring output, particularly adjustments for quality change, are not discussed here, but it should be noted that they may impart some downward bias to estimates of real product and productivity.

Labor input is frequently measured merely as the sum of hours worked. When data on hours paid for rather than worked are used, there is an upward bias to the extent that paid leave has risen. Some investigators (Denison, 1974) adjust labor input for the impact of increased education per worker on earnings and for other qualitative factors. Others (Jorgenson, 1980) have weighted labor hours by industry, occupation, sex, and educational attainment. The quality-adjusted hours have risen significantly faster in the United States and many other countries than have unweighted hours. If unweighted hours are used as input, then the increase in labor quality may be viewed as part of the explanation for the increase in the residual.

Similarly, nonhuman factor input may be measured in terms of the total real stocks of capital (plant, equipment, inventories, and land) multiplied by the base-period average rate of return. Or, the real stocks may be measured by industry and weighted by the base-period rate of return in each. In the latter case, relative shifts of capital to industries with higher rates of compensation mean that weighted capital input rises faster than the aggregate. If the aggregate is used in the denominator of the ratio, then interindustry shifts in capital become part of the explanation of productivity change.

Most specialists think the real gross stocks of depreciable capital goods are a better measure of output-producing capacity than the net stocks, which reflect the decline in value of fixed capital goods as they age. Some adjust the real stocks and inputs for changes in rates of utilization of capacity; others do not on the grounds that in an economy based on private property, capital carries a charge regardless of rates of utilization. If capital input is not so adjusted, changes in rates of utilization are a factor helping to explain cyclical changes in the productivity ratio.

Real input costs are added to obtain total input to be divided into the real value of output. If index numbers of the inputs are used, each is weighted by its base-period proportion of costs to obtain index numbers of total input. The quotients of index numbers of output and of inputs yield index numbers of productivity.

Causal Forces

The meaning of productivity changes (or differences) has been analyzed by a priori reasoning; by regression analyses relating differences in rates of productivity growth to differences in levels and/or rates of change of causal forces; and, at the aggregate level, by growth accounting studies, pioneered by Edward F. Denison.

When productivity is measured in terms of output per labor-hour, increases in nonlabor inputs per hour contribute to productivity gains, as noted previously. If the rate of change in the capital-labor ratio is weighted by the share of capital in factor cost, the resulting rate of substitution of capital for labor exactly explains the difference between the rates of change in labor productivity and in total factor productivity.

Denison's estimates show that more than half of the growth in total factor productivity in the United States since 1948 has been due to advances in technological knowledge as applied in production. A major part of these advances in the modern era stem from formal research and development programs. But there is still a significant amount of informal development of cost-reducing innovations and practices. Also, the rate of diffusion of innovations affects the pace of productivity advance. In part, this reflects the rate of investment in new plant and equipment which embody the latest technology.

If labor input is measured in terms of undifferentiated hours worked, then the effect of increased education and training per worker helps explain productivity growth. So, too, do other factors affecting the quality of labor, such as the average health status of workers, and conditions in the workplace. Changes in the ratio of actual to potential efficiency of workers can be important and reflect the skill of management in motivating workers to perform well. Shifts in the age-sex mix also affect productivity if there is a net shift toward groups with higher or lower average compensation and value added per hour. In the United States in the late 1960s, for example, the rise in youthful entrants into the labor force with less average pay and experience had a significant negative effect on productivity growth. Beyond some point, a declining average quality of land and mineral reserves also has a negative effect on productivity.

As labor and capital move from industries with lower rates of remuneration to higher-pay industries, this raises productivity if the factor inputs are not weighted on an industry basis. This factor is related to the degree of mobility of resources.

The rate of growth of demand and output itself affects productivity with respect to opportunities for economies of scale. The degree of cyclicality of demand also influences productivity—a relatively stable growth rate is more favorable than fluctuating demand. If growth is measured between years of different rates of utilization of capacity, this, too, will affect the rate unless adjusted for it.

Finally, if the productivity measure is confined to the business economy, the net impact of government may be important. Some governmental activities foster business; others, such as regulation, may increase real costs without increasing business output as measured. It is claimed that environmental, health, and safety regulations have had a negative impact on productivity in the United States during the past decade.

Behind the proximate determinants of productivity change stand the basic values, attitudes, and institutional forms and practices of a society. These generally change only slowly, and in any event affect productivity through the more immediate causes just discussed.

Economic Impacts

Growth of real income per capita is the product of increases in factor input per capita and of total factor productivity. In the United States since 1919 there has been no increase of input per capita—as declining hours worked per capita have offset rising real capital per capita—so all of the 2.3 percent a year average annual rate of growth of real income per capita has been due to increasing total factor productivity.

Productivity growth has also offset rising factor prices with respect to unit costs. Thus, from 1948 to 1966 in the United States, average hourly labor compensation and the price of capital together rose at an average annual rate of almost 5 percent, but productivity was rising by nearly 3 percent a year; consequently, unit costs and prices were going up by only around 2 percent a year, on average. After 1966, productivity growth decelerated and factor price increases accelerated so that inflation of unit costs and the general price level accelerated even more.

On an industry basis, relative changes in productivity and in prices are negatively correlated in the long run. That is, average factor prices show much the same rate of increase in most industries so that industries with the largest productivity gains show the smallest increases in unit costs and prices, and vice versa. To the degree that demand is price-elastic, and if price elasticities are not outweighed by income elasticities working in the opposite direction (or in extractive and service industries), relative changes in prices and in demand (output) are also negatively correlated. Therefore, relative changes in productivity and in output are positively correlated. This correlation is reinforced by scale economies. It is strong enough that there is not a significant degree of correlation between relative changes in productivity and in employment. In this sense, there is no technological unemployment, although there is obviously some temporary displacement of workers in particular occupations, industries, and localities.

Industries with relative increases in productivity and relative price declines also tend to fare better in international markets—unless their counterparts abroad are doing relatively even better. International differences in general productivity movements are only one factor influencing relative changes in price levels and currency values, however. Relative factor price movements can, and often do, counteract the effects of favorable relative productivity changes in comparative price level movements, and vice versa. The purchasing power of currencies depends not only on relative prices but also on the impact of financial flows on the supply of and demand for currencies. But it can be said that nations with relative productivity gains will be increasing their real consumption per capita, not only of domestic products but of imported goods as well.

References

Denison, Edward F., *Accounting for United States Economic Growth, 1948-1969*, Brookings, Washington, D.C. 1974; Kendrick, John W., *Understanding Productivity, An Introduction to the*

Dynamics of Productivity Change, Johns Hopkins Press, Baltimore, 1977; Kendrick, John W., and Beatrice Vaccara (eds.), *New Dimensions in Productivity Measurement and Analysis*, Studies in Income and Wealth, vol. 44, University of Chicago Press, Chicago, for the National Bureau of Economic Research, 1980; Nadiri, M. I., "Some Approaches to the Theory and Measurement of Total Factor Productivity: A Survey," *Journal of Economic Literature*, vol. 8, no. 4, December 1970, pp. 1137–1177.

(*See also* Economic forecasts; Economic growth; Employment and unemployment; Forecasting methods; Human capital; Index numbers; Innovation; Neoclassical economics; Production function; Research and development; Technology)

John W. Kendrick

Profits in economic theory

Profits are generally defined as the excess of total revenues of an enterprise over its total costs. On the revenue side, there are questions as to both the quality and the nature of the revenues and their timing. Revenues are not synonomous with cash payments. Goods and services sold are contributions to revenues at the time of sale, even if payment is not current. Sale of assets or other portfolio switches, such as the sale of securities for cash, do not in themselves constitute revenues. Even the excess of proceeds over cost in the sale of capital assets is generally considered capital gains rather than profits for accounting and tax purposes.

Costs present even more formidable problems. They do not include the purchases of assets. While omitting many cash expenditures, costs also include a number of accounting charges which do not involve out-of-pocket payments. The most important of these encompass depreciation or estimates of the exhaustion of values of existing capital.

Various Views

Profits in economic theory have been variously seen as the return to ownership or capital and the return to the entrepreneur. Where ownership and entrepreneurship coincide, as in a simple single proprietorship in which the owner's own capital is used to run the firm, this notion perhaps has some meaning. Most modern firms, however, are not of that sort. Capital is extensively borrowed, and most owners of equity have little to do with plant management or entrepreneurship. In practice, separate returns to ownership, management, and entrepreneurship are nevertheless difficult to identify.

Where capital is partly owned and partly borrowed, accounting conventions denote a return to borrowed capital as interest while including the return to the owned capital as profit. Where owners work in managing their firms, the value of their labor or managerial services is usually included in profit, except to the extent that owners formally pay themselves salaries.

Where capital and labor markets are perfect and where there is freedom of entry for new firms, the return to capital in equilibrium would be the market rate of interest adjusted for risk, and the return for labor performed by managers would similarly be the opportunity cost of their services elsewhere, perhaps again adjusted for risk. On the presumption that risk aversion is dominant and on the further assumption that owning a firm is relatively risky, the risk adjustment might make the income of owner-managers somewhat higher than what they would earn as employees and as lenders of their capital. To the extent that owner-managers prefer the independence that goes with entrepreneurship, however, they may actually continue in situations where their earnings are less than they could receive otherwise.

Under the conditions stated above, however, there is no further residual (other than the possible risk premiums) which would create profit in equilibrium, for even monopoly profit would be wiped out with free entry of competitors, reducing the industry to a situation of monopolistic competition with no profit beyond the return necessary to prevent capital from being withdrawn. Since entrepreneurship has no cost, new entrepreneurial talent embodied in new firms would enter an industry with profits, until the increased supply of product lowered prices (or pushed up costs) to the point where there were no profits. Profits thus become a transitory phenomenon of change or adjustment.

Profits: The Key Element in Innovation

Thus, as emphasized by Joseph Schumpeter, profits become the key element in innovation in a dynamic, changing economy. Profit seekers are driven to bring forth new processes and products. These profits from innovation are earned only at the introduction of the innovation, for after awhile others copy the changes and compete away the profits. Profits then are the lure that keeps the economy seeking new and more efficient ways of meeting real and potential human wants.

All this applies when there is freedom of entry. Entrepreneurship itself, however, is not homogeneous and in infinite supply. Some individuals or firms may possess or acquire through experience unique talents of organization which cannot be competed away by new firms led by new entrepreneurs because there are no new entrepreneurs with comparable talents. Further, combinations of costly information, imperfect capital markets, and risk aversion may make it difficult if not impossible for new firms to enter into successful competition with established industrial giants such as General Motors, General Electric, IBM, and AT&T. This difficulty may be compounded by economies of scale, in production or in marketing, which leave room for only one or two very large, really successful firms in an industry. In these situations there will be profits over and above the normal return to originally invested capital. If owners cannot exercise sufficient control to appropriate all of this extra return, some of it may well be distributed among management in the form of exceptionally high salaries and bonuses. Some may also be distributed to workers in higher wages.

Government frequently becomes the source of monopoly profits by offering contracts, franchises, and licenses to firms without seeking adequate competitive bidding. Along with this role of government may go regulations which interfere with entry and thus favor businesses already in the industry, as in the case of airlines, trucking firms, and taxicab companies.

Aside from these circumstances, profits in a competitive economy are the carrot that leads participants to the most efficient market solutions, occasionally requiring correction for externalities, that is, costs of market activities, such as pollution, which are not borne by the direct participants in the activity. Profits then, are, ever to be strived for, but never long enjoyed.

References

Kierstead, B. S., "Profit," in David L. Sills (ed.), *International Encyclopedia of the Social Sciences*, vol. 12, Collier and Macmillan, New York, 1968, pp. 547–552; Knight, Frank H., *Risk,*

Uncertainty and Profit, London School of Economics and Political Science Series of Reprints of Scarce Tracts in Economic and Political Science, no. 16, London, 1921, 1933; Robinson, Joan, *The Economics of Imperfect Competition*, St. Martin's, New York, 1933, 1961; Schumpeter, Joseph A., *The Theory of Economic Development: An Inquiry into Profits, Capital, Credit, Interest and the Business Cycle*, Harvard University Press, Cambridge, Mass., 1939.

(*See also* Capital, a factor of production; Capitalism; Financial statements; Innovation; Profits measurement; Return on investment; Risk premium on investment)

Robert Eisner

Profits measurement

Profits are defined simply as the excess of receipts over expenses. But the exact measurement of profits depends to a considerable extent on what is being measured and for what purpose it is being measured. Four principal measures predominate today, each subject to numerous variations: book profits, tax-return profits, national income profits, and so-called real profits. Depending on the choice of concept, both the magnitude and the direction of changes in profits can vary considerably.

However they are measured, profits are vital to our economic system. They provide compensation to the investor who has put capital into the corporation, they provide the incentive for further investment and risk taking, and they provide a measure of creditworthiness in obtaining additional funds for the conduct and growth of the business. For these reasons, it is highly important that the published data on profits present a meaningful and consistent picture.

Book Profits

Book profits are the figures reported by individual corporations to their stockholders. These represent management's official evaluation of the firm's performance and are a major factor in determining dividend policies and investment programs. They are the raw material for financial analysts' evaluations and the basis for price-earnings ratios and other stock-market criteria.

Corporate profits reports are compiled in conformity with generally accepted accounting principles consistently applied, under the watchful eyes of corporate auditors; of the accounting profession, which has set up a Financial Accounting Standards Board; of the Securities and Exchange Commission; and of other regulatory agencies. Nevertheless, there are still considerable differences in the way various corporations treat such items as valuation of inventories, depreciation of plant and equipment, installment sales, write-offs of discounted operations, fiscal years, etc. Because of mergers, acquisitions, and changes in accounting procedures, the profits reported by a major corporation may not be fully consistent over an extended period of time. Also, with diversification, changing technologies, and the growth of conglomerates, the grouping of corporate reports into industry totals has become less meaningful over the years.

Two-year comparisons of corporate profits as reported to stockholders are published each April by the economics department of Citibank (formerly First National City Bank) in its *Monthly Economic Letter*. These reports on industry profitability, including rates of return on net worth and profit margins on sales, have been appearing for over 50 years. For a smaller sample of firms similar tabulations with less industry detail but more accounting detail are published by *Business Week*.

The Federal Trade Commission (FTC) publishes quarterly estimates of profits and other balance sheet and earnings-statement data for major manufacturing industries and, since late 1974, for trade and mining as well. The FTC surveys an extensive, stratified sample from which it estimates industry aggregates. These figures are similar to those reported to stockholders, but differ in certain important respects, such as the exclusion of overseas branches and subsidiaries and of subsidiaries which engage in finance, insurance, and banking. The Citibank and *Business Week* tabulations merely add up the profits of specific reporting firms, but the FTC amplifies its sample corporations into an estimate for the whole industry.

Tax-Return Profits

Tax-return profits are the net income reported by corporations to the Internal Revenue Service (IRS). These data are the most comprehensive and most nearly uniform available, but they differ from profits reported to stockholders in several important respects, chiefly in the rate at which plant and equipment are depreciated, in treatment of investment tax credits, and in the way in which earnings of overseas subsidiaries are consolidated into the total. A firm can understandably and legitimately report to the IRS in a way which will minimize taxes, while at the same time reporting to stockholders what management and the accounting profession feel fairly presents the financial results of the firm's operations. For the year 1975, the IRS compared tax-return profits with book profits for 1.9 million corporations and found that book profits averaged 22 percent higher. The differences varied widely among individual industries.

National Income Profits

National income profits measure what corporations would earn if they kept their books in a manner consistent with the national income accounts, as published by the U.S. Department of Commerce. The Bureau of Economic Analysis (BEA) of the Commerce Department adjusts the IRS figures to the national income and product concepts. Some items, such as capital gains and losses and intercorporate dividends, are eliminated, while certain deductions, such as depletion allowances, bad debts, and state and local income taxes, are added back in to get pretax profits. Earnings of foreign subsidiaries and branches of U.S. corporations are excluded, and only the net income received from abroad by U.S. residents is included. Earnings of Federal Reserve banks and mutual thrift institutions are also included in the corporate total. These adjustments produce the estimate of pretax profits most commonly used.

To obtain the profits figure used in the national income total, the BEA makes additional adjustments in order to exclude inventory profits and to calculate depreciation on current replacement costs rather than historical costs. Because it usually takes the IRS 2 or 3 years to process the tax-return data, the Commerce Department must extrapolate its profits estimates with whatever data are available, usually book profits or figures from regulatory agencies.

Among the profits figures published by the Commerce Department are profits before tax, profits after tax, and profits adjusted for inventory profits and underdepreciation. These are presented for all corporations, including all domestic corporations and nonfinancial corporations. Limited industry estimates are published quarterly, and detailed annual industry estimates are also available, but only after a delay of several years.

These national income figures are probably the most widely used and quoted in assessing the financial well-being of corporations and the economy. They are also periodically subject to controversy, both because of sizable revisions—largely attributable to late reporting of IRS benchmark data—and because of the increasing role that inflation is playing in the growth and interpretation of profits.

"Real" Profits

Real profits are the earnings left after allowance has been made for the impact of inflation. Unfortunately, there is no general agreement on how this adjustment should be done. Efforts have ranged from a simple adjustment of book profits for changes in purchasing power to a detailed restatement of corporate balance sheets and earnings statements in constant prices.

Two adjustments for the effect of rising prices on profits have been incorporated into the national income accounts, as already noted. The inventory valuation adjustment (IVA) attempts to separate the change in physical volume of inventories, which should be part of the national product, from changes in book value due to price movements, which should not. The IVA is affected not only by prices, but also by composition of business stocks, turnover times, and the proportion of corporations using various accounting methods. The capital consumption adjustment (CCA) is really the net effect of two adjustments, one of which adjusts all corporate depreciation to a uniform straight-line basis and the other of which converts depreciation from an historical-cost basis to a replacement-cost basis. In effect, it assumes that measures of current output should reflect the current cost of the capital goods used up in the process of production.

Both these adjustments currently tend to reduce the profits figure used in the national income accounts relative to basic pretax profits. Much has been made of the fact that these reflect bookkeeping or "phantom" profits rather than profits arising from operations. Corporate income taxes must still be paid on such profits even though firms must eventually replace these assets at current costs. Prior to the 1970s, however, these adjustments were relatively small and few business executives took them into account in looking at profits.

The impact of inflation, particularly at today's rates, is far broader, affecting both sides of the balance sheet. Numerous proposals have been made for inflation adjustments, of which the most far-reaching is the ruling of the Financial Accounting Standards Board (FASB) which will require that large publicly held corporations provide supplemental reports on the effects of price changes. One aim of such adjustments is to provide an alternative measure of a corporation's fixed assets and inventories at current replacement costs and to figure both the cost of goods sold and depreciation on this basis. Another is to restate financial assets and liabilities in dollars of constant purchasing power. Thus, net holdings of monetary assets would show loss of purchasing power due to rising prices, and the reduced purchasing power needed to repay a fixed amount of debt would represent a gain. Such adjustments would not be part of the basic audited financial statements but would be separate unaudited material. Such adjustments can provide deeper understanding of the impact of inflation on corporate operations, but they may also be misleading, since the unrealized capital gains implied by replacement-cost pricing may prove to be unrealizable.

Profitability Measures

Profitability measures try to relate the dollar level of profits to sales or capital in order to measure the efficiency or investment potential of a corporation or industry. Profit margins are the number of cents of aftertax profits realized per dollar of sales. Rates of return usually relate aftertax profits to net worth or shareholders' equity. Industry averages for both of these measures are published annually by Citibank and quarterly by the Federal Trade Commission (FTC). The FTC also reports profits as a percentage of total assets. Other ratios frequently used are those of profits to total fixed assets or total capital investment (net worth plus long-term debt). Another measure, which rather than profitability is more properly termed total return on capital investment, is profits plus interest payments as a percentage of net worth and long-term debt. This adjusts for the difference in corporate rates of return due to leveraging, or the proportion of debt financing. Various inflation adjustments can also be introduced into these ratios.

The variety of measures of profits and profitability is vast and often bewildering, and care should be taken in order to choose the appropriate measure for a given purpose.

References

Cagan, Philip, "Inflation and Corporate Profits," *NBER Reporter*, June 1978, pp. 5–11; Citibank Economics Department, "Corporate Profits Tabulations, 1925–1978," Citibank, New York, October 1978 (also April issues of Citibank's *Monthly Economic Letter*); Cox, William, "A Perspective on Corporate Profits," *Business America*, U.S. Department of Commerce, June 4, 1979, pp. 21–23; Gorman, John A., "Aggregate Profit Measures, or Where Have All the Profits Gone?", *Business Economics*, January 1972, pp. 70–74; Kopcke, Richard W., "The Decline in Corporate Profitability," *New England Economic Review*, May–June 1978, pp. 36–60; Nordhaus, William D., "The Falling Share of Profits," *Brookings Papers on Economic Activity*, no. 1, 1974, pp. 169–217; Ture, Norman, *Corporate Profits in Company Financial Reports, Tax Returns, and the National Income and Product Accounts*, Financial Executives, Research Foundation, New York, 1978.

(See also Capital, a factor of production; Capitalism; Financial statements; Profits in economic theory)

Robert E. Lewis

Propensity to consume or to save and inducement to invest

The propensity to consume or to save and the inducement to invest were central to the Keynesian revolution. That revolution produced widespread acceptance of the view that a private enterprise economy, if left to itself, could not be relied on to attain stable full employment and that positive government action to that end would be needed. The revolution also maintained that such an economy would tend to save too much, so that it would suffer from chronic unemployment rather than inflation. The revolution took place in the 1930s, when full employment seemed to be a distant dream. Keynes' *General Theory* was not general, although it could be generalized.

Another way of describing the revolution is to state that it introduced into economics an explicit theory of aggregate demand consisting of the demand for consumption and the demand for investment. It is fair to say that pre-Keynesian theory generally adhered to Say's law, which held that aggregate demand was equal to aggregate supply at the full-employment level of output. Keynes disputed the position that automatic mechanisms in a free enterprise system would rapidly restore full employment. He asserted that there was no direct link between the propensity to save and the inducement to invest since the basic decisions were made by different people, responding in different ways to economic stimuli. Consequently, a period of unemployment could be prolonged.

The Keynesian system can usefully be considered by distinguishing between the short run and the long run. The analytic scheme of the *General Theory* is based on distinctly short-run assumptions, and conclusions drawn from it are strictly applicable to short-run situations. On the other hand, some of the most important policies and attitudes that are described as Keynesian, and which were supported by Keynes himself, relate to a much longer run of the economy. The famous stagnation thesis is a striking case in point.

The Short Run

Almost every modern textbook begins with an elementary Keynesian model of the form

$$C + \bar{I} = Y \qquad C = f(Y)$$

$$I = \phi(r) \qquad r = \bar{r}$$

or, alternatively,

$$S = Y - f(Y) \qquad \bar{I} = \phi(r)$$

$$I = S \qquad r = \bar{r}$$

Y, C, S, and I are all expressed in real terms. In Keynes' system, that means money values deflated by the wage rate. Y, S, and I are gross concepts. Y corresponds closely to GNP; S and I include private saving, net business saving, and depreciation allowances. The rate of interest is here taken as given. In the *General Theory* the interest rate depends on the quantity of money as determined by the government and on the interaction of the money market with the goods market.

One of the most important characteristics of the model is that it is constructed in real terms. Consumption depends on real income, and investment on the real rate of interest, that is, on the rate of interest that would exist under conditions of stable prices. The price level and the quantity of money enter the formal model only so far as they affect the rate of interest.

The rudimentary model is the one that Keynes presents at the beginning of the *General Theory*. The rest of the book discusses price, wage, and interest rate expectations, which influence both the propensity to consume and the inducement to invest.

Keynesian critics and admirers have sought to explain the formation of expectations in dynamic models and have not been wholly successful. Textbooks, in their opening chapters, still have to rely heavily on the static real model.

The model determines the level of income and output, and that determines the level of employment. As stated previously, it is generally assumed that the equilibrium so determined will be one of less-than-full employment. Whether it is will depend on the shape of the functions.

In this model, the government is ignored, or, alternatively, government consumption and investment are included in C and I. Also, the money market and the labor market are left out for the time being. The model determines the levels of output resulting from a given propensity to consume and an inducement to invest.

It deals essentially with a situation where the economy has entered a period of deep depression, as happened in the United States between 1929 and 1932. The stock of capital is assumed to be virtually unchanged, and current investment is assumed to be small in relation to the total stock. Moreover, consumers' tastes under these conditions are assumed constant.

With respect to the propensity to consume, Keynes considers in Chapters 8 and 9 the various objective and subjective factors. On the objective side, he considers factors such as the structure of the economy and depreciation allowances. On the subjective side, he recognizes motives for saving that he summarizes as "Precaution, Foresight, Calculation, Improvement, Independence, Pride and Avarice." He also recognizes the importance of business saving for the motives of enterprise, liquidity, improvement, and financial prudence. But these he considers long-run factors that change only slowly.

For the short period with which he was concerned, he maintained that consumption depends on income according to a psychological law which states that as income increases (decreases) consumption will increase (decrease) by a smaller amount. Under the law, as stated, consumption may be a constant proportion of income. But Keynes held, and most other investigators concur, that it will be a decreasing proportion.

The short-run function is frequently assumed to be linear and of the form

$$C = cY + d$$

In real terms, c is the marginal propensity to consume and is less than unity and d represents autonomous consumption, that is, the consumption that would be undertaken regardless of income. It should be noted that with this form the average propensity to consume will be

$$\frac{c}{y} = c + \frac{d}{y}$$

provided d and c remain unchanged. They will decrease as income increases.

Likewise, the average propensity to save S/Y will increase as income increases.

Given the propensity to consume, a decline in investment occurring for autonomous reasons brings about a determinate decrease in income, according to the multiplier.

The question then is whether in the short run there are factors in the economy that will bring about a recovery without government action directed to that end.

A depression is very unlikely to increase consumption. Consumers may keep up consumption by spending their reserves, but when reserves run out, consumption may decline further and the depression will worsen.

The possibility of automatic revival from a depressed level of income, therefore, depends on the possibility of an increase of investment. Is there any such possibility? That brings us to the problem of the short-run inducement to invest.

It must be emphasized that, in the short run, Keynes was dealing with a situation where there was widespread excess industrial capacity as well as widespread unemployment of labor. The capital stock was inherited from a previous state of prosperity when there was full employment of labor as well as reasonably full use of capacity.

When the economy is in a depressed state, there is an obvious depressing effect on investment since profits are low or nonexistent and the capital stock is redundant from the point of view of short-term requirements. In the short run these factors are given and are, therefore, not included as variables in the investment function. Consequently, the rate of interest is the short-term variable that affects investment incentives.

The decision to invest rests on the relation of the marginal efficiency of an asset to the rate of interest. Marginal efficiency according to Keynes, or the rate of return over cost according to Irving Fisher, is the rate of discount which will equate the expected future returns to an asset with its cost. At any time, the marginal efficiency of investment is supposed to decline with the amount of investment.

But Keynes' main emphasis was that the rate of investment depends on what he called the "state of confidence," which is a broad term that covers investors' assessment of the risk and uncertainty that surround their estimates of future profitability. Keynes considered that estimates of the future are themselves so unreliable that they are highly volatile under the influence of speculative moods. Also, the uncertainties of the future lead investors to place much more weight on the relatively certain present rather than on the highly uncertain future in making their estimates. Thus, a recession is likely to inhibit optimism concerning the future and to prevent recovery. Anyone who lived through the Great Depression can appreciate the force of that statement.

Under the circumstance of deep depression, there are some forces that may revive investment, but they are likely to be weak.

First, interest rates will fall from their boom levels because banks and the public will become more liquid. But a lower level of interest rates may be a weak incentive in view of the low level of profit resulting from the depression itself.

Second, as the capital stock grows older, some replacement expenditures will presumably be undertaken, although many may be deferred.

Third, some investments in improved and cost-reducing technology may occur as a survival strategy under the pressure of the depression itself.

The deeper the depression, the weaker these forces are likely to be. Not only are profits low but expectations of the future are gloomy. In the early 1930s investment decisions were not based on the expectation of returning to 1929 levels of prosperity.

If the depression is mild and expectations for the longer run are not impaired, the situation will be more promising. Consumption standards will not be eroded, and investors may welcome relief from the strains of a boom. In his chapter on the trade cycle, Keynes implies that some depressions arising from fluctuations in the marginal efficiency of capital can be mild and will be followed by recovery. His conceptual scheme, when dynamized, plays an essential role in most business cycle theories. But all this comes at the end of the book and is a very different matter from the low-level equilibrium that is described by the short-run model.

A deep depression did occur in the 1930s, and Keynes did establish his major thesis that positive government action was necessary to extricate the economy. With respect to that action, he believed that monetary policy alone would not be sufficient, both because of the depression itself and because of the inability of the banking system to reduce interest rates below a certain minimum (owing to liquidity preference). Consequently, he believed the remedy was fiscal policy designed to increase either the propensity to consume or the level of investment through direct government investment.

Keynes seemed to favor permanent intrusion of the government into the investment field. He believed that "pump priming" not only would get the economy back to a high level but also would restore favorable expectations of the future.

So far in this discussion, it has been assumed that the key economic problem is one of unemployment, where aggregate demand is insufficient to provide full employment. The Keynesian model can be adapted to deal with the opposite problem of inflation, where aggregate demand, in real terms, is excessive in relation to potential output. In that event, the price system must be introduced explicitly as the factor that eliminates the excess. But the *General Theory* did not explicitly deal with such situations, which seemed remote at the time it was written. Critics of Keynes have alleged that his theory of low-level equilibrium depends on wage rigidity, and they have argued that if money wages could be reduced, all would be well. Keynes countered this by saying that a wage cut, if it were possible, would result in a corresponding price cut; the effect of both would be to increase the real money supply and lower the rate of interest, which would stimulate investment. He argued that the same increase in the real money supply could be more efficiently achieved by central bank action and that in any case the consequent fall in the interest rate would be insufficient to realize full employment.

Pigou then came to the rescue of the critics by arguing that the real increase in the money supply would raise the propensity to consume by increasing the real balances held by consumers. He maintained that consumption depends not merely on income but also on wealth, particularly liquid wealth, and the wage cutting could continue until full employment was achieved.

Keynes could have argued, but did not, that the Pigou effect could also be achieved by direct money creation. This course commends itself since wages are in fact rigid.

In addition to the Pigou effect, which is now usually referred to as the real balance effect, there can also be a more general wealth effect raising the propensity to consume. Low depression interest rates or deliberate monetary policy may raise the capitalized value of fixed-interest securities. But a stock-market collapse, such as the one of which Keynes was aware, can produce an adverse wealth effect as it did during the 1930s and probably in 1945 as well. Keynes was aware of the real balance effect and the wealth effect. He referred to them in the *General Theory* but chose to ignore them. But the omission of the more general wealth effect may be a more important omission from the point of view of short-run diagnosis.

The Long Run

Keynes seriously damaged his position by using the short-term model as a basis for long-range predictions. He claimed to have shown that, unless corrected by government action, there will be a long-run deficiency of effective demand owing to both a deficient propensity to consume and a moderate inducement to invest. For example, in the *General Theory*, he states (p. 314), "Moreover, the richer the community, the wider will be the gap between its actual and its potential production, and, therefore, the more obvious and outrageous the defects of the economic system. . . . Not only is the marginal propensity to consume weaker in a wealthy community but owing to its accumulation being already larger, the opportunities for further investment are less attractive." These dramatic statements, which are embodied in the stagnation thesis, may or may not be correct, but they cannot be inferred from the short-term analytic model. The assumption that consumers' tastes are unchanging and the static assumptions concerning investment are particularly untenable.

The Long-Run Consumption Function

Extrapolation of the consumption function proved unreliable when economists attempted to forecast postwar consumption by extending a simple and unshifting linear function of the type noted above to the postwar period. A good statistical fit was found for the period 1929–41, but the formula yielded negative savings for earlier periods and excessive savings for the postwar period.

Moreover, there is a conflict in the empirical evidence. Budget studies which compare consumption of families with different incomes at the same time lend strong support to a Keynesian function with a decreasing average propensity to consume. On the other hand, Kuznets' long-term series from 1870 to 1955 shows no long-range tendency for the ratio of consumption to income to decrease. In fact, it tends to increase.

The resolution to this apparent conflict is that, assuming the short-run function to exist at any time, it must be shifting over time in such a way as to prevent a downward drift in the long-run consumption ratio. Consequently, we need an explanation of the long-run function.

The long-run function relates to the consumption that would occur if the economy stayed on its long-run growth trend, with capital, employment, productivity, and consumers' tastes changing. The short-run function is the Keynesian function where the growth factors remain substantially unchanged and income changes as a result of short-run fluctuations in aggregate demand.

Thus, if $\overline{Y}(t)$ represents the trend value and $Y(t)$ the current value of income, the consumption function would be of the form:

$$C(t) = \phi\{\overline{Y}(t) + \phi[Y(t) - \overline{Y}(t)]\}$$

or, if linearity and proportionality are assumed,

$$C(t) = a\{\overline{Y}(t) + b[Y(t) - \overline{Y}(t)]\}$$

Here, a is the long-run marginal propensity to consume and b is the short-run marginal propensity, provided we are dealing with periods sufficiently short.

A long-run wealth variable could also be included in the consumption function. It would represent the trend value of the capital stock of the economy. If economic growth involved a constant capital-output ratio, as it often seems to, the wealth effect would be included in $\overline{Y}$. If the ratio were increasing or decreasing over time, the long-run trend in wealth should be included separately. However, for the United States, Kuznets' long-run figures suggest that a constant capital-output ratio may be a sufficient approximation.

The question now is how the long-run function is determined. Various theories have been advanced, all of which are relevant but none of which is complete.

One is Friedman's permanent income hypothesis. Friedman maintains that consumers base their expenditures on expected permanent income rather than on current income. He argues that expected future income is a weighted sum of present and past levels of income. Consequently, a change in current income will have only a small effect on consumption if the change is considered transitory. However, if the change is persistent, it will affect permanent expectations. This theory is consistent with the formulation given above. What it does not do is explain the factor of proportionality between consumption and permanent income.

Another well-known theory is Modigliani's life-cycle hypothesis. This theory maintains that individuals attempt to maintain a constant or steady rate of increase of consumption over their lifetimes; they dissave when they are young and old and save during their earning years, and leave a fortune only because they cannot estimate when they are going to die. Again, this is a useful partial explanation. With a given age distribution of the population and a steady growth of the economy, it yields a constant ratio between consumption and income. This hypothesis, however, does not seem sufficient to explain the motives for accumulation.

A third theory is the relative income hypothesis of Duesenberry. This theory suggests that despite inequalities of income consumers at different income levels emulate each other in current consumption. As a consequence, low-income groups consume a higher percentage of their income than do high-income groups. This effect persists at any level of income. Thus, the ratio of consumption to income remains constant as income increases.

All these theories are useful in refuting the idea both advanced by Keynes and supported by crude econometrics that a rich country will have a lower propensity to consume than will a poor one.

A fruitful approach to the long-run problem is that of Modigliani's fluctuations in the income-savings ratio written in 1949. He arrived at the same consumption formula presented earlier, but he emphasized the fact that the shape of the long-run component depends on changing tastes, changing technologies, and the role played by durable goods, whereas the theories discussed previously are based essentially on the assumption of constant tastes.

How are changing tastes generated? They may come from the spontaneous desires of consumers generated by medical research, knowledge of foreign countries, and education; or they may come from the impact of producers on consumers through advertising and the introduction of new products, particularly durable goods. In fact, new tastes and consumers' desires emerge from the entire process of economic evolution. Schumpeter said that the essence of capitalistic development is that consumers are malleable in the hands of producers. Yet the standard theories of the consumption function assume a one-way causality between income and consumption. A plausible model could be constructed where the causality runs the other way. Our society, especially in modern times, is replete with examples of families earning extra income in order to buy houses or to pay for education (they used to buy extra automobiles). Part of the extra income earned is saved and spent on capital equipment (new houses) and part on consumption (education). This point of view was put forward by Ruth Mack in 1956 but has attracted little attention since. To quote briefly, "Income, in short, is a function of consumption via consumption standards, just as truly as consumption is a function of income."

The next question to consider is whether or not the prospective return on investment should enter as an explicit variable in the long-run consumption function. Will a country with abundant investment opportunities save more or consume less of its income than one with fewer opportunities?

The standard theories exclude any direct effect (they may include an indirect effect insofar as investment affects the growth of income, which in turn affects consumption). Kuznets also seems to hold that the desire to save is independent of the return on investment.

A notable authority on the other side of the argument is Schumpeter. For him the propensity to save is derived from and determined by investment opportunities. In an economy with no such opportunities, saving would be zero.

Most of the modern studies are concerned with the relation of personal consumption to disposable income. In that case there are conflicting possibilities. Under the life-cycle hypothesis, a fall in investment yields might induce increased saving in order to provide for old age. On the other hand, if the motive of the individual is accumulation, an increase in investment returns should increase savings.

However, business saving has been very largely ignored in modern discussion. Surely, the long-run state of business saving depends on opportunities for investment. And in the modern economy, business saving is as important as personal saving. Keynes himself would agree. In Chapter 9 of the *General Theory* he states that businesses save from the motive of enterprise "to secure resources, to carry out further capital investment." The spirit of this cursory discussion of the long run is a far cry from the crude extension of the short-term consumption function on which he bases his long-run predictions.

So far, the relation of net saving, individual and corporate, to net national product has been discussed. From the point of view of full employment, Keynes was properly concerned with the relation of gross saving to gross national product, both of which include depreciation allowances. He pointed out that during the Great Depression, depreciation allowances inherited from the previous prosperity helped to produce excessive saving. But from the point of view of long-run trend, this element of saving would be directly linked to investment opportunities. However, there may be some significant lag effects when the long-run rate of investment is increasing or decreasing.

The long-run considerations show that a simple extrapolation of the short-run propensity to consume or to save that depends on the behavior of consumers in relation to their incomes is illegitimate. Moreover, the notion that there is a decreasing long-run propensity to consume is not substantiated. An attempt to attach a value to the long-run propensity involves an excursion into the whole field of economic development.

The Long-Run Inducement to Invest

Extension of the short-run system is even more vulnerable when it comes to investment. It will be remembered that the short-run Keynesian inducement relates to a deep-depression situation where capital is redundant and excess capacity prevalent. Under those conditions it is indeed difficult to relate current investment to the increase of aggregate output on the supply side. Consequently, we are treated to a discussion of expectations and to the conclusion that successive additions to the already redundant stock of capital will yield diminishing profits. The role of investment in the short-run model is to contribute to demand but not to supply.

Keynes transferred his short-run conception bodily to the long run. He maintained that a rich country with a large stock of capital necessarily has a lower marginal efficiency of capital than does a poorer country with a smaller stock; and in a single country the marginal efficiency declines as the economy grows. Thus, he says (p. 31), "The Middle Ages built cathedrals and sang dirges. Two pyramids, two masses for the dead are twice as good as one, but not so two railways from London to York." Also (p. 219), "It follows that of two equal communities having the same technique but different stocks of capital, the community with the smaller stock of capital may be able for the time being to enjoy a higher standard of living than the community with the larger stock; though when the poorer community has caught up with the rich—as presumably it eventually will—then both alike will suffer the fate of Midas."

He did not seem to realize that if a country is short of transportation, two railroads may be more than twice as good as one or that the construction of an additional railroad may induce further economic development so that two railroads can again be more than twice as good as one and better than two pyramids. So far as the *General Theory* is concerned, investment is a factor that contributes to aggregate demand but not to supply in the long run as well as in the short run.

With this concept, increases in the rate of investment in a private enterprise economy can be achieved in the long run only by reductions in the rate of interest; and the possibility of achieving such reductions is limited by liquidity preference.

The fact is that Keynes did not have a long-run theory of the inducement to invest. He did not recognize as Harrod did in his *Dynamic Economics* (1948) that in the absence of limiting factors such as the labor supply or natural resources, a process of equilibrium growth with no diminution of the marginal efficiency of capital would continue indefinitely. Keynes maintained that there was something inherent in the process of accumulation that reduced the return on capital.

The Stagnation Thesis

The concept of diminishing investment opportunity has a long history. Adam Smith held that the extent of a country's market was limited and, consequently, so were its opportunities for increased division of labor. Consequently, a country could attain its full "complement of riches"—that would mean low investment and ultimately a stationary state.

Ricardo believed that diminishing returns in agriculture would raise wage costs, cut into profits, thus reducing both saving and investment and producing a stationary state. And it could be a stationary state of misery since population would obey the Malthusian law.

Mill recognized a tendency of profits to fall to a minimum because of diminishing returns. But he also recognized that the tendency can be counteracted by increasing productivity at home and foreign investment, both of which would sustain the inducement to invest.

Marshall proclaimed no long-run tendency toward falling profits and a stationary state. Presumably, he believed that increasing returns at home and inexpensive food from abroad would counteract any tendency toward diminishing returns. In this category must be included Keynes himself, but not the Keynes of the *General Theory*. In the *Economic Consequence of the Peace* (1919), he gives a dramatic account of the prosperity of pre-1914 Europe which resulted from accumulation of capital. He suggests that it was the inequality of the distribution of wealth in Europe which enabled vast accumulations of fixed wealth and capital improvements by the capitalist classes. They were least likely to increase consumption because of higher incomes.

But there were economic clouds on the horizon resulting from the war. Keynes believed that the war opened up the possibilities of consumption to all particularly the labor classes. He thought that the labor classes would want to expand their consumption, while the upper classes, less confident of the future, would merely want to maintain their high consumption levels. The trouble that Keynes foresaw in 1919 was an increased propensity to consume associated with diminished accumulation, investment, and, consequently, economic development. There was a trace of excessive saving. The *Economic Consequence* seems more like Schumpeter than the later Keynes.

In the *General Theory*, we have the Keynesian contradiction arising from the simple and unwarranted extension of the short-run model. In the long run, the participants in capitalism are supposed to generate, independently of each other, an increasing propensity to save and a decreasing inducement to invest. Possibilities of increasing inducements are limited; an economy could reach a state of full investment. Consequently, the emphasis should be placed on permanent fiscal action by the government to increase the propensity to consume he argues.

Alvin Hansen's contribution to the Keynesian revolution was his stagnation theory, including his argument for declining investment opportunity arising from declining population growth and the limitations on territorial expansion. When he propounded his theory in the late 1930s and early 1940s, he did not foresee, as did Marshall, the possibilities of technological advance that might revive those factors. His theory was really a reversion to Adam Smith with his full employment of riches and to Mill.

Hansen's weakness was that he accepted the notion of a long-range propensity to consume or to save that was independent of the inducement to investment. While he agreed that the saving-income ratio might be constant rather than increasing over the long run, he believed that declining investment opportunities would leave an unfilled gap that would be eliminated only be chronic unemployment. In short, he accepted the Keynesian contradiction with its implications for the need of government action, particularly to increase public and private consumption.

At the time it was propounded, the Keynesian stagnation thesis was rejected by eminent economists such as Schumpeter, Slichter, and Terborgh. It has now virtually disappeared from the textbooks. It is not even indexed in first-class Keynesian textbooks such as those by Samuelson, Gordon and Dornbusch, and Fischer. Why then examine the matter? The reason is that the influence of the thesis has extended beyond the field of economic analysis.

The Keynesian stagnation thesis resembled its predecessors in maintaining a long-run decline in the inducement to invest as a country moved toward its full complement of riches. But those theories ended in a stationary state of full employment. Keynesian stagnation produced chronic unemployment because of the failure of the propensity to save to decline pari passu with the inducement to invest. We were asked to believe that individuals and particularly businesses would want to save and hoard their accumulations as the country got poorer.

The remedy for classical stagnation was increased saving, investment, and foreign trade that would help overcome diminishing returns. The remedy for Keynes-Hansen stagnation was an all-out attack on the propensity to save.

The Keynesian Legacy

The *General Theory* did establish the proposition that an economy in a deep depression of the scale of the 1930s could not recover, at least in any tolerable time, without vigorous government action to increase aggregate demand. A deep depression can be described as one where excess capacity is so widespread as to destroy favorable long-term expectations as a stimulus to investment.

Keynes was not the first to advocate deficit spending in such a depression. Conservatives like Jacob Viner, Henry Simons, and Sumner Slichter had advocated and approved depression deficits. Keynes, however, did implant the idea of "low-level equilibrium" into economic doctrine, and the idea was carried over to mild depressions which might not need drastic corrective action.

The full-employment ideology which was enshrined in the United Nations Charter, the Employment Act of 1946, and similar legislation in the United Kingdom, Australia, and Canada was directly inspired by Keynesian influence. The basic idea was that skillful adjustment of the national propensity to consume (including the government propensity) and the inducement to invest (including public investment) would yield continuous full employment without lapses into unemployment and without inflation. These hopes have not been realized. Demand policies may be credited with avoiding anything like a deep depression, but they have also helped to produce inflation.

Disillusionment with stabilization on Keynesian lines has led to the monetarist counterrevolution. Monetarists hold that aggregate demand, both consumption and investment, can be most effectively and precisely controlled through controlling the quantity of money. But they also recognize the forecasting difficulty and hold that the uncertainties inherent in any stabilization policy may only increase instability. They, therefore, advocate fixed monetary targets. How such a policy deals with external disturbances such as the Vietnam war or the oil embargo is not made clear.

If monetarism does not work, there remains the ominous possibility that the country may resort to direct controls of wages, prices, and the rate of investment. Such a system, continued over an extended period, would effectively destroy the liberal economy that was Keynes' main objective.

The Keynesian long-run prognosis has entered the political mainstream, even though the stagnation thesis has been discarded from the textbooks. It has led to an emphasis on an aggregate demand and, until recently, to a neglect of supply. The implication of Keynesianism is that if aggregate demand is kept consistently at a high level, the rate of growth of output will look after itself. The idea is that high demand, and even a continued labor shortage, will provide greater investment incentives than a private economy that is left at the mercy of the business cycle. According to this view, there is no need to worry about the propensity to save. There will always be enough slack in the economy for the multiplier process to generate enough saving to cover both private investment and government deficits. There is, therefore, little likelihood that private investment will be crowded out by government financing. This point of view characterized the economic reports of the President in the early 1960s. There seems to have been enough slack in the economy to satisfy the aspirations of both consumers and investors. There is remarkably little in those reports concerning the investment requirements for sustained economic growth.

Keynesian demand policies seemed to provide a happy reconciliation of an egalitarian ideology with economic requirements. Democratic governments find it easy to vote for expenditures but difficult to support the fiscal and monetary measures needed to secure an adequate propensity to save. Some of the old ideologies that Keynes was at such pains to destroy, such as the value of thrift and the belief that public and private budgets should be balanced, could be useful today.

Keynes should not necessarily be charged with all our difficulties. It may be no more than coincidence that the United States and the United Kingdom have the lowest growth rates among advanced economics and are also the most Keynesian.

References

Ando, Albert, and Franco Modigliani, "The Life Cycle Hypothesis of Savings: Aggregate Implications and Tests," *American Economic Review,* vol. 53, no. 1, March 1963, pp. 55–84; Duesenberry, James S., *Business Cycle and Economic Growth,* Greenwood, Westport, N.Y., 1977; Friedman, Milton, *A Theory of the Consumption Function,* National Bureau of Economic Research,

New York, 1957; Hansen, Alvin H., *Fiscal Policy and Business Cycles*, Greenwood, Westport, N.Y., 1941; Harrod, R. F., *Towards a Dynamic Economics*, Macmillan, New York, 1948; Keynes, J. M., *Economic Consequences of the Peace*, Harcourt Brace Jovanovich, 1920; Keynes, J. M., *General Theory of Employment, Interest and Money*, Macmillan, New York, 1936; Kuznets, Simon, *Capital in the American Economy*, National Bureau of Economic Research, Arno, New York, 1961; Mack, Ruth P., "Trends in American Consumption and the Aspiration to Consume," *American Economic Review*, vol. 46, no. 2, May 1956, pp. 55–68, quote, p. 58; Modigliani, Franco, *Fluctuations in the Income-Savings Ratio*, Conference on Income and Wealth, National Bureau of Economic Research, New York, 1948; Schumpeter, Joseph A., *Capitalism, Socialism and Democracy*, Harper & Row, New York, 1941; Slichter, Sumner, *Economic Growth in the United States*, Louisiana State University Press, Baton Rouge, 1961; Terborgh, George, *The Bogey of Economic Maturity*, Machinery and Allied Products Institute, Chicago, 1945.

(*See also* Automatic stabilizers; Behavioral economics; Business cycles; Capitalism; Chicago school; Classical school; Consumption function; Depreciation allowance; Dynamic analysis; Dynamic macroeconomic models; Employment and unemployment; Expectations; Fiscal policy; General equilibrium; Great Depression; Income; Incomes policy; Inflation; Interest rates; Investment function; Keynesian economics; Marshallian economics; Monetary policy; Money supply; NeoKeynesian economics; Permanent income hypothesis; Post-Keynesian economics; Quantity of money; Real balance effect theory; Saving; Say's law of markets; Stagnation thesis; Static analysis; Technology; Wealth)

Arthur Smithies

Property taxation (*see* **Taxation, an overview**)

Protectionism

Protectionism, in the context of international trade, is a term used to describe any movement by a government to alter the flows of such trade. Narrowly interpreted, the term refers primarily to policies of taxing or otherwise limiting imports. Taken broadly, the term also encompasses such measures as direct subsidies or taxes on the production of traded goods, multiple exchange rates, and, indeed, all governmental intervention affecting trade flows (Corden, 1971, Chapter 1).

According to classical international trade theory, any such intervention reduces global economic welfare, a conclusion that has remained a tenet of virtually all orthodox theory since it was first articulated early in the nineteenth century by David Ricardo. By contrast, international trade, freely conducted among nations without governmental intervention, allows regional producers to specialize in the production of goods and services in which the region possesses comparative advantage. The resulting international specialization assures optimal use of the world's finite resources.

Benefits from Protectionist Policies

Economists recognize, however, that individual nations can in some cases benefit from protectionism. One such case is embodied in the optimal-tariff argument, which states that in the absence of retaliation by its trading partners, a nation can gain advantage by imposing a limited tariff on imports. But because world efficiency would be reduced, the optimal-tariff nation's gain would be exceeded by losses accruing to its trading partners. A second, and controversial, case is that of infant industries. Some economists, especially those advocating developing nations' interests, argue that in order to create competitive firms in new industries, governments must temporarily protect these firms from international competition. The protection is to be afforded only for as long as it takes the firm to learn the technologies and management skills required to compete.

Apart from optimal-tariff and infant-industry arguments, there are reasons why nations choose to pursue protectionist policies. The opening of an economy to external trade necessitates certain adjustments. Industries in which the economy enjoys comparative advantage can be expected to expand, while industries at a comparative disadvantage must contract and release resources for the expanding industries. Frictional costs of adjustment may cause laborers and holders of capital in the contracting industries to resist the change and, if these constituencies exert political influence, force the nation to adopt protectionist policies. The factor-price equalization theorem of neoclassical trade theory posits that as adjustment occurs, factors of production that are employed intensively in the expanding industries will gain in share of national income at the expense of factors of production employed intensively in contracting industries. (This theorem assumes, of course, that factors are at least partially substitutable and that different industries have different factor intensities.) If this theorem is correct and if the losing factor of production represents a political constituency, further political pressure for protectionist policies may arise.

Because freer trade leads to a net gain for an economy (except in those instances mentioned previously), the argument for avoiding protectionism is made on economic grounds. Although some constituencies may experience a welfare loss as a result of freer trade, the losses are more than offset by other constituencies' gains. Arguably, it is therefore preferable that a nation's government require gaining constituencies to compensate the losers for their losses than it is for the nation to adopt protectionist policies.

References

Balassa, Bela, et al., *The Structure of Protection in Developing Countries*, Johns Hopkins Press, Baltimore, 1971; Baldwin, Robert, "The Case Against Infant Industry Protection," *Journal of Political Economy*, vol. 77, May 1969, pp. 295–305; Bhagnati, J. N., et al. (eds.), *Trade, Balance of Payments, and Growth*, North-Holland, Amsterdam, 1971; Corden, W. M., *The Theory of Protection*, Oxford University Press, London, 1971; Ellis, H. S., and L. A. Metzler, *Readings in the Theory of International Trade*, Irwin, Homewood, Ill., 1950; Finger, J. M., "Substitution and the Effective Rate of Protection," *Journal of Political Economy*, vol. 77, November–December 1969, pp. 972–975; Johnson, H. G., *Aspects of the Theory of Tariffs*, Allen and Unwin, London, 1971; Lerner, Abba, "The Diagrammatical Representation of Demand Conditions in International Trade," *Economica*, no. 3, August 1934, pp. 319–334; Marshall, Alfred, *The Pure Theory of Foreign Trade*, London School of Economics and Political Science, London, 1930; Metzler, L. A., "Tariffs, the Terms of Trade, and the Distribution of National Income," *Journal of Political Economy*, vol. 57, February 1949, pp. 1–29; Myint, H., "The Gains from International Trade and the Backward Countries," *Review of Economic Studies*, vol. 22, no. 58, 1954–55, pp. 129–142; Ohlin, Bertil, *Interregional and International Trade*, Harvard University Press, Cambridge, Mass., 1933; Ricardo, David, *On the Principles of Political Economy and Taxation*, London, 1817; Samuelson, P. A., "International Trade and the Equalisation of Factor Prices," *Economic Journal*, vol. 58, June 1948, pp. 163–184.

(*See also* Barriers to trade; Exports; Imports; International economics, an overview)

Edward M. Graham

Psychological theories of the business cycle (see Juglar cycle)

Purchasing power of the dollar (see Value of the dollar)

Purely monetary theory of business cycles (See Juglar cycle)

Quantity theory of money

The quantity theory of money might more properly be called a family of theories which explain relationships among money, prices, and incomes. They assign a primary causal role to changes in money supply in explanations of changes in national incomes and prices. Quantity theories developed as early as the sixteenth century explained changes in a nation's price level by changes in the stock of money. Today, the term quantity theory refers to the theory of the demand for money, as developed in a synthesis of classical and Keynesian views by Milton Friedman and others. Modern quantity theory is used to explain business fluctuations as well as inflation.

Early History

The quantity theory has an extremely long history. Probably its earliest formal statement was in 1568, when Jean Bodin demonstrated by careful observation and analysis that the flood of gold and silver from the New World was the principal cause of the price revolution in Europe—the great inflation that followed the discovery of America. Although John Locke made one of the earliest clear formulations of the quantity theory in 1691, numerous English mercantilists preceded him by from 40 to 90 years in expressing simple versions of quantity theories to explain changes in the purchasing power of money in terms of goods and commodities.

In 1752, David Hume added the idea that an increase in the quantity of money would stimulate an increase in economic activity and trade in the interval between the money-supply increase and the time when it would be fully reflected in the resulting rise in prices. He argued that prices of different goods are affected in turn and that the "diligence of every individual" would be quickened before the increase in quantity of money increased wages of labor.

Adam Smith, David Ricardo, John Stuart Mill, and other classical economists explained changes in the general level of prices by changes in the quantity of money and its velocity of circulation. In general, they argued that an increase in the money supply—gold, silver, and bank notes—would be followed by a proportional rise in prices.

Irving Fisher's Theory

At the beginning of the twentieth century, Irving Fisher analyzed the relationships among money, prices, and other magnitudes in more detail than had been done before, in what he called "a restatement and amplification of the old 'quantity theory' of money." The equation of exchange, $MV = PT$, was one of his many substantive refinements. The equation is not the theory; it merely arranges the important variables to be explained: M, the quantity of money; V, velocity or rate of turnover of money; P, a price index covering all transactions; and T, total volume of transactions per unit of time. A later version of the equation of exchange was stated in terms of income, rather than in total transactions. In the income version, $MV = Py$, in which y represents total national real income and P is a price index, such as the GNP deflator, covering prices of all items comprising the flow of real income.

According to Fisher's theory, velocity was regarded as stable (but not constant) and was determined independently of the other terms of the equation. Consequently, changes in M, the quantity of money, would be reflected in prices or output or both. Fisher and his contemporaries focused most of their attention on the influence of money on prices. In common with the classical economists, they believed that prices and wages adjust rapidly, while adjustments in physical output and quantities of goods proceed slowly. However, they did not overlook the effects of money-supply changes on output; they expected short-run output changes to be triggered by price changes. During the transition period in which an economy adjusts to changes in prices caused by changes in money supply, Fisher said, the initial price changes touch off reverberations in interest rates, profits, and business activity that could culminate in booms and crises. Fisher and other early quantity theorists therefore believed that the way to stabilize business activity was to stabilize prices through controlling the money supply.

In another main strand in the development of the quantity theory, Alfred Marshall, A. C. Pigou, and other economists at Cambridge University argued that the quantity of real money balances people want to hold is a stable fraction of their real income. In the Cambridge cash-balance approach, as it came to be called, $M = kPy$, in which k is the fraction of real income people want to hold in the form of real balances. The Cambridge approach emphasized the demand for money as an asset, a store of value, rather than simply a means for carrying out transactions.

From the 1930s to the Mid-1960s

The quantity theory fell into disrepute during the Great Depression. Because the monetary authorities had failed to stem the Depression, it became widely believed that money does not matter. In Keynesian theory—which almost completely displaced the quantity theory for a time—money, and monetary policy, were important only as they were able to influence a narrow range of interest rates. Since the early 1950s, however, a reformulated and improved quantity theory of money has won many new adherents among professional economists, policymakers, and the general public in the United States and other countries.

One of the main reasons for the revival of the quantity theory was the experience with inflation following World War II. Countries that tried to hold interest rates down by increasing growth of their money supplies suffered inflation. Countries that curbed money growth succeeded in reducing inflation. The revival was supported by an explosion of economic research in universities and government agencies into the causes of inflation and recessions, especially after the advent of computers reduced the costs of doing large-scale econometrics work. Efforts of economists in banks and other businesses to improve their ability to forecast business activity, inflation rates, interest rates, securities prices, and foreign exchange rates also have done much to increase the emphasis on money in explanations of economic and financial developments.

The key reformulation of the quantity theory was Milton Friedman's "The Quantity Theory of Money—A Restatement," which he published in 1956. The central point in his restatement is that the quantity theory is not a theory of output, money income, or prices, but is a theory of the demand for money. He treated money as an asset or capital good, so that the demand for it is a problem in capital theory.

Whereas Fisher-type quantity theories emphasized the demand for money as a medium of exchange in transactions, the new quantity theory is more general. Money is treated as one asset in a whole portfolio ranging from land and other real assets through equities and other securities. In this view, money-supply changes influence output, employment, and prices through a portfolio-adjustment process. The modern quantity theory thus draws on Cambridge school approval and some of the monetary theories of John Maynard Keynes.

The key assertion of modern quantity theory is that people want to hold some command over real purchasing power in the form of money. How much money they want to hold depends on a stable way upon what their income is, what other assets they have, interest rates, and how much they expect prices of goods and services to change. The public, however, cannot change the total nominal amount of money, or number of dollars, pounds, marks, francs, rupees, or yen existing in the economy at a given time. The size of the nominal money stock is determined by the banks and the monetary authorities in most countries today. In earlier times, the discovery and depletion of gold and silver mines and changes in international trade balances caused large changes in national money stocks.

If the money stock grows faster than the amount people want to hold, they individually try to hold down their balances to their desired levels in two main ways: (1) They adjust their balance sheets by purchasing assets or paying off debts, or (2) they use current flows of income and expenditures to add to assets or to reduce indebtedness. Because one person's expenditure is another's receipt, individuals' attempts to adjust their cash balances put other people out of adjustment, causing repercussions throughout the economy. These attempts at adjustment increase the flows of expenditures and income and tend to raise the price level. The adjustments will continue until the real value of the existing nominal money stock is again equal to what people want to hold. If the money stock does not grow as fast as the demand for it, individuals trying to build up balances tend to reduce flows of expenditures and income and thus put downward pressure on prices. In this way, quantity theorists believe, changes in money supply influence income and prices in both directions.

Key Issues and Dispute

The quantity theory, in numerous versions, is being tested by an enormous volume of empirical research and intellectual debate in the United States and other countries. One key research issue is the stability of the demand for money. If the demand for money were proved to be highly unstable or volatile or it it were a simple function of interest rates alone, as some theories have asserted, changes in the supply of money would not have a predictable influence on income, employment, and prices. Keynesian theory, for example, implies that people are willing to vary the amounts of money they hold by large amounts in response to small changes in interest rates and that the velocity of circulation is, therefore, highly unstable. If this were true, changes in money supply would have little effect on spending. Nevertheless, tests over a great variety of circumstances and for many countries indicate that the demand for money does have the stability and other properties required for making reliable predictions.

The other key issue in dispute is the question of whether the supply of money and the demand for money are independent. A long-standing criticism of the quantity theory is that the quantity of money supplied responds passively to changes in the demand for it. The critics argue that the observed correlations between changes in money supply and changes in income reflect the influence of income on money supply rather than the influence of money supply on income. There are some effects of income changes on money supply because of the influence of business conditions on the operations of central banks and other monetary authorities. In mild business cycles, a tendency of central banks to accommodate changes in credit demands makes it difficult to determine whether changes in money supply initiate the changes in business activity or if the changes in business activity affect the money supply. Nevertheless, there is much evidence that the direction of influence is primarily, though not exclusively, from money to income and prices.

Much of the evidence in support of the independence of money supply and money demand is historical. For example, the massive work of Milton Friedman and Anna J. Schwartz (1963) and a companion study by Phillip C. Cagen (1965) demonstrated that money supply was determined independently of money demand, because the money supply of the United States has been controlled by a wide variety of institutional arrangements and forces, many of which could not conceivably have been much influenced by the state of the demand for money. These studies also demonstrated the powerful influence of money-supply changes on U.S. economic history by relating them to all the business cycles that have been identified by the National Bureau of Economic Research over that period.

Although there are many theoretical and empirical issues still to be settled, the quantity theory of money is gaining increasing influence in economic research and teaching and in public policy. It is particularly relevant to understanding and combating one of the most critical problems of the world today, inflation.

References

Cagan, Phillip, *Determinants and Effects of Changes in the Stock of Money, 1875–1960*, National Bureau of Economic Research, Columbia University Press, New York, 1965; Fisher, Irving, *The Purchasing Power of Money*, 2d rev. ed., Macmillan, New York, 1922; reprinted in Reprints of Economic Classics, Kelley, New York, 1963; Friedman, Milton, "The Quantity Theory of Money—A Restatement," Milton Friedman (ed.), in *Studies in the Quantity Theory of Money*, University of Chicago Press, Chicago, 1956; Friedman, Milton, and Anna Schwartz, *A Monetary History of the United States, 1867–1960*, National Bureau of Economic Research, Princeton University Press, Princeton, N.J., 1963; Gordon, Robert J. (ed.), *Milton Friedman's Monetary Framework: A Debate with His Critics*, University of Chicago Press, Chicago, 1974; Keynes,

John Maynard, *A Treatise on Money*, vol. I, Macmillan, New York, 1930, chap. 14; Laidler, David, *The Demand for Money: Theories and Evidence*, International Textbook, Scranton, Pa., 1970; Pigou, A. C., "The Value of Money," *Quarterly Journal of Economics*, November 1917, pp. 38–65; reprinted in F. A. Lutz and L. W. Mints (eds.), *Readings in Monetary Theory*, Irwin, Homewood, Ill., 1951.

(*See also* Business cycles; Chicago school; Federal Reserve policy; Inflation; Keynesian economics; Monetary policy; Money supply; Real balance effect theory; Velocity of circulation of money)

A. James Meigs

Radical economics

The term radical economics came into use in the United States in the late 1960s to describe a dissenting school of thought motivated by political opposition to contemporary capitalism and by intellectual dissatisfaction with contemporary mainstream economics. Although this school of thought has only recently become a significant force in American academic life, it belongs to an intellectual tradition that originated with the critical scholarship of Karl Marx and has long thrived in other countries. The growth of its appeal can be linked to the resurgence of the Left in American politics in the 1960s and to the faltering performance of American capitalism in the 1970s. The intellectual strength and staying power of radical economics has been confirmed by a steady growth in scholarly publications by radical economists and by increasing recognition of radical economics as a legitimate area of study and research at major American universities.

Radical political economy is essentially the same as Marxian political economy, provided that the word Marxian is construed broadly to reflect the general principles of Marxian analysis rather than the specific details of Marx's own writings.

In order to understand the meaning of radical political economy, one should recognize that it combines features of a radical and politico-economic approach to the study of society. Political economy is a term first used to describe the writings of the classical British economists (Smith, Ricardo, et al.), whose work—like that of Marx—drew upon and combined many of the disciplines into which the social sciences were subsequently divided. Political economists reject the compartmentalization of academic disciplines in general; they seek in particular to integrate into economic analysis the kinds of variables and relations that have largely become the intellectual property of sociologists and political scientists. A major concern of political economy is the analysis of power—the sources of political and economic power, and the ways in which different kinds of power interact with political and economic life.

Radical World View

Radical political economy unites the interdisciplinary orientation of political economy with a set of intellectual premises stemming from a radical world view. This
world view begins with a vision of a radically new social order that is both egalitarian
and liberating: differentials in individual economic well-being and decision-making
power are limited, and people are free to develop their full potential as human beings
without being dominated by others or locked into socially determined roles. Distant
as such a prospect may seem from the perspective of the contemporary real world,
radicals are optimistic about the possibility of ultimately achieving it. This optimism
derives from the perception that human behavior and socioeconomic institutions are
not based on inalterable aspects of human nature and inevitable technological imper-
atives but instead are significantly influenced by the socioeconomic environment—
an environment that is itself continually evolving and amenable to fundamental
change over time.

According to the radical world view, any given socioeconomic environment can
best be characterized by its particular structure of socioeconomic classes. In virtually
all past and present societies this structure has been highly unequal, with dominant
classes utilizing their superior power in an effort to maintain a social order in which
their interests tend to prevail in conflict with the interests of subordinated classes.
But such circumstances are inherently unstable: changes in the socioeconomic environment will eventually arise out of the struggle between classes, whose power relations change with the historical development of each society. From this general
analytical perspective, radicals draw the inference that it is not enough to curb the
excesses of existing socioeconomic environments in order to achieve significant progress toward a more humane social order; rather, it is essential to bring about fundamental changes in those environments. This conclusion leads to the radical political
commitment to support movements of subordinated classes that challenge the structural foundations of unequal social orders and the dominant classes that sustain
them.

Key Premises of Radical Political Economy

From this radical world view follow several key premises of radical political economy, which serve to differentiate it from contemporary mainstream economics. First,
economic behavior cannot adequately be analyzed in terms of universal human propensities and formal optimizing models; instead, the influence of historically specific
socioeconomic institutions on people's behavior patterns must be brought into the
analysis. Second, the most significant decision-making units are not individual persons, household, or firms. Groups and/or classes of people, exercising collective
power in conflictual situations, are often the critical determinants of economic outcomes. Third, economic processes should be modeled mainly in terms of marginal
changes from unchanging basic structures and tendencies toward equilibrium;
instead, continual change in basic structures should be recognized as the norm in
conflict-ridden class societies, and dynamic disequilibrium models are essential to
capture the dialectical and contradictory character of economic processes.

Any or all of these three methodological premises might well be shared by institutional economists with an historical and politico-economic orientation. But radical
political economists can be further distinguished by their effort to orient their scientific inquiry to the needs of political movements for fundamental social change. This

orientation influences the choice of topics for study, the kinds of questions asked, the manner in which knowledge is communicated, and the people to whom it is communicated. Much of the literature in radical political economy is therefore concerned with such issues as the sources of inequality in the distribution of income, wealth, power, and control; mechanisms of class conflict in both microeconomic and macroeconomic settings; tendencies toward crises within contemporary class societies; and transitions from one kind of socioeconomic system to another. Moreover, where a conservative perspective would lead to preoccupation with techniques for improving business efficiency, and a liberal perspective to concern with techniques of governmental social engineering, a radical perspective encourages study of the ways in which people can and must act collectively to promote their general welfare.

Criticism of Radical Economics

Criticism of radical political economy in the United States has been plentiful. Many mainstream economists have dismissed this school of thought as unscientific and polemical, an expression of political advocacy rather than an impartial search for truth. But other mainstream economists have accepted elements of the work of radical political economists as useful supplements to mainstream economics, capable of being absorbed into a somewhat more broadly defined discipline of economics. From a radical perspective, much of the hostile criticism reflects the differing world view (if not the vested interest) of the critic. The increasing extent to which mainstream economists have drawn upon radical scholarship to improve their own understanding of the world testifies to the insights that can be gained from alternative approaches to the study of economic issues.

References

Edward, Richard, Michael Reich, and Thomas Weisskopf, *The Capitalist System: A Radical Analysis of American Society*, 2d ed., Prentice-Hall, Englewood Cliffs, N.J., 1978 (a good general introduction to radical political economy in the context of the United States); Lindbeck, Assar, *The Political Economy of the New Left: An Outsider's View*, 2d ed., Harper & Row, New York, 1977 (a detailed critique of radical political economy); Union for Radical Political Economics, *The Review of Radical Political Economics*, published quarterly.

(*See also* Capitalism; Communism; Comparative economic systems, an overview; Marxism; Socialism)

Thomas E. Weisskopf

Random walk hypothesis

The random walk hypothesis originated in the 1960s. It states that successive stock price changes are identically distributed, independent random variables. If this is so, past security price movements cannot be used to forecast future prices. Hence, trading on new public information cannot earn profits in excess of what would be earned using a buy-and-hold policy.

If the random walk hypothesis holds for stocks traded in a particular capital market, this is a sufficient condition for that market to be called weakly efficient. Extensive tests for this type of efficiency by means of serial correlation and run tests were first undertaken by E. F. Fama (1965b), using 30 Dow Jones industrial stocks. In general, the tests supported the hypothesis.

Study of non-U.S. capital markets has been made by Dryden (1970) using prices on 15 stocks traded on the London Stock Exchange. Praetz (1969) tested Australian stocks, and Conrad and Juttner (1973) German stocks. C. W. J. Granger (1972) provides a full bibliography of these so-called weak-form tests. Not all of these tests in less active markets supported the random walk hypothesis because there was substantial serial correlation in regression residuals.

As Granger indicates, there are many ways to express the random walk hypothesis. Those tested include:

1. The RRW, or raw random walk model

$$P_t = E(P_{t+1} | P_{t-j}, j \geq 0)$$

in which the sequence P_t is a martingale.

2. The LRW, or log random walk model, which is a submartingale.

3. The CRW, or capital return radom walk, which is also a submartingale, where $a(T)$ is the expected or normal wealth ratio over T time units:

$$W(T)C_t = E(C_{t+T}^+ | P_{t-j}, j \geq 0)$$

where P_t = the price of security at time t, preferably dividend-adjusted
$\quad\quad c_t$ = captial returns, preferably including dividends at time t
$\quad W(T)$ = expected or normal wealth ratio over T
$\quad\quad T$ = time unit
$\quad W(T) > 1$

The vertical line and the term following it mean "given security prices at times less than j such that j is greater than or equal to zero."

Most investigators choose the LRW model because variability in price change depends to some extent on price level. For example, more absolute variability is likely in higher-priced stocks. This problem is eliminated when differences between log prices are used. Also, log P_t minus log P_{t-1} is the yield with continuous compounding from holding the stock over one period (less the yield attributable to dividends), so that the LRW model has some of the attractive attributes of the CRW model.

Generally, first serial correlation coefficients approaching zero are taken to indicate a lack of dependence between successive stock-market prices, but this conclusion depends on the conjecture that log stock price differences are normally distributed. Yet Fama, Dryden, and others have all found fairly large deviations from normality in stock price-change (and stock return) distributions in the direction of leptokurtosis—too many observations near the mean of distributions and too-fat tails.

This may have led Fama (1965a) to generalize the Sharpe-Lintner asset pricing model to markets where returns may have stable, nonnormal Paretian distributions, but in doing so he was forced to assume that distributions of random variables in the asset pricing model are symmetric, with three parameters instead of two, as compared with the Sharpe-Lintner model. Thus, a characteristic exponent was added to the mean (or expected) return and standard deviation of prices (or returns) in the portfolio selection process.

These objections have significance because stable and unstable Paretian distributions form a large class to which the normal distribution belongs, but all other members of that class have infinite variance. Hence, if stock return or stock price distributions are of this class, it is not possible to calculate correct standard errors. Moreover, variance enters into the denominator for the serial correlation coefficient, so that tests using this variable as a measure of randomness have little value.

In general, investigators have acknowledged this difficulty but have upheld the use of least squares when large samples are involved. Indeed, under these conditions, according to Granger, (1972), "the infinite variance property is remarkably unrobust, so that the more one becomes familiar with the statistical properties of random variables with infinite variance, the more relaxed one becomes about using standard techniques."

However, using more limited samples, Jennergren and Korsvold (1974) showed that serial correlation coefficients for Swedish stocks with lag 1 were generally much larger than serial correlation coefficients for Norwegian stocks, while serial correlation for more actively traded West German stocks, according to Conrad and Juttner, were substantially higher. Given the difference in size and activity in these markets, relative serial correlation coefficients did not support Granger's contention that inactive stocks in smaller markets might very well violate random walk.

On the other hand, nonparametric runs tests involving changes in signs, not magnitudes, showed mean absolute standardized variables for differencing at interval 1 that upheld Granger's supposition, with the amount of indicated dependence between changes increasing as the size of markets and trading activity declined. Runs tests were also used by Fama (1965b) to support the random walk hypothesis as early as 1965, and they are useful because they bypass some of the distribution problems involved in using least squares.

One reason, advanced by Jennergren and Korsvold, for the poor performance of serial correlation coefficients in determining the randomness of the returns of relatively inactive issues may have general applicability. They surmise that gaps in the series mean that the time series selected come from different populations because the number of trading days between transaction days changes from issue to issue. Moreover, this increases variance and decreases mean absolute serial correlations for less frequently traded stocks because variance enters the formula for calculating serial correlation coefficients in the denominator. One might also observe that, even in more active markets, many issues trade very little on most days, so that price changes are insignificant. However, in other periods, owing to news about these or related issues, there may be major price changes. If these periods of major price change vary from stock to stock, it might also be argued that the meaningful data in their time series come from different populations.

Spectral analysis can also test the randomness of stock price returns and stock prices. If the random walk hypothesis is correct, the spectrum of the error series should be completely flat. Granger and Morgenstern (1963), as well as Cootner (1964), present many estimates that support random walk using spectral analysis.

Challenging random walk in terms of weak-form tests of market efficiency, Alexander (1961) used various filter rules, claiming returns well in excess of buy-and-hold, but Fama and Blume, (1966) found his results to be biased by the assumption that stocks could be bought at the lows plus some assumed percent and sold at the highs minus the same percent—executions that could not have been made in actual markets. Bias was also introduced by the use of stock price indexes, which do not reflect dividends. Fama and Blume therefore used individual Dow-Jones industrial stocks, assuming they were bought or sold on the opening of the day selected by the filter rule. With execution problems eliminated as a possible source of bias, they showed that (when brokerage fees were included) most of the filters used by Alexander failed to produce returns in excess of buy-and-hold.

Nevertheless, filter sizes of 5, 1, and 1.5 percent produced average returns per security on long positions that were greater-than-average returns for buy-and-hold, indicating some positive persistence in small stock price movements. There was also evidence of negative dependence in intermediate-sized stock price movements (for filter sizes greater than 1.5 percent and less than 12 percent), so that average losses on short positions were greater than average returns from buy-and-hold.

The positive dependence that resulted from the use of small filters, according to Fama and Blume, could be used to outperform buy-and-hold by 2.5 percent if floor traders (who would pay no commission on the numerous transactions that would result) used only long positions and if no funds were idle. However, clearinghouse fees, operational expenses, and the cost of some idle funds would wipe out this advantage, especially if getting in and out at the times selected by the filters required orders to be placed with specialists.

Some caveats to this conclusion: Nothing prevents specialists from engaging in this sort of trading themselves, using excess funds that might otherwise be idle. Hence, specialists' fees might be avoided. Also, if trades using small filters were restricted to overnight transactions in volatile, high-priced issues, operational costs might be minimized. However, if this supposition is correct, we encounter a central argument in support of random walk, namely, that if excess returns from this operation were possible, other specialists would be likely after a short period to enter this market so that these excess-return opportunities would be extinguished.

The other technique that Fama and Blume found promising involved the use of large filters (perhaps 5 percent), executing short signals in reverse. In that case, any indicated large negative results from intermediate-sized price changes on short positions would become positive. However, this operation would be especially vulnerable to the "idle funds" constraint since such opportunities are relatively infrequent.

In the same vein, James (1968) as well as Van Horne and Parker (1967), found that trading rules based upon moving averages of past prices do not yield profits greater than buy-and-hold, although Levy (1967) claimed that "the theory of random walk has been refuted" on the basis of results from relative strength or portfolio upgrading rules. But Jensen showed that Levy's claims were overstated. Jensen and Bennington (1970) further deflated Levy's results by suggesting that even the remaining excess was due to "a subtle form of selection bias, namely that, given enough computer time, it should be possible to come up with a trading rule that works for a particular group of random numbers." But the same rule should not work on another set of random numbers. They therefore replicated Levy's results on a different body of data and showed them to be spurious.

In general, the random walk hypothesis provides "an extremely good approximation to whatever may be the truth," according to Granger. He adds, however, that "it is only an 'average' kind of law, and may not hold true for all securities at all times." One should add that only relatively simple, linear relationships have been investigated. Thus, chartists, stock-market technicians, and security analysts, who were first thought to be threatened, have survived perhaps because only relatively primitive forecasting devices have been proscribed by the advocates of the theory.

On the other side of the fence, in 1972 Granger outlined a random walk theory with reflecting barriers, i.e., the open buy-and-sell orders of specialists' books, a theory which is remarkably like chartism. Granger concluded that the correlation between adjacent price changes is negative since some time is spent "bouncing off reflecting barriers," and he talked of their being reduced in thickness and thus weakened, which chartists will recognize as penetration of a resistance or support area. Since open orders are often placed at particular levels on specialists' books to protect trading profits and at other levels to initiate trades after breakouts above resistence—generally in areas of heavy previous volume—it is clear that Granger is close to accepting a primitive form of chartism as an appropriate model for transaction prices in markets that permit the buildup of open orders.

So-called semistrong tests of market efficiency are concerned with the speed of price change in response to new information such as stock splits, quarterly earnings reports, and the like. Fama, Fisher, Jensen, and Roll (1969) showed that since stock splits were often associated with above-market-average earnings and dividend increases, the market used split announcements to "revaluate the stream of expected income from shares." Further, price changes as a result of split announcements were shown to be completed by the end of the split month, although there was substantial evidence that most of the reaction took place immediately after announcements. Finally, the evidence indicated that the market reacted only to the dividend implications of splits since, if dividend increases were not forthcoming, stock prices returned to the market-adjusted presplit level.

They also showed that the cross-sectional average residuals were positive for at least 30 months prior to splits, so that earnings improvements probably presaged split rumors and finally split announcements, but the high degree of persistence which this implies, which would also imply dependence in stock prices, was shown to be the result of averaging. There was no serial correlation between regression residuals of individual securities. Thus, if each stock was bought after its split announcement, no excess profits in excess of buy-and-hold would have been earned since individual stocks would have already reflected the "good news."

Little empirical work has been done on strong-form tests of market efficiency, which are concerned with whether all available price information, both public and private, is reflected in stock prices. But tests of results of mutual funds managers using average returns from funds support the conclusion that, as a group, fund managers are not able to outperform randomly selected portfolios. Thus, if these individuals, or other market professionals, had had access to privileged information or had had a special ability to interpret public or private information, either commission and clearance costs plus other expenses or an inability to act promptly would probably have prevented these advantages from making themselves felt.

According to Granger, however, there is limited evidence that corporate officers and other insiders, as well as specialists on stock exchanges, are able to use the information that is available to them to generate excess profits. If they have been able to do so, these returns have not been substantial enough to cause serial correlation of errors in tests of the various random walk models using data from the large markets of the United States, but such returns would help to explain the presence of substantial serial correlation in smaller and less well-regulated markets in other countries.

Many of the workers who have developed ingenious ways to test the random walk or efficient-market hypothesis have also been active in a related field, namely, the development of capital asset pricing models that (in the early models) equate market portfolio returns with a risk-free rate, sometimes given exogenously, plus a risk premium determined by the covariance of individual stock and stock market returns—the so-called mean-variance capital pricing models.

The general equilibrium models of Sharpe (1964) Lintner (1965), and Mossin (1966) for determining prices of capital assets under conditions of uncertainty evolved directly from the models of Markowitz (1959) and Tobin (1958) of the one-period investor as an expected one-period utility maximizer, which were in turn based on the expected-utility model of von Neumann and Morgenstern in *Theory of Games and Economic Behavior* (1953).

The literature of capital asset pricing models is extensive and beyond the scope of this article. However, according to Jensen (1972), "the models show promise of being of great help in addressing many important practical issues," including (among others) "valuation theory and the determination of the cost of capital."

An extensive literature challenges the random walk hypothesis, especially in the strong form that supports the capital asset pricing model (CAPM), much of it objecting to the theory's assumptions. For example, it has been shown that one consequence of the violation of the CAPM assumption that all investors are same-period, one-period utility maximizers would be that multiperiod investment horizons would take the market-clearing portfolio off the efficient frontier.

Many observers have also objected to the use of stock exchange data in proofs of the CAPM since, in theory, the CAPM consists of all capital assets, including foreign stocks and bonds, all real estate, tax hedges, art and collectors items, and so forth. Moreover, the correct market value of these other assets must be determined in order to calculate their proper percentage representation in the market portfolio, but this has not been attempted. However, if these less-liquid assets were included, the inefficiency of the market portfolio would probably increase substantially.

Other objections to the random walk hypothesis in its strong form include the fact that there is a spread between borrowing and lending rates that is not accounted for in most of the CAPM literature. Also, many institutional investors are barred from borrowing and tend to prefer high-yield issues for tax reasons compared with individual investors who prefer capital gains for the same reasons, which appears to violate the assumption of homogeneous expectations for market participants.

This fact suggests that there is not one, but a linear combination of several efficient portfolios that are nonadjacent corner solutions of the quadratic program used to calculate expected returns. If this is true, the linear combination of these portfolios will not constitute another efficient portfolio. Finally, many observers, including random walk proponents, have objected to the risk-free rate since this rate is not risk-free if it does not fully reflect inflation.

References

Alexander, S. S., "Price Movements in Speculative Markets—Trend or Random Walks," *Industrial Management Review*, vol. 2, 1961, pp. 7–26; Conrad, K., and D. J. Juttner, "Recent Behavior of Stock Market Prices in West Germany and the Random Walk Hypothesis," *Kyklos*, vol. 26, 1973, pp. 576–599; Cootner, P. H. (ed.), *The Random Character of Stock Market Prices*, MIT Press, Cambridge, Mass., 1964; Dryden, M. H., "A Statistical Study of U.K. Share Prices," *Journal of Political Economy*, vol. 17, 1970, pp. 369–389; Fama, E. F., "Portfolio Analysis in a Stable Paretian Market," *Management Science*, vol. 11, January, 1965a, pp. 404–419; Fama, E. F., "The Behavior of Stock Market Prices," *Journal of Business*, vol. 38, 1965b, pp. 34–105; Fama, E. F., and Marshall E. Blume, "Filter Rules and Stock Market Trading Profits," *Journal of Business*, vol. 39, no. 1, part II, January 1966, pp. 226–241; Fama, E. F., Laurence Fisher, Michael C. Jensen, and Richard Roll, "The Adjustment of Stock Prices to New Information," *International Economic Review,* vol. 10, no. 1, February 1969, pp. 1–21; Granger, C. W. J., "A Survey of Empirical Studies of Capital Markets," in G. Szego and K. Shell (eds.), *Mathematical Methods in Investment and Finance,* North-Holland, Amsterdam, 1972; Granger, C. W. J., and D. Morgenstern, "Spectral Analysis of New York Stock Market Prices," *Kyklos,* vol. 16, 1963, pp. 1–27; James, F. E., Jr., "Monthly Moving Averages—An Effective Investment Tool," *Journal of Finance,* March 1963, pp. 29–40; Jennergren, L. Peter, and Paul E. Korsvold, "The Non Random Character of Norwegian and Swedish Stock Market Prices," *Swedish Journal of Economics,* vol. 76, no. 2, June 1974, pp. 171–185; Jensen, Michael C., *Studies in the Theory of Capital Markets,* Praeger, New York, 1972; Jensen, Michael C., and George A. Bennington, "Random Walks and Technical Theories: Some Additional Evidence," *Journal of Finance,* vol. 25, no. 2, 1970, pp. 469–482; Levy, Robert A., "Random Walks: Reality or Myth," *Financial Analysts Journal,* vol. 23, no. 6 November–December 1967, pp. 69–77; Lintner, John, "The Valuation of Risk Assets and the Selection of Risky Investments in Stock Portfolios and Capital Budgets," *Review of Economics and Statistics,* vol. 47, February 1965, pp. 13–37; Markowitz, Harry, *Portfolio Selection: Efficient Diversification of Investments,* Wiley, New York, 1959; Mossin, Jan, "Equilibrium in a Capital Market Asset," *Econometrica,* vol. 34, October 1966, pp. 768–783; Praetz, P. D., "Australian Share Prices and the Random Walk Hypothesis," *Australian Journal of Statistics,* vol. 11, 1969, pp. 123–139; Sharpe, William F., "Capital Asset Prices: A Theory of Market Equilibrium Under Risk," *Journal of Finance,* vol. 19, September 1964, pp. 425–442; Tobin, James, "Liquidity Preference as Behavior Toward Risk," *Review of Economic Studies,* vol. 25, February 1958, pp. 65–68; Van Horne, J. C., and G. G. C. Parker, "The Random Walk Theory: An Empirical Test," *Financial Analysts Journal,* November–December 1967, pp. 87–92.

(*See also* Economic forecasts; Forecasting methods; Portfolio management theories; Statistical techniques in economics and business, an overview)

Arnold X. Moskowitz and George A. Harben

Real balance effect theory

The direct effect of changes in real money holdings upon the demand for goods and services is known as the real balance effect. Changes in real cash balances take place when changes in the quantity of money and/or in the price level occur. An increase (decrease) in real money holdings is presumed to increase (decrease) aggregate demand.

Accordingly, people are assumed to maintain a proportional relationship among the alternative forms in which they hold their wealth. When a change in the supply of one form of wealth occurs, people attempt to regain their former distribution of wealth holdings. Thus, the real balance effect theoretically is but one of many possible types of wealth effects.

How the Real Balance Effect Operates

Assume that, at a given price level, an increase in the nominal stock of money (M) occurs. People now have more real money (M/P) relative to their other wealth holdings than formerly. They have an excess supply of money balances and seek to divest themselves of a portion of their increased money holdings by increasing their demand for real goods and services. Additionally, they increase their demand for various financial assets, although most analysts confine the scope of the increase in demand to goods and services. Decreases in the nominal stock of money will have opposite results.

The real balance effect also operates when the price level changes. For example, a decrease in the price level (P), at any given nominal stock of money (M), will again increase the real stock of money (M/P) and disturb the optimal-wealth portfolio of individuals. There will again be an increase in real aggregate demand. Increases in the price level have opposite results.

Historical Background

The logic of the real balance effect is straightforward. Real balance effect theory preceded and then became part of the revival of the quantity theory of money initiated by Milton Friedman and culminating in the monetarist movement of the 1970s. First developed by A. C. Pigou (1943) and originally known as the Pigou effect, the real balance effect was later elaborated by Don Patinkin (1951, 1965) and used to resolve numerous theoretical problems important in classical and Keynesian monetary economics. Among the issues resolved were (1) the classical dichotomy, (2) the neutrality of money, (3) the unitary elasticity of demand-for-money curve, and (4) the possibility of simultaneous less-than-full employment and downward price flexibility.

Four Theoretical Issues Resolved
by the Real Balance Effect

First, according to the classical dichotomy, the monetary sector of the economy determines the general price level while the demand for and supply of goods and services determine relative prices. Hence, the price level has no effect on the demand for and supply of individual goods and services. The real balance effect denies the existence of this dichotomy, since any change in real balance will affect the demand for and supply of goods and services. While this dichotomization of the real and monetary sectors was apparently settled by Patinkin's refinement of the real balance effect, there are still some economists such as J. Niehans (1978) who deny that the dichotomy even existed in the classical literature except as an example of lack of clarity.

Second, closely connected with the issue of the classical dichotomy is the question of whether or not the stock of money is neutral in its real effects on the economy. Given a classical model producing at full employment, an increase in the nominal stock of money (M) creates an excess demand for goods and services through a positive real balance effect. By degrees the individual prices of various commodities must rise, and, accordingly, so must the general price level (P). The increase in the price level decreases the volume of real-money balances (M/P), which in turn generates a decrease in the demand for goods and services (a negative real balance effect). Ultimately, the price level rises in proportion to the initial increase in nominal money balances, and people have the same level of real money holdings with which they started. Thus, money has been neutral, the final behavior of people is unchanged, and the price level is higher.

Third, classical economists had argued that the demand for money balances (M) changes in proportion to the price level (P), that is, that the demand for money has unitary elasticity with respect to prices. The real balance effect demonstrated that this only follows when the stock of money (M) is changed. Were the stock of money unchanged and the price level increased, the amount of money demanded would increase by relatively less than the price level increase. Were people to increase their demand for money (M) in proportion to the rise in prices (P), they would sell off part of their holdings of goods. Were they successful in this effort, they would have fewer real goods and the same amount of real money balances (M/P) as they had prior to the price level change. Hence, their proportions of real money and goods would be disturbed. From this it follows that the increase in the demand for money must be less than in proportion to the price level increase.

And fourth, it had been argued by Keynesian economists that the attainment of full employment is impossible even if prices are flexible downward. The reasoning behind this view is that money affects the demand for good and employment only through its prior effect on the interest rate. According to the Keynes' effect, a decrease in the price level would increase the real stock of money and force interest rates down. If the demand for goods were insensitive to interest, a decrease in the price level would not stimulate the demand for goods and services. Even if aggregate demand responded to the interest rate, however, a decrease in the price level could still be ineffectual should there be some low interest rate (the liquidity-trap interest rate) at which people would no longer be willing to lend to borrowers. The real balance effect mechanism, on the other hand, transmits price level changes directly to changes in aggregate demand rather than indirectly through interest rate changes.

An Unresolved Issue

The real balance effect was developed as a theoretical construct. As such it has gained wide acceptance and use among monetary economists. Only one major theoretical issue appears to be unresolved, the nature of the monetary assets through which the real balance effect operates. Most economists feel that the real balance effect operates only through changes in the amount of currency issued by governments. They reject the idea that it works through the principal component of the money stock, i.e., checking deposit accounts. They reason that demand-deposit money is created when debt is created, and that a drop in the price level, for example, increases both real demand-deposit holdings and real outstanding debt. Any increase in aggregate demand coming from the rise in real money holdings would be offset by a decrease in aggregate demand coming from the rise in real debt. A few economists (B. Pesek and T. Saving, 1967) argue that net worth is increased in the creation of checking deposits and that deposit money should be included among the assets causing the real balance effect.

The Real Balance Effect Evaluated

How relevant is the real balance effect to the real world of economic policy? When real balances change as a result of nominal money-stock (M) changes, at any given price level, there is an abundance of empirical evidence that changes in the money stock and aggregate demand are positively related. However, most economists agree that the real balance effect associated with price level change is difficult to measure and that this real balance effect is likely to be offset in the real world by the effects arising from changing price expectations. For example, as prices rise, an anticipation of still further price rises will lead to increased spending rather than to the decreased spending called for by decreasing real balances. The changes in real balances associated with price change will have economic significance only when people expect future prices to remain about the same as current ones. That expectation is an explicit assumption of the theory. While this was a legitimate theoretical assumption and was empirically relevant for the 1960s, it did not apply to the inflation of the 1970s. Most economists now include price expectation effects in their models of the macroeconomic process. This is not to denigrate the significance of the real balance effect, since most contemporary macroeconomic models now include wealth effect variables.

The crux of the issue is as follows: Changes in the quantity of money have interest rate, real balance, and price expectation effects. The combination of these effects means that increases (decreases) in the growth rate of the money stock will in the short run increase (decrease) the growth of output, employment, and prices, but will in the long run only increase (decrease) the growth rate of prices.

References

Friedman, Milton (ed.), *Studies in the Quantity Theory of Money*, University of Chicago Press, Chicago, 1956; Gordon, Robert J (ed.), *Milton Friedman's Monetary Framework: A Debate with His Critics*, University of Chicago Press, Chicago, 1974; Klein, John J., *Money and the Economy*, 4th ed., Harcourt Brace Jovanovich, New York, 1978; Niehans, Jurg, *The Theory of Money*, Johns Hopkins Press, Baltimore, 1978; Patinkin, Don, "Price Flexibility and Full Employment," in F. A. Lutz and Lloyd Mints (eds.), *Readings in Monetary Theory*, Irwin, Homewood, Ill., 1951; Patinkin, Don, *Money, Interest, and Prices*, 2d ed., Harper & Row, New York, 1965; Pesek, Boris P., and Thomas R. Saving, *Money, Wealth, and Economic Theory*, Macmillan, New York, 1967; Pigou, A. C., "The Classical Stationary State," *Economic Journal*, vol. 53, 1943, pp. 343–351.

(*See also* Interest, economic theory; Interest rates; Keynesian economics; Money supply; Propensity to consume or to save and inducement to invest; Quantity theory of money; Wealth)

John J. Klein

Real estate investment trusts

Real estate investment trusts (REITs) are an investment medium which allows the small investor to participate in and share in the profits of a managed portfolio of real estate assets held by an REIT in the form of either properties or mortgages. There are two major types of REITs. Mortgage trusts invest in short-term mortgages, i.e., construction and development loans. They advance money to the builder as construction progresses. When the project is completed, a permanent lender assumes the long-term mortgage and pays off the construction loan. Equity trusts own or finance real estate directly.

Four Characteristics

For the U.S. investing public with limited wealth to invest, as well as for pension fund managers seeking to diversify into real estate without having to amass a huge realty-specialized staff, the REIT investment medium provides several advantages:

1. Daily, inexpensive pricing through market valuation of the shares with secondary market liquidity
2. Professional management through shared costs (usually pursuant to an advisory contract that is keyed to performance)
3. Provided the REIT remains qualified for tax purposes, a continued focus on income-operations or trading or a combination of these objectives
4. Prompt and accurate reporting, audited and subject to review by securities lawyers who ensure the many safeguards imposed by U.S. agencies charged with regulation of the public financial markets

The alternative methods of owning and deriving income from real estate (direct ownership, limited partnerships, fixed-income mortgage securities, or real estate operating companies) possess one or another of these attributes. Only the REIT has them all, distinguishing it from all other real estate securities.

History

In 1961, Congress attempted once more to provide real estate financing with a contracyclical intermediary. It granted unincorporated business trusts the same kind of tax treatment—i.e., no tax at the REIT level if virtually all income was passed along to investors as dividends—that was enjoyed by mutual funds. By the late 1960s, mortgage trusts had established a noticeably better dividend record than equity trusts. A combination of forces encouraged the investment banking community to heavily promote mortgage-lending trusts sponsored and separately advised by banks. For awhile, these new issues sold heavily on Wall Street during times of very high interest rates. The equity capital, invested in construction loans, competed favorably against the pinched banks, making it appear that the REIT was a contracyclical device. However, when rates came down, most of the mortgage-lending REITs began chasing earnings with borrowed money. Eventually, the double-digit prime rate of 1974 created chaotic market conditions, and the shakeout period for REITs occurred.

Current Focus

Today the REIT industry is once again focused primarily on the ownership and longer-term development of income-producing real estate, although some REITs still make construction loans. There are 216 REITs, with 160 of them having actively traded markets in their shares. Of those 160, as of mid-1979, 64 were traded on the New York or American Stock Exchange.

Industry assets grew from approximately $1 billion in the late 1960s to $21 billion at the peak; at mid-1979 the industry had just about finished its contraction, to roughly $12.5 billion. Of that total, more than $7.5 billion was in property owned, and less than $2 billion was in short-term mortgage loans, mostly construction financing at rates competitive with commercial banks.

Disclosure Problem

As Wall Street's window on the world of real estate, the REIT industry has drawn a lot of public attention. The institutional realty financiers (mostly banks and insurance companies) in competition with REITs for either loans or income-producing real estate projects have not been required to isolate and expose their real estate–financing departments or portfolios to the extent required of the REITs through the full-disclosure requirements of U.S. public securities laws. Consequently, when adverse developments of a possible material nature arise in a real estate transaction, none but the REITs have to report publicly. This competitive disadvantage exacerbates the industry's encounters with the known volatility of the cyclical real estate business, forcing the REIT industry to seek longer-term equity investments.

On the other hand, development of the industry and its emphasis on competitive pricing have caused, and continue to cause, increasingly widespread uniformity in the terms and conditions of major real estate financial transactions. While each parcel of real estate is unique, and, therefore, not readily interchangeable, the complex terms and conditions of major income-producing real estate transactions have been honed competitively. The subordinated land sale–lease back transaction, for instance, has become a highly competitive, much more standardized method of realty financing because at least three REITs decided to specialize in providing them.

REITs in Other Countries

While real estate trusts with similarities exist in other countries, the United States REIT is unique. Congress originally confined the special tax status to unincorporated business trusts—until 1976. Now, corporations can qualify so long as their affairs are conducted in conformity with REIT provisions of the tax code. Increasingly, REITs are becoming corporations because securities and business laws are much simpler for companies than for trusts. Thus, in time, the REIT industry may be primarily composed of corporations.

The British land trusts differ from American REITs in that their real estate holdings are revalued every year. In contrast, American REITs carry their assets at historic cost minus depreciation. The British land trusts also do not follow certain tax passivity rules that keep the REITs focused on investment, and not on profits from trading or land specualtion or from direct operation of reality business. In Canada, there are several forms of REITs, none of which is directly comparable, the chief difference being the Canadian government–imposed requirements that a certain portion of assets be held in home mortgages.

References

English, John, W., and Gray Emerson Cardiff, *The Coming Real Estate Crash*, Arlington House, New Rochelle, N.Y., 1979; Halpin, Michael C., *Profit Planning for Real Estate Development*, Dow Jones-Irwin, Homewood, Ill., 1977.

(*See also* Housing economics; Mortgage credit; Thrift institutions)

John B. Nicholson

Real theories of interest (see Interest, economic theory of)

Reform liberalism

Like the classical liberals, reform liberals are committed to the economic and spiritual improvement of the individual. Unlike classical liberals, reform liberals urge the state to take a more active role in creating opportunities in the market so that individuals, especially the poorest members of society, can improve their situation. Reform liberals such as Jeremy Bentham, John Stuart Mill, T. H. Green, Alfred Marshall, A. C. Pigou, J. A. Hobson, John Dewey, John Maynard Keynes, John Kenneth Gallbraith, and, most recently, John Rawls support progressive taxation of income and wealth, state-supported education, public health and sanitation provisions, public parks and urban planning, subsidization and taxation of various industries (depending upon whether the social cost of producing a marginal unit of supply is less than or greater than the social benefit), the taxation of inherited wealth, and the management of aggregate demand to avoid unemployment of resources. Reform liberals define individual freedom in positive terms and are not against using law as a tool of social reform. They hold that coercion as a political device is useful and socially justifiable if the social benefits exceed the social costs. Unlike the early group of classical liberals, reform liberals do not believe that individuals enter into society with certain natural rights such as the right to life and to personal property. Rather, they follow Jeremy Bentham and argue that private property, individual liberty, and open markets are justified because they are expedient and promote the "greatest good for the greatest number." According to Bentham, the greatest good can be enhanced by social experimentation even when this necessitates violating older traditions and norms.

As part of the larger liberal tradition, reform liberals cherish individual freedom and liberty and recognize that without genuine moral choice there can be little improvement in human character. They emphasize that individual freedom consists of much more than the absence of coercion in human affairs. Individual freedom requires the ability to enter professions, learn trades, develop refined tastes, and avoid a life of drudgery and boredom for oneself and one's children. Freedom of these sorts can be hastened by government reform so long as legislative solutions are based on a realistic appraisal of human nature in the market. Schemes that presuppose purely altruistic behavior on the part of individuals are suited for socialist visionaries and utopian dreamers, but reform liberals build their analyses on individuals as they actually behave in markets. Still, reform liberals hope for an eventual change in the refinement and tastes of the average citizen. If the reform liberal suffers from any obvious prejudice, it is the belief that middle-class values and aspirations are in some sense the index of individual and social improvement. During the 1960s this well-meaning attempt to impose middle-class values and behavior patterns on minority groups and welfare recipients, met with hostile and severe reaction on the part of the poor themselves. Many of these policies have not produced the results promised by the welfare state because they have dampened individual incentives and replaced competitive market processes with large, expensive government bureaucracies.

On analytic matters, reform liberals tend to view the social process as if production and distribution were separate activities carried out by separate groups for different purposes. But the economic system is not so simple as the parlor game Monopoly, where all players are dealt equal amounts of money and play until one person possesses all the wealth. To use the state to equalize individual's starting-out positions (so that all will have equal opportunities) means that the legal system is used to treat rich people differently from poor people. This means abandoning the older classical liberal ideal of equality before the law; however, the resulting economic redistribution may seriously dampen economic incentives. The poor may end up with a larger percentage share of a smaller total and, therefore, find themselves worse off than before.

Despite its vagueness and reliance on intuitive feeling for how much intervention is to be permitted and for what the limits of that intervention are, there can be no denying the enormous impact reform liberalism has had on Western democracies over the last 100 years. Unfortunately, much of reform liberalism has drifted toward the older socialist program of nationalizing industry. Policies that began promising quick results with a few controls for limited purposes have ended up requiring more and more controls until nationalization of the industry has become imperative. This trend toward escalation of government control of the economy was predicted by the older classical liberals such as Ludwig von Mises (*Socialism*, 1951) and Friedrich A.

Hayek (*The Road to Serfdom*, 1944). In the United States, large government bureaucracies have replaced private decision making in many areas of the economy, and entrepreneurial effort is at historically low levels. Some of John Maynard Keynes' schemes for demand-managed policies have degenerated into cheap money policies producing the severe inflationary environment that Keynes himself decried in the 1920s. Amidst the current chaos of welfare state, reform liberalism if not on the decline, has lost much of its original glamor.

References

Freden, Michael, "J. A. Hobson as a New Liberal Theorist: Some Aspects of His Social Thought until 1914," *Journal of the History of Ideas*, vol. 34, July–September 1973, pp. 421–442; Galbraith, John Kenneth, *Economics and the Public Purpose*, Houghton Mifflin, Boston, 1973; Keynes, Milo (ed.), *Essays on John Maynard Keynes*, Cambridge University Press, Cambridge, 1975; Nozick, Robert, *Anarchy, State and Utopia*, Basic Books, New York, 1974; Rawls, John, *A Theory of Justice*, Harvard University Press, Cambridge, Mass., 1971.

(*See also* Classical liberalism; Liberalism)

Laurence S. Moss

Regional economics

Regional economics addresses the challenge of understanding how a geographic subdivision of a national economy functions: what determines its level of output and employment, its industrial composition, its rate of growth, the level of productivity and income, and the rate of umemployment. The region is open in the sense that capital, labor, and commodities move freely across its borders. There are no trade restrictions and no barriers to migration. But the region is closed at any point in time in the sense that there is very little daily commuting to work across its borders. It may also be closed in the sense that it is bounded by subnational political jurisdictions. Thus, a region in practice could be a county, a group of counties (metropolitan or not), a state, or a group of states.

Regional Models

Regional economics has its roots in location theory and macroeconomics. In the simplest of formulations, a region is viewed as a place which is favored by some producers as a location for production to serve extraregional markets because of its unique resource endowments, its good access to markets, or the availability of labor and other inputs on more favorable terms. Based on this activity a region grows and develops beyond this base because other producers are attracted to serve the local market. The concept of the multiplier is adapted from macroeconomics. The key driving forces, therefore, are the growth of the basic industry, which in turn depends on the level of demand for that industry's output and the continuing competitiveness of that region as a location for that industry, and the value of the multiplier.

Missing from such a model of a region are the factors which operate on the supply side to affect both the region's competitive posture and the value of the multiplier in the process of growth and development. Location theory and macroeconomics do not shed light on these issues, which are becoming increasingly central to theoretical and empirical research in regional economics.

In the last 15 years much effort has been expended to develop more sophisticated regional models, some for specific regions, others for the country as a whole broken down by regions. "Region" is variously defined as a single county, a cluster of contiguous counties, a state, or a group of states. The indicators to be predicted or forecast relate to output, employment, income, interregional trade, and revenues and expenditures of the public sector. Some models pay lip service to supply factors; others develop them in considerable detail.

Regional Economics and Public Policy

Aside from intrinsic intellectual interest, regional economics is pursued for its relatively rich policy yield. It has potential value to many private and public decision makers within a region. Investments in physical capital—whether private or public—which support the production and the provision of goods and services to the region's households and enterprises must necessarily be informed by estimates of current and future levels of demand within the region. Thus, state and local governments, financial institutions, and public utilities have been prominently involved in the production and consumption of regional analyses and forecasts. The fiscal capacity of state and local governments, notwithstanding the growth of federal support in the last two decades, is still closely linked to the performance of the economy within these jurisdictions. Regional economics is, therefore, helpful in determining the amount of resources available for public investment. Finally, there is the complex relationship between local public policy and regional comparative advantage which extends to expenditures, taxes, and regulation.

Regional economics also informs national policy. The federal government invests heavily in infrastructure which is place- or region-specific: transportation, waste treatment, water supply, recreation, postal services. Acting in this role, the federal government takes its place alongside state and local governments as a consumer of regional economics. The increasing emphasis on geographic detail in the decennial census and the growth of a regional focus in the Bureau of Economic Analysis reflect the federal government's interest in regional data and the government's role as a producer as well as a consumer of regional economic analysis.

Regional economics is at the heart of federal policies and programs aimed at stimulating private investment in regions which are economically anemic. Thus, the Economic Development Administration has been a main source of support for research on the central questions of regional economics. Another stimulus to regional economics has been the need to understand and predict in different regions the impact of federal policies which have other primary objectives, e.g., energy policy, environmental policy, income maintenance policy.

Of all the subfields in economics, regional economics has probably had the most intimate contact with other disciplines. Geographers, of course, have been concerned for a long time with the economic map of the world and of specific countries. In earlier years, they tended to stress pure description. In recent years, they have become much more analytical, and they compete with economists for the attention of other researchers and policymakers. Sociologists, particularly demographers, have also interacted heavily with economists in the study of regions on such issues as migration and population forecasting. When the dynamics of regional growth are considered, there is natural contact with historians. When the focus is on the interplay between the regional economy and the public sector, political scientists often get involved.

The most significant reflection of the interdisciplinary nature of regional economics is the Regional Science Association, created in 1954 by Walter Isard, one of the pioneers in the field. The Regional Science Association meetings and publications serve as a forum for researchers in all the relevant disciplines, as well as for planners and policymakers. A worldwide network of regional science organizations and journals has developed during the last 25 years so that scholars working on regional issues in their respective countries have many opportunities to be in contact with each other.

Great impetus to the development of the field was also provided in the 1950s at Resources for the Future, a nonprofit research institute in Washington now heavily committed to energy and environmental issues.

References

Hansen, Niles M. (ed.), *Public Policy and Regional Economic Development: The Experience of Nine Western Countries*, Ballinger, Cambridge, Mass., 1974; Hoover, Edgar M., *An Introduction to Regional Economics*, 2d ed., Knopf, New York, 1975; Isard, Walter, *Introduction to Regional Science*, Prentice-Hall, Englewood Cliffs, N.J., 1975; Kain, John F., and John R. Meyers (eds.), *Essays in Regional Economics*, Harvard University Press, Cambridge, Mass., 1971; Richardson, Harry W., *Regional Growth Theory* (Halsted Press), Wiley, New York, 1973.

(*See also* Location theory; Macroeconomics; Urban economics)

Benjamin Chinitz

Regression analysis in business and economics

Regression analysis is a method of estimating functional relationships between two or more variables. Economic theory is largely concerned with such relations (production functions, demand functions, supply functions, consumption functions, and the like). Marginal product, marginal revenue, marginal cost, marginal propensity to consume, and similar concepts are defined as the slopes or derivatives of those functions at specified points. When economists in the early 1900s first attempted to estimate the demand functions of economic theory from market data on prices and consumption of farm products, regression analysis presented itself as the most logical and appropriate tool.

The most influential of these economists, Henry L. Moore, set out in 1908 to develop "the statistical complement of pure economics," and by 1917 he was convinced that multiple regression analysis was both necessary and sufficient for this task:

> No matter how complex the functional relations between the variables, it can derive "empirical laws" which, by successive approximations, will describe the real relations with increasing accuracy.... When the method of multiple correlation [we would now say regression] is thus applied to economic data it invests the findings of deductive economics with "the reality and life of fact"; it is the Statistical Complement of Deductive Economics.

In his last book, *Synthetic Economics* (1929), Moore proposed an implementation of the general equilibrium model of Walras. Its principal elements were to be comprehensive sets of empirical demand, supply, and production functions estimated by multiple regression techniques. Thus, Moore viewed the range of applications of regression analysis in economics as conterminous with the economy itself.

Simple Linear Regression

As a statistical technique, regression analysis is used in many disciplines and is generally associated with the method of least squares. The technique may best be illustrated for the case of simple linear regression.

Suppose Y is a variable that is functionally dependent on another variable X and that the relationship is believed to be linear. Given a set of n observations, each consisting of a pair of values Y_i and X_i, where $i = 1, 2, \ldots, n$, we wish to determine the parameters a and b of a straight line, $Y = a + bX$, which best expresses the assumed relationship.

We approach the problem by graphing the n observations with the values Y_i measured on the vertical axis and the corresponding values X_i on the horizontal. The resulting set of n points (dots) is called a scatter diagram. If all the points appear to lie exactly on a straight line, we can simply draw a line through them with a ruler and extend it until it intersects the Y axis. At this point, $X = 0$ and $Y = a$. The slope b can be calculated from the relationship $b = (Y - a)/X$; thus, if we choose $X = 10$ and find that the corresponding value of Y on the straight line is $a + 7$, then $b = 7/10$, or 0.7. If the value of the intercept a is 20, the equation of the line is $Y = 20 + 0.7X$.

In general, the points of the scatter diagram will not lie exactly on a straight line, and it is customary to estimate the parameters a and b by the method of least squares. We postulate that

$$Y_i = a + bX_i + u_i \qquad i = 1, 2, \ldots, n$$

where u_i is a random error with an expected value of zero. The expected value of Y_i is presumed to be an exact linear function of X_i, namely, $\hat{Y}_i = a + bX_i$, and the error term $u_i = Y_i - \hat{Y}_i$ expresses itself as a deviation of Y_i above or below this function. The method of least squares requires that the sum of the squared deviations be minimized.

The resulting regression line passes through the point of means at which

$$Y = \overline{Y} = \sum_{i=1}^{n} \frac{Y_i}{n} \quad \text{and} \quad X = \overline{X} = \sum_{i=1}^{n} \frac{X_i}{n}$$

The sum of the squared deviations of the Y_i from their mean, namely,

$$\sum_{i=1}^{n} (Y_i - \overline{Y})^2$$

is smaller than the sum of squared deviations of the Y_i from any other point. The regression line partitions the sum of squares

$$\sum_{i=1}^{n} (Y_i - \overline{Y})^2$$

into two additive components; one of these,

$$\sum_{i=1}^{n} (\hat{Y}_i - \overline{Y})^2$$

is regarded as "explained" by the regression relationship and the other,

$$\sum_{i=1}^{n} (Y_i - \hat{Y}_i)^2 = \sum_{i=1}^{n} u_i^2$$

as "unexplained."

To simplify notation, we may write deviations from the means as

$$y_i = Y_i - \overline{Y} \quad \text{and} \quad x_i = X_i - \overline{Y}.$$

Then the slope b of the regression line can be computed from the formula

$$b = \frac{\sum_{i=1}^{n} y_i x_i}{\sum_{i=1}^{n} x_i^2}$$

and the intercept a from the formula

$$a = \overline{Y} - b\overline{X}$$

The proportion of the sum of squares

$$\sum_{i=1}^{n} y_i^2$$

explained by the regression relationship may be written as

$$r^2 = \frac{\left(\sum_{i=1}^{n} y_i x_i \right)^2}{\sum_{i=1}^{n} y_i^2 \sum_{i=1}^{n} x_i^2}$$

where r^2 is called the coefficient of determination of y by x, or simply the squared correlation coefficient.

Multiple Regression

Many economic relationships involve more than two variables; for example, the quantity of meat (Q) demanded by consumers is a function of its retail price (P) and of consumer income (Y). This function could be linear in either arithmetic or logarithmic form, or it could be nonlinear (curvilinear) in various ways. When three or more variables are involved, the least-squares estimate of a function is called a multiple regression equation.

Moore had no special interest in agriculture, but he found that the most promising data available for his attempts to estimate empirical demand and supply functions were time series of prices, consumption, and production of farm products. His successes were followed up in the early 1920s by a group of young economists in the newly established U.S. Bureau of Agricultural Economics and in some of the agricultural colleges. Most notable of these economists were Moredecai Ezekiel, Frederick V. Waugh, Holbrook Working, Louis H. Bean, and Elmer J. Working. Moore's one direct disciple, Henry Schultz, also made impressive contributions from his vantage point at the University of Chicago. In their hands, the estimation of statistical demand functions using multiple regression techniques reached a high level of sophistication by the end of the 1920s. Their technical and empirical achievements are summarized in Ezekiel's *Methods of Correlation Analysis* (1930).

Some problems frequently encountered in regression analysis as applied to economic time series, including high intercorrelation among the independent variables and autocorrelation in the residuals, were clarified during the 1930s by Ragnar Frisch, Tjalling C. Koopmans, and Herman Wold. Paul H. Douglas began his work on production functions in the late 1920s, and Joel Dean made many regression estimates of statistical cost functions from 1937 on. Jan Tinbergen used multiple regression techniques (supplemented by the "bunch map analysis" methods of Frisch and Koopmans) to estimate his 45-equation model of the United States economy published in 1939. Henry Schultz's monumental work, *The Theory and Measurement of Demand* (1938), combined major presentations of economic theory and multiple regression techniques with detailed empirical studies of the demands for farm and food products.

During the 1920s and 1930s there were many arguments about the place of regression analysis in economics and business which now seem rather pointless. Few American economists active in those decades had much training in mathematics; many had studied economics as a verbal, historical, institutional, or descriptive subject; and most of those who had been exposed to a course in business or economic statistics had not advanced beyond "cookbook" recipes for fitting a least-squares trend to a time series. In this environment, some young economists who learned the techniques of freehand graphic curvilinear regression or of linear multiple regression analyses made extravagant claims and ridiculous mistakes. Thus, in 1934 Ragnar Frisch asserted that "a substantial part of the regression and correlation analyses which have been made on economic data in recent years is nonsense" because of the combined (and unrecognized) effect of random errors in and high intercorrelation among the explanatory variables. Chance correlations were sometimes mistaken for cause-and-effect relations, regression lines were extrapolated far beyond the range of the supporting data, and forecasts made on the implicit assumption of unchanging economic structures went awry when the structures did in fact change. It should be stressed that few such mistakes were made by the leading figures in the development of statistical demand analysis.

Currently, the place of regression analysis in economics and business may be summarized as follows:

Functional relations between economic variables may be technological (e.g., steel is an input in the production of automobiles); institutional (e.g., receipts from the personal income tax are a function of personal income and the schedule of tax rates); or behavioral (e.g., the quantity of beef demanded by consumers is a function of its retail price and their disposable income). Economists who take pains to stay informed about the technological, institutional, or behavioral factors relevant to a particular functional relationship and also about the sources, magnitudes, and natures of the errors that may be present in each variable can obtain useful knowledge by fitting a regression equation which approximates the function during the period to which the data refer. In doing so, they may obtain sufficient insight to adjust their regression coefficients when technology, tax schedules, or behavior change over time; and, thus, they can continue to make useful estimates or forecasts despite changes in structure.

References

Ezekiel, Mordecai, *Methods of Correlation Analysis*, 1st and 2d ed., Wiley, New York, 1930 and 1941; Ezekiel, Mordecai, and Karl A. Fox, *Methods of Correlation and Regression Analysis: Linear and Curvilinear*, 3d ed., Wiley, New York, 1959; Frisch, Ragnar, *Statistical Confluence Analysis by Means of Complete Regression Systems*, Universitet, DET Okonomiske Institutt, Oslow, 1934; Fox, Karl A., *Intermediate Economic Statistics*, vol. I: *An Integration of Economic Theory and Statistical Methods*, 2d ed., Huntington, N.Y. 1980, reprint of *Intermediate Economic Statistics*, Wiley, New York, 1968; Fox. Karl A., and Tej K. Kaul, *Intermediate Economic Statistics*, vol. II: *A Guide to Recent Developments and Literature, 1968–1978*, Krieger, Huntington, N.Y., 1980; Moore, Henry L., *Forecasting the Yield and Price of Cotton*, Macmillan, New York, 1917, quote, p. 173; Schultz, Henry, *The Theory and Measurement of Demand*, University of Chicago Press, Chicago, 1938; Seber, G. A. F., *Linear Regression Analysis*, Wiley, New York, 1977.

(*See also* Forecasting methods; Seasonal adjustment methods; Statistical techniques in economics and business, an overview)

Karl A. Fox and Tej K. Kaul

Rent (see Economic rent)

Research and development

Commonly abbreviated as R&D and used in the singular, research and development encompasses all systematic or organized endeavors aimed at the creation or furtherance of knowledge. The various types of activities within the R&D entity have been classified in a number of different and not always consistent ways, but the best known and the most widely used breakdown of R&D is basic research, applied research, and development.

Basic research, also called scientific or fundamental research, pertains to phenomena and relationships found in nature, including human nature, taken in an individual or collective context. Hence, the objective of basic research is to expand knowledge in the scientific disciplines, both natural and social.

Applied research, sometimes called technological or engineering research, has as its objective the formulation of concepts and methods and the invention of devices and techniques that can be used as inputs into some human-originated process, product, or event. Hence, applied research is more likely to be mission-oriented, i.e., to have predefined goals and objectives, than is basic research.

Development is the process of perfecting a new kind of product or activity that does not require or no longer requires the creation of new basic or applied knowledge. Development precedes the routine or mass introduction of new products or activities. Unforeseen problems and flaws are corrected during the development process, and in some classifications, pilot and prototype production is considered as the final stage of development.

In addition to this tripartition based on the substance of R&D, there are other types of classifications based on institutional or functional criteria. Hence, the literature has numerous references to industrial, academic, and defense R&D, or to offensive versus defensive R&D.

As indicated, the R&D entity, or at least many of its components, pertain to social as well as to natural or technological phenomena. They can also be interpreted to apply to management, the arts, or the humanities, but in most cases, the interest of economists in R&D is directed toward physical, chemical, biological, technological, or engineering endeavors. The potential of such endeavors can lead to the invention of new products and processes and to innovations in the process of production and consumption.

R&D and Economics

The integration of R&D into the conceptual structure of economics exemplifies a curious epoch in the history of economic thought. During that epoch, a set of new concepts were incorporated into an established philosophical and theoretical framework, one that was not fully prepared to accommodate those new concepts. Accordingly, modifications were in order, and the modifications, whenever deemed necessary, were applied to the R&D concept rather than to existing economic theory. As will be seen, some gaps and anomalies still remain in the economic interpretation of research and development.

Economists began to take serious and extensive interest in R&D shortly after World War II. This burst of interest is commonly attributed to three main causes: the devastation of the European scientific infrastructure during the war; the Sputnik-inspired international space race of the 1950s and 1960s; and a series of hot and cold wars during the same period. By the early 1970s, the momentum provided by the three causes was lost, and the actual performance of R&D ebbed, as did much of the interest of economists in the subject. There are many examples in the history of economic thought where interest in a given subject is closely linked to the coming and passing of current events. However, the case of R&D in the history of economic thought is noteworthy because of its acuteness as well as its brevity.

Nevertheless, the subject of R&D has come to occupy an important position in contemporary economics, particularly with regard to questions that relate to technological change, productivity, economic growth, and economic development. The surge of interest in the subject originated in the United States, but by the early 1960s, the international literature had become richly infused with economic treatments of research and development.

With a few notable exceptions, economists have accepted the conventional classification of R&D activities as basic research, applied research, and development and have made this tripartition the basis for the analysis of the incentives to undertake R&D. The incentive, of course, depends on an economic evaluation of expected returns from undertakings in comparison with the alternative employment of R&D resources. The accuracy with which returns from R&D can be predicted is widely agreed to be the highest in the case of development; it is believed to be lower for applied research; and the lowest, if it exists at all, for basic research. Hence, the incentive of profit-motivated private enterprise to undertake R&D is commonly ranked in the same order. Both this ordering and this historical performance put major responsibility for undertaking basic economic research in the hands of the federal government, as well as academic and nonprofit institutions. In addition, the federal government assumes responsibility for a considerable volume of applied research and development, aimed at the provision of social or collectively consumed goods, such as national defense, health, and environmental protection.

Within the conceptual framework of economics, R&D is commonly viewed as an investment, that is, the outlay of resources for the acquisition of some form of capital.

The definition of the invested resources and of the resulting capital, however, depends on whether the topic at hand is closer to the philosophical-theoretical or the empirical and policy-oriented end of the gamut of economic inquiry. At the philosophical-theoretical end, inputs into the R&D process are expressed as human creativity and intellectual effort, both direct and embodied in R&D plant and equipment. The output of R&D, viewed in the same context, is knowledge. Such abstractions are not useful in quantitative investigations, much less in policy-oriented empirical ones. Rather than attempting to mold the established edifice of economic theory and method to accommodate these abstractions, perhaps in a similar manner in which the abstractions of utility and welfare are accommodated, economists have decided to abandon the concepts of creativity, intellect, and knowledge and have adopted representative or surrogate concepts instead.

Accordingly, at the input end of the R&D process, the resources are represented by R&D expenditures, the employment of R&D personnel, and the use of plant and equipment. On the output side, the capital produced by R&D is taken to be represented by, or embodied in, increased productivity, new types of production processes, new types of goods and services, and more generally, economic growth and development, on both the macro and micro levels. In addition, the output of R&D activity is represented by patent, publication, and literature citation counts.

These formulations of the relevant R&D quantities still have not brought about complete compatibility between investment theory and the R&D phenomenon because some of the inherent attributes of the former, such as depreciation, capital replacement, and interest rates, have limited, if any, pertinence to investment in R&D. In spite of this, economists have made remarkable progress in identifying the connection between investment in and the output of R&D. Relying mostly on modern econometric techniques, including production function analysis, investigators have calculated both private and social returns from R&D in terms of productivity, profits, diffusion of innovations, technological progress, economic growth and development, and other selected economic variables. They have even tackled the difficult question of overinvestment in research and development activities.

Allocation of Resources for R&D

One core economic question continues to frustrate students of the R&D process. That question concerns the allocation of resources for R&D. In pure theory, with the freedom to define R&D inputs and outputs in any convenient way, it has been possible to construct equilibrium models for the optimal allocation of resources. Yet, whatever conceptual work may have been done on that level, concepts of optimal R&D inputs have had little impact on the actual input decisions either in private business or in government. Business R&D decisions are typically made on a project-by-project basis by the use of ad hoc criteria, by the extrapolation of past magnitudes, or by rules of thumb. In the government, the allocation of R&D resources remains largely a political process in the hands of the executive and congressional branches of the federal government.

The reasons why the market cannot be expected to bring about an effecient allocation of R&D resources and why it is so difficult to construct policy-oriented models of optimal allocation are inherent in the points made previously. They have to do with the uncertainty of return and with the persistent danger that any single R&D project may not be able to capture and to internalize the entire benefits of the undertaking. The latter point becomes particularly important toward the basic research end of the R&D gamut.

There is little doubt that the question of R&D resource allocation will continue to challenge the imagination of future investigators. Whether the solution, if one ever materializes, will be in the form of an optimizing equilibrium model or whether the search for such an equilibrium is a search in a blind alley remains to be seen.

References

National Science Foundation, *Science Indicators 1978*, National Science Board, 1979, published biannually; Nelson, Richard R. (ed.), *The Rate and Direction of Inventive Activity: Economic and Social Factors*, National Bureau of Economic Research, Princeton University Press, Princeton, N.J., 1962; Subcommittee on Domestic and International Scientific Planning and Analysis of the Committee on Science and Technology, *Selected Readings on Research and Development Expenditures and the National Economy*, U.S. House of Representatives, 94th Cong., 2d Sess. April 1976, serial Z; Subcommittee on Science, Research, and Development of the Committee on Science and Astronautics, *Selected Readings on Science, Technology, and the Economy*, U.S. House of Representatives, 92d Cong. 1st Sess., October 1971, serial E.

(*See also* Economic growth; Innovation; Productivity; Technology)

Theordore Suranyi-Unger, Jr.

Restraint of trade

Restraint of trade is primarily a legal concept used in reference to antitrust policy. Its classic expression is in the Sherman Antitrust Act of 1890: "Every contract, combination in the form of trust or otherwise, or conspiracy in restraint of trade or commerce among the several states, or with foreign nations, is declared to be illegal." Trade can be restrained in many ways, such as when persons or business firms agree by contract to limit competition among themselves or to prevent others from competing; or when they seek such limitations by a merger of actual or potential competitors, by any other joint action that can be called a combination, or by a secret conspiracy. An economist would usually speak of anticompetitive agreements, mergers, and collusion. In a society built on free enterprise and free competition, any interference with these free forces is suspect. The Sherman Act gives concrete expression to this suspicion.

The Concept of Reasonable Restraint

When individual trading emerged in the late Middle Ages, two kinds of restraint were deemed harmful. One was cornering the market on a necessity of life, thus raising its price; prohibition of this was a precursor of the Sherman Act's section 2, forbidding monopolizing. The other was agreeing not to compete: most typically artisans made this pledge when selling their trades to others. However, in suits for breach of contract under the common law, the courts developed the rule that an agreement limited in time and territory could be viewed as merely ancillary, or subordinate, to what was a lawful transaction. So the nineteenth century inherited a concept of reasonable restraints.

Public opinion was strongly stirred by the damage to competition it perceived as coming from the rise of big business in the 1870s and 1880s. There were mergers which created dominant corporations—unfair tactics made possible by size, which drove out small competitors—and even efficiencies of size which had the same effect. A companion development was the rise of price agreements, most noticeably among railroads. The Sherman Act followed, making restraints punishable, whereas the common law had left them unenforceable. Most states passed laws dealing with local restraint offenses.

Rule of Reason and Per Se Rule

In early Sherman Act decisions, against the Trans-Missouri Freight Association in 1897, the Joint Traffic Association in 1898, and the Addyston Pipe group in 1899, the Supreme Court declared that all agreements limiting competition were illegal. In 1911, however, its *Standard Oil* and *American Tobacco* opinions held that only unreasonable restraints, such as the mergers and competitive tactics in these two instances, were illegal. Public opinion was startled by this "rule of reason." Subsequently, the Clayton Antitrust Act and Federal Trade Commission Act of 1914 outlawed certain specific actions and "unfair methods of competition," respectively.

Four subsequent Supreme Court interpretations set the guidelines for the Sherman Act. In 1918 the Chicago Board of Trade's rules restricting the time of trading were allowed, as ancillary to an orderly market. But in 1927 the *Trenton Potteries* decision held that "the aim and result of every price fixing agreement, if effective, is the elimination of one form of competition"; the Court refused to apply the rule of reason. In *Appalachian Coals* (1933) a joint selling agency of 137 companies was allowed in view of the distress conditions in coal and the fact that one-fourth of producing tonnage remained outside, in competition. In the 1940 *Socony-Vacuum* opinion it was made clear that such cases would be exceptions: "Any combination which tampers with price structures is engaged in an unlawful activity. . . . raising, depressing, fixing, pegging or stabilizing the price of a commodity in interstate and foreign commerce is illegal *per se*."

The per se (in itself, or inherently) rule thus outlawed all agreements fixing prices or discounts, dividing the market, limiting production, or excluding other firms. Fines are now always imposed when such actions are proved, and jail terms are being given when the violation is deliberate.

It is accepted economic theory that in an oligopolistic situation the scarcity of competitors creates a psychological interdependence. Price-cutting is so much more certain to lead to quick retaliation in an oligopoly than in the case of many competitors that cuts are less likely to be made. Economists differ as to whether such a situation is to be deplored. The courts have not adopted a position that speaks of "tacit agreement" nor have they called it bad; on the other hand, they have not required the Department of Justice (or later, private parties seeking damages) to produce proof of conspiracy much more extensive than the identity of prices and trade practices of which the competitors are aware and which they want to keep.

Many court cases have resulted from attempts of the Justice Department to extend the antitrust law to business practices hitherto permitted and to experiments of business with new forms of contract or practice. Sometimes the business operation is held reasonable, sometimes not. The questioned agreements may be horizontal, i.e., between competitors, or vertical, i.e., between buyer and seller. Decisions have marked the limits of cooperation in voluntary retail chains and the limits of control over distributors by makers of machinery or transportation equipment and over franchise holders by restaurant chains and soft-drink producers. One use of the rule of reason by a trial court, not appealed to the Supreme Court, was in the *Investment Bankers* case of 1953: joint selling syndicates were judged reasonable in marketing new issues of securities. The *Standard Stations* decision of 1949 struck down contracts which let an oil refiner supply all the petroleum products and accessory supplies to service stations whose sales covered "a substantial share" of the market. But the *Tampa Electric* case of 1961 allowed a 20-year contract of this company to buy coal from a single supplier because of the security it gave both and because of the very small share of the market thus foreclosed.

There are also public restraints of trade, including licensing of occupations and regulation of certain industries. The trend of opinion among economists studying these issues in the late 1970s was to get away from such restraints by deregulation, where at all feasible, in the interests of free competition.

References

Handler, Milton, Harlan M. Blake, Robert Pitofsky, and Harvey Goldschmid, *Cases and Materials on Trade Regulation*, Foundation Press, Mineola, N.Y. 1975, with 1977 suppl.; Van Cise, Jerrold G., *Understanding the Antitrust Laws*, Practicing Law Institute, New York, 1976; Wilcox, Clair, and William G. Shepherd, *Public Policies Toward Business*, Irwin, Homewood, Ill., 1975.

(*See also* Antitrust policy; Competition; Government regulation of business; Mergers)

Simon N. Whitney

Return on investment

Return on investment (ROI) is a measure of the yield or return on invested capital, as in an existing business, or of the expected return on prospective investments, as in consideration of proposed plant or equipment purchases.

Return on invested capital (sometimes called ROE for return on equity) is usually a measure of the relative profitability of a firm or industry. A useful measure for analytical or comparative purposes, it is to be distinguished from perhaps the most popular measure of profitability, the sales margin, which is the percent of each sales dollar represented by profit.

Two Principal Measurements of ROI

The two principal measurements of ROI are ratios of net profit to net worth and of net profit to total assets.

The ROI ratio of net profit to net worth is commonly expressed as a percentage and shows the rate of return on equity capital, i.e., the original investment plus reinvested earnings. The percentage is derived by dividing net worth into net profit. The resulting percentage is an indication of the yield on the stockholders' accumulated investment.

$$\text{ROI for net worth} = \frac{\text{net profit (after taxes)}}{\text{net worth}}$$

For example

$$\frac{\$1,400,000}{\$10,000,000} = 14\%$$

The ROI ratio of net profit to total assets is also expressed as a percentage and is derived from dividing net profit by total investment, i.e., all assets. This percentage reveals the earning capability of the entire capital stock involved in the enterprise. The percentage can then be used to compare other potential investments open to management apart from further investment in the enterprise.

$$\text{ROI for total assets} = \frac{\text{net profit (after taxes)}}{\text{total assets}}$$

For example,

$$\frac{\$14,000,000}{\$200,000,000} = 7\%$$

Both ROI examples above enable management to get a better perspective on the profitability of the enterprise, especially in comparison with industry standards and the current cost of capital—e.g., interest rates.

Commonly, industrial firms attain their return on invested capital through high sales margins and low turnover, while retail firms make their ROI through low sales margins on high turnover. In broad industry numbers, the return on invested capital for industrial firms can be found in the *Quarterly Financial Report for Manufacturing Corporations,* published by the Federal Trade Commission.

Three Methods of Weighing Relative Profitability

ROI calculations on new investments are ways to plan fixed-asset expenditures, usually of large magnitude. They provide, in other words, methods of weighing the relative profitability of possible purchases of new plant or equipment against alternative investment opportunities over a span of years.

Three methods of weighing this profitability are payback, average rate of return, and discounted cash flow.

The popular payback method offers a means of determining the number of years of net attributable income required to recover a given investment. Payback calculations are simple to figure and easy to comprehend, and show the length of time of exposure to risk, including obsolescence. But the method is an indirect ROI. It does not tell of income generated beyond the payback time span nor does it take into account the way by which income is acquired i.e., the general pattern of cash throw-off over time. The accompanying table is illustrative of all three methods. It assumes the cost of Project X and Project Y to be $45,000 each and the estimated life of each project to be 8 years.

In the example, Project X would pay off in $1\frac{3}{4}$ years, and Project Y would pay off in $4\frac{1}{2}$; but in the fourth, fifth, sixth, seventh, and eighth years, Project Y would still be generating cash while Project X would not.

The relative profitability of each project is ignored by the payback method of ROI calculation; however, the average-rate-of-return method takes into account this profitability. Average cash flow under Project Y is $10,000, while under Project X it is only $7,500. By dividing the original investment of $45,000 into each of these figures, we find that the ROI, under the average-rate-of-return method, is 22.2 percent for Project Y and 16.7 percent for Project X. The average-rate-of-return method has the advantage of simplicity.

Payback on Projects X and Y

Year	Production gains before expenses		Expenses including depreciation* and taxes		Cash flow	
	X	Y	X	Y	X	Y
1	$70,000	$50,000	$40,000	$40,000	$30,000	$10,000
2	60,000	50,000	40,000	40,000	20,000	10,000
3	50,000	50,000	40,000	40,000	10,000	10,000
4	40,000	50,000	40,000	40,000	0	10,000
5	40,000	50,000	40,000	40,000	0	10,000
6	40,000	50,000	40,000	40,000	0	10,000
7	40,000	50,000	40,000	40,000	0	10,000
8	40,000	50,000	40,000	40,000	0	10,000

*Depreciation is treated differently under discounted cash flow.

The discounted-cash-flow ROI method not only considers the cost of capital funds over the life of the project but also allows for the differences in time during which the investments generate cash, which itself yields income. Thus, Project X generates $60,000 in 3 years during which time Project Y generates only $30,000. Allowing for these and the other income differences over the 8-year investment life, the ROI under the discounted-cash-flow method comes to 19.5 percent for Project X and 14.9 percent for Project Y.

References

Horngren, Charles T., *Cost Accounting: A Managerial Emphasis*, 4th ed., Prentice-Hall, Englewood Cliffs, N.J., 1977, especially pp. 375–423; Solomon, Ezra, *The Theory of Financial Mangement*, Columbia University Press, New York, 1963, especially pp. 120–137; Terborgh, George, *Business Investment Policy*, Machinery and Allied Products Institute, Washington, D.C., 1958; Weston, J. Fred, and Eugene F. Brigham, *Managerial Finance*, 6th ed., Dryden Press, Hinsdale, Ill., 1978; especially pp. 40–44, 283–340.

(*See also* Financial statements; Profits measurement; Risk premium on investment)

William H. Peterson

Right-to-work laws

Right-to-work laws are state laws which mandate that neither membership nor nonmembership in a labor union may be made a condition of new or continued employment. Such laws exist expressly in 20 states (Alabama, Arizona, Arkansas, Florida, Georgia, Iowa, Kansas, Louisiana, Mississippi, Nebraska, Nevada, North Carolina, North Dakota, South Carolina, South Dakota, Tennessee, Texas, Utah, Virginia, and Wyoming), plus American Samoa, and cover private-sector employment subject to a key federal statute, the National Labor Relations Act of 1935 (NLRA). More than 30 states offer right-to-work protections to at least some segment of their public employees. Finally, all federal (including postal) employees are protected by right-to-work legislative or executive order provisions.

The subject of considerable controversy in recent years, right-to-work laws have the practical effect of making illegal any closed shop, union shop, agency shop, or maintenance-of-membership clauses in union contracts. Indeed, where right-to-work protection exists, no person can be required as a condition of employment to join, assist, or support financially a labor organization.

History

Right-to-work laws are expressly provided for in section 14 (b) of the Taft-Hartley amendments (1947) to NLRA. Earlier, however, the National Industrial Recovery Act of 1933 (declared unconstitutional on other grounds in 1935) provided protections against compulsory unionism in section 7 (a), and the Railway Labor Act of 1926 was amended in 1934 to provide similar guarantees (amended later in 1951 to permit the union shop). The first state to provide express right-to-work protection was Florida in its 1944 constitutional amendments, thus preceding the passage of Taft-Hartley's section 14 (b) by some 3 years; the most recent state to pass such protective measures was Louisiana by statute in 1976.

Right-to-work political controversy occurred in 1965 when a concerted effort was made, with the active backing of President Lyndon Johnson, to repeal Taft-Hartley's section 14 (b). The effort failed, as have similar though less active attempts in later years. On the state level, right-to-work provisions have been enacted in a variety of ways (public referendum, statute, petition, constitutional amendment, etc). In only two cases has existing right-to-work protection in the private sector been removed (Indiana in 1965; Louisiana in 1956, but reenacted in broader form in 1976).

Union Benefit and Free-Rider Notions

Closely related to right to work as a phenomenon having economic implications are the concepts of union benefit and free rider. Proponents of compulsory unionism (in a sense, the antithetical position to right to work) argue that since unions supposedly benefit all whom they represent and since they must by law (with very few , limited exceptions) represent all employees in a bargaining unit (duty of fair representation) for which they are the certified agent, it follows that nonmember employees are free riders. Such employees enjoy the claimed benefits of union representation on terms and conditions of employment but, being nonmembers, pay none of the costs that the union incurs in representing them. Other arguments for compulsory unionism include the assertion that having all employees in the union brings stability to the work force, reduces the incidence of strikes (particularly unauthorized, or wildcat, strikes), enables the union to moderate its demands, furnishes members with psychic income, permits a grievance procedure, and provides the union with a steadier financial base.

Arguments for Right-to-Work Laws

Opponents of compulsory unionism (i.e., those who favor right-to-work laws) argue contrarily that stability is won at the expense of allegedly unchecked union discipline which interferes with the civil rights (e.g., the right not to join) of coerced members, that a union which doesn't need to perform services for employees as a means of convincing them that membership is a benefit may not be a responsible or responsive union, that strikes of all kinds appear not to have been reduced where compulsory unionism exists, and, generally, that too little factual evidence exists to support all the union proponents' claims. Most pertinently, right-to-work advocates have begun in recent years to challenge the fundamental factual basis of the union-benefit, free-rider argument by analyzing the employees' net returns attributable to union representation. Scholarly research, on the whole, had tended either to support these challenges or to erode the more extreme claims of economic harm allegedly stemming from right-to-work laws. Clearly, a considerable amount of research still needs to be done before these arguments can be sorted out by the thoughtful analyst or policymaker.

The right-to-work controversy is almost solely limited to the United States and Great Britain. The phrase may also be found in British political debates where it is solely a slogan of the radical left (particularly of Trotskyist factions), referring to an alleged responsibility of the government to provide employment to citizens.

References

Bennett, James T., and Manuel H. Johnson, "Free Riders in U.S. Labour Unions: Artifice or Affliction?", *British Journal of Industrial Relations*, vol. 27, no. 2, July 1979, pp. 158–172; Haggard, Thomas R., *Compulsory Unionism, the NLRB, and the Courts: A Legal Analysis of Union Security Agreements*, Labor Relations and Public Policy Series Report 15, Wharton School, Philadelphia, 1977; Hanslowe, Kurt, L., et al., *Union Security in Public Employment: Of Free Riding and Free Association*, Institute of Public Employment Monograph 8, New York State School of Industrial and Labor Relations, New York, 1978; Sultan, Paul, *Right to Work Laws: A Study in Conflict*, Institute of Industrial Relations Monograph 2, University of California, Los Angeles, 1958.

(*See also* Labor unions)

William H. Peterson

Risk premium on investment

The risk premium on investment is the incremental return required to compensate investors in projects with uncertain outcomes. In percentage terms, the risk premium is the difference between the rate of return required for a given project and a specified risk-free rate of return. The risk-adjusted rate of return on investment is the risk-free rate plus the risk premium.

Measurement of the risk premium has great practical importance for evaluating investment decisions in a world subject to random distances. Business executives and economists need a simple and accurate technique to quantify the risk premium. Such a technique must be grounded in sound economic principles to avoid a serious misallocation of capital.

Theorists and Risk Premium on Investment

The connection between risk and return on investment has been mentioned by classical economists from Adam Smith on. The primary emphasis of interest rate theorists such as Böhm-Bawerk and Fisher was the determination of an equilibrium rate of return in an environment of perfect foresight. The techniques of analysis of net present value and internal rate of return were developed in this classical framework.

Several economic theorists emphasized the importance of uncertainty in economic behavior. Frank Knight recognized the significance of random events in determining realized rates of return. Keynes stressed the role of expectations in selecting the level of investment. However, these economic theorists did not offer a model of a systematic relationship between risk and return.

Capital Asset Pricing Model

During the 1960s, research into the behavior of securities prices led to the formation of the Sharpe-Lintner-Mossin capital asset pricing model. This theory uses the variance in expected return of an investment as the measure of risk. Investors expect greater returns from higher-variance or riskier investment projects. Equilibrium among investors determines the risk premium associated with a given risk level. The securities markets reflect this equilibrium in the prices set for the claims to capital assets.

If the theoretical assumptions of this model can be accepted and if values can be assigned to a risk-free rate of return and the market price of risk, then the risk premium can be expressed as proportional to the expected rate of return on a market index:

$$E(R_i) - R_f = \beta_i[E(R_m) - R_f]$$

where $E(R_i)$ and $E(R_m)$ are the expected rates of return on project i and the market index, respectively; R_f is the risk-free rate of return; β_i is determined by the relative riskiness of the project in comparison with the market index. In empirical work β_i and $E(R_m) - R_f$ are frequently estimated using historical data on securities prices.

Importance of Risk Premium on Investment

The risk premium on investment is important in both theoretical and applied economics. In the theory of the firm, the risk premium refines the economist's understanding of optimal investment decisions. In macroeconomic theory, the connection is made between increased uncertainty and shocks to the economic system and the aggregate level of capital formation. On the applied side, the risk premium potentially offers an improved rule for the investment decision and an explanation for the different rates of return observed in various industries. In economic regulation, the risk premium has direct application in rate-setting cases.

Advantages and Disadvantages

Expression of the risk premium in terms of the capital asset pricing model has several advantages. The theory integrates the firm's evaluation of investment projects with the capital market's valuation of the claims to those assets. A numerical value for the risk premium can be estimated. Finally, the theory is buttressed by the empirical support for the capital asset pricing model.

Difficulties are found in this precise formulation of the risk premium. The capital asset pricing model specifies exactly the formation of expectations about the distribution of returns. Cash flows of a given project may not conform to this model. Even selection of the risk-free rate of return is complicated by expectations of future inflation rates. Several problems hamper calculation of β_i. For many projects adequate data on the cash flows are not available. Statistical methods used to estimate β_i are subject to errors, and controversy surrounds the choice of a market index.

Alternative approaches to the risk premiums have been suggested. Cash flows could be adjusted to their certainty-equivalent value and discounted at the risk-free rate of return. In practice, calculation of certainty equivalents can be cumbersome.

More elaborate models based on the pricing of stock options present similar computational problems.

The concept of the risk premium on investment is widely used in economics and is similarly defined in non-English dictionaries of economics.

References

Fama, Eugene F., "Risk-Adjusted Discount Rates and Capital Budgeting Under Uncertainty," *Journal of Financial Economics*, vol. 5, no. 1, August 1977, pp. 3–24; Hirschleifer, Jack, *Investment, Interest, and Capital*, Prentice-Hall, Englewood Cliffs, N.J., 1970; Knight, Frank H., *Risk, Uncertainty and Profit*, Houghton Mifflin, Boston, 1921; Knight, Frank H., "Interest," in Edwin R. A. Seligman and Alvin S. Johnson (eds.), *Encyclopedia of the Social Sciences*, vol. 7, Macmillan, New York, 1932, pp. 131–144; Knight, Frank H., "Profit," in Seligman and Johnson, ibid, vol. 12, pp. 480–486; Knight, Frank H., "Risk," in Seligman and Johnson, ibid., vol. 13, pp. 392–394; Myers, Stewart C., and Stuart M. Turnball, "Capital Budgeting and the Capital Asset Pricing Model: Good News and Bad News," *Journal of Finance*, vol. 23, no. 2, May 1977, pp. 321–332; Treynor, J. L., and F. Black, "Corporate Investment Policy," in S. C. Meyers (ed.), *Modern Developments in Financial Management*, Praeger, New York, 1976.

(*See also* Return on investment; Venture capital)

Joseph B. Starshak

Sampling in economics

The basis for most sampling work in economics is the statistical probability survey. A sample is selected from a particular population in such a way that every member of that population has a known probability of falling into the sample. This principle is refined in practice by stratifying a population into key segments and by clustering the sample selection process into relatively small geographic areas to save field costs.

For example, in a survey of manufacturing activity, the more than 3,000 counties in the country might be grouped into relatively homogeneous clusters, which then might be segmented into five categories on the basis of the extent of industrial activity in each segment. Then a few counties might be selected by some random probability process from each segment for inclusion in the sample. These probabilities of selection can be varied so that counties with very high industrial activity have a much higher probability of being included in the sample. The resulting stratified area probability sample can provide highly reliable, and statistically measurable, estimates of industrial activity for relatively low cost.

Without sample surveys, the study of economics as we know it today would not exist. In the United States, as in virtually all other countries, survey methods serve as the basis for the collection of basic data on the economic system and on the response of businesses and the consumers to government actions. For example, sample survey methods are used by the government to collect data on retail and wholesale prices, on employment and unemployment, on business investment, and on international trade to name a few target areas. Indeed, without the survey method, it would be impossible to collect such data since collecting data for an entire nation, or even for a small city, on employment and unemployment, for example, would be prohibitively expensive. As a result, a complete census (which technically is a 100 percent sample) is carried out only where absolutely necessary or when it is mandated by law, as with the decennial Census of Population in the United States. More-over, it may seem rather paradoxical that when the census is taken, survey methods are frequently used to supplement it, since such methods are the only efficient way to evaluate the reliability of the data and to estimate the extent of undercoverage of the census.

State, regional, and local governments also use sample surveys, though not as extensively as the federal government, since they obtain a great deal of data on their areas from the federal government surveys. When they do use survey methods, they are more likely to subcontract the work to a nonprofit or commercial survey agency since, unlike the federal government, they do not usually have their own survey resources. Types of economic data collected by these agencies include travel patterns of people within an area (such as origin-and-destination studies), tourist character-istics and expenditures, business employment practices, and farm-family expenses and living practices.

Survey Functions

Sample surveys fulfill four broad functions in economics.

1. They measure the state of the economy. The United States government, as well as governments in most other countries, uses sample surveys to collect contin-uing information on such key indicators as prices, retail sales, employment and unemployment, industry sales, business investments, and consumer income. Business and nonprofit organizations collect similar indicators on economic activity of special interest to themselves.

2. They gauge the effect of alternative policies. For example, no new product is put into full production by a manufacturer without first test marketing it on a sample basis and ascertaining consumer reactions. Government agencies test new policies by sampling consumers to ascertain their reactions. In recent years, this approach has been systematized in terms of the so-called social experiments on economic policy. These involve putting a new program into practice in a few selected areas for anywhere from 3 to 10 years and using sur-vey methods to measure the effects of this program. For example, a possible national program of cash housing allowances was tested during the late 1970s and early 1980s by actually making cash allowances to low-income families in selected parts of the country and studying the families' use of this money and its effect on the housing market.

3. They aid study of attitudes and the motivations for economic behavior. Obtain-ing so-called soft data, such as attitudes and intentions regarding buying, is now fairly common in economic analysis. Thus, in the United States, the Conference Board, as well as the University of Michigan Survey Research Center, collects continuing information on consumer attitudes and financial expectations. For business, the Bureau of Economic Analysis of the U.S. Department of Com-merce, as well as the McGraw-Hill Publications Company, collects information from samples of business firms on sales expectations, capital expenditure plans, and the investment outlook. Such data are used not only to analyze the current business situation but also to make short-run economic predictions, and they frequently appear in econometric models.

4. They develop more cost-effective methods of obtaining economic data. Empirical economists are continually seeking more reliable and economical ways of using sample surveys to improve knowledge of the economic system. While the amounts spent for methodological research are very small, such research is nevertheless carried out by various government agencies and university research centers. It involves such tasks as seeking cheaper ways of selecting samples for equal reliability, measuring biases due to nonresponse, and measuring the effect of question wording on responses to particular questions. As a result of such research it is possible, for example, to get highly accurate estimates of the extent of umemployment among particular population groups in the country with samples of only a few hundred or a few thousand people in each group.

Low-Cost High-Reliability Sampling Methods and Innovations

Monthly estimates of changes in economic indicators such as consumer prices or unemployment are made even more efficient by reinterviewing parts of a sample for several additional months on a rotational basis. This quasi-panel approach helps to reduce field costs even further and helps to eliminate errors due to sampling variability.

A major improvement in the efficiency of sample surveys in economics has been the growing use of the telephone to conduct interviews both with consumers and with business firms. With approximately 95 percent of the dwelling units in the United States having telephones, conducting a survey by telephone usually provides as much coverage as in a personal interview survey, and at a fraction of the cost. Moreover, the use of random-digit-dialing sampling techniques ensures that even unlisted telephone numbers have an equal probability of inclusion in a sample. While telephone surveys involve certain pitfalls of their own, such as inducing respondents to consult records in a financial study, they are especially effective in panel studies and in follow-up interviews on a regular study.

Another major innovation in the use of sample survey methods in economics, an innovation which is in its infancy, is the use of computers to simplify and increase the accuracy of all aspects of the survey operation. Thus, computers are being used to select probability samples from populations that are in computer files; computers are being used to instruct telephone interviewers as to what questions to ask in an interview, and in what sequence; and computers are being used to record immediately in a computer file responses to telephone and personal interview surveys. As a result, the traditional practice of handcoding survey responses may soon be obsolete for many types of surveys. The availability of the data in a computer file makes possible almost instantaneous checks for consistency of the replies and offers the possibility of providing the economists with tabulations virtually overnight.

Survey Agencies and Centers

Sample surveys in economics are generally carried out by government agencies, business organizations, and university survey research centers. The collection of national economic statistics in some countries is often concentrated in a so-called central statistical agency, as, for example, in Canada—all of its national government data are collected by a single agency known as Statistics, Canada. In the United States, the collection of economic statistics, whether by survey methods or by other methods, is decentralized. The principal data-collection agency, the U.S. Bureau of the Census, is responsible for the decennial censuses as well as for the periodic business and agriculture censuses. It also conducts monthly surveys on employment, unemployment, and retail sales, as well as annual surveys on a wide variety of activities including housing, transportation, and manufacturing. The Bureau of Labor Statistics collects information on consumer and wholesale prices and on working conditions; the National Center for Health Statistics of the U.S. Department of Health and Human Services collects information on the health status of the population; the U.S. Department of Agriculture collects information on farm prices and the economic status of farmers; and so on.

There is some coordination of these activities through the U.S. Office of Management and the Budget, an agency which is also entrusted with the review of regular survey programs, but such coordination is at best loose. In addition, regulatory agencies of the government, such as the Federal Trade Commission and the Food and Drug Administration, may survey businesses or consumers to obtain economic data relevant to their operations. Such surveys are in fact not subject to the review mechanism of the Office of Management and the Budget.

Business trade associations and nonprofit organizations are continually making economic surveys for the benefit of their constituents. Thus, the Conference Board makes surveys of business practices; the Institute of Life Insurance conducts surveys of both consumers and businesses on topics dealing with life insurance; the American Association of Advertising Agencies surveys activities in advertising; and so on.

Most major corporations, especially those handling consumer goods and services, engage in sample surveys of their own to find out how they are doing vis-a-vis their competitors and what consumers think of their products. They may do this through research departments of their own or by commissioning surveys through marketing research firms.

Various university survey research centers also engage in economic surveys. Some of these survey centers not only do survey research but also have nationwide samples and field staffs and collect economic data nationwide; these centers include the Survey Research Center of the University of Michigan, the National Opinion Research Center of the University of Chicago, and the Research Triangle in North Carolina. Other survey centers are more localized in nature and focus more on research on the methodology of economic surveys; these include the Survey Research Laboratory of the University of Illinois and the Survey Research Centers of the University of California at Berkely and at Los Angeles.

References

Lansing, John B., and James N. Morgan, *Economic Survey Methods*, Institute for Survey Research, University of Michigan, Ann Arbor, 1971.

(*See also* Computers in economics; Data banks; Marketing research and business economics; Statistical techniques in economics and business, an overview)

Robert Ferber

Saving

Saving is the process of withholding current income for future use and results in the accumulation of tangible and financial assets. The amounts so accumulated over past periods are referred to as savings. The reverse of saving, that is, when current expenditures exceed current income, is termed dissaving. Saving and dissaving occur within all three major groups of the economy-individuals, business, and government. Two concepts of saving are used in national income accounting—net saving and gross saving. On a net basis, individuals save when personal income after taxes exceeds personal outlays, business saves through retained profits, and governments save when current receipts exceed current expenditures. Gross saving includes, in addition, depreciation allowances covering the wear and tear on real assets for future replacement.

Gross Saving

Gross national saving is the source for additions to the stock of tangible assets, including investment in homes as well as in business inventories and plant and equipment. In fact, for the economy as a whole, gross saving equals gross investment. Although portions of the amounts spent on such investments during a period are provided directly by the savers purchasing the real assets, the bulk is usually borrowed from other savers in the capital markets, either directly or indirectly through financial intermediaries. The channels through which gross saving flows into gross investment, including financial intermediaries, are traced in the flow-of-funds accounts. The accompanying table shows the major categories of gross saving and gross investment from the income and output sides of the national income accounts:

Gross saving		Gross investment
Personal saving		Gross private domestic investment
Corporate profits (undistributed)		Plant and equipment
Capital consumption allowances		Residential buildings
Government surplus or deficit (−)		Business inventories
		Net foreign investment
Total gross saving	=	Total gross investment

By far the major portion of gross saving consists of capital consumption allowances, which accrue chiefly to the business sector; only a minor portion is attributable to owner-occupied homes. Together with undistributed corporate profits, the saving represented by business capital consumption allowances supplies funds for replacement, and some expansion, of plant and equipment. However, personal saving is the pivotal component of providing funds for the economy to grow through healthy rates of investment. Government saving covers the surplus or deficit, on a national income accounts basis, of the federal, state, and local governments combined and is subject to the host of political and other factors, including the state of the economy, which affect tax rates and collections and budget spending. Government saving is only a small part of gross saving or dissaving except in war or recession. A deficit reduces the total amount of saving in the economy (assuming that other factors remain the same), while a surplus increases saving on a net basis and, since no depreciation is assumed for the government sector, on a gross basis as well. Foreign-sector transactions do not add to national savings, but the resulting investment or disinvestment abroad represents a positive or negative use of saving.

Capital consumption allowances tend to rise year after year with the expansion of the capital stock and, since they are based on replacement cost, with the rate of inflation. Also, as economic conditions fluctuate, and as capital outlays or retirements are stepped up or cut back, the rate of growth may speed up or slow down. In contrast, the other component of business saving, undistributed corporate profits (noncorporate business profits are included in personal saving), show much wider variation from year to year with the state of the economy, and, even though inventory profits are excluded, with the rate of inflation, as business sales rise or fall faster than expenses. In addition, undistributed corporate profits may be affected by changes in tax provisions and rates and by increases or decreases in the proportion of profits paid out as dividends.

Personal Saving

Personal saving, in the national income accounts represents the residual obtained by subtracting personal outlays from disposable personal income. Disposable personal income consists of the aftertax income of individuals from wage and salaries (including fringe benefits or other labor income); from noncorporate businesses and professionals; and from rents, dividends, interest, and transfer payments, less social insurance contributions. Personal outlays include personal consumption expenditures, interest paid by consumers, and personal transfer payments to foreigners. The personal saving rate, i.e., the percentage of personal saving to disposable personal income, has varied widely over the years usually fluctuating with the ups and downs of the business cycle, but at times showing divergent movements. During the Depression years 1932-33, the personal saving rate was negative (there was dissaving), while during the war years 1942-45, the saving rate was around 20 to 25 percent. After wide fluctuations in the immediate postwar and Korean war years (8.5 to 2.9 percent), the range of fluctuation became more moderate, varying by only about $1\frac{1}{2}$ percentage points up or down from the 6.2 percent average over the years 1952 to 1979.

Conceptually, personal saving also represents the changes in net worth of individuals. Since individuals place the amounts saved from current income into tangible and financial assets and incur debts in the process of acquiring assets, the change in net worth should equal the amount of personal saving out of income. Statistics on changes in net worth of individuals are available from the flow-of-funds accounts. However, personal saving, as calculated from the changes in assets and liabilities of individuals in the flow-of-funds accounts, does not match the amount of personal saving as calculated from the national income accounts. The statistical discrepancies are larger than would be expected to arise from timing or other usual statistical difficulties and may represent underreporting of income (in the "underground" economy) or misreporting of some of the other aggregates involved. The reconciliation between personal saving on a flow-of-funds basis and on a national income accounts basis is illustrated by the accompanying table.

Personal Saving, 1979

(Billions of dollars)

Net increase in financial assets*	250.9
Plus: Net investment in tangible assets†	63.8
Less: Net increase in debt‡	208.6
Equals: Personal saving, flow-of-funds basis	106.1
Less: Discrepancy	33.3
Equals: Personal saving, NIA basis	72.8

*Demand deposits and currency; time and savings accounts; mutual and money-market fund shares; federal, corporate and municipal securities; private insurance and pension reserves; security credit; and miscellaneous financial assets of individuals.
†Gross investment, less capital consumption allowances, in nonfarm homes and noncorporate plant and equipment and inventories of individuals.
‡Mortgages, consumer credit, bank and other loans, security credit, and miscellaneous debt of individuals.

Saving Behavior of Individuals

Many theories have been advanced and empirical studies made to explain the saving behavior of individuals, both as separate entities or groups and in the aggregate. Basically, individuals forgo spending all of their income, and thus save, in order to have assets in the future to meet unexpected emergencies, to purchase goods and services in the future, to provide retirement income, or to leave to beneficiaries. Saving for a rainy day and habits of thrift have been extolled in the folklore. However, in practice, preferences for future over current consumption vary widely, with some groups being dissavers or low savers and others average or high savers. Empirical studies have shown that the percentage of income saved rises the older the age group up to the time of retirement. It has also been demonstrated that, not only the amount but also the percentage saved tends to be higher the higher the income group and that groups having generally more volatile incomes, such as salespersons and farmers, tend to have higher saving rates.

Classical economic theory related changes in the aggregate saving rate to the rate of interest, but recent theory revolves around the consumption function, that is, the percentage of income spent, or the obverse of the saving rate. Under Keynesian theory, it is assumed that consumption is a stable and dependable function of real income and that, as the aggregate real income of the economy increases, consumption does not rise proportionately, causing the saving rate to rise. The relative income hypothesis questions this formulation, holding that consumption is a social phenomenon, with interdependent spending patterns, as the result of "keeping up with the Joneses" and also as the result of past patterns of expenditure; thus, the aggregate saving rate is affected by many factors, including the age distribution of the population, the rate of growth of income, the distribution of income, and expectations of future income. The thesis that spending patterns change slowly as circumstances change was refined by the permanent income hypothesis, which holds that consumption is determined by longer-range income considerations, ie., consumption behavior is determined by perceptions of permanent income. A slightly different approach taken in the life-cycle theory argues that consumption is scaled according to perceived needs and expectations of income over the life cycle. The effects of changes in interest rates and of inflation on personal saving, which have recently come to the limelight, are acknowledged in these theories as factors if the changes are large.

The impact of wealth on saving has long been recognized in theory, but its effects on the aggregate personal saving rate have been considered to be overshadowed by other factors. Recently, however, with inflation causing prices of tangible assets to rise sharply and changes in net worth based on rising market values giving the illusion of well-being, the magnitude of the impact of wealth on the saving rate may have to be reassessed. The personal saving rate does not include either realized or unrealized capital gains or losses. Nor, on a national income accounts basis, does it include amounts spent on big-ticket consumer durable goods, such as automobiles, appliances, and jewelry (which are deducted from income as part of expenditures on consumer durable goods in obtaining personal saving). In the flow-of-funds accounts an alternate saving rate is provided which includes net expenditures on all consumer durable goods (including blankets, pillows, and eyeglasses), but this is also unsatisfactory as a basis for concluding how individuals assess their own net worth, a factor which may influence their spending and saving.

Savings Rates in Foreign Countries

Saving rates in countries abroad have been shown to be higher the higher the rate of economic growth, the higher the proportion of the working-age population, and the higher the per capita income. Retirement rates have also been found to have a bearing. Based on national income concepts, which differ somewhat from country to country, saving rates in other industrialized countries currently run much higher than in the United States. In the late 1970s, the published personal saving rates averaged over 15 percent in Italy, Japan, and France; 12.5 to 15 percent in West Germany, the Netherlands, and the United Kingdom; and around 10 percent in Canada, versus the current 4 to 5 percent in the United States. The variations arise not only because of differences in institutional arrangements (as well as in the statistical bases of the computations) but also because of different income and demographic factors and differing attitudes toward protection against the future.

References

Ando, Albert, and Franco Modigliani, "The Life Cycle Hypothesis of Saving: Aggregate Implications and Tests," *American Economic Review*, vol. 53, no. 1, March 1963, pp. 55–84; Board of Governors, Federal Reserve System, *Flow of Funds Accounts*, published quarterly; Bureau of Economic Analysis, *Survey of Current Business*, U.S. Department of Commerce, July: National Income issues; Duesenberry, James S., *Income, Saving, and the Theory of Consumer Behavior*, Harvard University Press, Cambridge, Mass., 1949; Feldstein, Martin, "Social Security and Saving: The Extended Life Cycle Theory," *American Economic Review*, vol. 66, no. 2, May 1976, pp. 77–86; Friedman, Milton, *A Theory of the Consumption Function*, National Bureau of Economic Research, Princeton University Press, Princeton, N.J., 1957.

(*See also* Chicago school; Classical school; Consumer theory; Consumption function; Disposable personal income; Flow of funds; Income; Keynesian economics; National income accounting; Permanent income hypothesis; Propensity to consume or to save and inducement to invest; Wealth)

Sally S. Ronk

Say's law of markets

The most popular and simultaneously most controversial definition of Say's law of markets is Keynes' concise dictum: supply creates its own demand. Keynes interpreted the classicists, i.e., pre-1930s orthodox economists, and J. B. Say in particular, as stating that production (supply) generates income which will be used completely and instantaneously to purchase (demand) commodities so supply creates its own demand at all times. Say's law holds in a barter economy where commodities are exchanged for commodities, but such is not the case in a monetary economy.

Production does indeed generate income for workers and capitalists. However, in a monetary economy income need not be spent completely and instantaneously on commodities. Individuals may prefer to hoard their income temporarily or expend it on financial assets. When this is the case, current supply exceeds the demand for commodities. Firms respond by curtailing production, and incomes fall. If Keynes' version of Say's law held, however, recessions would never occur since demand would always be sufficient to justify full-employment output, which is in the self-interest of firms to produce because full-employment output is also the profit-maximizing level of output. As technical progress and other factors cause output to increase over time, the economy would adjust automatically to its potential without need of government intervention. Economies unfortunately do not always produce maximum potential output. The existence of recessions is sufficient evidence to invalidate Say's law, as defined by Keynes. Government spending is the Keynesian remedy for recessions.

After being translated from the French, J. B. Say's *Treatise* quickly became one of the most popular economics textbooks in early-nineteenth-century America largely because it was easier reading than Adam Smith's *Wealth of Nations*. The expository skills which served Say well as a popularizer of Smith were unsuited to the precise and clear expression of complex theory demanded by the select circle of professional economists. Say spent more than a decade attempting to clarify and explain the law of markets, with little success. In large part Keynes was merely echoing charges levied earlier by Malthus and other so-called unorthodox nineteenth-century economists. On the basis of Say's writings alone, the Malthus-Keynes version of the law of markets is not an unreasonable interpretation. However, the Malthus-Keynes version clearly misinterprets the law as expressed by many of Say's supporters, most notably J. S. Mill (1844). Mill viewed his statement of the law as only an improvement in Say's exposition, without changing in any way Say's thought. The debate over the law of markets died from exhaustion without resolve, but the majority sided with Say and Mill.

When Keynes rekindled the debate approximately a century later, the weight of his international reputation, combined with the advantage of being the initial salvo, quickly convinced most economists, unaware of the original sources, of the validity of Keynes' interpretation. Most current elementary textbooks accept the Malthus-Keynes version of Say's law, thereby placing Say in a lower circle of economists. Keynes' interpretation did not go unchallenged for long, however. The universally respected historian of economic analysis Joseph Schumpeter strongly defended Say against the Malthus-Keynes criticisms and most advanced books now side with Schumpeter.

The alternative version of Say's law states that demand is and will remain insatiable, so demand cannot explain the growth of output over time. Growth is due to increasing productive capacity. Insatiable demands are not always manifested, so recessions occur temporarily. Ultimately, however, the insatiable demands are revealed, and increasing production is justified. This implies that developing countries can ignore demand and concentrate on transportation, education, and other supply-oriented policies. Workers in general need not be afraid of being permanently displaced by machines. Say's law also implies that recessions are not cured by curtailing supply or by make-work policies. While this may seem obvious, soil banks and featherbedding are but two policies indicating ignorance of Say's law.

References

Keynes, J. M., *The General Theory of Employment, Interest and Money*, Harcourt Brace Jovanovich, New York, 1936, chaps. 2, 3; Mill, J. S., *Essays on Some Unsettled Questions of Political Economy*, Parker, London, 1844, essay 2; Say, J. B., *Treatise on Political Economy*, Grigg R. Elliott, Philadelphia, 1834, chap. 15; Schumpeter, J. A., *History of Economic Analysis*, Oxford University Press, New York, 1954, pp. 615–625; Sowell, T., *Say's Law: A Historical Analysis*, Princeton University Press, Princeton, N.J., 1972.

(*See also* Classical school; Propensity to consume or to save and inducement to invest; Supply-side economics)

Paul A. Meyer

Scarcity

Scarcity and abundance are relative, and vague, descriptions of the availability of useful resources for human purposes. Any resource which commands a price in economic transactions—resources as diverse as fertile soil, machines, or human talent—may be called scarce. The rationale for this market-oriented definition is that at a lower price some economic agents would desire to employ more of the particular resource. In other words, when a resource commands a price in the market, some potential users will be induced to forgo otherwise rewarding applications of the resource.

The money price used in unrestricted economic transactions is a useful measuring rod for scarcity, but money prices are an artifact of social organization, while scarcity is a more basic aspect of the physical universe. A more precise concept is that of a physical limit to the availability of a productive resource during a given time interval. Such a limit may or may not be a constraint on human activities in the sense of not permitting all feasible and desired uses. For example, refined metal is generally scarce and constraining, while sunlight is not.

Allocation of Resources

A central feature of economic science is the analysis of how economic agents make constrained choices and how government actions or other social institutions influence the use of scarce resources. In a system of voluntary exchange, a resource will be allocated to uses that return the greatest value to the owner. When property rights are unclear and conflicting or when distortions of incentives occur owing to taxation and regulation, resources may not be allocated efficiently in a market system. Moreover, because the economic agents have imperfect knowledge, the forecasts and plans of all agents may be mutually inconsistent, giving rise to idle resources or other macroeconomic disturbance and instability.

When government takes more of a command role in the allocation of productive resources, some sort of central plan is formulated to decide the merits of alternative uses of a scarce resource. Since a major productive resource is human labor, government agents cannot take a complete command role in response to scarcity without costly overpowering of basic human instincts. When government takes an incomplete command role, it will incur costs of enforcing behavior contrary to private incentives. It may be suggested that under siege or other emergency conditions a central plan regulating in detail the use of a scarce resource tends to be faithfully accepted.

Prospects for Scarcity

In recent years some analysts have presented alarming forecasts of the consequences of growing human populations, growing levels of unhealthy environmental pollution, and acutely perceived limits on agricultural production and fossil fuel. Questions have been raised as to whether human societies will respond to depletion of particular resources and more acute scarcity in such a way as to avert catastrophic suffering and mortality. A presentation of these prospects by Meadows et al. (1972) has been reviewed and challenged by economist Robert Solow (1973). Since resources becoming more scarce in relation to demand will command higher prices, the development of substitutes and changes in lifestyle will be encouraged as economic agents find these methods of accommodation privately rewarding. Excellent historical examples involving such materials as lead, copper, and iron may be cited. Solow argues that prices of natural resources have shown no tendency to rise relative to other goods in the past 50 years. Are the new prospects really a radical break with history?

Economists have discussed the long-term relative scarcity of agricultural land since at least the work of Thomas Malthus. Fears of the eighteenth century that starvation was a primary check on human population and that all fruits of technical progress would be captured by landowners have proved unfounded in the developed nations. More recently, concerns about catastrophic food scarcity have been revived in light of rapid population growth in poorer nations. Death rates have declined very rapidly since 1945, but birthrates have not fallen to a corresponding degree. Some countries are, therefore, quite vulnerable to sudden food-supply reductions. This situation may pose a more serious long-term threat to international peace and human welfare than the more acute natural or artificial scarcity of petroleum.

References

Department of Economic and Social Affairs, *The Determinants and Consequences of Population Growth*, United Nations, New York, 1973; Meadows, Donnella, Dennis Meadows, Jorgen Randers, and William Behrens, III, *The Limits to Growth*, Universe Books, New York, 1972; Samuelson, Paul, *Economics*, McGraw-Hill, New York, 1976, chap. 1; Solow, Robert, "Is the End of the World at Hand?", *Challenge*, Vol. 16, no. 1, March–April 1973, pp. 39–50.

(*See also* Distribution theory; Malthusian theory of population; Zero economic growth; Zero population growth)

Bernard S. Friedman

Seasonal adjustment methods

The estimation of seasonal variations has always been a complex problem because seasonality varies and is not directly observable. Changes in economic phenomena result from many forces and, therefore, do not follow a set path with mathematical rigidity. The statistician's task has been to find methods that allow for constantly changing conditions. Estimations of the seasonal variations are currently mainly based on univariate time series models. The basic assumption for this approach is that the observed time series can be decomposed into a systematic part that is a well-determined function of time and into a random part that obeys a probability law. The random element is assumed to be identically distributed with constant mean, constant variance, and zero autocorrelation.

Most methods of estimation and their corresponding computer programs are based on regression methods or on linear smoothing filters such as moving averages. The optimality of each method depends on the fulfillment of the assumptions upon which it relies. Because there is no unique model applicable to all time series in all situations, no method of estimation should be used uncritically as the one given, unique optimal solution. This, however, does not preclude a larger scope of applications for some methods than for others. There are two main methodological approaches to which the majority of the methods belong.

Regression Methods

The use of regression methods is not new. In the late thirties, several statisticians proposed to fit polynomials by the least-squares method to estimate the seasonal adjustments. The regression methods assume that the systematic part of a time series can be approximated closely by simple functions of time over the entire span of the series. In general, two types of functions of time are considered. One is a polynomial of fairly low degree that fulfills the assumption that the economic phenomenon moves slowly, smoothly, and progressively through time (trend). The other is a linear combination of sines and cosines of different frequencies representing oscillations, strictly periodic or not, that also affect the total variation of the series (cycle and seasonals).

These functions are estimated by least-squares methods. For efficient estimates, the random component must be independent; otherwise, an appropriate version of generalized least squares must be applied. For certain regression functions, such as fixed periodic functions, polynomial time trends, and interaction of the two, ordinary least-squares estimates are asymptotically efficient if the random part is second-order stationary, that is, the mean and variance are constant and the covariance is a function only of the time lag. Therefore, if differences are taken to ensure stationariness, ordinary least squares are generally adequate. If the relationship among the components is multiplicative, the standard procedure is to take logarithms, and then differences, in order to transform the generating mechanism of the series into an additive form with a stationary random term.

The most common model specified for the decomposition of an economic time series by regression methods assumes a stable or linearly moving seasonality and a trend cycle represented by a polynomial of a relatively low degree. Unless the parameters are assumed to vary within the time span of the series, these models lack flexibility and imply a deterministic behavior of the components. For these reasons, regression methods have seldom been applied for time series decomposition; rather, they have been applied to estimate seasonality in econometric models by inserting dummy variables that capture the seasonal variations of the related variables.

Linear Smoothing Techniques

The seasonal adjustment of economic time series with linear smoothing filters, or moving averages, was known in the early twenties but seldom applied. One of the main reasons for this fact was that the best-known seasonal annihilator, the centered 12-month moving average, was found to be a poor trend-cycle estimator.

The majority of the seasonal adjustment methods today officially adopted by statistical agencies are based in linear smoothing procedures. These methods assume that systematic components of a time series do not fluctuate greatly in any small interval of time, but still cannot be well-approximated by simple functions of time over the entire range of the series. The assumptions are made for subintervals. They are of a local character, whereas those of regression methods concern the entire interval. Methods based on linear smoothing techniques can adequately estimate seasonal variations, trends, and cycles that change in a stochastic manner; that is, as new observations enter into the series, the level and/or the slope of the systematic components change adaptively.

The simplest method of smoothing data is to take a moving weighted average of the data and center the results. The weights are moved one position to the right of the observed data to obtain successive smoothed values. The weights can be obtained by fitting polynomials or by summation formulas developed by actuaries. In the first case, the weights are functions of the length of the moving average, say $2m + 1$, and of the degree of the polynomial to be fitted, say $p < 2m + 1$.

On the other hand, the basic principle of the summation formulas is the combination of operations of differencing and summation in such a manner that when differencing above a certain order is neglected, these formulas will reproduce the functions operated on. Today, the most widely applied methods of seasonal adjustment, the method II X-11 variant and the X-11-ARIMA (autoregressive integrated moving averages) method are based on moving-average techniques. The basic assumptions of these two methods are implicit in the kind of moving averages they use for the decomposition. These moving averages first detrend the data and then remove the seasonal variations. For central observations (approximately all the values of the series except those corresponding to the first and last 3 years), both methods make the assumption that the trend cycle follows a cubic within the span of 1 or 2 years depending on the amount of irregular variations, and that the seasonal variations, for each month separately, can be well-approximated by a straight line over the span of 7 years. These assumptions are adequate for a large class of economic time series. For current observations, however, the X-11 moving averages approximate well only a straight line for the trend cycle and a constant for the seasonals. On the other hand, the X-11-ARIMA uses a flexible combination of weights that adapts to the series in question. These weights capture the most recent movements of the series. They result from the combination of the extrapolation of ARIMA models that fit and extrapolate series with the fixed smoothing filters of the X-11 method. Contrary to regression methods, moving-average procedures are mainly useful for the decomposition of single time series, particularly for their seasonal adjustments.

References

Dagum, Estela Bee, *The X-11-ARIMA Seasonal Adjustment Method*, Statistics Canada, Catalogue No. 12-564 E, Ottawa, 1979; Kendall, Maurice G., and A. Stuart, *The Advanced Theory of*

Statistics, vol. 3, Hafner, New York, 1966; Shiskin, Julius, Allan A. Young, and John C. Musgrave, *The X-11-Variant of Census Method II Seasonal Adjustment*, U.S. Bureau of the Census Technical Paper 15, 1967; Zellner, Arnold (ed.), *Seasonal Analysis of Economic Time Series*, U.S. Bureau of the Census, 1978.

(*See also* Index numbers; Regression analysis in business and economics; Seasonal variations in economic time series; Secular trend; Statistical techniques in economics and business, an overview; Time series analysis)

Estela Bee Dagum

Seasonal variations in economic time series

A great deal of information on economic activity occurs in the form of time series where observations are dependent and the nature of this dependence is of interest in itself. The time series are generally compiled for consecutive and equal periods, such as weeks, months, quarters, or years.

Traditionally, four types of movements have been distinguished in the analysis of economic time series, namely, (1) the trend, (2) the cycle, (3) the seasonal variations, and (4) the irregular fluctuations. The feasibility of this decomposition is basic for time series analysis, the study of the cycle and economic growth, and the study of seasonality. The four components are not directly observable and, therefore, assumptions must be made on their behavioral pattern.

The trend corresponds to a variation persisting over a long period of time. It tends to be associated with the structural causes of the phenomenon in question. In some cases, the trend shows a steady growth; in others, it may move downward as well as upward.

The cycle is a quasi-periodic oscillation characterized by alternating periods of expansion and contraction. It is generally associated with the current state of the economy and referred to as the business cycle. It lasts from 3 to 4 years on average. For much analytical work, the trend and the cycle are combined because, for series covering relatively short periods, the trend loses importance.

The seasonal variations represent the effect of the climatic and institutional events that repeat more or less regularly each year. They affect the evolutions of economic time series recorded only for periods of less than a year.

The irregular fluctuations represent unforeseeable movements related to events of all kinds. They have a stable random appearance but, in some cases, extreme values may be present. These extreme values, or outliers, have identifiable causes, such as strikes or unseasonal weather, and, therefore, can be distinguished from the much smaller irregular variations.

Nature of Seasonal Variations

There is no important economic series which shows only trend, or only seasonal variations, or only irregulars. These components are interrelated and for most economic series they influence one another. Among these components, the influence of the seasonal fluctuations in human activity has long been recognized. The organization of society, the means of production and communication, the habits of consumption, and other social and religious events have been strongly conditioned by both climatic and conventional seasons. The seasonal variations in agriculture and construction, the high pre-Easter and pre-Christmas retail sales are well known. There are three main characteristics of seasonality. (1) The phenomenon repeats each year with certain regularity, but it may evolve; (2) it can be estimated and separated from the other factors that affect the total variations of the series; and (3) it is caused mainly by non-economic forces, exogenous to the economic system, that cannot be controlled or modified by decision makers, at least in the short run.

Changes in the seasonal patterns of a given series can be due to several reasons. A decline in the importance of the primary sector in the gross national product modifies seasonal patterns in the economy as a whole, as does a change in the geographical distribution of industry in a country extending over several climatic zones. Changes in technology alter the importance of climatic factors. For most economic time series, an evolving seasonality is more the rule than the exception. This is particularly true for long series of 20 years or more. The assumptions of stable seasonality, that is, of seasonality that repeats exactly every year, is good for a few series only. Depending on the main causes of seasonality the seasonal variations can change slowly or rapidly, gradually or abruptly, and in a deterministic manner or in a stochastic manner.

Various models have been proposed for gradual changes in seasonal variations, whether of a stochastic or of a deterministic type. These models have been grouped into two main categories—models that assume that the generating process of seasonal variations varies in amplitude only and those that assume it varies in both amplitude and phase. The assumption that seasonality changes gradually, slowly, and in a stochastic manner is, perhaps, the most widely applied one today.

A second characteristic of seasonality is that the phenomenon can be separated from the other forces—trend, cycle, and irregulars—that influence the movement of the series and that it can be estimated adequately. The seasonal variations are distinguished from trend by their oscillating character, from the cycle by being confined within the limits of an annual period, and from the irregulars by being systematic.

Finally, the third characteristic, i.e., that the main causes of seasonality are exogenous to the economic system, is the main reason for the removal of seasonality from the observed series to produce a seasonally adjusted series. The adjusted series thus reflects only variations in the trend, the cycle, and the irregulars. The removal of the seasonal variations from a time series, however, does not indicate how the series would have moved had there been no seasonal variations; rather, it shows more clearly the trend cycle abstracted from seasonality.

Seasonally Adjusted Data and Economic Analysis

The information given by seasonally adjusted series plays an important role in the analysis of current economic conditions, particularly in determining the stage of the cycle at which the economy stands. Such knowledge is useful in forecasting subsequent cyclical movements and provides the basis for decision making to alter the level of economic activity. It is particularly important around turning points because, for example, failure to recognize a downturn in the business cycle may lead to the adoption of policies to curb expansion when, in fact, a recession is under way.

In the absence of seasonally adjusted data, analysts who wish to get a picture of the economic situation undistorted by exogenous variables related to seasonal variations may make comparisons with the same month of the year before. Such comparisons however, show only what has happened a year after, not what was happening during the year and not what is happening currently. To evaluate the current state of the economy, the analyst should be able to measure cyclical changes for each month over less than a 1-year span, for example, to compare May with April or May with February (3-month span).

Decision making based on unadjusted data can lead to wrong policies, especially if the series is strongly affected by seasonal variations. The average absolute monthly percentage change in seasonal variation can be much greater than the corresponding changes in the irregular or trend cycle. Several studies of selected economic indicators for the United States show that the absolute average month-to-month percentage change in the seasonal component runs between three and seven times the absolute average percentage change in the trend cycle or in the irregulars over the same time spans.

The measurement of seasonality is also very useful for short-term decision making. The knowledge of the seasonal pattern of economic activities facilitates planning for the utilization of economic resources during periods of peak loads and inactivity. This knowledge can also be applied for better integration of economic activities characterized by opposite seasonal patterns. Resources which formerly served only one purpose can serve additional purposes and thus reduce the burden imposed by seasonality on the whole economy.

References

Dagum, Estela Bee, "The Estimation of Changing Seasonal Variations in Economic Time Series," in K. Namboodiri (ed.), *Survey Sampling and Measurement*, Academic Press, New York, 1978, pp. 217–228; Kendall, Maurice, G., and A. Stuart, *The Advanced Theory of Statistics*, vol. 3, Hafner, New York, 1966; Zellner, Arnold (ed.), *Seasonal Analysis of Economic Time Series*, U.S. Bureau of the Census, 1978.

(*See also* Seasonal adjustment methods; Secular trend)

Estela Bee Dagum

Secular trend

The concept of secular trend has been used in economics to represent smooth variations over a long period of years. The causes of this movement are mainly attributed to the growth of the population, technological progress, capital accumulation, and new ways of organization. For the majority of economic time series, the evolution of the trend tends to be smooth, gradual, and deterministic in character. There are cases, however, where the evolution changes abruptly its level and/or its slope. When this happens, the economic time series is said to have a structural change, that is, a new structural composition. To this type of phenomenon belongs what René Thom calls a catastrophe. Structural changes do not always manifest themselves in an abrupt manner. The higher the aggregation level of the phenomenon that the series represents, the more difficult it is for a structural change to produce sudden breaks in the trend. For example, the substitution of old firms by new ones that utilize a more advanced state of technology rarely will show abrupt changes at the industry aggregate level. On the other hand, a technological change affecting the mode of production of a firm will introduce discontinuity in its trend. The longer the period for which an economic series is recorded, the higher is the probability of structural changes affecting its trend.

The measurement of the secular trend is based on the assumptions that (1) the process has structural stability and (2) the data are homogeneous through time. The trend is not an isolated movement. Its presence in economic phenomena is affected by other movements that contribute to the total variation of the observations. The other best-known types of movements are (1) the cycle, (2) the seasonal variations, and (3) the irregulars. The cycle is a movement of quasi-periodic appearance related to the fluctuations of the economic activity, alternately increasing and decreasing. It takes the graphical form of a function that rotates around the trend. The seasonal variations represent the effect of climatic and institutional events that repeat with certain regularity over a year. The irregulars represent unforeseeable events of all kinds, and generally they have a stable random appearance, although some extreme values may be present. These components of the trend are not directly observable and assumptions must be made as to their behavioral pattern.

Methods of Trend Estimation

The estimation of the secular trend has always posed a serious problem to statisticians. The problem is not one of mathematical or analytical complexity but of conceptual complexity. This problem exists because the trend is not a directly observable variable, and its definition as a smooth, broad movement of an economic phenomenon over a long term is statistically vague. The concept of "long" in this connection is relative, and what is measured as trend for a given span might well be part of a long cycle once the series is significantly extended. To avoid this problem of complexity, statisticians have resorted to two simple solutions; one consists of estimating trend and cyclical fluctuations together, calling this combined movement the trend cycle; the other consists of defining the trend in terms of the series length, denoting it as the longest movement, periodic or not.

The simplest model assumed for an economic time series is the error model where the series is assumed to be composed of a smooth trend and an independent random component. The most common representation of the trend is by means of functions of times, whether polynomials of low degree or of transcendental functions. Polynomial trend equations take the form

$$Y_t = a + bt + ct^2 + dt^3 + \cdots + ht^n \tag{1}$$

The straight line is the particular case where only a and b are different from zero. In such a case, the trend has a constant slope; it changes by a constant amount per unit of time. When the term ct^2 is added, the trend follows a curve where c measures the rate of change in the slope at the origin. If the polynomial trend is a cubic, i.e., d is not zero, the curve changes direction twice.

The variate-difference method has been used primarily to examine the degree of the polynomial of best fit, a point reached when the sum of squares of the residuals does not change significantly for higher differences. This method provides a kind of lower limit of the degree of the polynomial which will represent the trend. Polynomial trends are generally used for series of up to 30 years, but for larger spans other functions seem to be more appropriate. Three of the most widely applied functions, called growth curves, are the modified exponential, the Gompertz curve, and the logistic.

The modified exponential trend is written as follows:

$$Y_t = a + bc^t \qquad \begin{matrix} c > 0 \\ c \neq 1 \end{matrix} \tag{2}$$

This function is a modification of the exponential function $Y = bc^t$ to which a constant has been added. For this type of function, the proportionate rate of increase or decrease of the trend is constant.

The Gompertz curve is expressed by the log-transformed representation

$$Y_t = ab^c c^t \qquad \begin{aligned} &a > 0 \\ &b > 0 \\ &c > 0 \\ &b \neq 1 \\ &c \neq 1 \end{aligned} \qquad (3)$$

and its log transformation becomes

$$\log Y_t = \log a + c^t (\log b) \qquad \begin{aligned} &c > 0 \\ &c \neq 1 \end{aligned} \qquad (4)$$

and the logistic function is

$$Y_t = \frac{1}{a + bc^t} \qquad \begin{aligned} &c > 0 \\ &c \neq 1 \end{aligned} \qquad (5)$$

These two types of functions have basically the same shape—an elongated S that indicates the pattern of growth. They are also called saturation curves because the growth converges with a finite upper limit.

The functions (1) through (5) are generally fitted to the observed series by least-squares procedures. If the trend is a smooth function of time but still cannot be well-approximated by simple functions over the whole range of the series, then linear smoothing techniques can be applied. Smoothing a time series provides a representation of the trend at a given point in time by a weighted average of the observed values over that point. The weighted average of the random elements will generally be a small value and, hence, the weighted average of the observed data will estimate the trend well. The weighted average is applied in a moving manner to obtain successive smoothed values. The longer the span of the average, the smoother is the fitted curve.

If the basic model of a time series is an error model, the trend is of a deterministic character in the sense that the irregular or random shocks do not affect the trend movement because of the assumptions of independence.

Another kind of model that can be postulated for trend estimation is a stochastic process. This model implies that the random disturbances are autocorrelated and that time affects both the systematic and nonsystematic part of the process. Trends subject to stochastic changes in level and/or slope can be approximated by stochastic processes models. The autoregressive integrated moving averages (ARIMA) processes have been intensively studied, and their application to concrete cases has increased significantly in recent years. They seem to be appropriate for trend estimation over a relatively short period of time.

Two simple models for trend estimation are the IMA (0, 1, 1) and the IMA (0, 2, 2), which take the form, respectively,

$$y_t = y_{t-1} + a_t - \theta a_{t-1} \qquad |\theta| < 1 \qquad (6)$$

or equivalently

$$(1 - B)y_t = (1 - \theta B)a_t \qquad \text{where } By_t = y_{t-1}$$

and

$$y_t = 2y_{t-1} - y_{t-2} + a_t - \theta_1 a_{t-1} - \theta_2 a_{t-2} \qquad \text{for } \begin{array}{l} \theta_2 + \theta_1 < 1 \\ \theta_2 - \theta_1 < 1 \\ 1 < \theta_2 < 1 \end{array} \qquad (7)$$

An equivalent representation of (7) is

$$(1 - B)^2 y_t = (1 - \theta_1 B - \theta_2 B^2) a_t$$

The a_t is a purely random process which may be regarded as a series of random shocks that drives the trend. The ARIMA models allow for the inclusion of a deterministic polynomial trend of any degree d.

For a crude approximation, θ can be interpreted as the extent to which the residuals incorporate themselves in the subsequent history of the trend. As θ approaches 1 in (6), the maximum impact of the residuals on the subsequent evolution of the series is approached.

References

Anderson, T. W., *The Statistical Analysis of Time Series*, Wiley, New York, 1971; Box, G. E. P., and G. H. Jenkins, *Time Series Analysis Forecasting and Control*, Holden-Day, San Francisco, 1970; Clark, C. T., and L. L. Schkade, *Statistical Analysis for Administrative Decisions*, South-Western, Cincinnati, 1974; Tintner, G., *The Variate Difference Method*, Principia Press, Bloomington, Ind., 1940.

(*See also* Index numbers; Regression analysis in business and economics; Seasonal adjustment methods; Seasonal variations in economic time series; Statistical techniques in economics and business, an overview; Time series analysis)

Camilo Dagum and Estela Bee Dagum

Securities and Exchange Commission

The Securities and Exchange Commission (SEC) is an independent federal administrative agency that regulates the securities industry. Composed of five members appointed by the President, the SEC was created by the Securities Exchange Act of 1934 to administer and enforce federal securities laws, which were designed to provide investors with adequate information about public offerings of stocks and bonds and to protect them from the malpractices of securities brokers and dealers.

After stock prices plummeted in the wake of the October 1929 crash (from 1929 to mid-1932 the Dow Jones industrial average dropped almost 90 percent), Congress undertook a massive investigation of the securities markets. Led by Ferdinand Pecora, the Senate Committee on Banking and Currency compiled thousands of pages of testimony that showed the existence of many abuses in the securities industry. For example, pooling operations had manipulated the prices of more than 100 New York Stock Exchange–listed stocks, and corporate insiders had profited by using information not available to stockholders and the general public.

These abuses seriously eroded investor confidence, hindering the capital investment vital to economic growth. Their revelation led Congress to enact several laws fashioned to restore the public's faith in the nation's financial markets. The first law passed—the Securities Act of 1933—requires full disclosure of all pertinent information pertaining to a public offering of securities. Its purpose is to provide potential investors with a firm foundation on which they may realistically judge the value of the stocks or bonds being offered. With the exception of state, local, and federal government securities and offerings under $1.5 million (which must comply with the SEC's regulation A), the act requires issuers of securities in interstate commerce or through the mails to file with the SEC a registration statement which contains all the relevant information. In addition, a prospectus including this information must be delivered to investors. Until the registration is in effect (which means that the SEC has not raised any objections, but which does not imply approval of the issue by that agency), it is unlawful to sell the securities. Violation of the law subjects the persons responsible to criminal as well as civil penalties.

The Securities Exchange Act of 1934 grants to the SEC broad regulatory powers aimed at promoting fair trading practices and protecting investors from fraud, manipulation, and other abuses. National securities exchanges (10 of them, as of January 1980) must register with the SEC and adopt rules governing the conduct of their members that conform with SEC regulations concerning investor protection. Brokers and dealers engaged in the over-the-counter securities market also have to register with the SEC, which monitors their activities. Specific trading activities, such as short sales, stabilization transactions, and options trading, on national securities exchanges are also regulated. Violators of federal securities laws are subject to SEC discipline, which includes revocation of registration, expulsion from national securities exchanges, and criminal prosecution.

Corporations whose stock is listed on a national securities exchange, or which have assets of $1 million or more and at least 500 shareholders, or which have issued securities under the Securities Act of 1933 must periodically report financial and other corporate information to the SEC. These companies must comply with SEC rules when soliciting proxies and other authorizations from holders of registered securities. Disclosure of the holdings and transactions by directors, officers, and holders of more than 10 percent of the equity securities of the companies must be made monthly to the SEC.

The Public Utility Holding Company Act of 1935 empowers the SEC to regulate electric and gas utility holding companies in order to limit them to single coordinated systems. Furthermore, the act calls for the simplification of the corporate and capital structures of these companies. This law reflects Congress's reaction to the concentration of economic power that resulted from extensive pyramiding within utility holding companies. The Investment Company Act of 1940 requires mutual funds and other investment companies to register with the SEC, which regulates their activities to protect investors. Under the Investment Advisers Act of 1940, persons who counsel others about security transactions, for compensation, have to register with the SEC. The act authorizes the SEC to issue rules prohibiting fraudulent or deceitful acts. Finally, the SEC participates as an adviser in corporate reorganizations (Federal Bankruptcy Act of 1978) and helps safeguard the interests of bond purchasers (Trust Indenture Act of 1939).

Along with its regulatory responsibilities, the SEC also collects, compiles, and publishes various financial and economic data, including weekly reports on New York and American Stock Exchange trading and monthly reports on insider trading.

References

Federal Register, *United States Government Manual, 1979–1980*, National Archives and Records Service, General Services Administration, May 1, 1979; Robinson, Gerald J., *Going Public—Successful Securities Underwriting*, Clark Boardman, New York, 1961.

(See also Bond; Government regulation of business; Stock; Stock exchange)

Henry C. F. Arnold

Selective credit controls

As most commonly understood, selective credit controls are restraints imposed directly on the extension of defined forms or categories of credit, in contrast with restraints imposed generally on the extension of credit through central bank manipulation of the volume of commercial bank reserves. In a broader view, selective credit controls include, in addition to the foregoing, interest rate controls, limits on the amount of credit extended either to individual borrowers or by individual lending institutions, and differential taxes and subsidies imposed on or available to borrowers and lenders.

Selective Credit Controls in the United States

Following the narrower of these concepts, experience with selective credit control in the United States began with the authorization under the Securities Exchange Act of 1934 for the Federal Reserve System to regulate credit used in buying or holding securities. Regulation was imposed initially on equity shares and convertible bonds traded on national stock exchanges but was subsequently broadened to cover securities traded off the exchanges. The control method is for the Federal Reserve to determine the maximum loan value of a specified group of securities, stated as a percentage of market value. Where, for example, the loan value is set at 60 percent, the purchaser or holder is required to have a margin, or equity, in the security serving as collateral for the loan of not less than 40 percent of market value.

In the control of stock-market credit, the purpose is to prevent crisis situations such as that which occurred in the stock-market collapse that preceded enactment of the 1934 legislation. Margin purchases of stock had been widespread, with securities dealers borrowing heavily from commercial banks to extend credit to customers. When declines in stock prices provoked demands from brokers for additional margin that customers could not supply, forced sales of stock to forestall credit losses by brokers intensified market disorder. It was also believed that the use of credit in stock-market transactions tended to drain it from the nonfinancial side of the economy.

In administering the regulation of stock-market credit, the Federal Reserve Board varies loan values not only with stock-market conditions and the volume of credit being used in security purchases but also with general economic and financial conditions in mind. Thus, if appropriate, loan values may be raised when credit is eased and lowered when it is tightened.

The second use of selective credit controls was authorized in August 1941, 4 months before the bombing of Pearl Harbor, when President Roosevelt issued an Executive order under the Trading with the Enemy Act of 1917 on the authority of which the Federal Reserve Board put into effect within a month a regulation (W) placing restraints on the extension of credit for the purchase of a designated list of consumer durable goods (automobiles, appliances, furniture, etc.). The regulation was designed to reduce consumption demand for goods utilizing materials and labor believed to be needed more urgently in defense industries, and applied to all types of lenders. It was also hoped that the regulation would moderate the increase of prices on scarce resources, supplementing the anti-inflationary effects of taxes and voluntary savings, and would create a backlog of consumer demand that would be useful in the post defense period.

Regulation W was first applied only to installment-type credit, whether granted as a cash loan or with a sales contract, but was extended later (May 1942) to charge account credit and single-payment loans. Restraints consisted of a minimum down-payment requirement and a maximum repayment period and were tightened twice in 1942, ultimately raising the minimum down-payment requirement to $33\frac{1}{2}$ percent for virtually all listed articles and lowering the maximum repayment period to 12 months. Restraints were subsequently relaxed by stages, in many cases by discontinuing altogether the listing of a commodity, and were abandoned entirely in June 1949.

Employing similar methods, regulation W was reinstituted in September 1950, incident to prosecution of the war in Korea, under authority of the Defense Production Act of 1950. Again, the major purpose was to facilitate the transfer of resources from civilian to defense use. Restraints continued until May 1952 when authority expired in keeping with the Defense Production Act Amendments of 1952.

During the Korean conflict, and under the same authority as permitted reimposition of regulation W, the Federal Reserve Board issued regulation X (October 1950) limiting the use of credit in purchasing homes and in financing home improvements. The major purpose was to reduce construction activity, thereby conserving scarce materials for defense purposes and moderating increases in their prices. As in regulation W, restraint was applied by setting minimum down-payment requirements and maximum repayment periods. Regulation X was discontinued in 1952 when authority lapsed.

At the request of President Eisenhower, the Federal Reserve Board undertook an extensive study in 1956 designed to evaluate the arguments pro and con for standby authority to impose relevant selective controls. Subsequently, the Board recommended against a grant of standby authority, and the matter lapsed until 1969 when legislation was enacted (Credit Control Act of 1969) with far wider scope than any previously contemplated. The 1969 law, designed specifically to control inflation generated by excessive credit extension, authorizes the President to regulate all terms on which credit is granted, including interest rates, as well as the amount of credit granted, and extends authority to all forms of credit. Also, it empowers the President to enlist banking and business interests in developing and deploying a system of voluntary credit controls, when needed.

Pro and Con for Selective Controls

Experience with selective credit controls has shown that they are difficult to administer effectively and equitably, though not to an extent that would render them clearly impractical, and there are widely divergent views on the merits of using them. Critics, who emphasize the difficulty of administration, maintain that the effectiveness of controls in war emergency situations is typically due as much to a physical shortage of materials as to the tightening of credit terms and assert that the inflation-restraining effect would be better achieved by the methods of conventional monetary policy. Proponents, who generally tend to put less emphasis than the critics on a monetarist approach to inflation control, view selective credit controls as a way of achieving allocations of credit, and possibly a limitation on its aggregate volume, more in keeping with perceived economic and social priorities. They maintain that there is also less upward pressure on interest rates than would result from the aggregative, indirect approach of monetary policy. Debate commonly concerns a far wider range of government intervention in credit markets than was involved in regulations W and X. Arrayed on the two sides of the argument are those who prefer less-interventionist forms of economic control against those who have greater confidence in the ability of central government to manage the economy constructively and equitably and who have a greater urge to move in that direction.

References

Board of Governors, Federal Reserve System, *Consumer Instalment Credit*, vol. 1, pt. I, 1957, chaps. 4, 6; *Credit Allocation Techniques and Monetary Policy*, Federal Reserve Bank of Boston, Boston, 1973, pp. 9–63; Young, Ralph, A., *Instruments of Monetary Policy in the United States*, International Monetary Fund, Washington, D.C., 1973.

(*See also* Business credit; Consumer credit; Credit, an overview; Federal Reserve policy; Federal Reserve System; Monetary policy; Mortgage credit)

Raymond J. Saulnier

Short-run forecasts (see Economic forecasts)

Short-term interest rates (see Interest rates)

Simulation in business and economics

Simulation is a set of techniques which can be employed to replicate processes or operations of systems. Its roots are ancient; and it has been practiced in various guises since antiquity. The primary purpose of simulation is to provide greater understanding of the characteristics of processes or systems so as to make possible improvements either in their structures or in the setting of external factors or strategies that influence results from their operation.

Simulation Forms

Simulation can take several forms. All involve creation, manipulation, and observation of a pseudo environment, usually a scaled-down or simplified depiction, that is intended to mirror an actual or hypothetical process or system. The pseudo environment can be a mathematical representation or a physical prototype. If the latter, it can include structures and machines, or individuals, or both. Examples, respectively, are automated process controllers (including robots with artificial intelligence or learning capabilities), experiments with individuals or groups of persons reacting to artificial market or incentive stimuli, and person-machine interactions such as in-flight simulations, piloting of model supertankers in artificial basins, and so forth. In general, no matter how the simplified artificial environment or analogue is created, simulation affords an effective means of controlled experimentation. Simulation techniques can be used for any complex representation of a system for which analytical solutions are not readily derivable or generalizable.

For analysis of operations and processes of systems in business and economics the pseudo environment or analog of the system in question typically is a set of formal mathematical expressions coded for purposes of simulation on a digital computer.

Physical analogs, such as electrical or hydraulic mechanisms which are postulated to have properties appropriate for the simulation pseudo environment, have also been utilized, primarily in the period predating rapid advances in digital computing technology of the past several decades.

The mathematical expressions of the simulation model are specified to reflect relationships between factors of interest that are hypothesized to exist in the environment. These relationships may be based, for instance, on technological considerations describing a production process. They may alternatively be behavioral in nature, determined by concepts of economic rationality or other notions of the characteristics of group or individual responses, or may be structural/institutional interactions which summarize and approximate a set of very detailed relationships dictated by law or custom.

The mathematical analog of the environment may be obtained by various techniques. If the simulation model is based on a set of econometric equations, parameters of the relationships are derived by use of appropriate statistical estimation methods from a body of observed data. Depending on the environment being described, the observations may be time series data—historical values observed for variables over a sample period; cross-sectional data—values observed for variables of a sample population; or longitudinal panel data—cross-sectional observations for multiple periods of a fixed population sample.

Analysis of variance methods such as factor analysis or principal components; decision theory; game theory; information theory; programming—linear, nonlinear, dynamic, or integer; systems dynamics; and other approaches to specifying or estimating relationships and determining their parameters, singly or in combination, may also be appropriate for simulation of particular processes. All have in common that they embody linkages of causal factors, that is, action-reaction, signal transmission-receipt, etc., as chains of simple or simultaneous cause and effect. The strength of the reaction depends on the strength of the cause (the forcing function or signal) and the structural characteristics of the system.

When an initial version of the analog (in mathematical terms, a model) is deemed to be appropriately specified and constructed, it is essential, if reliable simulation results are to be obtained, that it be tested and validated. This can be done by comparing data generated from model simulations with observations on the actual system or with a priori estimates of what such a system would produce. Rigorous statistical criteria, such as goodness-of-fit test statistics, likelihood ratios, or probability confidence bands, can be utilized to provide objective indications of the concordance of simulation with actual or hypothetical results. Alteration of factors exogenous to the analog system and its structure can be effected to ascertain the sensitivity of simulation outcomes to such changes. This, too, provides information on the analog's properties and realism. Specifications of the model may have to be reconsidered to attain properties which are in accord with those desired. Desirable properties are dictated by the nature of simulation results and by the uses for which experimentation with the analog is intended.

Two Types of Simulation Studies

Two types of simulation experiments normally are undertaken. In the first, values of exogenous or controllable factors (including structural characteristics of the analog) are altered and effects on other variables of the system are observed. The focus of all possible values of responses to all possible values of input factors, whether arising from controllable or from uncontrollable or natural sources, is called the response surface.

One purpose of conducting simulation experiments is to explore that response surface, particularly in the neighborhood of subjects of interest. For example, given a detailed model of a developed economy, analysts may wish to examine the consequences for consumption and investment patterns of alternative feasible changes in government tax and expenditure (fiscal policies) or monetary policies. Because an extremely large number of input alterations generally is possible, the design of the experiments should be such that the process of exploring the response surface is highly efficient. Otherwise, simulation could become extremely costly and, perhaps more importantly, major portions of the response surface with critical implications for input settings might be missed. For instance, with selected input values the system may tend toward extreme positions or paths or exhibit great degrees of instability. Rigorous methods for efficient search may be found in the literature on design of experiments.

The second type of simulation studies involves optimization or maximization. Both require specification of criteria and their statement in a form that can be used with the analog so that the degree to which the criteria are satisfied is manifest in the controllable variables of the system. The most common criterion is one of least cost or maximum profit. But more complex kinds and combinations of preferences can be used as long as they can be translated into cardinal or ordinal rankings. Thus, desirability of outcomes can be judged if marginal preference trade-off rates between variables of interest have been stated. For simulation applications with economic policies, this can be done by positing social welfare or utility functions where the arguments are variables such as consumption, government expenditures of different types, rates of unemployment, etc. Optimization with simulation models is akin to optimal control of engineering feedback systems. There is a large body of literature in that field, and some within economics, that describes how this technique effectively can be applied.

Construction of mathematical analogs for simulation on digital computers has been little standardized. Apart from use of common statistical methods of derivation of parameters of models, estimation and solution of models have been undertaken with a wide diversity of computer programs. Solution routines, especially, have been tailored for particular models in most instances. Few general-purpose simulation programs have gained wide acceptance. Among these, the best known are GPSS, originated by Philip Kiviat at the Rand Corporation, and DYNAMO, a product of the systems dynamics group headed by Jay W. Forrester at the Massachusetts Institute of Technology.

While computer-based and prototype simulation has been found highly useful for training, for increasing understanding of complex systems, for policy formulation, and for evaluation and other purposes, it has limitations. These stem mainly from divergences between behavior of the analog in response to changes in controllable and exogenous factors and behavior of the real-world system which is the object of study. Such divergence particularly may occur in exploring responses outside the range of past experience, even though simulation results seem intuitively satisfactory to the analyst. This may arise from specifications which diverge from the real-world system because of considerations of computational necessities or analytical convenience, because of poor-quality data for estimation of parameters or validation, or because of a basic lack of understanding of patterns of causality in the real-world system. Thus, caution is required in the design and execution of simulation experiments and in interpretation of their results for policy recommendations.

Since 1967 an Annual Simulation Symposium has been sponsored by the Association for Computing Machinery, the IEEE Computer Society, and the Society for Computer Simulation. The purposes of this nonprofit convocation are to provide a forum for interchange of ideas, techniques, and applications among practitioners and to offer grants for advancement of the art of simulation using computers.

References

Chow, Gregory, C., *Analysis and Control of Dynamic Economic Systems*, Wiley, New York, 1975; Lewis, Theodore, G., and B. J. Smith, *Computer Principles of Modeling and Simulation*, Houghton Mifflin, Boston, 1979; Naylor, Thomas H., *Computer Simulation Experiments with Models of Economic Systems*, Wiley, New York, 1971; Orcutt, Guy, H., et al., *Policy Exploration through Microanalytic Simulation*, Urban Institute, Washington, D.C., 1976.

(*See also* Computers in economics; Cross-sectional analysis in business and economics; Data banks; Dynamic analysis; Dynamic macroeconomic models; Econometrics; Economic models; Forecasting methods; Game theory, economic applications; Linear programming; Time series analysis)

Gary Fromm and Charles Movit

Simultaneous equations in business and economics

Simultaneous-equation estimation is a family of statistical techniques which proceeds from the assumption that the disturbances in different equations of an economic model are, or are likely to be, correlated with one another. This contrasts with the assumption almost universally made in economics prior to 1944 that the disturbances in different equations of a model were statistically independent (uncorrelated). Under this earlier assumption, each equation could be estimated separately by ordinary least squares—a single-equation technique.

Haavelmo's article "The Probability Approach in Econometrics" (1944) showed no evidence that he had heard of the 30 years of cumulative experience in applied econometric research prior to 1944 (much of it in the United States). Following its publication, there should have been passionate scholarly discussion and careful testing of its merits as a guide to applied econometric research. This did not occur because the scholarly community had been badly disrupted in Germany since 1933, in Austria since 1938, and in the whole of Europe since 1939. Some economists who might have moderated the discussion were in German-occupied countries, and others were working to capacity in war-related activities.

In order to concentrate on the implications of correlated disturbances in equations, Haavelmo and his equally brilliant associates neglected important problems that had long been recognized by applied econometricians:

1. At any given time, some of the variables that theoretically belong in a model may not yet have been measured.

2. Some of the variables measured are subject to substantial errors.

3. High intercorrelation among the independent variables in models fitted to economic time series is more nearly the rule than the exception.

Among the problems that were emphasized by Haavelmo and his colleagues, who apparently were unaware that the problems had been dealt with earlier by others were:

1. The "identification problem" in the case of Marshallian simultaneous demand and supply curves. This problem was formulated and solved explicitly by Marcel Lenoir in 1913 and E. J. Working in 1927, and it was well-understood by Mordecai Ezekiel and Holbrook Working in the mid-1920s.

2. The identification problem in the general case including both lagged and non-lagged variables. Moore in 1914 was seeking a causal explanation of business cycles in the following sequence: (1) Cycles in rainfall in the American Midwest cause (2) cycles in crop production, which cause (3) cycles in crop prices, which might cause (4) cycles in other sectors of the economy. Thus, rainfall (an exogenous variable) during the spring and summer determines the size of the crop harvested in the fall and sold during the fall and winter; hence, crop production is a predetermined variable in the demand functions for crops: $P_t = f(Q_t)$. In 1917, Moore also fitted a supply function for cotton in the form $Q_t = f(P_t - 1)$.

Moore contrasted his dynamic approach (which included lagged variables and a strong interest in prediction) with the static, simultaneous approach of Alfred Marshall. Moore's recursive supply and demand equations embodied a dynamic mechanism which later became known as the cobweb model. This mechanism was recognized independently and separately by Schultz, Ricci, and Tinbergen in 1930, described by Leontief and by Kaldor in 1934, and discussed in detail by Ezekiel in 1938. The cobweb model is an example of what Herman Wold later called a causal chain in which each equation can be estimated separately and without bias by least squares.

The identification problem was also solved and applied to more complicated models, some in economics and some in genetics, by Sewall Wright in 1921, 1925, and 1934.

Details of Haavelmo's Approach

The accompanying equations illustrate some elements of Haavelmo's simultaneous-equations approach in terms of the Marshallian demand and supply curves. Since P and Q are always synchronous in this model, the subscript t can be dropped.

Suppose we have a set of price-quantity observations which we believe to have been generated by the following model:

$$\text{Demand:} \quad Q = a + bP + u \tag{1}$$
$$\text{Supply:} \quad Q = \alpha + \beta P + v \tag{2}$$

where u and v are regarded as random disturbances. From a statistical point of view we have no basis for distinguishing between these two equations since both contain the same variables and both have random disturbances. It can be shown that the least-squares regression of Q upon P is, in an indefinitely large sample,

$$B = \frac{b\sigma_v^2 - (b + \beta)\sigma_{uv} + \beta\sigma_u^2}{\sigma_v^2 - 2\sigma_{uv} + \sigma_u^2} \tag{3}$$

where $\sigma_{uv} = r_{uv}\sigma_u\sigma_v$. If the demand curve has not shifted (i.e., if $\sigma_u = 0$), $B = b$; if the supply curve has not shifted (i.e., if $\sigma_v = 0$), $B = \beta$. But in general, B does not equal either of the structural coefficients, and neither of them is identifiable. If Equations

(1) and (2) constitute the true and complete model, there is, in general, no way by which b and β can be estimated from the data.

The situation is different if each equation includes a different predetermined variable (i.e., a variable which is statistically independent of u and v), say Y and Z, in the demand and supply functions, respectively:

$$\text{Demand:} \quad Q = a + bP + cY + u \tag{4}$$
$$\text{Supply:} \quad Q = \alpha + \beta P + \gamma Z + v \tag{5}$$

where u and v again are random disturbances; Q and P are now referred to as endogenous variables which are assumed to be correlated with u and v. Writing all four variables in lower-case letters as deviations from their respective means, we can express q and p as functions of the predetermined variables and the disturbances and obtain the reduced form of the model as follows:

$$p = -\left(\frac{c}{b - \beta}\right)y + \left(\frac{\gamma}{b - \beta}\right)z + \frac{y - u}{b - \beta} \tag{6}$$

$$q = -\left(\frac{c\beta}{b - \beta}\right)y + \left(\frac{\gamma b}{b - \beta}\right)z + \frac{bv - \beta u}{b - \beta} \tag{7}$$

The coefficients of the reduced-form equations may be estimated by least squares. The structural coefficient β can be estimated as the ratio of the coefficients of y in equations (6) and (7); b can be estimated as the ratio of the coefficients of z. Knowing β and b, we can readily derive c and γ from the coefficients of equation (6); a and α can be estimated from the other coefficents since the (sample) means of Q, P, Y, and Z are known. The model consisting of Equations (4) and (5) is just identified, i.e., our information is sufficient to make a unique estimate of each structural parameter.

In other models it may be possible to identify some of the structural equations but not others. The necessary and sufficient conditions for identifiability of a given equation in a set of m simultaneous linear equations can be summed up in three propositions:

1. At least $m - 1$ of the total number of variables in the system (counting lagged endogenous variables as separate variables) must be absent from the given equation.

2. Each of the other $m - 1$ equations in the system must contain at least one variable which does not appear in the given equation.

3. The matrix formed of the coefficients in the other $m - 1$ equations of variables absent from the given equation must be of rank $m - 1$ (i.e., it must contain at least one set of $m - 1$ columns and $m - 1$ rows which form a nonzero determinant).

The Haavelmo Bias

Haavelmo's approach was brilliantly conceived, but it rested on an untested assumption that nearly all econometric models were of the synchronous type, in which each equation contained two or more endogenous variables, the disturbances in different equations were correlated, and least-squares estimates of the structural coefficients were badly biased. If this assumption were true, it raised the possibility that nearly all results hitherto obtained by single-equation (least-squares) methods were invalid because they had ignored what Herman Wold referred to as the Haavelmo bias. As of 1945 this possibility was particularly alarming to Wold, for in that year he had nearly finished the statistical side of an investigation of consumer expenditures, all the numerical results of which might be subject to the Haavelmo bias.

Wold immediately undertook a critical examination of the traditional single-equation method and its logical foundations. Wold's conclusion (stated in a paper presented at a 1947 meeting of the Econometrics Society and published in 1949) was that the traditional method was free from Haavelmo bias when applied to a certain general class of models which was "wide enough to cover most, if not all, dynamic models used in econometric research up to 1940." Wold cited Jan Tinbergen's pioneer 1939 work in applying model sequence analysis or process analysis to statistical data in his 45-equation model of the U.S. economy during 1919 to 1932 and stated that "it is precisely this type of the systems, properly specified, which goes free from the Haavelmo bias." In his later work, Wold repeatedly and forcefully emphasized the importance of causal chain, or recursive, models in econometrics; the cobweb model is the earliest (and perhaps the simplest) representative of the type.

Wold's position was viewed as the correct one by most econometricians who had done serious work with data prior to 1944. Few or none of them adopted Haavelmo's approach. A younger group accepted Haavelmo's assumption of correlated disturbances at least provisionally and developed several additional techniques (two-stage least squares, instrumental variables, principal components, and others) for handling the first stage of estimation represented by the reduced-form Equations (6) and (7). As experience in applying such methods to data accumulated, it turned out that the estimates in many cases were so close to those obtained by least squares that the differences were not statistically (or economically) significant. It also turned out that the simultaneous methods were more sensitive than were ordinary least squares to high intercorrelation among predetermined variables and that specification errors in one equation could substantially affect the estimated coefficients of others. By the mid-1970s, applied econometricians felt free to use ordinary least squares or one of the simultaneous-equation methods depending upon the characteristics of particular equations and subgroups of equations in a complete model.

Koopmans (1945) and Marschak, who helped extend, explain, and popularize Haavelmo's approach, stated that errors in variables were disregarded in order to concentrate on the central problem of disturbances in equations. The computing instructions for applying Haavelmo's concepts to data embodied the assumption that all variables were measured without error, and these instructions were carried forward uncritically into a number of textbooks. As a result, several cohorts of graduate students were trained in the belief (sincerely held by instructors who had done no empirical research) that errors in variables were of no consequence. Only in the 1970s did econometricians trained in this tradition begin to recognize the need for dealing explicitly with errors in variables.

References

Christ, Carl F., *Econometric Models and Methods*, Wiley, New York, 1966; Ezekiel, Mordecai, "The Cobweb Theorem," *Quarterly Journal of Economics*, vol. 52, 1938, pp. 255–280; Fox, Karl A., and Tej K. Kaul, *Intermediate Economic Statistics, vol. II: A Guide to Recent Developments and Literature, 1968–1978*, Krieger, Huntington, N.Y., 1980; Haavelmo, Trygve, "The Probability Approach in Econometrics," *Econometrica*, vol. 12 (suppl.), 1944, pp. 1–118; Koopmans, Tjalling C., "Statistical Estimation of Simultaneous Economic Relations," *Journal of the American Statistical Association*, vol. 40, 1945, pp. 448–466; Lenoir, Marcel, *Études sur la Formation et le*

Mouvement des Prix, Giard and Brière, Paris, 1913; Moore, Henry L., *Economic Cycles: Their Law and Cause,* Macmillan, New York, 1917; Tinbergen, Jan, "Statistical Testing of Business Cycle Theories," vol. II: *Business Cycles in the United States of America, 1919–1932* League of Nations, Economic Intelligence Service, Geneva, 1939; Wold, H. O., "Statistical Estimation of Economic Relationships," *Econometrica,* vol. 17 (suppl.), 1949, pp. 1–21, (see also "Errata," *Econometrica* vol. 19, 1951, p. 227.); Working, E. J., "What Do Statistical Demand Curves Show?," *Quarterly Journal of Economics,* vol. 41, 1927, pp. 212–235; Wright, Sewall, "The Method of Path Coefficients," *Annals of Mathematical Statistics,* vol. 5, Institute of Mathematical Statistics, Hayward, Calif., 1934, pp. 161–215.

(*See also* Econometrics; Economic models; Regression analysis in business and economics; Statistical techniques in economics and business, an overview)

Karl A. Fox and Tej K. Kaul

Small business

A small business can be defined in many different ways, but essentially it is a business that entrepreneurs can manage and operate and in which they can make the critical decisions and retain the rewards or bear the losses of their risk taking and management. Small business is self-initiated, largely self-financed, and self-managed.

A more specific definition of small business is provided by the Small Business Administration, an agency of the federal government created in 1953 to promote and protect the small business section of the economy. This agency utilizes maximum sizes in its definitions of small businesses. In the retailing sector, a business is defined as small if its sales do not exceed $2 to $7.5 million, with the limit varying based on the specific type of business. In the services sector, a business is deemed small when its receipts are less than $2 to $8 million, depending on the type of service business. In the wholesaling sector, a business is considered to be small if the sales do not exceed $9.5 to $22 million, with the definition again varying based on the type of wholesaling business. In the manufacturing sector, the business qualifies as small if it employs less than 250 to 1500 employees, depending on the industry. In view of these definitions, over 95 percent of all private business firms in the United States may be classified as small. They account for 51 percent of the nation's business employment and furnish over 43 percent of the privately produced gross national product.

Most small businesses are proprietorships, the simplest and most flexible form, legally and administratively. In 1976, according to the Internal Revenue Service, there were some 11 million businesses in the United States, of which 7.9 million (72 percent) were owned by single individuals (proprietorships). Partnerships numbered almost another million, and corporations accounted for slightly fewer than 2.2 million of all the nation's businesses, of which nearly two-thirds held assets of less than $100 million.

Of the various definitions of a small business firm, probably the most meaningful and concise definition was developed in 1947 by the Committee for Economic Development. The definition is based on a firm's qualifying as a small business by fulfilling a minimum of two of the following four key factors:

1. Management of the firm is independent, with ownership and control normally held by the managers.

2. Capital is supplied by an individual or small group.

3. The operations are essentially local, with the employees and owners living in the same geographical vicinity. The markets served need not be local in scale.

4. The business firm must be small within its industry when compared with the largest firms in its field of operations. This measure can be in terms of sales volume, number of employees, or other significant comparisons.

Although large firms account for a large portion of the nation's gross national product, small firms exert an important role particularly in wholesale and retail trade and service industries.

The failure of small businesses is largely attributable to the lack of management skill. Many small businesses fail largely because of a lack of equity capital and/or difficulty or inability in securing credit or financing.

The Small Business Administration (SBA) has been credited with the recent success of many small businesses in the United States. This has been accomplished by providing financial and management assistance to the small business.

References

Bunzel, John H., *The American Small Businessman*, Arno, New York, 1962; Carosso, Vincent P., and Stuart Bruchey, *The Survival of Small Business*, Arno, New York, 1979; Carson, Deane, *The Vital Majority: Small Business in the American Economy*, U.S. Government Printing Office, Washington, D.C., 1973; Hollander, Edward D., *The Future of Small Business*, Praeger, New York, 1967; Hollingsworth, A. Thomas, and Herbert H. Hand, *A Guide to Small Business Management*, Saunders, Philadelphia, 1979; Phillips, Joseph D., *Little, Business in the American Economy*, University of Illinois Press, Urbana, Ill., 1958; U.S. Chamber of Commerce, *Small Business: Its Role and Its Problems*, 1962.

(*See also* Entrepreneurial ability, a factor of production)

Ronald W. Dickey

Smithsonian Agreement

The Smithsonian Agreement of 1971 represented a stage in the transition of the international monetary system from the fixed exchange rate, dollar-dominated pattern of Bretton Woods to the current system of a managed float.

Under the Bretton Woods Agreement of 1944, all member nations stated their currency values in terms of gold, with only the United States pledged to convertibility. With this unique status, the dollar became an international standard of value and the universally accepted asset for international payments. Aside from occasional devaluations of foreign currencies, the system worked quite effectively for about a quarter of a century.

By the early 1970s, however, with changed patterns of world trade, and particularly with the growing U.S. deficit, the Bretton Woods Agreement became increasingly unworkable. Even during the fifties and early sixties, although the United States generally maintained a comfortable surplus, the nation was losing gold. In 1965, with increasing dollar redemption, gold exchanges became restricted to foreign national monetary authorities.

Bretton Woods System Severely Tested

A solution to the problem of world payments, that is, the problem of maintaining stable exchange rates and providing liquidity to finance growing world trade, was problematical. One possibility was to increase the band, or the amount a nation's currency could move about its par value or gold definition. Under the Bretton Woods Agreement, currencies were permitted to move one percentage point above or below their par value. Rates were kept within the band primarily through the buying and selling of a nation's own currency with U.S. dollars. It was believed that a widening of the band would reduce speculative attacks on currencies as well as permit a nation greater flexibility and more time in executing domestic policies to stabilize its currency's external value.

In the spring and summer of 1971 the principles of the Bretton Woods system were severely tested. Increasing offers of dollars for deutsche marks forced Germany to move temporarily to a floating exchange rate. The Japanese central bank absorbed billions of dollars in an attempt to stay at dollar parity. Greater pressures were put on the United States to exchange its money liabilities for its gold assets. With U.S. domestic unemployment rising, American options to fight the dollar outflow were limited to curtailing U.S. foreign investment, cutting back its military posture, losing gold, or raising gold's price—a devaluation of the dollar. In a dramatic move on August 15, 1971, the United States suspended its currency convertibility, thereby breaking from the agreement set at Bretton Woods. Additionally, the United States imposed a punitive 10 percent surcharge on its imports. As an international bargaining device the surcharge was particularly onerous to America's trading partners.

After the announcement, and for the next 4 months, financial centers and international exchange markets were confused. With an undefined value of the dollar, the standard of the international currency system, nations sought to protect in different ways their currencies' international value. West Germany and the Netherlands allowed their currencies to float. Both England and Japan defended their currencies so as to maintain preexisting gold and dollar parity. France established a two-tier system, a fixed-dollar rate for commercial transactions and a floating rate for all other money exchanges.

Details of the Agreement

The diversity of national concerns kept the European Economic Community nations from unifying a position with respect to the dollar. Meetings under International Monetary Fund auspicies, as well as conferences of the Group of Ten (composed of the financial ministers of the industrialized nations of the free world), were unable to resolve national differences. Agreement on the exchange rate impasse was essentially reached in mid-December, as President Nixon and President Pompidou met to discuss the realignment of currency values.

These summit talks were quickly followed by a meeting of the Group of Ten in Washington, D.C., at the Smithsonian Institution on December 17 and 18, 1971. This 2-day conference succeeded in building a temporary raft from the flotsam of the shattered Bretton Woods arrangement. It was agreed that the dollar would be devalued. With its gold definition changed from $35 to $38 per ounce of gold, the dollar declined by 8.55 percent from its initial Bretton Woods parity. (The United States also removed its arbitrarily imposed 10 percent import surcharge.) With the dollar devaluation came changes by some of the other Group of Ten nations. With respect to the dollar all currencies rose by varying percentages: in Belgium, by 11.57; Italy, 7.54; Germany, 13.58; Japan, 16.88; the Netherlands, 11.57; and Sweden, 7.49. The French franc and the British pound maintained their gold parities, thus rising to the dollar by 8.55 percent. The Canadian dollar, which had been floating, retained its status.

The Smithsonian Agreement only embraced the Group of Ten. Other nations shortly followed exchange rate strategies that were in their own best interests, aligning themselves with other major currencies. All nations had the option of establishing new parity values or choosing a temporary, or central, rate.

In addition to the restructuring of currency values, the Smithsonian Agreement amended the Bretton Woods Agreement by widening the band about parity to $2\frac{1}{4}$ percentage points. This redefinition permitted greater flexibility of the new rates. It would also, it was believed, reduce speculative attacks by increasing the risk of buying or selling a currency on the assumption of further parity changes.

Since the U.S. dollar remained unconvertible, world finances were on a complete dollar standard, a holding action against further revisions to the Bretton Woods system. The fixed-rate system broke, however, under the weight of continued sizable U.S. balance of payment deficits. The patchwork revisions proved to be inadequate and the Smithsonian exchange rates unsustainable, so in March 1973, the era of the managed float replaced the Bretton Woods–Smithsonian Agreements.

The Smithsonian Agreement clearly showed that international agreements are only as good as their strongest link. The United States, without prior consultation with its trading partners, forced major revisions in the international payments network. The Smithsonian Agreement dramatically pointed to the inability of the Bretton Woods Agreement to adjust to changing trade patterns. The international economic environment of the 1970s was not to be governed by the economic relations existing in the 1940s.

References

The Smithsonian Agreement and its Aftermath: Several Views, Council on Foreign Relations, Inc., New York, 1972; Solomon, Robert, *The International Monetary System, 1945–1976,* Harper & Row, New York, 1977; Strange, Susan, in Andrew Shonfield (ed.), *International Monetary Relations,* vol. 2: *International Economic Relations of the Western World, 1959–1971,* Oxford University Press, London, 1976.

(*See also* Balance of international payments; Balance of international trade; Barriers to trade; Bretton Woods Conference; Foreign exchange rates; International economics, an overview; International Monetary Fund; Liquidity, international; Value of the dollar)

Bernard S. Katz

Social dividend (see Negative income tax)

Social overhead capital (see Infrastructure)

Social security programs

There are three federal social insurance programs. Two of them provide what are commonly called social security benefits. These are the old-age and survivors insurance program (OASI) and the disability insurance program (DI). The third program, which came later, is the medicare program of which part A is hospital insurance (HI) and part B is supplementary medical insurance (SMI).

The three programs provide one part of the nation's three-part income maintenance system. Social security provides for partial replacement of earnings lost because of death, retirement, or disability, and this is complemented by the HI and SMI programs for the aged and for certain disabled individuals. Private initiatives (private pensions, insurance, and savings) are expected to augment this "basic floor of protection," while needs-tested public assistance is available for those without sufficient income and resources.

Only the cash benefits programs (OASI and DI) are discussed here.

Enactment Description and Governance

The old-age (retirement) insurance program was enacted in 1935, with benefits scheduled to begin in 1942. In 1939, however, survivors insurance was legislated and the two were combined under an OASI trust fund, which became operational on January 1, 1940. On August 1, 1956, the DI trust fund was established. The OASI and DI programs provide monthly cash benefits to retired and disabled workers and their dependents and to survivors of insured workers. Each fund is held by a board of trustees composed of the Secretaries of the Treasury, Labor, and Health and Human Services. The Secretary of the Treasury is the managing trustee. The commissioner of social security is the secretary of the board for the OASI and DI funds.

Under the OASI and DI programs a person builds up protection through employment that is covered by the law. Current workers are required to pay contributions (taxes) on earnings and/or self-employment income up to a maximum stated in the law (in 1979, 5.08 percent on the first $22,900 of earnings). Employers match the contributions of their employees. The self-employed pay 7.05 percent. These contributions are then used to make benefit payments to current workers (or their dependents or survivors) whose earnings ceased because of retirement (at age 62 or after), death, or disability—thus making social security a huge pay-as-you-go, intergenerational transfer program. Current income not needed for benefit payments is deposited in the trust funds, which serve as a contingency reserve in the event outgo exceeds income.

The original legislation provided only retirement insurance and was limited to those in industrial and commercial employment. By December 1977, about 90 percent of all workers in paid employment were covered (85 million out of 94 million). Of the remaining 9 million, some 5 million were excluded by law. Half of those excluded were covered by a federal retirement system and half did not earn enough or work long enough to be covered (mostly self-employed, domestics, and farm workers). Coverage was optional for the other 4 million not covered, but the option was not exercised. These were mostly state and local government employees (almost all of whom were covered by a staff retirement system) and workers in nonprofit organizations.

Protection

Today, 93 percent of all people aged 65 and over are eligible for cash benefits. To qualify for retirement benefits for one's self and family, a worker must be fully insured. A worker who reached age 62 in 1975 or later is fully insured if he or she has at least one quarter of coverage (acquired after 1936), for each calendar year after 1950 (or after age 21, if later) up to the year in which the person attains age 62, dies, or becomes disabled. The maximum requirement is 40 quarters of covered work.

Survivors benefits are payable to the children and to the young widow (widower) of the worker if the worker was either fully insured or currently insured (had at least 6 quarters of coverage during the 13-quarter period ending with the quarter of death).

As of January 1978, 130 million people were insured for survivors benefits. About 95 of every 100 children under age 18 and the surviving parent of each of them have survivorship protection. Survivors benefits are also payable to aged widows (widowers), aged dependent parents, children aged 18 to 22 who are full-time students, and children 18 and over who were disabled before age 22.

Disability is defined as the inability to engage in any substantial gainful activity because of a physical or mental impairment which can be expected to last for at least 12 months or to result in death. To be insured, a worker aged 31 or over must be fully insured and, unless blind, must also have at least 20 quarters of coverage during the 40 quarters ending with the quarter of disability. For workers disabled before age 31, there is an alternative insured-status requirement. As of January 1978, 89 million workers under age 65 were so insured. Benefits may be paid to children of the disabled worker and to the spouse (if age 62 or more) if caring for an entitled child. People disabled before age 62 are protected in the event of death, disability, or retirement of an insured parent. Disabled widows (widowers) may receive reduced benefits as early as age 50. About four of every five persons aged 21 to 64 have this disability insurance protection.

Beneficiaries and Benefits

Over 34 million people (one in seven) were receiving cash benefits at the end of 1977. Of these, (1) 61 percent of the 34 million beneficiaries were retired workers and their spouses, (2) 15 percent were children of retired, deceased, or disabled workers, (3) under 2 percent were young widows (widowers) with children in their care, (4) under 1 percent were special age-72 beneficiaries, (5) 12 percent were widows (widowers), including disabled widows (widowers), (6) 10 percent were disabled workers under age 65 and their spouses, and (7) a minuscule number were dependent parents of deceased workers.

Effective June 1, 1979, the average monthly benefit for a retired worker alone was $283; for a retired couple, $482. A spouse's benefit, if also age 65, is one-half the worker's benefit unless entitled to more in his or her own right. The figures reflect the actuarial reduction for the many who take benefits before age 65. Surviving spouse benefits depend upon when they are taken (they are available as early as age 60) and upon whether or not the worker had a reduced retirement benefit. Such a benefit at or after age 65 is 100 percent of the benefit the worker was getting or would have gotten at age 65 or later. The average benefit for aged widows was $267 as of June 1979. For a disabled worker it was $320. A child's benefit is 50 percent of the worker's unreduced benefit if the worker is alive and 75 percent if the worker is dead. There is a maximum on the family benefit which ranges from 150 percent to 188 percent of the worker's unreduced benefit. The maximum monthly benefit for a worker retiring at age 65 was $553.30. The minimum benefit for a 65-year-old worker was $133.90. All benefits are tax-free and protected against inflation.

Indexed Earnings

For a person reaching age 62 in 1978 or earlier, actual earnings are used in the benefit calculation; for those reaching age 62 in 1979 or later, indexed earnings are used. To compute the latter, one must first count the number of years after 1950 (or age 21, if later) up to the year a person reaches age 62, becomes disabled, or dies. (The computation period will expand from 23 years for those reaching age 62 in 1979, up to 35 years for those reaching age 62 in 1991 or later.) Next, the actual taxable earnings are listed for each of the above years. Third, the actual earnings of each year are indexed by multiplying each one by the ratio of average wages in the second year before the person reaches age 62, becomes disabled, or dies to the average wage in the year being updated. (Actual earnings after age 62 or disability are counted and substituted for earlier years of indexed earnings if they increase one's benefit.) Fourth, the lowest 5 years are eliminated. Fifth, the indexed (and substituted actual) earnings are added for all included years, and sixth, that sum is divided by the number of months in the included years to obtain one's average indexed monthly earnings (AIME). A three-step formula is then applied (90 percent of the first $180 of AIME, 32 percent of the next $905 of AIME, and 15 percent of all AIME over $1085), which yields the retirement benefit (the primary insurance amount) for a person retiring at age 65.

For those reaching age 62 in 1978 or earlier, a more complicated formula is applied to unindexed average monthly earnings. The benefit is reduced by five-ninths of 1 percent for each month of retirement before age 65 (20 percent at age 62) and is increased by one-fourth of 1 percent for each month worked past age 65. The percentages in the three-step formula are fixed, but the dollar amounts are adjusted automatically each year to reflect the rise in average wage levels. This is necessary to keep replacement rates constant. A 5-year transition period for those reaching age 62 in 1979 through 1983 guarantees benefits no lower than those under the law before the 1977 amendments.

Replacement rates are the percentage of final earnings that benefits amounts replace. The benefit formula is tilted to yield a higher replacement rate, the lower one's earnings. Under the 1977 amendments, these rates are stabilized at about 52 percent for the low earner, 42 percent for the average earner, and 28 percent for the high earner (the one at the maximum taxable earnings base). If the spouse is also age 65, the rates are 50 percent higher.

The 1972 amendments provided, effective 1975, for benefits to be adjusted automatically for the rise in the consumer price index (guaranteeing that benefits would keep up with inflation) and for the contributions and benefit base to be adjusted automatically for the increase in average wages in the economy (maintaining the proportion of total payroll that is taxable). The 1977 amendments corrected an unintentional flaw in the 1972 amendments that permitted an overadjustment in the benefit adjustment. The benefit adjustments become applicable beginning in the year a worker becomes disabled, reaches age 62, or (in the case of survivors benefits) dies. If the benefits are not increased by the Congress, they are raised automatically each June whenever consumer prices rise 3 percent or more between specified annual base periods (usually the first quarter of the current and preceding years). The June 1, 1979, benefits quoted earlier reflect the 9.9 percent inflation adjustment effective on that date. The contributions and benefit base, scheduled at $22,900 for 1979, $25,900 for 1980, and $29,700 for 1981, is eligible for automatic adjustment thereafter. Such an adjustment will take place in any year following a year in which a benefit increase becomes effective.

Retirement Earnings Test

Since benefits are to replace lost earnings, an earnings test has always been part of the law. The test applies to beneficiaries under age 72 (age 70 in 1982). Earnings below a specified exempt amount have no effect on benefits received; for every $2 in earnings above the exempt amount, $1 in benefits is withheld. For beneficiaries age 65 to 72 (70 in 1980), the annual exempt amount is $4500 in 1979 and rises $500 per year to $6000 in 1982, with automatic adjustments thereafter to reflect increases in the general earnings level. For beneficiaries under 65, the annual exempt amount is $3480 in 1979, with similar automatic adjustments each year thereafter. Prior to 1978, there was also a monthly earnings test (one-twelfth the annual amount) which prevailed regardless of the amount of annual earnings received. This has been eliminated except for the initial year in which one receives a monthly cash benefit. This enables beneficiaries to receive monthly benefits upon retirement, despite the size of their annual earnings from work earlier in the year.

Financial

At the beginning of 1979, the OASDI funds, combined, had assets equal to 30 percent of expected 1979 outlays. Financing is adequate to maintain positive OASDI fund balances in the short range (1979 to 1983) under the trustees' intermediate and optimistic assumptions about future economic and demographic changes. Under the pessimistic assumptions, however, the DI fund balance will begin to experience cash flow problems in 1983, which will continue until a year or two after a scheduled increase in contribution rates in 1990. Over the next 25 years (1979 to 2003), the intermediate assumptions yield an average estimated actuarial surplus of 1.2 percent of taxable payroll; but over the next 75 years (1979 to 2053) a 1.2 percent average deficit is predicted (most of it in the last 25 years, 2009 to 2053).

Problems and Issues

Today, there are roughly three workers for every beneficiary. By the year 2025, there will be only two. This means that either more revenue will have to be raised (by increasing payroll tax rates or adopting additional alternative revenue sources) or less benefits will be paid (by raising the minimum age for retirement or actually paying smaller benefits than now assumed for the future). The declining worker-beneficiary ratio results from (1) the current labor-force participation by the large number of persons born in the post-World War II baby boom and their eventual retirement beginning about the year 2010, (2) the declining fertility rates since 1957, and (3) projected low fertility rates for the future.

There are many other problems and issues. One is the pressure for higher benefits for low earners. Current benefits for low earners are believed inadequate by some and too costly to correct at this time by others. Another issue is the liberalization of the disability definition for older workers (say, above age 55). Some want this change in order to help those who cannot get a job because of age or because of a disability severe enough to cause unemployment but not severe enough to merit eligibility for DI benefits. Others are opposed to this proposal, believing this is more properly an unemployment compensation problem, not a social security problem. Many want to eliminate the retirement earnings test to help beneficiaries who are hard-pressed financially, to encourage work, and to satisfy those who mistakenly believe the benefit is an annuity for which they have already paid. Opposed are those who want the earnings test to preserve the basic philosophy that benefits are to replace earnings lost because of retirement, death, or disability. Another proposal is to use general revenues to replace part or all of the payroll tax. Proponents argue that the payroll tax is regressive and already at its practical limits. They argue that future needs will require additional sources of financing. Those against the proposal fear that a runaway benefit program would ensue and that there would be a breakdown in public confidence in the system if the benefit-earnings relationship were so markedly broken.

There is also a drive underway to mandate universal coverage to prevent "double-dipping" by public pensioners who can qualify for the weighted minimum social security benefit with relatively small contributions, a benefit that was not designed for them but for career low earners. Some believe it is not fair for public employees to be excluded from sharing in the redistribution of income that takes place under social security. However, there is strong and powerful political opposition from the groups to be included. They argue that they are already making high payroll contributions under their own staff-retirement systems. They believe further that the technical difficulties in integrating their own staff-retirement systems with social security, without an increase in costs or reduction in benefits are too great.

Most women's organizations want more adequate benefits for aged widows, divorced wives, and young disabled wives. They want recognition for their contribution to the family's well-being when staying home to raise children (earnings credits and disability protection as homemakers). They also want to be entitled to benefits independently, not as dependents (separate earnings record and/or earnings-sharing of credits for benefits). They do not want benefit eligibility of a divorced wife to depend on the ex-husband's death or retirement or upon the duration of the marriage (10 years required now). They want the same benefit for all couples with the same combined preretirement earnings record (a one-earner couple gets more today than a two-earner couple). They want higher benefits from the contributions of the spouse with the lower earnings (not just the dependents benefits that most would receive if they had not worked and had not contributed).

These issues could be attacked individually or through a major restructuring of the social security system, such as earnings-sharing (crediting each spouse with 50 percent of the combined credit when married or divorced) or the establishment of a two-tier, double-decker benefit plan (a flat dollar amount payable to everyone upon eligibility regardless of earnings and an earnings-related benefit based solely on covered earnings). Depending on how they are structured, these proposals could prove costly. In any event they are controversial. Some fear and others want a needs test for the lower deck of the two-tier system, and some do not want to share earnings credits because they individually would not fare as well as they do under the present system. There are difficulties in designing either system without producing new inequities, and it may be technically difficult to make the change at this stage of development of the system.

Impact on Groups and the Economy

About 90 percent of the aged (65 and older) receive social security benefits. These benefits account for more than half of the total income of 56 percent of the married couples and 73 percent of the nonmarried persons. About 18 percent of the married couples and 34 percent of the nonmarried persons who were beneficiaries received almost all (90 percent or more) of their income from social security.

In 1976, 10.5 million households had money income below the official poverty level. These households contained 25 million persons, of whom 3.3 million were 65 and over. In the absence of social security benefits, the number of aged poor would probably have reached 10 million. Although social security goes largely to the aged, payments to aged and nonaged together probably kept 11 million persons of all ages out of poverty and certainly raised the income of others who still remained below the poverty level. The OASDI cash benefits cut the poverty gap in 1974 from $31 to $19 billion. About $11 billion represented payments to households which were raised above the poverty threshold and $6 billion to beneficiaries who remained below it.

Compared with whites, blacks benefit less from retirement insurance (their life expectancy is lower) and receive smaller benefits (their earnings are lower). However, they exceed whites in dependents and survivors benefits (they die earlier and leave larger dependent families) and in disability benefits (they are twice as likely to be disabled). Taken together, the system appears to provide roughly equal returns to blacks and whites.

In 1969, when social security was first included in the unified budget, OASDI taxes and outlays were each about 15 percent of total budget receipts and expenditures. The corresponding ratios for 1979 were estimated at 23 percent and 22 percent, respectively—and these taxes and outlays are part of a peacetime budget that has grown significantly relative to the gross national product. Social security taxes and outlays affect the size of the public sector and the economy in exactly the same way whether or not social security is part of the unified budget. Social security receipts and outlays are now so large that they must be increasingly considered by the nation's fiscal policymakers. But it would be better if policymakers made fiscal policy decisions elsewhere in the budget because the social security system is not an appropriate vehicle for discretionary, countercyclical fiscal policy. Unfortunately, this has not always been the case.

The social security system can also affect the nation's economic growth through its impact on savings and capital formation. Earlier empirical studies suggested that social security stimulated private savings. More recent studies suggest that a pay-as-you-go social security system has a significant depressive effect on private savings, but others are challenging the empirical analysis on which that conclusion is based.

Review of Social Security Programs

The social security program has been under serious review by several important groups. These include an HEW Study Group on the Treatment of Men and Women in Social Security (1979) in consultation with a Justice Department Task Force on Sex Discrimination (1978); the 1978–1979 Advisory Council on Social Security the HEW Universal Coverage Study Group (1979); the National Commission on Social Security (report due March 1981); and the President's Commission on Pension Policy (report due early 1981). Lively debate and possibly important legislation in the field of social security lies ahead.

Social Security Abroad

Most industrialized countries have some kind of social security system. The leading industrialized nations of Europe entered this field before the United States did and many have gone further. Comparisons are difficult to make because European social security systems are generally more broadly defined than the U.S. program (they include welfare programs, which we treat separately).

References

Ball, Robert M., *Social Security Today and Tomorrow*, Columbia University Press, New York, 1978; Myers, Robert J., *Social Security*, Irwin, Homewood, Ill., 1975; U.S. Social Security

Administration, *Social Security Programs throughout the World, 1975*, U.S. Department of Health, Education, and Welfare, 1976; U.S. Social Security Administration, *Social Security Handbook*, 6th ed., U.S. Department of Health, Education, and Welfare, July 1978; U.S. Social Security Administration, *Social Security Bulletin,* published monthly.

(*See also* Medicare program; Negative income tax)

Bernard Clyman

Socialism

Socialism has three different aspects: it refers to (1) a set of ideas or ideologies, (2) a set of political parties, and (3) a group of economic systems. The concept of socialism is both the criticism of capitalism and the idea of an alternative society. Socialist ideology has been mainly devoted to the criticism of capitalism. It holds that capitalism is primarily responsible for poverty, the exploitation of workers, pollution of the environment, unemployment and inflation, racial and sexual discrimination, and imperialist domination of other countries—which is the basic cause of war. Socialism, on the other hand, is described as producing a society of cooperation and collective ownership, in which there is a high degree of equality, no discrimination, no poverty, no exploitation, and no war.

Varieties of Socialist Ideology

The most widespread form of socialism is Marxism. Marxist socialism is the official dogma of over one-third of the world and has many adherents in the rest of the world. Marxism claims to be scientific in that it has a highly developed philosophy, economics, and historical view as well as a political program. Within Marxist ideologies, there are again many varieties, including the Soviet, Chinese, Yugoslav, and Eurocommunist views, as well as many independent Marxist views held by assorted scholars. Marxists view socialism as a stage in human social development that normally comes after a stage in economic evolution when capitalism has proved itself inadequate for human needs.

In addition to Marxism, there are many other views of socialism. In the early and mid-nineteenth century, the most popular view of socialism was that of a utopian colony of like-thinking and cooperative individuals, with no use for money and with completely democratic decision making on all issues. Throughout Western Europe there is a form of socialist ideology which labels as socialism any large amount of welfare reform within capitalism. In Western Europe, both the Socialist and the Communist parties agree that socialism must be democratic in its political forms.

The term socialism also applies to various political parties. From a few hundred adherents in the 1840s, Socialist and Communist parties have become a powerful force in most countries and rule over half the world. Karl Marx founded an International Workingmen's Association, lasting from 1864 to 1876, which included a number of small parties and many trade unions. A Second International was formed in 1889, which has united many social democratic parties from that time to the present.

The social democratic parties, mostly in Western Europe, advocate a limited amount of nationalization of industry; high welfare payments for unemployment, health care, and other purposes; but continued private capitalist ownership as the dominant economic form. They assume political democracy and very gradual changes. The Soviet Communist party advocates complete public ownership of all industry, central planning of all economic activities, and one-party political control. The Yugoslav communists want more decentralization, the Chinese want more equality of income, and the Western European communists want political democracy. Thus, even the various communist parties have major differences, sometimes leading to violence. There is also a vaguely defined socialism advocated by the leading political parties in much of Africa as well as in Cuba and Nicaragua.

Finally, the term socialism includes various kinds of noncapitalist economic systems. In Scandinavia, England, Germany, and France, socialism has brought cradle-to-the-grave welfare schemes plus a small amount of public ownership. In the Soviet Union and Eastern Europe, socialism has meant an entirely new economic system. All industry is owned by the government and run by government managers. Half of agriculture is government-owned; the other half is owned collectively by large groups of farmers (though with strong, government direction). Economic planners designate objectives for the whole economy, stating how much of every commodity is to be produced, what its price shall be, where labor is to be allocated, and where capital and materials are to be allocated. These plans are legislated into law and must be followed by every manager. Wages are paid according to the amount of work done, its degree of difficulty or skill, favorable or unfavorable geography (such as the Arctic in the Soviet Union), and so forth. Managers receive several times the salary of ordinary workers. Consumers may buy any commodity for which they have money. But it is illegal to own a factory or to produce anything for private profit by employing other people. Individual handicrafts, although legal, are mostly done in cooperatives.

China has followed the Soviet Union in government ownership and in one-party political control. The Chinese, however, have a much smaller spread of income, so that a manager will receive only two or three times the average wage—whereas a Soviet manager will receive eight or nine times the average wage. The Chinese also insist that most managers and intellectuals do some manual labor at times.

Yugoslavia has collective ownership or control by the workers in all enterprises through an elected workers council at each enterprise. Except for some wage and price regulations, all production and pricing decisions are made by the workers councils (and the managers appointed by them) according to the competitive conditions in the market. There is very little central planning.

References

Cole, G. D. H., *A History of Socialist Thought*, 6 vols., Macmillan, New York, 1953–1959; Dobb, Maurice, *Welfare Economics and the Economics of Socialism*, Cambridge University Press, Cambridge, 1970; Horvat, Branco, *An Essay on Yugoslav Society*, M. E. Sharpe, White Plains, N.Y., 1970; Sherman, Howard, *The Soviet Economy*, Little, Brown, Boston, 1970.

(*See also* Capitalism; Communism; Comparative economic systems, an overview; Maoism; Marxism)

Howard J. Sherman

Special drawing rights

The special drawing right (SDR) is an international financial asset created by the International Monetary Fund (IMF) and serves as an international unit of account, a means of payment among certain eligible official entities, and an international reserve asset. It is the agreed-upon objective of the IMF member countries to make the SDR the principal reserve asset of the international monetary system.

History

The Board of Governors of the IMF agreed at the 1967 annual meetings in Rio de Janeiro to create a new international monetary reserve asset to be named the special drawing right. SDRs can be created only by the IMF. The legal framework for their creation and allocation to member countries was established by the first amendments to the Articles of Agreement of the IMF adopted in 1968. The second amendment (1978) provided for a considerable liberalization of the rules governing the use of the SDR. On January 1, 1970, the first distribution of 3.4 billion SDRs was made to IMF member countries. Subsequent distributions of 3 billion SDRs each were made in 1971 and 1972, and 4 billion SDRs each were scheduled for allocation in 1979, 1980, and 1981, bringing the total amount of SDRs to 21.4 billion by the end of 1981.

Characteristics

The value of the SDR has been redefined several times. Initially, the value of the SDR was defined as equivalent to one-thirty-fifth of an ounce of gold. This value was the same as that of US$1, which also was pegged to gold. After the breakdown of the par-value Bretton Woods system, a new valuation procedure for the SDR was intro-duced. Effective July 1, 1974, the SDR was defined in terms of a currency basket. The currencies represented in the basket were those of the 16 IMF member countries whose exports of goods and services exceeded 1 percent of world exports in the 1962–1972 period. On July 1, 1978, the currencies represented were adjusted to take account of the changes in world trade patterns that had occurred in the meantime.

On January 1, 1981, the valuation of the SDR was simplified by basing it on the currencies of the 5 most significant countries in the world economy. The weight of the various currencies are as follows:

U.S. dollar	42 percent
Deutsche mark	19 percent
French franc	13 percent
Japanese yen	13 percent
U.K. pound sterling	13 percent

The weights reflect the relative international importance of these currencies based on the value of goods and services exported by the respective countries and use of the currency as an international reserve asset during the period 1975–79.

The interest rate on the SDR is determined by the weighted average of the short-term interest rates prevailing in the 5 countries.

There is a provision for a revision of the currency basket at 5-year intervals.

Uses

Currently the SDRs issued by the IMF can be used only in transactions among mon-etary authorities (central banks) and certain international institutions. That is, the SDR is transferable only among a limited number of official entities. SDRs may be used to purchase foreign currency from the IMF, to make payments to the IMF, or to engage in direct financial transactions among the official holders of SDRs.

References

deVries, M. G. (ed.), *The International Monetary Fund 1966–1971*, vol. 1, pts. I and II, International Monetary Fund, Washington, D.C., 1976; Polak, J. J., "The SDR as a Basket of Currencies," *IMF Staff Papers*, vol. 26, No. 4, December 1979, pp. 627–653.

(*See also* Balance of International payments; Bretton Woods Conference; Foreign exchange rates; International economics, an overview; International Monetary Fund; Liquidity, international; Smithsonian Agreement)

H. Robert Heller

Specialization (see Division of labor)

Spillovers (see Externalities)

Stages theory of economic development

A stage theory of economic development describes economic growth by a succession of clearly defined processes. Economic analysts generally seek to isolate the functional relationships which explain a nation's moving from low to higher incomes and from relatively simple to highly dependent means of production. Almost all such relationships implicitly specify movement through gradual processes.

A stage theory must move progressively forward over time. Any single stage must be clearly defined, with a limited number of characteristics distinguishing it from all other stages. The theory must correctly predict the successive stages. The characteristics that distinguish stages must be observable, and, ideally, measurable. A stage theorist must be able to identify an economic system at a given stage and compare the states of development among nations.

Under the contemporary analytical approach to economic development, stage theories have been analyzed as incomplete treatises. The standard criticism levied against most stage schemata is their inability to finely distinguish the turning points as a nation leaves one stage and enters another. It is argued that the stagists have, in fact, outlined economic, sociological, and institutional stages with blurred endings and beginnings.

The earliest stage theories were reactions against the interpretation of economic change based on individual decision-making adjustments to market conditions. These stage theorists questioned marginalist theory and relied almost exclusively on empiricism and social change in interpreting economic growth. While more contemporary stage analysts have incorporated the market action-reaction mechanism, they still heavily depend on historical socioeconomic changes to explain economic development.

Karl Bücher's Stages Theory

The first major works of stage theorists appeared in the late nineteenth century. Representative of the German historical school, Karl Bücher (1901) divided the economic growth of nations into three stages. The first stage is the closed household economy, characterized by the lack of any exchanges in the production of goods from raw material to final form. When exchanges take place between producer and consumer, the second stage, the town economy, has been attained. The transition from domestic to town economy, from nonexchange to exchange, is not abrupt and may take centuries to accomplish.

The third stage, the national economy, is characterized by the establishment of wholesale trade and markets—producer and consumer are estranged. The transition from town to national economy is based on the rise of political organization–permitting nation states.

Clark-Fisher Approach

Colin Clark (1940) and Allen G. B. Fisher (1940) viewed economic development through a triad of occupational stages. Nations beginning as initial primary goods producers (agriculture and fishing) move onto a higher level of development with the production of manufactured goods. This secondary stage comes through advancements in knowledge and skills. With the concomitant material accumulation, nations then seek greater welfare through higher forms of culture, and labor moves from a goods orientation to a service orientation. Representative of the tertiary stage is the growth in the transport, distribution, and public administration sectors. The highest levels of income are attained through nonmaterial output.

The Clark-Fisher stages approach has been criticized on two counts. Whereas the tertiary stage is last in their schema, for some low-income nations employment in the tertiary sector has exceeded the secondary sector's employment. Moreover, there is no theoretical basis to accept high employment in the service sector as representative of higher income levels. Conceivably the attainment of luxury manufacturers may be preferable to that of services or culture. However, the transition from primary to secondary employment has represented the development path of modern nations and is a good explanatory variable for income growth.

Marx's Stage Theory

A somewhat earlier, but an unquestionably more influential, stage theorist is Karl Marx. Marx, as economic historian, provided the key variable bridging his various epochs. In Marx's theories, economic systems reach higher stages through the strained relations that run between the dynamic forces of production (knowledge and technological change) and the slower-evolving social and political organizations which permit production. The social, psychological, and economic forces that are continually at work between the accumulators and owners of capital and their workers generate the evolution from feudalism to capitalism to socialism.

Marx gave a demonstrable measure for the decline of capitalism: a falling rate of profit and a rising army of the unemployed. Marx also provided the foundation for the most influential modern stage theorist, Walter W. Rostow.

Walter Rostow's Stages

As a noncommunist manifesto, Rostow's *Stages of Economic Growth* is a foray into positioning the sweep of modern economic history under capitalism into neat and hopeful epochs. Similar to the assimilation of Marx's ideas, Rostow's stages and language have entered our lexicon. Whereas Marx's "oppressed" and "exploited" are code words for revolutionary change, Rostow's terms "leading sectors," "takeoffs," and "drives to maturity" are hopeful banners of evolution.

Specifically, Rostow delegates the historical performance of modern industrial economies into stages of (1) the traditional, (2) the preconditions for takeoff, (3) the takeoff, (4) the drive to maturity, and, finally, (5) the age of mass consumption. While having a logical appeal to the historian, Rostow's five-stage schema is criticized for imprecisely defining the institutional and economic changes from stage to stage.

To Rostow's credit the most significant stage is set apart with concrete characteristics. The essential takeoff is marked by a doubling in the rate of investment. Within this stage there also emerge leading industrial sectors and a political system which together fuel expansion.

Rostow's takeoff and the requisite performance of the investment variable spurred researchers to study the investment history of the high-income nations. In these investigations a discernible jump of the investment ratio has not been universally detected. Moreover, the seemingly clear concept of leading sectors and their identification is seen as becoming mired in the links between industries under the impulse of growth.

Despite its lack of strict empirical verification, Rostow's work has provided the development economist with a recipe of the necessary ingredients for development. It has been suggested that Rostow's stages would be better read as a prospectus rather than a treatise.

Alexander Gerschenkron's *Economic Backwardness in Historical Perspective,* published in 1962, studied the economic performance of nations in Eastern Europe. Gerschenkron establishes six propositions based on a nation's extent of backwardness as the key elements in its future development pattern. While receiving general acceptance, his work tends to explain the recent growth of selected nations rather than to establish a historical long-range set of defined stages.

While no writer has presented a definitive stage theory of economic development, stage theorists have provided the development economist with avenues of research and with salient requirements for economic development. Whether the stage theorist can ever meet the strict tests drawn for a successful stage, theory may be contemplated in light of Henry Bruton's remark (1960), "It must be recognized that in a long period analysis the distinction between 'economic' and 'non-economic' factors loses significance and . . . that economic growth must be seen as a special aspect of general social evolution rather than as a process which can be factored out of the social system and studied in isolation."

References

Bruton, Henry, "Contemporary Theorizing on Economic Growth," in B. Hoselitz (ed.), *Theories of Economic Growth,* Free Press, New York, 1960, pp. 297–298; Bücher, Karl, *Industrial Evolution,* S. M. Wickett (trans.), Toronto University Press, Toronto, 1901; Clark, C., *The Conditions of Economic Progress,* Macmillan, New York, 1940; Fisher, Allen G. B., "Production, Primary, Secondary and Tertiary," *Economic Record,* vol. 15, 1939, pp. 24–38; Fishlow, A., "Empty Economic Stages," *Economic Journal,* vol. 75, no. 297, March 1965, pp. 112–125; Gerschenkron, Alexander, *Economic Backwardness in Historical Perspective,* Harvard University Press, Cambridge, Mass., 1962; Marx, Karl, and F. Engels, *The Communist Manifesto,* S. Moore (trans.), Washington Square Press, New York, 1964; Rostow, Walter W., *Stages of Economic Growth,* Cambridge University Press, Cambridge, 1960.

(*See also* Economic growth; Infrastructure)

Bernard S. Katz

Stagflation

Stagflation describes the condition of inflation's persistence and intractability when the economy's resources are utilized at below its potential. The condition is puzzling in the perspective of conventional economic theory because inflation traditionally has been described as caused by too much money chasing too few goods; i.e., either an excess of money or an excess of demand over available supply pushes up the general level of prices in sustained fashion.

Two major variants may be found: first, Milton Friedman's declaration that "inflation is always and everywhere a monetary phenomenon"; and second, in the alternative Keynesian expenditure-income approach, wherein an inflationary gap develops when the sum of money demands for goods and services is more than 100 percent of available or potential producible output, thereby generating rising prices. In the former approach, the causality of inflation lies primarily in an exogenously determined supply of money, in contrast with the latter's view that price levels are related to changes in aggregate demand, while influenced by an at least partly endogenously determined money supply (and its velocity). In each case, however, the phenomenon of significantly rising prices is inconsistent with low, zero, or negative economic growth that, in combination, is the hallmark of stagflation.

In the United States, the coexistence of slack demand and rising prices has been registered not only in periods of slow economic growth but also in recessions. Indeed, the failure of prices to decline during recessions and an upward drift of the inflation floor at recession lows have become increasingly evident in the post-World War II period, as shown in the accompanying table.

Business cycle, trough year	Unemployment rate, %	Consumer prices, % change, Dec.–Dec.
1949	5.9	−1.8
1954	5.5	0.5
1958	6.8	1.8
1961	6.7	0.7
1970	4.9	5.5
1975	8.5	7.0

Varied Explanations

Explanations of stagflation are varied and, increasingly, depend on the expectational behavior of labor and business. Indeed, it is the initiating causes of inflation which feed expectations of ever-rising wages and prices that are said to be essential for and to precede the condition of stagflation.

Among the initiating causes are those related to money-supply changes and excess aggregate demand, as noted earlier. However, independently, expectations may also be supported by so-called cost-push inflation arising from imperfections in the working of factor and product markets where monopolistic or oligopolistic practices prevail; imperfections resulting from shifts in the structure of demand whereby prices increase in sectors as demand rises without being accompanied by price declines in sectors where demand eases (because the mobility of resources is low); and arising from pricing behavior guided by long-run cost or rate-of-return considerations.

In the original classical-monetarist approach, stagflation could only be a transient phenomenon because assumptions of flexible wages and prices precluded other possibilities. Departures from full employment would result in competitively dictated declines in both wages and prices, a situation which eventually would establish conditions of revived demand in factor and product markets. In the interim phase, unemployment would rise and competition for jobs would increase, so that wages would decline more than prices. The resultant falloff in real wages would generate increased demand for labor (and reduced supply), which would eliminate any involuntary unemployment.

Monetarist Analysis

The modern monetarist analysis retains this inverse connection between changes in real wages and employment demand, while accepting the empirically established downward rigidity of wages and prices observed in the 1960s and 1970s. The modern monetarist also incorporates expectations in the theory of stagflation. Indeed, the expectations concept remains the basis for an explanation of the persistence of stagflation, possibly over several years, because that duration might be required for the dissipation of worker and company attitudes of resistance to lessened growth or to cuts in wages and prices. Thus, it is the doubt held by workers and companies that the condition of lessened aggregate demand is general and permanent which delays the wage and price reductions that would otherwise clear markets and restore equilibrium. As long as the more optimistic and irrationally held expectations are retained, both prices and employment rates may continue to rise.

Expansionary monetary policies might shorten the stagflation period but only at the cost of more inflation. If expectations of continuing high wage and price increases are validated by money-supply and demand growth, unemployment might be driven below the so-called natural rate—a so-called long-term sustainable level. The validation (through stimulated monetary growth) of successively higher expectations, as an alternative to stagflation, appears more politically palatable to governments and provides the basis for the accelerationist theory of inflation.

Momentum Theory

Allied but separately identifiable from the monetarist approach is the momentum theory of inflation and stagflation, which combines the elements of entrenched inflationary expectations with the sluggish response of manufacturing prices to short-run shifts in demand. Primarily reflecting market situations characterized by administered prices or competition among the few (which are said to predominate in manufacturing), the shared long-run interest of skilled workers and employers in continued employment relationships and in long-run sales and growth considerations looms more important than do short-run demand changes. This attitude thus leads to price strategies based on markups over unit costs of production at normal levels of output. Accordingly, prices may move higher during periods of slack demand in response to cost increases incurred previously during expansion periods but which as a matter of long-run company strategy were not at that time passed through into higher prices.

With wages and prices both geared to the long run, the acceleration of inflation which was associated with the demand-pull inflationary conditions of the late 1960s and early 1970s in the United States raised expectations of the magnitude of normal wage and price advances. This provided a momentum for expectations and inflation that extended into the middle 1970s, when aggregate demand was easing.

Under these circumstances, the economic policy prescription to thwart stagflation frequently is directed toward avoidance of overrobust expansion in economic growth for a period sufficiently long to lower expectations of inflation. However, this policy frequently has been characterized as neither politically acceptable nor feasible in the United States. Sometimes, the risk of large job losses over an extended period that this policy might cause by overdoses of fiscal and monetary restraint prompts proposals of an incomes policy to moderate the wage and price increases that develop in an expanding economy.

Cost-Push Explanation

Related to situations where high demand does not prevail, cost-push is a more familiar classification in describing the concurrence of inflation and low or zero economic growth. The major pressure is said to be rising wage costs imposed by powerful unions which are passed on into higher prices especially under conditions of inelastic demand for labor, rivalry among unions, etc. New elements on the cost or supply side in recent years have been both sharply higher prices caused by oil price increases mandated by the Organization for Petroleum Exporting Countries (OPEC) and rising food prices. These prompted labor on the basis of accelerated inflation to seek higher wage settlements, which in turn fed the wage-price (or, some say, the wage-wage) spiral.

An increase in costs ordinarily causes a reduction in output and employment in the standard case, unless validated by price advances via increases in the money supply. Under cost-push inflation, the macroeconomic policy recommendation of restraint in demand through fiscal and monetary means is said to be ineffective because its effects are concentrated more on reductions in production and employment than on the slowing of cost and price increases.

Closely allied with this is the view of Charles L. Schultze that changes in the structure of demand cause inflation in the United States. As shifts in demand for products and services develop, prices rise in industries experiencing increases without lowering them where sales decreases are occurring. As a result, even the demand-deficient industries may be required to pay higher wages and prices for resources to maintain production. As a result, average prices for all industries tend to rise secularly.

Critics charge that cost-push based on the monopoly power of union labor and paucity of firms cannot serve as an independent initiator of inflation. The latter is a continuing process, it is said, and so the exercise of monopoly power by firms could result merely in one-time price increases to obtain maximum profits. Without changes in the money supply or other macro-aggregate influences, increased claims for output in markets influenced by monopoly elements would be accompanied by reduced claims by competitive sectors—resulting in no change in average prices. Monetarists argue that only a steadily increasing degree of monopoly or oligopoly power could sustain the cost-push theory of inflation.

Nevertheless, cost-push does play an important though secondary role in the inflation theories of some monetarists. Price rises in slack markets are said still to be experiencing a step-by-step adjustment to a new equilibrium in a catch-up process following an initiating period of excess demand. Thus, continuously rising prices during slow economic growth or recession are said to reflect more a stretching out in time of the impact of the excessive demand in the preceding expansion phase of the business cycle. Accordingly, the policy prescription of the critics remains centered on curbing aggregate demand in the expansion phase, especially by control of the money supply. In this theory, the root of the accelerated inflation in the 1970s was validation of unusual cost increases (e.g., energy and food in the mid- and late 1970s) through increases in the money supply.

Other Theories

In still another view, theories of the delayed effects of demand-pull or of cost-push as explanations of stagflation are said to have been inapplicable in the 1970s. In this newer theory, the equilibrium full-employment unemployment rate—the lowest rate without accelerating inflation—has risen in the 1970s. Though the unemployment rate remained high during the business cycle expansion that began in early 1975 (clinging to $5\frac{1}{2}$ to 6 percent at the cyclical peak of 1978 to 1979 rather than returning to the low 4 percent rate of the 1950s), this did not reflect any deficiency of employment opportunities. Instead, such factors as increased search time for jobs, structural changes in the labor force, and involuntary unemployment have supported a higher full-employment unemployment rate. Because income transfers such as unemployment benefits and other public welfare payments are more generous, job search times have become prolonged, especially because multiworker households have increased in number. Also, the structural factor reflects a higher proportion of women and young adults (both of whose unemployment rate is typically higher than average) in the labor force. Higher legislated minimum wage rates also tend to increase the unemployment rate for unskilled, newer workers. Accordingly, a natural rate of unemployment at full employment would need to be revised upward—in a sense, denying that stagflation exists in the customary way.

The other side of this theory refers to the lowered potential real growth rate of the U.S. economy due to reduced productivity. Accordingly, measures to increase aggregate demand will generate inflation at lower economic growth rates than formerly in the post-World War II period.

References

Cagan, Phillip, *The Hydra-Headed Monster: The Problem of Inflation in the United States,* American Enterprise Institute for Public Policy Research, Washington, D.C., 1974; Gordon, R. J., "Recent Developments in the Theory of Inflation and Unemployment," *Journal of Monetary Economics,* vol. 2, 1976, pp. 185–219; Phelps, E. S., *Inflation Policy and Unemployment Theory: The Cost-Benefit Approach to Monetary Planning,* Norton, New York, 1972.

(*See also* Administered prices; Competition; Employment and unemployment; Expectations; Federal Reserve policy; Incomes policy; Inflation; Labor unions; Monetary policy; Money supply; Monopoly and oligopoly; Phillips curve; Velocity of circulation of money)

Herman I. Liebling

Stagnation thesis

The stagnation thesis is a theory which states that industrialized nations become mature because investment opportunities that could absorb savings are lacking and that, therefore, these nations' economies stagnate. The foremost advocate of the stagnation thesis was Alvin H. Hansen, who argued that four factors caused a marked decline in U.S. investment opportunities: (1) the rapid decline in population growth; (2) the closing of the frontier; (3) the lack of new industries, which would use up large amounts of capital funds; and (4) the increasing importance of depreciation reserves so that corporations did not have to tap new savings in order to finance replacement capital needs.

Other Economists' Views

By far the most important part of Hansen's theory was his argument that shrinking investment opportunity was due to declining population growth and the limitation on territorial expansion. When he propounded his theory in the late 1930s and early 1940s, he did not foresee, as did Marshall, the possibilities of technical advance that might revive these factors. Hansen's ideas were really a reversion to those of Adam Smith with his full-employment-of-riches notion and to Mill with his emphasis on increased productivity and foreign investment.

To this group of economists must be added Keynes —not the Keynes of the *General Theory*—but the Keynes of the *Economic Consequences of the Peace*. The trouble that Keynes foresaw in 1919 was an increased propensity to consume associated with diminished accumulation, investment, and, consequently, economic development. In the *General Theory*, we have the Keynesian contradiction rising from the simple and unwarranted extension of the short-run model. In the long run, capitalists are supposed to generate, independently of each other, an increasing propensity to save and a decreasing inducement to invest. The possibilities of increasing the latter are limited, and the economy could reach a state of full investment. Consequently, the emphasis should be placed on fiscal action by the government to increase the propensity to consume.

The Keynesian theory resembled its predecessors in maintaining a long-run decline in the inducement to invest as a country moved toward its full complement of riches. But those theories ended in a stationary state of full employment; however, Keynes' stagnation produced chronic unemployment because of the failure to save pari passu with the inducement to invest. He maintained that individuals and, particularly, businesses would want to save and hoard their accumulation as the country got poorer.

Hansen's weakness was that he accepted the notion of a long-run propensity to consume or to save that was independent of the inducement to invest. While he agreed that the savings–income ratio might be constant rather than increasing over the long run, he believed that declining investment opportunities would leave an unfilled gap that would be eliminated only by chronic unemployment. In short, he accepted the Keynesian contradiction with its implication for the need of government action, particularly to increase public and private consumption.

The remedy for classical stagnation was increased saving and investment, and increased foreign trade that would help overcome diminishing returns. The remedy for Keynes-Hansen stagnation was an all-out attack on the propensity to save.

References

Hansen, Alvin H., *Fiscal Policy and Business Cycles*, Greenwood, Westport, N.Y., 1941; Keynes, J. M., *Economic Consequences of the Peace*, Harcourt Brace Jovanovich, New York, 1920; Keynes, J. M., *General Theory of Employment, Interest and Money*, Macmillan, New York, 1936.

(*See also* Economic growth; Propensity to consume or to save and inducement to invest)

Arthur Smithies

Standard of living

Although the concept of standard of living has been used extensively since the turn of the century by economists and lay people alike, it has failed to achieve a precise meaning. In essence, it refers to a manner or way of living (i.e., level of living) which an individual or a society feels is important to attain (a standard). Nearly 35 years ago, J. S. Davis (1945) sought to reform the careless use of this term by economists, state leaders, business executives, and the average individual. In his benchmark article, he drew a chief distinction between level (what is) and standard (level wanted and worked for), and between consumption (goods and services consumed) and living (consumption plus intangible conditions of life). Although standard and level of living can be the same under conditions of satisfaction, apathy, or hopelessness, this is an unusual use of standard of living.

Standard of Living Versus Family Budget

Nevertheless, journalists especially have continued to confuse the issue and have used the term usually as level of consumption or, less frequently, as level of living. Researchers in acknowledging that most people use the term in this sense have defined standard of living for respondents in their surveys. For example, G. Katona (1975) defined it as "managing to live on your income pretty much the same (as you are now)," while J. L. Hafstrom and M. M. Dunsing (1973) defined it as "the things you have and the way you are living now."

The definition and measurement of standard of living perhaps has provoked as much attention in social science as has any other term. For example, expert committees in the United Nations and in the United States, as well as individual authors, have concerned themselves with this topic. Since 1967, the Bureau of Labor Statistics annually has developed standard-of-living budgets at designated lower, moderate, and higher levels for four-person families. These are an outgrowth of the earlier city worker's family budget developed for a modest but adequate living standard beginning in 1946. Currently, an Expert Committee on Family Budget Revision for the Bureau of Labor Statistics is revising the methodology for obtaining standard-of-living budgets.

Standard of living is used almost universally. It is included in the Charter of the United Nations as a general goal of international economic and social activity. It is used most often (in the sense of level of living) as a measure of progress in living conditions of nations at different points in time and for the comparison of these conditions in different nations at one point in time. In the United States, the hypothetical family budgets are used to compare the cost of attaining the three levels of consumption in selected urban areas. The budgets are based on actual expenditures of U.S. families. They are collected about every 10 years and are updated annually by using price changes reported in the consumer price index.

Higher or Lower Standard of Living

The rising standard of living has been one of the major goals of American society. It also has been stressed in American society to include continuous progress in the upgrading of many types of purchases (Katona, 1975). The idea embodied in this has led to criticism of Americans for being too easily manipulated, like puppets, by advertisers to buy more or better consumption goods, resulting in wasteful expenditures. Others, notably Katona, argue that the increase in expenditures for consumption goods brought about by the striving for a better standard of living results in consumer investment. Consumer investment itself acts, as does business investment, as a stimulus in the economy.

The onslaught of the energy shortage, high unemployment, and worldwide inflation, partially stimulated by the aspirations of people throughout the world for a higher standard of living, has resulted in some serious questions concerning whether the standard of living should be lowered drastically to help solve these problems. Katona argues that this solution would not work since he feels it is the wanting and striving for improvement in private living standards that form the solid basis of American prosperity.

Even more confusion has been added to the meaning of this term in recent years. Ideas such as quality of life and lifestyles have been equated with standard of living by some, while others have used standard of living as an influencing factor on quality of life and on lifestyles. Still others talk about the influence of quality of life and lifestyles on standard of living. As long as this confusion in the use of the term exists, it is important for economists to define standard of living in such a way that there will be no doubt as to its meaning.

References

Bureau of Labor Statistics, *Autumn 1978 Urban Family Budgets and Comparative Indexes for Selected Urban Areas*, U.S. Department of Labor Bulletin No. 79-305, 1979; Davis, J. S., "Standards and Content of Living," *American Economic Review*, vol. 35, no. 1, March 1945, pp. 1–15; Hafstrom, J. L., and M. M. Dunsing, "Level of Living: Factors Influencing the Homemaker's Satisfaction," *Home Economics Research Journal*, vol. 2, 1973, pp. 119–132; Katona, G., *Psychological Economics*, Elsevier, New York, 1975.

(*See also* Family budgets)

                                                                Jeanne L. Hafstrom

Static analysis

Static analysis refers generally to any analysis in which the passage of time does not play an essential role. A static analysis can be applied to flow variables (which are measured per unit of time) if the flows do not change any stocks which affect the equilibrium. In addition, a hybrid form of dynamic analysis uses the tools of static analysis to consider a sequence of short periods in which stocks change at the end of each period owing to flows within the period. With the notable exception of the *IS-LM* model, static analysis has been most fruitfully applied to microeconomic problems.

In a great many microeconomic problems, we can safely abstract from growth in the economy and deal with a model in which the equilibrium, once achieved, is unchanged period after period. Such an equilibrium is termed a stationary state. Further, we are very frequently interested only in the final effects of some change in a parameter of the model—say, in a tax or a price. In such problems, we need to examine the equilibrium only at one arbitrary point in time since the equilibrium is the same at any other time.

Two Types of Comparative Static Problems

Comparative static analysis examines the changes in the final equilibrium that result from some specified changes in the parameters of the model. Paul Samuelson (1948) observed that comparative static problems fall naturally into either of two types:

1. The first describes the optimizing behavior of individual economic agents (consumers, firms, or the like) as a function of the opportunities available to the agents. The solution of these problems normally involves finding a maximum or minimum of some objective function subject to the constraints which describe the opportunity set.
2. The second sort of problem studies an equilibrium involving the interaction (normally across markets) of a number of economic agents. In these cases, the equilibrium cannot be described as a maximum or minimum of some function. Instead, conditions for the stability of the equilibrium must be specified.

Samuelson's division of comparative static problems is fruitful because it focuses on the information required to make definite qualitative statements about the effects of a change in a parameter of the problem. It so happens that the ratio of the change in each endogenous variable to the change in the parameter generally can be expressed in terms of the determinants of certain matrices of partial derivatives. The conditions for achieving a maximum or minimum often restrict these determinants so that the sign of the ratio of changes can be inferred. The sign of this ratio indicates which direction the endogenous variable moves in response to a change in the parameter.

In the second sort of problem, Samuelson showed that a correspondence often exists between the conditions for stability of the equilibrium and conditions for definite results in a comparative statics problem. This duality, called the correspondence principle, allows one to find definite results for comparative static problems conditional upon observed stability or to infer stability given observed comparative statics results. Thus, it is frequently imperative to carry out a formal analysis of the conditions for stability in order to obtain definite comparative static results.

A stability analysis examines whether, beginning from a point away from the equilibrium, the model moves to the equilibrium as times goes to infinity. One may consider any feasible starting point or only points near the equilibrium (local stability). Stability analysis is a sort of abbreviated dynamic analysis in which the only important question is whether the model converges to the stationary-state equilibrium.

Although static analysis has a long history in economics (for example, Marshall, 1920), the modern form using differential calculus was popularized by John Hicks (1939). Samuelson's *Foundations* clearly demonstrated the usefulness of formal techniques and introduced the correspondence principle to extend the range of problems for which definite answers may be obtained. Today a static analysis is standard operating procedure whenever the problem at hand can be analyzed in terms of the final effects on a stationary state.

References

Hicks, John R., *Value and Capital*, Oxford University Press, Oxford, 1939; Marshall, Alfred, *Principles of Economics*, 8th ed., Macmillan, New York, 1920; Samuelson, Paul A., *Foundations of Economic Analysis*, Harvard University Press, Cambridge, Mass., 1947.

(*See also* General equilibrium; *IS-LM* model)

Michael R. Darby

Statistical techniques in economics and business, an overview

The basic concepts of economics can be stated as functional relationships among variables. In order for one to apply economic theory to real-life situations, appropriate statistical measurements must replace the mathematical symbols used by the theorist. Obtaining these measurements requires the use of statistical techniques in the gathering and analysis of these data. One of the principal areas of applied statistics is economic analysis and business management. Sample survey methods are widely used in data collection, involving applications of probability theory in the design of surveys and in the interpretation of the validity of the results. Regression analysis is the basic statistical technique in econometrics, the application of mathematics and statistics to economic analysis. Time series analysis, in its various aspects, is the basic statistical technique in forecasting for an economy, an industry, or a business firm. The special technique of index number methods is fundamental to the measurement of economic and business conditions and change.

Modern computer capability has made possible development of large-scale models of how economies and firms function and react to changing conditions. Development of large data banks, easily accessible by time sharing, has given statisticians access to quantities of data far beyond the reach of analysis prior to the 1960s. Development and dissemination of software packages have made available the newest and most sophisticated statistical techniques, economically and rapidly, to the academic and business community.

Regression Analysis

Econometrics, as a special branch of economic theory, has developed rapidly during the last half-century, and much of the theory has been reported in *Econometrica*, the journal of the Econometric Society. Economists such as Ragnar Frisch, Kenneth Arrow, and Joseph Schumpeter were among the pioneers. Regression analysis is the basic technique for measuring the relationships between economic variables. Regression is a term originated by Sir Francis Galton. His studies in heredity indicated a tendency of observations to regress toward the mean. The term now applies to methods of investigating relationships between variables.

Simple regression analysis seeks to estimate the relationship between the two variables X (independent) and Y (dependent). Once the relationship has been estimated, we may wish to determine the closeness of the relationship or the accuracy of any prediction made on the basis of the relationship. This is correlation analysis. Time does not enter into regression and correlation analysis, which may be likened to an instantaneous photograph.

In regression analysis, some assumption about the form of the relationship must be made. Varying assumptions give rise to linear and nonlinear regression functions. The regression of a dependent variable on more than one independent variable is termed multiple regression. A regression model consists of the relationship between the variables and the distribution of the error terms. The assumption may be that observed data are generated by a linear stochastic equation of the form $Y = a + bx + u$, or data = pattern + error. The forecast can vary from the expected pattern by an amount u which must be estimated in probabilistic terms. Since the statistician is usually working with samples, the parameter values must be estimated. The most commonly used method for fitting a line of regression (estimating line) is the method of least squares, which minimizes the sum of the squared deviations around the line. A measure of error may then be determined, called the standard error of estimate. The measurement of correlation is usually by means of the statistic r. The statistic r^2 measures how well the observations fit around the regression line.

A first step in linear regression analysis is to prepare a scatter diagram. Demand and supply curves, cost curves, and production and consumption functions may be estimated by regression analysis. In multiple regression there are one dependent variable (for example, sales) and two or more independent variables which are selected on the basis of their influence on sales. Thus, gross national product, volume of advertising expenditures, product prices, and so on could be tested for their influence on sales by using regression. Economic theory would suggest appropriate variables to test. If any or all of the selected variables in the regression analysis are found to influence sales, they can then be used to predict future levels of sales.

The Role of Data

The applied statistician is always conscious of the need to procure, prepare, and handle data. The role of data is critical to the accuracy and usefulness of predictions based on statistical methods. Data must provide information on those factors which are essential in decision making and planning. Much of the key data used by economists are complex aggregates such as gross national product. The spectacular increase in the quantity of data available in the last half-century has not necessarily been accompanied by improvement in accuracy.

Data can be collected from primary sources such as accounting records, or from secondary sources such as materials published by governmental agencies. Many of these data series are the result of sample surveys. Sampling theory is well-developed and relies on random methods which make possible procedures for estimating sampling error. However, measurement errors may also occur in the actual collection and processing of data; these may be called nonsampling errors. In practice, adequacy of public and private budgets for data collection is critical in providing an acceptable level of quality and quantity of basic data.

Index Numbers

An index number is a quantity which shows changes over time by its variations. Economists and business analysts frequently use index numbers not only for their simplicity as a statement of relative change over a base period but also as measures of magnitudes which are not susceptible to direct measurement, such as business activity, physical volume of production, and the general level of prices. Pioneer work in the development of index number formulas was done by Francis Y. Edgeworth and Irving Fisher.

Constructing an index number is as much a problem of economic theory as of statistical technique. An index number is limited to measurement of change in magnitude from one period of time to another. An index is expressed as a percentage of a reference base period (usually expressed as 100) chosen for its representative character.

While simple index numbers (relating to one series) may be useful, most index numbers are aggregates of several series, sometimes numbered in hundreds. The statistical techniques for combining series into an index number revolve around the appropriate weighting system. Base weighting (Laspeyres), given-period weighting (Paasche), and the so-called ideal index number proposed by Irving Fisher are major types. Complex weighting structures may be necessary in order to produce a suitably weighted index number. Thus, the determination of relative importance of the goods and services for which consumers spend their money requires sample surveys of consumers' purchases. Beginning with World War I the growth of industry and organized labor created interest in indexes of consumer prices, often improperly called cost-of-living indexes. Analogous indexes of wholesale or producers prices have been developed. Indexes of the level of industrial production, stock prices, farm prices, and the like are closely watched by economists and business analysts.

The development of a system of national income and product accounts for the United States in the 1930s and the theoretical thrust for the measurement of all the major macroeconomic variables playing a role in the business cycle greatly increased the resources allocated to index number construction. Considerable theoretical analysis as well as data development effort has been directed toward the validation of particular index numbers. Recently, for example, the Bureau of Labor Statistics has begun publication of several variants of the consumer price index to reflect demographic and economic changes in the structure of the body of consumers in the United States. Inflation has also contributed to renewed interest in appropriate measurement technique. Again, since most of the raw data are the product of sample surveys, sampling theory and practice are important.

Time Series

The increasing complexity of society, the competitiveness of business enterprise, and the acceleration of the rates of change in political and environmental factors have made the development of statistical techniques for the analysis of time series and for forecasting one of the most dynamic aspects of statistics. A time series is a set of observations of a quantitative characteristic of a phenomenon taken at different points of time, usually at fixed intervals. Thus, the monthly sales of automobiles, quarterly gross national product, and the daily index of stock prices are time series. The essential quality is that the series is ordered according to the time variable, as distinct from those variables which are not ordered at all (a random sample) or are ordered according to magnitude (a frequency distribution). Time now becomes the critical element, and its presence makes it impossible to apply classical statistical assumptions. Forecasting, planning, and decision making have become characteristic of modern business management and, politics permitting, of the administration of government agencies. Such processes are necessarily time-oriented. Time series forecasts involve the arraying of past observations into a time series and applying some mathematical function to obtain a forecast. The choice of the actual methods to be used is influenced by the level of skill of the forecaster, access to computer and software capability, the availability of data, the nature of the variable being forecast, and the best trade-off of accuracy and cost. The type of forecasting method to be employed is also influenced by the nature of the forecast required: immediate (next month), short-term (6 months), medium-term (2 years), long-term (5 to 20 years). In all cases the first step is a careful examination of available time series data, using arithmetic and semilogarithmic graphic plotting to help in the identification of patterns.

Techniques of Time Series Analysis

Techniques of time series analysis include smoothing methods, classical methods of statistical decomposition, autoregressive methods, and spectral analysis (frequency methods).

Smoothing Methods   Smoothing methods attempt to smooth or average a time series in order to eliminate fluctuations which are caused by randomness. While lacking in theoretical underpinning, they are widely used in practice because of their ease of application and the reasonable results achieved. The process can be carried out by freehand methods on charts, but usually use is made of moving averages. The objective is smooth data in the sense that first differences are regular and higher-order differences are small.

The simplest type of forecast is to use the last value as the forecast for the next period (naive forecast), but if the value is heavily influenced by random fluctuations, the forecast will be very inaccurate. One way of improving the forecast is to compute a moving average. The positive and negative random elements will tend to cancel each other out. The longer the period of the moving average the smoother the result, but fewer values will be left for analysis. Thus, if the statistician is working with monthly data heavily influenced by seasonal forces, the use of a 12-month moving average will (in theory) smooth out the seasonal variations. However, 6 months of values will be lost at each end of the time series.

Moving averages may be weighted. The method of exponential smoothing has gained wide acceptance. This method is based on the assumption that remote values have less importance than do more current values. The weights used with past data decline exponentially with time, that is, they decrease geometrically with age. A value α may be used as the weight, taking a value between 0 and 1. Storage problems are substantially reduced since only the most recent value, the most recent forecast, and a value α need to be stored. The forecaster may use the criteria of minimum squared error in selecting the level of α. The forecasting accuracy of exponential smoothing is much greater than that of moving averages. Exponential methods were developed by Robert G. Brown.

Classical Methods of Time Series Decomposition   Such methods attempt to break down the time series into constituent parts as contrasted with the extrapolation of the underlying pattern into the future as is done in smoothing methods. The basis for current methods was laid in the 1920s when the ratio-to-trend concept was developed. Classical procedures seek to identify three factors making up a time series—trend, seasonal, and cycle.

Trend is the long-term underlying movement of the time series. Least-squares regression methods may be used to identify the trend factor. The seasonal factor is the periodic (repetitive) pattern of a time series expressed in monthly, weekly, or shorter time periods. The increase in retail sales each December, the rise in automobile sales with the introduction of new models each year, and the higher volume of stock transfers each Monday are examples of seasonality. In general, monthly seasonal patterns can be expressed as a group of relatives called a seasonal index which is determined on the basis of a (centered) 12-month moving average. A seasonal index is made up of 12 monthly relatives, the sum of which is 1200. Widely used computer procedures incorporating many refinements such as trading day adjustment are available from the Bureau of the Census (X-11 program). The third component is the cyclical factor, which in economic time series is taken to be the business cycle.

The general mathematical representation of the decomposition method, in a multiplicative form, is $X = T \times S \times C \times E$, where E is the error or random component. In this form the seasonal and cyclical factors are indexes. The process of decomposition assumes that the trend factor may be determined by means of regression analysis and the seasonal by means of moving average. They can be removed by dividing the original time series values X by $T \times S$. The term $T \times S$ is frequently referred to as the statistical normal in the sense that both elements are expected. The residual is then assumed to be $C \times E$ in which C is a measure of the cyclical movement. This can be isolated reasonably well, in practice, by short-period smoothing to reduce the effect of the error term.

Using the classical method, the statistician can project the trend as described by a trend (regression) function, describe the seasonal factor by means of the seasonal index, and make some judgment about the cyclical pattern. In practice, the cyclical element may be the end product of most importance to the forecaster. Unfortunately, cyclical patterns do not have fixed periodicity. Historical datings of cycles in the United States since 1854 showing date of the peak and the trough in each cycle are published by the National Bureau of Economic Research. Using the classical methods, a forecaster can prepare a forecast on the basis of the expression $F_t = T_t + S_t + C_t$. The random element is not included since it obviously cannot be forecast. It is not possible to apply the usual statistical method of computing confidence limits to time series forecasts since statistical independence of the values may not be assumed.

Autoregressive Models   With widespread availability of computers (and detailed software packages), more general and theoretically more satisfactory methods of time series analysis called autoregressive moving average (ARMA) processes have been developed. The best known is the Box-Jenkins method, the most sophisticated approach to time series analysis. Usually it yields high forecasting accuracy, but the technique is complex. Also, the forecaster has to interact with the model and there is a need for considerable experience.

Autoregression is a procedure whereby the value of each observation in a series is partly dependent upon the values of those which have immediately preceded it, that is, each observation has a regression relationship with the previous value. If the autocorrelation coefficients of the original series drop rapidly to zero, the series is stationary (that is, without a significant trend factor present). First differences of the autocorrelations will probably show stationarity even if the autocorrelations do not. The autocorrelations are a summary of patterns existing in the data. Autoregressive models were introduced by G. Udney Yule and moving average models by Eugene Slutsky. The work of Abraham Wald laid the basis for the Box-Jenkins method, which is a combined ARMA procedure. The ARMA procedure includes the steps of identification of a suitable model, estimation of the parameters of the model, diagnostic testing of the model, followed by use of the model for forecasts and control purposes.

Spectral Analysis Spectral analysis offers another approach to time series analysis and is widely used in physical and engineering applications. It analyzes the frequency with which certain outcomes are observed rather than the magnitude of an outcome at a given period of time. Spectral analysis produces a spectrum (sometimes called a power spectrum since it reflects relative strengths of given frequencies) which is a graphic representation of the spectral density. C. W. Granger and M. Hatanaka (1964) have provided an introduction to spectral analysis as applied to economic time series.

In general, applications of spectral analysis have been limited because of difficulty in interpreting the spectra resulting from the procedures. In connection with the analysis of correlation between time series, the term "distributed lags" was introduced by Irving Fisher. It is based on the assumption that a given cause occurring at a point in time will produce its effect at various points of time in the future and thus be distributed. Phoebus J. Dhrymes (1971) has discussed problems of estimation in distributed-lag models.

Indicator Analysis

One spin-off from the classical methods of time series analysis which has attracted considerable interest on the part of economic and business statisticians is the concept of indicator analysis. During the pioneer work of the National Bureau of Economic Research under the leadership of Wesley C. Mitchell it was early recognized that the cyclical residuals of certain specific time series tended to lead, coincide with, or lag general business movements. While the definition of general business and, therefore, the specification of business cycles present many practical and conceptual difficulties, it is clear, even on the basis of economic theory, that certain series will have a varying relationship to general business movements. Thus, a time series reflecting manufacturing employment will tend to lead general business. A leading relationship also exists for a series on new orders, or business inventories.

Geoffrey H. Moore, Julius Shiskin, and others have prepared lists of selected series which historically have had a leading relationship and may therefore be called leading indicators of cyclical recessions and expansions. Economists working with cyclical residuals have selected the best indicators on the basis of economic significance, statistical adequacy, timing, conformity, smoothness, and currency. Such indicators for the economy as a whole and by economic process such as employment, income, orders, and the like provide useful analytical measures for the business forecaster.

Many indicators are published monthly by the U.S. Department of Commerce in *Business Conditions Digest*, which together with the *Survey of Current Business* provides the most readily available (and modestly priced) raw material for forecasters. Indicator analysis may be extended to economic regions and used in individual business firms. Indicators need to be revised periodically as the economic mix varies in the society or as institutional changes increase or reduce the significance of specific indicator series. There is considerable doubt that only one aggregate index made up of a few series can be consistently significant in the sense of always giving correct signals of cyclical turns. Thus, the widely publicized composite index of 12 leading indicators must be used with caution. In the use of any statistical technique the skill and judgment of the statistician will make a significant difference in the validity of the analytical result.

Input-Output Analysis

Input-output (I/O) analysis attempts to model a total economic or business system in terms of the relationship between the several variables present. This technique was developed by Wassily W. Leontief and has been applied in most major countries. Worldwide input-output models are now being developed. I/O analysis produces tables which show the transactions between component parts of the system and thus show the extent to which one industry purchases its inputs from and provides its outputs to other industries. Inputs can be classified by categories such as imports, labor, and commodities; and outputs, as exports, consumption, and investment. The process is essentially an accounting exercise.

I/O analysis has found its major applications in the planning process both for regional and national economies. Within large firms the method helps to trace the effects of changes in structural relationships. I/O analysis is most applicable in countries with economic plans and varying degrees of centralized economic planning. I/O accounting usually produces three basic tables: one reflecting interindustry transactions; another of direct requirements; and a third of total requirements, which summarizes direct and indirect requirements. From these tables final demand coefficients (in the form of a matrix) may be determined.

One of the restrictive assumptions of input-output analysis is that the technical coefficients remain constant. This is not valid over long periods of time and may be significantly invalid in particular industries even in the short term. Beginning with modest tables for 1919, 1929, and 1939 (prepared by Leontief) the federal government has undertaken construction of large-scale tables in the post-World War II period. Much of these data can be handled only by computer. There is no continuing program for periodic publication of I/O tables in the United States.

Computer Resources

Just as the preparation of large-scale (disaggregated) input-output tables would be impossible without modern computers because of the mass of statistical data in the matrix and the need to invert large matrices, so all aspects of statistical techniques in economics and business have been affected by the general availability of computer resources. Perhaps the most important aspect of the computer revolution from this point of view has been the establishment of large data bases accessible by means of time sharing.

In addition to data bases maintained by such governmental agencies as the Department of Commerce, the Bureau of Labor Statistics, and the Federal Reserve Board, private groups provide significant data bases. Two prominent vendors of data-sharing service are Data Resources, Inc., and Wharton Econometric Forecasting Services. Many large commercial banks maintain similar services. The work with large econometric models carried on by the Federal Reserve Board, many Federal Reserve banks, commercial banks, and academic research institutions would be impossible without large-scale computers. In addition, software packages, such as SPSS (statistical package for the social sciences), available generally or on a proprietary basis have facilitated the use of the statistical techniques.

References

Allen, R. G. D., *Index Numbers in Theory and Practice*, Aldine, Chicago, 1975; Butler, William F., Robert A. Kavesh, and Robert B. Platt (eds.), *Methods and Techniques of Business Forecasting*, Prentice-Hall, Englewood Cliffs, N.J., 1974; Dhrymes, Phoebus J., *Econometrics: Statistical Foundations and Applications*, Springer-Verlag, New York, 1974; Granger, G. W., and M. Hatanaka, *Spectral Analysis of Economic Time Series*, Princeton University Press, Princeton, N.J., 1964; Jenkins, Gwilym M., *Practical Experiences with Modeling and Forecasting Time Series*, GJP Publications, St. Helier, Channel Islands, 1979; Makridakis, Spyros, and Steven C. Wheelwright, *Forecasting Methods and Applications*, Wiley, New York, 1978; Theil, Henri, *Principles of Econometrics*, North-Holland, Amsterdam, 1971; Vatter, Paul A., et al., *Quantitative Methods in Management, Text and Cases*, Irwin, Homewood, Ill., 1978.

(*See also* Business cycles; Computers in economics; Data banks; Distributed lags in economics; Econometrics; Economic statistics; Forecasting methods; Index numbers; Input-output analysis; Leading indicator approach to forecasting; Regression analysis in business and economics; Sampling in economics; Seasonal adjustment methods; Time series analysis)

John I. Griffin

Statistics, economic (see Economic statistics)

Stochastic process (see Time series analysis)

Stock

Stock represents equity or ownership in a corporation. (In the United Kingdom, however, the term usually means debenture bonds issued by corporations or the government. The British use the term shares when they refer to stock.) In the United States, stock is classified as either common or preferred. Common stock gives the holder an unlimited interest in the earnings and assets of a corporation after all prior claims have been met. Preferred stock has preference over the common with respect to the payment of dividends and claims on residual assets in the event that the corporation liquidates.

History

It is uncertain as to when the corporate form of business organization was first established and stock issued to represent ownership. Late in the twelfth century, Italians devised a financial instrument that facilitated their trade at the fairs held in the northern French region of Champagne. The *commenda* was a piece of paper that described the agreement between the merchants who went to the fairs and the investors who remained in Milan, Venice, and other Italian cities. Some evidence indicates that mines in Italy and central Europe were jointly owned and shares in them were traded by the early sixteenth century. In 1553 London capitalists provided £6000 in £25 shares for "the discovery of the northern parts of the world." The Dutch East India Company was formed in 1602, followed a few years later by the English East India Company. From the outset, the Dutch company had a permanent capital structure which financed forts and munitions to protect its trading activities. The English company, on the other hand, financed voyages separately, splitting the profits, if any, after the ships returned home. However, by 1657 it was forced to raise permanent capital for reasons similar to those of the Dutch company.

Liabilities and Rights of Stockholders

Until the nineteenth century, the joint-stock company, or corporation, was used almost exclusively to undertake foreign ventures. However, the industrial revolution led to domestic business endeavors that required immense amounts of capital funds, which were too large for the sole proprietorship or partnership to raise. Thus, the corporation evolved. The corporation has two major advantages that enable it to raise the necessary funds. First, since in the eyes of the law the corporation is a legal entity separate from its owners, the stockholders' liability is limited to the investment they make in the corporation. Their personal assets are protected. Second, ownership can be transferred relatively easily—with actively traded stocks, in a matter of minutes. These advantages make corporate stock attractive to investors, who have thus provided the large amounts of capital funds that have allowed the corporation to become the vehicle for economic expansion in all the industrial nations outside the communist world.

In the United States, the laws of the state that charter the corporation and the provisions of the charter itself govern the rights that stockholders have. In general, as a group, common stockholders have rights that include the following: to adopt and amend the bylaws; to amend the charter; to elect the directors of the corporation; to change the amount of authorized stock; and to enter into mergers.

The most important right that the individual stockholder has is sharing in the corporation's earnings when dividends are declared. The stockholder also has the right to vote. But, since most shareholders in major U.S. corporations do not attend annual meetings, provision has been made that allows them to vote by proxy—a written power of attorney (usually temporary) that the stockholders give to another person (the proxy) to vote their shares. The stockholders have the right to share residual assets in the event of dissolution, but since they are the last claimants, this is a relatively weak right. They may sell their shares. And they may inspect the corporation's books, a right that is strictly limited. Obviously, a shareholder who works for a competing company would not be given carte blanche to look at all the books. In many corporations, stockholders have preemptive rights, which allow them to maintain their proportionate shares of ownership if new common stock is issued. For example, suppose a stockholder owns 100 shares of the outstanding 1000 shares of ABC Corporation. If ABC plans to issue an additional 1000 shares of common stock, the shareholder must have the first chance to purchase 10 percent, or 100 shares, of the new issue.

Preferred versus Common Stock

Preferred stock is frequently referred to as a hybrid security because it has some features similar to common stock and others that resemble bonds. Like common stock, the preferred represents ownership in a corporation—the holder is not a creditor. Preferred stock pays dividends, not interest, allowing the directors of the corporation to pass (to not declare) a dividend without the legal repercussions that would occur if they failed to meet interest payments on bonds. But, like bonds, preferred stock pays fixed-dollar amounts in dividends, and most preferred shareholders do not have the right to vote for the directors of the corporation.

Many preferred stocks are cumulative, that is, they carry the provision that all passed dividends from previous years must be paid to the preferred shareholders before the directors may declare a dividend to the common stockholders. Another feature that many preferred stocks have is convertibility—the right the holders have to convert the stocks into the common stocks of the same corporation.

Process of Issuing Stock

When corporations issue stock, they use the services of an investment bank, a financial institution that acts as an intermediary between the corporation and the investing public. Investment banks, or underwriters, perform three important functions: First, they offer financial advice to their clients. For instance, they help the company to decide what type of security to issue and what provisions it should contain. In many cases the financial counsel is continuing. Often the investment banker will sit on the board of directors of a client corporation. Second, acting as intermediary, the investment bank distributes the securities when a public offering is made. The underwriter has a marketing organization that presumably distributes the securities more efficiently than would be done if the corporation attempted to do it itself. Finally, and probably most important, investment banks bear the risk of price declines while the new issue of stock is being distributed. Once an underwriting agreement is reached between the issuing corporation and the underwriter, the latter guarantees that a certain amount of money for the securities will be turned over to the corporation on a specified date. If the price of the stock falls while the investment bank is marketing the securities, the underwriter suffers the loss.

Regulation of the Security Industry

Following investigations into the collapse of the stock market in 1929, Congress enacted several laws that regulate the securities industry. The Securities Act of 1933, for instance, governs the issuance of stock, covering all interstate public offerings of $500,000 or more. The major thrust of this law is to provide full disclosure of all relevant information regarding the stock being offered. This information and a record of representations are contained in a registration statement made to the Securities and Exchange Commission (SEC)—a government agency established by the Securities Exchange Act of 1934—and summarized in a prospectus, which must accompany the offering. If the SEC thinks that the information is inadequate or misleading, it will stop or delay the offering. Furthermore, if an investor suffers a loss because of misinformation, the investor may sue any of the parties who prepared the statement.

The Importance of Stocks to the Economy

Equity financing via common or preferred stock historically represented a major source of funds to corporations, but in recent years, corporations have conducted a relatively small amount of this type of financing. In a broader sense, stocks are an instrument used to bring savers and investors together, which is crucial for economic expansion. Industrial nations are highly specialized, and the people and institutions that save (consume less than their incomes) are usually different from those who invest (produce capital goods that increase the output of goods and services). Financial intermediaries, such as commercial banks, credit unions, and investment banks, bring savers and investors together, using various instruments including common and preferred stocks to do so. Stocks, therefore, are vital to a growing economy.

References

Bogen, Julius I. (ed.), *Financial Handbook*, 4th ed., Ronald Press, New York, 1968; Weston, J. Fred, and Eugene F. Brigham, *Managerial Finance*, 6th ed., Dryden Press, Hinsdale, Ill., 1978.

(*See also* Bond; Financial instruments; Securities and Exchange Commission; Stock exchange)

Henry C. F. Arnold

Stock exchange

A stock exchange is an organized marketplace in which securities such as bonds and common and preferred stocks are bought and sold. Because the origins of today's stock exchanges usually were informal gatherings of merchants and others who traded securities, it is difficult to pinpoint when the first organized marketplace began operations. Beginning in 1611, merchants met in Amsterdam to trade shares in the Dutch East India Company and, thus, may have formed the first stock exchange, or bourse, even though this exchange was not formally organized into the Association for Promoting Trading in Securities until 1785. The Paris Bourse was established in 1724, and in 1773 London brokers, who had been transacting business at Jonathan's (a coffee house), moved to a room in Sweeting's Alley and formally named it the Stock Exchange, the beginnings of what is today the second-largest stock exchange in the world. The Philadelphia Stock Exchange, begun in 1790, was the first organized marketplace in the United States, followed 2 years later by that historic meeting on May 17, 1792, when 24 merchants agreed to meet every day under an old buttonwood tree on Wall Street. The New York Stock Exchange (NYSE) traces its genesis to this agreement. Today, there are stock exchanges in virtually every industrial nation in the noncommunist world, including those in Zurich, Frankfort, Milan, Tokyo, Melbourne, and Toronto.

Regional Stock Exchanges

Eleven stock exchanges operate in the United States, ten of them registered with the Securities and Exchange Commission (SEC) as national securities exchanges (NYSE; American, Boston, Cincinnati, Midwest, Pacific, Philadelphia-Baltimore-Washington, Intermountain, and Spokane Stock Exchanges; and the Chicago Board Options Exchange, Inc.) and one (Honolulu) exempted from registration. At the end of 1976, these stock exchanges had 2926 issues of common stock listed, 820 issues of preferred stock, and 2923 bond issues. The market value of the common stock totaled nearly $860 billion, the preferred over $30 billion, and the bonds more than $400 billion. The market value of the NYSE's listed securities dwarfs the combined total of all other exchanges. At the end of 1976, the total value of the "big board's" listed common stock was more than $830 billion, almost 96 percent of that listed on all U.S. exchanges. Roughly three-fourths of the market value of all preferred stock was listed on the NYSE and 99.9 percent of the market value of bonds. The NYSE also dominates trading activity. Over the past few years, it has accounted for about 80 percent of all shares and 85 percent of the dollar amount of stock traded.

Although trailing far behind the NYSE, the American Stock Exchange (AMEX), also located in New York City, is the second-largest organized securities market in the United States. Established in the 1850s, the AMEX was called the New York Curb

Exchange because trading literally took place outside on the curb until 1921, when its operations were moved indoors. The name was finally changed in 1953. At the end of 1976, the market value of listed common stock on the AMEX totaled more than $34 billion and preferred stocks approximately $1.8 billion.

Of the remaining nine regional stock exchanges, the Boston, Pacific, Midwest, and Philadelphia-Baltimore-Washington exchanges are the most important, but only the Pacific Stock Exchange had listed stocks with a market value of more than $1 billion at the end of 1976. The Cincinnati Stock Exchange had only six common and three preferred stocks listed, with a total market value of slightly more than $30 million, and the Spokane Stock Exchange's listed stocks' value was roughly $2 million.

New York Stock Exchange

Since all the exchanges are organized and operate similarly to the NYSE, that exchange will be described in more detail. The NYSE is a corporation governed by a board of 21 directors: 10 chosen from the securities industry, 10 from outside that industry, and the presiding officer of the board, who is selected by the directors. The NYSE does not own securities, buy or sell stocks, or influence their prices. It provides a centrally located place for its members to buy and sell securities. Membership in the exchange numbers 1366 individuals who have bought seats, which allows them to trade securities on the floor of the NYSE. The value of a seat has fluctuated sharply over the years, reaching a high of $625,000 in 1929 and sinking to a low of $4000 in both 1876 and 1878. Since 1950, a seat's value has ranged from $515,000 in 1968 to $35,000 in 1977.

Members may be either general partners or holders of voting stock in one of the 473 member firms in existence at the end of 1977. Members perform different functions, which fall into four classifications. Roughly half are partners or officers of commission houses, firms that execute trades for the public for which they are paid commissions. Many of the larger firms have several commission brokers handling the public's trading on the exchange floor.

Approximately 200 members function as floor brokers. Popularly known as $2 brokers because at one time that was their commission for handling a 100-share transaction, these members help commission brokers by executing the latters' buy-and-sell orders when trading activity is high. Another 100 or so members are registered traders (or registered competitive market makers) who buy and sell for their own account, hoping to profit from their speculations. Their transactions must meet exchange requirements and allegedly increase the market's liquidity.

Finally, about one-fourth of the members are specialists, who act as both dealers and brokers. As dealers, the specialists are charged with maintaining an orderly market in the stocks in which they specialize. In carrying out this responsibility, specialists should be trading against the market—that is, buying if the prices of his stocks are declining and selling if they are rising. The object in both cases is to maintain price continuity and minimize the impact of a divergence of supply and demand. As brokers, specialists record other brokers' buy-and-sell orders that are away from the market—different from the prevailing prices—in their stocks. If and when the price of a stock moves up or down to the price on the order, specialists execute it and receive a commission for their services.

A corporation must meet certain requirements—more stringent on the NYSE than those on the other exchanges—before the NYSE will accept its stock for listing. It must have a demonstrated earning power of $2.5 million before taxes, a minimum of 1 million shares outstanding—with at least 2000 round-lot (100 shares) stockholders—and publicly held common stock with a market value of $16 million or more. The NYSE has other requirements, including voting rights for the common stockholders and periodic publication of financial statements.

Major Economic Function

The major economic function of securities markets is to help allocate capital resources efficiently—to direct these scarce resources to endeavors that offer the best return and to carry out this function at minimum cost. Organized securities exchanges presumably perform this function most efficiently because they closely resemble the classic textbook example of a purely competitive market. With numerous buyers and sellers transacting homogeneous financial claims and with information available to all, the theoretical outcome of pure competition should result: scarce resources should be allocated efficiently.

Although the evidence indicates that the stock exchanges have performed this function well, there have been some problems. For example, from its origins in 1792 until the 1970s, the NYSE both regulated the actions of its members and limited access to the trading floor. The NYSE maintained a schedule of fixed minimum commission rates, which led to a deleterious impact on the allocational efficiency of the exchange. Furthermore, NYSE members had to execute trades in listed stocks on the exchange floor unless they got permission—rarely given—from the governing authorities to use a regional stock exchange (which listed the stock) or the over-the-counter (OTC) market, the market for security transactions that are not made on an organized stock exchange.

Another problem has been the growth of block trading, which represents trades of 10,000 shares or more. Block trades are privately negotiated and do not depend to any significant degree upon either the facilities or procedures of the stock exchange.

Also, nonmember brokers and dealers had access to the exchange floor only through member firms. They had to pay the standard fixed commission that any other customer would pay, which obviously encouraged them to avoid the NYSE.

Major Changes

These monopolistic intrusions led to inefficiencies and distortions, the most important of which was a fragmentation of the stock market. At any given time, a stock might be trading at different prices in the various components of the stock market (the NYSE, the regional stock exchanges, and the OTC market), and customers might be deprived of receiving the best price when buying or selling stock. These restrictive practices came under a barrage of attacks from financial institutions, the SEC, the Antitrust Division of the Department of Justice, and the Congress in the late 1960s and early 1970s. These complaints led to major changes designed to increase competition and improve the efficiency of the securities markets and eventually lead to a national market system—which Congress ordered in 1975. In 1972, the SEC mandated a consolidated tape system, which now reports all stock transactions on the exchanges and the OTC market, providing up-to-date information to investors from all components of the stock market. Since May 1, 1975, commissions on all transactions, no matter what size, have been competitively negotiated. This action has benefited institutional investors most, but has also led to discount commission houses that attract small investors interested only in having their trades executed, not in the other services provided by the typical firm. The composite quotation system, initiated in 1978, provides bid and asked prices for all listed stocks from all components of the stock market, thus aiding the broker in getting the best price for customers. Finally, in 1978 the intermarket trading system (ITS) began functioning. The ITS electronically links the NYSE, the AMEX, and several regional exchanges and represents an important step on the road to a true national market system—one stock market covering the entire nation.

References

Amling, Frederick, *Investments: An Introduction to Analysis and Management*, 4th ed., Prentice-Hall, Englewood Cliffs, N.J., 1978.

(*See also* Bond; Securities and Exchange Commission; Stock; Stock price averages and indexes)

Henry C. F. Arnold

Stock-flow analysis

A stock-flow good can be produced, held, and consumed. Only stringent stipulations permit a good to be called a pure stock good or a pure flow good, i.e., not a stock-flow good. Thus the half-life of a pure flow good must approach zero. Still some goods can be produced and consumed but not held; personal services such as haircuts are pure flow goods.

When Alfred Marshall (1920) sought to analyze the properties of a factor of production that also was a pure stock good, he had to hypothesize his famous meteoric stones. Admittedly, works of art and the like, once produced, become pure stock goods: they cannot be replicated; the originals can only be copied. But there is enough substitutability between much artwork for stock-flow analysis to apply. Examples include contemporary music, painting, etc.

Stock-Flow and Portfolio Analysis

Once economists understood that stock-flow characteristics were common, portfolio analysis came to control serious studies of consumer and producer behavior. It has proved easy to apply the technique to the theory of the firm, subject to the following qualifications. First, it has been hard to supply a satisfactory theory of investment, i.e., of net acquisition and running off of holdings. J. M. Keynes (1936) sought to project expectations onto investment theory. And his notion of the aggregate supply price as the proceeds entrepreneurs must expect to receive is seminal for stock-flow analysis. More recently, theories of rational expectations, fulfilling conjectures of F. H. Knight, have led to creative turmoil. Secondly, full (stock-flow) equilibrium has been imperfectly specified, partly because macroeconomic steady states in the sense of Marshall and A. C. Pigou (1935) have been confused with microeconomic ones such as that formulated by G. C. Archibald and R. G. Lipsey (1958). Indeed, as economic theory has matured, the contrast between stationary and growth states, going back as far as Ricardo, has given way to one between linear and accelerated motion. (Motion can be linear in a semilog space.) In modern economics, the stationary state is a special case of unaccelerated motion —the genre encompasses all steady motions.

Stock-flow analysis has had a rougher passage in the pure theory of consumer choice, importantly because of perplexities of hedonic analysis. Any stock might yield a stream of services. G. S. Becker (1965) and K. J. Lancaster (1966) have built models in which service streams, yielding utility, are defined by qualities contributed by many goods. This approach has come rather to overshadow the more explicit stock-flow analysis of D. W. Bushaw and R. W. Clower (1957).

Stock-flow analysis has successfully penetrated study of the demand for consumer durables. Gregory Chow (1957) set the pace in his study of automobile demand; he associated demand for new cars with the difference between actual and desired stocks. The studies published in A. C. Harberger (1960) pushed on in the same direction; M. L. Burstein (refrigerators) and Zvi Griliches (automobiles) probed hedonics; Richard Muth (housing) developed a theme going back at least as far as J. M. Clark's (1917) accelerationist approach to investment. The more durable the good, the less important will be replacement demand and the more important will be investment demand, reflecting changes in demand for stocks, in turn reflecting shifting expectations of sales.

Stock-flow analysis has much enhanced econometric study of durable goods purchases: before due account was taken of stock-flow relationships, economists persistently underestimated price elasticities of demand.

When analysis of demand for consumer goods gets rooted in stock flow and so in a portfolio approach to behavior, monetary theory and the theory of real behavior intersect: houses and cars are fairly liquid assets and the former have been excellent inflation hedges. It is well-established that decisions to purchase consumer durables key on unexpected changes in income, just as do many securities purchases.

More exposition must precede full development of the stock-flow subject. Consumption should be distinguished from depreciation, a distinction clouded by such nomenclature as capital consumption allowances. And the widely known, but not widely understood, problem of dimensionality should be studied.

Households might hold stock-flow goods that do not depreciate, still consumption occurs in the sense that the goods yield desirable services.

Consumption versus Depreciation

The distinction of consumption from depreciation being made, consider a stock-flow good that does depreciate. Depreciation comprises part of holding costs, as do interest charges on invested capital. Service streams comprise a benefit. The scheme is like that found in Chapter 17 of Keynes' General Theory.

The theories of stock-flow goods and user cost intersect. A beautiful object, fungible and, so, a stock-flow good, might deteriorate independently of how much it is viewed. Contrast such an object with candy. One cannot have candy and eat it too. Bushaw and Clower (1957) implicitly model candy as they do the following hypothetical steel intermediate product. The amount incorporated into final products over a day contributes to the firm's payoff. So does the number held in stock at the beginning of the day: the chance of a shortage is a decreasing function of the amount in stock. Bushaw and Clower specify as an objective function

$$U = U(x_1, \ldots, x_n; D_1, \ldots, D_n) \qquad (1)$$

They remark:

*The flow demand (or supply) variables (x) represent quantities of various com-
modities purchased for current consumption (or sold as current "output"), and
the stock demand variables (D) represent corresponding quantities of the same
commodities which the consumer wishes to hold for future disposal (through use
or sale).*

Dimensionality

Turning to dimensionality, consider equation (1). The stock demands D refer to tons
of steel or numbers of cars desired to be held at time t. The flow demands x refer to
instantaneous time rates of change; x_r might be translated as purchase of the rth commodity at a rate per annum symbolized by x_r. So the numbers representing stock and
flow demand are incommensurable. Flow demand can be made commensurable with
stock demand by integration: $x_r \tau$ is the value of $f(t)$ at $t = \tau$; $f(t)$ describes the purchase plan; $\int f(t) \, dt$ has the dimension of a stock.

Not enough information has been supplied to map stock demands into flows. For
this to be done, desired holdings at date $t + h$ must be compared with holdings at t.
And the accumulation path must be specified. Stock-flow theory, in its inception, also
did not take account of Hamiltonians.

In period analysis, x and D both have the dimension of a stock. In period analysis,
x_r is the number of units of the rth commodity to be purchased during the day and
is perfectly commensurable with D_r, the number of such units desired to be held at
the end of the day.

Integration with Other Theories

The way in which stock-flow analysis integrates portfolio theory with the theories
both of the equilibrium of the isolated market and of real investment is illustrated by
the following simple model.

Model   Freight cars are to be hired out by source holders who make a market for
used cars and acquire new cars from manufacturers. Carriers rent equipment from
source holders and provide shipping services. Flow equilibrium requires that
replacement demand plus investment demand equal production of new cars. Investment demand will depend on the stock of sources at t relative to stocks planned for
future dates; stocks planned for future dates will depend on expected rents, interest
rates, and source prices; plans thus formed will map into investment demand at t, a
flow. The stock of sources is predetermined for the process determining flow equilibrium. In the special case of stock-flow equilibrium as a stationary state, investment
demand is nil. In that solution, source rentals and source prices, together with the
stock of sources, are such that the desired rate of production by source makers is
equal to replacement demand of source holders.

Equilibrium versus Disequilibrium   Flow disequilibrium is more straightforward
than stock-flow disequilibrium. If transactions occur in flow disequilibrium, so that
there is false trading, some transactors must be disappointed. Not all expectations
will be fulfilled. If there is flow equilibrium *cum* stock disequilibrium, no offer to sell
or bid to buy at market fails to be filled.

The concept of stock-flow equilibrium has become subsumed by a deep theory of
futures markets. And under rational expectations, transactors, knowing the structures

of the economy and the subeconomies in which they operate, will optimize relative to efficient estimates of future data. In the usual formulations of stock-flow disequilibrium, transactors fail to optimize even in deterministic models; in the nonstochastic world of standard stock-flow theory, rational transactors would achieve an equilibrium at the onset of a process spanning the phase space of the system. The insights of earlier stock-flow analysts would be supported but the analysis would require a quite different paradigm of market behavior. (Related discussion is found in Foley, 1975; Turnovsky and Burmeister, 1977; and Karni, 1979.)

The Stationary State

Proper stock-flow analysis must, like quantum physics, abandon "individual laws of elementary particles and state directly the statistical laws governing aggregations; its laws are for crowds and not for individuals" (A. Einstein and L. Infeld, 1942). Marshall and Pigou, anticipating this point, supplied parsimonious microeconomic foundations for the theory of stock-flow equilibrium. Pigou (1935) described three degrees of stationary states. "First, the system of industry as a whole may be stationary, while the several industries that compose it are in movement. Secondly [each] industry may be stationary, while the individual firms in it are in movement. Thirdly, individual firms, as well as individual industries may be stationary." J. S. Mill, Marshall, and Pigou all hugged the first degree in their macroeconomic analyses. Marshall, (1920) wrote, "This [stationary] state obtains its name from the fact that in it the general conditions of production and consumption, of distribution and exchange, remain motionless; but yet it is full of movement; for it is a mode of life. The average age . . . may be stationary; yet each individual is growing up towards his prime, or downwards to old age."

References

Archibald, G. C., and R. G. Lipsey, "Monetary and Value Theory; A Critique of Lange and Patinkin," *Review of Economic Studies,* vol. 26, no. 69, October 1958, pp. 1–22; Becker G. S., "A Theory of the Allocation of Time, *Economic Journal,* vol. 75, no. 299, September 1965, pp. 493–517; Bushaw, D. W., and R. W. Clower, *Introduction to Mathematical Economics,* Irwin, Homewood, Ill., 1957, quote, p. 128; Chow, Gregory, *The Demand for Automobiles in the United States,* North-Holland, Amsterdam, 1957; Clark, J. M., "Business Acceleration and the Law of Demand," *Journal of Political Economy,* vol. 25, 1917, pp. 217–235; Einstein, A., and L. Infeld, *The Evolution of Physics,* Simon & Schuster, New York, 1942; Foley, D. K., "On Two Specifications of Asset Equilibrium in Macroeconomic Models," *Journal of Political Economy,* vol. 83, April 1975, p. 303; Harberger, Arnold C. (ed.), *The Demand for Durable Goods,* University of Chicago Press, Chicago, 1960; Karni, Edi, "On the Specification of Asset Equilibrium in Macroeconomic Models: A Note," *Journal of Political Economy,* vol. 87, February 1979, p. 171; Keynes, J. M., *The General Theory of Employment, Interest and Money,* Macmillan, New York, 1936; Lancaster, K. J., "A New Approach to Consumer Theory," *Journal of Political Economy,* vol. 74, no. 1, 1966, pp. 132–157; Marshall, Alfred, *Principles of Economics,* 8th ed., Macmillan, New York, 1920, quote, pp. 366–367; Pigou, A. C., *The Economics of Stationary States,* Macmillan, New York, 1935, quote, p. 81; Turnovsky, S. S., and E. Burmeister, "Perfect Foresight, Expectations, Consistency and Macroeconomic Equilibrium," *Journal of Political Economy,* vol. 85, April 1978, p. 379.

(*See also* Firm theory; General equilibrium; Static analysis)

M. L. Burstein

Stock price averages and indexes

Arithmetic averages and indexes of selected stocks are designed to measure the level and trends of overall stock prices. Charles H. Dow, who founded the Dow-Jones Company, is reputed to be the first person to have measured the general level of securities prices by calculating the average price of a few representative stocks. His first list in 1884 comprised 11 stocks, including 10 railroad companies, which were the leading business enterprises of that day. In 1897, Dow-Jones expanded the original list to a 20-stock rail average, which has continued to the present, although many of the stocks have been replaced and the list's name has been changed to reflect the increasing importance of other means of transportation. In that same year, Dow-Jones introduced another average composed of 12 industrial stocks—the beginning of the Dow-Jones industrial average (DJIA). Since Dow-Jones's pioneering efforts, many firms at one time or another have computed and published stock price averages and indexes, but the DJIA has maintained its original prominence.

Major Averages and Indexes

Among those currently published on a daily basis in major newspapers are the following:

Dow-Jones Averages   These comprise four stock averages: The DJIA consisting of 30 industrial stocks (8 stocks were added to the original 12 in 1916 and another 10 in 1928), which is the best known and most popular measure of stock price trends; the transportation average of 20 stocks developed from the first of the Dow-Jones averages; the utility average of 15 stocks, which was introduced in 1929; and a composite average of the above 65 stocks. All stocks included in the Dow-Jones averages are listed on the New York Stock Exchange.

At the outset, the Dow-Jones averages literally represented the average price (arithmetic mean) of the stocks included in the group. But two major problems arose that distorted the averages. First, some companies included in the original list became less important and others not on the list became more important. Consequently, the publishers periodically substituted stocks in their averages. However, unless they were to replace a stock with another selling at the same price (which is highly unlikely), price trends would be misrepresented because the average would rise or fall even if stock prices remained unchanged. Fortunately, substitutions were made infrequently. Second, stock splits and stock dividends, which occur far more frequently, distorted the averages unless the editors made adjustments. For example: Suppose we have an average composed of three stocks whose prices per share are $25, $50, and $75, or an average of $50. If the company whose stock was selling at $75 decided to split the stock 5 for 1, the average would decline to $30—a 40 percent drop—obviously distorting stock price levels and trends.

Of the methods that could be used to prevent substitutions, stock splits, and dividends from affecting the averages, Dow-Jones uses the constant-divisor method. When computing the average after a split, for instance, it changes the divisor so as to negate the distortion that would occur from the split. In the aforementioned example, before the split the average was: 25 + 50 + 75 = 150, which divided by 3 yields 50. After the split: 25 + 50 + 15 = 90, which, if we divided by 3, would yield 30. Instead of dividing by 3, we solve the following equation so as to find that divisor which will keep the average unchanged, that is, at 50: $90/X = 50$; therefore, $X = 1.8$, which is the new divisor. This divisor is used until the next split, stock dividend, or substitution occurs. It should be stressed that the quotient computed is expressed in points, not dollars. The DJIA, for example, could rise 10 points without any of its 30 stocks increasing as much as a dollar.

Several criticisms have been leveled at the Dow-Jones averages. It is claimed that the number of stocks included in the averages is too small to be representative of the whole market. Furthermore, the stocks that are included are those of large, financially strong blue-chip companies, whose stock price trends might differ markedly from those of other companies. Most important, the Dow-Jones averages (and other averages) are not weighted. The higher the price of the stock, no matter how large the corporation or its importance to the economy, the greater the weight it carries in the average. At one time, for instance, Du Pont stock, because of its high price, influenced the DJIA more than the combined effect of the stock of United States Steel, General Motors, General Electric, and Westinghouse. The Dow-Jones averages, even with their serious deficiencies, have moved in tandem with other more technically correct indexes.

Standard & Poor's Indexes   The Standard & Poor's (S & P's) Corporation computes and publishes more than 130 stock price indexes, individually covering various industries such as cement, copper, chemicals, and so on. Better known, however, are the five S & P's indexes that are published in the daily newspapers: 400 industrial stocks; 20 transportation stocks; 40 utility stocks; 40 financial stocks; and, the best known, a composite index of the total 500 stocks. The base period for these indexes is the period 1941–43 equals 10, and they are weighted by the market value of the stocks. Standard & Poor's multiplies the price of each stock by the number of shares outstanding, adds the products, divides this sum by the value of the base period, and finally, multiplies this quotient by 10. The result is a market-value-weighted index of stock prices.

NYSE Common-Stock Index   In 1966, the New York Stock Exchange introduced a stock price index that covers all the common stocks listed on that exchange, currently around 1500 issues. It, too, is weighted by the market value of the stocks and its base is December 31, 1965, equals 50. The NYSE calculates the index continuously during trading hours and releases the data every half-hour. The exchange also computes and releases indexes for four maj\`r industry groups: industry, transportation, utilities, and finance.

AMEX Index   The American Stock Exchange also computes and publishes an index of the prices of its listed common stocks. It was started on August 30, 1973, which is also its base (equal to 100) and now includes approximately 1000 stocks. Like the other indexes, it is weighted by the market value of the stocks included.

NASDAQ Index   The National Association of Securities Dealers Automated Quotations index began in February 1971 and today includes some 2900 stocks that are traded over the counter. Its base is February 5, 1971, equals 100, and it is weighted by the market value of the issues included. Aside from the composite index, indexes for the following industry groups are also computed and published: industry, finance, insurance, utilities, banks, and transportation.

Designed to Correct Deficiencies

As evident from the preceding description of the various stock price indexes, they are designed to correct the deficiencies of the Dow-Jones averages. All include many more stocks in their coverage and, most important, all are weighted.

References

Eiteman, D. K., C. A. Dice, and W. J. Eiteman, *The Stock Market,* 4th ed., McGraw-Hill, New York, 1966.

(*See also* Index numbers; Stock)

Henry C. F. Arnold

Subsidies

Ordinary economic transactions occur between two parties, a buyer and a seller. A subsidy is a grant of money from an outside third party to either the buyer or the seller in the transaction. Subsidies generally allow a buyer to receive a good or service for less expense than would otherwise have been necessary. For example, in the United States payments to hospitals by government agencies allow many persons to receive medical care free or at charges much below the cost incurred by the hospitals. The effects of a subsidy are, in general, the opposite of the effects of a tax on transactions, in that a subsidy encourages transactions while a tax restricts them.

A business firm will not stay in operation very long unless revenue is great enough to cover cost outlays plus a return on equity and on managerial effort as large as could be earned in other pursuits. If revenue from buyers is insufficient, a subsidy from an outside agency may keep the firm in operation. It does not matter in theory whether the subsidy is paid directly to the firm. If the subsidy goes to the buyer, then it raises the price that the buyer is willing to bid for a specified good. Even if a firm does not operate for profit, revenue from buyers plus subsidies from philanthropists or government must be sufficient to meet cost outlays and to replace deteriorating structures and equipment.

Principal Forms of Subsidy

A subsidy can affect both the equilibrium quantity and the price in transactions of a specified good. The actual results depend on the form of the subsidy, on whether or not firms behave competitively, and on the elasticities of supply and demand. The principal forms of subsidy are the flat grant and the matching grant. Flat grants are fixed sums of money that are not dependent upon an exact volume of production. This is most common in private charitable giving, such as religious contributions. Other examples are government grants to universities for research or for student financial aid in meeting tuition. Matching grants employ some formula relating the amount of subsidy to the amount of production or costs incurred. Allowance of various deductions from taxable income is an important type of matching subsidy for socially favored expenses.

A flat grant increases the quantity of a good produced under two conditions. In one case the firm or activity may otherwise cease to exist. This case is relevant in grants for basic research which produce valuable information, but often with unenforceable property rights. In other cases, output and consumption are increased because the grant is combined with regulation to require that prices to consumers be low enough so that the activity just breaks even. A case of this sort is illustrated by local governments meeting the deficit of a mass-transit operator while requiring fares to be kept at some low level.

In the case of matching grants, we may assume that a government agency is set up to rebate to consumers some fraction of expense on a particular good. This is the same as offering a credit against income tax due from the individual (a refundable credit which would be received even if one were not to owe taxes). Demand for the good is increased because the net price—gross price less subsidy per unit—is less. If the supply is completely fixed, as may be the case in the short run, then the effect is to raise the income of producers. Potential buyers will bid against each other until the net price is restored to the preexisting gross price. If the supply is completely elastic with constant returns to scale and unchanging factor input prices, and this may better characterize the long-run possibilities, then the subsidy increases output with a net price permanently reduced by the amount of subsidy per unit. Intermediate supply elasticities imply that both the output and the gross price rise from the preexisting equilibrium.

A subsidy has a distributional impact relative to the taxes needed to balance the budget of the government program. Suppose, for example, that the program is financed by a general proportional tax on all consumption. People with especially strong tastes for the subsidized good or people receiving external benefits from its production are relatively favored. Note that if the share of this good in total family consumption rises with family income, richer families are disproportionately benefited. If some resources are not supplied elastically to this industry, owners of these resources will have their incomes raised relative to others. The case of doctors supplying subsidized medical care is a primary example.

Rationale for Subsidy Programs Is Controversial

Economists (Milton Friedman, for example) distrustful of political power have warned that concentrated producer interests seek to capture favors in the political process from diffuse and unorganized taxpayers. Taxation specialists such as Joseph Pechman have argued that many subsidies written into the tax laws erode the progressivity of the tax structure.

Martin Feldstein (1976) has articulated a more reassuring model of selection of subsidies. Suppose the production or consumption of some good generates positive externalities—where others in the community enjoy at little or no cost a good originally produced for another group—such that private markets are not induced to produce these goods in the appropriate quantity. Education, home ownership, and energy-producing inventions may be cited as candidates. Then a subsidy may be preferable to direct government production for several reasons: (1) There may be relatively less efficient managerial control in a bureaucratic agency than in a private corporation; (2) government may not produce the full variety and qualities of the good desired by individuals; and (3) the price elasticity of demand for the good may be greater than 1, in which case the revenue lost to the government is less than the private expenditures induced by the subsidy.

References

Feldstein, Martin, and Amy Taylor, "The Income Tax and Charitable Contributions," *Econometrica*, vol. 44, no. 6, November 1976, pp. 1201–1222; Friedman, Milton, *Capitalism and Free-*

dom, University of Chicago Press, Chicago, 1962, chap. 6; Musgrave, Richard, and Peggy Musgrave, *Public Finance in Theory and Practice,* McGraw-Hill, New York, 1976, chaps. 10, 11, 32; Pechman, Joseph, and Benjamin Okner, "Individual Income Tax Erosion by Income Classes," in *Economics of Federal Subsidy Programs,* U.S. Congress, Joint Economic Committee, 92d Cong. 2d Sess. 1972.

(*See also* Federal budget)

Bernard S. Friedman

Supply

The supply of any product or service consists of the quantities available or forthcoming, depending on possible prices and other factors. Supply is thus symmetrical with demand. The word supply, however, often refers to a single more or less definite amount, such as this year's crop, last month's inventories, etc. Such single amounts, or stocks, are the results of producers' decisions in the past as to what they expected prices to be. As a flow of products coming to market, the supply function for a commodity is the relation between quantities forthcoming and the possible current prices of the commodity, its expected future prices, the prices of alternative products or services, the costs of the producers, and time.

Elasticity of Supply

Supply functions are thus complex. From their components two can be selected that have much explanatory power. These are price and time. In the analysis of supply and price two simple tools can do much. One is the supply curve, the other the concept of elasticity of supply. The supply curve is a line on a diagram whose vertical axis measures price and whose horizontal axis is quantity. Elasticity of supply refers to the responsiveness of supplied quantity to a change in price. The coefficient of elasticity of supply is

$$e_s = \frac{\text{percentage change in quantity}}{\text{percentage change in price}}$$

Normally this coefficient is positive, meaning that a rise in price causes an increase in the quantity supplied. The supply curve slopes up and to the right. If for a 1 percent rise in price the increase in the quantity supplied is less than 1 percent, supply is said to be inelastic. If the increase in quantity is more than 1 percent, supply is elastic.

If supply is a single amount that can neither be increased by higher nor decreased by lower prices, the supply curve can be visualized as a vertical line. Elasticity here is zero. If supply is such that price increases, even if relatively large, call forth only very small relative increases in supply, the supply curve is steep and elasticity is very low. This is a common condition in periods of time so short that producers are unable to attain much additional output (bottlenecks). As the period of time lengthens, producers can bring more facilities and resources into production in response to higher prices. Thus the longer the time, the more supply curves swing from the nearly vertical toward the horizontal. The longer the time, the greater the elasticity of supply.

Changes in supply are shifts in supply curves. An increase in supply is a rightward movement of a supply curve, with more of the commodity being offered for sale at each possible price. An increase in supply can occur because sellers come to expect lower prices in the future, or because of bountiful crops or similar events, or because of declines in the prices of other products the sellers produce or could produce, or from combinations of these forces. Over periods of time long enough for production plans and processes to change, improvements in technology and changes in input prices are the leading causes of changes in supply.

Whatever the period of time, however, the supplies of products and services to any one individual consumer are all perfectly elastic, supply curves being horizontal. That is, the consumer can buy more of anything without, for that reason, having to pay a higher price. Perfectly elastic supplies also prevail for producers when there are many of them in markets for standardized products. Even land can be in perfectly elastic supply, e.g., to individual lessees of small parcels of fairly homogeneous land leased in active markets. Some types of labor can also be in perfectly elastic supply to a business firm that can hire more persons at prevailing wages. If, however, a firm expands its employment beyond some level, the firm might find that it must increase its wage offers. The supply curve for labor to such a firm is then horizontal for some distance after which the curve begins to rise to the right, perhaps becoming ever steeper.

Short-Run Supply Curves

For goods already produced and in the hands of sellers, costs of production have no influence on current supply. That supply is a function of current and of expected future prices. Current prices can be quite different from those producers had anticipated when they incurred the costs in the past. How far expected future prices influence current supply is a matter principally of storability and the costs of storage. Current supply curves, or supply curves in the immediate market as they are also called, slope steeply upward. But when viewed as a flow of production over time, supply becomes a function of producers' costs. Supply is then more elastic. Conventional theory distinguished between the short run and the long run in the relations among cost, output, and price. With varied chronological lengths in different industries, the short run is a set of conditions such that plant and equipment, management and skilled labor, etc., can be taken as fixed. Production in the short run can be increased or decreased by employing more or less of labor, materials, fuel, etc. If prices are depressed below full costs, firms will produce some output, provided that the prices cover at least their variable costs, because by continued production, firms minimize their losses. Short-run supply curves thus begin to take shape. At higher prices, firms are induced to produce more, provided again that such prices cover the added costs of additional output, i.e., the firms' marginal costs. Still more output is forthcoming at still higher prices, which begin to cover or more than cover full costs. As they expand under the stimulus of ever-higher prices, outputs begin to press against firms' capacities. The short-run supply curves are at that point steeper, becoming more so as marginal costs climb high. In sum, then, short-run supply curves typically rise to the right and then become steep as the limits of firms' capacities are reached.

Long-Run Supply Curves

In the long run producers can expand (and contract) the sizes of their plants, everything being variable, by standard definition of the long run. The prices to be received for planned outputs must cover the producers' full costs (which always include a minimal profit). The shape of the long-run supply curve is independent of changes in technology, of inflation and deflation, of the business cycle, and of other disturbances. The shape has to do with what happens to firms' full costs as plant capacities expand. An older view was that full costs per unit must increase with long-run expansion because of diminishing returns. This view is no doubt valid for many extractive industries, petroleum being a prominent example. Modern empirical investigations into production functions give strong support to the hypothesis that many long-run supply curves are actually flat over considerable ranges of output. Flatness means that the full cost per unit produced would remain constant if an industry were to double or quadruple in size. A horizontal supply curve for an industry is often assumed in applied theoretical work. This assumption bypasses many of the complications that pure theory delights in and is also probably fairly realistic.

Negatively Sloped Supply Curves

Supply curves with negative slopes, i.e., that go downward from left to right, can have several meanings. One such curve is often called backward-sloping because its upper part, at high prices, has a negative slope and its lower part, at low prices, has a positive slope. This curve can apply to the labor of an individual. At higher rates of earnings the individual will work fewer hours per week (month, etc.) than at lower rates. This is so if the income effect dominates the substitution effect in the individual's decisions. In other words, the higher rates of earnings multiplied by fewer hours, together with the added leisure made possible by the fewer hours, are preferred to the combination of less leisure and the income provided by the lower rates of earnings. It is less certain if such behavior of individuals can be generalized for groups, owing to differences among persons in their preferences for combinations of income and leisure. Thus, for example, generalizations about the effects of higher income tax rates on the supply of labor are controversial. On the other hand, economists mostly agree that the supply curve for the total labor force probably has a negative slope—that higher rates of earnings cause many adjustments (e.g., earlier retirement) whose net effect is the offer of fewer billions of hours of labor.

Another kind of negatively sloped supply curve applies to farmers who grow only one crop and who live and work in a context where they look upon a particular level of income as satisfactory. Lower prices cause such farmers to produce more in the effort to maintain their incomes. At higher prices they can achieve the desired incomes by producing less. For very short periods, a negatively sloped supply curve can also describe the actions of speculators in an organized commodity market. They could be caught in a position where they desperately need cash. Then, faced with declining prices, they sell more as prices fall. Still another supply curve with a negative slope is the long-run supply curve for a competitive industry whose unit costs diminish as the industry expands. But this supply curve is a construct surrounded with much theoretical controversy. Depending on how they are coupled with their relevant demand curves, negatively sloped supply curves can indicate unstable equilibrium in the functioning of competitive markets.

From time to time events in the economy bring about shortages of supply, or scarcities. Shortages occur when prices are at levels such that the quantities supplied are smaller than the quantities demanded at the same prices. These levels of prices exist under government price controls. Rent controls are another example. General price controls in periods of inflation can make shortages appear to be pervasive, even foreboding. Maximum prices, then, can transform the supply-price relation into shortages. Similarly, minimum prices of the kind often imposed in periods of general economic contraction can be causes of surpluses, gluts, and overproduction. When governments or producers' organizations establish minimum prices, the quantities supplied at those prices are nearly always greater than the quantities demanded at the same prices. The unsold quantities, the surpluses, may be destroyed or put into storage.

References

Hirschleifer, Jack, *Price Theory and Applications*, Prentice-Hall, Englewood Cliffs, N.J., 1976, chap. 10; Miller, Roger L., *Intermediate Microeconomics*, McGraw-Hill, New York, 1978, chap. 10; Watson, Donald S., and Mary A. Holman, *Price Theory and Its Uses*, 4th ed., Houghton Mifflin, Boston, 1977, chaps. 13, 14.

(*See also* Demand; Price theory; Production function; Scarcity)

Donald S. Watson

Supply-side economics

Supply-side economics constitutes a counterrevolution against both the theory and the related policy prescriptions of John Maynard Keynes. It is, in a broad sense, a return to the classical tradition of Adam Smith and Jean Baptiste Say, whose famous law of markets states that supply always creates its own demand. That was the proposition that Keynes was supposed to have laid to rest in demonstrating that capitalist economies had an inherent tendency toward underemployment, but supply-siders say that his argument was logically flawed. And they charge that government attempts to offset temporary weakness in private demand by deficit spending have become a major source of economic instability. Although they do not call for a return to laissez faire, they advocate a different framework for economic policy that replaces the Keynesian concept of demand management with concern for the effect of government on supply.

Remedy for Inflation

Just as Keynesian economics came into power because it offered a politically attractive remedy for unemployment, supply-side economics came into vogue in the 1970s because it offered a politically attractive remedy for inflation. According to Keynesian theory, inflation is the result of excess demand and can only be dealt with by slowing the rate of economic growth, generally by raising taxes. Supply-side economics holds that the proper approach is to stimulate production, generally by cutting taxes.

Underlying this startlingly different approach to inflation is a vastly different analysis of the effect of fiscal policy. Supply-siders completely reject the Keynesian idea of a "multiplier" that relates a tax cut to an increase in aggregate demand through successive rounds of an income-expenditure process. According to their theory, a tax cut works by enhancing the incentives to produce rather than by increasing the capacity to consume. And since it stimulates supply more than demand, a tax cut will reduce inflationary pressures while at the same time permitting a more rapid rate of economic growth. The obverse of this argument is the supply-side explanation for the unprecedented combination of large-scale unemployment and rapid inflation that has baffled Keynesian economists since it first appeared in the early 1970s. To supply-siders, the main problem is what is called "bracket creep." The interaction between inflation and a progressive income tax system means that taxes have been rising much more rapidly than real incomes. Because of its adverse effect on incentives, this unlegislated tax increase has reduced aggregate supply much more than it has restricted aggregate demand and hence has aggravated the problem of inflation while reducing the rate of economic growth.

Supply-Side Economics, Politicians and Monetarists

The supply-side approach first became politically important when a group of Congressional Republicans led by Representative Jack Kemp of New York began arguing for a massive 30 percent across-the-board tax cut in 1978. Their most effective rhetorical device was the Laffer curve (named after Arthur B. Laffer), which seemed to suggest that tax cuts could be so stimulative that they would actually pay for themselves through increased revenues. But for this relationship to hold mathematically, a tax cut would have to generate a supply response at least three times larger than itself. And although Ronald Reagan proposed a similar tax cut in 1981, he accompanied it with equally massive reductions in federal spending that allowed him to project a balanced budget without assuming strong supply-side effects. This approach was not inconsistent with supply-side theory, which holds that government spending tends to crowd out private spending in a way that leaves real output unchanged while raising prices. But it appeared to be less than a frontal attack on conventional economics than the original Kemp program.

Supply-side economics is in some respects an offshoot of monetarism, and like monetarists, most supply-siders do not think that the deficit has a direct impact on inflation. Since inflation is ultimately the result of an excessively rapid increase in the money supply, what counts is not the size of the deficit but whether the Federal Reserve monetizes it. According to the supply-side view, a tax cut has such a stimulative effect on personal savings that it creates the means of financing any deficit that it might generate.

Criticisms

Critics of the supply-side movement, which includes some monetarists as well as most Keynesians, argue that it is based on an exaggerated notion of the incentive effects of taxes. One way to look at the debate is as an argument over the relative size of the income effect of a tax cut and the substitution effect. The supply-siders say that a tax cut improves the work-leisure trade-off and leads to an increase in the supply of labor. Keynesians say that it increases disposable income and means that people do not have to work as hard to maintain their existing standard of living. Supply-siders say that by raising after-tax returns, a tax cut will induce additional savings. Keynesians maintain that since the income derived from past savings is augmented, current savings may well decline.

These questions are, of course, essentially empirical rather than matters of principle. But in many ways, the impact of supply-side economics has so far rested mainly on its ideological content. Keynesian economics provided a rationale not just for government intervention in the economy but for a large and growing public sector. The thrust of the supply-side argument is that a growing public sector will also inevitably lead to a reduction in the rate of growth of the private economy. Thus it presents a sophisticated argument for political conservatism that offers the public the prospect of less government while reconciling the seemingly inconsistent goals of rapid growth and price stability. And this threefold promise makes it a far more serious challenge to Keynesian economics than the more limited critique of the monetarists.

References

Gilder, George, *Wealth and Poverty*, Basic Books, New York, 1981; Keynes, John M., *The General Theory of Employment, Interest, and Money*, Macmillan, New York, 1936; Kristol, Irving, *Two Cheers for Capitalism*, Basic Books, New York, 1978; Laffer, Arthur B., and Jan Seymour, eds., *The Economics of the Tax Revolt*, Harcourt Brace Jovanovich, New York, 1979; Roberts, Paul Craig, "The Economic Case for Kemp-Roth," *Wall Street Journal*, Dow Jones, August 1 1978, p. 16; Say, J. B., *Treatise on Political Economy*, Grigg R. Elliott, Philadelphia, 1834; Smith, Adam, *The Wealth of Nations*, Random House, New York, 1937; Sowell, Thomas, *Say's Law: An Historical Analysis*, Princeton University Press, Princeton, N. J., 1972

(See also Federal Reserve policy; Fiscal policy; Keynesian economics; Laissez faire; Monetary policy; Propensity to consume or to save and inducement to invest; Say's law of markets)

Lewis Beman

Tableau économique (see **Physiocrats)**

Taxation, an overview

Taxation is the process by which governments secure funds by compulsory payments to pay for government expenditures. Taxes may be imposed directly on individuals or on impersonal legal entities such as corporations. Direct taxes may be set in fixed amounts or based on income, wealth, or other measures which are deemed to represent the taxpaying capacities of those subject to the tax. Alternatively, taxes may be imposed indirectly on transactions or on objects, tangible or intangible, regardless of the parties or the ownership of any property involved.

Income taxation is the most important form of direct taxation. Sales taxes—which may be general or specific to commodities such as liquor, tobacco, and gasoline—and stamp taxes to authenticate legal documents are the principal forms of indirect taxes. Customs duties are also indirect taxes but are typically classified separately because in major industrial countries the revenue provided, though sometimes substantial, is incidental to their main purpose, which is protection of national economic activities from foreign competition.

Social security contributions are also regarded as a separate category of taxes; they are a form of direct, but limited, income tax insofar as they are imposed on employees, and they are a form of indirect tax on a particular expenditure insofar as they are imposed on employers. These contributions are combined in a trust fund to pay social security benefits that are related to the taxes previously paid.

Though taxes are the principal source of government funds in most countries, revenues also are received from commercial and quasi-commercial activities. Substantial net profits are usually secured through sales from government monopolies on such products as tobacco and liquor. Proceeds from the sale of public lands have at

913

times been major sources, especially in the United States during the nineteenth century. North Sea oil is becoming important for some countries, and offshore leases provide modest receipts in the United States. Oil revenues, whether in the form of taxes, royalties, or simply sales prices, provide vast flows of funds to some of the small oil-rich countries.

In addition to raising revenue through taxes, almost all governments can and do borrow funds. State and local government debt is usually subject to limitations, with funds typically used for capital outlays. National governments have no real constraints on borrowing. Legal debt limits are waived or raised by legislation or decree.

The accompanying table shows the principal sources of federal revenue in the United States in 1975 and 1978. The increases in all items are conspicuous.

U.S. Federal Government Budget Receipts

(Billions of Dollars)

	1975	1978
Individual income taxes	$122.4	$181.0
Corporation income taxes	40.6	60.0
Social insurance taxes and contributions	86.4	123.4
Excise taxes	16.6	18.4
Estate and gift taxes	4.6	5.3
Customs duties	3.7	6.6
Miscellaneous receipts	6.7	7.4
Total	$281.0	$402.0

SOURCE: Budget of the United States government, fiscal year 1980 (summary figures by Tax Foundation, Inc.)

Criteria of a Tax System

A country's tax system is judged by many standards. Fundamentally, it must provide adequate revenue. It must also be regarded as equitable, but there is no agreed measure of equity in taxation. The principle of progressive taxation is widely accepted, though the degree of progression adopted inevitably depends on the interplay of political forces. There are no objective standards for measuring relative abilities to pay taxes.

A tax system should be simple and economical in the sense that it involves minimal waste and inconvenience for both taxpayers and the government. A tax system should also impose minimal restraints on economic growth and efficiency. It should mitigate rather than accentuate economic fluctuations.

All these criteria are generally recognized and accepted, though with different interpretations and weighting. However, these objectives frequently conflict with each other. What is regarded as equitable may have especially adverse effects on economic activity. What is simple and understandable for taxpayers may not correspond to theoretical concepts of equity. And relief provisions to increase fairness or to reduce tax barriers to economic growth or efficiency can be exceedingly complex.

During the 1960s, some writers reflecting an egalitarian point of view asserted that a principal purpose of taxation should be to redistribute income and wealth. With an increasingly large proportion of total government outlays as direct transfer payments for welfare and with social security and indirect benefits of medical programs, there is a good deal of redistribution downward from the expenditure side of government budgets alone. Taxation specifically designed to redistribute income and wealth is especially likely to reduce the supply and effective use of capital and discourage economic innovation. This conflict of objectives is particularly strong.

The fraction of national income taken by taxation has grown steadily in almost all countries since the late 1920s. In the United States, total taxation went from 10.8 percent of the net national product in 1929 to 34.5 percent in 1978.

It is generally agreed that the greater the total tax burden, the greater the likelihood that taxation will unduly discourage and distort private economic activity, savings, and investments. Opinions differ as to the relative importance of limiting the scale (and hence the cost) of government or of keeping taxes down. Opinions also differ as to the relative importance, with reference to the adverse effect on the private sector of the economy, of the total tax load or the structure of the tax system, that is, the choice of taxes imposed and the rates and definitions applied. There is probably general agreement that the greater the total tax burden the more important it is to design a tax system to limit its inevitable adverse effects.

Individual Income Taxation

The individual income tax was introduced in the United States in 1913 at rates ranging from 1 to 7 percent above an exemption of $4000. Despite assurances in congressional debates that the rates would never rise above 10 percent, the top rate had reached 77 percent by 1918 under the pressures for more revenue during World War I. The rates were reduced to a maximum of 25 percent in the 1920s. They were raised again during the depression period of the 1930s, with a range of 4 to 63 percent established in 1932. During World War II, a uniform personal exemption was established at $500 for a taxpayer, a spouse, and each dependent, with a bottom rate of 23 percent and a top rate of 94 percent, and withholding of taxes was required on wages and salaries. It was remarked at the time that the individual income tax was thereby changed from a class tax to a mass tax. After the war, rates were lowered to a range of 14 to 70 percent, and in 1972 the top rate was set at 50 percent for earned income.

The pattern of individual income tax rates is substantially similar in most major countries, though most of them have maximum rates below 70 percent. The incremental revenue derived from very high rates is relatively small; the rates are set for political purposes in spite of adverse economic effect. Great Britain for some years had conspicuously high top rates, 83 percent on earned income and 98 on investment. A top rate of 60 percent was established by the new government in 1979.

In all countries, income as defined for tax purposes conforms closely to the ordinary and popular concept of income. It includes wages, salaries, interest, dividends, and profits from individually owned businesses, farms, and ranches. The income of partnerships is imputed to and taxed to individual partners. Expenses immediately associated with earning income, such as a salesperson's nonreimbursed travel expenses, work clothes, and rentals of safe deposit boxes, are allowed as deductions in computing taxable income.

In the United States various deductions are also allowed as a matter of social or economic policy, or in response to effective political pressures from various groups. These include disproportionately high medical expenses and large casualty losses. Charitable contributions are also deductible, subject to strict definitions and limitations. Interest paid on debts, whether for business reasons or for personal reasons, state and local income taxes, and property and general sales taxes also qualify as deductions.

The principal difference between personal income as calculated in national income accounts and total taxable income arises from personal exemptions, which have been raised since World War II from $500 to $1000 effective in 1978.

The most controversial features in individual income taxation involve dividends and capital gains. The issue regarding dividend income is whether, how, and to what extent to give relief from the double taxation which arises from the fact that full taxation of dividends to stockholders represents double taxation in that they are paid from corporate income which has already been taxed to the paying corporations. Relief may be given at the corporate level by allowing, directly or indirectly, a deduction for some or all of the dividends paid. Alternatively, relief may be given to stockholders by letting them apply some of the corporate tax previously paid against their individual income taxes. The latter method is generally applied in the European Common Market.

The United States has usually given some nominal relief, always at the stockholder level. Substantial relief seemed in prospect by 1979, but the issue involves perennial controversy arising from economic uncertainty as to the actual extent of the double tax burden and from the political difficulty of voting relief for one class of investors regardless of the actual merits of the situation.

Capital gains in many countries have been wholly exempt from income taxation. In no country, including the United States, have they been included in full in taxable income. In the United States, usually one-half of long-term capital gains have been included in taxable income; for many years there was a ceiling rate of 25 percent. For a few years prior to 1978, the maximum rate under some circumstances exceeded 49 percent. In that year the administration proposed further increases in capital gains taxation. The Congress rejected the proposal and reduced the maximum rate to 28 percent by providing for inclusion of only 40 percent of long-term gains in taxable income.

The distinction between ordinary income and capital gains has become blurred as a result of ingenious maneuvers in financial and business transactions to try to convert ordinary income into something which will qualify as a capital gain under the letter of the law. The tax law has been complicated by various provisions to protect the differential taxation of capital gains.

Corporation Income Taxation

Virtually all countries tax the net income of corporations, at rates typically ranging from 30 to 50 percent. In the United States, the corporation income tax was adopted in 1909 at 1 percent. It was in the range of 10 to 13 percent during the 1920s and has varied from 46 to 52 percent since 1951. The definition of corporate taxable income conforms generally to income reported for financial purposes. A fundamental and pervasive divergence arises from the fact that taxpayers prefer deductions sooner rather than later. On the basis of present value it is better to save taxes if only for awhile to get the use of the funds until taxes are due subsequently. From the standpoint of the government the reverse is true. In tax law and tax administration there is a disposition to postpone the allowance of deductions and to pull forward items of income on which there may be questions of timing.

Differences of opinion on timing are particularly important on the recovery of the cost of machinery, buildings, and other depreciable assets and on the treatment of research and development expenses. Since World War II, most industrial countries have established periods for recovery of capital equipment much shorter than the actual useful lives of property. Though the United States has been among the laggards in this respect, in 1979 considerable bipartisan support developed to allow faster capital recovery. Under continuing inflation the replacement cost of capital equipment becomes much higher than the historical cost on which depreciation is allowed. Faster recovery of historical cost can give a rough offset to higher replacement cost.

The incidence of the corporation income tax is uncertain. Neither theoretical nor statistical analysis has given conclusive answers as to whether the ultimate burden rests on corporations, that is, on stockholders and, by a process of diffusion, finally on to all owners of capital, or is shifter forward in higher prices to consumers.

To the extent that the tax is shifted to consumers, it is a capricious excise tax. To the extent that it is not shifted, it discriminates against the more efficient firms and the more capital-intensive industries. It is, nonetheless, a major producer of revenue and perhaps because of the uncertainty of its incidence more acceptable politically.

During war periods, the United States and most other countries have had excess-profits taxes with rates ranging as high as 80 to 90 percent. The base of normal profits has been either a prewar level or an arbitrary selected rate of return on invested capital. For war periods, during which all resources must be directed, by allocation or otherwise, to war efforts, excess-profits taxes have been widely accepted as a reasonable feature of a mobilization economy. But under all other circumstances, they encourage waste and grossly distort business decisions. In no country have they been continued as a regular part of a tax structure.

A considerable part of the complications of income tax law arises from special rules necessary to deal with various special corporate situations such as mergers and reorganizations. In the United States, many special rules have been established to reduce the impediments which regular income taxation places in the way of new and small business concerns. International business also requires special treatment because two or more countries have the power and the right to tax income involved.

Payroll Taxes

In the period since World War II, payroll taxes to pay for some or all of the costs of social security systems have provided increasingly large proportions of total government revenues. In spite of the increases in tax rates, and in the income levels to which the taxes apply, benefit payments have run ahead of tax receipts. In the United States, payroll taxes are credited to a trust fund which, when the social security trust fund was established in 1935, was intended to operate as an insurance fund and accumulate enough to cover accrued liabilities. In fact, the fund is sufficient to cover only a few months of benefit payments at current levels. Increases in payroll taxes enacted in 1978 to become effective in subsequent years met such resistance that alternative revenue sources were sought.

Payroll taxes, by raising the cost of labor, discriminate against labor just as the corporation income taxes discriminate against capital. The two discriminations only rarely, and very roughly, offset each other.

Value-Added Taxation

A value-added tax, universally applied in the European Common Market, is a neutral tax in the sense that it falls uniformly on labor-intensive and capital-intensive industries, on small firms and large firms, and on integrated or independent companies. Furthermore, it neither penalizes efficient firms nor indirectly subsidizes inefficient firms. As the name implies, the tax base consists of the total value added by all firms. Though the concept thus stated seems abstruse, value added is measured simply by the total sales prices of a company's products or services less the cost of all its purchases from other firms subject to the tax.

It is usually calculated by applying its tax rate to a company's sales with a credit against its taxes for the taxes shown on the invoices for all its purchases. In that way it is self-policing because each successive purchaser will benefit by having the full tax due by its vendors correctly recorded. The tax may or may not be shown separately on invoices or sales slips to final consumers.

Value-added taxes are opposed on two principal grounds. Without some form of relief, they are regressive because they fall at a flat rate on all consumption, and those with lower incomes tend to consume a higher fraction of their incomes. Relief can be given either by exemption of certain products or by credits against income taxes, with credits paid outright to those not subject to income taxes. The second objection is that a value-added tax can produce so much revenue that, once adopted, the opportunity for increases in the rate of tax would reduce the pressure for curtailment of government expenditures. For those seeking to limit the scale of government activities, the second objection is significant.

Excise Tax

Federal excise taxes are levied on only a few commodities, principally liquor, tobacco, and gasoline; the latter is credited to a highway trust fund used to pay for highway construction. States also commonly impose both specific taxes at various rates on these same commodities and, in most states, general retail sales taxes as well. The taxes on liquor and tobacco, referred to as sumptuary taxes, are politically acceptable because of the nature of the products. Though these rates are high in relation to total cost, they are much higher in many other countries, constituting most of the retail prices. Gasoline and other major fuel taxes were first used here as a source of funds for highways, one of the few instances in which taxes have been related to and based on the costs of specific benefits to those paying the taxes. In most other countries gasoline taxes have been used as general sources of revenue. The very large special taxes proposed in 1979 on oil companies, occasioned by the price increases established by foreign producing countries, raise new and distinctive possibilities for special use.

Indirect taxes are imposed at specific amounts or as stated percentages of amounts involved in various transactions or events. As such, they have no direct relation to the total tax burden or taxpaying capacity of individual taxpayers.

Estate and Gift Taxation

Estate and gift taxes are imposed primarily to limit transfers of wealth to succeeding generations. Their social and economic importance is greater than their revenue significance. Some critics complain that death taxes should be more severe and more effective in redistributing wealth. Others complain that with rates as high as 70 percent they unduly reflect the politics of envy and adversely distort the forms of ownership and investment of property, especially through the use of trusts extending over many generations.

Property Taxation

Property taxation in the United States is the principal source of local revenue. In Colonial days it was imposed on all property; during the twentieth century it has come to apply almost entirely to land and buildings. The tax is collected annually on the basis of the assessed values of property which are revised periodically. A principal criticism of property taxation is that under inflation, it becomes an increasing burden on retired homeowners on fixed incomes. Various provisions have been adopted to relieve personal hardship under declining real incomes.

References

Groves, Harold M. *Financing Government*, 6th ed., Holt, Rinehart and Winston, New York, 1965; Musgrave, Richard A., and Peggy B. Musgrave, *Public Finance in Theory and Practice*, 2d ed., McGraw-Hill, New York, 1975; Peckman, Joseph A., *Federal Tax Policy*, 3d ed., Brookings, Washington, D.C., 1977.

(*See also* Capital gains; Federal budget; Fiscal policy; Value-added tax)

Dan Throop Smith

Technology

In the broadest sense, the term technology refers to the method of carrying out any activity that incorporates recurring acts, as well as the use of tools or implements. In a narrower and more common context, technology refers to the method of pursuing activities on a given minimum level of mechanical, engineering, or scientific sophistication. Accordingly, one may speak of the technology of Stone Age endeavors in one extreme, or of the high technology of modern-day undertakings in the other. Moreover, the technology concept can be used to describe a reservoir of knowledge, or it may be restricted to knowledge applied to actual procedures. In some countries technology is used synonymously with or in lieu of engineering; hence, schools of applied science are known as schools of technology.

The technology entity is commonly classified on any of the three following criteria: (1) the type of knowledge incorporated; (2) the type of broadly defined activity involved; or (3) the equipment used, or narrowly defined type of activity involved. Examples of the first category include science-based engineering or chemical technologies. The second category includes industrial, agricultural, communications, or space technologies. The third category consists of computer, laser, automotive, or even bolt-tightening technologies. In the last category, the concept of technology tends to become synonymous with the concept of technique.

Whereas the intermixing of the technology and concepts of technique is not permissible in exacting treatments, the practice is nevertheless quite common in the literature. A clear line of distinction between the two concepts might be attempted on some criterion of sophistication differential between the two, but specifying such criteria may be difficult, if possible at all. Alternatively, one might seek a distinction between technology and technique on the basis of the requirement for tools or implements. Hence, one may speak of techniques, but not of technologies, of athletes or performing artists.

In economics, technology is a concept linked most commonly to the process of production, but there is also a smaller, more recent literature on the technology of consumption. Pertaining to production, the concept of technology is analytically expressed via the production function, i.e., the quantitative cause-and-effect relationship between material and human inputs into a process at one end and the resulting output (product) at the other. In the case of consumption, the use of the concept of technology is analogous, whereby a functional relationship is specified between inputs into and the results or outputs of consumptive activity.

Although technology as a static concept and as expressed through the production function is one of the cornerstones of traditional economic analysis, the critical importance of technology is lodged in the dynamic aspect of the concept, i.e., technological change. Technological change, viewed as a change in an existing production function, or as the introduction of new types of production or of products, is commonly assumed to proceed in a forward direction, i.e., in the form of technological progress. Such progress, in turn, is usually assumed to bring about improvements when evaluated on criteria of efficiency, productivity, or welfare.

The phenomenon of technological change can be investigated on an individual, group, or aggregate scale. For example, if the change involves production functions, such functions can be postulated for the firm, the industry, or the economy as a whole. More generally, the phenomenon of technological change is always incorporated, in some form, in models of economic growth and development.

In economic history, important epochs of technological change have come to be associated with the key elements or ingredients of each case in point, such as mechanization, industrialization, or automation. In more focused historical contexts, one encounters the epochs of electrification, containerization, or computerization.

In the history of economic thought, technology and technological change have always had a place in the major writings. Adam Smith attributed considerable importance to technology, whereas John Stuart Mill underemphasized it. On the other hand, Karl Marx made technological progress one of the cornerstones of his system. In the decades following World War II, economic interest in technological progress was probably the highest throughout the entire history of economic thought. Until the late 1960s or the early 1970s, that interest was focused on the causes of innovation; the economic impacts of different kinds of innovation; the deliberate promotion of progress in technology, primarily by the government; the spillover or fallout effect of one type of new technology (e.g., military or space) on other types of endeavors; the deliberate promotion of domestic and international technology transfer via the exchange of know-how and materiel; and international differentials in technological potential, known as the technology gap.

By the early 1970s, domestic and international events changed the picture dramatically. As a result of growing public opposition to U.S. military operations abroad, which provided the stimulus for much of the government's technological initiative, technological progress as a social goal fell into widespread public disfavor. That disfavor also spilled over to the space effort. During the same time period, the environmental protection movement sprang up and brought with it calls and legislation for "technology assessment," i.e., a study and determination of the undesirable side effects of technological progress. Hence, the conducting of research into technology assessment became incorporated into the new subdiscipline of environmental economics.

Finally, as a result of developments in the international oil market, coupled with

the technology-assessment-motivated interest in nuclear energy and its consequences, the mid-1970s saw a vigorous upsurge of interest in energy economics, the
newest manifestation of economic interest in technology and technological change.

References

American Economic Association, *Papers and Proceedings of the Seventy-Eighth Annual Meeting*, Menasha, Wis., May 1966; Fellner, William, "Trends in the Activities Generating Technological Progress," *American Economic Review*, vol. 60, no. 1, March 1970, pp. 1–29; National
Science Foundation, *The Effects of International Technology Transfers on U.S. Economy*, July
1947; Terleckj, Nestor E., *Effects of R&D on the Productivity Growth of Industries: An Exploratory Study*, National Planning Association, Washington, D.C., December 1974.

(*See also* Automation; Economic growth; Innovation; Productivity; Research and development)

Theodore Suryani-Unger, Jr.

Theory of comparative advantage (see Comparative advantage theory)

Theory of interest (see Interest, economic theory)

Theory of the consumer (see Consumer theory)

Theory of the firm (see Firm theory)

Thrift institutions

Thrift institutions occupy a critical role in the nation's financial market structure.
Their primary objective is to attract savings from individuals and to channel these
funds into productive investments, largely mortgage instruments. There are two
major types of thrift institutions—savings and loan associations and mutual savings
banks. As of September 30, 1979, deposits held in these institutions totaled nearly
$750 billion—$575 billion in savings associations and $165 billion in savings banks.
This represented fully three-fourths of the total amount of consumer-type savings
and time deposits held by all kinds of financial institutions. Commercial banks and
credit unions account for the remaining one-fourth share.

Deposit Categories and Rates

During the post-World War II period, savings institutions have diversified savings
and time-deposit offerings to the public. Until the mid-1960s, only one type of account
was generally available to depositors—the passbook savings account which provided
the individual with a convenient, liquid outlet for surplus funds. By late 1979, the
saver could choose from as many as 14 different types of accounts carrying varying
terms of maturity and interest rates. In addition to ordinary passbook deposits, thrift
institutions are currently authorized to offer accounts having specified maturities
ranging from 3 months to 8 years or more. Time-deposit contracts typically include

among other things (1) the interest rate paid by the institution, (2) early withdrawal penalties which reduce the effective interest rate earned on the account if the depositor withdraws funds prior to maturity, and (3) the conditions under which the deposit can be renewed when the maturity date is reached.

Along with the broadening of deposit categories, rates of return paid on savings and time deposits have increased substantially over the past several decades, accompanying the rise in the overall level of interest rates in the economy. At the present time, a two-tier savings and time-deposit structure is in effect at thrift institutions. The more common type of deposit is the fixed-interest rate account which carries ceiling rates established by federal regulation. In recent years, two new market-linked types of accounts have also been created by federal supervisory agencies. These include a 6-month, $10,000-minimum money-market certificate of deposit with ceiling rates adjusted each week in line with changes in auction discount rates on 6-month Treasury bills, and savings certificates of 4 years or more carrying a ceiling rate 1 percentage point below yields on 4-year Treasury obligations.

In addition to these accounts, a relatively small but expanding group of special types of savings plans have been introduced by savings banks over the past decade. Among the most significant are (1) NOW accounts or interest-bearing nonpassbook savings accounts from which withdrawals may be made by negotiable orders of withdrawal; and (2) tax-sheltered retirement savings programs, of which the two most notable examples are individual retirement accounts designed for persons not otherwise covered by qualified pension plans and Keogh accounts for self-employed individuals. There are also pay-by-phone accounts which allow depositors to transfer savings deposit funds to third parties by means of a telephone transfer system.

Investment Patterns of Thrift Institutions

Since savings and time-deposit turnover is relatively slow, long-term capital-market instruments have proved to be particularly attractive investment outlets for savings institutions. Except during periods of severe financial-market stringency, long-term investments generally provide significantly higher yields than short-term ones. Partly reflecting historical orientation and partly legal restrictions, mortgage loans, especially on residential properties, have been the single most important long-term investment in thrift institution portfolios. These financial intermediaries currently hold about 70 percent of total home mortgage debt held by private financial institutions in the United States. They are also an important source of mortgage credit for the construction and purchase of commercial, industrial, and other types of nonresidential properties.

The dominant role of mortgages in the investment activity of these financial intermediaries can be seen in the 7:1 and 2:1 ratios of mortgage holdings to assets of savings associations and savings banks, respectively. Underlying their overall mortgage activity, however, are fairly pronounced differences in the composition of mortgage portfolios. Savings banks characteristically emphasize permanent long-term mortgage loans, while savings and loan associations allocate a larger proportion of their mortgage funds to construction loans. At the same time, savings banks have been a particularly important supplier of federally underwritten loans—essentially FHA-insured and VA-guaranteed mortgages. Savings associations, on the other hand, have concentrated their lending in the market on conventional home loans. Finally, because they have more flexible investment powers, savings banks have also acquired a wider variety of nonmortgage assets at times, particularly when real estate credit demands have fallen short of available investable funds or when needed for internal liquidity purposes.

Challenges and Problems

In recent years, the viability of thrift institutions in the nation's financial system has been severely tested by a climate of persistently high interest rates and inflation. On the liabilities side of the balance sheet, savings and loan associations and savings banks have found it increasingly difficult to compete in consumers' savings markets. This is a reflection of (1) below-market interest rate ceilings on many types of deposits which have generated shifts of funds away from thrifts into higher-yielding open-market investments; (2) intensified commercial bank competition, reflecting the narrowing, and in some instances, elimination of long-standing differentials on deposit ceiling rates between commercial banks and savings institutions; (3) increased saver access to new types of financial market instruments, such as money-market mutual funds offering instantly liquid, high-yielding outlets for individuals; (4) the growing ineffectiveness of newly authorized market-related savings instruments when interest rates are extraordinarily high; and (5) weakened consumer incentives to save in periods of substantial inflation. Such difficulties in attracting savings funds have severely hampered the ability of thrift institutions to maintain levels of mortgage lending adequate to meet the housing needs of the nation's population.

A fundamental reason underlying the problems of thrift institutions in competing for savers' funds is the large amounts of relatively low yielding mortgage loans remaining in their portfolios. As a result of these holdings, thrift institutions are unable to turn over assets and increase earnings rapidly enough to pay competitive rates on savings when market interest rates rise rapidly. At the same time, their efforts to strengthen earning power have also been frustrated by below-market usury ceilings in many states and by restrictions on lender issuance of mortgages carrying variable-rate provisions.

A variety of proposals aimed at increasing returns to savers have emerged calling for the elimination of all federal ceilings on savings and time deposits. This recommendation has been questioned, however, on the grounds that it should include measures to increase the long-run earning power of thrift institutions so that they can remain viable lenders.

As far as the future is concerned, the control of inflation and, hence, the creation of a more favorable interest rate climate remain the fundamental requirements for more effective thrift institution operations. Many observers also feel that increased savings bank and savings and loan access to nondeposit sources of funds and broadened family financial-service powers would enable them to maintain their vital importance in the financial structure.

References

Klaman, Saul B., *The Postwar Residential Mortgage Market*, Princeton University Press, Princeton, N.J., 1961.

(See also Banking system; Capital markets and money markets; Credit, an overview; Disintermediation; Financial institutions; Financial instruments; Interest rates; Mortgage credit; Saving)

Saul B. Klaman and Jack Rubinson

Time series analysis

When observations occur as a sequence in time, they are said to constitute a time series. There are many methods for analyzing series such as daily mean temperatures, weekly bank deposits, and monthly unemployment rates, in which the individual observations are separated by a constant interval and are given values of ..., $y_{t-1}, y_t, y_{t+1}, \ldots$, at times $\ldots, t-1, t, t+1, \ldots$.

The important distinguishing characteristic of time series is that successive observations are usually statistically dependent. This means in particular that the probability distribution of each new observation in a series depends on the values of previous observations. Time series analysis is aimed at deducing the nature of this dependence and exploiting it. Thus, some of the applications of time series analysis are (1) characterizing and modeling dependence within and between series, (2) forecasting future values of series, (3) smoothing and deseasonalizing series, (4) estimating the effects of interventions, and (5) deriving optimal-control equations.

Stochastic processes

As in other branches of statistics, we think of the data that we actually have as generated by some underlying hypothetical model. The theoretical probability model for a time series is called a stochastic process. A time series is then conceived as a particular realization of this stochastic process.

Stationary   A class of models of great theoretical and practical importance are stationary stochastic processes. A stationary process is one in a state of statistical equilibrium in which the probability relationship between different values in the series depends only on the time differences at which they were observed. In particular, a stationary process has a fixed mean, and the correlation between any two values in the series depends only on their distance apart in time. The correlation coefficient ρ_k between observations k intervals apart is called the theoretical autocorrelation function at lag k.

If, in addition to stationarity, it is assumed that all the individual and joint probability distributions of the observations are, to an adequate approximation, normal, then a stationary process is completely defined by its mean μ, variance σ^2, and the autocorrelation function $\rho_1, \rho_2, \rho_3, \ldots$, which defines the autocorrelation at all lags and is denoted by $\{\rho_k\}$. In practice the autocorrelations of a stationary process usually die out rather quickly as the lag is increased so that knowledge of the pattern followed by $\rho_1, \rho_2, \ldots, \rho_h$ will, for a moderate value of h, essentially characterize the process. Now, for any particular realized series, sample autocorrelations $\{r_k\}$ calculated from

$$r_k = \frac{\sum \tilde{y}_t \tilde{y}_{t+k}}{\sum \tilde{y}_t^2} \qquad \tilde{y}_t = y_t - \overline{y} \tag{1}$$

may be regarded as estimates of $\{\rho_k\}$.

Thus, a plot of the sample autocorrelation function (of r_k versus k) can suggest the pattern followed by the ρ_k's and is, thus, a basic tool in tentatively identifying (specifying) a model.

Economic series are seldom adequately modeled by stationary processes directly. The practical importance of the stationary normal model is that after suitable operations on a given time series such as differencing, the resulting derived series can often be approximated by a stationary normal process which can then be characterized and fitted fairly easily.

Spectral Analysis   A time series may show rather slow, irregular undulations or more rapid variations. In the first case we say that most of its variance is associated with low frequencies, and in the latter case with higher frequencies. This idea of associating variance with frequency gives rise to an alternative means of characterizing a stationary stochastic process. This employs not the autocorrelation function $\{\rho_k\}$ itself, but its Fourier cosine transform. The following function of frequency f, which can be computed knowing the autocorrelation function $\{\rho_k\}$ and the variance σ^2,

$$p(f) = 2\sigma^2 \left(1 + 2 \sum_{k=1}^{\infty} \rho_k \cos 2\pi \, fk \right) \tag{2}$$

is called the power spectrum of the stochastic process. It can be interpreted as measuring the variance of the process in a small frequency range between f and $f + df$.

The spectrum of an underlying stationary stochastic process may be efficiently estimated knowing the sample autocorrelation function $\{r_k\}$ and the sample variance s^2, but not, however, by direct substitution of $\{r_k, s^2\}$ for $\{\rho_k, \sigma^2\}$ in Equation (2).

Spectral analysis is particularly appropriate for problems which are most naturally thought about in terms of frequencies and where long series are available for analysis. In particular, cross spectral analysis between two or more series can indicate the frequencies at which maximum transmission from one series to the other is occurring.

Stochastic Difference-Equation (ARIMA) Models   In many economic problems, available time series tend to be short, and it becomes necessary to employ parsimonious models requiring a minimum number of adjustable parameters which need to be estimated. A valuable class of such models based on stochastic difference equations are called autoregressive moving-average (ARMA) models.

As an introduction to these models consider first an uncorrelated process . . . , a_{t-1}, a_t, a_{t+1}, . . . , consisting of random drawings from an approximately normal distribution having mean zero and variance σ^2. This is referred to as white noise or a random shock process.

Now consider the derived stochastic process defined by the stochastic difference equation

$$\tilde{y}_t = \varphi \tilde{y}_{t-1} + a_t \qquad |\varphi| < 1 \tag{3}$$

where $\tilde{y}_t = y_t - \mu$. This is called a first-order autoregressive process (AR$_1$). For an analogy $\tilde{y}_t$ might be the yearly deviation from the mean level of a reservoir. If φ were 0.6, the model would say that the deviation in the tth year consisted of a predictable part $0.6\tilde{y}_{t-1}$ depending on the deviation in the previous year plus an unpredictable gain or loss a_t.

For this AR$_1$ model $\rho_k = \varphi^k$, so that the theoretical autocorrelation function falls off exponentially (geometrically) as the lag is increased. An apparently stationary time series for which the sample autocorrelations $\{r_k\}$ fall off approximately exponentially would, thus, suggest that the underlying stochastic process was the AR$_1$ model of Equation (3).

Another simple model of interest is the first-order moving-average (MA$_1$) process in which $\hat{y}_t$ depends not only on a_t but also on the previous shock a_{t-1} entering the system.

$$\hat{y}_t = a_t - \theta a_{t-1} \qquad |\theta| < | \tag{4}$$

This stochastic process has the identifying characteristic that it produces series which are autocorrelated only at lag 1 $(\rho_k = 0 \qquad k > 1)$.

In general, suppose $\hat{y}_t$ depends not only on a_t but also on p previous y values $\hat{y}_{t-1}, \hat{y}_{t-2}, \ldots, \hat{y}_{t-p}$ and on q previous a values $a_{t-1}, a_{t-2}, \ldots, a_{t-q}$. Then the process is said to be an autoregressive moving-average process of order (p, q) or simply an $\text{ARMA}_{p,q}$ process. Thus

$$\hat{y}_t = \varphi_1 \hat{y}_{t-1} + \varphi_2 \hat{y}_{t-2} + \varphi_3 \hat{y}_{t-3} + a_t - \theta_1 a_{t-1} - \theta_2 a_{t-2} \tag{5}$$

in an $\text{ARMA}_{3,2}$ process.

An economic time series $\{y_t\}$ exhibiting nonstationary behavior might be such that its first difference $y_t = \nabla Y_t = Y_t - Y_{t-1}$ (or occasionally a higher difference of the series) was stationary. If after differencing the series d times $y_t = \nabla^d Y_t$ followed an $\text{ARMA}_{p,q}$ process, the model for Y_t would be called an autoregressive integrated moving-average process of order p, d, q, or an $\text{ARIMA}_{p,d,q}$ process. These processes, which are easily extended to model seasonal time series, seem to provide remarkably good models for a wide variety of economic series.

Model Building

Using the computer interactively, one can build ARIMA models according to the scheme

$$\text{Specification} \rightarrow \text{Fitting} \rightarrow \text{Diagnostic checking} \text{ ----,}$$

Specification (or identification) of the series (tentative choice of p, d, q) may be accomplished by first applying differencing or other similar simplifying operations to obtain approximate stationarity and, hence, to determine d. The pattern of sample autocorrelations in the resulting series can then suggest appropriate values for p and q. The process, tentatively identified in this way, is then fitted to the series. That is, values of the φ's and θ's are estimated using maximum likelihood. Finally, the residuals from the fitted model, which are estimates of the a_t's, provide the basis of diagnostic checks to seek out nonrandomness. Such checks can suggest whether, and how, the model needs to be modified.

Transfer Function (Distributed-Lag) Models   Suppose we are interested in monthly refrigerator sales Y_t and we believe that housing starts X_t serve as a leading indicator to determine a part $\mathcal{Y}_t$ of Y_t. The remaining part $N_t = Y_t - \mathcal{Y}_t$ we shall call the noise. Since houses take several months to build, we can expect to find a distributed-lag relationship

$$\mathcal{Y}_t = \omega_0 X_{t-g} + \omega_1 X_{t-g-1} + \omega_2 X_{t-g-2} + \cdots + \omega_n X_{t-g-n} \tag{6}$$

connecting $\mathcal{Y}_t$ and lagged values of X_t. Such relationships can often be economically described by simple difference equations. For example, suppose the weights ω in (6) fall of exponentially so that $\omega_j = \omega_0 \delta^j$, then the relation (6) can equally well be written as the first-order difference equation

$$\mathscr{Y}_t = \delta \mathscr{Y}_{t-1} + \omega_0 X_{t-g} \tag{7}$$

Thus a transfer function model for this example would be of the form $Y_t = \mathscr{Y}_t + N_t$ with $\mathscr{Y}_t$ determined by the difference equation (7) which related $\mathscr{Y}_t$ dynamically to X_t, and with the noise N_t determined by an ARMA (difference-equation) model relating N_t dynamically to a_t. The methods previously described have been extended to build such models.

Intervention Analysis   When transfer function models are adapted and used to provide estimates of the change in, say, Y_t, an economic indicator arising from an intervention such as a change of interest rate, the analysis is sometimes referred to as intervention analysis.

Optimal Control   When X_t is a variable that can be manipulated, transfer function models of the type previously described may be used to derive an optimal-control equation designed to maintain Y_t as close as possible to some desired target level.

Deseasonalizing Series   One of the most long-standing and difficult kinds of time series analysis attempts to facilitate understanding of economic indicators by removing the seasonal component. Traditional empirical approaches culminated in the development of the X-11 method which is very widely employed in government and business. It has been argued that model-based approaches which tailor the process of deseasonalization to the particular series could produce improved results.

Multiple Time Series   Autocorrelation analysis, spectral methods, and ARIMA models may all be generalized so that the interrelationships (including feedback relationships) between a number of associated series may be studied and exploited.

History

In the early twentieth century, time series studies were based on models containing deterministic terms plus independent shocks. In the 1920s the inadequacy of such models was pointed out by Yule and Slutsky, who introduced stochastic difference-equation models which were further developed notably by Walker, Wold, Kendall, and Bartlett. Stationary process theory and spectral analysis were developed in the 1930s and 1940s by Khintchine and Wiener and more recently, notably, by Tukey and his collaborators, and by Jenkins. Starting in the 1930s, use of stochastic models for prediction was developed in particular by Wold, Kolmogorov, Wiener, and Whittle. Methods for judging adequacy of fit of time series models were studied by Yule, Quenouille, Wold, Bartlett, and Whittle.

References

Anderson, T. W., *The Statistical Analysis of Time Series*, Wiley, New York, 1971; Box, G. E. P., and G. M. Jenkins, *Time Series Analysis, Forecasting and Control*, rev. ed., Holden-Day, San Francisco, 1976; Box, G. E. P., and G. C. Tiao, "Intervention Analysis with Applications to Economic and Environmental Problems," *Journal of the American Statistical Association*, vol. 70, 1975, pp. 70–79; *Seasonal Analysis of Economic Time Series*, Economic Research Report ER.1, U.S. Government Printing Office, Washington, D.C., 1978.

(*See also* Distributed lags in economics; Economic models; Economic statistics; Forecasting methods; Index numbers; Seasonal adjustment methods; Statistical techniques in economics and business, an overview)

George E. P. Box

Trade and professional associations

An association is a group of professionals or business people voluntarily organized to further their common objectives. These objectives include standards of professional conduct, standards of product and service quality, provisions for education and training, development of better communications among members, representation before other trade and professional organizations, and representation before government entities and to the general public.

Trade associations hire professional and clerical staff people on a part-time or full-time basis. The American Society of Association Executives estimates that there are 200,000 trade associations within the United States. Of these, 18,000 are identified as either national or regional in scope. The editor of the Kiplinger *Newsletter* estimates that there are 30,000 state, local, and national associations. The Columbia book list includes 6000 national, professional, and labor trade associations in the United States and Canada. The membership of trade and professional organizations may include different participants within the same business or social organization, e.g., the average firm of more than 200 employees may have employees participating in a dozen or more trade associations.

Trade and professional associations have been identified throughout recorded history. The histories of the ancient civilizations of China, Japan, India, and Egypt all make reference to such associations. The same is true of the time of the Roman Empire. Religious writings such as the Bible refer to trade and professional groups. The developing craft guilds and merchant guilds during the Middle Ages in Europe and up to the twentieth century were the forerunners of the labor organizations of today. While the guilds were less pronounced within the United States, remnants of these European guilds were brought to the United States during the colonial period and during the late eighteenth and the nineteenth centuries.

Government as Major Stimulus for Growth

During the twentieth century trade associations have been stimulated by the growth and power of government. Collective decision making accelerated during times of war and economic stress. During World War I the federal government's need for coordination of the war effort led to creation of industry-based trade associations to help the government achieve its war mobilization objectives. The Great Depression during the 1930s helped create unusual demand for industrywide responses to government requirements. This was particularly true with the passage in 1933 of the National Industrial Recovery Act, which created the National Recovery Administration to communicate and ensure effective action by industry—e.g., code authorities were instituted under the act and carried out through industry trade associations. World War II further stimulated trade associations for war mobilization, building upon the previous experience with such structures gained during World War I and the Great Depression. During the decades of the 1960s and 1970s, as government increased its control over business, trade and professional organizations expanded. The government role grew in pursuit of many objectives: health, safety, environment, equal opportunity, redistribution of income. These objectives were implemented through setting of standards and other regulations and through taxation and spending. Associations provided necessary information for achieving these objectives through the design of government regulations, taxes, and spending used for this purpose; and for ascertaining the point of view of its constituents. Associations also provided a channel for government to use in communicating its policies.

The development of the role of associations in recent years has been largely free from controversy about monopoly and price-fixing since such practices were legally prohibited long before the large and recent growth in associations.

While government has been the major stimulus for the growth of trade and professional associations in the United States during the twentieth century, it has in recent years also attempted to impose limitations on the role of associations, such as regulations concerning federal election laws and lobbying. The growth of associations in the United States indicates that they have become another avenue by which society achieves its objectives. The wide range of activities performed by associations reflects the inherent economic advantage of providing services whose costs can be widely shared by its members, but which would be beyond the means of individual association members to perform for themselves. Government has gained from the information and coordination. The membership and the general public have gained from higher professional standards through education and through training to achieve these standards.

References

Bradley, Joseph F., *The Role of Trade Associations and Professional Business Societies in America*, Pennsylvania State University Press, University Park, Pa., 1965; Colgate, Craig, Jr., and Patricia Broida (eds.), *National Trade and Professional Associations of the United States and Canada, and Labor Unions*, Columbia Books, New York, 1979; Israel, Jerry (ed.), *Building the Organizational Society*, Free Press, New York, 1972.

(*See also* Antitrust policy; Government regulation of business)

Jack Carlson

Transfer payments (see Poverty)

Underconsumption theory of the business cycle (*see* **Juglar cycle**)

Unemployment (*see* **Employment and unemployment**)

Urban economics

Urban economics is concerned with the patterns of location of households, business enterprises, and other institutions in densely developed areas: how these patterns evolve and change; how these patterns affect and are affected by federal, state, and local government expenditures, taxes, and regulations; and how these patterns affect the economic performance of enterprises and households.

Urban economics is less than a quarter-century old as a recognized subfield of economics. Before the late 1950s, there were no universities where a graduate student in economics could specialize in urban economics. Its roots, however, are older. Aside from classical and neoclassical economic theory, its antecedents are: location theory, regional economics, and public finance. Urban economics has enriched all of these antecedent fields, including microeconomic theory.

Residential Location Theory

The theory of residential choice—where to live and how much housing to consume—is a major component of urban economics and represents an extension of classical location theory because that theory dealt almost exclusively with the location decision of the business enterprise. On the other hand, the theory of residential choice treats the location of job opportunities as given. Income, family size, and transportation costs are the crucial factors determining the household's demand for space and housing at various distances from the workplace. Familiar patterns of urban settlement emerge. Well-to-do large families live further out (suburbs) because they want more space and can afford higher transportation costs. The poor live closer to the center of employment because they cannot afford high transportation costs. The competition for space restricts the size of their living quarters. The childless rich strike a compromise. They live closer to the center in large quarters.

The theory not only accounts for existing patterns, it also generates hypotheses about the sources of change. Rising affluence, reduced transportation costs, and the decentralization of workplaces predictably disperse the population and reduce the average density of settlements (people per square mile) in the metropolis.

Like every good theory in its formative stages, residential location theory abstracted from some hard realities which ultimately could not be ignored. One such reality is racial segregation. The classical variables of income, family size, and transportation costs, taking the workplace as given, would not predict the observed degree of racial segregation in urban areas. The ghetto phenomenon could only be explained in terms of racial discrimination, although the element of free choice was not totally absent.

The urban riots of the mid-1960s focused attention on this dimension of urban development and stimulated research on the consequences of restricted residential choice for the economic and social development of the affected groups: their income, employment, housing quality, access to public services, and other determinants of the quality of life.

A second and related reality which was missing in the early formulations of residential choice is the existence of a public sector and the multiplicity of local jurisdictions in the typical urban area. The latter phenomenon had been largely ignored in the field of public finance. The supply of locally produced public services and their cost (taxes) were not homogeneous throughout the urban area. It was reasonable to assume, according to Tiebout, that households would choose locations in respect of these factors as well and that their choices would be influenced by the importance they attached to the various services offered and by the price (tax) at which these services were offered at various locations. That choice might also be influenced by the posture of the jurisdiction with respect to the exclusion or inclusion of potential residents from various socioeconomic groups.

The simple theory of residential choice predicted the decentralization of population. The Tiebout hypothesis predicted the segregation of population into homogeneous suburbs, the core city gradually being abandoned to the poor, the victims of discrimination, and to the affluent single persons who valued proximity to their jobs and the classic urban amenities more than open space and quality public services.

Jobs and the Urban Area

How do urban economists explain the location of jobs within the urban area? For reasons which are readily perceived, the simplicity of the residential location model could not be replicated even in a rudimentary way. Location theory suggested some useful categories: market orientation, materials orientation, economies of scale, and agglomeration. Clearly, small shops serving local markets would have to be located nearby. (But where would the people be?) An enterprise serving the entire urban market might be expected to locate at some central point from which deliveries could be made in all directions (or customers could come from all directions), unless the location was dictated by the need to be near a port or rail terminal where bulky or heavy inbound materials could be received.

Only in the latter case could one view the location of jobs as largely independent of the location of population and, therefore, as a key determinant of the pattern of settlement. The enterprise which best fit that role was the one which sold its product or service in regional or national markets and did not process heavy or bulky materials such that its location would be dictated by the location of shipping terminals. The location choices of such unattached industries were seen as the key exogenous influence on urban form.

Why would such industries not locate randomly throughout the urban area? Why the seemingly excessive concentration of employment in highly congested downtown areas? The kernel of the explanation was found in conventional economic theory, namely, economies of scale. That concept had already been exploited by location theorists to account for the existence of cities in an otherwise featureless plain. But it was left to urban economists to articulate fully the nuances and implications of that concept for urban development.

The clustering of enterprises was seen as efficient not in terms of the scale of the firm but rather in terms of the scale of the industry and the scale of the local economy. The city was viewed as a device for maximizing productivity and profit by exploiting all the benefits of specialization at minimum transport cost. In line with Adam Smith's famous dictum, the clustering of enterprises enlarges the market and, hence, the potential for specialization.

Key Research Fields

Given the key role of transport costs in shaping urban form, it is not surprising that a major focus for research in urban economics has been urban transportation. On the demand side, a very substantial literature has developed under the heading of modal choice. Researchers have attempted to identify the price and service variables associated with each mode—car, bus, rail transit, taxi—which, when combined with variables describing the traveler—income, occupation, family size, location—serve to explain and predict modal choice. On the supply side, the effort has been directed at estimating average and marginal costs, both private and social, of alternative modes for alternative levels of capacity and utilization. This kind of research is critical for assessing alternative policies and projects designed to curtail the growth of auto travel and the decline of mass transit. Before 1973, the concern centered on the threat of the auto to the viability of the central city, to the quality of urban air, and to the containment of urban sprawl. Now, the top of the agenda is occupied by the linkage between the auto and imported oil.

Another major focus for research by urban economists has been housing. This is not a generic urban problem. In fact, the incidence of substandard housing is greater in rural areas. But because the residential location decision is also a housing decision and because the quality and cost of housing is central to public policy aimed at relieving poverty and reducing racial discrimination, urban economists have been heavily involved in research on the factors affecting the demand for housing, particulary price and income.

References

Chinitz, Benjamin (ed.), *City and Suburb: The Economics of Metropolitan Growth*, Prentice-Hall, Englewood Cliffs, N.J., 1964; Heilbrun, James, *Urban Economics and Public Policy*, St. Martin's, New York, 1974; Mills, Edwin S., *Urban Economics*, 2d ed., Scott, Foresman, Glenview, Ill., 1980; Muth, Richard F., *Urban Economic Problems*, Harper & Row, New York, 1974.

(*See also* Location theory; Microeconomics; Regional economics)

Benjamin Chinitz

User costs (*see* Opportunity cost)

Utility

After centuries of intellectual striving to arrive at a definition of utility, economists still have not completely settled on a meaning. Because the term is borrowed from ordinary vocabulary, it carries connotations that do not apply to the special field of modern economics. Jeremy Bentham, the modern architect of utilitarism, almost 200 years ago made the terminological transplant in the English literature. But, shortly before his death, Bentham lamented—and on good grounds—that "utility was an unfortunately chosen word." Indeed, what he had in mind and what economists now mean by utility is not some property of an object to produce pleasure or prevent pain, but the pleasure experienced by the individual in using that object. The snag is that in the ordinary usage utility is synonymous with usefulness, which is a property of a thing. The necessary distinction was clearly explained in an 1833 lecture by W. F. Lloyd, a Cambridge economist, using corn as an example. The usefulness of corn reflects its objective properties and, hence, is the same in time of famine as in a year of bumper crop. But in the discriminate sense, utility expresses "a feeling of the mind" that varies with the circumstances of the individual. However imprecise the old terms are, almost any specialist may speak of the "utility of corn" instead of the utility felt by an individual for corn in varying situations. Vilfredo Pareto proposed to replace the word utility with a specially coined word—"ophelimity"—in order to prevent such terminological bungles, but economists preferred (so it seems) convenience to scientific precision.

The importance of the concept of utility for economic science stems from the desire to find the cause of economic value. The search goes back to Plato and Aristotle, and beyond. Even the poet Pindar was intrigued by what we now call the paradox of value: why an important thing for life, such as water, has a practically null market value, whereas flimsy jewels always fetch very high prices. We still believe, with Aristotle, that things that are exchangeable must possess one and the same homogeneous "essence." Like Karl Marx centuries later, Aristotle argued that essence is the labor necessary for the production of a thing. In the case of the neoclassical school, the Aristotelian craving for a monist explanation simply shifted from one factor to another. As one of the founders, W. Stanley Jevons, taught, "Value in use equals total utility," a position shared by most members of that school.

Measuring Utility

It was Plato who first claimed that what we now understand to mean utility has a measure. As he explained, the life of one who does not plan on future pleasures is not the life of a human but the life of an oyster. These very ideas were revived 24 centuries later by Bentham. Pleasure and pain, Bentham preached, must be cardinally measurable, that is, just as milk or flour is. Just as milk is measured in quarts and flour in pounds, utility is measured in some proper units—in "utils," as was later suggested. In addition, Bentham strongly insisted that the sum of the utilities of all individuals represents the amount of happiness (of utility) of the entire community. He argued that if different utilities cannot be meaningfully added, all political science must come to a standstill. He even believed in the possibility of measuring utility by a "moral thermometer." The idea that utility would ultimately be measured by some such instrument was defended by several subsequent prominent writers, such as Francis Y. Edgeworth, who believed in a possible "hedonimeter," and Frank Ramsey, who counted on the discovery of a psychogalvanometer.

By now such hopes have been officially abandoned, together with the two basic Benthamite faiths: the cardinal measure of utility and the meaningful additivity of different utilities. Yet one still finds frequently in the literature arguments based on a measure of utility and on aggregate utility.

Principle of Decreasing Marginal Utility

Reaching the realization that subjective utility is one essential determinant of economic value was greatly hampered by the Aristotelian dogma that "the value of a thing lies in the thing itself," as J. B. Say insisted. The great appeal of that dogma stemmed from the ethical implications of its corollary: In a just exchange of things, no party must gain or lose. Not only the scholastic doctors but also classical economists, especially Karl Marx, were happy with it. David Ricardo explicitly dismissed the thought that the whims of the individuals may have any influence on economic value.

This position of subjective utility was all the more intriguing since the role of the consumers' preferences had already become obvious as a result of some economic progress in many European urban communities. By 1750, Ferdinand Galiani explicitly acknowledged the association between economic value and utility in his celebrated *Della moneta* (On Money). But that acknowledgment was not sufficient to spark a revolution in economic science. That came when a specific law, now known as the principle of decreasing marginal utility (PDMU), was set forth.

Prior to Galiani's work, Daniel Bernoulli, a famous mathematician and physicist, formulated the law in 1738. He was led to it by a gambling paradox in which the theoretical stake of the gambler playing against the bank is infinite. For its solution, Bernoulli introduced the idea that the "moral value" of an additional dollar is smaller for a millionaire than for one who is not as rich, i.e., it produces less felicity for the former. However, because of its mathematical nature, Bernoulli's paper remained unknown to economists for more than 100 years.

Some time around 1780, Bentham discovered the same principle. His precise formulation, if rephrased, reads: Successive units of wealth produce smaller and smaller additional utilities, all units of wealth being assumed equal.

Thus, the PDMU presupposes not only the measurability of utility but also the cardinal measurability of the thing that produces felicity. The principle does not apply, for instance, to successive additions of stamps in a collection.

Great though Bentham's influence was in Britain and elsewhere, economists still were unable to perceive the analytical importance of the PDMU. It was a German civil servant, Hermann Heinrich Gossen, who first related that principle to the behavior of an individual seeking to maximize happiness in life. But even Gossen's volume, published in 1854, remained ignored for some 30 years, until W. Stanley Jevons learned of it by chance. Yet the founding of utility theory is now attributed to

Jevons, Léon Walras, and Carl Menger, who independently rediscovered Gossen's idea in the early 1870s.

Actually, Gossen also formulated a second law, which states that utility also decreases if the same act of enjoyment is repeated too often. This law is still largely ignored in the literature, although it is well known that eating steak every day, for example, dulls the pleasure of eating it.

One theorem proved by Gossen (improperly called Gossen's second law) admirably shows the importance of the PDMU. It is as follows: In order to maximize utility, any individual must spend income in such a way that the utility of the last penny spent on any item must be the same as that of other pennies spent. In other words, the marginal utility of money must be the same for all expenditures.

The Independence Axiom

The first writers on utility assumed that the utility of any commodity depends only on the amount of that commodity in the possession of the individual in question, regardless of the amounts of other commodities the same individual may possess. According to this independence axiom, the utility felt by an individual I for some commodity C_k is a function $U_k^I(x_k)$ of the amount x_k in the possession of I; but when there is no danger of misunderstanding, we may simply write $U(x)$ instead.

The utility of a marginal increment Δx is $\Delta U = U(x + \Delta x) - U(x)$, which, however, is not the theoretical definition of marginal utility. The reason is that ΔU depends on the size of Δx. Marginal utility means the limit of the average marginal utility increment, i.e., the limit of $\Delta U/\Delta x$ for $\Delta x \to 0$, which is the first derivative, $U'(x)$, of $U(x)$. Therefore, the dimension of marginal utility is not utils, but a ratio of utils per amount of commodity. Also, since the PDMU means that $U'(x)$ is a decreasing function, it follows that the second derivative $U''(x) < 0$.

In diagrammatical analysis, it is the representation of $U'(x)$ rather than that of $U(x)$ that is used. In such a diagram, the utility $U(x)$ is represented by an area (shaded in Figure 1). This area, hence $U(x)$, may be infinite. Indeed, for the actions of an individual, just as for an ordinary navigator, it does not matter how deep is the ocean of utility on which one navigates: only the height of the waves counts.

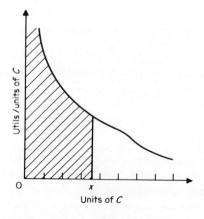

Units of C Figure 1

According to the independence axiom, the total utility corresponding to the amounts $x_1, x_2, \ldots, x_n$ of commodities $C_1, C_2, \ldots, C_n$ is the sum of simple functions

$$U_1(x_1) + U_2(x_2) + \cdots + U_n(x_n) \tag{1}$$

This unrealistic axiom was discarded by Edgeworth, who pointed out that the total utility is a function $U(x_1, x_2, \ldots, x_n)$ which rarely reduces to the sum shown in Equation (1). The marginal utility of C_1 (say, of potatoes) is $\partial U/\partial x_1$ (in a simpler notation, U_1'), which also depends on the amounts of the other commodities. This brought up the issue of the relationship between commodities. As Edgeworth and also two Viennese bankers, R. Auspitz and R. Lieben, argued, if an increase in x_2 increases the marginal utility U_1'—as is the case for potatoes and butter, for example—C_1 and C_2 are complementary. If on the contrary an increase in x_2 decreases U_1', the two commodities are competitive, or rival, in use (potatoes and bread, for instance). Finally, if U_1' is independent of x_2, C_1 and C_2 are independent in use. Two commodities are thus complementary, competitive, or independent according to whether $\partial^2 U/\partial x_1 \partial x_2$ is greater than, less than, or equal to 0.

Isoutility Curves

Utility analysis can then no longer make proper use of the diagram of Figure 1. As Edgeworth proposed, we can now visualize in the n-dimensional space an $(n-1)$-dimensional variety represented by $U(x_1, x_2, \ldots, x_n) = u$, u being any given amount of utility. This variety is the loci of all combinations of commodity amounts that produce the same utility; it is an isoutility variety. The commodity plane (for two commodities) is completely covered by a family of isoutility curves, as shown in Figure 2. This particular graph now dominates practically all economic arguments.

On this graph, a budget consisting of a given income m confronting given prices p_1 and p_2 is

$$p_1 x_1 + p_2 x_2 = m \tag{2}$$

and is represented by a straight line, such as $A_1 A_2$. The highest utility obtainable by that budget obviously corresponds to E, the point at which $A_1 A_2$ is tangent to an iso-

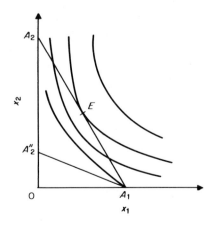

Figure 2

utility curve. The direction of a tangent to such a curve is given by $U_1' \, dx_1 + U_2' \, dx_2 = dU = 0$, whereas for the direction of $A_1 A_2$ we have $p_1 \, dx_1 + p_2 \, dx_2 = 0$. Therefore, in addition to (2), the coordinates of E must satisfy

$$\frac{U_1'}{p_1} = \frac{U_2'}{p_2} \tag{3}$$

a highly popular result. With some additions, ordinarily ignored, it is an equivalent statement of Gossen's theorem. The additions concern the fact that no actual individual ever buys all available commodities; hence, it is not correct to say that prices are proportional to the marginal utilities of every individual. For a simple illustration: If the budget is $A_1 A_2'$, the expenditure on C_2 is zero and (3) does not apply.

Theory of Binary Choice

In 1906, Vilfredo Pareto revolutionized not only utility theory but also all social sciences by replacing the fiction of measurable utility with a highly realistic theory, whose proper label is the theory of binary choice.

By asking an individual first whether he or she prefers the commodity combination P or Q, then P or R, P or S, and so on, one arrives at a division of the commodity space into three parts: (1) the domain of combinations preferred to P; (2) the domain of combinations such that P is preferred to them; and (3) the boundary between these two domains, which represents the loci of combinations indifferent to P (and indifferent among themselves). Even mathematicians did not present their arguments in axiomatic form then, nor did Pareto. But his argument implied the following:

1. The individual is rational (consistent), which means that if he or she prefers A to B and B to C, then the individual must prefer A to C (the postulate of the transitivity of preference).

2. In a continuous shift from a preference to a nonpreference relation one must necessarily pass through an indifferent state of mind (the postulate of the existence of indifference).

These two postulates lead to a map identical to that of Figure 2, the only difference being that the same curves now represent the loci of indifferent combinations. However, to each variety of indifference we can attribute a ranking number such as to indicate the preference ordering. Such a scale constitutes an ordinal measure. An ordinal measure differs from a cardinal one in that it is largely arbitrary. If $\phi(x, y)$ is an ordinal scale, $F(\phi)$ is also, if F is an arbitrary increasing function. For example, if xy is an ordinal measure, so is $(xy)^2$ or $\log x + \log y$.

It is, however, unthinkable that the states of mind of an individual when confronted with two different situations would be identical. The postulate of the existence of indifference is therefore a fallacy, the ordinalist fallacy. But we can drop it, too. The map of Figure 2 still retains its analytical validity. The indifference curves also lose their last meaning, but they still serve as "behavior lines," separating the preference from the nonpreference fields. Utility remains completely ordered but is no longer measurable in any sense. E is still the optional allocation of $A_1 A_2$ because it is the combination preferred to all others that are accessible.

Cardinalism versus Ordinalism

The craving for measure is so insatiable among modern scholars, Pareto's contribution notwithstanding, that some have tried to provide utility with a measure, if not like that of flour, at least like that of time or temperature. Utility would thus have a definite measure based on an arbitrary choice of the unit and of the origin of the scale. The seed of Daniel Bernoulli's solution of the St. Petersburg paradox reappeared in a 1926 essay of Ramsay and in 1944 in *The Theory of Games and Economic Behavior* by Oskar Morgenstern and John von Neumann. Instead of a hedonimeter, the instrument is the individual, who is supposed to be completely indifferent in a choice between some amount of ready cash M and a lottery ticket which wins either M_1 with probability p or M_2 with probability $q = 1 - p$. If the individual tells us how much M must be to create this indifference, then we have the equality (in utils)

$$U(M) = pU(M_1) + qU(M_2) \tag{4}$$

And if, for example, $U(M_1) = 0$ and $U(M_2) = 1$, then $U(M) = q$ utils. Varying all the parameters, we can determine the number of utils of any M.

The ordinalist camp has protested this theory, but cardinalism itself merely extends the use of the ordinalist fallacy. Both positions are thus open to the same criticism.

Revealed Preference

In a 1938 note, Paul A. Samuelson enunciated the following behavioral axiom:

If an individual chooses A as the optimal distribution of his or her budget when also B can be chosen, the same individual will never choose B in any budget for which A is also available.

The axiom is now called the weak axiom of revealed preference. However, the term "weak" is out of place. The axiom is an important landmark. It asserts in a simple and transparent manner the consistency of choice. In relation to Pareto's theory, it explains a basic property of the indifference curves—namely, their convexity—that previously had not been justified satisfactorily.

Samuelson went on to say that, by choosing A when B also is available through the budget, the individual reveals that he or she prefers A to B, by which Samuelson apparently meant that A is preferred to B in Pareto's sense. However, Samuelson, as well as numerous other economists, later took the position that the budget choice is not related in any way to the Paretian binary preference. It is only a brute market fact. The question then arose whether from the mere market data—i.e., from purely behavioral observations—we can derive the indifference map obtained by direct interrogation of the individual. This problem already had been considered in 1886 by Giovanni Antonelli, an Italian engineer, and in 1906 by Pareto (also an engineer). Pareto's solution involved a procedure of advanced calculus, namely, the integration of a total differential equation. That solution was sharply criticized by Vito Volterra, one of the mathematical authorities of that time, who objected that integration is not always possible if there are more than two commodities. A paradox, known as the integrability problem, was then introduced into utility theory. However, Volterra's criticism was based on a misunderstanding, although Pareto, apparently intimidated, accepted it. Like numerous mathematical economists who in recent times adopted his position, Volterra ignored the fact that even if integration is feasible, the varieties obtained by integration do not represent a Paretian preference map unless this map is known to exist already. And if it is known to exist, clearly it can always be reconstituted by integration from indirect (market) data.

Utility versus Wants

Neoclassical economists have criticized Marx's theory of value because it reduces concrete kinds of labor to an abstract notion—general labor. Yet neoclassicists have done the same; they have reduced concrete wants to one general and abstract want: utility. However, it is on concrete wants, not on the general want, that an individual bases economic choices.

Concrete wants are subject to various laws which, being dialectical in nature, cannot form the object of mathematical exercises. The most important law is their hierarchy within three distinct layers—biological wants with the same hierarchy for all humans, social wants with the same hierarchy for all members of the same society, and personal wants with no uniform hierarchy. The fact that concrete wants are so ordered and are also mutually irreducible lends additional support to the position (mentioned earlier) that preferences, although ordered, cannot have a measure. Still more important is the fact that the hierarchy of wants provides an objective basis for interpersonal comparison, the possibility of which is categorically denied by the conventional utility theory. This theory sprang out in a society in which most people were so well-to-do that they were interested mainly in personal wants. In general, however, humans will first satisfy their hunger, not the desire for fancy dress, if they have an income just sufficient to buy food. This is the objective basis for taxing the rich to aid the poor. Interest in studying wants flourished during the early nineteenth century but dwindled away with the advent of utility theory.

References

Interpretive Account of Historical Developments

Georgescu-Roegen, Nicholas, "Utility," *The International Encyclopedia of the Social Sciences,* vol. XVI, Free Press, New York, 1968, pp. 236–267; Stigler, George J., "The Development of Utility Theory," in J. J. Spengler and W. R. Allen (eds.), *Essays in Economic Thought: Aristotle to Marshall,* Rand-McNally, Chicago, 1960, pp. 606–665.

Basic Theory of Cardinal and Ordinal Utility

Hicks, John R., *Value and Capital: An Inquiry into Some Fundamental Principles of Economic Theory,* 2d ed., Clarendon, Oxford, 1946, chaps. I–III; Jevons, W. Stanley, *The Theory of Political Economy,* 5th ed., Kelley, New York, 1965; Pareto, Vilfredo, *Manual of Political Economy,* Kelley, New York, 1971.

Overview of Logical and Theoretical Problems

Arrow, Kenneth J., "Utilities, Attitudes, Choices: A Review Note," *Econometrica,* vol. 26, 1958, pp. 1–23; Chipman, John S., "The Foundations of Utility," *Econometrica,* vol. 33, 1960, pp. 193–224; Georgescu-Roegen, Nicholas, *Energy and Economic Myths: Institutional and Analytical Economic Essays,* Pergamon, New York, 1976, chap. 13.

Expectations and Measurability of Utility

Friedman, Milton, and L. J. Savage, "The Utility Analysis of Choices Involving Risks," in American Economic Association, *Readings in Price Theory,* Irwin, Homewood, Ill., 1952, pp. 57–96.;

Georgescu-Roegen, Nicholas, *Analytical Economics: Issues and Problems,* Harvard University Press, Cambridge, Mass., 1966, chap. 3; Marschak, Jacob, "Rational Behavior, Uncertain Prospects, and Measurable Utility," *Econometrica,* vol. 18, 1950, pp. 111–141.

The Integrability Paradox and Revealed Preference

Georgescu-Roegen, Nicholas, "Choice and Revealed Preference," *Analytical Economics: Issues and Problems,* Harvard University Press, Cambridge, Mass., 1966, chaps. 1, 4; Samuelson, Paul A., *Foundations of Economic Analysis,* Harvard University Press, Cambridge, Mass., 1947; Samuelson, Paul, A., "The Problem of Integrability in Utility Theory," *Economica,* vol. 17, 1950, pp. 355–380.

(*See also* Classical school; Neoclassical economics)

Nicholas Georgescu-Roegen

Value-added tax

Value-added tax (VAT) is the tax on the cost added in each stage of production and distribution. It treats all productive economic activity alike. It avoids dictation of the use of savings and does not treat the profits of success more harshly than wage or interest income. Also, VAT is a tax that does not attempt to favor one method of organizing a business over another. It is well-suited to an environment composed of competitive private enterprises.

The roots of the VAT idea and the theoretical support of the concept of value added as a tax base are American. Value-added tax was initiated by those with a desire to generate a neutral tax that would provide substantial revenues without reducing the effectiveness and efficiency of the market system in allocating capital, labor, and land. Because the United States is a free-market nation, it was appropriate that the early examining, explaining, and advocating of VAT be American. Also, U.S. economists were more interested in business statistics and analysis based on these data than were their European counterparts. German interest in VAT has always been considerable, but the concept did not attract German tax scholars as it did U.S. fiscal experts.

A Principal Tax in Western Europe

Value-added tax has become a principal tax of 12 Western European nations (France, Denmark, Germany, the Netherlands, Belgium, Luxembourg, Norway, Ireland, Italy, Great Britain, Sweden, and Austria), Korea, Brazil, and, in a modified form, in several developing nations. The tax was used in Michigan from 1953 to 1968. It was reintroduced as the single business tax in 1975. In addition, VAT has been proposed by a number of other states, including Alabama, Hawaii, Oregon, and West Virginia.

The federal government in 1965 and again in 1972 gave serious consideration to the introduction of VAT. Such was the case in 1979 as well.

The Brookings Institution, in 1932 and 1933, recommended the adoption of VAT in Alabama and Iowa. A little over 30 years later, the Brookings Center for Federal Government Tax Research published the proceedings of a conference titled *The Role of Direct and Indirect Taxes in the Federal Revenue System*. The conclusion of the conference was that VAT would not be helpful to the United States in developing sound domestic fiscal policy or an improved international economic balance. And since that time, more than 15 years later, Brookings has not undertaken a serious consideration of VAT as a major federal tax.

Dr. Gerhard Colm, a German-trained fiscal expert who became a leading tax specialist for the federal government and the National Planning Association, published in *Social Research* in 1934 an article entitled "The Ideal Tax System" recommending and describing VAT.

In 1940, Paul Studensky, a distinguished business taxation scholar, concluded VAT was the ideal business tax. He saw VAT as a neutral tax because wages, rent, interest, and profits—the return to the factors of production, labor, land, capital, and entrepreneurship—each bore the same direct tax burden. His analysis is of the additive-type VAT. Studensky saw government services benefiting each of the factors of production largely in proportion to gross income earned.

The early favorable reception given to VAT by the U.S. tax profession can trace its origins to the writings of T. S. Adams, who pioneered the 1913 federal individual income tax legislation. An article he wrote for the *Quarterly Journal of Economics* supported VAT as the best approach to the taxation of businesses. He had previously supported the basic concept of VAT in 1911.

After the defeat of Japan in World War II, the United States sent a group of tax experts to Japan to assist in the development of a democratic Japanese tax system. In 1949 the American Taxation Mission to Japan recommended the adoption of VAT. In 1950 the Japanese Diet adopted a local government VAT. A variety of circumstances prevented the legislation from being activated, and it was later repealed. Somewhat similar legislation is currently being used very effectively in Brazil.

VAT in France

The first French economic writer to seriously evaluate VAT was M. Lauré in 1952. France was the first nation to introduce VAT. The French VAT called *taxe sur la valeur adjoutée* (TVA) was introduced in 1954, a year after the Michigan VAT. The French, in the introduction of TVA, took an American and German tax idea based upon modern quantification of production and income sources and used it to meet a serious French fiscal crisis. France adopted VAT at first as a limited reform of a badly functioning tax system. Later, VAT typified the basic character of the French fiscal policy.

In 1936 the French introduced a single-stage production tax *(taxe à la production)*. This production tax used value added as its base and demonstrated a tendency to cover a broader and broader sweep of French production activity. Between 1953 and 1955, with April 10, 1954, given as the official date, the French production tax became TVA, a genuine value-added tax, albeit with quite a few exemptions, including retailing. In 1966, retailing was added. The French originators of TVA in 1954 saw it as a portion of an economic development plan. The tax grew out of a desire to make available for government purposes a stable portion of the new productiveness of French business enterprise.

In Western Europe VAT is called a subtractive consumption VAT. The tax rate is applied to the total sales of business firms. The tax collected is reduced by the amount of VAT shown on the invoices of all purchases, including capital equipment purchases. The remainder is the VAT payable to the government. It now provides about 25 percent of government revenues of the nations using it.

By being treated as an indirect tax under the General Agreement on Tariffs and Trade (GATT), value-added tax can be refunded to businesses making export sales. In addition, the VAT of a country can be applied as a border tax rate assessed on the price plus freight, insurance, and customs duties of exports. The international trade aspect of VAT under GATT rules explains much of the success of the Common Market in requiring a uniform VAT of its member states. It also provides a good economic reason for U.S. action.

References

Adams, T. S., "Fundamental Problems of Federal Income Taxation," *Quarterly Journal of Economics*, vol. 35, 1921, pp. 527–556; Colm, Gerhard, "The Ideal Tax System," *Social Research*, August 1934, pp. 319–342; Lindholm, Richard W., *Value Added Tax and Other Tax Reforms*, Nelson-Hall, Chicago, 1976; Studensky, Paul, "Toward A Theory of Business Taxation," *Journal of Political Economy*, vol. 48, October 1940, pp. 621–654; Surrey, Stanley, S., "A Value Added Tax: The Case Against," *Harvard Business Review*, vol. 48, 1970, pp. 86–94.

(*See also* Taxation, an overview)

Richard W. Lindholm

Value of the dollar

The dollar is the unit of currency and a measurement of economic value in the United States. It is also used as an unofficial currency in other parts of the world.

The value of a dollar can take on two quite different meanings, one in terms of goods and services, the other in terms of other currencies.

The value of a dollar in terms of some representative bundle of goods and services is always expressed in terms of changes in this value over some period of time. For example, in terms of the goods and services consumed by a typical American family, in March 1979 $1 purchased only 48 percent of what $1 purchased in 1967. Since the mixture of goods and services purchased by a typical family changes over time, comparisons such as this become more difficult the longer the period over which the comparison is made. But if we allow for this difficulty as best we can, $1 in 1979 purchased only 30 percent of what it purchased in 1939, just before the Second World War, and only 14 percent of what it purchased in 1914, just before the First World War. This decline in value reflects the great price inflation that has taken place during the twentieth century, particularly immediately after the two world wars and during the 1970s. Only the Great Depression of the 1930s produced a significant interruption of this trend. It should be noted, however, that this decline in the value of a dollar does not imply a decline in American living standards. On the contrary, the standard of living of a typical American family has grown enormously during the twentieth century. Earnings have grown more than enough to compensate for the declining value of each dollar. For example, per capita personal income in the United States, which was $324 in 1914 and $555 in 1939, had risen to over $8000 by 1979.

Value of Dollar Relative to Other Currencies

Value of the dollar has quite another meaning when the term is used to compare the dollar with other national currencies such as the British pound, the German mark (DM), or the Japanese yen. The history of each national currency is different, so that its value at any moment in time in terms of the U.S. dollar may vary greatly from one to another. For example, in mid-1980 one British pound was worth $2.34, whereas $1 was worth 835 Italian lira. These numbers are basically conversion units such as 1 meter equals 3.3 feet or 1 kilogram equals 2.2 pounds. In particular, these conversion units do not mean that the British pound is stronger than the dollar or that the dollar is stronger than the Italian lira. Strength in currencies refers to whether economic factors are tending to push up or down the value of one currency relative to another.

These conversion units, which are called exchange rates, are important for travelers or traders because they indicate how much of another currency travelers and traders can buy for a unit of their own currency and, hence, (given the prices in terms of foreign currencies) how much foreign goods or services cost in terms of their own currency. American travelers or traders can thus compare the dollar costs of foreign goods and services with what they would have to pay in the United States.

Unlike the conversion ratio between kilograms and pounds, the rate of conversion between currencies can change over time. For purposes of economic analysis, it is often of interest to compare how these external values of the dollar have changed. This can be done easily for a single foreign currency. For example, one British pound was worth $2.80 in 1965 and $2.34 in mid-1980, that is, the pound sterling depreciated relative to the dollar between 1965 and 1980. During the same period, in contrast, the German mark appreciated against the dollar, from $1 equals 4 DM to $1 equals 1.77 DM. Since there are about 140 different currencies in the world, we need some method for averaging if we are to speak of the external value of the dollar in comprehensive terms. One way to average, which is especially useful if the focus is U.S. foreign trade, is to give a weight to each major foreign currency relative to the value of that country's merchandise in United States trade. Another method of averaging is to compare the value of the dollar with the value of a special drawing right (SDR). The SDR is an international unit of account managed by the International Monetary Fund and is a composite of 16 different currencies, in which the U.S. dollar itself has a weight of 33 percent. (Effective 1981, the international unit of account was scheduled to be reduced to five currencies, with the U.S. dollar having a weight of 42 percent.)

The accompanying table illustrates the external value of the dollar in terms of various units for selected years since 1960.

Changes in the external value of the dollar are caused by many factors. One of the most important is the change in the value of the dollar, and of other currencies, in terms of goods and services, i.e., the rates of inflation in different countries. Thus, for the period 1960 to the end of 1978 inflation in Germany was 95 percent, while inflation in the United States was 129 percent. During this period, the U.S. dollar depreciated against the German mark by 56 percent, thus compensating for the higher rate of inflation in the United States, for lower productivity gains, and for U.S. balance of

	1960	1965	1970	1975	6/80
British pound ($/£)	2.80	2.80	2.40	2.22	2.34
German mark/$	4.20	4.00	3.66	2.46	1.77
Japanese yen/$	360	360	360	308	218
SDR ($/SDR)*	· · ·	· · ·	1.00	1.21	1.32
U.S. trade-weighted index (11 currencies, March 1973 = 100)	120	120	121	103	89

*SDR was created in 1970.

payments problems. In this fashion, movements in exchange rates help to compensate for divergent movements in national rates of inflation and help correct trade imbalances.

References

Fisher, Irving, *The Purchasing Power of Money*, Macmillan, New York, 1912, rev. ed., 1926; Shapiro, Eli, Ezra Solomon, and William W. White, *Money and Banking*, 5th ed., Holt, Rinehart and Winston, New York, 1968.

(*See also* Consumer price index; Foreign exchange rates; Inflation; International Monetary Fund; Liquidity, international; Special drawing rights)

Richard N. Cooper

Variable annuity

A variable annuity is a contract guaranteeing the annuitant—the individual covered by the insurance contract—a periodic income, based upon the investment performance of an underlying portfolio of securities, in return for a single payment or periodic payments that go into the buildup of the portfolio. Typically, the future annuitant builds the portfolio during the years spent working and receives annuity payments following retirement.

The main distinction between a variable annuity and the more common fixed annuity is implicit in the nomenclature. The present value of, and periodic payments from, the variable annuity change with current prices and earnings of the portfolio, while the fixed annuity is immune to such changes. The two contracts share the common characteristic of an insurance arrangement insofar as the duration of the payment period is typically related to actuarial mortality tables.

The Use of Units as a Measure

One's interest in a variable annuity is usually expressed in units with an assumed starting value of $10. This method enables the contract holder and the funding agent to distinguish between the effects of cash flows and of portfolio value changes. Thus, a portfolio initially purchased for $100,000 would contain 10,000 units, which are owned by the participants in proportion to their contributions to the purchase price. The value of each unit will change with the prices of the securities in the underlying portfolio, but the participant will continue to hold the same number of units originally purchased, plus any acquired subsequently.

Units are also used to compute payout benefits. Contract holders typically are entitled to the proceeds of a certain number of units per month or per year, the exact number depending both on their individual holdings at the time they begin to draw benefits and on their remaining life expectancy. The actual proceeds of this given number of units will continue to vary with investment experience. It is possible under most contracts to convert the proceeds from variable accumulations into fixed-dollar benefits during the payment period and vice versa.

Development and Growth of Variable Annuity

The development and growth of the variable annuity have been closely related to prevailing perceptions of common stocks as an inflation hedge. In a pathbreaking study published in 1951, William Greenough of the Teachers Insurance and Annuity Association (TIAA) examined the performance over long accumulation and payment periods of pensions funded through fixed-income as against common-stock portfolios. (Fixed income refers primarily to long-term bonds and mortgages.) He concluded that "contributions to a retirement plan that are invested partly in debt obligations and partly in common stocks . . . offer promise of supplying retirement income that is at once reasonably free from violent fluctuations in amount and from serious depreciation through price level changes."

Consequently, TIAA established an affiliated College Retirement Equities Fund (CREF) and began to offer a split-funding plan under which future annuitants could choose the proportion of their retirement contributions that would go into fixed-income versus common-stock investments. During the early 1960s, numerous life insurance companies began to offer variable annuities both through group pension contracts and through their individual annuity marketing mechanisms. In the mid-1960s, self-employed and small-group employee participation in variable annuities was facilitated by the Keogh plan legislation; and in the mid-1970s, a further avenue for individual participation was opened via individual retirement account (IRA) legislation.

Despite fairly rapid growth during the 1950s and 1960s, the variable annuity has captured only a small share of the total retirement benefit market. In the late 1970s, the number of persons covered by all private pension programs exceeded 40 million and the assets of private pension funds surpassed $250 billion. The number of persons with some variable feature in their pension and annuity contracts rose to slightly above 2 million, and the assets of plans with some variable feature to over $10 billion. Roughly two-thirds of all variable annuity plans arose from group contracts, the other one-third out of individual contracts.

Slow Growth of Variable Annuity

There are three reasons for the slow growth of the variable annuity. The first is the long legal and regulatory battles which accompanied its introduction. Throughout the early and mid-1960s, life insurance companies remained uncertain about the degree to which variable contracts would be subject to federal securities laws and regulations, over and above applicable state regulations. The matter was finally settled by court decisions and legislative compromises.

The second reason is the unfamiliarity of the public with the concept of a variable annuity. Uncertainty about the likely financial result, inherent in the concept, can be an adverse factor, perhaps overriding in many cases a better-than-even probability of its outperforming a fixed annuity contract.

The third and most important reason for the failure of the variable annuity to make much headway, however, is the generally disappointing performance of common stocks during the late 1960s and throughout the 1970s—a performance that is directly reflected in variable annuity unit values. The popular stock-market price indices fluctuated widely over this long period, yet remained essentially unchanged on balance. Thus, unit values of variable annuities changed sharply, often adversely, and trended upward for the most part only in reflection of dividends and their reinvestment. Simultaneously, the variable annuity experienced growing competition from fixed-income products that increasingly reflected generally rising interest rates.

Both the disappointing stock market and high interest rates can in turn be traced to inflation. (The inflation rate averaged about $6\frac{1}{2}$ percent annually during 1966 to 1979 compared with less than 2 percent in 1952 to 1965, and it worsened in the late 1970s.)

Inflation's adverse effect on common stocks has dashed the early hopes for the variable annuity as an inflation defense in old age. As noted, most variable annuity plans are flexible in terms of combining fixed with variable features. This fact, together with several sharp stock-market rallies in the late 1960s and the 1970s suggests that some discerning individuals may have benefited from the variable feature of their contracts through correct timing. Furthermore, it is inherent in the annuity concept that results should be appraised over long accumulation and payout periods—long enough to span several cycles of equity markets, interest rates, and inflation. Most important, past investment results are of limited relevance to investment decisions for the future. Thus, neither the favorable early years nor the unfavorable recent years provide a firm guide to the prospects for the variable annuity.

References

American Council of Life Insurance, *Life Insurance Fact Book*, Washington, D.C., published annually; American Council of Life Insurance, *Pension Facts*, Washington, D.C., published annually; Campbell, Paul A., *The Variable Annuity*, Connecticut General Life Insurance Company, Hartford, 1969; Conant, Roger A., "Inflation and the Variable Annuity," *CLU Journal*, American Society of Chartered Life Underwriters, October 1976, pp. 12–18; Greenough, William C., *A New Approach to Retirement Income*, Teachers Insurance and Annuity Association, New York, 1951.

(*See also* Inflation; Interest rates; Pension funds)

Francis H. Schott

Velocity of circulation of money

The velocity of circulation of money was defined by Irving Fisher in *The Purchasing Power of Money* as money's rate of turnover. He preferred to estimate it by dividing the total payments effected by money in a year by the total amount of money in circulation in that year. In modern usage, velocity is more commonly defined as the ratio of total income to the quantity of money. In the fourth quarter of 1979, for example, the income velocity of M-1A in the United States (GNP divided by the quantity of M-1A) was 6.66. To put it another way, the total stock of M-1A (demand deposits and currency) was being spent, or turned over, at a rate of 6.66 times per year for the goods and services included in the gross national product.

Economists have been concerned with the velocity of circulation for several centuries because the effects of a given change in the quantity of money on incomes and prices will vary with changes in velocity. In short, it is necessary to account for the rate at which money will be used in attempting to predict how a change in the quantity of money will affect incomes and prices.

Between the fourth quarter of 1978 and the fourth quarter of 1979, for example, the income velocity of M-1A increased by 4.32 percent, while the stock of M-1A increased 5.48 percent and GNP increased 10.03 percent. If velocity had remained constant, the increase in quantity of money would have increased GNP by only 5.48 percent. Thus, almost half of the increase in GNP over the period was contributed by the increase in velocity (4.32 + 5.48 + 4.32 of 5.48 = 10.03 percent).

Theories to Explain Behavior of Velocity

The key issue in dispute among economists is the stability, or predictability, of velocity. Before the 1930s, Irving Fisher and other classical monetary economists believed that velocity was not affected by the rate of growth of the money supply or by changes in the volume of transactions and prices. They believed that velocity was determined by slowly changing institutional factors affecting payments practices, such as the frequency of receipts and disbursements, use of checks, density of population, and speed of transportation. In practice, they considered velocity to be virtually constant over short periods, although they recognized that changes in interest rates and other factors affecting the desirability of holding money could affect it.

During the 1930s, large velocity changes and the general rejection of classical monetary theory shifted economists' attention to other influences on velocity, including interest rates and the availability of substitutes for money. One early, pessimistic conclusion from this discussion was that velocity changes would tend to offset changes in the quantity of money, thus making monetary policy impotent. In an extreme version of this argument, an increase in the quantity of money would reduce interest rates, thus reducing the cost of holding money, and velocity would decline by enough to prevent the increase in quantity of money from inducing people to increase spending. When the income expenditure theory of John Maynard Keynes became the predominant explanation of income and spending, many economists then assumed that velocity would adjust passively to income changes. In their view, velocity changes would enable a given quantity of money to accommodate the changes in income and spending induced by shifts in investment or government spending.

The emphasis on institutional factors affecting velocity reemerged in the discussion of new substitutes for money in the form of financial innovations, and technological changes, such as credit cards and electronic funds transfer systems, in the 1960s and 1970s. The 1960s and 1970s discussion raised the suspicion that financial innovations might make velocity so difficult to predict that the effectiveness of monetary policy would be impaired.

In modern quantity theory, often called the monetarist approach, velocity of circulation is determined by the factors that determine the demand for money. The demand for money, defined as the quantity people want to hold in relation to income, M/GNP, is simply the inverse of velocity GNP/M. The factors determining velocity in this approach include wealth, interest rates, inflation expectations, and other factors influencing the desirability of holding money, such as the availability of money substitutes and technological changes in payments practices. An increase in people's wealth in relation to their current income would induce them to hold more money in relation to income and thus would reduce the velocity of circulation. Increases in interest rates or inflation expectations would raise the opportunity costs of holding money and so would increase velocity. Financial innovations which increase the speed of making payments also should tend to reduce the quantity of money people want to hold and, thus, should increase velocity.

One of the most interesting implications of the monetarist view of velocity is that an acceleration or deceleration in rate of growth of money supply should induce a subsequent increase or decrease in velocity through its influence on incomes, interest rates, prices, and inflation expectations. Therefore, changes in velocity should reinforce the effects of changes in monetary growth rates on incomes and prices, instead of offsetting them. This view differs widely from both classical and Keynesian interpretations of velocity.

There now is a large body of evidence that the velocity of circulation is stable, in the sense of being predictable from a few variables which tend to change slowly. It should be possible, therefore, for a central bank or government to select a growth rate for the money supply that would contribute to stability in prices and economic activity.

Recent Behavior of Velocity in the United States

When the Board of Governors of the Federal Reserve System revised the definitions of the monetary aggregates it uses for policy purposes, it presented a comprehensive review of velocity behavior since 1959 for a wide variety of old and new monetary aggregates (*Federal Reserve Bulletin*, February 1980). This Federal Reserve evidence should be reassuring to those who fear that unpredictable changes in velocity will limit the power of monetary policy to reduce inflation.

Velocity of both old and new narrowly defined moneys (new M-1A, new M-1B, and old M-1) rose at a 3 to 3.2 percent annual rate from 1960 through 1979. Velocity of more broadly defined moneys, which include substantial proportions of interest-bearing deposits (new M-2, old M-2, old M-3, new M-3, old M-4, and old M-5), either grew or declined by less than a 1 percent annual rate over the period. Therefore, there was no evidence of secular trends in velocity that could not have been offset by small changes in growth rates of the monetary aggregates.

During each of the three recessions included in the period, velocity of all of the new and old monetary aggregates declined, or grew more slowly, from the cycle peak to the trough. During each of the three expansions, velocity of all the new and old aggregates either grew more rapidly or declined more slowly than during the recessions. This tendency for velocity to fall in recessions and to rise in expansions has been observed in the United States ever since the Civil War. Therefore, there is no evidence that the cyclical behavior of velocity has changed radically in recent years.

The final interesting bit of evidence is that velocity of all of the new and old aggregates either fell or grew more slowly in each of the three periods in which growth rates of the aggregates declined. Velocity of all the aggregates also grew more rapidly, or declined more slowly, in each of the three periods in which monetary growth rates accelerated. Therefore, there was no systematic tendency for velocity changes to offset changes in growth rates of the monetary aggregates. To the contrary, velocity changes systematically reinforced changes in monetary growth rates. Offsetting changes in velocity occurred for a quarter or two on several occasions in which there was a sudden, large change in growth rates of the money supply. These were soon followed, however, by changes in velocity in the same direction as the changes in monetary expansion rates.

In sum, changes in the velocity of circulation of money can and do affect the influence of changes in money growth rates on incomes, prices, and other variables. However, monetarists believe that these changes in velocity can be predicted or offset well enough for control of the money supply to contribute to achievement of stability in national incomes, price levels, interest rates, and exchange rates.

References

Burns, Arthur F., Statement before the Subcommittee on Domestic Policy of the Committee on Banking, Currency, and Housing, U.S. House of Representatives, February 6, 1975, *Federal Reserve Bulletin*, vol. 61, February 1975, pp. 62–68; Campbell, Colin D., "The Velocity of Money and the Rate of Inflation: Recent Experience in South Korea and Brazil," in David Meiselman (ed.), *Varieties of Monetary Experience*, University of Chicago Press, Chicago, 1970, pp. 341–386; Fisher, Irving, *The Purchasing Power of Money*, 2d rev. ed., 1922; reprinted in Reprints of Economic Classics, Kelley, New York 1963; Selden, Richard T., "Monetary Velocity in the United States," in Milton Freidman (ed.), *Studies in the Quantity Theory of Money*, University of Chicago Press, Chicago, 1956, pp. 179–275; Silber, William L. (ed.), *Financial Innovation*, Lexington Books, Lexington, Mass., 1975; Simpson, Thomas D., "The Redefined Monetary Aggregates," *Federal Reserve Bulletin*, vol. 66, February 1980, pp. 97–114; Warburton, Clark, "Monetary Velocity, Monetary Policy, and the Rate of Interest," *Review of Economics and Statistics*, vol. 30, no. 4, November, 1948, pp. 304–314, and vol. 32, no. 3, August 1950, pp. 256–257; reprinted in Warburton, *Depression, Inflation, and Monetary Policy, Selected Papers, 1945–1953*, Johns Hopkins Press, Baltimore, 1966, pp. 258–278.

(*See also* Chicago school; Classical school; Federal Reserve policy; Federal Reserve System; Interest rates; Keynesian economics; Monetary policy; Money supply; Propensity to consume or to save and inducement to invest; Quantity theory of money)

A. James Meigs

Venture capital

Venture capital is risk money, funds which are invested to pay for the initial risks of a new and potentially rapidly growing company or a newly developed growth product, not for the assets connected with the company or the product. It is used for the risk expenses which cannot usually be financed by a bank loan or a loan on inventory, plant, or equipment. Venture capital is not readily available in normal financial channels but is almost always a part of the total financing, which includes much borrowed money.

The Profit Motive

In addition to the 600 venture capital companies in the United States, which have as their main purpose investing their pool of money into newer and rapidly growing ventures for a profit, there are innumerable private individuals who, singly or in concert with others, make venture-type investments for a profit. Often entrepreneurs obtain investment funds from relatives, friends, or from their own savings or assets. In these deals neither the entrepreneur nor the relatives or friends usually expect to be paid back in a specific time or at a specific rate of interest. But venture capital companies and the venture groups do not advance funds because they are friendly or related to the entrepreneurs. They do it for a profit, and they expect to retrieve their investment along with their reward at some future time in order to continue the process of investing funds into other ventures. Venture capitalists are in the business of making smart investments, helping the company to grow to become a large and mature company. They expect to be paid back in 5 or 10 years at a rate which just about doubles their investment every $2\frac{1}{2}$ years or so.

Usually the investor (not lender) purchases the common or preferred shares of the company. Purchasing stock results in the shareholder being eligible for dividends if the board of directors so votes, but it also means that the company does not have to show a loan, either short- or long-term, on its balance sheet. This, of course, is of vital importance when banks are looking at the financial statements of new and growing companies to determine whether they are eligible for a loan.

Near Venture Capital

There is also what is known as near venture capital. There are banks—many with the Small Business Administration guarantees—which make long-term loans (5 to 7 years) where only the interest is paid in the early years and the principal is paid later on or in a balloon payment at the end of the term of the loan. This money behaves in a way similar to venture capital and is a popular method for a new venture to get started. Its one negative aspect is that it is listed on the balance sheet as a loan. Thus, bankers will want to see that there is provision made to begin the repayment of that loan.

Near venture capital also usually does not involve selling shares or ownership of the company (unless the lender requires an option to purchase stock). Many entrepreneurs do not want to give up shares in exchange for venture capital. As a general rule, most venture capitalists don't want to obtain majority ownership in an investment. They want the entrepreneur to be happily working toward his or her (and their) success as planned. It is only when the venture is not proceeding as planned that the venture capitalist wants to have more control over what is happening and to be able to affect the outcome of the venture. This is not significantly different from a bank's moves when a loan is in default. The bank can liquidate the assets and change the character of the company.

Venture Capital and the Return

Because they are using risk money, professional venture capitalists require a high return. If they were only lending the money out and it were collateralized by some valuable asset, there would be a much smaller risk of loss. But once they have extended their investment, there is no way that venture capitalists can get back their investment unless and until the company grows to the point where the stock can be bought back or sold on the over-the-counter market, or where another person or group wants to buy the stock.

Within the venture capital community it is estimated that an investment takes about 7 years from the time of the investment until it is capable of being retrieved. An entrepreneur can expect to pay back about three or four times the initial investment. In the meantime, this investment is illiquid, i.e., there is no market for the shares of the company, and the venture capitalist is stuck with the investment even if he or she wants to get out and use the money for some better investment.

When bankers make a loan, they expect to obtain quarterly reports and to get a full report on the progress of their loans once a year. In fact, the average commercial bank has 250 companies in its files to look after (about one per working day each year) while a venture capitalist has only between 5 and 10 companies on file. The venture capitalist expects to be on the board of directors of the company in which he or she has invested and expects to have a very close working relationship with the company.

The venture capitalist often is using other people's money to make the investment. Often, a group of well-to-do people pool their money into a venture capital project. Nowadays banks as well as pensions funds are in venture capital projects, and large corporations have also established venture capital pools. The managers of these pools know that if they invest their money in a manner similar to a mutual fund, they can expect to have a return of 12 to 16 percent, and at very little risk. The reason for the small risk is that such shares are in companies which have a proven track record, and if the conditions change, the fund manager can easily sell out. Venture capitalists, on the other hand, are stuck with their investments. Because these investments are much more risky, they want a higher return.

The Investor and the Business Plan

Professional investors will never make an investment unless and until they have a chance to study the business plan drafted by the entrepreneur. This plan is usually 20 to 50 pages long. It details what the business is all about and explores the prospects of the business for the foreseeable future. It then details how the company is and will be organized to obtain its share of the market. A good plan will also have financial projections showing the profit and loss statements for the next 3 years as well as expected balance sheets, etc. Even bankers expect to have some written planning documents as part of their file on a company.

Because the people involved in a venture project are important to the investor and banker, entrepreneurs generally have a competent management team ready and willing to get under way. The plan should have a fairly complete biographical history of the key people involved with the enterprise. Venture capital is much more available to people who have demonstrated competent work experience, relevant to their new enterprise. In fact, most venture capitalists believe that if an entrepreneur were to die in the first 3 years of a new enterprise, it would probably fail.

What the Entrepreneur Must Do

The entrepreneur makes contacts and seeks venture capital from a variety of sources. There are lists of venture capital companies for this search generally available in local libraries. Often the local bank has a list of contacts. In addition there are numerous private individuals ready and willing to make risky investments if they are convinced of the soundness of the entrepreneur's idea and of his or her ability to see it through.

It is indeed rare for a venture to obtain its investment in less than 90 days, and usually it takes 6 months or more to finally get the money. Also, if the business contemplated in the plan is not going to become a major nationwide business (only about 5 percent of companies have any possibility of becoming significant in size), then other, more private venture capital must be secured. Friends, relatives, trade suppliers, customers, bank contacts, and other professional contacts may provide investment funds of this nature.

SBICs

Small business investment companies (SBICs) are organizations which are licensed by the federal government and are permitted to borrow from the federal government to add to their own private money assets in order to make investments in small, growing companies. As of 1980 there were about 350 such companies operating in the United States. In addition there are minority enterprise small business investment companies (MESBICs). They operate very much like a regular SBIC except that they concentrate on minority businesses and have a few special privileges that regular SBICs do not have. These two licensed types of venture capital organizations contrast with private venture capitalists, who do not have and are not required to have any government license. In return for this freedom to operate, the private venture capitalist sacrifices the right to borrow from the government.

The American enterprise system was built on the ability of well-to-do people to make risky investments in new and growing companies. In fact, Queen Isabella provided the venture capital for Christopher Columbus to discover America. Finding risk money for a venture is difficult. However, using the money, once found, to make the business plan a reality is even more difficult.

References

Donaldson, Elvin F., et. al., *Corporate Finance,* 4th ed., Wiley, New York, 1975.

(*See also* Return on investment; Risk premium on investment)

John L. Komives

Wealth

The term wealth is used in two distinct but closely related senses. One usage relates to the tangible capital assets used in the process of production. The other concept is financial, equating wealth with net worth. The two concepts are the same for the total domestic economy, but they diverge with respect to individuals, organizations, and economic sectors.

Tangible wealth comprises the material means of production—land and other natural resources, structures, equipment, and inventory stocks. The term has also been extended to include the human factor of production, although balance sheets usually include only nonhuman capital goods which are bought and sold in organized markets, thus enabling an objective value to be assigned these goods. The economic value of human beings can be estimated only indirectly. But the inclusion of humans in the notion of tangible wealth means that they are part of the factors of production, representing capacity to produce income and product in the same sense as tangible capital. While most goods and services are sold to produce money income, some are not. Thus, owner-occupied dwellings and household durable goods represent wealth, although their services are rendered directly, as are the services of public infrastructure. The values of such nonmarket services may be imputed. And although wealth is tangible, its value reflects outlays for services designed to enhance its productivity—research and development in the case of nonhuman instruments, and education, for example, in the case of humans. The valuation of tangible wealth or capital reflects its expected future income, monetary or imputed. In the case of newly produced capital goods, the present value equals the purchase price, or cost of production including profit.

Net Worth

The concept of wealth as net worth represents the value of tangible assets plus intangible or financial assets, less liabilities. Balance sheets may, of course, be constructed for individuals or families, nonprofit organizations, firms, and governments—and combined, consolidated, or separately constructed for broad sectors: persons, business enterprises, and general government, as well as for the domestic or national economy. When the balance sheets of all sectors are consolidated, financial assets and liabilities wash out, and total domestic net worth equals the value of the productive tangible wealth. On a national basis, net worth equals the value of the domestic tangible wealth less the value of that portion owned by foreigners plus the claims by U.S. residents on foreign assets. In other words, national wealth (net worth) equals the value of domestic tangible wealth plus net foreign assets.

On a combined national balance sheet, the financial assets and liabilities are shown, but the difference equals the net foreign assets which, when added to the value of domestic tangible wealth, equal the net worth. Usually, balance sheets show only nonhuman wealth since human wealth is self-owned within the personal sector, and it is this sector to which labor compensation accrues.

For any one sector, net worth may be more (less) than the value of its tangible wealth to the extent that financial assets exceed (fall short of) liabilities. That is, the net worth of a sector, or of an individual or organization, equals the value of its tangible wealth plus its net financial claims on other sectors including the rest of the world. Thus, in an ultimate sense wealth represents tangible capital, either that owned by a sector or the net worth claimed, plus or minus, on the productive assets of other sectors. On a global basis wealth is productive capital since that is what produces income and product. The financial assets and liabilities are but evidences of ownership or indebtedness.

Valuation

On the balance sheets of firms, physical wealth is usually carried at original or acquisition cost. Accumulated depreciation reserves are also shown so that the net value may be computed. Balance sheets for the personal and government sectors have also been constructed using original cost valuation for comparability with the business sector. But for comparability with the national income and product accounts, in which market values are employed, it is necessary to revalue the various categories of physical wealth in terms of market prices, or proxies. For nonreproducible wealth, primarily land and natural resources (but also including art and other collections), market pricing is the direct approach, although appraisals or discounting actual and/ or expected future income may be resorted to.

Inventory revaluations require adjustment for changes in prices between the times goods are acquired and are sold or else charged to expense, which depends on methods of inventory accounting. To revalue net depreciable assets, one must obtain estimates of the various types of structures and equipment carried on the books by year of acquisition and revalue them to current prices using appropriate price indexes. Since the indexes are based on price data for new items, the revalued estimates represent depreciated replacement costs which are only an approximation to market prices of used assets, many of which are not traded in organized markets. Because of the difficulty of obtaining book values of depreciable assets by type and age, the perpetual inventory method of estimation may be used. This involves deflating annual fixed investments by type, depreciating over the estimated lifetimes of the various types of structures and equipment, summing net investments of all vintages for each year, and then revaluing the net stocks to replacement costs by use of the same price indexes used to deflate the annual investments.

For the corporate business sector, an alternative approach is to take the market value of equities, add liabilities, and subtract financial asset values. The deviations of these values from depreciated replacement costs fluctuate considerably and are significant in indicating changes in the state of business confidence and expectations.

Cash and short-term financial instruments are usually carried at face value. Long-term debt may be restated to reflect changing market values. If equities are carried on the left-hand side of business sector and combined national balance sheets, there should be an offsetting entry on the right-hand side so that net worth properly reflects the wealth of the property owners.

Since there is no market value of human beings, estimates may be made in terms of the costs of rearing, educating, and training members of the labor force, revalued to current prices, or by discounting actual or projected future labor compensation to obtain present values. In the United States, the latter values significantly exceed the costs, suggesting a higher rate of return on human than on nonhuman wealth.

Historical Review

Ever since the time of Sir William Petty (the latter part of the seventeenth century) and later mercantilist writers, the notion of wealth as a stock of goods and natural resources required for the production of goods and services has been an important part of economics. One reason Adam Smith in *The Wealth of Nations* defined national product in material terms was that he thought only tangible goods can be accumulated to increase national wealth, which he perceived as the source of economic growth and development. His lead was followed by David Ricardo and Karl Marx, and the national income accounting systems of communist countries still revolve around the concept of material product. Ever since the writings of Alfred Marshall, economists in the West have recognized the production of services as part of national product, and that certain service outlays—notably for research, education, training, health, and mobility—contribute to immaterial capital, embodied in human beings. The growth of human capital or wealth is considered coordinate with the growth of nonhuman wealth in contributing to economic progress.

Occasional estimates of national wealth have been made by individual investigators in many advanced countries. In 1955, the Japanese government conducted its first sample survey of the components of wealth. In 1959, the Soviet Union conducted a complete inventory of its structures and equipment, with valuations based on engineering appraisals. The United States government conducted eight censuses of wealth between 1850 and 1922, when the procedure was dropped because of the ambiguity created by a mixture of valuations. Since then, occasional estimates and time series have been prepared by individual scholars, notably R. Doane, S. Kuznets, R. Goldsmith, and J. Kendrick.

In recent years, the National Income and Wealth Division of the Bureau of Economic Analysis in the U.S. Department of Commerce has published estimates of real stocks of reproducible capital for the business sector and is in the process of extending these to cover the other sectors. When the tangible wealth estimates are completed, they can be combined with estimates of financial assets and liabilities, prepared by the Federal Reserve Board since the late 1950s as part of its flow-of-funds statistics, to provide complete balance sheets for the nation, by sector. It is important that balance sheets and wealth statements be prepared as part of an integrated set of national economic accounts in view of the close relationship between the stock and flow estimates. Other nations are also moving toward official preparation of balance sheets to accompany their national income and product accounts. Estimates of human wealth, however, are still the work of individual investigators.

Significance of Wealth:
Relationship to Other Variables

Tangible wealth, as the value of the factors of production, is the source of income and product. Indeed, economic growth—the rate of increase in real national product—may be viewed as a process of capital formation and thus of the rate of increase in real national wealth, human and nonhuman. Actually, in the United States since 1929 real product has grown somewhat faster than real wealth owing to economies of scale and other variables affecting total productivity. In current prices, however, net national income in 1973 was approximately the same percentage of net national wealth as in 1929 reflecting an increase in the price deflator for wealth relative to that for product. Although the average rate of return was around 10 percent per annum, it was somewhat higher for human wealth than for nonhuman.

Wealth is also related to aggregate demand. Its age composition is a factor in replacement demand for durables. The structure of the balance sheets of which wealth data are a part influences demand as households and firms attempt to adjust portfolios toward desired proportions. Also wealth, as a major indicator of permanent income, is an important determinant of consumption expenditures.

In reciprocal fashion, the growth of income and its allocation between saving for capital formation and consumption determine the growth of wealth. The increase in real wealth between the beginning and end of a period equals the real net investment during the period. In current prices, however, changes in net worth reflect changes in prices of assets and liabilities, as well as the volume of saving and investment. Thus, a revaluation account is required to supplement the capital (flow-of-funds) account in order to explain changes in balance sheets and wealth. The revaluations, resulting in realized and unrealized capital gains or losses, themselves influence expenditure decisions.

References

Conference on Research in Income and Wealth, *Measuring the Nation's Wealth,* Studies in Income and Wealth, vol. 29, National Bureau of Economic Research, New York, 1964; Goldsmith, R. W., and R. E. Lipsey, *Studies in the National Balance Sheet of the United States,* 2 vols., National Bureau of Economic Research, Princeton University Press, Princeton, N.J., 1963; Kendrick, John W., *The Formation and Stocks of Total Capital,* National Bureau of Economic Research, New York, 1976; *Provisional International Guidelines on the National and Sectoral Balance-Sheet and Reconciliation Accounts of the System of National Accounts,* ser. M, no. 60, United Nations, New York, 1977.

(*See also* Financial statements; Flow of funds; Saving)

John W. Kendrick

Welfare economics

Modern economics is divided into the two major areas of macroeconomics and microeconomics. Microeconomics, in turn, can be divided into the areas of positive microeconomics and normative microeconomics. The former deals with the explanation and prediction of actual resource allocation decisions made by consumers, producers, and (to some extent) governments. The latter deals with how those resource allocation decisions ought to be made: with the criteria for judging alternative resource allocations and with mechanisms for achieving them. Welfare economics, synonymous with normative microeconomics, is a collection of propositions and analytical devices useful for evaluating resource allocation decisions. Welfare economics should not be confused with government welfare programs. Although it can be used to evaluate such programs, as a scientific and politically neutral procedure it neither espouses nor opposes them. Welfare economics is the modern basis for economic policy prescriptions.

History

The distinction between welfare economics and positive microeconomics is a relatively modern convention. For the better part of the history of economic science, up until roughly the first quarter of this century, this distinction was not drawn. Welfare economics evolved gradually from the body of economic thought, and for this reason it is difficult to pinpoint its precise beginnings. Generally, the writings of such luminaries as Marshall, Edgeworth, Walras, Pareto, and Fisher can be thought of as containing the seeds of welfare economics. The publication of Pigou's *The Economics of Welfare* in 1920 might be considered the point at which welfare economics assumed its present independent identity. From 1920 to roughly 1950, the theoretical foundations of welfare economics were fashioned by such writers as Pigou, Hicks, Kaldor, and Scitovsky. During the fifties and early sixties, welfare economics and general equilibrium theory developed jointly, bringing sophisticated mathematical tools into the economists' arsenal. Arrow and Debreu were pathbreakers in this period. Most recently, welfare economics has taken an applied tack. That is, developments have focused on applying welfare economic theory to the resolution of practical and pressing economic problems. Applied welfare economics is often done under the rubric of cost-benefit analysis.

Discussion

Welfare economics, as the term suggests, deals with the welfare, or well-being, of the members of a society. It addresses the issue of deciding which of several alternative economic states of affairs (resource allocations and income distributions) is best. Much of the literature on welfare economics has dealt with exploring, proposing, and refining notions of what constitutes a better economic state.

Welfare economics is founded on two postulates. First, the individual is the one and only judge of his or her own well-being, and second, the welfare of society is influenced only by the welfare of each individual. These postulates reject the notion of an organic state independent of and greater than the sum of the individuals comprising it, and they reject the notion that the individual exists to further the goals of the state. Rather, the postulates adopt the view that the economic system exists to serve the needs and desires of the individual.

Five Criteria

Within this individualistic context, criteria are needed to judge economic states—to determine which of several states is best. Five criteria have come under scrutiny: unanimity, the Pareto rule, majority rule, the Bergson welfare function, and the potential Pareto rule. The unanimity rule declares that one state is socially superior to another if every member of society individually judges that the one state is preferable to the other. This criterion can evoke little dissent, yet it is of little use since the criterion is silent on realistic comparisons wherein unanimity does not prevail.

The Pareto rule is a slight weakening of the unanimity rule. It declares that state 1 is socially preferred to state 2 if no one prefers state 2 to state 1 and at least one person prefers state 1 to state 2. This criterion allows some individuals to be indifferent to the alternative states, and the social preference is then decided by those not indifferent. This rule suffers the same problem as the first—it is virtually inapplicable since all comparisons of interest will involve some preferences on both sides of the issue.

Majority rule declares that state 1 is socially preferred to state 2 if the majority of the members of society prefer state 1 to state 2. This rule does not suffer the weakness of its two predecessors—it is applicable to realistic situations. Its problem is lack of consensus. Recognizing the potential inequities inherent in majority rule (e.g., 50.1 percent of the people with weak preferences of state 1 over state 2 prevailing over 49.9 percent of the people with strong preferences of state 2 over state 1), few economists have been willing to embrace this criterion.

The Bergson welfare function assigns weights to individual preferences. This criterion is applicable in realistic situations, but it implies interpersonal utility comparisons. Since most economists feel interpersonal utility comparisons are not possible in practice, this criterion has not been widely adopted.

The final criterion is the potential Pareto rule. It declares that state 1 is socially preferred to state 2 if the gainers in state 1 could potentially compensate the losers so that no one would be worse off in state 1 compared with state 2. In other words, this rule establishes a potential compensation test. If the net gains in state 1 exceed the net gains in state 2, then it is potentially possible to distribute the net gains of state 1 so each person gets at least as much as he would in state 2. This criterion is applicable to real situations and has achieved the widest degree of acceptance of all the criteria. However, a recognized shortcoming of this criterion is the need for mere potential compensation; actual income transfers are not required. Thus, from the point of view of equity, perverse outcomes are possible.

The concepts of consumers' and producers' surpluses are two of the principal analytic tools in welfare economics. These concepts permit the estimation of net gains (or losses) associated with an economic state using estimated supply and demand curves.

Welfare economics has played a key role in the development of public-sector economics, an extension and outgrowth of public finance. Public-sector economics is concerned with the proper role of government in modern market-oriented economies. Welfare economics is the thread running through this field, tying together the concepts of public goods, externalities, regulation, and taxation. Important contributions to this field have been made by Baumol, Samuelson, Bator, Mishan, Musgrave, Coase, and Tiebout.

Current Status

Some years ago it was fashionable to suggest that welfare economics was dead. At that time the field was mired in apparently fruitless explorations for new and tractable welfare criteria. Since then, as mentioned earlier, the field has turned markedly toward an emphasis on applications. This new direction has breathed life into the field, and there is little doubt that the death of welfare economics was greatly exaggerated. Today, welfare economics provides the theoretical basis and analytic tools for such dynamic areas as cost-benefit analysis, public-sector economics, and policy science. Actual problems in areas such as public-utility pricing, deregulation, farm policy, government R&D, airport location, economic development, pollution control, energy policy, and many others have been and are being addressed using welfare economics. On the theoretical front, public choice theory now carries the banner of welfare economics. Public choice theory deals with the design and analysis of social choice mechanisms for achieving desired social states. A sign of the widespread acceptance of welfare economics is the fact that nearly all modern tests in microeconomics contain explicit treatment of welfare economics.

References

Arrow, K. J., *Social Choice and Individual Values*, Cowles Commission Monograph No. 12, Wiley, New York, 1951; Baumol, W. J., *Welfare Economics and the Theory of the State*, Harvard University Press, Cambridge, Mass., 1965; Little, I. M. D., *A Critique of Welfare Economics*, Clarendon Press, Oxford, 1950; Mishan, E., *Welfare Economics*, Random House, New York, 1964; Pigou, A. C., *The Economics of Welfare*, 4th ed., Macmillan, New York, 1932.

Recent Applications of Welfare Economics

Harberger, Arnold (ed.), *Cost Benefit and Policy Analysis*, vols. I–IV, Aldine, Chicago, 1972–1975.

(*See also* Cost-benefit analysis; Externalities; Microeconomics; Normative economics)

Peter G. Sassone

World Bank

The World Bank is the world's foremost intergovernmental organization concerned with the external financing of economic development in developing countries. Its loans help to finance the imports needed to complete approved development projects. Its advice helps to determine the priorities, the scale, and the nature of the projects financed, not only by the Bank itself but also by the development assistance programs of industrial countries, by private banks, by regional development banks, and by sources internal to the developing countries themselves. While the World Bank is a wholly independent international organization operating under its own Articles of Agreement, the staff of the bank coordinates its work with the relevant agencies of the United Nations and other international bodies.

History and Early Financing

The World Bank, officially the International Bank for Reconstruction and Development, opened its doors in 1946 as one of the two international institutions agreed to at the Bretton Woods Conference of July 1944. The other Bretton Woods institution is the International Monetary Fund. During the negotiations which preceded the Bretton Woods Conference, the British, led by Lord (John Maynard) Keynes, favored a single organization, an International Clearing Union, which might have managed the world money, it was thought, so as to reduce international economic fluctuations as well as the fluctuations in the balances of payments of member countries. Negotiators from the United States preferred to separate long-term (development) from a short-term (balance of payments) lending and advocated both a bank and a fund. The proposals of the United States, modified by Canadian, European, and Latin American suggestions, were ultimately accepted.

The Bank was designed in the first instance to assist in the external financing of the reconstruction of Europe at the conclusion of World War II. It became quickly apparent, however, that the resources of the Bank were too few and its organization too new for this task, which was then largely assumed directly by the United States. During the Bank's formative years, Bank lending also remained scanty for purposes of development. This low level of lending was due to its small lending capacity, to its conservative management and charter, and to the unsettled state of knowledge concerning the development process. Before recommending a Bank loan, the staff of the Bank must be satisfied that the productivity of the borrowing country will be increased and that the prospects for repayment are good. Thus, initially, Bank financing was largely confined to large infrastructure projects, such as transportation networks, and the Bank was criticized for being too cautious and insufficiently concerned with the development needs of its poor members. These criticisms are less frequent today, for the Bank has significantly increased both its lending capacity (subscriptions) and its lending and has approved increasingly large amounts of official development assistance.

World Bank Group

In 1950, an International Finance Corporation was established to supplement the World Bank by participating in equity financing in member countries, and in 1960, a third organization, the International Development Association (IDA), was created to round out the World Bank group. The IDA has the same officers and staff as the World Bank, but its separate charter enables it to offer loans to low-income member countries repayable at 0.75 percent of interest over 50 years (including 10 years' grace). This soft or concessionary assistance is made possible by contributions to (replenishments of) the IDA by the governments of high-income (industrial) countries. The management of the World Bank group is thus enabled to offer rates of interest and loan maturities which take into account the nature of the projects financed and the ability of borrowing governments to service the debt. It can also consider social issues, such as the distribution of income in developing countries.

While the International Development Association is financed by periodic government contributions, the Bank obtains the funds it lends (1) directly from the paid-in (10 percent) portion of the subscriptions of member governments and from earnings on past loans and (2) indirectly by selling its own bonds in the financial markets of its member countries. Its ability to sell its own bonds depends in turn on the commitment of member governments to support the bank in an emergency with that portion of their subscriptions not already paid in. In 1980, total subscriptions aggregated roughly $40 billion.

Authority and Management

The legal authority of the Bank resides with member governments represented by governors who meet at least annually to receive the annual report of the officers of the Bank and to conduct necessary business. Governors and executive directors vote in accordance with the voting power of the governments they represent. Voting power is related to the subscriptions of the member governments and is based on a formula which takes into account such factors as gross national product and volume of foreign trade. Virtually all the governments which belong to the United Nations also belong to the World Bank and the International Monetary Fund, except for the Soviet Union, the People's Republic of China, and some Eastern European countries.

References

Annual Report, World Bank, Washington, D.C.; Mason, Edward M., and Robert Asher, *The World Bank since Bretton Woods*, Brookings, Washington, D.C., 1973; Oliber, Robert W., *International Economic Cooperation and the World Bank*, Macmillan, New York, 1975.

(*See also* Bretton Woods Conference; International economics, an overview; International Monetary Fund)

Robert W. Oliver

Yield curve

The yield curve is a smoothly drawn curve that depicts the functional relationship between yield-to-maturity and years-to-maturity of fixed-income securities at a given point in time. Isolation of this relationship requires that all other factors affecting yield—risk of default, liquidity, cost of acquisition, and so on—be held constant; thus, yield curves are drawn only for securities that are identical except for maturity. For example, the most frequently used are those for U.S. Treasury securities because these debt obligations are available in a wide range of maturities, from a few days to more than 20 years, and are virtually identical in all other respects.

Varying economic conditions produce yield curves that have one of three basic shapes. A flat curve means that yields on short, intermediate, and long maturities are almost the same, suggesting that the supply of and demand for loanable funds are roughly in balance throughout the market. An upward-sloping curve indicates that yields are higher on longer maturities and suggests that the demand for short-term funds relative to supply is greater than it is for long-term funds. Finally, a downward-sloping curve shows that yields are higher on shorter maturities, indicating that the demand for longer-term funds relative to supply is greater than that for short-term funds.

Usefulness of Yield Curves

Yield curves are useful because they show geometrically the term structure of interest rates. Since yield curves assume flat, upward, and downward slopes at different times, the question arises: Why does the term structure of interest rates differ so markedly on different dates? Economists have put forth three hypotheses to explain the pattern of interest rates.

The Liquidity Preference Hypothesis   This hypothesis states that investors place a premium on liquidity, that is, the ability to convert an asset into cash quickly without loss. Since shorter maturities are somewhat more liquid than longer ones, they will command higher prices and, therefore, lower yields than longer maturities. However, scant evidence, if any, exists that liquidity-seeking investors dominate the fixed-income securities markets. In fact, investors might actually prefer paying a premium for an assured long-term rate rather than confront the uncertainty of what rate they will receive on funds reinvested each time the short-term obligations mature. Furthermore, and more damaging, although this hypothesis could explain what some people feel is a normal yield curve—upward-sloping—it obviously fails to account for the other two basic shapes.

The Market Segmentation Hypothesis   This hypothesis asserts that there are separate markets for short- and long-term fixed-income securities and that demand and supply in each determine yields on short and long maturities. Because the market is segmented, any pattern of yields could result depending upon the demand for and supply of short-term funds relative to that for long-term debt obligations. Thus, this hypothesis can explain why yield curves come in a variety of shapes. But, it denies that capital funds might be mobile among different maturities. In other words, it states that portfolio managers will only hold short- or long-term maturities and that governments and corporations will not vary the maturities of their debt issues. The evidence overwhelmingly argues against this position. Although perfect substitutability among various maturities does not exist, portfolio managers do alter the maturity composition of their portfolios, and governments and corporations behave similarly when issuing new debt claims, each responding to changing differentials between short- and long-term yields.

The Expectations Hypothesis   This hypothesis holds that investor expectations about future short-term rates determine the relationship between short- and long-term yields. If investors expect short-term rates to increase, the yield curve will slope upward; if they anticipate falling short-term rates, the curve will slope downward; and if they believe that these rates will remain at the same level, the curve will be flat. For example: Suppose you plan to invest funds for 2 years and that you have a choice between a 1- and a 2-year Treasury security, each yielding 6 percent. If you expect short-term rates to rise to, say, 8 percent, you would buy the 1-year security. Then, 1 year hence when it matures, you would reinvest the funds at 8 percent, raising your average annual rate of return above what you would have received on the 2-year security. Relatively greater demand for short-term securities will tend to push up their prices, reduce their yields, and result in a yield curve that slopes upward. The opposite occurs if you expect falling short-term rates. You would purchase the 2-year obligation, prices of longer maturities would tend to increase, their yields decline, and a downward-sloping yield curve would result. Finally, if you expect short-term rates to remain unchanged, you would be indifferent as to a choice between the two securities, and demand would be roughly even throughout the market, resulting in a flat yield curve.

The expectations hypothesis can also explain different yield curve patterns. But its fundamental assumption is opposite that of the market segmentation hypothesis: all maturities are perfect substitutes, that is, no market segmentation whatsoever exists. However, the evidence indicates otherwise. Some investors (e.g., commercial banks) tend to favor shorter maturities, while others (e.g., life insurance companies) tend to prefer longer-term obligations. Critics have also attacked the assumptions that investors can accurately forecast short-term interest rates and that they all will agree with the predicted direction and magnitude of movements. Obviously these assumptions are too emphatic.

Empirical studies suggest, however, that the expectations hypothesis, with modifications that take the above criticisms into account, best explains the term structure of interest rates and, therefore, the various yield curve patterns.

References

Conrad, Joseph W., *An Introduction to the Theory of Interest*, University of California Press, Berkeley, 1959; Malkiel, Burton, *The Term Structure of Interest Rates*, Princeton University Press, Princeton, N.J., 1966.

(*See also* Interest rates)

Henry C. F. Arnold

Zero economic growth

The proponents of zero economic growth (ZEG) advocate what the term suggests—no growth in national economic output because of the deleterious effects of uncurbed growth on the nation's welfare. In an age which is characterized by social and political unrest, ecological and environmental concern, and energy and nuclear crises, it is hardly surprising to find that the controversies surrounding the debate on the benefits and costs of economic growth are more often than not muddled, confused, and confusing where rational and scientific analysis is mixed with, and sometimes overshadowed by, passionate ideological arguments.

Most economists believe that net national product (NNP), as defined and computed in the national income and product accounts, is the most comprehensive yardstick for evaluating economic performance. But they also believe that NNP is not an adequate indicator of the level of economic welfare. For example, as now computed, NNP excludes the imputed values of goods and services not transacted in the market, e.g., leisure. It does not take account of externalities (the amount of which increases inevitably and concomitantly with the rise in production of most other outputs) that adversely affect consumers' well-being. Nor does it include psychic income stemming from ethical, moral, and religious considerations.

Proponents of ZEG conceive of an aggregate social indicator, gross national welfare (GNW), that would go far beyond the conventional income and product accounts by covering not only material items but also the spiritual aspects of life. Growth in GNW terms would by definition be beneficial to all concerned. The proponents of ZEG then argue that there must be a significant negative relationship between GNW and NNP and that there is no alternative available to alter such a correlation except to halt absolutely growth in NNP.

Arguments for ZEG

The typical no-growth advocate has two major propositions. The first is the observation that continuous exponential growth in population, physical output, and material consumption in a finite world will, if left unchecked, lead eventually to a disastrous collapse of the entire ecological as well as socioeconomic system, perhaps as early as some time in the next century. By that time, we would have so completely depleted the resource base of the earth and contaminated our environment that, even if life were possible under those circumstances, it would be a life of utter vice and misery. Implicit in the argument is the presumption that the prevailing global pro-growth attitude will have already caused us to overshoot the physical capabilities of our planet, and, hence, the swiftness of the ultimate decline will render the implementation of any countervailing policy impotent. What is more, this line of analysis does not regard technological progress and innovation, despite their impressive historical performance, as ways out of the grave danger; it places little faith in the ability of our socioeconomic system to generate automatically stabilizing forces before the doom draws near. The only prescription that is effective in averting the catastrophe, they argue, is to reorientate our values to accept and pursue a no-growth policy now so that the transition from the current exponential growth path to a steady state of global equilibrium, in which a balance is sustained between material output and physical limits, is smooth and orderly.

Secondly, ZEG advocates lament not only the fact that economic growth has promoted environmental decay, taken tranquillity from life, and robbed the world of its natural beauty but also the fact that the tyranny of growth has also rocked the basic foundation of our society, impeded the cohesive interrelationship among its important social institutions, and jolted the internal harmony of our psychological integrity. Economic affluence has brought about an unprecedented degree of labor mobility, and along with it the deterioration of stable family and personal relationships. The rise of national income has also bred high levels of violence, crime, and general discontentment of the masses, as the relative position of the poor has worsened rather than improved. The onslaught of technical advances has enabled the ownership of a large portion of total wealth to be concentrated in the hands of a few, giant multinational corporations, and the preferences of a modern consumer are seen to be increasingly subjected to manipulation by greedy corporate executives through well-orchestrated advertising campaigns in the media. Economic growth, thus, not only fails to produce a high level of aggregate welfare but also reduces it absolutely by acting as the most powerful destabilizing force in our society.

Criticism of ZEG

Most economists feel that no-growth advocates have greatly exaggerated the costs of growth while underestimating its benefits, that they are being unreasonably pessimistic about the adaptive capability of our economic system as well as the potency of technological progress, and that they have not adequately explored all available alternatives that are open to society to reduce the harmful effects often attributed to growth. To be sure, continuous exponential growth in a finite world cannot go on forever. Yet it would be equally absurd to argue that, given finiteness of our resource base, we should stop growth altogether immediately.

Others argue that a more rational approach would call for an optimal allocation of our remaining resources among their many uses. Under most circumstances, the market mechanism, in spite of its numerous imperfections, may still be the best rationing device to handle scarcity. In cases where the price system does not work efficiently, improved performance can be achieved by reinforcing it with intelligent government planning and regulations. It is, therefore, not true, opponents argue, that the result of such a rational approach would necessarily dictate a no-growth policy. Moreover, the capability of modern technology cannot be dismissed so easily. If recycling does not help the dwindling reserves of the earth's metallic deposits, synthetic substitutes might be found to substantially alleviate the problem, particularly regarding resources of the nonrenewable type. Failing that, it is not entirely inconceivable that, within the next century or two, our needs for minerals and fossil fuels can be largely satisfied by extraction from outer space. The successful tapping of solar energy on a massive scale would go a long way in solving our energy problems, and fusion energy may also be around the corner.

Opposition to growth based on ecological or environmental reasons is equally incomplete on logical grounds, since the validity of these depends on the special assumption that the composition and the technology used in the production of our national output remain fixed over time. It is certainly possible to have growth and at the same time to have pollution and other negative externalities reduced through the use of appropriately set effluent fees and regulations.

Arguments against growth that are couched in value terms are more difficult to defend. The assertion that economic growth has harmful social, psychological, and moral effects cannot be proved or disproved scientifically. However, some rather disturbing questions could be posed about the implications of a no-growth society. Will people in such a society be necessarily better off? If growth does not narrow the gap between the rich and the poor, it seems likely that zero growth would be worse, since one person's gain must now be another's loss. Beyond this possibility of intensification of distributional conflicts, will people feel more content in a stationary society in which creativity, innovation, and anything dynamic are discouraged? More importantly, will the sociopolitical system necessarily be more stable when growth is prohibited? These and other questions must be thoroughly analyzed, as critics of zero growth could contend, before a no-growth policy can be endorsed.

It is clear that both sides of the debate agree that there is a price to be paid for economic growth. The issue that must be resolved concerns the relative magnitudes of costs and benefits involved in the continued pursuit of growth. If anything is to be gained from the debate, it is that because of it we are now much more aware of the many complex problems, all of which require our urgent attention, that are inherent in the choice of a correct growth policy, an action that will surely have important and perhaps irreversible intergenerational consequences. It is also clear that any meaningful investigation of the subject must necessarily involve an interdisciplinary effort of both social and physical scientists.

References

Meadows, D. H., et al. *The Limits to Growth*, Universe Books, New York, 1972; Mishan, E. J., *The Costs of Economic Growth*, Staple Press, London, 1967; Nordhaus, W., and J. Tobin, "Is Economic Growth Obsolete?," in Milton Moss (ed.), *The Measurement of Economic and Social Performance*, National Bureau of Economic Research, 1972; Olson, Mancur, and Hans H. Landsberg (eds.), *The No-Growth Society*, Norton, New York, 1973.

(*See also* Energy costs; Environmental costs; Externalities; National income accounting; Normative economics; Welfare economics)

Hewell H. Zee

Zero population growth

The term zero population growth (ZPG) is associated primarily with those who urgently advocate the necessity of bringing to a halt, at an early date, the growth of world population. They oppose further population growth not only for the low-income, less-developed countries of Africa, Asia, and Latin America but also for the relatively rich industrialized nations, including the United States.

The rise of interest in ZPG as a specific target for public policy began in the middle 1960s and is roughly coincident with the emergence of greatly increased concern over environmental pollution. A nonprofit institution, Zero Population Growth, Inc., established in 1968 and headquartered in Washington, D.C., acts as a lobbying organization and presents testimony before congressional committees concerning population issues.

The study of the forces influencing population growth has long been a central concern within the field of economics. Among the academic community, however, enthusiastic support for ZPG has come more from natural scientists, particularly biologists, than from economists. However, there are a few well-known contemporary economists whose writings can arguably be claimed to place them on the side of the ZPG advocates—principally Kenneth Boulding, Nicholas Georgescu-Roegen, Robert Heilbroner, and E. J. Mishan.

History of ZPG

The origin of ZPG as a goal for humanity is attributed to Thomas Malthus, who published in 1798 his theory that the growth rate of population tends to outstrip the growth rate of food production. Malthus pessimistically expected ZPG to be reached soon, with starvation and disease holding population at the maximum number supportable, at a bare subsistence level, by a limited food supply. He expressed a faint hope, however, that humanity would eventually adopt a policy of population control through fewer and later marriages and sexual continence within marriage.

Malthusian theory fell out of fashion as the enormous increase in agricultural productivity and rapid advance in science and technology during the nineteenth and twentieth centuries made it possible for industrializing nations to support growing populations at rising levels of per capita real consumption. But by the 1960s, alarm over continued population growth was revived. The rate of population increase had accelerated in the less-developed countries through improved sanitation and disease control. World population, estimated at 2 billion in 1930, rose to 3 billion by 1960, and to 4 billion by 1975. The annual rate of increase was about 1.75 percent in the late 1970s. If maintained—assuming it to be maintainable—this rate would bring world population to over 6 billion by the year 2000, to 9.5 billion by 2025, and to almost 15 billion by 2050. The effort to improve nutrition and the material conditions of life in the less-developed countries appeared to have become a desperate race between agricultural productivity and exponentially rising population.

In the developed nations, increased attention to the population problem in the

1960s and 1970s did not arise from immediate concern over food supplies. Although the average population growth rate in these countries was below 1 percent per year, any continued rise in population was claimed to pose two threats. First, it would make it increasingly difficult to achieve and maintain a low level of environmental pollution, as more and more people occupied a fixed geographical area. Second, it would accelerate the rate of use of nonrenewable natural resources (fossil fuels and minerals). A smaller, stabilized population would be able to maintain over a longer time period a standard of living based upon high per capita consumption of these resources. It would thereby gain time in which to discover and develop new technologies which would rely upon nonexhaustible resources, such as solar energy.

Pro and Con Views

Like Malthus in his day, those who advocate ZPG now, or ZPG as soon as possible, are alarmed over the prospects for humanity within the not extremely distant future—the next 50 to 100 years. They see the planet Earth as having a maximum sustainable carrying capacity for a human population. A population which is allowed to exceed this limit will ultimately lower the carrying capacity—and, thus, eventually force a reduction in population to a level lower than otherwise could have been maintained—by damaging the environment in such ways as: conversion of arable land to urban use; deforestation through excessive lumbering; lowering of water tables through excessive reliance upon irrigation; creation of dust bowls from overgrazing and plowing of semiarid lands; depletion of the world's fisheries through overfishing and the buildup of water pollution; loss of topsoil from strip-mining; reduction of crop yields from air pollution and rapid depletion of nonrenewable resources for fertilizers; early exhaustion of recoverable deposits of fossil fuels and minerals; probable radioactive poisoning of the earth from accidents in nuclear power plants; production of possible adverse climatic changes from the increasing discharge of industrial heat and pollutants into the atmosphere.

Proponents of ZPG call upon economists to develop, in Kenneth Boulding's phrase, an "economics of spaceship earth," which recognizes the necessity of achieving a steady-state equilibrium between the world's population and its productive capacity from renewable natural resources. They do not claim ZPG to be a panacea for the complex problems of pollution and environmental damage, but they do claim that no policies for coping with these problems can succeed without ZPG. They believe that time is short and that world population, at its present growth rate, will soon be pressing upon the limits of the earth's carrying capacity.

In contrast to the ZPG advocates, most economists do not fear that a crisis is imminent unless population growth is stopped soon. They are more optimistic about humanity's problem-solving capacities. In their view, the advance of science and technology will almost certainly continue, for the reasonably foreseeable future, to allow more humans to live on the earth, with increased real material consumption per capita. The earth's potentially exploitable reservoir of resources is vast. They argue that, if allowed to operate, the price system can regulate satisfactorily the rate of consumption over time of those resources conventionally described as exhaustible. As relative prices of some of these resources rise, ways will be found to economize on their use, substitutes for them will be explored, and incentive will be provided both to discover new supplies and to develop techniques for lowering the costs of resource extraction. Science will eventually provide an abundant supply of energy, both nuclear and solar. Even with growing population and industrial output, pollution can be held to a tolerable level through technological innovation and a sophisticated use of such economic disincentives as taxes on the discharge of pollutants.

Moreover, most economists probably expect the population problem to be ameliorated gradually over time. In the advanced industrialized nations, the age-old economic incentives to raise children to provide labor for the family farm and support for parents in old age have almost vanished. As viewed by parents, children are now consumer goods. Rising real incomes would be expected to increase the demand for children through the income effect, but the substitution effect is working strongly to curtail demand. Expanded opportunities for employment of women outside the home, at increasing real wage rates, have greatly increased the opportunity cost of having children. By the late 1970s, the net reproduction rate in some European countries had fallen below unity, and many demographers considered it not improbable that the combined total population of the Western and Soviet bloc industrialized nations would grow slowly to a maximum within the next 40 to 60 years, and then begin to decline.

The 1979 net reproduction rate in the United States was very close to unity. If the rate soon reaches unity, if illegal immigration is choked off, and if legal immigration is greatly reduced, the population of the United States will grow from its current level of about 220 million and stabilize at a maximum of about 280 million soon after the year 2050.

Turning to the less-developed countries, few economists can complacently accept their present rate of population growth. However, birthrates in some of those countries, most notably in East Asia, have been cut sharply in recent years. Many observers are hopeful that birthrates in the less-developed countries will be reduced over the next 50 to 75 years to levels not far above those in the industrialized nations. Their hopes ride upon the effectiveness with which the governments of the less-developed countries carry out policies to increase literacy and education, raise real incomes, persuade their people to accept contraceptive techniques (including voluntary sterilization), and establish old-age security programs to reduce the incentives to have children.

Since the planet Earth is finite, the maximum number of people who can ever inhabit the earth at any one time is also finite. In that sense, zero population growth is inevitable. There will come a time at which the population of human beings upon the earth will reach a number that will never again be exceeded. The advocates of ZPG argue that since ZPG must come eventually, it should be deliberately and intelligently achieved by a plan of rigid population control, to avert the human suffering and the environmental damage which will result should ZPG arrive, instead, through the traditional controls of disease and famine. Those who see no need for adoption of a ZPG policy have more confidence that humankind will continue to find the means to support a growing population over many years into the future and that the rate of population growth will gradually subside without the adoption of coercive techniques to control human reproduction.

References

Daly, Herman E. (ed.), *Toward a Steady-State Economy*, Freeman, San Francisco, 1973; Frejka, Tomás, *The Future of Population Growth*, Wiley, New York, 1973; Malthus, Thomas R., in Philip Appleman (ed.), *An Essay on the Principle of Population*, Norton, New York, 1976; Olson, Mancur, and Hans Landsberg (eds.), *The No-Growth Society*, Norton, New York, 1973; Sauvy, Alfred, *Zero Growth?*, Praeger, New York, 1975; Simon, Julian L., *The Economics of Population Growth*, Princeton University Press, Princeton, N.J., 1977.

(*See also* Malthusian theory of population; Zero economic growth)

Robert E. L. Knight

Appendixes

General Economics; Theory; History; Systems   (Continued)

Incomes policy
Indexation
Industrial revolution
Input-output analysis
Institutional economics
Interest, economic theory of
Interest rates
Investment function
Keynesian economics
Labor, a factor of production
Labor theory of value
Laissez faire
Land, a factor of production
Liberalism
Macroeconomics
Manchester school
Maoism
Marginal cost
Marginal revenue
Marshallian economics
Marxism
Mercantilism
Microeconomics
Money illusion
Monopoly and oligopoly
Monopsony and oligopsony
Multiplier
National income accounting
Neoclassical economics
Neo-Keynesian economics

Normative economics
Opportunity cost
Permanent income hypothesis
Phillips curve
Physiocrats
Post-Keynesian economics
Price theory
Production function
Profits in economic theory
Propensity to consume or to save and
  inducement to invest
Quantity theory of money
Radical economics
Real balance effect theory
Reform liberalism
Saving
Say's law
Scarcity
Socialism
Stagflation
Stagnation thesis
Static analysis
Stock-flow analysis
Subsidies
Supply
Supply-side economics
Utility
Wealth
Welfare economics

Economic Growth; Development; Planning; Fluctuations

Accuracy of economic forecasts
Administered prices
Anticipation surveys, business
Anticipation surveys, consumer
Business cycles
Capital formation
Consumer price index
Cost of living
Council of Economic Advisers
Council on Wage and Price Stability
Dynamic macroeconomic models
Economic forecasts
Economic growth
Economic models
Economic planning
Energy costs
Environmental costs

Escalator clause
Expectations
Forecasting methods
Human capital
Implicit price deflator for GNP
Incomes policy
Indexation
Inflation
Infrastructure
Innovation
Input-output analysis
Joint Economic Committee of Congress
Juglar cycle
Kitchin cycle
Kondratieff cycle
Kuznets cycle
Leading indicator approach to forecasting

National Bureau of Economic Research
Price measurement
Producer price index
Productivity
Research and development
Secular trend
Stages theory of economic development

Stagflation
Stagnation thesis
Technology
Value of the dollar
Wealth
Zero economic growth
Zero population growth

Economic Statistics

Bayesian inference
Bureau of the Census
Bureau of Economic Analysis
Bureau of Labor Statistics
Business inventory
Business investment in new plants and
  equipment
Change in business inventories in GNP
Cross-sectional analysis in business and
  economics
Diffusion index
Disposable personal income
Distributed lags in economics
Dynamic macroeconomic models
Econometrics
Economic models
Economic statistics
Factor cost
Flow of funds
Game theory, economic applications
Government expenditures in GNP
Gross national product
Gross private domestic investment
Implicit price deflator for GNP
Index numbers
Industrial production index
Input-output analysis
IS-LM model
Isoquant
Leading indicator approach to forecasting
Linear programming

Lorenz curve
Marketing research and business economics
National income accounting
Net exports in GNP
Operations research
Personal consumption expenditures in GNP
Phillips curve
Potential gross national product
Price-earnings ratio
Producer price index
Productivity
Profits measurement
Random walk hypothesis
Regression analysis in business and
  economics
Sampling in economics
Seasonal adjustment methods
Seasonal variations in economic time series
Secular trend
Simulation in business and economics
Simultaneous equations in business and
  economics
Statistical techniques in economics and
  business, an overview
Stock-flow analysis
Stock price averages and indexes
Time series analysis
Value of the dollar
Wealth
Yield curve

Monetary and Fiscal Theory and Institutions

Automatic stabilizers
Bank deposits
Banking system
Bond
Bond rating agencies
Capital gains
Capital markets and money markets
Closed-end investment companies
Commodity exchanges
Consumer credit

Credit, an overview
Debt
Debt management
Depletion allowance
Depreciation allowance
Disintermediation
Eurodollar market
Federal budget
Federal budget process
Federal Reserve policy

Monetary and Fiscal Theory and Institutions   (*Continued*)

Federal Reserve System
Financial institutions
Financial instruments
Fiscal policy
Flow of funds
Gold standard
Housing economics
Interest, economic theory of
Interest rates
Monetary policy
Money markets
Money supply
Mortgage credit
Mutual funds
Open-market operations
Pension funds
Portfolio management theories

Price-earnings ratio
Quantity theory of money
Real balance effect theory
Real estate investment trusts
Securities and Exchange Commission
Selective credit controls
Stagflation
Stock
Stock exchange
Taxation, an overview
Thrift institutions
Value-added tax
Variable annuity
Velocity of the circulation of money
Wealth
Yield curve

International Economics

Arbitrage
Balance of international payments
Balance of international trade
Barriers to trade
Bretton Woods Conference
Comparative advantage theory
Dumping
Eurodollar market
European Economic Community
Exports
Foreign direct investment
Foreign exchange rates
General Agreement on Tariffs and Trade
Gold standard
Imports
Infrastructure

International economics, an overview
International Monetary Fund
Joint venture
Liquidity, international
Multinational corporation
Nationalization of industry
Net exports in GNP
Organization for Economic Cooperation and
    Development
Protectionism
Smithsonian Agreement
Special drawing rights
Stages theory of economic development
Value of the dollar
World Bank

Administration; Business Finance; Marketing; Accounting

Advertising, economic aspects
Break-even analysis
Business credit
Business investment
Business
Channels of marketing
Financial statements

Joint venture
Liquidity, corporate
Marketing research and business economics
Return on investment
Risk premium on investment
Venture capital

Industrial Organization; Technological Change; Industry Studies

Antitrust policy
Automation

Cartel
Computers in economics

Concentration of industry
Conglomerate
Countervailing power
Data banks
Energy costs
Environmental costs
Externalities
Federal Trade Commission
Firm theory
Government regulation of business
Housing economics
Industrial production index
Innovation

Integration
Joint venture
Linear programming
Mergers
Monopoly and oligopoly
Monopsony and oligopsony
Multinational corporation
Operations research
Productivity
Restraint of trade
Small business
Technology
Trade and professional associations

Agriculture; Natural Resources

Agricultural economic policy
Agricultural productivity

Agricultural revolution

Work Force; Labor; Population

Collective bargaining
Demographics and economics
Division of labor
Employment and unemployment
Fringe benefits
Human capital
Labor, a factor of production

Labor force
Labor-management relations
Labor unions
Malthusian theory of population
Productivity
Right-to-work laws
Zero population growth

Welfare Programs; Consumer Economics; Urban Economics; Regional Economics

Consumer theory
Consumerism
Consumption function
Discrimination economics
Family budgets
Income
Income distribution
Location theory
Lorenz curve
Medicare programs

Negative income tax
Permanent income hypothesis
Personal consumption expenditures in GNP
Poverty
Regional economics
Saving
Social security programs
Standard of living
Urban economics

APPENDIX II

A Time Table of Economic Events, Technological Developments, Financial Developments, and Economic Thought

Date	Events	Technology	Finance	Thought
400,000 B.C.	Homo Sapiens	Hunting, fishing, gathering wild fruits and vegetables, fire, stone implements		
8000	Neolithic period	Agricultural revolution Incipient cultivation and domestication in the Near East		
4000	Diffusion of agricultural revolution	Metals, ideograms, wheel, sail, calendar		
3000		Wooden plow		
1700				Code of Hammurabi
1400		Iron, alphabet		
1300				Ten Commandments
1000				Upanishads
700			Metal coins	Hesiod, Homer, Prophets
590				Laws of Solon
500	Early Mayan culture	Abacus		Buddha, Confucius
400		Horseshoe		Plato, Aristotle
A.D. 100	Pax Romana facilitates trade throughout the Mediterranean	Ships, ports, roads, other "social overhead" lower the transaction and transportation cost of this trade Watermill, horse collar harness	Roman mint ratio: copper to silver, 112:1; silver to gold, 12:1 Gold aureus Silver denarius (d.) Loses all silver by A.D. 275 Inflation of late Roman Empire	Roman law (codified in the Corpus Juris Civilis) defines the rules for the world market
190		Abacus		
300	Diocletian edict to fix prices			Fathers of the church: "Trade turns man away from the search for God"—St. Augustine

A Time Table of Economic Events, Technological Development, Financial Developments, and Economic Thought (Continued)

Date	Events	Technology	Finance	Thought
600	Social unrest, plurality of Germanic states, Moslem conquests shatter trade of Mediterranean: European feudalism	Windmill		
700		Gunpowder		
1066	Battle of Hastings		Coin age system of Charlemagne: pound (livre, libra) of silver divided into 20 shillings (sous, solidi), each in turn divided into 12 pence (deniers, denarii)—persists on European Continent to French Revolution; in England to 1968	
1100	First Crusade; Kingdom of Jerusalem in close alliance with Italian towns (Genoa, Pisa, later Venice)			
1150	University of Paris founded Oxford University founded			
1200	Champagne fairs Growth of medieval city merchant and craft guilds			
1215				Magna Carta
1250	Marco Polo in China Mongol invasion of Eastern Europe	Rudder for sailing into the wind; compass	Gold florin, deposit banking, partnership, and foreign exchange to circumvent usury	Summa Theologica: just price, usury, jus mercatorum, universities
1350	Black Death		Money for the commutation of labor services: from status to contract	Occam's separation of logic and metaphysics: divine action beyond any standards of human rationality

1400	Merchant Adventurers in Bruges Hundred Years' War (Jeanne d'Arc) ends English domination on European continent	Printing, mechanical clocks	Medici bank fiscal agent of the church	Oresme, in his *Treatise on Money* (1360), calls debasement of coins "worse than usury"
1450	French standing army, using artillery, victorious in Hundred Years' War Turks capture Constantinople: end of Byzantine Empire Prince Henry the Navigator	Caravel: gun-carrying sailing ships usher in 500 years of European world domination	Monts-de-Piété	
1492	Columbus in the Bahamas			
1494	Treaty of Tordesillas: longitude of 46°W demarcation line between Spain and Portugal			Pacioli on double-entry bookkeeping
1498	Vasco da Gama in Calicut			
1500	Intense rivalry among European nation-states in their struggle for overseas expansion and monopoly positions in the resultant commercial revolution Cabral lands in Brazil	Rifle		Humanism, Renaissance, Reformation All change the dominant world outlook and signal the end of "medieval" Europe.
1502		Leonardo da Vinci military engineer to Caesar Borgia		
1513				Machiavelli: *Il Principe* ("first social scientist of modern times")
1519			Fugger "thaler"	
1522			Copernicus on principles of a sound currency	
1531			Antwerp Bourse	

A Time Table of Economic Events, Technological Development, Financial Developments, and Economic Thought (Continued)

Date	Events	Technology	Finance	Thought
1539				Term "humanism" coined to indicate search for new authorities: from feudal nobility to elite of talent and intellect
1543				Copernicus: De Revolutionibus; Vesalius: Fabrica
1545			Silver mine of Potosi	
1546				Dumoulin defends interest on loans
1549				Hales's Discourse of the Common Weal
1560				Gresham's law
1568				Bodin's quantity theory of money to explain rising prices after silver exports to Europe from the new world
1571			London Exchange	
1580				Montaigne on nature's law of creative destruction
1581	Dutch independence: world trade center shifts from Antwerp to Amsterdam			
1588	Spanish Armada defeated	English naval arsenal at Chatham		
1589		Knitting frame in Nottingham		
1590		Microscope	Sixfold increase of European specie due to silver imports from the new world leads to	Mercantilism: economic policy to serve the needs of the nation-state in a period of intense

Year	Commerce / Politics	Technology	Finance / Economy	Economic Thought
1600	British East India Company		threefold price increase within half a century; Major financial centers of sixteenth century: Antwerp, Augsburg, Frankfurt, Lyons, Venice	rivalry for position in world markets when the total world economy was still viewed as a zero-sum game so that one country's gain was inevitably another country's loss
1602	Dutch East India Company	Telescope		
1609			Bank of Amsterdam	
1610				Galileo: pioneer of modern science
1611			Amsterdam Stock Exchange; Government bonds to finance the nation-state	
1616				Bacon: "balance of trade"
1620		Slide rule		
1621	Dutch West India Company (New Amsterdam)			
1623	Statute of Monopolies			
1625	Manhattan (New Amsterdam)			
1626				Misselden: The Circle of Commerce
1628	Petition of Right attacks royal monopolies (often granted to finance the royal household)			Grotius: De jure belli ac pacis
1630				Mun: "England's Treasure by Foreign Trade" to stress grievances against the Dutch and to plead for freedom of business from government regulation of specie movements (published 1664)

A Time Table of Economic Events, Technological Development, Financial Developments, and Economic Thought (Continued)

Date	Events	Technology	Finance	Thought
1635			Tulip Mania	
1637				Descartes: analytic geometry
1642		Digital calculator (Pascal)		
1643		Barometer (Torricelli)	Wampum legal tender in Massachusetts	
1649	Commonwealth of Oliver Cromwell			
1650			Amsterdam world money market	
1651	English Navigation Act: cause of first Dutch War			Hobbes: *Leviathan*
1652			Massachusetts mint	
1653				Pascal: theory of probability
1656		Pendulum clock (Huygens)		
1661	Louis XIV: L'état, c'est moi			Boyle: *Sceptical Chymist*
1662			Colbert controller general of French finances	Royal Society Petty: money not the blood but "the fat of the body politic, whereof too much does as often hinder its agility as too little makes it sick"
1664	New Amsterdam renamed New York			
1665	French woolen regulations			Spinoza: *Ethics*
1669				
1672			Stop of the Exchequer: Stuart government refuses repayment of debt	

990

Year	Economic thought / publications	Finance / money	Technology	Political / commercial events
1678	Petty: *Political Arithmetic*			
1687	Newton: *Principia Mathematica* "Century of genius"			
1688	Gregory King: "Observations upon the State of England" (detailed national income estimates)	Lloyd's in London		
1690	Locke: *Treatise on Civil Government*; North: *Discourse upon Trade*	First paper money in British Empire; Massachusetts Colony notes		Hudson Bay Company
1693		Beginning of English public debt: £1,000,000 at 10%		
1694		Bank of England: monetization of the debt within carefully specified limits		
1695	Boisguilbert: "laissez faire la nature et la liberté"			Darien scheme
1696	Bayle: *Dictionnaire*			
1697		Note monopoly for Bank of England		
1698	Davenant: *Discourses on the Trade of England*			
1700				Indian calicoes prohibited in England
1702		Massachusetts Province bills	Savery's "Miners' Friend, or an engine to raise water with fire"	
1705	John Law: *Money and Trade Considered* ("paper-money mercantilist")		Newcomen's steam engine	
1707	Vauban: *Projet d'une dime royale*			United Kingdom: Great Britain Fortnum and Mason

A Time Table of Economic Events, Technological Development, Financial Developments, and Economic Thought (Continued)

Date	Events	Technology	Finance	Thought
1708		Coke for smelting iron near Birmingham (Darby)		
1710	South Sea Company			Berkeley: *Principles of Human Knowledge*
1711				Shaftesbury: harmony between society and the individual
1713	Peace of Utrecht signals rise of the British Empire. Asiento gives Britain the sole right to the slave trade with Spanish America: ports of Bristol and Liverpool			
1714		Mercury thermometer (Fahrenheit)	Fiscal needs of the nation-state, and the goals of economic growth, leads to an appreciation of savings for capital formation.	Mandeville: "Private Vices, Publick Benefits" by the "skillful management of the clever Politician"
1720			"Mississippi Bubble": first stock-market crash	
1725				Hutcheson: "greatest happiness for the greatest numbers" Utilitarianism Vico: *Scienza Nuova* "First modern historian"
1730	Enclosures permit greater productivity of British agriculture, a precondition of the industrial revolution	"High farming" Horse-hoeing husbandry Lime and animal fertilizer Potato, clower, turnips, and alfalfa		Cantillon: *Essai sur la nature du commerce* (published 1755) "Real" theory of interest Specie-flow mechanism
1733		Flying shuttle (Kay)		Voltaire: *Letters sur les Anglais*
1740		Crucible steel at Doncaster		

Year	Technology / Industry	Politics / Economy	Finance	Ideas / Books
1748				Montesquieu: stage theory of history Hume: *Enquiry concerning Human Understanding*
1750	Cylinder-boring machine (Wilkinson), precondition of improved steam engine			
1752	Lightning rod (Franklin)			Franklin: *Poor Richard's Almanack* Hume: "On Money"
1754				Rousseau indicts private property
1758				Quesnay: *Tableau économique* Physiocracy
1759				Adam Smith: *Theory of Moral Sentiments*
1762	Soho metalworks (Boulton)			
1763		Treaty of Paris: British world hegemony established	Baring & Co.	
1764	Spinning jenny (Hargreaves)	Iron on enumerated list (could be exported from American only to English ports)		
1765		Stamp Act		
1766				Blackstone: *Commentaries* Sonnenfels: "Grundsätze der Polizey" (Austrian cameralist) Turgot: *Réflexions sur la formation et les distributions des richesses* Productivity of capital traced to the inherent fecundity of nature

A Time Table of Economic Events, Technological Development, Financial Developments, and Economic Thought (Continued)

Date	Events	Technology	Finance	Thought
1767	Colonial duties on tea Townshend Acts			Steuart: *Principles of Political Oeconomy* "Real bills" doctrine "Last of the mercantilists"
1768				*Encyclopedia Britannica* Du Pont: *Physiocratie* Theory of rent Influence on Jefferson
1769		Watt separates steam condenser: "steam is an Englishman" Spinning frame (Arkwright)		
1770	"Boston Massacre"			
1773			Stock Exchange building in London	
1774			Gold sole legal tender in Great Britain	
1776		Boulton-Watt partnership turns out first successful steam engine Steam blast for smelting iron	Beginning of U.S. Treasury	U.S. Declaration of Independence Adam Smith: *Wealth of Nations*—classic exposition of a market economy Bentham: *Fragment on Government* Utility basis of individual action and public policy The Age of Reason, or Enlightenment, expected a better world from the rational self-interest of free citizens.
1779		Grand Trunk Canal Spinning mule (Crompton) Iron bridge at Coalbrookdale		

1781	Bank of North America			Kant: *Kritik der reinen Vernunft*
1783		Balloon (Montgolfier)		
1784	Bank of New York (Hamilton)			Young: *Annals of Agriculture*
1785		Power loom (Cartwright)		
1787				U.S. Constitution
1788	Canal boom in England			
1790	Hamilton's fiscal program		First U.S. Census	Burke: *Reflections on the French Revolution*
1791				Hamilton: *Report on Manufactures*
1792	New York Stock Exchange U.S. coinage law			
1793		Cotton gin (Whitney) Textile mill at Pawtucket (Slater)		
1796		Vaccination against smallpox Decline of death rate		
1797	Bank of England suspends specie payments	Iron plow		
1798				Malthus: *Essay on Population*
1799			Anti-Combination Laws in England	
1800	Banque de France note monopoly	Electric battery (Volta)	World population about 900 million	
1801		Jacquard loom	First population census in England	
1802		Dupont near Wilmington		Thornton: *Paper Credit of Great Britain*
1803	London Stock Exchange issues first List			Say: *Traité d'économie politique* "Say's law"

A Time Table of Economic Events, Technological Development, Financial Developments, and Economic Thought (Continued)

Date	Events	Technology	Finance	Thought
1804		Steam-powered locomotive (Trevithick)		Lauderdale: *Nature of Public Wealth*
1805			Rothschild in London	
1807		High-pressure steam engine (Evans) for locomotive and steamboat		Hegel: *Phänomenologie des Geistes*
1810		Krupp in Essen		Ricardo: *The High Price of Bullion*
1811		Luddites smash power looms		
1812	U.S. declares war on Great Britain for "free trade and sailors' rights"		Short-term (1 year) Treasury notes	
1813		Interchangeable parts (North, Whitney)	Boston Manufacturing Company with capital stock of $300,000	Owen: *New View of Society*
1815	Corn Law excludes foreign grain from England. Act of the Congress of Vienna	New Jersey railroad. Miner's lamp (Davy)		Malthus, Ricardo, Torrens, and West independently formulate theory of rent
1816	Tariff to protect American manufacturers	Photography (Niepce). Lowell's factory at Waltham		
1817	English poor relief at peak: postwar unemployment	Cockerill near Liège		Ricardo: *Principles of Political Economy*—most influential contribution to the methodology of classical economics
1818	Free trade within borders of Prussia		First great American fortunes: Astor (fur, Manhattan real estate); Girard (Philadelphia banking and shipping)	The "classical school," a term coined by Marx, translates the spirit of Enlightenment into economics.
1819	British Factory Act bars employment of children under nine	Steamboat crossing from Savannah to Liverpool	Financial panic in U.S.: loss of export markets	Sismondi: *New Principles of Political Economy*

Year	Theory / Books	Economics & Finance	Science & Technology	Politics & Law
1820	Malthus: *Principles of Political Economy*	Gwathmey & Co. in Richmond: first U.S. cotton broker		
1821	James Mill: *Elements of Political Economy*	Resumption of specie payments by the Bank of England: prices fall at an annual average rate of 1.4% 1815–1847		
1822	Fourier: *Traité de l'association* (utopian socialist)		Faraday's magnetic pole	
1823	Monroe Doctrine		Digital calculator (Babbage); New York Gas Light Company	
1824	Clay's American System		Portland cement; Carnot: efficiency of steam engine	
1825	McCulloch: *Discourse on the Science of Political Economy*	Joint-stock companies	Erie Canal; Railway to carry coal from Darlington to Stockton	British Bubble Act repealed
1826	Thünen: *Der Isolirte Staat*		Menai suspension bridge	
1828			Baltimore & Ohio railroad	"U.S. Tariff of abominations": highest rates before the Civil War
1829			Braille	
1830	Cobbett: *Rural Rides*; Comte: *Cours de Philosophie Positive*		Liverpool and Manchester railway to carry cotton	
1831	Tocqueville in America		Revolver (Colt); Ring spindle; Reaper (McCormick); Electric transformer (Faraday)	
1832	Babbage: *On the Economy of Machinery* (economies of scale)	Bank veto by President Jackson: U.S. without central bank for the rest of the century	Rapid transit: horse car in New York; Baldwin & Co. in Philadelphia	British Reform Act: middle-class franchise

A Time Table of Economic Events, Technological Development, Financial Developments, and Economic Thought (Continued)

Date	Events	Technology	Finance	Thought
1833	Zollverein	Telegraph (Gauss)		
1834	British Poor Law reform		U.S. mint ratio 16:1	Longfield: *Lectures on Political Economy* Rae: *New Principles of Political Economy*
1835		Ludwigsbahn Nürnberg-Fürth	Liquidation of U.S. national debt: public land sales at peak ($25,000,000)	
1836	Cotton 20 cents	Mechanical thresher Schneider in Le Creusot	Specie Circular: only gold and silver accepted by U.S. government	Senior: *Outline of the Science of Political Economy*
1837	Drop in cotton prices: panic Procter & Gamble	Borsig in Berlin		Carey: *Principles of Political Economy*
1838	Manchester Anti-Corn Law League (Cobden) People's Charter in England	Stereoscope (Wheatstone) Regular trans-Atlantic steam travel: 1440-ton "Great Western," Bristol–New York		Cournot: *Principes Mathématiques* (mathematical theory of the business firm) Tooke: *History of Prices* (leader of the banking school)
1839		Maffei in München Daguerreotype (Daguerre) Midland Railway from Derby to Nottingham Vulcanization process for rubber (Goodyear)		Blanc: *Organisation du travail*
1840	Penny postage Cunard steamship line Silesian coalfield opened			Proudhon: *Qu'est-ce que la propriété?*
1841				List: *Das nationale System der politischen Ökonomie*

1843	British repeal law against exporting machinery			*The Economist* Roscher: *Grundriss der Staatswirtschaft*
1844	Factory Act extends protection to women Rochdale Society of Equitable Pioneers		Bank Charter Act: "currency principle" (Overstone) Hudson: English "railway king"	John Stuart Mill: *Unsettled Questions of Political Economy* Engels: *Die Lage der arbeitenden Klasse in England*
1845	Irish famine	Pneumatic tire (Thompson)		
1846	British Corn Laws repealed Walker Tariff Act: drastic reduction of American tariffs	Sewing machine Zeiss in Jena		
1847	Unemployment 40% in the English midlands	McCormick in Chicago Allis Chalmers in Milwaukee Deere in Moline Massey-Ferguson in Ontario Siemens and Halske in Berlin		Boole: *Mathematical Analysis of Logic*
1848	Revolutions in Europe Chicago Board of Trade Public Health Act in England (Chadwick)	Color photography (Becquerel) Roebling in Trenton	Discovery of gold in California	*Communist Manifesto* Mill: *Principles of Political Economy*
1849	British Navigation Laws repealed "Forty-Niners": beginning of gold rush to California Harrods in London			Macaulay: *History of England* Thoreau: *Civil Disobedience*
1850	New York Produce Exchange	Britannia Bridge (Menai Strait)	American Express Company Lehman Brothers	Carlyle: "dismal science" of economics Spencer: *Social Statics*
1851	Crystal Palace exposition: Britain "workshop of the world"	Illinois Central first U.S. land-grant railway		*New York Times*
1852	Anheuser-Busch	Elevator (Otis)	Discovery of gold in Australia Crédit Mobilier: French railroad boom	

A Time Table of Economic Events, Technological Development, Financial Developments, and Economic Thought (Continued)

Date	Events	Technology	Finance	Thought
1853	Rail connection from Atlantic seaboard to Chicago	Condensed milk (Borden)		*Dictionnaire de l'économie politique*
1854	Peak year (before Civil War) of U.S. immigration: 427,000 Reopening of Japan (Perry)	Horseshoe curve		Gossen: *Gesetze des menschlichen Verkehrs*
1855		Safety match (Lundstrom) First railroad bridge across the Mississippi (Rock Island)		Mangoldt: *Lehre vom Unternehmergewinn*
1856		Bessemer converter Organic chemical industry (Perkin)		
1857			Financial panic: cotton, 8 cents Comstock Lode in Nevada	Engel Gesetz
1858	Macy's department store in New York	"Great Eastern" largest steamship afloat: 20,000 tons Trans-Atlantic telegraph cable		
1859	Atlantic & Pacific grocery chain Bessemer Steel in Sheffield	Oil drilling at Titusville (Drake) Sleeping car (Pullman)		Darwin: *On the Origin of Species* Marx: *Critique of Political Economy* Mill: *Essay on Liberty*
1860	Cotton still two-thirds of all U.S. exports	Lenoir gas engine Baldwin Locomotive Works apply interchangeable parts	J. P. Morgan New York agent for his father's firm in London	Juglar: *Les Crises commerciales*
1861	Emancipation Edict in Russia Wanamaker in Philadelphia U.S. Civil War Congress adopts income tax		Jay Cooke ("The Tycoon") in Philadelphia Demand notes	
1862	Homestead Act Union Pacific charter	Machine gun (Gatling) Keystone Bridge Works (Carnegie)	Greenbacks Barclays converts to joint stock	Jevons: *General Mathematical Theory of Political Economy*

1863		Farbenfabriken Bayer in Elberfeld; Gasmotorenfabrik Deutz (Otto's gas engine); London Underground (Metropolitan)	U.S. National Banking system	U.S. Emancipation Proclamation: Lincoln declared all slaves "then, thenceforward, and forever free"
1864	"International" in London; Northern Pacific charter		New York Guaranty Co.	Laspeyres price index: Hamburger Warenpreise
1865	Thirteenth Amendment to the U.S. Constitution abolishes slavery	Antiseptic surgery (Lister); Siemens-Martin open-hearth steel furnace; Cylinder lock (Yale)	Credit Mobilier of America	Clausius: Die mechanische Wärmetheorie; Jevons: The Coal Question
1866	Chisholm Trail	Dynamite (Nobel); Aluminum (Hall); Skoda Works in Pilsen		Mendel: "quantum conception of biology"; Rogers: History of Agriculture and Prices in England
1867	Second Reform Bill in England; British North America Act creates Dominion of Canada		Kuhn and Loeb	Marx: Das Kapital
1868	Meiji restoration in Japan; Trades Union Congress in England	Air brake (Westinghouse)		
1869	Promontary Point (first transcontinental railroad); Knights of Labor; Suez Canal opened (Lesseps); Diamonds at Kimberley; Professional baseball (Cincinnati Reds)	Celluloid (first plastic); Caterpillar tractor	"Black Friday"; Royal Bank of Canada	Mendeleev: periodic table
1870		Standard Oil (Rockefeller); Stock ticker (Edison)	Deutsche Bank	
1871	New York Cotton Exchange	Mont Cenis tunnel; Compressed-air drill (Ingersoll); Frick & Co. in Connellsville	Dominion Bank; Sun Life Assurance; Germany on gold standard	Jevons: Theory of Political Economy; Menger: Grundsätze der Volkswirtschaftslehre

Date	Events	Technology	Finance	Thought
1872		Motion pictures		Verein für Sozialpolitik Mach: "Science is experience arranged in economical order"
1873			Panic: failure of Jay Cooke & Co. Silver demonetized "Crime of '73" Scandinavian countries on gold standard	Bagehot: *Lombard Street*— "money does not manage itself"
1874		Eads Bridge Barbed wire	Latin Monetary Union on gold standard	Walras: *Éléments d'économie politique pure* General equilibrium "Magna Carta of exact economics"
1875	British control of Suez Canal	Hoosac tunnel Thomas-Gilchrist process of making steel	Reichsbank	Gothaer Programm
1876	U.S. Centennial Exposition: "Gilded Age" Granger cases: public utility concept	Edison at Menlo Park		Walker: *The Wages Question*
1877	U.S. depression and discontent: Federal troops suppress railroad strike	Telephone (Bell) Hydroelectric power at Niagara Falls Phonograph (Edison)		Morgan: *Ancient Society*
1878			Household Finance Silver purchase by U. S. Treasury to stem steady price decline	
1879	Agricultural depression in Europe due to cheap U.S. imports	Incandescent light (Edison) Electric streetcar in Berlin Cash register	U.S. specie payments resumed: de facto gold standard	Henry George: *Progress and Poverty*

1880	U.S. regulates entry of Chinese immigrants	Synthetic indigo (Baeyer)	De Beers Mining Co. (Cecil Rhodes)	Edgeworth: *Mathematical Physics* Holmes: *The Common Law* Wharton School in Philadelphia
1881		Color photography		
1882	U.S. Tariff Commission	St. Gotthard tunnel	Midwest Stock Exchange Standard Oil Trust first industrial monopoly	*Wall Street Journal*
1883	Health insurance in Germany U.S. Civil Service Commission Brotherhood of Railroad Trainmen	AEG (Rathenau) Express d'Orient Brooklyn Bridge Cellulose (Swann)		Methodenstreit Fabian Society Ely: *Monopolies and Trusts* Sumner: *What Social Classes Owe Each Other* Toynbee: *Lectures on the Industrial Revolution* Sidgwick: *Principles of Political Economy*
1884	Agrarian discontent: decline of world farm prices		Money-market disaster	Böhm-Bawerk: *Kapital and Kapitalzins* Wieser: *Ursprung des wirtschaftlichen Wertes*
1885	American Telephone and Telegraph Company Lever Brothers Canadian Pacific Railway completed	Commercial adding machine (Burroughs) Daimler motorcycle Electric transformer (Stanley) Linotype and monotype (Mergenthaler) Automobile with internal combustion engine		American Economic Association John Bates Clark: *Philosophy of Wealth*
1886	American Federation of Labor Haymarket Riot	Phenacetin from coal tar Aluminum Severn railroad tunnel	U.S. Treasury surplus Discovery of gold in Transvaal: Johannesburg laid out First 1-million-share trading day in New York	Carnegie: *Triumphant Democracy* Newcomb: *Principles of Political Economy*

A Time Table of Economic Events, Technological Development, Financial Developments, and Economic Thought (Continued)

Date	Events	Technology	Finance	Thought
1887	Interstate Commerce Act	Comptometer (Felt and Tarrant)		Cheysson: cobweb theorem Sidney Webb: *Facts for Socialists*
1888	Miners' Federation of Great Britain	Montecatini Rubber tire Frash process of oil refining: First major achievement of chemical engineering in the United States Hand-held camera (Eastman)		Ashley: *English Economic History and Theory* Schmoller: *Literaturgeschichte der Sozialwissenschaften* Taussig: *Tariff History of the United States* Wieser: *Der natürliche Wert* coins term "marginal utility" ("Grenznutzen")
1889	Old-age insurance in Germany London dock strike Second "International" set up at Brussels	Tour Eiffel in Paris Rayon (de Chardonet)	Union Trust Company of Pittsburgh (Mellon)	Hobson: *Physiology of Industry* Pantaleoni: *Principi di Economia Pura* Shaw: *Fabian Essays*
1890	Sherman Antitrust Act Tobacco trust (Duke)	Steam turbine (Parsons) Forth Railway Bridge: world's first cantilever bridge	U.S. silver purchase stimulates continued debate about merits of bimetallism	Marshall: *Principles of Economics*, most influential contribution to neoclassical economics
1891	Russian famine Katanga Co. (copper)	Sarnia railroad tunnel: first international submarine tunnel Trans-Siberian railroad (Witte)		J. M. Keynes: *Scope and Method of Political Economy*
1892	Homestead strike General Electric Co.	Diesel engine Generator (Tesla)		*Journal of Political Economy* Fisher: *Mathematical Investigations into the Theory of Value and Price*
1893	Columbian Exposition in Chicago ALCOA Labor Party in Britain	Motion pictures (Edison) Zipper	Panic: "great depression"	Wicksell: *Über Wert, Kapital und Rente* Cannan: *Theories of Production and Distribution*

Year	Events		Science & Technology	Theory & Literature
1894	Pullman strike (Debs) Briey iron ore in France	IDS	Long-distance transmission of electricity (Steinmetz)	Wicksteed: *Co-ordination of the Laws of Distribution*
1895	U.S. income tax declared unconstitutional Anaconda Kiel Canal		Radio (Marconi) Wireless telegraphy (Marconi) X-rays (Röntgen)	London School of Economics Freud: *Studien über Hysterie* Le Bon: *Psychologie des foules*
1896	Klondike gold Hoffman-LaRoche in Basel	Dow-Jones industrial average Free silver speech of Bryan: "cross of gold"	"Horseless carriage" in Detroit Radioactivity discovered (Becquerel) Commercial motion picture: nickelodeon	Barone: *Studi sulla distribuzione* Pareto: *Cours d'économie politique* Taussig: *Wages and Capital*
1897	British preferential tariff		Müngstener railroad bridge: highest in Europe	
1898	Interurban streetcar Renault GATX		Radium isolated (Curie)	Wicksell: *Geldzins und Güterpreise*
1899	U.S. Panama Canal Commission Boer War Baghdad Railway concession FIAT founded by Agnelli		Bayer aspirin Electric home refrigerator Tape recorder	Bernstein: *Evolutionary Socialism* J. B. Clark: *Distribution of Wealth* Veblen: *Theory of the Leisure Class*
1900	Hejaz railway Hertie in Berlin	U.S. on gold standard	Zeppelin airship Tractor (Holt) Cellophane	Carnegie: "Gospel of Wealth" Planck: quantum theory
1901	U.S. Steel Co. Texas oil strike (Gulf Oil) Persian oil concession		Mercedes car Wuppertal Schwebebahn Balloon altitude of 35,000 feet	Spiethoff: *Theorie der Überproduktion*
1902	Opel Werke in Rüsselsheim		Bosch ignition Radio-telephone	Hobson: *Imperialism* Lenin: *What Is To Be Done?* Sombart: *Der Moderne Kapitalismus*

A Time Table of Economic Events, Technological Development, Financial Developments, and Economic Thought (Continued)

Date	Events	Technology	Finance	Thought
1903	Ford Motor Co. Menshevik and Bolshevik faction in Russia	Airplane flight of Wright brothers Bottle-making machine (Owens)		Cassel: *Nature and Necessity of Interest* Mitchell: *History of the Greenbacks*
1904		New York subway Vacuum tube for radio (Fleming)	Bank of Italy (renamed Bank of America 1930)	Veblen: *Theory of Business Enterprise* Max Weber: *Die Protestantische Ethik und der Geist des Kapitalismus*
1905	Russian general strike	Einstein: $E = mc^2$		Kautsky: *Theorien über den Mehrwert* Knapp: *Staatliche Theorie des Geldes*
1906	Stolypin: land reform in Russia	Simplon tunnel *Dreadnought* launched Vitamins		Pareto: *Manuale d'economia politica*
1907		Amplifying tube for radio (De Forest)	U.S. financial panic	Fisher: *The Rate of Interest*
1908	Persian oil strike	Sulfa drugs Tauern tunnel	C.I.T. Financial Co.	Sorel: *Réflexions sur la violence* Wallas: *Human Nature in Politics*
1909	Ford: Model T Anglo-Persian Oil Co.	Monoplane flight from Calais to Dover Nitrogen: Haber process	Merrill Lynch	Veblen: *The Limitations of Marginal Utility*
1910	Pennsylvania Station in New York Mexican revolution Brazilian rubber production at its height	Hydrogenation of coal Bakelite (Baekeland) Neon lamp		Hilferding: *Das Finanzkapital* Wicksteed: *Common Sense of Political Economy*

1911	IBM Chevrolet car U.S. Supreme Court outlaws "unreasonable" restraint of trade National Insurance Act in England Chinese revolution	Automobile self-starter (Kettering) Equivalence of gravitational and inertial forces Air conditioning (Carrier)	$MV = PT$ [Fisher] New York Curb Exchange	*American Economic Review* Institut für Weltwirtschaft Schumpeter: *Theorie der Wirtschaftlichen Entwicklung* Taylor: *Principles of Scientific Management*
1912	British coal strike	Isotopes X-ray diffraction (von Laue)		Luxemburg: *Imperialismus* Mises: *Theorie des Geldes* Pigou: *Wealth and Welfare*
1913	U.S. income tax Metro-Goldwyn-Mayer Woolworth building	Geiger counter Ford moving-assembly-line Helicopter (Sikorski) Multimotored airplane	Federal Reserve System	Keynes: *Indian Currency and Finance* Mitchell: *Business Cycles*
1914	U.S. Federal Trade Commission Ford raises daily wage rate to $5 Panama Canal World War I Clayton Antitrust Act	"Cat cracking" Military tank	Countries at war suspend specie payments	
1915		Fokker plane Submarine war	Debt finance by countries at war	Robertson: *Industrial Fluctuations* Slutsky: *Teoria del consumatore* Veblen: *Imperial Germany and the Industrial Revolution*
1916		Tanks and air support de Havilland and Sikorski planes	Allied war debts to U.S.	General theory of relativity Commons: *Principles of Labor Legislation* Pareto: *Trattato di sociologia generale* Lenin: *Imperialism, the Highest Stage Capitalism*

A Time Table of Economic Events, Technological Development, Financial Developments, and Economic Thought (Continued)

Date	Events	Technology	Finance	Thought
1917	U.S. enters World War I U.S. War Industries Board February and September revolutions in Russia	Bristol fighter		J. M. Clark: *Business Acceleration and the Law of Demand* Lenin: *Gosudarstvo i revolutsiya*
1918	Venezuelan oil fields			Cassel: *Theoretische Sozialökonomie* Kemmerer: *ABC of the Federal Reserve System* Spengler: *Untergang des Abendlandes*
1919	Treaty of Versailles Chrysler Co. U.S. steel strike Third International (Comintern)	Airplane crosses Atlantic	War reparations imposed on Germany	Bukharin: *ABC of Communism* Hawtrey: *Currency and Credit* Keynes: *Economic Consequences of the Peace* Schumpeter: *Soziologie des Imperialismus*
1920	U.S. transcontinental airmail U.S. commercial radio broadcast (Westinghouse) Grand Trunk Railway nationalized (CN) League of Nations first meeting	Disintegration of the atom (Rutherford)	Memo on the world's monetary problems (Cassel)	National Bureau of Economic Research Knight: *Risk, Uncertainty, and Profit* Phillips: *Bank Credit* Tawney: *The Acquisitive Society* Weber: *Universale Sozial-und Wirtschaftsgeschichte*
1921	Postwar depression U.S. immigration restricted "New Economic Policy" in Russia	Insulin	German reparation bill of 132 billion gold mark	Mitchell: *Income in the U.S.* Veblen: *Engineers and the Price System*
1922	Fordney-McCumber Tariff Fascist government in Italy		State Farm Mutual: automobile insurance	Fisher: *The Making of Index Numbers* Robertson: *Money*

1923	German inflation	1 trillion mark = $1		Brookings Institution Clark: *Economics of Overhead Costs* Keynes: *Tract on Monetary Reform* Marshall: *Money, Credit and Commerce* Willis: *The Federal Reserve System*
1924	U.S. immigration further restricted British Labor Government Firestone in Liberia Wrigley Building in Chicago	Dawes Plan		Bowley: *Mathematical Groundwork* Commons: *Legal Foundations of Capitalism* Tugwell: *The Trend of Economics*
1925	Mexican Petroleum Law	Reichsmark (Schacht) British pound sterling returned to gold standard at prewar parity of US$4.87.		Hitler: *Mein Kampf* Seligman: *Studies in Public Finance*
1926	British general strike National Broadcasting Co.	French franc devalued to 2 cents	Motion pictures with sound Black and white television (Baird and Jenkins)	Kondratieff: long-cycle theory Sraffa: *The Law of Returns*
1927	Lindbergh transatlantic flight Mao organizes landless peasants	German economy collapses	Transatlantic phone Moffat Tunnel Principle of indeterminacy (Heisenberg)	Cobb-Douglas production function Mitchell: *Business Cycles, The Problem and Its Setting* Pigou: *Industrial Fluctuations* Ripley: *Main Street and Wall Street*
1928	Russian Five-Year Plan (Stalin)		Mechanically operated computer (Bush) Penicillin (Fleming) Electric shaver (Schick)	Von Neumann: *Zur Theorie der Gesellschaftsspicle* (minimax theorem) Ramsey: *Mathematical Theory of Saving*

A Time Table of Economic Events, Technological Development, Financial Developments, and Economic Thought (Continued)

Date	Events	Technology	Finance	Thought
1929	U.S. Agricultural Marketing Act	Ambassador Bridge Cascade Tunnel	Stock-market crash Bank for International Settlements (Young Plan) DD Bank	Econometric Society Keynes: *Treatise on Money*
1930	U.S. Smoot-Hawley tariff U.S. commercial transcontinental flight (TWA)	Detroit International Tunnel Jet-propulsion aircraft (Whittle)		
1931	U.S. Davis-Bacon Act Brazil destroys coffee Trans-African railway	Cyclotron (Lawrence) Empire State Building George Washington Bridge Neoprene (synthetic rubber)	Austrian Credit-Anstalt fails Debt and reparations moratorium England suspends gold payments Pound falls to $3.49 Exchange controls lead to distinct trading blocs, such as sterling bloc	Fetter: *Masquerade of Monopoly* Hayek: *Prices and Production* Kahn: *Relation of Home Investment to Employment* (multiplier)
1932	"Great Depression" U.S. Reconstruction Finance Co. U.S. Norris-LaGuardia Act Insull utilities collapse Ottawa Imperial Economic Conference German unemployment 6,000,000 Dneproges in Russia Oil in Bahrain	Polaroid (Land)		Berle and Means: *The Modern Corporation* ("administered prices") Chamberlin: *Theory of Monopolistic Competition* Hicks: *Theory of Wages* Robbins: *Nature and Significance of Economic Science* Robinson: *Economics of Imperfect Competition*
1933	U.S. New Deal U.S. National Industrial Recovery Act (NRA) U.S. Tennessee Valley Authority	Drive-in movie	International Economic Conference at London tries to secure an agreement on currency stabilization; fails	Frisch: *Econometrica* Ohlin: *Interregional and International Trade*

Year	Events		Technology	Economic Theory / Publications
	World Economic Conference Russian famine Hitler, Chancellor of Germany	after message from President Roosevelt U.S. Securities Act (SEC) U.S. Banking Act (FDIC) U.S. Gold Repeal Joint Resolution: all contracts and debts payable in legal tender		Burns: *Production Trends in the U.S.* Douglas: *Theory of Wages* Hicks and Allen: *Theory of Value* (indifference curves) Kaldor: *Determinateness of Equilibrium* Wald: existence proof
1934	U.S. Reciprocal Tariff Act Hitler becomes Fuehrer	U.S. Gold Reserve Act: U.S. dollar redefined in terms of gold ($35 an ounce); U.S. continues to convert dollars held by foreign governments into gold German Schacht Plan provides for exchange controls and bilateral agreements with some 40 countries including two-thirds of German foreign trade		
1935	U.S. NRA declared unconstitutional U.S. National Labor Relations (Wagner) Act U.S. Social Security Act		Buna (synthetic rubber) Kodachrome film Nylon Parking meter	Fisher: *100% Money* Heckscher: *Mercantilism* Moulton: *Income and Economic Progress*
1936	U.S. Robinson-Patman Act		Hoover Dam San Francisco Bay Bridge	Keynes: *General Theory of Employment, Interest and Money* Lange: *On the Economic Theory of Socialism* Meade: *Economic Analysis and Policy*

A Time Table of Economic Events, Technological Development, Financial Developments, and Economic Thought (Continued)

Date	Events	Technology	Finance	Thought
1937	U.S. sit-down strikes	Lincoln Tunnel Shopping carts Jet engine		Allen: Mathematical Analysis for Economists Coase: The Nature of the Firm Dobb: Political Economy and Capitalism Haberler: Prosperity and Depression Hicks: Mr. Keynes and the "Classics" Morgenstern: The Limits of Economics Parsons: The Structure of Social Action Viner: Theory of International Trade
1938	U.S. Wages and Hours Law Mexico confiscates foreign oil companies Munich agreement	Bluewater Bridge Ball-point pen Nuclear fission Color television compatible with black and white (Valensi)		Temporary National Economic Committee (TNEC) Hansen: Full Recovery on Stagnation Kuznets: Commodity Flow and Capital Formation Myrdal: Population Schultz: Theory and Measurement of Demand Bergson: A Reformulation of Certain Aspects of Welfare Economics
1939	German invasion of Poland World War II	Trans-Iranian railway		Harrod: Essay in Dynamic Theory Hayek: Profits, Interest and Investment Hicks: Value and Capital

Year	Economics / Theory	Legislation & Finance	Science & Technology	Political & War Events
1940	Kalecki: *Theory of Economic Fluctuations*; Lindahl: *Theory of Money and Capital*; Schumpeter: *Business Cycles*	U.S. Investment Co. Act	Pennsylvania Turnpike; Queens-Midtown Tunnel; Styrene (plastics)	Battle of Britain; U.S. Selective Training and Service Act
1941	Clark: *Toward a Concept of Workable Competition*; Lösch: *Räumliche Ordnung der Wirtschaft*; Stigler: *Production and Distribution Theories*	U.S. Lend-Lease Act	U.S. Office of Scientific Research and Development: radar, proximity fuse, sonar, atomic bomb; Aerosol spray	Atlantic Charter; U.S. enters World War II
1942	Leontief: *Structure of the American Economy*; Rosa: *Multiplier Analysis of Armament Expenditure*		Nuclear energy released in Chicago	U.S. War Production Board; U.S. War Labor Board; U.S. Price Control Act; U.S. Office of Strategic Services
1943	Rosenstein-Rodan: *Problems of Industrialization*	U.S. withholding income tax		U.S. Board of Economic Welfare
1944	Lerner: *Economics of Control*; Von Neumann and Morgenstern: *Theory of Games and Economic Behavior*; Hayek: *The Road to Serfdom*	Bretton Woods plan for an International Monetary Fund	German rockets; *Mark I* (Aiken)	D-Day: Allied invasion of Europe from England across the English Channel
1945			Atomic bomb	Potsdam Conference; British Labor Government; People's Republic of Yugoslavia; U.N. Charter

A Time Table of Economic Events, Technological Development, Financial Developments, and Economic Thought (Continued)

Date	Events	Technology	Finance	Thought
1946	U.S. Employment Act: President's Council of Economic Advisers National Health Service in Britain	Electronic computer (Eckert)	Bank of England nationalized	Drucker: Concept of the Corporation Kuznets: National Income, A Summary of Findings
1947	Marshall Plan U.S. Taft-Hartley Act British coal mines nationalized Monnet Plan Benelux Truman Doctrine General Agreement on Tariffs and Trade (GATT)			Dantzig: linear programming Domar: Theory of Economic Growth Klein: The Keynesian Revolution Samuelson: Foundations of Economics Analysis
1948	ECA OEEC GATT Berlin airlift Communist coup in Czechoslovakia Escalator clause	Transistor Long-playing (LP) record	Deutsche mark	Hoover: The Location of Economic Activity Simons: Economic Policy for a Free Society
1949	Point Four program NATO Federal Republic of Germany People's Republic of China		British pound devalued from $4.03 to $2.80	Fellner: Competition Among the Few Mises: Human Action Orwell: 1984 Schneider: Wirtschaftstheorie
1950	Schuman Plan: EEC U.S. Celler-Kefauver Anti-Merger Act	Brooklyn-Battery Tunnel Hydrogen bomb		Feis: Diplomacy of the Dollar Little: Critique of Welfare Economics
1951	U.S. Mutual Security Agency Torquay Conference	Univac computer Color television in U.S.	Treasury-Federal Reserve Accord	Arrow: Social Choice and Individual Values

1952	Iranian oil industry nationalized	Long-distance "direct-dial" telephone service: area codes		Scitovsky: *Welfare and Competition* Arrow: *Le Rôle des Valeurs Boursieres pour la Repartition la meilleure des Risques* BLS input-output table Copeland: *Moneyflows in the U.S.* Galbraith: *American Capitalism* Nurkse: *Capital Formation in Underdeveloped Countries* Rostow: *The Process of Economic Growth* Schumpeter: *History of Economic Analysis*
1953		Polio vaccine (Salk)	New York Curb Exchange becomes American Stock Exchange	English translation of Walras by Jaffé Friedman: *Essays in Positive Economics* Rothenberg: *Conditions for a Social Welfare Function*
1954	SEATO U.S. Supreme Court holds unanimously that segregation in public education is a denial of equal protection	*Nautilus*: nuclear submarine Electronic data processing first employed for business data		Leibenstein: *Theory of Economic Demographic Development* Buchanan: *Social Choice, Democracy and Free Markets*
1955	AFL-CIO merger Bandung Conference		Federal Reserve System releases flow-of-funds accounts Toronto-Dominion Bank	Goldsmith: *Study of Saving in the U.S.* Lewis: *Theory of Economic Growth* Patinkin: *Money, Interest, and Prices*

A Time Table of Economic Events, Technological Development, Financial Developments, and Economic Thought (Continued)

Date	Events	Technology	Finance	Thought
1956	Egypt seizes Suez Canal Hungarian revolt	H-bomb test		Lachmann: *Capital and its Structure* Boulding: *The Image* Debreu: *Théorie de la valeur* Katona: *Consumer Expectations* Lancaster and Lipsey: *Theory of Second Best* Robinson: *Accumulation of Capital* Simon: *Models of Man*
1957	Eisenhower Doctrine	Mackinac Straits Bridge Sputnik Wankel engine	Deutsche Bank	Baran: *Political Economy of Growth* Bator: *Simple Analytics of Welfare Maximization* Becker: *The Economics of Discrimination* Downs: *An Economic Theory of Democracy* Koopmans: *Three Essays on the State of Economic Science*
1958	"Great Leap Forward" in China	Boeing 707 Explorer: first U.S. satellite	Congressional hearings on the national economic accounts of the U.S.	U.S. income and output (official estimates) Boulding: *The Skills of the Economist* Dorfman: *Linear Programming and Economic Analysis* Galbraith: *The Affluent Society* Hirschman: *Strategy of Economic Development* Phillips: *The Relation between Unemployment and the Rate of Change of Money Wage Rates*
1959	U.S. Landrum-Griffin Act	St. Lawrence Seaway	Morgan Guaranty Trust Co. Radcliffe Report	Chenery: *Interindustry Economics*

Year		Science & Technology	Business	Books
				Kantorovich: *Economic Calculation and the Best Use of Resources* Musgrave: *Theory of Public Finance*
1960	OPEC founded in Baghdad Communist China and Soviet Union split	Laser (Malman)	REITs	Buchanan: *The Public Finances* Gurley and Shaw: *Money in a Theory of Finance* Hitch and McKean: *The Economics of Defense in the Nuclear Age* Isard: *Methods of Regional Analysis* Kahn: *On Thermonuclear War* Mishan: *Survey of Welfare Economics* Schelling: *Strategy of Conflict* Triffin: *Gold and the Dollar Crisis*
1961	Alliance for Progress Berlin Wall LTV Corp. McDonald's Corp. Wage-price guideposts	First astronaut in space IBM Selectric typewriter	Certificate of deposit New headquarters buildings in New York for Chase Manhattan Bank and First National City Bank	McClelland: *The Achieving Society* Mumford: *The City in History* Muth: *Rational Expectations and the Theory of Price Movements*
1962	COMSAT Electronic Data Systems K-Mart discount stores U.S. Trade Expansion Act	Chesapeake Bay Bridge–Tunnel highway Color television		Friedman: *Capitalism and Freedom* Denison: *The Sources of Economic Growth* Kuhn: *The Structure of Scientific Revolution* Machlup: *Production and Distribution of Knowledge* Tinbergen: *Shaping the World Economy* Buchanan and Tullock: *The Calculus of Consent*

A Time Table of Economic Events, Technological Development, Financial Developments, and Economic Thought (Continued)

Date	Events	Technology	Finance	Thought
1963		First commercial nuclear reactor Valium		Barnett: *Scarcity and Growth* Friedman: *Monetary History of the U.S.* Schultz: *The Economic Value of Education* Pope John: *Pacem In Terris*
1964	U.S. "war on poverty" (OEO) U.S. food stamp program ITT largest conglomerate U.S. Civil Rights Act U.S. Tonkin Gulf resolution permits escalation of Vietnam war	Verrazano Narrows Bridge Zip codes		
1965	U.S. Medicare Act HUD Power failure affects 30 million people	DC-9	Fully automated quotation service of N.Y. Stock Exchange	Nader: *Unsafe at Any Speed*
1966	Laker Airways World food crisis as total food production falls 2% below last year Great Proletarian Cultural Revolution in China	Boeing 747 Implant of artificial heart (DeBakey)	BankAmericard issued nationally Interbank card: Master Charge	Heller: *New Dimensions of Political Economy*
1967	McDonnell-Douglas merger "Six-Day War"; Suez Canal closed	Microwave oven Montreal subway Adirondack Northway Steel arch bridge across St. Lawrence at Trois-Rivières World's largest hydroelectric power project completed in Siberia	Britain devalues the pound from $2.80 to $2.40	Kranzberg: *Technology in Western Civilization*

1968	Oil on Alaska's North Slope British-Leyland Motor Co. Data General Co. Penn-Central merger Norton Simon, Inc. United Brands "Prague spring" ended by Russian intervention	Supertanker	U.S. Truth-in-Lending Act	Leijonhufvud: *On Keynesian Economics and the Economics of Keynes* Mansfield: *The Economics of Technological Change*
1969	Italy's "economic miracle" grinds to a stop North Sea oil discovered Nuclear Nonproliferation Treaty	First walk on the moon Concorde supersonic jet John Hancock Center in Chicago Metroliner Mexico City's Metro		
1970	Burlington Northern, Inc.: longest U.S. railroad U.S. Postal Service U.S. Office of Management and Budget U.S. Environmental Protection Agency (EPA) U.S. Occupational Safety and Health Act (OSHA) Chilean president Allende Penn-Central bankruptcy Strategic Arms Limitation Treaty (SALT I)		Investors Overseas Services (IOS)	Georgescu-Roegen: *The Entropy Law and the Economic Process*
1971	Amtrak British postal strike Rolls-Royce bankrupt Berlin Accord Bangladesh independent		U.S. "New Economic Policy" suspends gold convertibility of dollars held by foreigners Breakdown of Bretton Woods international monetary system IMF special drawing rights (SDRs) become "paper gold" (Smithsonian Agreement) Listing of N.Y. Stock Exchange members: Merrill Lynch	Bronfenbrenner: *Income Distribution Theory* Commoner: *The Closing Circle* Forrester: *World Dynamics* Kuznets: *Economic Growth of Nations* Rawls: *A Theory of Justice* Tobin: *Essays in Macroeconomics*

A Time Table of Economic Events, Technological Development, Financial Developments, and Economic Thought (Continued)

Date	Events	Technology	Finance	Thought
1972	Watergate break-in EEC expands from 6 to 9 members New Mexican oil field estimated to be the largest in the Western Hemisphere	BART Washington Metro World Trade Center McGraw-Hill Building	Dow-Jones above 1000 IDS Center Reserve Funds in New York: first "money funds"	Friedman: *An Economist's Protest* Shackle: *Epistemics and Economics* Sik: *The Bureaucratic Economy* (Czechoslovakia) Lucas: "Expectations and the Neutrality of Money" Schultz: *Investment in Education*
1973	Allende government in Chile overthrown by military coup Yom Kippur war: Arab oil embargo Esmark		World monetary crisis: Second U.S. dollar devaluation within 14 months; floating exchange rates Dow-Jones industrial average peaks at 1052 Chicago Board Options Exchange (CBO) British bank rate 13%	Bergstrom: *Private Demands for Public Goods* Despres: *International Economic Reform* Kendrick: *Postwar Productivity Trends in the U.S.*
1974	"Stagflation": U.S. real GNP declines 2% with 7% of the work force unemployed, while inflation persists at 12%		Franklin National Bank insolvent: biggest bank failure in U.S. history "Indexation" U.S. begins consolidated stock exchange tape	Fogel and Engerman: *Time on the Cross* Fuchs: *Who Shall Live? Health, Economics, and Social Choice* Spengler: *Population Change, Modernization, and Welfare* Weidenbaum: *The Economics of Peacetime Defense*
1975	Suez Canal reopens Fall of Cambodia and South Vietnam Lebanese civil war		Fixed commission rates eliminated at U.S. stock exchanges	Minsky: *John Maynard Keynes* Okun: *Equality and Efficiency, the Big Tradeoff*

1976	Conrail "Gang of Four" arrested in China: Deng Xiaoping returns to power	Landings of *Viking* 1 and 2 on Mars	British pound sterling falls to $1.67	Hirsch: *Social Limits to Growth* Latsis: *Method and Appraisal in Economics* McCloskey: *Does the Past Have Useful Economics?* Ridker: *Population and Development* Scitovsky: *The Joyless Economy* Vernon: *Storm over the Multinationals*
1977	First oil from Alaska pipeline New York City blackout Seabrook nuclear plant protest in U.S. Sadat in Jerusalem		IMF approves largest single credit ever, $3.9 billion, to Britain	Frisch: *Inflation Theory 1963-1975* Weintraub: *The Microfoundations of Macroeconomics* Galbraith: *The Age of Uncertainty*
1978	Humphrey-Hawkins bill Cardinal Wojtyla elected Pope: John Paul II			North: *Structure and Performance, The Task of Economic History*
1979	Ayatollah Khomeini returns to Iran Three Mile Island nuclear accident Margaret Thatcher British Conservative Prime Minister Egypt and Israel sign peace treaty		British bank rate 17% British pound sterling rises to $2.28 Gold above $500	Simon: *Rational Decision Making in Business Organizations* Arrow: *The Future and the Present in Economic Life* Friedman: *Free to Choose* Hicks: *Causality in Economics*
1980	Russian troops in Afghanistan Indira Gandhi returns to power in India Trudeau returns to power in Canada World population 4.5 billion U.S. elects conservative president		Federal Reserve discount rate 13% Gold peaks at $875 U.S. prime rate 21½% U.S. inflation rate 18%	Sims: *Macroeconomics and Reality* Wallis: *Econometric Implications of the Rational Expectations Hypothesis*
1981	Supply-side economics popularized		Gold falls below $500	

Name Index

Subject Index

About the Editor in Chief

Dr. Douglas Greenwald is a consulting economist to governments and to several corporations and is an adviser on a new program for the teaching of Economic and Statistical Research in Business, Industry, and Government at Columbia University's Teachers College.

When he retired from the McGraw-Hill Publications Company in 1978, he was Vice President/Economics in the Publications Company and head of its internationally known Department of Economics.

He is the chief editor and coauthor of *The McGraw-Hill Dictionary of Modern Economics* and a coauthor of *New Forces in American Business,* published in 1959, and he contributed the chapter "Forecasting Capital Expenditures" in the first edition of the National Association of Business Economists' book *How Business Economists Forecast,* published in 1966. Dr. Greenwald was editor of a quarterly report, *Pulsebeat of Industry,* published by McGraw-Hill Publications Company and has prepared numerous articles on short- and long-run prospects for industries and economies of the world for financial, business, and industry magazines.

His surveys and judgments have earned him a prestigious place among the world's economists. He often speaks to business, professional, and government groups in the United States and abroad and is especially well known for his forecasts of business capital spending, which are widely quoted in financial circles as well as in the international press and are highly valued by business executives and government officials around the world.

He was a member of the board of directors of Standard & Poor's InterCapital Fixed Income Fund.

Dr. Greenwald was one of the organizers of the Federal Statistics Users Conference and was Business Community Trustee for the Conference and subsequently Chairman of the Conference and is currently an ex officio adviser to the Conference.

He is a Fellow of the American Statistical Association and was a member of its Board of Directors as well as Chairman of its Business and Economics Statistics Section. He was President of the New York Chapter of the ASA and Chairman of its Finance Committee. He has won ASA awards for accuracy in forecasting.

Dr. Greenwald is a Fellow of the National Association of Business Economists and a member of the American Economic Association and was President of the Metropolitan Economic Association. He was Vice President for economists in the Business Advisory Professions Society.

Dr. Greenwald was a member of the Regional Accounts Committee sponsored by Resources for the Future; an adviser to the National Wealth Planning Committee sponsored by George Washington University; a member of the American Statistical Association's Advisory Committee to the Bureau of the Census; a member of the Business Research Advisory Committee to the Bureau of Labor Statistics, concerned particularly with economic growth and productivity; a member of the Advisory Committee on Statistical Policy to the Statistical Policy Division of the Office of Management and the Budget; and an economic adviser to the Council of Economic Advisers to the President, to the Joint Economic Committee of Congress, to the Secretary of Commerce, to the Secretary of the Treasury, to the Congressional Budget Office, and to the Finance Department of the state of California.

He has testified many times before congressional committees on the economic outlook, prospects for capital expenditures, and the industrial operating rate. Dr. Greenwald was awarded a Certificate for Community Service. He is married to Mildred Janis Greenwald, President of Business Careers.